Written by the Editors at FL Memo with contributions from Philip Fontbin, ACA MBA.

FL Memo Limited

Original edition produced with the input, advice and collaboration of the UK office of

MAZARS

INTERNATIONAL BUSINESS ADVISERS AND ACCOUNTANTS

Important Disclaimer

This publication is sold on the understanding that the information provided within it is for guidance only, and that the publisher is not in business to provide accounting, tax or legal advice or any other professional services. Readers entering into transactions on the basis of, or otherwise relying on, such information should seek the services of a competent professional adviser.

Whilst every care has been taken to ensure the accuracy of the contents, the editors and the publishers cannot accept responsibility for any loss occasioned to any person acting or refraining to act as a result of any statement in it.

ISBN 978-0-9568162-0-7

FL Memo Limited
185 Park Street
Bankside
London SE1 9DY

Telephone: (020) 7803 4666
Fax: (020) 7803 4699
Email: flm@flmemo.co.uk
Website: www.flmemo.co.uk

British Library Cataloguing in Publication Data.
A catalogue record for this book is available from the British Library.

FL MEMO

Accountancy and Financial Reporting

2011

UK GAAP

Contents

Part 8: Smaller entities

Part 9: Group accounts

Part 10: Miscellaneous

Part 11: General information

Preface

Accountancy and Financial Reporting 2011 continues to provide clear, concise and accurate guidance on current accounting and financial reporting in the UK. This, the eighth edition, covers the provisions of Company Law and the requirements of Accounting Standards, UITF Abstracts, the Listing Rules and other Generally Accepted Accounting Practice (GAAP). Where relevant, the convergence of UK and International Accounting standards – and its effect – is discussed as well.

Accountancy and Financial Reporting 2011 has, unless otherwise stated, been updated and expanded to reflect regulations and practice in force at 31 January 2011.

As most readers will know, in October 2010 the Accounting Standards Board published its detailed proposals for the future of financial reporting in the UK. In short, UK GAAP – as a self-standing and separate regime – will soon give way to a new system: a hierarchical framework based on public accountability, in terms of which UK entities will be required to prepare financial statements according to their place within the hierarchy. Tier 1 is for publicly accountable enterprises, which are obliged to report using IFRS, while Tier 3 is for small companies that can report (and continue to report) under FRSSE. For the entities in between (i.e., Tier 2) the ASB is proposing a new standard based on the international standard for small and medium-sized entities. The exact timing of the new regime is not certain although it is likely that the changes will apply to accounting periods beginning on or after 1 July 2013. Thus, until the process is finalised, the existing body of UK GAAP retains its importance for those accounting entities that have not opted into the IFRS regime.

Accountancy and Financial Reporting 2011 is based on an internationally successful formula and is designed to keep readers abreast of changes affecting accountants in public practice and in industry. To this end, between editions, readers are able to access online updates, keyed by paragraph number, on our website, **www.flmemo.co.uk**, and at their option they can also receive periodic newsletters by email.

The editors welcome feedback from readers at: accountancy_editors@flmemo.co.uk

FL Memo Ltd
March 2011

Abbreviations

The following are the main abbreviations and terms used in this book:

ABI	Association of British Insurers
The Act	Companies Act
ACCA	Association of Chartered Certified Accountants
Accounts	Financial statements
AGM	Annual general meeting
AIM	Alternative Investment Market
APB	Auditing Practices Board, successor to the APC (Auditing Practices Committee)
ARD	Accounting reference date
ARP	Accounting reference period
ASB	Accounting Standards Board
ASC	Accounting Standards Committee
Cadbury Code	Code of Best Practice, issued by the Cadbury Committee
Cadbury Committee	Committee on the Financial Aspects of Corporate Governance
CA 1985	Companies Act 1985, as amended
CA 2006	Companies Act 2006
CASE	Committee on Accounting for Smaller Entities, a subcommittee of the ASB
CCAB	Consultative Committee of Accountancy Bodies, consisting of ACCA, CIMA, CIPFA, ICAEW, ICAI and ICAS
CIMA	Chartered Institute of Management Accountants
CIPFA	Chartered Institute of Public Finance and Accountancy
CISCO	City Group for Smaller Companies, now renamed Quoted Companies Alliance (QCA)
Code of Best Practice	Code of Best Practice issued by the Cadbury Committee
Combined Code	The principles of good governance and the code of best practice provisions annexed to the Listing Rules and derived by the Hampel Committee. Renamed *The UK Corporate Governance Code* in 2010.
Combined Code 2003	The Combined Code on Corporate Governance, published on 23 July 2003, including the Code and related guidance (the Turnbull guidance on Internal Control, the Smith guidance on Audit Committees and various items of good practice guidance from the Higgs Report)
DP	Discussion Paper
DRC	Depreciated replacement cost
DTI	Department of Trade and Industry
ED	Exposure Draft
EEA	European Economic Area
EPS/eps	Earnings per share
ESOP	Employee share ownership plan
EU	European Union
EUV	Existing use value
FAS	Financial Accounting Standard (USA)
FASB	Financial Accounting Standards Board (USA)
FIFO	First In, First Out
FRAG	Financial Reporting and Auditing Group
FRC	Financial Reporting Council
FRED	Financial Reporting Exposure Draft
FRRP	Financial Reporting Review Panel
FRS	Financial Reporting Standard
FRSSE	Financial Reporting Standard for Smaller Entities
FSA	Financial Services Authority
FTSE 100	Index: *Financial Times Stock Exchange* top 100 companies
GAAP	Generally Accepted Accounting Practice
GAAS	Generally Accepted Auditing Standards
GN	Guidance Note (issued by the Institute and Faculty of Actuaries)
Greenbury Committee	Study Group on directors' remuneration

Hampel Committee	Committee on corporate governance
Higgs Report	Review of the role and effectiveness of non-executive directors, by Derek Higgs, January 2003
IAS	International Accounting Standard
IASB	International Accounting Standards Board
IASC	International Accounting Standards Committee
ICAEW	The Institute of Chartered Accountants in England and Wales
ICAI	The Institute of Chartered Accountants in Ireland
ICAS	The Institute of Chartered Accountants of Scotland
IFRIC	International Financial Reporting Interpretations Committee
IGU	Income generating unit
IPO	Initial public offering
IRR	Internal rate of return
ISA	International Standard on Auditing
ISAE	International Standard on Assurance Engagements
ISMA	International Securities Market Association Ltd
JANE	Joint arrangement that is not an entity
LIBOR	London Inter-Bank Offer Rate
LIFFE	London International Financial Futures and Options Exchange
LIFO	Last In, First Out
Listed company	A company whose securities have been admitted to the Official List of the UK Listing Authority
LR	Listing rules of the UK Listing Authority
LTIP	Long-term incentive plan
NASDAQ	National Association of Securities Dealers Automated Quotations
NIC	National Insurance contributions
OEIC	Open-ended investment company
P&L	Profit and loss account
QCA	Quoted Companies Alliance
RIE	Recognised investment exchange
ROI	Return on investment
SAS	Statement on Auditing Standards
Sch	Schedule (to the Companies Act)
SEC	Securities and Exchange Commission
SFA	Securities and Futures Authority
SFAS	Statement of Financial Accounting Standards
SI	Statutory Instrument
SME	Small and/or medium-sized entity
SORP	Statement of Recommended Practice (recommendations of accounting practices for specific industries or sectors)
Smith Report	"Audit Committees; Combined Code Guidance-report and proposed guidance by an FRC-appointed group chaired by Sir Robert Smith"
SRO	Self-regulatory organization
SSAP	Statement of Standard Accounting Practice
STRGL	Statement of total recognised gains and losses
TR	Technical Release
TSR	Total shareholder return
Turnbull Committee	The Working Party set up the ICAEW to assist listed companies implement new internal control requirements of the Combined Code
UITF	Urgent Issues Task Force of the ASB
The UK Corporate Governance Code	New name (as of 2010) of the *Combined Code*
VAT	Value added tax
Walker Report	Sir David Walker's report on the corporate governance of banks and other financial institutions in November 2009

CHAPTER 1

Accounting rules and conventions

OUTLINE ¶¶

A. Introduction

This volume is concerned with accounting practice in the United Kingdom for those entities that have elected not to adopt International Financial Reporting Standards (IFRS). Although reference is frequently made to international standards, this is generally for the purpose of comparing their requirements to those prevailing in the UK. 1

The accounting principles and conventions currently in force in the UK have developed over many years and from various sources: legislation, accounting standards, and customs practised by professionals. However, as might be expected in a global business world, accounting in the UK cannot but be influenced by worldwide developments and practices as well.

The Accounting Standards Board, which establishes and issues financial reporting standards in the UK, in October 2010 issued far-reaching proposals that move away from the current UK GAAP reporting regime. These proposals will mark an important change for those entities that at present apply UK Financial Reporting Standards (FRS). Entities will be required to prepare financial statements according to how they slot into a tiered system based on whether they are publicly accountable or not, and (if not) how certain size-based criteria will then apply (see details at ¶252). Larger, publicly accountable enterprises already apply the IFRS regime while so-called small entities can elect to report under FRSSE (see ¶6000). Their position will remain largely unchanged. It is for those enterprises falling in between that the new framework will be relevant. 2

These proposals are still, at the time this book goes to press, under discussion (the consultation period runs until 30 April 2011) but it is anticipated that once finalised the changes will become effective in respect of accounting periods beginning on or after 1 July 2013.

The general framework and sources of authority for GAAP currently followed in the UK are discussed from ¶200. The overarching requirement of financial statements is that they give a true and fair view. 3

B. True and fair view

4 For over 50 years, company law in the UK has required financial statements to present a true and fair view of the reporting entity's financial position and the results of its operations. However, exactly what constitutes such a view is ultimately a matter of professional judgement – because its interpretation is governed by companies' legislation, accounting standards and generally accepted accounting practice. Moreover, "true and fair" is not a static concept, but one that is subject to changes over time. For instance, an accounting treatment that was considered to render a true and fair view as little as 10 years ago may now no longer do so because of changes in business practice or economic realities during the intervening period.

The **principle** that the financial statements present a true and fair view **applies** to all companies without regard to their size. Small and medium-sized companies (¶6000) can elect to adopt the Financial Reporting Standard for Smaller Entities (FRSSE), which – while it exempts them from the provisions of other accounting standards – still holds them to the requirement of true and fair presentation. Therefore, shorter-form and abbreviated financial statements prepared by these companies are expected to give a true and fair view.

5 s 393 CA 2006 The **Companies Act** states that the accounts cannot be approved by the directors unless they are satisfied that such financial statements "give a true and fair view of the assets, liabilities, financial position and profit or loss" of the company for the financial year.

For this purpose, accounts are required to comply with the provisions in regard to form and content of the balance sheet, the profit and loss account and any other additional information to be provided. The Act also requires companies to comply with prevailing accounting standards. This is generally sufficient to ensure that a true and fair view is given.

However, **in certain circumstances**, strict compliance may result in the unusual (and unexpected) situation in which readers are not given a proper appreciation of a company's financial statements – e.g., if additional information beyond the scope of what may have been required by the regulations (or formerly, under the 1985 Act, by Schedule 4) is necessary to explain an unusual transaction or to highlight a related party transaction (¶5000). In these cases, supplying the additional information will satisfy the true and fair requirement.

6 On the other hand, in special circumstances the accounting treatment required by the Act might not result in a true and fair view even if additional information is given. In these cases, the company is obliged to **depart from the relevant provisions** to the extent necessary to give a true and fair view and consequently follow an accounting treatment that is not in accord with the Act. Full details of any departure, including the reasons and the effect, must be given in the notes. This situation – where a company deliberately disregards a Companies Act requirement – is known as the **true and fair override**. It may be used only in special circumstances, such as where a company finds itself – in relation to a specific issue – in a situation that other companies facing a similar issue would not find itself. The same logic holds for companies in a particular industry, which may be considering issues that are specific to the industry concerned. For example, securities companies "mark to market" their current asset investments and take the resulting gains to the profit and loss account rather than the revaluation reserve, as the Act otherwise requires. This treatment is regarded as acceptable because, owing to the specific nature of the securities business, it gives a better view of such a company's performance. The point to be borne in mind is that before any company can invoke the true and fair override, it must be able to show special circumstances to justify it.

7 FRS 18 (4) The financial reporting standard **FRS 18, "Accounting policies"**, also prescribes a reporting entity's duty to ensure that its financial statements present a true and fair view, and adds that the accounting policies it adopts should be consistent with accounting standards, UITF (Urgent Issues Task Force) abstracts and company legislation. Thus, it is generally accepted

that true and fair presentation is inherently a question of compliance with accounting standards.

MEMO POINTS This idea was articulated in *Lloyd Cheyham & Co v Littlejohn* [1987] BCLC 303 as follows: "While the Statements of Standard Accounting Practice [SSAP] are not rigid rules, they are strong evidence of what is the proper standard to be adopted and, unless there is some justification, a departure from them will be regarded as a breach of duty."

Just as company law recognises a true and fair override, so too does FRS 18. Since all accounting standards have been specifically formulated with the objective of true and fair presentation in mind, departures from accounting standards are permitted only in the most **exceptional circumstances** and only to the extent necessary to give a true and fair view. **8** FRS 18 (15)

Companies that take advantage of the **true and fair override** must follow a step-by-step approach. The first step is to determine whether additional disclosure, beyond that ordinarily required under the accounting standards, would provide a true and fair view. Only if it does not should the company, as a last resort, depart from the accounting standards.

Disclosure of true and fair override

As stated, the Act requires that where a company uses the true and fair override, "particulars of any such departure, the reasons for it and the effects must be given in a note to the accounts." **10**

This requirement is not exhaustive, but FRS 18 provides greater clarity by prescribing the following: FRS 18 (62)
- a clear and unambiguous statement that there has been a departure from the requirements of an accounting standard, a UITF abstract or companies legislation and that the departure is necessary to give a true and fair view,
- a statement explaining the treatment that otherwise would be required in the circumstances and a description of the treatment actually adopted,
- a statement as to why the "normal" treatment would not give a true and fair view, and
- a description of how the position shown in the financial statements is different as a result of the departure, normally with quantification of the difference (except where this is self-evident or cannot reasonably be made, in which latter case the circumstances should be explained).

EXAMPLE *The following note should be given where a company includes exchange gains and losses in the profit and loss account under SSAP 20,* "Foreign currency translation".
In accordance with SSAP 20, exchange gains and losses on the translation of monetary items are taken to the profit and loss for the year. In the case of unrealised exchange gains arising on the translation of unsettled long-term monetary transactions, this treatment represents a departure from the Companies Act, which prescribes that only profits realised at the balance sheet date should be taken to the profit and loss account. However, consistent with SSAP 20, exchange gains on unsettled transactions can be determined at the balance sheet date no less objectively than exchange losses. Therefore, deferring the gains while recognising the losses would in effect deny that any favourable movement in exchange rates had occurred. This would also inhibit fair measurement of the company's performance during the year. Consequently, the directors consider that recognising such unrealised exchange gains is necessary to give a true and fair view of the company's affairs. The effect of this departure is to increase the profit before taxation by £xxx (previous year £xxx) and to increase the value of the asset involved by £xxx (previous year £xxx).

C. Accounting principles

Both the Act and the accounting standards require company financial statements to be prepared according to the following basic principles: **15**
- going concern
- consistency

- prudence and realisation
- accruals basis
- separate valuation of assets and liabilities
- substance over form (discussed in the following chapter from ¶110).

As a general rule, companies may depart from these only if there are special reasons to do so. In these cases, the notes to the financial statements must give details of the departure, the reasons for it, and its effect on the financial statements. Similarly, FRS 18 also requires disclosure of the particulars, reasons and effects.

1. Going concern

20 The preparation of financial statements on the going concern basis can be regarded as a general rule automatically followed by all business entities unless there are compelling questions as to the enterprise's continuity. The importance of this rule is underscored by the Act's specifically stating that companies "shall be presumed to be carrying on business as a going concern". Although the Act does not specifically explain the circumstances that might justify a departure from the going concern principle, where the company does prepare its accounts on another basis, it requires the particulars, reasons and effect to be disclosed in the notes. Again, FRS 18 concurs with this view but is more explicit. Thus, an entity should always prepare its financial statements on a going concern basis, unless:
- it has ceased trading or is in the process of liquidation,
- its directors have no realistic alternative but to cease trading or to liquidate the entity.

21 **All amounts recognised in financial statements** reflect the going concern principle: assets and liabilities are recorded at carrying amounts that are expected to be recovered or discharged in the normal course of business. Only if the business is no longer a going concern should the fixed assets be valued at their "break-up" value.

Where these circumstances are present, "the entity may, if appropriate, prepare its financial statements on a basis other than that of a going concern". These financial statements should reflect the amounts recoverable from a quick sale or scrap – i.e., the "break-up" value. As a practical matter, fixed and long-term assets and liabilities should be reclassified as current assets and liabilities, and provisions should be created in respect of anticipated further losses expected to be incurred to the date of termination of business.

EXAMPLE The details of a manufacturing company's assets are as follows:

	£	£
Factory buildings		
At cost	800,000	
Less: accumulated deprecation	100,000	
Net book value		700,000
Machinery and plant		
At cost	525,000	
Less: accumulated deprecation	265,000	
Net book value		260,000
		£ 960,000

The break-up values of the factory buildings, and the machinery and plant, are £500,000 and £125,000 respectively.

If the company is a going concern, the financial statements will show the fixed assets at their net book value of £960,000. Only if the company could no longer be regarded as a going concern would the fixed assets have to be written down to their break-up value of £625,000.

22 FRS 18 (23) Each year, at the time of preparing the financial statements, the board of directors must assess the entity's ability to continue as a going concern. However, even if they believe that there are significant doubts about the entity's ability to continue as a going concern, this does not automatically trigger the requirement to prepare financial statements on a basis

other than the going concern basis. In fact, unless the business is actually in the process of being terminated, or where termination of the business cannot be realistically avoided, the financial statements should continue to be prepared on the going concern basis. However, the details of any significant uncertainties regarding the entity's ability to continue as a going concern should be given and may be referred to by the company's auditors in their report.

In the case of **listed companies**, the UK Corporate Governance Code requires directors to actually "report that the business is a going concern, with supporting assumptions or qualifications as necessary". In other words, readers are not expected to infer this information in the absence of anything to the contrary. There are no similar positive going concern disclosure requirements for other entities. 23

The following table indicates the disclosures to be made as to a company's ability to continue as a going concern. FRS 18 (61)

Financial statements prepared on going concern basis	Financial statements not prepared on going concern basis
Any material uncertainties related to events or conditions that may cast significant doubt upon the entity's ability to continue as a going concern.	The fact that the statements were not prepared on the going concern basis, the basis on which they have been prepared, and the reason for not regarding the entity as a going concern.
Where the foreseeable future considered by the directors has been limited to a period of less than 1 year from the date of approval of the financial statements, that fact.	

MEMO POINTS If there is a fundamental uncertainty regarding the going concern basis, the company's auditors are obliged to draw attention to the notes to the accounts, where that uncertainty is explained.

2. Consistency

Accounting **policies** must be applied consistently from one accounting period to another. This requirement facilitates a logical correspondence with comparative figures for the previous accounting period. Comparability is essential to users' understanding and ability to evaluate financial performance over time – not only in respect of the same entity but even as regards different reporting entities. An important element of consistency, therefore, is the choice of suitable accounting policies that will allow for an adequate degree of comparability. 25

In this context, accounting policies are the principles, bases, conventions, rules and practices for: FRS 18 (4)
- recognising,
- selecting measurement bases for, and
- presenting

assets, liabilities, gains, losses and changes to shareholders' funds.

FRS 18 clearly differentiates between accounting policies and **estimation techniques**. Estimation techniques are methods used to make estimates of monetary amounts, under the various bases selected for assets, liabilities, gains, losses and changes in shareholders' funds when exact values are unknown. 26

Estimation techniques can be used to measure the following:
- depreciation and/or impairment of fixed assets
- provisions
- cost of stocks or work-in-progress
- turnover and profits attributable to the stage of completion on long-term contracts.

The concept of consistency does not preclude changes to accounting policies where changes are appropriate and of benefit to users (e.g., improvements in accounting or introduction of a new accounting standard whose treatment of certain items may differ from those employed by the entity under consideration). Likewise, the nature of an entity's operations or activities may change, making established accounting policies obsolete. When necessary, new accounting policies – and changes to existing policies – should be adopted in accordance with the latest accounting standards.

FRS 18 recommends that accounting policies should be regularly reviewed and adds that when considering whether a new policy would be more appropriate, account must be taken of the potential effect on comparability. Frequent changes could adversely affect comparability over the long term, so changes in accounting policies would be well-advised only when the benefits to users more than compensate for any disadvantages.

MEMO POINTS A change of accounting policy requires a prior year adjustment, in order to restate the comparative figures for consistency and comparability. A change of estimate affects the current year only and therefore comparative figures are not restated.

Selecting the most appropriate accounting policies

27 FRS 18 (17) Entities should always choose an accounting policy that is considered most appropriate to "the purpose of giving a true and fair view". Where an accounting standard allows more than one accounting policy or where a policy is not specified in an accounting standard, the ultimate choice will depend on these considerations. The most appropriate accounting policies should be selected on the basis of four **criteria**: relevance, reliability, comparability and understandability.

Relevance: Relevant information is information provided in a timely manner to assist readers in evaluating both their previous conclusions and their future decisions.

FRS 18 (35) **Reliability**: Reliable information faithfully represents (or can reasonably be relied on to represent) that which it is intended to represent, it is free from bias or error, it is in all material aspects complete and, where conditions are uncertain, is prudent.

Comparability: In the selection of accounting policies, directors should consider whether they are widely used in the industry. If the entity's policies deviate, the directors should be able to show why this is desirable and results in an enhanced level of presentation for users.

FRS 18 (41) **Understandability**: The information provided by financial statements must be capable of being appreciated and understood by users who have a reasonable knowledge of business, economic activities and accounting and who are willing to study the information with reasonable diligence. An appropriate accounting policy will enable such users to perceive the significance of the information given.

3. Prudence and realisation

30 Companies are required to use a prudent basis in determining the amount of any item included in its financial statements. It should be noted that, once the predominant influence in selecting an accounting policy, the importance of prudence has been downgraded.

Two factors play an integral part in the concept of a prudent basis:
– the recognition only of **profits** that have been realised at the balance sheet date, and
– all known **liabilities and losses** relating to the current or previous financial years – that have either already arisen or are likely to arise – must be taken into account in the financial statements.

31 Even though realisation is an accounting, rather than a legal, notion, directors must bear in mind their duties under the law. In the first place, departures from the principle of recognising realised profits are permitted only where it appears to the directors that there are special reasons to do so. However, the effect of the departure must be quantified and disclosed. In the second place, directors need to know which profits are realised so that they can determine the amount of profits legally available for distribution.

With regard to the recognition of all known liabilities, company law requires that these must be included even if they become apparent during the period between the balance sheet date and the date on which the directors sign the financial statements. It is important to note, however, that this requirement is in respect of losses and liabilities relating to the current and/or previous financial years. It is not intended to put the directors in the position of having to anticipate losses and liabilities relating to future years.

4. Accruals basis

Even before FRS 18 explicitly required the adoption of the accruals basis of accounting for all entities whose financial statements are intended to give a true and fair view, it had been a long-accepted accounting principle in both the Act and earlier accounting standards, which stated that revenue and costs should be recognised as they are earned or accrued rather than when their cash value is received or paid. The only practical difference likely to be felt since FRS 18 was issued is that its definition excludes any reference to matching revenues and costs. The reason given in the statement is that matching of revenue and expenditure should be restricted so that only items that meet the criteria of assets and liabilities should be recognised in the balance sheet. One effect of the change is that the former matching aspect of the accruals concept can no longer be used to justify deferring costs that are not assets. Such costs will now be recognised in the accounting period in which they occur. **35**

5. Separate valuation

The notion of separate valuation is that in determining the aggregate amount of any item, each individual asset or liability making up that item should be determined separately. **37**

In determining the value of "Investments", for example, those investments that are treated as fixed assets should be individually accounted for at cost, less write-downs for any permanent diminution in value. Historically, it was possible to consider them in the aggregate. For instance, if one investment had a market value that was lower than book value, but the market value of all the others exceeded book value to the extent that any shortfall on the first was more than compensated for, it was argued that the investments as a whole were not overstated and, therefore, that no provision against the one overstated investment was required.

Under the current regime, the only statutory exception to the separate valuation rule is that in certain circumstances tangible assets and raw materials and consumables may be included in the financial statements at a fixed quantity and value.

This should not be confused with the case of **legal right of set-off**, where assets and liabilities should be netted against one another. The reason is that in the particular circumstances, the assets and liabilities concerned do not constitute separate assets and liabilities.

D. Accounting conventions

The various accounting conventions observed in the preparation of financial statements are made up of different combinations of **basic accounting concepts**. Before discussing the most commonly adopted accounting conventions (¶50), it is first necessary to understand the nature and operation of these constituent basic accounting concepts. **40**

This is illustrated in the diagram below where the outer circles represent the basic accounting concepts, the choice of which influences the accounting convention adopted.

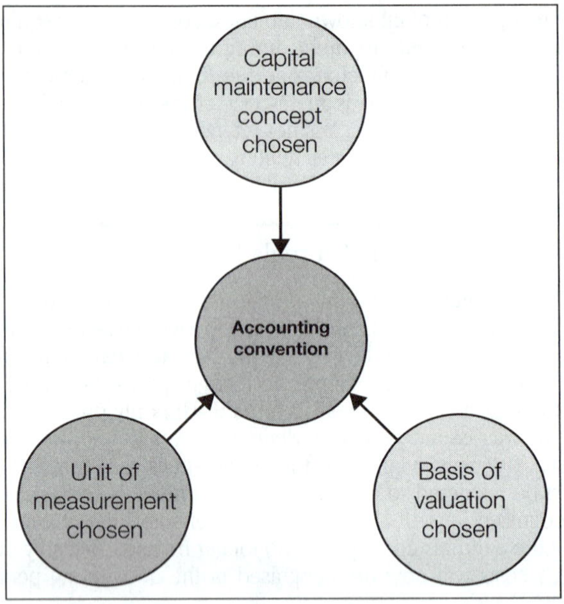

1. Basic accounting concepts

41 All accounting systems depend on the:
- capital maintenance concept adopted,
- basis used to value assets, and
- unit of measurement used.

These are discussed in turn, below.

Capital maintenance concepts

43 Capital maintenance is concerned with the measurement of accounting profit, which is the difference between a company's capital at the beginning and at the end of a reporting period. For these purposes, distributions from, additions to, and repayments of, capital are ignored.

The most widely used concept of capital maintenance is illustrated in the example below.

EXAMPLE In its first accounting period, a dealer in equipment for the construction industry purchases for resale a crane for £50,000, which it sells for £100,000. At the time of the sale, the cost of acquiring an equivalent item is £60,000. Assume there were no other transactions during the accounting period, and no other changes to capital.

	£
Sales	100,000
Cost of sales	50,000
Operating profit	50,000

The accounting profit of £50,000 represents also the amount in excess of the original capital of the business.

The above methodology seeks to preserve the value of the funds invested in the entity, and expresses it in pure monetary terms.

On the other hand, the value of £50,000 could be adjusted by a general purchasing-power index, so that the accounting profit is expressed in terms of its real purchasing power. Although this method is rarely used in statutory reporting and therefore has limited application, the following example explains the effect.

EXAMPLE Assume the same details as in the previous example. However, the factor for inflation between the dates of buying and selling is 5%.

Comparison: monetary capital and general purchasing power capital maintenance concepts		
	Monetary capital (as per previous example)	General purchasing power
	£	£
Sales	100,000	100,000
Cost of sales	50,000	50,000
Operating profit	50,000	50,000
Inflation adjustment – 5%	-	(2,500)
Profit – as adjusted	£ 50,000	£ 47,500

In this case, the inflation adjustment shows the effect of the general increase in prices on the opening financial capital of £50,000. It thereby seeks to ensure that profit is measured only after preserving the opening capital in the business in terms of its purchasing power.

Valuation bases

The basis on which the various assets employed in a business are valued (and revalued, where applicable) depends on the nature of those assets. These bases – such as historical cost, current cost, market value, net realisable value, etc – are discussed in the chapters dealing with the different types of assets. For the purpose of this discussion, however, the use of a specific basis – and the effect it has on measuring profits or losses – plays a part in the determination of the appropriate accounting convention to be adopted. 46

Units of measurement

The unit of measurement chosen affects how profit is determined and reported. Amounts can be reported either in units of monetary currency or in units of constant purchasing power. Financial statements for two years may be denominated in the same currency (e.g., pounds sterling) but as a result of inflation, the purchasing power of these units is not the same. Nevertheless, this is the basis that is used in historical cost accounts, which is the primary basis for accounts prepared under the Companies Act. 48

The use of a unit of constant purchasing power reduces the difficulty of non-comparability. For instance, if all non-monetary assets and liabilities relating to years before the current year (reporting date) are restated by reference to movements in a general price index, such as the retail price index, into the value of pounds at the reporting date. Although there had been attempts in years gone by, when inflation was particularly high, to present inflation-adjusted accounts in the UK, these are no longer required.

2. Most commonly adopted conventions

In theory, many different combinations of the options discussed in the section above are possible. However, most would not result in practical or satisfactory accounting conventions. Therefore, only those that are most widely adopted are discussed below. 50

Historical cost convention

The historical cost convention uses the following mix of basic accounting concepts: 51
- assets are valued at historical cost,
- capital maintenance is on the financial basis,
- unit of measurement is historical-cost pounds sterling.

Although it is the most common accounting convention, its major limitation is that in times of rising prices, certain values reported in the financial statements may be out-dated and not representative. For this reason it is best suited for preparing stewardship accounts and less suitable for investors or potential investors. Furthermore the directors should exercise caution in relying on the historical cost convention for purposes of determining amounts available for distribution. To illustrate, in the example at ¶43, if the directors had distributed the profit of £50,000 there would be insufficient funds remaining to continue trading in the same equipment.

Modified historical cost convention

52 Under this convention, the following mix of basic accounting concepts is used:
- capital maintenance is on the financial basis,
- unit of measurement is generally historical-cost pounds sterling,
- certain fixed assets are revalued and shown at an amount above historical cost.

While the modified historical cost convention gives a better indication of the value to the business of some of its the assets, not all companies revalue their assets. This has the effect of diminishing comparability between different companies.

Unrealised gains from the upward revaluation of assets are generally not recognised in the profit and loss account, suggesting that the gain is of a capital nature to be retained within the business that must be retained in order to ensure that its operating capacity is maintained.

Current purchasing power

53 Under this convention, the following is the mix of basic accounting concepts:
- assets are valued at historical cost,
- capital maintenance is on the financial basis,
- a unit of constant purchasing power is used instead of historical-cost pounds sterling.

All non-monetary items in the financial statements are adjusted by a general price index, which may give investors a better indication of what they can do with their funds in the general economy though not necessarily to the same extent for the specific business concerned.

Current cost accounting

54 In the case of current cost accounting, the mix of basic accounting concepts is more flexible. While assets are valued at their current value to the business, capital maintenance can be on the financial basis with measurement in terms of units of constant purchasing power. Or, capital maintenance is on the operating basis with measurement units in pounds sterling.

Current cost operating profit shows the entity's current trading margins by charging the costs incurred at prices applying when the sales are actually transacted. This provides an indication not only of the business's ability to generate profits from its current operations, but also of its current operating capacity.

Fair value accounting

55 Fair value accounting rules are relatively new, having first been introduced in respect of periods commencing on or after 1 January 2005. These rules allow certain financial instruments (and other assets, such as investment property) to be carried at fair value, with changes being recorded through the profit and loss account. One of the consequences of a company's electing to use the fair value accounting rules is that it will fall within the scope of FRS 26. These issues are discussed more fully in the relevant sections of this volume dealing with the financial instruments and assets concerned.

CHAPTER 2

The substance of transactions
(The principle of substance over form)

OUTLINE ¶¶

In general, financial statements should be provided in sufficient detail to enable users to understand and appreciate the commercial effects of transactions. If there exist any transactions that have resulted in the recognition of assets or liabilities that differ in nature from those of items that would normally be included under the relevant balance sheet captions (and which would therefore interfere with a user's ability to properly appreciate the effect of such transactions), the differences should be explained. **110** FRS 5 (30) – (31)

FRS 5, "The substance of transactions", was issued to answer the need for greater transparency when some companies began to finance their operations using complex arrangements that often resulted in a deliberate separation of the legal title to an asset from access to its benefits and risks. The effect of this so-called "off-balance sheet accounting" was to not only exclude transactions from the balance sheet but also provide a means of manipulating items in the profit and loss account. For instance, a particular transaction that results in a profit on the sale of an asset (with that profit being recorded in the accounts) might, in reality, be part of a larger transaction whose main purpose is to provide a loan. Examples of these arrangements can be found in the discussions of stocks, loans and leases respectively. **111**

Because a reporting entity's financial statements should both report and reflect the substance of the transactions into which it has entered, the provisions of FRS 5 were crafted to ensure that the **substance** of a company's transactions – **as opposed** to their strictly **legal form** – is reported in its financial statements. This is the principle of substance over form. **112** FRS 5 (14)

In the majority of cases, substance and form do not differ. Consequently, FRS 5 applies only to those transactions where there is a discrepancy or where the substance is not readily apparent, e.g., **113**
– legal title of assets and their benefits are separated (consignment stock, factored debts, etc.)
– options, in respect of which their exercise is almost certain, are granted
– a series of separate transactions that create a specific commercial effect only when taken as a whole (e.g., securitisations, project financing, circular finance structures, and take-or-pay agreements, etc.).

A. Scope of FRS 5

1. Entities concerned

115 FRS 5 applies to **all reporting entities** – i.e., companies as well as unincorporated entities such as partnerships – whose financial statements are required to give a true and fair view.

FRS 5 (13a) However, small and medium-sized reporting entities **applying the FRSSE** are exempt from FRS 5, unless they are preparing consolidated financial statements.

2. Transactions concerned

120 Except for a small number of specific exclusions, **all transactions** fall within the scope of FRS 5. The term "transaction" refers either to a single transaction or a series of legally separate elements that together achieve a particular commercial effect.

The **specific exclusions** are:
– forward contracts and futures (e.g., for foreign currencies or commodities)
– foreign exchange and interest rate swaps
– contracts under which a net amount will be paid or received based on a movement in a price or index
– expenditure commitments and orders placed, until the earlier of delivery and payment
– employment contracts.

If these contracts for future performance were not specifically excluded from the scope of FRS 5, the undesirable result would have been that certain transactions would be recorded at the time of ordering or agreeing to order, rather than at the time of payment or delivery (whichever is first).

121 FRS 5 (13) **FRS 5 in combination with other accounting standards** Particular transactions may be subject to various regulations in addition to FRS 5 – e.g., another FRS, SSAP, or by specific statute. Where this is the case, the more specific provisions should be followed.

EXAMPLE Under SSAP 21, "Accounting for Lease and Hire Purchase Contracts", specific rules apply to the measurement and disclosure of leases. The principles set out in FRS 5 are intended to ensure that leases are classified either as finance leases or as operating leases according to their substance – and not only in terms of the 90-percent test prescribed by SSAP 21 (see ¶3428).

B. Analysing transactions

125 In identifying and recognising assets and liabilities in the financial statements, FRS 5 provides rules that apply both to new transactions and in relation to prior transactions (i.e., amounts already reflected in the company's books and records). These are discussed in the paragraphs below.

1. New transactions

130 It is necessary to fully understand the rationale behind transactions in order to determine whether the provisions of FRS 5 apply to them. This involves the following:
– gaining a realistic appreciation of why a transaction is being entered into and why each party to it is involved;

– examining the transaction in the context of whether it is part of a bigger transaction, including the effect of conditional events such as options or guarantees resulting;
– assessing the outcome of the transaction (i.e., what has happened as a result of its having been entered into); and
– identifying which of the parties has borne the risks of the transaction.

The **commercial effect of a complex transaction** might change from year to year as the actual economic outcome becomes clearer over time. When the transaction is first entered into, it has to be analysed and the likely outcome in practice determined in the light of prevailing facts (or best estimates at the time). The substance of the transaction is then recorded in the accounts. Thereafter, the transaction should be monitored in case its practical effect changes. If such a change occurs, it must be accounted for.

An important element of determining the substance of a transaction is to **identify whether** 131
it has given rise to an asset or liability.

Assets are defined as rights or other access to future economic benefits controlled by an FRS 5 (2)
entity as a result of past transactions or events.

Liabilities are defined as an entity's obligations to transfer economic benefits as a result of FRS 5 (4), (18)
past transactions or events.

The following **aspects** of a transaction **can indicate** whether an item gives rise to an **asset** 132
or liability and whether it should, therefore, appear on the balance sheet:
– the legal rights of access to benefits and risks rather than the legal form of those rights,
– if the transaction is connected with other transactions the company might be entering into, and
– the options that may be available to the company.

Once an asset or liability has been **identified** it should be **recognised** in the entity's balance sheet if both of the following conditions are satisfied:
– there is sufficient evidence of the item's existence, and
– the item can be measured at a monetary amount with sufficient reliability.

Separation of title and risk of ownership

Complex transactions often include the separation of legal title from the benefits and risks. 133
It is possible that the legal title to an asset may remain with a company even if it enters into a transaction as a result of which the asset is sold.

For instance, in the case of goods sold under reservation of title until payment is received in full, the associated risks, benefits and obligations of ownership pass to the buyer. In this event, the selling company treats the transaction as a sale while the purchaser, recognising the substance of the arrangement, will account for the goods in its own balance sheet (even though strict legal title has not passed to it).

Similarly, where a lessor enters into a finance lease, it retains the legal title to the asset and in reality is merely receiving a lender's return on investment. The substance of the transaction is such that the asset and related obligation are recorded in the accounts of the lessee. The asset shown in the lessor's books is the amount recoverable under the lease contract rather than the asset itself.

Linked transactions

Transactions are often linked together in such a way that the commercial effect cannot be 134
appreciated without considering the effect of the various transactions as a whole. For **example**, a company sells an asset but enters into a separate agreement to repurchase the asset at a future time. The two transactions are inextricably linked and the commercial effect should be considered as if they were a single transaction. Depending on the repurchase conditions, the transactions could be accounted for as a financing arrangement rather than the sale of an asset.

Options

135 Simple options such as those to purchase shares can be seen as assets. The asset takes the form of the **right to purchase** the underlying shares at a future date, though not the actual shares themselves. However, more complex transactions often involve options in combination with other elements to give one party access to the future benefits associated with an asset despite its not necessarily having legal title to the asset.

FRS 5 (61) In endeavouring to determine the substance of a transaction that includes options, greater weight must be given to those aspects and implications that are more likely to have a **commercial effect in practice**. This involves considering the extent to which there is a genuine commercial possibility that the option will be exercised or, alternatively, that it will not be exercised.

Where there is no genuine commercial possibility that the option will be exercised, the existence of the option should be ignored. On the other hand, where there is no genuine commercial possibility that an option will fail to be exercised, its future exercise should be assumed.

In less extreme cases, further analysis is required to reveal the true commercial objectives of the parties and the commercial rationale for the inclusion of the options in the transaction – and whether the parties have, in substance, either outright or conditional obligations and access to benefits.

FRS 5 (62) In these analyses, it should always be assumed that each of the parties will act in accordance with its best economic interests.

EXAMPLE

1. Where the cost of exercising an option is expected to be lower than the benefits to be obtained by exercising it, it will generally be exercised. In analysing the transaction, the option's exercise should be assumed.

2. If the cost of exercising an option is expected to be higher than the benefits to be obtained in so doing, it can generally be assumed that the option will not be exercised and, thus, ignored when analysing the transaction.

3. Where the seller of an asset retains a call option over the asset and the buyer retains a put option, it is almost certain that either the seller will call back the asset or the buyer will put it back to the seller. If the asset is sold for £200,000 and the options are both priced at £220,000, then if the value of the asset decreases to £150,000, the buyer will put it back to the seller at £220,000. Conversely, if the value moves up to £250,000, the seller will call back the asset for £220,000. In this case the asset should remain on the seller's balance sheet as a financing arrangement as the seller continues to bear the risks and rewards of ownership.

4. Where the seller of an asset retains a call option over the asset and the buyer does not have an option to put the asset back to the seller, the intentions of the seller and the rationale for including the option will require careful consideration. As in **1**. and **2**., above, the price of the option might serve as an indicator of whether or not it will be exercised.

2. Existing assets or liabilities

140 FRS 5 (21) - (22) Assets that have been recognised previously in the financial statements will either:
- **continue to be reflected** therein if there has been no significant change in the entity's benefits or risks associated with it, or
- **be taken off balance sheet** (i.e., totally or partially derecognised) if a transaction involving the asset has the effect of transferring to another party all significant rights, benefits or risks.

a. Continued recognition

141 If an entity retains all significant benefits or risks in respect of an asset, the asset should remain on the balance sheet.

EXAMPLE A Ltd factors its debts in an arrangement with the factor, F Ltd, in terms of which A Ltd is responsible for both slow payment and bad debts.
The asset (debtors) cannot be derecognised because, clearly, A Ltd retains the significant risks associated with the transaction. Even though the legal title to the debts may have passed from A Ltd to F Ltd, in substance the transaction is simply one in which F Ltd supplies finance on which it receives a lender's return.
A Ltd is therefore exposed to the same benefits and risks as it was before the financing. However, it has an additional liability (to repay the finance), which must also be recognised on the balance sheet.

b. Derecognition – in full

Assets may be derecognised if both the rights and the risks in the assets concerned have been removed in their entirety. 143

It is also a condition for derecognition that any funds received in respect of the asset constitute neither a liability nor a form of non-recourse finance that will allow linked presentation (¶160).

EXAMPLE B Ltd sells its debts to F Ltd for a non-refundable amount. This means that F Ltd has no recourse to B Ltd even if the original debtors default on their payments.
In this case, the asset (debtors) should be removed from the books of B Ltd.

c. Derecognition – in part

In special cases, derecognition is allowed on a partial basis if, in respect of the assets concerned, there has been a significant change in the reporting entity's rights to benefits and exposure to risks. 145

This will apply under three circumstances where the description, classification and amount of a previously recognised asset may change – or where a liability may need to be reorganised – and full derecognition is not appropriate.

Transfer of part of the asset

An asset such as a loan might be transferred to another party either proportionately (i.e., including rights to interest and principal) such that cash flows and profits and losses are shared by the transferee and transferor in fixed proportions or by way of splitting the benefit stream (i.e., one party has the risks and benefits relating to the interest and the other has those relating to the principal). 146

Where the asset is **split proportionately**, the proportionate share transferred should be derecognised.

Where there is a **splitting of the benefit streams**, the party retaining the investment in the principal should derecognise the original asset and in its place recognise a new asset: the investment in the non-interest bearing principal. The original carrying amount should be allocated to the principal and the interest stream to determine the cost element of the interest stream. This is compared with the proceeds, to calculate whether there is a profit or loss (which, if applicable, will be reflected in the profit and loss account).

As for the "new" principal, it is generally recognised at a different amount than its original carrying value. The amount at which it is recorded should be such that, as it earns interest – which is added to the principal each year and credited to the profit and loss account – it will reach the amount at the end of its term for which it is to be redeemed.

Transfer of asset for part of its life

This arises where a company **sells an asset** reflected in its balance sheet, but **agrees to repurchase it** at a future time and at a value that fairly reflects the depreciation and use over the period concerned. The entity now has an interest only in the **residual** but, in addition, a new liability to repurchase the item. 148

The difference between the proceeds and the old book value is accounted for, at the time of the sale, as a profit or loss. Whether it is appropriate to account for the residual asset and liability depends on the likely commercial outcome of the arrangement. If repurchase is intended or likely, both residual asset and liability should be recognised. Furthermore, if a loss is likely on repurchase, it should be recognised at the start and accounted for by recording a residual liability in excess of a residual asset (i.e., by making a provision against the asset to reduce it to its recoverable amount).

On the other hand, if the company undertakes to buy back an asset after a set period but at a price so low that it is more likely that the entity to which it was sold will retain the asset (or sell it elsewhere at a higher price), it would not be appropriate for the company to record a residual asset or liability.

Transfer of asset for all of its life but where some benefit or risk is retained by the seller

150 An example of this situation is where a subsidiary is sold but part of the purchase consideration consists of an earn-out arrangement (i.e., an amount related to future earnings of the former subsidiary and to be paid at a later time). In this case, the investment in the subsidiary should be derecognised and a new asset (debtor) recorded in the amount of the company's best estimate of the amount to be received.

Another example is where an asset is sold subject to either a warranty of its condition at the time of sale, or a guarantee in respect of its residual value. Because the selling party has disposed of the benefits and risks associated with the asset, it is permitted to derecognise it; however, it should recognise a liability for any obligation that might arise under the warranty agreement.

3. Specific cases

a. Offset of assets against liabilities

155 In general, assets and liabilities may not be offset against one another.

FRS 5 (29) However, they may be aggregated into a single (net) item where the reporting entity:
– and the other party owe each other **determinable monetary amounts**, denominated in the same currency, or in different but freely convertible currencies, i.e., those for which quoted exchange rates are available in an active market that can rapidly absorb the amount to be offset without significantly affecting the exchange rate;
– has the ability, **assured beyond doubt**, to insist on a net settlement.

b. Linked presentation

160 The linked presentation is a specific type of offset and is used in the disclosure of certain transactions in which **non-recourse finance** is received in respect of specific assets and is repayable only out of the proceeds of those assets.

In this presentation, the asset is shown on the face of the balance sheet but from it is deducted the amount of the non-recourse finance. In this way, the two amounts are linked.

Transactions concerned

162 In general, the linked presentation is available in respect of a transaction that is in substance a financing transaction involving a specific, existing asset (or portfolio of assets) such that:

FRS 5 (26) – (27) – the finance will be repaid only from proceeds generated by the specific item it finances (or by transfer of the item itself) and there is no possibility whatsoever of a claim on the

entity being established other than against funds generated by that item (or against the item itself);
- there must be no provision granting the entity the **right to keep the item** upon repayment of the finance or, where title to the item has been transferred, creating an **obligation to re-acquire** it at any time.

Accounting treatment

Where the above conditions have been met in respect of the **entire amount of the finance** received, the linked presentation is permitted. 164

On the other hand, where these conditions hold for only **part of the finance**, a linked presentation should be used for only that part. In such cases, the amount deducted from the asset on the face of the balance sheet should not include any amount other than from funds generated by the specific item that the reporting entity might be required to make.

If a profit has been made in respect of an arrangement for which linked presentation is used, it should be recognised only to the extent that the non-returnable proceeds exceed the carrying value of the asset in question. Thereafter, any profit or loss should be recognised in the period in which it arises.

The following additional disclosures are required in financial statements where the linked presentation is used:
- the **directors** must state explicitly that the entity is not obliged to support any losses in connection with the transaction,
- that the **provider of the finance has agreed** in writing that it will seek repayment of the finance – as to both principal and interest – only to the extent that sufficient funds are generated by the specific item it has financed.

---

c. Transactions with quasi-subsidiaries

In certain situations, a relationship between two entities may exist which – though legally not a parent-subsidiary relationship – should, for purposes of "substance over form", be treated as such. In these situations, if a legal parent-subsidiary relationship would have required the preparation of consolidated accounts, these should also be prepared in this case. This type of relationship is referred to as "quasi-subsidiary". 170

A quasi-subsidiary (Q) is defined as a company, trust or partnership that – though not fulfilling the definition of a subsidiary – is directly or indirectly controlled by another reporting entity (E) and gives rise to benefits for E that are in substance no different from those that would arise if Q were a subsidiary. FRS 5 (7) - (8)

To determine whether a reporting entity controls a quasi-subsidiary, the criterion is **control** – i.e., the question of whether, in practice, it directs the financial and operating policies of the quasi-subsidiary with a view to gaining economic benefit from it. The rules are the same as those in FRS 2, "Accounting for subsidiaries", where control is defined in terms of the ability of a company to direct these elements. The ability to prevent others from deriving any advantage from the quasi-subsidiary's net assets is also evidence of control.

Where these financial and operating policies are predetermined, e.g., by way of a contract, and as a result the reporting entity enjoys benefits arising from its net assets, the other company should be accounted for as a quasi-subsidiary.

The rules for **excluding** a quasi-subsidiary from consolidation work in the same way as those for normal subsidiaries. Therefore, quasi-subsidiaries **need not be consolidated** if they are immaterial or where the quasi-subsidiary is held exclusively with a view to a subsequent resale and has not been previously consolidated. Similarly, where there are severe long-term restrictions that substantially hinder the exercise of the company's rights over the assets or the management of the other entity, this indicates that the company does not have the requisite control over that other entity for it to be considered a quasi-subsidiary. 172

EXAMPLE

1. B is a pension fund. Although A is significantly represented on its board of trustees, the benefits of the decisions made accrue to the pension-scheme members and not to A.

2. Although A has a participating interest in B, it can be shown that it does not actually exercise a dominant influence over it.

The exceptions from consolidation given in the Companies Act – i.e., situations where there is (1) disproportionate expense and undue delay, and (2) a significant difference between the activities of the quasi-subsidiary and the rest of the group – cannot be used under FRS 5 to justify the non-consolidation of a quasi-subsidiary, just as they cannot be used under FRS 2 for non-consolidation of legal subsidiaries.

Accounting for quasi-subsidiaries

175 There are two possible ways to account for a quasi-subsidiary:
- consolidation, or
- the linked-presentation basis.

FRS 5 (35) Where **consolidation** is used, the quasi-subsidiary should be consolidated into the group's financial statements in the same way as for other subsidiaries. The consolidated financial statements will therefore include the quasi-subsidiary's assets, liabilities, profits, losses and cash flows (after intra-group trading and profits have been eliminated).

If a company has no legal subsidiaries (and therefore does not prepare consolidated financial statements), it should provide, along with its individual financial statements, consolidated financial statements including the quasi-subsidiary. These consolidated financial statements should be presented with the same prominence as its individual financial statements.

176 In certain circumstances, a quasi-subsidiary's assets and liabilities may be included in the group's consolidated financial statements using the **linked presentation**. This is possible where, e.g., a quasi-subsidiary company (B) puts some of its assets into another entity (A) to be financed, and "ring-fences" the transaction. Thus, if there is no recourse at all to the group's other assets – and the other conditions for linked presentation are met (¶162) – the group may account for B in its consolidated financial statements using the linked presentation.

FRS 5 (38) The presence of quasi-subsidiaries must be disclosed in the financial statements and a summary given of each one in the notes. (However, if the reporting entity has more than one quasi-subsidiary of a similar nature, a combined summary may be given.) The summarised financial statements should show separately each main heading in the balance sheet, profit and loss account, statement of total recognised gains and losses and cash flow statement for which there is a material item, together with comparative figures.

C. Disclosure issues

180 The 2006 Companies Act brought about new statutory disclosure requirements for off balance sheet arrangements, and they are expressed differently from those of FRS 5. In general, FRS 5 requires that financial statements should give sufficient detail to allow users to understand the **commercial effects of transactions** irrespective of whether an asset or liability has been recognised (or ceased to be recognised).

181 s 410A CA 2006 The Act's requirements state that if a company has been party to arrangements that are not reflected in the balance sheet, and at the reporting date the risks or benefits arising out of such arrangements are material, the **nature and business purposes** of the arrangement, together with their **financial impact**, must be recorded in the notes. However, this informa-

tion need be given only to the extent necessary for enabling an assessment of the financial position.

While compliance with FRS 5 may not necessarily result in compliance with the Act, in most cases there is sufficient overlap. However, additional disclosure to satisfy company legislation may be required in the following cases: 182
- where the reporting entity is a party to a transaction that does not give rise to any assets or liabilities being recorded on the balance sheet, or
- where a complex transaction results in assets or liabilities that are different in nature from ones normally included under the relevant statutory balance sheet headings.

CHAPTER 3

Regulatory framework for financial accounting

OUTLINE ¶¶

SECTION 1

UK reporting

The system of accounting in the UK has been derived from a number of sources: statute, accounting standards, and precedent. In addition, accounting in the UK is increasingly being influenced by international practice. This latter development is discussed from ¶250. 200

Generally Accepted Accounting Practice (GAAP) is a widely used term that refers to the accounting system as synthesised from the various sources and components. Because there are many different classes or kinds of accounting entities, the rules applying to them are bound to differ from type to type. What they do have in common, however, is that they consist of two basic elements: mandatory rules and non-mandatory rules.

The **mandatory elements** include: 202

1. Legislation, i.e.,
- **Company law**,
- any **other rules** enacted by law or laid down by regulatory bodies.
2. Accounting standards, i.e.,
- **Financial Reporting Standards** (FRSs) and **Statements of Standard Accounting Practice** (SSAPs) issued originally, or adopted, by the Accounting Standards Board (ASB).
- **Abstracts** issued by the ASB's Urgent Issues Task Force (UITF).
- In respect of listed companies or those whose shares are traded on the Alternative Investment Market (AIM), the "**Listing Rules**" issued by the Financial Services Authority (FSA), and the "**AIM Rules**" respectively.

The **non-mandatory** sources – also referred to as the **advisory** sources – are: 204

- **Financial Reporting Exposure Drafts** (FREDs) issued by the ASB in advance of an FRS and which invite comments from practitioners. These generally indicate the thinking of the

ASB in relation to various areas, and they should be followed unless they contradict an existing FRS.
– The **Statement of Principles for Financial Reporting** issued by the ASB. This statement, which is not an accounting standard, and does not have the status of one, nevertheless provides a frame of reference. See ¶240.
– **Operating and Financial Review** (OFR) was published as a non-mandatory document although compliance was encouraged. The OFR is discussed in detail at ¶4700.
– Statements and recommendations from **professional or industrial bodies** – e.g., Statements of Recommended Practice (**SORPs**), which suggest accounting practices and policies to be followed by specialised sectors or industries, ICAEW **Technical Releases**, and ICAEW accounting recommendations.
– The **UK Corporate Governance Code** (see ¶5200) and **Reports** of various committees set up from time to time to report on specific matters (e.g., Hampel Committee, Higgs Review, Smith report, etc).
– Pronouncements of **international professional** bodies and committees.
– Established practice, i.e., practices that are **generally accepted**, even if they have not been officially codified in the literature.

A. The financial reporting infrastructure

210 The regulatory structure existing in the UK has its roots in the Dearing Report (issued in the late 1980s) on the setting of accounting standards. The key bodies entrusted with regulating and administering the financial reporting regime in place at present are discussed below.

Financial Reporting Council – FRC

212 Established in 1990, the FRC is instrumental in:
– setting, monitoring, and enforcing accounting and auditing standards,
– overseeing the regulatory activities of the professional accountancy bodies, and
– promoting high standards of corporate governance.

The FRC's original remit was extended to include a more active role in relation to corporate governance: it seeks a proactive role in relation to compliance with company law and accounting standards, and it assumes new responsibilities in relation to audit and auditing standards as well as oversight of the self-regulatory professional bodies.

In addition, the Companies Bill, currently with Parliament, will give the subsidiary bodies of the FRC new powers to exercise statutory functions in relation to accounting and auditing on behalf of the Secretary of State for Trade and Industry.

The FRC has two subsidiaries, the Accounting Standards Board (ASB) and the Financial Reporting Review Panel (FRRP). In addition, in April 2004, after a review of the UK regulatory framework by the Department of Trade and Industry (DTI), three new official regulatory boards were established under the umbrella of the FRC.

Accounting Standards Board – ASB

215 The ASB is the authority that has been prescribed by statutory instrument as the standard-making body under the Companies Act 1985. The accounting standards (designated FRSs) that it issues, amends and withdraws are "accounting standards" for the purpose of the Act's accounting requirements.

216 The ASB also collaborates with accounting standard-setters from other countries and the International Accounting Standards Board (IASB) in order to influence the development of international standards and to ensure that local standards are developed with due regard to international developments and thinking.

217 Another of its functions is to develop principles to guide it in establishing accounting standards. The ASB can issue accounting standards on its own authority, without the approval of

any other body. As a rule, the development of a new accounting standard involves at least two formal consultation documents: a Discussion Paper, and a Financial Reporting Exposure Draft (FRED).

The ASB initiated a programme to converge UK accounting standards with international accounting standards – see ¶250.

Urgent Issues Task Force – UITF

The main role of the UITF is to assist the ASB in cases where unsatisfactory or conflicting interpretations have developed (or may be likely to develop) about a requirement of an accounting standard or the Companies Act. The UITF fulfils its function not by writing new accounting standards, but in seeking to reach a consensus among its fifteen voting members who are drawn both from the accounting profession and from the wider business community. 220

While the UITF makes draft Abstracts available, it generally offers less time for comments than is the case with accounting standards, thus allowing it to respond more quickly to emerging issues than the ASB is able to. 221

The ASB regards UITF Abstracts as generally accepted accounting practice in the specific areas they deal with, and as part of the body of accounting pronouncements that should be followed. Generally, the expectation of the ASB is that it will adopt a UITF consensus – unless it finds that it conflicts with law, accounting standards, its own policy, or future plans. 222

Financial Reporting Review Panel – FRRP

The FRRP is empowered to examine material departures from the Act's accounting requirements – including departures from accounting standards. The FRRP was granted authority by the Secretary of State for Trade and Industry to discuss these departures with a company's directors and, if necessary, seek an order from the court to remedy them. 225

The FRRP restricts itself to the following: 226
- public limited companies, unless they are subsidiaries in small or medium-sized groups,
- companies within a group headed by a public limited company,
- companies not qualifying as small or medium-sized,
- companies within a group that do not qualify as small or medium-sized as defined by the Act.

Other companies, i.e., those that do not fall into any of the above categories, are dealt with by the DTI itself.

Professional Oversight Board for Accountancy – POBA

The remit of the POBA is: 230
- to provide an independent oversight of the regulation of the auditing profession by the recognised supervisory and qualifying bodies;
- to monitor the quality of the auditing function in relation to large companies; and
- to provide an independent oversight of the regulation of the accountancy profession by the professional accountancy bodies such as the Association of Chartered Certified Accountants (ACCA).

Auditing Practices Board – APB

The remit of the APB is to play an influential role in the development of auditing and assurance services standards including ethical standards governing the conduct of the industry. 233

Accountancy Investigation and Discipline Board – AIDB

The purpose of the AIDB is to offer an effective and transparent investigation and disciplinary scheme to handle cases of public (national) interest. Cases involving little public interest will continue to be dealt with by the individual accountancy bodies such as the ICAEW and the ACCA. 236

B. The Statement of Principles for Financial Reporting

240 The objective of financial statements is to provide financial information about the financial position, performance and financial adaptability of an enterprise so as to be useful to users in reaching decisions. In order to ensure that the requisite reliance could be placed in financial statements, basic standards need to be set and observed by all parties.

241 The ASB published its Statement of Principles for Financial Reporting in December 1999. Its primary purpose is to:
- provide a coherent **frame of reference** to help the ASB itself (and others who may, in conjunction with the ASB, play a part in the standard-setting process) in developing new accounting standards and reviewing existing ones,
- clarify the **concepts** underlying specific standards,
- ensure **consistency** in the preparation of standards.

242 The Statement of Principles is not an accounting standard; it describes fundamental principles but does not contain requirements on how financial statements should be prepared or presented. Its focus is on financial statements that are required to give a **true and fair view** (see ¶4). Company accounts should continue to be prepared under the requirements of company law and accounting standards.

243 The Statement's principles are also applicable to financial statements contained in the interim reports, preliminary announcements and summary financial statements of listed UK companies, although additional considerations (e.g., the Listing Rules, among others) may be relevant in the context of those statements.

The ASB's Statement of Principles for Financial Reporting is based on the IASB framework and is closely in line with it in identifying present and potential investors as the target users. The ASB includes in the objective the role financial statements can play in the assessment of the stewardship of management and their usefulness for making economic decisions.

244 The ASB has published for comment an exposure draft expanding on how the principles underlying financial reporting should be interpreted in the context of **public benefit entities**. It is intended to operate alongside the Statement of Principles, to underpin the preparation and presentation of public benefit entities' financial statements, just as the Statement of Principles does in respect of general purpose financial statements.

The exposure draft develops proposals relating to liabilities for commitments to provide public benefits; presentation of the residual interest and disclosure of restrictions over assets; voluntary gifts; capital contributions, and capital grants.

SECTION 2

International reporting

A. Convergence with IFRS

250 A major factor driving the development of new accounting standards is the requirement for international harmonisation and convergence with International Financial Reporting Standards (IFRS), an agenda the ASB has been following over the past number of years. Its intention has been not to independently issue new UK standards, but instead to work with

the IASB on its international projects and bring IFRS into the UK as accounting standards where appropriate. UK standard setting is now, therefore, firmly within the context of international convergence.

Differences between UK standards and IFRS have been reducing in the light of the ASB's agenda of alignment and the fact that the IASB is currently working extensively with national standard setters to achieve global convergence and reflect international practice. 252

UK companies have gradually been moving towards – and will have *de facto* adopted – international standards simply by remaining in compliance with UK GAAP.

Where there are differences between UK and International GAAP, these are likely to be reflected mainly in regard to **smaller companies**, particularly those to which FRSSE applies (for which an international counterpart – IFRS for SMEs – was issued in July 2009). These companies will be allowed to continue reporting under FRSSE and need not comply with international standards.

On the other hand, the issuing of the IFRS for SMEs does not mean that UK companies will be able simply to adopt it. The ASB has, after a long process of discussion and development, put forward its proposals for the future of financial reporting in the UK and the Republic of Ireland. The Exposure Draft issued in October 2010 sets out proposals for a three-tier reporting framework, which aims to balance the needs of preparers and users of accounts.

The Board's proposals envisage a differential reporting regime based on public accountability, as follows:

- Tier 1, consisting of publicly accountable entities, which would apply IFRS as adopted by the EU;
- Tier 2, representing all other UK entities with the exception of those eligible to apply the FRSSE – they may apply the IFRS for SMEs;
- Tier 3, small entities that elect to continue to apply the FRSSE.

In essence, these recommendations mean that there should be no change for quoted groups or those eligible to report under FRSSE. For those in between, the ASB is proposing a new standard based on the IFRS for SMEs, which preserves the overarching drive towards convergence.

The new reporting structure could be in place from 1 July 2013.

In the United States, the IASB together with the FASB have issued a discussion paper dealing with a common conceptual framework that both Boards can use in **developing new accounting standards**. The paper sets out the preliminary views of the two bodies on the objective of financial reporting and the qualities that make the information useful for decision-making. 253

B. Adoption of IFRS

The point in time at which a company is required to adopt international reporting standards depends on its particular circumstances. 256

Since 1 January 2005, **listed companies** have been required to produce their group accounts in accordance with IFRS. **Other companies** are free to choose whether to adopt IFRS or to continue to prepare their accounts in accordance with UK GAAP.

In point of fact, however, this choice is not entirely free because – for certain companies – electing to adopt IFRS may be advisable. For **example**, companies planning to list their shares or those belonging to groups in which fellow members are required to use IFRS would probably be well-advised to make the election to adopt IFRS.

UK **parent companies** should bear in mind that if they make the early, optional election, this choice will automatically invoke the election by all subsidiaries. Given that companies are not allowed to "undo" the election later and revert to UK reporting, this decision should be taken with due and careful consideration. 257

258 UK companies that do **adopt international standards for the first time** must apply the provisions of IFRS 1, "First time adoption of International Financial Reporting Standards", which applies to **first IFRS statements** and, for listed companies required to publish them, **interim financial reports**. These financial statements will require retrospective application of all IFRSs in force at the balance sheet date.

259 IFRS 1 (7) An entity must use the same **accounting policies** in its opening IFRS balance sheet and throughout all periods presented in their first IFRS accounts. These accounting policies must comply with each IFRS effective at the entity's first reporting date under IFRS.

261 First-time adopters must prepare an **opening balance sheet** at the date of transition to IFRS. This statement is not for publication but forms the starting point for its accounting under international standards.

263 IFRS 1 (10) Entities must, in their opening IFRS balance sheet:
– recognise all assets and liabilities whose recognition is required by IFRSs;
– not recognise items as assets or liabilities if IFRSs do not require such recognition;
– reclassify items that it recognised under UK GAAP as one type of asset, liability, or component of equity, but are a different type of asset, liability, or component of equity under IFRS; and
– apply IFRSs in measuring all recognised assets and liabilities.

265 The accounting policies used in the opening IFRS balance sheet may differ from those used before. The resulting adjustments should be taken directly to opening reserves (generally, retained earnings).

267 In addition, these financial statements must contain at least one year's **comparative figures**. However, where companies present historical information in respect of periods before the first period, this historical information need not comply with IFRS, although the company must:
– clearly label the earlier data as having been prepared under UK GAAP,
– disclose the nature of the main adjustments that would be necessary to make the information comply with IFRS, though the adjustments themselves need not be given.

269 IFRS 1 (38)-(39) The company must explain how the transition from UK GAAP to that under IFRS has affected its reported financial position, financial performance, and cash flows. To comply with this requirement, the first IFRS accounts should include:
– reconciliations of equity reported under UK GAAP with equity reported under IFRS for both the date of transition and the end of the latest period presented in the most recent financial statements under UK GAAP,
– a reconciliation of the profit or loss reported under UK GAAP for the latest period in its most recent annual financial statements with its profit or loss under IFRS for the same period, and
– where the company recognised or reversed impairment losses for the first time in preparing its opening IFRS balance sheet, any disclosures that IAS 36, "Impairment of Assets", would require.

These reconciliations must give sufficient detail to enable users to understand the material adjustments made.

PART 2

Profit and loss account

CHAPTER 1

Form and content of the profit and loss account

OUTLINE ¶¶

350 **Every company** has an obligation to prepare a profit and loss account that shows a true and fair view of the entity's results for the financial year. **All gains or losses** recognised in the financial statements for the period should be accounted for in an entity's profit and loss account, **except** gains or losses that are required (or permitted) to be taken directly to reserves.

A company **is free to select** one of four profit and loss account formats set out in Schedule 1 SI 2008/410 "The Large and Medium-sized Companies and Groups (Accounts and Reports) Regulations 2008", with additional alternative formats arrangements available to **small companies** (¶6000). The formats for banking and insurance companies are outside the scope of this book.

The formats incorporated in the Companies Act and the requirements of FRS 3 "Reporting financial reporting" are presented in this chapter, covering the **key disclosures required** on the face of the profit and loss account, or in the notes to the accounts. The profit and loss disclosure requirements of other accounting standards and pronouncements are also covered in this chapter, including developments on **revenue recognition**.

The **key differences** between UK GAAP and the requirements of the IAS (IFRS) are also reviewed.

SECTION 1

Profit and loss formats

352 The **general provisions** and formats for the profit and loss account in the financial statements are laid down in the Companies Act and apply to all companies.

These formats have been further modified by the requirements of FRS 3. In addition specific information must be provided by way of notes to the financial statements.

The formats and content of the financial statements will now be set out in regulations (Schedule 1 SI 2008/410) drafted under the framework of the Companies Act 2006. Although **some regulations** have been issued, they contain only minor adjustments to the formats contained in the Companies Act 1985. For instance, for small companies, the only adjustment is that the line "Operating profit and loss" has been omitted.

Choice of Companies Act formats

353

Type of format	Layout	Reference
Format 1 – Analysis of costs by type of operation and function	Vertical	¶361
Format 2 – Analysis of costs by type of expense	Vertical	¶552
Format 3 – Analysis of costs by type of operation and function	Horizontal	¶552
Format 4 – Analysis of costs by type of expense	Horizontal	¶552

Every profit and loss account **must adopt** one of the four formats, which must be in the order and under the headings and sub-headings given. The **choice of format depends on** a number of factors, depending on the nature of the company's activities and organisation of the accounting system. For example, Format 1 may be chosen by a manufacturing company whose major expenses are the cost of producing its goods, while Format 2 may be suited to a service company whose major expense is its staff costs.

MEMO POINTS Consolidated financial statements must comply with the provisions of Schedule 6 SI 2008/410 which governs the form and content plus the Companies Act 2006 Section 404 (1).

355 **Change of format** The company is required to adopt the same format for its financial statements for each financial year, unless the directors are of the opinion that **special reasons** merit a change. If this is the case, then details of the change and the reasons supporting it should be given in the notes to the accounts.

The following details must be disclosed:
- details of the change in format;
- reasons for the departure; and
- effects on the view given by the financial statements.

Companies Act formats

Format 1 is the most widely used in practice, and together with **Format 3** discloses the entity's cost of sales and gross profit, as well as classifying expenditure in terms of administration and distribution costs. 358

Format 1 is more suited to a manufacturing company, since **Format 2** does not allow for separate disclosure of cost of sales or gross profit, unless additional information beyond that required by the Companies Act is given.

Formats 1 and 3 contain the same headings, in a vertical and horizontal style respectively.

Format 1 is the only format that requires gross profit or loss to be shown as a separate item on the face of the profit and loss account. Gross profit or loss can also be derived in Format 3, but is not required to be shown in the profit and loss account.

Formats 2 and 4 tend to be less popular, both in terms of production and presentation.

Examples of Formats 2, 3 and 4 are shown in section 6.

FRS 3 requirements

FRS 3 has introduced a range of **additional disclosures** within the Schedule 4 formats, in order to highlight a number of important components of financial performance. Principally, FRS 3 requires **every profit and loss account** between turnover and operating profit (or loss), to be analysed between **continuing and discontinued operations**, with the results of acquisitions separately disclosed as a part of continuing operations. 360 FRS 3(b) (20)

Details of **exceptional items** should also be given, particularly concerning:
- profits or losses on sale or termination of an operation;
- costs of fundamental reorganisation or restructuring; and
- profits or losses on disposal of fixed assets.

The **analysis of turnover and operating profit** must be on the face of the profit and loss account while other headings (i.e. cost of sales) can be covered in the notes to the accounts. FRS 3 also requires additional headings (shown in bold in Format 1 below) to be given.

FRS 3 requests a sub-total for "operating profits" or "losses" and three additional format headings. FRS 3 stipulates that information be given in respect of any **exceptional transactions** in terms of value or size (see ¶474 for more detail).

MEMO POINTS A number of minor changes to FRS 3 have been proposed in FRED 22 "Revision to FRS 3, Reporting Financial Performance" (see ¶530).

Format 1

361

SCHEDULE 4	
PROFIT AND LOSS ACCOUNT: FORMAT 1 (Incorporating the requirements of FRS 3)	
1	**Turnover**
2	Cost of sales (A)
3	Gross profit or loss
4	Distribution costs (A)
5	Administration costs
6	Other operating income
	Operating profit and loss (1)
	Profits or losses on the sale or termination of an operation (2)
	Cost of a fundamental reorganisation or restructuring (2)

SCHEDULE 4	
PROFIT AND LOSS ACCOUNT: FORMAT 1 (Incorporating the requirements of FRS 3)	
	Profits or losses on disposal of fixed assets (2)
7	Income from shares in group undertakings
8	Income from participating interests (B)
9	Income from other fixed asset investments (B)
10	Other interest receivable and similar income (B)
11	Amounts written off investments
12	Interest payable and similar charges (C)
	Profit or loss on ordinary activities before taxation (3)
13	Tax on profit and loss on ordinary activities
14	Profit or loss on ordinary activities after taxation
15	Minority interests (D)
16	Extraordinary income
17	Extraordinary charges
18	Extraordinary profit and loss
19	Tax on extraordinary profit and loss
20	Minority interests (E)
21	Other taxes not shown under the above items
22	Profit or loss for the financial year
	Dividends paid and proposed (3)
	Amounts set aside or proposed to be set aside to, or withdrawn or proposed to be withdrawn from, reserves (3)

MEMO POINTS 1. Headings **in bold type** must be shown on the face of the profit and loss account. Headings with numbers 1 and 2 in brackets attached are required by FRS 3. Headings with number 3 in brackets are not included in the profit and loss formats, although these are required by the Companies Act.
2. Letters in brackets (A-E). For an explanation see ¶554.
3. All headings required by the Companies Act to be included in the profit and loss formats, have Arabic numbers. Items represented by Arabic numbers in any of the formats **may be combined if either**:
– their individual amounts are not material for assessing the results of the company for the financial year; or
– the combination facilitates the assessment of truth and fairness.
However, **in the latter case**, the individual value of any items so combined must be disclosed in a note to the financial statements.
4. A company **has the option** of showing any item in the profit and loss account in greater detail than that required by the format. A company's profit and loss account may include an item of income or expenditure, not otherwise covered in the format adopted.

SECTION 2

Primary disclosures

364 In this section, the key disclosures required on the face of the profit and loss account by the Companies Act and FRS 3 and, to a lesser extent, by FRS 9 are reviewed. This section will **mirror the structure of Format 1**, as this is the most common form of presentation adopted. Any detail supporting the key disclosures will normally be given not on the face of the profit and loss account itself but in the notes to the accounts.

a. Turnover

All Schedule 4 formats require disclosure of turnover. 368

Turnover is defined as amounts derived from the provision of goods and services falling within the company's ordinary activities, **after deduction of**:
- trade discounts;
- value added tax; and
- other taxes;

and in the case of consolidated financial statements:
- intra-group sales; or
- group share of turnover of associates and joint ventures.

Turnover **can also include** other immaterial income from other sources (see ¶383). Group turnover should include only sales made to external customers and all **intra-group sales** must be eliminated on consolidation.

There are a number of **different methods for recognising income**. As such, the accounting policy for recognising turnover must be stated in the notes to the accounts. In the majority of cases, a simple statement to the effect that turnover represents the amounts receivable, excluding VAT, in respect of goods and services supplied, has become the norm.

More **specialised businesses** should give additional information on turnover, to enable the reader of the accounts to better understand the nature of the income generated by the business. Examples include house builders, software companies, seasonal industries, or companies providing extended warranties on electronic goods, where the timing of recognition of the turnover is important (see ¶520).

Segmental analysis Where the company has supplied different geographical market segments that, in the opinion of the directors, **differ substantially** from each other, then the 370
amount of turnover attributable to each such market should be stated in the notes to the accounts. The **same criteria** applies to turnover by type of business activity.

Where classes of business and markets do not differ substantially from each other, the analysis of turnover can be treated as one class.

There may be circumstances where, in the opinion of the directors, the disclosure of any information required to be given in respect of geographical and market analysis of turnover would be **seriously prejudicial** to the interests of the company. In such cases, this information need not be disclosed but a note explaining this should be given in the notes to the accounts.

A more detailed treatment of segmental reporting and the requirements of SSAP 25 "Segmental Reporting" is given in ¶750.

Joint ventures In the **consolidated profit and loss account**, the investor's share of its joint 372
venture's turnover should also be shown, but not as part of the group turnover. In the FRS 9 (21)
segmental analysis too, the investor's share of its joint venture's turnover should be distinguished from the turnover for the group itself.

EXAMPLE **ABC Ltd**
Consolidated profit and loss account (extract)

	£ m	£ m
Turnover: group and share of joint ventures	320	
Less: Share of joint ventures turnover	(120)	
Group turnover		200
Cost of sales		(120)

The topic of joint ventures is covered in greater detail in ¶7410.

Associates In **consolidated financial statements**, group turnover should not include that 373
of a parent's associates. However, as a memorandum item in the profit and loss account, a

total combining the investor's share of its associates' turnover with the rest of the group may be shown, clearly distinguishing between group turnover and that of the associate.

Segmental analysis of turnover and operating profit, if given, should clearly distinguish between that of the group and that of its associates.

Associate undertakings are covered in greater detail in ¶7320.

374 FRS 3 (14) **Continuing and discontinued operations** Turnover should be analysed, on the face of the profit and loss account, between:
- continuing operations;
- acquisitions as a component of continuing operations; and
- discontinued operations.

The **specific rules** regarding the detailed analyses required in relation to continuing and discontinued operations are covered in detail in paragraphs ¶460 to ¶472 below.

b. Cost of sales

376 FRS 3 requires that cost of sales be analysed between the same categories as turnover, as set out in ¶374 above.

The costs of sales category **typically includes** the following costs generated from ordinary activities:
- purchases of direct materials;
- direct labour;
- production overheads;
- depreciation or diminution in value of productive assets; and
- research and development costs.

The cost of sales figure is also **subject to adjustments**, in respect of opening and closing stock, work in progress or own work capitalised.

376-1 **Negative goodwill** Where the amortisation of negative goodwill (¶1062) is material and has been deducted in arriving at the disclosed figure for cost of sales, distribution or administrative costs, it should be analysed separately on the face of the profit and loss account. It is a requirement of the Companies Act that positive and negative goodwill are not offset against each other.

376-2 **Directors' emoluments** The emoluments paid to directors should be included within the category most closely related to their function within the company. For example, the emoluments of the production director, under Format 1, typically would be included within cost of sales.

c. Gross profit or loss

378 **Under Format 1**, gross profit or loss, representing the difference between turnover and the cost of sales, should be shown as a separate category. The gross profit or loss can also be deduced from the information given in Format 3, but is not required to be shown in the profit and loss account.

Gross profit should be analysed, between continuing operations, acquisitions (as a component of continuing operations) and discontinued operations. This information may be disclosed in a note to the financial statements.

The manner in which expenditure is analysed under **Formats 2 and 4** makes it difficult to show gross profit or loss, unless additional information to that required by the Companies Act is given.

d. Distribution costs

Distribution costs generally comprise some or all of the following: 379

a. Sales related costs
- selling salaries, national insurance, and pension costs;
- sales commissions and other incentives;
- sales promotion costs; and
- cash discounts on sales.

b. Finished goods
- warehousing expenses;
- drivers' wages, national insurance, pension costs and expenses;
- transportation outwards, including vehicle running expenses;
- depreciation of vehicles; and
- repairs and maintenance of relevant premises, vehicles and equipment.

c. Direct overheads
- warehouse rent, rates, light and heat; and
- telephones.

The **inclusion of overhead items** such as printing and stationery, cleaning, staff expenses, and general expenses will depend on the sophistication of the accounting system, in identifying, analysing and allocating these costs to the correct distribution cost centre.

e. Administrative expenses

Examples of administrative costs are as follows: 380

a. Staff costs
- administration salaries;
- national insurance;
- pension costs; and
- other staff costs.

b. Equipment costs
- motor vehicle running expenses;
- hire of office equipment;
- depreciation of vehicles and equipment; and
- repairs and maintenance of relevant premises, vehicles and equipment.

c. Office overheads
- rent, rates, light and heat;
- telephones;
- printing, stationery and postage;
- legal and professional fees; and
- general expenses.

f. Other operating income

Other operating income includes all other income generated from ordinary activities of business, with the exception of income from investments and other income receivable. For the majority of companies this item is often not material and is included as part of turnover. Examples include royalties, commissions and sundry rentals. 383

g. Operating profit or loss

In addition to the heading required by the Companies Act, FRS 3 requires a sub-total for operating profit, which should be analysed on the face of the profit and loss account, between continuing operations, acquisitions (as a component of continuing operations) and 384 discontinued operations. Where an acquisition **has a material impact** on a major business segment, this should be disclosed and explained.

FRS 3 (14) **For most entities**, operating profit is normally profit before income from shares in group undertakings. However, income from associated undertakings or from other participating interests may be considered to be part of operating profit (e.g. investment holding companies).

FRS 9 (21) In the **consolidated accounts**, the group's share of operating profit of joint ventures and associates must be shown immediately after group operating profit.

---

h. Profits or losses on sale or termination of an operation

385 Profits or losses and **any provisions** relating to the sale or termination of an operation should be shown separately on the face of the profit and loss account, after operating profit and before interest, and included under the appropriate heading of discontinued operations. Only profits or losses **on a material disposal** of a business or business segment need be disclosed.

FRS 3 **does not provide specific guidance** in distinguishing which particular items should be included in the "trading" headings covering discontinued operations, as opposed to being presented under the heading of profits and losses on sale or termination of an operation. A practical approach would be to allocate the relevant income and expenses as follows:

a. Operating results of discontinued operations should include trading transactions of the sold or terminated entity up to the date of sale or termination carried out as part of the normal business of the entity (e.g. turnover and cost of sales from routine trading); and

b. Profit or losses on sale or termination of an operation should only include the financial effect of transactions arising as a result of the sale or termination, such as the proceeds on the sale of a part of the business and the legal fees involved in the sale.

386 FRS 3 (41) **Income and costs** Any income and costs **associated with a sale or termination** that has not been completed at the balance sheet date or within three months thereafter, or by the date on which the financial statements are approved, if earlier, should be included in the continuing category. In some cases, it may be appropriate to disclose separately in a note to the profit and loss account, the results of operations that although ongoing, are in the process of being discontinued. As such, the reader of the financial statements will have an appreciation of the consequences of the forthcoming termination/sale.

387 FRS 3 (15) **Material disposals** The profit or loss on each material disposal (or termination) should be disclosed in the financial statements.

There may be circumstances **where the net amount of profits or losses** on the sale or termination of an operation are not material, but the gross profits or losses are material. In such instances, the relevant heading should still appear on the face of the profit and loss account with a reference to a related note analysing the profits and losses.

388 FRS 3 (17) **Reorganisation or restructuring** The reorganisation or restructuring of continuing operations resulting from a sale or termination should be treated as part of continuing operations.

390 **Profit or loss on disposal of a subsidiary** Where a company **sells only part of its holding** in a subsidiary, with the retained holding classified as a subsidiary undertaking, a profit or loss on disposal will occur. In the **individual company's accounts**, the determination of the profit or loss will represent the difference between the proceeds received and the carrying value of the shares sold, reflecting the profit or loss on disposal of a fixed asset, which should be recognised on the face of the profit and loss account (see ¶398 below).

In the **consolidated accounts**, the group will still hold a subsidiary as it has not disposed of the operation itself. The operating profit is not affected by the sale as the subsidiary's operating profit will have been wholly reported within the group's operating profit. The issue is whether the profit or loss on disposal should be included before operating profit or treated as an exceptional item.

If the **undertaking is no longer a subsidiary** after the disposal of part of the holding by the parent company, and becomes an associate or simple investment, or where a complete disposal has taken place, then the associated profit or loss arising in the group accounts should be treated as an exceptional item.

i. Costs of a fundamental reorganisation or restructuring

The costs of a fundamental reorganisation or restructuring should be shown separately on the face of the profit and loss account after operating profit and before interest, and included under the appropriate heading of continuing or discontinued operations. **396** FRS 3 (20)

Where the costs of a fundamental reorganisation or restructuring **are not material**, but the gross profits or losses are material, the relevant heading should still appear on the face of the profit and loss account with a reference to a related note analysing the profits and losses.

Where companies have merged, **merger expenses** should be charged to the profit and loss account of the combined entity at the effective date of the merger, and classed as reorganisation or restructuring expenses. FRS 6 (19)

j. Profits or losses on disposal of fixed assets

Profits or losses on disposal of fixed assets **should be shown separately** on the face of the profit and loss account after operating profit and before interest, and included under the appropriate heading of continuing or discontinued operations. **398** FRS 3 (20)

The ASB approach, under FRS 3, is that **performance should be reviewed** by considering the profit and loss account and the STRGL together. A valuation surplus in one year should be recognised as an unrealised gain in that year in the STRGL as part of the financial performance for the year.

Accounting treatment 1. The **profit or loss on disposal** of an asset should be accounted for in the profit and loss account of the period in which the disposal occurs. This should be the difference between the net sale proceeds and the net carrying amount, whether carried at historical cost (less any provisions made) or at a valuation. **400** FRS 3 (21)

2. **Past revaluation surpluses or deficits** (for temporary diminution in value) in the revaluation reserve, concerning the disposal of a revalued asset, will be treated as realised when the related asset is sold. The appropriate treatment is to make a transfer from revaluation reserve to revenue reserves, which is then disclosed in the notes to the financial statements but not reflected in the statutory profit and loss account for the period (Companies Act formats).

3. **Where the gain is subsequently realised** in a later year, it should not be realised in the profit and loss account as it is not part of the performance of that year, but of a previous year. This is illustrated in the example below.

EXAMPLE A company owns an asset which originally cost £200,000, which was revalued upwards to £270,000 in year 2. In year 4 the company sold the asset for £300,000. Depreciation is ignored. The **accounting treatment** is as follows:

1. In year 2 the profit is calculated by reference to the carrying amount of £270,000 and the surplus of £70,000 is credited to the revaluation reserve and presented in the STRGL.

2. In year 4, the asset is sold and profit is calculated as the difference between the sale proceeds and the carrying amount (£300,000-£270,000 = £30,000). The profit is recorded in the profit and loss account as an exceptional item after operating profit and before interest. Under FRS 3, the previous revaluation reserve of £70,000 is taken to the profit and loss account reserve, and only £30,000 is shown in the profit and loss account.

3. If the taxation charge is calculated on the total surplus of £100,000, the charge would be split between the tax due on £30,000 realised in the profit and loss account and the tax due on the £70,000 recorded in the STRGL.

4. A **note of historical profits and losses** for the period should be presented immediately after the profit and loss account, where there is a material difference between the result as disclosed in the profit and loss account and the result on an unmodified historical basis.

MEMO POINTS 1. Under FRS 18 "Accounting policies", **entities are prevented from** changing their valuation policies prior to a disposal of an asset from a revaluation basis to a historic cost basis.
2. Any **tax arising** on the disposal of a revalued asset (where the revaluation was initially taken to the STRGL) could also be allocated to STRGL, so matching the tax charge to the original gain on disposal. The deferred tax charge will depend on whether the proceeds from the sale are reinvested in other assets or not. If this is the case, the tax charge can be rolled over. Deferred tax is covered in more detail in ¶9000.

k. Other income

404 **Income from shares in group undertakings** Individual company profit and loss accounts should include dividends received and receivable from subsidiary undertakings and dividends from fellow subsidiaries, where a company holds shares in a group undertakings. As intra-group transactions, these dividends will be eliminated on consolidation of the group results.

However, dividends received and receivable from **unconsolidated subsidiary undertakings** should be included in the consolidated profit and loss account.

405 **Income from participating interests** Participating interests are defined as an interest held by an undertaking in the shares of another entity, held on a long-term basis, for the purpose of contributing to the activities of the entity through the exercise of control or influence arising from that shareholding. For individual companies, items under this caption in the profit and loss account include dividends received and receivable from participating interests, such as associates and joint ventures.

In **consolidated profit and loss accounts**, joint ventures and associates should be accounted for under the equity method, so this heading must be replaced by the following two items:
- income from interests in associated undertakings; and
- income from other participating interests.

406 The **parent's share of** its **associates' operating results** should be included immediately after group operating result, but after the parent company's share of the results of any joint ventures. Any amortisation or write-down of goodwill arising on acquisition of the associates should be charged at this point and disclosed. In keeping with the general rules, the results of associates should be analysed between continuing operations, acquisitions and discontinued operations.

The **parent company's (investor's) share** of any **exceptional items** relating to an associate, included after operating profit, or of interest should be shown separately from the other exceptional items for the group. At and below the level of profit before tax, the investor's share of the relevant amounts for associates should be included within the amounts for the group, although for items below this level, such as taxation, the amounts relating to associates should also be disclosed.

407 **Income from other fixed asset investments** There should be separate disclosure of income and interest derived from group undertakings, or from other sources.

408 **Other interest receivable and similar income** As above, income and interest derived from group undertakings must be shown separately from income and interest derived from other sources.

l. Amounts written off investments

410 "Amounts written off investments" are disclosed separately between the headings "operating profit" and "profit on ordinary activities before interest".

In situations **where a provision has been made** to write an investment down to below its cost and that provision is subsequently found to be unnecessary and written back, the credit should be disclosed under this heading. Impairments on operating fixed assets are disclosed in the profit and loss account under the same heading as the related depreciation. Impairment losses are covered in greater detail in ¶1550.

m. Interest payable and similar charges

The **general requirement** is that there must be separate disclosure of interest payable in respect of: 412
a. the finance cost of borrowing or interest including:
- interest;
- amortisation of discount or premium on the borrowings; and
- amortisation of issue costs;

b. the interest element of finance leases and similar obligations;
c. fees for obtaining credit facilities; and
d. unwinding of the discount on long-term provisions.
It is normal for a single figure to be given on the face of the profit and loss account with a detailed analysis given in the notes to the accounts.
Where **interest or similar charges** are paid to group undertakings, the following disclosures are required analysed between both categories:
- bank loans and overdrafts;
- loans of any other type made to the company; and
- finance leases and similar obligations.

With the exception of loans to the company from group undertakings, the disclosure requirements apply to interest and charges on all loans, whether made on the security of debentures or not.
The investor's share of interest in respect of its joint ventures and associates should be shown separately from amounts for the group, unless the amounts are immaterial.

Repurchase or early settlement of debt Gains or losses arising on the repurchase or early settlement of debt should be: 413 FRS 4 (32) (64)
- recognised in the period during which the repurchase or early settlement is made; and
- disclosed in the profit and loss account as separate items within interest payable and similar charges.

Long-term provisions included on a discounted basis Provisions relating to cash outflows arising soon after the balance sheet date are more onerous, given the time value of money, than those where cash outflows arise at a later date. These provisions are discounted back to the present value of the amount that will be paid at some future date. **Discounting is only required** where its effect is material. The discount rate should be a pre-tax rate that reflects the time value of money and the specific risks attached to the liability. 414 FRS 12 (46)

The **unwinding of the discount** over time should be included as a financial item adjacent to interest, but should be shown separately from other interest either on the face of the profit and loss account or in a note to the financial statements. FRS 12 (48)

Finance costs

Finance costs **are defined as the difference between** the net proceeds of an instrument and the total amount of the payments (or other transfers of economic benefits) that the issuer may be required to make in respect of the instrument. Finance costs include interest as well as amortised issue costs or redemption premium. 418 FRS 4 (8)

The general rule is that finance costs should be expensed in the profit and loss account. In certain circumstances, finance costs can be capitalised as part the cost of an asset which is achieved by way of a transfer from the profit and loss account. Such transfers should be separately disclosed. FRS 4 (76)

Finance costs **disclosed under the heading of interest payable** and similar charges should be allocated for the period, including interest on finance leases (see also ¶496) and hire purchase contracts that have characteristics similar to finance leases.

The Companies Act permits interest on capital borrowed to finance the production of that asset, to be added to the production cost of the asset, to the extent that it accrues in respect of the period of production. **Where interest** on borrowed capital **has been capitalised**, this fact should be disclosed in the financial statements.

The treatment of finance costs is considered further in Part 5 Chapter 1 (see ¶3000).

MEMO POINTS The introduction of FRS 25 "Financial Instruments: Disclosure and Presentation", effectively supersedes the requirements of FRS 4, except for the material on the measurement of debt and gains or losses on the repurchase of debt. **FRS 4 is withdrawn for entities** applying the measurement requirements in FRS 26 "Financial Instruments: Measurement" and hence FRS 25, **but remains applicable** for other entities.

n. Profit or loss on ordinary activities before taxation

424 The profit or loss on ordinary activities is a **mandatory disclosure** on the face of the profit and loss account. The figure should include exceptional items (see ¶474) but exclude taxation and extraordinary items.

o. Tax on profit or loss on ordinary activities

426 Where applicable the following amounts **should be stated**:
- the charge for corporation tax;
- if the corporation tax charge would have been higher but for double taxation relief, a note of what that higher charge would have been;
- the charge for UK income tax, and;
- the charge for taxation imposed outside the UK on profits, income and capital gains.

These amounts **must be stated separately** in respect of the following items appearing on the profit and loss account; namely:
- tax on profit or loss on ordinary activities; and
- tax on extraordinary profit or loss (see ¶480, below).

428 FRS 3 (23) Any **special circumstances** which affect the liability in respect of taxation of profits, income or capital gains for the current financial year, or succeeding financial years, must be disclosed by way of a note to the profit and loss account and the individual effects quantified. Such disclosures should include any special circumstances affecting the tax attributable to the format headings specified in FRS 3.

p. Profit or loss on ordinary activities after taxation

430 This heading is included in all four Companies Act formats. However, if there are no amounts in respect of the format headings "Minority interests" or "Extraordinary items", in respect of the current or previous year, it is suggested that this heading be omitted by progressing to the next category, namely "Profit or loss for the financial year".

q. Minority interests (Non-controlling interests)

431 There is **a requirement to show** in each of the formats the amount of any profit and loss on ordinary activities attributable to minority interests. This requirement covers shares in subsidiary undertakings included in the consolidation, held by or on behalf of persons other than the parent company and its subsidiary undertakings.

The minority interests charge in the profit and loss account **should be analysed between** equity and non-equity minority interests. Where there are non-equity minority interests, a description should be given of any rights of holders of the shares against other group companies.

The sums attributed to non-equity minority interests and associated finance costs should be calculated in the same way as for non-equity shares. The finance costs associated with such interests should be included in minority interests in the profit and loss account. FRS 4 (51)

r. Dividends paid and proposed

The aggregate amount of any dividends proposed must also be shown separately on the face of the profit and loss account **if not shown** in the notes to the financial statements. 432

Aggregate dividends for each class of share should be disclosed including the total amount in respect of each of: FRS 4 (59)
- dividends on equity shares;
- participating dividends; and
- other dividends on non-equity shares.

Where **finance costs for non-equity shares** are not equal to the dividends, the difference should be accounted for in the profit and loss account as an appropriation of profits. Any **other appropriation of profit** in respect of non-equity shares should also be disclosed. Where there are amounts relating to non-equity shares and the above information is not given on the face of the profit and loss account, disclosure should be made in the notes to the accounts. FRS 4 (44)

In situations where the entitlement to **dividends on non-equity shares** is determined on a time basis, the dividends should be accounted for on an accruals basis, except where the ultimate payment is uncertain, such as where profits are insufficient to cover a dividend. All dividends should be reported as appropriations of profit. FRS 4 (43)

In terms of **dividend waivers** the following rules **apply to listed companies**: 434
a. details must be given of any arrangements in terms of which a shareholder has waived or agreed to waive any dividends. This applies to waivers of future dividends and waivers of dividends payable during the previous financial year;
b. waivers of minor amounts (less than one per cent of the total value of any dividend), may be disregarded, if some payment has been made concerning each share of the relevant class during the relevant calendar year.

The value of shares issued (or proposed to be issued), **as an alternative to cash dividends** should be deemed to be the amount receivable if the alternative of cash had been chosen. Where the number of shareholders who will elect to receive the shares is uncertain, the whole amount should be treated as a liability to pay cash dividends. FRS 4 (48)

s. Amounts set aside or withdrawn from reserves

The profit and loss account of a company must show separately any amount set aside or proposed to be set aside to, or withdrawn or proposed to be withdrawn from, reserves. This figure is often entitled "Retained profit" or "Transfers to/from reserves". 436

SECTION 3

Additional disclosures

There are a considerable number of disclosures required to the notes to the accounts as required by the Companies Act, FRS 3 and other accounting standards and pronouncements. 438

A. Companies Act disclosures

Depreciation

440 Formats 1 and 3 do not have a separate heading for depreciation and this item should be disclosed in a note to the financial statements as required by other provisions of the Act. Format 2, item 7 (a) and Format 4, item A4 (a) specify the disclosure of depreciation of fixed assets on the face of the Profit and Loss Account.

It is a requirement of FRS 15 "Tangible fixed assets" that the depreciation charge in the profit and loss account is based on the carrying value of the asset in the balance sheet, whether it is historical cost or revalued amount.

Where **assets are revalued** the amount of depreciation to be shown, irrespective of format, should be based on the revalued amount.

Provisions for diminution in value of fixed assets

442 The **following disclosures** are required either on the face of the profit or loss account or in the notes to the accounts:
- provisions for diminutions in value of fixed asset investments;
- provisions for permanent diminutions in value of other fixed assets; and
- previous provisions written back to the profit and loss account.

The **general rule** is that a provision for diminution in value should be made in respect of any fixed asset, if the reduction in its value is expected to be permanent, whether its useful economic life is limited or not.

443 FRS 11 (67) **Impairment** An impairment in the value of a fixed asset does not have to be permanent, before it is recognised and charged to the profit and loss account. Impairment losses should be recognised in the profit and loss account within operating profit, under the appropriate statutory heading and disclosed in the notes to the accounts. The topic of impairment is dealt with in greater detail in ¶1550.

444 **Alternative accounting rules** Tangible fixed assets may be included at a market value determined at the last valuation date or at current cost. Where the alternative accounting rules have been applied, a difference between the provision for depreciation based on the historical cost basis (historical cost amount) and the depreciation based on the alternative accounting rules (adjusted amount) will arise.

Where the **depreciation charge on a revalued asset** is greater than that which would have arisen from historical cost, the excess should be treated as a realisation of a part of the revaluation reserve. A transfer, equal to this excess depreciation charge, should be made from the revaluation reserve to cumulative profit and loss account reserves. This transfer should be disclosed in the notes to the accounts.

446 **Reversal of impairment loss** Where a provision for diminution in the value of a fixed asset ceases to apply, the Companies Act requires the provision be written back to the profit and loss account.

FRS 11 (56) FRS 11 is more detailed and requires that the resulting reversal of the impairment loss be recognised in the current period in the profit and loss account, to the point it matches what the carrying value of the fixed asset would have been had the impairment not occurred, with any balance carried in the STRGL.

Director's remuneration and other emoluments

448 Both the Companies Act and the Listing Rules require detailed disclosures in respect of director remuneration, pensions, compensation and payments to third parties. This topic is dealt with in greater detail in ¶4800.

Particulars of staff

The **following particulars must be given** in respect of the employees of the company: 449
- the average number of persons employed by the company in the financial year, and;
- the average number of persons employed within each category of employee by the company.

The **average number of employees** is calculated by dividing the relevant annual number by the number of months in the financial year. The "relevant annual number" is found by adding together the monthly totals of persons employed under contracts of service by the company. Service for part of a month should be taken as being for a full month.

As regards the employees taken into consideration in determining the employee numbers above, the following salary information must also be disclosed in the notes to the accounts:
- wages and salaries paid and payable;
- social security costs incurred by the company; and
- other pension costs incurred.

These items are shown on the face of the profit and loss account for **Formats 2 and 4**.

Social security costs refers to a contribution by the company to any state social security or pension scheme or fund or arrangement. 450

Pension costs include any:
- costs incurred by the company in respect of any pension scheme established for the purpose of providing pensions for current and former employees of the company;
- sums set aside for the future payment of pensions made directly by the company to current or former employees; and
- pensions paid to such persons without having first been set aside.

Auditors' remuneration

The amount of auditors' remuneration, including sums paid in respect of expenses, must be disclosed in a note in both the individual company and group financial statements. These disclosure requirements include the estimated money value and nature of benefits in kind. Group financial statements are also required to comply with this requirement. 452

The total audit fees for the group are disclosed in the consolidated financial statements and in addition, it is generally accepted practice to disclose the audit fee for the parent company.

Non-audit fees Regulations require the disclosure in the notes to a company's financial statements regarding the aggregate fees paid to auditors for non-audit work. In practice, this is likely to include fees in respect of tax advice, company secretarial and management consultancy. Such fees apply to services supplied to the company and any UK subsidiaries or associate undertakings audited by the same auditor, or any associates thereof. 453 SI 1991/2128

Companies that qualify as small or medium are exempt from these disclosure requirements in respect of non-audit fees. The auditors of a company have an obligation to furnish the directors of the company with the necessary information regarding the identify of audit associates.

Foreign currencies

Where sums originally denominated in foreign currencies have been brought into the balance sheet or profit or loss account in sterling, the basis on which those sums have been converted should be stated. This topic is dealt with in greater detail in Part 10, Chapter 3 (¶8000). 454

B. Required by FRS 3

In addition to the changes introduced into the format of the profit and loss account, FRS 3 imposes a number of **additional disclosure requirements** covering exceptional items, extraordinary items, prior period items and the discontinued and discontinued operations. 457

1. Continuing and discontinued operations

460 FRS 3 (38) Certain items appearing in the profit and loss account should be analysed between continuing and discontinued operations, with the results of acquisitions being shown separately within the continuing category.

The **objective of separate reporting** of the results of continuing operations, acquisitions (as a component of continuing operations) and discontinued operations, is to assist users in assessing the financial performance of these aspects of a reporting entity's operations and in forming a basis for the assessment of future income. **Separate presentation should assist** analysis of the significance of any operations that have ceased or of new operations that have been acquired.

FRS 3 (39) In order to avoid too much data on the face of the profit and loss account, the **minimum disclosures required** in respect of continuing operations, acquisitions and discontinued operations concern the analysis of turnover and operating profit. The disclosure of the other items, such as cost of sales, gross profit, distribution costs and administration costs, may be given in the notes to the financial statements.

Where practicable, this analysis should identify the amounts arising in respect of acquisitions.

FRS 3 (20) A **similar analysis is required** between continuing and discontinued operations for the items that should be disclosed in compliance with FRS 3 (see ¶360).

Discontinued operations

462 Discontinued operations are those that are sold or terminated and that **satisfy all of the following conditions**:

FRS 3 (4) **a.** The sale of termination is completed either:
- in the financial period; or
- before the earlier of three months after commencement of the subsequent period, and the date on which the financial statements are approved.

b. If a termination, when the former activities have ceased permanently.

c. The assets, liabilities and results of operations and activities are clearly distinguishable, physically, operationally and for financial reporting purposes.

d. The sale of termination has a material effect on the nature and focus of the reporting entity's operations and represents a material reduction in its operating facilities, resulting either from:
- its withdrawal from a particular market (i.e. specific class of business or geographical); or
- a material reduction in turnover in the reporting entity's continuing markets.

Operations **not satisfying all these conditions** should be treated as continuing.

FRS 3 (41) In some cases it may be appropriate to disclose separately in a note to the profit and loss account the results of operations, which although not discontinued, are in the process of being discontinued.

FRS 3 (42) The **nature and focus** of a reporting entity's operations refers to the positioning of its products or services in their markets, including aspects of both quality and location.

EXAMPLE A **hotel company** that had traditionally served the lower end of the hotel market sold its existing chain and purchased luxury hotels. While remaining in the business of managing hotels, the group effectively changed the nature and focus of its operations. A similar situation would arise if the same company were to sell for example, its luxury hotels in the United States of America and buy budget style hotels in South East Asia. In this case, the sale of the hotels would have a material impact on the nature and focus of the entity's operations.

This transaction is distinct from the regular sales and replacement of material assets that are undertaken by a reporting entity as part of the routine maintenance of its portfolio of assets, which should not be classified as discontinued or as acquisitions. In other words, the sale of hotels and the purchase of another chain of hotels within the same market sector and similar locations would be treated as wholly within continuing operations.

Profit and loss account Only **income and costs** directly related to discontinued operations should appear under the heading of discontinued operations. **463** FRS 3 (17)

If the financial results of a sold or terminated operation **are not identifiable separately**, from the accounting records or to a material extent can only be derived through making allocations of income or expenses, then the operation cannot be classified as a discontinued operation. **For example**, a manufacturing facility that is closed down but which lacks an external market price for its output cannot be classified as a discontinued operation.

Where the **turnover relates to an acquisition** that is **discontinued in the same period**, this should not be included under continuing operations. Where an acquisition has a material impact on a major business segment, this should be disclosed and explained in the notes. FRS 3 (44)

Where it is not practical to determine the post-acquisition results of an operation to the end of the current period, an indication should be given of the contribution of the acquisition to the turnover of the continuing operations. If an indication of the contribution of an acquisition to the results of the period cannot be given, this fact and the reason should be explained.

Provisions relating to sale or termination

The issue of provisions in general is covered in FRS 12 "Provisions, contingent liabilities and contingent assets". The **general rule** is where another accounting standard or SSAP with a more specific requirement exists, this should be applied in preference to FRS 12. The requirement in FRS 3 relates specifically to the decision to sell or discontinue an operation. **464** FRS 3 (8)

Provisions arising **from a decision to sell or terminate** an operation should cover obligations that have already been incurred in respect of that operation and that are not expected to be covered by the future profits of the operation. The provision should only cover the direct costs of the sale or termination, and any operating losses incurred up to the date of sale or termination.

"Demonstrably committed" The reporting entity should be "demonstrably committed" to the sale or termination, **as evidenced by**: **465**
- a binding sale agreement in the case of a sale; or
- in the case of a termination, a detailed formal plan from which the reporting entity cannot realistically withdraw.

Evidence of the "demonstrable" commitment might be:
- the public announcement of specific plans;
- the commencement of implementation; or
- other circumstances effectively obliging the reporting entity to complete the sale or termination.

Provisions Where an entity is "demonstrably committed" to the sale or termination of a business, provision should be made for the direct costs of sale or discontinuance of the business and any operating losses incurred by the entity up to the sale or closure date. The aggregate expected profit recognised in the profit and loss account from any further trading prior to closure or sale, should be deducted from the provision. These provisions should appear in the continuing operations category, unless the operation qualifies as a discontinued operation in the period under review. **465-1**

In **subsequent periods**, where the operation qualifies as discontinued, the provisions should be used to offset the results of the operation in the discontinued category.

Although FRS 12 **prohibits provisions for future operating losses**, the FRS 3 rules cover the situation where provisions relate to a decision to sell or terminate a business. In situations where a provision relating to the costs of terminating a business proved to be materially inaccurate, then an adjustment should be made in the period when the inaccuracy is discovered and should be classified in the profit and loss account as a "non-operating exceptional item".

A binding contract entered into after the balance sheet date may provide additional evidence of asset values and commitments at the balance sheet date. In the case of an intended sale for which no legally binding sale agreement exists, no obligation has been agreed by the reporting entity. Accordingly, provisions for the direct costs of the decision to sell and for future operating losses should not be made. In accordance with normal practice, however, any impairment in asset values should be recorded.

466 **Disclosure of provisions** The adoption or release of provisions and the actual profits or losses that occur should be classified into continuing and discontinued operations. For instance, if a company with a June 20X9 financial year end was "demonstrably committed" to terminating an operation at that date, but the closure was not affected until December 20X9, then the operation should be regarded as continuing in the 20X9 accounts and discontinued in the accounts for the following year. The comparative figures should also be restated.

Where **provisions have been utilised** in connection with a sale or termination of an operation, these should be analysed between the operating loss and the loss on sale or discontinuance of the operation. Disclosure should be made on the face of the profit and loss account, below operating profit for continuing operations.

Interest payable

468 FRS 3 (40) The analysis in respect of continuing operations, acquisitions and discontinued operations **is required only to the** profit before interest level, because interest payable is often a reflection of a reporting entity's overall financing policy. This involves both equity and debt funding considerations on a group basis, rather than an aggregation of the particular types of finance allocated to individual segments of the reporting entity's operations. Any allocation of interest would involve a considerable degree of subjectivity that could leave the user uncertain as to the relevance and reliability of the information.

FRS 3 (14) In those circumstances where a reporting entity considers it necessary to allocate interest (or tax) between continuing and discontinued operations, the method and underlying assumptions used in making the allocations should be disclosed.

Comparative figures

470 FRS 3 (30) Comparative figures relating to the profit and loss account **should include in the continuing category**, only the results of those operations included in the current period's continuing operations. No reference need be made to the results of acquisitions reported in the previous period, since they are not required to be presented separately in the current year.

FRS 3 (64) The analysis of comparative figures between **continuing and discontinued operations** is not required on the face of the profit and loss account.

The **requirement to restate comparative results** based on the status of an operation in the current period means that figures for acquisitions made in the prior period will not be shown separately in the comparative figures given with the results for the year under review.

The comparative figures **for discontinued operations** should include the previous period's results of business segments that were only discontinued during the current year. These results would in the previous period have been included within continuing operations.

472 **FRS 28 "Corresponding amounts"** FRS 28 "Corresponding amounts" consolidates the changes to company law. The **principal requirements** of this FRS can be summarised as follows:

– corresponding amounts should be shown in the primary financial statements and notes to the financial statements;

– the requirements of this FRS should be applied unless an accounting standard or UITF abstract permits or requires an alternative treatment;

– where corresponding amounts are not directly comparable with the amount shown in the current period, they should be adjusted.

The **majority of the exemptions** from disclosure of corresponding amounts, as set out in the Companies Acts, have been retained.

MEMO POINTS The ASB has published an amended version of FRS 28. The amendments do not alter the existing requirements of FRS 28, but update references to correspond with the Companies Act 2006 and the Large and Medium sized Companies Regulations 2008.

2. Exceptional items

The effect of any transactions that are exceptional, even where they fall within the ordinary activities of the company, must be disclosed. 474 FRS 3 (19) (20)

Exceptional items require separate disclosure in order to explain their impact on the entity's results and the longer term sustainable earnings of that entity. Exceptional items **of a similar nature** may be grouped together for the purposes of disclosure, except where they relate to discontinued activities, in which case separate disclosure is required.

Exceptional items **are defined** in FRS 3 as material items which: FRS 3 (5)

a. derive from events or transactions that fall within the ordinary activities of the reporting entity; and

b. individually or, if of a similar type, in aggregate, need to be disclosed by virtue of their size, if the financial statements are to give a true and fair view.

Exceptional items should be credited or charged in arriving at the profit or loss on ordinary activities, by inclusion under the statutory format headings to which they relate.

Examples of exceptional items **include**: 475 FRS 3 (46)
- redundancy and reorganisation costs unrelated to the discontinuance of a business segment;
- abnormal charges for bad debts, stock obsolescence or losses on long-term contracts;
- previously capitalised intangible assets written off other than as part of a process of amortisation;
- surpluses arising on settlement of insurance claims;
- the expropriation of assets;
- amounts received in respect of insurance claims for consequential loss of profits; and
- changes in basis of taxation, or significant change in government fiscal policy.

Separate disclosure compulsory Separate disclosure is compulsory for: 476 FRS 3 (20)
- profits or losses on sale or termination of an operation (see ¶385);
- costs of fundamental reorganisation or restructuring (see ¶396);
- profits or losses on disposal of fixed assets (see ¶398).

An adequate description of each exceptional item should be given to enable its nature to be understood and they should be disclosed (where material) after the operating profit for the year.

Tax effects and minority interests

Where an entity has disclosed on the face of the profit and loss account, after operating profit and before interest, exceptional items as required by FRS 3, relevant information regarding their effect on the taxation charge and, in the case of consolidated financial statements any minority interests, should be shown in the notes to the profit and loss account. 477

A **minimum requirement** is for the related tax and the minority interest to both be shown in aggregate in respect of the items referred to above. However, if the effect of the tax and minority interests differs for the various categories of items, further information should be given, where practicable. This would assist users in assessing the impact of the different items on the net profit or loss attributable to shareholders.

3. Extraordinary items

Particulars must be stated of any extraordinary income or charges arising in the financial year. 478 FRS 3 (48)

Extraordinary items **are extremely rare** as they relate to highly abnormal events or transactions that fall outside the ordinary activities of a reporting entity and which are not expected to recur. In view of the extreme rarity of such items, no examples are provided in FRS 3.

FRS 3 (2) **Ordinary activities** can be defined as any activities which are undertaken by a reporting entity as part of its business, and such related activities in which it engages in furtherance of, or that arise from these activities. Ordinary activities include the effects on the reporting entity of any event in the various environments in which it operates, including the political, regulatory, economic and geographical environments, irrespective of the frequency or unusual nature of the events.

Disclosure requirements

480 FRS 3 (22) An **extraordinary profit or loss** should be shown separately on the face of the profit and loss account, after the profit or loss on ordinary activities after taxation, but before deducting any appropriations such as dividends paid or payable. In the case of consolidated financial statements, it should appear after the figure for minority interests.

The amount of **each extraordinary item** should be shown individually, either on the face of the profit and loss account or in a note to the financial statements. An adequate description of each extraordinary item should be given to enable its nature to be understood as well as its impact on the results of the reporting entity.

4. Historical cost profits or losses

484 FRS 3 (26) Where an entity **has chosen to adopt** the alternative accounting rules, the situation may arise where there is a material difference between the result disclosed in the profit and loss account and the result that would have been calculated on an unmodified historical cost basis. In such a case, a note of what the profit or loss for the period would have been on the historical cost basis should be presented.

The **content of the note** of the historical cost profit or loss **should include**:

FRS 3 (54) 1. A reconciliation of the reported profit on ordinary activities before taxation to the equivalent historical cost amount.

2. A disclosure of the retained profit for the financial year reported on the historical cost basis. The note should be presented immediately following the profit and loss account or the STRGL.

3. Details of **any adjustments made** for items for such items as:

i. gains recognised in prior periods in the STRGL and realised in the current period. For example, the difference between the profit on the disposal of an asset calculated on depreciated historical cost and that calculated on a revalued amount; and

ii. the difference between an historical cost depreciation charge and the depreciation charge calculated on the revalued amount included in the profit and loss account of the period.

The note of historical cost profits and losses is a memorandum item; namely an abbreviated restatement of the profit and loss account, including any adjustments to the reported profit or loss.

Reasons for required disclosure

486 The **two reasons** usually advanced for disclosing the profit or loss for a period on the unmodified historical cost basis of accounting, are as follows:

FRS 3 (55) 1. As long as discretion exists on the timing or scale of revaluations included in financial statements, the unmodified historical cost basis will show the reported profits or losses of different reporting entities on a more comparable basis.

2. The wish of certain users to assess the profit or loss on sale of assets based on their historical cost, rather than, as FRS 3 requires, on their revalued carrying amount.

FRS 3 (26) Where full historical cost information is unavailable or cannot be obtained **without unreasonable expense or delay**, the earliest available values should be used.

5. Prior period items and adjustments

In any accounting period, the results will be effected by adjustments required in respect of transactions that were initially recorded in earlier years. 488 FRS 3 (60)

The **majority of these adjustments**:
- arise mainly from the corrections and adjustments which are the natural result of estimates inherent in accounting and more particularly in the periodic preparation of financial statements;
- are dealt with in the profit and loss account of the period in which they are identified and their effect is stated where material; and
- are not exceptional (or extraordinary) merely because they relate to a prior period; their nature will determine their classification.

Where adjustments are required, FRS 3 identifies **two specific situations** when adjustments that are required should be treated as "prior period adjustments". These are: 488-1
- items arising from changes in accounting policies; or
- from the correction of fundamental errors.

Where either of these two situations arises an entity should reflect the transaction in the results of prior period(s) and not in the current profit and loss account.

Any adjustments involve:
- restating the comparative figures for the preceding period in the primary statements and notes;
- adjusting the opening balance of retained profits or reserves for the cumulative effect;
- noting the cumulative effect of the adjustments at the foot of the STRGL of the current period; and
- where practicable, disclosing the effect of prior period adjustments on the results for the preceding period.

Where the prior period adjustment relates to a transaction that **spanned more than one period** previously and has no impact as such on the operating results for subsequent years, then the comparative figures for the profit and loss account itself will not be adjusted and the prior period adjustment will be reflected through the comparative figures in the balance sheet and, in particular, the accumulated reserves. 488-2

EXAMPLE A set of accounts for the year ended 31 March 20X9 is being prepared. It has been discovered that in the year ended 31 March 20X7 a material investment was erroneously written off through the profit and loss account. This error is to be corrected by way of a prior year adjustment. The profit and loss effect of the reinstatement of that investment will be reflected through the **cumulative reserves** and will not impact upon the results for the year ended 31 March 20X9.

6. Change of accounting policies

Accounting policies should be **applied consistently** within the same financial statements and from one financial year to the next, although situations may arise when a change in accounting policy is necessary. 490

However, Schedule 4 does allow departure from the principles used in preparing the financial statements in respect of any financial year, if it appears to the directors of the company that there are special reasons. In such cases, disclosure is required in the notes to the financial statements of:
- the particulars of the departure;
- the reasons for the change in accounting policy; and
- its effect on the results for the financial period.

FRS 3 specifies that a change in accounting policy **may only be made** if it can be justified on the grounds that the new policy is preferable to the one it replaces, because it will give a fairer presentation of the result and of the financial position of a reporting entity. It is a characteristic of a change in accounting policy, that it is the result of a choice between two 491 FRS 3 (62) or more accounting methods. Therefore, it does not arise from the adoption or modification of an accounting method, necessitated by transactions or events that are clearly different in substance from those previously occurring.

In those cases where the **effect of the change** on the current year **was either immaterial or similar** to the quantified effect on the prior year, a simple statement confirming this would suffice. Where it is not practicable to give the effect on the current year, that fact, together with the reasons, should be stated.

The **disclosures necessary** when a change of accounting policy is made should, in addition to the disclosure of the effect required by FRS 3, include an indication of the effect on the current year's results.

7. Correction of fundamental errors

492 In exceptional circumstances, it may be found that financial statements of prior periods have been issued containing **significant errors** that call into question the validity of the true and fair view assertion and, in turn, the accuracy of the financial statements. The corrections of such fundamental errors and the cumulative adjustments applicable to prior periods have no bearing on the results of the current period.

C. Disclosures required by other accounting standards and abstracts

495 There are a number of key disclosure requirements dictated by other accounting standards, covering leases, start-up costs, research and development and website development costs. These topics are covered briefly in this section and discussed more fully in the relevant chapters.

Leases

496 The following disclosures are required in the profit and loss account **of the lessee** in relation to operating lease costs:
- rentals charged to the profit and loss account split between plant and machinery and other operating leases;
- aggregate finance charges for finance leases; and
- total depreciation charged for the period under finance leases.

The **lessor should disclose** in the notes to the financial statements, the aggregate rentals receivable in the periods in respect of finance leases and operating leases, and details of any operating lease incentives.

An example of an operating lease incentive is an initial cash payment from a lessor in order to secure a lease contract. Under UITF 28 "Operating lease incentives", a **lessee** should account for the incentive as a reduction in rentals payable, and allocate this over the term of the lease, or the period before which the market rental will be payable.

The **lessor should account** for the incentive given to the lessee as a cost, by reducing the rental income through allocating the cost over the same period, ideally on a straight-line basis unless another allocation method is deemed more appropriate.

This topic is treated in greater detail in ¶3400.

Start-up costs

498 UITF 24 (4) Under FRS 15 it is not permissible to include start-up costs in the cost of a fixed asset. UITF Abstract 24 "Accounting for start-up costs" defines start-up costs as the cost of activities related to the opening of:
- a new business;

- a new production facility;
- a new product or service;
- a new process within an existing facility; or
- relocation or reorganisation of part or all of an entity.

The abstract recommends that items be expensed in the profit and loss account (i.e. training costs), unless they meet the criteria for recognition as assets under other accounting standards.

Research and development

SSAP 13, "Accounting for research and development" divides research and development expenditure into the following categories: **500** SSAP 13 (21)
- pure (or basic) research;
- applied research; or
- development research.

The key disclosures required by SSAP 13 are as follows: SSAP 13 (30)
1. The **total amount** of research and development expenditure charged in the profit and loss account, should be analysed between the current year's expenditure and amounts amortised from deferred expenditure.
2. The **accounting policy** on research and development expenditure should be stated and explained, in the notes to the financial statements.
3. In addition, **movements on deferred development expenditure** and the amount carried forward at the beginning and the end of the period, should be disclosed under intangible fixed assets in the balance sheet.

MEMO POINTS The disclosures in point 2 above are not required by entities that are not public companies, a parent company with a banking or insurance company as a subsidiary, or a company that satisfies the criteria for definition as a medium sized company.

Barter transactions

The accounting for barter transactions **is governed by** UITF Abstract 26 "Barter transactions for advertising". This abstract covers transactions, where advertising and related services are provided in exchange for reciprocal marketing services, such as in the internet industry, where advertising space is traded on reciprocal websites. The abstract also covers similar barter transactions involving advertising on television and posters, and in magazines. **501** UITF 26 (3)

The abstract **is not mandatory for** other industries although the same principles should apply.

The abstract recommends, that **turnover and related costs** in respect of barter transactions for advertising should not be recognised, unless there is persuasive evidence of its value, i.e. there is evidence of cash revenue being generated from other sales of similar advertising space to other customers.

Website development costs

The recognition of website development costs is governed by UITF 29 "Website development costs". Some costs can be capitalised as tangible fixed assets under FRS 15 "Tangible fixed assets", which are subject to depreciation and annual impairment reviews. **502**

Website development costs can be **categorised as follows**:
- planning;
- software costs;
- infrastructure costs; and
- design and content costs.

A **clear distinction** is drawn between planning cost and all other costs. Website planning costs should be expensed in the profit and loss account and all other costs capitalised, only where it can be demonstrated that the entity will derive economic benefits at least equal to the value of the capitalised costs.

For more detail on this topic see ¶1334.

Purchased goodwill

503 FRS 10 "Goodwill and intangible assets" stipulates that financial statements should disclose the profit or loss on each material disposal, of a previously acquired business or business segment.

FRS 10 (54), (71C) In the reporting period in which the business with which the goodwill was acquired, is **disposed of or closed**:
1. The amount included in the profit and loss account in respect of the profit or loss on disposal or closure should include attributable goodwill, to the extent that it has not previously been charged in the profit and loss account; and
2. The financial statements should disclose, as a component of the profit or loss on disposal or closure, the attributable amount of goodwill so included.

FRS 10 (71c) In determining the profit or loss on the **sale of a business previously acquired**, it is necessary to take into account that portion of purchased goodwill not yet charged to the profit and loss account. Where the **accounting policy** for accounting for goodwill has been to eliminate it against reserves and the related business is now either closed or has been disposed of, then the purchased goodwill included in the profit and loss calculation should be separately disclosed in the profit and loss account.

MEMO POINTS Where it is impractical or impossible to ascertain the goodwill attributable to a business that was acquired before 1 January 1989, this should be stated and the reasons given.

Amortisation and impairment of goodwill and other intangibles

504 Goodwill and certain intangible assets (see also ¶1550) should be capitalised and amortised and impairment reviews should also be conducted where appropriate. The Schedule 4 formats for the profit and loss account specify the headings for depreciation but not for impairment charges or goodwill amortisation.

The **general rules** are as follows:
- an impairment loss or reversal of a loss related to goodwill or other intangible assets should be disclosed in the profit and loss account (see memo point);
- material goodwill charges should be disclosed on the face of the profit and loss account, under the most appropriate statutory heading; and
- the amortisation charge for revalued intangible assets must be based on revalued amounts and the remaining useful economic life.

MEMO POINTS An impairment loss or reversal of a loss **related to goodwill or other intangible assets** should be disclosed in the profit and loss account under the following headings: In Format's 1 and 3 under "cost of sales", "distribution costs", or "administrative expense". For Format's 2 and 4, disclosure is required under "depreciation and other amounts written-off tangible and intangible fixed assets."

Contracts for the sale of spare capacity

505 The **rules governing contracts** for the sale of capacity are covered in UITF 36 "Contracts for sale of capacity". These types of contract are common in the telecommunications and utility industries such as electricity, where entities buy and sell capacity on their respective networks. The **general rules** are that the seller of the capacity should not account for the sale unless:
- the purchaser has an exclusive and irrevocable right to use of the capacity;
- the asset (or component thereof) is specific and clearly identifiable;
- the seller has no right to substitute for other assets;
- the cost of the capacity can be reliably measured;
- the contract term covers a significant part of the asset's useful economic life; and
- there are no significant risks retained by the seller, such as obsolescence risk or risk of marked change in the value of the asset.

Where the criteria as set out above have been met, then the sale proceeds can be reported as turnover, if the asset was previously classified under the heading of "stock" as "held for resale on acquisition/construction". Otherwise the sale should be reported as a disposal of fixed assets.

The **turnover and profits** on reciprocal contracts, where capacity on one network is exchanged for capacity on the network of another supplier, should only be recognised where the assets or services provided or obtained have a readily ascertainable value. The **substance of each transaction** should be reviewed.

Related parties

The requirements of FRS 8 "Related party transactions" include the disclosure of turnover arising from sales to a related party, if material and that are not covered by an exemption. 506 FRS 8 (6)

Employee share schemes

Disclosure is required of charges to the profit and loss account in respect of employee share schemes, which should be based on the fair value of the shares at the date they are awarded. 508 UITF 17 (13)

Details should also be given of the costs of operating any share schemes.

Earnings per share

FRS 22 "Earnings per Share" effectively implements IAS 33 in the UK. FRS 22 **is mandatory** for all entities whose ordinary shares (and potential ordinary shares) are publicly listed or are in the process of being listed. 509

The **key requirements** are set out in brief below and considered in greater detail in Part 2 Chapter 2.

1. FRS 22 requires that the basic and diluted earnings per share be disclosed on the face of the profit and loss account, for profits or losses **arising from continuous operations**. This is in addition to the current requirement for the EPS figures for net profit or loss for the period.
2. Basic or diluted EPS for **discontinued operations** (if reported) should be disclosed either on the face of the profit or loss account or in the notes to the accounts.
3. FRS 22 requires less disclosure in respect of additional share amounts presented. However, **where a component** of the income statement used for the additional earnings per share amount **is not reported** as a line item in the income statement, a reconciliation between the component and the line item should still be provided.
4. Both standards use profit and loss from continuing operations as the **control number** used to determine whether potential ordinary shares are dilutive or anti-dilutive. However, as FRS 3 "Reporting Financial Performance" requires an analysis of continuing operations, acquisitions and discontinued operations only down to the level of profit before interest, **additional guidance** on how to allocate interest and tax, and to calculate a reasonable estimate of profit or loss from continuing operations, is reproduced in the Appendix to the standard as non-mandatory guidance.

SECTION 4

Revenue recognition

The ASB has issued an amendment to FRS 5 "Reporting the Substance of Transactions – Revenue Recognition". The amendment is in the form of an Application Note appended to the standard, which deals with revenue recognition from the supply of goods and services by a seller to its customers. **Additional guidance** has also been issued in the form of UITF 40. 520

The relationship between the accounting standards, abstracts and Application Note is set out in the table below.

Standard	Scope
FRS 5 "Reporting the Substance of Transactions"	Principal standard on revenue recognition
SSAP 9 "Stocks and long-term contracts"	Specific guidance given on long-term contracts (see ¶2230) separation and linking of contractual relationships
Application Note G	General principles of revenue recognition. Does not amend the requirements of SSAP 9 (see ¶2263)
UITF 40	Additional guidance on accounting for revenue on service contracts (see ¶2264)
IFRS	(see ¶540)

MEMO POINTS The **IASB** plans to issue a **revised revenue recognition standard** in the form of an exposure draft. The objective is to provide a more consistent basis for reporting revenue that better reflects the underlying economics of complex transactions. Revenue is generally recognised when an entity satisfies a contractual performance obligation to deliver a good or provide a service to a customer at an agreed value. The exposure draft provides guidance on more complex contracts that involve the delivery of multiple goods or services, and in particular how the total consideration should be apportioned between the various performance obligations. More detail on this topic is available from the IASB website.

a. Application Note G – basic principles

521 The Application Note sets out the basic principles of revenue recognition to be applied in all instances, with **specific guidance** given for the following types of revenue:
- long-term contracts;
- separation and linking of contractual performance;
- bill and hold arrangements;
- sales with right of return; and
- presentation of turnover as principal or agent.

It **should be noted** that the standard has not been universally welcomed and is the subject of some controversy.

The application note **does not apply to revenues** arising from financial instruments and insurance contracts, issues dealt with more exclusively by FRS 5 or specifically by other accounting standards.

Entities **should only report turnover**, if they have performed services or supplied goods in accordance with the contractual terms agreed with their customers. Guidance is also given on the measurement of turnover in relation to deferred payments and where significant risks exist concerning payment by debtors. The **principles and requirements** of the Application Note are consistent with IAS 18 "Revenue".

Examples of sources of revenue covered by the application note:
- Barter transactions;
- Property sales;
- Sale or return;
- Software sales;
- Franchise fees;
- Interest;
- Royalties;
- Licences;
- Dividends;
- Revenue grants;
- Insurance recoverable;

- Sale of spare capacity (see also ¶505);
- Long-term contracts;
- Warranties
- Government grants (see ¶7900).

522

The basic principles of revenue recognition	
Condition	**Accounting treatment**
1. Revenue recognition	Seller recognises revenue under a contract with a customer, when it **obtains the "right to consideration"** (see memo point 3) in exchange for performance of the contract (see memo note 2). At the same time the seller, typically, recognises a new asset, usually a debtor.
2. Recognising contractual performance	1. **Goods**: delivery terms 2. **Services**: period over which service(s) is (are) provided (i.e. cleaning contract) Must consider what specific activities constitute performance of a contract.
3. Contracts comprising mixture of goods and services	Must consider the **terms of the contract**. For instance does the performance of the contract consist of clearly identifiable stages? If yes are these stages separable?
4. Contract consists of separable stages	1. **Is each stage** "an end product"? 2. **What benefit** does the customer gain at each stage of completion? 3. Where does the **balance of risk** lie at each stage of the contract?
5. Seller receives payment in advance from customer	The seller should **recognise a liability** equal to the payment received, representing its contractual obligation. When the seller obtains the right to consideration through performance on the contract, the liability should be reduced, with the reduction simultaneously reported as turnover.
6. Seller – partial consideration of contract	The seller should **recognise turnover** only to the extent that it has obtained the right to consideration through its performance.
7. Fair value	Revenue should be measured at **fair value of the right to consideration** (see memo note 1 below), normally the contract price, net of discounts, VAT and similar sales taxes.
8. Time-value of money	1. Where **material to reported revenue** – revenue recognised should be the present value of expected cash inflows. The unwinding of the discount should be credited to finance income as this is a gain from a financing transaction. **2. Subsequent adjustments** to a debtor to reflect time-value of money or credit risk should not be included within turnover.

MEMO POINTS **1. Fair value**: The amount at which goods and services can be exchanged in an arm's length transaction, between informed and willing parties. **2. Performance**: The fulfilment of the seller's contractual obligations to the customer through the supply of goods and services. **3. Right to consideration**: A seller's right to the amount received or receivable in exchange for performance of a contract.

b. Types of revenue recognition

Separation and linking of contractual arrangements

524 A contractual arrangement may require a seller to supply a number of different goods and services, which may not be related but which cannot be sold individually.

On the other hand, the components or goods may be closely related, so that it would be difficult to sell them separately. In this instance, the seller will often sell the goods and services as a package at a discount to the individual prices.

The **issue is to determine** whether as a result of the **performance of the contract**:
– the seller should recognise a change in its turnover and assets or liabilities, with regard to its right to consideration on each individual component in the contract (known as "unbundling"); or
– whether two or more components should be combined and turnover recognised on this basis ("bundling").

The **accounting treatment** for linked contracts is as follows:
1. "unbundled contract" – should be accounted for as two or more separate transactions, where the commercial substance indicates that the individual contract components operate independently of each other (different goods and services).
2. "bundled contracts" – are accounted for as a single transaction where the commercial substance of the contract so indicates.

524-1 Contracts with multiple components

Condition	Accounting treatment
Contract components **independent** of each other	1. A **reliable fair value should be assigned** to each component. Recognition of turnover and changes in assets or liabilities is on the basis of each component being accounted for separately. 2. Where **reliable fair values cannot be assigned** to either completed or uncompleted components of the contracts, the seller should recognise turnover and changes in assets or liabilities as a single, bundled contractual arrangement. 3. Where **fair values can only be assigned** to uncompleted components, these fair values should be deducted from the total fair value of the contract, to obtain the turnover for completed components.
Contract components **not independent** of each other (see example below)	The **seller should account** for components together, to reflect the seller's performance under the contract. Where the contract can be classified (under SSAP 9) as a long-term contract, it should be accounted for in accordance with that standard.

EXAMPLE **Software and related support service – recognition of turnover.**

A customer may purchase a **software package** "off the shelf" from a seller, with or without additional software support and maintenance. In this instance, the seller's performance comprises two components; namely, the software and the support package. The turnover on each part should be recognised separately.

Where a customer purchases **"bespoke" software** such as a management information system, this typically includes a maintenance and support element, needed to ensure continued operation of the system as well as development of the software to meet the specific requirements of the customer. The commercial substance of the arrangement is that the customer is often buying support over a period of time, which is not separable from the rest of the contract as the two elements are closely linked. In this instance, the **turnover should be recognised** on a long-term contractual basis.

Bill and hold arrangements

Under a bill and hold arrangement, the seller arranges a contract with a customer to supply goods, where although **legal title** is transferred immediately, physical delivery is deferred to a later date. The issue is whether the seller or purchaser should recognise the goods as assets or can the seller recognise the revenue and the right to consideration in the case where the goods have not been delivered to the buyer. 525

The criteria for **recognition of revenue** under these types of arrangement are considered below.

For the seller to be able to recognise the revenue arising from its **right to consideration** in respect of the bill and hold arrangement, or to continue to recognise the goods as stock, the terms of the contract between the seller and buyer should include all the **following characteristics**:

1. The goods should be complete and ready for delivery to the customer;
2. The seller should have relinquished all significant performance obligations, save safekeeping of the goods;
3. Subject to "Rights of Return", the seller should have gained the right to consideration, regardless of when the goods are subsequently shipped to the customer;
4. The commercial substance of any "Rights of Return" should be examined;
5. The goods should be separately identifiable from other stock held by the seller; and
6. The bill and hold arrangements should be in accordance with the commercial objectives of the buyer not the seller.

The **accounting treatment** is thus:

a. The seller should recognise the changes in assets or liabilities, and turnover when the "stock" is recognised as an asset by the buyer.

b. Where the substance of the transaction indicates that the goods are still an asset of the seller, it should be retained on the seller's balance sheet; any monies received from the customer (payments on account) should be included within creditors.

Principal benefits and risks The **principal benefits** of bill and hold arrangements for the customer are as follows: 525-1

- the right to obtain the goods when required;
- sole rights to the goods in terms of third parties and the associated cash flows; and
- guaranteed prices.

The **principal risks** relate to slow moving stock and the risk of obsolescence.

Sales with a right of return

Under the **terms of the contract** a buyer may be permitted to return goods that they have purchased, with the right to a refund or cancellation of an obligation to pay. The existence of "Rights to Return" goods could affect the seller's **"right to consideration"** under the contract and the recognition of revenue thereof. The seller's recognition of its "consideration" and contractual obligation to transfer economic benefits to its customer, in respect of "Rights of Return", are linked transactions. 526

As a consequence the **seller's turnover** should exclude the sales value of estimated returns and only include revenue for items not expected to be returned. Estimates of "returns" should reflect the maximum potential number of returns and other appropriate risks based on historical experience of comparable sales. **Where the risk of returns are significant** and effectively all risks associated with the goods are retained by the seller, no turnover or changes in assets or liabilities should be recognised, until such time as:

- the estimated "returns" can be reliably re-measured; or
- any associated time period for the returns has expired.

Any payments received should be included within creditors as payments in advance.

Estimates of returns should be reviewed at each balance sheet date, taking into account constructive as well as legal obligations.

EXAMPLE **Retail operation**

A retailer sells leather shoes over the internet to customers, who have the right to return the goods within 21 days, provided they are in a resaleable condition. The retailer can estimate the percentage of returns expected (i.e. 25%) based on experience and recognise the appropriate revenue accordingly (i.e. 75%). For each pair of shoes sold, part of the consideration will be recognised as revenue and the remainder as a provision. Cost of sales recognised on each sale should be adjusted for each item returned with a corresponding adjustment to stock. This accounting treatment is in accordance with FRS 12 "Provisions, contingent liabilities and assets".

Presentation of turnover as principal or as agent

527 A seller acting on its own when contracting with customers for the supply of goods is known as the principal. The seller is an agent where he acts as an intermediary on behalf of a principal in return for a commission.

The **general rule** is that for a seller to account for exchange transactions as a principal, it should have exposure to all **significant benefits and risks** associated with at least one of the following; namely the selling price or in respect of stock (i.e. exposure to risk of damage, slow moving stock). Other indications of principal status are that the seller assumes any credit risk and that the seller retains discretion over the choice of supplier.

Where the **seller acts as an agent**, it will not normally be exposed to the benefits and risks attached to the exchange transaction. Agency arrangements exhibit the following transactions:
- the seller has disclosed that it is acting as an agent; and
- the seller plays no further part in the transaction, once the agent has confirmed the customer's order to the principal;
- the seller's commission is pre-determined;
- the agent bears no credit or stock holding risk.

Summary Condition	Accounting treatment Based on substance of transaction
Seller acts as principal	Turnover should be based on gross revenue received or receivable in return for performance of the contract.
Seller acts as agent	Turnover represents the commission or other amounts received or receivable under the terms of the contract. Amounts received or receivable from the customer that are payable to the principal should not be included in the agent's turnover.

Disclosures

528 Application Note G does not include a requirement to list specific accounting policies so detailed disclosure should be made of revenue recognition policies adopted. For each principal source of revenue the following disclosures should be given:
- the timing of the revenue recognition;
- accounting treatment of discounts;
- measurement of sources of revenue; and
- methods used to allocate revenue in composite transactions where different revenue recognition policies are used.

EXAMPLE Retail

A retailer sells leather shoes over the internet to customers, who have the right to return the goods within 21 days, provided they are unworn and in resaleable condition. The retailer can estimate the percentage of returns expected (i.e. 25%) based on experience and recognise the appropriate revenue accordingly (i.e. 75%). For each pair of shoes sold part of the consideration will be recognised as revenue and the remainder as a provision. Cost of sales recognised on each sale should be adjusted for each item returned with a corresponding adjustment to stock. This accounting treatment is in accordance with FRS 12 "Provisions, contingent liabilities and assets".

SECTION 5

Proposed changes to UK GAAP

FRED 22

The ASB has **proposed limited amendments** to FRS 3 in the form of FRED 22 "Revision to FRS 3, Reporting financial performance". However, it is unlikely that FRED 22 will become a UK standard in its present form, as the ASB has postponed further development on this topic pending the outcome of its convergence programme with the IASB and the FASB. 530

The principal amendment was that the profit and loss account should be combined with the STRGL in a joint performance statement, divided into three sections; namely:
- operating activities from turnover to operating profit;
- financial and treasury including interest; and
- other gains and losses covering the STRGL as well as gains and losses on disposals of properties and profits or losses on disposal of continuing operations.

The FRED also proposes to **change the definition** in FRS 3 of a discontinued operation to that of a discontinuing operation.

Additional amendments would also be required to FRS 11 and FRS 15. All **impairment losses** would be reported as operating activities, compared to the current treatment of dividing the impairment between operating activities and other gains or losses, depending on whether or not there has been a consumption of economic benefits. 532

There is also a **potential conflict** in the accounting treatment between FRS 3 and FRS 23 "The Effects of Changes in Foreign Exchange Rates". FRS 3 specifies the accounting treatments of gains and losses for all assets. However, a problem can arise in connection with FRS 23 concerning the disposal of a foreign operation. FRS 23 requires that cumulative exchange rate differences recognised in the STRGL be recycled through the profit and loss account. The ASB has suggested a **limited amendment** permitting exemption from paragraphs 21 and 31a of FRS 3, for foreign exchange differences arising on the sale of a foreign operation. FRS 3 should be amended as FRS 23 is already convergent with IFRS. 534

Under FRS 26, unrealised gains and losses on **financial instruments** should be accounted for in the STRGL and then recycled through the profit and loss on realisation. Gains and losses are calculated by comparing sale proceeds with carrying value. The ASB has proposed that FRS 3 should no longer apply to these transactions. 535

SECTION 6

Comparison between UK GAAP and IFRS

There are a number of **key differences** between UK GAAP and IFRS in terms of presentation and disclosure issues. The relevant international accounting standards are IAS 1 "Presentation of Financial Statements (Revised), IAS 8 " Accounting Policies, Changes and Accounting Estimates and Errors (Revised)", IAS 18 "Revenue" and IFRS 5 "Non-Current Assets Held for Sale and Discontinued Operations". 540

In general, **UK GAAP requires more disclosures** on the face of the profit and loss account (Income statement), relating to exceptional items, discontinued operations and acquisitions, and is more specific in terms of formats and content of the financial statements, including the STRGL. IAS 1 sets out the minimum disclosures required on the face of the income statement but allows more scope in terms of the formats adopted. **The IAS rules** on the other hand require more detailed disclosures on the topic of discontinued operations.

Key differences between UK GAAP and IAS (IFRS)	
UK GAAP	**IAS**
1. Definition of **ordinary activities** more defined. (FRS 3 (2)) – prevents some items being classified as extraordinary	Definition in IAS 8 of extraordinary items is wider that FRS 3. The term "exceptional item" is not used.
2. FRS 3 (4) covers **discontinued operations**, although term is restricted to those operations that have been discontinued for more than 3 months after the balance sheet date, or if earlier, by the date financial statements approved	IFRS 5 (31) requires disclosures where an initial disclosure event occurs by the time the financial statements are approved
3. **Discontinued operations** – only disclosed if there is a material effect on the nature and focus of the operations (FRS 3 (4))	Discontinuing operations must be disclosed if discontinued (or are in the process of so being) by the time the financial statements are authorised (IFRS 5 (38))
4. **Dividends paid and payable** must be disclosed in the profit and loss account	Dividends – details need only be shown in the statement of changes in equity or in the notes to the financial statements (IAS 1 (96))

Issues dealt with more comprehensively in UK GAAP
1. Certain **exceptional items** must be disclosed on the face of the profit and loss account (FRS 3 (20)). (See also ¶360). Disclosures also required in notes of exceptional items that are material in aggregate, if not individually. IAS 8 does not refer to the term "extraordinary items".
2. **Extraordinary items** must be disclosed on the face of the profit and loss account after tax. Any interest in exceptional items applicable to minority interests should also be disclosed.
3. **Turnover and operating profit** (and other categories in between) relating to acquisitions should be included in continuing operations on the face of the profit and loss account. Discontinued operations – disclosures relating to turnover and operating profit to be shown on the face of the profit and loss account. This exceeds the requirements of IFRS 5 (33).
4. The Companies Act incorporates a **choice of standardised formats** for balance sheet and profit and loss account. The Act also requires disclosure in the notes of the segregation of assets and liabilities, distinguished between current and non-current. IAS 1 (53) allows an entity to decide on providing this information depending on the nature of its operations.
5. FRS 3 (26) requires disclosure of a **note of historical cost profit and loss** where there is a material difference between this and the profit disclosed
6. FRS 3 (23) also requires disclosure of **special circumstances** that may affect the **tax charge** of future periods

Issues dealt with more comprehensively in IAS (IFRS)
1. IFRS 5 (31) requires more extensive disclosures concerning discontinuing operations before completion of the discontinuance
2. Gains or losses must be included in the income statement (unless required to be included directly in equity by a specific accounting standard) as there is no equivalent to the STRGL under IAS
3. IAS 1 (95) requires disclosure of dividends per share for the period. In contrast, UK requirements only apply to listed companies making interim or preliminary announcements
4. Insurance companies are not exempt from disclosure requirements of IAS (IFRS)

IAS 18 deals with the **recognition and measurement of revenue** arising from the sale of goods, interest, royalties and dividends. There is no equivalent UK standard, although the ASB's Statement of Principles and FRS 5 generally cover the transactions addressed by IAS 18.

MEMO POINTS 1. The **IASB plans to issue** a revised revenue recognition standard in the form of an **exposure draft**, with the objective of providing a more consistent basis for reporting revenue that better reflects the underlying economics of complex transactions. Revenue is generally recognised when an entity satisfies a contractual performance obligation to deliver a good or provide

a service to a customer at an agreed value. The exposure draft provides guidance on more complex contracts that involve the delivery of multiple goods or services, and in particular how the total consideration should be apportioned between the various performance obligations. More detail on this topic is available from the IASB website.
2. In October 2010 **the ASB issued** a proposal to introduce **a financial reporting framework for medium-sized entities (FRSME)** not eligible to apply the FRSSE or full IFRS. The FRSME could replace current UK GAAP from July 2013 and is based on the principles underpinning full IFRS. If adopted there could be some key differences in the accounting treatment for revenue recognition.
3.The IASB and the US Financial Accounting Standards Board (FASB) have issued for public comment, a joint draft standard entitled "Revenue from Contracts with Customers", designed to align the financial reporting of revenue from customer contracts and related costs. The intention is to create a **single revenue recognition standard for IFRS and US GAAP** which would replace IAS 18 "Revenue", IAS 11 "Construction Contracts" and other related interpretations. The proposed standard should:
- remove inconsistencies in existing reporting requirements;
- provide a more robust framework for addressing revenue recognition issues;
- improve comparability across companies, industries and capital markets; and
- help clarify the accounting rules for contract costs.

The consultation period for the exposure draft expired in October 2010. Further developments in this topic are expected in 2011.

SECTION 7

Other Schedule 4 formats

The Schedule 4 formats 2, 3, and 4 are set out below with the accompanying notes, with additional disclosure requirements outlined in the table that follows (see also ¶352). 550

552

PROFIT AND LOSS ACCOUNT FORMAT 2	
1	Turnover
2	Change in stocks of finished goods and work in progress
3	Own work capitalised
4	Other operating income
5	a) Raw materials and consumables b) Other external charges
6	Staff costs a) Wages and salaries b) Other pension costs c) Social security costs
7	(a) Depreciation and other amounts written off tangible and intangible fixed assets (b) Exceptional amounts written off current assets
8	Other operating charges
9	Income from shares in group undertakings
10	Income from participating interests
11	Income from other fixed asset investments
12	Other interest receivable and similar income
13	Amounts written off investments
14	Interest payable and similar charges
15	Tax on profit and loss on ordinary activities
16	Profit or loss on ordinary activities after taxation *Minority interests* (E)

PROFIT AND LOSS ACCOUNT FORMAT 2	
17	Extraordinary income
18	Extraordinary charges
19	Extraordinary profit and loss
20	Tax on extraordinary profit and loss *Minority interests* (E)
21	Other taxes not shown under the above items
22	Profit or loss for the financial year

PROFIT AND LOSS ACCOUNT FORMAT 3	
A	**CHARGES**
1	Cost of sales (A)
2	Distribution costs (A)
3	Administration expenses (A) **Operating profit or loss (1)** **Losses on the sale or termination of an operation (2)** **Cost of a fundamental reorganisation or restructuring (2)** **Losses on disposal of fixed assets (2)**
4	Amounts written off investments
5	Interest payable and similar charges (E) **Profit or loss on ordinary activities before taxation (3)**
6	Tax on profit and loss on ordinary activities
7	Profit or loss on ordinary activities after taxation *Minority interests* (E)
8	Extraordinary charges
9	Tax on extraordinary profit and loss *Minority interests* (E)
10	Other taxes not shown under the above items
11	Profit or loss for the financial year **Dividends paid and proposed (3)** **Amounts set aside or proposed to be set aside to, or withdrawn or proposed to be withdrawn from, reserves (3)**
B	**INCOME**
1	Turnover
2	Other operating income **Operating profit and loss (1)** **Profits on the sale or termination of an operation (2)** **Profits on disposal of fixed assets (2)**
3	Income from shares in group undertakings
4	Income from participating interests (D)
5	Income from other fixed asset investments (B)
6	Other interest receivable and similar income (B) **Profit or loss on ordinary activities before taxation (3)**
7	Profit or loss on ordinary activities after taxation Minority interests (E)
8	Extraordinary income Minority interests (E)
9	Profit or loss for the financial year

PROFIT AND LOSS ACCOUNT FORMAT 4	
A	**CHARGES**
1	Reduction in stocks of finished goods and in work in progress
2	(a) Raw materials and consumables (b) Other external charges
3	Staff costs: (a) Wages and salaries (b) Social security costs (c) Other pension costs
4	(a) Depreciation and other amounts written off tangible and intangible fixed assets; (b) Exceptional amounts written off current assets
5	Other operating charges **Operating profit and loss (1)** **Losses on the sale or termination of an operation (2)** **Cost of a fundamental reorganisation or restructuring (2)**
6	Amounts written off investments
7	Interest payable and other charges
8	Tax on profit or loss on ordinary activities
9	Profit or loss on ordinary activities after taxation
10	Extraordinary charges
11	Tax on extraordinary profit or loss
12	Other taxes not shown under the above items
13	Profit or loss for the financial year
B	**INCOME**
1	Turnover
2	Increase in stocks of finished goods and in work in progress
3	Own work capitalised **Operating profit and loss** (1) **Profits on the sale or termination of an operation** (2) **Profits on disposal of fixed assets** (2)
4	Other operating income
5	Income from shares in group undertakings
6	Income from participating interests (D)
6	Or group accounts: (a) Income from interests in associated undertakings (a) Income from other participating interests
7	Income from other fixed asset investments
8	Other interest receivable and similar income **Profit or loss on ordinary activities before taxation** (3)
9	Profit and loss on ordinary activities after taxation *Minority interests* (E)
10	Extraordinary income *Minority interests* (E)
11	Profit or loss for the financial year

554

Notes regarding the Schedule 4 profit and loss account formats 1-4

(A) **Cost of sales: Distribution costs: Administration expenses**

- Format 1: items 2, 4 and 5
- Format 3: items A, 1, 2 and 3

These items must be stated after taking into account any necessary provision for depreciation or diminution in value of assets.

(B) **Income from other fixed asset investments: Other interest receivable and similar income**

- Format 1: items 9 and 10
- Format 2: items 11 and 12
- Format 3: items B.5, and 6
- Format 4: items B.7 and 8

Income and interest derived from group undertakings must be shown separately from income and interest derived from other sources.

(C) **Interest payable and similar charges**

- Format 1: item 12
- Format 2: item 14
- Format 3: item A.5
- Format 4: item A.7

The amount payable to group undertakings must be shown separately.

Formats 1 and 3

The amount of any provisions for depreciation and diminution in value of tangible and intangible fixed assets required to be shown under items 7 (a) A.4 (a) respectively in Formats 2 and 4 must be disclosed in a note to the financial statements in any case where the profit and loss account is prepared by reference to Format 1 and Format 3.

(D) **Income from participating interests**

Sch 4A para 21 (3) CA 1985

- Format 1: item 8
- Format 2: item 10
- Format 3: item B.4
- Format 4: item B.6

For consolidated profit and loss accounts, this heading must be replaced by the following two items:
- Income from interests in associated undertakings
- Income from other participating interests

(E) **Minority interests**

A further item headed "minority interests" must be added:
- In Format 1, between items 14 and 15
- In Format 2, between items 16 and 17
- In Format 3, between items 7 and 8 in both sections A and B; and
- In Format 4, between items 9 and 10 in both sections A and B

(E) A further item headed "minority interests" must also be added:
- In Format 1, between items 18 and 19
- In Format 2, between items 20 and 21
- In Format 3, between items 9 and 10 in section A and between items 8 and 9 in section B; and
- In Format 4, between items 11 and 12 in both sections A and between items 10 and 11 in section B

Notes regarding the Schedule 4 profit and loss account formats 1-4	
Other notes regarding the formats	
(1)	Required by FRS 3, paragraph 14.
(2)	Required by FRS 3, paragraph 20. In calculating the profit or loss in respect of these items, consideration should only be given to revenue and costs directly related to the items in question
(3)	Required by Schedule 4, paragraph 3, (6) and (7)

556

Additional disclosures required under Formats 2, 3 and 4	
Category	**Content**
Changes in stocks of finished goods and work in progress	Used by manufacturing companies. Show difference between opening and closing stock of finished goods and work in progress. Finished goods include components purchased as well as manufactured by the company.
Own work capitalised	Includes the value of direct materials and labour and relevant overhead costs relating to the in-house construction of fixed assets are capitalised.
Raw materials and consumables	Purchases of components should be included within the cost of raw materials. Difference between opening and closing stocks of raw materials and consumables is deducted from or added to the total cost of purchases of these items. Companies in the retail trade using this format use another wording for this heading; namely: "Goods for resale".
Other external charges	Includes production costs not included in stock and consumables heading such as: subcontractor's costs, equipment rentals etc.
Staff costs	The formats require a distinction be drawn between wages and salaries, social security costs and other pension costs. The detail classification can be provided in the notes to the accounts.
Depreciation and other amounts written off fixed assets	This information required is dealt with in ¶440.
Exceptional amounts written off current assets	Not often used.
Other operating charges	Other operating charges include selling and administration costs not included under other headings.

CHAPTER 2

Earnings per share (EPS)

OUTLINE ¶¶

This chapter details the rules for calculating and reporting earnings per share (EPS). The **general purpose** of the EPS figure is to allow the users of financial statements to make comparisons between the results of an entity from year to year, as well as between different companies in the same year, allowing for the limitations in the data resulting from the different accounting policies used to determine earnings. **600**

FRS 22, "Earnings per share", provides the necessary guidance on calculating and presenting EPS. It supersedes the older FRS 14 (which applied to years beginning before 1 January 2005). Note that there are **no requirements in company law** on the disclosure of earnings per share beyond the general requirement that companies should adopt generally accepted accounting practice – i.e., appropriate accounting standards.

MEMO POINTS FRS 22 is based on IAS 33, and was issued as part of the convergence process whereby UK and international GAAP are standardised.

FRS 22 differentiates between **basic EPS** and **diluted EPS**, requiring that each is disclosed on the face of the profit and loss account for both the net profit and loss for the period and also for the profit and loss from continuing operations. Basic EPS is the most common measure, derived by dividing net profit by the weighted average number of ordinary shares **602** in issue. Diluted EPS adjusts the basic EPS calculation to include the effects of potential ordinary shares that the company may be committed to issuing.

The focus of the standard is the **denominator** used in the calculations of both basic and diluted EPS.

603 FRS 22 (2) **Scope** The provisions of FRS 22 **apply to all entities**:
- whose ordinary shares are publicly traded;
- whose potential ordinary shares are publicly traded; or
- that file, or are in the process of filing, their financial statements with a securities commission or other regulatory information for the purpose of issuing ordinary shares in a public securities market.

A **potential ordinary share** is a financial instrument or right that may entitle its holders to ordinary shares, and includes share options and convertible debentures.

The phrase "publicly traded" does not refer only to shares that are *actually* bought and sold on a public market – as long as it is possible for the shares to be so traded, FRS 22 will apply to the entity.

FRS 22 (2a) Entities that apply the Financial Reporting Standard for Smaller Entities (FRSSE) are exempt from the EPS disclosure requirements of FRS 22. However, if an entity so exempted nevertheless chooses to disclose EPS, it should calculate and publish the EPS in accordance with the principles in the FRS.

FRS 22 (4) If an entity prepares both its own and **consolidated financial statements**, EPS information is required only in respect of the consolidated accounts. However, if it does choose to disclose EPS based on its own financial statements, this information must be prepared in accordance with FRS 22 and presented only on the face of its separate income statement. It must not present such information in the consolidated financial statements.

SECTION 1

Basic EPS

604 FRS 22 (10) **Basic EPS formula**

Basic EPS is calculated by dividing:

$$\frac{\text{Net profit or loss for the period attributable to ordinary shareholders (Numerator)}}{\text{The weighted average number of ordinary shares outstanding during the period (Denominator)}}$$

The EPS will change where there is an increase (or decrease) in the number of shares without a corresponding increase (or decrease) in profits.

EXAMPLE

Basic EPS

Net profit (Numerator)	£30,000
Ordinary shares outstanding (Denominator)	100,000
Basic earnings per share	**30p**

If the profits remain stable but the number of shares in issue increases to 125,000 then the EPS will become 24p.

605 This section is concerned with the **numerator** and **denominator** components of the formula for calculating basic EPS, and the key factors that influence them.

A. Numerator

The numerator represents the net profit or loss for the period attributable to ordinary shareholders, less dividends and other appropriations in favour of non-equity shareholders, such as dividends on preference shares. **606**

The **net profit or loss figure** for the period, as stated in the financial statements, is after:
- taxation;
- exceptional items; and
- minority interests.

Examples of **preference dividends** that are deducted from net profit are as follows: **607**
- actual preference dividends declared on non-cumulative preference shares; and
- the required preference dividend on cumulative preference shares, whether or not these have been declared, as the undeclared amount is still deductible. FRS 22 (14)

Similarly, because the dividend is always taken into account in the period during which it accrues, any **cumulative preference dividends** paid or deducted during the current period, but relating to prior period/s, are not taken into account.

B. Denominator

The denominator is the **number of ordinary shares** used in the EPS calculation (see ¶604). There are a number of factors that can influence the number of ordinary shares issued and hence the denominator. **610**

FRS 22 **characterises ordinary shares** as those that participate in the net profit for the period only after all appropriations in respect of other types of shares such as preference shares have been made. An entity may have **more than one class of ordinary shares**. If this is the case, the earnings for the period should be apportioned over the different classes of shares according to their dividend rights.

1. Calculation of the weighted average

In calculating basic EPS, the accounting standard specifies that the **number of ordinary shares** in the denominator should be the weighted average number of ordinary shares outstanding during the period. **612** FRS 22 (19)

The **weighted average** is the number of shares outstanding at the beginning of the period, adjusted by the number of shares issued and/or bought back during the period, multiplied by a time-weighting formula.

The weighted average number of ordinary shares outstanding during the period reflects the fact that the amount of equity capital may be varied during the financial year, as a result of share issues or share buy-backs. The **time-weighting factor** is the number of days that specific shares have been outstanding, as a proportion of the total number of days in the period. However, in most cases a reasonable approximation of the weighted average in terms of months is adequate. **613** FRS 22 (20)

Formula for calculating the weighted average

Ordinary shares outstanding at beginning of the period

+ New shares issued

× Time-weighting formula (A).

Each share issue is treated as a separate element of the formula.

(A) The time-weighting formula is as follows:

$$\frac{\text{Number of days (months) the shares are outstanding}}{\text{Number of days (months) in the year.}}$$

EXAMPLE If there are 90,000 shares in issue at the start of the year and a further 20,000 shares are issued halfway through the year, then the weighted average for the year would be 90,000 + (20,000/2) = 100,000. A more detailed example of calculating the weighted average number of shares is given later in this section.

2. Date from which shares should be included in the weighted average

614 FRS 22 (21) The **general rule** is that shares are included in the weighted average from the date the proceeds are receivable, as is the case in the most common scenario when shares are exchanged for cash. In other cases the applicable date is the date the shares are issued, although a reasonable estimate of the weighted average is permissible with months being used rather than days.

However, the date or timing of inclusion of the shares in the weighted average may be influenced by the specific terms and conditions attaching to the respective share issue.

The table below illustrates some **examples** of the **various circumstances** under which shares can be issued and gives guidance on the date they should be included in the formula for calculating basic EPS.

Ordinary shares issued	Date of inclusion in weighted average
1. For cash	Date when cash is receivable
2. On voluntary reinvestment of dividends (scrip dividends)	Dividend reinvestment date (¶616)
3. Shares issued as consideration for the acquisition of non-cash assets such as a merger or acquisition	The date on which the acquisition or merger is recognised (¶618)
4. Contingently issuable shares	Date on which conditions determining the share issue are met (¶620)
5. Changes in share capital not resources (i.e. bonus issues etc)	Number of shares adjusted to reflect the proportionate change from the beginning of the period reported (¶622)
6. On conversion of debt	The date interest on the debt ceases to accrue
7. In lieu of interest or principal on other financial instruments	The date interest on the instrument ceases to accrue
8. In exchange for the settlement of a liability	The settlement date

EXAMPLE **Exchange for cash plus share buy-back**

A Ltd had 50,000 ordinary shares outstanding at 1 January 20X5. During the year, the following changes in ordinary share capital occurred:

Date	Details
1 July 20X5	7,000 shares issued for cash
1 November 20X5	12,000 shares bought back for cash and cancelled

Calculation of weighted average number of shares

(50,000 × 12/12) + (7,000 × 6/12) – (12,000 × 2/12) = 51,500 shares

or

(50,000 × 6/12) + (57,000 × 6/12) – (12,000 × 2/12) = 51,500 shares

Scrip dividends

616 **Fully paid-up shares** are included in the EPS calculation from the date the consideration is payable whether they rank for dividends or not. At the same time, if there are shares in issue,

some of which are fully paid up and others not, as long as they are both eligible to receive the same level of dividends they are treated as being identical for EPS purposes.

Where **partly paid shares** have been issued to the extent that they are not entitled to receive a full dividend as compared to a fully paid share, they are, for EPS purposes, treated as a fraction of a fully paid-up share in terms of their entitlement to participate in dividends during the accounting period. **617**

Shares issued in lieu of cash in acquisitions or mergers

When ordinary shares are issued as part of a **business combination** that is accounted for as a merger, those shares are included in the weighted-average calculation for all periods presented in the first and subsequent financial statements after the merger has taken place. This information is given for the current and comparative period and the five-year summary. This treatment is consistent with the preparation of the group's combined financial statements, which are presented as if the group had always existed. Therefore, the number of ordinary shares to be used in the EPS calculation is the aggregate of the weighted average number of shares of the combined entities, adjusted to the equivalent shares of the entity whose shares are outstanding after the combination. **618** FRS 22 (22)

EXAMPLE On 1 October 20X6, C Ltd issued 200,000 ordinary shares to acquire the entire issued share capital of D Ltd. The company's year end is 31 December.

	C Ltd	D Ltd
	Number of shares	
1 January 20X5	200,000	80,000
1 July 20X4, shares issued for cash (market price)	–	20,000
31 December 20X5	200,000	100,000
1 October 20X6, shares issued to shareholders of D Ltd	200,000	–
31 December 20X6	400,000	100,000

Calculation of weighted average number of shares

20X6

200,000 + (100,000 × 9/12) + (400,000 × 3/12) = **375,000**

20X5 – comparative shown in the 20X5 financial statements

200,000 + [{80,000 + (20,000 × 6/12)} = **290,000**

Acquisitions When one entity acquires another and the consideration is in the form of ordinary shares in the investing company, then these ordinary shares are included in the weighted average number of shares **as of the date of acquisition**. This treatment is followed because the investing entity begins to incorporate the operating results of the purchased entity in its own profit and loss account from the date of acquisition. **619**

Contingently issuable shares

Contingently shares are shares that are issuable only upon the satisfaction of certain conditions. **620** FRS 22 (24)

The **general rule** is that when the events upon which the conditions were based have taken place and the issuing of the shares is definite, then the shares must be brought into the basic EPS computation even if, at the reporting date, they have not yet actually been issued. This is because the shares are no longer dilutive, as illustrated in the following example.

EXAMPLE **E Ltd** had 100,000 ordinary shares outstanding at January 20X5. In terms of a **deferred consideration agreement** relating to a recent acquisition, 3,000 additional ordinary shares are issuable in respect of every new retail branch opened between 1 January 20X5 and 31 December 20X7.

E Ltd opened new branches on 1 October 20X5 and 1 April 20X7.

Calculation of weighted average number of shares	20X5		20X6		20X7
Ordinary shares	100,000		103,000	(see 2)	103,000
New branch contingency	750	(see 1)	–		2,250
Weighted average number of shares	100,750		103,000		105,250

1. 3,000 × 3/12 (Oct-Dec).
2. In 20X6, shares relating to the branch opened on 1 October 20X5 are included from their date of issue.
3. 3,000 × 9/12 (Apr-Dec)

Where the events referred to above have not taken place, the **dilutive effects** of the ordinary shares must be accounted for in diluted EPS (¶635). Examples of contingently issuable shares are as follows:
- shares issued under the terms of a profit sharing or employee remuneration scheme;
- warrants and options; and
- convertible securities such as debentures, loan stock or preference shares.

Contingently issuable shares are dealt with in greater detail in ¶670.

Changes in share capital not resources

622 FRS 22 (26) The weighted average number of shares outstanding during the period and for all periods presented **should be adjusted for** events that have increased or reduced the number of ordinary shares outstanding, without a corresponding change in resources.

Examples of these events include:
- bonus issues;
- share splits; and
- share consolidations.

624 **Bonus issues** In a bonus issue, ordinary shares are issued to existing shareholders for no additional consideration, and as such there is no increase in the entity's resources. However, treating a bonus issue in the same way as an issue of ordinary shares for cash would result in a distorted impression of the company's profitability. Therefore, the number of shares outstanding before the event should be adjusted for the **proportionate change** in the number of ordinary shares outstanding, as if the event had occurred at the beginning of the earliest period reported.

EXAMPLE **D Ltd** had 600,000 shares outstanding from its incorporation on 1 January 20X1 until 30 September 20X4.
On 1 October 20X4, shareholders received a bonus issue of 2 ordinary shares for each ordinary share they held at 30 September 20X4.

Calculation of weighted average number of shares
Since the bonus issue results in shares being issued for no consideration, in the financial statements for the year ended 31 December 20X4, it is treated as if it had occurred before the beginning of 20X3, the earliest period reported.

Shares outstanding before bonus issue	600,000
Bonus issue: 2 for 1; therefore	1,200,000
Weighted average number of shares	**1,800,000**

This figure would be used to calculate the EPS for 20X3 and for the comparative figures.

626 **Share splits** In the case of a share split, as with a bonus issue and share consolidation, the number of shares outstanding is adjusted as if the share split had taken place at the beginning of the earliest period presented. No new capital is generated and the profits for the year should be divided by the number of shares in issue after the stock split. If an EPS figure has been disclosed for the previous year, this should be recalculated using the revised number of shares in issue.

For example, an equity share with a nominal value of $1 is split into four shares with a nominal value of $0.25. This technique is often used when a company wishes to increase liquidity in its shares if the market price is deemed too high, thus deterring small investors.

EXAMPLE E Ltd has opted for a stock split of four £0.25 shares for every one £1 share held. Its year end is 31 December.

Shares in issue at 1 January 20X4	100,000
Share split 4: 1 on 31 May 20X4	400,000
Total shares in issue after share split	400,000

Weighted average number of shares:
100,000 + (400,000 × 7/ 12) = 333,000
The weighted average would be used in the 20X4 financial statements for calculating the EPS for the current year and for the comparative period.

Share consolidation A share consolidation has the effect of **reducing the number of shares** outstanding without a reduction of resources. Therefore, the number of ordinary shares outstanding **should be adjusted** for the proportionate change in the number of ordinary shares outstanding, as if the event had occurred at the beginning of the earliest period reported in the financial statements. 628

If a share consolidation is combined with a **special dividend**, so that the net effect is that of a repurchase at fair value, no adjustment is made to the number of ordinary shares before the event.

However, the **weighted average number of ordinary shares** outstanding for the period in which a repurchase at fair value takes place is adjusted for the reduced number of shares from the date of payment of the special dividend.

EXAMPLE **F Ltd** had 900,000 ordinary shares outstanding. On 30 June 20X7, halfway through the financial year, it consolidated its shares 3: 1, thereby reducing its issued share capital to 300,000 shares.

Weighted average number of shares outstanding

(1)	As originally reported in 20X7	900,000
(2)	In **20X8**, for both 20X8 and 20X7	300,000

Assume, however, that the share consolidation was accompanied by a **special dividend** paid on 30 September 20X8.

Weighted average number of shares outstanding

(1)	As originally reported in 20X7	900,000
(2)	In 20X8:	
	(900,000) – (600,000 × 3/12)	750,000
Comparative figure shown for 20X7		900,000

Rights issues

In general, when **potential ordinary shares are converted** into actual shares and issued at full value, the change in the entity's resources is proportionate to the change in number of issued shares and no bonus element arises. In a rights issue, the **exercise price** is often less than the fair value of the shares. This difference represents a bonus element. 630

MEMO POINTS Quoted companies raise capital in exchange for shares. Under "pre-emption rights", existing shareholders are offered new shares in proportion to their existing shareholdings. For example, a 1: 4 rights issue means that shareholders will be asked to buy 4 new shares for each existing share held. The "rights" are usually issued at a discount to the "market price" of existing shares. Shareholders are not obliged to take up these rights.

The number of ordinary shares to be used in calculating basic EPS for all periods before the rights issue is the number of ordinary shares before the issue **multiplied by the following factor**:

Formula

$$\frac{\text{Fair value per share before the rights are exercised}}{\text{Theoretical ex-rights fair value per share}}$$

where the denominator is calculated as follows:

Total fair value of shares before exercising the rights;

Plus proceeds from the rights issue;

Divided by the total number of shares outstanding after the rights issue.

The calculation of the theoretical ex-right value per share is illustrated in part A of the example below and the calculation of the adjustment factor in part B.

EXAMPLE **E Ltd** had 500,000 shares outstanding before a rights issue, in terms of which shareholders would receive 1 new share for every 5 held at £5 per share.
Last day to exercise rights: 1 March 20X9
Fair value of one ordinary share immediately before this date: £11

A) Computation of theoretical ex-rights value per share

$$\frac{\text{Total fair value of outstanding shares + proceeds of rights issue}}{\text{Total number of shares outstanding after the rights issue}}$$

$$= \frac{(£11 \times 500{,}000 \text{ shares}) + (£5 \times 100{,}000 \text{ shares})}{(500{,}000 \text{ shares} + 100{,}000 \text{ shares})}$$

Theoretical ex-rights value per share = £10

B) Calculation of the adjustment factor

$$\frac{\text{Fair value per share before the rights are exercised}}{\text{Theoretical ex-rights fair value per share}}$$

$$= \frac{£11}{£10}$$

= 1.1

Weighted average number of shares
As originally reported in **20X8**, the weighted average number of shares would have been **500,000**. In **20X9**, the comparative EPS for 20X8 is restated for the rights issue. Therefore, the weighted average number of shares is 500,000 × 1.1(adjustment factor) = 550,000 shares.
EPS for 20X9 is calculated using the following formula for weighted average number of shares:
= (500,000 × 1.1 × 2/12) + (600,000 × 10/12)
= 591,667 shares.
As can be seen, the weighted average for 20X4 is calculated in the normal manner but for the weighting of the pre-issue element by the adjustment factor.

Ordinary shares excluded from basic EPS

632 If any of the following shares are outstanding during the period, an adjustment is required to exclude them from the computation of the weighted average number of shares:

1. **Shares in issue that are held by a group member** should be treated as if they had been cancelled from the date issued.
2. **Shares held by an employee share ownership plan (ESOP) trust** If these shares are reflected in the company balance sheet then, similarly, they are to be treated for basic EPS purposes as if they had been cancelled. This treatment remains in force until the shares vest unconditionally with the employees. If the transfer into the ESOP takes place during the year, the amount of shares to be excluded is adjusted on a time weighted basis.

EXAMPLE **ESOP Trust**

B Ltd has 100,000 ordinary shares in issue on 1 January 20X4. On 30 June 20X4, it set up an ESOP trust, which acquired 20,000 company shares on that date at the prevailing market price.
At year end, 31 December 20X4, the shares had not been vested in the employees and they were reflected as a deduction from shareholders' funds.
In accordance with UITF 38 (10), the shares are treated as if they are cancelled.

SECTION 2

Diluted EPS

While basic EPS can be considered to give some indication of an entity's capacity to generate future earnings on a per-share basis, where changes in the number of shares in issue are (or can be) anticipated, it is useful if readers of financial statements can be given a mechanism by which to take the potential effect into account. 635

Accordingly, diluted EPS reflects the future effect of **dilutive potential ordinary shares** (¶644) outstanding during the period on net income attributable to ordinary shareholders. In particular, it recognises the post-tax effects of dividends or interest included in the current period relating to dilutive potential ordinary shares that, on conversion to ordinary shares, will no longer be incurred.

The objective of diluted earnings per share is consistent with that of basic earnings per share, i.e., to provide a measure of the interest of each ordinary share in the performance of the company while giving effect to all dilutive potential ordinary shares outstanding during the period.

The **general rule** is that if an entity has any potential ordinary shares that are dilutive and outstanding during the period, then the diluted EPS must be calculated and disclosed. For the purpose of calculating diluted earnings per share, the net profit attributable to ordinary shareholders and the weighted average number of shares should be adjusted for the effects of dilutive potential ordinary shares. 636 FRS 22 (31)

The **general formula** for calculating diluted EPS is consistent with that used to calculate basic EPS, but it **adjusts** both the net profit attributable to ordinary shareholders and the weighted average number of shares outstanding for the effects of dilutive ordinary shares. 637

These adjustments are made as if the dilutive potential ordinary shares had been converted to ordinary shares at the beginning of the period.

Formula

$$\frac{\text{Earnings per basic EPS adjusted for the dilutive potential ordinary shares (Numerator)}}{\text{No. of shares per basic EPS adjusted for the dilutive potential ordinary shares (Denominator)}}$$

It should be noted that a **potential ordinary share is regarded as dilutive** only if its conversion to an ordinary share would reduce profit per share or increase the loss per share. If a potential share is not dilutive, it should be excluded from the diluted EPS calculation.

A. Numerator

For the purpose of calculating diluted earnings per share, the profit or loss attributable to ordinary equity holders must be **adjusted** by the after-tax effect of: (a) any dividends or other items related to dilutive potential ordinary shares deducted in arriving at profit or loss attributable to ordinary equity; (b) any interest recognised in the period related to dilutive potential ordinary shares; and (c) any other changes in income or expense that would result from the conversion of the dilutive potential ordinary shares. 638 FRS 22 (33)

The conversion of potential ordinary shares may lead to consequential changes in income or expenses. The reduction of interest expense related to potential ordinary shares could, for instance, lead to an increase in the expense related to a non-discretionary employee profit sharing plan. For the purpose of calculating diluted earnings per share, profit or loss attributable to ordinary equity holders should be adjusted for any consequential changes in income or expense of this type. 639

Factors affecting the numerator

640 After the dilutive potential ordinary shares are converted into ordinary shares, the dividends, interest and other income or expense associated with the financial instruments or rights through which they are generated will no longer be incurred.

642 The new ordinary shares will be entitled to participate in the net profit attributable to ordinary shareholders, which should be increased by the savings referred to above. The expenses associated with potential ordinary shares include fees, discounts and premiums allocated to periods over their term at a constant rate. The amount of dividends, interest and other income or expense are adjusted for any tax effects attributable to them.

In the following example, bonds are convertible into ordinary shares, which subsequently affects both reported EPS and the number of ordinary shares in issue. The example illustrates the process of calculating diluted earnings per share and the effect of dilutive potential ordinary shares on EPS.

EXAMPLE **Bonds convertible into ordinary shares**

The following information was extracted from the financial statements of **J Ltd**:

Net profit	£1,000
Ordinary shares outstanding	10,000
Basic EPS	10p
Convertible 10% bonds	1,000

Each block of 10 bonds is convertible to 15 ordinary shares

Interest expense for the year relating to the liability component of the convertible bonds (Includes amortisation of the discount arising on initial recognition of the liability component)	£100
Current and deferred tax on the interest expense	£40

Calculation of diluted EPS

1. Adjusted net profit: Net profit £1,000 + £100 interest – £40 tax = £1060

2. Number of shares resulting from conversion of bonds 1,000 × 15/10 = 1,500

Ordinary shares in issue	10,000
Conversion of bonds to ordinary shares	1,500
Total	11,500

3. Diluted EPS

Adjusted net profit/total number of ordinary shares (including conversion)

£1,060/11,500	**9.2 p**

B. Denominator

643 FRS 22 (36) For the purpose of calculating diluted earnings per share, the number of ordinary shares is the weighted average number of ordinary shares as computed for the basic EPS calculation, plus the weighted average number of ordinary shares that would be issued on the conversion of all the dilutive potential ordinary shares into ordinary shares.

Dilutive potential ordinary shares are, as a general rule, deemed to have been converted into ordinary shares at the beginning of the period or, if later, the date of the issue of the potential ordinary shares. They are determined independently for each period presented. The number of dilutive potential ordinary shares included in the year-to-date period is not a weighted average of the dilutive potential ordinary shares included in each interim computation.

Potential ordinary shares are weighted for the period during which they are outstanding. Those that are cancelled (or allowed to lapse) during the period are included in the calculation of diluted EPS only for that portion of the period they are outstanding. Potential ordinary shares that are converted into ordinary shares during the period are included in the calculation of diluted earnings per share from the beginning of the period to the date of conversion. From the date of conversion, the resulting ordinary shares are included in both basic and diluted EPS.

The number of ordinary shares that would be issued on conversion of dilutive potential ordinary shares is determined from the terms of the potential ordinary shares. Where there is more than one basis, the calculation must assume the most advantageous from the holder's point of view.

A **subsidiary**, **joint venture** or **associate** may issue to parties other than the parent, venturer or investor potential ordinary shares that are convertible into ordinary shares of either (1) the subsidiary, joint venture or associate, or (2) the parent, venturer or investor (i.e., the reporting entity). Where these potential ordinary shares have a dilutive effect on the basic earnings per share of the reporting entity concerned, they must be included in the calculation of diluted earnings per share.

C. Dilutive potential ordinary shares

Potential ordinary shares must be treated as dilutive when, and only when, their conversion to ordinary shares would have the effect of decreasing earnings per share (or increasing loss per share) from continuing operations. **644** FRS 22 (41)

Companies must use profit or loss from continuing operations attributable to the parent entity as the control number to establish whether potential ordinary shares are dilutive or antidilutive. Potential ordinary shares are antidilutive when their conversion to ordinary shares would increase earnings per share (or decrease loss per share) from continuing operations. The calculation of diluted earnings per share does not assume conversion, exercise, or other issue of potential ordinary shares that would have an antidilutive effect on earnings per share. (In other words, antidilutive shares are disregarded in the calculation of diluted EPS.)

The following are **examples** of dilutive potential ordinary shares: **646**
- convertible debt or equity instruments, including preference shares (¶654);
- share warrants and options (¶660);
- rights granted under employee or other share purchase plans (¶666);
- contingently issuable ordinary shares (¶670) i.e., rights to ordinary shares that are contingent upon the satisfaction of specific conditions.

1. Determining whether potential ordinary shares are dilutive

For purposes of determining whether potential ordinary shares are dilutive, **each issue or series** of potential ordinary shares is considered separately. The sequence in which potential ordinary shares are considered also may affect whether they are dilutive. Therefore, in order to maximise the dilution of basic EPS, each issue or series of potential ordinary shares is examined to determine the most dilutive through to the least dilutive (see ¶684). **647** FRS 22 (44)

Potential ordinary shares are weighted for the period they were outstanding. If potential ordinary shares **were cancelled or allowed to lapse** during the reporting period, they are included in the calculation of diluted EPS only for that part of the period during which they were outstanding.

Potential ordinary shares **that have been converted** into ordinary shares during the reporting period are included in the calculation of diluted earnings per share, from the beginning of the period to the date of conversion. From the date of conversion, the resulting ordinary shares are also included in the basic earnings per share.

Timing of deemed conversion For purposes of the calculation, potential ordinary shares are deemed to have been converted into ordinary shares **at the beginning of the period**. If, **649**

however, they did not exist at that time, the date of issue of the financial instrument or the granting of the rights by which the potential ordinary shares are generated should be used instead.

2. Types of dilutive potential ordinary shares

Convertible debt and shares

654 Companies often issue capital instruments such as preference shares, loan stocks or debentures that are convertible into equity shares when **certain criteria are met**. The **terms attached** to the issue will detail the dates, number of shares, and the conversion or issue price of the securities and determine the impact in terms of diluting earnings per share.

655 **Adjustment to earnings (Numerator)** represents the following in respect of debt instruments and non-equity shares:
- interest or dividends charged;
- amortisation of issue costs; and
- amortisation of redemption premium (or discount).

656 **Adjustment to the number of shares (Denominator**) assumes that holders of all convertible instruments exercise their rights to convert to ordinary shares. In situations where different conversion ratios are allowed on different dates, then the ratio should assume the maximum number of new ordinary shares will be issued. The most advantageous conversion rate or exercise price should be factored into the calculation.

In the following example the **convertible shares** have the **effect of diluting earnings per share**.

EXAMPLE **Dilution of earnings per share**

A company with an issued share capital of 1,000,000 ordinary shares (nominal value £1) issued £500,000 of 6% convertible loan stock, convertible at the rate of £100 nominal value into 150 ordinary shares. Trading profits for 20X4 were £650,000 and corporate tax was 30%.

Calculation of basic EPS

	20X4 £
Profit before interest and tax	**650,000**
Interest on 10% convertible stock	50,000
Profit before tax	600,000
Tax (30 %)	180,000
Profit after tax	**420,000**
Equity shares	1,000,000

Basic EPS
£420,000/ 1,000,000 = 42.0p

Calculation of diluted EPS – effects of the convertible stock.

Profit for basic EPS calculation	**420,000**
Plus: the interest saved	50,000
Less loss of tax relief on interest saved at 30%	(15,000)
Adjusted equity earnings	**455,000**

Adjusted number of shares.
1,000,000/ 100 × 150 = 1,500,000 ordinary shares
£455,000/ 1,500,000 = diluted EPS of 30.3p

Share warrants and options

660 FRS 22 (45) Share warrants and options give the beneficiary of the financial instrument the right to purchase or subscribe for ordinary shares, at a particular price at a future date. **Only dilutive options are of interest here**, although the accounting treatment of more complex dilutive options is beyond the scope of this book.

When calculating diluted EPS, the first step is to assume that all dilutive options and other dilutive potential ordinary shares are exercised on either the first day of the accounting period or the date granted if later.

The **proceeds of these assumed transactions** should then be regarded as having been from the issue of shares at fair value, which is calculated on the basis of the average price of the ordinary shares during the reporting period. The difference between the number of shares issued and the number of shares that would have been issued at fair value should be treated as an issue of ordinary shares for no consideration.

Options and other share purchase arrangements Options and other share purchase arrangements that result in the issue of ordinary shares for less than fair value are considered dilutive. The extent of the dilution will depend on the difference between the fair value and the issue price. In order to calculate diluted EPS, each contract or arrangement is deemed to consist of: 662

a. Adjustment to earnings (Numerator) The general rule is that for contracts concerning share warrants or options, adjustments to earnings are not required, except concerning ESOP trusts. Contracts for the issue of a certain number of ordinary shares at average fair value are normally considered neither dilutive nor antidilutive and are ignored in the calculation of diluted EPS.

b. Adjustment to number of shares (Denominator) Where shares are issued for no consideration they have no effect on the net profit attributable to ordinary shares outstanding. As such these shares are dilutive and are added to the number of ordinary shares outstanding in the calculation of the diluted EPS. The number of shares is adjusted by the number of shares deemed to be issued free of charge.

Determining the dilutive impact of share options on EPS

Calculate the following in this order: 664

1. The **cash proceeds** if all options exercised at contracted exercise price.
2. The **number of shares** which, if issued at fair value, would raise the same capital; namely calculate the average fair value of ordinary shares for period and divide by proceeds if all options exercised at contracted exercise price.
3. The number of shares deemed **issued for no consideration** by determining the total number of shares deemed created if all options exercised, then deducting from this figure the total number of shares issued at fair price; the remaining number of shares are deemed to be issued for no consideration.

EXAMPLE **Impact of share options on diluted EPS**

The following assumptions have been made for financial year 20X4

Net profit for the year	£1.2 million
Weighted average number of ordinary shares outstanding during the year	5 million
Average fair value of 1 ordinary share	£4.00
Weighted average number of shares under option	1 million
Exercise price for shares under option	£3.00

Computation of earnings per share

Net profit for the year (A)	£1,200,000
Weighted average number of shares (B)	5,000,000
Basic earnings per share (A ÷ B)	**24 p**
Number of shares under option	1,000,000
Less: Number of shares that would have been issued at fair value of £4 to generate the total proceeds earned if all options exercised at £3 = (1,000,000 × £3/£4)	– 750,000
Number of shares for denominator (C)	5,250,000
Diluted earnings per share (A ÷ C) (£1.2m/5,250)	**22.9 p**

Employee share and incentive plans

666 FRS 22 (47a) Share-based payment and other incentive schemes are increasingly a constituent of employee remuneration packages. When dealing with these arrangements, the issue and exercise prices should include the fair value of any goods or services to be supplied to the entity as part of the share-based payment.

667 FRS 22 (48) In the calculation of diluted EPS, employee share options with fixed or determinable terms and non-vested ordinary shares are treated as options (even though they may be contingent on vesting). They are treated as outstanding on the grant date. Performance-based employee share options are treated as contingently issuable shares because their issue is contingent upon satisfying specified conditions in addition to the passage of time.

Contingently issuable shares

670 Contingently issuable shares are shares issued at a future date, subject to certain conditions such as earnings, market price etc. being met. Contingently issuable shares are an example of potential ordinary shares that are sometimes included in the calculation of basic EPS, although the main impact is often on diluted EPS. The various types of contingently issuable shares are considered below.

672 **General rules** A number of general rules or conditions apply to contingently issuable potential ordinary shares, as well as contingently issuable share options, warrants, convertibles and any other potential ordinary shares.

Contingently issuable shares are **included in the calculation** of diluted EPS as of **the earlier of**:

FRS 22 (52)
- the beginning of the reporting period; or
- the date that the relevant financial instrument granting the rights came into existence.

673 **1. Adjustment to earnings (Numerator)** Contingently issuable shares have no impact on the earnings figure used to calculate diluted EPS, even where the condition itself is earnings related. The reason for this is that the number of contingently issuable shares included in the diluted EPS calculation is always based on the condition(s) existing at the balance sheet date.

674 **2. Adjustment to number of shares (Denominator)** The number of shares to include in the calculation of diluted EPS is based on the number of shares that would be issued under the **terms of the contingency**, based on the assumption that the current status of the contingency remains unchanged until the end of the agreement. In other words, the number of shares that would be issued if the end of the reporting period was the same as the end of the contingency period.

If a condition is expressed as an average over a period it has the same effect as a cumulative amount over the period.

> EXAMPLE If the condition depends on whether profits average £200,000 over two years, it is the same as expressing a cumulative target of £400,000 for the whole period. Therefore, if at the end of the first year, profits are £150,000, no additional shares are brought into the diluted EPS calculation. This is because the assumption is made that at the end of the reporting period the contingent condition will not be satisfied, [the profit for the year for £150,000 is less than the average required of £200,000] and it is assumed that this will prevail until the end of the contingency period.

675 **3. Market price** If the number of shares to be issued at some point in the future depends on the market price of the shares of the issuing company at that point (or the average over a specific period), the number of shares to include in the diluted EPS calculation should be based on the market price at the end of the current reporting period.

If the event upon which the shares will be issued is **not related to earnings or market price**, the shares should be included in the calculation, on the assumption that the status of the condition at the end of the reporting period will remain unchanged until the end of the contingency period.

If, for instance, a further issue of shares will be generated on the occurrence of a specific condition, such as the opening of a fifth retail outlet and, by year end, only four stores have been opened, no contingently issuable shares are included in the diluted earnings per share computation.

4. Deferred consideration agreements In the case of deferred consideration agreements where the consideration is fixed but the number of shares issuable is not yet known, the number of shares to be included in the calculation is based on the market price at the balance sheet date (i.e., as if it were the end of the contingency period). 676

5. Combination of factors If the number of shares to be issued is dependent on a combination of factors, the number to be included should be based on the status of all relevant conditions at the end of the reporting period. No shares are to be included if one of the above conditions is not met. 677

6. Consistency If an entity has contingently issuable potential ordinary shares in respect of the same class of ordinary shares and on the same terms as, e.g., warrants already in issue then, for consistency, the contingently issuable warrants should be included in diluted earnings per share only if the conversion or exercise of the warrants already in issue is also assumed. 678

EXAMPLE H Limited has 1,000,000 ordinary shares outstanding at 1 January 20X3. The terms of a **deferred consideration agreement**, related to a recent business acquisition, provide for the following contingently issuable shares:

a. **20,000 additional ordinary shares** for every new retail outlet opened in each of 20X4, 20X5 and 20X6.

b. **2,000 additional ordinary shares** for each £1,000 of total net income in excess of £700,000 over the 3 years ending 20X6.

Assume that additional shares are issued on 1 January in the accounting period following that in which the relevant condition is met.

H Limited's results during the period were as follows:

1. New retail outlets opened on 1 April 20X4 and 1 February 20X6
2. Net income

- 20X4 – £300,000
- 20X5 – £475,000
- 20X6 – £350,000

		20X4		20X5		20X6
Calculation of basic EPS						
Numerator:		300,000		475,000		350,000
Denominator:						
Ordinary shares		1,000,000	C	1,020,000		1,020,000
Retail outlet contingency	A	15,000		-	E	18,333
Earnings contingency	B	-	D	-	D	-
Total shares		1,015,000		1,020,000		1,038,333
Basic EPS		29.6 p		46.6 p		33.7 p
Calculation of diluted EPS						
Numerator:		300,000		475,000		350,000
Denominator:						
Ordinary shares in basic EPS		1,015,000		1,020,000		1,038,333
Additional shares for:						
Retail outlet contingency	F	5,000			F	
Earnings contingency	G	-	H	150,000	I	850,000
Total shares		1,020,000		1,170,000		1,888,333
Diluted EPS		**29.4 p**		**40.6 p**		**18.5 p**

A 20,000 × 9/12
B In 20X4, the earnings contingency does not affect EPS because the condition is not satisfied (see also D, below).
C In 20X5, shares relating to the retail outlet opened on 1 April 20X2 are included in basic EPS from date of issue.
D In 20X5 and 20X6, the earnings contingency does not affect basic EPS because it is not certain that the condition is met until the end of the period.
E 11/12 × 20,000
F Additional shares included in diluted EPS, which includes contingently issuable shares from the beginning of the period.
G Ltd did not have £700,000 net income at 31 December 20X4.
H (£775,000 – £700,000)/1,000 × 2,000
I (£1,125,000 – £700,000)/1,000 × 2,000; the shares will be included in basic EPS as of 1 January 20X7, their date of issue.

680 **7. Settlement by way of shares or cash** When an entity issues a contract that may be settled either in shares or in cash at the election of either party, it may not be known at the reporting date which method of settlement will be used. The FRS recommends that if a stated policy or past experience provides a reasonable basis on which to determine what the outcome will be, this should be followed. However, if both past experience and a stated policy are absent, it should be assumed instead that the contract will be settled by the more dilutive method.

681 **8. Subsidiaries, joint ventures or associates** may issue potential ordinary shares **exchangeable for either**:
- their own ordinary shares; or
- ordinary shares in the reporting entity.

If these potential ordinary shares have a dilutive effect on the **consolidated basic EPS** of the reporting entity, they are to be included in the calculation of diluted EPS.

D. Ranking dilutive potential ordinary shares

684 Each category of potential ordinary shares should be considered separately. This is illustrated in the example below.

EXAMPLE Determining the order in which to include **dilutive potential ordinary shares**:
The following information relates to **K Ltd** in respect of the accounting year ended 31 December 20X4.

Net profit attributable to ordinary shareholders	£12 million
Net profit attributable to discontinued operations	£2 million
Ordinary shares outstanding	20 million
Average fair value per ordinary share during year	£7.50
Tax rate	40%

Potential ordinary shares

(A) – Options	Number: 5 million Exercise price: £6.00
(B) – Convertible preference shares	Number: 800,000 Each entitled to a cumulative dividend of £8.00 Each convertible to 2 ordinary shares
(C) – 2% Convertible bond	Nominal amount: £100,000,000 Each £1,000 bond is convertible to 40 ordinary shares Assume no amortisation of premium or discount affecting the determination of interest expense

Stage 1

Calculate diluted EPS for each category of potential ordinary shares

1. First, determine the effect on earnings should the potential ordinary shares have been converted to ordinary shares at the beginning of the period.
2. Next, determine the number of shares that would have to be issued.
3. Finally, for each category of potential ordinary shares, calculate the additional earnings per additional share.

Stage 1	**Increase in earnings**	**Increase in number of ordinary shares**	**Additional earnings per share**
A – Options			
Increase in earnings	Nil		
Incremental shares issued for no consideration		1,000,000	Nil
5,000,000 × (£7.50 – £6.00)/£7.50			
B – Convertible preference shares			
Increase in net profit	Nil		
Preference dividend no longer payable on conversion			
(£8 × 800,000 preference shares)	6,400,000		
Incremental shares 2 × 800,000		1,600,000	£4.00
C – 2% convertible bonds			
After-tax effect of reduction in interest	1,200,000		
(£100,000,000 × 2%) × (1-0.4 %)			
Incremental shares 100,000 × 40		4,000,000	30p

Stage 2

Diluted EPS – ranking of dilutive potential ordinary shares

1. In the next stage, rank the additional earnings per additional share in order from the highest to the lowest.
2. Then, adjust "continuing earnings per share" for each category of potential ordinary shares based on the increased earnings and number of shares.
3. If the resulting EPS is less, the potential ordinary shares are dilutive. If more, the shares are anti-dilutive and are excluded from the EPS disclosure.

Stage 2	**Net profit attributable to continuing operations**	**Ordinary shares**	**Earnings per share**
A. Options	**£**	**Number**	**£**
As reported	10,000,000	20,000,000	0.50
Options		1,000,000	
Totals	10,000,000	21,000,000	0.48 Dilutive
B. 2% Convertible bonds	1,200,000	4,000,000	
Totals	11,200,000	25,000,000	0.45 Dilutive
C. Convertible preference shares	6,400,000	1,600,000	
Totals	**17,600,000**	**26,600,600**	**0.66 Anti-dilutive**

Stage 3

Computation of basic earnings per share:

Net profit	£12 million
Weighted average number of shares	20 million
Basic earnings per share	60p

Computation of diluted earnings per share:

Net profit (£12m plus £1.2m convertible bond interest)	£13.2 million
Weighted average number of shares outstanding	25 million
Diluted earnings per share	52.8p

SECTION 3

Presentation

690 Entities are required to present, on the face of the income statement, both basic and diluted earnings per share for profit (or loss) from continuing operations attributable to the ordinary equity holders of the parent entity, and for profit or loss attributable to the ordinary equity holders of the parent entity, for the period in respect of each class of ordinary shares that has a different right to share in profit for the period. Basic and diluted earnings per share are to be shown with equal prominence for all periods presented.

As a practical matter, EPS is usually expressed in pence though this is not specifically required by FRS 22. Disclosure of EPS is required even where it is a negative amount, i.e., a loss per share.

692 FRS 22 (70) For entities that fall within the scope of FRS 22, the following information must be disclosed in their financial statements.

Category	Compulsory disclosure requirements
Basic EPS	Must be shown on the face of the profit and loss account for each class of ordinary share.
Diluted EPS	As per basic EPS (equal prominence).
Numerators	The numerator must be disclosed in the notes to the accounts for both basic and diluted EPS. A reconciliation of the numerator with the net profit or loss for the year is required.
Denominators	The weighted average number of shares used in the calculation of basic and diluted EPS must be shown in the notes to the accounts and excepting figures given in respect of different classes of ordinary share, a reconciliation of these denominators to each other is required.
Discontinued operations	Companies reporting discontinued operations must disclose the basic and diluted EPS for the discontinued operations in question. (This can be shown on the face of the income statement or in the notes.)
Potentially dilutive instruments	Instruments (including contingently issuable shares) that could potentially dilute basic earnings per share **in the future**, but were not included in the calculation of diluted earnings per share because they are antidilutive for the period(s) presented.
Transactions after balance sheet date	A description of ordinary share transactions or potential ordinary share transactions occurring after the balance sheet date (even if these have not been taken into consideration in computing the published EPS figures). However, this disclosure is required only if the transaction is of such significance that non-disclosure could affect users of the financial statements in their evaluation or decision making.

694 **Consolidated financial statements** When a parent entity presents both its own and consolidated financial statements, only the consolidated EPS need be disclosed. For disclosure purposes of EPS, ordinary shares carrying the same dividend rights are regarded as one class of share.

Both basic and diluted EPS must be disclosed in respect of each class of ordinary share. Diluted EPS must always be disclosed, even if basic EPS is negative (i.e. a loss per share) and the difference between basic and diluted EPS is not material. If they are identical, a single amount may be shown as follows:

Earnings per share

Basic and diluted (pence)... xx.xx

EXAMPLE

P Ltd – Annual Report and Accounts	Profit (numerator)	Shares (denominator)	Earnings per share
Notes to the accounts	£		£
Net profit for the year	125,000		
Less: Preference dividends	5,000		
1. Basic EPS			
Profit attributable to ordinary shareholders	120,000	200,000	60p
2. Diluted EPS			
Effect of dilutive potential ordinary shares, namely convertible preference shares	5,000	40,000	
Profit attributable to ordinary shareholders and assumed conversion.	**125,000**	**240,000**	**52p**

When circumstances dictate, the following **additional disclosures** should be made. 696

Additional earnings per share

If an entity chooses to disclose additional EPS information (other than basic and diluted EPS) using as the numerator a component of reported net profit, other than net profit or loss for the period attributable to ordinary shareholders, the **weighted average number** of shares used in the calculation (i.e. the denominator) should still be determined in accordance with the FRS. 700 FRS 22 (73)

The reason that additional EPS information has been presented should be given. This information should also be: FRS 14 (74)
- presented on a consistent basis over time; and
- reconciled with the relevant basic and diluted EPS, listing the amounts that have been adjusted and showing their individual effect on the calculation:
  - changes in assumptions used; or
  - conversion of potential ordinary shares into ordinary shares.

Both the reconciliation and the explanation must appear adjacent to each other or clearly referenced as a note to the EPS disclosure.

Retrospective adjustments

If the number of ordinary (or potential ordinary) shares outstanding increases as a result of a capitalisation, bonus issue or share split, or if it decreases as a result of a reverse share split, the calculation of basic and diluted earnings per share for all periods presented must be adjusted retrospectively. 702 FRS 22 (64)

If these changes have taken place **after the balance sheet date** but before the financial statements have been approved:
- the calculations should be based on the new number of shares; and
- the fact should be stated.

The basic and diluted earnings per share of all periods presented should be adjusted for the effects of errors and adjustments resulting from changes in accounting policies accounted for retrospectively.

Special dividend If a share consolidation was combined with a special dividend and the overall effect is of a **share repurchase at fair value**, no adjustment is necessary. However, the fact that EPS has not been restated in these circumstances should be disclosed. 704

Prior period Diluted EPS for any prior period presented should not be restated for either: 706
- changes in assumptions used; or
- conversion of potential ordinary shares into ordinary shares.

CHAPTER 3

Segmental reporting

OUTLINE ¶¶

Many entities conduct a range of different business activities, serve various markets, and operate in more than one geographical location. Each of these business units, irrespective of how they may be categorised or organised, have their own unique commercial characteristics: for instance, different rates of profitability, different opportunities for growth and different degrees of risk. As more and more businesses trade on a world-wide basis, growing and diversifying their activities, so the users of their financial statements need to understand the varying economic, political and business risks – as well as opportunities – that exist in the individual segments, and the effect they have on overall growth, profitability, and financial position. The user groups most likely to benefit from segmental information include shareholders, investment analysts and major creditors. 750

The **general purpose** of SSAP 25, "Segmental reporting", is to assist users of financial statements by providing segmental analysis of the information they contain, in particular the disclosure of turnover, results, and net assets by class of business and by geographical sector.

No less importantly, the accounting standard seeks to ensure as far as possible that the segmental information reported is disclosed consistently over time and to minimise the possible danger, when comparing the results of similar segments in different entities, of differences in accounting policies adopted, bases of accounting for inter-segment sales, and the treatment of common costs.

Two broad categories of segment are distinguished: **business** and **geographical**. SSAP 25 provides guidance on how to determine the segments and what information should be 752 disclosed. The directors can therefore exercise considerable discretion when compiling segmental information.

753 If a company operates in two or more significant markets or classes of business, and these differ substantially from one another, it is obliged to comply with the **statutory** disclosure requirements on segmental reporting contained in the Companies Act. Broadly, these are that the turnover attributable to the different classes and markets should be shown individually in the notes. The regulations to the 2006 Act allow that only those classes of business or markets that make a **material** contribution need be disclosed; amounts that are not material may be combined with other classes and markets and shown as such. A total exemption from the disclosure requirements of the Companies Act is possible but difficult to justify. One such exemption would be where, in the opinion of the directors, the disclosure of segmental information would be harmful to the company's interests. However, the fact that the information has not been given must be clearly stated.

754 Additional non-statutory (i.e., required by **GAAP**) disclosure requirements are required for certain entities under SSAP 25 and FRS 3 "Reporting financial performance". Further specific disclosure rules apply to certain industries (such as Oil and Financial Services), which have issued their own statements of recommended practice (SORPs). Segmental information may also be included in the interim reports published predominantly by listed companies.

As a general rule, the disclosure of segmental information is encouraged even if the entity is able to claim **exemption** from some or all of the additional disclosure requirements of SSAP 25. The majority of companies present their segmental information in the notes to the accounts.

This chapter provides an overview of some of the general difficulties associated with the compilation of segmental data and the need for consistency in presentation. A comparison with IAS 14, "Segmental reporting", is given at the end of the chapter.

756 **Exempt Companies** The following entities are specifically exempt from SSAP 25, though not from the Companies Act:
- reporting entities reporting under the dispensation for smaller entities (FRSSE);
- a subsidiary company (that is not a public limited company or a banking or insurance company), where its parent publishes segmental information in compliance with this standard or in accordance with International Accounting Standards (see *Memo Point*, below); and
- particular types of entity that are subject to different statutory rules and that are outside the scope of this manual (e.g., building societies, among others).

MEMO POINTS (1) The exemption in respect of subsidiaries whose parent entities provide segmental information was previously applicable only to those complying wih SSAP 25. In 2010 the ASB, in its annual review of financial reporting standards, decided to extend the exemption to parent entities that comply with IFRS. (2) The amendment applies to annual periods beginning on or after 1 January 2011, with earlier application permitted.

SECTION 1

Determination of significant segments

760 Beyond giving general suggestions for determining classes of business, the Act leaves it to the directors to decide on the matter. Similarly, SSAP 25 identifies a number of factors that the directors might consider in their determination of what constitutes a geographical or business segment and, again, allows them to exercise their judgement as to what comprises a significant segment. SSAP 25 does, however, require "material segments" to be disclosed, irrespective of the directors' opinion.

General factors

The directors, in trying to identify reporting segments, should consider those operations that have different: 762 SSAP 25 (8)
- returns on investment, disproportionate to the rest of the business;
- degrees of risk;
- comparative scales of operation;
- rates of growth; and
- potential for future development.

The selection of segments should be based on an assessment of any of these factors either individually or in combination. The accounting standard advises that these **criteria** should be reviewed annually and redefined as appropriate because of the likelihood that no single set of characteristics will continue to apply or remain dominant indefinitely. However, as far as is practicable, the directors should maintain consistency of approach so that segmental results will be comparable year on year.

Business segments

A business segment is defined as a separate division that provides a different product or service and can be based on any of the following criteria: 764 SSAP 25 (12)
- type of the **product or service**
- nature of the **production process**
- **markets** in which the products or services are sold
- **distribution channels** for the products
- any particular **legislative framework** relating to the segment – e.g., bank or insurance company
- the manner in which **activities are organised**.

The business segments of some major listed companies are shown in the following example by way of illustration.

EXAMPLE

Company	Reported business segments
United News and Media	Business services; consumer publishing; broadcasting.
WPP Group plc	Advertising & media planning; information & consultancy; public relations; buying & research.
United Utilities plc	Water and wastewater; electricity distribution; energy supply.

Geographical segments

A geographical segment is generally defined as an area comprising an individual country or group of countries in which an entity either physically operates, or markets and supplies, goods or services. This might also cover a group of countries linked through the adoption of a currency zone such as the euro. 766 SSAP 25 (14)

Geographical segments should reflect the extent to which an entity's operations are affected by:
- the **political climate** in the country of operations,
- any **exchange control** regulations, and
- fluctuating **exchange rates**.

However, it is not practical to define a method of grouping that would reflect all the differences between international business environments or that would apply to all entities.

Materiality

A geographical or business segment would also be considered significant if one of the following criteria apply, irrespective of the judgement of the directors: 768
- its **turnover** is 10 percent or more of the total turnover (excluding inter-company sales) of the entity;

– the **segmental profit** or loss is 10 percent or more of the combined results of all the entities' profit- or loss-making segments; or
– its **net assets** are 10 percent or more of the total assets of the entity.

In practice, some companies also disclose information on segments that are below the materiality limits stipulated in the standard because of historical considerations or the growing significance of such a segment. It is also important to note that additional disclosures are required of **associates and joint ventures** (¶7300), which are triggered at a specific threshold.

SECTION 2

Compliance

774 A number of **compulsory disclosures** are prescribed by the Companies Act; additional disclosures are required under SSAP 25, which seeks to ensure that the disclosure and presentation of segmental information is undertaken on a consistent basis, so as to facilitate comparison over time.

The issue of voluntary disclosure and the problems inherent in compiling segmental information are also covered.

A. Compulsory disclosures required by the Companies Act

776 Under the Companies Act, companies that operate in two or more major markets must provide a **description** of each class of business, as well as an **analysis** of:
– turnover and profit or loss before tax between substantially different classes of business;
– turnover between significant geographical segments; and
– the amount of profit or loss of the company before tax, attributable to each business segment.

In analysing segmental information, the directors must give due consideration as to how the business activities are organised. Furthermore, classes of business or markets that do not differ substantially from each other should be treated as one class, and amounts that are not material may be included in another class of business or market segment.

The Companies Act 2006 **exempts medium-sized companies** from this disclosure.

778 **Exemptions** An exemption from the Companies Act disclosure requirements is available only where, in the opinion of the directors, the disclosure of information would be **seriously prejudicial** to the interests of the company. An **example** might be the case of a company that trades with neighbouring countries that are in conflict with each other.

This non-disclosure exemption cannot be used simply to avoid disclosing information that the entity would prefer **competitors** not to know. If the exemption is invoked, this fact must be disclosed in a **note to the accounts** although the **reasons** need not be given. In practice, the exemption is rarely used.

780 SSAP 25 (20) The Companies Act contains provisions exempting **banks and insurance companies** from the requirement to disclose segmental turnover in certain circumstances. In spite of this, it does not appear that banks enjoy a similar exemption under SSAP 25.

B. Additional disclosures required by SSAP 25

Under SSAP 25, which extends the statutory disclosure requirements, an entity should disclose in its financial statements the **basis** on which it **defines** its geographical and business **segments**. For each segment it should then disclose all of the following information: **790** SSAP 25 (34)
- turnover split by group companies, joint ventures and associated companies;
- turnover split by geographical segment but excluding inter-company transactions and VAT;
- turnover analysed by reference to customer location (source) or destination and by its origin;
- operating results after tax, minority interests and extraordinary items; and
- net operating assets.

Turnover

The users of the financial statements should gain a better understanding of the entity's exposure to geographical factors if turnover is disclosed according to the location of both operations and markets. **792** SSAP 25 (18)

The **origin** of turnover is the geographical area from which products or services are supplied to a third party or another segment. The **destination** of turnover is the geographical area to which goods and services are supplied. Where there is no material difference between the origin and destination of sales, separate disclosure is not required although a statement to this effect must be provided.

Where segmental turnover is **not required to be disclosed by statute**, it is likewise not required by the accounting standards. However, the fact that segmental turnover has not been disclosed must be clearly stated. SSAP 25 (20)

Operating results and net assets

Disclosures relating to segmental results and net assets are generally based on the locations of operation because this will enable the user to match turnover, operating results and net assets on a consistent basis. It will also allow comparisons to be made between the perceived risks and opportunities within each segment. **796** SSAP 25 (24)

Aggregate disclosures

The aggregate figures given for each segment should equal the total as disclosed in the profit and loss account. Where this is not the case, because for example certain common costs have not been apportioned to a particular segment, a **reconciliation** should be provided. The reconciling items should be clearly explained. **Comparative figures** for the previous accounting period should also be disclosed. **798**

Further disclosure requirements are imposed where an entity has associated entities that form a **material part of the group's results or assets**. These additional disclosures are required where associates account for 20 percent or more of the total operating results or the total net assets of the group (including the group's share of the associates' results or net assets). The information disclosed should represent the aggregate of all the associate undertakings. The same criteria apply to joint ventures.

If the **materiality threshold is exceeded**, the entity must supply certain segmental information – i.e., its share of:
- profits (or losses) before tax, minority interests and extraordinary items; and
- total net assets.

Where practicable, the value of net assets of associates should be restated to incorporate their fair values as at the date the entity acquired its interest in the associate.

Changes to group composition

804 FRS 3, "Reporting financial performance", requires that when the composition of a group changes through an **acquisition, sale or termination** that has a material effect on a significant business segment, this fact should be disclosed.

The following example illustrates the disclosure of segmental information concerning the termination of a business operation; the discontinued operation is shown as a residual category with continuing operations analysed by segment. This format can be adapted for either a major sale or acquisition requiring disclosure.

EXAMPLE

Discontinued operations	Total £m	UK £m	Europe £m	Americas £m	Pacific £m
Sales	76	35	6	20	15
Trading profit	12	5	1	3	3
Continuing operations – current year	**Total £m**	**UK £m**	**Europe £m**	**Americas £m**	**Pacific £m**
Sales:					
Beverages	2500	20	400	1600	480
Confectionary	3000	1000	1000	500	500
Totals	**5500**	**1020**	**1400**	**2100**	**980**

Voluntary disclosures

806 A number of companies also report in excess of the current requirements by publishing additional voluntary information on, **for example**:
- fixed assets and capital expenditure by business segment,
- employees by geographical location, and
- exceptional items.

Exceptional items

808 SSAP 25 does not specifically require that specific disclosure be made of the segment to which exceptional items relate. However, FRS 3 does require an **adequate description** of an exceptional item to be given so as to enable the reader to understand its nature. It would also be appropriate for that description to indicate the segment(s) to which the item corresponds.

EXAMPLE **Extract from accounts**

A Ltd

Notes to the financial statements – 31 December 20X4

The segmental analysis of operating profit includes continuing and discontinued operations, but excludes exceptional operating items of £49.5m (20X3: £43.8m), in respect of the restructuring provisions for the group's Australian manufacturing companies and for the company's UK operations in 20X4.

Entities required to disclose additional segmental information

810 SSAP 25 (41) SSAP 25 requires the following entities to provide additional (mandatory) segmental information to that required by the Companies Act:

a. public limited companies (or companies with a subsidiary that is a public limited company – i.e., **group**), or

b. banking or insurance companies, or

c. companies that **meet two** of the following criteria:
- turnover exceeds £259m (*before 6 April 2008* – £228m);
- balance sheet total £129m (*before 6 April 2008* – £114m); and
- the average number of employees exceeds 2500.

Stock exchange requirements

The London Stock Exchange requires a geographical analysis of both net turnover and contribution to trading results of those trading operations carried on by the company (or group) outside the United Kingdom. No analysis of the contribution to trading results is required unless the contribution is "abnormal" in nature. "Abnormal" is defined as being substantially out of line with the normal ratio of profit to turnover. 812 SSAP 25 (54)

C. Difficulties in compiling segmental information

A number of difficulties can arise when compiling and presenting segmental information. 820

Comparative data

Difficulties comparing similar segments in different entities can result from the: 822 SSAP 25 (19)
- **basis** of accounting adopted for inter-segment sales;
- **differences** in accounting policies and standards;
- treatment of common costs being **inconsistent** between entities; or
- **changing** composition of segments.

In order to achieve consistency within a set of accounts, if a company should, e.g., decide to alter the scope of a particular business segment, adopt a new accounting standard, diversify its activities, or isolate an operation previously aggregated within another segment, it should amend the comparative figures for the previous year.

Inter-segment sales

SSAP 25 stipulates that turnover should be split between external and internal sales and shown separately with the **geographical analysis** grouped by origin rather than destination. The standard does not require the disclosure of the basis on which inter-segment sales are conducted. Some companies disclose the basis of their transfer pricing, i.e., whether: 824 SSAP 25 (23)
- market price;
- established internal prices; or
- prices derived from arm's length negotiations.

Common costs

Operating costs that relate to more than one segment should be apportioned by the directors on a basis consistent with their internal reporting structures. **Central administrative overheads** are an example of common costs that should be allocated to business or geographical segments using an acceptable basis such as a proportion of direct costs. However, other methods are acceptable. For instance, a listed confectionary company stated in its annual report that common or corporate costs were allocated equally between the company's two business segments, beverages and confectionery. 826

Common costs should not be apportioned over segments if to do so would be misleading. In these cases the cost element that is not apportioned should be deducted from the aggregate of the segment results.

Allocation of interest

In most companies, different classes of business or geographical segments are financed by different proportions of **interest-bearing debt and equity**. Where all, or a significant part, of the entity's business revenue or costs is interest earned or incurred, or where interest income or expense is central to the business (e.g., the travel industry), interest should be accounted for in arriving at the segmental results. This applies particularly in the case of companies in 828 SSAP 25 (22) the financial sector (e.g., loan companies) as well as conglomerates in which some cash-rich divisions finance other businesses within the group.

In the absence of the above situations, the allocation of interest earned or incurred is usually the result of group policy and, consequently, interest is generally excluded from the segmental disclosures so that the net assets of each significant segment should represent the non-interest-bearing operating assets less the non-interest-bearing operating liabilities.

Common assets

830 SSAP 25 (24) Assets or liabilities that do not belong to a specific segment should be allocated on a reasonable basis. The total net assets that cannot be allocated in this manner should be shown as a reconciling item between the total of all segments' net assets and the net asset figure appearing in the balance sheet.

Net assets

832 SSAP 25 (18) Net assets are not defined in SSAP 25 but are generally considered to be non-interest-bearing operating assets less non-interest-bearing liabilities. Different companies may be justified in interpreting net assets in different ways (as long as the chosen definition is applied consistently). As a result, comparisons between returns on capital employed might have limitations.

Operating assets and liabilities may relate to a specific segment or jointly to more than one segment.

Change of policy

834 If segmental definitions or reporting policies have changed, the nature of the change, its effect, and the reasons, must be stated by way of the notes.

SECTION 3

The international situation

840 The International Accounting Standards Board (IASB) has issued IFRS 8, "Operating Segments", which replaces the earlier international standard, IAS 14.

The Standard requires entities to adopt the "management approach" to reporting on the financial performance of its operating segments. Generally, the information to be reported would be the same as is used by management internally for evaluating segment performance and deciding how to allocate resources to operating segments. This information may therefore differ from that which is used to prepare the income statement and balance sheet. Consequently, the IFRS requires explanations of the basis on which the segment information is prepared and reconciliations to the amounts recognised in the income statement and balance sheet.

PART 3

Balance sheet – Fixed assets

CHAPTER 1

Overview of the balance sheet

OUTLINE ¶¶

It is a requirement of the Companies Act that every balance sheet should give a true and fair view of a company's state of affairs at the end of the financial year. The Companies Act details the form and content of the balance sheet with additional requirements contained in the accounting standards. The balance sheet formats for **small and medium sized companies** are covered in ¶6000. Listed companies must prepare their accounts using international financial reporting standards and formats (IFRS), although it is not a regulatory requirement for their subsidiaries to follow suit. 960

A **choice between** two balance sheet formats is permitted, although the most common presentation is format 1, in which the balance sheet headings are presented vertically in the following order: Assets, Liabilities, and Capital and Reserves. Under format 2, the presentation is horizontal with assets on one side and liabilities, capital and reserves on the other. 962

The **two formats** together with the supplementary notes given in Schedule 4 are reproduced in the Appendix to this chapter. It should be noted that the formats do not specify where in a vertical balance sheet presentation, the "balance" should be struck. The norm is to strike a balance for net assets (after item J in the formats illustrated below) which matches the aggregate of capital and reserves. However, FRS 4 requires that the total amount of shareholders funds, analysed between equity and non-equity interests, must be shown irrespective of where a company decides to "strike the balance".

MEMO POINTS The formats and content of the financial statements will now be set out in regulations drafted under the framework of the Companies Act (2006). Two sets of regulations have been issued; one set being exclusively for small companies (SI 2008/409) (see ¶6000) whilst the other covers large and medium-sized companies and groups (SI 2008/409). The drafts **restate the form and content requirements** contained in the Companies Act 1985. The **main difference** is that the small company regulations include simplified sub-headings.

Balance sheet headings

In the formats laid down by the Companies Act, each major classification of asset, liability and capital and reserves is assigned a balance sheet heading, which in turn is **assigned either a letter or a Roman numeral**. The headings must be presented in the order in which they appear in the formats given in the Act and the headings given in the formats must be followed. Under each major classification are various sub-headings, which are accompanied by Arabic numerals and which can be adapted to meet the requirements of particular companies. 966

Where considered necessary, the directors of a company may chose to give more detail than is generally required by the format.

In practice, those **items assigned Arabic numerals** are, as permitted by the Act, not usually shown on the face of the balance sheet but are instead aggregated under the relevant asset heading [identified by a roman numeral] and the analysis of the individual items included in that aggregated amount shown in the notes to the financial statements.

A small number of items have **alternative positions** within the formats and these are discussed in the following paragraphs.

Classification of assets and liabilities

970 The **definition of fixed and current assets** is based on the intended use of the asset in the business. The distinction is that fixed assets are intended to be used on a continuing basis, whilst current assets are not. In FRS 5 "Substance of transactions" and the ASB's **Statement of Principles**, assets are defined as "rights or other access to future economic benefits controlled by the entity as a result of past transactions or events".

All assets must be classified under the headings of "Fixed assets" or "Current assets", except for the following which can either be shown separately as a main heading (i.e. one that is assigned a letter) in the formats or as subheadings (i.e. one that is assigned an Arabic numeral); namely:

- Debtors;
- Prepayments and accrued income; and
- Called-up share capital not paid.

There is **no statutory requirement** to classify current assets into those realisable within one year or after more than one year.

972 **Current liabilities** are split into two categories in the formats dependant upon when the liability falls due for payment. The two categories are Creditors; "amounts falling due within one year" and "Creditors and amounts falling due after more than one year".

"Accrual and deferred income" may be shown separately as a main heading or as a subheading under one of the two "Creditor headings".

Liabilities are defined in FRS 5 and the ASB's statement of principles, as "obligations of an entity to transfer economic benefits as a result of past transactions or events".

974 **Net current assets or liabilities** is a subtotal for current assets and liabilities under format 1, which must include "Prepayments and accrued income", even where this item is shown under a separate heading from current assets.

975 **Defined benefit pension assets or liabilities** must be presented separately on the face of the balance sheet. Under format 1, this asset or liability should be included between item J "Accruals and deferred income", and item K "Capital and reserves". For format 2, a pension asset should appear after Assets item D "Prepayments and accrued income" and any pension liability after "Liabilities, Accruals and Deferred income".

Rules for valuing assets

976 The rules for valuing assets are set out in the Companies Act, and are generally consistent with the requirements of the accounting standards. A distinction is drawn between the **historical cost accounting rules** and the **alternative accounting rules**, which permits for certain asset categories the revaluation of assets or the use of current cost in statutory financial statements. A mixture of both sets of rules (i.e. cost and valuation) is permitted although certain restrictions have been imposed by FRS 15 "Tangible fixed assets", where consistency of accounting treatment by class of asset is required.

The **general valuation rules** are set out in the table below along with the respective chapter references.

Overview of asset valuation rules		
	Historical cost	**Alternative accounting rules**
Cost	Purchase or production cost	Separate requirements: 1. **Tangible fixed assets**: – market value at last valuation date or at current cost (see ¶1200). 2. **Intangible assets** (excluding goodwill) – at current cost (see ¶1000). 3. **Fixed asset investments**: – market value at last valuation date or directors valuation (see ¶1750). 4. **Current asset investments**: – current cost (¶2700). 5. **Stocks**: – current cost (see ¶2000).
Depreciation	Carrying amount of asset is written down to residual value over useful economic life through provisions for depreciation	As under **historical cost**
Impairment – fixed assets (see ¶1550)	Provision required if reduction is permanent (assets recoverable amount falls below carrying value)	1. Assets carried at **market value** – as under historical cost. 2. **Assets** carried **at current cost** each year. Provision required for any diminution in value if current cost falls. 3. **Fixed asset investments** – provision for diminution in value. 4. **Current assets** – written down to net realisable value if lower than cost or alternative valuation.

MEMO POINTS The ASB's "Statement of principles for financial reporting" also permits the use of **an alternative valuation method** known as **"value to the business"**. There is a choice of valuation bases based on determining what the entity would lose if deprived of the use of an asset; namely:
- entry value (replacement cost);
- market value; or
- value in use (present value of future cash flows).

Companies Act formats – individual company

984

Format 1	
A	**Called up share capital not paid** (1)
B	**Fixed assets**
B-I	Intangible assets 1. Development costs 2. Concessions, patents, licences…etc (2) 3. Goodwill (3) 4. Payments on account
B-II	Tangible assets 1. Land and buildings 2. Plant and machinery 3. Fixtures, fittings… 4. Payments on account and assets in the course of construction

Format 1	
B-III	Investments 1. Shares in group undertakings 2. Loans to group undertakings 3. Participating interests (13) 4. Loans to undertakings in which the company has a participating interest 5. Other investments other than loans 6. Other loans 7. Own shares (4)
C	**Current assets**
C-I	Stocks 1. Raw materials, etc. 2. Work in progress 3. Finished goods/goods for resale 4. Payments on account
C-II	**Debtors** (5) 1. Trade debtors 2. Amounts owed by group undertakings 3. Amounts owed by undertakings in which the company has a participating interest 4. Other debtors 5. Called up share capital not paid (1) 6. Prepayments and accrued income (6)
C-III	**Investments** 1. Shares in group undertakings 2. Own shares (4) 3. Other investments
C-IV	**Cash at bank and in hand**
D	**Prepayments and accrued income**
E	**Creditors: amounts falling due within one year** 1. Debenture loans (7) 2. Bank loans and overdrafts 3. Payments received on account (8) 4. Trade creditors 5. Bills of exchange payable 6. Amounts owed to group undertakings 7. Amounts owed to undertakings in which the company has a participating interest 8. Other creditors including taxation and social security (9) 9. Accruals and deferred income (10)
F	**Net current assets (liabilities)** (11)
G	**Total assets less current liabilities**
H	**Creditors amounts falling due after one year** 1. Debenture loans (7) 2. Bank loans and overdrafts 3. Payments received on account (8) 4. Trade creditors 5. Bills on exchange payable 6. Amounts owed to group undertakings 7. Amounts owed to undertakings in which the company has a participating interest 8. Other creditors including taxation and social security (9) 9. Accruals and deferred income (10)

Format 1	
I	**Provision for liabilities and charges** 1. Pensions and similar obligations 2. Taxation, etc 3. Other provisions
J	**Accruals and deferred income (10)**
K	**Capital and reserves**
K-I	Called up share capital (1)
K-II	Share premium account
K-III	Revaluation reserve
K-IV	Other reserves 1. Capital redemption reserve 2. Reserve for own shares 3. Reserves provided for by articles 4. Other reserves
K-V	Profit and loss account
M	Minority interests (alternative position – before K) (14)

Format 2	
Assets	
A	**Called up share capital not paid** (1)
B	**Fixed assets**
B-I	Intangible assets 1. Development costs 2. Concessions, patents, licences…etc (2) 3. Goodwill (3) 4. Payments on account
B-II	Tangible assets 1. Land and buildings 2. Plant and machinery 3. Fixtures, fittings… 4. Payments on account and assets in the course of construction
B-III	Investments 1. Shares in group undertakings 2. Loans to group undertakings 3. Participating interests (13) 4. Loans to undertakings in which the company has a participating interest 5. Other investments other than loans 6. Other loans 7. Own shares (4)
C	**Current assets**
C-I	Stocks 1. Raw materials, etc. 2. Work in progress 3. Finished goods/goods for resale 4. Payments on account

Format 2	
Assets	
C-II	**Debtors** (5) 1. Trade debtors 2. Amounts owed by group undertakings 3. Amounts owed by undertakings in which the company has a participating interest 4. Other debtors 5. Called up share capital not paid (1) 6. Prepayments and accrued income (6)
C-III	**Investments** 1. Shares in group undertakings 2. Own shares (4) 3. Other investments
C-IV	**Cash at bank and in hand**
D	**Prepayments and accrued income**
	Liabilities
A	**Capital and reserves**
I	Called up share capital (1)
II	Share premium account
III	Revaluation reserve
IV	Other reserves 1. Capital redemption reserve 2. Reserve for own shares 3. Reserves provided for by articles 4. Other reserves
V	Profit and loss account
	Minority interests
B	**Provision for liabilities and charges** 1. Pensions and similar obligations 2. Taxation, etc. 3. Other provisions
C	**Creditors** 1. Debenture loans (7) 2. Bank loans and overdrafts 3. Payments received on account (8) 4. Trade creditors 5. Bills on exchange payable 6. Amounts owed to group undertakings 7. Amounts owed to undertakings in which the company has a participating interest 8. Other creditors including taxation and social security (9) 9. Accruals and deferred income (10)
D	**Accruals and deferred income** (10)

986

Notes to the balance sheet formats

1. Called-up share capital not paid may be shown in either of the two positions shown in Formats 1 and 2.
2. Concessions, patents, licences, trade marks and similar rights and assets should only be included in the company's balance sheet under this heading if:
a. the assets were acquired for a valuable consideration and not required to be shown under goodwill; or
b. the assets were created internally by the company.
3. Goodwill should only be included if acquired for a valuable consideration.
4. Own shares The nominal value of the shares should be shown separately.
5. Debtors falling due after more than one year should be shown separately for each item under debtors.
6. Prepayments and accrued income can be shown in either of the two positions shown in Formats 1 and 2.
7. Debenture loans The amount of any convertible loans should be shown separately.
8. Payments received on account of orders should be shown for each item were not shown as a deduction form stocks.
9. Other creditors The amount for creditors in respect of taxation and social security shall be shown separately from the amount for other creditors.
10. Accruals and deferred income The two positions in Format 1 at E9 and H9 are an alternative to the heading under position J. In Format 2 the two positions given are alternatives.
11. Net current assets (liabilities) should include amounts shown under 'prepayments and accrued Income'.
12. Creditors falling due after more than one year should be shown separately for each item under creditors.
13. Participating interests should in group accounts be replaced by "interests in associated undertakings" and "Other participating interests".
14. Minority interests only arises in group accounts. The two positions given in Format 1 are alternatives.

Consolidated formats

Parent companies preparing consolidated financial statements must comply with the provisions of the Companies Act, on the basis of the group being a single company. In addition, the parent company must also satisfy the provisions of the Act in terms of their own form and content. 988

The format selected by the parent company for its individual balance sheet, will usually be adopted for the consolidated balance sheet.

The **following headings** can be shown in alternative places in the consolidated formats:
- Called-up share capital not paid (A and C.II.5);
- Prepayments and accrued income (C.II.6 and D);
- Accruals and deferred income (E9, H9 and J); and
- Minority interests (K and M).

For group accounts, a category of "Interests in group undertakings" can be inserted after "loans to group undertakings".

Presentation requirements of IAS (IFRS)

There are a number of international standards governing the presentation of financial statements, containing the formats, fundamental principles and basic rules on presentation and disclosure requirements. 990

Although the **IAS formats** are broadly consistent with the formats contained in the EU 4th Directive, there are some differences in balance sheet presentation between IAS and UK GAAP.

The IASB are currently reviewing the presentation standards although any change is not envisaged before 2012 at the earliest.

The **key international standards** governing presentation of the balance sheet are:
- IAS 1 "Presentation of financial statements;

- IAS 10 "Events after the balance sheet date";
- IAS 24 "Related party disclosures";
- IFRS 5 "Non-current assets held for sale and discontinued operations".

MEMO POINTS An overview of the developing relationship between international accounting standards and UK GAAP can be found on the Department for Business, Innovation and Skills (BIS) website.

992 **Minimum disclosures on face of balance sheet** The following headings are the minimum required on the face of the balance sheet:

1. Property, plant and equipment
2. Investment property
3. Intangible assets
4. Financial assets (excluding items shown under 5, 8 and 9)
5. Investments accounted for under the equity method
6. Biological assets
7. Inventories
8. Trade and other receivables
9. Cash and cash equivalents
10. Trade and other payables
11. Provisions
12. Financial liabilities (excluding amounts under 10 and 11)
13. Liabilities and assets for current tax (IAS 12)
14. Deferred tax liabilities and deferred tax assets, as defined in IAS 12
15. Minority interests
16. Issued capital and reserves

MEMO POINTS Issued share capital and reserves requires the following disclosures (IAS 1 (76)): authorised, issued and fully-paid, and issued but not fully-paid share capital; nominal value of share capital; reconciliation of shares at the beginning and end of the financial year; description of rights, preferences and restrictions; treasury shares, shares held by subsidiaries and associates; shares to be issued under options or contracts; and a description of the nature and purpose of each reserve.

Other line items should be presented on the face of the balance sheet when presentation is relevant to an understanding of the entity's position, for example as:
- total assets held for sale; or
- assets and liabilities included in groups held for sale in accordance with IFRS 5.

Further **sub-classifications** of items presented in the balance sheet will depend on the requirements of the IFRS and the materiality of the amounts.

993 **Minimum disclosures on face of the income statement** As with the balance sheet the international accounting standards do not specify a prescribed format, but set out the minimum disclosures that must appear on the face of the balance sheet.

1. Revenue
2. Finance costs
3. Associates and joint ventures: Share of profit (loss): equity method.
4. Discontinued operations: total gross and net profit (loss) + any post-tax gains on disposal of associated assets or companies.
5. Taxation
6. Profit (loss)

CHAPTER 2

Intangible assets and goodwill

OUTLINE ¶¶

Intangible assets **are defined as** identifiable assets that do not have a physical substance, but where the controlling entity has access to future economic benefits generated by the asset, either through custody or legal protection of the asset. Examples include trademarks, franchises and copyrights. 1000 FRS 10 (2)

Intangible assets can either be **purchased separately**, as part of a business acquisition, **or developed internally** by the business. Intangible assets range from those that are readily available and can be measured separately from goodwill to those that are similar in substance to goodwill. Only intangible assets **capable of separate recognition** can be capitalised. **Revaluation** under the alternative accounting rules is permitted, although strict criteria must be met.

Goodwill may be purchased or generated internally. Purchased goodwill is defined as the difference between the cost of an acquired entity and the aggregate fair values attributed to the individual identifiable assets and liabilities acquired. 1001

The **statutory requirements** relating to accounting for intangible assets and goodwill are covered in the Companies Acts. The **principles of accounting** for intangible assets and goodwill are principally contained in FRS 10 "Goodwill and Intangible Assets" and the amendments proposed in FRED 37 "Intangible assets". 1002

The topics of intangible assets and goodwill were covered in the same accounting standard, as the **basic principles** covering initial recognition, amortisation and impairment of intangible assets are similar to goodwill.

The impairment of intangible fixed assets and goodwill is covered by FRS 11, which although touched on briefly in this chapter, is covered in greater detail in ¶1550. The key differences between UK GAAP and IAS 38 "Intangible assets" are outlined as are the current developments in this standard.

Scope of FRS 10

1003 The **objective of FRS 10** is to ensure that intangible assets and purchased goodwill are charged to the profit and loss account, for the periods in which they are depleted, and that sufficient information is disclosed in the financial statements to enable users to determine the impact of intangible assets and goodwill on the financial position of the reporting entity.

The **requirements of FRS 10 apply** to all intangible assets (and goodwill), **except where** specifically addressed by another accounting standard or SORP, such as research and development costs and oil and gas exploration.

Small and medium-sized companies **applying the FRSSE** are currently exempt from applying FRS 10, unless preparing consolidated financial statements. For those companies permitted to and opting to apply the FRSSE, there are provisions contained therein relating to the treatment of goodwill and intangibles, which broadly follow the same principles as those set out in FRS 10.

A. Intangibles other than goodwill

1010 This section covers the initial treatment of intangible assets and the problems inherent in their valuation.

1012 **Types of intangible assets**

Definitions	
Franchise	A franchise is a concession or rights granted to a party to sell a company's goods or services in a particular area, usually to an agreed format, covering corporate style or branding. Examples include car dealerships and fast food outlets.
Licences	A licence is a contract, in which a company enters into an agreement with another party, concerning a particular trading arrangement. Examples include brewers who obtain a licence to brew a beer from another manufacturer and licence agreements for the use of software and computer technology produced by a third party.
Copyrights	Copyrights are designed to protect the holder's exclusive right for a specified period of time to produce copies or control a piece of artistic work, including, for example, original music or literature. Publishing companies often control the rights to exclusively print the works of an author, in the expectation of future income streams from those works.
Patents	Patents are granted by the government to an inventor protecting his sole right to produce, use and sell the invention for a specified period of time
Trademarks	Trademarks are used to differentiate the products of competing manufacturers and protect the investments made by companies in their brands
Internet domain names	Internet domain names are hostnames that help identify a computer on the internet
Emissions allowances	Granted by the government in form of licences with emission limits pre-determined.

MEMO POINTS Accounting practice on emissions allowances varies considerably. Some entities classify emissions allowances purchased from the government as intangibles assets and account for them "at cost". Allowances gifted by the government are recorded at nil cost. For emissions allowances accounted for at "fair value", the difference between fair value and cost is recognised as a government grant and classified as deferred income in the balance sheet.

1. Initial recognition

The **general rules** for the recognition of intangible assets (and goodwill) are set out in the table below. 1018 FRS 10 (9)

Intangible assets	Accounting treatment – initial recognition
1. Purchased separately	Capitalised at cost
2. Business acquisitions	Where intangible assets can be separately identifiable from goodwill – record at fair value
3. Internally generated	Not capitalised. Exception is where they have a readily ascertainable market value such as brands or products
Goodwill	
1. Purchased	Classified as an intangible asset and capitalised as part of a business combination
2. Internally generated	Not recognised or capitalised

Each of these situations is discussed in more detail below. In addition, an **alternative treatment** is permissible under the Companies Act, where intangible assets, except goodwill, can be included in the balance sheet at **current cost**.

Intangible assets purchased separately

An intangible asset should initially be capitalised and recorded at cost. 1020 FRS 10 (10)

Once intangible assets have been **capitalised**, they should be dealt with in the same manner as goodwill and amortised over their useful economic lives.

Under FRS 10 there is a **rebuttable presumption** that the useful economic life of goodwill and intangibles will not exceed 20 years. However, when **certain conditions are met**, a longer economic life may be used. The amortisation of intangibles and goodwill is discussed more fully in ¶1086.

Control of access to economic benefits may also be obtained through custody; namely the protection of technical or intellectual knowledge. Where control over the expected future benefits from intangible assets is insufficient due to the absence of legal rights or custody rights, they should not be recognised as assets. 1021

Business acquisitions

The **identifiable assets** of an acquired undertaking should be included in the consolidated balance sheet at "fair value" at the acquisition date, including intangibles such as purchased brands or publishing titles. 1022

The exception is where the asset does not have a readily ascertainable market value. In this instance, the fair value should be limited to an amount that does not create or increase any negative goodwill arising on the acquisition. 1023 FRS 10 (10)

There are a **number of specific problems** inherent in valuing certain intangible assets obtained through a business acquisition, which are outlined in ¶1035 below.

MEMO POINTS 1. An **identifiable asset** is defined by companies legislation as one that can be separately identified and sold off without having to dispose of the entire business. If an asset can be sold only as part of the revenue generating activity of which it forms a part, it is deemed to be indistinguishable from the goodwill relating to that activity and accounted for as such.
2. FRS 7 "Fair values in acquisition accounting" **stipulates that** "fair values" should be placed on identifiable assets and liabilities, in allocating the purchase consideration for a business to its separable net assets. Any balance should be attributable to goodwill. The fair value should be based on the estimated market value and be capable of reliable measurement.

Internally developed intangible assets

1025 The **general rule** is that the cost of developing intangible assets internally should not be capitalised, but charged as an expense as they are incurred. The aim is to align the accounting treatment of intangible assets that are similar to goodwill, with that of goodwill.

1026 FRS 10 (14) The **exceptions** are intangible assets that are clearly identifiable and have a readily ascertainable market value.

1028 **Brands created internally and other unique intangible assets** Although the Companies Act allows the production cost of intangibles to be included in the balance sheet, this treatment is prohibited by FRS 10 in relation to brands and publishing titles created internally.

The reason is that internally generated goodwill **may only be capitalised if** it has a readily ascertainable market value, and as intangibles such as publishing titles and brands are unique, their value is not readily ascertainable.

Exceptions

1030 The **general rule** is that intangible assets cannot be revalued after having initially been recognised at cost or fair value on acquisition. The **exceptions are** intangible assets that have a readily ascertainable market value.

These intangible assets can be included in the balance sheet at market value, provided that:
- all intangible assets in the same class are revalued; and
- regular revaluations are conducted to ensure that the carrying value is the same as the market value at the balance sheet date.

Where an intangible fixed asset is valued at current cost, the **depreciation rules** are different. The amortisation charge should be based on the balance sheet value and not the historical cost.

FRED 37 proposals

1031 FRED 37 "Intangible assets" was issued in July 2005 and is based on IAS 36. It proposes **new criteria for recognising intangible assets**, namely where assets:
- can be separated from the entity and either sold, transferred, licensed, rented or exchanged, either individually or together with a related contract asset or liability; or
- arise from contractual or other legal rights, regardless of whether the rights are transferable or separable from the entity or other rights and obligations.

This definition differs from that in FRS 10, which defines intangible assets as those that are capable of being disposed of or discharged separately, without having to dispose of the business. FRED 37 extends this definition to include recognition of contractual and other legal rights that would not be recognised under the "separable requirement in FRS 10".

The latest position regarding this FRED is that the comments from respondents are still being analysed by the ASB. No announcement is expected in the immediate future.

Taxation

1032 A number of changes to the tax treatment of intangible assets over the last few years means it now more aligned with the accounting treatment for these assets. In general, debits and credits in respect of intellectual property and other intangibles are only recognised for the purpose of taxation when they are taken to the profit and loss account. A detailed explanation of taxation requirements relating to intangibles is beyond the scope of this book.

2. Difficulties in valuing intangibles

1035 Where intangible assets are **purchased separately**, valuation is generally not an issue as there is a purchase price that is used for initial recognition. However, where intangible assets are purchased as part of a **business acquisition or are generated internally**, they can be much more difficult to value.

For **certain types of intangibles** (given their unique nature) it may be difficult to determine a value.

The **principal difficulty** is establishing a **readily ascertainable market value** at which the asset could be exchanged in an arm's length transaction. 1036 FRS 10 (2)

The standard requires that the value of an intangible fixed asset could be established by reference to a market for a similar intangible asset or group of assets, that are equivalent in all material aspects and where there is an active market for that group of assets. Intangible fixed assets fitting this definition include licences, quotas or franchises.

EXAMPLE **Readily ascertainable market.**

1. **Taxi licences** granted within a city limit may give identical rights to each licence holder. As such, the licences are traded actively at all times and there is a defined market price and a readily ascertainable market value.
2. The **cable television licence** for each region in the UK is different. The population demographics are different and as such the value of the licences will vary. The cable broadcasting licence for a rural area, for instance, will have a different cost structure from that of a more densely populated urban area. As such, these licences are unlikely to have a readily ascertainable market value.

Determining the initial value of intangible assets

Initial recognition The rules governing **acquisition accounting** (¶6820) require that the fair value of an intangible asset, when recognised, should normally be based on its replacement cost; this is predominately the asset's estimated market value. 1038

Difficulties in determining initial value In certain industries or entities, methods for determining the market value of intangible assets have been developed, which can be used for the initial recognition of such assets at the time of purchase. However, for some intangible assets, where it may be difficult to determine a market value or replacement cost, **other valuation methods** may be employed. FRS 10 (12)

When measurement is unreliable Where the **initial value** of an intangible asset purchased as part of the acquisition of a business cannot be measured reliably, it should be subsumed within the portion of the purchase price attributed to goodwill. FRS 10 (13)

Valuation methods

Valuation methods are many and varied and are usually applied for commercial transactions rather than accounting purposes. It is beyond the scope of this book to discuss the merits of the various valuation methods and the suitability of the values they produce for inclusion in financial statements. However, a small number of the more **common valuation methods** for intangible assets are summarised below. 1044 FRS 10 (12)

Valuation methods	Characteristics
Royalty method	This method is used to determine the value that could be obtained by licensing out the right to exploit the intangible asset, or to estimate the royalties the owner of the licence does not have to pay to a third party. A **notional royalty rate** is calculated as a percentage of the projected revenues, with the resulting royalty revenue stream capitalised by discounting at a risk adjusted market rate, to arrive at an estimated market value.
Premium profits method	This method is used to determine the value of an intangible asset by capitalising the additional profits attributable to the intangible asset, such as a market leading brand, and deducting the profits earned by comparable unbranded competitor products. The estimated profits are then capitalised by discounting at a risk adjusted market rate to arrive at an estimated market value.
Capitalisation of earnings method	This method is used to estimate the sustainable earnings expected from the intangible asset. A capitalisation factor or multiple of earnings is then applied to the earnings, adjusted for future prospects and risk.

1049 A **number of factors** must also be considered, when determining risk and valuing intangible assets such as brands using the above methods, including:
- the market sector;
- customer loyalty;
- market share;
- export markets;
- marketing support;
- competition;
- changes to legislation; and
- technological changes.

B. Goodwill

1054 Goodwill may be purchased or generated internally. **Internally generated goodwill** should not be capitalised. In this section, the initial recognition and accounting requirements for purchased goodwill and negative goodwill are considered.

The rules governing the determination of the useful economic life, the amortisation of goodwill and the requirements for impairment reviews, are also covered. Certain **transitional arrangements** for goodwill previously eliminated against reserves are included within FRS 10 and reviewed below.

MEMO POINTS For guidance on the application of this accounting standard to associates and joint ventures, see ¶7300.

1057 Goodwill is seen as a bridge between the cost of an investment, as shown in the purchaser's own financial statements and the values attributed to the acquired assets and liabilities in the consolidated statements by the purchaser.

Goodwill **is distinguished from other assets** because of the following characteristics:
- valuations of goodwill are subjective;
- goodwill cannot be sold as an asset separately from the rest of the business; and
- there is no reliable correlation between goodwill and the costs incurred in creating it.

Goodwill is generated through **a number of factors**, such as the expertise of the workforce, product reputation, or location. The factors that generate goodwill also make it difficult to value objectively. For this reason, the Companies Act contains a provision that **goodwill may only be recognised** as an intangible fixed asset, if acquired for a valuable consideration as part of the purchase of a business or business segment.

MEMO POINTS 1. HMRC has issued guidance on the apportionment of goodwill for transactions involving the sale of a business run from **trade related premises**, such as public houses, cinemas, restaurants, care homes, petrol stations or hotels. When a business operated from a trade related property is sold as a going concern, the sale price usually includes an element of goodwill. The relevant question is what is the value of that goodwill? The answer will depend on the facts of each individual case. In some cases the value of the goodwill may be nominal but in others it may be substantial.
2. HMRC has given guidance on how the consideration received should be apportioned between goodwill and other assets. This represents a **change of policy**, which was previously based on the assumption that there is unlikely to be any significant element of goodwill, because the occupation of a particular building was deemed essential to the functioning of the business and its revenue generation. In general, companies are now being advised to take an accounting based approach when calculating goodwill, as opposed to simply interpreting previous legal rulings. HMRC has also simplified its **classification system** for goodwill.

Purchased goodwill

1058 FRS 10 (7) Purchased goodwill arises when the cost of an acquired entity exceeds the aggregate fair values attributable to the identifiable assets and liabilities acquired.

1. Purchased goodwill should be capitalised and classified as an intangible asset on the balance sheet.

2. Purchased goodwill **can arise from the following**:
– business combinations in which a parent undertaking acquires a subsidiary undertaking which it accounts for by acquisition accounting;
– unincorporated businesses acquired by the entity; and
– investments such as associates and joint ventures accounted for using the equity method.

Accounting treatment The **most common instance** of purchased goodwill is that arising on consolidation by a parent undertaking of an acquired subsidiary. 1060

1. Although purchased goodwill **is not in itself recognised as an asset** in an individual entity's accounts, it is included in consolidated intangible fixed assets rather than as a deduction from shareholders' equity, in recognition of the fact that goodwill is part of a larger group of assets represented by the acquired business. Goodwill is unique in the sense that it is incapable of being recognised without selling the whole business or business segment.

2. **Purchased goodwill diminishes over time** as the factors generating it change and it is replaced by internally generated goodwill. However, where goodwill is capable of continued measurement, it can in some very limited circumstances be retained indefinitely in the balance sheet.

The Companies Act requires that goodwill be capitalised as an intangible fixed asset and amortised over the appropriate period, as illustrated in the following example.

EXAMPLE **MNO Plc – Annual report and accounts**
Notes to the balance sheet

10. Purchased goodwill

The acquisition of the shares of Bunting Defence Systems in June 20XX was for a consideration of £16m. The table below sets out the fair value of the identifiable assets and liabilities of Bunting at the date of its acquisition by MNO plc. The goodwill is capable of continued measurement and will be amortised over a useful economic life of 15 years.

	£'000
Tangible fixed assets	2,003
Stocks and work in progress	236
Debtors	7,881
Cash in bank	740
Creditors: amounts falling due within one year	(585)
Bank overdrafts	(250)
Bank loans	(125)
Finance lease obligations	(200)
Other creditors	(6,500)
Net assets	**3,200**
Cash	13,000
Costs	3,000
Total consideration paid	**16,000**
Goodwill arising	**12,800**

Amortisation £16M – £12,8m/ 15 = £853,333 per annum.

Negative goodwill

Negative goodwill **occurs when the consideration paid** is less than the fair value of the identifiable assets because, either: 1062
– the seller requires a quick sale and has sold at a "bargain" price;
– the purchase price has been reduced to take account of future expected costs such as reorganisation costs; or

– the seller decides to divest of a business that no longer fits with the strategic direction of the company.

Negative goodwill **can also arise** where an acquired business is expected to generate losses in the immediate future. In these circumstances, it is expected that the value of the net assets of the business will fall as the losses are incurred. However, the requirement to perform **impairment reviews** (¶1550) will eliminate much of the negative goodwill that would otherwise be attributed to future costs or losses.

1063 FRS 10 (48) **General rules** Negative goodwill **usually relates** to valuation differences in respect of **non-monetary assets** and FRS 10 seeks to limit situations where negative goodwill is recognised through applying the following rules:

Intangible assets	General rules
Impairment	In situations where an acquisition appears to generate negative goodwill, the fair value of the acquired assets and liabilities should be tested for understatement or impairment
Single transaction	Purchased goodwill resulting from a single transaction that contains both positive and negative goodwill should not be divided into the two categories. Negative goodwill and intangible assets should not be recognised in respect of a single transaction.
Fair values	Negative goodwill, up to the fair values of the non-monetary assets acquired, should be accounted for in the profit and loss account in the periods (through depreciation or sale) that are expected to benefit from that negative goodwill, as illustrated in the example below
Negative goodwill	Where negative goodwill is recognised, it should be shown on the face of the balance sheet, immediately below the heading for goodwill. Where both positive and negative goodwill from different acquisitions are shown in the balance sheet, a sub-total showing the net goodwill figure should be added.

EXAMPLE **Negative goodwill**
Accounting treatment – charge to the profit and loss account.

A company that has net assets with a **fair value** of £30m is purchased for £27 million. The negative goodwill is £3m. The non-monetary assets at the acquisition date total £25m, comprising stocks of £5m and £20m of tangible fixed assets. In the year following acquisition, all the stocks were sold and £5m depreciation was charged on the tangible fixed assets.
Therefore, of the **non-monetary assets** of £25m at the date of purchase, £10m was recognised in the profit and loss account in the year following the purchase of the business. As a result, negative goodwill of £1.2m should be written back to the profit and loss account. The £1.2m is calculated as follows:
£10m [assets acquired now recognised in the profit and loss account in the year] **/**
£25m [total assets acquired] × £3m [total negative goodwill arising on the original acquisition].

Transitional arrangements

1064 FRS 10 (67) FRS 10 does not have a retrospective effect, so any purchased goodwill previously written off to reserves does not have to be reinstated and amortised over its useful economic life. However, **there is an option** for companies to reinstate previously written goodwill as a prior year adjustment. Prior period adjustments and required disclosures are governed by FRS 3 "Reporting financial performance" and FRS 18 "Accounting policies".

MEMO POINTS Companies were obliged to apply FRS 10 in the first accounting period on or after 23 December 1998, in respect of all existing goodwill and other intangible assets. Companies were given a choice on how to deal with **goodwill previously eliminated against reserves**, relating to acquired businesses that had not subsequently been terminated or disposed of. An entity could reinstate all or part of the goodwill previously eliminated against reserves.
For **most practical purposes**, therefore, other than for a **small number of provisions** that still have a potential impact on a parent undertaking's financial statements, these transitional provi-

sions no longer have any impact on an ongoing basis. Those remaining provisions that have any practical effect are discussed below.

Goodwill not reinstated Where goodwill written off to reserves, prior to the implementation of FRS10, **remains eliminated** against reserves, the financial statements should include **disclosure** of: 1065
- the accounting policy adopted in respect of goodwill;
- the cumulative amounts of positive goodwill eliminated against reserves and negative goodwill added to reserves, net of any goodwill attributable to business disposed of before the balance sheet date; and
- the fact that this goodwill had been eliminated as a matter of accounting policy and that it will be charged to the profit and loss account on any subsequent disposal of the business to which it related.

Subsequent disposal of a business When an acquired business is subsequently disposed of or closed, the following accounting treatment is required in the accounting period in question: 1065-1 FRS 10 (71)
- the amount included in the profit and loss account concerning the disposal or closure should include attributable goodwill to the extent that it has not previously been charged to the profit and loss account; and
- the financial statements should disclose, as a component of the profit or loss on disposal or closure, the attributable amount of goodwill so included. Where it was difficult or impractical to determine the goodwill attributable to a business acquired before 1 January 1998, this should be stated and the reasons given.

C. Useful economic life

As with other fixed assets, the **cost of goodwill or other intangibles**, less its expected residual value, should be amortised over its expected useful economic life. Intangible assets that have been valued at current cost; namely, the most recent production cost or valuation, should also be amortised over their remaining useful economic life. 1066 FRS 10 (19)

The **basic premise** set out in FRS 10, is that goodwill and intangible assets have a useful economic life of not more than 20 years. This **presumption can be rebutted** in certain circumstances. The determination of the useful economic life of goodwill and intangible assets and circumstances in which it can exceed 20 years or indefinite, are set out below.

FRS 10 recognises that **intangible assets other than goodwill may** have a residual value at the end of the useful economic life. No residual value may be assigned to goodwill. 1068

The issue of when the **carrying value** of these assets should be subject to an impairment review and the types of amortisation methods permitted are covered in this section.

1. Determining useful economic lives

The useful economic life of purchased goodwill **is defined as** the period over which the value of an acquired business is expected to exceed the values of its identifiable assets and liabilities. 1070

Both **economic and legal factors** can influence the useful economic life of an asset. Economic factors, such as technological progress, can affect the period over which the expected future economic benefits will arise, whilst legal factors could restrict the period over which the entity can control the benefits. 1071

Intangible assets/goodwill:	Accounting treatment
With **finite** economic lives	intangible assets should be amortised on a systematic basis over life of asset, so recognising the reduction in value of the goodwill over time
Where **continued measurement** of goodwill not possible	an asset's depletion should be recognised over a prudent time period
Where intangible assets and goodwill are deemed to have **indefinite useful economic lives**	they should not be amortised. Where a company adopts a policy of non-amortisation, this must be justified in terms of presenting a true and fair view, with disclosure of the reasons for and effect of such a policy. It must also subject the carrying value of goodwill to an impairment view each year.
Residual value	1. No residual value may be assigned to **goodwill**. 2. **Amortising an intangible**: RV may be attributed to the asset only if it can be measured accurately. The residual value of an intangible asset is often negligible and **only likely to be material** when: – there is a legal or contractual right to receive a certain sum at the end of the period of use of the intangible asset; or – there is a readily ascertainable market value for the residual asset.

Finite useful economic life

1074 FRS 10 (19) The **general rule** is that the useful economic lives of purchased goodwill and intangible assets should not exceed 20 years from the date of acquisition. The belief is that the premium paid on acquiring a business over its net asset value will not be maintained indefinitely.

The cost of the licences, copyrights and patents should be amortised over the period of the agreement. Where the **licences** have been acquired as part of a business acquisition, they should be capitalised separately from goodwill where they can be reliably measured and amortised over the expected useful economic life.

1076 FRS 10 (24) **Legal factors** Where access to the economic benefits derived from an intangible asset are governed by legal rights granted for a finite period, the useful economic life of the asset may extend beyond the end of that finite period, if the legal rights can be renewed or extended and the renewal or extension is assured. Any costs incurred in extending the legal protection or rights should be excluded from the value of the asset amortised.

In terms of intangible assets, legal protection **takes the form of**:
- a franchise;
- time related protection through licence, quotas, or copyright; or
- a patent or trademark restricting access to others.

1077 **Renewal of legal rights may be assured only if**:
- the value of the intangible asset does not decline as the initial expiry date approaches, or reduces only by the amount of the legal costs incurred in extended the underlying legal rights;
- it is reasonable to assume that the legal rights will be extended (based on past experience); and
- where the entity is required to abide by any conditions under the terms of the legal right and where the breaching of such terms may prevent renewal, no evidence exists that these terms have been or will be breached.

Indefinite useful economic life

1078 The **non-amortisation** of goodwill constitutes a departure from the requirements of the companies' legislation, to depreciate the value of goodwill over a limited period not exceeding its useful economic life. This treatment reflects the depletion of purchased goodwill over time and its replacement by internally generated goodwill. However, the strict requirements of FRS 10 and FRS 11 relating to an indefinite useful economic life must be met.

A policy of non-amortisation is permitted in **special circumstances**, where following the normal rules of amortisation would not give a true and fair view. The "true and fair view override" cannot be applied freely and must be considered on an acquisition by acquisition basis and not as a general accounting policy. FRS 10 (18)

The **general rule may be rebutted** and the useful economic life extended indefinitely **only where** all of the following conditions apply: 1080
- the durability of the acquired business or intangible asset can be determined so justifying the extension for a period exceeding 20 years;
- the goodwill or intangible asset is capable of continued measurement; and
- it is possible to conduct annual impairment reviews.

Where the useful economic life is **deemed to be indefinite**, this will not affect the initial treatment of the intangible asset.

Durability In some circumstances, the durability of the premium or goodwill paid for an acquired business can be maintained over **a period exceeding 20 years**, depending on: 1081 FRS 10 (20)
- the nature of the business;
- the stability of the industry in which the acquisition operates;
- the lifecycle of the products to which the goodwill relates;
- where the acquisition scales market barriers to entry that persist; and
- the expected future impact of competition.

EXAMPLE **Blackstones Brewing Plc**
Annual report and accounts
Note. Intangible assets

The Kronnenborg brand was initially recognised at its fair value on acquisition. The brand has a long history in an established industry and enjoys a significant share of the UK beer market. The brand receives continued marketing support in all regions. These factors together with the scale of the business contribute to the durability of the brand. As such, the directors are of the opinion that the useful economic life is indefinite and therefore no annual amortisation is provided. The carrying value of the brand is subject to an annual impairment review.

Continued measurement The useful economic lives of goodwill and intangible fixed assets should be reviewed at the end of each reporting period and any revisions made and reflected in the carrying value of goodwill or intangible asset should be amortised over the remaining useful economic life. 1082 FRS 10 (20)

Where **the cost of** continued measurement of goodwill and intangible assets is unjustifiably high, ongoing measurement may not be possible. This could mean that deemed economic lives in excess of 20 years will not be permissible. Circumstances where this arises include, for example: 1083 FRS 10 (23)
- where acquired businesses are merged with existing businesses in such a way that the associated goodwill cannot be tracked;
- the management information systems cannot identify and allocate cash flows at an income generating level; or
- where the amounts involved are immaterial and do not justify annual impairment reviews.

EXAMPLE **Wrightsbury Publishing Plc**
Annual report and accounts
Note. Intangible assets

The goodwill in the Company arose as a result of the transfer of assets, liabilities and trade of Grant Rollins Publishing Limited to Wrightsbury Publishing Limited, at market value on 30 April 20XX. Since the acquisition, the business acquired has been fully integrated into the operations of the Company, making it difficult to identify the ongoing value of associated goodwill. The Company has taken the view that it is appropriate to write off goodwill to the profit and loss account during the year and this policy has increased the charge to the profit and loss account by £550,000.

Revision of useful economic life

1084 UITF 27 (10) Abstract 27 "Revision of useful economic lives" covers the specific situation where a company that has not previously amortised goodwill or intangible assets subsequently changes this policy. The important point is that this does not represent **a change in accounting policy** requiring a prior-year adjustment. Where the estimated economic life of goodwill or other intangible sets are revised, the carrying value at the date of the revision should be amortised over the revised remaining useful economic life.

2. Methods of amortisation

1086 FRS 10 (30) Although the method of amortisation selected should reflect the pattern of depletion of the goodwill or intangible asset, the **straight-line method** of depreciation must be used except where it can be shown that another method is more appropriate.

An **alternative method** of amortisation that may sometimes be appropriate is the unit of production method. This could be used where, for example, a licence permits the production of a finite quantity of a product. This method should not be used, however, if it proves less conservative than a straight-line method.

MEMO POINTS 1. The ASB has also issued an exposure draft, "Amendment to FRS 15 and FRS 10: Interest methods and depreciation", which proposes to prohibit the use of interest methods of amortisation of intangible assets and goodwill. The amendment can be downloaded from the ASB website.
2. FRS 10 **forbids the use of** amortisation methods that aim to produce a constant rate of return on the carrying value of an intangible asset, such as the annuity method. The reverse "sum of digits" method is also prohibited, as it effectively transfers the amortisation charge to later periods and is not related to depletion of the goodwill.

3. Impairment of intangible assets and goodwill

1090 An asset is recognised as being impaired, if the **recoverable amount** (the higher of net realisable value and value in use (i.e. income stream)) falls below its carrying value. Impairment reviews should be conducted to ensure that intangible assets and goodwill are not carried at values exceeding their recoverable amount.

The **requirement to conduct impairment reviews** differs depending upon whether goodwill or other intangible assets have been assigned useful economic lives of less than or more than 20 years. The revaluation and restoration of past impairment losses is also considered.

Systematic amortisation should ensure that the carrying value of an asset is reduced to reflect the reduction in the recoverable amount of the asset over its useful economic life. Therefore, the asset is less likely to be materially impaired, unless the valuation on initial recognition was erroneous or where subsequent events have resulted in a sudden fall in the estimate of the recoverable amount.

The **impairment process** can be complex and subjective and is dealt with in greater detail in ¶1550.

Useful economic life less than 20 years

1092 FRS 10 (34) **Impairment reviews** should only be conducted on intangible assets and goodwill, amortised over a period not exceeding 20 years from the date of acquisition:
- at the end of the first full accounting period following the date of acquisition; and
- thereafter, when events or changes in circumstances indicate that the carrying values may not be recoverable.

1093 **End of first full accounting period** 1. If, at the end of the first full accounting period following acquisition, there are **no indicators of impairment**, no additional work is required and the carrying values of intangible assets are unaffected.
2. Where an **acquisition takes place part way through an accounting period**, the impairment review does not have to be undertaken at the end of that period but at the end of the subsequent period, that being the first full accounting period after acquisition.

The **requirement to perform an impairment review**, at the end of the first full financial year after the initial recognition of intangible assets and goodwill, ensures that any impairment arising on acquisition is recognised as a loss at the time, rather than amortised over the life of the asset. FRS 10 (39)

Subsequent impairment reviews Impairment reviews should be performed in accordance with the requirements of FRS 11. The **exception is** that the first year impairment review for goodwill and other intangible assets may be performed in two stages; namely: **1094**

1. Identify any possible impairment by comparing post-acquisition performance in the first year with pre-acquisition forecasts used to support the purchase price. FRS 10 (40)
2. Perform a full impairment review in accordance with the requirements of FRS 11, only if the initial review indicates that the post-acquisition performance has failed to meet pre-acquisition expectations or if any unforeseen events indicate that the carrying value may not be recoverable.

Where an **impairment is identified** at the end of the first full accounting period, this will result from one of the following circumstances:
- an overpayment;
- an event that occurred between acquisition and the first year review; or
- depletion of the acquired goodwill or intangible asset between the acquisition date and the first year review that exceeds the value recognised through amortisation.

A **number of indicators** that could underpin the circumstances outlined above are: **1095**
- operating losses or net cash outflows resulting from, for instance, a decline in market share or profit margins, increased competition, or increased marketing support to sustain present market share;
- the loss of key employees;
- adverse changes in the regulatory market; or
- adverse changes to any of the factors affecting fair values of intangible assets on acquisition.

Where any factors exist that indicate that the carrying amount of an intangible asset may not be recoverable, a full impairment review should be undertaken (as illustrated in the example below). Where **impairment in value is confirmed**, then the asset should be written down to its recoverable amount.

EXAMPLE **Dundee Marketing International Plc**
Report and accounts
Note. Amortisation of goodwill

Gross goodwill in respect of subsidiary companies and associated undertakings of £235.2m (20X9: £265.3m) is subject to amortisation over periods of up to 20 years. The group **tests annually** the carrying values of indefinite life goodwill and other intangible assets for impairment. Goodwill subject to periodic amortisation is tested for impairment if there is a change in circumstances that suggests that the carrying value may not be recoverable.

The 20XX **impairment review** was completed in December and assessed whether the carrying value of goodwill was supported by the net present value of future cash flows derived from assets using a projection period of up to 5 years for each income generating unit (IGU). After the projection period, growth rates of nominal GDP have been assumed for each IGU.

The impairment review relating to Ballack and Scholl Plc (£175.5m) was carried out using a 10 year projection. This time period is deemed prudent by the directors and reflects the current estimates of economic viability for this particular investment. The projections for the initial three years are derived from existing budgets and form the base period.

Projections for the remaining 7 years assume an annual growth rate of 4.4% in revenues and an improvement in operating margins to 13%. At the end of the 10 year period, growth is assumed to be in line with nominal GDP. The projections include assumptions for taxation and have been discounted using the group's weighted average cost of capital of 7.5%.

The **estimates and assumptions** made in connection with impairment testing could differ from actual results of operations and cash flows. Further, future events could result in the Company concluding that impairment indicators exist and that the certain asset values have become impaired. Any resulting impairment loss could have a material impact on the Company's financial position. The carrying value of goodwill and other intangibles will continue to be reviewed annually for impairment and adjusted to the recoverable amount where necessary.

Useful economic life exceeding 20 years or non-amortisation

1096 Intangible assets and goodwill amortised over a period exceeding 20 years from the acquisition date, or that are not amortised, should be viewed for impairment at the end of each reporting period.

The reason that **annual impairment reviews** are required where the amortisation period exceeds 20 years, is that the longer the useful economic lives are assigned to intangible assets and goodwill, the higher the risk that the recoverable amount will fall below the carrying value over time.

Impairment losses

1098 FRS 10 (36) Impairment losses **must be recognised by** reference to the expected future cash flows. Any assumption that it might not be possible to continue to measure the future value of goodwill will not in itself justify the goodwill balance being written off at the first impairment review.

The **first impairment review** should be based on updating initial investment appraisal calculations, with the remaining carrying value amortised over a period not exceeding 20 years.

Where an **impairment loss is confirmed**, the impairment should be recognised immediately through a charge to the profit and loss account. The revised net book value should be amortised over the estimated remaining useful economic life of the intangible asset. If goodwill arising on consolidation is found to be impaired, then the carrying amount of the investment recorded in the parent company accounts should also be reviewed for impairment.

1100 **Revaluation and restoration of past losses** The **general rule** is that goodwill and intangible assets should not be revalued, either to increase the carrying value above original cost or to reverse prior period losses arising from impairment or amortisation. Revaluation has the effect of recognising values that have been developed internally.

1102 However, intangible assets with readily ascertainable market values may be revalued by reference to those market values.

If one intangible asset is revalued, then all other capitalised intangible assets in the same class should be revalued. After an intangible asset has been revalued, **further revaluations** should then be carried out regularly to ensure that the carrying value does not differ greatly from the market value at the balance sheet date.

The **amortisation charge** for revalued assets should be based on the revalued amounts and the remaining useful economic lives of the assets. Amortisation charged before the revaluation should not be written back to the profit and loss account.

FRS 10 (43) Where previously an impairment loss has been recognised as a result of an external event and that **impairment has now reversed**, as a result of other external events that were not foreseen in the original impairment calculations, that reversal should be recognised in the current period.

Past impairment losses may not be reversed when the restoration in value is generated internally.

D. Disclosures

1116 A significant number of disclosures are required by FRS 10 covering recognition, amortisation and revaluation of intangible fixed assets and goodwill.

Classification

The standard classifications of intangible assets are contained in Sch. 1 to The Large and Medium-sized Companies and Groups (Accounts and Reports) Regulations 2008 (SI 2008/410) are as follows: **1117**

EXAMPLE **B Fixed assets** (extract)

Intangible assets
1. Development costs (¶1150)
2. Concessions, patents, licences, trademarks and similar rights and assets
3. Goodwill
4. Payments on account

Assets included under the category of "Concessions, patents, licences, trademarks and similar rights and assets" **can only be shown** if they:
– were acquired for a valuable consideration; and
– are not required to be shown under goodwill, or the assets were created internally by the company itself.

Further **sub-divisions** of intangible assets are permissible where, for example, different types of licence have different functions within the business segments or divisions.

For small companies, only two standard classifications are required under the above-mentioned regulations; namely:
– Goodwill; and
– Other intangible assets.

Recognition

The **following information** should be **disclosed separately** for positive and negative goodwill as well as for each class of intangible asset recorded in the balance sheet; namely: **1118** FRS 10 (53)
– the cost or revalued amount at the beginning of the financial period and at the balance sheet date;
– the cumulative provisions for amortisation or impairment at the beginning of the financial period and at the balance sheet date;
– a reconciliation of the movements, with separate disclosures for additions, disposals, revaluations, transfers, amortisation, impairment losses, reversals of past impairment losses and amounts of negative goodwill written back in the financial period;
– the net carrying amount at the balance sheet date; and
– the profit or loss on any material disposal of a previously acquired business or business segment.

In respect of **negative goodwill** the following should also be disclosed: **1120**
– the period(s) in which negative goodwill is being written back to the profit and loss account; and
– where negative goodwill exceeds the fair values of the non-monetary assets, the amount and source of the "excess" negative goodwill and the periods in which it is to be written back should be given.

Amortisation disclosures

The following disclosures are required covering the amortisation of goodwill and intangible assets: **1122** FRS 10 (56)

a. The **methods and periods** of amortisation of goodwill and intangible assets and the reasons for choosing these time periods.

b. Where there has been a **change in the method** of amortisation used, the reason and the effect if material.

c. If the **amortisation period is changed** following a review of the useful economic life of any goodwill or intangible assets, the reason and any material effect.

d. Where goodwill or intangible assets are amortised **over a period greater than 20 years**, the grounds for rebutting the 20 year rule should be given, and the particular circumstances supporting the durability of the acquired business or intangible asset.
e. Where **goodwill** in the financial statements **is not amortised**, a note to this effect should be given, stating that the company has departed from the specific requirement of the companies legislation to amortise goodwill over a finite period, in order to give a true and fair view. The specific reasons for the departure and its effect should be disclosed.

Accounting policies

1124 FRS 10 (60) FRS 18 (62)

FRS 18 "Accounting policies" specifies that disclosures are required to provide the user of financial statements with a clear account of the **reasons for any departure from a statutory requirement**, including when it is not possible to quantify the effect of the departure.

The following disclosures are required where the "**true and fair view override**" is invoked; namely:
- a statement that the financial statements depart from the specific requirements of the Companies Act to amortise goodwill over the estimated useful economic life;
- details of the accounting treatment actually adopted and reasons why departure from the Companies Act is necessary; and
- a description of the specific factors supporting the durability of the acquired business.

EXAMPLE **Slangram Plc – Annual report and accounts**
Notes to the accounts (extract)

Accounting policies (extract) – amortisation of intangible fixed assets and goodwill
Brands are valued independently as part of the fair value of assets acquired from third parties where the brand has a value which is substantial and long term and where brands can be sold separately from the rest of the business acquired. Brands are amortised on a straight-line basis over the estimated useful economic lives, although no longer than 20 years, except where it is not possible to estimate the useful economic life of the brand.

Goodwill capitalised relating to other group acquisitions is based on a useful economic life of 20 years.
The goodwill arising on the acquisition of Tallydrum Ltd, amounting to £124.2m, has, in the opinion of the directors, an indefinite useful economic life. As such, amortisation is not provided. The Company's main operations are in the UK market, where barriers to entry are high and the company has exclusive rights of operation under ownership rights in perpetuity. As a consequence, the goodwill element is deemed to be durable and there are no plans to merge this business with the existing business as it is deemed capable of **continued measurement** (FRS 10).
As required under FRS 10, an impairment review was carried out in February 20XX, which confirmed that the value of goodwill does not exceed its **recoverable amount**. The accounting treatment is a departure from the requirements of the Companies Act and is adopted in order to present a **true and fair view** of the Group's results. If the goodwill had been amortised over 20 years, the amortisation charge for the year to June 20XX would have been £3.2m and the net book value of goodwill equals £121m.

EXAMPLE **ABC Ltd – Annual report and accounts**
Accounting policies (extract)

Trademarks and brands
The Group has registered trademarks throughout the world and is the owner of many licences, patents, technology and know-how relating to its products and production processes, packaging and the operation of various processes and equipment. An amount of £2,456,000 has been included in the Group's balance sheet at 30 June 20XX reflecting the cost of brands acquired since 20X2. The Group does not amortise this cost in its UK GAAP accounts; an appropriate charge against income is made where there is a confirmed diminution in value.

Notes to the accounts
Intangible assets represent significant owned brands acquired since 20X5 valued at historical cost. **No amortisation is charged** as the annual results reflect significant expenditure in support of these brands and the carrying value are reviewed on an annual basis for any impairment in value. Where there is a split between goodwill and brands, this is calculated using the Group's valuation methodology.

Prior to 20X5, goodwill, being the excess of the consideration over fair value, was written-off against reserves on consolidation. Upon disposal of a previously acquired business the attributable amount of goodwill previously written-off to reserves is included in determining the profit or loss on disposal. Since 20X5, **acquired goodwill** has been capitalised and, through annual impairment reviews or an annual amortisation charge, its subsequent measurement determined based on the individual circumstances of each business acquired. Goodwill written-off to reserves prior to 20X5 has not been recorded on the balance sheet.

The Group has concluded that goodwill arising on its associate, Sveno Cola and Bottling Group (SCBG), should not be amortised as it has an indefinite useful economic life that can be demonstrated and the value of the investment can be readily measured.

SCBG operates in the profitable US soft drinks market sector. The sector has high market barriers to entry due to the nature of the licence agreements with soft drink concentrate owners and the capital requirements needed to operate as a bottler and distributor. As an associate, the company is managed separately from the Group and can be valued on a discounted cash flow basis.

The Group does not amortise this goodwill, representing a **departure from the Companies Act**, for the overriding purpose of giving a true and fair view of the Group's results. If the goodwill arising on SCBG and DHS Industries had been amortised over a period of 20 years, operating profit and investment in associates would have decreased by £20m in 20XX (20X9 £15m).

Balance sheet (extract) 20XX	**Goodwill** **£m**	**Intangibles** **£m**	**Total** **£m**
Cost			
At 1 July 20X9	xx	x, xxx	x, xxx
Exchange rate adjustments	(xx)	xxx	xx
Goodwill arising on acquisition of subsidiaries in the year	xxx	–	xxx
Intangibles arising on acquisition of brands		xxx	xxx
Cost at 30 June 20XX	**xxx**	**x, xxx**	**x, xxx**
Amortisation			
At 1 July 20X9	(x)		(x)
Charge for the year	(xx)		(xx)
Amortisation at 30 June 20XX	(xx)		(xx)
Net Book Value 30 June 20XX	**xx**	**x, xxx**	**x, xxx**
Net Book Value 31 June 20X9	**xxx**	**x, xxx**	**x, xxx**

Revaluation (alternative accounting rules)

The **following disclosures** are required in the financial statements where a class of assets has been revalued, namely: 1126 FRS 10 (61)
- the year the assets were valued, the values and the valuation bases;
- the original costs, or fair value, of the assets and any provision for amortisation that would have been recognised had the assets been valued at their original cost;
- the difference between the historical cost amount and the value stated in the balance sheet;
- where any asset has been revalued during the year, the name and qualification of the valuer and reason for revaluing the intangible asset and quantification; and
- a statement of the treatment usually adopted.

E. Comparison between UK GAAP and IAS (IFRS)

In **general terms** IAS 38 requires intangible assets to be recognised where it is probable that the future economic benefits attributable to the asset will be reaped by the entity. 1130

The **key requirements of** IAS 38 are as follows:

1. Intangible assets (e.g. brands, internet domain names or construction permits) acquired as **part of a business combination** must be accounted for separately from goodwill, where

the fair value can be reliably measured or the assets arise from contractual or other legal rights.

2. The **rebuttable presumption** that the useful economic life of intangible assets should not exceed 20 years no longer applies. Intangible assets are now regarded as having indefinite useful economic lives, as it is recognised that there is no pre-determined limit to the period over which an asset can generate revenues.

3. Intangible assets with **indefinite useful economic lives** are no longer amortised but should be measured initially at cost less any accumulated impairment losses. Instead intangible assets must be **tested annually** for impairment, or where events or circumstances indicate that impairment has occurred.

MEMO POINTS 1. The International Valuation Standards Council (IVSC) has issued an exposure draft, updating the recommendations in earlier guidance notes, concerning the principal methods for valuing intangible assets such as brands, and intellectual property. The IVSC has also issued revised guidance on the valuation of intangibles for IFRS reporting purposes, including the principal accounting requirements underpinning valuations (i.e. methodology, most common methods etc). GN4 is effective from March 2010 and copies can be downloaded from the IVSC website.

2. The ASB has issued **two amendments to IAS 38**. The first relates to intangible assets acquired as part of a business combination and which are separable or result from contractual or legal rights. The purpose of the amendment is to ensure that intangible assets are not simply subsumed within goodwill and that their fair value is accurately assessed. The **second amendment** clarifies the descriptions of valuation techniques used to determine the fair value of intangible assets.

3. Under the small company IFRS, intangible assets and goodwill are assumed to have a **maximum finite useful economic life** of 10 years, meaning that tax relief would be available on the amortisation of qualifying assets. This is in contrast to full IFRS, which assumes an infinite useful economic life (thereby restricting the tax relief available), and UK GAAP, which advocates a maximum term of 20 years, which in turn is rebuttable if certain criteria are met.

4. In October 2010 the ASB issued a proposal to introduce a financial reporting framework for medium-sized entities (FRSME) not eligible to apply the FRSSE or full IFRS. The FRSME would replace current UK GAAP from July 2013 and is based on the principles underpinning full IFRS. If adopted there could be some key differences in the accounting treatment of intangible assets and in particular goodwill, development costs and revaluation.

Key differences

1134 There are a **small number of important differences** between IAS 38 "Intangible fixed assets" and UK GAAP which can be summarised as follows:

- the criteria for recognising internally-generated intangible assets;
- differences in terminology which can result in assets meeting the definition of an intangible asset under IAS 38 may not do so under FRS 10; and
- SSAP 13 "Accounting for research and development" permits a choice between capitalisation and recognition as an expense for certain development costs. IAS 38, on the other hand, requires capitalisation of development costs which meet certain criteria.

First-time adoption

1136 There are **no specific transitional rules** contained in IFRS 1 "First time adoption of IFRS". A brief outline of other requirements related to the opening IFRS balance sheet are given below.

The entity's opening IFRS balance sheet should exclude all intangible assets that do not meet the recognition criteria under IAS 38, at the transition date to IFRS. This requirement also covers intangible assets, acquired as part of a business combination, that were not originally recognised in the acquirer's consolidated balance sheet under UK GAAP and that would not qualify for recognition under IAS 38 in the balance sheet of the acquiree.

1137 **Recognition criteria** The criteria for recognising an intangible asset under IAS 38 are as follows:

- that the future economic benefits attributable to the asset are expected to flow to the entity; and
- that the original cost of the asset can be reliably measured.

Other adjustments 1. If an **internally-generated** intangible asset qualifies for recognition at the transition date to IFRS, it may be included in the opening IFRS balance sheet, even where it was earlier recognised as an expense under UK GAAP. If the asset qualifies at a later date, its cost will be the total of the expenditure incurred on the asset at that date. 1138

2. Intangible assets acquired as **part of a business combination** prior to the transition to IFRS are recorded at its carrying amount under UK GAAP.

3. **Where the amortisation methods** adopted under UK GAAP **are acceptable** under IFRS, the accumulated amortisation need not be restated in the IFRS opening balance sheet. Instead, the entity accounts for any change in amortisation periods or estimated useful life prospectively, from the period it changes its estimates.

4. **Where the amortisation methods** adopted **are not acceptable** under IFRS, such as where the useful economic lives are unrealistic, and the differences have a material effect on the financial statements, the entity is required to adjust accumulated amortisation in the opening IFRS balance sheet.

5. An entity **adopting IFRS for the first time** may select either of the following as the deemed cost of an intangible asset:
- the fair value at the date of transition to IFRS; or
- the cost resulting from a revaluation under UK GAAP that meets the criteria in IFRS 1.

CHAPTER 3

Research and development

OUTLINE ¶¶

The key reporting standard is SSAP 13 "Accounting for research and development", which distinguishes the costs of research and development from other non-research expenditure based on the presence or absence of an appreciable element of innovation. Reporting entities applying the Financial Reporting Standard for Smaller Entities (FRSSE) are subject to the same accounting requirements as those stipulated in SSAP 13. 1150

A. Classification

Research and development expenditure can be defined and grouped as follows: 1152 SSAP 13 (21)

Research classification	Characteristics
Pure research	Pure research is experimental or theoretical work undertaken primarily to acquire new scientific or technical knowledge for its own sake as opposed to research directed towards a specific aim
Applied research	Applied research is an original or critical investigation undertaken to obtain new scientific or technical knowledge or develop existing knowledge directed towards a specific commercial objective
Development costs	Development costs are the costs of using scientific or technical knowledge in order to: – produce new or improved materials, products or services; – install new processes or systems prior to the commencement of commercial production or commercial applications; – design, construct and test pre-production prototypes, pilot plants, models and development batches; – design and test products, services, processes or systems involving new technologies or that substantially improve those already produced or installed; or – that substantially improve existing processes or systems

Exclusions The **costs of the following activities** should not be classified as research and development expenditure: 1154 SSAP 13 (7)
- testing analysis either of equipment or product for purposes of quality or quality control;
- periodic alterations to existing products, services or processes;

– operational research not directly linked to a specific research objective;
– repairs and renewals expenditure relating to processes during normal commercial production;
– legal and administrative work connected with patent applications, records and litigation or the sale or licensing of patents;
– market research;
– design or construction engineering relating to the construction, relocation, rearrangement or start-up of facilities or equipment not directly connected to any particular research activity.

1155 **Extractive industries** The development of **new surveying methods and techniques**, as an integral part of research on geological phenomena, should be included in research and development, as they are within the jurisdiction of SSAP 13. However, expenditure related to the actual exploration of oil, gas and mineral deposits in the extractive industries does not fall within the definition of research and development, and should be treated in accordance with the relevant SORP.

MEMO POINTS The Statement of Recommended Practice (SORP) "Accounting for oil and gas exploration and development activities" covers the accounting treatment of expenditure incurred in exploring, developing and extracting oil and gas.

B. Accounting treatment

1160 SSAP 13 (1) The **general rule** is that research and development expenditure should be expensed as incurred, although certain development costs can be deferred if strict criteria are met. It should be noted that whilst the standard permits the capitalisation of development costs that satisfy the relevant criteria this is optional and not a requirement. The accounting policies to be adopted for research and development expenditure are based on the "accruals concept", by which revenue and costs are accrued, matched and dealt with in the period to which they relate.

1. Pure and applied research

1162 SSAP 13 (8) Expenditure on pure and applied research should be considered part of the continuing operations required to maintain the competitive position of the company. These costs should be expensed in the profit and loss account as incurred.

2. Development costs

1164 SSAP 13 (9) Expenditure on development should be commissioned with the expectation of commercial success and future benefits from revenues and related profits or reduced costs. To the extent that this type of expenditure meets the capitalisation criteria below, it may be deferred and then expensed against future revenues.

Capitalisation criteria

1166 SSAP 13 (11) If an **entity wishes to defer** development expenditure it must be able to demonstrate in respect of the costs to be deferred that:
a. there is a clearly defined project;
b. the related expenditure is separately identifiable;
c. development costs including related production, selling and administrative costs incurred on a project are expected to be covered by future revenues;

d. adequate resources exist, or are reasonably expected to be available, to enable the project to be completed; and
e. the project is deemed technically feasible and commercially viable depending on:
- likely market conditions, including competing products and services;
- public opinion; or
- consumer and environmental legislation.

Application of criteria

Where all the **criteria for recognition have been met**, development expenditure can be deferred instead of writing it off as it is incurred. Where some of the capitalisation **criteria have not been met**, or have ceased to apply, then the development expenditure should be expensed in the profit and loss account. 1167

A number of other issues should be considered including amortisation, annual reviews for diminution in value, and taxation.

Amortisation The directors should be realistic in their assessment of the period over which development expenditure should be written-off, and whether the benefits will accrue evenly. 1168 SSAP 13 (28)
The amounts amortised should commence with the commercial production or application of the product, service, process or system.

The **straight-line method** of depreciation is often used but other methods can often be more appropriate.

> EXAMPLE A new hi-technology product may have an estimated life span of three years – but with 50% of sales anticipated in year 1, 35% in year 2 and 15% in year three. Half a million pounds in development expenditure has been deferred in respect of the product. In this case it would be inappropriate to use the straight-line method and the amortisation of the deferred development costs should match the anticipated sales profile. This would therefore result in amortisation of £250,000 in year 1, £175,000 in year 2 and £75,000 in year 3.

Reinstatement SSAP 13 is silent on the question of reinstating development expenditure that has been written-off, should circumstances change and the criteria set out in the standard be satisfied. Whilst it is theoretically possible to reinstate the costs previously written-off, this is not regarded as best practice and is not recommended. 1169

This does not, however, preclude the deferral of **additional expenditure** incurred from the point at which the relevant criteria are satisfied.

Diminution in value A company must review the development expenditure it has deferred at the end of each financial year. If the circumstances that underpinned the original deferral of development costs no longer apply, or are considered doubtful, then to the extent that unamortised expenditure is considered irrecoverable, it should be charged to the profit and loss account in the accounting period concerned. Deferred development costs fall within the scope of FRS 11 "Impairment of fixed assets and goodwill". 1170 SSAP 13 (15)

Tangible fixed assets The use of tangible fixed assets acquired, or constructed, to provide facilities for research and development activities usually extends over a number of accounting periods; accordingly, they should be deferred and written off over their useful economic lives. 1172 SSAP 13 (16)

Third party contracts Where companies enter into a firm contract to undertake development work on behalf of third parties, any expenditure not reimbursed at the balance sheet date will usually, depending on the nature and length of the contract, be accounted for in accordance with the provisions of SSAP 9 in respect of **long-term contract** work in progress. 1174 SSAP 13 (17)

Where the development **costs are fully reimbursed** or there is an agreement to develop and manufacture at an agreed price calculated to reimburse expenditure on development and on manufacture, then these costs should not be deferred and should also be dealt with as contract work in progress.

Complexities arise where there is "**risk-sharing**" within a development contract with third parties. In this case it is necessary to:
- examine the element of cost retained within the company and assess to what it relates to;
- determine whether it qualifies as development expenditure; and
- whether it satisfies the SSAP 13 criteria for carrying it forward.

This may be difficult to justify where the final commercial development of a product being developed lies with another entity.

1175 **Forecasting profitability** A problem with the recognition criteria is that companies have to justify the commercial profitability of a project before capitalisation of the costs is permitted. Revenue must exceed costs. For some projects, this could involve revenue projections covering a considerable number of years. As such, the longer the forecast, the more subjective the assumptions are likely to be.

C. Taxation

1176 There are a number of tax issues relating to research and development expenditure; namely:
- qualifying expenditure;
- availability of capital allowances; and
- disposal of research and development assets.

1177 **Qualifying expenditure** The following expenditure could qualify for R & D relief:
- staffing costs;
- payments to volunteers in clinical trials;
- subcontracted R & D costs; or
- software or consumable items.

However, **certain conditions apply**. Firstly, the R & D must help develop and grow the existing business or help improve working conditions including the health and safety of employees. Secondly, the relevant costs must total at least £10,000 in any 12 month accounting period.

The **staff costs** that can be attributed to R & D differ according to the nature of the research. For instance, the costs of directors and staff (e.g. salaries, pension costs, NI contributions) actively engaged in research projects can be claimed. Where the directors or staff are not 100% engaged in research the costs must be apportioned on a "just and reasonable" basis. For **external workers** (non subcontractor) used on research projects, a maximum of 65% of the costs can be attributed to R & D expenditure. Different rules apply where the company supplying the external workers is a connected (related) company.

There are also rules governing pre-trading qualifying R & D expenditure.

MEMO POINTS R&D expenditure will also qualify where the funding is provided by government (national, local & EU) in the form of grants or subsidies.

1178 **Capital allowances** Any **capital expenditure** incurred on research and development could qualify for allowances with the exception of expenditure on land and buildings. Revenue expenditure may be deducted as an expense of the trade.

Additional relief is available to certain other companies, incurring qualifying research and development expenditure, entitling them to deduct an amount greater than the actual expenditure in computing the trading profits. For example, under certain conditions, SME's could claim up to 175% and larger companies 130% of qualifying expenditure as trading deductions against taxable profits.

Alternatively, a R & D tax credit may be available from the Inland Revenue where the company has traded at a loss..

A more detailed analysis of the tax treatment of research and development expenditure can be found in the **tax memo**.

MEMO POINTS 1. The Finance Bill 2010 removes the restriction on small and medium-sized entities claiming tax relief on research and development (R&D) expenditure, where they do not own the intellectual property rights (IPRs). The legislation applies to any relevant R&D expenditure incurred in the accounting period ending on or after 9 December 2009.
2. The Government is currently consulting on incentives to attract and preserve Intellectual Property (IP) in the UK. The plan is to modifying the existing system of R&D tax reliefs and introduce of a new scheme for patents commercialised after 29 November 2010. The consultation will focus on examining the current definition of R&D and in particular qualifying costs, as well as how to:
- improve targeting of R&D tax reliefs for genuine innovative developments;
- encourage greater investment by small companies in R&D; and
- simplify the claims process and make it more accessible.

D. Disclosures

Considering the problems inherent in defining research and development, disclosure is restricted to the following companies: **1180** SSAP 13 (20)
- a public limited company;
- a bank or insurance company;
- a parent company that has either a public limited company or a banking or insurance company as a subsidiary; or
- a company that exceeds by a multiple of 10, the criteria for defining a medium sized company.

The following **key disclosures** are required: **1181** SSAP 13 (19)
1. the accounting policy adopted;
2. the total research cost charged to the profit and loss account;
3. the period over which development costs originally deferred are to be written off;
4. the reasons for capitalising development costs;
5. the total development cost charged to the profit and loss account, split between:
- the current expenditure and the amounts amortised from deferred expenditure;
- the movements on deferred development expenditure during the year.

The **general disclosure requirements** are illustrated in the following examples.

EXAMPLE **X Ltd. - Notes to the financial statements 2010**

Accounting policies (extract)

Research and development: Research expenditure is written off as it is incurred and charged to the profit and loss account. Development expenditure is written off, except where there is a separate project that is technically, commercially and financially viable. In these cases, the identifiable expenditure is deferred and amortised over the period the company is expected to derive benefit.
Product T: Development costs are capitalised and carried forward as the product is not yet in commercial production. The costs are to be amortised over five years from 2010.

EXAMPLE **X Ltd. - Notes to the financial statements**

Development costs

	£
Cost	
As at 1 January, 2010	xx, xxx
Additions	x, xxx
Disposals	x, xxx
Exchange adjustments	xx
As at 31 December, 2010	xx, xxx

Aggregate amortisation	
As at 1 January, 2010	x, xxx
Charge for the year	xxx
Impairment losses	xxx
Reversal of past impairment losses	xx
Exchange adjustment	xx
As at 31 December, 2010	x, xxx
Net book value	
As at 31 December, 2010	xx, xxx
As at 31 December, 2009	xx, xxx

Development costs relate to specific projects utilising technical knowledge to increase the company's range of products. They are capitalised and written off over a period of five years, commencing in the year of commercial production.
Development costs are capitalised in accordance with SSAP 13 and hence the amount of unamortised development expenditure is not treated as a realised loss for the purposes of calculating distributable profits.

1182 **The Directors' Report** should contain general information on the research and development activities of the company and its subsidiaries.

1183 **Realised revenue loss** The Companies Act requires development costs, carried in a company's balance sheet as an asset, to be treated as a realised revenue loss. If **special circumstances** exist, which the directors believe justify treating these amounts as unrealised losses, then additional disclosures are required in the notes to the financial statements.

The **notes should disclose**:
– the fact the unamortised development expenditure is not to be treated as a realised loss for the purpose of calculating distributable profits; and
– the reasons justifying the directors' decision not to treat the unamortised development expenditure as a realised loss.

Research and development costs must not be carried forward indefinitely.

Exemptions

1184 Some disclosure exemptions are available to small and medium-sized companies. These small companies need not disclose the total research and development costs charged to the profit and loss account, **unless a parent or other group member** belongs to one of the categories set out in ¶1180.

1185 **Private companies** The majority of private companies do not have to disclose any research and development expenditure charged in the profit and loss account, although they will still be required to disclose information regarding the accounting policy adopted and the total of any agreed deferred development expenditure.

E. Comparison between UK GAAP and IAS (IFRS)

1188 IAS 38 (54) – (64) Broad compliance with the content of SSAP 13 will ensure compliance with IAS 38 "Intangible assets".

The **key differences** are that:

1. SSAP 13 allows development costs which meet certain criteria (see ¶1166) to be either capitalised or recognised as an expense. IAS 38, on the other hand, does not offer the choice and requires capitalisation of development costs meeting the said criteria.

2. IAS 38 prohibits the reinstatement in the balance sheet of development costs expensed in periods before the asset recognition criteria were met.

Under IAS 38, the **option of the immediate write-off** of development expenditure is not available where the item qualifies as an intangible asset. This could have an effect on some UK companies switching to IFRS, particularly where significant development costs are incurred such as in the motor industry or in telecommunications.

Expenses incurred prior to a project satisfying the criteria for recognition as an intangible asset must be charged to the profit and loss account. Furthermore, these costs cannot be capitalised if the project later satisfies the criteria for an intangible asset. The **problem is knowing at what stage** the recognition criteria for intangible assets have been met. The recognition criteria must be applied to each stage of the product life cycle.

Impairment Where a new product is developed that replaces an existing product or 1190
system, the issue of impairment must be addressed. In addition to estimating the future economic benefits to be obtained from the new product, the entity will also need to reassess whether the benefits, from the existing systems or products that have been replaced or affected, have been impaired. The **primary indicators** of impairment are covered in IAS 36 (see ¶1718).

CHAPTER 4

Tangible fixed assets

OUTLINE ¶¶

Tangible fixed assets **have been defined** by the Accounting Standards Board (ASB) as assets that have physical substance and are either held for use: **1200**
- in the production or supply of goods and services;
- for rental to others; or
- for administrative purposes on a continuing basis in the reporting entity's activities.

The Companies Act 2006 and FRS 15 "Tangible Fixed Assets" contains for all entities, the consistent principles that must be applied in accounting for the initial **classification, valuation, revaluation and depreciation** of tangible fixed assets. Disclosures sufficient to enable the users of the financial statements to understand the impact of the accounting policies selected in this area should also be given. FRS 15 (1)

Subsequent expenditure on tangible fixed assets, the accounting treatment of related finance costs and the impact of the alternative accounting rules on the valuation of tangible fixed assets are also covered.

MEMO POINTS The legal framework now includes the CA 1985 Sch 4 para. 31; Sch. 1 to The Large and Medium Sized Companies and Groups (Accounts and Reports) Regulations 2008 (SI 2008/410) and Sch. 1 of the Small Companies and Groups (Accounts and Directors' Report) Regulations 2008 (SI 2008/409).

1202 **All reporting entities** are subject to the provisions of FRS 15, **except those small entities** applying the Financial Reporting Standard for Smaller Entities (FRSSE).

FRS 15 is likely to be revised as part of the ongoing **convergence programme** with international accounting standards. The proposals contained in FRED 29 "Property, Plant and Equipment" are outlined in this chapter, as are the key differences between FRS 15 and IAS 16 "Property, Plant and Equipment" and IAS 23 "Borrowing Costs".

SECTION 1

Classification

1210 FRS 15 (2) Fixed assets fall into a variety of categories, each requiring classification in order to determine the appropriate accounting treatment and disclosures.

A classification can be defined as a "category of tangible fixed assets having a similar nature, function or use within the business of the entity."

FRS 15 (62) Tangible fixed assets should be classified under the following **broad categories**:
- land and buildings;
- plant and machinery;
- fixtures, fittings, tools and equipment; and
- payments on account and assets in the course of construction.

1212 Within the broad statutory categories, classifications can be narrowed to meet the requirements of **specific industries**. Where it is industry practice to adopt narrower classifications, the disclosures required may be given by **class of asset** and not just the main categories as defined in the Companies Act.

Land and buildings

1213 Land and buildings which are usually classified as freehold, short or long-leasehold (50 years or more to run at the balance sheet date), and can be **further sub-divided** into specialised properties (see ¶1400) and non-specialised properties (see ¶1388). The issue of **separable assets** and whether they should be classified as land and buildings or not is covered in ¶1484.

Plant and machinery

1214 Plant and machinery can be defined as the equipment that enables a business to function. The **definition used in the tax legislation** is that plant and machinery represents whatever apparatus is used by a businessman for the conduct of his business, as opposed to his stock in trade which he buys or makes for resale.

Plant and machinery includes "all goods and chattels, fixed or moveable, live or dead, which the businessman keeps for permanent employment in the business." (*Yarmouth v France 1887*). For example, where fixtures and fittings are immaterial, it may be possible to consolidate them in with plant and machinery, for disclosure purposes.

1216 **Motor vehicles** The Act does not stipulate a separate category for motor vehicles. Therefore, the category in which they should be placed is a matter of judgement. A distinction can be drawn between motor vehicles grouped as production assets (e.g. vans, trucks and cranes), which are typically included within plant and machinery and other vehicles for staff or the sales force, which could be included within fixtures and fittings. If the number of vehicles involved is significant, then a **separate classification** for motor vehicles may be added to the financial statements.

Fixtures, fittings, tools and equipment

This **group of assets** includes such items as: 1218
- showcases;
- counters;
- shelving;
- display fixtures;
- safes; and
- office equipment and furniture, including computer equipment.

Tools are generally divided into two categories: namely machine tools and hand tools. Typically machine tools are expensive and are usually capitalised as fixtures, fittings and equipment, whilst hand tools are normally expensed. Non-production companies often classify all their assets in "other property" under fixtures, fittings, tools and equipment. 1220

Payments on account and assets under construction

This category includes payments the company has made in relation to assets that are in the process of construction or installation, but that are not in service at the balance sheet date. A company **will not normally charge depreciation** or impair an asset that is in the course of construction, except in exceptional cases. 1222

Often the amounts involved are immaterial and do not require separate disclosure. However, significant amounts relating to assets under construction (e.g. property) or development should be separately disclosed within fixed assets, until the asset is bought into use, when the costs should be transferred to the appropriate asset categories.

SECTION 2

Initial valuation

This section outlines the **general rules** contained in FRS 15 and the Companies Act for the initial valuation of tangible fixed assets, the recognition of directly attributable costs and the rules governing the capitalisation of finance costs. The rules governing the valuation of specific tangible fixed assets such as donated assets, historical assets, and website development costs are also covered. 1226

A. General rules

A tangible fixed asset is ready for use when its physical construction is complete. 1230 FRS 15 (6) (13)

A tangible fixed asset **should initially be** accounted for at cost irrespective of whether an asset is purchased or produced in-house. Subsequent valuations may be carried at market value under the **alternative accounting rules** as discussed further in ¶1358.

For tangible fixed assets either **purchased or constructed in-house**, there are a number of rules governing the costs that must be capitalised (see ¶1240 and ¶1290) and costs that must be expensed (see ¶1270). The **capitalisation of costs** is only permissible, in respect of the period in which the activities necessary to bring the asset into use are undertaken.

Where initial recognition of tangible fixed asset is based on:	
Purchase price	The purchase price of an asset includes the actual price paid plus any expenses directly attributable to its acquisition, in order to bring the asset to its present location and condition
Production cost	The production cost of an asset includes the purchase price of raw materials and consumables used and other directly attributable costs

1234 FRS 15 (33) **Impairment** On **initial recognition** the asset should only be reviewed for impairment if there is a good indication of a diminution in value or it is specifically required by another accounting standard. This may occur where for instance, there is a sudden slump in demand for a product, that the asset helps produce.

The key requirement is that **the value** of the tangible fixed asset originally recognised in the accounts, **should not exceed** the recoverable amount of the asset. Where the capitalisation of directly attributable costs results in the initial cost of the tangible fixed asset, being greater than its recoverable amount, the asset is impaired and should be written down to the lower value. Impairment is treated in greater detail in Part 3 Chapter 5.

1. Attributable costs

1240 The general rules covering attributable costs are set out in the table below.

Directly attributable costs	These costs should be capitalised and can be grouped as either labour or incremental costs
Labour costs	Only labour costs (e.g. site works, in-house architects, surveyors) arising from the construction, acquisition or installation of the tangible fixed asset should be capitalised
Costs resulting from potential acquisitions or development that did not proceed	These costs must be excluded. For example, where a company is looking to buy new land survey costs on land examined but not purchased may not be included within the cost of the piece of land that the company ultimately purchases

Incremental costs

1242 FRS 15 (9) Incremental costs **can be defined as** costs to the entity that would have been avoided if the tangible fixed asset had not been constructed or acquired. Incremental costs include start-up costs, decommissioning provisions and finance costs.

1244 UITF 24 (5) **Start-up costs** Start-up costs should be treated in the same way as similar costs incurred by the entity as part of its ongoing activities. The **key issue is whether** specific costs that result from start-up activity should be recognised as an asset or expense when incurred. The Urgent Issues Task Force (UITF) concluded that start-up costs could only be recognised as assets if they meet the **specific recognition criteria**, under a recognised accounting standard such as FRS 15, FRS 10 "Goodwill and intangible assets" or SSAP 13 "Accounting for research and development".

Start-up **costs not meeting** the asset recognition criteria should be expensed in the profit and loss account. Start-up costs that meet the definition of an exceptional item under FRS 3 should be disclosed separately in accordance with the requirements of that standard.

1246 The following are some **examples** of activities **that generate start-up costs**:
- the opening of a new facility;
UITF 24 (4)
- starting of a new operation;
- initiation of a new process in an existing facility;
- the introduction of a new product or service;

- development of new business in a new territory; and
- relocation or reorganisation of all or part of the entity.

Examples of start-up costs include: 1248
- costs of site clearance and preparation;
- initial delivery and handling costs;
- installation costs;
- acquisition costs (import duties, stamp duty); or
- professional fees (legal, architect, engineers etc.).

Specific costs associated with a **start-up or commissioning period** before an asset is bought into use, should only be included in the cost of the tangible fixed asset, when the asset is available for use but incapable of operating at normal levels, without such a period of commissioning. For instance, costs incurred during a commissioning period required to test a machine, in order to ensure it works to a particular specification and is capable of normal use, could be capitalised even though it is physically incomplete. 1250 UITF 24 (6) FRS 15 (14)

Commissioning costs should be distinguished from the costs of an initial operating period, in which a tangible fixed asset is not used to full capacity because demand for its output is not yet sufficiently high. For example, a new hotel for instance, will normally take a period of time to build up occupancy levels. Insufficient demand in itself is not an acceptable reason for treating operating costs as start-up costs and capitalising them. 1252

Provision for decommissioning costs

Decommissioning costs include the **dismantling and removal** of a facility and the restoration of a site arising from the construction or acquisition of an asset. 1260 FRS 12 (66)

If any anticipated costs qualify as a provision before they are actually incurred, then they can be capitalised as a directly attributable cost of the relevant asset on **initial valuation** and depreciated over the life of the asset.

A provision should only be recognised and capitalised when the **obligation incurred** is deemed to give access to future economic benefits.

Even where expenditure of this type emerges only some time after the original capitalisation of the asset, this may not prevent its capitalisation.

Examples of decommissioning costs that may be capitalised as part of the cost of the tangible fixed asset are: 1262
- removal of machinery;
- abandonment costs in mining and other extraction industries;
- restoration of sites (e.g. landfill, mines); and
- environmental clean up costs.

Where an **obligation arises later in the life of an asset** as a result of legislative, obsolescence or technological change, then any original provision should be adjusted. 1264

EXAMPLE **A number of provisions** relating to the decommissioning of an asset with a useful economic life of 20 years were capitalised at the time of construction. However, legislative changes after 5 years meant that further obligations totalling £500,000 arose in respect of decommissioning costs. Further provisions were made to cover the additional obligations.
Accounting treatment: The **provision** should be capitalised in full as an addition to the original costs of the tangible fixed asset and depreciated over the remaining useful economic life of 15 years.

2. Excluded costs (non-direct)

All **costs not classified as directly attributable** should be excluded from the capitalised cost of the asset and include the following: 1270
- trade discounts or rebates;

- employee costs not directly related to the specific asset (initial site selection costs);
- administration costs;
- obligations arising from damage through use that do not meet the criteria discussed above under decommissioning costs;
- indirect production overhead included in cost of stock transferred to fixed assets;
- operating losses resulting from the suspension of revenue generating activities during construction of an asset, not directly connected to bringing the asset into use;
- other general overheads; and
- abnormal costs (i.e. design errors, idle capacity, waste materials or labour or other resources and production delays).

1274 **Indirect production overheads** When an item of stock is transferred to fixed assets (from current assets), the indirect production costs previously included in the cost of stock, that do not meet the criteria laid down in FRS 15 for inclusion in the cost of the tangible fixed asset, should be expensed in the profit and loss account at the time the transfer is made.

3. Capitalisation of finance costs

1280 FRS 15 (19) Both FRS 15 and the Companies Act permit companies to capitalise finance costs incurred during the production of a fixed asset, where they can be specifically identified. Finance costs relating to **leased tangible fixed assets** should be accounted for in accordance with SSAP 21. The process for determining the capitalisation rate is considered in ¶1310 whilst the disclosures required are outlined in ¶1512.

1281 FRS 15 (4) Where a property company constructs its own investment properties, the **capitalisation rules** in FRS 15 must be applied during the construction phase.

Finance costs **can be defined as** the costs of procuring and servicing the funds for construction of tangible fixed assets. This definition has been widened by the accounting standards to mean "the difference between the net proceeds of an instrument and the total number of payments that the issuer may be required to make in respect of the instrument."

Directly attributable finance costs

1282 FRS 15 (20) Directly attributable finance costs are those costs that would have been avoided, had the borrowings to fund the asset not been required or if the funds tied up in the asset were used to repay existing loans.

Finance costs **are incurred on** either:
- specific external borrowings to fund the construction of a particular tangible fixed asset; or
- on funds allocated from the general external borrowings of the company, in which case FRS 15 requires that a calculation be performed to determine the appropriate amount to be capitalised. This is discussed in ¶1306 below.

1284 **An entity has the option** of capitalising directly attributable finance costs or it can choose to write them off immediately. If an entity chooses to capitalise finance costs this policy should be applied on a consistent basis to all tangible fixed assets, where finance costs apply.

Capitalisation is **not confined to interest** alone but covers all the finance costs associated with the relevant borrowings. The justification for capitalising finance costs is that they are an integral part of the cost which should be reflected in the market price of the asset.

General rules

1290 FRS 15 (26) 1. **The capitalisation of finance costs** should start when finance costs are actually being incurred and other expenditures and activities that are necessary to prepare the asset for general use are also in progress.

2. Where **specific funding costs** are being capitalised, the company must ensure that it can adequately record the timing of activity and expenditures involved in the construction of the tangible fixed asset. The activities necessary to bring the asset into general use include (in addition to its physical construction) certain technical or administrative work (i.e. permits) undertaken prior to construction.

3. **Time-span** Finance costs should be capitalised only for the period in which the activities necessary to prepare the asset for use, are in progress. Costs incurred after the asset is in use should generally be expensed in the profit and loss account.

4. **Assets constructed in stages** Where a tangible fixed asset is constructed in stages and each part is capable of being used independently, and construction continues on the remainder of the asset, then the capitalisation of finance costs relating to any completed part should cease. This requirement is intended to prevent companies including costs for periods in which the asset was available for use, but was not actually being utilised.

EXAMPLE An example of an asset that can be divided into component parts is a business park comprising several buildings, each of which can be used individually. Some units can be operable while others are still under construction. In this instance, the capitalisation of directly attributable costs on the completed units should cease. FRS 15 (26) (29)

5. **Cessation** The capitalisation of directly attributable costs should cease when the asset is brought into use or when its physical construction is complete.

6. **Alterations to assets** Where an asset is purchased and then altered to meet the specific requirements, any borrowing costs incurred should be capitalised, but only on the borrowings incurred to make the alterations and not on the initial purchase cost. Furthermore, where companies hold assets for alterations but are not actually altering them, then any related borrowings should not be capitalised.

EXAMPLE Finance costs incurred while the land is under development may be capitalised. However, finance costs incurred while land acquired for building purposes is held without any associated development activity may not be capitalised. Where land has been purchased and the architects have begun the process of drawing up plans and obtaining permits, these are relevant activities for capitalisation purposes.

7. **Maximum amount that can be capitalised**. If the entity has borrowed funds to fund the purchase or construction of a tangible fixed asset, the total of the finance costs is **limited to** the actual costs incurred on the borrowings during the construction period. The total finance costs capitalised during a period should not exceed the total amount of finance costs incurred during that period.

Construction could include either the use of outside contractors or any construction completed by the company itself.

8. **Exchange rate** Differences arising on exchange rates, on funds borrowed to finance the construction or purchase of a tangible fixed asset are deemed to be an adjustment to interest costs. Any exchange rate "losses" should be capitalised as part of finance costs. Exchange gains will reduce the finance costs.

9. **Taxation** Finance costs should be capitalised gross of tax before the deduction of any related tax relief.

10. **Intra-group borrowing**

i. Subsidiaries can capitalise interest in their own financial statements on finance provided by other group companies. However, at a consolidated level, **intra-group interest** must be eliminated because the group itself has not incurred external interest (only notional interest) on these internal borrowings.

ii. Where the **group borrows finance externally** and lends to another group member, any interest capitalised in the subsidiary's accounts will remain capitalised on consolidation.

iii. However, **where intra-group interest rates** and other finance charges **vary significantly** from the group's weighted average borrowing rate, consolidation adjustments will be required to bring the amount capitalised by the subsidiary into line with that which would be allowed, based on the group's finance rate.

iv. **Where the inter-group rate is higher** than the group's actual borrowing rate, the carrying value of the relevant fixed assets in the consolidated accounts will be less than the amount shown in the subsidiary accounts.

11. **General borrowings** If the funds used to finance the construction of a tangible fixed asset form part of the entity's overall borrowings, the level of finance costs capitalised is determined by applying a weighted average capitalisation rate to the capital expenditure on that asset.

1306 FRS 15 (24) There is a **choice of how to calculate the costs** of general borrowing included in the weighted average for a group; either: .

– all the borrowings of a parent and its subsidiaries can be included when calculating the weighted average finance cost; or

– where subsidiaries within a group organise their own treasury function, they should calculate their own weighted average cost of capital, applicable to its own borrowings.

The capitalisation rate

1310 FRS 15 (24) The relevant capital expenditure figure is the **weighted average carrying amount** of the asset during the period, including finance costs previously capitalised. The capitalisation rate is based on the weighted average of rates applicable to the entity's general borrowings (the weighted average cost of capital or WACC), outstanding during the period.

The borrowings included in the **weighted average** should be directly attributable to the construction or purchase of the asset. It is important to ascertain a capitalisation rate that is a fair reflection of the costs incurred in the financing of the construction of the asset.

The **method of determining** the capitalisation rate will depend on how the company or group is structured and how its activities are financed. Where **funds are pooled in a group** and finance is considered at the group level, then the capitalisation rate should be determined at group level, as illustrated in the following example.

EXAMPLE **Capitalisation of interest on general borrowings.**

A company with a June 30 financial year-end finances the construction of a tangible fixed asset from its general borrowings. The level of capitalised expenditure is shown in row 1. The amount brought forward from the previous year (including interest) is £7,000. The balances of capitalised expenditure (excluding interest) during the year are: Oct. 1 £10,000; at Jan. 1 £15,000; at April 1 £21,000 and June 1 £23,000.
The company's general borrowings are shown in row 7. They total £20,000 on 1 July; £25,000 on Oct. 1; £18,000 on Jan. 1; and £25,000 on 1 April.

		Annual average £	1 July b/fwd. £	Oct. 1 £	Jan. 1 £	April 1 £	June 30 £
1	Capitalised expenditure	13,250	7,000	10,000	15,000	21,000	23,000
2	Weights			0.25	0.25	0.25	0.25
3	Capitalised interest						**1,656**
4	**Total**						**24,656**
5	Tranches	13,250	7,000	3,000	5,000	6,000	2,000
6	Weights		1	0.75	0.50	0.25	
7	Total borrowings outstanding		20,000	25,000	18,000	25,000	
8	Borrowing costs during the period		2,200	2,500	2,000	4,500	
9	**Capitalisation rate**	**0.1225**	**0.11**	**0.10**	**0.11**	**0.18**	

The **interest costs** for the year total £1,656 and is calculated by multiplying:
a. the annual average balance of expenditure of £13,250 by
b. the annual average capitalisation rate of 0.1225
The costs are then added to the total capitalised expenditure of £23,000 to be carried forward to the following year.

Calculation.
a. The **annual average capitalisation expenditure** (Row 1) is calculated by totalling the borrowings of £53,000 (£7,000 + £10,000 + £15,000 + £21,000) and dividing this figure by 4 (quarters) = £13,250. Each balance of capitalised expenditure lasts for three months and the annual average is the time-weighted average, using the weights in row 2.
b. The **capitalisation rate** (Row 9) is found for each quarter by dividing the borrowing costs by the total outstanding borrowings for each quarter (i.e. Quarter 1 £2,200/£20,000 = 0.11). The quarterly rates are then totalled and averaged using the weights given in row 2 of the table (0.11 + 0.10 + 0.11 + 0.18/4 = 0.1225).

Prohibited finance costs

Certain types of finance costs are prohibited from being capitalised, such as: **1314**
- loans to hedge foreign investments;
- notional finance costs, such as interest foregone on cash deposits used to finance the purchase or construction of the tangible fixed asset; or
- for the purpose of capitalisation, any interest earned on borrowed funds temporarily reinvested should not be offset against finance costs incurred.

Suspension Finance costs incurred during a period in which the activities required to prepare any asset for use are suspended, do not qualify for capitalisation as they relate to the cost of holding partially completed assets. **Development** of a tangible fixed asset **may be suspended**, where a company discontinues or mothballs development in the face of falling demand projections or other external constraints such as government policy. **1316** FRS 15 (27)

4. FRSSE provisions covering tangible fixed assets

A brief summary of the main provisions of the FRSSE applicable to tangible fixed assets is covered below. **1318**

The FRSSE incorporates a simplified version of the requirements of FRS 15 relating to the cost of tangible fixed assets. The **basic requirements** are as follows:
1. Tangible fixed assets should initially be valued at cost, then written down to its recoverable amount, where necessary.
2. Only costs directly attributable to bring the tangible fixed asset into use should be included in the cost of the asset. The FRSSE does not contain detailed rules covering costs to be included or excluded in the cost of the tangible fixed asset.
3. The FRSSE permits the capitalisation of finance costs directly related to the cost of the asset but does not mention specific or general borrowings or the use of a capitalisation rate.
4. The FRSSE requires that the capitalisation of directly attributable costs including finance costs, should be suspended during extended periods where active development is interrupted. Capitalisation should cease when the tangible fixed asset is essentially ready for use.
5. The FRSSE contains slightly simpler rules than FRS 15 regarding subsequent expenditure as it does not require major inspections or overhauls of assets.

B. Initial valuation of specific types of tangible fixed assets

Particular types of tangible fixed asset such as donated assets, historic assets and websites require special consideration in terms of their initial valuation. **1324**

Donated assets

Tangible fixed assets by charities received as **gifts** or **donations** should initially be carried at the current value of the assets, at the date they are received. Where the asset is deemed to be impaired, the current value should be the replacement cost for existing use. **1326** FRS 15 (17)

Problems can arise when these assets:
- cannot be disposed of without external consent;
- the assets are of a particular historic, scientific or artistic importance; or
- when conventional valuations are not sufficiently reliable.

Further guidance on these issues is given in the SORP for the charity sector issued by the Charities Commission (see ¶9500).

1328 Even where conventional valuations are practical, significant costs may be involved that effect an assessment of the management of these assets. However, where these factors are significant or if an **alternative valuation basis** is deemed more appropriate, adequate disclosure of the reason for the different treatment, and the age, nature and volume of the assets should be given in the notes to the accounts.

Any gain on the recognition of a donated asset should be recognised in the financial statements.

Heritage assets

1330 FRS 15 (18) Heritage assets are defined as assets of historical, artistic or scientific value, held to further the preservation, conservation and educational activities of charities, and include land, buildings, collections, exhibits or artefacts.

The **normal cost rules** apply to historic assets owned by companies.

Historic and similar tangible fixed assets owned by a charity should be carried in the balance sheet where:
- the assets give rise to future economic benefits;
- the entity has stewardship of the assets; and
- the owner may have invested funds in the acquisition, maintenance and restoration of the assets.

However, for assets that were not previously capitalised or which were donated, **the costs of obtaining a valuation** may outweigh the benefits. In these instances the appropriate disclosures should be made in the notes to the accounts. **Further guidance** can be found in the relevant sector guidance notes or SORPs. The accounting treatment will be as for donated assets.

MEMO POINTS The ASB has issued FRS 30 "Heritage Assets", applicable to accounting periods beginning on or after 1 April 2010. The new standard includes more detailed disclosure requirements (see ¶9586).

Asset purchases with a foreign currency

1332 Where an asset is purchased with a foreign currency, it is the **exchange rate** at the date on which the transaction is originally recorded (historic rate), that should be used for calculating the cost of the asset. If the exchange rate on this date differs from the rate prevailing on the invoice date, the exchange gain or loss should be taken directly to the profit and loss account.

Websites

1334 UITF 29 (3) Companies that have established a website may have incurred significant costs in the process. The **general rule** is that **a distinction must be drawn between** planning costs (expenses) and development costs (capitalised).

Planning costs comprise the costs of feasibility studies to determine the objectives for the website as well as identifying hardware and software needs. Planning costs should be expensed in the profit and loss account.

1336 **Development costs** Development costs include the costs associated with the following:
- purchasing specialist hardware;
- purchasing or designing specialist software;
- creative design and graphics;

- content of web pages;
- registration of domain names; and
- other infrastructure costs such as e-commerce systems and encryption software.

Recognition criteria The **key requirement** is that in order **to capitalise** development costs a direct link must be established between the website and any revenues generated. In addition, website development expenditure **can only be capitalised if** the following criteria are also met; namely: 1337

- the expenditure should be separately identifiable;
- the technical and commercial viability of the website should have been established with reasonable certainty;
- the website is expected to generate sales or revenues directly through orders placed or payments made via the website or from selling advertising space; and
- that adequate resources exist to complete, launch and maintain the website.

Accounting treatment **Expenditure to maintain or operate** a website once it has been developed and constructed should be charged to the profit and loss account as incurred, in accordance with the requirements of FRS 15. 1338 UITF 29 (11c)

Where capitalisation of website development costs **is justified**, the following accounting treatments apply: UITF 29 (17)

1. The asset should be **amortised** over its estimated useful economic life (which may well be short given the pace of technological change), which should be reviewed at the end of each accounting period and revised if appropriate.
2. **If the design or content** of the website **is changed frequently**, a different (shorter) depreciation charge should apply to these costs rather than the rest of the asset (see ¶1484).
3. The asset should be **reviewed regularly** for impairment. For instance, if the website is "refreshed", any new design and content costs may be capitalised. However, any design or content costs previously capitalised and not yet written-off should be reviewed for impairment.

Where the website is used only for **promotional purposes** and as a database for customers or the general public, it may be difficult to prove conclusively that sales or revenue are generated direct from the website. In these situations all design and content costs should be written off to the profit and loss account. 1340

Revenues generated from the development of a website, **that previously flowed from** other tangible assets, may mean that these assets have become impaired as a result.

Where website development costs **are reclassified from** intangible assets to tangible fixed assets, this represents a change in accounting policy. The first set of financial statements issued after adopting UITF 29, should detail the change in accounting policy and where material, explain the prior year adjustment.

Low value assets retained at a fixed amount

Certain types of tangible fixed assets can be valued at a fixed amount (initial measurement) provided that they: 1342

- are not material in value;
- are constantly being replaced; and
- are not subject to material fluctuations in terms of value, quantity or composition.

Examples of this type of asset include low value, short-life assets such as small tools.

Motor vehicles

The **purchase price** of the majority of tangible fixed assets will normally be capitalised exclusive of VAT. Motor cars are an exception and should be capitalised at the invoice price inclusive of VAT as the input tax on cars cannot usually be reclaimed by the company. 1344

SECTION 3

Revaluation

1348 This section covers the rules governing the revaluation of tangible fixed assets (principally property), the revaluation process and selection of valuation bases, the treatment of depreciation as well and the treatment of revaluation gains and losses on revalued tangible fixed assets. **Special revaluation rules** apply to non-specialised properties. The revaluation policy for **charities** and other not-for-profit organisations, which are beyond the scope of this book are treated in the relevant sector guidance notes or SORPs.

Overview of revaluation policy

1350 Tangible fixed assets are **more likely to be revalued** in times where asset values rise sharply or where a company may wish to strengthen the appearance of its balance sheet. Whilst the Companies Act permits the revaluation of an entity's fixed assets under the **alternative accounting rules**, the detailed rules governing the revaluation process are set out in the provisions of FRS 15.

MEMO POINTS 1. The term "revaluation" does not cover either the write-down of the carrying amount of a tangible fixed asset held at historical cost for an impairment, or the determination of the cost of an asset acquired as a result of a business combination stated at its fair value at the date of acquisition, in accordance with FRS 7 "Fair Values in Acquisition Accounting".
2. The legal framework includes the CA 1985 Schedule 4 para. 31; Sch. 1 to The Large and Medium Sized Companies and Groups (Accounts and Reports) Regulations 2008 (SI 2008/410) and Sch. 1 of the Small Companies and Groups (Accounts and Directors' Report) Regulations 2008 (SI 2008/409).

FRS 15 (42) Tangible fixed assets **should initially be measured** at historical cost and **only revalued** when the entity adopts a formal policy of revaluation. Such a policy is optional for all companies.

1352 **General rules**

FRS 15 (100)

	Revaluation rules
Initial measurement	Tangible fixed assets **should initially be measured** at historical cost and **only revalued** when the entity adopts a formal policy of revaluation. Such a policy is optional for all companies.
Subsequent revaluations of a tangible fixed asset	This should be applied to all assets within that class of assets. Individual assets cannot be selected or "cherry-picked" for revaluation purposes, as the aim is to reduce the scope for selecting individual assets for revaluation that have increased in value
Specific industries	An entity may depending on the requirements of a particular industry, **adopt other narrower classes of assets**, provided they meet the definition of a category of tangible fixed asset having a similar nature, function or use in the business of the entity. For example, land and buildings can be sub-divided into specialised properties, non-specialist properties and short-leasehold properties. Separate disclosures are required for each class of asset.
Where a realistic market value cannot be obtained	For particular assets within a specific class that is being revalued, i.e. if the asset is located overseas, it may be excluded from the valuation, although the carrying amount and the fact that it has not been revalued should be stated in the notes to the accounts
Impairment indicated	An impairment review should be carried out in accordance with the requirements of FRS 11. The asset should be recorded at the lower of the revalued amount and the recoverable amount; namely the higher of net realisable value and value in use.

Alternative accounting rules

The alternative accounting rules in the Companies Act permit tangible fixed assets to be valued at market rate, determined as at the date of their last valuation or at their current cost. However, this policy could lead to a **mix of assets** carried at historical cost and others at market value. There is also no requirement under the alternative accounting rules for the revaluations that are performed to be kept up to date. 1358

Therefore, to help introduce an element of consistency, FRS 15 **sets out the conditions that must exist** in order for the alternative accounting rules to be adopted, covering:
- which types of tangible fixed asset should be revalued;
- when assets should be revalued;
- the valuation bases that may used; and
- who is permitted to revalue assets.

It should be noted that there is **no obligation** under either FRS 15 or the Companies Act for an entity to revalue its tangible fixed assets. They merely set out the rules that have to be followed if an entity should chose to revalue them.

In general, the only widespread use of the alternative accounting rules is for the valuation of **freehold and leasehold properties**.

The value to a business of a tangible fixed asset in current use is usually its **replacement cost**, (see ¶1384) unless the asset is impaired, in which case the recoverable amount will be lower. The replacement cost means the cost of replacing the capability of the asset. 1362 FRS 15 (54)

A. Frequency

Where a tangible fixed asset is revalued its **carrying amount** should represent the current value at the balance sheet date. In order to satisfy this requirement, a full valuation of previously revalued assets should be conducted at least every 5 years, with a formal interim valuation after 3 years. 1364 FRS 15 (43)

In addition to the two aforementioned mandatory revaluations, **interim valuations** in years 1, 2 and 4 should be carried out, where it is likely there has been a material change in value. All valuations should be carried out as close to the financial year-end as possible. FRS 15 (45)

The accounting standard does not insist on **annual revaluations**, although the objective of revaluation policy is to replace the current valuation at the balance sheet date.

Material changes in value Valuations must be updated where there is perceived to be a material change in value, which is defined in the standard as "a change in value that would reasonably influence the decisions of as user of the accounts." In determining whether a material change in value is likely, the combined impact of all relevant factors should be considered. Situations that may give rise to a material change in value, include physical deterioration in the property or a general movement in market prices. 1367 FRS 15 (52)

Non-specialist properties An exception to the general rules set out above exists for non-specialised properties, where an annual valuation may be completed on only a part of the property portfolio. 1370 FRS 15 (46)

Non-specialised properties should be the subject of a full valuation on a **rolling basis**, designed to cover the entire portfolio over a five-year cycle, together with an interim valuation on the remaining portfolio every year, where a material change in value is deemed likely.

This approach is appropriate where the property portfolio consists of a number of **broadly similar properties** impacted by the same market factors, that can easily be divided into groups. 1372

For instance, a portfolio comprising of sports clubs, hotels and restaurants could be divided into the following classifications:
- business units;
- regions; or
- groupings by size.

B. Revaluation process

1374 FRS 15 (47) The **majority of revaluations** involve property although the process involved is applicable to other tangible fixed assets.

A formal revaluation should be carried out at both the interim and full five yearly valuation, and normally involves the following stages:
- a detailed inspection of the property;
- inspection of the locality;
- enquiries of local planning and similar authorities (legal rights, planning permission etc); and
- research on market prices or trends for similar properties.

1376 **Full valuation** The full valuation should be conducted by:
- a qualified external valuer with no financial interest in the entity; or
- FRS 15 (48) a qualified internal valuer, provided it is then reviewed by a qualified external valuer.

A **qualified valuer** is defined as a person who:
- holds a relevant professional qualification;
- has recent post-qualification experience; and
- knows the market, location and category of tangible fixed asset concerned.

1377 An **external review** often involves the valuation of a sample of the entity's properties by the external valuer, for comparison with the internal valuer's figures. The external valuer must be satisfied that the sample represents a genuine cross-section of the entity's property portfolio. An external valuer cannot be a director, officer or employee of the company.

1378 FRS 15 (49) **Interim valuation** An interim valuation should be conducted by a qualified internal (or external valuer) involving essentially the same process as the full valuation. The **main difference** in the requirements of a full and interim valuation, is that where the interim valuation is performed by a qualified internal valuer, there is no requirement for it to then be reviewed by an external qualified valuer.

The revaluation process **at the interim date is** also less rigorous **and consists of** the following:
1. Research into market transactions involving similar properties, analyses of market trends and application thereof, to determine the value of the property;
2. A physical inspection of the property and locality by the valuer; and confirmation that:
- the property has not been radically altered;
- legal rights and obligations are unchanged; or
- local planning regulations have not been infringed.

Tangible fixed assets other than properties

1380 FRS 15 (50) For tangible fixed assets **other than properties**, where an active second-hand market exists as evidenced by frequent activity, or where there are appropriate measurement indices that allow the value of an asset to be ascertained with reasonable certainty, then an annual valuation conducted by the directors may be sufficient (as opposed to using a qualified external surveyor). Examples include company cars and office equipment.

The **indices** must be appropriate to the class of asset to which it is applied, as well as to the asset's location and condition and have a proven record of publication and use.

If the **directors are not able** to obtain a reasonable valuation on an annual basis because an active second hand market or indices do not exist, then they must commission a full or interim valuation. It is the **directors' responsibility to ensure** that the carrying values are accurately described as current at the end of each financial year. 1382

C. Valuation bases

Different valuation bases **must be applied** to the revaluation of properties, and the revaluation of other tangible fixed assets. A company that has revalued its fixed assets must maintain records of both historical costs and revaluation of fixed assets, and calculate depreciation on both historical cost and revaluation. 1384 FRS 15 (53)

Valuation basis – all categories Type of tangible fixed asset	Valuation base	Notes
Non-specialised properties	Existing use value (EUV) (¶1390)	Include notional directly attributable acquisition costs
Specialised properties	Depreciated replacement cost (DRC) (¶1404)	
Surplus properties	Open market value (OMV) (¶1390)	After deducting material directly attributable selling costs
Non-property tangible fixed assets	OMV or depreciated replacement cost where market value not available	Include notional directly attributable acquisition costs

1. Non-specialised properties

Non-specialised properties **are defined as** all properties, for which there is a general demand, with or without adaptation, and which are generally bought, sold or leased on the open market for their existing or similar uses, either with vacant possession for occupation or as investments or for development. 1388

Examples of non-specialised properties **include**: FRS 15 (Appendix I)
- residential properties;
- shops;
- offices;
- industrial and warehouse buildings;
- public houses;
- petrol stations;
- hotels;
- cinemas, theatres and gaming clubs;
- private hospitals and nursing homes; and
- sports and leisure facilities.

Existing use value

The **general rule** is that non-specialised properties should be valued on the basis of existing use value (EUV), with the addition of notional directly attributable acquisition costs; namely dealing costs such as professional fees and non-recoverable taxes and duties. In practical terms, EUV will typically correspond to Open Market Value (OMV). Where the EUV **differs materially** from the OMV, the EUV and reasons for the difference should be disclosed. 1390 FRS 15 (56)

The existing use value of a property takes account of its current function rather than the potential it has to be used in a more beneficial way. For example, a site that is used as an office block may have planning permission for use as luxury housing. On an EUV basis it will be valued as an office block which may be materially different to the OMV if it were sold, potentially, for redevelopment as houses.

MEMO POINTS The **open market value** is defined as the best price at which the sale of an interest in a property or tangible fixed asset would be completed, for cash at the valuation date. OMV is the only basis that is appropriate for investment properties surplus to the company's requirements.

1393 The existing use value is **the best price** at which the **sale of an interest in property** would have been completed for cash on the date of valuation assuming that there is a willing seller, and that:
- the state of the market, level of values and other circumstances were, on any earlier assumed date of exchange of contracts, the same as on the date of valuation;
- account is taken of any additional bid by a prospective purchaser with a special interest;
- both parties conducted the transaction at arm's length;
- the property can be used for the foreseeable future only for the existing use;
- vacant possession is provided on completion of the sale of all parts of the property occupied by the business; and
- prior to the date of valuation, there had been a reasonable period (having regard to the nature of the property and the state of the market) for the proper marketing of the interest, for the agreement of the price and the terms and for the completion of the sale.

1394 FRS 15 (Appendix I) **Certain types of non-specialised properties** can be valued separately as businesses on the basis of their existing use value (EUV).

1. The EUV of a property valued as an **operational entity** takes account of the trading potential of the property. Personal goodwill created in the business by the present owners, that is not expected to remain in the business when the property is sold, is excluded. The EUV reflects the **service potential** that is used by the owner rather than the alternative uses to which the building may be put.

2. In the majority of cases where a non-specialised property is being utilised for its most beneficial use, the EUV should equal the OMV (with vacant possession). The EUV **generally will not exceed** the open market value (OMV), as the latter reflects the additional possible uses ignored in arriving at EUV. For instance, a factory located on the edge of a town may have a greater value as a residential site than as an industrial site.

1396 FRS 15 (Appendix IV.22) **Where EUV exceeds OMV** In some cases however, EUV will exceed OMV where for instance:
- planning consent is personal to the present occupier;
- there are restrictive alienation clauses in the head leases; or
- there is known contamination that does not affect the existing use of the non-specialised building.

All these examples would result in a lower OMV but would be disregarded in determining EUV, as they do not affect the cost of a replacement. The FRS requires that further information concerning the OMV be disclosed in the notes to the accounts, where this materially exceeds the EUV.

1397 FRS 15 (57) **Excluded costs** Expenditure for **enhancing the value** of a site such as costs associated with planning applications, site preparation and clearance and other costs already reflected in the existing use value (EUV) should be excluded. In practical terms, notional acquisition costs that are not material should be ignored.

Where EUV is deemed unreliable for valuation purposes

1398 FRS 15 (57) In the following circumstances, the EUV may not be a reliable measure of the replacement cost of a non-specialised property.

1. **Adaptation works** such as structural changes made to the shell of a property often lower the OMV and EUV below replacement cost, because the individual nature of the works will generally not be required by other companies. Because there is no market for the adaptation

works they are held at either cost or depreciated historical cost, and the shell of the building is valued using EUV. Adaptation works often have a low or nil market value as a result of their specialised nature and include shop fittings or fascias.

2. An entity with an **exceptionally large property** may have to divide the assets into saleable units, as it may be difficult to sell the asset to a single purchaser in its existing condition. In this situation it is unlikely that there are other similar market transactions to benchmark the value against.

2. Specialised properties

Specialised properties are defined in FRS 15, as properties of a specialist nature that are **rarely sold on the open market**, for single occupation for a continuation of their existing use, except as part of a sale of a larger business operation. **1400** FRS 15 (57)

The specialised nature of these properties **may arise from** the construction, arrangement, size or location of the property, or a combination of these factors. It may also be due to the nature of the plant and machinery and items of equipment that the buildings are designed to house, or the function or purpose for which the buildings are provided.

Specialised properties **include the following**: FRS 15 (Appendix I)
- oil refineries;
- chemical works;
- power installations;
- docks;
- schools, colleges, and universities;
- hospitals and other specialist health care institutions;
- museums, libraries, and other similar premises; and
- standard properties in particular geographical areas (i.e. remote areas), located there for specific business reasons.

Depreciated replacement cost

Specialised properties are primarily valued using depreciated replacement cost (DRC), where the OMV is not available due to the specialised nature of the properties. **1404**

However, in certain other cases specialised properties may be valued as **fully operational entities**, given their own trading potential (i.e. docks). If this basis for valuation is adopted this should be disclosed in the financial statements.

The DRC of property **is defined** as the total amount of the value of the land for the existing use or a notional replacement site in the same locality, and the gross replacement cost of the buildings and other site works from which appropriate deductions may be made. FRS 15 (Appendix I)

All of these factors might result in the existing property being worth less to the undertaking in occupation than a new replacement building.

The **objective of DRC** is to permit a realistic estimate of the: **1405**
- current cost of constructing an asset that has the same service potential as the existing asset; and
- the net realisable value attributable to the service potential of the asset over its remaining useful economic life, after deducting the estimated residual value.

The costs **directly attributable** to bringing the property into working condition for its intended use are included in the depreciated replacement cost. Examples include the costs of: **1406**
- installation (e.g. water, electricity);
- commissioning;
- consultants fees; and
- non-recoverable taxes and duties.

1407 In calculating DRC, the **deductions from gross replacement cost** should cover:
- the age and condition of the asset;
- economic and functional obsolescence; and
- environmental and other factors.

3. Surplus properties

1410 **Properties surplus to requirements** should be valued by taking the open market value (OMV) (see ¶1390) less any material directly attributed selling costs. Selling costs are deducted to reflect the net realisable value of the asset to the entity. Similar valuation bases are used for tangible fixed assets other than properties.

The OMV **is defined** as the best price at which the sale of an interest in a property or tangible fixed asset would be completed, for cash at the valuation date. OMV is the only basis that is appropriate for investment properties surplus to the company's requirements.

1412 The **criteria that apply** to determining the open market value are the same as those for EUV, except that two conditions do not apply; namely that the property:
FRS 15 (Appendix 1) – will only be used for the same purpose for the foreseeable future; and
- that it will be sold with vacant possession.

4. Non-property assets

1414 FRS 15 (59) Tangible fixed assets other than properties that are used in a business should be valued using the **open market value base**; namely what it would cost the entity to replace the asset.

Notional directly attributable acquisitions costs such as professional fees, non-recoverable taxes and duties, should be added to market value where material.

Where market value is not obtainable, assets should be valued on the basis of **depreciated replacement cost**, as determined by a qualified valuer or on the basis of an appropriate index. The cost of replacing an existing asset with a similar new asset with similar production or service capacity is depreciated to reflect the value of an existing remaining useful economic life.

1415 FRS 15 (Appendix I) The **value of non-property plant and machinery** to the business is defined in FRS 15, as the price at which an interest in the plant or machinery would have been transferred at the date of valuation given:
- that the plant and machinery will continue in its present uses in the business;
- the continuing viability or profitability of the undertaking having due regard to the value of the total assets employed and the nature of the operation; and
- the transfer is part of an "arm's length sale" of a business.

MEMO POINTS An "**arm's length transaction**" entered into by unrelated parties, each acting in their own interests in paying or charging prices based on fair market values. This may not be the case with companies belonging to the same group, who may transact with each other for taxation or other reasons.

5. Treatment of revaluation gains and losses

1418 This section covers the accounting treatment for revaluation gains and losses and the possible impact of deferred taxation.

Revaluation gains

1420 A revaluation gain is the positive difference between the revalued amount and the carrying amount of the tangible fixed asset, net of cumulative depreciation.

General rules 1. **All revaluation gains** on tangible fixed assets **should be recognised in** the STRGL, as they generally represent gains from rising prices and are valuation adjustments and not realised profits, as illustrated in the example below. **1421** FRS 15 (63)

EXAMPLE An entity has a tangible fixed asset that cost £15,000 at the start of year 1; it has a useful economic life of 10 years, a residual value of £3,000 and is being depreciated on a straight-line basis. At the end of year one, the asset was revalued upwards to £17,500.

Accounting treatment Year	**Year 1**
	£
Cost of the asset	15,000
Depreciation charge	(1,200)
Adjusted book amount	13,800
Gain on revaluation	3,700
Closing book amount	**17,500**

The revaluation gain of £3,700 should be reflected in the STRGL.
The **initial depreciation charge** is credited to reserves and the asset depreciated over the remaining useful life of the asset.

Accounting entries

	Dr.	**Cr.**
Fixed assets – cost	2,500	
Revaluation reserve		2,500
Fixed asset – depreciation	1,200	
Revaluation reserve		1,200

2. Revaluation gains **should only be recognised in the profit and loss account** (net of the impact of depreciation that would have been charged to the profit and loss account had the property not previously have been revalued downwards), to the extent that they reverse revaluation losses on the same asset, previously recognised in the profit and loss account.

3. Any **gain is reduced by** the same depreciation charge that would have been levied had the loss previously taken to the profit and loss account not been initially recognised, as illustrated in the example below. FRS 15 (64)

4. On revaluation, **material gains (or losses)** on individual assets in a class should not be aggregated. FRS 15 (67)

MEMO POINTS For a discussion of the accounting treatment regarding the profit (or loss) on the disposal of fixed assets – see ¶398.

EXAMPLE An asset costs £15,000 at the start of year 1; it has a useful economic life of 10 years, a residual value of £3,000 and is being depreciated on a straight-line basis. At the end of year one the asset was revalued downwards to £10,500 (the recoverable amount). In year two the asset has been revalued upwards to £17,500. The accounting treatment is as follows.

Accounting treatment	**Yr 1**	**Yr 2**
	£	**£**
Cost/valuation brought forward	15,000	10,500
Depreciation charge	(1,200)	(833)
Adjusted book amount	13,800	9,667
Gain (loss) on revaluation	**(3,300)**	**7,833**
Closing book amount	**10,500**	**17,500**

Year 1
The revaluation loss of **£3,300** should be reflected in the profit and loss account, because it represents the fall in value below depreciated historical cost.

Year 2
The revaluation gain of **£7,833** should be accounted for as follows:
– **£2,933** (£3,300-£367) should reverse the loss posted to the profit and loss account at the end of year 1. The figure of £367 represents the additional depreciation charge that would have been taken in year 2 had the opening balance been £13,800 and the loss not been recognised.
– **£4,900** should be accounted for in the revaluation reserve and disclosed in the STRGL.

Accounting entries

	Dr.	Cr.
Fixed assets	£7,833	
Profit and loss account		£2,933
Revaluation reserve		£4,900

Revaluation losses

1426 A revaluation loss **is defined as** the negative difference between the revalued amount of the tangible fixed asset and the net book value of the asset. A revaluation loss **may result from**:

FRS 15 (69)
- a consumption of economic benefits, as evidenced by a decline in service provided by the asset or the physical destruction of the asset (impairment);
- a result of a general fall in the level of prices; or
- a combination of a fall in prices or consumption in economic benefits.

1427

Revaluation losses: causes	Accounting treatment
Resulting from a clear **consumption of economic benefits** (impairment)	Revaluation losses should be recognised in the profit and loss account, in line with the requirements of FRS 11. Losses cannot be netted off against gains arising on other assets.
Other general revaluation losses	The revenue loss should be recognised in the STRGL until the carrying amount reaches its depreciated historical cost; and thereafter, in the profit and loss account, unless it can be demonstrated that the recoverable amount of the asset is greater than its revalued amount. In this case the loss should be recognised in the STRGL, to the extent that the recoverable amount of the asset is greater than its revalued amount.

1428 **Accounting treatment** 1. **Where the reason** for the **fall in value of the asset is not clear**, then splitting the revaluation loss between the STRGL and the profit and loss account is an arbitrary allocation, because it depends whether the fall in value is above or below depreciated historical cost.

FRS 15 (65)

FRS 15 (66) 2. However, **where** it can be demonstrated that **the recoverable amount is greater than its revalued amount**, the loss should be recognised in the STRGL, to the extent that the recoverable amount of the asset is greater than its revalued amount. The recoverable amount of the asset should be calculated in accordance with the requirements of FRS 11.

3. Where there is **difficulty in allocating an impairment loss**, it is assumed that the fall in value from the previous carrying value of the asset to the depreciated historical cost is due to a general fall in prices, which should be accounted for in the STRGL as a valuation adjustment.

4. Thereafter, a **further fall in value** from depreciated historical cost to **revalued amount** is due to the consumption of economic benefits and the impairment should be recognised in the profit and loss account.

Revaluation gain followed by a revaluation loss

1436 The example below illustrates the **recognition and accounting treatment** of a revaluation gain followed by a revaluation loss.

EXAMPLE A **non-specialist property** costs £1m, has a useful economic life of 10 years and no residual value. The company's policy is to depreciate buildings on a straight-line basis and revalue the property annually.
Depreciation is calculated based on the opening book amount. At the end of years 1 and 2 the asset has a EUV of £1,080,000 and £700,000 respectively.
At the end of year 2, the **recoverable amount** of the asset is £760,000 and its depreciated historical cost is £800,000. There is no obvious consumption of economic benefits in year 2, other than that allowed for in the normal depreciation charge.

Scenario A – Accounting treatment under historical cost

	Year 1	Year 2
	£'000	£'000
Opening book value	1,000	1,080
Depreciation	(100)	(120)
Adjusted book amount	900	960
Revaluation gain (loss)		
- recognised in the STRGL	180	(220)
- recognised in the profit and loss account	-	(40)
Closing book value (EUV)	1,080	700

Year 1. Revaluation gain
After a depreciation charge of £100,000, a revaluation gain of £180,000 is recognised in the STRGL.

Year 2 Revaluation loss
After a **depreciation charge** of £120,000, the revaluation loss on the property totals £260,000. As this has not resulted from the clear consumption of economic benefits but a fall in prices, revaluation losses should be recognised in the STRGL until the carrying amount reaches the level of its depreciated historical cost. As a consequence, the fall in value from the adjusted book amount (£960,000) to the depreciated historical cost (£800,000) of £160,000 is recognised in the STRGL.
The **depreciated historical cost** of £800,000 represents the opening book amount minus two years depreciation charge (2 x £100,000).
The remainder of the **revaluation loss** of £100,000 (resulting from the fall in value from depreciated historical cost £800,000 to **revalued amount** £700,000) should be recognised in the profit and loss account.

Scenario B – Alternative treatment
However, if it can be demonstrated that the **recoverable amount** is greater than the **revalued amount**, a different treatment is applied. In this example, the recoverable amount of £760,000 is greater than the revalued amount of £700,000 by £60,000, which should be recognised in the STRGL and not the profit and loss account. The total revaluation loss of £220,000 (£60,000 + £160,000) is recognised in the STRGL. The remaining loss of £40,000 (derived from the fall in value from depreciated historical cost of £800,000 to recoverable amount of £760,000) is recognised in the profit and loss account.

Limitations on use of a revaluation reserve

Once a revaluation has taken place, the use of a revaluation reserve is limited. An amount may be transferred from the revaluation reserve to the profit and loss account, only if the amount: 1437
- was previously charged to the profit and loss account;
- represents realised profit;
- is applied in paying up (wholly or in part) unissued shares in the company (this is often referred to as capitalisation); or
- is in respect of taxation relating to a surplus credited to the revaluation reserve.

The revaluation reserve must be disclosed on the face of the balance sheet as a separate amount.

Deferred taxation (timing differences)

Deferred taxation results from timing differences between capital allowances and the depreciation charge. The revaluation of an asset will generate a deferred tax timing difference insofar as the profit or loss that would result from the asset's realisation at the revalued amount is taxable at that later date, rather than at the point of revaluation. 1438 FRS 19 (2)

Where a deferred taxation liability is recognised the revaluation surplus should be reduced by that amount. The deferred tax is not therefore recognised in the profit and loss but in the STRGL.

It should be noted, however, that under FRS 19, entities should not usually recognise within its deferred tax provision, the potential tax that will arise on revaluation surpluses. The revaluation reserve will not therefore normally be reduced by the potential tax payable.

The company is obliged to disclose the **taxation effect** of the revaluation in its financial statements. Where the potential amount of deferred tax on a revalued asset is not shown, because the revaluation does not constitute a timing difference, this fact should be stated.

Deferred taxation is discussed more fully in ¶9000.

Restatement of comparatives

1440 The **option to value** tangible fixed assets at cost or valuation is considered a choice of accounting policy under FRS 18 "Accounting policies". As such a change of policy from cost to valuation will require a restatement of comparatives as follows:
- assets in the comparative balance sheet must be restated to current values at the balance sheet date; and
- depreciation must be recalculated, to reflect any changes to estimates of UEL or residual value at the balance sheet date.

Historical cost information must still be prepared in order to comply with the disclosure requirements of the Companies Act. This information is also useful should an entity reverse its policy of valuation to one of cost.

SECTION 4

Depreciation

1444 FRS 15 (81) This section details the various **methods of depreciation** and the concepts that underpin them as well as the special rules that apply to the provision of depreciation in relation to revalued tangible fixed assets, subsequent expenditure and separable assets.

1445 The general disclosure requirements covering depreciation are covered in ¶1510. For depreciation of **specific categories** of tangible fixed assets covered by other reporting standards such as investment properties or leases, refer to the specific chapters covering these topics.

1446 The **concept of depreciation** is defined in the accounting standards as the cost resulting from the wear and tear, consumption or other reduction in the useful economic life of a tangible fixed asset, whether arising from use, passage of time or obsolescence through technological change.

The **purpose of depreciation** is to charge to the profit and loss account a notional sum that reflects on a consistent basis the costs of using tangible fixed assets during a particular financial period. Depreciation is also a measurement of the loss in value of tangible fixed assets over a given time period.

1448 The **general rule** is that all tangible fixed assets with the exception of freehold land have a finite life not exceeding 50 years. Tangible fixed assets should be depreciated according to an appropriate method, which is underpinned by the concepts of useful economic life, materiality and residual value.

The implications for companies who **choose not to depreciate** an asset or select a depreciation period in excess of 50 years are dealt with below (see ¶1488).

A. Concepts

1450 The concepts of materiality, useful economic life and residual value are inter-linked but not necessarily inter-dependent, as they are based on individual judgements and are therefore subjective by nature.

In general however, **changing the parameters and assumptions** underlying an assessment of either materiality, useful economic life or residual value will probably impact on one or more of the other concepts. For instance, if an entity chooses to increase the useful economic life of one of its tangible fixed assets, this could in turn reduce its residual value and increase the total depreciation charged albeit over a longer period of time.

Materiality

An asset and related depreciation charge would be deemed material, if its omission from the financial statements would be misleading for users of the accounts. Materiality is not an absolute concept as it is, in turn, **based on an assessment** of a number of primary factors including the asset's useful economic life and estimated residual value. 1452

When an entity seeks not to depreciate an asset on the grounds that it is immaterial, it must be able to justify that the omitted charge for the year and accumulated depreciation is not significant for an appreciation of both the results for the year and the financial position shown by the balance sheet. As a consequence, it would be difficult for an entity to defend a policy of non-depreciation on an expensive asset.

Residual value

The residual value of an asset is the **expected disposal proceeds** from the sale of an asset (net of costs), at the end of its useful economic life and should be deducted from the cost of the fixed asset when determining the appropriate depreciation charge. It should be noted that when assessing residual values, they should be based on prices prevailing at the time the asset is purchased. An assessment of residual value should not take into account anticipated price increases over the life of the asset. 1453

The residual value of an asset can be **influenced by a number of factors** including its useful economic life or second hand market value. Any material change in the estimated residual value should be accounted for through the depreciation charge over the remaining useful life of the asset.

High residual value In terms of a high residual value, the depreciation charge may be deemed insignificant as a result of one or more of the following: 1454
- the asset is immune to economic or technological obsolescence resulting from changes in demand patterns;
- the entity has a policy of disposing of similar assets, with high residual values well before the end of their useful economic lives;
- where the disposal proceeds of similar assets are not significantly less than their carrying value; or
- a policy of regular maintenance and repair (charged to the profit & loss) that sustains previously assessed performance levels and useful economic lives.

EXAMPLE A hotel group does not provide for depreciation in respect of freehold hotels, as it is considered that the useful economic lives and residual values of these buildings are such that any depreciation charge would be immaterial. The logic supporting this decision is that the hotel group regularly refurbishes its hotels, thereby extending the useful economic lives more or less indefinitely and preserving the residual values of the group's assets.

Where the residual value is revised it should where possible be restated in terms of the price that prevailed when the asset was purchased or revalued. If this is neither possible nor practicable, the residual value should be restated in terms of current values only where the residual value at current prices is below the original estimate of residual value. Events or changes in circumstances that **result in a fall in the residual value** may indicate the asset is impaired, in which case an impairment review should be conducted in accordance with the requirements of FRS 11. 1455 FRS 15 (96)

Useful economic life

Initial recognition The **general rule** is that the useful economic life of an asset is determined when the asset is either purchased or (if self-constructed), commissioned for use and 1456 FRS 15 (93)

represents the period over which the owner will derive economic benefits from its use. The assessment should, where appropriate take into account the following:
- contractual or legal restrictions, as in the case of a lease or its covenants; or
- consumption or extraction, which in turn is restricted by capacity or identifiable reserves as in the case of a mine or oil field.

A projection of the useful economic life of a tangible fixed asset **should also include** an estimate of the impact upon its life of such factors as repair costs and the cost of replacement assets. High repair costs may shorten the useful economic life of a tangible fixed asset as may the falling cost of replacement assets.

1458 **Revisions** **Where material in value**, the estimates of useful economic lives should be renewed and revised if appropriate (particularly where a policy of non-depreciation is followed).

1. The useful economic life **can be revised** on an on-going basis reflecting any:
- deterioration in the physical characteristics of the asset through use or the passage of time, which may result from the entity's asset maintenance programme; or
- economic or technological obsolescence resulting from improved technology or changes in market demand for the product or service.

2. **If the useful economic life** of a tangible fixed asset **is revised**, the carrying value at the date should be depreciated (after allowing for any impairment that may have occurred) over the remaining useful economic life of the asset. It should be noted that a change of estimated useful life is not in itself a change of accounting policy and does not give rise to a prior period adjustment.

EXAMPLE ABC plc owns a paint spray machine which originally cost £200k in January 20X6. The useful economic life of the asset was estimated at 10 years with a residual value of £10k. Annual depreciation was calculated at £19k p.a. on a straight-line basis (£200k-£10k/ 10 years. However after two years, a reassessment of the useful economic life of the spray machine highlighted the fact that changes in technology had **reduced the residual value** to zero and the useful economic life of the asset to 7 yrs, of which five years remained. The revised annual depreciation charge was determined as follows:
The net book value at January 20X8 was £162k (£200k- £38k (2 years depreciation charge)). This should now be depreciated over 5 years (7-2) giving an annual depreciation charge of £32.4.
The issue of subsequent expenditure and the possible impact on the UEL of an asset is discussed in ¶1498.

B. Methods

1460 The entity can select from a number of different methods of **calculating depreciation** over the life of the asset, although the straight-line and the reducing balance methods are the most common.

The **choice of method** (and related assumptions of useful economic life and residual value) can have a significant impact on reported profits and asset values in the balance sheet. Furthermore, two companies operating in the same industry can depreciate similar assets differently, thus making comparisons between them difficult.

The **depreciation method adopted is** largely dependent upon the type of asset and its function within the entity and should reflect a realistic, phased charge that matches the consumption of the economic benefits derived from the asset.

1461 A **change from one method** to another is only permissible if it provides a better reflection of the way in which the economic benefits associated with an asset are consumed. However, the use of a **different depreciation method** does not constitute a change in accounting policy, but is simply a change in estimate. The carrying amount of the tangible fixed asset will simply be depreciated using the new depreciation method over the remaining useful economic life of the asset, beginning in the period that the change is made.

If the change in the method of depreciation **has a material effect** on the reported profit for the year, this must be disclosed in the financial statements.

The **annuity method** of depreciation is not often used as it relies on assumptions of future profitability, which is fraught with complications.

1. Common methods

Straight-line method

The straight-line method **is defined as** the original cost of the asset less its residual value, divided by the estimated number of years comprising its useful economic life. The asset is written off in equal instalments, based on the assumption, that the economic benefits derived therefrom are evenly consumed over the useful life of the asset. 1462

EXAMPLE An asset such as a motor vehicle with a useful economic life of 5 years, costing £25,000 and with a residual value of £5,000 would result in an annual depreciation charge of £4000 per annum (25,000-5,000/5).

Although this method **is the simplest to apply** and is very widely used, it may not be the most appropriate as it is most suited to assets with a short but fixed working life e.g. leasehold property, or plant and equipment including computers. The disadvantage of this method is that an average annual depreciation charge may not reflect the actual consumption of economic benefits derived from the asset.

Reducing balance method

This is a method by which the **annual depreciation charge** diminishes as the asset ages. The depreciation charge is calculated by determining a fixed percentage annual rate, which is applied to the net book value of the asset at the beginning of the period, to arrive at the depreciation charge for the ensuing period. 1463

This **method is designed to** reflect the theory that the consumption of economic benefits derived from the asset reduces as it gets older. Therefore, depreciation is higher in the early years of the asset's life and lower in subsequent years.

Higher initial depreciation charges are offset by low maintenance costs, the reverse of which applies as the asset ages. **Certain assets may become obsolete** quickly and therefore the reducing balance method may be more appropriate.

This method is often used for motor vehicles, in order to match the net book values (NBV) of second hand vehicles to their market values.

The **disadvantages of this method** are: 1464
- that the depreciation charge in the early years can be very high and that it is more complicated to calculate an appropriate depreciation rate; and
- that it will ensure the asset is written down to its residual value by the end of its useful economic life.

EXAMPLE If a reducing balance rate of 27.5% is applied to a motor vehicle costing £25k with a useful economic life of 5 years and a residual value of £5k, the following depreciation charges will arise.

Year	NBV Start of year £	Depreciation charge (27.5 %) £	Closing NBV £
1	25000	6875	18125
2	18125	4984	13141
3	13141	3614	9527
4	9257	2620	6907
5	6907	1907[1]	5000 (RV)

1. Rounding

Except for assets that will be sold before the end of their economic life and are expected to have a material residual value, **there is some doubt** as to whether this is an appropriate method to use.

The sum-of-the-digits method

1466 This method of calculating depreciation is **similar to the reducing balance method**. The estimated life of the asset is first expressed in terms of years, which are then allocated a digit. If an asset is estimated to have a life of four years, year one will be allocated the digit 4, year two the digit three, year three 2 and year 4 digit 1. The sum of the digits is then 4 + 3 + 2 + 1 = 10.

This method front loads the depreciation charge in the earlier years of the asset's life, where cash flows earned by the tangible fixed asset might be highest or the consumption of economic benefits greatest.

One difference between the sum of the digits and reducing balance, is that after a predetermined period, the net book value under the sum of the digits method could reduce to nil.

1467 The **proportion of the assets cost** (less the residual value) to be written off as depreciation in a particular year is determined by the number of years remaining before the asset is decommissioned, expressed as a proportion of the sum of the years.

EXAMPLE For an asset with an estimated economic life of 5 years, the sum of the digits will be 5 + 4 + 3 + 2 + 1 = 15. Therefore, 5/15 of the cost (or valuation) is written off in the first year, 4/15 in the second year, 3/15in year 3 and so on.

If the asset cost £25k and has a residual value of £5k total depreciation of £20,000 is required and the depreciation profile will be as follows:

Year	NBV Start of year	Sum of digits	Depreciation charge	Closing NBV
	£	£	£	£
1	25000	5/15	6667	18333
2	18333	4/15	5333	13000
3	13000	3/15	4000	9000
4	9000	2/15	2666	6334
5	6334	1/15	1334	5000

Where the economic benefit to be derived from an asset is not expected to reduce in a linear fashion, as assumed in the above example, the "digits" applied to each year of the asset's estimated useful economic life do not have to follow a linear series. It should be noted that this method is not widely used.

Production-unit method (output or usage method)

1468 This method of computing the depreciation charge **is appropriate where** the economic life of an asset is more linked to consumption or usage than to time, such as certain types of machinery and extractive land (i.e. coal, quarries).

1. An estimate is made of the total number of units to be produced over the estimated useful economic life of the asset.

2. A depreciation rate per production unit is then estimated and applied to the production levels for each year of the asset's life.

EXAMPLE The **formula** for calculating the depreciation rate per production unit is as follows: **C – R/P = PU**

Where: C is the original cost;
R is the estimated residual value;
P is the estimated number of production units; and
PU is the rate per production unit.

If we take the asset profile adopted in the previous example and estimate the total output from the asset as 6000 units analysed over its useful economic life as follows:

Year	Production units (estimate)	Depreciation charge
1	2500	2500/6000 * £20000 = £8333
2	1500	1500/6000 * £20000 = £5000
3	1000	1000/6000 * £20000 = £3333
4	750	750/6000 * £20000 = £2500
5	250	250/6000 * £20000 = £834
Total	6000 units	

EXAMPLE In the extractive industries a **number of variations** on the production unit method are used, where estimates are made of the units mined within the accounting period as a proportion of the total reserves.
a) At RXB Mining plc depreciation on mine development is not charged until full production commences or the assets are utilised. On commencement of full production, depreciation is charged on a tonnage-extracted basis over the estimated useful life of the recoverable reserves.
b) Another variation of this method is utilised by a large public utility company, where depreciation on a landfill site is based on the average cost per cubic metre of landfill space, consumed in a given accounting period.

Care must be taken where the production-unit method of calculating depreciation is used as actual production may vary considerably from that originally anticipated. This can result in significant over or under depreciation provision over the useful economic life of the asset. It is important therefore, that at the end of each accounting period, the estimated total production over the remaining useful economic life of the asset is reassessed and if necessary, a revised depreciation rate per unit of production applied. **1469**

It should be noted that this method is not widely used.

The **revised depreciation rate** per unit of production should be calculated as follows: **1470**

(Net book value at the date of reassessment – estimated residual value)/ estimated remaining units of production over the remaining useful economic life of the asset.

This does not constitute a change in accounting policy, simply a change in accounting estimate and should not therefore result in a prior-year adjustment.

2. Less common methods

Renewals accounting

Renewals accounting **is defined as** the method of estimating depreciation on a group of **infrastructure assets** with finite lives, where the assets making up the infrastructure cannot (except with great difficulty) be separately identified in a fixed asset register and depreciated over their useful economic lives. It may be appropriate to treat such a group of fixed assets or network of systems as a single infrastructure asset. **1472** FRS 15 (97)

The **use of renewals accounting** is permissible where all the following conditions are satisfied: **1473**
– the infrastructure asset is a system or network that is required to be maintained at a specific level through the continued replacement and refurbishment of its component parts;
– the annual expenditure required is based on an asset management plan and certified by an appropriate independent qualified person; and
– the infrastructure system is in a mature or steady state (i.e. if the annual cost of maintaining the assets is relatively constant).

Where tangible fixed assets or components within an infrastructure system **have determinable finite lives**, they should be separately accounted for and depreciated over their useful economic life.

Renewals accounting is a relatively new depreciation method where the rules are still being tested. The **key feature** of renewals accounting, is that the level of annual expenditure required to maintain the operating capacity of the infrastructure asset is taken as the depreciation **1474** charge for the year and deducted from the carrying value of the asset. The actual expenditure is capitalised (as part of cost of the asset) in the normal way.

Examples of such infrastructure assets and how they were treated for depreciation purposes can be found in the rail, water, and electricity industries.

EXAMPLE

a. Railtravel plc adopted renewals accounting, whereby the **annual asset maintenance plan** charge, including efficiencies and an allowance for economic obsolescence of £504m, was treated as the depreciation charge for the year, for assets classified as track, route, structure and depots. The group stated that it operates an independently certified 10 year rolling asset maintenance plan for maintaining the operating capability of its assets.

b. East Narnia Water plc has defined infrastructure assets as those assets comprising a network of systems (i.e. sewers, mains, reservoirs, pipelines). Expenditure on enhancing or increasing the operating capacity of infrastructure assets is treated as an addition for capital expenditure purposes.

1475 Expenditure on maintaining the **operational capability** of the network infrastructure, in accordance with previously assessed standards of performance, is charged as an operating cost and classified as infrastructure renewals expenditure, (as opposed to depreciation).

Revaluation method

1476 A method of depreciation, whereby the asset to be depreciated is revalued each year at the end of the accounting period and any fall in its value reflected in the depreciation charged to the profit and loss account.

This method, although not widely used, **is suitable for assets** with short economic lives such as small loose tools and minor low value fixed assets, where there are practical problems in recording each asset individually, and which do not meet the criteria for renewals accounting.

3. Summary of depreciation methods

1478 The summary table **reflects the annual impact** of the depreciation charge on profits using the most widely recognised methods.

In all cases the asset costs £20,000, the estimated useful economic life is assumed to be 5 years, and the estimated residual value is nil. The charge for the production unit method is illustrative only (and uses the same production profile as in the example in ¶1468) and the charge would in practice depend on the actual production profile over the life of the asset.

Summary table comparing depreciation methods

Method	Depreciation charge by year (£)					
	1	2	3	4	5	Total
Straight-line	4000	4000	4000	4000	4000	20000
Reducing balance	6875	4984	3614	2620	1907	20000
Sum-of digits	6667	5333	4000	2666	1334	20000
Production unit method	8333	5000	3333	2500	834	20000

C. Specific depreciation issues

1480 In this section, the accounting treatments are considered for the calculation of depreciation for the following:
- revalued tangible fixed assets;
- assets which have separable components; and
- assets with useful economic lives exceeding 50 years.

The consequences of adopting a **policy of non-depreciation** are also considered.

Revalued tangible fixed assets

For tangible fixed assets that are **subject to periodic revaluation** there is still a requirement to charge depreciation. 1482

The **general rule** is that depreciation charged must be based on the new valuation (less estimated residual value, divided by the remaining useful economic life), rather than the historical cost and must be debited to the profit and loss account.

EXAMPLE At 1.1.20X9, the freehold buildings of ABC plc, (acquired on 1.1.20X4) have been recorded in the accounts at historical cost and are being depreciated over 40 years. It is estimated that there will be no residual value.

	Cost	Accumulated Depreciation	Net Book value
	£'000	£'000	£'000
Freehold property	2500	312.5	2187.5

The freehold properties were then revalued at £3m.
A revaluation surplus of £812.5k arises being the difference between the net book value of £2817.5k and the revalued amount of £3000k.
The revaluation surplus of £812.5k (£3m – £2187.5k) will be accounted for as a credit to the revaluation reserve.
The **original depreciation charge** was £2.5m/40 = £62.5 p.a. The accumulated depreciation charge at 1.1.20X9 was £312.5k covering 5 years. The remaining useful economic life is therefore 35 years (40 – 5). The **revised depreciation charge** based on the revalued amount is £3m/ 35 years = £85.7 p.a.

Where an asset has been revalued and the **depreciation charge** in the profit and loss account is **based on the revalued amount**, then in subsequent years there should be a transfer from the revaluation reserve to the profit and loss account. This transfer should represent the difference between the depreciation charge based on historical cost and the charge based on the revalued amount. This transfer is made as a movement on reserves shown in the notes to the financial statements and is not reflected in the entity's profit and loss account.

Separable components

If a tangible fixed asset comprises **two or more significant components** each with substantially different useful economic lives, then each part should be depreciated separately. 1484 FRS 15 (38)

Each component is then depreciated over its useful economic life so that the depreciation profile of the entire asset more accurately reflects the actual consumption of the asset's economic benefits.

Any subsequent expenditure incurred in replacing or renewing the component is accounted for as an addition to the tangible fixed asset and the carrying amount of the replaced component is removed from the balance sheet.

However, the separation of an asset into its individual component parts (including expenditures on overhauls or inspections) for depreciation purposes may not always be necessary, and will be **based on a number of factors including one or more** of the following: FRS 15 (83)
– whether the useful economic lives of the components are substantially different from the remainder of the asset;
– the materiality (in terms of cost) in the context of the financial statements;
– the regularity (and type) of expenditure required to maintain the asset in different accounting periods; or
– type of asset component.

EXAMPLE

a. **Land and buildings**, even if acquired together are treated differently for depreciation purposes. Buildings are deemed to have a finite life and are depreciated, whereas land typically does not require a provision for depreciation, unless for example it is subject to depletion through the extraction of minerals.

b. **Buildings and general fixtures and fittings**.
A building could be depreciated, for example over 50 yrs on a straight-line method which far exceeds the useful economic life of assets acquired within the building, (e.g. the heating systems or the lifts). The element of the purchase price attributable to the provision of the heating system/lifts should be identified separately and depreciated over their own, shorter, estimated economic life.
c. **Ships**
A ship contains different component parts (e.g. the hull or engine) some of which may have varying economic lives and be measured by different means such as mileage or hours of service. In this way the depreciation profile of the whole asset will more accurately reflect the consumption of its various economic benefits.

EXAMPLE **Lofgren Haulage Ltd**
Annual report and accounts

Accounting policy

Depreciation
Depreciation is provided on operational assets, with the exception of land, over the useful economic lives of the assets as detailed below:

Fixed assets	
Buildings	50 yrs
Fixtures and fittings	7-20 yrs
Plant and equipment	10 yrs
Office equipment	5-8 yrs
Motor vehicles	5 yrs
Computers	
– hardware	4 yrs
– software	5 yrs

Separable assets
The company owns a fleet of articulated distribution lorries and applies the following accounting policy with regard to the depreciation of separable assets.

Cab structures	5 yrs
Truck containers	10 yrs
Flat bed trailers	15 yrs
Air conditioning systems	5 yrs
Freezer units	4 yrs

Maintenance expenditure is charged to the profit and loss account, except where this results in the improvement in the asset's service potential, in which case the cost is capitalised and written-off over the useful economic life of the asset.

1486 Where the **trading potential is inseparable** from a property such as a public house or restaurant it should not be treated as a separate asset.

Non-depreciation or depreciation over periods in excess of fifty years

1488 FRS 15 (89) In general, all tangible fixed assets are deemed to have a finite economic life and should be depreciated over a period of not more than 50 years. However, the following tangible fixed assets **are generally not depreciated**:
- freehold land; or
- assets capitalised at a fixed amount.

Directors often argue that assets with a high residual value and long economic lives do not need depreciating. FRS 15 recognises that this may be the reality of the situation in some circumstances, but dictates that the **only permissible reason** for non-depreciation of an asset is that the depreciation charge and accumulated depreciation are "immaterial", in that they would not reasonably influence the decisions of users of financial statements.

FRS 15 (91) An entity **must be able to justify** that a policy of non-depreciation is acceptable on the grounds of immateriality, both in aggregate and in terms of individual assets. Depreciation may be immaterial due to:

- a long useful economic life; or
- high residual value (or both).

A **high estimate of residual value** may be justified on the following grounds: 1489

i. the entity has a policy of regular maintenance and repair (charged to the profit and loss account), so that the asset maintains its performance standards;

ii. the asset is not expected to suffer from economic or technological obsolescence resulting from for example, changes in patterns of demand; or

iii. where estimated residual values are material, because:
- the entity has a policy of disposing of similar assets before the end of their useful economic lives; or
- the disposal proceeds of similar assets have been similar to their carrying amounts.

An **impairment review**, in accordance with FRS 11, must be performed annually on tangible fixed assets (other than non-depreciable land), at the end of each accounting period, where: 1490
- no depreciation is charged as it is deemed immaterial because of the length of the remaining useful economic life or where the estimated residual value is not markedly different from the carrying amount; or
- the tangible fixed asset's estimated useful economic life exceeds 50 years.

If there are **difficulties performing an impairment review** on individual assets then assets may be grouped as income generating units (IGUs) (See ¶1550).

MEMO POINTS This approach is conceptually consistent with FRS 10's treatment of intangible assets and goodwill, although annual impairment reviews must be conducted where useful economic lives exceed 20 rather than 50 years.

For all other tangible fixed assets, an impairment review need only be conducted where: 1491
- expectations of future cash flows or discount rates have changed significantly; or FRS 15 (92)
- there are adverse changes in other key assumptions and variables.

Where the recoverable amount was previously, substantially in excess of the carrying amount, it may be possible to ascertain immediately that the asset is not impaired.

Where **depreciation is not charged** because it is considered immaterial, there is a risk that at some future point the recoverable amount will fall below the carrying value of the asset.

SECTION 5

Subsequent expenditure

Subsequent expenditure on tangible fixed assets can be categorised as either **maintenance or performance enhancing** expenditure, although a precise allocation between the two may sometimes be difficult. The issue of depreciation on subsequent expenditure is considered in ¶1484. 1494

Maintenance expenditure

Maintenance expenditure will be incurred in maintaining the standard of performance of the asset over its estimated useful economic life. The **general rule is** that this type of subsequent expenditure on a tangible fixed asset should be expensed as incurred. 1495 FRS 15 (34)

Where tangible fixed assets are accounted for as several components or one element of the asset is depreciated over a different time scale from the rest of the asset, the cost of replacing, restoring, overhauling or inspecting the asset, or component parts is not capitalised, but expensed in the profit and loss account.

Examples include the routine overhaul of plant and equipment. Without such expenditure the depreciation charge would increase, because the useful economic life or residual value of the asset would be reduced.

Performance enhancing expenditure

1496 FRS 15 (39) Some tangible fixed assets require, in addition to routine repairs and maintenance, substantial periodic expenditure for refits, refurbishment, replacement or restoration of major components.

The **accounting treatment** for subsequent expenditure should reflect the circumstances accounted for on initial recognition of the asset and the depreciation profile adopted.

Where the initial rate of depreciation is based on the asset life assuming no additional expenditure, then any subsequent expenditure which enhances its life beyond that original estimate will be capitalised.

Where the estimated life has been adjusted to the extended life expectancy, the additional expenditure should be treated as maintenance required to achieve the original estimated life expectancy and written-off immediately to the profit and loss account.

1497 FRS 15 (36) **Capitalisation of subsequent expenditure** Subsequent expenditure on a tangible fixed asset can also be recognised as an addition to the asset, and capitalised where:

i. it enhances **the economic benefits** derived from the tangible fixed asset in excess of the previously assessed standard of performance;

ii. a **component** part of a tangible fixed asset has been **treated separately** for depreciation purposes and depreciated over its useful economic life is replaced or restored; or

iii. it relates to a **major inspection or overhaul** of a tangible fixed asset that restores the economic benefits of the asset that have been consumed by the entity and reflected in its depreciation charge.

FRS 15 (37) **Examples** of subsequent expenditure that enhances the economic benefits derived from a tangible fixed asset, include the modification of a plant to increase its capacity or extend its useful economic life or the upgrading of machine parts, in order to improve the quality of outputs or reduce the operating costs of the asset.

EXAMPLE Some assets require a regular service overhaul by law (e.g. aircraft), without which it cannot be licensed for service. Therefore, the costs of the overhaul should be capitalised as they restore the economic benefits of the tangible fixed asset. The depreciation charged should be expensed over the time period until the next inspection.
Care must be taken that, over a period of years, the gross cost of the assets is not inflated by ensuring that the cost and accumulated depreciation of previous inspections/overhauls are reflected in the asset values.

1498 **Revision of useful economic life** Subsequent expenditure that enhances the economic benefits of an asset could lead to a revision in the estimate of the asset's useful economic life, residual value or the depreciation method adopted.

The **capitalisation of further expenditure** should depend on the revised assessment of the standard of performance of the asset. For instance, the cost of converting storage space into retail space to increase sales capacity should be capitalised. Although this type of subsequent expenditure does not extend the useful economic life of an asset, it may impact on its residual value.

Other types of subsequent expenditure may impact on either the useful economic life or residual value. For instance, technical developments may result in subsequent expenditure that triggers a revision of the originally assessed standard of performance of a tangible fixed asset, affecting either the useful economic life, residual value or impairment of the carrying value.

Euro conversion costs

1499 The **general rule** is that all conversion costs relating to **modifying systems** to deal with the introduction of the Euro, should be expensed or possibly treated as exceptional items. The exceptions to the rule are where the company has a policy of capitalising software and system costs and that the asset's useful economic lives have been enhanced beyond the previously assessed limit, rather than merely maintaining its current service potential.

Other examples of conversion costs include:
- administrative and planning costs;
- staff training; or
- the adaptation of relevant hardware such as vending machines, cash registers etc.

MEMO POINTS UITF 21 addresses the issue of subsequent expenditure needed to enhance or maintain existing accounting systems in order to cope with the introduction of the Euro.

SECTION 6

Gains and losses on disposal

Profits or losses on disposal of tangible fixed assets should be treated in accordance with FRS 3 (the rules of which are repeated in FRS 15) and accounted for in the profit and loss account for the period in which the disposal occurs (see ¶398). **1500** FRS 15 (Appendix IV)

The profit or loss on the disposal of a tangible fixed asset **represents the difference** between the net sale proceeds and the carrying amount, whether carried at historical cost or at a valuation.

It should be noted that **this is inconsistent with the treatment** for revaluation gains and losses, which are carried in the STRGL, even though it is the result of the same factors; namely rising prices.

EXAMPLE **Replacement asset**

Gain on disposal

A new tangible fixed asset valued at £100,000 was acquired from insurance proceeds after a previously held asset was destroyed by fire.
The carrying amount of the destroyed asset was £85,000, which was then removed from the balance sheet and the resulting gain on disposal of £15,000, representing the difference between the insurance proceeds and the carrying amount, was recognised in the profit and loss account. The new tangible fixed asset should be recorded at replacement cost.

Replacement asset Where an asset (or component of an asset) is replaced, its carrying amount is removed from the balance sheet by eliminating its cost (or revalued amount) and related accumulated depreciation. The resulting gain or loss on disposal is accounted for in the profit and loss account.

Anticipated sale of assets

If a company wishes to dispose of a fixed asset, then the asset is no longer intended for use on a continuing basis in the business. The asset **can either be reclassified** under a separate subheading under fixed assets of "assets held for resale" or reclassified as a current asset. **1502**

Within **current asset investments** only stocks and current asset investments can be revalued under the alternative accounting rules.

Furthermore, a decision to dispose of an asset may trigger an impairment review. If a loss is identified, **it must be determined** whether this is the result of the decision to sell the asset, in which case it should be treated as a loss on disposal, or whether it results from other events.

SECTION 7

Disclosures

1508 This section covers the general disclosures for tangible fixed assets required under FRS 15 and the Companies Act, as well as the specific disclosure requirements relating to any revaluation and subsequent expenditure on tangible fixed assets, and the capitalisation of finance costs and leased assets held under finance lease or hire purchase agreements.

General disclosures

1510 FRS 15 requires, that adequate information be disclosed in the financial statements, to enable the user to understand the impact of the entity's accounting policies for the initial measurement, valuation and depreciation of tangible fixed assets on the financial performance on the entity.

FRS 15 (100) There are **extensive disclosures required** in the financial statements for **each category** of tangible fixed asset.

The following **cumulative disclosures** are required:

1. Cost or revalued amount at the beginning and end of the financial year;
2. Total depreciation charged for the period;
3. Cumulative depreciation charge (or impairment) at the beginning and end of the financial period;
4. Carrying amount (net book amount) at the beginning and end of the financial year;
5. Methods of depreciation adopted;
6. Useful economic lives or the depreciation rates used;
7. The financial effect of a material change in either estimate of useful economic lives or residual values;
8. A reconciliation of the movements on depreciation with separate disclosures for additions, disposals, impairment losses, leases, revaluations, and transfers;
9. Any change in the depreciation method or policy adopted as well as the reason for the change;
10. The amount of any interest capitalised; and
11. The difference between the carrying amount and market value of interests in land, where in the opinion of the directors the difference is significant. This disclosure should be given in the directors' report.

EXAMPLE ABC Ltd
Report and Accounts
31 December 2010

Notes to the accounts	**Tangible fixed assets**				
	Freehold £m	**Long lease £m**	**Short lease £m**	**Plant & machinery £m**	**Total £m**
Cost					
Balance as at 1.1.2010	9.8	3.5	2.4	76.6	92.3
Additions	4.7	0.1	0.4	9.4	14.6
Disposals	(3.2)	–	(1.7)	(10.2)	(15.1)
Transfers	–	–	–	(5.0)	(5.0)
Balance as at 31.12.2010	**11.3**	**3.6**	**1.1**	**70.8**	**86.8**
Depreciation at 31.01.2010	0.1	–	0.6	49.6	50.3
Charge for year	0.3	0.1	0.5	8.9	9.8
Disposals	(0.1)	-	(0.7)	(9.0)	(9.8)
Transfers	-	-	–	1.5	1.5
Total depreciation	0.3	0.1	0.4	51.0	51.8
NBV as at 31.12.2010	**10.8**	**3.5**	**0.7**	**19.8**	**35.0**

Example of an accounting policy note.

Depreciation is based on historic cost or revaluation, less the estimated residual values, and the estimated economic lives of the assets concerned. Freehold land is not depreciated. Other tangible fixed assets are depreciated in equal annual instalments (straight-line method) over the period of their useful economic lives. Allowance has been made for technological and commercial obsolescence.

Freehold land and buildings	2%
Short and long lease properties	Period of lease
Equipment:	20%
Furniture, fixtures and fittings	10%
Motor vehicles	25%

Capitalisation of finance cost disclosures

If a policy of capitalisation of finance costs **is adopted**, then the financial statements should disclose the following: **1512**
- accounting policy adopted; FRS 15 (31)
- aggregate amount of finance costs included in the cost of tangible fixed assets;
- total finance costs capitalised during the period;
- total of the finance costs recognised in the profit and loss account during the period; and
- capitalisation rate used to determine the total finance costs capitalised during the period.

The disclosures required by FRS 15 governing the capitalisation of finance costs are similar to the requirements of the Companies Acts. **Companies must disclose** in the notes to the accounts, that the interest is included in determining the production costs of particular assets and the amount of interest. **1514** LR 12.43

The **listing rules** require listed companies to disclose the amount of interest capitalised in the year, together with an indication of the amount and treatment of any related tax relief.

Where finance costs are capitalised by way of simultaneous transfer from the profit and loss account, they should be separately disclosed. The **interest charge** in the profit and loss account will be the net amount, but in the notes to the accounts this should be expanded to show the gross figure with the amount capitalised deducted.

Revaluation disclosures

There are a **number of general disclosures** required for revalued tangible fixed assets and for each class of tangible fixed asset, both under FRS 15 and under the alternative accounting rules in the Companies Act. The **principal disclosures** cover the accounting policies adopted by the company regarding revaluation, and include details on depreciation and any diminution in value of the assets. **1518**

Where any **class of tangible fixed assets** of an entity have been revalued, the following disclosures are required for each class of asset, per the balance sheet formats set out in the Companies Act; namely: **1519** FRS 15 (74)
- name and qualifications of the valuer(s) or organisation;
- valuation bases adopted (including whether notional directly attributable acquisition costs have been included or selling costs deducted);
- the date and amounts of the valuations;
- whether the valuation is internal or external;
- the date of the previous valuation;
- the cumulative historical cost by class of asset; and
- carrying value including cumulative provisions for depreciation or diminution in value.

These disclosures are given in the notes to the accounts.

Valuation policy A concession is permitted upon the **first application** of FRS 15, allowing an entity to retain previously revalued assets at carrying value. When this policy is adopted, the following disclosures are required up until the date of any disposal: **1520**

- that the transitional rules have been adopted;
- that values have not been updated; and
- the date of the last valuation.

This **concession allows** entities to retain any "cherry-picked valuations". However, the above disclosures are required in each year that use is made of this concession. Likewise, additional disclosures will also be required under the Companies Act.

Where **an entity restates to historical cost** a previously revalued asset, this should be treated as a change in accounting policy, resulting in a prior-year adjustment. Disclosure is required of:
- the reason for the change in accounting policy;
- the cumulative effect on reserves; and
- the impact on profits for the current financial year.

1521 FRS 15 (74b) **Revalued properties** Additional disclosures are required for revalued properties including:
- a statement that a property has been revalued as a fully equipped operational entity regarding their trading potential, and the carrying amount of these properties; and
- where material, the total notional directly attributable acquisition costs included in the carrying value.

1522 FRS 15 (75) **Other professional bodies** including the RICS request additional disclosures in financial statements to those listed above. For example, the RICS requires confirmation in published documents containing references to valuation reports, stating that the valuation has been conducted in accordance with the RICS Appraisal and Valuation Manual; any departure from this must requirement must be disclosed.

The **following example** illustrates the required revaluation disclosures as discussed above.

EXAMPLE **BHI Ltd**
Report and accounts – 31 December 2010
Notes to the accounts (extract)

Movements in cost and depreciation

	Land & buildings	Machinery & plant	Tools & fittings	Assets in course of constr'n	Total
	£'000	£'000	£'000	£'000	£'000
Cost					
Balance as at 1.1.2010	800	350	150	85	1,385
Additions	100	50	25	20	195
Disposals	(15)	(22)	–	–	(37)
Transfers	–	15		(15)	–
Revaluation	65	–	–	–	65
Balance as at 31.12.2010	**950**	**393**	**175**	**90**	**1,608**
Depreciation:					
Balance as at 1.1.2010	120	210	70	–	400
Charge for the year	40	53	15	–	108
Eliminated on disposal	(15)	(18)	–	–	(33)
Revaluation	(55)	–	–	–	(55)
Balance as at 31.12.2010	**90**	**245**	**85**	–	**420**
Net book value:					
At 31.12. 2010	860	148	90	–	1,188
At 31.12.20X9	740	140	15	90	985

Report and accounts – 31 December 2010
Notes to the accounts (extract)

5. Land and buildings

Revaluation policy
During each of the last 5 yrs a sample of the freehold and long-leasehold properties owned by the Group's property subsidiary, Rappur Properties, have been valued by external qualified valuers (R. Bittan & partners). The sample taken on 30 June 20X9 has been valued by the external valuers which then formed the basis of the internal valuations performed on the remainder of the group's property valuers by the group qualified internal valuers.

Properties occupied by the Group are valued on an **existing use basis (EUV)**, whilst properties not occupied by Group companies are valued on the basis of **open market (OMV)**. These valuations comply with the RICS Appraisal and Valuation Manual. There is no material difference between the existing use value and open market value. In the opinion of the Directors, there would be no tax payable if all the properties were realised at these values.
The relevant revaluation adjustments have been taken to the revaluation reserve, a surplus totalling £28m (20X9 £19m).

Alternative accounting rules The **following disclosures** are required for tangible fixed assets revalued under the alternative accounting rules, either on the face of the balance sheet or in the notes to the accounts: **1524**
- comparative amounts based on historical cost; and
- differences between alternative valuation and historical cost valuation.

Comparable amounts are defined as the total amount that a entity would have disclosed under historical cost, including cumulative provisions for depreciation or diminution in value, for each class of revalued assets. FRS 15 (74)

Assets held under hire purchase and finance lease agreements

The **following disclosures** are required of tangible fixed assets held under finance leases or hire purchase agreements: **1525** SSAP 21 (49)
- the gross amounts of assets held under finance leases;
- related accumulated depreciation by major class of asset; and
- the total depreciation allocated for the period by major class of asset.

This information may be shown separately from that concerning owned assets or integrated with the total for each major class of owned assets. **1526**

Where the **alternative accounting rules** are adopted, the net amount of assets held under finance leases included in the overall totals should be separately disclosed. The depreciation allocated for the period in respect of assets held under finance leases, included in the overall total, should also be disclosed.

For a more detailed review of the disclosure requirements concerning hire purchase agreements and finance lease arrangements see ¶3400.

SECTION 8

FRED 29 – review of proposals

FRED 29 "Property, Plant and Equipment; Borrowing Costs" was issued as part of the ASB's convergence programme with international accounting standards. The exposure draft is based on IAS 16 "Property, Plant and Equipment" and IAS 23 "Borrowing Costs". The current position is that the exposure draft is still at the consultation stage with the ASB. **1530**

FRED 29 **sets out the requirements** for the initial recognition, measurement, valuation and depreciation of tangible fixed assets. FRED 29 **applies to all** tangible fixed assets, except investment properties (where construction is complete), which are regulated by SSAP 19

"Investment Properties". The disclosure requirements in FRED 29 are similar to those required by UK Company Law and FRS 15.

The approach in FRED 29 to **revaluation losses** is simpler than that adopted in FRS 15, where losses are charged to the STRGL until the carrying amount reaches depreciated historical cost, with any further losses charged to the profit and loss account.

The other **key differences** between FRS 15 and the exposure draft are set out in the table below.

Subject	FRS 15	FRED 29
Revalued assets	Revaluation to current value based on "value to the business model"	1. Revaluation to fair value. 2. Where a revaluation policy is adopted, then all the assets within that class should also be revalued on a regular basis to ensure that the carrying amount matches the asset's fair value at the balance sheet date.
Valuations	5 year valuations – interim updates Detailed guidance	No maximum period between valuations. Guidance on valuations less detailed.
Residual values	Residual values based on prices at date of acquisition or most recent valuation.	Residual values revised using current prices (fair values) – could impact significantly on depreciation charge
Subsequent expenditure	1. Depreciation should be charged. 2. Annual impairment review required for assets with a useful economic life of 50 years or where no depreciation is charged as it is deemed immaterial.	1. Depreciation should be charged. 2. No such requirement for impairment review.
Renewals accounting	Use of renewals accounting permitted if certain criteria are met (see ¶1472)	Excludes the "Renewals accounting rules" adopted in the UK, and which would effectively be prohibited under the new IAS
Borrowing costs	1. The requirements of FRS 15 confined to tangible fixed assets. 2. Capitalisation of borrowing costs restricted to interest on funds actually used to purchase assets. 3. Interest paid or received on unused tranches of borrowings accounted for in the profit and loss account. 4. If borrowings capitalised two disclosures specific required: the total finance cost included in cost of assets and amount of finance costs charged to the P & L.	1. FRED 29 mirrors IAS 23 – applies more widely to "qualifying assets", including inventories. 2. Interest paid or received on total borrowings can be capitalised (Optional). Policy must be persistently applied. 3. No such requirement.
Exchanged assets	No guidance on measurement of exchanged assets	Property, plant or equipment acquired in exchange for another asset should be measured at fair value
Donated assets	Specific guidance given (see ¶1326)	No specific guidance given

SECTION 9

Comparison between UK GAAP and IAS (IFRS)

The **principal requirements** for the recognition, measurement and depreciation of tangible fixed assets are included in IAS 16 "Property, Plant and Equipment", with some additional requirements contained in IAS 23 "Borrowing costs". 1532

Key differences

Meeting the requirements of FRS 15 leads to compliance with IAS 16 and the relevant requirements of IAS 23, in terms of the scope and measurement of tangible fixed assets. However, for those enterprises that choose to revalue their assets, the revaluation methods and treatment of revaluation losses differ between IAS and UK rules. **These and other differences** are outlined in the tables below. 1534 FRS 15 (Appendix III)

Key differences between UK GAAP and IAS	UK GAAP	IAS 16 & 23
1. Revaluation of property	"Value to the business model" requiring valuation at existing use, replacement cost or open market value. (FRS 15 (53)). (See also ¶1384). Reference to RICS definitions.	Fair value – usually market value at revaluation date less accumulated depreciation (IAS 16 (31))
2. Revaluation losses due to consumption of economic benefits	Charge to Profit and loss account	First charge to an existing revaluation reserve, thereafter to the profit and loss account
3. Revaluation losses – no clear consumption of economic benefits	Charge to STROLL, until the carrying amount falls to depreciated historical cost, thereafter in the profit and loss account, to the extent that the recoverable amount exceeds the revalued amount. (FRS 15 (65))	Charge to equity (Revaluation reserve) where a related surplus for that asset exists (IAS 16 (38)). Any loss in excess of that surplus goes to the profit and loss account.
4. Capitalisation of borrowing costs	1. Capitalisation only allowed on borrowings related to expenditure on the asset completed. (FRS 15 (19)). 2. Exchange differences on foreign currency borrowings cannot be treated as borrowing costs. 3. Consistent application of capitalisation policy required.	1. If funds are borrowed specifically to finance construction or purchase of a tangible fixed asset – finance costs on the total borrowing can be capitalised, followed by a deduction of interest income on invested funds. (IAS 23 (15)). 2. Exchange differences on borrowing costs can be capitalised. 3. As with FRS 15, except that policy should apply not only to tangible fixed assets but qualifying assets within stocks and intangible assets.
5. Residual values	Prices at acquisition date or most recent valuation should be used – enables depreciation to be calculated on a consistent basis	Current prices at date of revision should be used
6. RICS valuation guidelines	The FRS draws heavily on the RICS valuation guidelines and definitions	No parallel classification in IAS
7. Government grants	UK company law requires government grants to be treated as deferred income	Government grants for the acquisition of tangible fixed assets may be offset against the cost of the asset

1535

Topics dealt with more comprehensively by UK GAAP	Reference
1. **Regenerative and non-regenerative materials** (e.g. forests and mineral rights) are dealt with under FRS 15, but not specifically considered under IAS	
2. **Revaluation** should be at least every five years with more detail required on frequency and reliability of valuations. Under IAS 16 the fair value of land and buildings is determined by market based evidence provided by qualified valuers.	FRS 15 (45)
3. Both the FRS and IAS state that the need for **depreciation** to be charged on **subsequent expenditure** is not negated. The FRS is more comprehensive and requires an annual impairment test, if assets have a depreciable UEL in excess of 50 years or no depreciation is charged on grounds of immateriality. There is no similar requirement under IAS.	FRS 15 (89)
4. Under UK GAAP there is a **yearly review of useful economic life.** Under IAS there is only a periodic requirement.	FRS 15 (93)
5 FRS 15 includes the concept of renewals accounting; this is not recognised in IAS 16	FRS 15 (97)

MEMO POINTS In October 2010 the ASB issued a proposal to introduce a financial reporting framework for medium-sized entities (FRSME) not eligible to apply the FRSSE or full IFRS. The FRSME would replace current UK GAAP from July 2013 and is based on the principles underpinning full IFRS. If adopted there could be some key differences in the treatment of revaluation of tangible fixed assets and borrowing costs.

Additional disclosures under IAS 16

1536 FRS 15 (Appendix III) IAS 16 requires the following additional disclosures to those stipulated in FRS 15:

a. General disclosures

- property, plant and equipment pledged as security for liabilities and any restrictions on title;
- expenditure on property, plant and equipment under construction;
- details of any commitments for the acquisition of property, plant and equipment; and
- details of valuation bases for determining the gross carrying amount of property, plant and equipment.

b. For **each revalued class** of property, plant and equipment:

- the nature of any indices used to determine the replacement cost; and
- the revaluation surplus and the movement for the period (if any) and any restriction on the distribution of the balance to shareholders.

First-time adoption of IFRS 1

1538 This section briefly outlines the key areas in the first time adoption process, covering tangible fixed assets, for entities moving to IFRSs.

The **interaction** of IFRS 1 **with IAS 16 and IAS 23** is considered in the tables below.

IAS 16	Accounting treatment
Deemed cost of property, plant and equipment	An entity **should use** one of the following bases to measure the assets in its opening balance sheet. 1. Cost (or deemed cost) less accumulated depreciation and impairment losses under IAS 16 benchmark treatment (cost model) (IAS 16 (30)); or 2. Fair value (revaluation model-alternative treatment) at transition date to IFRSs, less depreciation and impairment losses (IAS 16.(31)). The following disclosures are required under IFRS 1(para 44); namely the aggregate of the fair values and the aggregate adjustment to the carrying amounts reported under UK GAAP.

IAS 16	Accounting treatment
Revaluation (alternative treatment)	Where an entity revalues an asset, all assets in that class must be revalued (IAS 16.(36)). The cumulative revaluation surplus at the transition date to IFRSs, is based on a comparison of the carrying amount of the asset at that date, with its cost.
Depreciation methods (IAS 16.(60))	1. Methods acceptable under UK GAAP. Entity accounts for any changes in UEL or pattern of depreciation prospectively. 2. Methods acceptable under UK GAAP **but not under IFRS**. If material, the entity should adjust accumulated depreciation in its opening IFRS balance sheet retrospectively, in order to comply with IFRS.
Obligations attached to construction or commissioning of an asset	Where construction of commissioning of an asset generates an obligation to dismantle the asset or restore a site at some future date, the following must be considered: 1. IAS 37 "Provisions, contingent liabilities and contingent assets" to be applied in recognising the provision. 2. IAS 16 applied in determining the total provision to be included in the cost of the asset, prior to depreciation and impairment losses (IAS 16 (16c)).

IAS 23	Accounting treatment
Borrowing costs	Two treatments possible: – Capitalisation = alternative treatment (IAS 23.(10)). – Non-capitalisation = benchmark treatment (IAS 23.(7)). Option selected **must be applied** consistently in opening IFRS balance sheet and first financial period under IFRS **Exception**: If deemed cost is used – borrowing costs incurred before the date of measurement as a deemed cost are not capitalised **Disclosures** required of interest capitalised during the financial period. IFRS 1 or IAS 23 do not require disclosure of cumulative interest capitalised.
Transitional provisions	**Retrospective application** encouraged – adjust financial statements in accordance with IAS 8 "Accounting Policies, Changes in Accounting Estimates and Errors." (IAS 23.(30)). An entity can adopt the **alternative treatment** of capitalising prospectively, but only those borrowing costs incurred after the effective date for IAS 23, that meet the capitalisation criteria (IAS 23.(13)).

MEMO POINTS The IASB has issued a number of amendments to IFRS 1, which covers the retrospective application of IFRSs, with the objective of reducing the costs of the transition process. The amendments principally cover exemptions regarding leasing contracts, based on an exposure draft issued back in September 2008.

CHAPTER 5

Impairment of fixed assets and goodwill

OUTLINE ¶¶

Impairment **is defined as** a reduction in the recoverable amount of a fixed asset or goodwill below its carrying value in the balance sheet. An impairment charge is in addition to normal depreciation. **1550** FRS 11 (2)

The **principles of accounting** for the impairment of tangible and intangible fixed assets (including fixed asset investments) and purchased goodwill are contained in FRS 11 "Impairment of fixed assets and goodwill".

MEMO POINTS FRED 38 "Impairment of fixed assets", has been issued in order to bring FRS 11 more into line with IAS 36 (see ¶1734). However, the ASB has postponed a decision concerning implementation of this FRED pending the completion of its convergence strategy for UK GAAP and IFRS.

Fixed assets and goodwill are generally only tested for impairment on the basis of a **number of indicators**, used to determine whether a fixed asset (or goodwill) or the environment in which the asset operates might be impaired and whether as a result an impairment review is required. However, **in certain circumstances** fixed assets and purchased goodwill automatically require annual impairment reviews irrespective of whether there is impairment or not.

A number of other related topics such as the impairment of **financial instruments**, are addressed by other accounting standards and abstracts (see table in ¶1572).

1552 **All reporting entities** are subject to the provisions of FRS 11, except those smaller entities applying the Financial Reporting Standard for Smaller Entities (FRSSE) unless preparing consolidated financial statements, in which case they should apply the accounting standard to such financial statements as required by the FRSSE (¶6000).

The **general rules** for the treatment of impairment losses and more specific issues such as the reversal of past impairment losses must are be considered.

MEMO POINTS The terms impairment and impairment losses are more or less synonymous.

Objective of FRS 11

1554 FRS 11 (1) The objective of FRS 11, is to ensure that intangible, tangible fixed assets and goodwill are not carried in the financial statements at more than their recoverable amount, and that:
- any resulting impairment is recognised and measured on a consistent basis; and
- sufficient information be disclosed in the financial statements to enable a proper understanding of the impact of the impairment on the entity's performance.

The Companies Act requires that a **provision be made** for any permanent diminution in value. Under FRS 11, however all diminutions in value, whether temporary and permanent, should be recognised immediately. These **impairment losses** should be recognised in the profit and loss account, unless they represent the reversal of a previously recognised revaluation surplus that has been credited to a revaluation reserve, in which case it may be permissible to charge the impairment through the statement of total recognised gains or losses (STRGL) and reduce the revaluation reserve.

SECTION 1

Impairment reviews - overview

1558 An automatic impairment review may be required each year or only where certain factors indicate that an impairment has occurred; namely that the carrying value of a fixed asset or goodwill may not be recoverable.

Impairment in relation to **specific fixed assets** and goodwill are addressed by other accounting standards (see table in ¶1572). Irrespective of where another primary accounting standard stipulates that an impairment review is required, the review itself should be conducted within the guidelines of FRS 11.

Measurement of impairment

1560 The **recoverable amount** of an individual fixed asset or Income Generating Unit (IGU) will be determined by reference to the higher of net realisable value (NRV) and **value in use**. If the **carrying value** of the asset exceeds its recoverable amount, it is impaired and should be written down to the recoverable amount.

1562 FRS 11 (22) (25) As an assessment of recoverable amount is to look at the higher of NRV and value in use. It is common to look initially at an **estimate of the NRV** of the fixed asset or goodwill. This figure can often be derived relatively easily if there is an active market for the sale of the type of asset under review.

If this estimate of NRV **proves inconclusive** or turns out to be less than the carrying value, then it will be necessary to perform a more detailed calculation of value in use in order to determine whether an impairment has occurred.

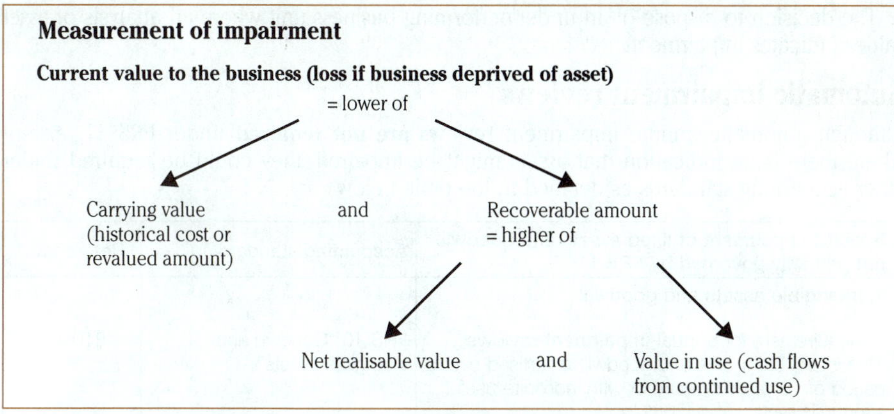

MEMO POINTS 1. The **carrying value** is defined as the value at which an asset (or liability) is recorded in the balance sheet. For example, a fixed asset such as a building will be shown at historical cost less accumulated depreciation to-date. Under the alternative accounting rules the carrying amount is the revalued amount less accumulated depreciation.
2. The **recoverable amount** is defined as the higher of the cash flows generated by the fixed asset or income generating unit either through a sale (net realisable value) or by continued use (value in use). The definition of recoverable amount is drawn from the Statement of Principles published by The Accounting Standards Board (ASB).
3. **Net realisable value (NRV)** is defined as the estimated net sale proceeds from a sale of a fixed asset or IGU.(¶1576).
4. **Value in use** is defined as the discounted present value of future cash flows (i.e. income stream) obtainable as a result of an asset's continued use, including those resulting from its ultimate disposal (¶1582).

Impairment indicators

A review may not necessarily be required every year, as the systematic **charging of depreciation** should ensure that the carrying amount of the fixed asset or goodwill is reduced throughout its useful economic life, so reflecting the reduction in the recoverable amount of the asset, arising from the consumption of economic benefits. **1564**

A **review for impairment** of a fixed asset or goodwill **should only be undertaken** if events or changes in circumstances indicate, that the carrying value of an individual fixed asset (or IGU) (see ¶1590), or goodwill may not be recoverable. **Impairment occurs when** something happens to affect the value of the fixed asset itself or has altered the environment in which it operates. FRS 11 (8)

Common events that indicate impairment include the following: **1566**
– a current operating loss or net cash outflow from operating activities;
– expectations of continuing operating losses or net cash outflow from operating activities;
– evidence of physical damage or obsolescence;
– a reorganisation or restructuring of the business; or
– the company has suffered a loss of key employees.

Other **less common indicators of impairment** indicators of impairment are:
1. A significant increase in market interest rates or other market rates of return that are expected to materially affect the assets recoverable amount.
2. There are significant adverse changes in any of the following:
– developments in the market or business segment in which the company operates (i.e. new competitors, new products);
– the regulatory environment governing the business;
– any indicator of value such as multiples of turnover, used to measure the fair value of a fixed asset on acquisition; or
– a significant devaluation of a currency in which the entity denotes its cash flow.

3. The decision to dispose of an under-performing business unit where an analysis of asset values indicates impairment.

Automatic impairment reviews

1568 Although automatic annual impairment reviews **are not required** under FRS 11, except where there is an indication that assets might be impaired, they could be required under other accounting standards as detailed in the table below.

Specific impairment of fixed assets and goodwill not primarily governed by FRS 11	Accounting standard	Reference
1. Intangible assets and goodwill		
a. Requirement for **annual impairment reviews** – on intangible assets and goodwill amortised over a period of 20 years or more or with indefinite useful economic lives.	FRS 10 "Goodwill and intangible assets"	¶1090
b. **Purchased goodwill** written off to reserves under the transitional arrangements.	FRS 10 "Goodwill and intangible assets"	¶1090
c. A **special first year** impairment review (end of first year) for goodwill and intangible assets relating to **new acquisitions**.	FRS 7 "Fair values in acquisition accounting"	¶6864
2. Tangible fixed assets		
a. Tangible fixed assets **other than non-depreciable land**, should be reviewed at the end of each financial year: – when either no depreciation is charged (deemed immaterial); or – the asset's useful economic life exceeds 50 years.	FRS 10 "Tangible fixed assets"	¶1490
b. Impairment resulting from **a fair value exercise** on new acquisitions.	FRS 7 "Fair values in acquisition accounting"	¶6864

Specialist areas covered by other accounting standards

1572 There are a number of specialist areas **exempt from the requirements** of FRS 11, which are covered by other accounting standards.

Specialist areas dealt with by other accounting standards or pronouncements	Reference
1. Financial assets/instruments Financial assets such as investments in equity and non-equity shares and debt instruments.	¶3400
2. Investment properties	¶1900
3. ESOP Trusts Entity's own shares held in an ESOP and carried as a fixed asset.	¶1784
4. Oil and gas exploration Oil and gas exploration costs capitalised pending confirmation of commercial development of reserves.	See industry SORP

SECTION 2

Impairment review process

Impairment reviews should be a detailed assessment of whether the present value of future cash flows justifies the carrying value of the fixed assets or goodwill. It should be noted that as the underlying **cash flow assumptions** supporting asset valuations **are subjective in nature** as they are based on estimates of future events, any such impairment write-downs can only reflect broad estimates of impairment losses. 1574

1. The **initial stage** of the impairment review is to estimate the net realisable value of the individual asset or group of assets (IGU).

2. **If this initial review indicates** that the NRV is lower than the carrying value of the individual asset or IGU or that no reliable estimate of NRV is available, then the value in use should be calculated.

3. Initially, an estimate of value in use at a post-tax level can be used, although **if this is inconclusive or indicates impairment** then a more detailed calculation (pre-tax level) of value in use is required, involving the calculation of discounted future cash flows.

A. Net realisable value

1576

NRV of:	Based on
Tangible fixed assets	Market value (e.g. commercial vehicles, computers, plant and machinery).
Other tangible assets – e.g. specialist plant and machinery or buildings	Benchmark may not be available-valuation based on experience or negotiation.
Intangible fixed assets	Difficult to determine where no comparative market exists. For some intangibles such as brands sophisticated valuation techniques have been developed.

1. Where **an asset is being sold**, the expected sale proceeds (less direct selling costs) should equal a reliable estimate of NRV.

2. Where a **business is being sold** subject to a binding contract, the expected sale proceeds may reflect the NRV of the net assets and goodwill.

In determining net realisable value, **selling costs directly related** to the disposal of the asset (e.g. legal costs, commissions) or business should be deducted from the expected disposal proceeds. 1580

Costs or provisions associated with **reducing or reorganising the business**, including redundancy, prior to a sale are not deemed direct selling costs, and so should not be deducted in calculating net realisable value. Provisions for certain costs of re-organisation can be recognised as liabilities, if certain criteria in FRS 12 "Provisions, contingent liabilities and contingent assets" are met; namely, where a company has a constructive obligation to undertake the re-organisation. If the obligation does not exist at the time of the impairment review, no provision should be set aside.

Having determined NRV

Where the NRV has been determined, **one of three conditions** applies as illustrated in the table below. 1581

FRS 11 (15)

Estimated net realisable value Condition		Accounting treatment
1.	If the NRV is **higher** than the carrying amount of the asset.	The asset is not impaired and no further investigation is required.
2.	If the NRV is **lower** than the carrying amount of the asset.	Estimate the value in use to determine whether the it is higher or lower than NRV (see table conditions 2 & 3. ¶1584). If NRV **is below the carrying amount** of the asset it should not automatically be written down to this value. This is because, although some assets could only be sold for this lower amount, their value in use may be higher – so this should be calculated.
3.	No **reliable estimate** of NRV available.	The recoverable amount should be based on value in use except for specific tangible fixed assets (e.g. fixed asset investments).

EXAMPLE **Based on the conditions stated in the table above.**
Net realisable value

Condition 1 – NRV higher than carrying amount
Company X estimates the value of a tangible fixed asset to be £75,000 less direct selling costs of £5,000, resulting in estimated net sale proceeds (NRV) of £70,000. The carrying value of the asset is £60,000. As the NRV is higher than the carrying amount there is no impairment and no further action is required.

Condition 2 – NRV lower than carrying amount
If the carrying value of the tangible fixed asset were £80,000, so exceeding the NRV of £70,000 Company X would be required to calculate the value in use to determine whether this is higher of lower than NRV.

MEMO POINTS In determining whether the recoverable amount should be based on value in use, or net realisable value, the **deferred tax** that would arise on the potential disposal of each asset should also be considered. The topic of deferred tax is dealt with in greater detail in ¶9000.

B. Value in use

1582 Value in use **is calculated where**:
– it has not been possible to measure accurately the net realisable value of an asset or group of assets. As such the only means of determining the recoverable amount is by estimating its value in use; or
– the NRV is lower than the carrying value of asset. In this latter case, value in use will be taken as the recoverable amount where it is greater than the NRV.

FRS 11 (25) The **general rule** is that the value in use should be calculated for individual assets wherever possible. **Where this is not the case**, the value in use of an Income Generating Unit (IGU) will suffice.

In reality, it is **often difficult to calculate** the value in use of a single fixed asset as it is the use of groups of assets (and liabilities), together with associated goodwill that generate cash flows. As such, value in use is often determined in total for groups of assets or groups of IGU's, where only material impairments need identification.

1. Quick estimate of value in use (post-tax)

1584 The **carrying value** of each asset or IGU reviewed should be compared with the higher of its value in use or the NRV of the asset or IGU. The possible outcomes are set out in the table below.

It may be possible to dispense with the additional work involved in grossing up a post-tax rate to a pre-tax discount rate, by determining whether an asset is impaired at a post-tax level. Companies need only transfer to a **pre-tax analysis** if impairment is indicated and more detailed calculations are required, as shown by conditions 2 and 3 in the table below.

Estimated value in use Condition		Accounting treatment after determining value in use
1.	Where estimated value in use is higher than the carrying value.	No impairment has occurred and no further testing is required.
2.	If estimated value in use is lower than the carrying value but higher than NRV.	Impairment has occurred but the impairment charge will be based on the difference between carrying value and value in use.
3.	Where estimated value in use is lower than net realisable value.	Impairment is measured by reference to net realisable value, and not value in use.

EXAMPLE **Based on the conditions stated in the table above**
Value in use

Condition 1 If the value in use of a tangible fixed asset is £65,000 and the carrying value is £60,000 then no impairment has occurred.

Condition 2 If the value in use is £65,000, the carrying value £80,000 and the NRV of £60,000 then the impairment charge should be calculated with reference to the value in use and not the net realisable value (£80,000-£65,000 = £15,000).

2. Detailed calculation of value in use (pre-tax)

Where a **post-tax analysis indicates impairment** then a more detailed calculation of value in use is required, to determine the pre-tax discount rate (see ¶1638) and the pre-tax value in use of the asset or IGU, from which the impairment loss and related deferred tax effects can be calculated. **1586**

Where a detailed calculation of value in use **is required**, a **number of steps** should be followed as set out in the table below. This process is the same for individual assets or groups of assets. **1588**

	Determination of value in use and comparison with carrying value	Reference
1.	Identify the **individual assets or income generating units** (individual or group of assets) comprising net assets and allocated goodwill.	¶1590
2.	Estimate the expected **future cash flows** for an asset/IGU (including effects of taxation).	¶1614
3.	Determine the **pre-tax discount rate** and discount the **future cash flows** of an asset/ IGU to determine the value in use.	¶1638
4.	**Compare the value in use** of the discounted cash flows **with the carrying value** of the individual asset or net assets attributable to the IGU (comprising fixed assets and goodwill) and allocate any impairment.	¶1656

a. Identification of individual assets or IGU's

An income generating unit (IGU) **is generally defined** as a group of assets, liabilities and associated goodwill that generates income largely independent of the reporting entity's other income streams. An IGU could also represent a single asset such as a brand. **Examples include** major products or services. **1590** FRS 11 (30)

Assets tested individually Wherever possible, **assets should be tested individually** when there is an indication that impairment has arisen. In some cases however, impairment may **1591**

be tested only for **groups of assets** because the cash flows supporting the calculation do not arise from a single asset, but from groups of assets (and liabilities). In these instances, impairment is measured for the smallest group of assets deemed to produce an independent income streams; namely an IGU.

The **IGU's** will generally mirror the structure of the business and its products and services. Income-generating units **can be identified by** dividing the total income of the entity into as many independent income streams as reasonably practical and that are capable of separate measurement.

1592 **Level of aggregation** However, the higher the **level of aggregation** of assets and liabilities, the greater the risk that impairment losses on some assets may be obscured by increases in the value of other assets. However, it is possible to aggregate the IGU's for the purpose of calculating value in use, provided that the level of aggregation is reasonable in the circumstances of the impairment review.

MEMO POINTS Impairment of **fixed asset investments** such as subsidiaries, associates and joint ventures (¶7300) fall within the compass of FRS 11. As their respective cash flows can be measured individually, their value in use should be based on the future net cash flows of the underlying entities that are attributable to the group, rather than on dividend flows. In the case of **associates and joint ventures** the carrying value of the group's interest reflects two elements; namely the group's share of net assets and any purchased goodwill. Any impairments in the underlying fixed assets should have been accounted for in the financial statements of the associate or joint-venture.

Allocation of assets to income-generating units

1594 The assets (and liabilities) allocated to IGU's could include:
- those assets **directly involved** in generating the income:
- an appropriate proportion of those **central assets** used to generate more than one income stream; and
- **purchased goodwill** which if present, should also be apportioned across the IGU's.

The **form and content** of an income generating unit will vary from industry to industry, as illustrated in the following examples.

EXAMPLE **Types of income generating-units**

1. Bus company

A long-distance bus company operates a travel network comprising a number of **major routes fed by subsidiary routes**. Decisions about adding or closing any of the subsidiary or feeder routes, are based on the revenues generated by the contribution they make to the revenues derived from the trunk routes; the revenues are not considered in isolation. Each main route and associated subsidiary routes comprise an IGU as the cash flows generated by the major routes are not independent of the subsidiary routes.

2. Brewer-continuous production

A company produces different quantities of beer at a **number of different sites**, not all of which are used to full capacity. In this scenario there is not enough surplus capacity to enable one site to be closed. The cash flows generated by one site will be dependant on the allocation of production across the other breweries. The IGU will therefore, comprise all the sites at which the product can be made.

3. A chain of restaurants

A nationwide chain of restaurants with a large number of outlets can be separated into individual (and small) IGU's. The **cash inflows of each restaurant** can be monitored individually and a sensible allocation of central costs made to each restaurant. Any material impairment is only likely to occur when a number of restaurants within the chain are affected by the same economic factors. In this case it might be possible to group a number of restaurants together in one IGU, such as on a regional basis. However, individual restaurants can also be affected by local factors such as planning, in which case specific restaurants could be accounted for as independent IGU's.

4. Furniture manufacturer

An entity comprises **three stages of production** encompassing the growing and felling of trees, the production of furniture parts and their assembly into finished furniture goods. The output from the first stage is partly transferred to the production of semi-finished goods and partly sold on the

open market. The output from the production of semi-finished goods has no external market and is passed in its entirety to the production of semi-finished goods.
The first stage forms an IGU as its cash flows can be separately identified; namely sales to the open market and the transfer price to the second production stage. The second and third stages of production comprises one IGU as there is no external market for the production from the second stage.

Excluded assets and liabilities

All the assets and liabilities of the entity, should be allocated to the IGU's, **except for** the following: 1596
- deferred tax balances;
- interest-bearing debt;
- dividends payable;
- other items relating to financing; and
- disposal of a fixed asset.

In addition, where the **disposal of a fixed asset** is planned, the income stream from such an asset should be determined and excluded from the cash flows generated by the IGU. Where the asset is an independent IGU this does not represent a problem, but where the asset is part of a larger IGU, revenues and associated costs must be apportioned.

These assets and liabilities are excluded because the **related cash flows** are also excluded from the impairment calculation, but are taken into account when determining the appropriate discount rate used to discount future operational cash flows in calculating value in use.

The issue of impairment losses **on asset disposal** is considered in ¶1686.

Treatment of central assets in relation to IGU's

Central assets such as group or regional head offices, working capital, or computer and research centres, should be identified and apportioned across the IGU's in a logical and consistent manner, so that the total value of the IGU's is equal to the total carrying value of the net assets of the entity. Central assets are included in the IGU's because they are expected to generate sufficient cash flows to recover the carrying amounts of all the entity's assets. 1600

The **non-allocation** of central assets to IGU's, could result in impairment losses on some assets being obscured by other more profitable IGU's. This is because at a combined level there is no impairment of the central assets, as long as the combined assets in aggregate earn a market related return on the carrying values of all assets.

There are **two principal methods** of dealing with central assets, as illustrated in the following examples. However, each of these methods will probably result in different impairment calculations. The first example deals with a situation where central assets are allocated to IGU's and the second where they cannot be allocated on any meaningful basis. 1602

EXAMPLE **Method 1- Allocation of central overheads to income generating-units on the basis of net assets per IGU.**

An entity has three independent income streams X, Y and Z, with separable net assets of £100 million, £150 million and £200 million respectively. In addition head office net assets total £18 million. The relative proportion of the head office resources utilised by the income streams is 2.3.4, (based on net assets of 100: 150: 200) resulting in the apportionment of central overheads across the three units as illustrated.

Income-generating unit	**X**	**Y**	**Z**	**Total**
Net assets directly attributable to IGU (£m)	100	150	200	450
Head office net assets (£ million)	4	6	8	18
Total (£ million)	**104**	**156**	**208**	**468**

Impairment review If there was an indication that a fixed asset in IGU Z was impaired, the recoverable amount of Z should be compared with £208 million. The cash flow of Z should include the relevant proportion of any cash outflows resulting from its apportionment of £8 million in central overheads.

1604 The above example illustrates a basis of apportionment that might be appropriate. Central assets could also be apportioned across income-generating units using **other methods** such as number of staff employed in each IGU (service organisations) or turnover per IGU.

FRS 11 (32) Where it is **not possible to allocate** central assets accurately over the individual IGU's, then these assets should be excluded from the IGU's. However, entities are still required to conduct an impairment review on the **excluded central assets**. This is done by aggregating the total net assets of the IGU's to which the central assets contribute, which are then compared with the combined carrying amount of the combined value in use, as illustrated in the following example.

EXAMPLE **Method 2 – Exclusion of central assets from net assets of individual Income generating units.**

Based on the figures in the previous example, the recoverable amount of the income generating unit Z would be compared with £200 million and not £208 million. A **further impairment test** would then be required on the whole entity, in effect treating it as a single IGU, to compare the recoverable amount of £450 million with the total carrying value of £468 million, including central office overheads.

Apportionment of capitalised goodwill

1607 FRS 11 (34) Capitalised goodwill should be attributed to (or apportioned between) IGU's or groups of similar units. There is little guidance in FRS 10 and FRS 11 on how to allocate any purchased goodwill to different business units, except that impairment in goodwill in one business cannot be offset against an increase in value in another dissimilar business acquired subsequently.

Apportioning goodwill **is difficult in complex group structures**, especially where business are merged with existing operations or are restructured, as FRS 10 does not permit the division of purchased goodwill into positive and negative amounts and FRS 7 requires any impairment be reflected by reducing the fair values of assets on acquisition.

Group companies should keep detailed records of the composition of any purchased goodwill, in order that it can later be allocated (if required) to individual IGU's if required by an impairment review, and for:
- tracking elements of goodwill with different useful economic lives; and
- allocating goodwill to business units subsequently disposed of.

MEMO POINTS 1. **A number of methods** have been devised to apportion goodwill to different IGU's on acquisition, the choice of which should reflect the basis on which the business was valued by the market at the time of acquisition. **Earnings-based methods** are appropriate for businesses acquired for their future profit flows whilst asset based methods are more appropriate for asset-based acquisitions such as property companies. A detailed review of these methods is beyond the scope of this book.
2. **FRED 38 "Impairment of fixed assets"** proposes some changes to how goodwill is accounted for (see ¶1734).

1610 **Recoverability** Where IGU's are combined for the purpose of testing goodwill, a **two tier review process** is required similar to that used for central assets.

1. Impairment reviews for fixed assets require a **lower level of aggregation** at the level of the IGU to be tested for impairment. A lower level of aggregation means that fixed assets are reviewed at the level of individual IGU's.

2. A **higher level of aggregation** for goodwill is allowed, providing the combined IGU's were acquired as part of the same investment and constitute similar segments of the business. A higher level of aggregation refers to groups of IGU's summed together for the purpose of allocating goodwill.

The **process of recoverability** is as follows:

1. The IGU's are **first reviewed individually** for the purpose of assessing the recoverability of any capitalised intangible assets and tangible fixed assets, and any impairment identified is allocated to individual assets.

2. The **second stage** is that the combined IGU's are then reviewed to determine the recoverability of the goodwill. The review compares the carrying amounts of the net assets of the combined IGU's and the purchased goodwill of the combined IGU's with their combined value in use; any further impairment identified at this level is allocated to goodwill, as illustrated in the following example. FRS 11 (35)

EXAMPLE Allocation of goodwill at a higher level of aggregation

A group of companies acquired in a single transaction and which resulted in purchased goodwill that is to be amortised over a period exceeding 20 years, can for the purpose of the annual review required under FRS 10, be aggregated as one IGU. However, if there are reasons to believe that some or all of the assets have become impaired, then an impairment review will be required at the level of individual IGU's.

An entity acquires a business consisting of four IGU's: A, B, C and D. After 4 years, the carrying value of the net assets in the IGU's and the purchased goodwill compares with the value in use as follows:

Income-generating unit	**A**	**B**	**C**	**D**	**Goodwill**	**Total**
Carrying value (£m)	80	100	120	140	80	520
Value in use	**100**	**120**	**140**	**120**		**480**

There is an apparent impairment overall of £40m. An impairment loss of £20 million is recognised in respect of income-generating unit D, reducing its carrying value to £120 million. A further impairment loss of £20 million is recognised in respect of goodwill, which is reduced to £60 million. The total carrying value will be reduced from £520 million to £480 million.

An **alternative approach** to allocating goodwill to IGU's is also permitted as illustrated in the following example. 1611

EXAMPLE **Allocation of goodwill at a lower level of aggregation**

An entity acquires a business consisting of four IGU's A, B, C and D. After 4 years, the carrying value of the net assets in the IGU's and the purchased goodwill compares with the value in use as follows:

Income-generating unit	**A**	**B**	**C**	**D**	**Total**
Carrying value (£million)	80	100	120	140	440
Goodwill	23	23	24	10	80
	103	123	120	150	520
Value in use	**100**	**120**	**140**	**120**	**480**

There is an impairment of £40m. An impairment loss of £30 million is recognised in respect of income-generating unit D, reducing its carrying value to £120 million. A further impairment loss of £10 million is recognised in respect of goodwill, which is reduced to £70 million. The total carrying value will be reduced from £520 million to £480 million.

b. Estimating future cash flows (recoverable amount)

The expected future cash flows of an individual tangible fixed asset or IGU subject to an impairment review, including any allocation of central overheads, should be based on realistic assumptions encompassing the latest budgets or plans. 1614 FRS 11 (36)

There are a **number of constraints** applicable to initial cash flow forecasting for IGU's and **special rules** that apply to the forecasting of cash flows for newly acquired IGU's. The impact of taxation must also be taken into consideration.

Component cash flows

Where the **recoverable amount** of an asset is based on value in use, the asset will be impaired if it does not generate sufficient cash to recover its carrying value including where appropriate, its cost of capital. If interest rates rise, the asset will need to generate higher cash flows to cover financing costs, as such this could trigger a further impairment review. 1616

The cash flows used to estimate value in use **should include the following**:
- cash inflows from the asset or IGU;
- cash outlays directly attributable to the asset or IGU;
- allocation of any overheads attributable to central overheads;
- net cash inflows from disposal of the assets or IGU's subject to the impairment review; and
- cash outflows to maintain operating capacity of existing fixed assets.

Specific exclusions

1618 FRS 11 (38) Future cash flows **should only be estimated** for IGU's or individual fixed assets in their current condition and with the exception of newly acquired assets or IGU's, should not include:
a. cash outflows or related cost savings such as reducing the number of employees, or benefits that are expected to arise from a future reorganisation for which provision has not yet been made.
b. capital expenditure that will improve the IGU's or assets in excess of their planned or budgeted standard of performance or enhance the future benefits derived from this expenditure.

EXAMPLE **Capital expenditure included within (excluded from) the cash flow forecasts**

The assets comprising an IGU comprise a factory and plant and machinery. The factory is expected to last 50 years, but will need a new roof in 30 years, whilst the machinery needs to be replaced every 10 years. The company expects to be in a position to reduce unit costs of production by extending the factory in order to double production in two year's time.
The replacement expenditure for the 50 years (i.e. for the machinery and roof) should be included in cash flows, but neither the expenditure on factory expansion nor the additional income and revenue expenditure derived from that expansion should be included.

FRS 11 (20) Where a **fixed asset is not held** for the purpose of generating cash flows either by itself or collectively with other assets, such as assets held for charitable purposes, the use of expected future cash flows is not an appropriate forecasting method. Neither should the asset be written down to its recoverable amount; in this case an alternative measure of service potential may be more realistic.

Constraints on forecasting

1624 Forecasts of future cash flows used as a basis for determining value in use of a business are subjective by nature. In order to reduce the risk of over-optimistic forecasting being used to in order to disguise impairment losses and to ensure the reliability of cash flow forecasting, FRS 11 incorporates **two important controls**; namely:
- constraints on the level of **growth rates** used in forecasting; and
- the **requirement to monitor** the cash flow projections for five years following an impairment review.

1625 FRS 11 (37) **Growth rates** **a.** Longer-term cash flow projections should not assume a rate of growth that normally exceeds the **long-term average** growth rate for the country in which the entity operates.

b. Higher rates can be used in forecasts covering a shorter period, but only in **exceptional cases** can higher rates be used in forecasts exceeding five years, principally where:
- the long-term growth rate for the relevant industry (the industry growth rate) is expected to be higher than the average growth rate for the country; and
- the business concerned is expected to grow in line with projected industry growth, even allowing for the possibility of new entrants.

c. Where an industry growth rate for a **period exceeding five years** has been used, this fact should be disclosed in the notes to the accounts.

d. Furthermore, although the long-term average growth rates in specific industries may exceed the average growth rates for the country, **this does not mean** that all entities within an industry will grow at the same rate. Progressive industries often attract new entrants so reducing the opportunities for high growth rates for existing businesses.

e. The period before a **steady or declining** growth rate is used should not be longer than five years.

Subsequent monitoring The **second principal constraint** on estimates of future cash flow projections is the need to monitor the accuracy of cash flow forecasts, for the five years following an impairment review. 1626

Certain **specific issues** are required to be addressed where relevant.

Issue	Accounting treatment
1. Where the actual cash flows are found to be in line with estimates	– no further action is required.
2. Where cash flows are lower than estimated	– an additional impairment loss may need to be provided for in the current period's profit and loss account.
3. Where cash flows are higher than forecast	– a reversal of the original impairment (if recognised) could be permitted.
4. If the monitoring process identifies impairments that would have been recognised in previous years but which have since been reversed	– then the non-recognition of this impairment from a previous year must be disclosed, in order to deter management from building its forecasts on unrealistic assumptions.
5. Where any planned investments or reorganisation assumed at the time of acquisition do not materialise	– the cash flow projections should be revised and any associated benefits embedded in the forecast removed from forecasts used to support future impairment reviews.

Special rules for newly acquired IGU's In the case of a newly acquired IGU such as a subsidiary, the purchase price should reflect the synergies for making better use of the assets as a result of the acquisition. This may mean the purchaser reorganising the operations of the subsidiary or investing in capital equipment in order to obtain the benefits of the acquisition. 1627

Consequently, when assessing the future cash flows of the investment, any **planned reorganisation** or **capital expenditure costs** known at the time of the impairment reviews, (up to the end of the first full year after acquisition), may be accounted for in the first and subsequent impairment reviews, provided they are consistent with the budget formulated by the end of the first year of acquisition. FRS 11 (39)

Effects of taxation

The standard identifies **two situations** in an impairment review where taxation needs to be considered. 1628

1. **The first of these is** where value in use and net realisable are compared to determine which should be taken as the recoverable amount of a fixed asset or goodwill.

In this situation, the standard requires that the **deferred tax balances** that would arise on both the value in use and the net realisable value be calculated and then deducted from the gross amount. It is the net value arising in each case which should then be compared to determine which is the recoverable amount.

EXAMPLE **Impact of deferred taxation on recoverable amount of asset or AGUE.**

If the net realisable value of a AGUE is £110 and gives rise to a deferred tax liability of £45 and the value in use £100 and gives rise to a deferred tax liability of £30, then the recoverable amount should be based on value in use as follows:

	NRV	Value in use
	£	£
Asset value	110	100
Tax	(45)	(30)
Net	65	70

At first, NRV appears to be higher than Value in use (£110 v £100), but after the tax effects are taken into account, one can see that the recoverable amount should be based on Value in use (£70) and not NRV (£65).

2. The **second situation relates to** the cash flows used in order to arrive at the value in use of an IGU. The accounting standard requires that the discounted cash flows are pre-tax cash flows and the discount rate should be a pre-tax discount rate. Once the impairment process has been completed and, for example, any provisions for impairment losses made then the extant standards relating to tax should be applied to the resulting financial statements and thus the tax effects of the impairment, if any, will be taken into account.

c. Determining pre-tax discount rates

1638 The discount rate **is defined as** the **rate of interest** or **cost of capital** used in discounted cash flow appraisal calculations and is used to estimate:
- the time value of money;
- the effect of risk in the valuation of a stream of future cash flows; and
- reflects the rate of return an entity requires on its assets.

1639 The discount rate should be calculated on a **pre-tax basis**. The required pre-tax rate of return is that, which after tax has been deducted gives the required post-tax rate of return.
1. The **pre-tax rate is estimated by** grossing-up the post tax discount rate to reflect the effective rate of corporation tax levied on the operating profits of the particular asset or IGU.
2. The estimated pre-tax rate should then be **adjusted to allow for any special factors** that might distort the relationship between the post-tax and pre-tax discount rate, such as the timing of cash flows due to accelerated capital allowances.
3. The estimated **pre-tax cash flows** expected from the asset or IGU **are then discounted** by the estimated pre-tax discount rate, to give an estimated value in use, which should then be compared with the carrying value.
4. Where the impairment loss is estimated on a pre-tax basis, the **deferred tax effect** can be calculated by applying the current tax rate to the impairment loss.

1640 The pre-tax rate can be derived from the post-tax rate and the post-tax cash flows as illustrated in the following example.

EXAMPLE **Calculation of pre-tax rate of return and value in use**

An asset is required to generate a post-tax return of 14%. Therefore, if the asset cost £100, it would be expected to generate post-tax cash flows of £114. The tax rate is 30%.

	£
Pre-tax cash flows	114
"tax value" of capital allowances	30
net post tax cash flows	84

This £84 is then grossed up to determine the pre-tax cash flows that would be required to leave post tax cash flows of 114.
Therefore £84 × £100/£70 = £120
The **required pre-tax cash flows** would be £120, and the pre tax rate of return would be 20%.
Assuming pre tax cash flows of £120 and post tax cash flows of £114 the value in use assigned to the asset would be £100, irrespective of whether it was calculated by discounting the pre-tax cash flows of £120 by:
1. The pre-tax cash required discount rate (20 %); or
2. By discounting post-tax cash flows of £114 by the post-tax required rate of return of 14%.
It should be noted that in this example it has been assumed that the cost of the asset is fully deductible for tax purposes, due to the capital allowances of 100% that are available and, therefore, there are no deferred tax considerations. There is therefore a £30 "tax credit" in effect in respect of these capital allowances which is taken into account in determining the pre-tax cash flow required.

The **relationship between** the post-tax rate and pre-tax rate is more complicated when multi-period cash flows are considered, causing timing differences between pre-tax cash flows and related tax cash flows.

Discount rate adjusted for risk

The discount rate should be adjusted to reflect specific risks associated with the entity or industry in which it operates. The purpose is to calculate the value in use of a tangible fixed asset or IGU, by discounting the cash flows derived from their use, at the rate of return the market would expect from a similar asset. 1644 FRS 11 (Appendix I)

The **market rate** can be estimated based on the following **three options**: 1645 FRS 11 (42)

1. The weighted average cost of capital (WACC) for the entity adjusted for the specific risks associated with the IGU;
2. The current WACC of a listed company whose cash flows are of a similar risk profile to those of the IGU; or
3. The market rate used in transactions of similar assets.

Whichever method of determining the market rate is adopted it must be disclosed in the notes to the accounts.

Where the **first option** is selected, the following conditions are of note: 1646

1. Where the cash flow forecasts assume a growth rate that exceeds the long-term average growth rate for more than five years, the discount rate should be increased to reflect the higher level of risk.
2. The discount rates applied to individual IGUs should, when aggregated, equal the entity's overall WACC.

The **second option** is restricted in use as there will be few listed companies that offer a useful comparison, because they generally have a wider product or service base, larger markets and, potentially, a lower risk profile. The **third option** is seldom used due to the unique nature of these types of transactions.

Problems using a pre-tax discount rate based on WACC The problem is how to calculate a pre-tax rate from a post-tax starting point. 1648

Adjusting a post-tax rate to a pre-tax rate involves consideration of a **number of issues** as follows.

1. When basing the discount rate on the WACC, and **where the company has only one IGU**, then the WACC for the company can be used.
2. Where the **company comprises many IGU's**, the discount rate for any one IGU will be higher or lower depending on the relative difference in risk elements within that IGU as compared to other IGU's, such as durability, liquidity, asset versatility etc. For instance, a higher rate of risk will apply to intangible assets.
3. The **weighted average discount rates** for all IGU's should equal the overall WACC for the entity.

Impact of taxation in the determination of the discount rate The **tax consequences** of different cash flows vary and as such the pre-tax rate of return is not always the post-tax rate of return grossed up by the standard rate of tax. However, it might be possible to avoid the complexity involved in grossing-up to pre-tax rates, except where impairment is indicated. 1650

In the absence of impairment, the **pre-tax method** produces the same value in use as the post-tax method, because no deferred tax balances arise from the carrying value established on a pre-tax basis.

When an **asset becomes impaired**, the relationship between pre-tax and post-tax rates of return changes, because as future pre-tax cash flows are impaired or reduced, the associated tax relief may not. This problem is overcome by providing for deferred tax on any timing differences created by recognition of the impairment loss, and not by making any adjustment to the pre-tax discount rate.

FRS 11 (Appendix I)

EXAMPLE **Recognition of a deferred tax asset**

Following on from the first example, were £100 was paid for an asset expected to generate pre-tax cash flows of £120. Circumstances changed and the expected pre-tax cash flows were deemed to be impaired and downgraded to £60.

	£	£
Pre-tax cash flows		**60**
Tax at 30% of £60	(18)	
Allowance for cost of asset (£100 at 30%)	30	
		12
		72

The pre-tax cash flows have halved to £60 but the post-tax cash flows have not been reduced as much. Therefore, discounting the pre-tax cash flows of £60 by 20 per cent (value £50) does not produce the same value for the asset as would the result of discounting the post-tax cash flows of £72 by 14% (value of £63).

The difference is not eliminated by making adjustments to the pre-tax rate of return, but by providing for deferred tax on the timing difference created by the recognition of the impairment loss:

	£
Impaired carrying value of the asset (£60 discounted by 20%)	50
Deferred tax asset – impairment of £50 at 30%, discounted by 14%	13
Total amount recognised in respect of the asset	63

Cash flows adjusted for risk

1654 As **an alternative** to using the market rate, the cash flows can be adjusted for risk and then discounted at a risk-free discount rate. Where a risk-free discount rate is used, an indication of the risk adjustments made to the cash flows should be disclosed in the financial statements along with details of the **underlying assumptions** on which they were based.

The discount rate should exclude the effect of any risks for which the cash flows have already been adjusted.

---

d. Discounting future cash flows to determine value in use

1656 FRS 11 (41) After a stream of future cash flows has been calculated for an individual asset or group of assets, they must be discounted at the agreed pre-tax discount rate, in order to determine the value in use as illustrated in the following example. The value in use is then compared with the carrying value to assess the extent (if any) of the impairment.

EXAMPLE **Discounting future cash flows to determine the value in use.**

XYZ Ltd. comprises two IGU's for which the cash flow projections for the next six years have been made. The cash flows have been discounted as follows: The **discount rate** is assumed to be 10% for IGU 1 and 12% for IGU 2.

The **net realisable value** of the assets of IGU 1 and IGU 2 are £5 million and £7 million respectively.

The **discounted cash flows** are then totalled to determine the present value in use (i.e. £3,940.5 for IGU 1 and £9,359.7 for IGU 2). These figures are then compared with the carrying value in order to determine whether the IGU has suffered impairment.

The **carrying value** of IGU 1 and 2 is £6m and £8.5m respectively.

	IGU 1 Cash flows: £000	Discount Rate 10%	**Present value £000**	IGU 2 Cash flows: £000	Discount Rate 12%	**Present value £000**
Year 1	800	0.909	**727.2**	2,000	0.893	**1,736.0**
Year 2	600	0.826	**495.6**	2,200	0.797	**1,753.4**
Year 3	900	0.751	**675.9**	2,700	0.712	**1,922.4**
Year 4	1000	0.683	**683.0**	2,400	0.636	**1,526.4**
Year 5	1100	0.620	**682.0**	1,500	0.567	**850.5**
Year 6	1200	0.564	**676.8**	3,000	0.507	**1,521.0**
Value in use			3,940.5			9,359.7
NRV			5,000.0			7,000.0
Recoverable amount [greater of Value in use and NRV]			**5,000.0**			**9,359.7**

In **IGU 1**, the value in use of £3,940.5m is less than the NRV, so **recoverable amount** is based on NRV of £5m. The carrying value of the IGU is £6m so the impairment loss is £1m.
In IGU 2, the recoverable amount of £9,3597m based on value in use exceeds the NRV of £7m. The recoverable amount of £9,3597m exceeds the carrying amount of £8.5m so there is **no impairment loss**. The entity may be able under the alternative accounting rules and FRS 15 to revalue the asset to reflect the higher value in use.

SECTION 3

Treatment of impairment losses

The **general rule** is that where an impairment loss on a fixed asset or goodwill is recognised, for instance through physical damage or deterioration in the quality of service provided, the remaining useful economic life and residual value should also be reviewed and where appropriate revised. The new carrying amount should be depreciated over the revised estimate of the asset's useful economic life. **1670** FRS 11 (21)

Where a fixed asset or IGU is impaired it will always be the case that both the value in use and the NRV will be below carrying value. Although this does not mean that a loss is permanent, it is prudent in relation to fixed assets held at depreciated historical cost, that this be regarded as permanent and charged to the profit and loss account. FRS 11 (Appendix II)

Particular care should be taken regarding impairment relating to acquisitions, mergers, asset disposals and revaluations. The reversal of impairment losses also requires special consideration.

General rules

A number of general rules apply as detailed below. **1674** FRS 11 (49)

a. A tangible asset with a net realisable value that can be **measured reliably** should not be written down below this value.

b. The **carrying amount** of an IGU that is reviewed for impairment should be calculated as the net of the carrying amounts of the assets, liabilities and goodwill allocated to the unit.

c. The **IGU is impaired where** the carrying amount of the IGU exceeds its recoverable amount, and the extent of the impairment reflects this difference in value.

i. Where there is **obvious impairment of specific assets** then the impairment loss should be allocated against these assets first. (Part A of Table below).

ii. Where there is **no impairment of specific assets** then the aim in allocating an impairment loss, is to write down the assets with the most subjective valuation first. (Part B of Table below).

Allocation of impairment losses within an income generating unit	
A) Obvious impairment of specific assets	**B) No obvious impairment of specific assets**
	(Most subjective valuations first)
The impairment should be **initially allocated to** the specific assets in the IGU, and thereafter: – to any capitalised goodwill asset within the IGU; and – thereafter to any tangible assets in the IGU on a pro-rata basis.	The impairment should be allocated initially to any goodwill in the unit, and thereafter on a pro-rata basis to: – any intangible asset within the IGU; and – any tangible assets in the IGU on a pro-rata basis.
This process is illustrated in scenario 1 below.	This process is illustrated in scenario 2 below.

EXAMPLE **Scenario 1**

Impairment of specific assets

Comparison of value in use to carrying value

An impairment loss of £60 million has been identified and allocated first against specific tangible fixed assets in IGU B, where total carrying value exceeds value in use. The remaining £50 million has been allocated against capitalised goodwill of £40 million with the balance (£10m) allocated against head office assets.

Income-generating unit:	**A**	**B**		**Unallocated central assets and cash flows**		**Sub Total**	**Impairment**	**Total**
Carrying values:								
Direct net assets	£100m	£150m	(i)			£250m	(£10m)	£240m
Goodwill				£90m	(ii)	£90m	(£40m)	£50m
Head office assets				£40m	(iii)	£40m	(£10m)	£30m
Total carrying value	**£100m**	**£150m**		**£130m**		**£380**	**(£60m)**	**£320m**
Value in use	**£200m**	**£140m**						

Summary

A total **impairment of £60 million** (£10m direct assets, £10m head office assets and £40 goodwill) has been identified is allocated as follows:

1. IGU A. No action required as value in use exceeds carrying value.
2. IGU B plus central assets and overheads:

i) £10 million apportioned against specific assets in IGU B; assuming no intangibles carried.
ii) £40 million is allocated to capitalised goodwill.
iii) £10 million is allocated to head office assets.

If head office assets were carried at NRV, then the £10 million would be allocated between assets in the IGU's on a pro-rata basis

Scenario 2

No obvious impairment of specific assets – allocate to assets whose recoverable amount is most subjective first.

Calculation of an impairment loss and subsequent allocation

In this example the comparison of carrying value with recoverable amount means that **IGU 1** has suffered no impairment.

In the case of **IGU 2** there is an impairment of £6,140.3 allocated between the different asset categories as illustrated below.

The **carrying value** of the assets in IGU 1 and IGU 2 are as follows:

	IGU 1 £'000	**IGU 2 £'000**
Goodwill	–	2,100
Trademarks	1,000	400
Tangible fixed assets	1,600	10,700
Stocks	2,200	2,300
Carrying amount	**4,800**	**15,500.0**
Recoverable amount	5,000	9,359.7
Lower of carrying value and recoverable amount	4,800	9,359.7
Impairment loss	**0**	**6,140.3**

Allocation of the impairment loss – IGU 2

		Impairment loss	Recoverable amount
Goodwill		2,100.0	0
Trademarks		400.0	0
Tangible fixed assets	(1)	2,996.2	7,703.8 (3)
Stocks	(2)	644.1	1,655.9 (4)
Total		**6,140.3**	**9,359.7**

Notes

(1) Tangible fixed assets – impairment: £6,140.3 – £2,500 (£2,100 + £400: goodwill + trademarks) = £3,640.3 × (£10,700/£13,000 = tangible fixed assets + stocks)) = £2,996.2
(2) Stocks – impairment £3,640.3 × (£2,300/ £13,000) = £644.1
(3) Tangible fixed assets revised carrying value – £10,700/£13,000 x £9,359.7 = £7,703.8
(4) Stocks revised carrying value – £2,300/£13,000 × £9,359.7 = £1,655.9

a. Allocation of impairment when acquired businesses are merged with existing operations

There are **specific requirements** regarding the measurement of an impairment arising after a purchased business has been merged with existing operations. 1680

1. A single IGU that results from the merger of an acquired operation with an existing operation includes assets and liabilities of both acquired and existing business, will also combine both purchased and internally generated goodwill arising from previous operations.
2. If an impairment review of the combined IGU is later required, its value in use will be compared with the carrying value. The value in use of the IGU will comprise:
- carrying values of the recognised net assets of the acquired and existing businesses; and
- the carrying value of the purchased goodwill relating to the acquired business.

Notional carrying amount

Any future impairment of the combined business will need to be apportioned between the purchased and internally generated goodwill, by notionally adjusting the carrying amount of the IGU, to take account of the internally generated goodwill of the existing operation at the date the businesses are merged. 1682 FRS 11 (51)

Even **where an impairment review is not required** at the point of the "merging" of the two elements of the business the distinction should still be drawn between internal and purchased goodwill, in order to provide an accurate basis for any future impairment reviews that might be required.

Notional carrying value of a combined IGU.		
	Net Assets	**Goodwill**
Acquisition	Fair value	Purchased
Existing businesses	Carrying value	Internally generated Purchased (i.e. earlier acquisitions) Purchased (previously written-off to reserves under FRS 10 transition rules).

Notional value of internally generated goodwill 1. The notional carrying amount of the internally generated goodwill is first estimated, by deducting the fair value of the net assets and purchased goodwill within the existing IGU, from its estimated value in use before the businesses are combined. 1683 FRS 11 (52)

2. The notional value of internally generated goodwill of the existing business is added to the carrying amount of the newly combined IGU for the purpose of performing an impairment review on that combined IGU. The notional goodwill is assumed to be depreciated on the same basis as purchased goodwill, even though it is not recognised in the financial statements.

Recognition of impairment

At the date an acquired businesses is merged with an existing business, and the **aggregate carrying value** of the net assets and goodwill, (including the notional internally generated 1684 FRS 11 (50)

goodwill) exceeds the **recoverable amount** of the IGU, the resulting impairment should recognised as follows:
a. Any impairment should **first be allocated** entirely to the purchased goodwill within the newly acquired business and recognised in the consolidated profit and loss account. The logic for this is that any impairment relating to notional internally generated goodwill will have been identified when the fair value exercise was undertaken on acquisition. Therefore, any further impairment identified must relate to the purchased goodwill of the acquired business.
b. Subsequent impairments should be allocated pro-rata reflecting the current carrying values, between the goodwill of the acquired business and the existing business;

1. the impairment allocated to the existing business should be first apportioned to the internally generated goodwill; and

2. only the impairments allocated to purchased goodwill (or recognised intangible or tangible assets) should be recognised in the profit and loss account.

FRS 11 (53)

EXAMPLE **Where an acquired operation is merged with existing operations – allocation of impairment losses**

Initial allocation
1. An entity acquires a business for £60 million with net assets with a total fair value of £80 million, resulting in **purchased goodwill** of £20 million. The acquired business is merged with an existing operation that has net assets with a fair value of £100 million and a carrying amount of £70 million. Purchased goodwill is amortised over ten years.
The **value in use** of the existing operation at the time of the acquisition is £150 million, resulting in internally generated goodwill of £50 million. The comparison with the value in use may have resulted in the recognition of any impairment of the existing business at the time it was merged with the acquired operation.

2. **Subsequent impairments** must be attributed between the internal goodwill and the purchased goodwill on a pro-rata basis reflecting their current carrying values.

3. **After five years**
The carrying amount of the net assets of the combined IGU is £105 million and the carrying amount of the purchased goodwill is £10 million. Value in use is calculated at £119 million. There is no reliable estimate of net realisable value.

4. **Calculation of the impairment loss**	**£m**
Carrying amount of acquired assets	105
Carrying amount of goodwill	10
Notional carrying amount of the internally Generated goodwill at acquisition date – calculated on same basis as purchased goodwill.	25
i.e. The purchased goodwill has been amortised by 50% therefore for the purposes of the impairment review so too should the notional internally generated goodwill identified at the date of the merger.	
Total	**140**
Value in use	119
Impairment	21

Accounting treatment
Scenario A) The impairment of £21 million should be **allocated** on a pro-rata basis as follows:
– purchased goodwill £10 million (10/25 = 2/7) = £6m
– internally generated goodwill £25 million (25/35 = 5/7) = £15m
Purchased goodwill should be written down to £4 million (£10m – £6m).
(£21m x 2/7 = £4m).
Internally generated goodwill should notionally be "written down" to £10 million (25m –£15m) (£21m x 5/7).

But as the internally generated goodwill is not recognised in the financial statements this aspect of the impairment is entirely notional and does not impact upon those financial statements.

Scenario B) If the **value in use** were calculated at £98 million, the resulting impairment loss of £42 million would be allocated as follows:
- first against purchased goodwill and notional internally generated goodwill) £35 million,
- then to any intangible assets,
- then any tangible fixed assets in the IGU.

The resulting impairment loss of £42 million (£140m – £98m) should be recognised as follows:
- a write down of purchased goodwill of £10 million.
- a notional write down of internally generated goodwill of £25 million.
- a write down of intangible and tangible assets of £7 million.

b. Disposal of assets

Where an asset is to be disposed of it should be regarded as an IGU in its own right and not part of any other IGU. The **estimated disposal proceeds** should be factored into the calculation of its recoverable amount as opposed to using cash flows from continued use. If the carrying amount of the asset for sale exceeds the recoverable amount, the asset is impaired. Impairment losses arising on the intended disposal of an asset should be recognised as soon as a decision to dispose of an asset has been taken. **1686** FRS 11 (31)

MEMO POINTS FRS 12 "Provisions and liabilities" forbids the recognition of provisions for liabilities in respect of the sale of a business or disposal of an asset, unless:
- there is binding contract for sale; or
- a constructive obligation to transfer resources has been incurred.

EXAMPLE **Disposal of a group of assets**

XYZ Ltd. intends to dispose of a group of assets whose recoverable amount of £95,000 is below their carrying values of £140,000. The recoverable amount of £95,00 is the value in use to the group. This results in an estimated loss of £45,000 which should be taken to the current period profit and loss account.

c. Revalued fixed assets

Impairment **losses arise on revalued fixed assets** when the asset's recoverable amount falls below its carrying amount. **1690** FRS 11 (63)

The **general rules** are as follows:

1. An impairment loss on a revalued fixed asset should be recognised in the profit and loss account where it is caused by a **clear consumption of economic benefits**, such as physical damage or a decline in the quality of service provided by the asset.
2. Other impairments of revalued fixed assets **caused by a general fall in market prices** should be recognised in the STRGL until the carrying amount reaches its depreciated historical cost, and thereafter in the profit and loss account.
3. Where an **impairment loss has been recognised** it is important that detailed records are kept, in order that any reversal (see ¶1694) of an impairment loss can be substantiated and recognised in later years.
4. Where **assets are revalued upwards**, the historic cost is adjusted to reflect the revalued amount.

The accounting treatment for any **impairment in subsequent years** is illustrated in the following example.

EXAMPLE **Impairment loss on a revalued fixed asset – accounting treatment**

A **fixed asset** costs £3 million and has a useful economic life of 10 years with no residual value. It is depreciated on a straight-line basis and **revalued annually**. At the end of years 1 and 2 the asset is revalued and has a market value of £3.6 million and £2.1 million respectively. The historical costs are shown for comparison.

	Historical cost £	Revaluation £
Year 1		
Opening carrying value	3,000,000	3,000,000
Depreciation	(300,000)	(300,000)
Revaluation surplus		900,000
Closing carrying value	**2,700,000**	**3,600,000**
Year 2		
Opening carrying value	2,700,000	3,600,000
Depreciation	(300,000)	(400,000)
Impairment loss		(1,100,000)
Closing carrying value	**2,400,000**	**2,100,000**

Depreciation on historical cost is calculated £3.6m/10 years = £300,000 per annum. After revaluation the new carrying value of £3,600,000 is depreciated over its remaining useful economic life of nine years.

The resulting impairment loss of £1.1 million should be recognised in year 2. The accounting treatment will depend on the reason the impairment arose.

a. If the impairment was due to the consumption of economic benefits, such as physical damage, then the loss of £1.1 million should be charged to the profit and loss account.

b. In other circumstances the carrying amount based on the revaluation policy immediately before impairment, needs to be compared with what the depreciated historical cost would have been immediately before impairment:

	£	
Carrying amount based on revaluation	3,200,000	(£3.6m-£400,000)
Depreciated historical cost	(2,400,000)	(£2.7m- £300,000)
Total	800,000	

£800,000 of the impairment can be deducted from the **revaluation reserve**, leaving £300,000 (Impairment loss of £1.1 million – £800,000) to be charged to the profit and loss account. £300,000 equals the loss where the asset to be carried at historical cost.

d. Reversal of impairment losses

1694 FRS 11 contains different rules covering the recognition and reversal of an impairment loss for tangible fixed assets and investments, and for intangible assets and goodwill.

Tangible fixed assets and investments

1696 The reversal of past impairment losses can be recognised, when the recoverable amount of a tangible fixed asset (or investment in a subsidiary, an associate or joint-venture) has increased because of a change in economic conditions or in the expected use of the asset. This will normally be the reverse of the economic conditions that triggered the original impairment.

General rules	
1. A **reversal** of an impairment loss should be recognised in the profit and loss account	**– to the extent that** it increases the carrying amount of the asset up to the amount at which it would currently be carried, had the original impairment not been recognised. This is after taking into account the annual depreciation charges that would have arisen between the date of the impairment and the date of the reversal.
2. Any **balance remaining** of the reversal of impairment	– should be recognised in the Statement of Total Recognised Gains and Losses (STRGL).

General rules	
3. Provisions for **diminutions in value**	– must be written back if the reasons for the impairment provision cease to apply. There may be practical problems in applying these rules as it may be difficult to distinguish between increases in the value of a fixed asset or IGU, because the reasons for the impairment no longer apply or as a result of increases in value through other reasons.
4. The **reason** an impairment loss has been recognised	– should be disclosed in the accounts (see Table B ¶1710).

Exceptions The **general rules** outlined above **do not apply to the following**: 1700
a. Where the asset was previously revalued in which case the reversal should be accounted for as stated in ¶1690.
b. The recognition of an increase in the recoverable amount of a tangible fixed asset, above the amount that its carrying amount would have been had the original impairment not occurred, is a revaluation and not a reversal of an impairment.
c. Increases in value in use should not be recognised as reversals of impairment losses if they: FRS 11 (58)
i. reflect the passage of time (increases in the discounted value of future cash flows as they become closer) rate; or
ii. the occurrence of forecast cash outflows which once they have happened no longer form part of the value in use calculation and as a result, the value in use increases.

In such cases, the increases in value should be treated as revaluation surpluses and taken to the revaluation reserve.

Intangible assets and goodwill

The accounting treatment under FRS 11 regarding intangible fixed assets; is consistent with principles laid down in FRS 10 "Goodwill and intangible assets"; namely that the revaluation of goodwill is prohibited, but that the revaluation of intangible assets is permitted in certain circumstances. Increases in the value of internally generated intangible assets should not be recognised. 1704

The **general principle** is that the reversal of an impairment loss relating to goodwill or intangible assets, resulting in an increase in the recoverable amount, should be recognised in the current period only if: 1705 FRS 11 (60)
a. An **external event** caused the recognition of the impairment loss in previous periods, and subsequent events clearly reverse the effects of the original event, in a way that was not foreseen in the original impairment forecast (as with tangible fixed assets); or
b. The impairment loss arose on an intangible asset with a readily ascertainable market value and net realisable value based on that **market value**, has increased above the assets impaired carrying amount.

Where an impairment loss (recognised) has been reversed, the carrying amount of the asset should be increased up to the pre-impairment level (after adjusting for depreciation), and an increase recognised in excess of this level is regarded as a revaluation and may not be recognised unless it satisfies the conditions set out in FRS 10.

EXAMPLE **Impairment losses – allocation and subsequent reversal**

An IGU consisting of a factory, plant and equipment and purchased goodwill becomes impaired, because the products it manufactures have become outdated compared with a competitors product.
The recoverable amount of the IGU falls to £60 million, with an impairment loss of £80 million recognised, but not attributable to identifiable tangible fixed assets.

	Carrying amounts Before impairment £m	Impairment £m	Carrying amounts after impairment £m
Goodwill	40	(40)	-
Patent – no market value	20	(20)	-
Tangible fixed assets	80	(20)	60
Total	140	(80)	60

The impairment loss is first allocated to goodwill (£40m), then other intangibles (£20m) with the balance of £20m set against tangible fixed assets.
After four years the entity makes its own technological breakthrough and the recoverable amount of the IGU increases to £90 million. The carrying amount of the tangible fixed assets had the impairment not occurred would have been £70 million (£80m – £10m depreciation charge).

Reversal of impairment and allocation
1. The impairment loss is reversed to the extent that the carrying amount of the tangible fixed asset is increased to the **pre-impairment value**, i.e. a reversal of £10 million of the original impairment loss of £20 million is recognised (the other £10 million represents depreciation) and the tangible fixed assets written back to £70 million which is what their carrying value would have been had their not been an impairment recognised in the first place.
2. Reversal of the impairment is not recognised **in respect of** the goodwill and patent, because the event causing the reversal was not reversed; the original product has still been overtaken by a superior model and the original goodwill and patent is still therefore impaired. As such £20m of the £30m revaluation is not recognised.

SECTION 4

Disclosures

1710 FRS 11 (67) Impairment losses recognised in the profit and loss account should be included within operating profit under the appropriate statutory heading and disclosed as an **exceptional item** if appropriate. Impairment losses recognised in the STRGL must be disclosed separately on the face on that statement.

FRS 11 (68)

Table A Presentation and disclosures for impairment losses arising on revalued fixed assets	
1. Assets carried on a **historical cost basis.**	Impairment loss included within cumulative depreciation. The cost of the asset should not be reduced.
2. Revalued assets held at **market value** (e.g. existing use or open market value).	Impairment loss included within the revalued carrying amount.
3. Revalued assets held at **depreciated replacement cost**.	**a.** Impairment loss charged to **profit and loss account** should be included within cumulative depreciation. The carrying amount of the asset should not be reduced. **b.** An impairment loss charged to the **STRGL** should be deducted from the carrying amount of the asset.

FRS 11 (69)

Table B	Additional disclosures concerning impairment losses
Discount rate	Where the impairment loss is measured with reference to the **value in use** of a fixed asset or IGU, then the discount rate applied to the cash flows should be disclosed. If a risk-free discount rate is used a note of the adjustments made to the risk profile of the cash flows should be given.
Value in use-measurement	Where the period before a steady or declining long-term growth rate has been assumed, extends to more than five years, the longer period adopted and the reasons justifying it should be given.

Table B	Additional disclosures concerning impairment losses
Recognition in previous period	Where an impairment loss would have been recognised in a previous period if the forecasts of future cash flows had been more accurate, but the impairment has reversed and recognition of the reversal is permitted, the impairment loss now identified and its subsequent reversal should be disclosed.
Reversal of impairment loss	Where an impairment loss recognised in a previous period is reversed in the current financial period, then the reasons for so doing should be disclosed, including the revised assumptions upon which the new calculation of recoverable amount is based.
Forecasting	Where the **long-term growth rate** used in the measurement of value in use exceeds the long-term average growth rate for the country or countries in which the entity operates, disclosure is required of the assumed growth rates and the reasons for their selection.

The ASB has amended FRS11 "Impairment of Fixed Assets and Goodwill" by strengthening the disclosure requirements to bring it more into line with IAS 36 "Impairment of Assets". Where an impairment loss is measured by discounting cash flows, in order to estimate the value in use or net realisable value of a fixed asset or income generating unit (IGU), the following disclosures are required: **1711**
- the discount rate applied to the cash flows;
- an indication of any risk adjustments made to cash flow forecasts;
- the period covered by the projections; and
- the growth rate used.

SECTION 5

Comparison between UK GAAP and IAS (IFRS)

IAS 36 "Impairment of assets" covers the recognition, measurement and disclosure of impaired assets, including capitalised goodwill. IAS 36 **applies to all assets** (including investments in subsidiaries, joint-ventures and associates), except assets covered by other standards such as inventories, investment properties and financial assets. **1714**

The **basic approach** taken in IAS 36 is similar to that adopted in FRS 11, namely that impairment is measured by comparing the carrying value of fixed assets and goodwill with the higher of net selling price (net realisable value) and value in use. Value in use is calculated by discounting the cash flows expected to be generated by the assets. **1715**

However, FRS 11 embodies **some restrictions not present in IAS 36**, particularly concerning the requirement for "look-back tests" and the calculation of notional internally generated goodwill. Furthermore, the terminology in IAS 36 is different to FRS 11, referring to cash-generating units rather than income generating units.

IAS 36 was revised as part of the IASB's project on **business combinations** (see ¶6800), designed to promote international convergence on accounting for business combinations and the subsequent accounting treatment of goodwill and intangible assets.

There are no **specific transitional rules** in IFRS 1 relating to the revised version of IAS 36.

1. IAS 36

The intention of the IASB in revising IAS 36 was to incorporate only those changes relating to the project on Business Combinations and not to reconsider all aspects of the existing standard. **1718**

Annual impairment testing

1720 IAS 36 (IN5) The revised version of IAS 36 requires an annual impairment test **to determine**:
– the recoverable amount of an intangible asset with an indefinite useful economic life, irrespective of whether there is an indication of impairment;
– the recoverable amount of an intangible asset not yet in use, irrespective of any indication of impairment; and
– any goodwill acquired as part of a business combination.

Measuring value in use

1722 IAS 36 (IN6) IAS 36 requires that the **following elements** be considered when calculating the value in use of intangible assets:
– an estimate of the future cash flows the asset is expected to generate for the entity;
– the time value of money, representing the current market risk-free interest rate;
– expectations concerning possible fluctuations in the timing of future cash flows;
– the price reflecting the uncertainty inherent in holding the intangible asset; and
– other factors such as poor liquidity, should be priced into the future expected cash flows.

IAS 36 (IN8) The **cash flow projections** used to calculate value in use must be based on reasonable assumptions, representing the best estimates (by management) of the economic conditions expected to exist over the useful economic life of the asset. Furthermore, it is expected that management should review the reasonableness of the assumptions on which the future cash flow forecasts are made.

Care must be taken to **exclude the following cash flows** from the projections:
– cash flows expected to arise from future restructuring to which the entity is not committed; or
– cash flows arising from improvements in the assets performance.

Identifying the cash generating units (CGU)

1724 IAS 36 (IN10) The **principle** is that where an active market exists for the output produced by an asset or group of assets, then the asset or asset grouping should be identified as a cash-generating unit, even where some of the input is used internally. This requirement is carried forward from the previous standard

Where any cash flows generated by an asset or cash generating unit are affected by **internal transfer pricing**, the entity should adopt the best estimates by management of future prices achievable in arm's length transactions when estimating:
– future cash inflows used to calculate the value in use of an asset or CGU; and
– future cash outflows used to calculate the value in use of other assets or IGU's affected by internal transfer pricing.

MEMO POINTS An amendment to IAS 36 clarifies that a cash generating unit should represent the lowest level within an organisation, at which goodwill is monitored for internal management purposes; namely at the level before the aggregation of similar operating segments. It is expected that this amendment will result in an increase in the number of impairment losses recorded.

Allocating goodwill to CGU's

1726 IAS 36 (IN12) Under the previous version of IAS 36, goodwill acquired as part of a business combination had to be tested for impairment, as part of the CGU to which it related. **This requirement has been incorporated** into the new standard with the **following caveats**:
1. The goodwill should be allocated, at the acquisition date, to each of the acquirer's CGU's (or group of CGU's), expected to benefit from the synergies of the business combination.
2. **Each CGU (or group of CGU's)** to which the goodwill is allocated should:
– equal the lowest level within the entity at which goodwill is monitored by the management; and
– be no larger than a reporting segment determined in accordance with IAS 14 "Segmental Reporting".

3. If an **entity reorganises its reporting structure** and in so doing changes the composition of any CGU's to which goodwill has been allocated, the goodwill should be reallocated to the units affected.
4. The **initial allocation of goodwill acquired** in a business combination should be completed before the end of the financial year in which the acquisition was completed.
5. Where an **entity disposes of an operation that includes a CGU** (or group of CGU's), to which goodwill has been allocated, then the goodwill should be included in the carrying amount of the operation when calculating the gain or loss on disposal.

Timing of impairment testing for goodwill

The annual impairment test for a CGU to which goodwill has been allocated **can be completed** at any time during the financial year. The CGU should then be subjected to future impairment tests at the same time each year. Different CGU's can be tested for impairment at different times of the year. **1728** IAS 36 (IN13)

Where goodwill has been allocated to a CGU acquired as part of a business combination during the current period, the impairment test should be conducted before the end of the current financial reporting period.

Reversals of impairment losses for goodwill

Under the revised IAS 36, the reversal of impairment losses for goodwill is prohibited. This is different from the previous version of IAS 36, which permitted the reversal of an impairment loss resulting from a specific external event not expected to recur and for which subsequent events reversed the effect of that event. **1729** IAS 36 (IN15)

Disclosures

The following **additional disclosures** are required under the revised standard: **1730**
- the amount of any goodwill acquired in a business combination that is not allocated to a CGU, and the reasons for non-allocation;
- information (including key supporting assumptions) on each CGU, for which the carrying value of goodwill or intangible assets with indefinite useful economic lives allocated to that CGU, is significant in relation to the total carrying amount of goodwill or intangible assets with indefinite lives; IAS 36 (IN 18)
- information on goodwill or intangible assets with indefinite lives that are allocated across a number of CGU's, and where the amount allocated to each CGU is significant in comparison with the total carrying value of goodwill or intangible assets.

First-time adoption

An **entity applying** IAS 36 for the first time must: **1731**
- determine if any impairment loss exists at the transition date to IFRS;
- determine the extent of the impairment loss at the transition date;
- reverse any impairment loss that no longer applies; and
- include in the first IFRS financial statements, details of impairment losses or reversals, recognised in the period beginning with the date of transition to IFRS.

Where an entity's opening IFRS balance sheet **reflects impairment losses**, the entity should charge any reversals of those losses to the income statement, except where the reversal is treated as a revaluation. This rule applies to both impairment losses recognised under previous GAAP and additional impairment losses recognised on the transition to IFRS's.

2. Key differences

The key differences between FRS 11 and IAS 36 are outlined in the tables below. **1732**

Key differences between FRS 11 and IAS 36	
FRS 11	**IAS 36**
1. Impairment losses on **revalued fixed assets** should be charged to income if caused by a clear consumption of economic benefits. FRS 11 (63)	1. Impairment losses on revalued fixed assets are first set off against previous surpluses. IAS 36 (60). However, where a previous impairment loss on the same asset was recognised in the profit and loss, so any reversal of that impairment loss is also recognised in the profit and loss account.
2. Losses relating to **income-generating units** should be allocated to obviously impaired specific assets, then goodwill, then intangibles, then tangibles. FRS 11 (48)	2. Losses are allocated first to goodwill and then pro-rata to other assets. IAS 36 (104)
3. The **reversal of impairment losses** on intangibles is restricted to those with readily ascertainable market values. FRS 11 (60)	3. No restriction under IAS 36.
4. In **future cash flows estimates**, after a five year period, the steady or declining growth rates should not exceed the long term average growth rate for the country.	4. IAS 36 relates the growth rates to relevant products industry or country.

1733

Issues dealt with in more detail in FRS 11
1. Requirements concerning the **allocation of impairment losses** after the creation of a new IGU, through a business combination. FRS 11 (50). The loss should be first allocated to purchased goodwill of the newly acquired business, with subsequent impairments allocated pro-rata to the acquired and existing businesses.
2. Impairment losses shown in the **profit and loss account** must be included in operating income. FRS 11 (67)
3. Details on how the **discount rate** has been estimated when the entity's weighted average cost of capital is used as a reference. FRS 11 (42)
4. **Comparisons of cash flow** "actuals" with forecasts over a five year period are required, sometimes with re-calculation and recognition of impairment losses. FRS 11 (54)
5. **Certain costs** relating to reorganisation and related expenditures can be accounted for in the estimation of cash flows of a newly acquired IGU. FRS 11 (39). This treatment is not permitted under IAS 36.
6. **Additional disclosures** are required for: – the treatment of impairment losses within the figures. For example, for assets held on a cost basis, impairments should be included within cumulative depreciation; – where growth rates exceed five years, the term and justification for this should be provided; – the growth rate for measuring value in use, plus the justification thereof, where this exceeds the long-term average growth; and – longer term cash flows that do not assume steady or declining growth rates.

1734

Issues dealt with in more detail in IAS 36
1. More guidance is required on the calculation of **net selling price** with or without an active market. IAS 36 (18-23)
2. Guidance is required on how the estimation of **net cash flows** related to expected eventual cash flows from disposals. IAS 36 (39) (53)
3. The allocation of **goodwill** to cash-generating units is dealt with in greater detail. IAS 36 (80)
4. On the reversal of **impairment losses** for an IGU, allocation should start pro-rata with assets other than goodwill. There are also limits set on the carrying amounts of individual assets. IAS 36 (122): Reversal of impairment losses for goodwill now prohibited.
5. Details are required **by segment**, of the location of impairment losses and any reversals.
6. For each **material loss or reversal**, disclosure of the causes, amounts and methods are required. IAS 36 (126). If the individual sums involved are not material they may be aggregated.

MEMO POINTS 1. **FRED 38 "Impairment of fixed assets"** is based on IAS 36 "Impairment assets" and covers goodwill carried without systematic amortisation, and where an impairment test is required to determine the annual reductions in the carrying amount of acquired goodwill.
2. The **two principal differences** between FRS 11 and FRED 38 are:
i) that the tests in FRS 11 attempt to distinguish between acquired and internally generated goodwill and to recognise goodwill only on the acquired part and
ii). FRS 11 includes a test designed to assess to accuracy of impairment by comparing the actual cash flows against projections. The FRED does not contain a similar test.
The current position is that the ASB continues to postpone a decision on implementing this FRED until completion of its convergence programme between UK GAAP and IFRS.

CHAPTER 6

Fixed asset investments

OUTLINE ¶¶

Fixed asset investments **are defined as** assets which are intended for use on a continuing basis in the company's activities; thus, distinguishing them from current asset investments (¶2700) which are held for the short-term. **1750**

There is no one specific UK or international accounting standard that deals with fixed asset investments and there is also a choice of measurement (valuation) bases.

1. Classification

Investments should be classified as fixed where the company can demonstrate that it intends to hold them on a **long-term basis**, depending on: **1755**
- the nature of the investment;
- the investment strategy of the company; and
- whether there are restrictions on the investor's ability to dispose of the investment.

Investments that are **not intended to be held for the long-term**, should be classified as current asset investments. If the value of the investments held by a company is material, the accounting policies should provide details of the criteria applied in determining whether an investment is a fixed asset. **1756**

Investments is a **main heading** which appears on the face of the balance sheet under fixed assets. A number of subheadings are required for fixed asset investments as set out in the Companies Acts, with different requirements for small companies. **1757**

Balance Sheet formats (extract) **Large & medium-sized companies**	**Small Companies**
B Fixed Assets **III Investments** – Shares in group undertakings (Subsidiaries) – Shares in participating interests (Associates, Joint-ventures, Qualifying Partnerships) – see ¶7300. – Loans to participating interest – Loans to group undertakings – Other loans – Other investments (non-loans) – Own shares	**Fixed Asset Investment** – Shares in group undertakings and participating interests – Loans to group undertakings and participating interests – Other investments (non-loans) – Own shares

Shares in group undertakings

1760 Shares in group undertakings are investments by a parent company (be it the ultimate or the intermediate parent within a group) in a subsidiary undertaking.

Shares in participating interests

1762 A participating interest is defined in the Companies Act as an interest in the shares of another undertaking that are intended to be **held on a long-term basis**, for the purpose of seeking to **exercise control** or influence the activities of the entity. Participating interests include holdings in qualifying partnerships, unlimited companies and associates and joint-ventures, but exclude interests in subsidiary undertakings.

MEMO POINTS 1. A **qualifying partnership** or **unlimited company** is an entity governed by the laws of the United Kingdom, each of whose members are a limited company or another unlimited company, whose members are a limited company.
2. The term "**associate**" is defined in FRS 9 "Associates and joint-ventures" as an entity (other than a subsidiary) in which another entity (investor) holds a participating interest and over whose operating and financial policies, the investor exercises a significant influence. This definition is also consistent with the definition of an associate given in the Companies Acts.

1764 SI 1996/189 A participating interest is deemed to be a **holding of 20% or more** of the nominal value of share capital or where the value carried in the investing company's accounts exceeds one-fifth of the assets of the investing company.

A holding of less than 20% is considered to a participating interest if the investor exerts considerable influence over the strategic policies of the company.

An interest includes any convertible rights and options or interests held on behalf of the company.

1765 **Classification** Where the investing company **does not prepare** consolidated financial statements, but holds a 20% or more shareholding in another entity, that investment should be shown as a participating interest. This category also includes interests in associates and joint ventures.

Where the investment is included in the consolidated balance sheet, any shareholding in excess of 20% should be shown under a sub-heading of fixed asset investments, termed "interests in associated undertakings" or "interests in joint-ventures".

If the shareholding relates to non-voting shares then the investment should be classified under "other participating interests".

Loans to group undertakings and participating interests

1770 The balance sheet formats include categories for amounts owed to and from group undertakings. The **classification of loans** to group and participating undertakings will depend on the terms of each loan agreement and in particular the repayment terms of the loan.

1772 **Group undertakings** Many types of loan between companies in a group are often not governed by a formal agreement, having been made on an informal basis, with no agreed repayment terms. These loans may be intended to meet the capital requirements of various group companies and are often **long-term in nature**, representing investments that will be used on a continuing basis in the group. If that is the intention they should be classified as fixed asset investments. Loans made to group undertakings on a **short-term basis** and routine trading balances should be classified as current asset investments and shown under debtors.

1774 FRS 5 (29) Where a **parent company has loans both to and from** its subsidiary companies, it may not offset these loans against each other in arriving at the amounts to be disclosed in the parent's balance sheet.

The loans to and from each group undertaking should be considered separately and classified appropriately, according to their terms.

Loans to 3rd parties

Loans to third parties should be classified as fixed asset investments if: **1776**
- the term of the loan would be regarded as long term; or
- they are related to the company's activities such as establishing a new trading venture with a partner or supplier.

MEMO POINTS Determining whether a loan is long-term or not is somewhat of a grey area and therefore, the purpose behind the loan is as important as the length of the loan period.

These types of loans should be covered by a **formal agreement** stipulating payment dates and interest arrangements. Other types of loan that are **less than 12 months** or are unrelated to the company's activities should be included in debtors.

EXAMPLE **Notes to the financial statements**
Fixed asset investments – Loans to BX. Com (US Company)

The company owns a US $25m convertible loan note in Bx.com, due for conversion in 20XX. Bx.com is a business venture set up to develop internet healthcare portals in the USA. Interest is payable half-yearly on 1 January and 1 July.

Other investments (non-loans)

Fixed asset investments other than group undertakings and participating interests can include: **1778**
- listed and unlisted shares;
- time deposits with banks and building societies;
- life insurance policies; and
- unusual investments (e.g. debenture holdings, entitling the holder to tickets at a major sports grounds).

The **classification** of other investments as either a fixed or current asset investment **will depend on** the rationale behind making the investment.

"Own shares"

The **general rule** is that a company (including a subsidiary company) is not permitted to own its own shares, except where it is acting as a personal representative for a third party or trustee, and where either the holding company or subsidiary has no beneficial interest. **1780**

The rules governing the accounting treatment and disclosure requirements of different types of "own shares" are dealt with in share capital and reserves (¶3600).

Under UK legislation, there are a number of instances where **shares can legally be held by a subsidiary in a parent**. These include situations where shares in the parent were acquired: **1782**
- by forfeiture, surrender or way of a gift;
- by a company before it became a subsidiary of that parent; or
- where a subsidiary company has held the shares since prior to the Companies Act 1948.

Furthermore, if shares have been acquired by a trust under an **employee share ownership scheme (ESOP)**, these shares could be included in the issuing company's own balance sheet. Although the shares are legally held by the ESOP they are disclosed in the issuing company's own balance sheet as "own shares". **1784**

Where a company owns shares in **an entity that subsequently purchased it**, then any shares so held will not carry voting rights at company meetings. If the shares are held for the continuing benefit of the sponsoring company, they must be accounted for as "own shares" within fixed assets or as current assets.

---

2. Measurement

Fixed asset investments can be recorded in the financial statements using different valuation regimes as set out in the table below. **1786**

Regime choice – initial recognition	Regulation
Historical cost	Companies Act (SI 2008/410 Sch 17)
Alternative accounting rules	Companies Act (SI 2008/410 1 Sch. 32 (3))
Statement at fair value (Listed companies)	Companies Act + FRS 26 (some exceptions)

a. Historical cost

1788 In determining the cost of an investment, any **expenses incidental to its acquisition**, such as stamp duty and broking fees, can be added to the purchase cost as long as this does not result in a value that exceeds the value of the investment.

In some instances, the **incidental costs of purchase** can be significant as with the purchase of an investment in a subsidiary, where the costs incurred in issuing shares, or other capital instruments, due diligence and legal costs, need to be considered.

Excluded costs However, depending upon the nature and structure of the purchase, some costs, such as issue costs related to capital instruments used to finance the purchase of the investment, should be excluded. Issue costs should be deducted from the proceeds of the debt instrument or for share issues written off to the share premium account or other reserve.

1790 **Shares in group undertakings** that are retained as fixed asset investments should be recorded in the investing company's balance sheet at historical cost less provision for any permanent diminution in value.

1792 **Shares in participating interests** include associates and joint-ventures carried in the company's own balance sheet at historical cost, less any provision for permanent diminution in value (equity method).

1794 **Provisions for a diminution in value** The **general rule** is that fixed asset investments are initially measured at historical purchased cost.

Where there is a subsequent diminution in value of a fixed asset investment, a provision may be made against the carrying value which should be charged to the profit and loss account. The Act does not make the creation of a provision compulsory, except where the diminution is considered to be permanent.

1796 There is therefore, considerable judgement to be applied when assessing the nature of a diminution in value and the appropriate accounting treatment. When the **reasons for the provision no longer apply** it should be written back to, and separately disclosed in, the profit and loss account and in the notes to the accounts.

In determining the need for any provisions each investment should be valued separately.

1798
FRS 11 (5)
Further guidance is provided by FRS 11, which does not distinguish between a temporary and permanent diminution in the value of fixed assets, but adopts a single approach to measuring the value of fixed assets, with **some exceptions**; namely:
– investment companies permitted to take a permanent diminution in the value of tangible fixed assets to the revaluation reserve;
– "own shares" held in ESOP trusts and investments;
– investments that fall within the jurisdiction of FRS 13 "Derivatives and other financial instruments"; and
– investments that fall within the scope of FRS 25 "Financial instruments: measurement"

(e.g. investments covered by FRS 13 plus contracts that can be settled by an entity's own equity instruments (FRS 25 (11)).

Alternative accounting rules

Under the alternative accounting rules, investments **classified as fixed assets** may be valued either: **1800**
- at market value at the date of the most recent valuation; or
- at a more appropriate value as determined by the directors.

Directors' valuation The provision in the Companies Act to allow a directors' valuation does not give guidance on permitted valuation bases. Considerable flexibility is allowed in the valuation of investments and it may be the case that the valuation derived by the directors, may be neither the historic cost nor the current value, but some intermediate value. **1802**

The Act does, however, require that the reasons for adopting a directors' valuation and the valuation bases used must be disclosed in a note to the accounts.

---

b. Statement at fair value

Listed companies are now required to adopt FRS 26 "Financial Instruments: measurement". **1803**
The standard **is also compulsory for** all other **entities that elect to adopt** fair value accounting (now incorporated into the Companies Acts) and state fixed asset investments at fair value. However, as not many UK companies are expected to adopt these rules, only a brief summary of the recognition and subsequent measurement requirements is given here.

Also under FRS 26, **an exception** is permitted; namely that **unquoted equity investments** whose fair value cannot be measured reliably, can be stated at cost less impairment.

Initial recognition and subsequent measurement Financial assets are initially recognised at fair value and fall into four main classifications as set out in the note below. **1803-1**

MEMO POINTS 1. **Held for trading (HFT)**: typically short-term in nature and are revalued at fair value at the end of the financial year (e.g. derivatives).
2. **Held for maturity (HTM)**: Investments with fixed payments and maturity dates are held at amortised cost. The difference between original cost and maturity value is amortised to the profit and loss account over the life of the asset. If impaired, assets should be written down.
3. **Originated loans and receivables (OLR)**: Accounted for as HTM assets except where they are not of fixed maturity, in which case they are measured at amortised cost and written down if impaired.
4. **Available-for-sale (AFS)**: Stated initially at fair value and revalued at the end of each financial reporting period, with changes in value taken either to reserves or the income statement.

Reclassification 1. Fixed assets cannot be reclassified in and out of the "fair value" regime through the profit and loss account. **1803-2**
2. However, reclassification within the "fair value" regime is permitted. For example, an asset originally classified as HTM can be redesignated as AFS.
3. Where as asset formerly stated at fair value is restated at amortised cost, the previous fair value becomes its deemed cost.
4. For HTM assets, any gain or loss previously accounted for in equity is released to the profit and loss account over the period to maturity. For other assets, gains or losses remain in equity until the asset is disposed of.
5. An asset originally stated at cost because no reliable valuation measure was available, but which should be valued at fair value, must be restated if and when an accurate valuation becomes possible.

Impairment The rules for recognising impairment are covered in greater detail in ¶1550. **1803-3**

The emphasis is on ensuring that entities do not make excessive impairment provisions. For assets carried at fair value, impairment should be carried in the profit and loss account as should reversals, except where arising on AFS assets.

c. Revaluation

1805 A profit (or loss) arising on revaluation **under the alternative accounting rules** must be credited (or debited) to the revaluation reserve, after which the normal rules regarding that reserve apply.

The **exception is investment companies** which take revaluation gains or losses to another reserve. In addition, investment companies can also take permanent diminutions in the value of fixed asset investments to that same reserve, whilst **other companies** must take such diminutions to the profit and loss account.

d. Gains or losses on disposal

1806 The profit or loss on the disposal of an asset should be accounted for in the profit and loss account in the period, in which the disposal takes place. The gain (or loss) should represent the difference between the net sale proceeds and the net carrying amount of the investment at the date of disposal; namely historical cost less any provisions for impairment valuation.

1808 **Surpluses on revaluation** previously credited to the revaluation reserve do not therefore flow through the profit and loss account when the asset is subsequently sold. However, the amount held in the revaluation reserve in respect of that investment should be released to the profit and loss account as a movement on reserves.

1810 **Individual shares** or similar types of investment **may not be easily identifiable**; therefore, a basis for identifying the cost of particular holdings is required for part-disposals. In the example of a company in which a shareholding is managed through **piecemeal acquisition and disposal**, the following methods can be used for determining the cost of the investment at any particular time:
- first in first out (FIFO); or
- weighted average.

These valuation methods are described in greater detail in the chapter on inventories.

Summary

1813

Initial recognition	Revaluation	Gain/loss on disposal
Historical cost	Diminution in value – provision charged to P & L	Charge to P & L
Alternative accounting rules	Cr (Dr) to revaluation reserve. Some exceptions permitted	Cr (Dr) to P & L Amounts previously held in revaluation reserve – to P & L (movement on reserve)
Fair value	Cr (Dr) to P & L	Dr. (Cr) – P & L. Exception is AFS assets – STRGL

3. Disclosures.

1814 There are a number of general disclosures that are required for all investments (including those investments valued under the alternative accounting rules), in respect of their cost and any diminution in the value recorded. There are also additional disclosure requirements relating to listed investments, subsidiaries, participating interests, qualifying partnerships and "own shares".

a. General disclosures

1816 The Companies Act model formats for the balance sheet include headings for investments under the general heading of both fixed and current assets.

Under each **sub-heading** of fixed asset investments, the following information should be disclosed either on the face of the balance sheet or, more usually, in the notes to the accounts: 1817
- the balances at the beginning and end of the financial year;
- any revaluation revisions made during the year;
- acquisitions and disposals during the year;
- details of any provisions made in respect of fixed asset investments;
- transfers of assets to or from fixed asset investments; and
- details of listed investments.

Permanent diminution in value

Where there is a permanent diminution in value, the following disclosures are required in the notes to the accounts: 1818
- the balances at the beginning and end of the year;
- provisions made during the year;
- adjustments from provisions arising from disposals; and
- other adjustments made in respect of provisions during the financial year.

Comparative figures for the preceding year are not required.

If a **diminution in value is expected to be temporary** then a provision may be made at the discretion of the directors. This fact must be disclosed in the notes to the financial statements.

The disclosure requirements are more comprehensive for **listed companies** and are detailed below. Companies listed on the Alternative Investment Market (AIM) are not listed companies for the purpose of this classification.

b. Additional disclosure requirements

Listed investments

Listed investments refer to any investment that is quoted either on all "recognised" **investment exchanges in the UK** and certain other countries (Table 1) or only the stock exchanges of repute in specific other countries (Table 2). All other investments are regarded as unlisted and no additional disclosures are required. 1820

MEMO POINTS 1. There is **no legal definition** of a "stock exchange of repute" in the Financial Services and Markets Act (FMSA) 2000 (Part 18), as this will depend on the status of an individual stock exchange within its own country. A recognised investment exchange as defined by the FSMA 2000, is one in which a recognition order is in place. This definition is also addressed in The Large and Medium-sized Companies and Groups (Accounts and Reports) Regulations 2008 (SI 2008/410, Para 8, Sch 10) and The Small Companies and Groups (Accounts and Director's Report) Regulations 2008 (SI 2008/409, Para 5. Sch 8).
2. **The Alternative Investment Market (AIM)** is a subsidiary of the London Stock Exchange that provides small companies with access to capital and a market for the trading of their shares without the expense and restrictions of a full stock exchange listing.

Table 1 Designated UK Investment exchanges	All official exchanges in the following countries
London Stock Exchange (inc. AIM)	The European Union
London Securities and Derivatives Exchange Ltd.	USA
The London Metal Exchanges (LME)	Switzerland
The International Petroleum Exchange (IPE)	Japan
The London International Financial Futures Exchange (LIFFE)	Norway

Table 2 Specific Stock Exchanges	
Alberta	Singapore
Australia	Thailand
New Zealand	Toronto
Mexico	Vancouver
Cayman Islands	
Hong Kong	
Johannesburg	
Kuala Lumpur	

1822 The **following information** regarding listed investments is required in the notes to the accounts:
- the total carrying value of listed investments included in each subheading;
- the aggregate market value of listed investments, where this differs from the amount stated in the financial statements; and

SI 1996/189 – details of any differences between the market value and the stock exchange value, where for instance, a sizeable shareholding could be deemed more valuable than a smaller shareholding.

EXAMPLE XYZ Ltd.
Notes to the accounts (extract)
Listed investments

	Company	Balance Sheet Value £'000	Market Value £'000	Stock Exchange Value £'000
Listed on the London	F	130	220	285
Stock Exchange	G	210	175	175
	I	50	60	60
		390	455	520
Listed on the Frankfurt	A	100	120	140
Stock Exchange	B	75	45	45
		175	165	185

Subsidiaries

1830 Holdings in subsidiary undertakings should distinguish separately holdings by the parent company and by the group (if different). Where a company **does not prepare consolidated accounts**, but has subsidiary companies, then certain disclosures are required in the financial statements of the investing company. In addition, a company is required to state why it is not required to prepare consolidated financial statements.

MEMO POINTS A company may not be required to prepare consolidated financial statements because its subsidiaries come within the scope of the exclusions from consolidation provided in Section 229 of the Companies Act. The precise reason for the exclusion should be disclosed for each subsidiary.

1832 The disclosures are required for **each individual subsidiary** company and include:
- the name of each subsidiary;
- its place (country) of incorporation;
- if unincorporated, the address of its principal place of business;
- the identity and proportion of the nominal value of each class of shares held;
- the profit and loss for the year; and
- the aggregate amount of the capital and reserves of the undertaking as at the end of the financial year.

The above disclosures are also required for **investments held by subsidiary companies**. As such the identity and number of shares in each class held by the investing company and its subsidiaries in a subsidiary undertaking must be disclosed, and classified between those shares held by the investing company and those held by any of its subsidiaries. 1834

Additional disclosures are required under FRS 2, for each subsidiary company whose results or financial position substantially affect the figures in the consolidated financial statements. 1836 FRS 2 (33)

The disclosures required include the:
- nature of the business;
- number of shares that the subsidiaries or their nominees hold;
- proportion of voting rights held by the parents and its subsidiaries; and
- details of own shares held by the subsidiary or held in the parent company.

Exemptions Some companies are exempt from the disclosure requirements outlined above; where: 1840
- where the company is exempt due to section 228 of the Companies Act from preparing group accounts (parent company included in the accounts of a larger group);
- the investment is accounted for by way of the equity method and is shown in aggregate in the notes to the accounts;
- the undertaking is not required by the Act to deliver a copy of (or publish) its balance sheet in Great Britain or elsewhere; and
- the shareholdings to be disclosed are immaterial.

Furthermore, information on own shares is not required where the subsidiary holds the shares as a **personal representative** or as **trustee**. If the company or any of its subsidiaries is a beneficiary under the trust, then this exemption is not available for a subsidiary acting as a trustee, unless the beneficial interest is a security for a normal business transaction such as a loan. 1842 SI 1996/189

If the **number of undertakings** involved **are numerous**, then the directors need only give the information for undertakings which materially affect the figures shown in the individual or group accounts and undertakings which have been excluded from consolidation. A note to this effect should be given. 1844

Significant interests

If a company has significant interests through exercising **considerable influence but owns less than 20%** of the share capital of the undertakings concerned, then no additional disclosure beyond the separate categorisation of the investment and income is required. 1846

Where the company owns 20% or more of the share capital of a significant interest, the disclosures required in respect of each undertaking, in the notes to the accounts, are as set out in ¶1832. 1848

Shares held by the company **on behalf of a third party** should not be attributed to the company for disclosure purposes, but shares held by third parties on behalf of the company should be disclosed. 1850

The following **additional disclosures** are also required in the notes to the financial statements for amounts: 1852
- owed by undertakings in which the company has a significant interest should be disclosed under debtors; and
- owed to undertakings in which the company has a significant interest should be disclosed under creditors.

Separate figures are required in both cases, for amounts due for payment after more than one year.

Qualifying partnerships and unlimited companies

The disclosure requirements for qualifying companies and partnerships were laid down in The Partnerships and Unlimited Companies (Accounts) Regulations (1993). 1854 SI 1993/1820

Where a company **holds a material interest in a qualifying company** or partnership [an undertaking] at the end of the financial year, the disclosures required in the notes to the company or group accounts are:
- the name and legal form of the undertaking; and
- the registered office, or if not applicable, the head office.

If a fixed asset investment relates to a qualifying partnership then the **following disclosures are required**:
- a copy of the latest accounts for the qualifying partnership has or will be appended to the investing company's financial statements to be filed with the Registrar of Companies; or
- the name of at least one body corporate (including the investing company) in whose group accounts, the results of the partnership are to be or are already consolidated.

The **accounting treatment** for qualifying partnerships is dealt with in greater detail in (¶7600).

1856 SI 1993/1820 **Exemption** A company need not provide the disclosures listed above, if it has taken advantage of the exemption permitted under regulation No. 7 of The Partnerships and Unlimited Companies Regulations 1993.

Own shares

1858 Where a company owns its own shares or shares in its parent, the number and nominal values of the shares, the subsidiaries or their nominees hold and the carrying amount or value must be disclosed in the notes to the accounts.

EXAMPLE **XYZ Group Plc**
Notes to the financial statements 20XX
Fixed asset investments

Own shares	**Group**	**Company**
Cost and net book value	**£'000**	**£'000**
As at January 20XX	485.0	346.0
Additions	10.0	
Disposals	(145)	-
As at December 20XX	350.0	346.0

The number of own shares totals 250,000 with a nominal value of £100,000.

c. Alternative accounting rules

1864 Where fixed asset investments are valued in accordance with the alternative accounting rules, the following disclosures are required in the notes to the accounts:
a. the investments concerned and the valuation bases.
b. for fixed asset investments excluding listed investments:
- the name of the valuers and qualifications;
- the values; and
- the basis of the valuation. If any valuation base other than market value is used the reason for adopting the alternative valuation must be given.

c. the comparable historical cost for those investments and any provision for any diminution in value that would have been made under the historical cost convention, or the difference between these amounts and the alternative valuation.

4. Comparison between UK GAAP and IAS (IFRS)

1870 The requirements of international financial reporting regarding fixed asset investments are principally covered in IAS 27 "Consolidated Financial Statements and Accounting for Investments in Subsidiaries", IAS 28 "Accounting for Investments in Associates" and IAS 31 "Financial Reporting of Interests in Joint Ventures". The table below reflects the accounting treatment in the parent company's individual financial statements whilst the accounting treatment in the group accounts is dealt with in ¶7300.

The **differences between** UK GAAP and IFRS have narrowed with the publication of FRS 25 "Financial instruments: presentation" and FRS 26 "Financial instruments: measurement".

TABLE

	IAS (IFRS)	Accounting treatment in financial statements of investing company
Subsidiaries	IAS 27, IAS 39	Accounted for either at: – cost; – use of the equity method; or – categorise as available-for-sale (AFS) under IAS 39. IAS 39 applies where subsidiaries are held exclusively for resale or long-term restrictions apply.
Associates	IAS 28, IAS 39	As for subsidiaries. IAS 39 applies where subsidiaries are held exclusively for resale or long-term restrictions apply.
Joint ventures	IAS 31 IAS 39	Not addressed in IAS 31 As for subsidiaries
Other investments	IAS 39	Classify as either: – Held for trading (HFT); – Held to maturity (HTM); – Originated loans and receivables (OLR); or – Available-for-sale (AFS) (see ¶1803-1).

CHAPTER 7

Investment properties

OUTLINE ¶¶

Investment properties are **defined as** an interest in land and or buildings in respect of which construction or development work has been completed and which is held for its investment potential, with any rental income being negotiated on an arm's length basis. **1900** SSAP 19 (7)

Investment properties may be held by all companies, but **are typically held by** an entity that specialises in this type of asset, such as an investment trust or property investment company.

A property which is **owned and occupied** by a company **for its own purpose** is not an investment property, as is a property let and occupied by another group company, except where rent is determined on an arm's length basis and charged accordingly. **Partial owner-occupation** of an investment property is not addressed in SSAP 19, although a significant level of occupation will prevent the assets classification as an investment property.

The **principles of accounting** for investment properties are contained in SSAP 19 "Accounting for investment properties". The application of this standard represents a departure from the requirement of the Companies Act to give a true and fair view, arising from the non-provision of depreciation on a fixed asset with a useful economic life. Reporting entities applying the Financial Reporting Standard for Smaller Entities (FRSSE) are exempt from this accounting standard, although provisions broadly similar to those of SSAP 19 are included in the FRSSE. **1901** SSAP 19 (17)

An overview of the requirements of IAS 40 "Investment property" is also given.

Classification	Reporting regime
Small companies	Choice of adopting FRSSE; SSAP 19 or IFRS for small companies
Medium and large companies	Choice of SSAP 19 or IAS 40
Listed companies	IAS 40

1. Accounting treatment

The **general rule** for investment properties is that they should be recorded in the balance sheet at their **open market value (OMV)**, at the balance sheet date. This contrasts with **property owned by an entity**, that is held as a fixed asset, and recorded in the financial statements at cost, or valuation, and that is subject to an annual depreciation charge that reflects the loss of value, arising from use, passage of time or technological or market changes. **1904** SSAP 19 (11)

Investment properties **are not subject to** an annual depreciation charge, except where the property is a leasehold property. The rationale for this, is that a **different treatment** is called SSAP 19 (2) for where a significant proportion of an entity's fixed assets are held as investments and not for use within the operations of the business, and where the disposal of such assets would not materially affect the trading position of the entity. In these circumstances, the current value of these investments and changes in current value are of more importance, than the calculation of an annual depreciation charge. **Leased properties** can be classified as investment properties if let to unrelated third parties.

1905 SSAP 19 (10) **Short leasehold properties** There is an important **exception to the rule** that investment properties should not be subject to depreciation charges; namely, properties held on a lease with a term of 20 years or less. It is necessary in such cases to recognise the annual depreciation charge in the financial statements, to prevent the scenario whereby a short lease is amortised against the investment revaluation reserve, whilst the rental income is taken to the profit and loss account.

The **problem of** accounting for property **leases originally in excess of 20 years**, but which still have 20 years to run from the current accounting period, is not covered by SSAP 19.

1906 **Reclassification** Where an investment property loses its status the balance on the investment revaluation reserve should be transferred to the revaluation reserve for non-investment properties.

Recognition of gains and losses

1909 The determination of whether a **deficit is permanent or temporary** may not be so obvious. For a diminution in value to be deemed temporary there must be a reasonable expectation that the value will reverse in the near future. Each investment property must be judged on its individual circumstances. For instance deficits arising from structural damage, obsolescence, or changes to local infrastructure, that render the property unattractive, should be deemed permanent. Deficits that arise from short term fluctuations in market sentiment or that arise from damage that is repairable, should be regarded as temporary.

Temporary changes in market value of investment properties from one balance sheet date to the next, should be taken to the statement of total recognised gains and losses (STRGL), and not the profit and loss account, as this represents a movement on an investment revaluation reserve. The amount taken to the **revaluation reserve** will ordinarily be the gross revaluation surplus, without a deduction for any potential deferred tax liability that might arise on that surplus.

EXAMPLE **Annual report and accounts**
Statement of total recognised gains and losses
Year ended 30 September 2010

	2010			2009		
	Group	Associated undertakings	Total	Group	Associated undertakings	Total
	£m	£m	£m	£m	£m	£m
Profit on ordinary after taxation	195.2	4.5	199.7	165.2	6.2	171.4
Revaluation of properties	(0.3)	(1.0)	(1.3)	–	–	–
Currency translation differences	(20.2)	–	(20.2)	(10.5)	–	(10.5)
Total recognised gains and losses for the year	174.7	3.5	178.2	154.7	6.2	160.9

1910 **Permanent changes in value** Where a **deficit (or reversal of a deficit)** on an individual investment property **is expected to be permanent**, it should be charged (or credited) to the profit and loss account for the financial period in question.

MEMO POINTS Investment properties are exempt from the requirements of FRS 11 "Impairment of fixed assets".

Exceptions However, the above requirement **does not apply** to: 1912 SSAP 19 (14)
- **insurance companies and groups** (and consolidated financial statements incorporating these entities) where changes in the market value of investment properties are carried in the profit and loss account;
- **pension funds** where changes in the market value of investment properties are included in the relevant fund account; and
- **investment companies and property unit trusts** – valuation deficits are shown in the STRGL.

Status of Valuer

SSAP 19 does not require the valuation of investment properties to be made by a qualified or independent valuer, although certain disclosures are required in the financial statements (see ¶1922). However, where investment properties represent a **substantial proportion of the assets** of the entity, a valuation should be: 1916 SSAP 19 (6)
- undertaken annually by suitably professionally qualified persons with recent post-qualification experience in the location and type of properties concerned; and
- at least every five years by an external valuer.

Development costs

Investment properties cover buildings in which development and construction work has been completed. As such when a property company or group constructs its own investment properties, the capitalisation rules set out in FRS 15 apply, as the buildings can not classified as investment properties until completed. 1917

Sale of investment property

The general rule is that when an asset that has previously been revalued is sold, the resulting gain or loss, which has now been crystalised, is based on the net carrying amount (rather than historical cost), and should be taken to the profit and loss account (see ¶400). 1918

Taxation

Where investment properties are reclassified as non-investment properties (or vice versa), there may be capital gains tax implications, particularly concerning rollover reliefs. 1919

2. Disclosures

The general disclosures requirements relating to the **true and fair view override** contained in FRS 18 "Accounting policies" are set out in ¶2. 1920

Other key disclosures include: 1922 SSAP 19 (12)
- details of the valuers including names, qualifications and bases of valuation;
- the valuation bases;
- where the valuation is conducted by an employee or officer of the company or group that owns the property, this fact should be disclosed in the financial statements; and
- the carrying value of investment properties and the investment revaluation reserve should be prominently displayed in the financial statements.

EXAMPLE **Example**
ABC Group ltd
Annual Report and Accounts – September 2010
Tangible fixed assets (extract)

Land and buildings including investment properties	Group £m	Company £m
Valuation as **at 1 October 2009**	120.7	105.3
Additions	25.0	22.0
Reclassification	(3.0)	(3.0)
Revaluation surplus	(15.0)	(13.0)
As at 30 September 2010	127.7	111.3

Investment properties were valued on the basis of open market value (OMV) as at 30 September 20X9 by the group's internal qualified personnel. In accordance with SSAP 19, no depreciation is charged in respect of investment properties. This policy represents a departure from the requirements of the Companies Act 1985, to provide systematic annual depreciation for fixed assets. However, as these properties are held for investment and not consumption, the directors consider the adoption of this policy necessary to give a true and fair view.

EXAMPLE **Example**

XYZ Groupl ltd
Annual report and accounts – September 2010
Investment revaluation reserve

	Group £m	Company £m
As at 1 October 2009	270.5	170.3
Currency exchange differences	(20.2)	
Revaluation of property	(1.3)	(0.3)
Revaluation surplus realised on disposal	(45.3)	(15.0)
As at 30 September 2010	203.7	(155.0)

3. Comparison between UK GAAP and IAS (IFRS)

1924 IAS 40 (28) Investment property is defined in IAS 40 "Investment properties" as property (land and buildings) held by the owner (or lessee under a finance lease), that earns rental income or is held for capital appreciation or both. The recognition and measurement of **owner occupied property** is dealt with in IAS 16 "Property, plant and equipment". Small companies can adopt the IFRS for small entities.

There are **no current proposals** for full UK convergence.

MEMO POINTS In October 2010 the ASB issued a proposal to introduce a financial reporting framework for medium-sized entities (FRSME) not eligible to apply the FRSSE or full IFRS. The FRSME would replace current UK GAAP from July 2013 and is based on the principles underpinning full IFRS. If adopted there could be some key differences in the treatment of investment properties.

Key differences

1925 SSAP 19 (11) The key differences between IAS 40 and SSAP 19 are set out in the table below.

Subject	SSAP 19	IAS 40
Valuation	Carried at open market value (OMV). Recognition at depreciated historical cost is not permitted.	Choice of: 1. fair value model which reflects market values at balance sheet date; or 2. depreciated cost.
Treatment of gains or losses	Revaluation gains or losses taken to STRGL	1. Arising from changes in fair value of investment properties should be recognised in the P & L account. 2. Depreciated cost- properties recorded at cost less accumulated depreciation and impairment losses.
Guidance on determining fair value	Only recognises OMV – adopts guidance used by Royal Institute of Chartered Surveyors (RICS)	Standard gives guidance – IAS 40 (33-55)
Subsequent expenditure	Not considered	Standard covers recognition, measurement and accounting treatment

Subject	SSAP 19	IAS 40
Operating leases	Leases with short unexpired terms: – depreciation recognised in the P & L; – lease not amortised against revaluation reserve where rentals taken to the P & L. SSAP 19 (5)	Permits properties **held under operating leases** to be recognised as investment properties, where certain criteria are met; namely: – the property meets the definition of an investment property; – it is accounted for as a finance lease; and – the fair value model is adopted for all investment properties. IAS 40 (6).
Ancillary services	Not specifically covered	Where ancillary services (e.g. cleaning, security, maintenance services) supplied by property company are insignificant part of the arrangements-can still be classified as an investment property.

MEMO POINTS 1. The IASB has increased the scope of IAS 40 to cover investment properties under construction. As properties are rarely traded whilst under construction, they were not previously covered by this IFRS.
However, companies are now required to calculate the fair value of investment properties under construction. As a general rule, entities should take the estimated market value of the property, as if it were completed at the valuation date, less estimated costs to completion and an allowance for risk. The International Valuations Council (IVSC) has issued an interim position statement setting out the new requirements.
2. The IVSC has published an updated guidance note (GN17) covering the valuation of investment properties under construction. The update reflects changes made to IAS 40 and now requires investment property companies to classify property under construction as investment property and not as property, plant and equipment.

IAS 40 requires the following **additional disclosures**: **1926**
- details of whether the fair value or cost model has been adopted;
- where the fair value model has been adopted, the methods and significant assumptions applied in determining the fair value of investment property;
- amounts recognised in the profit and loss account for rental income and direct operating expenses such as repairs and maintenance;
- details of any restrictions on the sale of investment property or remittance of rental income; or
- details of contractual obligations to purchase or construct investment property or for repairs and maintenance.

PART 4

Balance sheet – Current assets

CHAPTER 1

Stock (Inventories)

OUTLINE ¶¶

2000 This chapter sets out the **general guidelines** and rules for determining the valuation of stock, including the determination of historical cost, net realisable value and the replacement cost of stocks.

All reporting entities, except unincorporated entities, are subject to the provisions of SSAP 9 "Stocks and Long-term contracts" and the Companies Acts. Companies applying the Financial Reporting Standard for Smaller Entities (FRSSE), should apply the provisions that relate to stock within the FRSSE.

MEMO POINTS The terms **stock** and **inventories** are interchangeable. "Stock" is the terminology used in the Companies Act and SSAP 9, while "inventories" is used in international accounting standards.

2001 SSAP 9 (1) It is a key principle that the revenues generated from sales are matched with the related costs incurred in earning them. Therefore, the **costs of unsold or unconsumed stocks** at the end of one financial year should be carried forward into the next financial period and matched with the revenue recognised on their future sale. Furthermore, the **choice of stock valuation method** can have a significant impact on the entities' reported profit for the period.

2002 **Specific requirements** apply to disclosures in respect of stocks. Less disclosures are required from small companies, including those who elect to submit shorter form or abbreviated accounts. The detailed treatment of **consignment stock** and the **sale and repurchase of stock agreements** is also covered in this chapter, based on the provisions of FRS 5 "Reporting the substance of transactions".

The procedures that have evolved for the costing and valuation of stock in **specialist industries** such as agriculture, are beyond the scope of this book. The relevant international financial reporting standards are IAS "Inventories" and IAS 18 "Revenue".

SECTION 1

Classification

2005 Stock is classified in SSAP 9 as set out in the table below.

SSAP 9 (16)

Classification	Examples
Consumable stores	Consumables are materials used in the production process that do not form part of direct material cost. Examples of direct consumables include the cooling fluids and lubricating oils used for production machinery and items of small value such as nails, nuts and bolts.
Raw materials and components	Purchased for incorporation into finished goods. Raw materials are direct materials used in the production process which are at a low level of completion, relative to the final product, e.g. steel plate, wood, chemicals.
Semi-finished goods (Work in progress)	Includes products and services in the intermediate stages of completion
Finished goods	Represent products that have completed the manufacturing process and are available for distribution or sale

Classification	Examples
Goods or other assets purchased for resale	Includes trading stock, which covers products available for sale that have either been produced in-house or purchased externally
Long-term contracts (¶2200)	Defined as a contract that falls into two or more accounting periods and are commonplace in the construction industry

A company may hold a combination of the stock classifications listed above, each potentially requiring different **valuation methods**. In their disclosures in the accounts, companies can adapt the **standard classifications**, if this provides a better understanding of the type of stock they hold (see ¶2115). Alternatively, the standard classifications can be supplemented with additional categories that fit the profile of the industry in which the reporting entity operates. **2006**

SECTION 2

Valuation

Stock valuation is a subjective exercise which has resulted in a **number of valuation methods** (¶2064) being adopted. The statutory regulations embodied in the Companies Act and SSAP 9, are designed to promote uniformity in the valuation methods used and in their disclosure in the financial statements prepared under the historic cost convention. The **key valuation issues** are as follows: **2012** SSAP 9 (21) (26)

1. Stocks are valued for inclusion in the balance sheet at **historical cost**; namely the purchase price or production cost.

2. If, however, the **net realisable value** (NRV) (see ¶2090) is less than historical cost, the stock should be written down to (and stated at) the net realisable value. The comparison of cost with net realisable value should be completed for each line of stock individually and not in aggregate.

MEMO POINTS The NRV is defined as the actual or estimated net selling price (net of trade but excluding settlement discounts), less additional costs to completion and marketing, distribution and selling costs.

3. Stock may also be stated in the financial statements at **replacement cost** but only where this is lower than the net realisable value; this approach is not often adopted in practice.

4. Where a company adopts the **alternative accounting rules**, stock may be stated at the lower of current replacement cost and net realisable value, with any permanent diminution in value (i.e. obsolete) provided for. However, this method is not often used in practice.

5. Adjustments may be required in respect of stock items where there are **transfers of assets** (¶2085) from fixed assets to stock or vice versa and also on the cessation of a trade.

6. There are also a number of important areas that must be considered when adjusting accounting profits for **tax** issues; namely trading stock, appropriations of stock and cessation of trade.

There are a **number of methods for valuing closing stock** which impact on the reported profit for the year, so care must be taken not to over or undervalue the stock. Stocks meet the definition of assets as the entity holding any unsold stocks at the year end will expect to earn revenues from them at some future date. **2014** SSAP 9 (4)

A. Historical cost

2015 SSAP 9 (17) **Cost is defined** in relation to the different categories of stocks, as expenditure incurred in the normal course of business, required to bring the product or service to its present location and condition. The cost should include the purchase cost plus an appropriate proportion of any conversion costs.

The **value of stocks carried forward** represents the expenditure incurred in purchasing or producing the goods. In many cases, it will be difficult to identify the exact production or purchase cost for each item held in stock at the year end, and in reality, an element of averaging, costing and allocation of overheads will be required to determine the "cost" of stock.

2017 The **cost of trading stock** is simple where goods are purchased for resale in the same condition, such as where a wholesaler buys goods in bulk and then divides the stock for further distribution to smaller retail or production outlets. The cost is the price of the goods purchased plus the additional costs of bringing the goods to market.

For others types of stock, the valuation may be more complex, especially in a complicated industrial process involving conversion costs and apportionment of both direct and indirect overheads.

1. Cost categories

2022 SSAP 9 (17) On an **historical cost basis**, the cost of the different categories of stocks includes various elements of expenditure incurred in bringing the product or service to its present location and condition.

The **calculation of the costs** of stock for a company involves **two principal stages**; namely:
- an assessment of the material and direct costs (e.g. labour) attributable to each item of stock; and
- the calculation of the proportion of total direct overhead costs attributable to that item.

Calculation of attributable overhead is an important element of cost especially when the stock item is generated through a complex manufacturing process.

Direct material cost

2025 Direct material costs consist of the actual invoice price of material purchased plus any additional charges such as:
- import duties;
- transport; and
- handling and other amounts directly attributable to the acquisition of the direct materials.

Trade discounts, rebates and other subsidies should be deducted.

2026 **Other related costs** include the costs of normal levels of scrap and wastage where these are unavoidably incurred as part of the production process, and may be included either as part of the material cost or treated as an overhead.

Conversion costs

2028 SSAP 9 (19) Conversion costs (direct costs) consist of expenses that are **specifically attributable** to units of production:
- direct labour;
- direct expenses and sub-contracted work;
- production overheads; and
- other overheads incurred in bringing the product to its present location and condition.

Costs of **direct labour** should be allocated to production based on normal operating conditions.

Direct production overheads

Production overheads **are costs based on** "normal levels of activity" incurred in respect of materials, labour or services for production and will vary with the level of production. 2030

The **general principle**, is that production overheads should be included in the cost of stock but only where they are directly related to the process of generating stock. As such, general company overheads should be excluded from the cost of stock. The allocation of overheads is not a precise exercise and inevitably involves a degree of subjectivity or judgement.

In determining what is deemed "normal", the **following factors** should be considered for the financial year in question; namely the: 2032
- production capacity (volume);
- budgeted level of activity; and
- actual level of activity.

Some of these overhead costs, e.g. depreciation of manufacturing plant and equipment, are included even though they may accrue wholly or partly on a time basis. **Temporary changes in activity** may be ignored but persistent variations should result in a revision of any overhead allocation.

The **allocation of overhead costs** must be based on the level of activity, so enabling the costs of excessive wastage, inefficiency or idle time, to be written off in the current period and not carried forward to future years in the stock valuation.

Indirect overhead costs

Overhead costs comprise the total cost of indirect materials, labour and expenses (e.g. rent, rates, insurance). Only those overhead costs that arise from the "normal commercial activity" of the entity can be included in the cost of stock, except in special circumstances as outlined below. 2034

Overheads **not directly attributable** to a specific product or service are not normally included in the costs of stocks. If, however, firm sales contracts have been entered into for goods or services made to customers' specifications, **overheads incurred before the manufacturing process** begins can be included, **if they relate to** the following: 2036
- design;
- administration (e.g. central administrative departments);
- marketing; or
- selling costs.

Only where **central administrative costs** can be **reasonably apportioned** to production, should they be included in the cost of conversion. 2037

Central service departments, such as accounting, usually support the following functions:
- production (paying salaries, controlling purchases, and preparing financial analysis for the production units);
- marketing and distribution (analysing and controlling sales); or
- general administration (preparing management accounts and annual financial statements or preparing budgets, controlling cash resources and planning investments).

The **costs of general management** are not directly related to current production and should be excluded from the cost of conversion, except in smaller organisations, where the separation of duties between production and administration is not so clearly defined. Where management is involved in the daily supervision of various functions, it may be permissible to allocate these costs using appropriate bases. 2038

Absorption bases for apportioning general overheads There are a **number of methods** of apportioning overheads to production. The method selected should be appropriate to the nature of both the product and the process of production and include: 2040
- by labour hour or machine hour rate;
- as a proportion of direct labour costs;

– as a proportion of material costs; and
– by unit of production (possible only if a single product is produced in the relevant cost centre).

Whichever **allocation method** is selected, the overheads should be applied on the basis of the company's usual level of production activity.

A detailed treatment of these absorption bases is beyond the scope of this book.

Production costs excluded from stock valuation

2044 There are a number of production costs that should be excluded from the stock valuation figure where they do not relate to "normal" levels of activity.

1. All **abnormal costs** generated from spare capacity, exceptional spillage or other losses, other than normal loss, should be excluded from the stock valuation.
2. Labour costs resulting from **operating inefficiencies** such as abnormal idle capacity, spoilage or rectification work should not be included in the stock valuation.
3. **Distribution costs** from the sales point to the customer should not be included in the production cost. However, distribution costs relating to the transfer of goods from the factory to the sales depot represent costs incurred in bringing the product to its present location, and are included in cost.
4. As a general rule, **interest is not included** in the costing of stock because capital is usually borrowed to finance the activities of the enterprise as a whole. If, however, in the rare situation where borrowed capital can be identified as financing specific stocks, the interest payable during the period can be charged to these contracts as a direct expense.

An **example is in the whisky distilling industry**, where stocks often include a classification for "maturing whisky stocks", to cover units that are neither work in progress or ready for resale. The interest charges involved in holding this stock can be included in the valuation.

2. Methods of overhead cost allocation

2046 SSAP 9 (Appendix 1.11) The **costing methods** adopted by an entity are designed to capture and charge on a reasonable basis, overhead costs for the purposes of valuing stock. There are a number of methods of apportioning overhead costs to stocks.

The main costing methods in **general use** include:
– job (contract) costing;
– batch costing;
– process costing;
– standard costing; and
– other variations on the above.

2047 Often it is not practical to relate expenditure to **individual units of stock**. Therefore, the use of costing methods often requires judgements be made to ensure that the method selected provides the fairest approximation to cost. **Once a method has been adopted**, the company must be consistent in its application from one accounting period to the next. If an entity adopts a different method, this must be stated in the note on accounting policies adopted in the financial statements. Also, **where a change in methodology** is implemented, consideration needs to be given to the impact of the change.

2048 The choice of the most **appropriate costing system** will depend on the nature of the company's product or service or the volume of the goods produced. A general outline is provided of each of the principle cost allocation methods.

Where possible, stocks should be valued by attributing costs to specific units of production using either the **job costing**, **contract costing** or **batch costing** methods. This requires the identification of each stock item referenced to a particular purchase invoice or specific costs of production. Standard costing can be used especially where costs are relatively constant and the standard cost is therefore likely to be a close approximation to actual costs.

Where individual **stock identification is not practicable** or a number of similar items have been purchased or form part of a continuous process, then costs can be determined and allocated by using process costing.

Job costing

A job costing system can be used to collect costs on **specific jobs or individual units of stock** being produced. It is adopted in organisations producing different products or making bespoke items to order and in service companies, in order to cost each service provided. 2050

An **effective job costing system** requires:
- identifiable cost centres;
- detailed documentation for materials or stores issues;
- detailed labour analysis;
- a method of catching time costs; and
- appropriate absorption bases for overheads.

As the "job" progresses through a number of stages and departments (cost centres), costs are collected. Materials requested from stock are costed to the "job card", along with the cost of labour and the related overheads.

MEMO POINTS A job card is a computerised or manual record of all the costs posted to a particular job or project.

The **accounting treatment** is to debit the work in progress account with the cost of direct materials, as raw material stock is being converted into work-in-progress (stock), and credit the stores ledger control account. In addition to these entries in the **control accounts**, individual jobs should be charged with the cost of materials issued, so that job costs can be calculated. Indirect costs such as factory overheads are collected and pooled before being transferred to the stores ledger control account. 2051

In service industries, many "job cards" do not generally show an overhead absorption rate but an inflated labour rate, which includes both the direct labour costs plus an allocation for the production overhead and the profit margin. However, it should be noted that this "inflated labour cost" method is only appropriate where there is a close correlation between labour costs and the production overhead.

Contract costing Contract costing is a form of job costing, often large scale, long-term in nature and undertaken to meet specific customer requirements. **Examples include** large civil engineering projects (i.e. motorways or bridges), shipbuilding, and aircraft manufacture. This subject is dealt with in greater detail in the chapter on long-term contracts (see ¶2200). 2052

Batch costing

Batch costing is more appropriate to production processes that produce a large number of identical units or "**fungible items**", which are defined as being indistinguishable from each other, such as stocks of nuts, bolts, pens and pencils. Batch costing is used extensively in the printing, packaging, clothing and building products industries. 2054

This method **differs from job costing** in that production costs are charged to one production order which covers a quantity of cost units. When the batch is complete, the unit cost is found by dividing the quantity produced into the total batch cost.

The **key principle** is that the longer the production run, the lower the **unit costs**, although the risk of obsolescence is greater. There are a number of considerations involved in the determining the size of a batch; namely: 2055
- the financing of the stock, including interest;
- demand for the product; and
- other production demands and competition for resources.

Process costing

2057 Process costing is a method of cost accounting used by companies whose production consists of **continuous or operational stages, or processes** such as those used in the chemical and oil industries. The costs are accumulated for the whole production cycle and the average unit production costs are computed for each stage.

Special rules are applied in process costing to the valuation of work in progress, normal losses and abnormal losses. It is also common to distinguish between the main product of the process, by-products and joint products.

Joint products are defined as two or more products separated in the course of processing, each having a sufficiently high saleable value to merit recognition as a main product in its own right. Any costs incurred need to be identified and matched with revenues.

Standard costing

2059 Standard costs, are **pre-determined estimates** based on expected levels of costs, production and efficiency. Standard costs are based on "normal levels of production" and should be reviewed on a regular basis to ensure that they reflect current prices, while any abnormal costs or costs arising from inefficiencies should be written off in the period. Also, standards should be adjusted for new products in order to take account of new production techniques.

Standard costing **is often used for internal purposes** such as stock valuation for management accounting purposes. It can also be the basis for stock valuation in published financial statements where the standard cost provides a close approximation to actual costs.

2060 **Accounting treatment** Where purchases are valued at standard cost, any difference between the standard and actual cost is written off to the profit and loss account. All issues from stores are at the same standard price.

The table below illustrates the management accounting treatment for materials received, materials variance and issues from stores.

Table	Debit	Credit
Materials received	Stock a/c at standard cost	Purchase ledger at cost
Materials variance	Debit variance posted to manufacturing profit/loss.	Credit variance posted to manufacturing profit/loss.
Issue of materials	Work in progress at standard cost	Stock a/c at standard cost

Where the materials variance is significant this may indicate that the standard cost is not sufficiently accurate to form an acceptable basis for use in published financial statements.

2061 **Specialist industries** In certain industries such as farming, specialist **valuation techniques** have been devised for valuing stock. For instance, it can be difficult to determine the true cost of livestock and the stock valuation is generally derived by taking the market price less estimated profit. Because of the varying methods applied and their limited application, a detailed review of valuation methods for specialist industries is beyond the remit of this book.

3. Methods of valuing closing stock

2064 There are **two principal methods** of valuing closing stock; namely the first-in-first out (FIFO) and the weighted average price method. There are also a **number of other methods** whose usage is restricted. When selecting a method for valuing stock, the directors must ensure that it provides the fairest approximation to "actual cost".

Whichever method has been adopted requires a disclosure to this effect to be given in the notes to the accounts. The method selected could impact on trading profit, as illustrated in the following examples.

a. Principal valuation methods

FIFO

Under the first in first out (FIFO) method, stocks at the end of the financial period to be represented by the most recent purchase price or cost of production. The logic is that the method reflects the **physical flow of goods** from production or purchase to sale; it assumes that the goods purchased or produced first will have been used first and that the remaining stock at the period end will represent the latest purchases or production. **2066**

The **profit and loss account** should then provide a close approximation to the actual costs incurred in the production or purchase of each unit of sales. This method is the most widely used.

EXAMPLE **Scenario 1**

In this example closing stocks total 300 units. The FIFO method assumes that the stock is appropriated from the **most recent stock purchase** which was at £36 per unit.
The total value of the stock will be 300 × £36 = £10,800.

Gross profit (extract)	£	£
Turnover		108,500
Purchases	90,000	
Less: closing stock	10,800	
Cost of sales		79,200
Gross profit		**29,300**

Scenario 2

The second scenario illustrates how the FIFO method is applied to **multiple stock purchases** throughout the financial year.

Date	Quantity Units	Price per tonne £	Value £
25 May	500	41.00	20,500
18 June	500	32.00	16,000
7 August	800	34.00	27,200
19 September	500	38.00	19,000
3 November	200	36.50	7,300
Total	**2,500**		**90,000**

At the end of the accounting period on 30 October, the entity has 300 units of raw material in stock.
Using a FIFO basis, the year-end stocks are assumed to relate to the latest purchases and will be valued as follows:

200 units [purchased on 3 November] at £36.50 =	£7,300
100 units [out of the batch of 500 units purchased on 19 September at £38 =	£3,800
Totals 300 units	**£11,100**

Profit and loss account (extract)

Gross profit	£	£
Turnover		108,500
Purchases	90,000	
Less: closing stock	11,100	
Cost of sales		78,900
Gross profit		**29,600**

The **advantages** of the FIFO method are as follows: **2067**
- the oldest items are issued from stock first;
- closing stock should represent the current value of stock (matches pricing); and
- this valuation method is accepted by the inland revenue.

The **principal disadvantage** of the FIFO method is that the issue price may not reflect current economic values.

Weighted average price

2070 Under the weighted-average price method, the cost is determined by dividing the total cost of the units by their number. This price may be arrived at through a continuous, periodic or a moving average.

The weighted average method **does not reflect the costs incurred** in the production of individual stock units. However, in many instances the differences are unlikely to be significant. Situations where the use of weighted average is unlikely to be appropriate, include times of high inflation or where, for example, purchases are made in foreign currencies with fluctuating exchange rates.

2071 The **advantages** of the weighted average method are:
- issue prices from stores need only be computed on the receipt of new deliveries and not with each issue, as required by FIFO;
- receipts tend to be less frequent than issues, so the method is less cumbersome to operate;
- price fluctuations are "ironed out" over time; and
- the costs computed will be somewhere between the figures derived from the LIFO and FIFO methods.

The **disadvantage** is that issues from stock may be priced at a level different from current economic value or prices. The required accounting entries are illustrated in the example.

EXAMPLE As with the example used in the FIFO method, the closing stock is 300 units and the financial year-end is 31 October 2010.

Date 2010	Quantity Units	Price per tonne £	Total cost £	
25 May	500	41.00	20,500	
18 June	500	32.00	16,000	
7 August	800	34.00	27,200	
19 September	500	38.00	19,000	
3 October	200	36.50	7,300	see 1.
	2,500		**90,000**	

The **average cost** should be based on normal stockholding and usage patterns. In this example, the total cost is divided by the total units (£90,000/2,500 = £36.00 or an average can be taken over another time period (i.e. the latest quarter or half year) and the resulting value applied to the year end stock holding. The **year end closing stock valuation** method would be 300 units × £36.00 = £10,800.

1. Accounting entries
Stock receivable

		Dr £	Cr £
Debit:	Stock (materials at cost)	20,000	
Credit:	Purchase ledger (at cost)		20,000

Issues from stock – 20 Oct 2010

		Dr £	Cr £
Debit:	WIP (weighted average) 400 x £33.33	13,332	
Debit:	Profit/loss a/c variance ((400 x 50) – £13,332)	6,668	
Credit:	Stock		20,000

Profit and loss account (extract)
Gross profit

	Dr £	Cr £
Turnover		108,500
Purchases	90,000	
Less: closing stock	9,999	
Cost of sales		80,001
Gross profit		**28,499**

Summary of primary valuation methods

£	FIFO	Weighted average
Turnover	108,500	108,500
Purchases	90,000	90,000
Closing stock	11,100	9,999
Cost of sales	78,900	80,001
Gross profit	**29,600**	**28,499**

2075

b. Other valuation methods

Unit production cost method The unit production cost of each item in stock is the actual cost of its production. Unit cost is a practical method of calculating cost used by retailers and wholesalers who specialise in low volume, high-value goods (e.g. jewellery manufacture), where the allocation of overheads is relatively straightforward and is likely to be an immaterial part of the overall cost. 2076

The **method is not suitable** for most types of manufacturing companies where the costs of collecting the relevant information may often be prohibitive. Where there are high levels of production it will be difficult and costly to determine the costs of each production unit.

Retail method Under this method, the total stock in hand is valued at current selling price which is then adjusted to an approximate purchase cost by deducting the gross margin. For example, this method is sometimes used in department stores, where a large number of different stock lines can be identified and adjusted for any difference in gross profit margins. 2077

EXAMPLE **DEF Ltd – Annual report and accounts**
Accounting policies (extracts)
Stocks – Retail method

Stocks comprise goods held for resale and are valued at lower of cost and net realisable value. Stocks in stores are calculated at retail prices and reduced by appropriate margins to the lower of cost and net realisable value.

Fixed amount method The Companies Act allows items to be included in stocks of raw materials at a fixed quantity, if the value is immaterial or the quantity, valuation and composition, are not subject to material variation. 2078

The cost of the stocks are calculated on the basis of a fixed unit value ascribed to a predetermined number of units of stock. Any excess number over above this stock quantity is valued on the basis of one of the other methods.

Marginal costing Marginal costing may be used as a basis of stock valuation for management accounting purposes only, by adding a proportion of production overhead not already included in marginal cost. For financial accounting purposes, the method is deemed unacceptable under SSAP 9. 2080

Base stock method This is similar to the fixed amount method but is generally discouraged. The problem with this method is that it often results in stocks being stated in the balance sheet, at amounts that are very different to current prices. The method relies on a buffer stock that does not change and which is accounted for in the stock-take at its original purchase price. 2081

Latest invoice price method Under this method the latest invoice price is applied to the number of items in retained stock. The problem is, that this is not necessarily the same as 2082 the actual cost of previously acquired stock, and in times of rising prices will result in "unrealised" profits being taken. In addition, closing stock valuations will be higher, resulting in higher gross profits. The **exception** is if price fluctuations during the period have been insignificant and the calculated value is a reasonable approximation of cost.

4. Transfers from current to fixed assets

2085 There are **different rules** for valuing fixed assets and stocks. Fixed assets are valued at cost less depreciation and provisions for permanent diminution in values. Current assets are carried at lower of historical cost or net realisable value. Companies could, theoretically, avoid charging write downs to the profit and loss account on **unsold trading assets** by transferring them to fixed assets at a figure exceeding net realisable value. However, situations do arise where such transfers are legitimate, as in the example below.

2086 **Accounting treatment** FRS 5 requires an entity to account for stock under the current asset accounting rules, up to the effective date the asset is transferred, at the lower of cost or net realisable value. Any **diminution in value** up to that date should be charged to the profit and loss account, covering the loss to the entity while the asset is held as a current asset. Accurate records should be kept of any transfers and external valuations should be undertaken for material items which should be disclosed in the notes to the accounts.

EXAMPLE A property company constructed an office block with the intention of selling it on the open market. However, due to the expansion of its own operations it decided to use the building for its own headquarters and not sell it. The building cost £1.5m and the NRV was £1.2m. The transfer from current to fixed assets should be at the NRV of £1.2m, with the diminution in value charged to the profit and loss account.

MEMO POINTS UITF 5 "Transfers from current assets to fixed assets" covers current assets included in the balance sheet at the lower of cost or net realisable value. The abstract does not apply to assets accounted for under the alternative accounting rules.

B. Net realisable value (NRV)

2090 SSAP 9 (5) The net realisable value or "market value" is the estimated proceeds from the sale of stock items minus all further costs to completion, including the costs of marketing, distribution and selling. Where the net realisable value of the stock is less than cost, the stock should be written-down to that value.

In assessing NRV, there may be a **number of specific issues** to consider such as provisions, stocks of spare parts, post-balance sheet events, group stocks or by-products.

2091 The net realisable value is likely to be less than the cost, **where one or more of the following events** has occurred; namely:
- an increase in costs;
- a fall in selling price;
- physical deterioration of stocks;
- product obsolescence;
- a strategic decision to produce goods at a loss; or
- production or purchasing errors.

2092 In addition, **when excess stocks are held** which are unlikely to be sold within the current period, the impending delay in converting stocks to sales, could result in one or more of the situations listed becoming significant.

Where materials are purchased for use in the **production of a larger product** that is to be sold (e.g. the cost of a radio to be included within a new car), the NRV of that item on a stand alone basis may be less than its cost. However, no reduction need be made to the cost of that individual component, provided that the goods into which the materials are to be incorporated, can still be sold at a profit after incorporating the material at cost price.

If there is **no reasonable expectation** that retained stocks will be able to generate sufficient revenue to cover the costs incurred in purchasing or manufacturing, then these costs, to the extent that they are irrecoverable, should be written-off in the current year.

Provisions

If a provision is required **to reduce the value of finished goods** below cost, the stocks of parts and "sub-assemblies" comprising such goods, together with committed orders for stocks, should also be reviewed. **2094**

Even if a company uses a pre-determined formula (see example below) to determine the value of its stocks, the calculation of provisions to reduce stocks from cost to net realisable value must take account of the following: SSAP 9 (Appendix 1.16)

- age of the stock;
- expected future stock movements; or
- estimated scrap values.

Consideration must be given to other **any special factors** that may influence the value of the stock.

If **stocks in hand** have **previously been written down** to net realisable value, but in the current period it is determined that the reasons for doing so no longer apply (whether in full or in part), then that part of the provision should be written back through the profit and loss account.

EXAMPLE **Basis of the provision for slow-moving goods (predetermined formula based on the frequency of stock usage).**
Company X calculates on the basis of experience that the following year-end provision is required for slow-moving goods.

Last movement	**Provision (%)**
Goods that have not moved in the last:	
– 3 months	nil
– 6 months	15%
– 9 months	30%
– 12 months	50%
– Over 12 months	100%

Stocks of spare parts

Where stocks of spares are held for resale, **special consideration** of the factors listed in ¶2094 is required in the context of the: **2098** SSAP 9 (Appendix 1.18)

- number of units sold to which stock is applicable;
- estimated frequency with which replacement spares are required; or
- estimated useful life of the unit of production to which the stock applies.

The demand for spares is strongly correlated to the demand for the underlying product, and so should be so considered when calculating the net realisable value for the stock.

EXAMPLE Motor vehicle dealerships generally incorporate a spare-parts department that holds large stocks of car parts. There is generally a **high turnover of general parts** such as air filters, or spark plugs or other components that fit a range of cars across the fleet. These stocks are usually replenished on a frequent basis to meet the demand for servicing, MOTs etc.

Consumable stores and other stocks not intended for resale must be stated at lower of cost or net realisable value. As there is often no anticipated net realisable value they will often be written off as purchased.

Stock write-offs – post balance sheet

2100 SSAP 9 (Appendix 1.19) Events that occur between the financial year end and the signing of the financial statements, when considering net realisable values at the balance sheet date, should be considered.

EXAMPLE The company estimated future demand for product X as 50,000 units per annum, at £10 per unit. At the year end 40,000 units were still in stock at a cost of £5 per unit. Initially, no provision against the carrying value was considered necessary.

Following the year end, a major contract of 30,000 units per annum was lost and the company does not anticipate finding a replacement customer. Therefore, based on revised sales forecasts, 20,000 units have been deemed surplus to requirements and will be scrapped for nil consideration. As such, a provision of £100,000 [20,000 units at a cost of £5 per unit] has been made in the financial statements.

Groups of stock items

2102 Ideally, the comparison of cost with net realisable value should be made on an item-by-item basis. However, this is usually not practicable and in such cases it is permissible to consider groups of similar items together.

EXAMPLE **Trading stock**

A company holding trading stock in a warehouse suffered some damage from flooding. Although the stock had deteriorated it was deemed saleable through discount channels. The stock was originally valued at £100,000, but is now deemed to have a net realisable value of £25,000.

By-products

2104 SSAP 9 (Appendix 1.15) By-products are recovered incidentally from the materials used in the manufacture of the main products or may be further processed to create joint products. In industries **where the cost of** minor or by-products **is not separable** from the cost of the principal products, stocks of such by products may be stated in the financial statements at net realisable value. The cost of the main product is then calculated after deduction of the NRV of the by-product.

EXAMPLE **Refining Plc – Annual report and accounts**
Accounting policies (extract)
By-products

The company produces by-products from its refining process. The costs incurred in processing prior to the separation of the products are known as joint costs. The proceeds from the sale of the by-product are treated as pure profit and stocks held are stated at net realisable value; namely selling price less marketing, selling and distribution costs.

C. Replacement cost

2108 SSAP 9 (6) Replacement cost is the cost of replacing stock at current prices, either purchase or production. The use of replacement cost **is not acceptable where** the effect is to take account of a loss greater than that originally expected. The **estimated replacement value** of stock may be used in certain circumstances where the replacement cost is below net realisable value.

For example, in the case of materials whose prices are fluctuating and which have not formed part of sales contracts agreed at the date the financial statements are prepared, the replacement cost may be the best measure of net realisable value. It is the responsibility of the directors to determine whether replacement cost is the best measure.

If the value of stocks reflected in the accounts at historical cost **differs materially** from the replacement cost, that difference must be disclosed in a note to the accounts. Where the actual purchase price or production cost of stock items has been calculated on an individual basis and not using one of the stock valuation methods, then this disclosure need not be given.

EXAMPLE **Disclosure of replacement cost**

Notes to the accounts (extract)

The following note would be appropriate when the replacement cost of stocks is materially greater than the historical cost at which they are stated:
Included in the amount shown for stocks of raw materials are items valued at cost on a first in, first out basis (FIFO). The replacement cost of these items at 31 December 2010 exceeds by £225,000 (20X8 – £180,000), the amount at which they are included in the financial statements.

Also, where a company adopts the **alternative accounting rules** as permitted under the Companies Act, items of stock may be stated at the lower of current replacement cost and net realisable value. Any permanent diminution in value should be provided for. However, it may be difficult to estimate the cost if the asset in question cannot be replaced. 2109

SECTION 3

Disclosure framework

"Stocks" is a main heading under current assets and must be shown on the face of the balance sheet. Additional disclosures are required under the Act of various sub-categories of stock. The **accounting policies** adopted with regard to stocks should also be disclosed. The disclosure requirements for all stock classifications are the same. 2112

Formats

As **required by the Companies Act**, the stock categories listed in ¶2005 should be grouped and disclosed under the following sub-categories of "stocks": 2113
- raw material and consumables;
- work in progress;
- finished goods and goods for resale; and
- payments on account.

These details can be given either on the face of the balance sheet or in the notes to the accounts.

Where a **small company** chooses to prepare and file shorter-form accounts it can condense the disclosures to just stocks and payments on account. The detailed requirements for small companies electing to adopt the FRSSE are dealt with in the chapter on small companies. If the FRSSE is not adopted then the requirements of SSAP 9 apply to shorter form accounts. 2115

Should a company **decide to file abbreviated accounts**, then only the total (combined) stock figure need be disclosed. Any difference between the stock figure disclosed in the accounts and the replacement cost of the stock need not be disclosed. Although a **medium-sized company** may file abbreviated accounts, none of the permitted abbreviations relate to the balance sheet.

MEMO POINTS Small companies are not required to give a sub classification of stock, except to distinguish between stocks and payments on account. The reference to Schedule 4 of the Companies Act has now been replaced by Schedule 1 to the Large and Medium-sized Companies and Groups (Accounts and Reports) 2008/SI 2008/410. Schedule 8 to the Companies Act 1985 has been replaced by Schedule 1 to the Small Companies and Groups (Accounts and Director's Reports) Regulations 2008/SI 2008/409.

Alternative formats

In certain circumstances, the **special nature** of a company's business will mean that the formats adopted in the company's financial statements may need to be amended. 2117

The following example is of a building development company that holds significant stocks of residential land. The information supplied in the notes to the accounts highlights the fact that it has the capacity for future building projects and associated revenues.

EXAMPLE **Barge Developments Ltd**

Notes to the accounts (extract)

10. Stocks

	2010	**2009**
	£m	**£m**
Raw materials and consumable	2.4	2.8
Finished goods and goods for resale	6.8	5.4
Residential developments		
– Land	435.1	345.8
– Development and construction costs	220.7	175.4
Commercial, industrial and mixed development properties	185.4	212.4
Total	**850.4**	**741.8**

Accounting policies

2119 SSAP 9 (32) It is a further requirement of the Companies Act, that accounting policies for stocks (and long-term contracts) and the method of calculating turnover and attributable profit be disclosed and applied consistently within the business from year to year. If **different bases** have been adopted for valuing different types of stock, this fact must be disclosed as illustrated in the following example.

EXAMPLE **Notes to the accounts** (extract)

15. Disclosure of general accounting policies

Weighted average cost

Stocks are valued at the lower of weighted average cost or estimated net realisable value.
Cost comprises direct material and labour costs together with relevant factory overheads (including depreciation) on the basis of normal activity levels. The cost of cocoa also reflects the use of the futures market on the basis of forecast physical requirements.
The following are examples of different accounting policy notes that highlight that at different stages of production, different valuation methods are appropriate for dealing with the **treatment and valuation** of stocks:

1. **Stocks and work in progress** are stated at the lower of cost and net realisable value.
2. **Finished goods and goods for resale** are stated at the lower of cost, including appropriate production overheads, and net realisable value. Distribution and administrative expenses are not included in the stock valuation.
3. **Work in progress** is valued at cost of materials plus manufacturing labour and overheads.
4. **Raw materials** are valued at purchase price but reduced to net replacement cost if this is lower.
5. Provision is made for **slow moving or obsolete** items.

Hedging of stock transactions in foreign currencies

2120 The gain or loss should be disclosed once a foreign exchange transaction has been recorded, at the rate specified in the forward contract used to hedge the stock items.

The **deferred gain or loss** should be calculated by re-translating the stock at the spot rate at the transaction date and comparing the value to the carrying amount. The recognition of the deferred gain or loss will depend on stock utilisation through the production process or its subsequent resale.

Replacement cost

2121 Where a **significant difference** exists between the value of stock recorded in the balance sheet and the replacement cost of the stock (production or purchase cost), this fact should be disclosed in the notes to the accounts.

SECTION 4

Taxation

In general the requirements of HMRC regarding the valuation of stock, are aligned with those of SSAP 9 and IAS 2, with a small number of exceptions as set out in the table below. The treatment of depreciation is also considered. **2122**

Discontinued business	Unsold stock and work in progress is included in taxable trading profit, as if sold at market value on the date the business ceases trading
Stock sold to connected persons	If the seller and buyer are connected persons (e.g. family members) the stock must be valued at the prevailing market price, as if the sale had been made at arm's length
Stock sold to another trader who continues with the business	Where the stock is sold to another trader who will continue the business, the stock should be valued in the final accounts at the agreed consideration for the sale
Appropriations of trading stock for private use	Market value should be used for tax purposes rather than cost, where stock is appropriated for private use. This requirement is based on case law (Sharkey v Wherner 1955), which was subsequently codified in the Finance Act 2008.

MEMO POINTS **Special rules exist** for certain trades or industries such as motor dealers or farming. HMRC issue regular tax bulletins updating their guidance in these areas.

Depreciation For financial statements to accurately reflect business costs they should include a cost element ("depreciation – ¶1444) covering the reduction ("wear and tear") in the useful economic life of fixed assets. The depreciation charge for each period is recognised as an expense in the profit and loss account for the period unless it can be included in the carrying amount of an asset. **2123**

This depletion charge against income should be added back in the tax computation.

The determination of profit for an accounting period requires the matching of costs with related revenues and as such, a business should ensure that it has appropriate mechanisms in place to ensure that depreciation is added back in the computation for each year/period of disposal of stock.

Where there are only a **small number of relatively large items in stock**, it is easier to track the depreciation within stock and so ensure that on the disposal of the stock in question, the relevant depreciation is correctly included in the tax computation.

Where the stock comprises a **large number of individual items each of relatively modest value**, the record keeping requirements for depreciation in stock are rather more burdensome.

The relationship between the accounting treatment for depreciation and the requirements of tax law is encapsulated in a ruling handed down by the House of Lords in the case of the joint appeal by Mars UK Ltd and William Grant & Sons Distillers Ltd in 2007, and provides guidance for companies in this area.

MEMO POINTS A ruling in the House of Lords dated 28 March 2007 in the case involving joint appeals by Mars UK Ltd. and William Grant & Sons Distillers Ltd. was based on the generally accepted accounting practice, that costs be matched with related revenue. The costs of stock may have been incurred in the year in question, or in earlier years and carried forward in accordance with the general principle that they be matched with the related sales when they occur. The Judge concluded that both Mars and Grant had prepared their accounts in accordance with SSAP 9 as they had apportioned the depreciation into two parts:

- the first part related to depreciation of fixed assets regarding the production of goods sold during the year and which was deducted from the revenue for the year, and
- the second part reflected the depreciation in fixed assets related to the production of unsold stocks which was carried forward.

Lord Hoffman agreed that the appellants had only deducted the first part of the depreciation charge in arriving at the profit for the year. The **tax effect** resulting from this accounting analysis is that ICTA88/S74(1)(f) does not require the second part of depreciation to be added back as this should occur when the stock is disposed of and the depreciation deducted in arriving at the profit for the year of the disposal.

SECTION 5

Consignment stocks

2126 Consignment stocks are a **type of stock financing arrangement** predominately used by car manufacturers and dealers, although it does apply to other industries. Application Note A to FRS 5 "Reporting the substance of transactions", details how the principle of recognising assets and liabilities should be applied to these arrangements.

2127 FRS 5 (A1) Consignment stock is held by one party (the "dealer") **whilst still the legal property** of another (the "manufacturer"), on terms that give the dealer the right to sell the stock in the normal course of its business, or to return it unsold, without penalty, to the legal owner. Consignment stock may be physically located on the premises of the dealer or held at another site.

This type of arrangement can provide the following **commercial advantages** to both parties; namely:
- the dealer can hold or have quicker access to a larger range of stock;
- the manufacturer can avoid stock building up on its premises by moving it closer to the customer; and
- the sales potential of the product may be enhanced.

2128 The **terms of consignment agreements** can vary considerably concerning key aspects such as:
- the right of return by the dealer (¶2134);
- determination of the sale (transfer) price; or
- the deposit terms required by the manufacturer of the dealer.

Characteristics of consignment stock arrangements

2129 FRS 5 (A2) The **main features** of a consignment stock arrangement are as follows:

1. The **manufacturer** passes goods to the dealer but **retains legal title** to the stock until one of a number of events takes place; namely:
- the dealer sells the goods to a third party;
- a specified time period elapses triggering the return of the goods; or
- the dealer uses the goods as demonstration models.

Until such a qualifying event occurs, the dealer is entitled to return the goods to the manufacturer or the manufacturer is able to require their return or insist that they are passed to another dealer.

2. As soon as the **legal title** to the goods **passes**, the transfer price becomes payable by the dealer:
- which may be fixed at the date the goods are delivered to the dealer;
- it can vary with the period between delivery and transfer of title; or
- it may be the manufacturer's list price at the date of transfer of title.

3. The **dealer may** be required to **pay a deposit, display or financing charge** to the manufacturer, which may be fixed for a period and may bear interest. In other cases, a finance company will pay the deposit or charge to the manufacturer and will charge interest when recharging the dealer.

4. **Other items** include inspection rights or insurance for loss or damage.

A. Benefits and risks

The **substance of each agreement** should be determined to see where the principal risks and benefits lie by examining all commercial aspects of the agreement. The **general rule**, is that the stock should appear on the balance sheet of the dealer when he has access to its principle benefits, but at the same time it carries the principal risks inherent in these types of transaction. The aim is to determine whether, at any given time, the **dealer has acquired an asset** in the form of stock and a corresponding liability to the manufacturer, where the legal title has passed to the manufacturer. 2131

The **principal benefits** of consignment stocks for **dealers** are: 2132 FRS 5 (A3)
- the future cash flows from a sale to a third party and the right to retain the items of stock in order to achieve such a sale;
- insulation from changes to the transfer price charged by the manufacturer for its stock; and
- the right to use the stock (e.g. as a demonstration model).

The **principal risks** are being compelled to retain stock that is not readily saleable or obsolete and the risk of slow movement, resulting in increased financing costs and possible write downs.

The accounting standard identifies **four principal sources** of benefits and risks associated with consignment stocks; namely, 2133
- the manufacturer's right of return;
- the dealer's right of return;
- the stock transfer price; and
- the dealer's right to use stock.

Manufacturer's right to demand the return of stock

The **dealer's access** to the benefits of the stock will be restricted if the manufacturer can demand the return of the goods or their transfer to another dealer. If for instance, a high proportion of the stock meets this definition, this indicates that the stock remains an asset of the manufacturer. 2134 FRS 5 (A5)

Alternatively, if the dealer is not obliged to comply with the request of the manufacturer to return stock, this would indicate that the stock is an asset of the dealer. A number of different scenarios are considered in the table below.

Asset of the manufacturer	Deemed an asset of the dealer
Manufacturer can require the dealer to return or transfer stock without compensation	Manufacturer cannot demand the dealer return or transfer the stock
Manufacturer can levy penalties on a dealer for non-return or transfer of stock at the manufacturers request	Financial incentives provided to persuade the dealer to return or transfer stock

Dealer's right of return

Where the dealer has a right to return stock **without penalty**, it does not bear any obsolescence risk, thereby indicating that the dealer has neither the asset "stock" nor the liability (to the manufacturer). The **commercial effect** of this arrangement should be considered. For instance, if the right of return is exercised frequently or the manufacturer provides an incentive such as price discounts, in order to persuade the dealer to retain the stock, this would indicate that the stock is in substance, not an asset of the dealer. 2135 FRS 5 (A6)

Conversely, **if the dealer has no right to return the stock** or is charged a penalty for so doing, this would indicate that the dealer bears significant commercial risks regarding the stock; thus making the stock an asset. The dealer also has a corresponding liability to the manufacturer to pay for the stock.

Dealer's right of return	
Dealer has unfettered right to return stock to the manufacturer without penalty and actually exercises the right to practice	**Dealer has no right to return stock** or is commercially compelled not to exercise its right of return
Manufacturer bears obsolescence risk, e.g. – obsolete stock is returned to the manufacturer without penalty; or financial incentives given by manufacturers to prevent stock being returned to it (e.g. model change or if it becomes obsolete)	**Dealer bears obsolescence risk**, e.g. – penalty charged if dealer returns stock to manufacturer; or – obsolete stock cannot be returned to the manufacturer and no compensation is paid by the manufacturer for losses due to obsolescence

Stock transfer price and deposits

2136 FRS 5 (A7) Where the stock transfer price is the manufacturer's list price at delivery, then the dealer is protected from any price changes imposed by the manufacturer. This would indicate that the stock is an **asset of the dealer** at the delivery date.

Alternatively, if the price charged to the dealer is the manufacturer's list price at the date the legal transfer of the goods take place, this could indicate that the stock is an asset for the manufacturer, until such a transfer takes place.

2137 **Slow movement risk** The price at which the stock is transferred may also affect who absorbs the slow payment risk and the financing costs until the stock is sold. The **manufacturer bears** the slow payment risk when there is no deposit and the charge to the dealer is simply the list price, payable when legal title is transferred.

Conversely, the **dealer bears the slow payment risk** whenever the transfer price is determined by the length of time for which the stock is held. For instance, the arrangement may include a clause that the price to the dealer increases over the time the stock is held, or where the transfer price is the list price at the transfer of the legal title and not simply the delivery date.

2138 FRS 5 (A9) **Where a deposit is provided by the dealer** to the manufacturer, the question arises as to whether the dealer bears any variations in stock financing costs due to slow movement, such as where a large interest-free deposit is related to stock levels held by the dealer. Alternatively, a finance company could provide a deposit to the manufacture and charge interest to the dealer.

FRS 5 (A8) EXAMPLE

Stock transfer price	
Asset of the manufacturer	**Asset of the dealer**
Stock transfer price charged by the manufacturer is based on the manufacturer's list price at date of transfer of legal title	Stock transfer price charged by manufacturer is based on manufacturer's list price at date of delivery
Manufacturer bears slow movement risk, e.g. transfer price set independently of time for which dealer holds stock, and there is no deposit	**Dealer bears slow movement risk** – dealer is effectively charged interest as transfer price or other payments to manufacturer vary with time for which the dealer holds stock; or – dealer makes substantial interest free deposits that vary with the levels of stock held

Dealer's right to use the stock

Where the dealer exercises a right to use the consignment stock in its business, this will usually make it an asset of the dealer; the legal title will be transferred to the dealer and give rise to an obligation to pay the manufacturer. 2140 FRS 5 (A10)

B. General accounting treatment

Varying treatments in respect of the same transaction are possible depending on the terms underlying the transaction. 2142 FRS 5 (A12)

Where the **substance of the transaction** indicates that the **stock is an asset of the dealer**, the stock should be recognised on the dealer's balance sheet, together with the corresponding liability.

Any **deposit should be deducted** from the liability to the supplier. The notes to the financial statements should detail:
- the nature of the arrangement;
- the value of the consignment stock included in the balance sheet; and
- the main terms, under which the stock is held, including the terms of any deposits.

Where the substance of the transaction indicates that the **stock is not an asset of the dealer**, the stock should not be included on the dealer's balance sheet until the transfer of title has crystallised. Any deposit paid by the dealer to the manufacturer should be classified under "other debtors". The notes to the financial statements should include information similar to that required where the stock is deemed to be an asset of the dealer.

A **typical consignment arrangement** is illustrated in the example below. 2145

EXAMPLE **Consignment stock**

Terms and conditions, accounting treatment and disclosure requirements.
A motor manufacturer may conclude an agreement with its dealer network to consign stock to them. These agreements are often very detailed; a typical consignment agreement will consist of some of the following **terms and conditions**:
1. The dealer is **allocated stock** by the manufacturer which is to be stored at the dealer's premises.
2. The manufacturer can **reward or penalise** the dealer through the allocation of consignment stock, with preferred dealers gaining favourable access to new models etc.
3. **Legal title** to the stock does not pass until the dealer has paid for the stock, which for example could be the earlier of:
- the date of sale of a vehicle to the custom; and
- the date the stock is appropriated for demonstration purposes; or 90 days.
4. The manufacturer and dealer may conclude a deal with a third party finance house to finance the vehicles consigned to a dealer, who pays a **finance cost** based on the value of the consignment. The manufacturer receives a payment from the finance house for all the vehicles consigned to the dealer.
5. Until the dealer **sells or adopts the stock** with the agreed time limit (e.g. 90 days), the stock may be returned to the manufacturer, exchanged or transferred to another dealer in the network. This increases the stock availability to the dealer.
6. Where a particular model is slow moving and is approaching the limit of the agreed time period, the dealer has the **following options**:
- exchange or transfer the vehicle to another dealer;
- negotiate an extension of the consignment deal; and
- provide incentives to generate sales.
7. The stock **transfer price** is based on the manufacturer's list price.

Accounting treatment for the dealer
The **agreement** should be assessed to ascertain where the **principle risks and benefits of ownership** lie. In this example the manufacturer appears to carry the risk of obsolescence, with the risk of slow payment falling on the dealer after the free stocking period has expired.
The dealer should recognise the **obligation** (equal to the principal on which interest is paid) in its balance sheet at the end of the free stocking period. The **related asset** of similar value should be

accounted for as an "interest in consignment stock". At the point the stock is adopted by the dealer for either sale or demonstration, it should be recorded as stock of the dealer.

In this example, the **interest payments payable** by the dealer to the finance house represent an obligation to transfer economic benefits; namely a liability in the form of a loan.

Revenue recognition In this example **the manufacturer** recognises revenue at the date the consignment stock is adopted; namely, at the point all the risks and rewards of ownership are transferred. In the free stocking period the manufacturer still holds the stock and the dealer does not recognise the asset. In the period between the end of the free stocking period and adoption of the stock, the manufacturer will continue to hold the stock whilst the dealer also holds an "interest" in the consignment stock.

Disclosure requirements

Year-ended 30 June 2010

Accounting policies (extract)

Stocks of motor vehicles have been valued at the lower of cost or net realisable value. Part stocks are valued at cost on a weighted average or first-in first out basis (FIFO). Provisions have also been made against slow-moving, obsolete and surplus stock. **Consignment stocks** from the manufacturers that are the subject of interest or other charges are included at cost. Vehicles subject to repurchase agreements are included at the contracted repurchase price. In both cases, the associated liability is accounted for in creditors.

Stocks

	2010 £	2009 £
Goods for resale	2,750,000	1,620,000
Repurchase agreements	150,000	105,000
Consignment vehicles (interest bearing)	98,000	65,000
Total	**2,998,000**	**1,790,000**

Accounting treatment for the manufacturer

2146 In relation to the example above, the accounting treatment for the manufacturer is not discussed in FRS 5. Whereas the dealer might register an "interest in the consignment stock" on its balance sheet, the manufacturer could register the **physical stock** in its balance sheet. Also, the manufacturer is not required to make any specific disclosures in its financial statements other than the need to provide sufficient information on the commercial effect of the transaction.

There are **three possible dates** under a typical agreement that a sale might be registered:
- the date the stock is assigned to the dealer;
- the date from which interest is payable by the dealer under a related financing arrangement; or
- the date the dealer adopts or sells the stock.

The most appropriate date for the purposes of **derecognition** is the latter option.

Disclosure requirements

2147 In general, the FRS 5 criteria permitting a **linked presentation** will not be satisfied, where the terms of the consignment agreement allow for the vehicle to be retained by the dealer.

C. Sale and repurchase of stocks

2150 Stock is sometimes sold with an **option to buy it back** at a later date. Options have different terms and conditions and run for different time periods, during which time the company that sold the stock uses the sale proceeds as a form of finance.

2151 The **substance of each option** must be examined and the accounting treatment will be dependent upon where the risks and benefits associated with the stock lie. For example, **options may be structured** so that the purchaser agrees with the lender for them to buy back the stock at the original sale price, without genuine exposure to, or benefit from, changes in the value of underlying assets. Such an agreement should be accounted for as a financing arrangement not as the sale of an asset.

EXAMPLE Company A agrees to sell stock for £50,000 to Company B, with whom Company A enters into an agreement to buy back the stock 10 months later for £55,000. The additional £5,000 should be accounted for as the finance cost or interest and not as part of the cost of the stock, and should be charged to the profit and loss account of Company B.
The **substance of this agreement** is that of a secured loan that requires the presentation of the original asset (stock) at an agreed future date. The receipt of £50,000 should be accounted for by Company A on its balance sheet as a finance liability. For the 10 month period the stock should be carried on the balance sheet of Company B.

SECTION 6

Goods with reservation of title

Companies may sell goods to other companies with reservation clauses included in the sale contracts, so enabling the seller to retain ownership of those goods until the debtor is settled. These clauses are sometimes referred to as "**Romalpa clauses**". 2160

The **principal advantage** of trading with reservation of title is that if the purchaser becomes insolvent, a creditor may be able to reclaim the stock from their insolvent customer. In practice, it has been shown to be difficult to enforce these "reservation of title clauses" and they no longer have the prominence that once had.

MEMO POINTS The case of *Aluminium Industrie Vaassen B.V. v Romalpa Aluminium Limited* (1976) gave rise to what is known as the "Romalpa clauses", which govern contractual relationships.

Accounting treatment

These **legal clauses only come into effect** when a company becomes insolvent and as accounts are prepared on a going concern basis, the **general rule** is that the purchaser recognises the stock and the corresponding liability in its balance sheet, even though the supplier usually retains legal title to the goods. This is consistent with FRS 5, as it is the purchaser who bears the risks and enjoys the benefits from the asset. A note to this effect should be given in the financial statements. Disclosure will be necessary where there are doubts as to the going concern status of the purchaser. 2162

EXAMPLE **ABC Ltd – Annual report and accounts**
30 September 2010
Notes to the accounts

Creditors – amounts falling due within one year (extract)
Trade Creditors includes a sum of approximately £30,000, which is secured by the reservation to the supplier of a legal title to goods supplied and the proceeds from their sale. However, the amount secured in this manner depends on the legal interpretation of individual contracts and so cannot be determined exactly.

SECTION 7

Comparison between UK GAAP and IAS (IFRS)

The key reporting standards are IAS 2 "Inventories" and IAS 18 "Revenue". 2165

Both IAS 2 and SSAP 9 require that inventories be measured at cost or net realisable value and that cost should comprise all costs of purchase, costs of conversion and other costs incurred in bringing the inventories to their present location and condition.

MEMO POINTS In October 2010 the ASB issued a proposal introducing a financial reporting framework for medium-sized entities (FRSME) not eligible to apply the FRSSE or full IFRS. The FRSME would replace current UK GAAP from July 2013 and is based on the principles underpinning full IFRS. If adopted there could be some key differences in the treatment of stocks.

Definitions

2166 Inventories are defined in IAS 2 as assets:
- held for sale in the ordinary course of business;
- in the process of production for sale; and
- in the form of materials or supplies destined for the production process or supply of services.

First-time adoption

2167 There are no specific rules contained in IFRS 1 "First time adoption of International Financial Reporting Standards", in respect of IAS 2. As such the general rule of retrospective application will apply.

Key differences

2168 Although the requirements of SSAP 9 are broadly similar to those of IAS 2, there are a few significant differences, including structural differences in the presentation of IAS 2 and SSAP 9.

A summary of the differences between the international and the UK standard is given in the table below.

Key differences between UK GAAP and IAS	
Treatment **under SSAP 9**	**Treatment under IAS 2**
SSAP 9 covers **producer's inventories** of livestock, agricultural and forest products and mineral stocks, which should be valued at lower of cost or net realisable value, rather than net realisable value	IAS 2 includes **guidance on the application** of the lower of cost or net realisable value to individual items or groups of similar items (IAS 2.1). Does not cover biological assets or agricultural produce (IAS 41). Prohibits **write-downs on broad classifications** of inventories or industry or geographical segments. Inventories purchased on **deferred payment terms** – the difference between the price payable under normal credit terms and actual sum paid should be accounted for as an interest expense over the financing period.
Use of the **retail method** is permitted for determining the cost of inventories (SSAP 9.4)	IAS 2 includes **additional guidance** on the gross margins used in applying the retail method
Subsidies should be deducted from cost of purchase of inventories (SSAP 9.18)	IAS 2 makes no reference to issue of subsidies
Guidance is provided on the **allocation of costs** of general management and central service departments to production overheads	IAS 2 offers no such guidance
All costs incurred in **marketing, selling and distribution** of the stocks should be deducted when calculating the 'net realisable value' (SSAP 9.21), except where firm sales contracts have been concluded to a customers specification	IAS 2 refers only to "costs necessary to make the sale". IAS 2 requires that selling costs be excluded from cost (IAS 2: 16d). There is **no specific reference** to marketing costs.

Key differences between UK GAAP and IAS	
Treatment **under SSAP 9**	**Treatment under IAS 2**
Borrowing costs SSAP 9 does not deal with this issue, although some companies follow the approach adopted in the IAS, as permitted by the Companies Act	IAS 2 deals with the inclusion of **borrowing costs** in the cost of inventories, that are in an early stage of production and which need a considerable period of time to bring them to a saleable condition
SSAP 9 does not cover the issue of **annual reviews or write-down reversals**	IAS 2 requires a re-assessment of **net realisable value** of inventories at the end of the financial period and possible reversals of write-downs
Joint products. This issue is not dealt with in SSAP 9, although the use of net realisable value as a means of valuing joint products is included in the appendix	IAS 2 requires that costs be allocated between **joint products** on a consistent basis, such as on the sales values of the products
By-products Where the costs of minor by-products are not separable from the cost of the main products, stocks of by-products are calculated after deducting the NRV of the by-products	

Additional disclosure requirements

The Companies Act requires disclosure of the difference between the replacement cost (or most recent purchase price) and the carrying amount of the stocks. 2170

IAS 2 requires the following disclosures not expected by SSAP 9:
- the cost formula used;
- carrying amount of inventories carried at net realisable value;
- reversal of write-downs to net realisable value and details of circumstances that permitted the reversal; and
- cost of inventories recognised as an expense or other operating cost applicable to revenues (in addition to cost of sales).

CHAPTER 2

Long-term contracts

OUTLINE ¶¶

This chapter sets out the general guidelines, rules and principles governing the determination of turnover and profit on long-term contracts, as well as the disclosures required. **2200** SSAP 9 (22)

A long-term contract **is defined as** a contract that typically falls into two or more accounting periods, for the construction of a substantial asset or provision of a service. The test is whether the reported turnover and profits represent a true and fair view of the contract activity in the relevant accounting period. The **choice of accounting treatment** for long-term contracts will have a significant impact on the entity's reported results for the period.

The accounting treatment and disclosure requirements for long-term contracts are covered in the following:
- SSAP 9 "Stocks and long-term contracts",
- the Companies Acts,
- FRS 5 "Reporting the substance of transactions (Application Note G)",
- UITF 40 "Revenue recognition and Long-term Contracts",
- FRED 28 "Inventories and Construction and Service Contracts", and
- the FRSSE.

SSAP 9 gives specific guidance on the accounting treatment for all aspects of long-term contracts. Application Note G deals with the general principles of revenue recognition, while UITF 40 is narrower in scope providing additional guidance for accounting for revenue on service contracts.

SECTION 1

Types of long-term contract

2206 The **main types** of long-term contracts include:
SSAP 9 (22)
- the design, manufacture or construction of a single asset (e.g. civil engineering projects);
- the provision of a service (e.g. catering contract); or
- a combination of assets and services that make up a single project (e.g. refurbishment of a chain of retail outlets).

2208 A **distinction needs to be drawn** between long-term work in progress for a third party and that for the contracting company itself. For example, a company building an office block for sale to a third party will, assuming the relevant criteria are met, account for it as a long-term contract. A company building the same office block for its own use, will treat the partly completed building as an asset in the course of construction and include it within fixed assets at cost.

SSAP 9 **does not specify** particular types of contract. The **most common types** of long-term contracts are fixed-price or cost-plus contracts.

Fixed-price contracts

2210 Under fixed-price contracts, the **computation** of the amount **of turnover** is quite independent of the issue of how much profit should be taken. This is because even if a contract is loss making the turnover will still be generated. The amount of the profit or loss to be recognised will then be a function of the level of turnover recognised and the level of actual costs to date and anticipated costs to completion of the contract. There are **numerous types** of fixed-price contract with different penalty regimes or cost escalation clauses.

EXAMPLE An engineering company agreed a fixed-price contract to upgrade track and signalling on a major section of the national rail network. The contract price agreed was in the region of £2.5bn, but delays and cost overruns have forced the company to revise its cost estimates for the project to around £3bn. Under the terms of the contract the contractor is liable for any excess costs, which should be provided for when recognised.

Cost-plus contracts

2212 After all legitimate costs have been authorised, an **agreed profit percentage** is applied to determine the appropriate turnover figure. All the costs that have been incurred, including those that are not approved, should be included in the cost of sales figure to derive the profit or loss to date on the contract. Provisions should be made for **known additional costs** not yet incurred, that will not be approved under the contract.

SECTION 2

Accounting treatment

2214 This section covers the accounting treatment for long-term contracts including recognition of turnover, identifying profit, loss making contracts and treatment of legal claims or pre-contract expenses.

A. Overview

2216 On long-term contracts in progress, it is appropriate to take credit for ascertainable turnover,
SSAP 9 (28)
associated costs and profit, in keeping with the requirement for financial statements to

present a true and fair view. **A separate contract account** should be opened for each long-term contract although different treatments may apply to different parts of the contract. As a result, individual contracts may be treated differently regarding the timing of the recognition of revenue, costs and profits. Once **a particular accounting treatment has been adopted** it must be applied consistently to each individual contract from one accounting period to the next.

Some **contracts lasting less than one year** should also be accounted for as long-term contracts, if they are material to the activity of the accounting period and the omission of turnover and the related costs in respect of those contracts, could impair the truth and fairness of the financial statements. This requirement has been reinforced by the introduction of UITF 40.

General rules

1. Where the **outcome of the contract** can be assessed with **reasonable certainty**, even though it is not complete, then the part of the profit attributable to the work performed at the accounting date should be included in the profit and loss account for the year. 2218
2. Where the outcome of the project is **less than certain** or **losses** are envisaged then a different accounting treatment is required. **Where it is not possible** at any stage in the contract **to assess the degree of profit** with any certainty, then turnover and costs recognised should be equal and a profit should not be recognised. It is relatively common, therefore, not to recognise profits in the early stages of long complex projects.
3. Where it can be foreseen that **a loss will be made** the costs recognised should include full provision for that future loss.

As the **estimated outcome** of a contract that extends over **several accounting periods** could vary with changes in circumstances, then the estimated profit on the contract should also be revised. The results for the year will not necessarily represent the proportion of total profit on the contract, appropriate to the amount of work actually carried out in a relevant accounting period, as they will also incorporate the impact of adjustments made to profits recognised in previous periods, as a result of any revision to estimated profits. However, by recognising the proportion of each contract attributable to the accounting period, the **costs and revenues generated** can be matched more accurately.

B. Recognition

The **general rule** under which turnover and profit are recognised on the sale of goods and services is, that the seller's full performance under terms of the contract must have been completed when the turnover is recognised. **Where that stage has not been reached**, the cost of work completed to date is included in work in progress and no turnover recognised. 2230 SSAP 9 (7)

However, simply applying the above rule to businesses that enter into long-term contracts would not necessarily result in a fair presentation of the level of activity in the year.

Basis of recognition The basis on which turnover and costs are recognised should be appropriate to the nature of the particular contract. A **common approach** is to assess the percentage of work completed to date and apply that to the total value of the contract, in order to determine the cumulative value of the turnover on that contract. This is then matched against the costs incurred to date to assess the profit that should be recognised. 2232

In order to determine the amounts at which long-term contracts should be included in the financial statements, the following accounting treatment for the recognition of turnover, costs and profit (or loss) should be applied.

Recognition	
Category	**Accounting treatment**
Turnover to date	% of contract completed based on valuation or estimate (¶2248)
Cost of sales	Costs transferred from work in progress (¶2266)
Profit – indentifiable	Prudent (matching) (¶2276)
Profit – unidentifiable	No profit recognised (¶2284)
Loss – realised or anticipated	Full loss taken to P & L (¶2310)

1. Turnover

2240 SSAP 9 (8) SSAP 9 does not give a definition of turnover in view of the different methods of determining it. The turnover on long-term contracts taken to the profit and loss account in an accounting period, must relate to either **separate or measurable parts** of the contract completed in that period.

SSAP 9 (23) **Companies should calculate turnover** on long-term contracts in a way that is **appropriate to**:
- the stage of completion of the contract (e.g. 30%);
- the nature of the contractual relationship with the client; and
- the particular business and industry concerned (e.g. construction).

FRS 5 "Reporting The Substance of Transactions: Revenue Recognition" and UITF Abstract 40 provide **additional guidance** on the recognition of turnover derived from long-term contracts (¶2262).

a. Stage of completion

2242 SSAP 9 (13) The determination of the stage of completion **can be derived from**:
- an actual valuation of the contract work carried out to date;
- an estimate of contract completion; and
- values attributable to specific stages or agreed dates (multi-stage) as specified in the contract.

2244 In some contracts, **interim payments** are agreed on certain dates or at certain points in the contract (or milestones as they are termed). These payments are not necessarily related to the value of work completed when a milestone is reached, so care must be taken not to simply accept the value of payments received as being a fair reflection of the value of the turnover to be recognised.

Actual valuation

2248 On certain contracts, particularly in construction, valuations are prepared by **independent surveyors**. However, the accounting standard does not specify that an independent valuation be undertaken, although the use of appropriately qualified individuals is to be recommended as best practice. Accounts prepared by the construction agent and agreed by the client or their advisors form the basis of the turnover recognised on the contract.

> EXAMPLE A long-term contract worth £300,000 has been independently valued as 45% complete at the end of the first accounting period. Assuming the value of turnover accrues evenly throughout the contract, the recorded turnover should be £130,500.

If the valuation is conducted some time **prior to the financial year end** an adjustment reflecting additional turnover on work completed should be made.

2250 **Certification** Remuneration for the building contractor is usually based on architects' certificates or an engineer's certificate for engineering contracts. Work certified will usually include a figure for retentions, which represent monies withheld until rectification work has been completed. The value of turnover recognised should therefore be the gross figure before any deductions for retentions.

EXAMPLE The value of work on a long-term contract was assessed at £350,000 with a figure of 10% for retentions. The payments to date total £300,000 with the outstanding debtor balance of £35,000 representing the retention fee.

Estimates

In some cases it is not possible to conduct an independent valuation or it is not required under the terms of the contract. The entity therefore estimates the **value of the work completed** by reference to milestones in the contract or the judgement of the directors, and calculates the **percentage completion** achieved to date, before multiplying this figure by the contract value to ascertain the turnover. 2252

This **method is only appropriate** where:
- costs are incurred evenly over the life of the contract; and
- where there is a strong correlation between costs incurred to date and the stage of completion of the contract.

Example. On a contract worth £35,000 the company has incurred actual costs of £15,000 and estimates further costs of £10,000 to completion of the contract. The company should **determine its turnover** based on the following formula: 2254

$$\frac{\text{costs incurred}}{\text{total expected costs}} \times \text{estimated contract value}$$

$$= \frac{£15{,}000}{£15{,}000 + £10{,}000} \times £35{,}000 = £21{,}000$$

EXAMPLE This example illustrates a single contract that spans three financial years using the **percentage cost completion method**. The costs of £10,464 in year one represent 24% of the total estimated costs of £43,600. The cost percentage is then applied at the end of each accounting period to the total contract turnover to derive the profit for the period.

Contract – Alpha **Year ending December 2010**	**Yr. 1** **£** **2008**	**Yr. 2** **£** **2009**	**Yr. 3** **£** **2010**
Turnover per contract	55,000	55,000	55,000
Costs incurred to date	10,464	30,520	43,600
Costs to complete	33,136	13,080	0
Total estimated costs	43,600	43,600	43,600
Total estimated profit	**11,400**	**11,400**	**11,400**
Stage of completion (%)	24%	70%	100%

The profit and loss account for the three financial years 20X8-2010 are shown below.

Contract – Alpha **Profit and loss account 2008**	**Cumulative profit** **£**	**Profit previous year** **£**	**Profit current Year** **£**
Year 1 2008 (cumulative)			
Turnover (£55,000 × 24%)	13,200		3,200
Costs (£43,600 × 24%)	**10,464**		10,464
Profit	2,736		2,736
Year 2 2009 (cumulative)			
Turnover (£55,000 × 70%)	38,500	13,200	25,300
Costs (£43,600 × 70%)	**30,520**	10,464	20,056
Profit	7,980	2,736	5,244
Year 3 2010 (cumulative)			
Turnover (£55,000 × 100%)	55,000	38,500	16,500
Costs (£43,600 × 100%)	**43,600**	30,520	13,080
Profit	11,400	7,980	3,420

Multi-stage contracts

2258 SSAP 9 (Appendix 1.22) On some long-term contracts, for example, the construction and delivery of a number of large capital items, the contract price may be determined and invoiced according to separate parts (or performance) of the contract (e.g. the number of aircraft or trains delivered). The most **appropriate method** of accounting for this type of contract is to match the costs of each distinct part of the contract, with the corresponding sales value.

b. Cumulative turnover

2260 The cumulative turnover on the contract recorded in the profit and loss account for all accounting periods is compared with the total payments on account. If **turnover exceeds** "payments received on account", then an "amount recoverable on contracts" is determined and separately disclosed within debtors. **For example**, if the cumulative turnover over three accounting periods is £60m and the payments on account total £45m, then the balance of £15m should be accounted for as "amounts recoverable on contracts".

2261 Where **payments on account** exceed turnover, the excess is classified as a deduction from the contract balance in long-term contract balances, if the contract is still work in progress. **If the contract is complete**, then **any residual balance** in excess of cost should be accounted for in creditors.

c. Additional guidance

2262 SSAP 9 gives specific guidance on the accounting treatment for all aspects of long-term contracts. Application Note G deals with the general principles of revenue recognition, while UITF 40 is narrower in scope providing additional guidance for accounting for revenue on service contracts.

Application Note G (AN G)

2263 FRS5 (G18) The ASB issued an application note to FRS 5 setting out the **principles of revenue recognition** to be applied in specific areas such as long-term contracts. The application note does not amend the requirements of SSAP 9.

Under SSAP 9, the seller recognises turnover as the contract progresses where the value can be assessed with reasonable certainty. The seller should recognise changes in its assets or liabilities and turnover that reflect the accrual (of the right to consideration) over the term of the contract.

The right to consideration is, in turn, derived from an assessment of the fair value of the goods or services provided to date under the contract as a percentage of the total contract value. The fair values should be determined using the prices in force at the beginning of the contract unless the contractual terms allow for price changes to be passed on to the customer.

The **guiding principle** for all contracts is to determine the stage of completion of each project, in order to determine the seller's right to consideration. A consequence of this is that profitability may vary for different stages of a project.

It should be noted, however, that even with the introduction of Application Note G, there is still no single universally applied (or agreed) method of determining turnover on long-term contracts. The **most acceptable methods** are those based on calculating cumulative turnover by multiplying an estimated percentage of completion by the agreed value of the contract (see ¶2294).

UITF 40

2264 The ASB issued UITF 40 "Revenue Recognition and Service Contracts" to assist in the interpretation of FRS 5 AN G, and applies to all entities including those adopting the FRSSE.

The **principles** contained in the Abstract **apply to all contracts for services**, including those rendered by professional service firms such as accountants, solicitors and estate agents.

UITF 40 addresses the issue of whether SSAP 9 or AN G requires or permits revenue to be recognised as contract activity progresses or only on completion of the contract. As the **terms and commercial substance of service contracts vary** considerably, it is difficult to provide specific guidance for all types of contract. Each company will be required to develop an appropriate income recognition policy, taking into consideration the requirements of SSAP 9, AN G or UITF 40.

Companies **may be required to recognise profits** on contracts at an earlier stage. There is also a related tax issue in terms of the possible impact on taxable profits and the timing of the related tax charge.

UITF 40 reinforces the general principles contained in AN G; namely that there is no difference between the accounting treatment required for long-term contracts and other contracts for services. The **prime consideration** is whether the seller has performed, or partially performed, their contractual obligations. If the seller has performed some, but not all, of its contractual obligations, it is required to recognise revenue only to the extent that it has obtained the "right to consideration" through performance.

MEMO POINTS 1. The tax faculty at the ICAEW has compiled a tax guide (08/06) on this topic, which can be viewed at www.icaew.co.uk/taxfac. 2. Work in progress is valued on the basis of the lower of cost or net realisable value (NRV). This principle applies to incomplete service contracts with the consequence that a profit or loss is not recognised for tax purposes until all the relevant contract obligations have been fulfilled.

Key elements The key elements of UITF 40 are as follows: 2265

1. The Abstract **applies to** all contracts for services.

2. Where a single contract may be divided into **separate clearly identifiable stages**, it may be appropriate to account for them as separate transactions.

3. Where a contract for services **falls into separate accounting periods** and is deemed material it should be accounted for as a long-term contract. Where a number of such contracts exist, the aggregate effect should be assessed in relation to their impact on the financial statements.

4. **Where the substance of a contract** is that the seller's obligations are **performed over time**, revenue should be recognised as contract activity progresses, to reflect the seller's partial performance of the contract. The revenue recognised should reflect the accrual of the "right to consideration" as the contract activity progresses.

5. Where the substance of the contract is that a "**right to consideration**" does not arise until a critical event has occurred (or condition fulfilled), then revenue should not be recognised until such time.

6. The **accounting policy** should be applied consistently to all similar contracts and from one accounting year to the next.

2. Cost of sales

The costs associated with the turnover recorded in the profit and loss account should be deducted from the total costs incurred on the contract to date (under work in progress) and charged to the profit and loss account. The costs of sale relate directly to the **performance of the contract** and include: 2266

- construction material costs;
- labour costs;
- transport costs for plant and equipment;
- depreciation of plant and machinery;
- design and technical costs;
- rectification and guarantee costs; and
- miscellaneous costs (e.g. insurance, general overheads).

2268 Traditionally, the cost of sales is matched with turnover with the balance representing profit. However, where the **recognition of profit** is uncertain, the cost of sales could represent the balancing figure, after turnover and profit are calculated at the end of each financial period prior to completion of the contract.

The costs expensed should accurately reflect that part of the contract completed at the accounting date, and should be transferred from total contract costs incurred to cost of sales in the profit and loss account. **If format 2** of the balance sheet **is adopted**, then the cost transfer should be to the more detailed but appropriate headings.

2270 **Cost overruns** should be expensed in the relevant accounting period. In considering future costs, it is necessary to take account of likely increases in wages and salaries, and the price of raw materials and general overheads that are not recoverable.

2272 **Allocation of overheads** Administration overhead expenses that are not directly traceable to a specific contract are often split on an arbitrary basis and charged to each contract. The **alternative approach** is to omit these costs from the contract accounts and offset them against the total contribution to profit from contracts.

3. Identifiable profit

2276 SSAP 9 (23) Identifiable profit is the total profit estimated to arise over the **duration of the contract**, after allowing for:
- estimated remedial and maintenance costs; and
- increases in costs that are not recoverable under the terms of the contract.

The overall profit calculation may be independent of the valuation of turnover allocated to different accounting periods on a long-term contract. SSAP 9 aims to prevent the **arbitrary allocation** of profits between accounting periods.

Reasonable certainty

2278 The general rules are as follows:

1. The **overriding principle** is that profit cannot be attributable until the profitable outcome of the contract can be assessed with reasonable certainty. SSAP 9 does not give any guidance on how to determine reasonable certainty, although a **contract completion figure** of 30% may generally be regarded as the earliest point at which profit should be recognised.

2. When the outcome of long-term contracts can be assessed with reasonable certainty, the identifiable profit should be calculated on a **prudent basis** and included in the results of the period under review.

3. It is necessary to define the **earliest point for each contract** at which profit should be taken.

4. In deciding whether a **stage in the contract** has been reached, at which it is appropriate to take profit (as with turnover), account should be taken of the nature of the business concerned.

5. The profit should not only reflect the proportion of the work completed at the accounting date but also take into account any known **inequalities in profitability** over the various stages of a contract's life cycle, thus resulting in a better match of costs and revenues.

6. If the contract **is not split into stages or** where the **costs attributable to certified work** are not readily identifiable, then the profit attributable to completed work can only be estimated.

2284 SSAP 9 (10) **Profit uncertainty** If the outcome of a long-term contract **cannot be assessed with reasonable certainty**, then no profit should be reflected in the accounts. Nevertheless, as long as it can be reasonably assumed that no loss will arise, it may be appropriate to show a proportion of the total contract value as turnover, using a zero estimate of profit.

> EXAMPLE If a zero profit (or loss) is expected on a long-term contract with a projected value of £200,000 that is 80% complete, it may be appropriate to reflect £160,000 as turnover. The transfer to cost of sales will equal the amount recorded as turnover.

Methods for determining identifiable profit

The two main methods for determining identifiable profit are: 2290 SSAP 9 (9)
- the percentage cost completion method; and
- valuation of the work authorised at the balance sheet date (¶2300).

In addition, there are a **number of variations** on these methods that may be used to arrive at identifiable profit.

The **choice of method will depend on** the difficulty of ascertaining costs and the type and scale of the project. The method selected should: 2292
- be appropriate to the nature of the contract;
- be used consistently; and
- accord with the methods adopted by other companies within the industry.

Percentage cost completion method Under this method, the **cost of the work** completed to date is determined and then compared to the total estimated costs of the project. The total anticipated profit to completion is then calculated by multiplying the budgeted contract profit by the percentage of completed costs, as illustrated in the example below. 2294

A **variation** on the completion method is illustrated in the subsequent example, where the turnover is calculated by comparing actual costs to an agreed "bill of materials", derived from the contractor's project costings.

EXAMPLE **Completion method – percentage cost basis**

An aircraft manufacturer has agreed a fixed-price contract for £5m to supply components to a large commercial airline. The contract is for two years and the total estimated costs are £3.8m. The contractor ascertains the **stage of completion** of the contract by measuring the costs of work to date with the estimated total costs. The turnover was determined through an external valuation.

	Year 1	**Year 2 Cum**
	£m	**£m**
Turnover	3.0	5.0
Costs to date	1.5	3.0
Balance on costs	2.3	0.8
Total estimated costs	3.8	3.8
Estimated profit	1.2	1.2
Completion	**39%**	**100%**

The **completion rate** of 39% is derived by dividing costs to date by total estimated costs (£1.5m/£3.8m = 39 %). A profit of £468,000 would be taken in year one (estimated profit of £1.2m × 39%) with the balance in year two. These figures can be presented as follows:

		£
Turnover in year 1		**3,000,000**
Less:		
costs to date	1,500,000	
cost provisions (Balancing figure)	1,032,000	
Total cost		**2,532,000**
Profit		**468,000**

The cost provisions are found by deducting costs to date and profit from turnover.

An example of the **alternative cost completion method** based on budgeted costs is given below.

EXAMPLE **Alternative cost completion method – based on budgeted costs**

A construction company that has a contract to refurbish a number of car showrooms with new branded elements including signage and entrance facia, has agreed to invoice the client on a completion based method. At the year end the costs for each site are computed and compared with the agreed "bill of materials" for each showroom. For instance, the costs incurred for showroom 1 total 75% of the budgeted costs which represents the turnover billed.

Under this contract the **profit element** (cost plus) for the contractor **is invoiced separately** on the basis of an agreed percentage fee for each completed showroom.

	Showrooms			
	1	**2**	**3**	**4**
Budgeted costs (£000's)	100	250	165	312
Actual costs to date (£000's)	75	158	122	200
Completion (%)	**75**	**63**	**74**	**64**
Turnover billed (£m)	75	158	122	200

2300 **Valuation method** The valuation method may be based on either an independent **external valuation** or on **internal costings** prepared by the company. The procedure adopted will depend on the nature of the contract and the terms agreed with the client.

1. Profit is recognised by taking an agreed proportion of the total contract value as turnover and using the formula stated in the example immediately below.

2. However, **profits may fluctuate considerably** over the life of a project (see example in ¶2302), thus requiring a different treatment. The valuation should also incorporate any known contingencies such as legal claims as illustrated in the example in ¶2306.

Care needs to be taken that the estimated profit is based on current levels of expenditure and not simply on initial profit estimates.

EXAMPLE **Valuation method**

Formula

$$\frac{\text{External (internal) surveyor's valuation}}{\text{Total estimated contract value} \times \text{estimated profit}}$$

A company has a three year contract valued at £500,000 with current estimated profits of £75,000. The recognition of turnover and profits is calculated using an **external** valuation at the end of each accounting period.

At the **end of the first accounting** period the external valuation of the contract is agreed at £258,750 (52% complete). A profit of £39,000 is determined as follows:

$$\frac{£258,750}{£500,000 \times £75,000} = £39,000 \text{ (approx)}$$

The cost of sales totals £219,750 with the balance of total costs of £55,250 (£275,000-219,750) representing work in progress. In **year 2** the project is 80% complete with cumulative turnover of £400,000. Profits of £60,000 are recognised.

Contract – Beta	Year 1 £	Year 2 £	Year 3 £
External valuation of turnover (cumulative)	**258,750**	**400,000**	**500,000**
Percentage completion	52%	80%	100%
Profit taken (cumulative)	**39,000**	**60,000**	**75,000**
Costs to date (WIP)	275,000	385,000	425,000
Costs transferred to cost of sales	219,750	340,000	425,000
Work in progress	**55,250**	**45,000**	**0**

2302 All **direct costs** are debited to the contract account as are overheads which are apportioned using one of a number of costing methods (¶2040). **Revenues** are credited to the contract account which is effectively a trading profit and loss account. As contracts usually span a number of accounting periods, the turnover and profit attributable to each financial year must be apportioned as illustrated in the following example.

EXAMPLE **Gamma Construction Ltd.**

A construction contract valued at £250,000 is expected to take two years to complete yielding a profit of £30,000. The contract accounts for the two years are as follows. Certified revenues totalled £120,000 in year 1.

For the purpose of the annual accounts the **depreciation charge** for plant was calculated (using the straight-line method) with reference to the expected value of the plant when the contract is complete. The estimated cost of the plant over two years is £16,000 (£18,000 – a residual value of £2,000). The **stocks** of materials on site, not utilised at the year end, were carried forward to year 2 at cost price.
Costs not transferred to cost of sales form **work in progress** balances transferred to the profit and loss in year 2.

Credit is taken in year 1 for part of the estimated total profit on the completed contract (see note 2).

Gamma Construction Ltd.			
	Dr. £		Cr. £
Plant purchased	18,000	Certified work See 1.	120,000
Materials purchased	47,950	Plant c/d	10,000
Plant hire	8,500	Stock c/d	2,000
Materials issued from stores	12,500	Work in progress c/d	27,181
Wages	32,045		
Subcontractors	10,000		
Direct expenses	15,786		
Gross profit – transferred to P/L	**14,400**	See 2.	
	159,181		**159,181**
Year 2			
Plant b/d	10,000	Work certified	130,000
Stock b/d	2,000	Sale of plant	2,000
Work in progress b/d	27,181		
Materials purchased	44,691		
Wages	17,960		
Direct expenses	14,568		
Gross profit – to p/l	**15,600**	See 2.	
Totals	**132,000**		**132,000**

1. Valuation of turnover
Year 1 The work completed to date was certified at £120,000.
Year 2 The contract was completed in year 2 and the balance of the contract's value (£130,000) was certified and invoiced. A retention fee of 5% (£15,000) was withheld at the year end and is reflected in debtors.

2. Calculation of profits (Valuation method)
Year 1
Work certified / total contract price × total estimated profit

£120,000 / £250,000 × £30,000 = 14,400

The contract is 48% complete so it is reasonable to take an element of profit in year one.
Year 2
£130,000 / £250,000 × £30,000 = 15,600

Fluctuating profits

Profits may not be generated evenly over the life of a project, for instance where the project is divided into a number of distinct stages each generating different levels of profit. The **relationship between costs and profit** in the valuation method is not based on a fixed percentage. Profits generated over the life of a contract may be uneven due to unexpected variations in cost and should reflect the activity undertaken in the period. **Factors other than** the percentage of contract completion should also be considered, such as contract variations or legal claims. 2304

EXAMPLE **Fluctuating profits**

This example illustrates a contract in which the **level of profits** varies over the life of the contract, without profit smoothing. A contract spanning three years has a value of £350,000 and a profit of

£70,000. The **profits are not recognised** in proportion to costs but are based on an external valuation, with the costs matched subsequently. For instance in year one, the costs total 41% of the total costs although only 34% of the contract was valued as complete.

	Year 1 £	Year 2 £	Year 3 £	Totals £
External valuation (cum)	**120,000**	**275,000**	**350,000**	**350,000**
Turnover recorded	120,000	155,000	75,000	350,000
% of total contract turnover	34%	45%	21%	
Costs (actual) – by period	115,000	105,000	60,000	280,000
% of total costs	41%	38%	21%	
Profit by period	**5,000**	**50,000**	**15,000**	**70,000**
% of total contract profit	7%	71%	22%	

Adjustments to valuation

2306 The profit recorded in an accounting period should incorporate any variations in the estimated profitability of the contract and not just factors relevant to the period in question.

EXAMPLE A contract worth £500,000 spanning two years was expected to yield a profit of £50,000. At the commencement of the project the profit was estimated to accrue evenly over the life of the project.
After the first year, the project was 60% complete with an estimated profit of £30,000. However, due to expected cost overruns resulting from legal claims, the cumulative profit on the project has been downgraded to £30,000. As a result, the profit for year 1 should be reduced to £18,000.

Conversely, the profits calculated at previous accounting year ends may have been formulated on expectations of **cost overruns** that subsequently did not materialise, thus requiring an adjustment to the initial valuation.

Other factors that can affect the profits from a contract are considered in ¶¶2320 to ¶2328.

4. Contract losses

2310 SSAP 9 (24) **Foreseeable losses** are those losses that are estimated to arise after the commencement of a contract after allowing for all remedial and maintenance work and cost overruns, not recoverable under the terms of the contract. An **estimate is required** for foreseeable losses **irrespective of**:
- whether or not work has yet commenced on such contracts;
- the proportion of work completed at the accounting date; or
- the level of profits expected to be generated from other contracts with the same client.

If the outcome of a long-term contract is expected to be a loss, then the full loss should be taken in the accounting period in which it first becomes apparent.

SSAP 9 (11) 1. The foreseeable loss should be deducted from the work in progress figure of the relevant contract, thus reducing it to the net realisable value.

2. Any loss in excess of the work in progress figure should be classified as an accrual within "**Creditors**" or under "**Provisions for liabilities and charges**", depending on the circumstances.

However, the accounting standard is not clear as to the exact nature of these circumstances. **One interpretation could be**, that if a loss arose on a long-term contract because of an event that had already occurred, such as an overrun on material costs, then this would represent an accrual. If, however, the loss was estimated based on forecast levels of costs and remedial work, then a provision would be more appropriate, as set out in the following example:

EXAMPLE **Loss recognised in full in the profit and loss account.**

The estimated loss for **Project Z** is as follows:

	£
Value of work done and recognised as turnover	200,000
Total direct costs incurred	250,000
Total contract value	320,000
Expected total costs (including administrative overheads of £20k)	380,000
Estimated loss	60,000

The amount shown as a provision for foreseeable losses is:

		£
Actual costs incurred		250,000
Less: Transferred to cost of sales	250,000	
Foreseeable loss on contract as a whole	**60,000**	
Total costs		310,000
Classified as: Provision for foreseeable losses		**60,000**

3. Where the **expected loss** on a contract **is of such a magnitude** that it will utilise a considerable part of company resources for a substantial period, any related administrative overheads incurred during the period to completion of the project should be included in the calculation of the provision for the losses.

5. Private Finance Initiatives (PFIs)

PFIs **are defined as** a contract covering the creation or maintenance of an asset by a private company which it legally owns, but then leases to a public sector body. Examples include roads, bridges, hospitals, prisons and educational establishments. In recent years there has been an increase in the number of these partnership or joint financing arrangements between the public and private sectors. **2314**

Both central and local government departments are now required to report under IFRS and the impact of this changeover for reporting PFIs is still being assessed.

The **main features** of a PFI contract are set out below:

1. A contract to provide services is awarded by the purchaser (public sector body) to the operator (private sector entity), specifying type and level of service required and time period. Often "unitary" payments are made in each period covering performance and usage levels etc.
2. The private company takes responsibility for the design, construction, financing and operation of the asset. The contract details the special features, requirements and level of service to be provided over a given time period and the payment schedule reflects factors such as service volume, capacity, performance levels etc.
3. Normally, details of any special arrangements for the asset at the end of the contract term are given. For instance, legal title may pass to the purchaser for a fixed price, or the procedure to be followed for retendering for a contract extension or hand-over to a new operator.
4. An analysis of how the project would be more cost effective if operated solely by the private sector. Normally, this is achieved through transferring the project risk to the private sector.

Accounting treatment The accounting treatment for PFIs is set out in FRS 5 "Reporting the Substance of Transactions" (Application Note F) and SSAP 21 "Accounting for Leases and Hire Purchase Contracts". The key issue is to determine whether the purchaser (public sector authority) has a capital asset and a corresponding liability to pay the operator of the asset/facility. The contracts can be complicated and take a variety of forms. Application **2315**

Note F may also be applicable to certain contracts that have the characteristics of a PFI contract between private sector entities. These include contracts in the warehousing and distribution sector.

Contracts for services Current practice is not to capitalise contracts for services. However, **where a property is required** to fulfil a contract for services, then the property may have to be recognised as an asset. The rules for determining the appropriate accounting treatment are set out in the table below.

MEMO POINTS 1. Another type of PFI is the public private partnership (PPP). 2. Both central and local government departments have now adopted IFRS, from April 2009 and April 2010 respectively. Under UK GAAP, PFIs and other joint financing arrangements have traditionally been accounted for by determining the risks and rewards, whereas under IFRS the onus is on who has effective control. This could result in the majority of PFI, PPP or other outsourcing arrangements now being recorded on the public sector balance sheet.

Contract	Action
1. Can the contract be divided into property and service elements?	**No** – Apply FRS 5 – review the profit (or losses) **(see table below)** **Yes** – see point 2 below
2. Where the residual element of a payment covers asset and non-separable services	**Analysis under FRS 5** – review the split of profit or losses on assets and non-separable services. **7 main risks** are identified, including: demand; third party revenue; nature of the asset; technological changes; residual values; penalties for under-performance; and level of operating costs.
3. Where the residual element of payment does not include any service costs	**Apply SSAP 21**. Application note includes guidance on application of a test ("90%"), choice of discount rate and assessment of minimum lease payments

MEMO POINTS The Treasury has issued a Technical Note (1) "How to account for PFI transactions", which provides practical guidance for public sector bodies on the use of Application Note F issued by the ASB. The guidance advocates a two-tier approach involving a qualitative and a quantitative analysis. The former should be conducted first and should this prove inconclusive, then the quantitative analysis should be conducted.

2316 FRS5 (APP NOTE F51-F60)

	Action
Purchaser – has a property asset	1. Asset = property + liability to pay for it. Record in balance sheet 2. Initial amount recorded at fair value of property 3. Subsequently, asset depreciated over its useful economic life 4. Liability reduced as payments made 5. An imputed finance charge on the liability in subsequent years should be used 6. Remaining PFI payments should be recorded as an operating cost (i.e. full payment less capital repayment/financing charge) 7. Other obligations – account for under FRS 12 "Provisions, Contingent Liabilities and Contingent Assets"
Purchaser – no property asset but other assets or liabilities	**A. Contributions to a PFI contract** (e.g. advance cash payments, contribution of existing assets) **Key question is**: Do contributions give rise to future benefits for the purchaser? **Yes** - if contribution results in lower service payments, carrying amount of asset should be reclassified as a prepayment (current asset) and subsequently recharged as an operating expense over the period of reduced PFI payments. **No** - contribution charged as an expense (e.g. short-life assets)

	Action
	B. Acquisition of the residual – where property is transferred at the end of PFI contract: i. At market value at date of transfer – any difference between market and amount specified in the contract. ii. During life of contract-expected residual value falls, but payment schedule is not changed, must consider if asset is impaired. A provision may be required accounted for under FRS 12.
Operator – has an asset in form of property	**1.** Operator should record asset in the balance sheet initially at cost, then depreciated to its expected residual value over its estimated economic life. **2.** Where a residual transfer value is stipulated in the contract – PFI payments can be varied over life of the contract to reflect changing estimates in expected residual value. **3.** Where the operator incurs liabilities as a result of the contract (e.g. environmental clean-up costs), these must be recorded separately within liabilities.
Operator – does not have an asset of a property	Then it has a financial and not a physical asset, as it represents a debt due from the purchaser for the fair value of the property. **1.** Financial asset is reduced in subsequent years as payments received. **2.** Finance income on the financial asset should be recorded using a property specific rate. **3.** Remaining element of PFI payments (i.e. full payments, less capital repayments and imputed finance charge) are recorded within operating profit.

6. Miscellaneous issues

Treatment of interest

In determining the value of long-term contracts it is not normally appropriate to include interest payable on borrowed money as this is charged separately to the profit and loss account. Financing is often agreed in tranches and may not be project specific. In circumstances where the finance procured can be identified as contract specific, a proportion of the related interest may be included in cost. The disclosure requirements are as for stocks. **2320** SSAP 9 (Appendix 1.21)

Contract variations

Examples of variations to long-term contracts include changes to: **2322**
- the scope or design requirements;
- the contractual completion period; or
- legal requirements (e.g. health and safety). SSAP 9 (Appendix 1.26)

Where **approved variations** have been made to a contract in the course of its execution and the amount receivable in lieu of the alterations is material, it is necessary to make a conservative estimate of the revenue which should be included in the total sales. Alternatively, provision should be made for any foreseen losses or penalties arising out of delays in completion or from other sources.

Legal claims

The settlement of claims arising from circumstances not foreseen in the **original contract** or that result from approved variations can result in a high level of uncertainty. It is generally prudent to recognise receipts in respect of such claims only when: **2324** SSAP 9 (Appendix 1.27)
- negotiations are at an advanced stage;
- the value of the claims have been agreed.

2326 Where **additional contract costs** are expected to be incurred as a result of a dispute or losing a legal case, then the normal recognition of liabilities under FRS 12 apply. If the liability is recognised then this should be added to the contract costs and the estimated profit revisited. Where the **potential loss is considerable** it may be prudent not to recognise further profit until any dispute or legal claim is resolved.

Pre-contract costs

2327 UITF 34 (15) Companies bidding for contracts can incur significant costs before the contract is secured. **The issue is** whether these costs should be expensed in the profit and loss account or recognised as an asset and charged to expenses over the term of the contract. The **general rule** is that directly attributable pre-contract costs should be recognised as an asset only when it is sufficiently certain that the contract has been secured.

MEMO POINTS The Accounting Standards Board (ASB) has issued Abstract UITF 34 covering the consistency of the accounting treatment of pre-contract costs, pertaining to **costs incurred in tendering for contracts** to supply goods and services. The Abstract discusses whether pre-contract costs should be recognised as an asset and if so, which particular costs.

2328 **Directly attributable costs** should be interpreted as the range of costs that can be included in the cost of a tangible fixed asset, under FRS 15 "Tangible fixed assets". Pre-contract costs incurred during the competitive tendering stage, up to the point at which it becomes reasonably certain that the contract has been secured, should be recognised as expenses and not subsequently reinstated as an asset. Further pre-contract costs are then recognised as an asset (within debtors) and charged as an expense over the period of the contract.

Amounts recovered in respect of **costs written off** are deferred and amortised over the life of the contract.

EXAMPLE A marketing services company incurred considerable cost in tendering for a multinational services account. The costs incurred covered creative design and management time and were expensed as incurred.

From the time the company expects to win the contract, costs incurred (e.g. management time, additional creative work, production materials and market research) can be recognised as an asset under work in progress (stocks) and later transferred to cost of sales.

SECTION 3

Disclosure requirements

2334 Long-term contract balances are disclosed under the balance sheet heading of "Stocks". The requirements of the Companies Act and the accounting standards cover the general accounting policies to be disclosed, as well as the specific disclosures relating to key aspects of the accounting treatment for long-term contracts.

a. Accounting policies

2336 SSAP 9 (32) It is a key requirement of SSAP 9 that accounting policies for long-term contracts and especially **the method** of calculating turnover and identifiable profit (on a prudent basis) are disclosed in a note to the financial statements. The accounting policies must be applied consistently within the business from year to year.

2338 SSAP 9 (14) **Where different bases have been adopted** for various types of long-term contracts, the amount included in the financial statements in respect of each type should be stated.

The first example below illustrates the general information to be disclosed relating to the valuation and ongoing control or review procedures on long-term contracts. The **following examples** illustrate accounting policies relating to turnover, profits, and costs.

EXAMPLE **Accounting policies - Valuation policy**

Valuation Long-term contract balances are valued at costs incurred on specific contracts, net of amounts transferred to cost of sales in respect of work recorded as turnover, less foreseeable losses and payments on account. If the ultimate profitability of a contract can be assessed with reasonable certainty, after having made prudent allowance for future risks and uncertainties, then profit is recognised in proportion to the contract work completed. Immediate provision is made for all foreseeable losses.

EXAMPLE **Disclosure of accounting policies**

Turnover. Contract turnover includes the value of work completed during the financial year, after reference to the total sales value and stage completion of the project and including the settlement of claims arising from previous years.

Profits on long-term contracts are calculated in accordance with industry standard accounting practice and do not directly relate to turnover. Profit on current contracts is only taken at the stage near enough to completion for that profit to be reasonably certain. Provision is made for all losses incurred to the accounting date, together with any further losses that are foreseen in bringing contracts to completion.

Costs for this purpose include valuation of all work done by subcontractors, whether certified or not, and all overheads other than those relating to the general administration of the relevant companies. For any contracts where receipts exceed the book value of the work done, the excess is included in creditors as payments on account.

EXAMPLE **Profit recognition on contracting activities**

Profit on individual contracts is taken only when their outcome can be foreseen with reasonable certainty, based on the lower of the percentage margin earned to date and that prudently forecast at completion, taking account of agreed claims. Full provision is made for all known or expected losses on individual contracts, taking a prudent view of future claims income, immediately such losses are foreseen.

b. Other important disclosures

The table below **summarises the key classifications** and balance sheet locations for disclosure requirements relating to long-term contracts. For companies undertaking many long-term contracts, the appropriate balance sheet disclosures should be determined contract by contract and not on an aggregate basis. 2342

Classification	Locations
Amounts "recoverable on contracts" (¶2344)	Debtors
Payment on account (¶2348)	Offset against Stocks
Provisions for losses (¶2352)	Creditors or provisions for liabilities
Long-term contract balances (¶2356)	Stocks
Profit and loss disclosures – turnover, cost of sales or losses (¶2360)	Profit and loss a/c

Amounts "recoverable on contracts"

Amounts "recoverable on contracts" is a classification specific to long-term contracts and represents the amount by which **turnover exceeds payments received on account**; it is shown separately under debtors. 2344

An "amount recoverable on contracts" **does not have the contractual status** of a debtor in the strict legal form, although it represents accrued income receivable and has all the attributes of a debtor. This is because once a transaction has been recorded as turnover and invoiced to the client, then any amounts remaining unpaid represent debtors and not stock.

2346 Also, the balance may, in effect, include an **element of profit** recognised on contracts still in progress. Therefore, it would be inappropriate to include the balance within stock, which is required by company law and the accounting standards to be shown, normally at the lower of cost and net realisable value. This treatment is well established under the **accrual concept** of cost and revenue recognition and the requirement under FRS 5 to reflect the substance of a transaction.

EXAMPLE **Project X**

	£
Turnover recognised	265,000
Cumulative payments on account received	220,000
Excess – recoverable on contracts	**45,000**
– included in Debtors.	
Total costs incurred	230,000
Costs transferred to cost of sales	190,000
Balance to work in progress	**40,000**

The amount to be included under "Amounts recoverable on contracts" in the balance sheet and disclosed separately under debtors is £45,000, being the amount by which turnover of £265,000 exceeds payments on account of £220,000.
The balance of costs not yet transferred to cost of sales is included in work in progress.

Balance sheet (extract)
Note – Debtors Amounts recoverable on contracts

	Group 2010 £'000
Amounts falling due within one year	
Trade and other debtors	360
Amounts recoverable on contracts	**45**
Amounts falling due after one year	
Trade and other debtors	35
Contract retentions	25
Totals	**465**

Accounting policy note

Amounts "recoverable on contracts" which are included in **debtors** are stated at cost, plus attributable profit to the extent that this is reasonably certain after making provision for contingencies, less any losses incurred or foreseen in bringing contracts to completion, and less amounts received as progress payments.

Payments on account

2348 SSAP 9 (30) If payments on account **are greater than** the amount of **turnover recognised**, then the excess balance should initially be offset against the amount disclosed as long-term contract balances under stocks for the project concerned.

If the excess is greater than the contract balance, the residual amount should be shown as "Payments on account" under creditors.

Payments on account may also be listed as "Payments received in advance of turnover".

EXAMPLE Assume that payments on account for **Project X** in the example above were £320,000. The result, after deducting the value of work completed of £265,000, is a credit balance of £55,000. This represents the balance of costs not transferred to cost of sales (£40,000) and recorded in Stocks and the £15,000 accounted for as "excess payments on account".
This figure should be set off against the amount carried under stocks for the project and the balance remaining shown separately as "Payments on account" under creditors:

	£	
Value of work completed	265,000	
Total costs incurred	230,000	
Transferred to cost of sales	190,000	
Included under stock	**40,000**	
Offset: excess payments on account	55,000	(320,000 – 265,000)
Included in creditors	**15,000**	(55,000 – 40,000)

Balance sheet (extract)
Note – Creditors

	Group 2010 £'000	Group 2009 £'000
Amounts falling due within one year		
Trade and other creditors	180	158
Contracts – payments received on account	**15**	**12**
Amounts falling due after one year		
Trade and other creditors	35	30
Totals	**230**	**190**

Provision for foreseeable losses

The amount by which the provision for foreseeable losses exceeds costs incurred (after transfers to cost of sales) must be shown under provisions for "liabilities and charges" or "creditors", as appropriate. **2352** SSAP 9 (30)

EXAMPLE **Balance sheet**

Provisions for liabilities and charges

	Deferred Tax £m	Losses on contracts £m	Total £m
Group			
Balances at 1 April 2009	55	15	70
Charged against profit for the year	15	25	40
Total provisions at 31 March 2010	**70**	**40**	**110**

Long-term contract balances

2356 Long-term contract balances **represent** the cost of works in progress, after deducting any foreseeable losses and payments on account not matched with turnover; they are classified as "long-term contract balances" and disclosed separately under stocks.

By **way of note**, the following should be also be **disclosed separately**: SSAP 9 (30)
- net cost less foreseeable losses; and
- applicable payments on account.

The first example is of a contract expected to produce a profit whilst the second example following illustrates the accounting treatment and disclosures required for a loss-making contract.

EXAMPLE **Profitable contract**

	£
Value of work completed	245,000
Total costs incurred	267,000
Payments received on account	215,000
Contract value	320,000
Estimated total costs	307,000
Estimated Profit	13,000

Accounting treatment

Profit and loss account	**2010**
Turnover	245,000
Cost of sales	(235,050)
Profit	**9,950**

Profit calculated as follows: (245,000/320,000 × 13000)

Balance sheet	**2010**
Total costs	267,000
less costs transferred to profit and loss	(235,050)
Long-term contract balances	**31,950**

Disclosures

Annual Report and Accounts (extract)

Notes to the accounts – Stocks & long-term contracts

	2010
	£'000's
Raw material and consumables	10.0
Long-term contract balances:	
– Net costs less foreseeable losses	246.9
– Applicable payments on account	(215.0)
Total stocks	**41.9**

EXAMPLE **Loss making contract**

Assume the following details for **Project Y**, a long-term contract in progress undertaken by B Ltd. as at 31 December 2010. The directors are of the opinion that there will be a loss of £25,000 on the contract as a whole.

	£
Value of work done and recognised as turnover	255,000
Payments on account	260,000
Total costs incurred	310,000
Costs transferred to cost of sales	265,000

The amount to be included under long-term contract balances is calculated as follows:

	£
Total costs to date	310,000
Less: transferred to cost of sales	265,000
	45,000
Less: foreseeable losses on contract as a whole	(25,000)
	20,000
Less: Excess payments on account (£260,000 – £255,000)	(5,000)
Long-term contract balances	**15,000**

The notes to the balance sheet must disclose separately:
1. the net cost less foreseeable losses of £275,000 (£255,000 + 25,000-£5000); and
2. payments on account of £260,000

Balance sheet extract – B Ltd

Notes to the accounts – Stocks

	2010
	£m
Raw material and consumables	4
Properties in development	45
Long-term contract balances:	
– Net cost less foreseeable losses	**275**
– Applicable payments on accounts	(260)

Disclosure of losses in the profit and loss account

Where an **expected loss has crystallised**, the gross loss to be shown in the profit and loss account is the difference between amounts recognised as turnover and the amounts transferred to cost of sales plus provisions for foreseeable losses. 2360

EXAMPLE If for example a project is expected to yield a loss of £40,000 and costs of £250,000, then the profit and loss account should be charged with the following:

2010 Profit and loss account

		£
Included in turnover		250,000
Less: Included in cost of sales	250,000	
Foreseeable loss on contract as a whole	40,000	290,000
Loss		**40,000**

Summary of key disclosures

Below is a summary of the application of the provisions of SSAP 9 as they affect the disclosure of long-term contracts. The example illustrates the disclosures for turnover and profit recognition in the profit and loss account and balance sheet, for three projects at the end of the financial year. 2364

EXAMPLE C Ltd. is engaged in **three long-term projects**: P, Q and R. The following transactions took place during the current financial year in respect of these projects.

As at 31 December 2010		£'000	
	P	Q	R
	£	£	£
Value of work done/turnover	570	200	720
Costs to date	670	250	550
Transferred to cost of sales	550	220	510
Payments on account	600	100	800
Loss to completion		**80**	

The computation of amounts to be disclosed in the financial statements is as follows:
Profit and Loss Account (extract) 2010

		£'000		
	P	Q	R	Total
Turnover	570	200	720	1490
Less: Cost of sales	550	300	510	1360
Amounts transferred to cost of sales	550	220	510	1280
Loss to completion		80		80
Gross profit (loss)	**20**	**(100)**	**210**	**130**

		£'000	
Balance sheet	P	Q	R
Payments on account	600	100	800
Amounts recoverable on contracts [see 1];		**100**	
Excess payments on account to apply against work in progress	30		80
Costs to date	670	250	550
Transferred to cost of sales	550	220	510
Work in progress	**120**	**30**	**40**
Further loss to completion of project		80	
Provision for foreseeable losses [see 2]		**50**	
Excess payments on account calculated above	30		80
Long-term contract balances [see 3]	**90**		
Payments on account (see 4)			**40**

1. Disclosed separately as **debtors.**
2. Disclosed within either **provisions for liabilities and charges** or **creditors**, as appropriate. Note that this credit balance is not offset against the debit balance amounts recoverable on contracts under debtors.
3. Disclosed under **stocks**; in addition the following additional information to be shown: Gross work in progress amounted to £120,000 before the deduction of excess payments on account amounting to £30,000.
4. Disclosed under **creditors**.

SECTION 4

Comparison between UK GAAP and IAS (IFRS)

2376 IAS 11 is more specific in its scope than SSAP 9, which also covers contracts for the provision of services, which are in turn dealt with in IAS 18 "Revenue". There is no specific guidance contained in IFRS 1 "First-time adoption of IFRS", covering IAS 11.

Similarities

2377 1. IAS 11 and SSAP 9 permit the use of the **percentage completion method** for the recognition and measurement of profits, revenues and expenses on long-term contracts. However, there are some differences in the application of this method between the two standards (see table below).
2. Both standards also require the **immediate recognition of** expected losses.
3. IAS 11 requires **contracts to be combined when** part of a package, or treated separately when the commercial substance of each contract is separate and the revenues and costs can be separately identified. SSAP 9 has similar rules where fair values can be attributed to each part of the contract. **Where the criteria is not met** both standards permit the use of the "zero profit method", under which profit is recognised only after costs have been recovered (or are expected to be).

Key differences between SSAP 9 and IAS 11

2378

Issue	IAS 11	SSAP 9
Principles underpinning the determination of attributable profit	Probability Reliable measurement	Prudence
Classification of balance sheet items – debtors, WIP	Limited guidance	Extensive guidance
Contract revenue (components)	Defined/specified	Not defined/specified
Use of percentage completion method	Used where outcome can be estimated reliably	More emphasis on prudence
Project – stage of completion	Based on costs incurred to date, valuation or completion of work	Permits similar methods
Contract costs and cost measurement	Specified	Limited guidance given
Pre-contract costs	Capitalised – when it is probable contract has be awarded. Costs initially incurred cannot be re-instated	UITF 34 stricter – only permits recognition when it is certain contract will be awarded

Issue	IAS 11	SSAP 9
Presentation in balance sheet	Gross amount due for contract work	Asset split between "amounts recoverable on contracts" and "long term contract balances"
Specific contracts (fixed-price or cost-plus)	Recognised	Type not distinguished

Disclosures required under IAS 11

IAS 11 does not concern itself with presentation of contracts unlike SSAP 9 "Stocks and long-term contracts", but **it does require details of** segmentation and combined contracts. 2382

Additional disclosures are required by IAS 11, namely:
- contract revenue recognised as revenue in the period;
- methods used to determine contract revenue;
- methods used to determine the stage of completion;
- the aggregate costs and recognised profits, payments on account and retentions for contracts in progress;
- the gross amounts due to/from (liability/asset) customers for contract work; and
- details of contingent assets and liabilities (e.g. warranty costs, penalties, possible losses) in accordance with requirements of IAS 37.

FRED 28

The ASB issued FRED 28 "Inventories and construction contracts" in 2002. This FRED is still being discussed and forms part of an ongoing convergence programme with IFRS, being undertaken by the ASB. As at March 2010 there are no further developments to report and conversion to a full standard is not expected anytime soon. 2384

FRED 28 **proposes that** IAS 11 replaces that part of SSAP 9 concerning long-term contracts and incorporates related elements of IAS 18 "Revenue", which is also in the process of being amended by the IASB.

Although the FRED proposes no significant changes to the rules contained in SSAP 9, there are some **minor differences**, which are outlined as follows:

1. Under SSAP 9, profits can be attributed to projects when there outcome can be assessed with reasonable certainty. Under FRED 28, profits can be recorded where they can be reliably estimated.
2. FRED 28 seeks to remove the detailed disclosure rules contained in SSAP 9, except the requirement to separately record payments in advance of completed work on contracts.
3. FRED 28 also contains more stringent rules governing the aggregation and disaggregation of contracts.

CHAPTER 3

Debtors

OUTLINE ¶¶

Debtors **are defined as** monies owed to an organisation for the sales of goods or services and amounts paid to third parties in advance of goods and services. 2400

The classification, accounting treatment, and disclosure requirements relating to debtors are contained primarily in the Companies Act. The legislation is supported by a number of accounting standards and pronouncements.

In general, all debtors should be disclosed as current assets, no matter when they fall due. Additional disclosures are also required for **material debtors** due more than one year from the end of the financial period. 2404

Small companies that adopt the financial reporting standard for smaller entities (FRSSE) are exempt from the reporting requirements of the other accounting standards. **Specific rules** also apply to small companies who elect to submit short-form or abbreviated accounts.

1. Classification

"Debtors" is a **main statutory heading** under current assets and must be shown on the face of the balance sheet. Various subcategories of debtors are also required to be shown either on the face of the balance sheet or in the notes to the accounts. 2408

The **statutory subcategories** of "debtors" are as follows: 2410
- trade debtors;
- amounts owed by group undertakings;
- amounts owed by undertakings in which the company has a participating interest;
- called-up share capital not paid;
- prepayments and accrued income; and
- other debtors.

Further items **not covered** by the statutory format but which are covered by financial reporting standards may be shown separately in the financial statements and include amounts: 2412
- receivable in respect of finance leases;
- receivable in respect of hire purchase contracts;
- factored debts; and
- recoverable on contracts (i.e. long-term contracts).

2. Accounting treatment

2416 The Companies Act **requires all debtors** to be stated at the lower of cost and net realisable value, after deducting any provision for doubtful or bad debts. The accounting treatment for the different categories of debtors is outlined in this section.

Trade debtors

2420 Trade debtors represents the aggregate of amounts due from customers in respect of goods and services supplied, but not yet paid for. It will also include the **VAT payable** by customers on invoices raised but not yet paid.

The category "trade debtors" typically consists of:
- amounts invoiced to customers;
- goods delivered but not yet invoiced;
- retentions on contracts; and
- suppliers debit balances.

2422 Each individual **sales ledger account** records sales, cash received, discounts given and details of goods returned. The totals of the individual debtor balances should be reconciled to the debtors ledger control account.

If the **net realisable value** of the total debtors is likely to be less than the amount recorded in the company's accounts, a provision should be made against the carrying value of the debt to reduce it to the estimated realisable value.

2426 **Provisions** Such provisions made are needed in respect of the following:
- bad and doubtful debts;
- credit notes issued for returns; or
- settlement discounts.

2427 **Bad debts** All debtors balances should be assessed prior to the finalisation of the annual statutory accounts, in order to determine the "recoverability" of each debt. Particular attention should be paid to debtors outstanding **in excess of the current credit terms**. Where a debtor is not expected to pay either in whole or in part, a specific provision should be made against the balance to cover the anticipated shortfall. **General provisions** as a percentage of the total outstanding debtor balance may also be provided based on past experience. Such general provisions may not, however, attract tax relief.

2428 **Credit notes** Provision should be made for any credit notes issued after the year end (post-balance sheet) in respect of invoices included in end of year balances, as the debtors figure in the balance sheet will not be fully realised.

2430 **Credit balances** If a material credit balance arises on a debtor account, for instance where a customer has paid an invoice twice, then this amount should be transferred to creditors.

2432 **Settlement discounts** A company may give a discount to customers for prompt payment of invoices. The discount is deducted from the payment remitted and must be removed from trade debtors and charged to the profit and loss account.

Amounts owed by group undertakings

2436 All amounts owed by group members, namely the **parent, subsidiary and fellow subsidiary undertakings**, are required to be shown separately under debtors, as amounts due from group undertakings. These amounts include:
- loans;
- current accounts; and
- dividends receivable.

Inter-company balances due from one group undertaking should not be set off against those due to another group undertaking, unless a **legal right of set-off** exists. For example, if Company A has a debtor balance of £30,000, due from a subsidiary company with whom it also has a creditor balance of £25,000, but no legal right of set-off, then it cannot offset one account against the other. 2438

The **disclosure requirements** for group undertakings and participating interests are illustrated in the example below.

EXAMPLE **A Ltd – Annual report and accounts 2010**
Notes to the accounts (extract)

Debtors

	2010 **£'000**	**2010** **£'000**
Due within one year		
Trade debtors	56,500	48,750
Amounts recoverable on contracts	15,785	11,786
Amounts owed by subsidiaries	**5,785**	**1,567**
Amounts owed by associated undertakings	**2,789**	**-**
Amounts owed by joint ventures	**3,568**	**1,256**
Prepayments	687	2,568
Other debtors	1,473	899
	86,587	**66,826**
Due after one year		
Trade debtors	5,786	2,457
Amounts owed by joint ventures	**-**	**287**
Prepayments	2,023	1,602
	7,809	**4,346**
Totals	**94,396**	**71,172**

Amounts owed by participating interests

Participating interests include any **associates or joint ventures** of the company. Under FRS 9, amounts owed by participating interests should be analysed between amounts relating to loans and amounts consisting of trade balances. 2444

Other debtors

Other debtors that result from **non-trading activities** include: 2450
- amounts due from the sale of fixed assets (e.g. sale of building, land);
- insurance claims (e.g. fire, theft);
- refundable deposits (e.g. land purchase);
- tax balances; or
- loans to finance the acquisition of the company's own shares.

Although principally trading related, this category also includes advances or partial payments for the construction of stocks or fixed assets (e.g. long-term contracts).

Tax balances Tax balances listed under other debtors include VAT repayments or corporation tax recoverable. 2454

Debtor tax balances do not need to be shown separately, except where they are material to an appreciation of the balance sheet. It should be noted that deferred tax assets, which are not netted off against deferred tax liabilities, should also be included within debtors and shown separately if material.

EXAMPLE B Ltd – Annual report and accounts – 2010
Notes to the financial statements (extract)

Debtors

	2010 £'000	2010 £'000
Trade debtors	499	353
Other debtors	366	153
Corporation tax	**49**	**21**
Other taxes and social security	**15**	**10**
Advance corporation tax recoverable	**12**	
Prepayments	32	26
Totals	**973**	**563**

2456 **Loans to finance acquisition of own shares** If a company has provided loan capital to fund the purchase of its own shares, the **aggregate amount of such loans** should be disclosed in the notes to the accounts. The degree to which a company can provide loans for the acquisition of its own shares is limited and there are specific conditions that must be satisfied before they are permitted. The **relevant rules** are discussed in greater detail in Part 5 chapter 5.

The following are examples of the **types of loans** made by a company to finance the acquisition of its own shares:

a. financial assistance to an **employee share scheme** or to facilitate transactions in the company's shares between employees, former employees, their spouses, infant children or stepchildren;

b. loans to **bona fide employees** to enable them to purchase shares in the company or its holding company to be held by them by way of beneficial ownership; and

c. loans **made by a private company** to acquire its own shares or those of its holding company, or to reduce any liability incurred as a result of acquiring these shares.

Called-up share capital not paid

2460 Any amounts outstanding at the balance sheet date in respect of called-up share capital can be shown either as a **subcategory** of debtors or as a **main heading** in the balance sheet before fixed assets. It is usual for an explanation to be given in the share capital note concerning the amounts outstanding.

EXAMPLE Company A has a called-up share capital of £6m of which £4.5m has been paid in two stages. The balance outstanding as at 30 June 2010 of £1.5m was stated in its financial statements under debtors and represents the following:
- £0.5m called-up share capital not paid from the second "call"; and
- £1m representing the third and final call in respect of the original flotation terms.

Prepayments and accrued income

2462 Prepayments and accrued income may be disclosed as a subcategory of debtors or under a separate heading on the face of the balance sheet. Factors that will influence how they are disclosed include the materiality of the amounts concerned and whether they fall due after more than one year.

When determining profit or loss for a period, it is important that revenues earned are matched against the costs incurred in earning them. Therefore, any costs incurred in respect of future revenue streams should be disclosed as prepayments.

2464 In order **to carry forward expenditure** as a prepayment, the **following criteria** should be satisfied:

a. the expenditure should not relate to income that has been included in the profit and loss account;

b. the expenditure should generate future revenues sufficient to cover the amortisation of these costs (otherwise they will result in losses that should be recognised immediately);

c. the period during which the expenses should be amortised should be short enough to allow for reasonable certainty of recovery; and

d. prepayments should be subject to continuous review and written off immediately their "recoverability" becomes doubtful.

Examples of prepayments include: 2465
- rent paid in advance;
- unexpired portion of insurance premiums;
- unexpired portion of interest payments; and
- advertising costs paid in advance (but only if the specific campaign has not commenced at the accounting date).

In practice, if the enterprise is deemed to be a going concern and the element prepaid is not in respect of an onerous contract, for example, rent not paid on a factory that is no longer operational, it is usual to assume that the necessary conditions have been met.

EXAMPLE **C. Ltd – Annual report and accounts**
Notes to the financial statements 2010 (extract)

Debtors

	2010 £000's	**2010 £000's**
Due within one year		
Trade debtors	589	478
Other debtors	399	153
Prepayments	**40**	**41**
	1028	**672**
Due after more than one year		
Amounts recoverable on contracts	530	125
Pension prepayment	28	
	558	**125**
Totals	**1586**	**797**

The prepayments of £68,000 include a payment in advance for materials under a ten year agreement which was signed this year, totalling £40,000 and £28,000 for a receivable due after more than one year resulting from a bond posted in the US in lieu of litigation.

Exemptions and exclusions UITF Abstract 24, "Accounting for start-up costs", **specifically prohibits** the treatment of certain start-up activities as prepayments, except where similar costs as part of a company's ongoing activities would also be deferred. 2466

Start-up costs cover costs relating to:
- the establishment of a new entity;
- a new operation within an existing business; or
- the launching of new products or the reorganisation of all or part of an enterprise.

Accrued income includes amounts earned at the end of the accounting period but which the reporting entity has not yet invoiced or received. Examples are rental income, interest and goods despatched but not invoiced. Goods despatched but not invoiced, are usually included in trade debtors, since the transaction has legally taken place although the invoice has yet to be raised. 2468

Amounts recoverable on contracts

Enterprises engaged in **long-term contracts** are required by SSAP 9 "Stocks and long-term contract", to include turnover within debtors as "Amounts recoverable on contracts" where turnover exceeds payments on account. SSAP 9 requires that these amounts be disclosed separately within debtors and is an additional heading to those normally required by the Companies Act. 2470

Any amounts actually invoiced to customers, including requests for progress payments are included under trade debtors.

Finance leases and hire purchase agreements

2472 Where a finance lease is in place, SSAP 21 "Lease and Hire Purchase Contracts" requires that the lessor follows "substance over form". Instead, therefore, of showing an asset, which is the subject of the lease within fixed assets, the lessor includes a "debtor" in their balance sheet, representing the net investment in the lease; namely, the fair value of the asset at the beginning of the agreement less the present value of the lease payments received.

2473 The **lease rental payments**, representing the income stream over the life of the agreement must be apportioned between:
- the repayment of the principal capital; and
- the interest element on the outstanding finance provided.

2474 The **lease debtor** should not include any unearned interest, leaving only the principal balance to be disclosed. In the case of finance leases, the lessor's net investment in the lease is recorded under debtors as an additional heading "Amounts receivable under finance leases". This heading is in addition to those required by the Companies Act.

2476 The **net investment** in finance leases should be disclosed separately under "amounts receivable under finance leases", within debtors. Where hire purchase agreements have also been agreed, these should be disclosed separately under a subheading, detailing:
- the outstanding lease payments due under the terms of the agreement; and
- the residual values of "leased" assets.

The figures should also be analysed between amounts due within one year and after one year.

EXAMPLE **D. Ltd – Annual report and accounts 2010**
Notes to the financial statements (extract)

Finance leases

	2010 £'000	2010 £'000
Amounts due within one year		
Trade debtors	652	385
Capital grants receivable	285	178
Other debtors	199	93
Prepayments	27	31
Net investment in finance leases	14	13
	1,177	**700**
Amounts due after more than one year		
Other debtors	18	20
Net investment in finance leases	53	68
	71	**88**
Totals	**1,248**	**788**
Net investment in finance leases comprises		
Total lease payments receivable	96	116
Less finance charges allocated to future periods	(43)	(48)
Totals	**53**	**68**

2478 **Hire purchase agreements** Hire purchase agreements are similar in nature to finance leases and are therefore accounted for in the same way.

Under a hire purchase agreement, the buyer takes possession of the goods, usually following the payment of an initial deposit and ownership is obtained when all the agreed number of subsequent instalments have been paid. Hire purchase agreements often involve a finance company as a third party. The manufacturer of the goods often sells them to a finance company which then enters into a hire purchase agreement with the customer.

EXAMPLE **D. Ltd – Annual report and accounts.**
Notes to the financial statements 2010 (extract)

Hire purchase debtors

	2010 **£m**	**Due after more than one year** **£m**
Amounts due within one year		
Instalments and hire purchase debtors	999.7	203.6
Provision for unearned finance charges	(60.1)	(17.2)
Other debtors	380.0	25.2
Total trade debtors	**1,319.6**	**211.6**
Book value of finance leases in lessor subsidiaries	16.5	15.2
Prepayment and accrued income	120.5	18.2
	1,456.6	**245.0**

3. Debt factoring

Debt factoring comes in many guises, but typically **allows companies to** convert debtors into cash quickly and can help mitigate the risk of slow payment or bad debts. However, in most cases it is the company entering the factoring arrangement, and not the debt factor, that is still exposed to the risk of bad debts. In general, therefore, applying the principles inherent in FRS 5, "Substance of Transactions", means factored debts are usually accounted for as trade debtors, although the presentation will differ depending on the type of debt or agreement. 2480

FRS 5 gives guidance in Application Note C on the applicable accounting treatment and disclosure requirements as they affect debtors.

a. Overview

Debt factoring is a popular method of raising funds from the **sale of debtor balances** to a third party, before the debts are collected. The transactions can take many forms with the simplest involving a clear sale at a fixed price without recourse, or where the factor takes over the administration of the sales ledger and collects the debts on behalf of the company. 2482 FRS 5 (C1)

In **more complicated arrangements**, the buyer (factor) may have recourse to the seller in the event of non-payment and, in addition, the price received for the debts may vary depending upon how long they remain unpaid, to reflect any possible slow payment risk. Under these types of arrangement where the seller retains a significant economic interest in the underlying debts, they should be accounted for as financing arrangements, with the debtors remaining on the balance sheet. 2483

Debt factoring agreements may require different accounting treatments as dictated by the terms of each individual agreement, the main characteristics of which are usually as follows: 2484
a. a company sells or assigns specific debts to the factor;
b. the factor provides finance to the company selling the debt based on a percentage of the value of the debt transferred; and
c. the factor will charge for the factoring services which may be a fixed amount, or based on actual sums collected from the debtors. Alternatively, it could represent an amount based on the sum advanced and the time taken to collect from the debtor.

b. Principal factoring methods

There are **three principal accounting treatments** for companies factoring their debtors: 2486 FRS 5 (C3)
– Derecognition;
– Separate presentation; or
– Linked presentation.

Each of these options is discussed below.

A detailed understanding of the **commercial terms** (as well as the practical and theoretical detail) of each factoring agreement is necessary in order to determine which of the accounting treatments is most suitable. It is **important to ascertain**:
– which party retains the benefits and risks of each agreement; and
– the basis of the factoring charges.

2488 **Benefits** The benefits of the agreement include future cash flows derived from the settlement of monies due by the debtors and the risks will be of default or slow payment. It will often be **the nature of the risk** that determines the appropriate accounting treatment.

Summary table	
Accounting treatment	**Characteristics**
Derecognition	No significant risks/benefits retained Factor has no recourse to the company
Linked presentation	Company retains significant benefits/risks Exposure to losses restricted to a fixed amount
Separate presentation	Factored debts and related finance shown separately (not linked) on balance sheet where a company retains significant risks/benefits. Conditions for linked presentation not met.

Derecognition

2490 An entity may only use this accounting treatment where all the **following criteria** exist:
FRS 5 (C11) – a sale of the debtors to the factor at arm's length;
– the company receives fixed, non-returnable funds from the factor for the debts;
– there is no recourse to the company selling the debt (in terms of slow payment or bad debts); or
– the company will not benefit or suffer in any way if the debts perform better or worse than expected.

2492 Where **debts are sold without recourse** and all further risks to the seller are effectively eliminated, the accounting treatment is termed "derecognition". The debts can be credited with the sale proceeds and the effect is the same as if the respective debtors had settled the debts themselves. These debtors are then removed from the balance sheet and no liability to the factor is recorded.

However, an entity would be required to record a loss on the disposal of the debts which represents the difference between the face value of the debts and the payment received from the factor. **Where any of these features is not present**, this means the seller has retained the risks and benefits relating to factored debts and either a separate or linked presentation should be used.

EXAMPLE **Wortley Ltd**
Notes to the accounts
Derecognition

A company opts to factor debtors valued at £300,000 for £270,000. No further sum is receivable from the factor company who in turn has no recourse to the company for bad debts or slow payment. In this instance, the company has sold the debtors for a fixed sum and does not retain the right to any benefits from the payments made by the debtors or bear any further risk in relation to the debts.
The entity will be required to post a charge of £30,000 to the profit and loss account representing the factor's fee for purchasing the debtors.

Separate presentation

2494 The **following characteristics** indicate that a separate presentation is the appropriate
FRS 5 (C17) accounting treatment:
– the cost of factoring varies with the speed of payment by the debtors;

– there is full recourse to the seller for losses; and
– the seller is required to repay a fixed amount on a specified date, regardless of timing or debtor balances collected.

Where the company retains **significant risks** in respect of the factored debts, these debts remain under debtors on the balance sheet with the amounts disclosed by way of note. The proceeds received from the factor are reflected as a liability and shown separately as a creditor, as it represents the finance provided by the factor for the debts. The **interest element** of the factor's charges should be charged in the profit and loss account on a basis consistent with the terms of the financing. 2496 FRS 5 (C20)

EXAMPLE **B. Ltd – Separate presentation**

Funding from a factoring agent has been arranged totalling £125,000 against a debtors ledger balance of £155,000. These monies are repayable to the factor in three months' time, when any outstanding debtors are transferred back to the company. In this instance the company has retained all the **benefits and risks** in respect of the debts.

Accounting Treatment The problem will be if the debtors are slow in paying then the company will have to find alternative funding in order to repay the factoring agent after three months. Furthermore, all potential bad debts will be returned to the company after the agreement has expired. The notes to the financial statements should detail the total of the factored debts **discounted with recourse** that are outstanding at the balance sheet date.

B. Ltd – Annual report and accounts – 2010
Notes to the accounts (extract)
10. Debtors
Following the adoption of FRS 5, "Reporting the Substance of Transactions", trade debtors and bank loans and overdrafts as at 30 June 2010 include £125,000 of invoices discounted with recourse.

EXAMPLE **S Ltd – Separate presentation**

S Ltd enters into the following factoring arrangement with F Ltd.
– S transfers all its trade debts to F, with a limit placed on the total due from any one debtor;
– F administers S's sales ledger and collects debtors in return for an administration charge of 2% based on the outstanding balance at the year end;
– S may draw up to 75% of the gross debtors factored;
– S assigns and sends invoices to F on a weekly or monthly basis;
– any debts not recovered after the 90 days are reassigned to S for immediate cash settlement;
– F pays for all debts less any advances and interest charges 90 days after the date of their assignment; and
– on termination of the agreement the balance on the factoring account is settled in cash.

Accounting treatment
The debts have been legally transferred to F although the benefits and risks have been retained by S as it continues to bear the risk of slow payment. S must pay for any **debts not settled after 90 days**. S Ltd therefore has an **unlimited exposure** to loss.
S also has an obligation to repay amounts received from F on or before a set date (i.e. 90 days), irrespective of the level of collections from the factored debts, either out of the monies collected from debtors or from other resources. In this case separate presentation should be adopted in the balance sheet.

Linked presentation

A linked presentation **is defined** as the presentation in the balance sheet of an asset that is in substance a financing arrangement. The asset can be shown gross on the face of the balance sheet with the finance liability deducted from the same asset caption. 2498 FRS 5 (C15)

A linked presentation will be appropriate where, although the seller has **retained significant benefits and risks** concerning the factored debts, there is no doubt that the exposure to a loss is limited to a fixed monetary amount. A linked presentation **should only be used where** there is no doubt that the factor's claim extends solely to collections from the factored debts and no provision for the seller to reaquire the debts in the future. 2500

Where the company **retains significant risks and benefits** in respect of the factored debts but the downside exposure to losses are limited to a fixed amount, the debts concerned may be recorded as a linked presentation.

2502 However, in order that a linked presentation may be adopted, **a number of criteria must be met**; namely:

FRS 5 (27) 1. The financing (principal and interest) must be repaid from the proceeds of the item;
2. The entity should not have the option of retaining the title to the asset on repayment of the financing or be able to reacquire the item at some point in the future;
3. The entity does not have the right to retain the item upon repayment of the finance or to reacquire it at any time;
4. The finance relates to a specific item and, in the case of a loan, is secured on that item and not on any other asset;
5. The finance provider has no recourse to the other assets of the entity for losses and the entity has no obligation to make good the losses;
6. The directors of the entity must disclose in the financial statements that where a linked presentation has been adopted, the entity is not required to make good any losses incurred by the finance provider;
7. If the revenues generated by the item are insufficient to repay the finance provider, this does not constitute a default by the entity; and
8. Where all of the above conditions hold for only a part of the finance, a linked presentation should be used only for that part.

2504 The **following conditions** also apply when considering the **accounting treatment** of a financing arrangement as a linked presentation.

a. a linked presentation should not be used where the debts that have been factored cannot be separately identified; and

b. the factor agrees in writing that there is no recourse, and such an agreement is noted in the financial statements.

FRS 5 (C16) Where debts are **factored on an ongoing basis**, the arrangements for terminating the agreement must be scrutinised to ensure that the conditions for a linked presentation are met. It is a requirement that although the factor does not take on further debts, it continues to bear the risk of any losses on debts already factored and is not able to transfer them back to the seller. Where this is not the case, the factor may have the option of returning the debts that it suspects will be bad, by terminating the factoring arrangement. In this situation the seller's exposure is not limited and a linked presentation inappropriate.

The **mechanics of** linked presentation are illustrated in the examples below.

2506 **Profit recognition** Where a **linked presentation** is adopted, profit should be recognised only to the extent that the non-returnable proceeds received exceed the previous carrying value of the item. Thereafter, any profit or loss arising from the item should be recognised in the period in which it relates. The net profit or loss recognised should be included in the profit and loss account, with separate disclosure of its gross components given in the notes to the accounts.

2508 **Disclosures** Under the linked presentation, the company continues to reflect its factored
FRS 5 (27) debts (after deducting the finance element and providing for bad debts) on the balance sheet. **In addition**, the notes to the financial statements should include the following:
- the main terms of the agreement;
- the gross amount of the outstanding factored debts;
- the factoring charges recognised during the period (analysed as to interest and other charges);
- a statement that the company is not obliged to support, or intends to support losses beyond the specified recourse in respect of specific debts under the arrangement; and
- confirmation that the factor has agreed in writing to seek recourse to interest and principal only to the extent that sufficient funds are generated by the specific debts it has agreed to finance.

The accounting treatment and key disclosure requirements for **three different examples** are given below.

EXAMPLE **Linked presentation**

C Ltd has factored debts of £745,000 in return for an initial non-returnable payment from the factor of £520,000, plus further deferred sums, based on the amounts actually collected from the debtors.

Accounting treatment In this example C Ltd has retained:
- some of the benefits of future payments from debtors as further sums will be receivable from the factor, depending on the level of payment by the debtors; and
- a proportion of the risks of non-payments by the debtors.

C Ltd has limited its potential exposure to the risk of slow payment or bad debts to £225,000. The company should adopt a linked presentation in its disclosure in the balance sheet.

EXAMPLE **Linked presentation**

D Ltd enters into a factoring agreement with **F Ltd** under the following terms:
- D will transfer by assignment to F such trade debts as D shall determine, subject only to a credit approval by F who levies a charge of 5% of turnover, payable monthly;
- D will continue to run the sales ledger and handle all aspects of debt collection;
- D may draw up to 75% of the gross debts assigned;
- D assigns and forwards copy invoices as and when they are raised;
- F provides protection from bad debts. Any debts not recovered after 90 days are passed to F. A charge of 1% of the gross value of the debts is levied for this service; and
- F pays the debt less advances, interest and credit protection, 90 days after the date of purchase.

Accounting treatment Although the debts have been legally transferred to F, D continues to bear significant benefits and risks, such as a slow payment risk, as the interest charged by F varies with the speed of debt collection. The gross amount of the debts should be shown on the front of the balance sheet until they are either collected or all of the risks are transferred to F after 90 days. For D, the maximum downside loss is limited since any debts not recovered after 90 days are paid by F which then assumes all slow payment and credit risks. Therefore, a linked presentation should be adopted.

Disclosures The amount deducted on the face of the balance sheet should be the lower of the proceeds received and the gross amount of the debts less all charges to the factor. For example, debtors of £500,000 would be shown less proceeds from the factoring arrangement, credit protection and finance charges.
Assume proceeds of £375,000 and costs of £10,000.

Balance sheet (extract) – 30 June 2010

Current assets		**£'000**
Stocks		**X**
Debts factored without recourse:		
Gross debtors after credit protection and accrued interest (£500k-£490k)	490	
Less: non-returnable proceeds	(375)	
		115
Other debtors		**X**
Cash		**X**
		XX

The non-returnable proceeds of £375,000 would be accounted for in cash and the profit and loss account will be charged with the interest and credit protection expenses of £10,000.

Notes to the accounts
Debtors – linked presentation
Trade debtors **subject to limited recourse financing** represent debts discounted with financial institutions, subject to strictly limited recourse in that the majority of the cash received on discounting is not returnable. The returnable portion of these proceeds is recorded as loans due within one year and more than one year, as appropriate. The company **does not intend to make good any losses** over the agreed recourse limit and the financial institutions concerned have confirmed their acceptance in writing.

EXAMPLE **Global Plastics Ltd**
Linked presentation

Balance sheet (extract) as at 30 June 2010

	Note	£'000	2010 £'000	£'000	20X9 £'000
Current assets					
Stocks			395.6		275.6
Debtors			1,765.3		1,435.6
– **due within one year**					
– due after more than one year			345.2		282.6
Securitised receivables	**16**	545.2		909.7	
Less: non-recourse borrowing	**17**	(324.5)	220.7	(677.7)	232.0
Investments			65.2		35.4
Cash at bank			275.2		326.8
			3,067.2		**2,588.0**

Securitised receivables
Global Plastics has securitised a significant portion of its debtor book, with the proceeds being used to reduce bank borrowings. Within current assets, non-recourse borrowings are linked with the securitised element of receivables. Turnover and profits before taxation are reduced by financing costs in respect of non-recourse borrowings.

Note 16 **Interest in securitised receivables:**	**2010** **£'000**	**2009** **£'000**
- due within one year	315.6	595.6
- due after more than one year	219.6	334.1
Bank balances		
Amounts owed (to)/ by group undertakings		(20.0)
	545.2	**909.7**

Note 17 **Non-recourse borrowings**		
- due within one year	181.0	478.2
- due after more than one year	143.5	199.5
	324.5	**677.7**

Non-recourse borrowings In the Group balance sheet, non-recourse borrowings are shown after the deduction of unamortised issue costs incurred by Global Plastics of £0.6m.

Bills of exchange

2510 A bill of exchange **is defined as** an unconditional order in writing, addressed by one person (drawer) to another (drawee), requiring the drawee to pay on demand or on a fixed date a specified sum of money.

FRS 5 prescribes the **treatment and disclosure** of bills of exchange received from debtors that have been discounted. Where the bank has full recourse to the company in the event that the bill is not honoured, it is clear that the risks in respect of the underlying debts have remained unchanged. Therefore, following the **treatment of factored debts**, the debtor should remain on the company's balance sheet while the cash received for discounting the "bill" should be shown as an asset with the finance provided shown as a liability.

Bills of exchange **can be either short or long-term** so care must be taken to ensure that the correct debtors classification is applied (i.e. after one year). Furthermore, if the bill of exchange is settled after the year end, this does not constitute a separate post-balance sheet adjusting event.

4. Disclosure framework

The **general rule** is that the total debtors figure must be disclosed within current assets on the face of the balance sheet. However, different formats are permitted and more detailed information can be provided in the notes to the accounts. The disclosures required of small companies filing shorter-form or abbreviated accounts can be reduced. 2520

Small companies

Shorter-form accounts Should a company elect to prepare and file shorter-form accounts then it can reduce the level of disclosures in respect of debtors. The only categories required are: 2522
- trade debtors;
- amounts owed by group undertakings;
- amounts owed by participating interests; and
- other debtors.

Disclosure is also required of the aggregate amount of debtors due after more than one year.

FRSSE If a small company chooses to adopt the FRSSE, then it is not bound by either FRS 5 or UITF 4 "Presentation of long-term debtors in current assets". 2526

Abbreviated accounts Where a company files abbreviated accounts only the aggregate debtors figure need be disclosed. However, called-up share capital not paid and prepayments and accrued income can either be included in debtors or shown as a separate heading on the balance sheet. 2528

If a small company files abbreviated accounts, a complete set of accounts or shorter-form accounts must still be presented to the members. These accounts should include a detailed analysis of debtors.

Balance sheet

2532

EXAMPLE **Alpha Ltd**
Annual report and accounts 2010

Balance sheet (extract)		**2010 £'000**		**2009 £'000**
Current assets				
Stocks		250		195
Debtors				
Due within one year	125		169	
Due after one year	85	210	71	240
Cash resources		155		85
		615		**520**

Debtors falling due after one year Any amounts in respect of each category of debtors that fall due after one year should be shown separately. The Act does not require this information to be given on the face of the balance sheet itself, but may be given in the notes to the accounts. In determining whether an amount is due **within or after more than one year**, it is normal practice to take the earliest date at which payment is expected. 2534

It is a requirement of UITF Abstract 4, therefore, that debtors due after more than one year are disclosed on the face of the balance sheet, if the amount is material in the context of total net current assets. UITF 4 (3)

The following are **examples of items** that potentially may fall due after more than one year and which may require separate disclosure:
- amounts due to lessors by lessees under finance leases; and
- deferred payments in respect of the disposal of fixed assets or investments.

2536 **Notes to the accounts** The examples below illustrate the most common disclosure presentations adopted in the notes to the accounts.

EXAMPLE **Presentation of debtors**

Method 1
Beta Ltd Annual report and accounts 2010
Notes to the accounts (extract)

	2010 £'000	2009 £'000
Debtors		
Due within one year:		
Trade debtors	100	120
Less: Amounts provided for doubtful debts	(11)	(10)
	99	**110**
Other debtors and prepayments	12	30
	111	**140**
Due after one year:		
Owing by subsidiary companies	17	12
Other debtors and prepayments	16	-
	33	**12**
Totals	**144**	**152**

Method 2
Delta Ltd – Annual report and accounts 2010
Notes to the accounts (Extract)

Debtors	2010 £'000	2009 £'000
Debtors		
Trade debtors	541	560
Amounts owed by subsidiaries	25	15
Amounts owed by joint ventures	15	26
Tax recoverable in one year	14	11
Other debtors	107	87
Prepayments	55	72
Totals	**757**	**771**
Included within the above amounts falling due after one year:		
Trade debtors	27.6	20.2
Other debtors	11.4	9.8
Totals	**39.0**	**30.0**

CHAPTER 4

Cash

OUTLINE ¶¶

This chapter explains the rules governing the accounting treatment and disclosure of cash at bank and in hand. An overview of the key differences between UK GAAP and IAS (IFRS) is also given. **2600**

Cash **is defined** in FRS 1 "Cash flow statements" as cash in hand and deposits repayable on demand with any qualifying financial institution, less overdrafts repayable on demand. FRS 1 does not, however, define the treatment of bank and cash balances within the balance sheet which is addressed to a limited extent by the Companies Act. **2602** FRS 1 (2)

Classification The term "**cash**" includes the following: **2610**
- legal tender;
- amounts due by banks;
- cheques;
- bank credit card vouchers;
- short-term deposits (up to seven days);
- other demand deposits such as those denominated in foreign currencies;
- overdrafts; and
- short-term loans.

A **more expansive definition** of "cash at bank" includes the total amount of cash on deposit with other financial institutions (e.g. building societies) and term deposit funds. This definition does not restrict cash to demand deposits; the rationale being that cash should include all "monies" available on demand as this gives a better indication of the liquidity of a company. **2614**

Deposits **are deemed repayable on demand**, if they can be withdrawn at any time without notice or penalty, or if a maturity or period of notice of not more than 24 hours or one working day has been agreed. Deposits **may also be accounted for** as investments depending on the terms attached to each deposit account.

Cash advances to employees on account of expenditure to be incurred are not considered cash and should be shown under debtors. **2616**

1. Accounting treatment

2620 The **two principal** methods of accounting for cash in the financial statements are the cash-book and bank statement methods. According to the circumstances of the company either method could be selected, although the company should be **consistent in its choice**. In practice, however, the cash book method is almost universally adopted by companies although care needs to be taken that it is not manipulated by delays in despatching cheques. It is not common to see an accounting policy for bank and cash in a set of financial statements, but one should be considered where the statement method is adopted. A **change of method** should also be accompanied by a note of the comparative figures and an explanation for the change.

Cash book method

2622 In general, the amount to be shown under "Cash" should be the figure recorded in the company's cash book, including cheques issued and despatched but not yet presented for payment and receipts lodged which have not yet been credited by the bank. This is considered an appropriate treatment which represents the substance of the payment/receipt, with the reverse side of the double entry for the lodgements and issued cheques being reflected in debtors and creditors. Where cheques in settlement of liabilities or cheques received have, at the reporting date, been drawn but not yet despatched, then they should be added back to both the cash balances and the outstanding creditor balances.

Bank statement method

2624 Under this method, the company records the balance per the bank statement at the end of the reporting period. A company **may adopt this method where**, in practice, a considerable period of time elapses between the date on which cheques are drawn (or received) and posted to the cash book and the date they cleared the company's bank account. The rationale for this method is that the company does not recognise the cash transaction until it is reflected in the bank balance.

2626 A **different accounting treatment** may be appropriate if the sums involved are material, which involves disclosing the transactions as either "Cash in transit" or "Uncleared banking terms". The balance per the bank statement represents the cash balance disclosed in the financial statements, and debtors and creditors are adjusted to incorporate cheques drawn or received prior to the year-end (but not reflected in the bank statement), with the opposite entries being in "Cash in transit" or "Uncleared banking items".

2. Set-off of bank balances

2630 It is a **general requirement** of the Companies Act and FRS 25 "Financial instruments: Presentation" that assets may not be offset against liabilities in the financial statements, except when there is a **legally enforceable right** of set-off between the balances.

An agreement can be reached between parties, involving the set-off of one debt against another or a loss against a gain. For instance, a bank may match a credit balance with a company on one account against a debit balance on the other, if:
- the accounts are in the same name; and
- denominated in the same currency or in other freely convertible currencies.

2640 **Criteria for set-off** Offset is required only when:
- the entity has a legally enforceable right to set off the asset and liability; and
- the entity intends to settle on a net basis the asset and associated liability simultaneously.

A **net presentation should only be used** if this reflects the future cash flows expected to arise from the settlement of the separate financial instruments. The existence of a legally enforceable right is not enough to justify the use of net presentation in the financial statements. Likewise, the stated intention of two parties to settle on a net basis without a legally enforceable right to do so does not justify use of a net presentation, as the rights and obligations of the underlying financial instruments remain unaffected. Use of net presentation in this case would not be a true reflection of the agreement. Special care is needed when preparing consolidated accounts.

Offsetting is **not an appropriate policy, where**:
- financial assets and liabilities arise from financial instruments with the same risk profile but that are comprised of different underlying components;
- financial assets have been pledged as collateral for non-recourse financial liabilities; and
- insurance proceeds are expected to be recovered from a third party that cover related obligations.

3. Restricted funds

Restricted funds in specially designated bank accounts, which may only be used for certain specific or restricted purposes, as is often the case with charities (see ¶9500), should be shown separately. 2650

Examples of restricted funds include:
- monies held in countries whose currency is **subject to exchange regulations** which could delay repatriation; or
- deposits **subject to** either **a legal assignment** or a charge in favour of a third party.

EXAMPLE **Alpha Ltd – Report and accounts 31 December 2010**
Notes to the accounts (extract)

10. Cash at bank and in hand

£25m of the cash balances of £65m (20X9 £356m) are held in countries subject to exchange controls which may delay repatriation of these funds. A further £5m represents cash deposits subject to a legal assignment in favour of a third party.

4. Disclosures

The disclosure requirements for cash are set out in the balance sheet formats contained in the Companies Act and illustrated in the following example of a balance sheet extract for current assets. Additional disclosures are required in the notes to the accounts. Overdrafts and short-term loans are disclosed separately within creditors. 2654

Balance sheet (extract)

2655

EXAMPLE **Alpha Ltd – Report and accounts – 2010**
Balance Sheet (extract)

Current assets	**2010**	**2009**
	£'000	**£'000**
Stocks	361.2	102.2
Debtors	568.3	324.5
Investments	145.6	89.0
Cash at bank and in hand	**62.9**	**40.9**
Total current assets	**1138.0**	**556.6**

Notes to the accounts

The **first example** of a note to the financial statements illustrates cash and a separate category of short-term deposits. The **second example** shows the option of showing deposits under current asset investments (see ¶2700), while the **third example** depicts an alternative 2656 presentation of a combined balance sheet extract with an accompanying note detailing cash inflows and outflows.

EXAMPLE **Alpha Ltd – Annual report and accounts – 2010**
Notes to the accounts (extract)

15. Cash and short-term deposits

	2010 £'000	20X9 £'000
Cash at the bank	42.9	25.3
Short-term deposits	20.0	15.6
Totals	**62.9**	**40.9**

EXAMPLE **B Ltd – Annual report and accounts – 2010**
Notes to the accounts (extract)
Current assets

	Note	2010 £'000	20X9 £'000
Investments and deposits	5	758.3	589.2
Cash at bank and in hand		18.2	14.1
		776.5	**603.3**

Notes – No 5 Current asset investments

	2010 £'000	2009 £'000
Listed investments	587.2	475.5
Short-term deposits	171.11	113.7
	758.3	**589.2**

EXAMPLE **C Ltd – Annual report and accounts – 31 December 2010**
Notes to the accounts (extract)
Current assets

	Note	2010 £'000
Cash at bank and in hand	14	3,427

14. Notes to the accounts

	Cash £'000
Balance b/fwd. Jan. 1 2010	1,546
Net cash inflow	4,210
Net cash (outflow)	(2,905)
Deposits	586
Cash at bank per the balance sheet	**3,437**

5. Comparison between UK GAAP and IAS (IFRS)

2660 IAS 1 requires disclosure of "**cash and equivalents**", which are defined under IAS 7 "Cash flow statements" as "short-term, highly liquid investments", that are readily convertible to cash and with little risk of significant changes in value.

The IAS differs from UK GAAP which requires these "cash equivalents" to be disclosed as current asset investments.

CHAPTER 5

Current asset investments

OUTLINE ¶¶

This chapter **covers the rules** determining the classification, accounting treatment and disclosure requirements for current asset investments, which are defined as assets retained by an investor for a short period of time. 2700

The reporting framework for companies adopting **historical cost** is governed by the requirements of the Companies Act, whilst entities electing to value current asset investments at **current value** must adopt FRS 26 "Financial Instruments: Measurement".

A. Classification

Investments can be classified either as fixed assets or as current assets under the Companies Act. Investments are treated as current assets when they are **short-term in nature** and where there are no restrictions on the company's ability to dispose of them. Investments are classified as fixed when the investing company's intention is to hold them on a continuing basis over the longer term. 2704

Statutory headings

The Companies Act formats prescribe certain subheadings for current asset investments, which can be shown either on the face of the balance sheet itself or in the notes to the financial statements. 2706

The **required "subheadings"** for investments under current assets are as follows:
- Shares in group undertakings;
- Other investments; and
- Own shares.

For small companies only the first two categories are required.

Group undertakings Shares in group undertakings should be classified as current assets only in exceptional circumstances, for example, if they were acquired for the express purpose of resale. 2708

When an entity or business is **purchased solely for resale**, such as when acquired as part of a larger acquisition, it should be valued at the estimated sale proceeds and included under current asset investments. Depending on the nature of the investment, the interest may also be regarded as a financial asset under FRS 13 "Derivatives and other financial instruments", and therefore subject to additional disclosure requirements.

Investments that satisfy the definition of associated undertakings, partnerships and joint ventures should be treated as **fixed asset investments** (¶1750).

2716 **Other investments** Other investments include the following:
- bank or building society deposits;
- quoted and unquoted securities; and
- short-term loans to institutions (e.g. banks).

Bank and building society deposits can be disclosed as either current asset investments or as cash in hand, depending on the precise terms attached to the deposits. If the figures involved are material in value, a policy note should detail where the investments have been included in the accounts.

2718 **Quoted investments** are defined in the Companies Act as any investment listed on either:
- a recognised investment exchange other than an overseas investment exchange; or
- any stock exchange of repute outside Great Britain.

MEMO POINTS Recognised investment exchanges in the UK include:
- The London Stock Exchange;
- The London Commodity Exchange;
- The London Metal Exchange;
- LIFFE Administration and Management; and
- The International Petroleum Exchange.

B. Accounting treatment

2724 The **general rule** is that current asset investments should be valued under the historical cost regime and stated at the lower of purchase price or net realisable value. Companies can elect to revalue current asset investments at market value (fair value under FRS 26).

Certain **specialist sectors**, such as charities, **have different rules** which require even current asset investments to be included in the financial statements at market value.

1. Historical cost

2726 Current asset investments are **normally recorded** at the lower of their purchase price or net realisable value. The cost of current assets can be calculated using a cost-flow assumption such as FIFO, provided the replacement cost or latest purchase price is disclosed.

Where the net realisable value (NRV) of an investment **is lower than its historical cost**, the diminution in value should be debited to the profit and loss account and the carrying value of the investment is reduced accordingly.

If, in a subsequent period, any part of **this diminution in value is reversed**, any provision made earlier should be written back to the profit and loss account.

EXAMPLE **A Ltd – Annual report and accounts**
Notes to the financial statements (extract)

Current asset investments
A Ltd had previously made a number of short-term loans to institutions in the construction sector. However, due to difficult trading conditions the prospect of default on the loans became a serious possibility and a provision was made at the end of the financial year 2009 to reflect the revised estimated net realisable value of the investments. In 2010, these loans were repaid in full to A Ltd. and the provision released to the profit and loss account.

Where the cost of an investment, which is **a listed investment**, is less than its market value, the market value should also be disclosed. 2728

Companies **can voluntary elect** to disclose the market value of their current asset investments, even where there is no strict requirement for them to do so.

2. Current cost

Certain assets can be valued under so-called alternative accounting rules. **These rules modify** the historical cost accounting convention and allow current asset investments to be included in the balance sheet at current cost. A **variation of current cost** is fair value accounting (see ¶2744). 2730

However, **except where a specific standard** (e.g. the Charities SORP) requires current asset investments to be revalued, it is not general practice to adopt the alternative accounting rules.

Best practice on revaluation is indirectly reflected in FRS 15 "Tangible fixed assets", which prohibits the cherry-picking of assets for revaluation. This accounting treatment supports the line taken in the Companies Act, that any surpluses and deficits on the revaluation of assets should be treated line by line and not on a portfolio basis.

MEMO POINTS Current cost is the lower of net current replacement cost and recoverable amount, which in turn is the higher of net realisable value and value in use.

Determining current cost

Where a revaluation to current cost is undertaken, the following rules apply: 2732

1. **Any surplus arising** on restating current asset investments to current cost should be taken to the revaluation reserve.
2. Any **subsequent diminution in value** should first be debited against the revaluation reserve, and to the extent that the diminution takes the value below cost, that element should be charged through the profit and loss account.

Market value is often taken as the current cost of current asset investments. However, account should also be taken of other issues that could affect the value of the underlying investment. 2734

Quoted investments The market value to be used is usually the mid-market share price at the financial year-end, although the directors should adjust the market price to take into account any additional factors that could affect the proceeds from the disposal of the shares. 2736

EXAMPLE B Ltd has acquired a large holding of shares in S Ltd but less than the 20% barrier that represents a significant interest. At the end of the accounting period, B Ltd classified its investment in S as a current asset, on the basis that it was a strategic short-term investment. The mid-market price of the shares was £8.50. If the directors of B Ltd were planning to dispose of part of the company's holding in S Ltd (e.g. 5%), this could cause the value of its remaining shareholding to fall. This should be reflected in the valuation of current asset investments at the financial year-end and disclosed by way of a note to the accounts.

Unquoted companies Where an **investment is not listed** and has no readily ascertainable market value, the directors may determine the value using other methods. The **directors are responsible for** identifying a suitable basis for identifying the current cost. Where the alternative accounting rules are to be applied to unquoted current asset investments, the company should disclose in the notes to the financial statements details of the basis they have adopted. 2738

The directors may wish to record unquoted investments at a value **other than historical cost** in the financial statements. A commonly used method of determining the market value in these circumstances, is to apply the **price earnings ratio (P/E)** of a similar listed company to the company in question. The P/E is often used for valuing small parcels of shares in trading companies.

EXAMPLE The **price earnings ratio** is the current market price of a company share divided by the earnings per share (EPS). The P/E ratio is expressed as a number and reflects the number of years it would take a company to earn profits matching its market value. High multiples are synonymous with growth stocks and low multiples with no-growth stocks. The ratio enables comparisons between companies in the same sector.

A company which is listed has made profits of £10m and its shares currently trade at £15. The number of shares in issue is 5 million.
The EPS is calculated as follows: £10m/ 5m = £2.0
The P/E ratio is therefore: £15/ 2 = 7.5 times (multiple).

The **unquoted company** can then use this P/E ratio as a benchmark, against which to value its unquoted investments after adjusting for any additional factors such as risk, size of holding and, if not quoted, lack of marketability.

2742 **Other methods used to determine current cost** Other valuation methods include:
- the accounting rate of return;
- net asset method;
- dividend yield; or
- discounted cash flow valuations (DCF).

A detailed discussion of these methods is beyond the scope of this book.

Fair value accounting

2744 The requirements of the Companies Act have been amended by the EU Fair Value Directive, and FRS 25 and FRS 26 "Financial Instruments: Measurement", which allow assets to be included in the balance sheet at fair value and any changes in value to be recorded in the profit and loss account. This is a variation on the alternative accounting rules.

These **new provisions apply predominantly to** financial instruments, but now mean that certain current investments can be carried as "marked to market". The new provisions are optional rather than mandatory. Fair value accounting covers both individual and consolidated accounts and is available to all companies including smaller companies preparing shorter-form accounts.

A number of companies hold considerable portfolios of highly liquid (readily marketable) investments. Under the alternative accounting rules all **revaluation gains or losses** must be credited or debited to the revaluation reserve.

However, **some exceptions** are permitted. Companies such as commodity brokers (market makers) can elect to carry their investments at market value where there is a ready or active market for the investments.

The **key difference** is that the investments are considered to be the equivalent of cash with any profit recognised in the profit and loss account.

3. Other valuation issues

Recognition of gains or losses on disposal

2754 FRS 3 (21) The profit or loss on disposal of a **revalued current investment** should be accounted for in the profit and loss account for the period in which the disposal occurs and should represent the difference between the net sale proceeds and the net carrying value, whether that be historical cost or revalued cost.

Where an investment that is sold **has previously been revalued**, that element of the revaluation reserve relating to those investments should be released to the profit and loss account as a movement on reserves.

Reclassification of investments

2756 Under Abstract UITF 5 "Transfers from current assets to fixed assets", assets should be accounted for under the relevant rules until the date of the transfer, and transferred at the lower of cost or net realisable value, unless the alternative accounting rules have been applied. This rule is designed to prevent companies avoiding a write-down of current assets to net realisable value, simply by reclassifying them as fixed assets.

Composite valuation

If a company has a series of current asset investments resulting from a number of purchases at different prices, it is not necessary for each investment to be recorded at its actual price. One of the methods of valuing stock such as **FIFO or Weighted Average** can be used for the purposes of valuing current asset investments, with the caveat that the replacement cost or most recent purchase price should be disclosed, if it is materially different from the figure in the balance sheet. 2758

Investments held exclusively for resale

Where an entity is acquired exclusively with the intention of subsequently being disposed of, such as where it forms part of a larger acquisition, then the interest in that investment should be accounted for at fair value (estimated sale proceeds) under the heading of "Investments". 2760

Such investments are not excluded (unlike subsidiaries, joint ventures and associates) from the scope of FRS 13 "Derivatives and other financial instruments: disclosures". As such these investments are categorised as **financial assets available-for-sale (AFS)** (see ¶1803-1), which must be revalued at each reporting date at fair value. Any movements in fair value must be accounted for in the profit and loss account or in reserves.

C. Disclosures

The key disclosure requirements for current investments, including the specific disclosures required of **listed investments**, are set out below. 2764

Entities adopting fair value accounting will be required to adopt FRS 25 "Financial instruments: disclosure and presentation", as FRS 13 will no longer apply to these entities. The disclosure requirements of FRS 25 have now been superseded by FRS 29 (see ¶3400).

MEMO POINTS **Equity instruments**, **and other investments** such as bonds, **held by one reporting entity in another**, whether classified as fixed or current assets, are also regarded as financial instruments/financial assets under FRS 13 "Derivatives and other financial instruments: disclosures", thereby triggering additional disclosure requirements. It should be noted that **FRS 13 only applies to companies which** have one or more of their capital instruments listed or publicly traded on a recognised stock exchange or market.

General disclosures

The examples listed below cover the disclosure requirements for balance sheet extracts, accounting policies and notes to the accounts. "**Investments**" is a primary heading that should appear on the face of the balance sheet under current assets. 2766

EXAMPLE **Brimar Ltd**
Annual report and accounts – 31 December 2010
Current assets (extract)

	2010 £'000	**2009 £'000**
Stocks	15.9	9.2
Debtors	353.4	274.2
Investments	**690.6**	**254.3**
Cash at bank and in hand	125.4	85.9
Totals	**1,185.3**	**623.6**

Details of **accounting policies** relating to current asset investments should also be disclosed, as illustrated in the following example.

EXAMPLE **Ashridge Ltd – Annual report and account 31 December 2010**

Accounting policies (extract)
Investments held as current assets are stated at market value at the balance sheet date and the difference between cost and market value is taken to the profit and loss account. This treatment is a departure from UK accounting rules which stipulate that unrealised profits be credited to the revaluation reserve. In the opinion of the directors, this treatment is necessary to adopt a true and fair view.

True and fair override

Marketable securities held as current trading assets are stated at market value. The resulting profits and losses have been accounted for in the profit and loss account. This treatment is not in accordance with Schedule 4 of the Companies Act, which requires that (1) these assets be stated at the lower of cost and net realisable value, and that (2) any revaluation differences be taken to a reserve account.

The directors consider that these requirements would fail to give a true and fair view of the company's profit during the year because the marketability of the securities in question allows the economic measure of profit to be made by reference to the market values.
The effect of this departure is an increase in profits before taxation of £90,000 (20X9 – £50,000) and an increase in the value of current assert investments of £90,000 (20X9 – £50,000).

Notes to the accounts

2768 The first example illustrates listed investments included in the balance sheet at cost and market value, whilst the second example illustrates a more detailed accompanying note.

EXAMPLE **Note to the accounts**
Current asset investments – disclosure of market value

	2010 £'000	2009 £'000
Listed investments	85	5
Short-term loans to subsidiary undertakings	10	7
Other short-term deposits and investments	245	58
Total current asset investments	**340**	**70**
Market value of listed investments	**90**	7

EXAMPLE **Notes to the accounts** (extract)
Current asset investments

Liquid resources comprise treasury investments that are readily convertible into known amounts of cash close to their carrying value or are traded in an active market. Liquid resources included as current asset investments are stated at the lower of cost and market value.

Investments (extract)

	Note	2010 £'000	2009 £'000
Listed:			
– UK		353.3	145.6
– Overseas		78.2	55.6
Other		102.5	85.3
	10	**534.0**	**286.5**

Note 10.
Analysis of investments

	2010 £'000	2009 £'000
Commercial paper	158.4	87.6
Floating and variable rate notes:		
– issued by banks	75.4	55.3
– issued by building societies	24.3	15.8
– mortgage backed	98.4	36.1
– other asset backed	145.6	48.0
– issued by corporates	15.0	10.0
Term deposits	6.0	15.0
Other	10.9	18.7
	534.0	**286.5**

Specific disclosures for listed investments

Investments in listed companies should be disclosed separately for each subheading. In addition, the following information must be given: 2770
- the **aggregate market value** if this is different from the amount at which they are stated on the balance sheet; or
- in cases **where the market value** of listed investments is used in the preparation of the financial statements and this value exceeds the stock exchange value, both must be disclosed.

EXAMPLE

South Downs Ltd
Annual Report and accounts 2010

Details of listed investments

	Name of company	Balance sheet value	Market value	Stock Exchange Value
		£'000	**£'000**	**£'000**
Listed on the London Stock Exchange	X Ltd	270	230	230
	Y Ltd	200	275	250
	Z Ltd	110	85	80
		580	590	560
Listed on the New York Stock Exchange	P, Inc.	130	220	210
	Q, Inc.	100	125	120
		230	345	330
		810	935	890

The shareholdings should also be disclosed in summary format.

Listed investments	**£'000**
Balance sheet value	810
Market value	930

Certain listed investments included in the market value figure above are stated at a value greater than the stock exchange value. The details are as follows:

Market value (£'000)	660
Stock exchange value (£'000)	540

Exemptions

Where the disclosure in respect of current asset investments would be either excessively long or prejudicial to the interest of the company, then a company may take advantage of exemptions from the normal disclosure requirements. 2774

Disclosures of excessive length If a company **has significant holdings** in a number of undertakings that would result in disclosure requirements of excessive length, the company need not comply with the detailed disclosure requirements. Instead the company can supply in the notes to the accounts, brief information relating to the undertakings whose results or financial position principally affect the results shown in the company's financial statements. 2776

If the exemption is invoked, a statement should be given in the notes to the accounts, explaining that the information provided relates only to those investments that are material in terms of the financial results. In addition, the information that would otherwise have been disclosed must be annexed to the company's next annual return.

2778 **Prejudicial information** Where disclosures concern investments in undertakings established outside the UK and the directors believe that such disclosures will be seriously prejudicial to the business or any of its subsidiaries, they may apply to the Secretary of State to waive the disclosure requirements. Where the agreement of the Secretary of State has been obtained, this must be stated in the notes to the accounts.

PART 5

Balance sheet – Liabilities

CHAPTER 1

Financial instruments

OUTLINE ¶¶

The term "Financial Instruments" comprises all **financial assets** and **financial liabilities** – including cash, amounts payable and receivable in cash, debt instruments, investments in equity, and derivatives such as swaps, options and forward contracts. Many large companies routinely make use of **derivatives** to control their exposure to risk. **3000**

Until January 2005, there were no dedicated reporting standards relating to financial instruments. Even the term itself was new; previously the term used was "capital instruments" to refer to a means of raising finance.

It was only after FRS 25, "Financial instruments: disclosure and presentation" and FRS 26, "Financial instruments: measurement", were issued by the ASB as part of its ongoing policy to converge UK and international accounting standards, that the more inclusive concept of financial instruments – financial assets and financial liabilities – came to be recognised.

FRS 26 applies to accounting periods commencing on or after 1 January 2005 for all listed entities following UK standards, and to accounting periods commencing on or after 1 January 2006 for unlisted entities whose financial statements are prepared in accordance with the fair value accounting rules set out in the Companies Act. The presentation requirements of FRS 25 apply to all entities for accounting periods beginning on or after 1 January 2005. For accounting periods beginning on or after 1 January 2006, all entities that fell within the scope of FRS 26 were subject to the disclosure requirements of FRS 25. However, for accounting periods beginning on or after 1 January 2007, FRS 29, "Financial instruments: disclosures" replaces the requirements in FRS 25. FRS 25 **disclosures** are therefore not dealt with in this chapter as they have fallen away.

FRS 25 and FRS 26 have the effect of withdrawing certain provisions of FRS 4, "Capital Instruments", except for those on the measurement of debt and gains and losses on the repurchase of debt. This material is withdrawn for entities applying the measurement requirements in FRS 26, but remains applicable for other entities. FRS 13, "Derivatives and other financial instruments: disclosures" applies only to listed entities and to banks and similar institutions. Most of these entities will be required to adopt the measurement rules of FRS 26 and accordingly fall within the scope of FRS 29's disclosure requirements. For such entities, FRS 13 is withdrawn. FRS 13 remains in force for any banking or similar institution that does not fall within the scope of FRS 26 and does not voluntarily adopt that standard. It is, however, not discussed in detail in this chapter as it is relevant to only a small number of entities.

Because the rules applicable to financial instruments differ according to whether the reporting entity is **listed** or **unlisted**, and – if listed – according to the reporting period, this chapter is arranged according to those criteria.

As a result of all these different possibilities, as well as the complexity of the various transition rules affecting them, reporting entities must, as a first step, determine which regime applies to their specific circumstances.

These application dates – and the regime that applies – are summarised in the table below.

	Reporting entity	
I	Listed companies Unlisted companies applying fair value rules	FRS 26 and FRS 29, as well as the presentation requirements of FRS 25
II	Other unlisted companies	FRS 4, FRS 13, as well as the presentation requirements of FRS 25

Creditors fall into the general definition of financial liabilities but, as they are treated in the same way by all companies, are discussed in a separate chapter – beginning at ¶3200.

SECTION 1

Unlisted companies not applying Fair Value rules

3001 Unlisted companies not applying fair value rules are required to comply with the provisions of FRS 4, FRS 13 and the presentation requirements of FRS 25.

FRS 4, "Capital Instruments", regulated the manner in which capital instruments were to be classified and presented in financial statements. FRS 13, "Derivatives and other financial instruments: disclosures", applied principally to listed companies and banks, and it prescribed specific narrative and numerical disclosures in relation to those entities falling within its scope. The presentation requirements of FRS 25 deal with the **classification** of capital instruments issued between debt and equity and the implications of that classification for dividends and interest expense. These requirements are discussed in detail in Section 2, ¶3060.

MEMO POINTS FRS 25 has the effect of withdrawing certain requirements of FRS 4 – except for those on the measurement of debt and gains and losses on the repurchase of debt, as included below.

A. Debt instruments

1. Types

Capital instruments that are classified as debt – and therefore disclosed as liabilities – can take different forms, ranging from debentures and loans with basic, uncomplicated repayment terms, to more complex arrangements such as convertible debt, subordinated debt, perpetual debt or limited recourse debt. 3005

Debentures and loans

A debenture is generally taken to refer to a loan carrying a fixed rate of interest and repayable at a fixed date. Under the Act, the term "debenture" includes debenture stock, bonds or any other securities of a company, whether or not constituting a charge on the assets of the company. 3006 s 738 CA 2006

For companies wishing to raise finance, issuing debentures is advantageous. Compared to overdrafts, interest rates are usually lower, and the repayment term much longer.

Convertible debt

Convertible debt confers on the lender the option to convert the loan into shares in the issuing company usually at the end of a specific period. Sometimes, the conversion right is exercisable not at one specific point in time but during a **conversion window** that could last several months or even several years. In practice, this form of debt carries a lower rate of interest than straight debt, and generally results in cheaper financing. In addition, convertible debt can provide a cash-flow advantage to the issuer, which has the opportunity to increase equity rather than repay cash when the instrument matures. 3008

For the holder, convertible debt provides not only a fixed interest rate as well as a fixed repayment at maturity, but also – by electing to convert rather than redeem – the possibility of benefiting from any future appreciation in the value of the company's share price.

MEMO POINTS If a company has issued any convertible debt that carries a redemption option, the company has a contingent liability to transfer economic benefits. The possibility of conversion should not be anticipated. Note 7 to the balance sheet formats requires convertible debt, if material, to be shown separately on the face of the balance sheet within liabilities. (Where the amount is not material, it may be shown in the notes.)

Bonds with detachable warrants

A bond issued with a warrant attached allows the holder to use the warrant at any time to subscribe for equity shares while still retaining the bond. These compound capital instruments differ from ordinary convertible debt in that, with ordinary convertible debt, the bond has to be surrendered at the time that the option is exercised. 3010

The two constituents of this type of instrument can be independently and separately transferred, cancelled or redeemed. Therefore, the proceeds on the issue of the instrument should be allocated between the debt portion (i.e., included in liabilities) and the warrant portion (i.e., included with shareholders' funds).

Subordinated debt

Subordinated debts are those that are ranked behind other loans and debts for purposes of repayment if the borrowing company is liquidated. Note, however, that holders of such debt rank ahead of shareholders on liquidation. Although holders always retain the **right to repayment**, these payments may be effectively postponed for the long term. 3012

From the company's point of view, its obligation to transfer economic benefits remains in force and, consequently, subordinated debts are classified as part of liabilities.

Perpetual debt

3014 Perpetual debt is debt issued with no redemption date and on which interest payments are made in perpetuity. Clearly this debt contains **an ongoing obligation to transfer economic benefits** and FRS 4 therefore requires it to be shown as a liability.

The finance charge for each period will be the actual interest payable and the debt will be carried in the balance sheet at the amount of the net proceeds. Any difference between gross and net proceeds (i.e., discounts on issue or costs of issue) are not amortised, but reflected in the carrying value from period to period. This treatment applies whether the interest is fixed or variable.

Limited recourse debt

3016 Limited recourse debt arises where a company obtains a loan subject to the condition that, if it should default on the loan, its liability will be limited to the particular asset financed by the loan or to the particular security specified in the loan agreement.

Because this limited recourse does not diminish the company's legal duty to transfer economic benefit to the lender (by repaying the loan), it should be accounted for as a liability.

Limited recourse debt is an unusual type of debt and not commonly encountered.

---

2. Maturity

3020 Sch 4 para 85 CA 1985 Disclosures given in the financial statements, and the recognition of finance charges associated with the debt, are influenced by the date of maturity of that instrument. It is therefore important to correctly establish the maturity profile.

General rule

3021 The maturity date of a **loan** is the earliest date on which lenders are entitled to call for repayment under the rights and options available to them.

Early redemption

3022 FRS 4 (74) Ordinarily, the term of the debt should be taken as the earliest date that the instrument could be redeemed, unless there is no realistic commercial possibility that the early redemption would be exercised. For instance, if a lender can require early redemption, but, on exercising that right, would receive substantially less than the full redemption value, it is most likely that such a lender would not normally choose to redeem unless the issuer's ability to repay the debt was in question. In such a case, the term of the debt should be taken to extend to its final maturity date because, though this date comes after the theoretical first redemption date, it represents the lender's earliest opportunity to require repayment without suffering a penalty.

Commercial paper arrangements

3026 Under commercial paper arrangements, funds are raised from lenders who are not parties to an agreement providing finance beyond the maturity of existing indebtedness. As these lenders are not the same as the original lenders, the date of maturity of these arrangements should be taken to be the maturity date of the **existing debt**.

---

3. Carrying amount

3030 FRS 4 (27) Immediately after issue, debt should be recorded at the amount of net proceeds of the issue, i.e., the fair value after deducting **issue costs**.

FRS 4 (29) At the end of the year and during later accounting periods, the amount of the debt is increased by the finance costs for the period and reduced by any payments made in respect of the debt (e.g., interest and any capital payments) in that period.

Finance costs are discussed from ¶3035, together with examples showing how the carrying amount is calculated and shown from year to year.

a. Issue costs

Issue costs are often incurred specifically and directly in connection with the issue of a capital instrument. 3031 FRS 4 (11)

The following are **examples of issue costs**:
- underwriting fees,
- arrangement and registration fees, and
- certain legal, merchant bank and accounting fees incurred in producing a prospectus in respect of a public offering of shares or in relation to documentation drawn up to cover a debt instrument.

They are accounted for as a **reduction in the proceeds** of a capital instrument and released into the profit and loss accounts over the life of the debt as part of the total finance charges. The carrying value of the debt is increased each year by the amount charged to the profit and loss account.

Costs that do not qualify as issue costs should be written off immediately to the profit and loss account. The effect of this treatment is to account for such costs in the year they are incurred. 3032

Examples are: FRS 4 (96)
- costs of researching and negotiating sources of finance or of ascertaining the suitability or feasibility of particular instruments,
- allocations of internal costs that would have been incurred irrespective of whether the instrument had been issued, e.g., management time, and
- costs incurred in connection with a financial restructuring or renegotiation.

Where **shares and debt are issued together**, the total issue costs should be apportioned on an appropriate basis (e.g., in proportion to gross proceeds) to the two categories.

Where an entity **issues debt that has an indeterminate life**, the issue costs should not be taken to the profit and loss account until the instruments are redeemed or cancelled. FRS 4 (95)

b. Finance costs

Definition

Finance costs are **defined** as the difference between the net proceeds of an instrument and the total amount of the payments (or other transfers of economic benefits) that the issuer may be required to make in respect of the instrument. 3035 FRS 4 (8)

Finance costs therefore incorporate both interest payments and any costs associated with the issue of the instrument that were not charged immediately to the profit and loss account.

Allocation

As a general rule, finance costs must be allocated to profit and loss – and included together with interest payable – over the **term of the debt** at a **constant rate of return** on the carrying amount. 3036 FRS 4 (28)

Term of the debt

In order to properly apportion the finance charges, an accurate determination of the term of a capital instrument must be made. 3037

The term is defined as the period from the date of issue to the date at which it will expire, be redeemed or cancelled. Thus, the term of a capital instrument is not necessarily the same as its life, and rules of the FRS for establishing the term are summarised in the following table. 3038 FRS 4 (16)

	Term of capital instrument is from date of issue to:
If neither party has the option to redeem or cancel	date of expiry
If either party has a **genuine option to redeem or cancel** – and it is not certain whether the option will be exercised	the earliest date on which the instrument may be redeemed or cancelled (but see ¶3040 and ¶3041 for exemptions)
If either party has the **right to extend the period** of the instrument, and	
• there is a genuine commercial possibility that the period will not be extended	the earliest date on which the instrument will expire
• it is certain that the period will be extended	the end of the period of the extension

As the table shows, the term and therefore the carrying value of capital instruments are affected by options that attach to them. Options held by holders and issuers do not always have the same result.

3040 FRS 4 (73), (74) **Holder's option** In general, if the holder has the option to redeem early, the term of the debt should be taken to be the earliest exercise date of the option. An exception to this rule is where there is no commercial possibility that the holder will exercise the option (such as if, by doing so, the holder will receive an amount that is disproportionately lower than the redemption value). In such a case, as it is so unlikely that the holder will exercise the option, in determining the term of the debt, the early redemption date is ignored.

3041 UITF 11 (6) **Issuer's option** Where a capital instrument is issued subject to the issuer's option to redeem early on payment of a premium, UITF Abstract 11, "Capital instruments: issuer call options", does not consider it appropriate to account for the premium as an element of finance charges. The reason for this treatment is based on the definition of what constitutes finance charges (i.e., those that the issuer may be required to make). Therefore, should the issuer decide to exercise the option, the premium payable will be treated as an elective payment to be reflected as a gain or loss arising on early redemption.

EXAMPLE C Ltd issues 1,000 £100 bonds at par redeemable in 10 years at a premium of 10%. Issue costs amount to £2,000.
Interest is payable at 5% per annum. C Ltd has the option to redeem the bonds at the end of 5 years at a premium of £15.
Under UITF Abstract 11 (6), the term of the bonds will be taken as 5 years.
If C Ltd redeems the bonds at the end of 5 years, the premium of £15,000 will represent a loss on early settlement.
During the first 5 years, the finance costs to be allocated will be £32,000, i.e.

Interest (5 × £5,000)	£ 25,000
Half of the premium	5,000
Issue costs (in total)	2,000
	£ 32,000

These finance costs must be allocated at a constant rate on the outstanding balance over the period. To achieve this, a rate of 6.36% should be used.

Year	Balance at beginning of year	Finance cost allocated at 6.36%	Cash paid	Balance at end of year
1	98,000	6,233	5,000	99,233
2	99,233	6,311	5,000	100,544
3	100,544	6,395	5,000	101,939
4	101,939	6,483	5,000	103,422
5	103,422	6,578	5,000	105,000
		£ 32,000		

Assuming that at the end of 5 years C Ltd does not exercise its option, for the remainder of the term the interest rate will reduce to 5.61% (because the issue costs will have been fully amortised by year 5).

Year	Balance at beginning of year	Finance cost allocated at 5.61%	Cash paid	Balance at end of year
6	105,000	5,894	5,000	105,894
7	105,894	5,944	5,000	106,837
8	106,837	5,997	5,000	107,834
9	107,834	6,053	5,000	108,887
10	108,887	6,113	*115,000	0
		£30,000		

* This final payment consists of the capital repayment of £100,000 plus premium of £10,000 plus interest for the year of £5,000.

The UITF applies only to genuine options and not to situations where it is clear that the issuer would be **commercially obliged to exercise the call option**. The UITF gives an example of a case in which the instrument's terms and conditions give the issuer the option of early redemption, but it is clear even at the time of issue that in all conceivable circumstances it would be to the issuer's advantage to exercise the option rather than allow the debt to remain in issue. Such an option is therefore not a genuine option and in this case the premium would be considered a finance charge and accounted for accordingly. **3042** UITF 11 (8)

Where the effective **rate of interest increases after the date on which the option may be exercised**, the premium may be seen as compensation to the investor for the increased return that it will forgo as a result of the issuer's decision to exercise the option. The UITF rule (not to regard the premium as finance charges) does not apply in these circumstances and, as an exception to the rule, the premium payable on exercising the option should be regarded as being part of the finance costs. **3043** UITF 11 (9)

EXAMPLE Using the same facts relating to C Ltd in the example above, but assuming that the interest rate after exercising the option is such that the premium is regarded as a finance charge, the term should be taken to be 5 years. During this period, the finance charges to be allocated are £42,000 – i.e.,

	£
Interest (5 × £5,000)	25,000
Early redemption premium	15,000
Issue costs	2,000
	£ 42,000

To allocate these finance costs at a constant rate on the outstanding balance, a rate of 8.06% should be used.

Year	Balance at beginning of year	Finance cost allocated at 8.06% (rounded)	Cash paid	Balance at end of year
1	98,000	7,900	5,000	100,900
2	100,900	8,130	5,000	104,030
3	104,030	8,380	5,000	107,410
4	107,410	8,650	5,000	111,060
5	111,060	8,940	5,000	115,000
		£42,000		

MEMO POINTS UITF Abstract 11 "Capital instruments: issuer call options" is superseded by FRS 26 for those entities applying FRS 26.

Constant rate of return

3044 The constant rate of return is the discount rate that equates the present value of the net proceeds of the instrument with the present value of the total amount that will be repaid on the instrument over its term. In practice, it may be calculated by using the internal rate of return function on most computer spreadsheet programmes or financial calculators.

While this calculation is relatively straightforward when a fixed interest rate is charged over the term of the debt, it becomes more complex when, for instance, there is **an interest-free period** at the start of the term of the debt or where the rate of interest is stepped and changes at predetermined dates over the term of the debt. Further complexities arise when the rate of interest for the term of the debt is **variable over the period** of the debt as at any time there will be considerable uncertainty over the total amount of payments to be made. However, in this regard it is important to remember that even though in cash terms there may be an interest-free period or low-start interest rate attached to the instrument, in terms of the profit and loss account, finance charges should start affecting it from date of inception and that the charge is based on the whole cost of the borrowing over the life of the debt.

3045 FRS 4 (75) It would therefore generally not be acceptable to use the straight-line method to allocate finance costs unless it produced a similar result to that which would be obtained using a constant rate. Only where the two results are essentially the same may the nominal interest rate on the loan be charged to the profit and loss account.

MEMO POINTS A nominal interest rate will not differ materially from the amount computed at a constant rate where:
- issue costs on a debt instrument are immaterial, and
- there is no redemption premium to be accrued over its term.

This is the usual situation in the case of simple bank loans or overdrafts, and the actual charge is taken to the profit and loss account.

EXAMPLE A Ltd issues convertible debt on 1 January 20X1 for 5 years, redeemable at £350,000. Interest is payable at £12,000 per annum. Assume that there are no options for early redemption. Total finance charges are:

£12,000 × 5 = £60,000 plus the premium on redemption of £100,000, therefore, a total of £160,000.

Finance charges are required to be allocated at a constant rate on the carrying amount. This can be achieved using a rate of 11.2%. Thus, the carrying value over the term of the debt is as follows:

Year	Balance at beginning of year	Finance cost allocated at 11.2% (rounded)	Cash paid	Balance at end of year
31.12.01	250,000	28,000	12,000	266,000
31.12.02	266,000	29,700	12,000	283,700
31.12.03	283,700	31,775	12,000	303,475
31.12.04	303,475	34,000	12,000	325,475
31.12.05	325,475	36,525	*362,000	0
		160,000		

* £350,000 on redemption, plus £12,000 interest for the year.

Premium or interest subject to contingencies

3046 Sometimes, the payments required under a debt instrument are **linked to external factors**, such as an interest rate index or the **occurrence of uncertain future events**. This produces uncertainty over the total future payments that will have to be made over the term of the debt. In these circumstances, the calculation of expected total future payments will be based initially on the information known when the calculation is first performed – e.g., the total estimated interest payable on a variable rate loan will usually be based on the current interest rate. When one of these factors changes, the estimated payments for the whole term of the debt will have to be recalculated. Moreover, the annual finance charge to be made to the profit and loss account should also be recalculated.

Charges made in prior periods are not recalculated nor is a prior period adjustment made. The changes in total cost arising from the change in a variable factor are in effect therefore absorbed over the period of the debt remaining at the date the change takes place.

EXAMPLE B Ltd receives a loan of £1,250 on 1 January 20X0 on which interest of 4% is payable (£50). The principal amount repayable on 01.01.20X5, is based on an index.
The balance at the end of each year is calculated by multiplying the original principal amount by the index at the end of the year; the change in the amount is treated as additional finance costs.

Year ending	Balance at beginning of year (A)	Index at end of year (B)	Balance at end of year (C)	Cash paid (interest) (D)	Finance cost for the year [(C) + (D) - (A)]
31.12.X0	1250	106	1325	50	125
31.12.X1	1325	110	1375	50	100
31.12.X2	1375	112	1400	50	75
31.12.X3	1400	120	1500	50	150
31.12.X4	1500	130	1625	50	175

Note: This example is based on one given in the application notes to FRS 4.

SECTION 2

Listed companies and unlisted companies applying Fair Value rules

I. Financial instruments – defined

A financial instrument is defined as any **contract** that gives rise to **a financial asset** of one entity and a **financial liability** or equity instrument of another entity. It is therefore a contract expected to lead ultimately to the receipt or payment of cash, or to the acquisition or issue of shares. **3050** FRS 25 (11)

FRS 26 specifies four categories of financial instrument:

1. Financial assets or liabilities at fair value through profit or loss – assets and liabilities which are either classified as held for trading or are designated by the entity as at fair value through profit or loss upon initial recognition.

2. Held-to-maturity investments – non-derivative financial assets with fixed or determinable payments and fixed maturity that an entity has the positive intention and ability to hold to maturity other than:
– those that the entity designates as at fair value through profit or loss upon initial recognition;
– those that the entity designates as available for sale; and
– those that meet the definition of loans and receivables.

3. Loans and receivables – non-derivative financial assets with fixed or determinable payments that are not quoted in an active market, other than:
– those that the entity intends to sell immediately or in the near term and those that are designated as at fair value through profit and loss upon initial recognition;
– those that are designated as available for sale upon initial recognition; or

– those for which the holder may not recover substantially all of its initial investment, other than because of credit deterioration, which must be classified as available for sale.
4. Available-for-sale financial assets – non-derivative assets that are designated as available for sale and are not classified as financial assets at fair value through profit or loss, held-to-maturity investments or loans and receivables.

An entity must not classify any financial assets as held to maturity if the entity – during the current financial year or during the two preceding financial years – sold or reclassified more than an insignificant amount (in relation to the total amount of held-to-maturity investments) of held-to-maturity investments, other than sales or reclassifications that:
– are so close to maturity or the asset's call date that changes in the market rate of interest would not have a significant effect on the asset's fair value;
– occur after the entity has collected substantially all of the asset's original principal through scheduled payments or prepayments; or
– are attributable to an isolated event that is beyond the entity's control, is non-recurring and could not have been reasonably anticipated by the entity.

3051 **Financial assets** are any assets in the following form:
– cash;
– an equity instrument of another entity;
– a contractual right:
– to receive cash or another financial asset from another entity; or
– to exchange financial assets or financial liabilities with another entity under conditions that are potentially favourable to the entity; or
– a contract that will or may be settled in the entity's own equity instruments and is:
  – a non-derivative for which the entity is or may be obliged to receive a variable number of the entity's own equity instruments; or
  – a derivative that will or may be settled other than by the exchange of a fixed amount of cash or another financial asset for a fixed number of the entity's own equity instruments. For this purpose, the entity's own equity instruments do not include puttable financial instruments classified as equity instruments, instruments that impose on the entity an obligation to deliver to another party a pro-rata share of the net assets of the entity only on liquidation and are classified as equity instruments, or instruments that are contracts for the future receipt or delivery of the entity's own equity instruments.

3052 **Financial liabilities** are any liabilities in the following form:
– a contractual obligation:
  – to deliver cash or another financial asset to another entity; or
  – to exchange financial assets or financial liabilities with another entity under conditions that are potentially unfavourable to the entity; or
– a contract that will or may be settled in the entity's own equity instruments and is:
  – a non-derivative for which the entity is or may be obliged to deliver a variable number of the entity's own equity instruments; or
  – a derivative that will or may be settled other than by the exchange of a fixed amount of cash or another financial asset for a fixed number of the entity's own equity instruments. For this purpose, the entity's own equity instruments do not include puttable financial instruments that are classified as equity instruments, instruments that impose on the entity an obligation to deliver to another party a pro-rata share of the net assets of the entity only on liquidation and are classified as equity instruments, or instruments that are contracts for the future receipt or delivery of the entity's own equity instruments.

In certain circumstances, an instrument that meets the definition of a financial liability can nevertheless be classified as an equity instrument if it has all the features described above. See ¶3065.

3053 An **equity instrument** is any contract that evidences a residual interest in the assets of an entity after deducting all of its liabilities.

A puttable instrument is a financial instrument that gives the holder the right to put the instrument back to the issuer for cash (or another financial asset) or is automatically put back to the issuer on the occurrence of an uncertain future event or the death or retirement of the instrument holder.

Financial instruments also include **derivatives**. FRS 26 **defines** a derivative as a financial instrument or other contract with all three of the following characteristics: **3055** FRS 26 (9)
– its value changes in response to the change in a specified interest rate, financial instrument price, commodity price, foreign exchange rate, index of prices or rates, credit rating or credit index or other variable, provided in the case of a non-financial variable that the variable is not specific to a party to the contract;
– it requires no initial net investment or an initial net investment that is smaller than would be required for other types of contracts that would be expected to have a similar response to changes in market factors; and
– it is settled at a future date.

An **embedded derivative** is a component of a hybrid (combined) instrument that also includes a non-derivative host contract. The embedded derivative must be separated from the host contract only if: **3056** FRS 26 (10)-(12)
– the economic characteristics and risks of the embedded derivative are not closely related to the economic characteristics and risks of the host contract;
– a separate instrument with the same terms as the embedded derivative would meet the definition of a derivative; and
– the combined instrument is not measured at fair value (with changes in fair value being recognised in the profit and loss account).

If an entity is required to **separate an embedded derivative from its host contract**, but is unable to measure the embedded derivative separately either at acquisition or at a subsequent financial reporting date, it should treat the entire combined contract as a financial asset or financial liability that is held for trading.

MEMO POINTS In September 2009, the ASB published amendments to UITF Abstract 42 "Reassessment of Embedded Derivatives" and FRS 26 "Financial instruments: recognition and measurement", which clarify the treatment of embedded derivatives when an entity reclassifies a financial asset out of the fair value **through profit or loss category**.
Under these amendments, if an entity is required to separate an embedded derivative from its host contract, but is unable to measure the embedded derivative separately either at acquisition or at the end of a subsequent financial reporting period, it must designate the entire hybrid (combined) contract as at fair value through profit or loss. Similarly, if an entity is unable to measure separately the embedded derivative that would have to be separated on reclassification of a hybrid (combined) contract out of the fair value through profit or loss category, that reclassification is prohibited. In these circumstances, the hybrid (combined) contract remains classified as at fair value through profit or loss in its entirety.
These amendments are applicable to accounting periods ending on or after 31 December 2009. Earlier application is permitted.

II. General presentation rules

The presentation requirements of FRS 25 apply to all entities for accounting periods beginning on or after 1 January 2005, which corresponds with the amendments to the Companies Act 1985 resulting from the EU Accounts Modernisation Directive. One of the conceptual differences under FRS 25 is that while FRS 4 concentrated on the **legal** form of capital instruments, FRS 25 follows a **substance over form** approach. **3060**

Arising out of an amendment to FRS 25, issued in August 2008, certain financial instruments are to be classified as equity instruments despite their meeting the definition of a financial liability. Entities are required to apply the amendments for reporting periods beginning on or after 1 January 2010. Earlier application is permitted only for periods beginning on or after 1 January 2009. Where an entity applies these changes in respect of an earlier period, it must disclose that fact and apply the measurement requirements of FRS 26 and the disclosure requirements of FRS 29.

A. Classification

3062 FRS 25 (15) One of the key requirements of FRS 25 is that the issuer of a financial instrument must **classify** it – or its component parts – on initial recognition as:
- a financial liability,
- a financial asset, or
- an equity instrument

in accordance with the substance of the contractual arrangement and the respective definitions of each.

3063 The Standard considers how these definitions should be applied as well as:
- whether an instrument contains a **contractual obligation** to deliver cash or another financial asset;
- the way in which a contract is **settled** – e.g., by way of its own equity instruments; and
- the way in which contingent **settlement provisions** or settlement options are treated.

3064 A financial instrument can be regarded as **equity** (rather than a **financial liability**), only if **both** of the following conditions are satisfied:
1. The instrument includes no contractual obligation to:
- deliver cash or another financial asset to another entity; or
- exchange financial assets or financial liabilities with another entity under conditions that are potentially unfavourable to the issuer.
2. If the instrument will, or may, be settled in the issuer's own equity instruments, it is:
- a non-derivative that includes no contractual obligation for the issuer to deliver a variable number of its own equity instruments; or
- a derivative that will be settled only by the issuer exchanging a fixed amount of cash or another financial asset for a fixed number of its own equity instruments. For this purpose the issuer's own equity instruments do not include instruments that have all the features and meet the conditions described below or instruments that are contracts for the future receipt or delivery of the issuer's own equity instruments.

A contractual obligation, including one that arises from a derivative financial instrument, that could result in the future receipt or delivery of the issuer's own equity instruments, but does not meet both of the conditions above, is not an equity instrument.

3065 The ASB, following the lead of the IASB, introduced a change to the above general rule. The need for the amendment arose out of the global financial crisis, which saw an increase in the number of entities using **rights issues to raise capital**.

Under prior rules, rights issues that were denominated in a foreign currency were classified as derivative liabilities. The reason was simply that a financial instrument could not be presented as equity unless settlement of the contract resulted in the entity's delivering a fixed number of its own equity instrument in exchange for a fixed amount of cash or other asset. Settlement in a foreign currency did not satisfy the strict "fixed for fixed" criterion. The unintended result was that the financial instrument was classified as a liability, whereas the underlying substance of a rights issue would better suggest classification as equity.

The amendment now changes this rule so that if a fixed number of rights, options or warrants are issued pro rata to an entity's existing shareholders for a fixed amount of foreign currency, these should be classified as equity **regardless of the currency** in which the exercise price is denominated.

3067 FRS 25 (16a) - (16e) As another exception, FRS 25 requires that certain puttable financial instruments or instruments that impose on the entity an obligation to deliver to another party a pro-rata share of the net assets of the entity only on liquidation are classified as equity rather than financial liabilities. In order to be classified as equity, the instrument must meet all of the following conditions:

1. It entitles the holder to a pro-rata share of the entity's net assets in the event of the entity's liquidation. The entity's net assets are those assets that remain after deducting all other claims on its assets. A pro-rata share is determined by:
– dividing the entity's net assets on liquidation into units of equal amount; and
– multiplying that amount by the number of the units held by the financial instrument holder.
2. The instrument is in the class of instruments that is subordinate to all other classes of instruments. To be in such a class, the instrument:
– has no priority over other claims to the assets of the entity on liquidation, and
– does not need to be converted into another instrument before it is in the class of instruments that is subordinate to all other instruments.
3. All financial instruments in this class have identical features. For example, they must all be puttable, and the formula or other method used to calculate the repurchase or redemption price is the same for all instruments in that class or they must have an identical contractual obligation for the issuing entity to deliver a pro-rata share of its net assets on liquidation,
4. Apart from the contractual obligation for the issuer to repurchase or redeem the instrument for cash or another financial asset, the instrument does not include any contractual obligation to deliver cash or another financial asset to another entity, or to exchange financial assets or financial liabilities with another entity under conditions that are potentially unfavourable to the entity, and it is not a contract that will or may be settled in the entity's own equity instruments as set out in ¶3052.
5. The total expected cash flows attributable to the instrument over the life of the instrument are based substantially on the profit and loss, the change in the recognised net assets or the change in the fair value of the recognised and unrecognised net assets of the entity over the life of the instrument.

Note: **4** and **5** apply to puttable instruments only.

In addition to having all the above features, the issuer must have no other financial instrument or contract that has:
– total cash flows based substantially on the profit or loss, the change in the recognised net assets or the change in the fair value of the recognised and unrecognised net assets of the entity (excluding any effects of such instrument or contract), and
– the effect of substantially restricting or fixing the residual return to the instrument holders.

For the purposes of applying this condition, the entity must not consider non-financial contracts with a holder of an instrument described above that have contractual terms and conditions that are similar to the contractual terms and conditions of an equivalent contract that might occur between a non-instrument holder and the issuing entity. If the entity cannot determine that this condition is met, it must not classify the instrument as an equity instrument.

An entity must classify an instrument as an equity instrument as set out above from the date when the instrument has all the features and meets the conditions specified and must reclassify a financial instrument from the date when the instrument ceases to do so. Disclosure should be made of the amount reclassified into and out of financial liabilities or equity and of the timing and reason for the reclassification.

The **substance** of a financial instrument, rather than its legal form, **governs its classification** in the entity's statement of financial position. While substance and legal form are generally consistent with one another, some financial instruments take the legal form of equity but in substance are liabilities. Others may combine features associated with both, for instance: **3068** FRS 25 (18)
– a **preference share** that provides for mandatory redemption by the issuer for a **fixed or determinable amount** at a **fixed or determinable future date**, or gives the holder the right to require the issuer to redeem **it at or after a particular date** for a **fixed or determinable amount**, is a financial liability;

– a financial instrument that gives the holder the right to put it back to the issuer for cash or another financial asset (a "**puttable instrument**") is a financial liability, except for those instruments classified as equity instruments as explained in ¶3067.

3069 FRS 25 (21) A contract is not an equity instrument for the sole reason that it may result in the receipt or delivery of the entity's own equity instruments. An entity may have a contractual right or obligation to receive or deliver a **variable number** of its own shares (or other equity instruments) that varies in such a way that the amount equals the amount of the contractual right or obligation. Such a contract is a financial liability despite the fact that the entity can or must settle it by delivering its own equity instruments. It is not an equity instrument because the entity uses a variable number of its own equity instruments as a means to settle the contract.

FRS 25 (22) On the other hand, a contract that is to be settled by the entity's delivering (or receiving) a **fixed number** of its own equity instruments in exchange for a fixed amount of cash or another financial asset is regarded as an equity instrument. For example, an issued share option that gives the other party the right to purchase a fixed number of the entity's shares for a fixed price or for a fixed stated principal amount of a bond is an equity instrument. As stated in ¶3065, this principle now applies also to transactions in foreign currencies.

FRS 25 (22a) However, if the entity's own equity instruments to be received, or delivered, by the entity upon settlement of contract are financial instruments with all of the features and meeting the conditions described in ¶3064, the contract is a financial asset or a financial liability.

3070 FRS 25 (25) A financial instrument may require the entity to deliver cash or another financial asset (or otherwise to settle it in such a way that it would be a financial liability), in the event of the occurrence or non-occurrence of **uncertain future circumstances** that are beyond the control of both the issuer and the holder of the instrument. (Examples are a change in a stock market index, consumer price index, interest rate or taxation requirements, or the issuer's future revenues, net income or debt-to-equity ratio.)

Because the issuer of such an instrument does not have the unconditional right to avoid delivering cash or another financial asset (or to settle it in such a way that it would be a financial liability), the instrument is a financial liability unless:
– the part of the contingent settlement provision that could require settlement in cash or another financial asset is not genuine; or
– the issuer can be required to settle the obligation in cash or another financial asset only in the event of the issuer's liquidation; or
– the instrument has all of the features and meets the conditions in ¶3067.

3071 FRS 25 (26) When a derivative financial instrument **gives one party a choice** over how it is settled (e.g., either the issuer or the holder can choose settlement net in cash or by exchanging shares for cash), it is a financial asset or a financial liability.

B. Compound financial instruments

3072 FRS 25 (28) The issuer of a non-derivative financial instrument must evaluate its terms in order to determine whether it contains **both a liability and an equity component**. Where both components are present, they must be classified separately as financial liabilities, financial assets or equity instruments – as the case may be.

3073 FRS 25 (29) The entity must recognise separately the components of a financial instrument that:
– **creates a financial liability** of the entity, and
– **grants** an **option** to the holder of the instrument to convert it into an equity instrument of the entity.

For instance, a bond or similar instrument convertible by the holder into a fixed number of ordinary shares is a compound financial instrument. From the perspective of the entity that issues it, the instrument comprises two components: a financial liability (i.e., the contractual arrangement to deliver cash or another financial asset) and an equity instrument (i.e., a call option granting the holder the right, for a specified period of time, to convert it into a fixed number of ordinary shares in the entity). The economic effect of issuing an instrument of this type is in substance the same as simultaneously issuing a debt instrument with an early settlement provision and warrants to purchase ordinary shares, or issuing a debt instrument with detachable share purchase warrants. In these cases, the entity must present the liability and equity components separately on its balance sheet.

Where there is a **change in the likelihood** that a **conversion option will be exercised**, classification of the liability and equity components of a convertible instrument is not revised even if it appears that exercise of the option has become economically advantageous to some holders. Assumptions cannot be made about how holders will act because their particular circumstances can differ widely (e.g., the tax consequences that are applicable to them). In addition, the likelihood of conversion will change over time. 3074

C. Treasury shares

Where an entity reacquires its own equity instruments ("treasury shares"), these are required to be deducted from equity. No gain or loss is recognised in profit or loss on the purchase, sale, issue or cancellation of an entity's own equity instruments; consideration paid or received is recognised directly in equity. 3075 FRS 25 (33)

The amount of treasury shares held is disclosed separately either on the face of the balance sheet or in the notes.

MEMO POINTS Where an entity holds its own equity on behalf of others (e.g., a financial institution that holds its own equity on a client's behalf) there is an agency relationship in effect and, therefore, these holdings are not included on the entity's balance sheet.

D. Interest, dividends, losses and gains

Interest, dividends, losses and gains relating to a financial instrument or a component that is a financial liability must be recognised as **income or expense**. 3077 FRS 25 (35)

Distributions to holders of an equity instrument must be debited directly to equity, net of any related income tax benefit.

Transaction costs of an equity transaction, other than costs of issuing an equity instrument that are directly attributable to the acquisition of a business, must be deducted from equity, net of any related income tax benefit.

Whether a financial instrument has been classified as a financial liability or an equity instrument determines how interest, dividends, losses and gains relating to it are recognised. Therefore, dividend payments on shares wholly recognised as liabilities are recognised as expenses (i.e., in the same way as interest on a bond). Gains and losses associated with redemptions or refinancings of **financial liabilities** are recognised in **profit or loss**, while redemptions or refinancings of **equity instruments** are recognised as **changes in equity**. 3078 FRS 25 (36)

E. Offsetting

3080 FRS 25 requires an entity to present its financial assets and financial liabilities on a net basis (i.e., offset against one another) if doing so reflects the expected future cash flows from settling two or more separate financial instruments. Where an entity has the right to receive or pay a single net amount – and intends to do this – it has, in effect, only a single financial asset or financial liability.

3081 FRS 25 (42) A financial asset and a financial liability may be offset and the net amount presented in the balance sheet when, and only when, the entity concerned:
- currently has a legally enforceable right to set off the recognised amounts; and
- intends either to settle on a net basis, or to realise the asset and settle the liability simultaneously.

In other circumstances, financial assets and financial liabilities are presented separately from each other consistently with their characteristics as either resources or obligations of the entity.

III. Measurement of financial instruments

3085 FRS 26, "Financial instruments: measurement", implements the measurement and hedge accounting requirements of the international standard IAS 39. It requires:
- all **derivatives** and all **financial assets** and **financial liabilities** that are held for trading to be measured at fair value (with all changes in those fair values recognised immediately in the profit and loss account);
- all **loans and receivables held as assets** and all financial assets that are being **held to maturity** by the reporting entity to be initially recognised at fair value but subsequently measured at cost-based amounts;
- **all other financial assets** (so-called "available-for-sale" financial assets) to be measured at fair value with gains and losses recognised immediately in the STRGL; and
- **all other financial liabilities** to be initially recognised at fair value but subsequently measured at cost-based amounts.

However, there are two exceptions:
- the entity can, at its option, elect to measure any financial asset or financial liability that would otherwise be measured at a cost-based amount at fair value instead – as long as this choice is made on **initial recognition**. (If this "fair-value option" is chosen, all changes in fair value should be recognised immediately in the profit and loss account.); and
- the requirements may be modified by the use of **hedge accounting techniques**.

MEMO POINTS Entities applying FRS 26 remain subject to the provisions of the Companies Act, which restricts the use of fair value measurement for some liabilities. These entities might not, as a result, be able to take advantage of the fair value exception.

3086 A debtor and a creditor can renegotiate the terms of a financial liability in such a way as to result in the debtor's being able to settle the liability to the creditor by issuing equity instruments (so-called "**debt for equity swaps**"). The question that arises is how the debtor accounts for the transaction.

In July 2010 the ASB issued UITF Abstract 47 to address it. The consensus reached is that where an entity issues its own equity instruments to extinguish all or part of a financial liability, it must measure these equity instruments at fair value, unless the fair value cannot be reliably measured. In this case, the equity instruments must be measured to reflect the fair value of the financial liability extinguished.

If only part of the financial liability is extinguished, the entity must carefully consider whether some of the consideration paid relates to a modification of the terms of the liability that remains outstanding. If that is the case, the entity must then allocate the consideration paid between that part of the liability that was extinguished, and that part still outstanding.

A final question in relation to these transactions is the treatment of the **difference** between the **carrying amount** of the liability extinguished and the **consideration paid**. In accordance with FRS 26, this difference must be taken to profit and loss, where it should be disclosed as a separate line item (or separately in the notes).

FRS 26 deals with the measurement of financial assets and financial liabilities. Equity instruments are instruments that evidence a residual interest in the assets of an entity after deducting all of its liabilities. Therefore, when the initial carrying amount of a compound financial instrument is allocated to its equity and liability components, the equity component is assigned the residual amount after deducting from the fair value of the instrument as a whole the amount separately determined for the liability component. The value of any derivative features (such as a call option) embedded in the compound financial instrument other than the equity component (such as an equity conversion option) is included in the liability component. The sum of the carrying amounts assigned to the liability and equity components on initial recognition is always equal to the fair value that would be ascribed to the instrument as a whole. No gain or loss arises from initially recognising the components of the instrument separately. 3089

Under this approach, the issuer of a bond convertible into ordinary shares first determines the carrying amount of the liability component by measuring the fair value of a similar liability (including any embedded non-equity derivative features) that does not have an associated equity component. The carrying amount of the equity instrument represented by the option to convert the instrument into ordinary shares is then determined by deducting the fair value of the financial liability from the fair value of the compound financial instrument as a whole. 3090

3091

EXAMPLE A Ltd issues 2,000 convertible bonds at the beginning of 20X1. The bonds have a three-year term, and are issued at par with a face value of £1,000 per bond, giving total proceeds of £2,000,000. Interest is payable annually in arrears at a nominal annual interest rate of 6%. Each bond is convertible at any time up to maturity into 250 ordinary shares. When the bonds are issued, the prevailing market interest rate for similar debt without conversion options is 9%.

The liability component is measured first, and the difference between the proceeds of the bond issue and the fair value of the liability is assigned to equity. The present value of the liability component is calculated using a discount rate of 9% – i.e., the market interest rate for similar bonds having no conversion rights.

Present value of the principal - £2,000,000 payable at the end of 20X3	1,544,367
Present value of the interest - £120,000 payable annually in arrears in each of the three years	303,775
Total liability component	1,848,122
Equity component (by deduction)	151,878
Equity component (by deduction)	£ 2,000,000

The above illustration is based on Example 9 in FRS 25

Hedge accounting is a special type of accounting that generally involves deferring the recognition of gains and losses that would otherwise be taken immediately to the profit and loss account. FRS 26 permits the use of hedge accounting in accounting for financial instruments, but only if: 3092

– the hedging relationship involved was designated at the outset as a hedge and the hedge meets certain requirements; and

– the hedge accounting techniques that are adopted are those prescribed by FRS 26.

A. Initial measurement

3095 FRS 26 (43) When a financial asset or financial liability is first recognised, the entity must measure it at its **fair value** plus, in the case of a financial asset or financial liability not at fair value, **transaction costs** that are directly attributable. For these purposes, the fair value of a financial instrument on initial recognition is normally the transaction price (i.e., the fair value of the consideration given or received). However, if part of the consideration given or received is for something other than the financial instrument, the fair value of the financial instrument must be estimated, using a valuation technique.

B. Subsequent measurement

3097 After initial recognition, an entity must, in general, measure financial assets at fair value without any deduction in respect of transaction costs it may incur on sale or other disposal. Some assets, however, are excluded from this rule; the following table summarises the position.

Type of asset:	Measure at:
Financial assets including derivatives (general rule)	Fair value
Loans and receivables	Amortised cost
Held-to-maturity investments	Amortised cost
Investments in unquoted equity instruments (where fair value cannot be reliably measured), and derivatives that are linked to these unquoted equity instruments	Cost

Financial assets that are designated as hedged items are subject to be measured in accordance with the hedge accounting requirements. (¶3092)

All financial assets except those measured at fair value through profit or loss are subject to review for impairment.

3098 After initial recognition, an entity must measure all financial liabilities at amortised cost using the effective interest method, except for:

Type of liability:	Measure at:
Financial liabilities at fair value through profit or loss, including derivatives that are liabilities	Fair value
Derivative liabilities linked to (and which must be settled by delivery of) unquoted equity instruments whose fair value cannot be reliably measured	Cost

Reclassifications

3100 FRS26 (50) – (54) An entity:

– must not reclassify a derivative into or out of the fair value through profit or loss category while it is held or issued;

– must not reclassify any financial instrument out of the fair value through profit or loss category if upon initial recognition it was designated by the entity as at fair value through profit or loss; and

– may, if a financial asset is no longer held for the purpose of selling or repurchasing it in the near term, reclassify that financial asset out of the fair value through profit or loss category if certain requirements are met.

An entity must not reclassify any financial asset into the fair value through profit or loss category after initial recognition.

If it is no longer appropriate to classify an investment as held to maturity, it should be reclassified as available-for-sale and remeasured at fair value.

Whenever sales or reclassification of more than an insignificant amount of held-to-maturity investments do not meet any of the conditions set out in ¶3055, any remaining held-to-maturity investments must be reclassified as available for sale.

If a reliable measure becomes available where it was not previously, and the asset or liability is required to be measured at fair value if a reliable measure is available, the asset or liability must be remeasured at fair value. If it becomes appropriate to carry a financial asset or liability at cost or amortised cost rather than at fair value, the fair value carrying amount on that date becomes the new cost or amortised cost, as applicable.

MEMO POINTS Amendments made to FRS 26 by "Reclassification of Financial Assets (Amendments to FRS 26 and FRS 29)", issued in October 2008 – regarding reclassification of non-derivative financial assets and transfers from the available-for-sale category to the loans and receivables category – are applicable from 1 July 2008. Any reclassification made on or after 1 November 2008 takes effect from the date of reclassification. Any reclassification made before 1 November 2008 can take effect from 1 July 2008 or a subsequent date.

Gains and losses

Any gain or loss arising from a change in the fair value of a financial asset or financial liability that is not part of a hedging relationship are to be recognised as follows: 3101

Gain or loss arising on:	Recognition:
Financial asset or financial liability classified at fair value through profit or loss	Recognised in profit or loss
Available-for-sale financial asset	Recognised through the STRGL
Foreign exchange losses and/or impairment losses	When asset is derecognised, amounts previously recognised through STRGL to be recognised in profit and loss account
Non-hedged financial assets and financial liabilities carried at amortised cost	When the financial asset or liability is derecognised or impaired, recognised in profit or loss

Impairment of financial assets

A financial asset or a group of financial assets is considered to be impaired only where there is objective evidence of impairment occurring after the initial recognition of the asset (a loss event) and the loss event affects the estimated future cash flows of the financial asset/s concerned. 3103

Where such objective evidence exists, the entity must determine the amount of the impairment loss as follows:

Type:	Measurement and treatment:
Financial assets carried at amortised cost	The loss is measured as the difference between the asset's carrying amount and the present value of estimated future cash flows discounted at the original effective interest rate (i.e., the effective interest rate computed at initial recognition); the carrying amount of the asset is reduced and the amount of the loss is recognised in profit or loss.
Financial assets carried at cost	The impairment loss is measured as the difference between the carrying amount of the financial asset and the present value of estimated future cash flows discounted at the current market rate of return for a similar financial asset.
Available-for-sale financial assets	The cumulative loss that had formally been recognised through the STRGL is removed from reserves and recognised in profit or loss even though the financial asset has not been derecognised.

C. Hedging

3105 Some entities use financial assets and financial liabilities as hedges to manage their risk profile. When instruments are used in this way, they are usually accounted for using hedge accounting. There are three types of hedging relationships:

3106 **Fair value hedge** – a hedge of the exposure to changes in fair value of a recognised asset or liability (or identified part thereof) or an unrecognised firm commitment, or an identified portion of such an asset, liability or firm commitment, that is attributable to a particular risk and could affect profit or loss.

3107 **Cash flow hedge** – a hedge of the exposure to variability in cash flows that is attributable to a particular risk associated with a recognised asset or liability or a highly probable forecast transaction and, in either case, could affect profit or loss.

3108 **Hedge of a net investment in a foreign operation** – i.e., a hedge in the amount of an entity's interest in the net assets of its subsidiary, associate, joint venture or branch, the activities of which are based or conducted in another country or currency.

3109 FRS 26 lays down no restrictions on the circumstances in which a derivative may be designated a hedging instrument, as long as the following conditions are met:

FRS 26 (88)

- At the inception of the hedge there is formal designation and documentation of the hedging relationship and the entity's risk management objective and strategy for undertaking the hedge.
- The hedge is expected to be highly effective in achieving offsetting changes in fair value or cash flows attributable to the hedged risk, consistently with the originally documented risk management strategy for that particular hedging relationship.
- For cash flow hedges, a forecast transaction that is the subject of the hedge must be highly probable and must present an exposure to variations in cash flows that could ultimately affect profit or loss.
- The effectiveness of the hedge can be reliably measured, i.e., the fair value or cash flows of the hedged item that are attributable to the hedged risk and the fair value of the hedging instrument.
- The hedge is assessed on an ongoing basis and determined actually to have been highly effective throughout the financial reporting periods for which the hedge was designated.

The accounting treatment is shown in the following table.

Type of hedge:	Accounting:
Fair value hedge	– The gain or loss from re-measuring the hedging instrument at fair value must be recognised in profit or loss; – The gain or loss attributable to the hedged risk must be used to adjust the carrying amount of the hedged item and be recognised in profit or loss; Any adjustment to the carrying amount of a hedged financial instrument for which the effective interest method is used must be amortised to profit or loss.
Cash flow hedges, and hedges of a net investment in a foreign operation	– The portion of the gain or loss that is determined to be effective is recognised through the STRGL; and – The portion judged as ineffective is recognised in the profit or loss account.

3110 If a hedge of a forecast transaction subsequently results in the recognition of a financial asset or liability, the associated gains or losses that were recognised directly in reserves must be reclassified into profit or loss in the same period or periods during which the asset acquired or liability assumed affects profit or loss. However, if an entity expects that all or a portion of a loss recognised directly in reserves will not be recovered, it must reclassify into profit or loss the amount that is not expected to be recovered.

FRS 26 (97) - (100)

If a hedge of a forecast transaction subsequently results in the recognition of a non-financial asset or non-financial liability, or if a forecast transaction for a non-financial asset or non-financial liability becomes a firm commitment for which fair value hedge accounting is applied, the entity must adopt one of two accounting policies:
1. It reclassifies the associated gains and losses that were recognised directly in reserves into profit or loss in the same period or periods during which the asset acquired or liability assumed affects profit or loss. However, if an entity expects that all or a portion of a loss recognised directly in reserves will not be recovered, it must reclassify into profit or loss the amount that is not expected to be recovered.
2. It removes the associated gains or losses that were recognised directly in reserves and includes them in the initial cost or other carrying amount of the asset or liability.

For all other cash flow hedges, amounts that had been recognised directly in reserves must be recognised in profit or loss in the same period or periods during which the hedged forecast transaction affects profit or loss (e.g., when a forecast sale occurs).

An entity must discontinue prospectively the accounting treatment for a fair value hedge if: **3111**
- the hedging instrument expires or is sold, terminated or exercised,
- the hedge no longer meets the criteria for hedge accounting, or
- the entity revokes the designation.

The entity must discontinue the accounting treatment for a cash flow hedge if:
- the hedging instrument expires or is sold, terminated or exercised,
- the hedge no longer meets the criteria for hedge accounting,
- the forecast transaction is no longer expected to occur, or
- the entity revokes the designation.

IV. Disclosure of financial instruments

Company legislation requires disclosure by all companies of financial commitments inasmuch as they affect or contribute to a proper understanding of the company's affairs (e.g., outstanding forward contracts). The following sample disclosure satisfies the requirements of the Act. **3120**

EXAMPLE NOTES TO THE FINANCIAL STATEMENTS (extract)

Outstanding Forward Contracts

The company had outstanding forward contracts to hedge foreign currencies and purchases at 31 December 20X5 as follows:

	Foreign currencies		Sterling equivalent	
	20X5	20X4	20X5	20X4
	'000	'000	£ '000	£ '000
Maturing within 1 year				
To cover future capital commitments in U.S. dollars	$ 225	$ 155	£ 160	£ 115
To hedge future purchases in U.S. dollars	$ 75	$ 69	£ 55	£ 46
To hedge debt in euros	€ 100	€ 150	£ 60	£ 100
Maturing after 1 year				
To cover future capital commitments in U.S. dollars	$ 180	$ 65	£ 96	£ 33

To this layer of disclosure, FRS 29 "Financial Instruments: disclosures" adds various other requirements which are intended to enhance the user's understanding of the significance of financial instruments for an entity's financial position and performance and to provide **3125** information about exposures to risks arising from financial instruments and about an entity's objectives, policies and processes for managing capital.

FRS 29 replaces the disclosure requirements of FRS 25, and applies to entities applying FRS 26 (i.e., companies that are listed and those that use the fair value accounting rules). The provisions of the new standard are mandatory in respect of accounting periods commencing on or after 1 January 2007. Although entities not applying FRS 26 are not required to comply with FRS 29, voluntary compliance is permitted.

3127 In May 2009 the ASB issued "Amendments to FRS 29: Improving disclosures about financial instruments". The amendments require **enhanced disclosures** about fair value measurements and liquidity risks. They also set out disclosure requirements for the credit risk of loans and receivables designated at fair value through the profit and loss. The amendment is applicable for accounting periods beginning on or after 1 January 2009. In the first year of application, entities do not have to provide comparative information for the disclosures required by the amendments. Earlier application is permitted. If an entity applies the amendments for an earlier period, it must disclose that fact. See ¶3167, ¶3168 and ¶3175.

3129 In November 2010 the ASB, in response to amendments by the IASB to IFRS 7, issued amendments to FRS 29, which are intended to provide clarity regarding issues of classification, measurement and impairment. All of these are discussed from ¶3171 and are designed to enable users to better understand the nature and extent of risks arising from financial instruments. The amendments apply to periods beginning on or after 1 January 2011, with earlier application permitted.

3133 FRS 29 (6) - (7) As a general rule, entities are required to **classify** financial instruments into classes that are appropriate to the nature of the information disclosed and that take into account the characteristics of the financial instruments concerned. Sufficient information must be provided in order to:
- permit **reconciliation** with the line items presented in the balance sheet, and
- allow users to evaluate the significance of financial instruments to the entity's **financial position and performance**.

A. Balance sheet disclosures

3140 The **carrying amounts** of each of the following must be disclosed – either on the balance sheet itself or by way of note:
1. financial assets at fair value through profit and loss, showing separately those
- designated as such on initial recognition;
- classified as held for trading;
2. held-to-maturity investments;
3. loans and receivables;
4. available-for-sale financial assets;
5. financial liabilities at fair value through profit and loss, showing separately those:
- designated as such on initial recognition;
- classified as held for trading;
6. financial liabilities measured at amortised cost.

Where the entity has designated a financial liability as at fair value through profit and loss, it must disclose:
1. the amount of change (both during the period and cumulatively) in the fair value that is attributable to changes in the credit risk relating to the liability – either
- as the amount of change in its fair value that is not attributable to changes in market conditions affecting market risk; or
- by another method if this more faithfully represents the amount of change attributable to credit-risk fluctuations.

2. the difference between its carrying amount and the amount the entity would be required to pay at maturity to the holder of the obligation.

In addition, it must disclose the methods used to comply with these disclosure requirements.

EXAMPLE If the only changes in market conditions giving rise to changes in market risk are changes in benchmark interest rates, the amount can be estimated as follows:

Step 1. The entity computes the liability's internal rate of return at the beginning of the period using the market price of the liability and its contractual cash flows. From this, it deducts the benchmark interest rate at the start of the period to arrive at an instrument specific component of the internal rate of return.

Step 2. The entity calculates the present value of the liability's cash flows at the end of the period and a discount rate equal to the sum of the benchmark rate at the end of the period and the internal rate of return determined in Step 1.

Step 3. The difference between the observed market price of the liability at the end of the period and the amount determined in Step 2 represents the change in fair value not attributable to changes in the benchmark interest rate. This is the amount to be disclosed.

If an entity has designated a loan or receivable (or group of loans or receivables) as at fair value through profit or loss, it must disclose: 3142 FRS 29 (9)
a. the maximum exposure to credit risk of the loan or receivable (or group of loans or receivables) at the end of the reporting period;
b. the amount by which any related credit derivatives or similar instruments mitigate that maximum exposure to credit risk;
c. the amount of change, during the period and cumulatively, in the fair value of the loan or receivable (or group of loans or receivables) that is attributable to changes in the credit risk of the financial asset determined either:
- as the amount of change in its fair value that is not attributable to changes in market conditions that give rise to market risk; or
- using an alternative method the entity believes more faithfully represents the amount of change in its fair value that is attributable to changes in the credit risk of the asset;
d. the amount of the change in the fair value of any related credit derivatives or similar instruments that has occurred during the period and cumulatively since the loan or receivable was designated.

Changes in market conditions that give rise to market risk include changes in an observed (benchmark) interest rate, commodity price, foreign exchange rate or index of prices or rates.

Where an entity **reclassifies** a financial asset from cost (or amortised cost) to fair value – or vice versa – it must disclose the amounts reclassified into and out of each category and explain the reasons. 3145 FRS 29 (12)

Where it reclassifies a financial asset out of the fair value through profit or loss category or out of the available-for-sale category in accordance with FRS 26, it must disclose: 3146
- the amount reclassified into and out of each category;
- for each reporting period until derecognition, the carrying amounts and fair values of all financial assets that have been reclassified in the current and previous reporting periods;
- if reclassified due to a rare situation, this fact and the circumstances indicating the situation was rare;
- for the reporting period when the financial asset was reclassified, the fair value gain or loss on the financial asset recognised in profit or loss or the statement of total recognised gains and losses in that reporting period and in the previous reporting period;
- for each accounting period following the reclassification until derecognition of the financial asset, the fair value gain or loss that would have been recognised in profit or loss or the statement of total recognised gains and losses if the financial asset had not been reclassified and the gain, loss, income and expense recognised in profit or loss; and
- the effective interest rate and estimated amounts of cash flows the entity expects to recover, as at the date of reclassification of the asset.

3147 FRS 29 (14) Where an entity has made a **pledge** of financial assets as collateral, it must disclose the
- carrying amount, and
- terms and conditions relating to the pledge.

3148 FRS 29 (15) Where an entity **holds collateral**, which it is permitted to sell or repledge even in the absence of default by the owner, it must disclose:
- the fair value of the collateral held,
- the fair value of the collateral sold or repledged, and whether the entity is obligated to return it,
- the terms and conditions in relation to its use of the collateral.

3149 If financial assets are impaired by credit losses and these are accounted for via a separate account (i.e., rather than directly reducing the carrying value of the assets in question), a reconciliation must be provided.

3150 FRS 29 (17) In respect of compound financial instruments that contain both liability and equity components in which there are multiple embedded derivatives whose values are interdependent, full disclosure of these features must be made.

3151 FRS 29 (18) In respect of loans payable, the following disclosures must be made:
- details of any defaults during the period (whether relating to principal, interest, sinking fund or redemption terms);
- the carrying amount of loans payable in default; and
- whether the default has been remedied – or the applicable terms renegotiated – before the financial statements were authorised for issue.

3152 FRS 29 (19) In respect of any other breaches that have permitted the lender to demand accelerated payment, the same information is required to be disclosed unless the breaches were remedied, or the terms of the loan renegotiated, on or before the reporting date.

B. Income statement disclosures

3155 The following items must be disclosed – either on the face of the financial statements or the notes:

1. net gains or losses on
- financial assets or liabilities at fair value through profit and loss, showing separately those on financial assets and financial liabilities designated as such on initial recognition, and those classified as "held for trading"
- available-for-sale financial assets, showing separately gains or losses recognised directly in equity over the period
- held-to-maturity investments
- loans and receivables
- financial liabilities measured at amortised cost;

2. total income or expense relating to interest (calculated using the effective interest method) on financial assets or liabilities that are not at fair value through profit and loss;
3. fee income and expense arising from
- financial assets or liabilities that are not at fair value through profit or loss
- trust and other fiduciary activities resulting in the holding or investing of assets on behalf of others;

4. interest income on impaired financial assets;
5. the amount of any impairment loss for each class of financial asset.

C. Accounting policies

For entities that choose to apply FRS 29 but not FRS 26, it is important to provide adequate information so that users of financial statements can fully understand the basis on which financial assets and financial liabilities have been measured. Disclosures of accounting policies should therefore indicate not only whether cost, fair value, or some other basis of measurement has been applied to a specific class of asset or liability, but also the method of applying that basis. **3160** FRS 29 (21a)

MEMO POINTS For financial instruments carried at cost, an entity should disclose how it accounts for:
- costs of acquisition or issuance;
- premiums and discounts on monetary financial assets and financial liabilities;
- changes in the estimated amount of future cash flows associated with a monetary financial instrument;
- changes in circumstances that result in significant uncertainty about the timely collection of all contractual amounts due from monetary financial assets;
- decreases in the fair value to below carrying amount of financial assets;
- restructured financial liabilities.

For financial assets and liabilities carried at fair value, the entity must indicate how these carrying amounts were determined – e.g., from quoted prices, independent appraisals, discounted cash flow analysis, etc – and disclose any significant assumptions made in applying these methods.

In respect of **hedge accounting**, the following must be disclosed: **3161** FRS 29 (22)
- a description of each type of hedge;
- a description of the financial instruments designated as hedging instruments and their fair values at the reporting date; and
- the nature of the risks being hedged.

For **cash flow hedges**, the following disclosures must be made: **3162**
- the periods when the cash flows are expected to occur and when they are expected to affect profit or loss;
- a description of any forecast transaction for which hedge accounting had previously been used, but which is no longer expected to occur;
- the amount that was recognised in equity during the period;
- the amount that was removed from equity and included in profit or loss for the period, showing the amount included in each line item in the income statement; and
- the amount that was removed from equity during the period and included in the initial cost or other carrying amount of a non-financial asset or non-financial liability whose acquisition or incurrence was a hedged highly probable forecast transaction.

An entity must disclose separately: **3163**

a. gains or losses in fair value hedges
- on the hedging instrument, and
- on the hedged item attributable to the hedged risk.

b. the ineffectiveness recognised in profit or loss that arises from cash flow hedges; and

c. the ineffectiveness recognised in profit or loss that arises from hedges of net investments in foreign operations.

Except in the following three circumstances, disclosure is required of the **fair value** of that class of financial assets and liabilities in a way that permits it to be compared with its carrying amount. For these purposes, financial assets and financial liabilities can be grouped into classes, but offset only to the extent that their carrying amounts are offset in the balance sheet. **3164** FRS 29 (25) – (26)

The three circumstances in which these **disclosures are not required** are: **3165** FRS 29 (29)
- when the carrying amount is a reasonable approximation of fair value (e.g., short-term trade receivables and payables);
- in respect of investments in equity instruments that do not have a quoted market price in an active market (or derivatives linked to them);

– for contracts containing a discretionary participation feature if the fair value of that feature cannot be measured reliably.

However, in the latter two cases, the entity must disclose sufficient information to help users of the financial statements make their own judgements about the extent of possible differences between the carrying amount of the financial assets or financial liabilities and their fair value. (See ¶3168 for examples.)

3166 FRS 29 (27) In **all other cases**, the entity must disclose:
– the methods and – when a valuation technique is used – the assumptions applied in determining fair values (e.g., information about the assumptions relating to prepayment rates, rates of estimated credit losses, and interest rates or discount rates);
– whether fair values are determined by reference to published market prices or are estimated using a valuation technique;
– whether the fair values are determined using a valuation technique based on assumptions that are not supported by prices from observable current market transactions in the same instrument and not based on available observable market data. If changing one or more of those assumptions to another set of reasonable assumptions would make a significant difference to the fair value determined, this fact – and the effect – should be disclosed.

3167 Under the amendments to FRS 29, applicable to accounting periods beginning on or after 1 January 2009, an entity is still required to disclose in respect of each class of financial instruments the **method** and, when a valuation technique is used, the **assumptions** applied in determining fair values of each class of financial assets or financial liabilities. In addition, if there has been a **change in valuation technique**, the entity must disclose that change and the reason for making it. Disclosures are categorised according to a fair value hierarchy. The hierarchy has three levels:

FRS 29 (27a) 1. quoted prices (unadjusted) in active markets for identical assets or liabilities (Level 1);
2. inputs other than quoted prices included within Level 1 that are observable for the asset or liability, either directly (i.e. as prices) or indirectly (i.e. derived from prices) (Level 2); and
3. inputs for the asset or liability that are not based on observable market data (unobservable inputs) (Level 3).

The level in the fair value hierarchy within which the fair value measurement is categorised in its entirety is determined on the basis of the lowest level input that is significant to the fair value measurement in its entirety. For this purpose, the significance of an input is assessed against the fair value measurement in its entirety. If a fair value measurement uses observable inputs that require significant adjustment based upon unobservable inputs, that measurement is a Level 3 measurement. Assessing the significance of a particular input to the fair value measurement in its entirety requires judgement, considering factors specific to the asset or liability.

3168 FRS 29 (27b) For fair value measurements recognised in the **balance sheet**, an entity is required to disclose for each class of financial instruments:

a. The level in the fair value hierarchy into which the fair value measurements are categorised in their entirety, segregating fair value measurements as set out above.

b. Any significant transfers between Level 1 and Level 2 of the fair value hierarchy and the reasons for those transfers. Transfers into each level are to be disclosed and discussed separately from transfers out of each level. For this purpose, significance must judged with respect to profit or loss, and total assets or total liabilities.

c. For fair value measurements in Level 3 of the fair value hierarchy, a reconciliation from the beginning balance to the ending balances, disclosing separately changes during the period attributable to the following:
– Total gains or losses for the period recognised in profit or loss, and a description of where they are presented in the profit and loss account;
– Total gains or losses recognised through the statement of total recognised gains or losses;
– Purchases, sales, issues and settlements (each type of movement disclosed separately); and
– Transfers into or out of Level 3 (e.g. transfers attributable to changes in the observability of market data) and the reasons for those transfers. For significant transfers, transfers into Level 3 must be disclosed and discussed separately from transfers out of Level 3.

d. The amount of total gains or losses for the period in (a) above included in profit or loss that are attributable to gains or losses relating to those assets and liabilities held at the end of the reporting period and a description of where those gains or losses are presented in the profit and loss account.
e. For fair value measurements in Level 3, if changing one or more of the inputs to reasonably possible alternative assumptions would change fair value significantly, the entity must state that fact and disclose the effect of those changes. The entity must disclose how the effect of a change to a reasonably possible alternative assumption was calculated. For this purpose, significance shall be judged with respect to profit or loss, and total assets or total liabilities, or, when changes in fair value are recognised through the statement of total recognised gains and losses, total equity.

FRS 29 specifies that these quantitative disclosures should be presented in tabular format unless another format is more appropriate.

Where an entity establishes a fair value for a financial instrument using a valuation technique (because, e.g., there is no active market for it), the best evidence of fair value at initial recognition is the transaction price. However, if there is a difference between the fair value at initial recognition and the amount that would be determined at that date using the valuation technique, the entity must disclose, by class of financial instrument: **3169** FRS 29 (28)
- its accounting policy for recognising that difference in profit or loss, and
- the aggregate difference still to be recognised in profit or loss at the beginning and end of the period and a reconciliation of changes in the balance of this difference.

Examples of the type of information referred to in ¶3165 are: **3170**
- the fact that fair value information has not been disclosed for these instruments because their fair value cannot be measured reliably;
- a description of the financial instruments, their carrying amount, and an explanation of why fair value cannot be measured reliably;
- information about the market for the instruments;
- information about whether and how the entity intends to dispose of the financial instruments; and
- if financial instruments whose fair value could not previously be reliably measured are derecognised, that fact, their carrying amount at the time of derecognition, and the amount of gain or loss recognised.

Risk

In general, reporting entities are required to disclose information that enables users of their financial statements to evaluate the **nature and extent of risks** arising from financial instruments to which the entity is exposed at the reporting date. These disclosures can be given in the financial statements or cross-referenced to another statement and are required to focus on the **risks that arise** from financial instruments and how they have been **managed**. **3171**

In its amendments to FRS 29 (November 2010), the ASB added that the interaction between qualitative and quantitative disclosures enables users to better evaluate an entity's exposure to risk.

For each type of risk arising from financial instruments, the following must be disclosed: **3172**
- the exposures to risk and how they arise;
- the entity's objectives, policies and processes for managing the risk and the methods used to measure the risk;
- any changes from the previous period;
- summary quantitative data about its exposure to that risk at the reporting date based on the information provided internally to key management personnel of the entity;
- a quantitive disclosure of the concentration of risk arising from financial instruments having similar characteristics and subject to being affected in a similar way by changes in economic conditions.

The various types of risk are discussed below.

Credit risk

3173 FRS 29 (36) For each class of financial instrument, the entity must disclose:
- the amount that best represents its maximum exposure to credit risk at the reporting date, without taking account of any collateral held or other credit enhancements (e.g., netting agreements that do not qualify for offset); however this disclosure is not required for financial instruments whose carrying amount best represents the maximum exposure to risk;
- a description of any collateral held as security and of other credit enhancements, and their financial effect (e.g., a quantification of the extent to which collateral and other credit enhancements mitigate credit risk) in respect of the amount that best represents the maximum exposure to credit risk; and
- information about the credit quality of financial assets that are neither past due nor impaired.

MEMO POINTS The November 2010 amendment removed a fourth requirement to disclose the carrying amount of financial assets that would otherwise be past due or impaired whose terms have been renegotiated. While this change is effective for years beginning on or after 1 January 2011, early adoption is permitted.

3174 FRS 29 (37) If financial assets are past due or impaired, the following must be disclosed:
- an analysis of the age of financial assets that are past due as at the reporting date but not impaired;
- an analysis of financial assets that are individually determined to be impaired as at the reporting date, including the factors considered in determining that they are impaired.

MEMO POINTS The November 2010 amendment addressed a concern that the disclosure of the fair value of collateral was potentially misleading, since in a particular class of assets, some might be over-collateralised while others may be under-collateralised. As a result, disclosure of an aggregate amount is no longer required. While this change is effective for years beginning on or after 1 January 2011, early adoption is permitted.

Liquidity risk

3175 FRS 29 (39) In respect of liquidity risk, the following should be disclosed:
- a maturity analysis for non-derivative financial liabilities (including issued financial guarantee contracts) that shows the remaining contractual maturities;
- a maturity analysis for derivative financial liabilities, which must include the remaining contractual maturities for those derivative financial liabilities for which contractual maturities are essential for an understanding of the timing of the cash flows;
- a description of how it manages the liquidity risk inherent in the above.

Market risk

3176 Entities must disclose:
- a sensitivity analysis for each type of market risk to which the entity is exposed at the reporting date, showing how profit or loss and equity would have been affected by changes in the relevant risk variable that were reasonably possible at that date;
- the methods and assumptions used in preparing the sensitivity analysis; and
- changes from the previous period in the methods and assumptions used, and the reasons for such changes.

3177 Where the entity prepares a sensitivity analysis that reflects interdependencies between risk variables (e.g., interest rates and exchange rates) and uses it to manage financial risks, it may use that sensitivity analysis instead. However, it must also give explanations of:
- the method used in preparing such a sensitivity analysis, and of the main parameters and assumptions underlying the data provided; and
- the method used and of limitations that may result in the information not fully reflecting the fair value of the assets and liabilities involved.

3178 If the entity's sensitivity analysis disclosures in accordance with ¶3176 or ¶3177 are unrepresentative of a risk inherent in a financial instrument (e.g., because the year-end exposure does not reflect the exposure during the year), this fact, and the reasons, must be given.

CHAPTER 2

Creditors

OUTLINE ¶¶

A. Classification and accounting treatment

Creditors are defined as entities to which an organisation owes money. The amounts can be owing in respect of purchases, loans or any other indebtedness. The relationship with a creditor may arise as a result of a capital instrument (as in the case of a loan) but this is not a necessary condition (e.g., as in the case of trade creditors). The accounting treatment of the various types is discussed below. 3200

1. Statutory formats

Creditors is a main statutory heading under both Formats 1 and 2 of the Accounting Regulations (formerly the Schedule 4 formats under the 1985 Companies Act). 3201

Under Format 1, creditors falling due within one year are set off against "Current assets" in the calculation of "Net current assets" while those due after one year are shown separately after "Total assets less current liabilities".

Under Format 2, creditors are shown on the face of the balance sheet under "Liabilities". For each subheading under "creditors", amounts falling due within one year must be shown separately from amounts falling due after one year.

A company's "net assets" and "shareholders funds" is a question of fact and will be the same irrespective of the balance sheet format it adopts. However, for those users of financial statements who may be less sophisticated, the differing presentation of the amount for "creditors" can affect their perception of the apparent overall position. The example on the following pages illustrates how the balance sheets of the same company will differ under the two formats.

EXAMPLE Comparison of **Balance Sheet** under **Format 1** and **Format 2** for the current year (20X1) and the previous year (20X0)

Format 1	**20X1** £'000	**20X0** £'000
Fixed assets		
Tangible assets	12,932	10,221
Investments	1,284	1,190
	14,216	11,411
Current assets		
Stocks	38,540	35,217
Debtors	16,849	18,044
Cash in hand and at bank	27,636	25,625
	83,025	78,886
Creditors due within one year		
Borrowings	(10,000)	–
Other creditors	(29,624)	(23,951)
	(39,624)	(23,951)
Net current assets	43,401	54,935
Total assets less current liabilities	57,617	66,346
Creditors due after more than one year		
Borrowings	(5,000)	(10,000)
Other creditors	(3,547)	(10,386)
Provisions for liabilities and charges	(6,500)	(4,000)
Net assets	£ 42,570	£ 41,960
Capital and reserves		
Called up share capital		
Ordinary shares	21,455	21,455
Preference shares	6,000	6,000
Share premium account	8,500	8,500
Profit and loss account	6,615	6,005
Shareholders' funds	£ 42,570	£ 41,960

2. Sub-categories

3202 Both Format 1 and Format 2 provide for various sub-categories, which may be shown either on the **face** of the balance sheet or in the **notes** to the accounts. If, however, the individual amounts are not material, they may be added together.

These sub-categories are explained below (except **debenture loans**, which are discussed at ¶3006).

Format 2	20X1 £'000	20X0 £'000
ASSETS		
Fixed assets		
Tangible assets	12,932	10,221
Investments	1,284	1,190
	14,216	11,411
Current assets		
Stocks	38,540	35,217
Debtors	16,849	18,044
Cash in hand and at bank	27,636	25,625
	83,025	78,886
Total assets	£ 97,241	£ 90,297
LIABILITIES		
Capital and reserves		
Called up share capital		
Ordinary shares	21,455	21,455
Non-equity share capital		
Preference shares	6,000	6,000
Equity reserves		
Share premium account	8,500	8,500
Profit and loss account	6,615	6,005
Shareholders' funds	42,570	41,960
Creditors		
Due within one year	39,624	23,951
Due after more than one year	8,547	20,386
Provisions for liabilities and charges	6,500	4,000
Total liabilities	£ 97,241	£ 90,297

a. Bank loans and overdrafts

Most bank loans and overdraft facilities are extended subject to the agreement that the bank has the right to **demand payment in full at any time**. If this is the case, the overdraft should be treated as repayable within one year, even if other arrangements have been made for periodic repayments. **3203**

If bank accounts with both debit and credit balances are maintained at the same bank and there is a **right of set-off** (¶2630), the net amount may be shown under current liabilities (or current assets, as the case may be). If there is no right of set-off, the debit and credit balances should be shown in full under respective headings. **3204**

b. Payments received on account

Payments received on account represent payments received in advance of work being undertaken (or a service provided) and are therefore accounted for as a liability and not **3206** income of the receiving company. Only when the work has been performed is the creditor released and the income recognised.

In the case of **long-term contracts**, SSAP 9 prescribes that progress payments should be set off against amounts recoverable on the contract concerned included in debtors. Any excess not absorbed should be set off against any balance in stocks relating to the contract. Finally, only if there is still a balance remaining should it be included in creditors and shown as payments received on account.

c. Trade creditors

3208 Trade creditors are amounts owed to **suppliers of goods and services**. While in theory it can be argued that only "trade creditors" relate to these, in practice most entities include all outstanding balances in the creditors' ledger under trade creditors.

Occasionally, suppliers of trade goods try to protect themselves with "reservation of title" clauses as part of their terms and conditions – these clauses seek to establish that the goods remain the property of the seller until paid for in full. Certainly from an accounting point of view (and possibly from a legal perspective as well), these clauses have no practical effect. Therefore, both the goods, and the liability in respect of amounts owing, should be accounted for in the ordinary way.

3209 Where there are **debit balances** on suppliers' accounts, and these are material, they should be shown instead with debtors.

d. Bills of exchange payable

3210 Bills of exchange normally represent agreements entered into to obtain **extended credit terms** or to facilitate transactions with **overseas-based suppliers**. If material, these should be stated separately.

Where bills of exchange payable and accruals are not material and do not justify being shown separately, they can be included with trade creditors.

e. Amounts owed to group undertakings

3212 Amounts owed to companies within the group, whether trading balances or loans, should be included under this caption. The normal rules apply; therefore these amounts must be analysed between balances falling due within one year and subsequently. One of the characteristics of inter-company indebtedness is that there is often **no formal agreement** concerning the debtor company's right to demand repayment. In such cases, it is usual for the balance to be treated as due within one year in the accounts of the creditor company.

f. Amounts owed to undertakings in which the company has a participating interest

3214 FRS 9 (55) Where these amounts relate to participating interests in **associated undertakings** or **joint ventures**, FRS 9 requires additional disclosures over and above those prescribed by the Companies Act. The total creditor balance must be analysed between amounts relating to loans and amounts relating to trading balances.

As a matter of good practice, the analysis should be given separately for the amounts due within, and after more than, one year as well as for the total amount.

g. Other creditors including taxation and social security

Note 9 to the balance sheet formats states that "other creditors including taxation and social security" should be analysed between "other creditors", and amounts in respect of "taxation and social security". 3216

Items that will be shown as "**other creditors**" include loans (other than debenture loans and bank loans), dividends declared but unpaid, and any other creditor that cannot be appropriately shown elsewhere.

MEMO POINTS Dividends that have been proposed or recommended but not yet declared are not a liability in law. It would therefore not be appropriate to include them under this heading. Such dividends, if undeclared at the year end, may be shown instead under "Creditors, amounts falling due within one year".

The following amounts can be aggregated and shown as "**taxation and social security**": corporation tax, VAT, PAYE, NI contributions, excise duties, ACT payable on dividends, and any other amounts owing to central governments.

Deferred tax is excluded from this subheading as the balance sheet formats require it to be disclosed as part of "Taxation, including deferred taxation" under the separate statutory heading "Provisions for liabilities and charges".

h. Accruals and deferred income

The balance sheet formats permit companies to show accruals and deferred income under "Creditors" or a **separate heading** after "Creditors" or "Provisions for liabilities and charges" – depending on the format being used. Where disclosure is made under "Creditors", the amounts that will fall due within one year should be shown separately from amounts that will fall due after one year. However, when disclosure is made under a separate heading, this analysis is not specifically required. 3218

Accruals

Generally, accruals consist of items such as estimated liabilities in respect of goods and services for which invoices have not yet been received, unpaid salaries, pension costs, employees' accrued holiday pay, bank interest not yet charged, or royalties due for payment. All such expenses should be included here, except accrued taxes, which should be shown under "taxation and social security" discussed at ¶3216. 3219

Deferred income

Certain items of income – such as rent, interest or government grants – may have been invoiced and received in advance of the period to which they relate. According to the matching principle, such amounts should not be recognised as income but disclosed as a liability until they fall due and the company has a legal right to the amounts as income. 3220

B. Disclosure

The general and specific disclosure requirements are outlined below along with the different types of balance sheet layout permissible and forms of presentation used in the notes to the accounts. Small companies preparing short-form accounts are exempt from certain disclosure requirements. 3222

1. General rules

3223 In disclosing "creditors" in the balance sheet, the Companies Act formats must be adopted and an aged analysis of the total debt must be given, specifying amounts falling due as follows:
- within one year or less
- after one year but not more than two years
- after two years but not more than five years
- after five years.

This analysis may be shown on the face of the balance sheet or, as is more usual, in the notes.

3224 In respect of the aggregate of items shown under creditors, the following must be shown:
- debts falling due **after five years** from the balance sheet date and which are not paid by instalments,
- where debts are repayable by instalments, the amount of instalments that fall due after five years.

In respect of each debt, the terms of payment and rates of interest payable must be shown. If the number of debts is large, a general indication of the terms and rates of interest may be given.

Note that the Companies Act 1985 required the above disclosures to be made in respect of **each item** shown under creditors; under the 2006 Act the **aggregate of the items** is required.

3225 EXAMPLE Creditors – amounts falling due after one year

	2X08 £'000	2X07 £'000
9% Debentures	540	600
(2X02 to 2X11, repayable £60,000 annually)		
Bank loans		
Interest at 0.75% above base lending rate, repayable 2X09	100	100
Interest 1.25% above base lending rate, repayable 2X10	50	50
	690	750
Analysis of repayments:		
Due in 1 year or less	60	60
Due after 1 year but not more than 2 years	120	120
Due after 2 years but not more than 5 years	280	280
Due after more than 5 years	230	230
	£690	£690
Amounts payable after 5 years		
Debenture loans	180	180
Bank loans	50	50
	£230	£230

Debentures are secured by a floating charge on all the assets of the company. Bank loans are secured by first mortgages over the company's land and buildings.

2. Specific rules

3227 In respect of debentures and trade creditors additional disclosure requirements apply.

Debenture loans

3228 Disclosure of the following is required in respect of **issues** of debentures **during the year**:
- the classes of debentures issued
- for each class, the amount issued and the consideration received.

The balance sheet formats require that the amount of **convertible debt** (which almost always falls within the definition of debentures) must be shown separately. 3229

FRS 4 extends this requirement by stating that convertible debt should be stated separately from other liabilities. Generally, it is taken to mean that the disclosure should be made on the face of the balance sheet if material, but allows disclosure in the notes if not material. However, in the latter case, the caption on the face of the balance sheet should make it clear that convertible debt is included. FRS 4 (25)

In either event, the following must be shown in the notes: FRS 4 (62)
- date and amount payable on redemption
- number, description and class of shares into which the loan is convertible
- whether conversion is at the option of the issuer or the holder.

EXAMPLE **Extract from financial statements**
Balance Sheet
31 December 2X08

Creditors – amounts falling due after one year

	2X08	2X07
	£'000	£'000
9% Debenture loans, including convertible loans (Note 25)	1,350	1,600

Notes

Note 25

Convertible unsecured loans stock may be converted at the company's option into fully paid ordinary shares of £2 each in any year up to and including 2X09 at the rate of one ordinary share for every £5 of convertible loan stock. Full conversion of the outstanding rights will result in the issue of 270,000 ordinary shares. If the company does not exercise the conversion option, it will redeem the loan stock on 1 January 2X10 at a premium of 5 per cent.

Trade creditors

Public companies, and companies that do not qualify as small or medium-sized companies (¶6000) that at any time during the year were part of a group of which the parent company was a public company, are required to state the following in their directors' reports: 3230
- the creditor payment policy, and
- the number of days represented by trade creditors as at the year end.

3. Sample disclosure

The following sample disclosure follows Format 1. 3235

EXAMPLE **Extracts from financial statements**
Balance Sheet
31 December 2X08

	Note	2X08 £'000	2X07 £'000
Fixed assets	xx	xxx	xxx
Current assets	xx	xxx	xxx
Creditors – amounts falling due within one year	12	523	455
Total assets less current liabilities		xxx	xxx
Creditors – amounts falling due after more than one year	13	688	577
Net assets		xxx	xxx

Notes to the Accounts
31 December 2X08

12. Creditors – amounts falling due within one year

Debenture loans (note 21)	-	38
Bank loans and overdrafts (note 21)	169	92
Payments received on account	27	11
Trade creditors	256	207
Other creditors, including taxation and social security	16	27
Proposed dividend	55	80
	£523	£455

13. Creditors – amounts falling after more than one year

Bank loans (note 21)	150	20
Obligations under finance leases (note 21)	475	502
Accruals and deferred income	63	55
	£688	£577

21. **Debenture loans** (3 %; 20-year term ending 2X10) are secured by first mortgages over the company's freehold property

Bank loans and overdrafts are secured by first mortgages over the company's freehold property

Obligations under finance leases and hire purchase contracts are secured by related leased assets and bear finance charges ranging from 5% to 10% per annum

Directors' Report
31 December 2X08

Policy on payments to creditors
The Company's policy is to agree payment terms with its suppliers when it enters into binding purchase contracts. The Company seeks to abide by such terms whenever it is satisfied that the supplier has provided the goods or services in accordance with the agreed terms and conditions. The Group seeks to treat all of its suppliers fairly and has a standard dealing specifically with the payment of suppliers.
The Company had 34 days' purchases outstanding at 31 December 2X08 based on the average daily amount invoiced by suppliers during the year then ended.

CHAPTER 3

Provisions and contingencies

OUTLINE ¶¶

SECTION 1

Introduction

In general, an entity's balance sheet reflects all the assets and liabilities that are known to exist at the balance sheet date. There are, however, circumstances in which, for various reasons, it may **be unclear whether an obligation actually exists**. Moreover, even where the existence of an obligation is known, there may still be some uncertainty regarding the amount or the timing of the payment required to discharge it. 3250

In these cases, the obligation should be classified either as a provision or as a contingency, depending on the circumstances. The accounting treatment of both of these sub-categories of liability is covered in the Companies Act and by FRS 12, "Provisions, contingent liabilities and assets". 3251

Entities that report under the FRSSE are exempt from FRS 12. However, the FRSSE's rules for provisions and contingencies, though more succinct than those under FRS 12, replicate most of its key provisions.

Liabilities and losses that have arisen or are likely to arise in respect of the financial year – even those that become apparent between the balance sheet date and the date on which it is signed – should be taken into account.

3252 In July 2005, the ASB issued FRED 39, which sets out revisions to FRS 12 to bring it in line with corresponding international requirements proposed by the IASB. Although the comment period has expired, according to its website, at the time of writing, neither the IASB nor the ASB have reached final conclusions. It is not therefore expected that changes based on FRED 39 will affect FRS 12 for the time being.

FRED 39 no longer uses the terms "contingent liabilities" and "contingent assets" but instead views contractual rights and obligations as either "conditional" or "unconditional". The term "contingency" is now used to refer to uncertainty about the **amount** that will be **required to settle a liability**, rather than the uncertainty as to whether a liability exists.

An unconditional right or obligation meets the definition of an asset or liability; therefore a reporting entity would recognise a liability on the basis of its unconditional nature even if there is some inherent uncertainty about the future event. Any such uncertainty is reflected in the **measurement** of the liability. For example, the supplier of a product warranty has an unconditional obligation to provide warranty cover and a conditional obligation to repair the goods should a fault arise. The supplier recognises a liability in respect of the unconditional obligation to provide warranty cover.

The FRED also amends the definition of "**constructive obligations**" to clarify that an entity's actions must result in other parties having a valid expectation that they can reasonably rely on the entity to discharge its responsibilities.

FRED 39 also raises a new issue in relation to **termination benefits**, for which previous UK accounting standards have not required specific accounting treatment. Under the exposure draft, termination benefits are defined as either "voluntary" (i.e., those offered for a short period in exchange for an employee's decision to accept termination) or "involuntary" (i.e., those provided where the entity terminates the employment). A liability and expense for **voluntary** termination benefits are proposed to be recognised when the employee accepts the employer's offer, while those in respect of **involuntary** benefits would be recognised only when the employer has a plan of termination and also has communicated it to the employees concerned.

SECTION 2

Provisions

A. Definition

3255 The word "provision" as used in FRS 12 has a narrower meaning than is ascribed to it by normal, everyday usage – even among accountants.

FRS 12 (2) Provisions are defined as liabilities "of uncertain timing or amount." Liabilities are defined as obligations of an entity to transfer economic benefits as a result of past transactions or events.

Though the FRS clearly regards provisions as a type of liability, it considers them separately from other liabilities because of the element of uncertainty as to their timing and/or amount.

MEMO POINTS The Standard is concerned with **provisions for liabilities**. It does not apply to items that arise in the context of **adjustments to the carrying amounts of assets**, which are sometimes referred to as provisions (e.g., provisions for depreciation, impairments, bad debts, stock write-downs).

Comparison with liabilities and accruals

In the case of "strict" **liabilities**, such as creditors, the reporting entity will have received goods or services at the balance sheet date and can therefore easily determine the amount owing to settle the obligation. In addition, because payment terms will most likely have been agreed in advance, the timing is also known. 3256

In the case of **accruals**, the underlying goods or services will have been supplied, but not invoiced, at the balance sheet date. Therefore, in the absence of an invoice, the reporting entity may have to make an estimate of the amount. While this treatment may be similar to that of provisions, there is much less uncertainty in the case of accruals.

MEMO POINTS In practice, the difference between provisions and other liabilities is not always clear and reclassification from "provisions" to other classes of liabilities is not uncommon.

Exclusions

The FRS applies to all provisions and contingencies, except those: 3257 FRS 12 (3)
- in respect of **financial instruments** that are **carried at fair value** (FRS 12 applies to instruments, e.g., guarantees, that are not carried at fair value);
- resulting from **executory contracts** (unless the contract is onerous, see ¶3275);
- in the case of insurance entities, arising from **contracts with policy-holders**; or
- covered specifically by another FRS or a SSAP.

MEMO POINTS An **executory contract** is one under which (i) neither party has performed any of its obligations or (ii) both parties have partially performed their obligations to an equal extent (e.g., contracts with employees in respect of continuing employment, obligations to pay council taxes and levies, supplier purchase contracts or capital commitments).

B. Criteria for recognition

A provision **must be recognised** in the financial statements when all three of the following criteria are met: 3260 FRS 12 (14)
- an entity has a **present obligation** (legal or constructive) as a result of a **past event**,
- it is **probable** that a **transfer of economic benefits** will be required to settle the obligation, and
- a **reliable estimate** can be made of the amount of the obligation.

If all of these are **not met**, the provision should not be brought into the accounts. However, it is still possible that the obligation is a **contingent liability**, depending on its characteristics (see ¶3280).

Present obligation

Before a present obligation can exist, an **obligating event** must have taken place. An obligating event is one that results in the entity's having no realistic alternative but to settle the obligation created. The obligations will be **legal** (i.e., enforceable by law) or **constructive** (i.e., it creates a valid expectation in the other party that the entity will settle the obligation). 3261 FRS 12 (15)

It is not always immediately clear whether a particular event is an obligating event. In practice, it may become apparent only after some time has passed that the event was, in fact, the obligating event. For example, a legal claim might be received after the balance sheet date alleging damage as a result of an event that occurred during the financial year. At the time, though, the damage had not manifested itself. Another example is a change in the law that, when passed, has retroactive effect on existing circumstances.

Past event

Only those obligations **arising from past events** and **existing independently of an entity's future actions** are recognised as provisions. For example, penalties or clean-up costs for 3263 FRS 12 (18)-(19)

unlawful environmental damage caused before the balance sheet date will lead to a transfer of economic benefits in settlement regardless of the future actions of the entity. On the other hand, the situation is different where, as a result of commercial pressures or legal requirements, an entity may intend or need to carry out expenditure to **operate in a particular way in the future**. An example of this might be a new law requiring the installation of health or safety equipment in factories where specified manufacturing processes are to be undertaken in the future. Because it is theoretically possible for the company to avoid the future expenditure by its future actions (for instance by changing its method of operation), it has no present obligation for that future expenditure. Where this is the case, no provision should be recognised.

Probable transfer of economic benefits

3265 FRS 12 (23) The obligation to transfer economic benefits is an integral component of the definition of a liability. Similarly, in determining whether a provision in respect of a liability should be recognised, there must be a probability that such a transfer will take place. For the purpose of the Standard, an occurrence is regarded as "probable" if it is more likely than not to occur (i.e., a probability greater than 50 percent).

3266 FRS 12 (24) Where an entity has a **number of similar obligations** (e.g., in respect of product warranties) the probability that a transfer will be required in settlement is determined by considering the class of obligations as a whole. Although the likelihood of outflow for any one item may be small, it may be probable that some transfer of economic benefits will be needed to settle the class of obligations as a whole. Where this is the case, and the other recognition criteria are also met, the entity should recognise a provision.

Reliable estimate

3268 FRS 12 (25)-(26) The use of estimates is an essential part of the preparation of financial statements. Provisions, by their nature, are more uncertain than most other balance sheet items. Entities are normally able, in respect of likely situations, to determine a range of possible outcomes and make a sufficiently reliable estimate of the obligation that will arise. Instances in which a liability is known to exist but no reliable estimate can be made are unusual. However, where this does happen, the liability cannot be recognised as a provision but, instead, must be disclosed as a contingent liability (see ¶3325).

Application of criteria to specific cases

a. Future operating losses

3270 FRS 12 (68)-(69) Provisions should not be recognised in respect of future operating losses because there is no present obligation, and therefore no liability, existing at the balance sheet date.

FRS 12 (87) There is also a specific prohibition against recognising future operating losses up to the date of a **restructuring** unless the losses relate to an onerous contract.

b. Onerous contracts

3275 FRS 12 (71) If an entity is a party to an onerous contract, the present obligation under the contract should be recognised and measured as a provision.

An onerous contract is one under which the **economic benefits** to be received are less than:
- the costs of fulfilling it, or
- the penalties arising or compensation owing as a result of failing to fulfil it.

Before a separate provision for an onerous contract is established, an entity must recognise any impairment loss that has occurred on assets dedicated to the particular contract. FRS 12 (74)

c. Restructuring programmes

FRS 12 provides specific guidance on how the general recognition criteria for provisions apply to restructuring programmes. 3280

Definition

The FRS **defines** a restructuring programme as: 3281 FRS 12 (2)

"A programme that is planned and controlled by management, and materially changes either:

a) the scope of a business undertaken by an entity; or

b) the manner in which that business is conducted."

This definition includes events such as: FRS 12 (75)

- the **sale** or **termination** of a line of business;
- the **closure** of business locations in a country or region or the **relocation** of business activities from one country or region to another;
- changes in **management structure** (e.g., eliminating a layer of management); and
- fundamental reorganisations that have a material effect on the **nature and focus** of the entity's operations.

Requirements triggering recognition

Where a provision in respect of restructuring costs falls within the general criteria for provisions (¶3260), it is appropriate to recognise the provision. It is also necessary that at the balance sheet date a **detailed formal plan** for the restructuring was in place, and there is a **valid expectation** that the plan will be implemented. 3283

The following must be specified as part of a detailed formal plan:

- the business or part of a business concerned,
- the principal locations affected,
- the location, function, and approximate number of employees who will be compensated for terminating their services,
- the expenditures that will be undertaken, and
- when the plan will be implemented.

MEMO POINTS 1. A valid expectation will exist for those affected either when the company actually begins to implement the plan or announces its main features in a sufficiently detailed manner to make it clear that the company will not be able to withdraw or otherwise fail to move forward with the plan.

2. The existence of a valid expectation relates to the situation **at the balance sheet date**. Therefore, if by the balance sheet date no event has taken place to give rise to a valid expectation, then even if the implementation had commenced by the time the financial statements are approved, no provision should be made.

3. To constitute a constructive obligation, therefore, there would have to have been – at the balance sheet date – some action such as dismantling plant, the sale of assets or the making of a public announcement in such a way that it reasonably gives rise to an expectation in customers, creditors, employees, etc that the restructuring will be carried out.

No obligation arises for the **sale of an operation** until the entity is committed to the sale by way of a binding sale agreement. 3284 FRS 12 (83)

When a **sale is only one element of a restructuring**, a constructive obligation can arise concerning the other parts of the restructuring before a binding sale agreement exists. Where this is the case, the assets of the operation should also be reviewed for impairment under FRS 11. FRS 12 (84)

Expenditures included in the provision

3290 FRS 12 (85) The standard specifies that only the direct expenditures arising from the restructuring may be included in the provision. Such expenditures must be both:
- **necessarily entailed** by the **restructuring**, and
- **not associated** with the entity's **ongoing or future activities**.

The following table indicates whether specific expenses can be included within a provision for restructuring.

Expenses that may be included	Expenses that are excluded
Costs of making employees redundant	Costs of retraining or relocating continuing staff
Costs of terminating leases and other contracts (where the termination results directly from the restructuring)	Investment in new systems and new distribution networks
Remuneration of staff engaged in dismantling plant	Gains on the expected disposal of assets (even if the sale is part of the restructuring) cannot be taken into account
Remuneration of staff involved in disposal of surplus stocks	Future operating losses up to the date of restructuring (unless relating to an onerous contract)
	Marketing expenses
Note that items in the second column are excluded because they relate to future activities of the business and do not arise as an obligation from a past event.	

C. Measurement

1. Best estimate

3295 FRS 12 (36) The amount recognised as a provision should be the best estimate of the expenditure required to settle the obligation at the balance sheet date.

FRS 12 (37) The best estimate is the amount that an entity would "rationally pay to settle the obligation at the balance sheet date or to transfer it to a third party at that time." Of course, it will often be either impossible or prohibitively expensive to actually settle or transfer the obligation at the balance sheet date; nevertheless this approach gives the best indication under the circumstances.

The FRS suggests that there are different methods of dealing with the uncertainties surrounding the amount to be recognised as a provision. Some of these are:
- The **most likely outcome** (i.e., the outcome with the highest probability). The problem with this method is that it ignores the effects of other possible outcomes and can result in a misstatement of the entity's obligations.
- The **maximum amount** (i.e., the highest possible outcome). The disadvantage of this method is that it can lead to excessive provisions where the likelihood of the outcome is small.
- **At least the minimum amount** (i.e., a value falling between the lowest possible outcome and the highest possible outcome). This problem here is that the wide range of possible estimates could impair comparability between financial statements.
- The **expected value** (i.e., an amount that takes account of all possible outcomes using probabilities to weight them). Where the provision involves a **large population** of items, the obligation is best estimated using this method, which weights all possible outcomes by their probability of occurring. This method is commonly used.

EXAMPLE A Ltd sells goods with a warranty under which customers are covered for the cost of repairs of any manufacturing defects that become apparent within the first year after purchase. If minor defects were detected in all products sold, repair costs of £500,000 would result. If major defects were detected in all products sold, repair costs of £2 million would result. The entity's past experience and future expectations indicate that, for the coming year, 75 per cent of the goods sold will be defect free, 20 per cent of the goods sold will have minor defects and 5 per cent of the goods sold will have major defects.
The expected value of the cost of repairs is:
(75 % of nil) + (20 % x £0.5m) + (5 % x £2m)
= 0 + £100,000 + £100,000
= £200,000

Alternatively, if a **single obligation** is being measured, the individual most likely outcome may be the best estimate of the liability. However, the entity should still consider other possible outcomes. 3296

EXAMPLE B Ltd built a major item of manufacturing plant for a customer. If the company is called upon to rectify a serious fault, the single most likely outcome is that the repair will succeed at the first attempt at a cost of £1 million. However, a larger provision should be made if there is a significant chance that additional attempts will be necessary to solve the problem.

Provisions are measured **before tax**. The consequences, if any, of tax are dealt with in accordance with SSAP 15, "Accounting for deferred tax" (¶9060). 3297 FRS 12 (41)

2. Adjustments to amounts

The following factors may further affect any estimate of the amounts to be provided for. 3300

Time value of money

Where the effect of the time value of money is material, the amount of a provision should be the present value of the future expenditures expected to settle the obligation. The discount rate used should be a pre-tax rate that reflects current market assessments of 3301 FRS 12 (45)
- the time value of money, and
- the risks specific to the liability.

MEMO POINTS Most provisions will reverse in the short term, usually within the subsequent financial year and the one following. Therefore, because the FRS is clear that it does not require cash flows to be discounted except in cases where the effect is material, the effects of discounting can be ignored.

Risk

Inherent in estimating the amounts to be provided is an element of uncertainty. The effect of adjusting cash outflows for risk is that the provision will be greater than otherwise would have been the case. The FRS states that one way of taking a risk factor into account is to use a discount rate that reflects current market assessments of the time value of money. In such a case, the cash flows themselves should not be adjusted for risk as this would be duplicative. 3303

On the other hand, it would be appropriate to adjust the cash flows to take account of risk but then the rate used must be a discount rate (e.g., a government bond rate). A risk-adjusted rate for estimating the present value of provisions will be lower than a risk-free rate. Theoretically, risk-adjusted cash flows discounted using a risk-free rate should arrive at the same net present value as cash flows that have not been adjusted for risk, but have been discounted using a risk-adjusted rate. Where the cash flows arising under an obligation are certain in monetary terms, there is no element of risk in the discounting rate.

EXAMPLE A Ltd is obliged to provide for a liability that is expected to be payable two years after its current financial year. Its best estimate of the amount payable at that time is £20,000, although the actual liability will fall into the range of values between £19,000 and £21,000.
The company has ascertained that it can pass the obligation on to another party for a fixed payment of £20,500 in two years' time. Assuming that a fair, risk-free rate is 4.5%, the fixed cash flow of £20,500 will render a net present value of £18,780.
However, the obligation arising at the balance sheet date for which provision must be made should be the same net present value amount irrespective of whether the best estimate, or the fixed equivalent, is used.
To arrive at a net present value of £18,780 on the basis of a payment in two years of £20,000, the rate to apply is 3.2% (the calculation is easily done on a financial calculator or PC spreadsheet). This rate therefore represents a risk-adjusted rate.

	Cash flow at end of:		Net present value	Rate
	Year 1	Year 2		
Certain cash flow (i.e., on the fixed amount)	0	20,500	18,780	4.5% (risk-free)
Expected/best-estimate cash flow	0	20,000	18,780	3.2% (risk-adjusted)

Future events

3305 FRS 12 (51) Where future events, such as changes in legislation and technology, are expected to affect the amount required to settle an obligation, the provision should be adjusted to reflect these events. However, this treatment can be applied only if there is sufficient objective evidence that the changes will occur. It must be remembered that we are considering the impact of future events on conditions that already exist at the balance sheet date and not on conditions arising thereafter.

For **example**, an entity may believe that the cost of cleaning up a site at the end of its life will be reduced by future changes in technology. The amount recognised should reflect the reasonable expectation of technically qualified and objective observers that the new technology will be available at the time of the clean-up. Similarly, the expected cost reductions associated with increased experience in applying existing technology, or the expected cost of applying existing technology to a larger or more complex clean-up operation than has previously been carried out, may also be taken into account. However, an entity must not anticipate the development of a completely new technology unless there is sufficient objective evidence to support that view.

FRS 12 (53) Where new legislation is "virtually certain to be enacted", the effect it is expected to have on an existing obligation should be taken into account. Evidence is required both of what legislation will demand and of whether it is virtually certain to be enacted and implemented in due course. In practice, this evidence is not available until the new legislation is actually enacted.

Reimbursements from third parties

3307 FRS 12 (56), (58) Where an entity is able to look to a third party to pay either part or all of the amount required to settle a provision, it should reduce the amount of the provision accordingly, but only if the entity:
– would not be liable for the costs even if the third party failed to pay them, or
– will be liable for the full amount of the costs not reimbursed, but the reimbursement is virtually certain to be received when the entity discharges the obligation.

In the second instance, the reimbursement should be treated as a separate asset. The amount recognised for the reimbursement should not exceed the amount of the provision.

Examples of circumstances in which an entity is able to expect a recovery from a third party are insurance contracts, indemnity clauses or suppliers' warranties. It does not make any difference whether the third party reimburses amounts paid by the entity or whether it pays the amounts directly.

Disposal of assets

Gains expected to be made on the disposal of assets should not be taken into account in measuring a provision. 3309 FRS 12 (54)

The FRS states clearly that no such gains may be recognised even if the expected disposal is closely linked to the event that gives rise to the provision.

Changes in provisions

Existing provisions should be reviewed at each balance sheet date and adjusted to reflect the current best estimate. 3311 FRS 12 (62)

Adjustments are usually required as a result of:
- revisions to estimated cash flows,
- changes to present values as a result of the passage of time, and
- revision of discount rates used to bring them in line with current market conditions.

In cases where it appears to be no longer probable that a transfer of economic benefits will be required to settle the obligation, the provision should be reversed.

D. Uses of provisions

Provisions should be used only for expenditures in respect of which they were originally created. Where the purpose for which the provision was created no longer exists, it should be eliminated. Provisions that are no longer required should not be used to absorb other unrelated, possibly unexpected, expenditure. 3313 FRS 12 (64)-(65)

E. Accounting consequences of recognising provisions

Once it has been established that an entity should recognise a provision, the question that arises is how to treat the other side of the accounting entry (i.e., the debit side). There are two choices: to create an asset account, or to charge the amount to the profit and loss account. The correct treatment will depend upon how probable the access to economic benefits is considered to be. 3315

FRS 12 requires that when a provision (or a change in a provision) is recognised, an asset can be recognised **if** (and only if) **the obligation incurred gives access to future economic benefits**. Where this is not the case and the transfer of economic benefits is merely probable, the provision should be charged to the profit and loss account. 3316 FRS 12 (66)

From a practical point of view, in the majority of cases the debit entry will be a charge to the profit and loss account and only occasionally will it give rise to the creation of an asset – such as where the provision is in respect of costs relating to the purchase of a fixed asset.

For **example**, in the oil and gas industry, an obligation for decommissioning costs arises as a consequence of commissioning an oil rig. The commissioning of the rig also gives access to an income stream from oil reserves over the years that the rig operates. Therefore, it would be appropriate to recognise the decommissioning costs as part of the total cost of the rig and capitalise them to the asset account. They would then be amortised over the useful life of the rig.

Another reason to create an asset rather than make a charge to the profit and loss account might be where an insurance recovery may be possible. This situation could arise where a provision is made in respect of injury to an employee covered by an insurance policy.

F. Disclosure requirements

3318 The sources of the rules relating to the disclosure of provisions are the Companies Act and FRS 12. The Act requires that all liabilities and losses that either have already arisen or are likely to arise in respect of the accounting period under review (or a previous year, if appropriate) must be taken into account.

3319 FRS 12 (90) For each class of provision recognised by the company, the following must be disclosed:
- a brief description of the nature of the obligation, and the expected timing of any resulting transfers of economic benefits,
- an indication of the uncertainties about the amount or timing of those transfers of economic benefits and, where necessary to provide adequate information, details of the major assumptions made concerning future events, and
- the amount of any expected reimbursement, stating the amount of any asset that has been recognised for that expected reimbursement,
- particulars of any material provision included in "other provisions".

The following table indicates the information to be provided when a transfer is made to or from a provision.

3320

	Authority: FRS 12 ¶
The carrying amount at the beginning and end of the period	89 (a)
Additional provisions made in the period, including increases to existing provisions	89 (b)
Amounts used (i.e., incurred and charged against the provision) during the period	89 (c)
Unused amounts reversed during the period	89 (d)
The increase during the period in the discounted amount arising from the passage of time and the effect of any change in the discount rate	89 (a)
The source and application of funds transferred	-

Note: Comparative figures are not required by either the Companies Act or FRS 12.

3321 The principal disclosure requirements are usually satisfied by way of a summary of movements in the notes to the accounts in a format similar to the following.

	Pensions	Deferred taxation	Other	Total
	£	£	£	£
Balance at beginning of year	**50,000**	**22,000**	**4,000**	**76,000**
Used during the year	(9,000)	–	–	(9,000)
Reversed during the year	–	(4,500)	–	(4,500)
Provided during the year and charged to profit and loss			1,000	1,000
Balance at end of year	**£ 41,000**	**£ 17,500**	**£ 5,000**	**£ 63,500**

Note that the number of columns required will depend on whether items need to be separately disclosed or whether they can be grouped together by class.

SECTION 3

Contingent liabilities

A. Definition

The FRS differentiates between "provisions" (which are liabilities) and "contingent liabilities" (which are not). **3325** FRS 12 (2)

Contingent liabilities are:

1) possible obligations that cannot be recognised as liabilities because they have not **yet come into existence** – and may never do so unless some future event takes place; and

2) obligations that have **arisen** from past events but cannot be recognised because either the **amount cannot be measured** or there is **little probability that a transfer of economic benefits** will settle them.

Contingent liabilities are therefore potential liabilities that do not meet the **recognition criteria** for provisions. The question then is whether the users of the entity's financial statements should be made aware of them by way of **disclosure in the notes**. The answer to this will depend on the circumstances, as discussed below. FRS 12 (27)-(31)

B. Criteria for disclosure

Contingent liabilities should be disclosed in the notes to the accounts **unless the probability of a transfer** of economic benefits is **remote**. **3327** FRS 12 (28)

In certain circumstances, an entity might be **jointly and severally liable** for an obligation (such as may arise in joint venture arrangements). The portion of the obligation for which the entity itself may be liable should be recognised as a provision or disclosed as a contingency depending on whether the transfer of economic benefits is probable – i.e., according to the general rules. The part of the obligation that the entity expects the **other parties** to meet should be treated as a contingent liability and disclosed if appropriate. FRS 12 (29)

From **year to year**, the status of contingent liabilities should be monitored for any changes that may require their being recognised as provisions instead. Should it become probable that a transfer of future economic benefits will be made in respect of an item previously treated as a contingent liability, a provision should be recognised in the financial statements relating to the **period in which the change in probability occurs**. The exceptions to this rule are those cases in which it is not possible to make a reliable estimate. **3328** FRS 12 (30)

Conversely, where the likelihood of a transfer of economic benefits becomes remote, it may no longer be necessary to disclose the contingency at all.

The following table summarises the possible outcomes of reviewing annually any amounts previously disclosed in the financial statements as contingent liabilities. **3329**

If the outcome of the future event giving rise to the contingency is –	Contingent liabilities should –
virtually certain	be recognised
probable	be recognised
possible	be disclosed by way of note
remote	not be disclosed

C. Disclosure requirements

3330 FRS 12 states that unless the possibility of any transfer in settlement is remote, for each class of contingent liability an entity should disclose a brief description and, if practicable, the following:
- an estimate of its financial effect,
- an indication of the uncertainties as to amount or timing, and
- the possibility, if any, of reimbursement.

3331 The Companies Act requires disclosure of:
- the amount (or estimated amount) of any contingent liability,
- its legal nature, and
- whether any security has been provided in connection with it and, if so, the nature of the security.

Where there has been a charge on the assets of the company to secure the liabilities of any other person, details should be given. However, this requirement will not be necessary if the existence of the charge creates a contingent liability that will in any event have to be disclosed.

Guarantees and other financial commitments (e.g., bills discounted) undertaken on behalf of:
- parent or fellow subsidiary undertakings, or
- any subsidiary

of the company should be disclosed separately.

SECTION 4

Contingent assets

3333 FRS 12 (31), (33) In general, entities should choose against recognising contingent assets in their financial statements. The reason is simple: recognising such assets could result, in turn, in the recognition of profits that may never be realised. However, in situations where it is **virtually certain** that the profit will arise, then the related asset is not a contingent asset – but in fact a real one – and its **recognition is appropriate**.

3334 FRS 12 (32), (94) Contingent assets generally come about from unplanned or other unexpected events that give rise to the possibility of an inflow of economic benefits to the entity. Where such an inflow of economic benefits is **probable**, an entity should **disclose the nature of the contingent asset** at the balance sheet date and, if practicable, an estimate of its financial effect.

Disclosure

3335 FRS 12 (94) Where an inflow of economic benefits is probable, a brief description of the nature of the contingent assets at the balance sheet date should be given together with an estimate of their financial effect, if practicable.

FRS 12 (95) Care should be taken that disclosures for contingent assets do not give a misleading indication of the likelihood that a profit may arise from contingent assets.

FRS 12 (96) As in the case of contingent liabilities, if any of the disclosures relating to contingent assets are not made because it is not practicable to do so, that fact should be stated.

SECTION 5

Schematic summary

The following diagram, adapted from Appendix II to FRS 12, illustrates the steps to be taken in deciding whether an obligating event gives rise to a provision or a contingent liability, or whether neither provision nor disclosure should be made. 3340

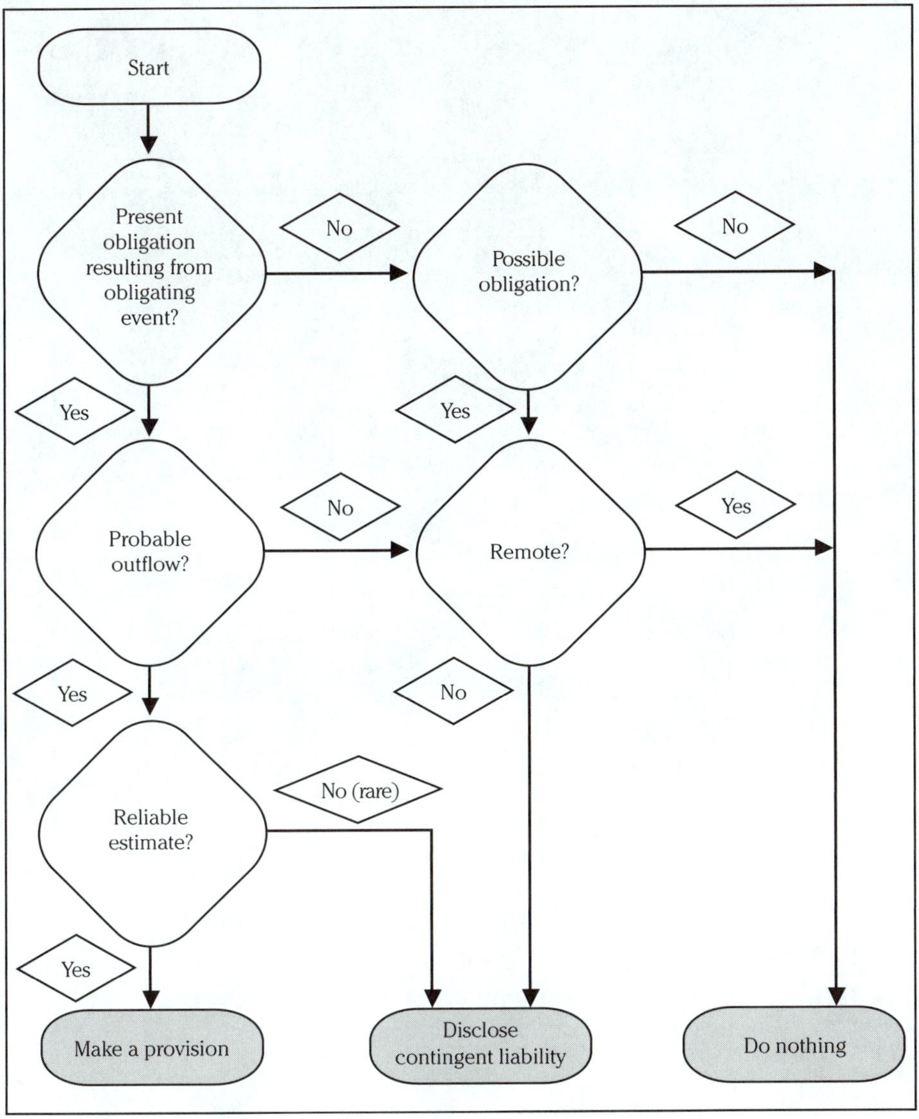

CHAPTER 4

Leasing and hire purchase contracts

OUTLINE ¶¶

Leases and hire purchase contracts are a major source of finance for businesses in the UK because they provide the mechanism by which to (i) obtain the **right to use** assets, or (ii) **buy** them without a possible adverse effect on liquidity that a cash transaction might entail. **3400**

SSAP 21 "Accounting for leases and hire purchase contracts" does the following: SSAP 21 (1)

- codifies the **principles to be applied** in accounting for leases and hire purchase contracts;
- draws a **distinction** between hire purchase contracts, finance leases and operating leases;
- specifies standard accounting practice through a comprehensive series of **guidance notes**; and
- sets out the **disclosures** required to be observed in addition to those specified by company law.

All leases transfer some of the **risks and rewards of ownership** to the lessee, and the distinction between an operating lease and a finance lease is essentially one of degree, as discerned from the **terms of the contract** between the lessor and lessee. Assets held under both finance leases and operating leases are not legally owned by the lessee because the rights granted relate to use, and not ownership. **3402**

Hire purchase contracts are structured in a similar way to leasing arrangements. However, there is one fundamental difference: at the end of the contract there is a further payment by the hirer, sometimes optional and often for a notional amount, which the hirer pays to acquire ownership of the asset he has been "hiring". In spite of this, the accounting for hire purchase contracts is essentially the same as that for leases.

3403 In **accounting for leases**, one must determine whether the lease in question is, in the context of the life of the asset, a relatively short-term hire contract with most risks associated with the asset remaining with the lessor and with rentals charged to the profit and loss account (operating lease), or whether it is a financing arrangement for the use of fixed assets (finance lease), where the accounting requirements are based on the **substance of the transaction**.

MEMO POINTS The Finance and Leasing Association (FLA) issued a SORP in April 2000 entitled "Accounting issues in the asset finance and leasing industry", which endorses the requirements of FRS 5 and SSAP 21, in that lease transactions should be accounted for in accordance with the substance of the transaction and not simply their legal form. Under FRS 5, the classification of a SSAP 21 transaction can be challenged if the resulting treatment contradicts the substance of the transaction.

The **key differences** between UK GAAP and IAS (IFRS) are addressed in this chapter as are the **proposals** contained in a discussion document published by the IASB.

SECTION 1

Classifications and terminology

3405 SSAP 21 provides a detailed list of definitions and terminology relating to the accounting for leases and hire purchase agreements, which are set out in the table below and the notes that follow.

Classification	Definition
Lease	A contract between a lessor and a lessee for the use of a specific asset for a specified period of time, in return for a stream of rental payments. Legal title to the asset remains with the lessor.
Lessor	The entity holding the legal title to an asset that it leases to another entity.
Lessee	A party who leases an asset from a lessor.
Finance lease	A lease that transfers substantially all the risks and rewards of ownership of an asset to the lessee. SSAP 21 (18). Finance leases are recorded on the balance sheet.
Operating lease	A lease other than a finance lease, which usually involves the lessee paying a rental for the hire of an asset for a period of time, normally substantially less than its useful economic life. Operating lease payments are recognised as an expense over the lease term.
Hire purchase contract	A method of buying goods where the purchaser takes immediate possession on payment of an initial instalment of the price (deposit). Legal title passes to purchaser when all instalments have been paid.
Sale and leaseback transaction	A sale and leaseback transaction is a linked arrangement (¶3485), typically involving a property, in which the owner of the asset sells that asset and then leases it back from the purchaser.

Terminology

3406 SSAP 21 (19) **1. Lease term** The period for which the lessee has contracted to lease the asset and any further terms for which the lessee has the option to continue to lease the asset (secondary lease period, with or without further payment). It should be reasonably certain at the inception of the lease that the lessee will exercise the option if that period is to be included in the lease term for the purposes of assessing the nature of the lease.

2. Present value The present value of a leased asset should be calculated using the interest rate implicit in the lease. 3407

3. The interest rate implicit in a lease is the discount rate that at the inception of a lease, when applied to the amounts that the lessor expects to receive and retain, produces an amount (i.e. the present value) equal to the fair value of the leased asset. 3408 SSAP 21 (24)

The amounts the lessor expects to receive and retain consist of:

a. the minimum lease payments to the lessor, as defined above, *plus*

b. any residual value not guaranteed, *minus*

c. any part of (a) and (b) for which the lessor will be accountable to the lessee.

If the interest rate implicit in the lease is not determinable, it should be estimated by reference to the rate that a lessee would be expected to pay on a similar lease.

4. Minimum lease payments are classified as the minimum payments over the remaining part of the lease term, excluding charges for services and taxes to be paid by the lessor, and: 3409 SSAP 21 (20)

- in the case of the **lessee**, any residual amounts guaranteed by him or by a party related to him, or;
- in the case of the **lessor**, any residual amounts guaranteed by the lessee or by an independent third party.

5. Early termination Where the lease contains an option for early termination, any calculation of the minimum lease payments that accounts for the exercise of the option should also include any penalty payments attached to the termination. 3410

6. Fair value The price at which an asset could be exchanged in an arm's length transaction less, where applicable, any grants receivable towards the purchase or use of the asset. 3411 SSAP 21 (25)

7. Finance charge The amount borne by the lessee over the lease term, representing the difference between the total of the minimum lease payments, including any residual amounts guaranteed, and the amount at which the leased asset is recorded in the balance sheet at the inception of the lease. 3412 SSAP 21 (27)

8. The gross investment in a lease represents the total of the lease payments and any residual value (not guaranteed) accruing to the lessor. 3413 SSAP 21 (21)

9. Net investment in a lease comprises the gross investment in a lease less gross earnings allocated to future periods. 3414 SSAP 21 (22)

10. Net cash investment in a lease is the total funds invested in a lease by the lessor, including the cost of the asset plus or minus the following payments and receipts: 3415 SSAP 21 (23)

- grants (i.e., government grants, see ¶7900) towards the purchase price of the asset;
- rentals receivable;
- taxation payments and receipts (including capital allowances);
- residual values at the end of the lease term;
- interest payments on loans to finance asset purchases;
- interest receivable on cash surpluses; and
- profit extracted from the lease.

SECTION 2

Accounting: Lessees

This section covers the accounting treatment for hire purchase contracts, operating leases and finance leases. 3417

SSAP 21 requires **assets held under finance leases** and the **related leasing obligations** to be capitalised on the lessee's balance sheet. A hire purchase is normally accounted for in a SSAP 21 (10) similar way. However, under an **operating lease**, the lessee accounts only for the rental as a charge to the profit and loss account.

3418 **Non-material leases** that would otherwise be accounted for as finance leases may be accounted for as **operating leases**. The size criteria for a lease, or aggregate of a number of leases, is in relation to:
- total fixed assets,
- total borrowings,
- the gearing ratio, and
- the profit or loss for the year.

MEMO POINTS Gearing ratios express a company's capital gearing. There are a number of ratios that can be calculated from the balance sheet or profit and loss account. Ratios based on the balance sheet usually express debt as a percentage of equity, or a percentage of debt plus equity.

3419 When **assessing materiality**, a lessee should assess the lease both individually and in aggregate with other similar leases. For example, where a company leases a single computer on a finance lease, this would not be deemed material. However, if that company leases 100 individual computers on finance leases, then their treatment as operating leases may materially distort the balance sheet and the finance lease rules should be applied.

A. Operating leases

3420 SSAP 21 (8) An operating lease is a **lease other than a finance lease**, which usually involves the lessee's paying a rental charge for the hire of an asset for a period of time, normally substantially less than its useful economic life. The lessor retains most of the risks and rewards of ownership of an asset in the case of an operating lease.

3421 SSAP 21 (37) **Basis for allocating rentals** The rentals under an operating lease should be charged as an **expense** on a straight-line basis over the lease term, even if the payments are for differing amounts, unless another basis is more appropriate, such as where the rentals of an asset are based on:
- the actual usage of that asset,
- periodic revisions that reflect market rates (e.g., property leases), or
- the efficiency of the asset.

3422 **Property leases** A **lessee** may be offered various incentives, for instance a rent-free period, as an inducement to enter into a new lease transaction (see also ¶3466). Other incentives include contributions to service costs, relocation costs or refurbishment. UITF 28 requires that any lease benefits or inducements should be accounted for as a reduction in rental costs. The **value of the benefits** should be allocated on a straight-line basis over the shorter of the lease term or the period to the first rent review date.

B. Finance leases

3424 SSAP 21 (32) Assets held under a finance lease should be recognised on the balance sheet of the lessee as both an **asset** and an **obligation (liability)** to pay future rentals. Such assets should be described as "leased assets" in order to distinguish them from owned assets and they should be **depreciated** over the shorter of the lease term or their useful economic life.

3425 SSAP 21 (8) A finance lease is a lease that **transfers substantially all the risks and rewards of ownership** of an asset to the lessee. A finance lease usually involves payment by a lessee to a lessor of the full cost of the asset together with a return for the finance provided by the lessor. It is the transfer of risk that distinguishes the finance lease from an operating lease.

The **terms and conditions** attached to each lease agreement must be reviewed to determine whether it is a finance lease, and in particular a test (see ¶3428) should be applied to determine the net present value (NPV) of the minimum lease payments relative to the fair value of the leased asset. SSAP 21 uses this assessment of the NPV of minimum lease payment as a benchmark in determining whether substantially all the risk and rewards of ownership have been transferred to the lessee.

At the **inception of the lease**, the sum to be recorded as an asset should be the present value of the minimum lease payments, derived by discounting them at the rate of interest implicit in the lease. The lease is deemed to start at the earlier of: **3426**
- the date on which the asset is first used by the lessee; or
- the date from which lease rentals first accrue.

For **example**, if a lease provides for an initial rent-free period at the start of the lease term, the lessee should adopt, as the inception date, the date on which it first used the property.

Rationale for capitalisation

If a company were to **lease an asset** in preference to purchasing it outright and not capitalise it and its associated obligations, then potentially large off-balance sheet liabilities could be accumulated of which a user of the accounts would be unaware. In addition, the leased assets employed would not be reflected on the balance sheet, and as such, these omissions may mislead both internal and external users of a company's accounts in various ways, as follows: **3427** SSAP 21 (Foreword)

1. **External users** may use a company's accounts when making investment or credit decisions. The capitalisation of assets held under finance leases means that the company's assets and obligations are more readily apparent than if leased assets and obligations are not recognised.
2. **Internal users** such as divisional managers may in some cases not be aware of, nor involved in, the choice of finance for the assets that they use. Without capitalisation, the choice of leasing or buying could result in a divisional manager's performance being assessed by reference to a misleading figure of capital employed. At the group level, both assets and obligations, and thus gearing, would be similarly understated.

The 90-percent test

There is a presumption that if the net present value of minimum lease payments exceeds 90 percent of the fair value of a leased asset, the lease is a finance lease (see ¶3444, below). **3428**

Further, the presumption is that a **transfer of risks and rewards** occurs if – at the inception of a lease – the present value of the minimum lease payments, including any initial payment, amounts to substantially all, i.e., 90 percent or more, of the fair value of the leased asset.

Rebuttal of presumption In **exceptional circumstances**, this presumption may be rebutted if it can be clearly demonstrated that although the lease in question exceeds the 90-percent threshold test, it does not transfer substantially all the risks and rewards of ownership, other than legal title to the lessee, as other factors may indicate otherwise. **3429** SSAP 21 (16)

Likewise, **where the threshold is not met** the lease could still be classified as a finance lease if other terms and conditions of the lease support this. However, SSAP 21 does not state that a minimum value less than 90 percent automatically represents an operating lease as greater emphasis may need to be placed on other factors.

Other factors The classification of a lease should be based on the most likely course of events. Therefore, **evaluation of a lease** requires an examination of the **lease agreement** including supporting schedules, covering rental payments, and rebates to which the 90-percent test can be applied and arrangements applicable if the lease runs its full term; namely the inclusion of: **3430**

– options,
– balloon payments,
– guarantees,
– process of disposal of asset,
– break clauses with the option to return equipment and cancel further rentals, and
– the useful economic life of the asset relative to the term of the lease.

Other relevant clauses cover insurance, maintenance procedures, and insolvency. For instance, with property leases, the present values of rentals often exceed 90 percent of the fair value of the property.

However, they are often not classified as finance leases but operating leases, because:
– the useful economic life of the asset is expected to be considerably longer than the term of the lease; and
– the lessor retains the right (reward) to raise rents (rent review) during the term of the lease.

The financial consequences of **terminating a lease contract** must be taken into account.

3431 SSAP 21 (34) **Impact of grants and capital allowances** The benefit to a lessor of regional development and other grants together with capital allowances (which reduce tax liabilities) may enable the minimum lease payments under a finance lease to be reduced to a total that is less than the fair value of the asset. In these circumstances, the amount to be capitalised and depreciated should be restricted to the minimum lease payments. A **negative finance charge** should not be shown.

Apportioning rentals between capital repayments and finance charges

3435 Rental payments should be apportioned between the finance charge and a reduction of the outstanding obligation for future amounts payable.

SSAP 21 (35) The **total finance charge** under a finance lease should be allocated to accounting periods during the lease term so as to produce a constant (or a reasonable approximation) periodic rate of charge on the remaining balance of the lease obligation for each accounting period.

3436 **Methods of apportioning rentals** The table below illustrates the **main methods** used by lessees for apportioning the rental payments between the finance charge and capital obligation under a **finance lease**. The methods of apportioning rentals under other types of leases are shown for comparison.

As will be seen in the examples below, the different methods can produce significantly different results; care must therefore be taken when selecting the method.

Type of lease	Method of apportioning rentals
Finance lease	Straight-line method Sum-of-the-digits method Actuarial method
Hire purchase contracts (¶3447)	As for finance leases
Sale and leaseback (¶3485)	Depends on whether classified as finance or operating lease
Operating leases (¶3420)	Straight-line method

3440 **1. Straight-line method** This method writes off finance charges evenly over the lease term and as such does not take into account the reductions on the outstanding obligation for future amounts payable.

3441 **2. Sum-of-the-digits method** This method writes off finance charges over the lease term approximately in proportion to the reducing obligation for future amounts payable.

3. Actuarial method This method writes off the finance charges over the lease term based on the actual interest payable on the outstanding obligation for future amounts payable. This is based on the internal rate of return that will effectively discount the minimum lease payments to the carrying cost at which the asset is recorded. 3443

Of these methods, the actuarial method most closely accords with the objectives and requirements of SSAP 21.

The **first part** of the example below illustrates the method of determining whether the minimum lease payments equate to or exceed 90 percent of the fair value of the asset. The **second part** then compares the way the rentals would be apportioned under each of the methods outlined above.

3444

EXAMPLE **Finance lease – allocation of finance costs**

A quarrying company leased a cement mixer truck on 1 January 20X2 under the following terms:

- **Annual rental** of £10,000, for four years, first payment due on 31 December 20X2.
- **Cash price** is £28,550.
- The lease can be **extended indefinitely** after the primary period, at a nominal rental.
- The lessee is required to **maintain and insure** the mixer.
- The **interest rate** implicit in the lease is 15%.

Stage 1: 90-percent test for finance lease

1. Minimum lease payments = £10,000 × 4 = £40,000.
2. Present value of minimum lease payment, using 15% (interest rate): £10,000 x 2.855 (derived from discount tables) = £28,550
3. Fair value, taken as cash price = £28,550

As the rentals in the **secondary period** are purely nominal, they are unlikely to have a material impact on the calculation; as such, they have not been taken into account. If the secondary rentals were set at a more commercial level (but sufficiently beneficial to the lessee) to make it probable that the option for the secondary rental period would be taken up, they should be brought into the calculation.

Hence, as the present value of minimum lease payments of £40,000 is greater than 90% of the fair value of the asset, this arrangement should be treated as a **finance lease**.

Stage 2: Allocation of rental payment between finance charge and capital repayment

The total rental charge to the profit and loss account over the term of the lease will be the same for all three methods. The difference lies in the **spread of the payments** over the term of the lease.

a) Straight-line method

	£
Total minimum lease payments	40,000
Fair value of truck	28,550
Total finance charges over 4 years	11,450
Finance charges per annum	2,862.50

The **charge to the profit and loss account** under the straight-line method is **spread evenly** over the term of the lease as follows:

Instalment	**Annual rental repayment**	**Finance charge**	**Repayment of obligation**
Year ended	**£**	**£**	**£**
31 December 20X2	10,000	2,863	7,137
31 December 20X3	10,000	2,862	7,138
31 December 20X4	10,000	2,863	7,137
31 December 20X5	10,000	2,862	7,138
Total	**40,000**	**11,450**	**28,550**

b) Sum-of-the-digits method

The sum of the digits is calculated as follows:

Instalment	Digit	Relevant fraction	Total finance charges	Annual finance charge
Year ended	**£**	**£**	**£**	**£**
31 December 20X2	4	4/10	11,450	4,580
31 December 20X3	3	3/10	11,450	3,435
31 December 20X4	2	2/10	11,450	2,290
31 December 20X5	1	1/10	11,450	1,145
Total	**10**	**10/10**		**11,450**

The charge to the profit and loss account and reduction of the obligation under this method results in **higher charges in the earlier years** of the lease term as follows:

Instalment	Annual rental repayment	Finance charge	Repayment of obligation
Year ended	**£**	**£**	**£**
31 December 20X2	10,000	4,580	5,420
31 December 20X3	10,000	3,435	6,565
31 December 20X4	10,000	2,290	7,710
31 December 20X5	10,000	1,145	8,855
Total	**40,000**	**11,450**	**28,550**

c) Actuarial method

Instalment	Obligation at beginning of year	Finance charge at 15%	Subtotal	Annual repayment	Obligation at end of year
Year ended	**£**	**£**	**£**	**£**	**£**
31 December 20X2	28,550	4,282	32,832	10,000	22,832
31 December 20X3	22,832	3,425	26,257	10,000	16,257
31 December 20X4	16,257	2,439	18,696	10,000	8,696
31 December 20X5	8,696	1,304	10,000	10,000	– 0 –
Total		**11,450**		**40,000**	

Under the actuarial method, the charge to the profit and loss account is **higher in the early years** of the lease. The reduction in the outstanding lease obligation is loaded towards the end of the lease term, as follows:

Instalment	Annual repayment	Finance charge	Repayment of obligation
Year ended	**£**	**£**	**£**
31 December 20X2	10,000	4,282	5,718
31 December 20X3	10,000	3,425	6,575
31 December 20X4	10,000	2,439	7,561
31 December 20X5	10,000	1,304	8,696
Total	**40,000**	**11,450**	**28,550**

The relevant obligation in the balance sheet would be as follows:

Instalment	Total obligation	Non-current obligation	Current obligation
Year ended	**£**	**£**	**£**
31 December 20X2	22,832	16,257	6,575
31 December 20X3	16,257	8,686	7,561
31 December 20X4	8,696	-	8,696
31 December 20X5			

Summary

The following table summarises the profile of finance charges over the three available methods.

Method	Year ended 31 December 20X2	20X3	20X4	20X5	TOTAL
	£	£	£	£	£
Straight-line	2,863	2,863	2,863	2,863	11,450
Sum-of-the-digits	4,580	3,435	2,290	1,145	11,450
Actuarial	4,282	3,425	2,439	1,304	11,450

As this example demonstrates, the **straight-line method** produces a significantly different spread of finance charges to the sum-of-the-digits and the actuarial methods. This is generally the case in actual lease situations. 3445

In practice, while it is the **actuarial method** that is theoretically most pure, the sum-of-the-digits method will often produce a spread of finance charges over the life of the lease that is sufficiently close to the actuarial method to be acceptable.

When SSAP 21 was first implemented, the lack of readily available simple computer programs meant that the sum-of-the-digits method was widely used because of its relative arithmetic simplicity. The increasingly sophisticated computer programs now readily available to lessees means the actuarial methodology is increasingly being adopted.

C. Hire purchase contracts

A hire purchase contract has **similar features to a lease**, except that the hirer may acquire **legal title** by exercising an option to purchase the asset upon fulfilment of certain conditions (most commonly the payment of an agreed number of instalments). A hire purchase agreement often involves a finance company as a third party; the seller sells the goods to the finance company, which in turn enters into a hire purchase agreement with the hirer. 3447 SSAP 21 (1)

Purchase options

Purchase options at a favourable price are often included in hire purchase contract agreements. Where it is certain at the inception of the lease that the lessee will take up the option, it is therefore expected that the depreciable economic life of the asset will extend beyond the current term of the contract. While leased assets are depreciated over the period of the lease, assets held under hire purchase agreements will normally be depreciated over the full expected life of the asset. 3448

Except for that principal difference, the accounting for hire purchase contracts is to all intents and purposes the same as that for leases, usually finance leases.

It has long been accepted that **assets held under hire purchase contracts** should be recognised on the balance sheet of the hirer of the asset and this is reconfirmed in SSAP 2. Assets leased under hire purchase contracts that have the character of finance leases should be depreciated over their useful economic lives.

D. Summary

3450 The table below summarises the key requirements for accounting for finance leases and operating leases (lessees) and for hire purchase contracts (hirers).

Finance lease	
	BALANCE SHEET
Inception of the lease	**Leased asset and related lease obligation** capitalised where the net present value of minimum lease payments exceeds 90% of the fair value of the asset. This presumption is **rebutted** if other terms and conditions of the lease contradict this.
Leased assets	Describe as "**leased assets**" to distinguish them from owned assets.
Depreciation	1. Leased assets should be **depreciated** over the shorter of the lease term (including secondary lease periods), and their useful life. 2. In respect of a hire purchase contract that has the **characteristics of a finance lease**, the asset should be depreciated over its useful life.
Effect of government grants or capital allowances	The receipt of grants or capital allowances could mean that an asset is available on a finance lease such that the **minimum lease payments** are less than the fair value of the asset. Consequently, the leased asset and related lease obligations should be recorded at inception of the lease at the total of the minimum lease payments.
Rental variation clauses	**Rentals** are adjusted to reflect movements in interest rates or changes in taxation rates. Any increase or reduction in rentals should be accounted for first as an increase or reduction in finance charges; further reductions in excess of the finance charge should be reflected in the depreciation charge.
	PROFIT AND LOSS ACCOUNT
Charge to profit and loss account	1. The difference between total minimum lease payments and their present value at inception of the lease represents the finance charge to be allocated to accounting periods over the term of the lease. 2. Any difference between planned rentals at inception of lease and actual rental payments is charged to profit and loss account.
Operating lease	
Inception of the lease	Lessee pays a rental for hire of asset for a specific period of time. Lessee retains risks and rewards of asset ownership.
Allocation of rentals	Rentals should be allocated on a straight-line basis over term of the lease, unless another basis is more appropriate (¶3421).
Hire purchase contract	
Inception of the HP contract	HP contracts are similar to leases, except inasmuch as the hirer may acquire legal title through exercising an option to purchase the asset. HP agreements often involve third party finance.
Depreciation	Assets held under HP contracts should be recognised on the balance sheet of the hirer and depreciated over the full economic life of the asset.

SECTION 3

Accounting: Lessors

This section covers the accounting treatment required of lessors for leases and hire purchase contracts. 3460

Lessors fall into three broad categories, namely entities (including banks and finance houses) that: SSAP 21 (4)
- **provide finance** under lease contracts to enable a single customer to acquire the use of an asset for the greater part of its useful life,
- operate a business that involves the **renting out of assets** for varying periods and probably to more than one customer, or
- are **manufacturers or dealer lessors** (¶3480) and who use leasing as a means of marketing their products, which involves leasing a product to one customer or to several customers.

Tax-free grants – available to the lessor against the purchase price of assets acquired for leasing – should be accounted for as non-taxable income and spread over the period of the lease. Usually, some of the benefit of the grant is passed on to the lessee through reduced rentals. 3461 SSAP 21 (41)

Classification of leases As with lessee accounting, a lessor should classify a lease as operating or finance depending upon the risks passed to the lessee. It can happen that the same lease may be classified as a finance lease by the lessor but as an operating lease by the lessee. This might result from differences in cash flows and the fact that in calculating the minimum lease payments, the lessor accounts for third-party income (e.g., grants, residual values) whereas the lessee accounts only for payments made. 3462

Operating leases

For **operating leases**, the lessor treats the leased asset as a fixed asset and **depreciates** it over its useful life. Rental income from an operating lease, excluding charges for services such as insurance and maintenance, should be recognised on a **straight-line basis** over the lease period. 3463 SSAP 21 (43)

Depreciation The depreciation method adopted should reflect the usage pattern of the asset. Typically, the **straight-line method** is used especially where the use of the asset over its useful economic life takes place evenly. 3464

In order to smooth profit over the term of the lease, The Finance and Leasing Association permits the use of the **annuity method** for operating leases provided the following conditions are applicable:
- the asset is leased for a considerable part of its useful economic life;
- the lease terms protect the lessor against early termination of the lease; and
- sufficient income is retained in the lease to cover projected realisable values.

The annuity method better reflects the **time value of money** and results in a lower depreciation charge in the early years of the lease, and more even net profit after interest.

MEMO POINTS The Finance and Leasing Association has issued a SORP covering the use of the annuity method for operating leases.

Rental incentives A lessor may grant a rent-free period or an up-front cash payment or contribution to costs, as an incentive to encourage a prospective tenant to take up a lease (see also ¶3422). These incentives should be accounted for by reducing the lease income. UITF Abstract 28 requires that **reimbursement of expenditure** that does not relate solely to lessee's use of the property, but enhances the value of the property, from which the lessor will benefit beyond the term of the lease, should not be classified as a lease incentive. 3466

SSAP 21 (44) **Initial direct costs** such as commissions, or legal costs incurred by a lessor in arranging a lease, may be apportioned over the period of the lease on a systematic basis.

Finance leases

3470 A lessor generates **two types of income** from a finance lease: namely, the finance income generated by the lease and any profit on the "sale" of the asset. In accounting for **finance leases** the lessor should recognise the substance of the transaction, namely that the lessor is supplying finance to enable the lessee to use a specific asset. It is the rental income due under the finance lease that should be recognised as an asset in the balance sheet, rather than the asset itself.

SSAP 21 (38) In the balance sheet of a lessor this should be shown as a debtor at the amount of the net investment in the lease (¶3411) after making provisions for items such as bad and doubtful rentals receivable.

3471 **Lessor rentals** The rentals received by the lessor should be apportioned between finance income to the lessor and repayment of the debtor balance, so reducing the net investment in the lease by the lessor over the term of the lease. Over the period of the lease the finance income represents the gross earnings. **Total gross earnings** under a finance lease should normally be allocated to accounting periods to give a constant periodic rate of return to the lessor's net cash investment in the lease in each period.

3472 **Methods of allocating rental payments** The guidance notes in SSAP 21 propose two methods by which lessors allocate gross earnings on finance leases, namely:
- the actuarial method; and
- the investment period method.

The latter method is deemed the more prudent although both methods require complex calculations.

Hire purchase contracts

3475 SSAP 21 (31) A hire purchase contract with **characteristics similar to those of a finance lease** should be accounted for on a similar basis to that used for finance leases as set out in ¶3470 to ¶3472 above. Other hire purchase contracts should be accounted for on a similar basis to that adopted for operating leases as covered in ¶3463 to ¶3466.

SSAP 21 (39) The allocation of gross earnings so as to give a constant periodic rate of return on the finance company's net investment will in most cases be an approximation to an allocation based on the net cash investment. This is because the **capital allowances** under a hire purchase contract are claimed by the lessee and therefore the lessor's net cash investment will not be significantly different from its net investment.

The guidance notes in SSAP 21 give examples of two methods applicable to hire purchase contracts, namely:
- the actuarial method; and
- the sum-of-the-digits method.

The detail behind these methods is beyond the scope of this book.

3476 SSAP 21 (40) As an **alternative treatment**, an allocation may first be made out of gross earnings of an amount equal to the lessor's estimated cost of finance included in the net cash investment calculation, with the balance being recognised on a systematic basis.

Special requirements for a manufacturer/dealer lessor

3480 SSAP 21 (45) A manufacturer or dealer lessor should not recognise a **selling profit under an operating lease** because the legal rights to the asset have been retained in order to generate rental income. Therefore, the asset should be included in the balance sheet initially at production cost or purchase price.

The **selling profit under a finance lease** should be restricted to the excess of the fair value of the asset over the manufacturer's or dealer's cost, less any grants receivable by the manufacturer or dealer towards the purchase, construction or use of the asset. The profit on the sale of the asset should be recognised at the commencement of the lease.

SECTION 4

Sale and leaseback transactions

Where a company owns an asset but subsequently sells that asset to a third party – typically a finance company – and leases that asset back, the accounting treatment of the sale will depend upon whether the leaseback is in the nature of a finance lease or an operating lease. **3485** SSAP 21 (46)

The leaseback itself will then be accounted for in accordance with the rules for operating and finance leases outlined above.

Where a sale and leaseback transaction results in a **finance lease**, any apparent profit or loss (i.e., the difference between the sale price and the previous carrying value of the asset) should be deferred and amortised in the financial statements of the seller/lessee over the shorter of:

- the lease term, and
- the useful life of the asset.

An example of a sale and leaseback transaction that should be classified as a finance lease is a long lease on a property at a fixed rental.

Where the leaseback arrangement is an **operating lease** – i.e., where significant risks and rewards of ownership have been transferred to the purchaser – the fair value of the asset should be determined and compared with the price of the sale contract. Any differences are accounted for as follows: **3486** SSAP 21 (47)

Condition If:	Accounting treatment
a. Sale price is equal to the fair value but above book value	Any profit or loss on the sale should be recognised immediately.
b. Sale price is below fair value	No action is required.
c. Sale price exceeds fair value	The difference between the book value and the fair value should be taken to the profit and loss account. Any excess of the sale price over fair value should be deferred and amortised over the shorter of the remainder of the lease term and the period to the next rent review, if any.
d. Sale price is also below the book value	The shortfall resulting from lower lease rental income should be carried forward and charged to the profit and loss account over the period to the next rent review, or end of the lease period.

EXAMPLE **a. Sale price is EQUAL TO fair value**

	£
Book value	350
Fair value	400
Sale price	400
Profit to be recognised	**50**
Profit deferred	**-**

b. Sale price is BELOW fair value

	£
Book value	350
Fair value	400
Sale price	370
Profit to be recognised	**20**
Profit deferred	**-**

c. Sale price is HIGHER THAN fair value

	£
Book value	350
Fair value	400
Sale price	450
Profit to be recognised	**50**
Profit deferred	**50**

The deferred profit of £50 is deferred and spread over the remaining period of the lease.

SECTION 5

Disclosures

3490 The principal disclosures required by both lessees and lessors for hire purchase contracts and the different types of lease are set out below.

A. Disclosures required of lessees

3491 The accounting policies adopted by lessees for operating leases, finance leases and hire purchase contracts should be disclosed.

Finance leases

3492 SSAP 21 (48) A finance lease should be shown in the lessee's balance sheet as both an **asset** and a corresponding **obligation**. At the inception of the lease these figures will be the same, but may well differ in subsequent years as, for example, the lease obligation is reduced on an actuarial basis whilst the asset may be amortised on a straight-line basis.

There are **two principal forms of disclosure** for fixed assets held under finance leases – namely, class of asset and cumulative disclosure.

3493 SSAP 21 (49) **Class of asset** For each class of asset the following disclosures in respect of finance leases are required:
– the gross amounts of assets;
– related accumulated depreciation; and
– the total depreciation allocated for the period in respect of assets held under finance leases for each major class of asset.

EXAMPLE **Finance leases**

Extract from balance sheet of D Limited at 31 December 20X4

Fixed assets	£
Plant and equipment under finance leases	28,550
Less: Accumulated depreciation	3,570
Net book value	24,980

Cumulative disclosure The alternative treatment afforded by SSAP 21 is to include the information set out in ¶3492, within the **overall totals of fixed assets**. The totals of 3494 SSAP 21 (50)
- gross amounts,
- accumulated depreciation,
- net amount, and
- depreciation allocated for the period for each major class of asset

are included with similar amounts in respect of owned fixed assets and not separately disclosed.

Where this **alternative treatment** is adopted, the **net value of assets** held under finance leases included in the overall total should be disclosed. The amount of depreciation allocated for the period in respect of assets held under finance leases included in the overall total should also be separately disclosed. This latter treatment is widely adopted in practice.

Net obligations The amounts of obligations related to finance leases, net of finance charges allocated to future periods, should 3495 SSAP 21 (51)

a. be disclosed separately from other obligations on the face of the balance sheet or in the notes to the accounts; or

b. where the total of these items is combined on the balance sheet with other obligations and liabilities, give the equivalent analysis of the total in which it is included.

Net obligations under finance leases should be **analysed between**:
- amounts payable in the next year;
- amounts payable in the second to fifth years inclusive from the balance sheet date; and
- the aggregate amounts payable thereafter. SSAP 21 (52)

If the analysis is presented according to (a) above, a lessee may, as an alternative to analysing the net obligations, analyse the gross obligations, with future finance charges being separately deducted from the total.

EXAMPLE **Finance lease – disclosure of lease obligations**

X Limited

Balance sheet (extract) at 31 December 20X1

Liabilities	£
Current obligations under finance leases	6,575
Non-current obligations under finance leases	16,257
	22,832

Notes to the accounts

The company's commitments at 31 December 20X1 to future **minimum lease payments** are as follows:

Finance charges	£
Amounts payable within one year	10,000
Amounts payable in the second to fifth years	20,000
Amounts payable after five years	-
	30,000
Less: Finance charges allocated to future periods	7,168
	22,832

Alternative disclosure – Notes to the accounts

The company's commitments at 31 December 20X1 in respect of **future net obligations** are as follows:

	£
Amounts payable within one year	6,575
Amounts payable in second to fifth years	16,257
	22,832

Aggregate finance charges allocated for the period in respect of finance leases should be disclosed, as should the amount of any commitments existing at the balance sheet date in respect of finance leases which have been entered into but whose inception occurs after the year-end. 3497 SSAP 21 (53)

EXAMPLE **ABC Group Ltd**
Notes to the accounts 31 December 20X1

15. Finance leases
The Group has contracted to lease an asset under a finance lease, under which the asset will be supplied and rental obligations incurred from April 20X2. The minimum payments under the lease amount to £18,000 over a period of three years.

3500 The Regulations to the Companies Act require that particulars should be given of any financial commitments that have not been provided for and that are relevant to assessing the company's state of affairs. While finance leases are capitalised by lessees, the obligations under finance leases should be provided for in the accounts. The Regulations also require disclosure of the amount charged to revenue in respect of sums payable for the hire of plant and machinery.

The balance sheet formats require that:
- creditors falling due within one year should be shown separately from creditors falling due after more than one year; and
- amounts falling due after more than one year shall be shown separately from each item included under debtors. This is relevant to the disclosure of amounts receivable by a lessor.

Operating leases

3504 SSAP 21 (55) The total of **operating lease rentals** charged as an expense in the profit and loss account should be disclosed, and analysed between amounts payable in respect of (1) hire of plant and (2) other operating leases.

3506 The lessee should disclose the payments it is committed to make during the next year regarding operating leases, and analyse between those in which the commitment expires:
SSAP 21 (56)
- within that year;
- in the second to fifth years inclusive, and;
- more than five years from the balance sheet date.

It should be noted that this disclosure is of the amount payable in the next year and not the cumulative amount payable over the remaining lives of those leases.

Commitments should be shown separately in respect of:
- leases of land and buildings, and
- other operating leases.

EXAMPLE **ABC Group Ltd**
Notes to the accounts (extract)

At 31 December 20X1, the company had annual commitments in respect of **operating leases** as follows:

	Land and buildings £	Other assets £
Operating leases that expire:		
- Within one year	-	5,000
- In the second to fifth years inclusive	50,000	7,000
- Later than five years	30,000	-
Total annual commitment at 31 December 20X1	80,000	12,000

B. Disclosures required of lessors

Finance leases and hire purchase contracts

The following key disclosures are required: 3510 SSAP 21 (58)
1. The net investment in finance leases, and hire purchase contracts, at each balance sheet date should be disclosed under debtors as "Amounts receivable under finance leases (and hire purchase contracts)". This is an additional sub-heading over and above that required by the Act.
2. The cost of assets acquired, whether by purchase or finance lease, for the purpose of letting under finance leases.

Operating leases

The gross values of assets held for use in operating leases and the related accumulated depreciation charges should be disclosed. 3512

Other disclosures should also be made of: 3514 SSAP 21 (60)
1. The **accounting policy** adopted for operating leases and finance leases and, in detail, the policy for accounting for finance lease income;
2. The **aggregate rentals receivable** in respect of an accounting period in relation to finance leases, and operating leases; and
3. The **cost of assets acquired**, whether by purchase or finance lease, for the purpose of letting under finance leases.

EXAMPLE **Annual Report and Accounts – (extract)**
Q Ltd
Accounting policies

Finance leases Assets obtained under finance leases are included in tangible fixed assets at cost and are depreciated over their useful economic lives, or the term of their lease, whichever is the shorter. Future instalments under such leases, net of finance charges, are included within creditors. Rental payments are apportioned between the financial element, which is charged to the profit and loss account, and the capital element, which reduces the outstanding obligation for future instalments, so as to give a constant rate of charge on the outstanding obligation.
Hire purchase transactions are treated similarly, except that the assets are depreciated over their useful economic lives.
Operating leases Rental payments under operating leases are charged to the profit and loss account on a straight-line basis over the term of the lease, even if the payments are not made on such a basis. Assets held for leasing under operating leases are included in tangible fixed assets at cost less accumulated depreciation.

SECTION 6

Key differences between UK GAAP and IAS (IFRS)

SSAP 21 is similar in most respects compared with IAS 17 "Accounting for leases". Both IAS 17 and SSAP 21 define leases as leases that transfer all the risks and rewards of ownership to the lessee, although some **significant differences** exist as explained below. Both accounting standards also require lessees to capitalise assets subject to a finance lease and to recognise the matching obligation, and lessors to account for the asset as a receivable and allocate the finance income over the lease period. 3520

The **significant differences** between the two accounting standards are that:
– the definition in IAS 17 of a finance lease does not contain a rebuttable presumption equivalent to the 90-percent test.

– under IAS 17, the net cash method is not recognised; lessors must therefore recognise income based on the **net** investment method.
– IAS 17 requires more detailed disclosures as set out below.

MEMO POINTS Note that the IASB is working on a project to replace IAS 17, see ¶3528.

Additional disclosures required under IAS 17

3524
IAS 17 (23) (27)

Additional disclosures required under IAS 17 by Lessees
In respect of finance leases
1. A reconciliation between the total minimum lease payments at the balance sheet date and their present value.
2. Any contingent rents recognised in the period.
3. A general description of leasing arrangements including the basis of contingent rents, renewal and purchase options and restrictions imposed by leasing arrangements.
In respect of operating leases
1. The total of future sublease payments expected to be received under non-cancellable subleases.
2. A general description of leasing arrangements including the basis for contingent rents, renewal and purchase options and restrictions imposed by leasing arrangements.
3. Lease and sublease payments recognised in the financial period, including separate disclosure of minimum lease payments, contingent rents and sublease payments.

3526
IAS 17 (39) (48)

Additional disclosures required under IAS 17 by Lessors
In respect of finance leases
1. A reconciliation between the total gross investment in the lease and the present value of the minimum lease payments receivable at the balance sheet date.
2. The total gross investment in the lease and the present value of the minimum lease payments receivable, for each of the following: not later than one year; between one year and five years; after five years.
3. Unearned finance income.
4. Contingent rents recognised in income.
5. A general description of leasing arrangements.
6. Details of any accumulated provisions for minimum lease payments receivable but not collectable.
In respect of operating leases
1. A general description of leasing arrangements.
2. Details of any accumulated impairment losses, for each class of asset.
3. Impairment losses and reversals for the financial period.
4. Total depreciation charged for the financial period.
5. Contingent rents recognised in income.
6. Future minimum lease payments under non-rescindable operating leases in aggregate, for each of the following: not later than one year; more than one year and not later than five years; after five years.

SECTION 7

Current developments

The International Accounting Standards Board (IASB) is undertaking a project to replace IAS 17, "Leases". The project is being carried out jointly with the US Financial Accounting Standards Board (FASB). 3528

Under existing accounting standards, leases are **classified** as either finance leases or operating leases. If a lease is a finance lease, the transaction is treated as if the leased asset has been sold by the lessor to the lessee. As a result, the lessee recognises the leased asset and an obligation to pay for it, and the lessor derecognises the leased asset and recognises a receivable. If a lease is classified as an operating lease, the lessor continues to recognise the leased asset and a receivable for any lease payments due for the lease period to date but not yet received, and the lessee simply recognises an obligation for any lease payments due for the lease period to date but not yet paid.

Over the years, this accounting model has attracted criticism from users of financial statements, whose needs are not being satisfactorily met. In particular, the following has been argued: 3529

– operating leases give rise to assets and liabilities that should be recognised in the financial statements of lessees, and

– the existence of different accounting models for finance leases and operating leases means that similar transactions can be accounted for in substantially different ways. This reduces comparability and provides opportunities to structure transactions so as to achieve a particular accounting effect.

Because of these concerns, the Boards decided to review the existing lease accounting model from first principles, in order to ensure that accounting standards require **all assets and liabilities** that arise from leases to be **recognised** in the balance sheet. 3530

The IASB issued an Exposure Draft in August 2010, proposing a "right-of-use" accounting model in terms of which lessees and lessors record all leases on the balance sheet. However, the proposals go beyond the mere elimination of operating lease accounting, as they include far-reaching changes to the recognition, measurement and disclosures for assets and liabilities arising from leases.

For **lessees**, the proposals are based on the premise that a lessee has acquired a "right-of-use" to use the underlying asset, and it pays for that right with the lease payments. A lessee would record: 3531

– an asset for its right to use the underlying asset (the right-of-use asset); and

– a liability to pay rentals (liability for lease payments).

For **lessors**, the accounting would reflect the exposure of a lessor to the risks or benefits of the underlying asset: 3532

– when the lease transfers significant risks or benefits of the underlying asset to the lessee, a lessor would apply the derecognition approach. This approach requires the lessor to take part of the underlying asset off its balance sheet (i.e., to derecognise it) and record a right to receive lease payments. It is possible that a lessor could record a gain on commencement of the lease under this approach;

– when the lessor retains exposure to significant risks or benefits of the underlying asset, the lessor would apply the performance obligation approach. This approach requires the lessor to keep the underlying asset on its balance sheet and to record a right to receive lease payments and a liability to permit the lessee to use the underlying asset (a lease liability). The lessor records income over the expected life of the lease.

CHAPTER 5

Share capital and reserves

OUTLINE ¶¶

3600 The objectives of the Companies Act in relation to share capital and reserves are twofold:
1. **recording their issue** and the consideration received, the **maintenance** of share capital and reserves, and the **protection of the rights** of shareholders and creditors,
2. providing a framework for the **presentation** of useful information about the share capital and reserves.

This chapter summarises the legal issues surrounding share capital and reserves. It also explains the general requirements for the calculation of the relevant amounts and how they are required to be disclosed in the financial statements with reference not only to the Companies Act but also Financial Reporting Standards and the Listing Rules.

SECTION 1

Issue of share capital

I. First issue of shares

3602 Under the Companies Act 1985, all companies incorporated in the UK with the exception of companies limited by guarantee are obliged to have an authorised share capital and a minimum number of members.

As of 1 October 2009, when the relevant provisions of the Companies Act 2006 came into force, the requirement for an authorised share capital was discontinued on incorporation.

A. Types of shares

3604 Shares can be of various types and classes, including **ordinary** shares, **preference** shares, **redeemable** shares and non-voting shares. The differences between each type depend on the rights they confer on their holders. While companies are, in general, free to issue the types and classes of shares in the numbers and ratios they choose, they may not issue redeemable shares unless:
- they are authorised to do so in the Articles, and
- there are also non-redeemable shares in issue.

MEMO POINTS

In October 2009, when the relevant provisions of the Companies Act 2006 came into effect, the requirement for prior authorisation in the Articles for a proposed allotment of redeemable shares was removed. The members may, however, restrict or prohibit the company's ability to issue redeemable shares by including a provision to this effect in the Articles.

Equity and non-equity shares – an historical perspective

3605 Both the **Companies Act** and **FRS 4**, "Capital Instruments", differentiate between equity and non-equity share capital.

s 548 CA 2006 The Act describes **equity shares** as those conferring unrestricted rights to shareholders to participate in distributions – both by way of dividends and on winding up. In general, **ordinary shares** meet this definition.

FRS 4 defines equity shares as "shares other than non-equity shares" and describes **non-equity shares** as those possessing any of the following characteristics: 3606 FRS 4 (12)
- **rights to receive payments** (e.g., dividends, on redemption or otherwise) are limited to a certain amount that is not dependent on the company's assets or profits, or the dividends on any class of equity share;
- **rights to participate in a surplus** on winding up are limited to a specific amount that does not depend on the company's assets or profits and the limitation had a commercial effect in practice either when the shares were issued or, if later, when the limitation was introduced;
- they are **redeemable according to their terms of issue** or at the option of the holder (or a party other than the issuer).

EXAMPLE A Ltd has three classes of shares in issue:
- "A" shares with a right to receive dividends as recommended by the directors,
- "B" shares, which also carry the right to dividends as recommended by the directors but only if profits before dividends are in excess of a certain amount, and
- "C" shares, which entitle holders to a fixed dividend plus a percentage of the dividend paid on ordinary shares.

The "A" shares are clearly equity shares because there is no limitation on their rights to participate in a distribution.
The "B" shares are also equity shares because the restrictions on their rights are dependent upon the company's profits.
The "C" shares (participating preference shares) are non-equity shares because of the fixed element of the dividend they carry.

Equity and financial liabilities

For accounting periods beginning on or after 1 January 2005, FRS 25, "Financial Instruments: Disclosure and Presentation" has the effect of withdrawing FRS 4 (except for material on the measurement of debt and gains and losses on the repurchase of debt) for all entities applying the measurement requirements of FRS 26. FRS 25 requires all financial instruments to be classified as equity, financial liabilities, or financial assets and therefore FRS 4's **distinction between equity and non-equity** falls away and becomes instead a **distinction between equity and financial liabilities**. As a result, some shares are no longer classified as share capital but as financial liabilities instead, even though their legal status remains the same as before (see examples at ¶3778). These requirements correspond with the amendments to the Companies Act that also require the classification of items on the balance sheet to follow the approach of substance over form. 3607

Equity is defined in FRS 25 as "any contract that evidences a residual interest in the assets of an entity after deducting all of its liabilities". A financial liability is defined as any liability that is:
a. a contractual obligation to deliver cash or another financial asset to another entity, or to exchange financial assets or financial liabilities with another entity under conditions that are potentially unfavourable to the entity; or
b. a contract that will or may be settled in the entity's own equity instruments and is either a non-derivative for which the entity is or may be obliged to deliver a variable number of the entity's own equity instruments, or a derivative that will or may be settled other than by the exchange of a fixed amount of cash or another financial asset for a fixed number of the entity's own equity instruments.

As an **exception**, certain puttable financial instruments and certain instruments that impose on the entity to deliver to another party a pro rata share of the net assets of the entity only on liquidation are classified as equity instruments despite meeting the definitions of a financial liability. (For details, see ¶3067.)

MEMO POINTS For the purpose of (b) above, the entity's own equity instruments do not include puttable financial instruments that are classified as equity instruments, instruments that impose on the entity an obligation to deliver to another party a pro rata share of the net assets of the entity only on liquidation and are classified as equity instruments, or instruments that are contracts for the future receipt or delivery of the entity's own equity instruments.

B. Payments for shares

1. Issue price

3609 Companies may issue shares either at nominal value or at a premium.

At nominal value When shares are issued at an **amount equal to the nominal value** (also called "par value"), the amount received must be recorded in the balance sheet as "called up" or "issued" share capital.

At a premium Shares can be issued by the company at a **price that is higher** than their nominal value. Again, the nominal value will be shown as explained, but the excess over nominal value is usually credited to a separate **share premium** account. In certain circumstances, the Companies Act permits the premium not to be recognised.

Matters relating to shares issued at a premium are discussed in further detail at ¶3745.

s 580 CA 2006 Shares may not be allotted at a discount – i.e., they cannot be issued as **fully paid** for an amount less than their nominal value.

2. Payment terms

3610 In the majority of cases in the UK, first issues of shares are paid for **in full** when issued. However, the Act does allow shares to be issued partly paid. Similarly, the issue price is usually settled in **cash**, but non-cash considerations are possible. These points are discussed below:

Partly paid up shares

3611 s 581 CA 2006 It is not obligatory that shares are paid for in full (i.e., the amount of the nominal value) at the time of issue. They may be paid for in part but the shareholder will be liable to settle the balance later when it is called up.

In the case of **private companies**, there are no rules that stipulate the minimum amount that has to be paid in respect of each share at the time of issue.

For **public companies**, there are two possibilities:

- **Issue of shares to the subscribers to the Memorandum of Association**. In this case, these shares must be paid in full.
- **Other issues of new shares**. In these cases, payments must be equal to **at least** 25 per cent of the nominal value **plus** 100 per cent of any share premium.

Any amounts owing from shareholders should be recorded as, and shown together with, assets in the balance sheet.

EXAMPLE **B Ltd** plans to issue shares with a nominal value of £1 at a premium of 50p. The company intends asking shareholders to pay 60p per share. Whether this is acceptable will depend on the company's status as either private or public, as follows.

If **B Ltd** is a **private company**, there is no minimum amount of consideration imposed by the Act and the arrangement will be acceptable.

On the other hand, if **B Ltd** is a **public company**, and the share issue is not to subscribers to the Memorandum, the Act requires that at least 25 per cent of the nominal value (i.e., 25p) plus the full amount of the premium (i.e., 50p, making a total of 75p) must be paid and allocated to share capital and share premium accordingly. Unless the potential shareholders are willing to pay this amount, the company may not go ahead with the issue.

Considerations not in cash

In general, companies may accept payment for shares (including any share premium) either in the form of cash or in the form of assets other than cash. Non-cash payments can be tangible, such as assets or shares, or intangible, such as goodwill or services. 3612

For **private companies** there are no restrictions on this rule.

For **public companies**, the following restrictions apply:
- **In respect of services**. An undertaking for services to be performed is not permitted as a form of non-cash payment.
- **In respect of payment by long term undertaking**. If the consideration for the allotment of shares includes an undertaking which is to be, or may be, performed more than five years after the date of allotment, the consideration must be in the form of cash.
- **In respect of valuation**. To be acceptable as payment for shares, a non-cash consideration must be independently valued within the six-month period before allotment. This valuation must be made by a person qualified to be the company's auditor (who may rely on the valuation of an independent expert). A copy of the valuer's report must be given to the proposed allottee. s 593 CA 2006

A valuation is not required where shares are issued:
- as a **bonus issue** and the company uses any balance on an appropriate reserve account to transfer to share capital and share premium;
- in connection with a **takeover** or **merger**;
- as payment for the **transfer** or **cancellation** of shares in another company – provided the arrangement is open to all the shareholders of the same class of shares in the other company.

C. Share capital denominated in foreign currencies

It is permissible that UK companies issue share capital denominated in foreign currencies. 3613
Public companies are required by the Act to have an authorised minimum allotted share capital of 50,000 in pounds sterling or the prescribed euro equivalent. Once a company has obtained a trading certificate, there is no requirement for the authorised minimum to remain denominated in sterling or euros and, if it wishes, a public company may subsequently redenominate all of its share capital. Private companies are not restricted and may issue any amount of shares in foreign currencies. s 763 CA 2006

Difficulties are sometimes encountered when companies that have previously issued share capital in foreign currencies wish to purchase, redeem or cancel them – assuming that they have fulfilled all the necessary conditions.

EXAMPLE On 1 January 19X7, F Ltd, a UK company, issued 10,000 shares denominated in US dollars when the exchange rate was $2: £1. The shares have a nominal value of $1. On issue, and in the accounts, the share capital of $10,000 was translated to £5,000.

Because it is not the policy of F Ltd to retranslate the share capital in subsequent years, at 31 December 20X2, the share capital was still shown at £5,000. On this date, however, the company repurchased the shares at nominal value.

For the sake of illustration, assume that the rate was
- $1.50: £1 (i.e., sterling had weakened against the dollar and, therefore, to purchase the shares would require more pounds than the carrying value of the shares), or
- $2.50: £1 (i.e., sterling had strengthened against the dollar and, therefore, to purchase the shares would require fewer pounds than the carrying value of the shares).

In the first case, the repurchase of the shares stated at £5,000 costs £6,667. The question arises as to which account should be debited with £1,667. Clearly, because the shares were issued at par, there is no balance in the share premium account to offset the debit. The entry will therefore have to be debited against distributable profits.

Similarly, in the second case, the amount required to repurchase the shares is £4,000. The "profit" on redemption of £1,000 will be credited to distributable profits.

As discussed above, where shares are repurchased out of distributable profits, an amount equal to their nominal value must be transferred to the capital redemption reserve. Once again, there is a question about the exchange rate to use. The company can use either the historic exchange rate, representing the nominal value of the shares when they were issued, or it can use the rate prevailing at the time of redemption and representing the nominal value of the reduction in share capital. The answer to this question has not been definitively decided upon and therefore companies finding themselves in this situation should seek legal advice.

D. Financial assistance for the acquisition of own shares

1. Public companies

3615 s 678 CA 2006 The Companies Act prohibits public companies from giving **direct or indirect** financial assistance to any entity for the purpose of acquiring either the company's own shares or those of its holding company.

There are, however, situations in which financial assistance is permissible: the Act does not prohibit transactions in which the giving of financial assistance for acquiring shares may be **incidental** to some larger purpose, where the assistance is given in good faith and in the company's interests.

In the following cases, the prohibitions against financial assistance do not apply to public companies that can show their assets are not reduced as a result (or, if they are reduced, the assistance is provided out of distributable profits):
- where **lending** of money is part of the **ordinary business** of the company and a loan is made in the normal course of business;
- where the financial assistance is given in respect of an **employees' share scheme** or to enable or facilitate transactions in the company's shares between employees, former employees, their spouses, widows, infant children or stepchildren;
- where a loan is made to bona fide **employees** (but not directors) to enable them to purchase shares in the company or its holding company to be held by them by way of beneficial ownership.

MEMO POINTS **Indirect assistance** includes loans, gifts, guarantees, indemnities or any other mechanism that would allow the other entity to receive financial assistance. Financial assistance also refers to the provision of funds (whether directly or indirectly) to enable another party to reduce or discharge any liability it has incurred in the acquisition of the company's and/or its holding company's shares.

2. Private companies

3617 In general, private companies were prohibited, under the Companies Act 1985, from giving direct or indirect financial assistance to any entity for the purpose of acquiring either the company's own shares or those of its holding company. However, from 1 October 2008, this prohibition was repealed by the Companies Act 2006 and private companies are now able to provide financial assistance for the purchase of their own shares.

3618 In the case of **groups**, where a private company takes advantage of the exceptions in order to give assistance in connection with the acquisition of shares in its **parent**, the following rules apply:
- the parent must also be a private company
- a private company (A) may not give assistance for the acquisition of shares in its private parent (B) if B has a subsidiary that is a public company (C) and C is a parent of A.

– special resolutions and statutory declarations are required from the company giving the assistance, the company whose shares are the subject of the financial assistance, and any other company that is an intermediate holding company of the company giving the assistance.

II. Increases in share capital

Share capital can be increased in various ways including: 3622
– **issuing additional shares** for cash or other consideration,
– **converting loan capital** into share capital,
– using reserves to **make bonus issues** of additional shares to existing holders, and
– various **combinations** of the above.

A. Issue of new shares

The rules that apply to the initial issue of shares also apply to subsequent issues. However, additional factors must be taken into account. 3623

1. Pre-emption rights

When a company **wishes to allot** additional ordinary shares (or securities that are convertible into ordinary shares) for cash, it must first offer them to **existing holders** of the same class of shares or securities on terms that are either similar to, or more favourable than, the terms being offered to outsiders. These are called pre-emption rights. 3624

Private companies can dispense with pre-emption rights entirely by means of a provision in the Articles of the company. **Public** companies can, by **special resolution**, authorise directors to issue shares without regard to pre-emption rights.

2. Warrants and options

Warrants and options are securities that give their owners the right to subscribe for ordinary shares in the company at a fixed future time and usually at a fixed price. 3625

When a company issues warrants or options, the proceeds are treated as shareholders' funds and allocated as equity or non-equity according to the rights that attach to the underlying shares. Thereafter, the accounting depends on whether the warrants or options are exercised.

If exercised, the amount of the proceeds should include both the amount previously recognised when they were issued and the additional consideration received at the time of exercise.

Both warrants and options can lapse **if** their holders choose **not** to exercise them. This will represent a realised gain to the company and should be reflected in the STRGL (¶4300).

B. Utilisation of reserves to finance new issues

Companies may **use the available balances on reserves**, such as distributable profits, share premium, revaluation reserve or capital redemption reserve, out of which to issue additional 3630 shares to existing members. These are called **bonus shares**. Where the profit and loss account is used, the company is in reality reallocating some of its distributable profits to the capital base. Similarly, where the share premium or capital redemption reserve is used, the company is effectively exchanging one set of non-distributable reserves for another.

Sometimes companies offer **additional shares** to shareholders **in place of a cash dividend**. This is called a **scrip dividend**. The consideration to be used in recording the transaction is the value of the cash alternative (i.e., the cash dividend that could have been taken) and is treated as an appropriation of profit. To the extent that the total consideration for the shares (in other words, the dividend foregone) exceeds the par value of the shares issued in lieu thereof, the excess should be credited to the share premium account.

Scrip dividends are often treated for legal purposes as bonus issues. In this case the appropriation of profit should be written back as a movement on reserves and a transfer made from distributable profits to share capital (for the nominal value of the shares issued) and to share premium (for any excess).

If a company has offered a scrip dividend and is preparing annual financial statements before it knows the extent to which shareholders will take them up, it should treat the whole amount as a liability to pay a cash dividend. In the next accounting period it will effectively treat any amount of scrip dividend as a conversion of debt.

MEMO POINTS When debt is converted into shares, the **carrying amount** of the debt at the date of conversion is treated as the consideration received for the shares. (See ¶3805.)

SECTION 2

Reduction of share capital

3635 Companies may for various reasons **choose** to reduce their issued share capital. There are different ways in which they can do this: by a reduction of capital, by redeeming redeemable shares, or by purchasing non-redeemable shares, usually on the open market. Redemption and acquisitions of shares are discussed in the next section (¶3645).

In some cases, reductions in share capital can result from transactions the company enters into with the co-operation of members and creditors. These are discussed in this section.

3636 A reduction of capital is most commonly undertaken where:
– The company's **share capital exceeds the fair value of its underlying assets**. In this situation, it would be to the company's benefit to reduce the share capital to more closely represent the employment of its capital.
– The company has **liquid assets surplus to its needs**. Typically, in situations where a company has excess cash or other liquid resources (i.e., it has assets that are no longer needed), it may be appropriate to reduce its capital by returning these excess funds to shareholders.

3637 The freedom of a company to reduce its capital depends on its status as either **limited** or **unlimited**.

In general, **unlimited** companies are free to make distributions of capital to members. For **limited** companies, however, the **principle of capital maintenance** requires that, if any part of the permanent capital base is repaid to members, it must be:
– replenished by a transfer out of profits, or
– replaced by new capital.

3638 s 641 CA 2006 A limited company having a share capital may reduce its share capital:
a. in the case of a private company limited by shares, by special resolution supported by a solvency statement;
b. in any case, by special resolution confirmed by the court.

A company may not reduce its share capital by special resolution supported by a solvency statement if as a result of the reduction there would no longer be any member of the company holding shares other than redeemable shares.

Reduction of capital supported by solvency statement

The directors of the company must make a statement of the solvency of the company not more than 15 days before the date on which the resolution is passed and the resolution, solvency statement and a statement of capital must be delivered to the registrar within 15 days of the resolution being passed. The solvency statement must be made available to the company's members when they vote on the resolution to reduce capital. In making the solvency statement, the directors have to form the opinion that at the date of the statement there are no grounds on which the company could then be found to be able to pay or otherwise discharge its debts; that in the event of any winding-up within the following twelve months the company will be able to pay its debts in full within twelve months of the commencement of the winding-up, and that in any other case the company will be able to pay its debts as they fall due during the twelve months following the date of the statement. In doing so, the directors are required to take account of all of the company's liabilities. **3639**

Registration of resolution and supporting documents

Within 15 days after the resolution for reducing share capital is passed the company must deliver to the registrar a copy of the solvency statement and a statement of capital. The statement of capital must state with respect to the company's share capital as reduced by the resolution: **3640**

a. the total number of shares of the company,
b. the aggregate nominal value of those shares,
c. for each class of shares:
- prescribed particulars of the rights attached to the shares,
- the total number of shares of that class, and
- the aggregate nominal value of shares of that class, and

d. the amount paid up and the amount (if any) unpaid on each share (whether on account of the nominal value of the share or by way of premium).

Reduction of capital confirmed by the court

Where a company has passed a resolution for reducing share capital, it may apply to the Court for an order confirming the reduction. Before the Court will confirm the transaction, it must first consider whether the cancellation or reduction of capital would prejudice the **rights of creditors**, who are normally entitled to look to the share capital in the event that debts owing to them are not paid. The Court will usually require an undertaking from the company that it will not distribute the special reserve until all creditors outstanding at the time of the transaction have been settled. Alternatively, if new capital is being raised, the special reserve may be distributed on a pound-for-pound basis with the new issue. **3641**

Co-operation with members and creditors

The following are **examples** of transactions that, while not setting out specifically to bring about a reduction in the share capital, may nevertheless have that result: **3642**

- the **transfer** of a going-concern business (i.e., its assets and liabilities) to one or more companies followed by the dissolution of the transferor company without a winding up,
- the **variation** of shareholders' rights including the consolidation or division of shares into other classes, and
- the **cancellation** of one class of shares and replacing it with new shares.

The mechanism by which these transactions are completed often requires the company to obtain the agreement not only of the shareholders but also of creditors before the court will sanction the capital reduction. Where three quarters of shareholders and creditors vote in favour of any such scheme, the court will usually direct that it is binding on them all. s 899 CA 2006

SECTION 3

Acquisitions of own shares

Transactions authorised

3645 s 658 CA 2006 In general, the Companies Act does not permit a limited company to acquire its own shares – whether by purchase, subscription or otherwise. In contrast, unlimited companies are not subject to these restrictions and may purchase their own shares as long as their Articles of Association do not preclude it.

However, the general prohibition on limited companies is not absolute, and if the proposed transaction falls within one of the following **exceptions** specifically provided for, it will be allowed:
– the redemption of redeemable shares;
– the acquisition of shares under an authorised reduction of capital;
– the purchase of shares is made under a court order, such as in a reconstruction;
– the purchase of qualifying shares to be held as treasury shares (see ¶3689);
– specific shares are forfeited or surrendered as a result of calls on them not having been paid;
– the shares are acquired by way of a gift or bequest without the payment of a consideration (e.g., to nominees to hold on trust for the company).

An unlawful acquisition (i.e., one that is not covered by the above exceptions) is void and will be considered not to have taken place. The company and its officers are liable to criminal sanctions.

MEMO POINTS The most common reasons for a company to find it desirable to acquire its own shares include:
– to allow shareholders of shares that are **restricted** as to their transfer to other shareholders to sell them to the company instead;
– to **return surplus funds** to shareholders;
– to **increase earnings** or **net asset value** per share.

Legal conditions

3646 s 690 CA 2006 Both public and private companies will be permitted to purchase any of their own shares (including redeemable shares that have not yet reached redemption date) if the following conditions can be satisfied:
– there are no prohibitions in the company's **Articles of Association**;
– where there are **restrictions on transfers** of shares (in practice, a situation that arises mainly in the case of private companies), the specific consent of shareholders will be required before the transaction can be entered into:
– after the purchase or redemption of its own shares, the company must have other non-redeemable shares in issue (two or more shares in the case of a **public** company; one share if the company is **private** or **limited by guarantee**);
– the company cannot purchase or redeem any of its own shares that are not fully paid.

The legal requirements and procedures are discussed at ¶3670.

Funding conditions

3647 A purchase or redemption can be made only out of:
– **distributable** profits,
– **proceeds of a fresh issue** of shares – but only up to the nominal value of the shares being purchased,
– **share premium** (where there is a fresh issue at a premium and the shares being purchased were also issued at a premium),
– **capital** (but only in the case of a **private company** and where the above three sources have been exhausted) – see ¶3661.

MEMO POINTS 1. Distributable profits are those profits out of which a company would be lawfully able to make a distribution equal in value to the payment. 3648
2. A company may purchase or redeem its own shares only out of distributable profits or the proceeds of a fresh issue of shares made for that purpose. Further, any premium payable on the transaction must be paid out of the company's distributable profits – unless the premium arose on the original issue of the shares now being acquired, in which case it may be funded out of a fresh issue of shares made for that purpose.
3. Most expenses relating to the acquisition are regarded as part of the overall cost of acquisition and treated in the same way as the purchase cost itself. However, payments in consideration for varying a contract for an off-market purchase of a company's own shares or for the release of any obligations under a contract to purchase a company's own shares, can be made only from distributable profits.
4. A private company may, only if the total of distributable profits and the proceeds of any fresh issue do not cover the purchase or redemption price, make up the shortfall by a payment from capital.

Payment of consideration

The consideration for a company's own shares must be paid in cash at the time of purchase and cannot be paid for by instalments or by way of a loan extended by the seller to the buyer. In addition, the payment cannot be in the form of an asset other than cash (for instance, land). 3649 s 691 CA 2006

Effects and consequences

If a company intends purchasing its own shares but this is not done in proportion to existing shareholdings, there may be unexpected or undesired effects for the remaining shareholders. As an example, a particular shareholder or group of shareholders may, as a result of their shareholding becoming proportionately larger, be in a position to control the voting in a way that they could not before. 3650

As soon as a company purchases or redeems any of its shares, it must treat them as cancelled. They will not be able to be reissued in the future. The effect will be to permanently reduce the issued share capital by the nominal amount of the shares purchased, though the authorised share capital will not be affected. If, however, the company is not willing to see this permanent reduction, at the time that it is about to purchase or redeem its own shares, it has a special power to issue shares up to the nominal value of the shares about to be purchased. In practice this could mean that for a short period (i.e. between the issue of the new shares and the cancellation of the purchased shares) the authorised share capital is exceeded, but this is specifically permitted in the circumstances. 3651 ss 688, 706 CA 2006

MEMO POINTS The reference to the effect of the redemption on authorised share capital is not replicated in the Companies Act 2006, the relevant provisions of which became effective in October 2009.

1. Accounting procedures

Acquisition out of distributable profits

The following example explains the steps that must be taken in a typical case of an acquisition by a private company of its own shares out of distributable profits. 3652

EXAMPLE Mr A is the chairman and a shareholder of A Ltd. As he is approaching retirement age, he wishes to sell his shares in the company. He originally paid £20,000 for his 20 percent stake in the company's authorised and issued share capital of £100,000.
The other directors (who between them own all the other shares in A Ltd) have agreed that the company will purchase Mr A's shares for £250,000. The company will make the payment out of distributable profits.

The transaction will be reflected in the books by way of the following entries:

Dr: Share capital	20,000	
Dr: Distributable profits	230,000	
Cr: Cash		250,000
Purchase of 20,000 £1 shares at a premium of £230,000		

Dr: Distributable profits	20,000	
Cr: Capital redemption reserve		20,000
Transfer to maintain the capital of the company		

Balance sheet	**Before transaction**	**Purchase of own shares**	**Transfers to maintain capital**	**After transaction**
	£'000	**£'000**	**£'000**	**£'000**
Share capital	100	(20)		80
Capital redemption reserve	-		20	20
Capital	100	(20)	20	100
Distributable reserves	300	(230)	(20)	50
	400	(250)	-	150

Thus the company's capital remains £100,000.

3653 The accounting for the debit to distributable reserves will depend on how the shares had been presented in the balance sheet immediately before the purchase took place.

If the shares are regarded as **debt** (by FRS 25), the loss on the repurchase of the shares should be recognised in the profit or loss for the period. On the other hand, if the shares meet the definition of **equity**, the loss should be taken directly to reserves and shown in the reconciliation of movements in shareholders' funds.

Acquisition at a premium out of fresh issue

3654
s 692 CA 2006

The **nominal value** of the shares being acquired can be funded out of the proceeds of a fresh issue of shares made for the specific purpose. In addition, if the shares had originally been issued at a premium, any premium now being paid on the reacquisition may – subject to the following limitation – also be funded out of the proceeds of a fresh issue.

The amount of premium that can be met by the fresh issue is the lower of:
– the aggregate of the premiums the company received when it first issued the shares it is now purchasing, and
– the amount of the company's share premium account after crediting the premium, if any, on the new issue of shares it makes to fund the purchase or redemption.

EXAMPLE The following is an extract from the balance sheet of B Ltd, which intends to purchase the 10 percent shareholding (i.e., 20,000 shares) of Mr B, at a premium of 50p.

Ordinary shares of £1	200,000
Preference shares of £1	100,000
Share premium	80,000

Additional information
The preference shares and share premium arose as a result of a fresh issue that was intended to fund the purchase of Mr B's 20,000 ordinary shares.
The following two cases will be considered:
Case (a) – the shares, when originally issued, were issued at nominal value; and
Case (b) – the shares were originally issued at a premium of 5p but the resulting share premium was later used in full to make a bonus issue to existing shareholders.

Determination of how the purchase will be funded	**Case (a)**		**Case (b)**	
From the proceeds of the fresh issue of shares:				
Nominal value shares to be purchased		20,000		20,000
Premium on purchase:				
The lower of:				
– balance on share premium account; or	80,000		80,000	
– initial premium on issue of the shares now being purchased (20,000 at 5p)	N/A	-	1,000	1,000
Amount that can be funded from fresh issue		20,000		21,000
Total amount payable on purchase		30,000		30,000
Therefore, balance to be funded out of distributable profits		£ 10,000		£ 9,000

The transaction will be reflected in the books by way of the following entries:

	Case (a)		**Case (b)**	
	Dr	**Cr**	**Dr**	**Cr**
Dr: Cash	180,000		180,000	
Cr: Preference share capital		100,000		100,000
Cr: Share premium		80,000		80,000
Issue of 100,000 £1 preference shares at a premium of £80,000				

	Case (a)		**Case (b)**	
	Dr	**Cr**	**Dr**	**Cr**
Dr: Share capital	20,000		20,000	
Dr: Share premium			1,000	
Dr: Distributable profits	10,000		9,000	
Cr: Cash		30,000		30,000
Purchase of 20,000 £1 shares at a premium of £10,000				

Note that there is no transfer to capital redemption reserve because the nominal value of the shares purchased (£20,000) is less than the proceeds of the fresh issue. Therefore, the company's capital has been maintained and there is no need for a transfer.

Capital maintenance

Except for the case of a private company making an acquisition of its own shares out of capital, all other companies are required to **maintain their capital** before and after the acquisition of shares. This generally requires the company to transfer to a capital redemption reserve an amount that is equal to the nominal value of the shares that it acquires, or on cancellation of shares held as treasury shares. **3656** s 733 CA 2006

The reason for the capital maintenance rule is to safeguard the interests of creditors and others by ensuring that the company's legal capital is maintained.

Where, however, the acquisition is funded wholly or partly by a fresh issue of shares, the amount to be transferred to the capital redemption reserve is the difference between the proceeds of the fresh issue and the nominal value of the shares being purchased. The reason is that the company's share capital is being maintained (even though some of the capital before the transaction is now represented in part by share premium and the amount that was transferred to the capital redemption reserve). **3657**

3658 The capital redemption reserve is restricted in much the same ways as to its use as share capital, though with some exceptions. For instance, it can be used to pay up unissued shares allotted as fully paid bonus shares. Also, in certain circumstances, a private company may be able to use its capital redemption reserve to fund the purchase or redemption of shares.

The following table summarises the rules for public and private companies:

Circumstances surrounding purchase, cancellation or redemption of shares	Transfer to capital redemption reserve that must be made
Company purchases or redeems shares wholly out of **distributable profits**	An amount equivalent to the nominal value of the shares it purchased. In addition, it must reduce the issued share capital by the nominal value of the shares purchased.
Company purchases or redeems shares wholly or partly out of a **fresh issue** with no payment being made out of capital, where the nominal value of the shares purchased or redeemed exceeds the amount of the proceeds of the fresh issue	The difference between the nominal value of the shares purchased/redeemed and the proceeds of the fresh issue (see example, immediately below).
Company cancels shares held as **treasury shares**	An amount equivalent to the nominal value of the shares cancelled. In addition, the company must reduce the amount of its issued share capital by the nominal value of the shares cancelled.

EXAMPLE C Ltd purchases 10,000 £1 "A" ordinary shares at a premium of £1.20 partly out of the proceeds of a fresh issue of shares and partly out of distributable reserves. C Ltd issues 5,000 "B" ordinary shares with a nominal value of 20p at a premium of £1.00 (the total proceeds therefore being £6,000).

The amount to be transferred to the capital redemption reserve is:

Nominal value of shares redeemed	10,000
Proceeds of fresh issue	6,000
Transfer to the capital redemption reserve	£ 4,000

Determination of how the purchase will be funded	
From the proceeds of the fresh issue of shares:	
Nominal value shares to be purchased, limited to the proceeds of the fresh issue	6,000
Total amount payable on purchase	22,000
Therefore, balance to be funded out of distributable profits	£ 16,000

Acquisition at a discount out of fresh issue

3659 In certain circumstances, it is possible to make acquisitions of shares at a discount.

Where a company makes a fresh issue of shares for the purpose of acquiring its own shares, it may still be necessary to maintain the company's capital in accordance with the capital maintenance rules discussed at ¶3656 by transferring to the capital redemption reserve the difference between the amount raised on the fresh issue of shares and the nominal value of the shares being redeemed (if greater).

EXAMPLE D Ltd has no distributable reserves. Nevertheless it wishes to purchase 200,000 of its £1 shares for £180,000 (representing a discount of 10 percent) and for this purpose makes a fresh issue of 90,000 £1 redeemable preference shares issued at a premium of £1 (i.e., £180,000 total proceeds).

Amount to be transferred to capital redemption reserve	
Nominal value of shares to be purchased, limited to the proceeds of the fresh issue	200,000
Proceeds of fresh issue	180,000
Amount to be transferred	£ 20,000

Acquisitions out of capital

The Companies Act 2006 permits **private companies** to purchase or redeem their own shares out of capital, but unlike the 1985 Act, does not require, as a condition, that the articles allow it. This means that permission exists unless it has been specifically excluded. Members may, if they wish, restrict or prohibit such transactions by including a provision to this effect in the articles. 3660

The statement required when a company makes a payment out of capital in respect of a redemption or purchase of its own shares must specify the amount of the permissible capital payment for the shares in question. It must also state that, having made full inquiry into the affairs and prospects of the company, the directors have formed the opinion that the company will be able to continue to carry on business as a going concern (and will accordingly be able to pay its debts as they fall due) throughout that year. In forming this opinion, the directors must take into account all of the company's liabilities, including any contingent or prospective liabilities. 3661

The statement must have annexed to it a report addressed to the directors by the company's auditor stating that: s 714 CA 2006
- he has inquired into the company's state of affairs,
- the amount specified in the statement as the permissible capital payment for the shares in question is in his view properly determined in accordance with the relevant sections of the Companies Act 2006, and
- he is not aware of anything to indicate that the opinion expressed by the directors in their statement is unreasonable in all the circumstances.

Permissible capital payment (PCP) The maximum amount of payment that may be made out of capital is limited to the "permissible capital payment" or PCP, which is equal to the price of the shares being purchased less the total of any available profits and proceeds of a fresh issue made to fund the purchase. The effect of this rule is to require a private company to use its available profits and any proceeds arising from a new issue before looking to capital. The calculation of the permissible capital payment is represented by the following formula: 3662

PCP = acquisition price – (available profits + proceeds of fresh issue)

MEMO POINTS "Available profits" refer to those that are available for distribution within the meaning of the Companies Act, i.e., its accumulated realised profits, to the extent they have not been used in distributions or capitalisations, less its accumulated realised losses, so far as they have not been previously written off in a reduction or re-organisation of capital.

EXAMPLE E Ltd has the following balances in its balance sheet:

Share capital	£ 500,000
Share premium	£ 200,000
Distributable reserves	£ 125,000

The company intends to purchase 200,000 £1 shares from one of its shareholders at a premium of £1. (These shares were originally issued at par value.) The company issues 100,000 ordinary shares of £1 each at a premium of 75p per share for the purposes of purchasing the shares in question.
The PCP is calculated as follows:

200,000 £1 shares at a premium of £1 per share		400,000
Less: Proceeds of fresh issue (100,000 £1 shares at a premium of 75p)	175,000	
Distributable profits	125,000	300,000
PCP		£100,000

The purchase would be made as follows:

Out of the proceeds of the fresh issue:		
(a) Nominal value of shares purchased	200,000	
(b) Share premium account	-	200,000
Out of distributable profits		125,000
		325,000
Total cost of purchase		400,000
Therefore, balance out of capital		£ 75,000

Transfer to capital redemption reserve

3663 s 734 (2) CA 2006 When a private company purchases its shares wholly or partially out of capital, a transfer must be made to the capital redemption reserve represented by the following formula:

Transfer to capital redemption reserve = Nominal value of shares purchased – (payment out of capital + proceeds of fresh issue)

EXAMPLE X Ltd, Y Ltd, and Z Ltd are private companies. Each purchases 40,000 of their own shares that were originally issued at their nominal value of £1 per share. In each case, a premium of £1.20 per share is payable on purchase. Y Ltd issues 28,000 redeemable preference shares at par and Z Ltd issues 16,000 redeemable preference shares at par. In both cases, the shares are redeemable at par. The companies' retained profits are: X Ltd £64,000; Y Ltd £120,000; and Z Ltd £60,000. The purchase price to be paid is determined as follows:

	X Ltd	Y Ltd	Z Ltd
Out of proceeds of new issue:			
(a) Nominal value of shares purchased – restricted to proceeds of fresh issue	-	28	16
(b) Share premium	-	-	-
	-	28	16
Available from distributable profits	64	60	60
	64	88	76
Therefore, balance out of capital	24	-	12
Total amount to be paid	88	88	88

Amount to be transferred to the capital redemption reserve is as follows:

	X Ltd	Y Ltd	Z Ltd
Nominal value of shares purchased	40	40	40
Less:	24	28	28
Proceeds of fresh issue	-	28	16
Permissible capital payment (PCP)	24	-	12
Transfer to the capital redemption reserve	16	12	12

3664 s 734 (3) CA 2006 When the PCP **exceeds the nominal value of the shares** purchased or redeemed, the company may use the excess to reduce one of the following:
- the capital redemption reserve
- the share premium account
- fully paid share capital
- the revaluation reserve.

Similarly, where shares are purchased out of the proceeds of a new issue, if the nominal value of the shares being purchased is **less than** the sum of the permissible capital payment and the proceeds of the new issue, the company may use the excess to reduce the above. This is represented by the following formula: 3665

Debit to reduce capital = (payment out of capital + proceeds of fresh issue) – (nominal value of shares purchased)

EXAMPLE S Ltd and T Ltd are private companies. They intend to purchase, at a premium of £1.50 per share, 200,000 of their own £1 shares (originally issued at a premium of 20p per share). To help fund the purchase, T Ltd issues 8,000 £1 preference shares at par (redeemable at par). The distributable reserves of S Ltd and T Ltd are £25,000 and £18,000 respectively. The purchases are made as follows:

	S Ltd	T Ltd
Out of proceeds of fresh issue of shares:		
Nominal value of shares purchased – limited to the proceeds of the fresh issue	-	8,000
Share premium account	-	-
	-	8,000
Out of distributable profits	25,000	18,000
	25,000	26,000
Total cost of purchase	50,000	50,000
Therefore, balance out of capital	£ 25,000	£ 24,000

The amount by which the companies may reduce their capital redemption reserve, the share premium account and/or the fully paid share capital is as follows:

	S Ltd	T Ltd
PCP	25, 000	24,000
Proceeds of new issue	-	8,0004
	25,000	32,000
Nominal value of shares purchased	20,000	20,000
Excess available	£ 5,000	£ 12,000

Disclosure requirements

Any company that purchases its own shares during the year must disclose in its financial statements the details of such share purchases during the year, the rights of redemption of any redeemable shares, and the authority under which the company acquired the shares in question. 3667

The directors' report in respect of the year in which the purchase of a company's own shares takes place must include the following: 3668
– the number and nominal value of the shares purchased or redeemed,
– the aggregate consideration paid,
– the reason/s for their purchase,
– the percentage of the called-up share capital that the shares purchased or redeemed represent.

For **listed** companies, the directors' report should, in addition to disclosing the details in respect of a purchase of own shares, give similar information in respect of any **purchases or options or contracts** to make such purchases it has entered into in respect of its own shares **since the end of the year** covered by the report. The company must also include in its financial statements: 3669 LR 9.8.6
– Particulars of any shareholders' authority for the purchase by the company of its own shares in force at the end of the period under review.

- In the case of off-market purchases or those made other than by tender to all shareholders,
  • during the period under review, the names of the sellers of the shares purchased or proposed to be purchased,
  • subsequent to the end of the period under review, information equivalent to that required by ¶3668, above.
- In the case of sales of treasury shares for cash made other than through the market, or in connection with an employees' share scheme, or other than pursuant to an opportunity that was available to all shareholders on the same terms, particulars of the names of the purchasers of such shares sold (or proposed to be sold) by the company during the period under review.

2. Legal procedures

3670 One of the important legal procedures relating to a company's purchasing its own shares is to first determine whether the purchase will be a market purchase or an off-market one.

3671 s 693 CA 2006 An "**off-market**" purchase is one in which either of the following applies:
- the shares are not purchased on a recognised investment exchange (such as the Stock Exchange and AIM), or
- the shares are purchased on a recognised investment exchange, but they are not subject to a marketing arrangement on that exchange (in other words, where they are not listed or where they cannot be traded without prior permission for individual transactions and without constraints as to timing).

Any other purchase is a "**market**" purchase.

Purchases by public companies

3672 s 701 CA 2006 A **market** purchase by a listed public company of its own shares must first be authorised by **ordinary resolution** of the company in general meeting. The authority, which may be general or specific to a class or description of shares, must:
- specify the maximum number of shares authorised to be acquired,
- determine both the maximum and the minimum prices that may be paid for the shares. It may do this by specifying a particular sum or providing a basis or formula for calculating the amount of the price as long as the amount can be calculated without reference to any person's discretion or opinion,
- specify a date not more than 18 months from the date of the resolution on which the authority is to expire. The terms of the authority may permit a purchase to be made after its expiry if the contract of purchase was concluded before the authority expired and the terms of the authority permitted the company to make a contract of purchase that would or might be executed wholly or partly after its expiration.

3673 The authority may be varied, revoked or renewed at a company's general meeting by an ordinary resolution, as long as it still complies with the above conditions. A copy of such a resolution must be lodged with the Registrar of Companies within 15 days.

3674 Under the Companies Act 1985, a company could make an off-market purchase of shares only if its shareholders approved the contract by special resolution before the contract was entered into. The special resolution conferring the authority to enter into an off-market contract to purchase its own shares was not effective:
- if the shares in question were being voted on by the shareholder who owned them where, if he had not voted, the resolution would not have passed;
- unless a copy of the contract (or, if it was not in writing, a written memorandum setting out all the terms, including the names of the members whose shares are to be purchased) was available for inspection by members at the company's registered office for not less than 15 days.

Under the Companies Act 2006, effective October 2009, a company can enter into a contract for an off-market purchase of its own shares, subject to the contract's being approved by the shareholders. The effect is to save valuable time as it is possible for directors to negotiate and agree the terms of a contract for an off-market purchase of shares ahead of seeking shareholder approval. However, should the shareholders not subsequently pass a special resolution approving the contract, the company will not have the authority to purchase the shares in question and the contract will lapse.

Returns and contracts

After a company, whether public or private, has purchased its own shares, it is required to submit, no later than 28 days after the delivery of shares to it, a return in the prescribed form to the Registrar of Companies stating: 3678
- the number and nominal value of the shares purchased,
- the date they were delivered to the company.

In the case of a **public company** the return must also state:
- the aggregate amount paid by the company for the shares, and
- the maximum and minimum prices paid in respect of shares of each class purchased.

A public company must, in addition, state the aggregate amount paid for the shares and the maximum and minimum prices paid in respect of shares of each class purchased. 3679

Failure to file the form is a criminal offence.

Both private and public companies must keep a copy of each contract for an **off-market** purchase or contingent purchase contract they enter into, together with any variations to any such contracts. These documents must be kept at the company's registered office (or elsewhere, as specified in accordance with section 1136 of the Companies Act 2006) from the date the contracts are concluded until the end of a period of ten years from the date of the purchase to which they relate. 3680

A private company must make a copy of such a contract available for inspection by any member without charge, while a public company must do so for any interested party. Companies must give notices to the registrar of the place where the contract is kept available for inspection. 3681

A public company that makes a **market** purchase must keep a copy of each contract for a purchase authorised by the company in general meeting, together with any variations to it. Again these must be kept at the company's registered office (or as specified in section 1136 of the Companies Act 2006) for ten years from the date of the purchase to which it relates. Similarly, a public company must make any such contract available for inspection not only by members, but also by any other person. Notice must be given to the registrar of the place where the contract is available for inspection.

Contingent purchase contracts

A contingent purchase contract is a contract under which a company becomes either entitled or obliged to purchase its own shares. Contingent purchase contracts can be used to give a company the option to purchase its shares. Alternatively they can be used to give a shareholder the right to require the company to purchase the shares – where, for instance, a shareholder is prepared to maintain an investment in a company only if there are arrangements in place that enable him to sell his shares back to the company at some future time. 3683

MEMO POINTS Another way of achieving this might have been for the company to issue redeemable preference shares but this contractual arrangement may be more convenient in certain circumstances. Similarly, a contingent purchase contract might provide for a situation in which a company is obliged to purchase an employee's shares on his retirement.
Because the use of contingent purchase contracts to buy a company's own shares may be open to abuse, the Act provides a safeguard by treating contingent purchase contracts as off-market contracts – i.e., subject to the rules and regulations that apply to off-market contracts.
Similarly, the prohibition on a company's assigning its rights under a purchase contract applies to contingent purchase contracts.

Liability on winding up

Under the Insolvency Act 1986, if a company proves to be **insolvent** and is wound up within a year of making a payment out of capital, both the shareholders whose shares were purchased or redeemed, and the directors who signed the statutory declaration, will be called 3685 upon to contribute to the assets of the company. However, directors will be exempt from such a liability if they can show that there were reasonable grounds for their opinion stated in the statutory declaration.

Such a person's liability will be limited to the amount he received out of capital in respect of his shares, and the company's directors are jointly and severally liable with the past shareholder for that amount.

Failure to acquire shares

3687 s 735 (2) - (3)CA 2006 If a company agrees to purchase or redeem any of its shares but fails to do so, the affected shareholder cannot rely on the courts to order specific performance of the contract, especially in a case where the company is not able to meet the costs of purchasing the shares out of distributable profits. Neither can the shareholder sue the company for damages.

s 735 (4) CA 2006 Where, however, the company's failure to perform under the contract happens at the same time as it faces going into liquidation, the terms of the purchase can be enforced – but only if:
- the purchase was to take place before the winding up commenced, and
- there would have been distributable profits equal to the purchase or redemption price.

Treasury shares

3689 s 725 CA 2006 Companies with "qualifying shares" – i.e., those that are listed on the London Stock Exchange or that of another EEA state, traded on AIM or similar market in an EEA state – may purchase them out of distributable profits and hold them in treasury for resale, transfer, or cancellation at a later date.

3690 Where a company has only one class of shares, the aggregate nominal value of shares held as treasury shares may not exceed 10 percent of the nominal value of the issued share capital. Similarly, if the company has more than one class of shares, the aggregate nominal value of the shares of any class held as treasury shares must not exceed 10 percent of the nominal value of the issued share capital of the shares in that class at that time.

3691 The company may not exercise any rights (including voting rights) over the treasury shares. In addition, it may not pay a dividend or make any other distribution including any distribution of assets to members on a winding up to itself in respect of the treasury shares.

3692 s 690 CA 2006 A company is not permitted to purchase its shares in a situation where, as a result of the transaction, there would no longer be any member of the company holding shares other than redeemable shares or shares held as treasury shares.

3693 s 724 (4) CA 2006 Where shares are held in treasury, the company must be entered in the register of members as the member holding those shares.

Sale

3695 s 731 CA 2006 When a company sells treasury shares, if the **proceeds** are **equal to or less than** the **purchase price** paid for the shares, the proceeds are treated as realised profit. If the proceeds **exceed** the purchase price, the excess over the purchase price must be transferred to the share premium account.

The purchase price paid by the company for the shares is determined by the use of a weighted average price method. If the shares were allotted to the company as fully paid bonus shares, the purchase price is deemed to be nil.

Cancellation

3697 s 729 (4) CA 2006 If a company cancels shares held as **treasury shares**, it must reduce the amount of its issued share capital by the nominal value of those cancelled shares.

s 733 (4) CA 2006 The amount by which the company's issued share capital is reduced on the cancellation of treasury shares must be transferred to a capital redemption reserve.

If shares held as treasury shares cease to be "qualifying shares" for any reason other than if they are suspended from listing, the company must immediately cancel them. 3698

Filing of returns

Where a company purchases its own treasury shares, it must lodge a return with the Registrar of Companies no later than 28 days after the delivery of shares, stating in respect of each class of shares purchased: 3700 s 707 CA 2006
- the number and nominal value of each,
- the date on which they were delivered to the company.

In the case of a **public company**, the return must also state:
- the aggregate amount paid by the company for the shares, and
- the maximum and minimum prices paid in respect of each class of shares purchased.

Redeemable shares

The redemption of redeemable shares is one of the **exceptions to the general rule** that a company may not purchase its own shares. Much of the legislation relating to redemptions is similar to the rules for purchases of own shares. 3702

Historically, companies needed authorisation in their articles of association in order to issue redeemable shares. The situation changed in October 2009 and private companies no longer require prior authorisation. A company's members may, however, prohibit or restrict the authority of the company to issue redeemable shares by including a provision to this effect in the articles. In addition, directors of both private and public companies alike are permitted to determine the terms, conditions and manner of a redemption of redeemable shares. The power conferred on the directors requires prior authorisation by the company's members, either by resolution of the company or through the articles. The terms and conditions of the redemption must be stated in the statement of capital. If the directors are not authorised to set the terms of the redemption, then they must be set out in the company's articles. 3703 s 685 CA 2006

Another difference is that the legal procedures relating to both market and off-market purchases (see ¶3671) do not apply to redeemable shares. 3704

MEMO POINTS Even though redeemable shares will often meet the definition of debt in IAS 32 and FRS 25 and be accounted for as such, in the legal sense they are shares and their redemption is governed by the provisions of the Act.

SECTION 4

Distributions

"Distributions" include all **payments to members**, whether in the form of cash or other assets. The following are **not** distributions: 3710
- issues of bonus shares;
- the redemption or purchase of shares out of capital or unrealised profits;
- the reduction of share capital by reducing or extinguishing amounts owed;
- distributions of assets on winding up;
- repayments of loans to members made not in their capacity as members.

1. Profits available for distribution

The amount of profits that are available for distribution depends on the type of company wishing to make the distribution. For companies other than investment companies (discussed at ¶3714) or insurance companies (discussed at ¶3715), available profits consist of **accu-** 3711 s 830 CA 2006

mulated realised profits less **accumulated realised losses**. The origin of these profits can be either capital or revenue.

3712 **Private companies** enjoy the greatest freedom in making distributions; they may distribute the whole of their accumulated realised profits not previously distributed or capitalised less any accumulated realised losses not previously written off in a reduction or reorganisation of capital. Private companies are not required by the Act to take unrealised losses into account. However, under common-law principles, the duty of directors to act in the best interests of the company means that in practice unrealised losses cannot simply be ignored if, as a result, the company's financial standing is compromised.

3713 s 831 CA 2006 **Public companies** are subject to the condition that they may not make any distribution to the extent that the distribution would reduce their net assets below the sum of their called up share capital and non-distributable reserves. This means that they, unlike private companies, are required to take into account net unrealised losses.

The following example illustrates the difference between the amounts allowed to be distributed by private and public companies.

EXAMPLE

	A Ltd £	B Ltd £
Share capital	300,000	300,000
Net realised profits	90,000	50,000
Realised profits	120,000	70,000
Realised losses	(30,000)	(20,000)
Net unrealised losses	(25,000)	(75,000)
Unrealised profits	10,000	14,000
Unrealised losses	(35,000)	(89,000)
Share capital and reserves	**£ 365,000**	**£ 275,000**
Amount permitted to be distributed if		
– private company (total of net realised profits)	£ 90,000	£ 50,000
– public company (net realised profits less net unrealised losses)	£ 65,000	£ 0

3714 **Investment companies** may distribute only **the excess of their accumulated realised revenue profits** over their accumulated **revenue losses** (both realised and unrealised). The advantage is that **capital losses** may be ignored when making distributions.

In addition, an investment company must satisfy the following **conditions** before making a distribution:

a) its assets must be at least equal to 150 percent of the aggregate of its liabilities, and the distribution will not reduce the company's assets to a level below 150 percent of the aggregate of its liabilities;

b) the company's shares are listed on a recognised investment exchange other than an overseas investment exchange;

c) the company did not, during the preceding accounting period, distribute any of its capital profits or apply any unrealised profits or capital profits (realised or unrealised) in paying up debentures or any amounts unpaid on any of its issued shares. However, since Statutory Instrument SI 1999 No 2770 was issued, investment companies are allowed to use **capital profits** for the purpose of repurchasing their own shares. Note that this change has no effect on any other prohibitions on distributions out of capital profits for investment companies.

3715 **Insurance companies** whether public or private, have an **additional restriction** to take into account. Any amounts transferred to the profit and loss account from a surplus on the long-term business fund must be treated as a realised profit, while any deficit in that fund must be treated as a realised loss. Any other profit or loss in that business fund should be disregarded.

2. Reference to financial statements

Before a distribution can be made, the company must first ensure that it is lawful, i.e., that sufficient distributable reserves are available. For this purpose, reference is usually made to the company's most recent audited financial statements. **3717**

Effect of audit report

The first step is to examine the audit report on the previous financial statements. An **unqualified audit report** gives rise to the following possibilities: **3718**
a) If there are **sufficient distributable profits** to cover the distribution, the distribution can be made;
b) If the last annual accounts show insufficient distributable profits to cover the proposed distribution, **interim accounts** should be prepared. There is no requirement for interim accounts to be audited. If the statements show adequate distributable profits, the company, if a **private** company, can make the distribution.

Public companies must comply with the following additional requirements:
- the accounts must have been prepared in accordance with the same accounting policies as used in the preparation of annual accounts,
- the balance sheet must be signed by a director,
- the balance sheet and profit and loss account must give a true and fair view,
- the accounts must be delivered to the Registrar of Companies.

A **qualified audit report** gives rise to the following possibilities: **3719**
a) If the auditors' report stated that **the financial statements do not give a true and fair view**, no distribution may be made.
b) If, in the auditors' opinion, **the financial statements were not properly prepared**, their report will reflect that opinion. In this event, there is a requirement that the auditors state in writing, either at the time of their report or later, whether the qualification is material for purposes of determining the legality of any proposed distribution. If the qualification is not material for these purposes, the next step is to look at the available distributable profits.

Effect of previous distributions in the current period

If, since the last financial statements, a company, public or private, has already made a distribution or has entered into an arrangement such as the purchase or redemption of shares, which may reduce distributable reserves, it may continue to rely on the last annual accounts as long as it takes into account the cumulative effect of such earlier transactions on the available profits. **3721**

First accounting period

Where a company wishes to make a distribution during its first accounting period or before it has prepared its first annual accounts, it must publish **initial accounts** for the purpose of justifying the distribution. If the company is a **public** company, these accounts must be audited and filed with the Registrar of Companies. **Private** companies do not have to meet the audit and filing requirements. **3723**

3. Realised profits and losses

The Act **defines** realised profits and losses as: **3725** s 853 CA 2006
"profits or losses of the company as fall to be treated as realised in accordance with principles generally accepted at the time when the accounts are prepared."

In areas not covered by accounting standards, it may prove difficult to show that any particular treatment is sufficiently generally accepted to ensure compliance. The following provide guidance:

3726 FRS 18 (28) **The principle of prudence** One obvious solution is to look to the principle of prudence, in terms of which **profits** should not be anticipated but recognised in the profit and loss account only when realised in the form of cash or, if in the form of other assets, where the realisation of those assets into cash can be assessed with reasonable certainty. **Losses** should be provided for whether the amount is known with certainty or even if it can only be estimated based on available information. (See also ¶30.)

3727 **Technical Releases** Guidance has also been issued on realised profits and losses in Technical Release (TR) 1/08.

In addition to those situations in which a profit is "readily apparent", the following would constitute a realised profit:

a) the receipt or accrual of investment or other income receivable in the form of qualifying consideration;

b) a gain arising on a return of capital on an investment where the return is in the form of qualifying consideration;

c) a gift (such as a "capital contribution") received in the form of qualifying consideration;

d) the release of a provision for a liability or loss that was treated as a realised loss;

e) the reversal of a write-down or provision for diminution in value or impairment of an asset that was treated as a realised loss.

3728 Examples of realised losses include:

a) a cost or expense (other than one charged to the share premium account) that results in a reduction in recorded net assets;

b) a loss arising on the sale or other disposal or scrapping of an asset;

c) the writing down, or providing for the depreciation, amortisation, diminution in value or impairment, of an asset;

d) the creation of, or increase in, a provision for a liability or loss that results in an overall reduction in recorded net assets. However, when assets are revalued to their fair value, with any unrealised gain being included in the profit and loss account (for instance, by insurance companies), the deferred tax on that gain should be treated as a reduction in that unrealised gain rather than as a realised loss;

e) a gift made by the company (or the release of all or part of a debt due to the company or the assumption of a liability by the company) to the extent that it results in an overall reduction in recorded net assets;

f) a loss arising from fair value accounting where profits on remeasurement of the same asset or liability would be treated as realised profit.

Asset revaluations

3730 A **surplus on revaluation** of a fixed asset is credited to the **revaluation** reserve and is not distributable.

s 841 CA 2006 In general, **provisions for depreciation and write-downs** are treated as realised losses, except where a company **revalues all of its fixed assets**, in which case these provisions and write-downs in value of the revalued assets are unrealised.

However, where only certain classes of assets have been revalued (e.g., properties), **assets that have not been revalued** can be treated as having been revalued if they are worth as least as much as the aggregate amount at which they are stated in the accounts. The effect is to permit a provision for diminution in value of a fixed asset to be treated as an unrealised loss, but only if the directors make the following disclosures in the accounts:

– the directors have considered the value of the fixed assets without revaluing them;

– they are satisfied that the aggregate value of the assets in question is not less than their net book value; and

– they are treating their consideration of the fixed assets as a revaluation.

Where fixed assets have been revalued and the **annual depreciation charge is higher than it would otherwise have been**, an amount equal to the cumulative additional depreciation should be treated as a realised profit. This restores the amount of profits available for distribution as if the assets had not been revalued. This will be effected by making a transfer, as a reserve movement between the revaluation reserve and the profit and loss account, of an amount equal to the increase in the annual depreciation charge resulting from the revaluation. 3731 s 841 (5) CA 2006

Profits before 22 December 1980

If the directors are **unable to determine**, in respect of particular profits or losses made before 22 December 1980, whether they are realised or unrealised, they may treat any profit as realised and any loss as unrealised. 3732

Development costs

Development costs **included as assets** in a company's balance sheet should be treated as realised losses, unless there are special circumstances that provide the directors with sufficient justification not to treat them as such. In this case, the circumstances must be explained in a note to the accounts. 3733

Goodwill

Goodwill **arising on consolidation** does not affect realised (and, therefore, distributable) profits because distributions are made by individual companies and not by the group. However, in the case of purchased goodwill that has been **capitalised** in a company's balance sheet, amortisation charges will reduce distributable profits. 3734

Non-cash distributions

Where a company makes a **distribution in the form of an asset** other than cash, any unrealised profit relating to that asset must be treated as realised. Under the Companies Act 2006, a company that has revalued assets showing an unrealised profit in the accounts will be able to treat that profit as a realised profit if it makes a distribution that includes a non-cash asset. 3735

4. Transactions between group companies

Although the question of whether a distribution can be made is decided by reference to the distributable profits of individual companies within a group, certain inter-company transactions may have an effect on the distributable reserves of such companies. 3740

Great care should be exercised when making distributions based on profits generated through inter-company transactions – for two reasons:

1. the profit, although technically realised, may not be supported by the liquid resources to make the payment of a dividend commercially viable; and
2. intra-group transfers can be used to manipulate profits in individual companies and may not reflect the same results as would have been achieved had the transactions been done on an arm's-length basis.

a. Sales of fixed assets

There are questions as to how to treat the profit that is made within a group if one company sells an asset to another. The following example illustrates two possible scenarios. 3741

EXAMPLE Scenario 1

A Ltd sells an asset to B Ltd, a fellow subsidiary. Although A Ltd had carried the asset in its books below market value, B Ltd bought it at its market value.
The profit should be considered realised or unrealised. The answer will depend on all the circumstances surrounding not only the transaction itself but also the companies, and legal advice may be needed.

If B Ltd has **net liabilities** and the consideration is added to an inter-company account with no realistic possibility of its being settled, it is likely that the profit arising in A Ltd's books should be treated as unrealised. On the other hand, if B Ltd is trading profitably and pays for the asset with cash, there is a strong case for A Ltd to regard the profit as realised.

Scenario 2

S Ltd sells an asset to H Ltd, its holding company. The asset is sold at its book value of £5,000. It has a market value of £12,000. The difference of £7,000 may be deemed to be a dividend from S Ltd to H Ltd. If S Ltd does not have sufficient distributable reserves, the dividend will be a return of capital, which is unlawful.
See also ¶3742 regarding inter-company dividends.

MEMO POINTS In the past, it was unclear under company law when intra-group transfers of assets could be conducted by reference to the asset's book value rather than its market value (frequently higher than the book value). The Companies Act 2006 clarifies this situation: where a company has distributable profits, the amount of any distribution consisting of or arising from the sale, transfer or other disposition by a company of a non-cash asset to a member of the company should be calculated by reference to its book value. Thus, if an asset is transferred for a consideration not less than its book value, the amount of the distribution is zero, but if the asset is transferred for a consideration less than its book value, the amount of the distribution is equal to that shortfall (which will therefore need to be covered by distributable profits).

b. Inter-company dividends

3742 The dividends paid and received within a group can also affect distributable reserves. There are two issues that need to be considered: the **method of payment** and the **timing of recognition** in the receiving company's accounts.

A parent company should regard dividends as realised whether they are paid in cash or passed through a current account – provided that a proper assessment of the realisable value of the current account balance is made.

With regard to the question of timing, dividends receivable from subsidiaries and associates with respect to accounting periods ending on or before that of the parent company are normally **accrued** in the parents' financial statements. This is so even if the dividends are declared after the parent's year end. In other words, while it would not be normal practice for a company to accrue dividends receivable from another company unless they were declared before the receiving company's year end, this rule is not observed in the case of companies within a group.

5. Unlawful distributions

3743 s 847 CA 2006 Before a distribution can be made, the company must first ensure that it is lawful, i.e., that sufficient distributable reserves are available. Where an unlawful distribution is made by a company to one of its members who knows, or has reasonable grounds for believing, that it is so made, the member is liable to repay to the company a sum equal to the value of the distribution at that time. This is not applicable in the case of financial assistance given in contravention of the rules governing financial assistance for the acquisition of a company's own shares or in the case of any payment made by a company in respect of the redemption or purchase by the company of shares in itself.

SECTION 5

Reserves

A. Share premium account

If a company **issues shares for a consideration that exceeds their nominal value**, the difference is accounted for in the share premium account. Where the consideration is paid in cash, this value is easily measured. If the consideration is composed of assets other than cash, the consideration must be valued in order to properly determine the amount, if any, in excess of nominal value that must be credited to the share premium account. 3745

Uses of the share premium account

The share premium account can be used: 3747 s 610 CA 2006
- to issue new fully paid **bonus shares** to members;
- where, on issuing shares, a company has transferred a sum to the share premium account, to write off the **expenses** or **commission** on the issue of those particular shares.

For purposes of **reducing share capital**, the share premium account is treated as forming part of a company's capital. It can therefore also be used for the following:
- a reduction of capital sanctioned by the court;
- repayment of original share premium to shareholders if there has been a fresh issue of shares;
- payment of a permissible capital payment (see ¶3662).

MEMO POINTS

The Companies Act 2006 made some changes to the uses of the share premium account under the previous Act. For one, it restricts the application of the share premium account and companies can no longer use this account to write off preliminary expenses. Companies are still able to use the share premium account to write off any expenses incurred, or commission paid, in connection with an issue of shares but the application of the share premium account in these circumstances is limited so that the company is able to use the share premium account arising on a particular issue of shares only to write off commission paid or expenses incurred in respect of that issue.

B. Revaluation reserve

A revaluation reserve will arise in a company's books if it revalues any of its assets under the 3748 Sch 1 para 32 SI 2008/410
alternative accounting rules. Any profit or loss arising on the revaluation must be credited or debited, as the case may be, to the revaluation reserve.

An exception to the rule is provided for **investment companies**, which need not transfer the profit or loss to the revaluation reserve.

The **initial surplus** credited to the reserve on revaluation represents the difference between the revalued amount and the previous carrying value of the asset.

EXAMPLE The historical cost of an asset was £150,000. Its book value, after accumulated depreciation of £50,000, is £100,000. The asset is revalued at £180,000. The amount to be credited to the revaluation reserve is £80,000.

Uses of the revaluation reserve

3749 The balance on the revaluation reserve represents an unrealised profit and is therefore not distributable. However, the balance on the revaluation reserve may be used for the following purposes:
- wholly or partly paying up unissued shares in the company that will be allotted to members as fully or partly paid shares (e.g., bonus shares),
- recognising taxation relating to any amount credited or debited to the reserve,
- eliminating amounts no longer necessary for the purposes of the valuation method used,
- transfers to the profit and loss account of amounts either previously charged there or representing realised profits.

Adjustments to the revaluation reserve

3751 Two adjustments are considered: the **adjustment for depreciation** and the **adjustment for impairment losses**.

3752 The **depreciation** charged in the profit and loss account in respect of assets that have been revalued is based on the revalued amount. However, the amount by which this depreciation exceeds the depreciation that would have been charged on the historical cost represents a realised profit. Therefore, the excess should be transferred annually from the revaluation reserve to the profit and loss account – in effect reducing the total depreciation charge to the amount that would have been charged on the asset's historical cost.

EXAMPLE An asset with a book value of £16,000 is revalued to £25,000. At the date of revaluation the remaining useful life was estimated at 10 years. The annual depreciation charge based on the revalued amount is therefore £2,500. Assuming that the historical-cost depreciation amounted to £1,600 per annum, the excess, i.e., £900, should be transferred every year from the revaluation reserve.

3753 An **impairment loss** is a permanent diminution in value of an asset. Where the impairment is in respect of an asset that has been revalued upwards, the loss is recognised in both the profit and loss account and the revaluation reserve.

EXAMPLE An asset with a cost of £20,000 is revalued to £30,000 when its book value is £16,000. It is estimated that the asset has a useful life of 10 years. Two years later, the asset is deemed to have suffered an impairment. Its carrying value is reduced to £6,000.

Initial amount transferred to revaluation reserve on revaluation (£30,000 – £16,000)	£ 14,000
Excess annual depreciation charged over the 2 years (2 × £1,400)	2,800
Balance on reserve	£ 11,200
Carrying value of asset at date of impairment (£30,000 – [2 × £3,000])	£24,000
Transfer from revaluation reserve	11,200
	12.800
Carrying value	6,000
Impairment loss to be recognised in profit and loss account	£ 6,800

If amounts have been transferred from the revaluation reserve in connection with a bonus issue and, later, certain of the assets which had been revalued and which had given rise to the revaluation reserve are sold, the amount to be transferred to the profit and loss account should be limited to the balance remaining on the revaluation surplus in respect of those assets. 3754

C. Capital redemption reserve

When a company uses **distributable profits** out of which to purchase or redeem its own shares, it is required to transfer to the capital redemption reserve an amount equal to the nominal value of the shares concerned. The capital redemption reserve is specifically required by the Act to be shown under "Other reserves" – either on the face of the balance sheet or in the notes. 3756

If a redemption is **funded in part by a fresh issue** of shares, the amount required to be transferred to the capital redemption reserve is the difference between the nominal value of the shares redeemed and the proceeds of the fresh issue. 3757

The **capital redemption reserve may be used** to pay up fully paid **bonus** shares.

EXAMPLE Scenario 1 – No fresh issue of shares

D Ltd redeems shares with a nominal value of £110,000 (originally issued for £120,000) for £140,000.

The journal entries to give effect to the transaction and the requirements of the Act are as follows:

To record the redemption:	Dr.	Cr.
Distributable reserves	140,000	
Cash		140,000
To transfer to the capital redemption reserve:		
Called up share capital	110,000	
Capital redemption reserve		110,000

Scenario 2 – Fresh issue of shares

E Ltd makes a fresh issue of ordinary shares to finance the redemption of redeemable shares as follows:

Shares issued		
Nominal value		£ 75,000
Issue price		£150,000
Shares redeemed		
Nominal value of shares		£150,000
Originally issued at a premium of		£ 7,000
Premium on redemption		£ 30,000

Immediately before these transactions took place, the salient balances in the books of E Ltd were:

Issued share capital		£ 450,000
Share premium (including the original premium on the shares to be redeemed)		35,000
		£ 485,000
Distributable profits		180,000
	£ 665,000	

Redemption of shares

The total amount to be redeemed is £180,000, being nominal value of £150,000 and premium on redemption of £30,000. The premium on redemption may be funded out of the fresh issue to the extent of the premium originally received (£7,000) or the balance on the share premium account after the new issue (£35,000 + £75,000 = £110,000) – whichever is the lower.

	Nominal value	Premium
Redemption to be financed	150,000	30,000
Premium on redemption – out of fresh issue		7,000
Therefore, amount to finance from distributable profits		£23,000
Proceeds of fresh issue already applied to redemption premium	7,000	
Redemption of nominal value financed by fresh issue	£143,000	

Following a strict interpretation of the Act, there is no difference between the aggregate proceeds of the fresh issue and the nominal value of the shares redeemed. Therefore, no transfer to the capital redemption reserve is required. Thus, the balance sheet after redemption will reflect the following:

Issued share capital	[450,000 – 150,000 + 75,000]	£375,000
Share premium	[35,000 – 7,000 + 75,000]	103,000
		478,000
Distributable profits	[180,000 – 23,000]	157,000
		£ 635,000

The rules can be interpreted another way. The proceeds of the fresh issue used to finance the redemption of the share premium (£143,000) is different from the nominal value of the shares redeemed (£150,000). There is thus an argument that this difference should be transferred to the capital redemption reserve. In this case, the post-redemption balance sheet will appear as follows:

Issued share capital	[450,000 – 150,000 + 75,000]	£375,000
Share premium	[35,000 – 7,000 + 75,000]	103,000
Capital redemption reserve		7,000
		485,000
Distributable profits	[180,000 – 23,000 – 7,000]	150,000
		£ 635,000

D. Reserves provided for by the Articles of Association

3759 Reserves under this heading will be those specifically required by the company's Articles of Association. For example, the Articles of an investment trust may require that profits on the sale of investments be transferred to a non-distributable capital reserve.

E. Other reserves

3761 The finance costs in respect of non-equity shares, accrued over the term of such shares, may appear under this heading. Another example may be translation differences arising on the consolidation of foreign subsidiaries.

SECTION 6

Disclosure in the accounts

The Companies Act – in particular, the balance sheet formats given in Schedule 1 to SI 2008 No. 410 – prescribes the headings that must be shown on the face of the balance sheet under **Capital and reserves**, as follows: 3770

I	Called up share capital
II	Share premium account
III	Revaluation reserve
IV	Other reserves 1. Capital redemption reserve 2. Reserve for own shares 3. Reserves provided for by the articles of association 4. Other reserves
V	Profit and loss account

Additional disclosure requirements are set out in FRS 4, FRS 25, FRS 29, and the Listing Rules. However, the disclosure provisions of FRS 25 apply for accounting periods beginning on or after 1 January 2005 only for those entities that are also applying FRS 26 requirements on measurement and hedging. From 1 January 2007, FRS 29 replaces the disclosure requirements of FRS 25 for all companies applying FRS 26.

As FRS 4 remains applicable to unlisted entities not applying the measurement requirements of FRS 26, references to FRS 4 have been retained in this chapter. Full details of FRS 29 are included at ¶3140.

While the Act refers specifically to shares and debentures many companies issue other types of capital instruments as a means of raising finance. These include loans, other debt instruments, warrants and options.

A. Share capital

1. Under the Companies Act

On the face of the balance sheet, the respective amounts of **allotted** share capital and **called up** share capital that has been paid must be shown separately under "Share capital and reserves". 3775

In the notes, the following must be stated:

1. for each **class** of share that has been allotted, the **number** and **nominal value**.

2. where shares are held as treasury shares, the number and aggregate nominal value of the treasury shares and, where shares of more than one class have been allotted, the number and aggregate nominal value of the shares of each class held as treasury shares.

3. if the allotted capital includes **redeemable** shares:

– the earliest and latest dates on which the company can redeem the shares;

– whether the company is obliged to redeem the shares or whether the shares are redeemable at the option of either the company or the shareholders;

– whether any premium is payable on redemption and, if so, the amount.

4. if any shares have been **allotted during the current year**: Sch 1 para 48 SI 2008/410

– the class of shares allotted;

– for each class, the number allotted, their aggregate nominal value and the consideration received;
– the reason for making the issue.
5. if there are **options** to subscribe for shares or other rights that require the allotment of shares:
– the number, description and amount of shares for which the rights are exercisable;
– the period during which the rights are exercisable;
– the price to be paid.

MEMO POINTS Under the Companies Act 1985, a company was required to have an authorised share capital. Accordingly, there was a requirement to state the amount of authorised share capital in the notes to the accounts.

2. Under FRS 4

3777 FRS 4 (56) FRS 4 requires the presentation of a brief summary of the rights attaching to the different classes of **non-equity shares**, (¶3606) including:
1. the rights to dividends
2. the dates on which the shares are redeemable and the amounts payable on redemption
3. the priority and amounts receivable on a winding up
4. voting rights.

If, in respect of any class of shares for which the above disclosures are made, additional information is necessary to explain why the shares have been classified as non-equity, this information should be given.

FRS 4 (58) Where warrants or convertible debt in issue may result in the company's issuing a class of shares not already in issue, the above information should be set out for those shares.

EXAMPLE X Ltd has ordinary and "A" class preference shares in issue. It also has warrants in issue entitling the holders to one "B" class share for every 2 warrants held. The notes to the balance sheet should disclose the following regarding "B" shares:
Class "B" shares, when issued, will carry the following rights:
1. one vote per share
2. a cumulative preference dividend of 8 per cent
3. ranking after "A" class preference dividends in a winding up, with a per-share entitlement limited to £3.

3. Under FRS 25

3778 FRS 25 requires all financial instruments – or their component parts – to be classified as equity, financial liabilities, or financial assets. As a result, certain types of shares will no longer be classified under share capital but as financial liabilities (see definition at ¶3607). Furthermore, some shares may actually be **compound financial instruments** and, accordingly, must be split into their respective "equity" and "financial liability" components.

Ordinary shares are treated as equity and are disclosed as part of shareholders' funds. Preference shares can either fall into the same category or be classified as a financial liability depending on the rights and characteristics attaching to them. For example, **non-redeemable** preference shares, whose dividends are payable at the **company's option**, are regarded under FRS 25 as equity instruments and would be disclosed together with ordinary shares.

On the other hand, **cumulative preference shares** will be treated differently. Because the dividend accumulates if not paid in any year, they do not fall into the category of dividends payable at the company's option, as described above; on the contrary, they remain a liability until paid. Therefore, these financial instruments must be divided into their components so that the equity component is shown in the balance sheet under "Shareholders' funds" while the liability component would be shown under "Creditors: Amounts payable after more than one year".

4. Under the Listing Rules

Where a listed company **allots shares for cash during the year** under review and the allotment: 3779 LR 9.8.4 (7)
– was not made to the company's shareholders in proportion to their shareholdings, and
– was not specifically authorised by the shareholders,
the Listing Rules require the following to be disclosed:
– the classes of shares allotted and for each class of shares, the number allotted, their aggregate nominal value and the consideration received by the company for the allotment,
– the names of all the allottees if less than six in number or, if six or more, a brief generic description of each new class of equity holder,
– the market price of the securities concerned on the date that the terms of issue were fixed, and
– the date on which the terms of the issue were fixed.

If a listed company is a **subsidiary** of another company, any participation by the parent company in any placing during the period under review must be disclosed. LR 9.8.4 (9)

5. Example

The following serves as an example of prevailing disclosure requirements in respect of share capital in the notes. 3780

20. Share Capital

	Ordinary shares	Preference shares	Total share capital	Share premium	Total
	£000	**£000**	**£000**	**£000**	**£000**
At 1 January 20X5	100	12	112	10	122
Proceeds from shares issued	10		10	5	15
At 31 December 20X5	110	12	122	15	137
Preference shares reclassified to borrowings	-	(12)	(12)	-	(12)
At 1 January 20X6	110	-	110	15	125
Proceeds from shares issued	20		20	20	40
At 31 December 20X6	130		130	35	165

	20X6		20X5	
	Shares	**£000**	Shares	£000
Authorised ordinary shares of £1 each	250,000	250	250,000	250

	20X6		20X5	
	Shares	**£000**	Shares	£000
Allotted, called up and fully paid ordinary shares of £1 each:				
At start of year	110,000	110	100,000	100
Proceeds of issue	20,000	20	10,000	10
At end of year	130,000	130	110,000	110

During the year, the company issued 20,000 ordinary shares (20X5 – 10,000) at a premium of £1 each (20X5 – 50p)

B. Reserves

1. Disclosure on the face of the balance sheet

3782 Companies may have any of the following reserves. Unless the balance sheet is in deficit, the reserves, in aggregate, represent the excess of assets over liabilities after called up share capital has been deducted.

The following reserves must be shown on the face of the balance sheet:
- share premium account
- revaluation reserve (or similar title)
- other reserves
- profit and loss account.

The revaluation reserve is the only reserve that companies are allowed to call by another name.

3783 The main heading "other reserves" has the following constituents, which can be shown on the balance sheet itself or by way of a note:
- capital redemption reserve
- reserve for own shares
- reserves provided for by the articles of association
- other reserves (realised and unrealised that do not fit elsewhere in the formats).

3784 Sch 1 para 59 SI 2008/410 For each reserve in respect of which there have been transfers either in or out during the year, the following must be shown:
- opening and closing balances
- amounts transferred to or from reserves during the year
- the source and application of the amounts transferred.

3785 Companies can provide the required information for each reserve separately or in a combined note, as illustrated below. When there have been transfers between reserves, a combined note will often give readers a clearer view of the overall movements.

Comparative figures for the preceding year are not required.

2. Statement of movements on reserves

3787 The Companies Act requires companies to reconcile the opening and closing balances of individual reserves. Where the entity's reserves structure is complex, it may be useful to show the information in a statement of movements on reserves.

EXAMPLE **Statement of movements on reserves**

	Profit and loss account	Share premium	Revaluation reserve	Total
	£	£	£	£
At beginning of year	200	120	450	770
Surplus on revaluation of investment properties	-	-	42	42
Decrease in value of trade investment	-	-	-27	-27
Transfer of realised profits	58	-	-58	-
Profit retained for the year	110	-	-	110
At end of year	368	120	407	895

3. Distributable reserves

If, in the context of **group accounts**, there are any significant statutory, contractual or exchange control restrictions on the parent undertaking's access to distributable profits, FRS 2, "Accounting for subsidiary undertakings", requires the consolidated financial statements to disclose both the nature and extent of those restrictions. 3789 FRS 2 (53)

EXAMPLE **The following is an example of a note envisaged by FRS 2:**

The Group has certain reserves that are not freely distributable and represent amounts of foreign tax exempted under non-UK investment-incentive programmes. These reserves cannot be distributed to shareholders without incurring liability for payment of the previously exempted taxes, interest and penalties. The reserves are currently reinvested in the business and there is no intention to remit them. At 31 December 20X1, these non-distributable reserves amounted to £25 million (20X0: £32 million).

4. Items charged or credited direct to reserves

Items should be charged or credited direct to reserves (without going through the profit and loss account) only if: 3791
- it is specifically required by an accounting standard, or
- it is required or permitted by law.

Examples are items charged directly against share premium account (such as issue costs on shares) or **contributions from owners**.

C. Shareholders' funds

1. Disclosure on the face of the balance sheet

Although FRS 25 effectively rendered FRS 4 obsolete in most respects for those entities applying the measurement requirements of FRS 26, the old standard remained applicable in the case of the measurement of debt and the measurement of gains and losses of the repurchase of debt. 3793

Because FRS 25 does not recognise non-equity shareholders' funds, an analysis is no longer required either on the face of the balance sheet or the notes to the accounts. In the main, shares that in the past were disclosed as non-equity shareholders' funds will be presented as liabilities instead.

2. Reconciliation of movements in shareholders' funds

FRS 3 prescribes a reconciliation of the opening and closing totals of shareholders' funds to highlight those items that do not appear in the profit and loss account or **the statement of total recognised gains and losses** (STRGL). The reason is to ensure that attention is drawn to matters that are important for a proper appreciation of the company's affairs. These include dividends as a deduction from the year's net profit/loss as well as other movements in shareholders' funds such as goodwill written off and share capital issued or redeemed. 3795 FRS 3 (28), (59)

This reconciliation should, however, be **shown separately** from the STRGL.

EXAMPLE The following is an example of a reconciliation of movements in the **STRGL**:

	20X2 £'000	20X1 £'000
Profit for the year	£ 49	£ 41
Dividends	-23	-19
	£ 26	£ 22
Other recognised gains and losses for the year (net)	15	-9
New share capital subscribed	12	0
Net increase in shareholders' funds	£ 53	£ 13
Shareholders' funds at beginning of year	243	230
Shareholders' funds at end of year	£ 396	£ 243

3796 Where only a small number of movements on reserves has taken place during the year, it is permissible to **combine** the statement of movements in shareholders' funds with the statement of movements on reserves.

EXAMPLE **Combined Statement of Movements in Shareholders' Funds and Statement of Movements on Reserves**

	Profit and loss account	Issued share capital	Share premium account	Revaluation reserve	20X2	Total 20X1
	£	£	£	£	£	£
At beginning of year	200	500	120	450	1270	1195
Profit for the year	112	-	-	-	112	98
Dividends	-56	-	-	-	-56	-43
Surplus on revaluation of investment properties	-	-	-	42	42	-
Increase (decrease) in value of trade investment	-	-	-	-27	-27	20
Capital subscribed	-	20	2	-	22	-
Transfer of realised profits	25	-	-	-25	-	-
At end of year	281	520	122	440	1363	1270

3. Capital contributions

3798 If a parent makes funds available to a subsidiary in the form of a non-returnable gift, the transaction is deemed to be a contribution of capital. The subsidiary has no obligation to transfer economic benefits and the contribution should be taken directly to shareholders' funds. The item should be shown in the reconciliation of movements in shareholders' funds.

As to where, within shareholders' funds, a capital contribution should be shown, the following possibilities exist:

– unless otherwise provided by the Articles, if the contribution was received in cash it can be considered realised and therefore taken to the profit and loss reserve;

– if the contribution was received in a form other than cash, until such other assets have been realised they should not be considered as part of distributable profits. In this case, showing the contribution under "other reserves" is more appropriate.

MEMO POINTS As to the treatment of the capital contribution by the **parent** company (i.e., the donor), no formal reporting guidance has been given. It is most commonly capitalised as part of the cost of the investment in the subsidiary.

4. Share issue expenses

3800 When shares are issued, any expenses that can be treated as share issue costs must be taken into account in determining the net proceeds of the issue and shown in the reconciliation of movements in shareholders' funds. They should not be shown in the statement of total recognised gains and losses.

For non-equity shares, the total finance costs recognised in the profit and loss account over the term of the shares must include the share issue expenses.

D. Carrying amounts

The carrying amount is the amount at which shares are stated in the balance sheet and is of particular importance where, for instance, the shares in question are redeemed. The amount at which the transaction is recorded is based on the carrying value of the shares at the time. **3805**

1. Amount recorded on issue

When shares are first issued, the net proceeds are reported in the reconciliation of shareholders' funds. The Act requires the nominal value of shares to be shown as share capital and any premium (excess of proceeds over the nominal value) in the share premium account. **3807**

The Act prescribes further that the share premium account can be used to write off share issue expenses. However, if the amount in the share premium account is insufficient to absorb them, these costs should be taken to an "other" reserve. Although it is also permissible for these share-issue expenses to be taken to the profit and loss account reserve, this is a less desirable option because:
- share issue costs do not represent a realised loss, which means that charging profit and loss reserves could create a potentially misleading view of profits available for distribution, and
- for purposes of establishing legally distributable reserves, separate records will have to be kept of the unrealised loss included within the profit and loss account reserve.

2. Subsequent adjustments

In the case of **equity shares**, no adjustments are made to the value at which they are carried. **3809** FRS 4 (45)

The treatment of **non-equity shares** differs in that the carrying value is increased each year by the **finance costs** (¶3035) for the period and reduced by the amount of any dividend or other payment made during the year. FRS 4 (41)

3. Conversion of debt or non-equity shares to equity share capital

When **debt** is converted to equity share capital, the amount at which to record the new issue is the carrying value of the debt at the date of conversion. No gain or loss is recognised. **3811** FRS 4 (26)

In cases where **non-equity shares** are converted to equity shares, the conversion can take the following forms:
- the non-equity shares can be cancelled and new equity shares issued in their place;
- the non-equity shares are not cancelled but the rights attaching to them are altered so that they fall under the definition of equity shares.

Under both methods the net total reserves will remain the same; however, individual reserves may be affected.

EXAMPLE To raise funds, **C Ltd** issues 1000 redeemable convertible preference shares as follows:

Nominal value	£1
Issue price	£1.40
Dividend rate	8.5%

The issue costs amounted to £270.

The shares can be redeemed at a premium of 30p on the nominal value after 5 years. Alternatively, holders may elect to convert their preference shares into £0.50 ordinary shares in the ratio of 1: 1 at any time after the first 2 years.

Finance costs are to be apportioned at a rate of 10 per cent on the carrying amount.

The net proceeds of the issue, £1130, will be recorded as follows:

Share capital	£1000
Share premium (premium of £400 less issue expenses of £270)	£ 130

Over 5 years, the carrying amount of the shares will accumulate to equal the amount of the redemption payment as follows:

Year	Beginning-of-year balance	Finance Charge	Payments	End-of-year balance (carrying value)
1	1130	113	85	1158
2	1158	115	85	1188
3	1188	119	85	1222
4	1222	122	85	1259
5	1259	126	85	1300
			*1300	0

* Final redemption payment

Annual finance costs in excess of dividends paid should be taken to a separate reserve (£113 – £85 in Year 1; £115 – £85 in Year 2, and so on).
If any of the preference shares are converted before their redemption date, the proceeds of the ordinary shares issued (or their issue price) is the carrying value of the preference shares at the time. This amount will have a nominal value element and a share premium element.
To illustrate, assume that all the shares are converted – into 1000 50p ordinary shares – at the end of year 3, when the carrying value is £1,222. The following journal entries will record the transaction:

	Dr.	Cr.
Preference share capital	1000	
Preference share premium	130	
Other reserves (reserve for premium on redemption)	92	
Ordinary share capital		500
Ordinary share premium		722

E. Finance costs of non-equity shares

3813 The cost of financing non-equity shares is the difference between the net proceeds received by the issuer and any payments it makes to the holders over the term of the shares. Specifically, the financing charge for the company includes all dividend payments and the premium payable on redemption. In addition, any issue costs on converting the non-equity shares to equity shares are included as finance costs.

3814 In general, the total finance costs of non-equity shares should be spread over the term of the shares. The term of the share will end on the earliest date that the provider of the finance (i.e., the shareholder) can demand repayment.
Where options for early redemption are available, the term should be taken to the first date at which the option can be exercised. The term should not include any period for which the share may be extended, unless it is known at the time the shares are issued that the term is **certain to be extended**.

F. Warrants and options

Warrants and options are similar instruments generally requiring the issuer to issue shares but not to transfer economic benefits. Options are usually granted to specific individuals while warrants are generally transferable. Where a company **issues** warrants, the treatment under FRS 4 was that proceeds were credited directly to shareholders' funds. Provided that the purchase relates to equity shares, a similar treatment after 1 January 2005 (from which date FRS 25 supersedes FRS 4) should apply. 3816

FRS 25 introduces the requirement that where an entity issues a compound financial instrument, it must account separately for the components that create a **financial liability** and those that grant an option to the holder to convert it into **equity**.

When warrants are **exercised** the net proceeds must be transferred out of shareholders' funds to share capital (and share premium account, if appropriate). 3817

The disclosures required in respect of warrants and options are: the number, description, and amount of shares; the period during which the option is exercisable; and the price to be paid. Where the warrants are convertible into a class of shares not already issued, the rights attaching to them should also be disclosed. 3818

PART 6

Other primary statements

CHAPTER 1

Cash flow statements

OUTLINE ¶¶

4000 FRS 1 (5) There is **no statutory requirement** for companies to prepare a cash flow statement. However, FRS 1, "Cash flow statements", requires that all reporting entities preparing financial statements intended to give a true and fair view include a cash flow statement, unless specifically exempted. The cash flow statement comprises a number of **standard classifications**, within which the cash inflows and outflows should be shown separately in accordance with the substance of the underlying transactions.

4002 The **purpose of the cash flow statement** is to:
– report the cash generation and absorption of an entity by highlighting the significant components of cash flow; and
– provide information enabling users to assess an entity's liquidity and solvency and hence the financial risk.

4004 A cash flow statement is usually reviewed in conjunction with the profit and loss account and balance sheet and is supported by a number of **key reconciliations** and **disclosures**. Group cash flow statements and foreign currency cash flows require additional disclosures.

FRS 1 (2) **Cash flows are defined as** increases or decreases in cash and comprise cash in hand and deposits, or an overdraft repayable on demand at a qualifying financial institution such as a bank, building society or other business that grants credits and receives deposits or other repayable funds.

MEMO POINTS Deposits "repayable on demand" qualify if they can be withdrawn at any time without penalty, or if a maturity or period of notice of not more than 24 hours or one working day has been agreed. Cash also includes deposits denominated in foreign currencies.

The **key differences** between FRS 1 and IAS 7 are covered. The cash flow statements prepared by banks and insurance companies are beyond the scope of this book.

Exempt entities

4010 The **following entities** are exempt from the requirements of FRS 1 to produce a cash flow statement:
– subsidiary undertakings where 90% of the voting rights are controlled within the group and consolidated accounts are publicly available;
– companies satisfying the small company criteria under the Companies Act 2006;
– mutual life assurance companies;
– pension funds; and
– open-ended investment funds meeting certain criteria.

MEMO POINTS "Publicly available" means disclosure in a national registry or national gazette.

4012 Exemption **is not available where a small company** is:
– a public company;
– a bank or insurance company;
– a person authorised under the Financial Services Act 1986 (2010); or
– a member of a group containing one or more of the above entities.

MEMO POINTS The Financial Services Act 2010 received its Royal Assent in April 2010.

4014 **Small groups** may be excluded from preparing cash flow statements if the parent company qualifies as a small company, and claim exemption from preparing consolidated financial statements.

4016 **FRSSE** The FRSSE **encourages but does not require** smaller entities to prepare a cash flow statement, but when they so do, the use of the indirect method is recommended (¶4042). Small **unincorporated entities** that satisfy the criteria (see ¶6017) for a qualification as a small company are exempt from preparing a cash flow statement. An example of a cash flow statement for a small company is given in ¶4120.

4018 **Medium-sized companies** Medium-sized companies should produce a cash flow statement, irrespective of whether or not they choose to file full financial statements with the Registrar of Companies. **Medium sized groups** are not entitled to claim exemption under the Companies Act from preparing consolidated financial statements and hence a cash flow statement, unless the parent is itself a small company, in which case it is entitled to exemption in its own right.

Open-ended investment funds For open-ended investment funds to be granted exemption, substantially all of the fund's investments should be highly liquid and carried at market value and the entity must provide a statement of changes in net assets. **4022**

SECTION 1

Format

The accounting standard stipulates how cash flow information should be presented under the following **standard headings** in the order shown below: **4024**
- operating activities; FRS 1 (c)
- dividends from associates and joint ventures;
- returns on investments and servicing of finance;
- taxation;
- capital expenditure and financial investment;
- acquisitions and disposals;
- equity dividends paid;
- management of liquid resources; and
- financing.

The **cash flow classifications** may be further divided into inflows and outflows to provide a more detailed breakdown of the entities operations. In addition to the standard headings, certain reconciliations, as discussed in section 3 below, must be provided along with other information in the notes to the cash flow statement. There is also a requirement to detail any **exceptional cash flows**. **4026**

All the headings should be in the sequence set out above **with the option** of the last two being combined under a single heading, provided that the cash flows pertaining to each are shown individually with sub-totals. The format is the same for both individual company and group cash flow statements. Including **a sub-total** after any of the other standard headings is neither required or prohibited, but is a useful device for highlighting the level of net cash flows under a particular category.

In general, there is **a degree of flexibility allowed** in the reporting of cash flows. Companies may elect to report all significant gross cash flows on the face of the cash flow statement under the appropriate standard headings, or the information can be detailed in the notes to the cash flow statement, with only the main headings being shown on the face of the cash flow statement itself. **4028** FRS 1 (8)

The standard classifications adopted in the FRS **can be changed only** in exceptional circumstances and where failure to do so would mislead readers of the financial statements.

The standard classifications are intended to improve the comparability of cash flow statements of different entities. Entities are encouraged to provide further information in the notes to the cash flow statement that better reflect the particular circumstances of their industry. Reporting the division of cash flows between **continued** and **discontinued operations** is also required. **4030**

A. Content by classification

The **general rule is** that each individual cash flow should be classified according to the substance of the underlying transaction that gives rise to it. Where the reason for adopting a particular classification is not readily apparent from the nature of the transaction, additional detail should be provided either in the form of notes or a reconciliation. **4034**

Operating activities

4036 FRS 1 (11) Cash flows from operating activities are the cash effects of transactions and other events relating to operating or trading activities, as shown in the profit and loss account in arriving at operating profit. Operating cash flows can be presented by either the **direct method** or the **indirect method**.

FRS 1 (Appendix IV.18) Although the Accounting Standards Board (ASB) advocates the use of the direct method where the information is not too costly to obtain, the information supplied in the indirect method is still required. Therefore, there is little incentive to adopt the direct approach and in practice most companies use the indirect method.

4040 FRS 1 (58) **Direct (gross) method** Under the direct method of preparing a cash flow statement, the operating cash receipts and payments are aggregated to show the net cash flow from operating activities. This method reports individual company cash flows, **based on an analysis** of the cash book and tabulates the actual cash received or remitted, to show the net cash flow from operating activities. This method is considered more costly and time consuming to prepare. The **principal advantage** of the direct method is that it shows operating cash receipts and payments.

EXAMPLE **Direct method**
ABC Ltd
Notes to the cash flow statement

Operating activities	**£'000**
Cash received from customers	28,000
Cash payments to suppliers	(12,000)
Cash paid to employees	(4,000)
Other operating cash payments	(3,000)
Net cash inflow from operating activities	**9,000**

4042 **Indirect (net) method** The cash flow statement prepared on the basis of the indirect method indicates the relationship between profitability and the cash generating ability of the business. The indirect method arrives at the same net cash flow from operating activities as the direct method, by working back from operating profit in the form of a reconciliation (as illustrated in ¶4134). The **operating profit is adjusted** for charges such as depreciation, amortisation, and profits and losses on the disposal of fixed assets. The reconciliation should also include adjustments for movements in stocks, debtors and creditors.

Dividends from joint ventures and associates

4044 Dividends for joint ventures and associates **are shown separately because** of the high degree of influence that an investing entity may exercise over joint ventures or associate companies. Also in the consolidated financial statements, the dividend received figure for individual companies is not readily apparent from the consolidated profit and loss account.

Cash flows from a group's operating activities are different from the cash flows resulting from returns on its investments and, as such, should be separately identified. FRS 1 intends that although there should be a single heading, this should be analysed further into the two separate categories for associates and joint ventures.

Other cash flows from associates and joint ventures, such as those arising from trading or loan interest, should be included under the appropriate heading in the statement.

EXAMPLE **ABC Ltd**
Notes to the cash flow statement (extract)

	2010	**2009**
	£m	**£m**
Dividends from joint ventures and associates	**10.5**	**6.8**
Dividends received from joint ventures	7.5	4.2
Dividends received from associates	3.0	2.6

Returns on other investments and servicing of finance

Returns on investments and servicing of finance **are receipts resulting from** the ownership of an investment, other than an associate or joint venture and payments to providers of finance, non-equity shareholders (e.g. preference shares) and minority interests. **Dividends paid** to equity shareholders are shown under a separate heading because they are discretionary by nature whereas other finance costs such as interest are contractual. 4046 FRS 1 (13)

Cash inflows include interest received, including any related tax recovered and dividends received. 4050

Cash outflows include:
- interest paid, even if capitalised;
- finance costs, including issue costs on debt and non-equity share capital; FRS 1 (15)
- the interest element on finance lease rental payments;
- dividends paid on non-equity shares of the entity; and
- dividends paid by subsidiaries to minority interests.

The **capital element on finance lease rental payments** is included under the separate heading of financing.

It is worth noting that because of the method of calculating finance costs under FRS 4, the charge in the profit and loss account may not represent the cash flows actually arising in that year. The amount included within the cash flow statement may well be different from the charge in the profit and loss account.

EXAMPLE **ABC Ltd**
Notes to the cash flow statement (extract)
Returns on investments and servicing of finance

	2010 £m	2009 £m
Interest received	11.0	8.8
Interest paid	(3.5)	(2.7)
Interest element of finance lease rental payments	(1.4)	(1.3)
Dividends received from other investments	5.0	2.0
Dividends paid to minority shareholders	(2.2)	(1.8)
Preference dividends paid	(1.1)	(0.8)
Total	**7.8**	**4.2**

Taxation

The cash flows under this heading represent taxation on the profits of the entity. Payments in respect of other taxes paid by the entity, such as PAYE, should be shown as part of the cash flow to which the taxation relates. 4052 FRS 1 (16)

Cash inflows include tax rebates and returns of overpayments. For **subsidiaries**, payments received from other group companies for group relief, should be included as cash inflows.

Cash outflows cover tax payments and for subsidiary undertakings, payments made to other group companies for group relief.

EXAMPLE **ABC Ltd**
Notes to the cash flow statement (extract)
Taxation

	2010 £m
UK Corporation tax paid	(69.0)
Non UK tax paid	(10.2)
Total	**(79.2)**

Value added tax Cash flows should be shown net of any attributable VAT unless the tax is recovered by the reporting entity. The net movement on the amount payable to, or receiv- 4058 FRS 1 (39) able from, the taxing authority should be allocated to cash flows from operating activities unless a different treatment is more appropriate.

Where **restrictions apply** to the recovery of VAT, the **irrecoverable amount** should be allocated to those expenditures affected by the restrictions. If this is not practicable, the irrecoverable tax should be included under the most appropriate standard heading.

Capital expenditure and financial investment

4060 The cash flows included under this heading relate to the acquisition or disposal of fixed assets (other than those to be disclosed under the heading "acquisitions and disposals"), and current asset investments not regarded as liquid resources.

Cash inflows include receipts from:
- the sales or disposals of property, plant and equipment;
- the repayment of the reporting entity's loans to other entities; and
- sales of debt instruments of other entities.

FRS 1 (20)

Cash outflows include:
- payments to acquire property, plant or equipment;
- loans made by the reporting entity; and
- acquisition of debt instruments.

Also included in this category are cash flows relating to development costs that have been capitalised.

EXAMPLE **ABC Ltd**

Notes to the cash flow statement (extract)

Net cash inflow (outflow) for capital expenditure and financial investment

	2010 £'000	**2009 £'000**
Purchase of intangible fixed assets	(4,208)	(1,710)
Purchase of tangible fixed assets	(4,756)	(2,150)
Sale of tangible fixed assets	440	375
Purchase of fixed asset investments	(93)	(80)
Disposal of fixed asset investments	175	135
Total cash inflow (outflow)	**(8,442)**	**(3,430)**

4064 **Assets acquired under finance leases** are not shown separately but included in the total addition to fixed assets figure for the year. However, as the purchase of fixed assets does not involve a cash outlay at the start of the lease, the fair value of the leased asset included in fixed asset additions should be eliminated, in order to reflect the true cash outflow.

The finance lease rental payments should be analysed between interest and capital, and shown under "Returns on investments and servicing of finance" and "financing" respectively.

Acquisition and disposals

4068 **Cash inflows** comprise receipts from sales of:
- investments in subsidiary undertakings;
- investments in associates or joint ventures; and
- minority interests.

FRS 1 (22)

Other cash inflows result from:
- the take up of shares resulting from a **rights issue** by a subsidiary; or
- a **capital contribution** from a parent to a subsidiary (non-returnable gift).

For the subsidiary, non-returnable gifts are included in the financing section of the cash flow statement. The parent should treat the gift in its cash flow statement under acquisitions and disposals.

Cash outflows cover payments to acquire:
- investments in subsidiary undertakings;
- investments in associates and joint ventures; and
- minority interests.

EXAMPLE **ABC Ltd**

Notes to the cash flow statement (extract)

Acquisition and disposals

	2010 £'000	**2009 £'000**
Purchase of subsidiary undertakings	(14,450)	3,605)
Investments in joint ventures	(3,750)	(1,800)
Investments in associates	(5,720)	(3,250)
Repayment of loan to joint venture	(750)	(250)
Disposal of subsidiary undertakings	4,250	1,116
Sale of investments in joint ventures	500	125
Net cash (outflow) for acquisitions and disposals	**(19,920)**	**(7,664)**

The presentation above can be included on the face of the cash flow statement or detailed as a note to the accounts. Cash flows for any subsidiary disposed of should be added to the cash flow statement for the period its results were included in the group profit and loss account. **4069**

Information should also be supplied by way of note, covering net assets acquired and net assets disposed of.

The following information for disposals should be given in the notes:
- cash received;
- a summary of the effect of the disposal on each category of asset and liability;
- where material, the effect on the cash flow position of the parent company resulting from the disposal of the subsidiary. Comparative figures for the previous year are not required.

Similar information covering the impact of any acquisitions on the group cash flow statement should also be disclosed.

Equity dividends paid

This classification includes equity dividends paid by the reporting entity or, if part of a group, the parent's equity shares. Dividends paid by subsidiaries to shareholders outside the group (minority shareholders) must be shown under "Returns on investments and servicing of finance". **4074** FRS 1 (25)

Management of liquid resources

This section of the cash flow statement is designed to reflect the profile of a reporting entity's cash and liquidity management. Liquid resources are **current asset investments** (¶2700) held as disposable stores of value readily convertible into cash at, or close to, their carrying amount. An entity is required to detail the investments it has included as liquid resources and any change in accounting policy. **Charges in the market value** of current asset investments included under liquid resources do not have an immediate impact on cash flow but may affect the carrying value of the investment at the balance sheet date. **4076** FRS 1 (26)

Unlisted investments held as current assets are unlikely to qualify as liquid resources and are more appropriately included under capital expenditure and financial investment. **Fixed asset investments** (¶1750) do not qualify because they are held as a ready store of value for continuing use in the business and are not readily disposable. **4077**

Cash inflows include withdrawals from short-term deposits not qualifying as cash and inflows from disposal or redemption of any other investments held as liquid resources. **4080**

Cash outflows cover payments into short-term deposits not qualifying as cash and outflows to acquire other investments held as liquid resources.

The cash inflows and outflows in this section may be "netted-off" against one another if the following apply: FRS 1 (26)
- the cash flows relate in substance to a single transaction; or

– are due to short maturities and high turnover occurring from the rollover or reissue of short-term deposits. Simply **renewing overnight deposits** with the company's bankers would not be regarded as a separate inflow and outflow of cash.
Unlisted investments held as current assets are unlikely to qualify as liquid resources and are more appropriately included under capital expenditure and financial investments.

EXAMPLE **ABC Ltd**
Notes to the cash flow statement (extract)
Management of liquid resources

	2010 £'000	2009 £'000
Purchase of government securities (treasury bills)	(1,555)	1,023)
Short term deposits over 3 months	(345)	(255)
Sale of government bonds	1,265	952
Withdrawals from short-term deposits	1,002	520
Sale of corporate bonds	50	
Net movement of short-term investments and deposits under 3 months not repayable on demand.	(450)	(390)
Net cash inflow (outflow) from management of liquid resources	(33)	(196)

Financing

4082 FRS 1 (29) Financing cash flows consist of receipts from or repayment to external providers of finance. Only the principal amounts of finance should be included in this category with any interest element or dividend dealt with under the appropriate category.
Cash inflows covers receipts from issuing:
– shares or other equity instruments; and
– debentures, loans, notes, and bonds and from other long-term and short-term borrowings (excluding overdrafts).
Cash outflows:
– repayments of amounts borrowed (excluding overdrafts);
– the capital element of finance lease rental payments;
– payments to require or redeem the entity's shares; and
– payments of expenses or commissions on any issue of equity shares.

4083 It should be noted that **because of the basis of recognising capital instruments** under FRS 4, for example showing a debenture in the balance sheet net of issue costs, recognition of amounts in the balance sheet and therefore the profit and loss account, may differ from the cash flows arising. Movements in the amount recorded in financial instruments and other liabilities in the balance sheet may not therefore correspond with the amounts shown in the cash flow statement. This is partly why certain reconciliations (see ¶4128), are required by FRS 1.

EXAMPLE **ABC Ltd**
Cash flow statement (extract)
Financing

	2010 £'000	2009 £'000
Issue of ordinary share capital	175	110
Issue of shares to minorities	25	
Issue of debentures 2010	2,000	1,200
New loans	7,500	5,430
Redemption of preference share capital	(350)	(125)
Repayment of secured loans	(2,175)	(1,175)
Net increase (decrease) in short-term borrowings	(2,200)	(1,356)
Repayment of unsecured loans	(125)	(68)
Initial element of finance lease rentals	(1,342)	
Net cash inflow (outflow) from financing	**3,508**	**4,016**

B. Exceptional cash flows

A cash flow may be deemed exceptional due to its value, size or incidence, or it relates to an item treated as exceptional in the profit and loss account. Cash flows deemed exceptional should be shown separately under the relevant standard heading or by way of a note to the accounts. In addition, sufficient information should be provided to allow the users to understand the underlying transactions generating the cash flows. **4085** FRS 1 (37)

Examples of exceptional cash flows include: **4086**
a. Cash inflows arising on the sale of fixed assets;
b. Restructuring or reorganisation costs; resulting from:
- the costs of training;
- new systems development;
- the downsizing of operations;
- elimination of product lines; or
- the mothballing or relocation of production facilities.

Exceptional profits or losses from a **sale of operations** should be included under "acquisitions and disposals", whilst proceeds from a **sale of fixed assets** should be categorised under "capital expenditure and financial investment". **4088**

Where cash flows are exceptional, because of the size or incidence, but are not related to items in the profit and loss account, sufficient disclosure should be given in the notes to explain the cause and the nature of the cash flow. A large prepayment against a future pension liability is an example of an exceptional cash flow unrelated to an exceptional item in the profit and loss account.

SECTION 2

Foreign currency cash flows

The accounting treatment of foreign currency activities in cash flow statements is relatively complex and FRS 1 gives minimal guidance on the treatment required. Foreign currency transactions for **individual companies** are dealt with in this section and can be divided into a number of categories. **Group foreign currency cash flows** are covered in ¶4218 whilst for a more detailed review of the accounting treatment for foreign currency transactions, see ¶8000. **4090**

Companies may enter directly into business transactions denominated in foreign currencies or conduct foreign currency operations through overseas subsidiaries, associates or branches. A distinction should be drawn between **settled** and **unsettled foreign currency transactions** at the balance sheet date. **Special rules exist** for non-operational transactions and hedging transactions.

FRS 23 "The Effects of Changes in Foreign Exchange Rates" **only applies to entities** that prepare their financial statements in accordance with FRS 26 "Financial Instruments: Measurement", to which a number of further conditions apply, as set out below and in greater detail in ¶3400. **Where FRS 26 and hence FRS 23 are not applied**, existing UK GAAP in the form of SSAP 20 still applies. **4092**

MEMO POINTS 1. FRS 23 and FRS 26 form part of a package of standards including FRS 24 "Financial Reporting in Hyperinflationary Economies", and FRS 25 "Financial Instruments: Disclosure and Presentation". FRS 23 is covered in greater detail in ¶8382.
2. FRS 26 **applies to all listed entities**. **Other entities** are free to adopt the standard with the proviso that all standards in the package (FRS 23-26) are adopted. **Unlisted entities** that have adopted fair value accounting policies must also apply the new standards.

3. Most of FRS 4, with the exception of material relating to the measurement of debt and gains and losses on the repurchase of debt, is withdrawn when an entity opts to adopt FRS 25. The remainder of FRS 4 is withdrawn on implementation of FRS 26.
4. The ASB has plans to issue improvements to FRS 24-26 in 2011.

Settled currency transactions

4094 For **direct transactions** in foreign currencies the entity must assess the basic components of each transaction in order to determine the relevant cash flows.

Examples of operational transactions **include**:
- purchase or sale of trading items, such as stock, in a foreign currency;
- settlement by a foreign currency trade debtor; or
- settlement of a foreign currency trade creditor.

The results of the foreign currency transaction are translated into the reporting currency of the company, at the rate ruling at the transaction date. **Exchange differences** arise because of differences in the exchange rate at the transaction date and settlement date.

4096 The **profit or loss arising on exchange differences**, resulting from operational foreign currency transactions, will be reflected in the profit and loss account and included in the cash flow statement as part of "Net cash flow from operating activities". No specific adjustments are required.

EXAMPLE **Settled transactions**
Notes to the cash flow statement
Repayment of foreign currency trade creditor

A UK Company was set up in 2008 and had only two transactions in the first financial year. It raised £350,000 through a share issue. The company purchased goods for resale from Germany in March 2009 for €300, 000 at an exchange rate of £1 = €1.50. The purchase was entered in the accounts as €300, 000/1.5 = £200,000. Under the terms of the contract, the company paid the outstanding creditor in June 20X9 when the exchange rate has moved to £1 = €1.45. The amount paid in settlement was: €300, 000/1.45 = £206,897. An exchange rate loss of £6,897 should be recorded when calculating operating profit for the year.
A simplified cash flow statement would be as follows assuming no other transactions in the year.

Cash flow statement: 2010

	£
Net cash flow from operating activities (payment for stock)	(206,897)
Financing	350,000
Increase in cash	143,103

Note to the accounts
Reconciliation of operating profit to net cash flow from operating activities

	£
Net operating profit/ (loss)	(6,897)
Increase in stocks	(200,000)
Net cash flow from operating activities	(206,897)

The cash flow statement will reflect the amount of sterling that has flowed in or out of the business a result of the transaction, irrespective of how that has ultimately been recorded in the profit and loss account and balance sheet.

Unsettled currency transactions (operational)

4100 Foreign currency transactions that remain **outstanding at the balance sheet date** can give rise to exchange differences, where the asset was recorded at the actual exchange rate prevailing at the time of the transaction and then re-translated at the rate prevailing at the balance sheet date.

Any differences arising from the translation of **short-term working capital items** denominated in foreign currencies, such as cash and bank balances, debtors, creditors and loans, will generally be included in the profit and loss account. Therefore, **no adjustment is necessary**

when preparing the cash flow statement. This is due to the fact that increases or decreases in the debtor or creditor balances will include exchange differences on their re-translation at the balance sheet date, and the total movement in debtors and creditors constitutes an adjusting item in the reconciliation of operating profit to operating cash flows.

Any **exchange differences on long-term monetary items** reported as part of profit and loss account and included in operating profit, should be eliminated in arriving at net cash flow from operating activities. This is because the actual movement on long-term monetary items, which includes the exchange difference, is not reported in the reconciliation of operating profit to operating cash flow. Any exchange difference should be reported instead in the reconciliation of net cash flow to net debt (funds) (¶4144). **4104**

Non-operational transactions

Transactions that fall outside the scope of operations require the profit or loss arising to be matched and included as part of the cash flow arising from the related transaction. Examples include the following: **4112**
- **dividends** received from a foreign investment; and
- repayment of **foreign currency debt** (i.e. loan).

The dividend received plus any conversion profit or loss should be included under "Returns on investments and servicing of finance" or "Dividends from associates and joint ventures". Where foreign debt is repaid the capital repayment should be included under "Financing". **Any profit or loss on conversion** should not be shown separately but included in the reconciliation of "Net cash flow from operating activities".

Hedging transactions

Companies enter into hedging transactions as a protection from financial loss that can result from variations in price or exchange rates. This topic is introduced in this chapter in the context of cash flow statements, with greater detail given in ¶8300. **4116** FRS 1 (66)

The **general rule** is that where a **futures, forward, option or swap contract** is accounted for as a hedge, the cash flows of the contract should be reported under the same standard heading as the transaction that gives rise to the hedge. This treatment ensures that the cash flows resulting from the hedging instruments are paired with the cash flows arising from the items being hedged. **4117**

For example, the reporting entity may purchase a futures contract to reduce its exposure to increases in the price of planned stock purchases. Any cash flows generated by the futures contract should be reported in operating cash flows.

Another example is that an entity wishing to convert an existing fixed rate borrowing into a floating rate equivalent might enter into an interest rate swap, by which it receives fixed rates but pays floating rates. All the cash flows under this transaction should be reported under "Returns on investment and servicing of finance", because they are equivalent to interest or are hedges of interest payments.

SECTION 3

Small company format

Small companies **are exempt** from the requirements of FRS 1 and a cash flow statement is not required by the FRSSE, although **voluntary compliance** is encouraged. The main elements of the statement are as follows: **4120**

1. The **indirect method** should be used for calculating cash flows from operating activities.

2. The **cash flows from operating activities** should be reconciled to the cash position in the balance sheet, as opposed to the net debt position as required by FRS 1.

3. The **definition of cash** is simplified to that of "cash at bank and in hand, less overdrafts repayable on demand". FRS 1 widens the definition to include "deposits or overdrafts with qualifying institutions" and "deposits in foreign currencies".

An example of the format for a small company cash flow statement is set out below.

4121 EXAMPLE **NOP Ltd – 31 December 2010**

Cash flow statement

	2010	
	£	£
Cash generated from operating activities		
Operating profit (loss)	(25,500)	
Reconciled to cash generated from operations:		
Depreciation		
Increase in stocks	(34,000)	
Decrease in trade debtors	72,000	
Decrease in trade creditors	(27,000)	–
Increase in other creditors	26,000	
		11,500
Cash from other sources		–
Interest received	1,000	
Issue of shares for cash	30,000	
New long-term borrowings	2,500	–
Sale of tangible fixed assets	2,500	
		36,000
Application of cash		–
Interest paid	(3,000)	
Tax paid	(9,500)	
Dividends paid	(10,000)	–
Purchase of fixed assets	(8,500)	
		(31,000)
Net increase in cash		**16,500**
Cash at bank and in hand less overdrafts at beginning of the year		(3,250)
Cash at bank and in hand less overdrafts at end of year		**13,250**

SECTION 4

Reconciliations to other primary statements

4124 In addition to the main cash flow statement, a number of reconciliations **are required** to link the cash flow statement to the balance sheet and profit and loss account. Additional disclosures are required in the notes to the cash flow statement.

A. Compulsory reconciliations

4128 The information provided in the cash flow statement should be viewed in the context of information given in the other primary financial statements and not in isolation. In order to reconcile the cash flow statement to key components in the balance sheet and the profit and loss account, **two important reconciliations** are required, namely that between:

– the operating profit and net cash flow from operating activities; and

– the movement in cash in the period to the movement in net debt.

The reconciliation of movement in cash to movement in net debt (¶4144) should also include an analysis of both the **changes in net debt** and **total closing net debt**. Both reconciliations should be clearly labelled to highlight the fact that they are not part of the main cash flow statement. The reason for this is that some of the reconciling amounts may not be actual cash flows, so to include them in the cash flow statement would be inappropriate. **4130** FRS 1 (12)

1. Operating profit to net cash flow from operating activities

A **reconciliation between** the operating profit reported in the profit and loss account and the net cash flow from operating activities, forms part of the **indirect method**. The analysis should disclose separately the movements in stocks, debtors and creditors related to operating activities and other differences between cash flows and profits. This reconciliation should either adjoin the cash flow statement or be shown by way of note. However, some companies choose to include the reconciliation at the top of the cash flow statement. **4134**

The reconciliation adjusts operating profit for **non-cash charges** (e.g. depreciation) and **credits** in the profit and loss account, in order to reconcile it with the net cash flow from operating activities. It also recognises that some transactions in the profit and loss account which will ultimately result in "cash flows", for example purchases of goods and services, may not yet have generated cash flows, so that at any given point in time there are debtors and creditors. The **cash flow information is obtained by** analysing the movement in the figures in the balance sheet that correspond to the standard headings in the cash flow statement.

Increases in work in progress, stocks, and debtor balances represent cash outflows, as does a decrease in creditor balances. Conversely, a decrease in WIP, stocks or debtors represents cash inflows, as does an increase in creditor balances. **Depreciation charges** do not represent cash flows and as such are added back to operating profits in the reconciliation, as illustrated below. **4138**

EXAMPLE **XYZ Ltd**
Reconciliation of operating profit to net cash flow from operating activities
Indirect method

	2010	2009
	£'000	**£'000**
Operating profit	**759.5**	**625.0**
Depreciation and amortisation	191.3	152.0
Increase in work in progress	(25.3)	(20.0)
Increase in stocks	(272.3)	(299.0)
(Increase)/ decrease in debtors	(119.6)	(99.0)
Increase/ (decrease) in creditors	326.0	250.0
Payments against provisions	(22.0)	(11.0)
Net cash inflow from operating activities	**837.6**	**598.0**

Discontinued operations

Where an entity has reported discontinued operations in the profit and loss account, it is recommended that a note is provided, showing the division of cash flows into continued and discontinued operations. The reconciliation is generally positioned directly under the cash flow statement or by way of note. The **two principal methods** of presentation are illustrated in the example below. **4140** FRS 1 (56)

EXAMPLE **Notes to the cash flow statement**

Method 1

OPERATING ACTIVITIES	**£'000**
Net cash inflow from operating activities	16,662
Net cash outflow in respect of discontinued operations	(990)
Net cash inflow from operating activities	15,672

Method 2

	Continuing operations £'000	Discontinued operations £'000	Total £'000
Operating profit/ (loss)	18,829	(1,616)	17,213
Depreciation charges	3,108	380	3,488
Restructuring provisions	-	(560)	(560)
Increase in stocks	(11,193)	(87)	(11,280)
Increase in debtors	(3,754)	(20)	(3,774)
Increase in creditors	9,672	913	10,585
Net cash inflow – continuing operations	16,662	–	–
Net cash outflow – discontinued operations	–	(990)	
Net cash flow from operating activities			15,672

2. Reconciliation to net debt (funds)

4144 FRS 4 (6) FRS 1 (33)

A note reconciling the movement of cash in the period to the movement in debt should be given either adjoining the cash flow statement or in a note to the financial statements. The FRS emphasises that the reconciliation is not part of the cash flow statement and as such should be clearly labelled. The purpose of the analysis is to provide information about the **impact of changes in debt** on the liquidity of an entity.

Where cash and liquid resources exceed the borrowings of the entity reference should be made to "net funds" rather than "net debt".

MEMO POINTS **Net debt** is defined as the borrowings of the entity, including debt as defined in FRS 4, together with derivatives and obligations under finance leases less cash and liquid resources. Total net debt is the cumulative total of net debt for the financial period with net debt bought forward at the beginning of the financial year.

4146 The **changes in net debt** arising from both cash flows and non-cash items, should be separately analysed and then reconciled with the opening and the closing net debt balances per the balance sheet. The reconciliation **starts with the closing cash position** for the period as shown at the foot of the cash flow statement. This figure will include cash flows relating to the management of liquid resources and borrowings included in financing, which should be added back to give the total change in net debt resulting from the cash flows in the period. Non-cash movements include assets acquired under finance leases and exchange rate differences.

EXAMPLE **XYZ Ltd**

Notes to the cash flow statement

Reconciliation of net cash flow to movement in net debt

	2010 £'000	£'000
Decrease in cash in the period	**(6,752)**	
Increase in debt	(2,347)	
Decrease in liquid resources	(700)	
Change in net debt resulting from cash flows		**(9,799)**
Loans and finance leases acquired with subsidiary		(3,817)
New finance leases		(2,845)
Exchange movements		643
Increase in net debt in the period		**(15,818)**
Net debt at 1.1.2010		**(15,215)**
Net debt at 31.12.2010		**(31,033)**

Analysis of total change in net debt

This analysis should contain the following information, where material: 4150
- the general cash flows of the entity relating to net debt;
- debt movements arising as a result of the acquisition or disposal of subsidiary undertakings;
- other non-cash changes; and
- the recognition of changes in market value and exchange rate movements.

The cash flows **relating to the acquisition or disposal** of subsidiaries include borrowings acquired or transferred, as part of the sales or acquisitions, which are not included in the financing section of the standard, but impact on the closing net debt balances. **Other non-cash** charges include the acquisition of fixed assets under finance leases.

Where several balance sheet amounts or proportions thereof **have been combined** to form the components of opening and closing net debt, sufficient detail should be shown to enable the cash and other components, to be traced back to the amounts shown under the relevant captions in the balance sheet. For example, bank loans or overdrafts included as a single figure within current liabilities should be identified separately, because overdrafts should be included within the cash component of net debt. 4152

Examples of two different methods of presenting an analysis of changes in net debt (funds) are given below.

EXAMPLE **XYZ Ltd** FRS 1 (Appendix 1)

Notes to the cash flow statement
Analysis of changes in net debt

Method 1

	At 1 Jan. 2010 £'000	Cash flows £'000	Other changes £'000	At 31 Dec. 2010 £'000
Cash at bank	42	847		889
Overdraft	(1,784)	1,784		
		2,631		
Debt due within 1 year	(149)	149	(230)	(230)
Debt due after one year	(1,262)		230	(1,032)
Current asset investment	250	450		700
Total	**(2,903)**	**3,230**	-	**327**

Method 2

XYZ Ltd.
Notes to the cash flow statement
Detailed analysis of changes in net debt

	At 1 Jan. 2010 £'000	Cash flows £'000	Acquisition ex.cash/ overdraft £'000	Other non-cash charges £'000	Foreign exchange movements £'000	At 31 Dec. 2010 £'000
Cash at bank and in hand	235	(1,250)	–	–	1,392	377
Overdrafts	(2,528)	(5,502)	–	–	(1,422)	(9,452)
		6,752				
Debt due after 1 year	(9,640)	(2,533)	(1,749)	2,560	(792)	(12,154)
Debt due within 1 year	(352)	(1,156)	(837)	(2,560)	1,465	(3,440)
Finance leases	(4,170)	1,342	(1,231)	(2,845)	–	(6,904)
Current asset investments	1,240	(700)	–	–	–	540
Total	**(15,215)**	**(9,799)**	**(3,817)**	**(2,845)**	**643**	**(31,033)**

B. Supplementary notes

4160 There are a number of supplementary notes required including non-cash transactions, a commentary and comparative figures, examples of which are set out below.

Non-cash transactions

4162 FRS 1 (67) Material transactions **not resulting in movements of cash** should be disclosed in the notes to the cash flow statement, if the disclosure is necessary for an understanding of the underlying transactions, such as:
- finance lease arrangements;
- exchange of assets for non cash consideration; and
- shares issued for the acquisition of a subsidiary.

4164 **A finance lease** is one of the more common non-cash transactions. The transaction is reflected in the balance sheet but not reflected in the cash flow statement, because the reporting entity neither remits or receives cash.

The **conversion of debt to equity** is the equivalent of repaying debt in cash and receiving cash for new shares, although as the transaction represents only notional cash flows it does not appear in the cash flow statement. However, this information should be disclosed by way of note. Similarly, a note detailing the value of shares issued in exchange for a controlling interest in a subsidiary should be given.

Restrictions on remitting funds

4165 FRS 1 (47) A consolidated cash flow statement should identify and explain the circumstances and effect of the **restrictions preventing** a transfer of cash from one part of the group to meet the obligations of another. The requirement also applies to overseas branches and subsidiaries.

The note to the accounts should only include details of circumstances, where access is severely restricted by external factors beyond the control of the group, such as cash balances:
- in escrow;
- retained within employee share ownership trusts; or
- deposited with an industry regulator.

Commentary

4166 The provision of information in addition to the cash flow statement is recommended by the **Operating and Financial Review (OFR)** (see also ¶4700). The discussion should form part of the "financial review" section and cover "funds from operating activities", other sources of "cash" and current liquidity, as illustrated in the example below.

The commentary in the OFR should highlight the level of borrowings and whether they are seasonal, as well as the maturity profile of commitments. Although useful to the reader there is no formal requirement to disclose the following:
- borrowing facilities not utilised;
- restrictions on possible transfer of funds from one part of the group to another;
- any breaches of borrowing covenants; and
- assets and liabilities denominated in foreign currencies.

EXAMPLE **Ameira Property Development Ltd**
Financial review (extract)

Cash flow and borrowings

Net Group borrowings at 30 June 2010 were £20.6m (2009 12.6m net funds), representing a negative movement of funds of £33.2m. The cash outflow was due to a reduction in turnover, reorganisation costs and the funding of losses. Assets employed by Ameira Property Developments increased by £26m but profits of £38m resulted in a positive cash flow for the property division. The cash outflows were in associated activities.

In 2009 the Group took steps to align the **maturity profile of debt facilities** to the profile of the assets employed. A private placement of US $56m of loan notes in the USA, on terms averaging seven to ten years, provided longer-term finance to match the infrastructure investment portfolio as well as a currency hedge against US housing assets. The Group also arranged medium-term debt facilities of £45m in order to fund seasonal working capital requirements and acquisition of investments.

In February 2010, the Group purchased Northwood Investments Limited. The **purchase consideration** was £60.0m, but the assets included £23m of cash, resulting in an expansion to the asset infrastructure portfolio of £40.6m. Of this £16m was deferred consideration pending third party consent to the change of ownership of certain assets. **In addition to the purchase consideration** the Group acquired commitments to pay £27m of deferred equity, on projects held by Northwood Investments Ltd. The acquisition was financed out of existing debt facilities. The Group will now seek to further align the debt profile with the underlying assets, and additional short and medium-term banking facilities will be arranged to increase flexibility.

With the acquisition of Northwood investments, the continuing regular infrastructure investment programme of the Group in housing assets and property developments, the Group will now face higher underlying levels of balance sheet gearing.

Disclosure of **segmental cash flows** that are materially out of line with segmental profits, for example as a result of capital expenditure, should also be highlighted. FRS 1 encourages the provision of segmental cash flow information, in order to expand on the segmental disclosures required by SSAP 25, but does not specify the how this should be achieved; neither does the OFR. **4170**

A typical presentation of segmental cash flows is given in the following example.

EXAMPLE **Pub Retailing Group Ltd**
Notes to the financial statements

12. Operating cash flow	**2010 £m**	**2009 £m**
Hotels	134	120
Leisure retailing	89	49
Games division	23	16
Branded drinks	100	75
Miscellaneous	9	5
Totals	**355**	**265**

Comparative figures

Comparative figures **should be given for** all items reported in the cash flow statement and supporting notes, except: **4172** FRS 1 (48)
- a note to the statement that analyses changes in balance sheet amounts comprising net debt; and
- the note of the material effects of acquisitions and disposal of subsidiary undertakings on each of the standard headings.

Treatment of non-trading gains and losses

Gains or losses **that do not give rise to cash flows** should be excluded from the cash flow statement and reported in the profit or loss account or STRGL as appropriate. If gains or losses are included in arriving at operating profit, they should be adjusted (gains deducted, losses added) in the reconciliation between operating profits and net cash flow from operating activities (¶4134). **4174**

For instance, a gain on the sale of plant of £10,000 included in operating profit should be excluded from cash flow from operating activities, if it forms part of the proceeds of the sale that was disclosed under the capital expenditure section of the cash flow statement.

Refinancing of borrowings

4176 Companies may decide to **renegotiate the terms** of existing borrowings. If the borrowings are renegotiated with the same lender there may not be any immediate cash flow issues. However, if a new lender is involved then there will be cash inflows and outflows that will be reflected in the increase or decrease in cash for the period.

Reconciliation of net cash inflow from operating activities to free cash flow

4178 In addition to the reconciliation provided in ¶4134 above, a reconciliation of net cash inflow from operating activities to free cash flow, as illustrated in the example below, can also be given.

EXAMPLE **ABC Ltd**
Notes to the cash flow statement

Reconciliation of net cash inflow from operating activities to free cash flow

	2010 £'000	2009 £'000
Net cash inflow from operating activities	423	372
Capital expenditure net of sale of tangible fixed assets	(73)	28
Dividends received from associated undertakings	9	8
Operating cash net of fixed assets	**359**	**408**
Taxation paid	(34)	21
Net interest paid	(72)	(77)
Dividends paid	(167)	–
Free cash flow	**86**	**352**

SECTION 5

Consolidated cash flow statements

4180 The preparation of a consolidated cash flow statement will be similar in many cases to that of single companies. However, there are some **general rules governing** this process and a requirement for a number of additional disclosures.

The group cash flow statement should be built up from the statements prepared by the individual subsidiaries, with intra-group cash flows being eliminated as part of the consolidation process. The group cash flow statement **should present only** cash flows between the group and the outside world.

4182 Particular **care should be taken** where a subsidiary undertaking **joins or leaves a group** during a financial year, in that the group cash flow statement should only include the cash flows of the subsidiary undertaking for the same period as that for which the subsidiary's results are included in the group's consolidated profit and loss account.

Intra group cash flows

4184 **Examples** of internal cash flows are payments and receipts of:
- management charges;
- dividends;
- interest; or
- intra-group sales.

Where intra-group cash flows are **denominated in a currency other than** the parent company's reporting currency, and they are separately identifiable, and the actual rate of exchange at which they took place is known, then that rate may be used to translate the cash flows in order to ensure that they cancel out on consolidation. If the rate used to translate intra-group cash flows is not the actual rate, any exchange rate differences arising should be included in exchange rate movements, as part of the reconciliation to net debt. FRS 1 (41)

Minority interests

The **group represents a sole entity** for financial reporting purposes. Cash flows relating to minority interests should be shown under the heading "Returns on investments and servicing of finance". Where minority interests in a subsidiary are consolidated as part of a group, the treatment in the consolidated cash flow statement should be consistent with the overall approach adopted in preparing the group's financial statements. 4186

Minority interests should be shown as a liability, **where a parent or fellow subsidiary undertaking** has guaranteed their dividends or redemption of shares or undertaken to purchase the minority shares, if the subsidiary fails to make expected dividend payments. In such cases the dividends should be shown as interest paid and not as dividends to minorities, but still included under the classification "Returns on investment and servicing of finance". 4188

EXAMPLE **Example**

ABC Ltd

Notes to the cash flow statement

A parent company that has a number of subsidiaries that are not wholly owned who have minority interests should present the cash flow information as follows.

Returns on investments and servicing of finance (£m)

	2010	**2009**
Dividends paid by subsidiaries to minorities	(27.9)	(20.0)

Subsidiaries

Parent companies require detailed information from their subsidiaries in order that the parent company can present the correct analysis of group cash flows and to ensure that gross cash flows are not "**netted-off**", but recorded under the correct heading. An example would be information on debtors and creditors which are vital to ensure that movements included in the "Reconciliation of operating profit to cash inflow from operating activities" relate only to operating debtors and creditors. 4200

Where a **parent company acquires or disposes** of a subsidiary undertaking, then the related cash flows are reported under acquisitions and disposal in the cash flow statement.

In addition, the **notes to the cash flow statements** should include: 4204
- details of cash paid or received from the purchase or sale of subsidiary companies;
- an indication of how much of the consideration comprised cash; and FRS 1 (45)
- a breakdown of the subsidiaries assets and liabilities, including purchased goodwill, underlying the purchase consideration.

Any **shares issued** as part of the consideration in exchange for the net assets acquired do not generate cash flows, and are therefore disclosed by way of a note to the cash flow statement.

The **material effects** of any reported amounts under each of the standard headings within the cash flow statement, reflecting the cash flows of the subsidiary company purchased or sold, should also be shown (as far as is practical), where the post acquisition cash flows of the subsidiary acquired can be clearly identified and segregated. 4206

Care should be taken to eliminate all cash flows between the group and the subsidiary acquired or disposed of, for the period the subsidiary's results (and cash flows) are included in the consolidated figures. Any cash or overdraft balances transferred should be shown separately, as illustrated in the following example.

EXAMPLE **XYZ Ltd**
Notes to the cash flow statement

Purchase of subsidiary undertakings

	£'000
Net assets acquired:	
Tangible fixed assets	12,195
Stocks	9,384
Debtors	13,856
Investments	1,309
Cash at bank	1,439
Creditors	(21,715)
Bank overdraft	(6,955)
Loans and finance leases	(3,817)
Deferred taxation	(165)
Minority interest	(9)
Goodwill	16,702
	22,224
Shares allotted	9,519
Cash	12,705
Total	**22,224**

The subsidiary undertaking acquired during the year contributed £1,502,000 to the group's net operating cash flows, paid £1,308,000 in respect of interest, £522,000 in respect of taxation and utilised £2,208,000 for capital expenditure.

Notes to the cash statement
Purchase and sale of investments (including cash balances transferred on acquisition)

	£'000	**£'000**
Purchase of subsidiary	(22,224)	
Net cash acquired with subsidiary	1,439	
		(20,785)
Sale of business		120.0
Purchase of an interest in a joint venture		(75.0)
Total		**(20,830)**

Associates and other equity investments

4210 FRS 1 (44) Where a group has investments such as associates or **unconsolidated subsidiaries** that are accounted for under the equity method, the consolidated cash flow statement should include only the cash flows between these entities and not the cash flows of those entities. Any dividends, loans and interest on loans should be shown under "Dividends from associates and joint ventures" or "Returns on investments and servicing of finance" as appropriate. Cash flows from sales or purchases between group and associated undertakings or joint ventures should, however, be included in arriving at net cash flow from operating activities.

Joint arrangements that are not entities

4212 FRS 1 (41) The **group's share of cash flows** from joint arrangements that are not an entity (JANE) should be included in the cash flow statement and notes on a line-by-line basis. The relevant proportion of each of the "JANE's" cash flows should be aggregated with the corresponding cash flows of the group. In addition the opening and closing net debt balances will include the relevant percentage of the JANE's balances. As there is therefore effective consolidation, on a proportional basis of the JANE's cash flows, adjustments are required to eliminate cash transactions between the investor and the JANEs.

Foreign currency

Where business is transacted through a foreign entity, such as a subsidiary, associate or branch, then the cash flows of that entity should be converted into sterling for inclusion in the group cash flow statement. The cash flows of the foreign entity are considered as a whole rather than a series of single transactions. 4218

There are **two methods** of preparing a consolidated group cash flow statement including overseas subsidiaries; namely:
- the net investment method (closing rate); or
- the temporal method (actual rate).

Entities **are free to choose** either of the two methods although they must be consistent in the approach adopted. A brief outline of both methods is given below; for a more detailed treatment refer to the chapter on foreign currency (¶8000).

Net investment method This method involves the following: 4224

Stage 1. The **foreign entity** prepares a cash flow in its own currency. SSAP 20 (54) FRS 1 (41)

Stage 2. The cash flow is then converted into sterling at either the **closing or average rate of exchange**. The exchange method chosen must be the same as that used for converting the profit and loss account. All the cash flows of the foreign subsidiary must be included in the consolidated cash flow statement at the same rate.

Stage 3. The **sterling cash flow** is then consolidated with the group cash flow statement, after eliminating any intra-group items such as dividends payments, loans, and asset sales. Such items plus any exchange differences should be reported in the reconciliation to net debt.

This method uses the exchange rate prevailing at the balance sheet date and any exchange gain or loss on translation is taken directly to reserves. An average rate may be used if rates do not fluctuate significantly.

Temporal method The temporal method is used when the operations of the foreign entity are more dependent on the economic environment of the investing company. Under this method all non-monetary items and profit and loss account items of the foreign entity are translated at the rate of exchange prevailing at the transaction date or an average rate if the exchange movements are not material. The financial statements of the foreign enterprise should be included in the **consolidated financial statements** as if all the transactions had been entered into by the investing company itself in its own currency. With the temporal method, the **average rate** is only used when the relevant exchange rate is relatively stable and results in only minor exchange rate differences. 4228 SSAP 20 (21)

The procedure is as follows:

1. Translate the individual entity's results and balances into sterling, using the actual or an average rate.
2. Consolidate with the results of the parent company.
3. Prepare a group cash flow statement from the consolidated financial statements.

Practical example of a group cash flow statement

The example given below illustrates a group cash flow statement prepared under the indirect method, complete with reconciliations of net cash flow to movement in net debt and analysis of net debt. 4240

EXAMPLE **Cash flow statement as at 30 June 2010**

Indirect method

	Year to 30 June 2010 £'000	Year to 30 June 2009 £'000
Net cash inflow from operating activities (see 1)	423	372
Dividends received from associated undertakings	9	8
Returns on investments and servicing of finance (see 2)	(76)	(81)
Taxation (see 3)	(34)	21
Capital expenditure and financial investment (see 4)	(118)	(11)
Acquisitions and disposals (see 5)	(635)	(217)
Equity dividend paid	(163)	–
Management of liquid resource	(6)	52
Financing (see 6)	488	(68)
Decrease in cash in the period	**(112)**	**76**

Reconciliation of net cash flow to movement in net debt

(Decrease)/ increase in cash this year	(112)	76
Increase/ (decrease) in liquid resources	6	(52)
(Increase)/ decrease in loan capital	(488)	68
Movement in net debt resulting from cash flows	**(594)**	**92**
Exchange adjustments	(8)	(29)
Movement in net debt during the year	**(602)**	**63**
Opening net debt	(1,252)	(1,315)
Closing net debt	**(1,854)**	**(1,252)**

Analysis of changes in net debt

	Cash at Bank	Borrowings within 1 year	Loan capital within 1 year	Loan capital within 1 year	2010 Net debt
	£'000	£'000	£'000	£'000	£'000
At 1 July 20X8	112	(558)	–	(806)	(1,252)
(Decrease)/ increase in cash	(5)	(107)	–	–	(112)
Increase/ (decrease) in cash	6	–	–	–	6
(Increase)/ decrease in loan capital	–	–	(110)	(378)	(488)
Exchange adjustments	(2)	5	–	(11)	(8)
Balance as at **30 June 2010**	**111**	**(660)**	**(110)**	**(1,195)**	**(1,854)**

Notes to the cash flow statement

1. Reconciliation of operating profit to net cash inflow from operating activities:

	2010 £'000	2009 £'000
Operating profit	547	420
Depreciation	56	51
Goodwill amortisation	12	3
Increase in stocks	(72)	(43)
Increase in trade debtors	(55)	(97)
(Decrease)/Increase in creditors	(43)	39
Expenditure against provisions for reorganisation and restructuring costs	(34)	(54)
Other costs	12	53
Net cash inflow from operating activities	**423**	**372**

2. Returns on investments and servicing of finance

	2010	2009
Interest received	6	4
Interest paid	(78)	(81)
Dividends paid to minority shareholders	(4)	(4)
	(76)	**(81)**

3. Taxation	**2010**	**2009**
UK Taxation	15	77
Overseas taxation	(49)	(56)
	(34)	21

4. Capital expenditure and financial investment	**2010**	**2009**
Purchase of tangible fixed assets	(97)	(87)
Sale of tangible fixed assets	24	115
Purchase of intangible fixed assets	(19)	–
Purchase of ordinary share capital for employee trusts	(26)	(39)
	(118)	**(11)**

5. Acquisitions and disposals	**2010**	**2009**
Purchase of subsidiary undertakings	(442)	(103)
Borrowings acquired with subsidiary undertakings	(193)	–
Disposal of subsidiary	4	(162)
Cash and overdrafts disposed of with subsidiary undertakings	(4)	48
	635	**217**

6. Financing	**2010**	**2009**
Redemption of debt	(637)	–
Increase in long-term debt	944	–
Increase/ (Decrease) in other debt	181	(68)
	488	**(68)**

SECTION 6

Comparison between UK GAAP and IAS (IFRS)

FRS 1 "Cash flow statements" **focuses on** movements in cash, whereas IAS 7 "Cash flow statements" concentrates on cash and cash equivalents (short-term highly liquid investments readily convertible into cash, which are included in "management of liquid resources"). **4250** FRS 1 (6) IAS 7 (7)

Cash **is defined** in the UK standard as cash and balances at central banks and loans and advances to banks repayable on demand. Cash is defined in IAS 7 as cash on demand and demand deposits. The FRS **focuses more narrowly** on changes in cash that are hidden in the narrower classifications of IAS 7, which is deemed more flexible that FRS 1 in terms of the diversity of presentations permitted. FRS 1 requires that cash flow statements should reconcile to "cash" whereas under IAS 7, the statement should reconcile to "cash equivalents". FRS 1 (2)

Entities applying IFRS 1 "First-time adoption of international financial reporting standards" are required to comply with IAS 7 in full. An example of a group cash flow statement prepared under IFRS is given in ¶4260.

MEMO POINTS The IASB has amended IAS 7, in order to clarify the differing accounting treatments adopted for classifying cash flows related to expenditure incurred for the generation of future cash flows. Some entities currently classify these expenditures (e.g. marketing, research) as cash flows from operating activities and others as investing activities. The IASB advocates that only expenditures that result in a recognised asset should be classified as investing activities. These reporting requirements take effect for accounting periods beginning on or after 1 January 2010. Earlier adoption is permitted although this must be disclosed in the notes to the financial statements.

Key differences

IAS 7 **applies to all entities** irrespective of size, as the exemptions applicable under FRS 1 (see ¶4010) are not permitted. Although not impacting on listed companies, it does affect those small companies that elect to voluntarily adopt. IAS 7 differs from FRS 1 in terms of the focus and presentation of cash flow statements. **4254**

Table 1 illustrates the areas that are dealt with more comprehensively in the UK standard than the IAS whilst **Table 2** outlines the areas treated in greater detail in IAS 7.

Table 1		
Topic	**FRS Treatment**	**IAS Treatment**
Classification/presentation	The FRS has 9 classifications, the first 7 of which must be presented in sequence. Definitions and classifications more prescriptive than the IAS.	IAS 7 has three categories – there is no standard sequence. 1. Cash flow from operating activities (Revenues). (IAS 7.10) 2. Cash flows from investing activities (acquisitions and disposals). (IAS 7.6) 3. Cash flows from financing activities (transactions affecting size and composition of equity capital and borrowings. (IAS 7.6)
Bank overdrafts	Should be deducted in determining cash (FRS 1.2)	Choice of deducting overdrafts from cash or cash equivalents or included in financing cash flows
VAT	Cash flows reported net of VAT where recoverable (FRS 1.16)	
Provisions	Provisions should be classified as operating cash flows irrespective of whether the provision was included in operating profit (FRS 1.11)	
Substance of the transaction	Cash flows should be reported according to the substance of the underlying transaction. (FRS 1.10). For instance, cash flows associated with a hedge transaction should be reported under the same heading as the related cash flows.	
Acquisitions and disposals	Cash outflows relating to acquisitions disclosed separately from cash inflows from disposals (FRS 1.22)	Cash received or paid from sales and purchases reported net of cash and cash equivalents acquired or disposed of (IAS 7.42)
Dividends paid	Accounted for under specific heading (FRS 1.7)	Can be accounted for as operating or financing cash flows (IAS 7.34)
Interest paid or interest and dividends received	Accounted for under specific heading "Return on investments and servicing of finance" (FRS 1.13). Includes receipts from investments and payments to non-equity shareholders, minority interests and providers of finance. Dividends received from joint ventures and associates included as separate items in between operating activities and returns on investments (FRS 1.12A)	Can be accounted for as operating, investing or financing cash flows (IAS 7.31)

Table 1		
Topic	**FRS Treatment**	**IAS Treatment**
Reconciliation of movement in cash for the period to net debt	Required (FRS 1.33). Provides information about company's treasury's activities	Not required
Reconciliation of Net profit to net cash flows from operating activities	Presented separately from the cash flow statement irrespective of whether the direct or indirect method is used (FRS 1.12)	Disclosed on face of cash flow statement or in notes

4256

Table 2		
Topic	**IAS Treatment**	**FRS Treatment**
Small companies	Applies to all small companies	Does not apply (FRS 1.5)
Foreign subsidiaries	Foreign subsidiaries – cash flows should be translated at historical rate or weighted average (IAS 7.26)	FRS also allows the closing rate or average rate. Historical rate used for intra-group transactions (FRS 1.41)
Foreign exchange differences	On cash and cash equivalents must be reported on face of profit and loss account – for reconciliation of opening and closing cash positions	Exchange differences on cash are treated as non-cash items- disclosed in notes to the accounts
Subsidiary undertakings	Applies to subsidiary undertakings	The FRS does not apply to 90% or more of subsidiary enterprises provided the subsidiary is included in consolidated financial statements
Joint-ventures using proportional consolidation	Disclosure required of aggregate amounts for operating, investing and financing cash flows (IAS 7.50b)	Proportional consolidation not permitted under UK GAAP
Cash receipts and payments	Can be presented net for items for which turnover is immediate, and the amounts are material (i.e. credit card receivables, purchase and sale of investments)	Does not allow this treatment except where items relate to a single financing transaction or the maturities are short
Liquid resources	Reported as cash equivalents (IAS 7.6)	Separate presentation required (FRS 1.2)
Taxation	Tax cash flows are reported under operating activities, unless a financing or investing activity (IAS 35.27)	Taxation covers cash flows to and from the tax authorities in terms of revenue and capital profits (FRS 1.16)
Discontinued operations	Separate disclosure required of cash flows relating to discontinued operations (IAS 35.27)	Disclosure only encouraged
Insurance and mutual companies	Applies to mutual fund assurance companies, pension funds and open-ended investment funds	Does not apply (FRS 1.5b)

Group cash flow statement (IAS/IFRS)

4260 The example given below is a consolidated cash flow statement prepared under IAS 7. The supporting reconciliations are not provided as this example is for comparative purposes only (see also ¶4240).

EXAMPLE **Cash flow statement as at 30 June 2010**
Indirect method

	Year to 30 June 2010 £'000	
Cash flows from operating activities		
Profit before taxation	3,350	
Adjustments for:		
Depreciation	450	
Foreign exchange differences	40	
Finance cost	400	
Investment income	(500)	
	3,740	
Increase in trade and other receivables	(500)	
Decrease in inventories	1,050	
Decrease in trade payables	(2,000)	
Cash generated from operations	2,550	
Interest paid	(270)	
Income tax paid	(900)	
Net cash from operating activities		1,380
Cash flows from investing activities		
Acquisition of subsidiary net of cash acquired	(550)	
Property, plant and equipment purchases	(350)	
Sale of equipment	20	
Interest received	200	
Dividends received	200	
Net cash used in investing activities		(480)
Cash flows from financing activities		
Proceeds from share capital issue	250	
Proceeds from long-term borrowings	250	
Finance lease liabilities	(90)	
Dividends paid	(1,200)	
Net cash used in financing activities		(790)
Net increase in cash and cash equivalents		110
Cash and net equivalents at beginning of period		120
Cash and net equivalents at end of period		230

CHAPTER 2

Statement of total recognised gains and losses (STRGL)

OUTLINE ¶¶

A. Scope and objective

The statement of total recognised gains and losses (STRGL) is a **primary statement** required by FRS 3, "Reporting financial performance". The purpose of the STRGL is to show the extent to which shareholders' funds have increased or decreased during the year from **all gains and losses**, whether realised or not. (Some gains may be recognised in one period but realised in another.) **4300** FRS 3 (56)

Not all gains and losses will have flowed through the profit and loss account, especially those arising out of movements on reserves. Therefore, to satisfy the requirements of full and proper disclosure, these gains and losses must be captured and reflected elsewhere. FRS 3 prescribes using the STRGL for this purpose.

Certain **gains and losses** are specifically **permitted** or, in some cases, **required** by law or an accounting standard to be taken directly to reserves, e.g., unrealised gains arising on the revaluation of fixed assets. These are not reflected in the profit and loss account but are expressly required to be taken directly to the revaluation reserve. **4301**

Any company, including **smaller companies** reporting under the FRSSE (see ¶6000), that intends to give a **true and fair view of its financial position**, and its profit or loss for the period under review, must include the STRGL in its financial statements. **4302**

No corresponding obligation is imposed by the Companies Act.

Because the STRGL is a primary statement, it should be presented separately and with the same prominence as the other primary statements (i.e., balance sheet, profit and loss account and cash flow statement). Therefore, it is unacceptable to include it with the notes to the financial statements. **4303** FRS 3 (27)

If there are **no recognised gains or losses** in both the current and prior periods – other than those already reflected in the profit and loss account – the STRGL may be omitted. However, a statement to this effect must be given at the foot of the profit and loss account. **4304** FRS 3 (57)

EXAMPLE PROFIT AND LOSS ACCOUNT (extract)

There were no recognised gains and losses, both in the current year and in the previous year, other than the profit [or loss, *as applicable*] for the year as shown above in this profit and loss account. As a result, no statement of recognised gains and losses is presented.

4305 FRS 3 (58) In the case of a material recognised movement in the amounts attributable to **different classes of shareholders** that has no effect on **total shareholders' funds** (e.g. an appropriation of profit to accrue a premium on redemption of preference shares), an explanatory footnote to the statement may be appropriate.

4306 In respect of **consolidated financial statements**, the requirements of FRS 3 must be satisfied by presenting a Consolidated Statement of Total Recognised Gains and Losses.

B. Content

4307 FRS 3 imposes no strict **format** for the STRGL. Reporting entities are therefore permitted to use their own discretion in determining the disclosure most appropriate to their circumstances. The items most commonly included are explained in ¶4310 below.

4308 The opening entry in the STRGL is usually the profit or loss for the period. The other items are the gains and losses that were taken directly to reserves and therefore not reflected in the profit and loss account. Because the STRGL, like the profit and loss account, is regarded as a performance statement, gains and losses are taken to reserves through one or the other of these statements. Consequently, any item recognised in the STRGL in one period cannot be recognised again ("recycled") in the profit and loss account in a subsequent period.

MEMO POINTS Although the general rule states that an amount recognised in the STRGL in one period cannot be recycled in the profit and loss account subsequently, there is an exception in respect of gains and losses that FRS 23 and FRS 26 **specifically require to be recycled**. In these cases, to avoid mis-stating total recognised gains and losses, the STRGL must include a separate line item to reverse the amount previously recognised.

4309 If there has been a prior period adjustment, the **comparative figures** should be restated and the cumulative effect of the adjustment shown at the bottom of the STRGL of the current period. The logic behind this treatment is that the adjustments represent gains and losses recognised in the current period even though they **relate to previous periods**.

1. Items most typically included

4310 The following items are most typically encountered in the STRGL.

4311 **a) Profit or loss before dividends attributable to shareholders for the year** – this figure is taken as the starting point for the STRGL.

4312 **b) Gains and losses on revaluation of assets during the year** – certain gains and losses arising on the revaluation of tangible fixed assets are required by FRS 15, "Tangible fixed assets", to be recognised in the STRGL rather than being taken to the profit and loss account. See also ¶1421.

4313 **c) Unrealised currency translation differences** – in other words, differences in net values of investments in foreign enterprises resulting from exchange rate fluctuations not reflected in the profit and loss account.

4314 **d) Gains arising from lapsed warrants** – see discussion at ¶3625.

4315 **e) Impairment losses arising on fixed assets and goodwill** – FRS 11, "Impairment of fixed assets and goodwill", requires certain impairment losses relating to previously revalued assets to be recognised in the STRGL. Similarly, if the impairment is reversed, and the reversal is permitted under FRS 11, it should be recognised in the STRGL.

4316 **f) Unrealised gains on the sale of assets to associated companies.**

4317 **g) Tax attributable to those gains or losses recognised in the statement** – under FRS 16, "Current tax", the **current taxation** for a period should be recognised in the profit and loss account – unless it is attributable to a gain or loss that has been recognised directly in the STRGL. The reasoning is that if any transaction that results in a profit or loss is recognised directly in the STRGL, the attributable tax should be recognised there as well.

Any tax shown in the STRGL should be **analysed** into UK and foreign tax. Each of these should be further analysed to differentiate between:
- tax estimated for the current period, and
- tax adjustments recognised in respect of previous periods.

With regard to **deferred tax**, FRS 19, "Deferred tax", requires it also to be recognised in the current period's profit and loss account – unless it is attributable to a gain or loss that has been recognised directly in the STRGL. Where this is the case, the deferred tax should likewise be recognised there. **4318**

The amount of deferred tax recognised directly in the statement of total recognised gains and losses should be disclosed and, where the amounts are material, **analysed** into: **4319** FRS 19 (60)
- the origination and reversal of timing differences;
- changes in tax rates and laws;
- adjustments to the estimated recoverable amount of deferred tax assets arising in previous periods.

2. Items not included

The following items are not shown in the STRGL: **4320**
- contributions from or distributions to shareholders; and
- goodwill written off directly to reserves or reinstated on the subsequent sale of the business.

These items are excluded because they are not elements of a company's performance. Consequently, the best place for their disclosure is in the **reconciliation of movements in shareholders' funds** (¶3795).

3. Special case – investment companies

Previously, investment companies were obliged to include only **distributable profits** in their profit and loss account – and if they had made any non-distributable profits (irrespective of whether realised or unrealised), these had to be shown in the STRGL. This requirement was withdrawn by FRS 25 in respect of periods commencing on or after 1 January 2005, with the result that investment companies are now subject to the same rules as other companies as to where they report these gains and losses. **4325** FRS 3 (31)

4. Sample statement

The following is an example of the form and content of a typical STRGL. **4330**

Statement of Total Recognised Gains and Losses
For the year ended 31 December 20X1

	20X1	20X0
	£m	£m
Profit for the year attributable to shareholders of the company	320	285
Unrealised surplus [1]/ (deficit) on revaluation of properties in associate	50	(19)
Foreign exchange translation adjustments [2]	(35)	(22)
Total recognised gains and losses for the year	335	244
Prior year adjustment [3]	(10)	–
Total gains and losses recognised since last annual report	325	244

1. Amount credited to the revaluation reserve during the year.
2. Unrealised losses or gains on translation of net foreign-currency investments, translated at rate at end of year.
3. The £10m represents the cumulative adjustment to reserves in 20X1. The comparative year's profit (i.e., £285m) will have been adjusted by the amount that relates to 20X0.

PART 7

Reports and other disclosures

CHAPTER 1

Directors' report

OUTLINE ¶¶

This chapter deals with the content of the directors' report and the reporting framework that underpins the disclosure requirements. The **objective of the directors' report** is to provide details of the company's principal activities, development and future prospects, as well as the non-financial issues affecting the entity and stakeholders. **4500**

It is a requirement of the Companies Act, that a directors' report is included in the financial statements of all companies for each financial year. Recent **changes changes to this legislation**, mean enhanced disclosure requirements for large companies and, to a lesser degree, medium-sized companies. There are also new provisions covering directors' liability for statements made in the directors' report (see ¶4508).

MEMO POINTS 1. Although the **Companies Act 2006** predominantly restates the requirements of the Companies Act 1985, it does contain some **new provisions** covering disclosures. Additional disclosure requirements are included in SI 2008/409 (Sch 5), "The Small Companies and Groups (Accounts and Directors' Report) Regulations 2008 and Sch 7, "The Large and Medium-sized Companies and Groups (Accounts and Reports) Regulations 2008.
2. Although there is no specific accounting standard covering the directors' report, there is interaction between a number of standards and the requirements of the Companies Act. Examples include SSAP 13 "Accounting for research and development" (¶1150) and FRS 21"Events after the balance sheet date" (¶5700).
3. The **coalition Government** has published a consultation paper discussing how to improve the quality of company reporting and encourage more effective shareholder involvement. The consultation process seeks feedback on whether the current regulatory framework is considered adequate or whether further improvements are needed. Particular focus is given to the business review required by large and medium-sized companies, the significance of the Operating and Financial Review (OFR) and directors' remuneration. The consultation paper can be accessed on the Department for Business, Innovation and Skills (BIS) website.

A **parent company that prepares group accounts** must also produce a group directors' report, covering all entities included in the consolidation. Individual directors' reports are not required for each company. Certain small and medium-sized companies (SMEs) are permitted to take advantage of certain exemptions under EU Accounting Directives, including those that are part of a group. For **listed companies** further disclosures are required under the Combined Code and a separate directors' remuneration report is also required. **4501**

MEMO POINTS 1. Small companies (including those that are part of an ineligible group (s 415A CA 2006) are exempt from preparing the enhanced directors' report under CA 2006,
2. An group is defined as ineligible if any of its members is (s 384(2) CA 2006):
– a public company;
– a body corporate other than a company whose shares are traded on a regulated market in the EEA;

– a person other than a small company authorised to undertake a regulated activity under FSMA 2000;
– a small company that is an authorised insurance company, banking company, e-money issuer, or
– a person who carries on insurance market activity.

4503 The disclosures in the directors' report must be consistent with the information given in the financial statements. Most companies tend to meet only the **minimum statutory disclosure requirements**, which may also be provided at the discretion of the individual company, in other areas of the financial statements such as the Operating and Financial Review (OFR) (¶4700) or the Chairman's Statement. A copy of the directors' report must be filed with the Registrar of Companies, **except for companies** entitled to the small companies exception (¶4512), including those who elect to file abbreviated accounts.

MEMO POINTS Small companies can elect to voluntarily file a directors' report with the Registrar of Companies.

Penalty for non-compliance

4504
s 416 CA 2006 The directors' report must be **approved by** the board of directors and signed and dated on their behalf by a director or the company secretary, before being sent to the Registrar of Companies. The name of the signatory must be clearly stated on the report. There are penalties for failure to comply with the requirements covering the preparation, content and signature of the report.

The directors **holding office at the date** the financial statements are approved, have a responsibility to produce and approve a directors' report, even if none of the directors were actually in office during the time covered by the report. This requirement cannot be avoided on the grounds that the directors were not responsible for the activities covered in the report.

In situations where the company **does not fully comply** with the requirements for the **approval and signing** of the directors' report, the company, and every director who is in default, will be guilty of an offence, punishable by a fine. Furthermore, if the directors' report does not comply with requirements for preparation and content, then any director who knew of this and failed to take reasonable steps to ensure compliance, will be guilty of an offence and liable to a fine.

4506 **Enforcement** The **legal mechanism** for enforcing the new regulations, will be the extension of the existing administrative enforcement regime, to cover directors' reports. Responsibility for **enforcement will be undertaken**:
– for small companies by the secretary of state; and
– for large and medium-sized companies by the Financial Reporting Review Panel (FRRP).

The FRRP now reviews the directors' reports of public companies and large private limited companies, thereby extending its current remit. The requirements of the directors' reports, encompassing the **new business review**, are set out in the Companies Act 2006. The aim will be to see if the directors' report is consistent with the financial statements and that it reflects the development and performance of the business.

Directors' liability (safe harbour)

4508 Provisions contained in the new Companies Act, covering directors' reports sent to shareholders, are now in force. A director will be required to compensate the company for losses incurred arising from:
– known false or misleading pronouncements in the directors' report; or
– material omissions intended to conceal important information.

The directors are only liable to the company and not third parties wishing to make claims against them.

A "**safe harbour clause"** has been included in the new Companies Act enabling directors to omit information covering current developments, including negotiations and contracts, where disclosure is deemed seriously prejudicial to the interests of the company.

A. Companies Act disclosures

The **minimum disclosure requirements** in the directors' report for all companies (irrespective of size), are set out in the table below. 4510

Disclosure requirements				
Type of company	**Disclosure**	**Chapter Reference**	**s 415-6 CA 2006**	**Sch 5 SI 2008/409 Sch 7 SI 2008/410**
All companies	Names of directors	¶4514	✓	
	Principle activities of company + subsidiary undertakings	¶4520	✓	
	Political donations	¶4532		✓
	Charitable donations	¶4546		✓
	Purchase by company of "own shares"	¶4548		✓
	Statement as to disclosure of information to the auditors		✓	
	Additional disclosure requirements		**s 416-7 CA 2006**	**Sch 7 SI 2008/410**
Large/ medium-sized companies	Enhanced business review (including key performance indicators)	¶4554	✓	
	Dividend payments	¶4558	✓	
	Research & development	¶4560		✓
	Post balance sheet events	¶4562		✓
	Employee policies (companies with more than 250 employees)	¶4576		✓
	Overseas branches	¶4572		✓
	Creditor payment policies	¶4564		✓
	Use of financial instruments	¶3400		✓
	Carbon emissions (see ¶3400)			
			Other	
Large companies only	Valuation of land and buildings	¶4568		✓
	Directors statement of responsibilities	¶5250	SAS 600	
	Remuneration report	¶4865	SAS 600	
	Audit committees	¶5276	SAS 600	
	Financial instruments	¶3400		✓
	Introduction of the Euro	¶4618	UITF 21	
	Overview of likely future developments	¶4554		✓

Exemption for small companies

A company is entitled to certain exemptions regarding the directors' report, if for the financial year in question it qualifies as a small company (¶6000), or would have done so if not 4512 s 415-417 CA 2006 a member of an ineligible group. The exemptions cover the content of the business review, dividend recommendations and filing obligations.

If the **directors have taken advantage** of the disclosure exemptions available to small companies in the preparation of the directors' report, they must disclose this fact in a prominent position above the signature on the directors' report.

EXAMPLE **ABC Ltd – Annual Report and accounts**
Directors' report (extract)

This report has been prepared in accordance with the special provisions of section 415 A Companies Act 2006 relating to small companies.

Approved by the board of directors on 5.2.2010 and signed on its behalf by
...
B. Kavanagh
Secretary

A company entitled to the small company exemptions outlined above, must still deliver a copy of their financial statements to the Registrar of Companies, although submission of the directors' report is optional.

MEMO POINTS Small companies (including those that are part of an ineligible group (s 415A CA 2006) are exempt from preparing the enhanced directors' report under CA 2006. For a definition of ineligible group see ¶4501.

1. All companies

Names of the directors

4514 s 416 CA 2006 The following **statutory information** is required in the directors report:
– names of the persons who were directors of the company at any time during the financial year;
– the dates of any appointments or resignations of directors during the financial year;
– details of any appointments or resignation of directors since the end of the financial year; and
– retirement of directors at the AGM and whether they offer themselves for re-election.

EXAMPLE **Smithsony Ltd**
Annual report and accounts – December 2010
Directors' Report (extract)

Directors
Biographies of the directors of the company are shown on pages xx to xx. Lady Thornton retired as a director on 31 May 2010, Steven Spencer retired on 30 June 2010 and Paul Rodgers resigned from the board on 31 August 2010.
In accordance with Article 68 of the Articles of Association, Ian Smith (appointed May 20X9); Martha Reeves, Carmen Zapata (both appointed March 20X9) and David Ferrer (appointed July 20X9) **only hold office until** the AGM and, being eligible, offer themselves for re-election. In accordance with Article 70 of the Articles of Association, Jan Bolinger, and Neil Cook retire by rotation at the annual general meeting and being eligible, offer themselves for re-election.
The company has received **special notice** in accordance with the Companies Act 2006 of the intention to propose the re-election of Bruce Manning, who attained the age of 72 years on 31 May 2010, as a director of the company. Accordingly in the notice of the annual general meeting there is a resolution proposing to reappoint Bruce Manning as a director for a further year. The board is supporting this resolution because it considers that Mr Manning provides an invaluable source of knowledge and personal experience in European and international business affairs.
Details of directors' interests in company shares are shown on page xx. No director was materially interested in any significant contract entered into by the company. Ted Smith is, however, a non-excutive director of Superdeals Limited (a travel and leisure company) and Tangrame publishing.

In the **group financial statements**, disclosure is only required of the names of the parent company's directors. It is common for a list of the directors to be placed at the beginning of the report. If the names of the directors are not listed in the directors' report then details of where these disclosures are located must be given. 4516

Details of **non-executive directors** and the committees on which they sit (i.e. audit committee) need not be supplied in the directors' report, although a reference to where this information can be located, should be provided.

Principal activities

The directors' report should detail the principal activities and progress of the **company and its subsidiaries** during the financial year and details of any significant changes in these activities. However, the Companies Act does not specify a format or dictate the precise content of this review. 4520 s 416 CA 2006

EXAMPLE **ABC Group Ltd – Annual report and accounts**
Directors' report (extract)

Principal activities
The group trades principally as Home Improvement, Electrical and Furniture and General Merchandise retailers across the UK and Continental Europe. In addition, the group has extensive property interests in the UK.
On 30 September 2010, the group acquired DAB electronics AG, the second largest electrical retailer in Germany, which in turns owns and manages a significant distribution company. During the year the group's activities have also been expanded further by its entry into the UK double glazing market, with the purchase of Glazedover Ltd.
A **review** of the group's principal activities and its financial position at 31 December 2010 are reported in the chairman's statement and in the financial, operational and business reviews on pages xx to xx.

Principal activities are not defined in the Companies Act, but can generally be interpreted as the different **industry segments** or **classes of business** in which the entity operates. Classes of business are defined as "a separate product or service or a separate group of related products or services". No single group of characteristics is universally applicable in determining industry segments or classes of business, although there should be consistent presentation with the requirements of **segmental reporting** (¶750) in the financial statements. The judgement of the directors is required to determine what business segments or classes of business are significant, although the general rule is that any segment breaching the 10% barrier (i.e. turnover) requires separate disclosure. Broad classifications such as manufacturing or wholesaling should be avoided. 4522

Political donations

The requirements of the Companies Act relating to political donations, require companies including subsidiaries, to obtain **shareholder approval** for the following: 4532
- political donations (subject to certain de-minimis limits); and
- political expenditure in the UK and other member states.

Provisions relating to political donations contained in the new Companies Act, largely restate existing provisions and are consistent with the framework established by the Political Parties, Elections and Referendums Act 2000.

There are also **special rules** for subsidiaries and for parent companies of non-UK subsidiaries.

A company is deemed to be treated as giving money for political purposes, if it provides a donation or subscription to a political party, or a division or officer thereof.

Contributions and donations to a political party are defined as follows: 4534
- any gift of money or property;
- sponsorship;
- subscription paid for affiliation or membership of the party;
- contributions to expenses incurred either directly or indirectly by the party;

– loans to the party (except on commercial terms); and
– provisions of property or services to a political party (unless on commercial terms).

4536 Where **a payment is made by a subsidiary company**, prior approval must be obtained from the shareholders of the parent company. This requirement is designed to prevent companies from circumventing the approval provisions by channelling payments through a subsidiary. The **same rules apply** to overseas subsidiaries of a UK parent company.

The directors of the company are personally liable to reimburse the company for political contributions or donations made, where prior shareholder approval has not been sought. In the case of non-compliance by a subsidiary, the directors of the holding company will also be personally liable.

Exemptions

4538 s 374-378 CA 2006 **Shareholder approval is not required** for the following donations:
– contributions to trade unions, including provision of facilities and services;
– membership subscriptions to EU trade associations;
– payments to all party parliamentary groups;
– political donations below the threshold disclosure limit of £5,000; and
– political donations exempted on the authority of the Secretary of State.

4540 **Disclosures** Separate disclosure is required in the directors' report of political donations within the EU and the rest of the world.

4542 The following disclosures are required in the directors' report, of any political donations made by both parent and subsidiary companies to **parties within the EU**:
– the name of each person or political party within the EU to whom a sum in excess of £2,000 was given;
– disclosure of the aggregate amount paid or donated to EU political parties by a company or group; and
– where prior shareholder approval was given for political donations within the EU (including aggregate donations) in excess of £2,000 during the financial year.

MEMO POINTS **1. EU political donations** are defined as any expenditure committed in respect of:
– the preparation, publication or distribution of promotional material that is designed to generate support for any EU political party;
– activities that can be construed as providing support for any EU political organisation; and
– any activities that can be regarded as helping to influence voters in a national or regional election held in a EU member state.
2. An **EU political organisation** is any party registered under Part II of the Political Parties, Elections and Referendums Act 2000, any political party registered in another EU state, or any independent candidates standing in EU elections.

4544 Disclosure is required of the total contributions made by a company or group of companies to political parties **outside the EU**. There is **no threshold** for these disclosures. Wholly owned subsidiaries of companies incorporated in the UK are exempt from this requirement on the basis that the details will be given in the parent company's financial statements.

Charitable donations

4546 The directors' report must disclose the total amount that the company has provided for charitable concerns, during the financial year, **unless the donation** is less than £2,000. If a company makes a number of charitable donations that in aggregate exceed £2,000, then disclosure is still required. The **same threshold applies** to both individual companies and groups.

The **donation threshold has been increased** to £2,000 through regulations issued under the Companies Act 2006.

Companies making payments to a **company trust**, which then has discretion to donate funds to individual charities, should disclose the sums and charities involved.

EXAMPLE **Annual report - June 2010**
Directors' report (extract)

Charitable donations
During 2010 the company made charitable donations totalling £367,000. The annual donations budget is administered by a committee of the Board and by local site committees. The policy is predominantly directed towards assisting charities working in the educational field and other community based projects.

Exemption from the disclosure requirement to disclose charitable donations is available: 4547
- to wholly owned subsidiaries of a company incorporated in the UK, on the basis that the information will be supplied in the directors' report of the parent company;
- where payments to a charity are of a commercial nature; or
- for payments to a person ordinarily resident outside the UK at the time the donation was made.

Purchase by company of "own shares"

Where a company acquires its own shares **through the following methods** it is required to make certain disclosures in the directors' report: 4548
- through a share purchase;
- by forfeiture or surrender in lieu of forfeiture;
- by purchase in compliance with a court order;
- by redemption;
- through a reduction of capital;
- indirect purchases by a nominee, where the company will have a beneficial effect; and
- charges or lien on own shares for an amount that is payable in respect of those shares.

The **following disclosures** are required for own shares acquired by the company:
- the number and nominal values of the shares purchased in the financial year;
- the percentage of the called-up share capital that any purchase represents;
- the consideration paid for the shares;
- the reasons for the purchase;
- the number and nominal values of any such shares disposed of in the financial year; and
- the reasons for the disposal.

Similar disclosures are required for shares acquired by a **nominee company or a third person** on behalf of the company. Additional disclosures are required for listed companies.

EXAMPLE **STL Ltd**
Annual report and accounts - 2010
Directors' report (extract)

Interests in own shares
STL Group Ltd repurchased 1,325,000 of its ordinary shares of 20p each, representing a total of 0.3% of the total called-up share capital. The aggregate consideration paid was £350,000. These shares were acquired by two trusts in the open market using funds provided by the company to meet obligations under the Performance Share Plan and Long-Term Incentive Plans.

---

2. Large and medium-sized companies

The disclosure requirements for large and medium-sized companies are extensive and comprise an enhanced business review and research and development initiatives, as well information regarding creditor payment, employment and dividend policies and carbon emissions, 4552

Enhanced business review

All companies, **except those classified as** small companies, must produce an "enhanced fair review" of their business in the directors' report, although listed companies are not required 4554 to duplicate information already contained in the OFR, the Chairman's statement or chief executive's review. New regulations have expanded the existing requirements, that the directors' report provide a comprehensive and balanced review of how the business has developed over the course of the financial year, including that of its subsidiaries, associates and joint ventures.

Subsidiaries that qualify as medium or large must prepare a business review, even where a group report is prepared by the parent company.

MEMO POINTS 1. The ASB issued a review of the narrative reporting of 50 listed companies in 2008-2009. The general findings were positive with key weaknesses highlighted, including lack of disclosure regarding principal risks, non-financial KPIs and corporate social responsibility. **2**. The Financial Reporting Review Panel (FRRP) has published a list of business sectors it will focus on in the coming year, including commercial property, insurance, and support services. The Panel will monitor entities operating in niche markets or those outside the FTSE 350, as they are deemed to be more at risk in the current economic climate, with added emphasis on those companies with significant exposure to public sector spending cuts. The Panel will increasingly **target the business review** and in particular the identification and description of principal risks and uncertainties and areas where management has made key judgements. The Panel will also review whether the information given is sufficiently specific to enable shareholders to assess the key threats facing the business.

4556 The **type of information** disclosed under this heading includes:
- any material changes in turnover during the financial period;
- a brief review of the results for the year;
- the overall return on assets that the company or group obtained during the year;
- any positive or negative changes in markets or products;
- details of any major restructuring or reorganisation; and
- details of any significant foreign exchange gains or losses.

4557 s 417 CA 2006 The **content and analysis** should be consistent with the size and complexity of the business and cover selected key performance indicators (KPIs) and the principal risks and uncertainties facing the business. Key performance indicators (KPIs) are defined as factors that measure the development, performance or position of the business.

4558 **Selected KPI's include** those covering:
- financial results (e.g. ROCE; average revenue per user); and
- non-financial information (e.g. employee statistics; environmental performance standards).

There is **no definitive list** of KPIs, but more detailed guidance is given for large non-listed companies and medium-sized companies in an appendix to "The Operating and Financial Review" (OFR) (see also ¶4785). The number and choice of KPIs included in the report is at the discretion of each individual company.

Medium-sized companies need only include financial KPIs, unless they have adopted international financial reporting standards (IFRSs), in which case they should, along with large companies, provide details of important non-financial KPIs.

Medium-sized companies are not required to include details of non-financial KPIs in financial statements prepared under IFRS.

4559 The ASB has recommended more detailed disclosures be given in the business review, concerning the company's **financial capital and how it is managed**, even though this is not required under the Companies Act 2006. This is because investors require reassurance that a company has sufficient capital to meet its current and future funding needs, and offers adequate protection for creditors. The ASB has advised that information concerning financial capital management is important for all companies and not just those in the financial services sector.

Capital management is a key discipline as adequate capital underpins growth and provides a security buffer against significant economic shocks, thereby reducing the risk of a liquidity crisis. This discipline is particularly important in the current economic climate given the pressures on particular sectors facing the impact of reduced government spending.

Dividends

Although only the proposed dividend need be disclosed, details are usually given for both the interim dividend paid during the year and the proposed final dividend as illustrated in the following example. 4560

EXAMPLE **ABC Ltd**
Annual report and accounts - 30 June 2010

Directors' report (extract)
The directors recommend a **final dividend** of £2.50 a share to be paid on 15 April 2011, to shareholders registered on 24 February 2011. This, together with the interim share payment of £1.75 a share, paid on 7 August 2010, makes a total dividend payment of £4.25 per share for the year. The total (aggregate) dividend payment for the financial year 2010 is £13.5m.

Where the directors **decline to propose** a dividend this fact should be stated in the directors' report. Details of any shareholder agreements to waive rights to dividends payable during the last year should be disclosed. This requirement applies to waivers of future dividends. **Dividend waivers** totalling less than 1% of the value of any dividend disregarded, on each class of share, need not be disclosed.

Research and development

The directors' report should contain an overview of the company's research and development activity during the financial year and details of the accounting policy adopted as required by SSAP 13 "Accounting for research and development". 4561

The disclosures **should focus on** the commercial direction of the research and development expenditure, in order to provide some indication of **future revenue streams** for the benefit of current and potential investors, as well as the impact this may have on the activities of the company.

The **information disclosed** typically covers:
- a broad indication of the nature and level of research and development activity;
- a brief analysis of specific research and development projects; and
- an overview of any major contracts or joint research and development projects.

EXAMPLE **ABC Ltd**
Report and accounts - 30 June 2010
Directors' report (extract)

The group engages in research and development activities (R & D) relating to the introduction of new products and production processes and to the improvement of existing products and processes.
The business is supported by high quality technical facilities for R & D led by group facilities in Liverpool, Nottingham and Norwich, supporting the group's global activities.
The **principal research activities** include:
- the assessment of safety and toxicology;
- the improvement of flavour, colouring and texture;
- the development of packaging techniques; and
- the application of micro-technology to the process control procedures.

The group spent £42.5m in 2010, (£23.1m 2009) on research and development. Included in this figure is £5m spent on a joint research project with the Science Research Council.

Post balance sheet events

The Companies Act requires that the directors' report for companies (other than small companies), contain important post balance sheet events which have affected the company since the end of the financial year. In order to avoid duplication this information is often provided in the notes to the accounts. 4562

Creditor payment policy

4564 Public Limited Companies (PLC) and large private companies which are members of a group whose parent is a PLC, are required to disclose their payment policy regarding suppliers. The provisions apply to each individual company and not to the group as a whole; therefore subsidiary companies do not have to disclose the creditor policy of the parent company and vice-versa.

The **directors must state** in their report:
a. Whether it is company policy to follow any code or standard on payment practice; this should be done with reference to the year following the period covered by the last financial statements.
b. If a particular standard or code is adopted by the company, details of the code and from where copies can be obtained should be disclosed.
c. Whether the policy applies to all or some of the creditors, and if different the class of suppliers should be identified.
d. The terms of payments should be agreed with suppliers prior to each transaction.
e. The average number of days taken to settle trade creditors accounts as illustrated in the following example.

MEMO POINTS Creditor payment codes include the CBI's "Prompt Payers Code of Good Practice".

EXAMPLE **XYZ Ltd**
Annual report – August 2010
Directors' report (extract)
Creditor payment policy

The company's policy concerning the payment of its trade creditors is as follows:
Distribution suppliers are paid monthly, for costs incurred in that month, based on estimated annual contracts, and payments are adjusted quarterly to reflect any variations against estimate.
Trade creditor days for the year ended 31 August 2010 were 16.5 days, based on the ratio of company trade creditors at the end of the year to the amounts invoiced during the year by trade creditors.
For all trade creditors, it is company policy to:
- agree the terms of payment at the commencement of business with that supplier;
- ensure that the suppliers are aware of the terms of the payment;
- pay in accordance with its contractual and other legal obligations.

Valuation of land and buildings

4568 Where the valuation of the directors of land or buildings owned by the company **materially exceeds the value** recorded in the balance sheet, then this difference should be disclosed. The disclosure should be based on a recent valuation although there is no requirement for this to be a professional valuation.

Where the value of land or buildings is **less than the book value** and the directors determine that a write-down is not required, some justification for this policy should be stated in the directors' report.

MEMO POINTS Where a company adopts a policy of **revaluing assets** under FRS 15 "Tangible fixed assets", any gains or losses should be incorporated into the accounts.

EXAMPLE **Handel Plc**
Report and accounts – 30 October 2010
Directors' report (extract)

Property
The directors have reviewed the current value of the premises portfolio and estimate that there is a shortfall of £6.5m, compared to the balance sheet value. The shortfall relates to UK properties and the directors are of the opinion that this will not prove to be permanent; therefore no adjustment has been made in the balance sheet.

Overseas branches

The directors' report must, unless the company is unlimited, contain details of business establishments it operates outside the United Kingdom. Overseas establishments operated by its subsidiaries should be disclosed in the directors' report of the subsidiary companies. 4572

Employee policies

Companies employing an **average of more than 250 people** throughout the year must disclose details relating to: 4576
- the dissemination of information to employees on matters concerning them (i.e. health and safety, employee welfare policies);
- employee consultation procedures;
- employee share schemes; and
- employment of disabled persons.

If a company prepares consolidated financial statements, the director's report need only contain the employee information (dictated by Schedule 7) for the parent company.

The Companies Act requires that the **average number of employees** be calculated, by first determining the number of people employed by the company in each week of the financial year, totalling the individual weekly totals before dividing by the number of weeks in the financial year. 4578

The threshold applies to **individual companies**; there is no requirement to aggregate figures for persons employed by a group of companies. Disclosures are not required for persons wholly or primarily employed outside the UK. Therefore, where a parent company is purely a holding company with a small number of employees, then employee policy disclosures are not required in the group accounts. However, it is regarded as **best practice** to disclosure employee numbers, where the group employs in excess of 250.

The **format of the disclosures** is usually in **narrative form** and may for example cover discussion of: 4582
- the use of internal seminars and training programmes to supply information to employees;
- details of in-house newsletters;
- relationships with recognised trade unions;
- details of employee share schemes; and
- action to promote equal opportunities.

Disclosures are not required for persons wholly or primarily employed outside the UK.

EXAMPLE **PQR Ltd**
Annual report and accounts 2010
Directors' report (extract)

Employee involvement
The Board continues to place emphasis on high standards of customer care and service by each operating company. The commitment of every employee to this business requirement is considered to be critical. Accordingly, operating companies have continued to develop their arrangements for **employee information, consultation, communication and involvement**, including attitude surveys, briefing groups, internal magazines and newsletters on matters relating to business performance and objectives, community involvement and other related issues.
Training and links with the educational sector reinforce our commitment to employee involvement and development. Employees are represented on the trustee board of the Group's pension arrangements.

The Group has an **Employee Savings Related Share Option Scheme** to which all UK employees are entitled to participate, regardless of hours worked but provided certain service criteria are met. For our overseas companies a similar savings scheme operates although reflecting the different tax and legal requirements.

Equal opportunities The Group is committed to the principle of equal opportunity in employment and to ensuring that no applicant or employee receives less favourable treatment on the grounds of gender, race, age, colour, nationality, religion, HIV status, disability, sexuality, or unrelated criminal convictions or other unjustified requirements or conditions.

The Group applies employment policies that are fair and equitable and which ensure entry into, and progression within the Group, is determined solely by application of job criteria and personal ability and competency.

4584 **Disabled persons** The statutory disclosures regarding company policy, in respect of the employment of disabled persons, include the following:
- equal employment opportunities for disabled people;
- continued employment and training of staff becoming disabled, whilst employees of the company; and
- general training, career development and promotion of disabled persons.

The same **threshold rules** as for general employee policies apply.

Carbon emissions

4586 Under the Climate Change Act 2008 provisions exist for regulations (or secondary legislation) to be introduced, imposing a mandatory obligation on large and medium-sized companies to disclose their carbon emissions in their directors' reports. The Act requires the Government to introduce such regulations, or lay a report before Parliament if this has not happened, by April 2012. In the meantime, guidance has been published by the Department for Environment, Food and Rural Affairs (DEFRA) (in partnership with the Department for Energy and Climate Change (DECC)) on how companies can measure and report their greenhouse gas emissions, as well as set targets to reduce them. The guidance is available from DEFRA's website along with separate guidance for small companies.

2. Quoted companies are required to provide more detailed information as part of the business review (see ¶4554).

B. Additional disclosures required by listed companies

4590 Listed companies are required to make further disclosures in the directors' report (or separately) in addition to those required under company law. These disclosures principally arise out of the Listings Rules issued by the Financial Services Agency (FSA) and the Combined Code published by the Committee on Corporate Governance.

Listed companies must disclose how they have applied the principles and provisions of the **Combined Code** either in the directors' report or within a separate report on corporate governance. These disclosures cover directors' responsibilities, shareholder relations, internal control and audit. In addition, there are a number of other important disclosures required in the directors' report and which are listed below.

4594 **Directors' service contracts** Details of the unexpired part of directors' service contracts must be stated in the directors' report, for any director offering themselves for re-election at the forthcoming AGM. Directors' service contracts should not exceed three years without shareholder approval and details of the unexpired period should be disclosed in the directors' report.

4598 **Related party transactions** For a detailed treatment of this topic see ¶5000.

4599 **Financial instruments** Additional disclosure requirements are required covering the use of financial instruments. For a more detailed treatment of this topic see ¶3400.

4600 **Variance from published forecasts** Where a company or group has published forecasts that cover the accounting period on which they are reporting, the directors' report must detail any material variances (10 % +).

Note on future developments The wording of any note on forecast future developments should be carefully chosen, in order that it should not be construed as a profit forecast. If the directors' report is seen to include a profit forecast that relates to a period during which a take-over bid arises, then the forecast should be included in any offer or defence document and accountants will be required to report: 4602
- that the forecast has been properly prepared in accordance with the accounting policies of the company or group; and
- any differences (exceeding 10%) between the actual results as stated in the financial statements and the forecast results that exceeds 10%.

Interest capitalised Interest capitalised during the period and the amount and treatment of any tax relief, should be included in the directors' report. 4604

Waiver of emoluments Details of any arrangement by which a director has waived or agreed to waive, any current or future emoluments from the company or any subsidiary, must be disclosed. 4606

Purchase of own shares The directors' report should disclose **details of any authority granted** to a company to acquire its own shares, either directly or indirectly via a nominee company or person with or without financial assistance from the company, in addition to the normal disclosures required under the Companies Act. This information should include details of any authority given by the shareholders in general meeting, still effective at the year end. 4608

The disclosures required **should also include details** of the actual or proposed seller of any purchases or proposals made, excluding offers through the market, by tender, or through a partial offer to all shareholders. The disclosures required in respect of the purchase of one's own shares should also cover the purchase or acquisition of a company's own shares, made since the end of the financial year.

Placing Where a listed company which is a subsidiary makes a placing of shares, details of the parent company's participation in the event must be disclosed. 4610

Substantial holdings Disclosure is required of any person other than a director of the company, who holds or has a beneficial interest in 3% or more of the share capital of the company, on a date not exceeding one month prior to the date of the annual meeting. 4612

EXAMPLE **Coneyfisher PLC**
Annual report and accounts
Directors' report (extract)

Major shareholders
As at 5 April 2010, the Company has been notified of the following interests, in 3% or more of the Company's shares:

	No. of shares	% holding
Beechers Bank Plc	42,014,132	3.00
CTYV and certain subsidiaries	49,521,170	3.55
P & B Investment Management Ltd	52,108,750	3.73

Transactions with a controlling shareholder(s) who control 30% or more of the voting power in the company, or who are able to control the appointment of directors who exercise a majority of the votes at board meetings, should be disclosed in the directors' report. 4614

Special business Where the directors of a company request special business to be discussed by the members prior to the AGM, they must supply details of the relevant special business in a separate report and give details in the directors' report. 4616 LR 14.17

Examples of special business include:
- amendments to the Articles of Association;
- renewal of the directors' authority for the company to purchase its own shares; and
- approval of Senior Management Incentive Plan.

4618 UITF 21 (7) **Euro** Where the potential impact of any expenditure relating to the change over to the Euro is likely to be significant, this should be discussed in the directors' report.

4620 LR 12.44 **Significant transactions** The Listings Rules require disclosure of significant contracts entered into by the Company or one of its subsidiaries, in which a director has or had a material interest. A significant contract is deemed to be equal to 1% or more of:
- the aggregate of the group's share capital and reserves; or
- the group's total purchases, sales, payments or receipts.

4622 **Environmental reporting** The disclosure of environmental information is **currently voluntary**. There is an increasing demand for information about an entity's impact on the environment, to be included in the financial statements and in the directors' report in particular.

Some listed companies (e.g. British Petroleum) have produced separate detailed reports on the impact and risks that their operations pose to the environment. Other listed companies, such as the major high street banks, have stressed their involvement in community projects.

MEMO POINTS Guidance on environmental reporting is given in the "Statement of good practice – Environmental Reporting in Annual Accounts (1991)", issued by the Hundred Group of Finance Directors. Developments in corporate social responsibility and environmental reporting in general (CSR) are covered in more detail in ¶4760-¶4761.

EXAMPLE **LMO Ltd.**
Report and accounts 2010
Directors' report (extract)

Community affairs and environmental issues
The Company and its subsidiaries contribute to a number of **community projects**, either in cash or in kind by donation of human resources. The value of this year's contribution is estimated at £3.2m (2009 £1.7 million).
The Group continues to identify the key **environmental impacts** of the operational element of the business and its products. Progress has been made to reduce that impact and the Group is committed to making further improvements.
The Group celebrated 10 years of environmental achievement by winning the Business in the Environment award for its stores and supplies. These have saved more than £2 million in energy use and £750,000 in waste management, as well as impacting on overall business performance.

New environmental targets include a commitment to be "toxic safe" by the end of 2010 and to reduce carbon dioxide emissions through store operations by 25% and from logistics by 45%. The electricity supply at our head office in London has switched to renewable resources from green energy.

Recycling electrical goods The Group trains unemployed young people to repair white goods with a two-fold purpose. Firstly, the young people gain a valuable qualification in the NVQ Service Repair and secondly, waste products are removed from the waste stream.

Ethical trading During the year, we have introduced an ethical business code implemented throughout the supply chain.

MEMO POINTS Quoted companies are required to provide more detailed information on carbon emissions as part of the business review see ¶4586.

4626 **Membership of committees** In addition to the requirements of the Companies Act covered briefly in ¶4516, the Combined Code recommends the disclosure of the names of the directors of the following:
- the audit committee;
- the nominations committee; and
- the remuneration committee.

Directors' statement of responsibilities The directors' reports of companies **subject to audit**, should include a statement from the directors that no information has knowingly been withheld, that would affect the auditor's opinion of the annual financial statements. The directors' report should also include a statement of directors' responsibilities, arising out of the International Standard on Auditing 700, "The Auditors' Report on Financial Statements". 4628

EXAMPLE **LMO Ltd.**
Report and accounts 2010
Directors' report (extract)

Directors' statement of responsibility
The directors are responsible for preparing the Directors' Report and the annual financial statements in accordance with UK company legislation and generally accepted United Kingdom accounting practice. The directors are satisfied that the financial statements give a true and fair view of the state of affairs of the company and the profit or loss for the period in question. In preparing the financial statements the directors have:
- selected suitable accounting policies and applied them consistently;
- made prudent and reasonable accounting estimates;
- have followed UK accounting standards and explained any material departures in the notes to the accounts;
- prepared the financial statements on a going concern basis;
- taken adequate measures to ensure that proper accounting records have been maintained; and
- put in place effective safeguards to protect company assets from fraud and misappropriation.

Operating and financial review The statutory requirement **for listed companies** to provide an OFR (see ¶4700), has been repealed. Instead, Reporting Standard RS 1 has mutated into a statement of best practice. The extended business review section should cover the principle risks and uncertainties facing the business and be consistent with the size and complexity of the entity. Less detail will be expected of small companies. 4629

CHAPTER 2

Operating and Financial Review (OFR)

OUTLINE ¶¶

An Operating and Financial Review (OFR) is a voluntary statement included within the annual report of both listed and large private companies. A **statement of best practice** (Operating and Financial Review RS (OFR)) issued by the ASB, continues to provide influential guidance following the Government's decision to repeal legislation (Regulations) requiring a mandatory OFR. At present **all companies**, except those meeting the small companies' criteria, must include a business review in the enhanced directors' report (see ¶4500). However, further reforms in this area of financial reporting can be expected. **4700**

MEMO POINTS The new coalition Government has outlined plans to make the provision of an OFR in company reports compulsory, and replace the current requirement for a non-mandatory business review covering performance indicators and social and environmental issues. The new proposals are designed to improve corporate accountability and reporting transparency, particularly with regard to the entity's social and environmental obligations.

The **rationale** behind the OFR, is that it should provide **a consistent reporting framework** for investment and form an integral part of the annual report and accounts. The OFR gives directors the opportunity to interpret the financial statements and discuss the performance of the business, the structure of its finance, the nature of any significant risks, known or forecast changes in the environment in which it operates and additional analysis using financial and non-financial key performance indicators. In addition to the shareholders, the OFR should address the needs of other stakeholders such as employees or suppliers. **4702**

The OFR **should focus on those issues** that are of greatest significance to the business in the reporting period. Detailed guidance is provided in RS (OFR) on the layout and content of the OFR, although major corporations are also expected to provide a lead in developing and adapting this statement to the individual circumstances of their own company or industry. **4704**

The **emphasis** in the OFR is on a review of **business objectives and the strategies** for achieving them, although the directors may decline to provide a detailed narrative of some aspects of the business, if they believe that the disclosure of confidential information would be of benefit to their competitors. However, the **directors have a duty** to ensure that any such omissions do not mislead the user of the accounts. Information contained in the OFR that would otherwise be required in the directors' report, need not be duplicated. **4706**

There is currently **no requirement** to produce an OFR under IFRS, although this is being reviewed.

MEMO POINTS The ASB has updated its guidance clarifying the use of cross-references where the directors' report and OFR are published in the same report (see ¶4554).

A. Principles

4720 The **preferred structure** is not compulsory and the disclosure requirements of the OFR can be included within existing formats such as the directors' report as a business review or the chairman's statement. Although a great deal of discretion is allowed, the OFR should be written in a concise and balanced style, and be objective in its presentation of both the positive and negative aspects of financial performance.

4721 The following principles are regarded as essential to the preparation of a good OFR.

1. **Purpose**. The OFR should assist the user's assessment of the future performance of the business, by covering the directors' analysis of the business, including:
- the nature of the business;
- the objectives and the strategies required to achieve them;
- the performance of the business in the period and the main influences on performance such as trends and potential risks; and
- the financial position, including capital structure and treasury policy.

2. **Audience**. The OFR should focus on issues relevant to investors and should not assume users have a prior knowledge of the business, or the significant features of its operating environment.

3. **Time frame**. The important factors identified as being relevant to the business within the relevant financial period, as well as those factors that are expected to affect future performance, should be discussed.

4. **Reliability**. The information given in the OFR should be neutral, free from bias and balanced. Where a significant matter is discussed elsewhere in the annual report, such as the chairman's statement, a cross-reference should be provided.

5. **Comparability**. The disclosures given in the OFR should be sufficient to enable the user to compare the information presented with similar information on other entities in the same industry.

6. **Financial and non-financial measures**. Any financial and non-financial measures used must be disclosed including those widely used within the same industry sector or more generally, including details of:
- key performance indicators used in running the business;
- any calculation methods used;
- sources of data and any assumptions used, including a reconciliation where information has been adjusted for inclusion in the OFR;
- comparative amounts; and
- any changes to accounting policies applied in the financial statements or to the basis of key performance indicators with the comparative amounts restated.

4722 The **directors are now obliged** to include a confirmation of the **level of compliance** with the principles set out in RS (OFR). Any fundamental departures from the standard should be disclosed. The directors should also discuss the adoption for the first time of any new financial reporting standards.

B. Disclosure framework

1. Operating review

4725 The operating review should be an **objective discussion** that both analyses and explains the dynamics underlying the results and financial position of an entity, how they interrelate, and are expected to change in the near future. Information is often grouped under the headings listed below.

Operating results

The operating review should cover all sections of the profit and loss account down to the level of profit on ordinary activities before taxation, and focus on the overall business with particular emphasis given to important business segments and their interaction. The directors should also indicate: 4726
- any **special factors** that have affected performance in the period under review, including exceptional items reported in the financial statements; and
- **whether the financial results** cover a complete financial reporting year or only a part thereof.

The **key areas** covered would typically include: 4728
- the structure of the business, including an overview of the main operating facilities and their location;
- changes in market conditions, share or position;
- its main products and services, business processes and distribution methods;
- new products, activities or services introduced;
- changes in turnover and operating margins;
- changes to significant features of the legal or regulatory environment; and
- an overview of discontinued activities, exceptional items, and any acquisitions or disposals.

Material acquisitions The OFR should review the extent to which the expectations relating to an acquisition have been realised. Where a seasonal business has been acquired in the period under review, or the results are not for a full period, this should also be indicated. 4730

Intangible assets

The OFR should also give a commentary on the strengths and resources of the business that it draws on in the pursuit of its objectives, that are not easily valued, including: 4732
- corporate reputation and brand equity;
- intellectual capital;
- research and development;
- websites and databases; and
- proprietary business processes.

This information should be augmented by the disclosure of **additional non-financial data** such as customer satisfaction or productivity levels, in order to provide an insight into the scale of the business and the key stakeholder relationships.

Business risks

The **principal risks** facing the business and the method of managing them should be identified and, where possible, their impact on the results (in qualitative terms) should be disclosed. The **two principal categories** are commercial and social risk. 4734

Some examples of **commercial risk** include the following:
- cost pressures resulting from a scarcity of one or more of the factors of production (i.e. land, labour, materials);
- the expiry of patents, licences or franchises;
- undue dependence on major suppliers or customers;
- product liability (i.e. warranties);
- technological change (i.e. warranties); or
- threat of new competition.

MEMO POINTS 1. The Combined Code (¶5200) deals with the director's approach to risk management and any disclosures would normally be included within a separate corporate governance statement.

2. The Financial Reporting Council (FRC) is canvassing company directors, audit and risk committee chairpersons, investors and advisors on how companies are responding to the new UK Corporate Governance Code provision, regarding their determination of the nature and the extent of the risks they are willing to take in order to achieve their strategic corporate objectives. Feedback will be sought on the following issues:
– what are the respective roles of the board, board committees and management, and how do they interact?
– where does oversight end and operational management begin? and
– how do boards assess their attitude to risk and reassure themselves that their risk management and internal control systems are functioning effectively at an operational level?
The FRC will then consider whether the Turnbull Guidance on risk and internal control should be adjusted as a result of their consultations.

4738 **Social risk** covers areas such as:
a. health and safety;
b. environmental protection and (potential) environmental liabilities including:
– clean-up costs from oil spillages; and
– landscape restoration costs in the extractive industries.
Other regulatory issues include changes in political or macro-economic conditions (i.e. exchange rates).

Business dynamics

4742 The operating review should also **cover the major factors** that will influence future results of the entity, whether or not they are fundamental to the period under review. It is intended that the OFR should not contain any profit forecasts. It is not possible to give a definite list of all the business dynamics, as this will depend upon the nature of the business concerned.

4744 **All forms of investment** undertaken should be discussed.

The operating review should include details of **future investment plans** and how the directors aim to maintain and improve performance, in respect of the following:
– the defence of existing income and profit streams through marketing, refurbishment or maintenance initiatives;
– the development of new products or services (i.e. e-commerce);
– capital expenditure, covering the major business and geographical segments; or
– details of any proposed significant projects and the benefits that are expected to ensue.

The **potential impact** of any proposed investment on future profits should also be disclosed.

4746 **Capital expenditure** The OFR should discuss the benefits expected to accrue from the capital expenditure, including benefits arising during the present period from previous capital expenditure as well as those expected in the future. The OFR should also explain how any investment is to be directed in order to achieve the objective of the business, as well as an analysis of how changes in the levels of such activity and expenditure impact on the performance of the business.

EXAMPLE HRT Group Ltd

Operating and financial review
Capital expenditure

Capital expenditure for the period was £40.5m compared to £32m in 2009. This increase reflects our continued demand for increased capacity to satisfy sales growth and to automate some of our key manufacturing processes. In 2010 we invested some £10million in new manufacturing facilities at Smitherly. Net capital expenditure of £38.5m reflects the one-off sale of three properties which realised proceeds of £8m.
All capital expenditure goes through a rigorous evaluation process prior to its approval and is subject to constant review both during and after completion to ensure that the resultant project delivery is in line with expectations.

4748 **Other investment expenditure** Examples of other activities or expenditure that can enhance future profits include:
– training programmes;

- marketing and advertising campaigns to improve brand equity;
- technical support to customers;
- pure and applied research leading to potential new products and services; or
- business rationalisation and restructuring programmes.

Returns to shareholders

The OFR should discuss returns to shareholders, including: 4750
- distributions and share repurchases;
- increases or decreases in share price in the period in comparison with that of its peers;
- comparison between profit and dividends for the financial period, both in total and in per share terms; and
- basic and diluted earnings per share (see ¶600).

Dividend policy The operating review should discuss the overall return attributable to shareholders in terms of the dividends and capital growth resulting from operating profit performance. 4752

The dividend policy of the entity should also be outlined, confirming the directors' proposed final dividend on the ordinary shares of the company and the date it will be paid to shareholders.

Valuation It is not intended that an overall valuation of the business be given or, in the case of listed companies, for net asset value to be reconciled to market capitalisation. 4754

Accounting policies Within the operating review, the directors should explain any sensitive, subjective judgements and arbitrary financial allocations included in the financial statements (as well as any significant effects), arising from the application of specific accounting policies, where key to an understanding of the business. 4756

The adoption of FRS 12 "Provisions, contingent liabilities and assets" requires an entity to report, by way of note, the consequences of transactions such as provisions for onerous contracts or restructuring costs, whose life extends beyond the timescale of the current financial reporting period.

Stakeholder interests A number of leading companies are seeking to include in the operating review, a section covering the interests of stakeholders other than the investment community. This section covers the contribution made to the company's performance by other stakeholders such as employees, customers, suppliers and the local community and seeks to **highlight activities** that are often **not quantifiable** in financial terms, such as: 4758
- improvements in customer service;
- educational programmes in schools and universities;
- the company's health and safety record; or
- equal opportunity policies and employee development schemes.

Other initiatives include co-operative ventures with local suppliers on quality initiatives or product design.

Corporate social responsibility (CSR)

A growing number of **listed companies** are now producing a CSR report, usually forming part of the operating and financial review. The Department of Trade and Industry (DTI) has published proposals outlining its position concerning corporate social responsibility at a global level. These proposals are in addition to existing initiatives and proposals such as those covering ethical trading. At present companies are not legally required to publish information about CSR. 4760

A **sample framework** for CSR is given in the table below.

Corporate social responsibility **Area of responsibility**	**Accountability**
1. Business ethics	Standards of conduct Policy on political contributions
2. Food safety	Risk assessments and secure provenance of raw materials Purchasing and procurement controls Routine audits of business units and supply chain Key performance indicators on food hygiene, customer complaints and food safety
3. Health and safety	Objective to reduce accidents by 10% health and safety training programmes Internal health and safety audits – performance v measurable targets
4. Environment (see below)	Reduction in emissions of pollutants (e.g. pesticides) Impact of Climate Change Levy Agreement Introduction of recycling programmes (e.g. packaging)
5. Sourcing/supplies	Business conduct with suppliers Supply chain employment policies Environmental purchasing (e.g. ethical purchasing)
6. Customers	Performance targets such as orders delivered on time
7. Employees	Employee welfare and human rights Company values (i.e. teamwork, customer care, innovation) Equal opportunity policies Employee retention policies Disabled policies Flexible working Training, staff appraisals and career development
8. Community interests	Charities Support of local causes – school projects, community schemes

EXAMPLE **BWWO Group Plc**

Annual Report and Accounts 2010
CSR Report

Investors are paying increasing attention to ways in which social, environmental and ethical issues are managed in order to preserve and grow shareholder value. This section of the OFR concentrates on CSR governance, CSR risks, and environment and community policies. More detailed disclosures of our CSR policies and procedures are available on-line in our independently verified social and environmental report.

Environmental accounting

4761 There are a **number of developments** in the area of environmental reporting both in the UK and within the European Commission, that are expected to lead to a significant increase in the level of environmental disclosures by listed companies, in the operating and financial review section of the annual report, as well as increased reporting requirements for small companies. Attempts are currently being made by a number of organisations to overcome the current limitations of conventional financial reporting in this area.

In a **separate development** the UK Environment Agency, in co-operation with the ACCA, has also published a number of papers detailing recent developments in environmental accounting practice, covering issues such as climate change, emissions trading and product disposal legislation. The Environment Agency recommends more disclosures and discussion of the possible impact of these activities on the balance sheet.

Although directors of listed companies currently **have the discretion** to decide whether or not to include environmental information in the OFR, the process by which this choice is made will be subject to review by the auditors. Any inconsistencies between the OFR and the financial statements should be reported. The Environment Agency can also **impose fines and pollution abatement costs** and can withdraw permits and operating licences from listed companies and their subsidiaries. The **following example** is representative of a company whose activities have a high impact on the environment. The level of disclosure is expected to increase over time with more detail expected on environmental policies and quantifiable performance targets.

EXAMPLE **Hoppy Smith Brewing Plc**

Annual report and accounts
Environmental policy

The company considers compliance with current environmental legislation and the adoption of responsible standards as an integral part of its business operations. The company is also committed to introducing new measures to limit any adverse effects its business operations may have on the environment and shall promote best practice in accordance with the latest techniques. Overall responsibility for environmental policy rests with the board although divisional managing directors are responsible for the sound environmental management of their particular operations.

In 20X6 we monitored our energy consumption, as a base from which to set our target for reduction in energy as part of the "Climate Change Levy Agreement". We have set a target of reducing our kilowatt hour per tonne rate by 10% over the next ten years with five key milestone targets every two years. We are on course to meet the 2011 milestone target. Targets have also been set for improvements in reducing waste disposal and use of pesticides.

EXAMPLE **Premier Industries Ltd**

Environmental report – climate change

We have adopted a comprehensive environment policy and publish an annual report tracking our performance. Our Environment Management Committee includes three external members to oversee performance. Our activities include our contribution to cleaner rivers, energy efficiency projects and landscape/wildlife protection programmes.

Kyoto Protocol As a company we contribute to the national target for reducing carbon dioxide emissions through reducing our energy consumption, through renewable generation and investment in customer energy saving programmes. At present we generate out 15% of our total energy consumption from renewable resources.

Business in the Environment Index We have implemented the Environmental Management System (EMS) throughout the group. The Index was initiated in 1996 to monitor the progress of the FTSE 100 companies in establishing coherent environmental management. Our score in the Index has risen to 80% against an FTSE average of 75%.

Rio declaration We are attempting to enhance the bio-diversity of our estates through careful land and habitat management, resulting in increased survival prospects for rare species. We are also on target to plant a million trees by 2012, to add to the five million that we already manage. Our partners in these projects include various Government agencies and charities.

MEMO POINTS 1. **A new emissions trading scheme**, known as the Carbon Reduction Commitment Energy Scheme (CRC Scheme), came into force in the UK in April 2010. The scheme will be administered by the Environment Agency and applies mainly to public sector organisations (e.g. schools, hospitals) and large companies such as retail chains, supermarkets, and hotels. The scheme will be phased in over a 3 year period until April 2013, during which the government will sell emission allowances in order to encourage these entities to reduce their trading emissions. A penalty regime will be established to cover misdemeanours such as making false or misleading statements in the annual reports relating to participation in the CRC Scheme, and failure to register for the scheme or submit compliance reports when required. More information concerning this trading emissions scheme can be found on the Environment Agency's website.

2. The IASB and the US Financial Accounting Standards Board (FASB) have discussed the measurement of allowances for assets and liabilities in an **emissions trading scheme**. A cap and trade scheme, as it is also known, is a market-based approach used to control pollution by providing economic incentives for achieving reductions in pollutant emissions. The joint proposal outlines four measurement models for further consideration and stresses the need for additional analysis, including quantitative examples that outline the effect of the different measurement techniques. The IASB plans to issue an exposure draft on emissions trading in 2011.

3. **The Global Reporting Initiative (GRI)**, a not for profit organisation, has called for better integrated financial and environmental reporting through wider use of its Sustainability Reporting Framework (SFR) and guidelines. The SFR provides help for organisations, regardless of size or sector, regarding the disclosure of sustainability performance using a universally-applicable, comparable reporting framework. The guidelines, including examples of standard disclosures, are available from the GRI website.

4762 **UK GAAP** There are at present **no reporting standards** dealing specifically with environmental accounting, although a company with environmental provisions or contingent liabilities is required to disclose the amounts and circumstances surrounding them in its annual financial report. **Further disclosures**, detailing the treatment of material changes in asset values arising from environmental factors, **may be appropriate under**:
- FRS 10 "Goodwill and intangible assets" (IAS 38 "Intangible assets"); and
- FRS 11 "Impairment of fixed assets and goodwill" (IAS 36 "Impairment of assets").

4763 The EU Modernisation Directive states that annual reports should where appropriate include "an analysis of environmental and social aspects necessary for an understanding of the company's development, performance and position" and also that the analysis shall include both financial and non-financial KPIs, including information relating to environmental and employee matters.

The **type and scale** of environmental reports are dependent on the activity of the individual entity and the industry sector to which it belongs, and should correlate with the scale of the environmental impact. For instance, a higher level of disclosure is required of resource intensive companies such as the oil and gas sectors under International Accounting Standards. A greater recognition of natural resources as natural assets in annual reports is also expected.

4763-1 The **EU Trading Emissions Scheme** is also expected to give rise to environmental assets in the form of rights to emit greenhouse gases. Under this scheme, which came into effect in January 2005, the level of environmental reporting under the accounting standards listed above will increase.

4763-2 **Another work-in-progress report** is the EU Commission Recommendation (2001/453), which covers the recognition, measurement and disclosure of environmental expenditures, liabilities and other risks and assets as well as the company's attitude to the environment.

MEMO POINTS The International Federation of Accountants (Ifac) has issued a paper on environmental accounting, entitled "Why Sustainability Counts for Professional Accountants in Business". This paper provides advice on how to deal with the risks and rewards offered by sustainable development and offers general guidance on measuring, recording and assessing sustainability related information.

4763-3 **Summary**

Environmental accounting	Internal management accounting tool
Objectives	Identify cost savings Improve financial performance Minimise environmental risk Measure environmental impacts (energy use, waste, sustainability, recycling policies, transportation) Stakeholder involvement (employees, suppliers, Government etc) Aid investment decisions
Legal framework	Companies Act European legislation UK Environment Agency OFR
Environmental costs	Identify types of environmental costs (e.g. product design/engineering costs, production facilties, waste management, compliance costs) Key performance indicators (KPI's) – by industry sector Supply chain management Internal control systems Offsetting environmental costs through developing by products

Techniques	Cost accounting Depreciation of natural capital (resources) Risk assessments
Taxation	Environmental tax obligations Environmental taxes – levies (e.g. aggregates, climate change, landfill taxes) Tax breaks. capital allowances for plant-machinery (ECA) Tax credits Penalties

2. Financial review

The financial review should be an overview of the **capital structure** that supports an entity, its treasury policy and sources of liquidity and their application, and the implications of the financing requirements arising from any capital expenditure plans, delivered in narrative form, and supported by figures where this assists understanding. The financial review is **typically structured** under the following headings. **4764**

Capital funding and treasury policy

This section of the OFR should cover the following: **4766**
- internal financial controls surrounding treasury activities;
- maturity profile and type of company debt;
- currency profile of borrowings (i.e. cash and paper equivalents);
- exposure to currency exchange rate fluctuations;
- use of financial instruments for hedging purposes (i.e. swaps, derivatives); or
- use of financial instruments for purposes other than hedging.

EXAMPLE ABC Group Ltd

Financial Review

Our treasury activities are controlled and monitored by the Group Finance Director and are carried out in accordance with the policies approved by the Board. The purpose of the treasury policies is to ensure that adequate cost-effective funding is available to the company at all times and that exposure to financial risk is minimised. The risks managed by the Group Treasury department are funding risk, interest rate risk and currency risk.

A detailed treasury manual is used across the Group which clearly defines policies governing the management of these risks. These policies have remained unchanged throughout the period.

The Treasury department does not operate as a profit centre and no speculative transactions are permitted.

The financial review **should also include comment** on: **4768**
- the interest cover ratio;
- the debt/equity ratio;
- short plus long-term funding plans; and
- an explanation of the effects of any major transactions undertaken, up to the date the financial statements are approved.

Cash flow from operating activities and other sources of cash

The **following information** should be **disclosed**: **4772**

a. the principal sources and applications of cash generated from operations and other cash inflows during the period under review;

b. segmental cash flows that are significantly out of line with segmental profits;

c. the entity's liquidity position including the level of (and fluctuations in) borrowings and their maturity profile;

d. an overview of funding requirements for capital expenditure commitments;

e. an assessment of any constraints on the following:

– the transfer of funds between group companies through exchange controls or potential tax liabilities; or

– the general terms of any restrictive covenants on the level of credit facilities, level of dividend or sale of key assets. Known or expected breaches of covenants and any proposed remedial measures should also be disclosed.

4774 **Current liquidity** The level of liquidity within the business at the end of the financial period under review should also be discussed, including an overview of:
– the level of borrowings;
– the seasonality of borrowing requirements; and
– the maturity profiles of both borrowings and undrawn but committed borrowing facilities.

Interest rate and exchange rate risk

4776 This section of the OFR should cover the following:
– the interest rate profile (i.e. fixed or floating);
– the effect of interest costs on profits and the potential impact of changes in interest rates;
– exposure to exchange rate fluctuations; or
– the effect of different exchange rates between revenues and costs or between different market or business segments.

EXAMPLE ABC Group Ltd

Financial Review – Interest rate management
At the end of the financial period our core borrowings were approximately £68m. We have a policy of managing our exposure to interest rate fluctuations by keeping approximately 30% and 65% of our borrowings at a fixed rate of interest for two to four years, with the remainder held at floating rates.

Foreign currency risk
We have four large overseas trading operations and their receipts and payments are predominately in their local currencies and so are not hedged. We do have a dollar/sterling exposure from our operations in the United States that we hedge via short-term contracts. In order to protect our sterling balance sheet from the effect of currency fluctuations on our continental European assets, we utilise euro denominated borrowings. This form of hedging accounts for approximately 40% of our year-end debt position.
On purchases of goods in foreign currency, we eliminate currency exposure on transactions through the use of forward exchange contracts.

Taxation

4780 Significant differences between the standard UK rate of tax (i.e. the normal UK rate applied to profit before taxation) and the overall tax charge should be explained. The disclosure requirements are now covered by FRS 19 "Deferred tax" (¶9000).

EXAMPLE ABC Group Ltd – Operating and Financial Review

The tax charge for the period was £5.3m on pre-exceptional costs, an effective rate of tax of 16% (2009: 25%), compared to the standard UK corporation tax of 30%. During 2010, agreement was reached with the Inland Revenue on the tax treatment of two different transaction in the previous financial year. The recognition of these assets is the principle reason for the low effective rate in 2009.

Other disclosures

4782 **Going concern** The Combined Code on Corporate Governance proposed that the directors of listed companies state in the annual report (in the OFR), their opinion that the company is a going concern.

MEMO POINTS The FRC has issued updated guidance for all company directors, covering the going concern statement required in annual reports. The following key areas were addressed:
– the process directors should follow in determining whether the entity is a going concern:
– the period covered by the assessment; and
– the disclosures required, including the key underlying assumptions supporting the going concern and liquidity risk assessments. The new guidance is applicable from 31 December 2009 and applies also to interim reports.

Shareholders' funds The review should discuss how shareholders' funds have grown or declined in the period covered by the review and the principal reasons for the change, i.e. increased profits or surpluses that may have arisen from the sale of assets. 4784

Details of the share price and shareholder services such as preferential share dealing should also be included.

Key performance indicators (KPIs)

KPIs are factors that aid measurement of the performance, growth or position of the company or group. An entity should provide information to enable users of the financial statements to understand each KPI or other form of performance measure referred to in the report as follows: 4785
- the definition and method of calculation method should be disclosed;
- its purpose;
- the source of the supporting data and any assumptions explained;
- quantification or commentary on future targets;
- corresponding amounts for the preceding financial year; and
- any changes to KPIs.

The topic of accounting ratios is covered in ¶5900.

C. Audit of the OFR

Audit requirements

The Government has removed the statutory requirement for quoted companies to publish an OFR has implications for the Auditing Practices Board (APB), which has developed draft standards and guidance in respect of the auditor's new statutory reporting responsibilities concerning the OFR and directors' report. 4788

Audit guidance (best practice) is provided in the Statement of Auditing Standard (SAS) 160.

Checklist

The following checklist provides an aid to the preparation of the OFR. 4792

CHECKLIST		Yes/ No
1	Do you understand the interests and concerns of your members and other stakeholders?	
2	Have your objectives and strategy been clearly defined?	
3	Do your KPIs support your strategy and objectives?	
4	Are your KPIs clearly defined, measurable and comparable?	
5	Have you incorporated OFR reporting into your reporting processes?	
6	Have your current reporting systems been adjusted to ensure the timely collection of quality OFR data?	
7	Have all relevant risks been assessed?	
8	Have the company's assurance processes been reviewed to incorporate the OFR?	
9	Do you have policies that reflect the concerns of other stakeholders (e.g. environmental, employee, suppliers)?	
10	What are the costs of compliance?	£

D. Comparison between UK GAAP and IFRS

4794 There is currently no mandatory international reporting standard covering the OFR. However, the IASB has commissioned a team of national standard setters to develop a discussion paper on a "management commentary". The working group comprises standard setters from the UK, Canada, New Zealand and Germany.

The working group has produced a Discussion Paper, the conclusions of which are as follows:
- the IASB should issue a principles based statement, together with non-mandatory implementation guidance;
- the objectives, principles and qualitative characteristics of the management commentary should be outlined; and
- the disclosures in the management commentary should coalesce around five key areas: nature of the business; objectives and strategies; resources, risks and relationships; performance measures and results and prospects.

The working group is still in the process of updating the Discussion Paper following feedback from the IASB.

MEMO POINTS The International Accounting Standards Board (IASB) has issued a Practice Statement, setting out a broad, non-compulsory presentation framework for narrative reporting in financial statements. The Practice Statement came into effect on 8 December 2010 and includes a requirement for more informative disclosures in the shape of an expanded Operating and Financial Review (OFR), covering the key resources, risks and relationships impacting on the business and information regarding the entity's social and environmental policies.

CHAPTER 3

Directors' remuneration

OUTLINE ¶¶

SECTION 1

Introduction

The term "director" includes any person who occupies the **position of director** by whatever name called. From this definition it is clear that it is an individual's functions – and not his or her title – that determines whether he or she is a director. 4800

The **three sources** of requirements relating to the disclosure of the remuneration paid to directors are: the Companies Act, the Listing Rules, and the UK Corporate Governance Code (formerly the Combined Code).

The provisions of company law relating to directors' remuneration came into force on 6 April 2008 – and apply to financial years beginning on or after this date. Under the 2006 Act, regulations set out the information needed to be given in the accounts. (These supersede 4801

Schedules 6 and 7A to the Companies Act 1985.) Separate regulations have been published for small companies on the one hand, and medium-sized and large companies on the other. These regulations are:
- The Small Companies and Groups (Accounts and Directors' Report) Regulations 2008 (SI 2008/409); and
- The Large and Medium-sized Companies and Groups (Accounts and Reports) Regulations 2008 (SI 2008/410).

MEMO POINTS Small companies are exempt from certain requirements concerning directors' remuneration. Where provisions in this chapter apply to small companies, references to Schedule 3 of SI 2008/409 are given.

4802 The statutory rules relating to disclosure of directors' remuneration fall into the following categories:
- those applying to all companies;
- those applying to quoted companies
- those applying only to unquoted companies.

4803 A **quoted company** for the purposes of the above is one whose equity share capital:
s 385 CA 2006 a) has been included in the official list in accordance with the Financial Services and Markets Act 2000; or
b) is officially listed in an EEA State; or
c) is admitted to dealing on either the New York Stock Exchange or the Nasdaq.

Although AIM companies are treated with unquoted companies, they are nevertheless obliged to give more information in respect of **share option gains** and **long-term incentives received in shares** than other unquoted companies are obliged to do.

This chapter is concerned only with the earnings of directors. The provision of loans or other credit, guarantees, and any other transactions entered into between companies and their directors, whether permitted or not, are dealt with in the chapter on **related party transactions**.

4804 The UK Corporate Governance Code sets out standards of good practice in relation to issues such as board composition and development, remuneration, accountability and audit and relations with shareholders.

In its May 2010 revision of the Code, the FRC set out to implement a number of changes dealing with remuneration. These include a clearer statement of the need for performance-related elements to be aligned to the long-term interests of the company and new references to alignment with risk policies and systems. In particular, provisions have been amended to clarify that the remuneration of non-executive directors should not include any performance-related element. In addition, all payouts under incentive schemes should be subject to non-financial performance criteria and compatible with the company's risk policies.

Note that the Code does not deal with disclosure; these requirements are set out in the Regulations to the Companies Act.

SECTION 2

General disclosures required by the Act

4805 In general, the Act places upon companies a duty to make full disclosure in the notes to the financial statements of all amounts paid to directors in respect of their **services as directors** – i.e., their qualifying services (¶4810).

The Act provides further that, if the directors fail to disclose the required information, the company's auditors are bound by duty to include it in their own report – to the extent they are reasonably able to do so.

There are separate disclosure requirements for amounts paid to **third parties** in respect of the services of a director.

A. Remuneration for qualifying services

Qualifying services are defined as those services rendered: 4810 Sch 3 para 12 SI 2008/409 Sch 5 para 15 SI 2008/410
- as a director of a company or of the company's subsidiaries (while a director of the company), and
- otherwise in connection with the management of the affairs of the company or any of its subsidiaries (while a director of the company).

Whether any particular remuneration is paid to a director for **services as a director** or otherwise in connection with the management of the company's affairs is purely a question of fact. Unless it can be unambiguously shown that a particular payment was made in some other capacity, it should be regarded as a payment for services as director. For instance, if one of a company's non-executive directors who practises as a solicitor performed a professional service (or whose firm performed that service) for the company, it may be assumed that this service does not fall within the ambit of directors' remuneration. However, it is likely that the provision of legal services will be required to be disclosed as a related party transaction under the provisions of FRS 8.

The amounts to be disclosed must include **all payments made** in respect of qualifying services – not only by the **company** itself, but also by the company's **subsidiaries** or any other person/s.

The provisions that apply to directors also apply to "**connected persons**" (¶5018). Therefore, amounts receivable by a director will include amounts receivable by a connected person (which might also be another company or body corporate), as long as the amount concerned is not caused by such treatment to be counted twice. For example, where one of the spouses is a director of a company, amounts receivable by the other spouse are taken into account in the computation of director-spouse's emoluments; on the other hand, where a husband and wife are directors of the same company, they are still connected parties but their earnings are counted only once. 4811 Sch 5 para 5(3) SI 2008/410

The amount to be shown in respect of a particular **financial year** is the total of all sums receivable by directors during that year even if they have not yet been paid. If a payment made to a director does not relate to a particular reporting period, it should be reported in the **year** it is **approved for payment** (because that is when the liability is created). 4812

EXAMPLE At the end of its financial year, 31 December 20X1, **A Ltd** proposes directors' fees payable to its board in the sum of £200,000. This payment will not become due until approved in general meeting. The company also proposes a special bonus, not in respect of any particular financial year, payable to its Chief Executive. Because the board does not have the authority to approve such payments, the bonus will not become due until it is subsequently approved in general meeting.

In the financial statements, the directors' fees should be recorded at their proposed amount despite the fact that they will be paid in the following year. The special bonus, however, should be reported in the year ended 31 December 20X2, the year in which the liability to pay the bonus was created.

If the financial statements cover a period that is either less or more than 12 months, the remuneration disclosed must be in respect of that shorter or longer period.

If a director is appointed during the year, only that part of his remuneration earned while he was a director is regarded as being in respect of qualifying services.

EXAMPLE Mr A has been employed by C Ltd for 5 years. His salary was £100,000 p.a. Midway through the financial year, he was appointed to the board of directors and received a salary increase of £50,000 effective from that date.

In the financial statements for the year, directors' remuneration of £75,000 is shown in respect of Mr A, i.e., the amount earned during the six months since becoming director.

4814 Only information relating to the remuneration of people who are the directors of the **reporting entity** is required to be given. Thus, in the consolidated accounts of a parent and its subsidiaries, only payments to the directors of the parent must be reported. Amounts paid to individuals who are directors of subsidiaries only – even if the parent company makes payments to them – need not be disclosed in the **group** financial statements.

EXAMPLE B Ltd has two subsidiaries, Y Ltd and Z Ltd. Ms P is a director of all three companies and receives a salary of £20,000 from each. Mr Q, a director of Z Ltd, receives director's fees of £5,000. In the financial statements of B Ltd, only Ms P's earnings of £60,000 are required to be disclosed. Mr Q's remuneration is not shown because he is not a director of the reporting entity.

If a company is a **member of a group** but is not the parent of that group, it must disclose only the remuneration it pays to its own directors in its financial statements. Therefore, amounts of remuneration in respect of services to its parent company or fellow subsidiaries are excluded, even if the director concerned is also a director of those companies.

EXAMPLE D Ltd has a subsidiary, E Ltd. Mr X is a director of D Ltd, from which he receives a salary of £30,000. He also earns £20,000 from E Ltd. Ms Y is the general manager of D Ltd and a director of E Ltd. Her salary from D Ltd is £18,000 and from E Ltd is £4,000.

Disclosure: E Ltd
In the financial statements of E Ltd, directors' remuneration of £20,000 for Mr X is shown only if he is a director. If he is not, no amount needs to be shown. In respect of Ms Y, her salary of £4,000 must be disclosed.

Disclosure: D Ltd
In the financial statements of D Ltd, directors' remuneration to be disclosed is £50,000 for Mr X. As Ms Y is not a director of D Ltd, her earnings are not disclosed.

4816 Where directors are paid a single amount in respect of their services to the group, the board may apportion these salary payments in any manner that is appropriate to the circumstances.

Sch 3 para 5(6) SI 2008/409
Sch 5 para 7(6) SI 2008/410
Sch 3 para 4(2) SI 2008/409
Sch 5 para 6 SI 2008/410

If information (other than the aggregate of gains made by the directors on the exercise of share options) that is required to be disclosed is readily ascertainable from other information shown elsewhere in the financial statements, the Act's requirements are satisfied. Therefore, if in accordance with the **Listing Rules**, the individual total of each director's remuneration is shown, and from the information provided it is clear which among them is the highest paid director, then this disclosure is sufficient and need not be repeated elsewhere.

B. Elements of remuneration

4819 "Remuneration" is a broad category made up of various subcategories. The Act expressly provides that certain of these subcategories must be shown separately under specific headings. These are discussed in turn, below.

1. Remuneration

4820 Companies legislation uses the term "emoluments", rather than "earnings" as is used, for example, in tax legislation. (The new Companies Act prefers the term "remuneration".)

In general, remuneration **includes**:
– salaries,
– fees,
– bonuses,

Sch 5 para 9 SI 2008/410

- expense allowances, and
- the value of any non-cash benefits given to directors.

Excluded from remuneration are items that are disclosed under other categories - for instance, share options and pensions.

MEMO POINTS Remuneration also does not include amounts of cash or other **advances** that a director must account for, or pay back, to the company or any of its subsidiaries. However, if a director is granted a round amount for expenses and this amount is subject to income tax, then this amount is treated as part of remuneration. Sch 3 para 5(5) SI 2008/409 Sch 5 para 7(5) SI 2008/410
If any such payments are not treated as remuneration (and therefore not disclosed in the year they were paid) but in a subsequent accounting period they are charged to tax, the relevant amount should be included under remuneration, and shown separately in the first financial statements in which it is practical to do so.

Annual bonus schemes

Awards under annual bonus schemes are included under remuneration whether payable in cash, shares, or any other asset. **4822** Sch 3 para 7(1) SI 2008/409 Sch 5 para 9(1) SI 2008/410

If a bonus is awarded in respect of one accounting period but is payable only in the event that the director concerned is still in employment at some point in a future accounting period, there are two possible alternatives. On the one hand, the **continuing-employment requirement** can be regarded as a criterion on which the bonus depends. In this event, the bonus should be reported in the year it is paid. On the other hand, if the bonus is regarded as **having accrued to the director** in one year but merely paid during the next, it should be reported in the year to which it relates.

Golden hellos

When recruiting new directors, some companies offer **incentives** in the form of cash, shares, options, or a combination of these. Even though these so-called golden hello payments may not seem to relate to the individual's services as director, the Act specifically treats them as remuneration and requires their disclosure as such. Therefore, any element paid in cash will be shown together with salaries, bonuses, etc., while any element related to shares and options will be shown under the appropriate subcategory. **4824** Sch 3 para 12(2) SI 2008/409 Sch 5 para 15(3) SI 2008/410

Benefits not paid in cash

Specifically included under remuneration is the estimated money value of benefits not paid in cash. Estimates of this kind can be difficult and the company providing such benefits may have to consider the following in attempting to provide proper disclosure: **4825**

- if the company has incurred an **identifiable and direct cost**, this actual cost should be used;
- if there is no identifiable cost, such as when a director enjoys the use of a company-owned asset, an **estimate of the market value** of this benefit should be made;
- if neither of the above methods can be used, the **taxable value** of the benefit should be used (for further information, refer to *Tax Memo*);
- if there is **no reasonable method** to value the benefit, the relevant facts should be disclosed.

MEMO POINTS In cases where the market value, rather than an actual cost to the company, is used for disclosure purposes, the amounts required to be disclosed under the Act in respect of directors' emoluments will not agree with the figures in the company's accounting records.

2. Long-term incentive plans

The Act requires companies to disclose separately the aggregate amounts paid under long-term incentive schemes. Long-term incentive plans are those in terms of which cash or other assets are receivable subject to certain **qualifying conditions** that cannot be fulfilled within a single accounting period. These qualifying conditions relate to **service** or **performance**. **4826**

Sch 5 para 11 SI 2008/410 The definition of long-term incentive plans specifically excludes the following, as they are shown elsewhere under other categories:
- bonuses determined by reference to a single year only;
- payments for loss of office and related amounts;
- retirement benefits.

In general, the amount to be disclosed includes the value of both cash and non-cash assets (excluding share options, which are disclosed separately). However, in the case of unlisted companies, if an award is made in shares, it is not their value that must be shown but, instead, the number of directors in respect of whose qualifying services the shares were received.

3. Shares and share options

4830 Because the Act expressly provides that share options are excluded from the definition of emoluments, they are required to be disclosed separately in the financial statements. The nature of the information that needs to be disclosed varies according to whether the company is quoted or not.

4835 Sch 5 para 1(3) SI 2008/410 Companies that are **neither quoted nor listed on AIM**, in respect of which a market price for shares is not readily available, are required to show:
- the number of directors who exercised share options, and
- the number of directors who became entitled to shares under long-term incentive schemes.

Neither the number of shares nor the exercise price paid needs to be disclosed in respect of unlisted companies.

The requirements for quoted companies are discussed from ¶4871.

4. Pension contributions

4838 The Act requires both listed and unlisted companies to disclose information relating to the number of directors to whom benefits are accruing, as well as contributions paid by the company – depending on the **type of pension fund**.

Companies are also required to disclose other details relating to pensions in respect of the highest-paid director.

MEMO POINTS Small companies are required to disclose information relating to the number of directors to whom benefits are accruing, as well as contributions paid by the company. They are, however, exempt from the requirements to disclose details in respect of the highest-paid director.

Types of pension schemes

4840 There are two main types of pension schemes:
- defined contribution schemes, and
- defined benefit schemes.

Under a **defined contribution scheme** (sometimes also called a money purchase scheme), the benefits that will accrue to the director are based on the contributions made to the scheme. Under a **defined benefit scheme**, the rules specify the benefits that will be paid (these usually being based on the director's average or final pay).

Some schemes pay either money purchase benefits or defined benefits – depending on which is higher. This gives rise to a third type of scheme, which is actually a hybrid scheme.

For purposes of disclosure, the Act allows companies to classify hybrid schemes according to the type of benefits that appear most likely at the financial year-end.

The following are required to be disclosed:

Money purchase/defined contribution pension schemes:	Defined benefit pension schemes:
– contributions paid on behalf of directors, and – the number of directors who are accruing retirement benefits	– the number of directors who are accruing retirement benefits

EXAMPLE H Ltd operates a company pension scheme. The scheme is funded as if it were a defined benefit scheme, paying out a maximum pension of 60 percent of basic salary after 20 years of service. However, the actual pension payable will be the higher of:
- the above defined benefits, and
- the pension that would have accrued had the company instead paid contributions equal to 6 percent of basic salary into a money purchase scheme that would have invested the contributions.

In respect of the financial statements for the year ended 31 December 20X2, the company must determine which benefits are likely to be higher and make appropriate disclosures.

(1) If the defined benefits are higher, the following must be disclosed:
a. the number of directors who are members of the scheme, and
b. the amount of the accrued benefit for the highest-paid director.

It is advisable, though not mandatory, to add an explanation that the scheme is a hybrid scheme and that the directors have classified it as a defined benefits scheme because the benefits on this basis appear to be higher.

(2) If the money purchase benefits are higher, the following must be disclosed:
a. the aggregate of the contributions upon which the money purchase benefits are calculated,
b. the number of directors that are members of the money purchase scheme, and
c. the amount of the contributions made in respect of the highest-paid director.

In this case again, it is advisable to explain that the scheme is a hybrid scheme and that the directors have classified it as a money purchase scheme because the benefits on this basis appear to be higher.

5. Pensions and other retirement benefits

The financial statements must disclose the amount of retirement benefits receivable by both directors and past directors under pension schemes to the extent that these benefits exceed the amounts such directors were entitled to on the later of: **4842** Sch 5 para 3(1) SI 2008/410
- when they first became eligible for benefits, and
- 31 March 1997.

Retirement benefits for these purposes are far ranging and include pensions, lump sums, gratuities and other benefits, payable in cash or otherwise. The details of any benefits in kind must be given in the notes. Sch 5 para 3(4) SI 2008/410

If a director or former director who is already receiving retirement benefits is awarded an increase in these benefits, this must be disclosed in each subsequent financial statements until these additional benefits cease to be paid. However, this disclosure need not be made if: Sch 5 para 3(2) SI 2008/410
- the pension scheme does not require additional funding in order to make the payments, and
- additional amounts are paid or made available to all pensioner members of the scheme on the same basis.

MEMO POINTS In addition to the requirements of the Act specifically relating to director's remuneration in Schedule 3 of SI 2008/409 and Schedule 5 of SI 2008/410, companies are obliged in any event under Schedule 4 to disclose particulars of any commitments to pay pensions to past directors. Sch 1 para 57(4) SI 2008/409 Sch 1 para 63(4) SI 2008/410

6. Compensation for loss of office

General requirements

4844 Sch 3 para 2 SI 2008/409 Sch 5 para 4 SI 2008/410

All companies are required to disclose the aggregate amount of any compensation, including the value of any benefits in kind, to directors or past directors for loss of office.

If any non-cash benefits in kind are included in the amounts to be disclosed, they must be explained in the notes.

Loss of office as a result of a takeover

4846 s 219 CA 2006

Under the Companies Act 2006, for a payment for loss of office to a director in connection with the transfer of shares in the company or in a subsidiary of the company resulting from a takeover bid, approval is required of the holders of the shares to which the bid relates and of any other holders of shares of the same class. If a payment for loss of office is made and the payment is in connection with a takeover bid, and the required member approvals are not obtained, then the payment is held on trust for the persons who have sold their shares as a result of the offer.

Loss of office as a result of breach of contract

4848 Sch 5 para 4(3) SI 2008/410

Where payments are made to a director in respect of his retirement resulting from a **breach of contract**, any damages, settlements or compromises in respect of the breach are to be treated as compensation for loss of office and disclosed under this category.

If, as a consequence of a director's ceasing to be a director, his pension entitlement is increased, there are two possibilities as to where this should be disclosed – i.e., under:
– "compensation for loss of office", or
– "pensions to directors and former directors".

Where the increase is made **as part of the director's loss of office**, the capital cost of the increase should be disclosed as compensation for loss of office. However, any increase in pension entitlement that takes place after a director has **already ceased to be a director** is disclosed as part of pensions.

7. Amounts paid to third parties

4850 Sch 5 para 5 SI 2008/410

Any consideration paid to or receivable by third parties for making available the services of a director must be disclosed. This applies when the person's services have been made available:
– as a director of the company, or
– while a director, as a director of any of its subsidiaries or otherwise in connection with the management of the company or any of its subsidiaries.

The amounts paid include **non-cash benefits**. Both the nature and value of such benefits must be disclosed.

The Act's **definition of third parties excludes**:
– the director himself,
– any person connected with him or a body corporate controlled by him, and
– the company and any of its subsidiaries.

> EXAMPLE J Ltd enters into a joint venture with K Ltd. As part of the arrangement, K Ltd appoints one of its directors to the board of J Ltd. In respect of the services of the director, J Ltd pays K Ltd £20,000 per annum.
>
> Notwithstanding that the director is remunerated separately by K Ltd and does not receive the £20,000, J Ltd must disclose the payment as sums paid to third parties in respect of directors' services.

C. Highest-paid director

For companies **other than quoted companies**, the Act requires details of the highest-paid director's emoluments and other benefits to be given. 4855

If the sum of the following three elements of remuneration attributable to the directors of an unquoted company, payable in any accounting period (irrespective of its length), is £200,000 or more, details relating to the highest-paid director's emoluments and other benefits must be disclosed in the financial statements: Sch 5 para 2 SI 2008/410
- **emoluments** paid to or receivable by directors **in respect of qualifying services**;
- gains made by directors on **exercising their share options** (applicable to AIM-traded companies only);
- money and the net value of other assets (other than share options) paid to or receivable by directors **under long-term incentive schemes** in respect of qualifying services.

The highest-paid director is the director to whom the greatest part of the total of the items listed above is attributable. Frequently, the person who is defined as the highest-paid director in one year is not the same person who met the definition in the previous year. Where this happens, the comparative figures to be given for the previous year are those relating to the other director. There is no need to state the prior year earnings of the individual who is the highest paid director in the current year.

MEMO POINTS For unquoted companies, gains made on the exercise of share options and the value of shares received under long-term incentive schemes are not taken into account, because these amounts are neither calculated nor disclosed by unlisted companies (¶4835).

Where the **disclosure** is needed, the following details are to be presented: 4856
- the total emoluments, excluding pension contributions, of the highest-paid director;
- the amount of any company contributions paid to money purchase pension schemes in respect of the director's qualifying services;
- if the director is a member of a defined benefit scheme, the amount of his **accrued pension** at the end of the year as well as any **accrued lump sum**;
- whether the highest paid director exercised any share options;
- whether any shares were received or receivable by that director under a long-term incentive scheme.

The **accrued pension** and **accrued lump sum** are the amounts that would be payable to the director on reaching normal retirement age (i.e., the earliest date at which the director is entitled to receive a full pension). They are calculated on the following assumptions: 4858
- the director left the company at the end of the year,
- there is no inflation from the end of the year to the director's pension age,
- there is no commutation of the pension or inverse commutation of the lump sum, and
- any amounts attributable to voluntary contributions made by the director to the scheme and any money purchase benefits payable under the scheme were disregarded.

In the determination of the amounts to be shown as accrued lump sums, disclosure is made only where, under the pension scheme rules, the director will automatically receive a lump sum on retirement. If the lump sum is one that would arise only if the director elects commutation of rights to an annual pension, such a lump sum is not disclosed. Similarly, an accrued pension should not include any amount of inverse commutation of a lump sum (i.e., where the director might elect to reduce all or part of his entitlement to a lump sum by taking a larger annual pension).

EXAMPLE As of the end of the reporting period, the highest-paid director of L Ltd is 10 years away from retirement age. He joined the company as a director 15 years ago. His maximum pension is 25/50 of his final salary after 25 years. (His salary for the current financial year was £100,000.) He is also entitled to a lump sum of 75/50 of final salary after 25 years. If he so elects, however, he may commute the lump sum by taking a larger annual pension.

The accrued pension to be disclosed is:
15/50 × £100,000 = £30,000.

The accrued lump sum to be disclosed is
45/50 × £100,000 = £90,000

The effects of any inverse commutation of the lump sum are ignored, even if the director has already decided to commute the entire lump sum when he retires.

D. Sample disclosure

4860 A sample disclosure is given below.

		20X7	20X6
		£	£
Directors' remuneration			
Aggregate emoluments		700,000	640,000
Amounts receivable under long-term incentive schemes (excluding shares)		80,000	60,000
Company pension contributions to money purchase schemes		17,000	12,000
Compensation for loss of office		-	125,000
Sums paid to third parties for director's services		45,000	-
Excess retirement benefits	– current directors	5,000	5,000
	– past directors	8,000	8,000

Three directors exercised share options during the year and one became entitled to receive shares under the company's long-term incentive scheme.
Retirement benefits are accruing to three directors under the company's money purchase pension scheme and to two directors under a defined benefit scheme

	20X7	20X6
Highest paid director		
Aggregate emoluments and benefits under long-term incentive schemes (excluding gains on share options exercised and value of shares received)	195,000	150,000
Company pension contributions to money purchase schemes	5,000	5,000
Defined benefit scheme:		
Accrued pension at end of year	55,000	45,000
Accrued lump sum at end of year	88,000	75,000

The highest-paid director, Mr A, exercised share options during the year and received shares under the executive long-term incentive scheme.

SECTION 3

Additional disclosures for quoted companies

4864 The Directors' Remuneration Report Regulations 2002 (SI 2002/1986) introduced requirements for quoted companies, contained in Schedule 7A to the Companies Act 1985, that duplicated many of the requirements of the Listing Rules, which prescribe additional disclosures in respect of companies whose shares are quoted (see ¶4803). The disclosures required are both complicated and specialised; they are dealt with only insofar as the scope of this book allows. Readers are advised to seek expert opinions on these matters if required.

Schedule 8 to The Large and Medium-sized Companies and Groups (Accounts and Reports) Regulations 2008 (SI 2008/410) re-enacts the provisions to Schedule 7A to the Companies Act 1985 and is applicable to accounting periods beginning on or after 6 April 2008.

Quoted companies must comply with the disclosure requirements that are applicable to all companies and, in addition, to those specifically added by Schedule 8 to SI 2008/410 and the Listing Rules.

A. Remuneration report

The annual report and accounts of quoted companies should include a **remuneration report** from the board of directors to the shareholders. Though this report is usually presented as a separate report, it can also form part of the directors' report. 4865

In addition, the Combined Code contains principles relating to the remuneration of directors. Companies are therefore obliged to disclose whether, and the extent to which, they have applied these principles.

Certain elements of the remuneration report **fall within the scope of the auditors' report**. These are:
- individual directors' emoluments and compensation
- share options
- long-term incentive schemes
- pensions
- excess retirement benefits of directors and past directors
- compensation for past directors
- amounts paid to third parties in respect of directors' services.

MEMO POINTS The Act requires the auditors to determine whether the financial statements and (in the case of quoted companies) the auditable part of the directors' remuneration report are in agreement with the accounting records. Should this not be the case, the auditors are required to include a statement to this effect in their report.

If the directors include the required information in the notes to the financial statements and make clear cross-references to it from the remuneration report, readers of the financial statements will be able to tell which information is subject to the review of the auditors. However, companies are free to choose the best way of presenting the required information in their financial statements.

The remuneration report must **disclose** the following: 4866
- the company's policy of executive directors' remuneration
- details of each element of each director's remuneration package
- information on share options
- details of long-term incentive schemes
- explanation of pensionable remuneration other than basic salary
- long-term service contracts or pre-determined compensation clauses
- the unexpired term of service contracts of directors proposed for election or re-election at the next AGM
- the company's policy on granting options or awards under employee share schemes and other long-term incentives
- directors' pension entitlements
- emoluments waived
- the names of members of the remuneration committee
- sums paid to third parties in respect of directors' services
- performance graph
- service contracts
- compensation for past directors
- consideration of conditions elsewhere in the company and group.

MEMO POINTS "Consideration of conditions elsewhere in the company and group" is a new requirement of the Companies Act 2006.

Sch 8 para 2 SI 2008/410 To the requirements of the Listing Rules concerning the remuneration report, the Act adds that if anyone, including a director who was not a member of the remuneration committee, provided advice or services that materially assisted the committee, their name should be given. If that person is not a director of the company, the following further information should be disclosed as well:
- the nature of any other services that the person provided to the company during the year
- whether the person was appointed by the committee.

EXAMPLE **Remuneration Report (extract)**

Membership and Responsibilities (extract)
The Remuneration Committee consists exclusively of independent non-executive directors. The members are: Mr A (Chairman), Mr B, Ms C, Ms D, and Mr E. Biographical details appear on page *xx*.

Advice
Advice is provided to the committee by the company secretary's office, which is independent of executive management and reports to the non-executive chairman. Mr F, who is an independent consultant within the company secretary's office, was appointed during the year by the committee as its secretary and special adviser. He does not provide any other services to the group.
The committee also appoints external professional advisers to provide specialist advice and services on particular remuneration matters. During the year, the following provided advice or services on specific matters:
Ms H (Chief Executive) was consulted on matters relating to the other executive directors who report to her and on matters relating to the performance of the company. She was not present when matters affecting her own remuneration were considered.
Mr I (Director of Human Resources), who provided to the committee some of the company's calculations for the performance-related pay which were then subject to independent verification.
Only Mr F was appointed by the committee.

1. The company's policy of executive directors' remuneration

4867 Sch 8 para 3(1) SI 2008/410 The remuneration report should contain a statement of the company's policy on directors' remuneration for the following year and subsequent years. This statement is not subject to audit.

Sch 8 para 3(2) SI 2008/410 The policy statement should include, in respect of those directors who are serving as directors at any time in the period from the end of the financial year to the date on which the directors' remuneration report is laid before the company in general meeting:
- for each director, a detailed summary of any performance conditions to which the director's entitlement to share options or long-term incentive awards is subject, together with an explanation of why those conditions were chosen;
- a summary of the methods used to assess whether the performance conditions are met, and an explanation of why those methods were chosen;
- if any of the performance conditions involves comparison with external factors, a summary of those factors; if any of the factors relates to the performance of other companies (or of an index on which a company or companies are listed), the identity of the company or of the index must be given;
- a description of, and explanation for, any significant amendment proposed to the terms and conditions of any entitlement of a director, either to share options or under a long-term incentive scheme;
- if no performance conditions are attached to the entitlement of a director to share options or under a long-term incentive scheme, the reasons why;
- Sch 8 para 3(3) SI 2008/410 in respect of each director's terms and conditions relating to emoluments, explain the relative importance of those elements that are related to performance, and those that are not.

The policy statement must summarise and explain the company's policy on: Sch 8 para 3(4) SI 2008/410
– the duration of contracts with directors; and
– notice periods and termination payments under such contracts.

2. Details of each element of each director's remuneration package

The details of each element of the total remuneration paid to each director should be disclosed in respect of the current period. The details include: 4869 Sch 8 para 7 SI 2008/410
– the name of the director
– the basic salary and fees
– the estimated value of benefits in kind
– annual bonuses
– deferred bonuses
– expenses paid that are subject to income tax and are paid in respect of qualifying services
– compensation for loss of office, payments for breach of contract, and/or any other payments on termination
– in respect of former directors, any significant payments made to them during the period under review.

For each director, a total should be shown for both the current and the previous period. The details making up the comparative figures are not required.

The above information is required to be presented in tabular format unless it is inappropriate to do so.

The following is an example of appropriate disclosure.

EXAMPLE **Alpha plc**
Year ended 31 December 20X7
Extract from: Remuneration report

DIRECTORS' EMOLUMENTS

	Salary	Bonus	Benefits (estimated value)	Total 20X7	Total 20X6
	£ 000	£ 000	£ 000	£ 000	£ 000
Chairman					
Ms A	250	200	39	489	433
Executive directors					
Mr B	180	155	22	357	295
Mr C (appointed 1 July 20X7)	75	100	20	195	
Ms D	150	135	14	299	220
Ms E	200	179	15	394	308
Non-executive directors					
Mr F	95	12	-	107	91
Ms G	65	10	-	75	60
Retired director					
Mr H (retired 31 May 20X7)	120	-	6	126	292
Total emoluments	**1,135**	**791**	**116**	**2,042**	**1,699**

Mr C was appointed to the board on 1 July 20X7. Included in his benefits is compensation of £14,000 for loss of future benefits from his previous employer.
Mr H retired on 31 May 20X7. In terms of his contract with the company, his salary includes a payment in lieu of notice equal to six months' salary.
Benefits relate mainly to the provision of company cars, fuel and travel, and to the use of company property at reduced charges.

3. Information on share options

4871 **Quoted companies** are required to disclose the aggregate amount of gains made by directors on the exercise of share options. For these purposes, gains are calculated by comparing the price paid for the shares with the market price on the date the options were exercised.

It is usually a feature of share options granted to directors that they are not exercisable until the director has remained with the company for a certain period. The options are typically exercisable at a price equal to the market price of the shares at the time the options were granted.

In many cases, options are granted to directors at zero cost as part of their remuneration packages. Where a director has paid a price for options (e.g., by purchasing them on the open market), this cost should probably be deducted from the gross gain for purposes of calculating the gain to be disclosed. Although the Act is not specific on this point, it states that "the price actually paid for the shares" should be used in the computation of the gain.

4872 The Act also does not specifically refer to **qualifying services** in connection with share options. It is therefore reasonable to assume that companies are obliged to disclose the gains made by directors on options:
- purchased on their own account, or
- acquired before their appointment as directors.

EXAMPLE Mr F was appointed to the board of directors of G Ltd on 1 June 20X7. During the year ended 31 December 20X7, he exercised options as follows:

Date of exercising options	Number of options exercised	Exercise price	Market price at date of exercise	Gain on exercise of options
31 March 20X7 (options acquired in 20X0 at no cost)	3,000	£ 3.00	£ 4.50	£ 4,500
30 September 20X7 (options acquired in 20X0 at no cost)	6,000	£ 4.00	£ 5.00	£ 6,000
Total				**£ 10,500**
Only the gains made by Mr F **after** the date of his appointment as director must be disclosed, i.e., £6,000.				

4873 LR 9.8.8(2)(d) The Listing Rules state that the report to the shareholders by the Board must contain information, together with explanatory notes as necessary, on any share options, including save-as-you-earn options, for each director, by name, in accordance with the requirements of the Directors' Remuneration Report Regulations. As stated earlier, the requirements of the Directors' Remuneration Report Regulations were contained in Schedule 7A to the Companies Act 1985. This schedule is re-enacted by Schedule 8 to SI 2008/410.

4874 Sch 8 para 9 SI 2008/410 The information required to be given in terms of Schedule 8 is as follows.

a) Number of shares subject to a share option at the beginning of the financial year or, if later, at the date of appointment as a director (differentiating between options having different terms and conditions).

b) Number of shares at the end of the financial year or, if earlier, at the date of ceasing to be a director (differentiating between options having different terms and conditions).

c) Details of options awarded, options exercised, options expiring unexercised and options whose terms and conditions have been varied in the financial year.

d) For each share option that is unexpired at any time in the financial year:
- price paid for its award
- exercise price
- date from which the option may be exercised
- date on which the option expires.

e) A description of any variation made in the year to the terms and conditions of a share option.
f) A summary of any performance criteria on which the award or exercise of an option is conditional and a description of any variation in such performance criteria made in the year.
g) For each option that has been exercised in the financial year, the market price of the shares in relation to which the option was exercised, at the date of exercise.
h) For each option that is unexpired at the end of the financial year, the market price of the related shares at the end of that year and the highest and lowest market prices of the related shares in that year.

MEMO POINTS In respect of items (a) and (b), share options having different terms and conditions should be separately identified. The information in (a) to (d) is required to be given in tabular form.

If the information to be given would be excessive in length, a more concise disclosure may **4875**
be given. One alternative is to use weighted average prices instead of the actual different prices at different dates. However, there may need to be additional information given, such as showing separately options that are "out of the money" (i.e., where the exercise price is higher than the market price) and those that are "in the money".

4. Details of long-term incentive schemes

The Listing Rules require the disclosure of any long-term incentive schemes **other than** share **4877**
option information, which is disclosed as discussed under "Information on share options" at LR 9.8.8(3)-(6)
¶4871.

Long-term incentive schemes can take many forms and can be called by different names. What is, however, common to all such schemes is that they require certain conditions relating to performance or service to be satisfied over a period exceeding one financial year. The awards under long-term incentive schemes can be paid out in cash, in shares or in a combination of both.

The following information should be disclosed in respect of each director, by name, who, at any time during the year under review, was involved in the scheme:
- the interests in schemes at the beginning of the year,
- entitlements and awards granted and commitments made under the schemes during the period, showing which came to fruition during the period and which afterwards,
- the money value and number of shares, cash payments or other benefits received during the period,
- the interests in schemes at the end of the year.

Certain long-term incentive schemes are set up especially to facilitate, in unusual circum- **4878**
stances, the recruitment or retention of a **particular person's services**. If the sole participant LR 9.4.3
in such a scheme is a director of the company, the following should be disclosed in the first annual report after he has become eligible to participate in the arrangement:
a) the name of the director
b) the date on which he became eligible to participate
c) an explanation of the unusual circumstances
d) the conditions to be satisfied under the arrangement
e) the maximum awards under the arrangement or (if there is no maximum) the basis of determining the awards
f) the information required by the Listing Rules, which is as follows: LR 13.8.11
1. the principal terms of the scheme (or the full text thereof)
2. if the trustees of the scheme are directors or have an interest (direct or indirect) in the trustees, the relevant details of the trusteeship or interest
3. a statement that any provisions relating to:
- the persons for whom securities, cash or other benefits are provided under the scheme

– limitations on the number or amount of the securities, cash or other benefits subject to the scheme
– the maximum entitlement for the participant
– the basis for determining the participants' rights to benefits and to any adjustments thereto in the case of a capitalisation issue, rights issue or open offer, sub-division or consolidation of shares or any other variation cannot be altered to the advantage of the participant without the prior approval of a general meeting (except in the case of minor administrative matters).

EXAMPLE The following is an illustration of the disclosure required. Assume the current financial year is 20X2.

Beta plc
Extract: Directors' Report for the year ended 31 December 20X2

Long-term incentive plan
Potential share awards held by the executive directors under the Plan at the beginning and end of the year, as well as details of actual awards during the year are:

	Potential awards held at beginning of year	Potential awards for the 3-year performance period ended 31/12/20X5 (1)	Actual awards for the period ended 31/12/20X1 (2)		Potential awards held at end of year
			Number of shares	Value £	
Mr A	23,212	8,222	2,802	18,886	28,632
Mr B	13,953	5,574	1,494	13,008	18,033
Mr C	19,494	7,247	2,086	18,194	24,655
Mr D	21,612	7,665	2,564	13,163	26,713

(1) The share price used to calculate the potential awards for the three-year performance period ending 31/12/20X5 was 546.3p
(2) The value shown is that of the actual awards to each director on the date he called for his shares

Note
For the performance period ended 31/12/20X2 the company's TSR (total shareholder return) performance was ranked 48th (20X1 – 64th) relative to companies in the FTSE 100 Index. Consequently, no awards lapsed.
The company funds an employee share ownership plan trust (ESOP) to enable it to acquire and hold the necessary shares. The ESOP currently holds 158,996 shares; the executive directors each have a technical interest in all these shares. All dividends on shares in the ESOP are waived by the trustees.
During the period 31 December 20X2 to [date of the accounts] no directors have exercised their options to call for the transfer of shares out of the Plan.

5. Explanation of pensionable remuneration other than basic salary

4880 LR 9.8.8(7) Normally, only basic salary is pensionable. If, therefore, any other element of a director's remuneration is pensionable – e.g., annual bonuses – an explanation and justification should be given as part of the remuneration report.

The following is an example of appropriate wording:

EXAMPLE **Post retirement benefits**

Executive directors participate in pension schemes established by Group companies to provide pensions to staff in retirement. Pensions are normally equivalent to two-thirds of final salary, excluding bonus and other forms of remuneration, assuming approximately 20 years' service at senior executive level. In the case of the Chairman, Mr X, his pension entitlement is based on salary plus annual bonus, which is in accordance with prevailing practice in the United States of America.

6. Long-term notice periods or pre-determined compensation clauses

The large compensation payments to directors on loss of office arising out of service contracts longer than one year (rolling contracts) often attract criticism. 4882 LR9.8.8(8)

It is beyond the scope of the Listing Rules to require notice periods to be set at (or reduced to) one year. However, where there are in existence service contracts with a notice period exceeding one year, or contracts under which compensation payments are in excess of one year's salary and benefits in kind, these are to be disclosed. The reasons for such notice periods are also required to be given.

An illustration is given in ¶4884.

7. Service contracts

In respect of any director proposed for election or re-election at the forthcoming Annual General Meeting, the Listing Rules require the unexpired periods of their service contracts to be disclosed. If such directors do not have service contracts, then that fact should be disclosed. 4884 LR9.8.8(9)

The following details of any contract for services in respect of each director who has served at any time during the financial year must be disclosed: Sch 8 para 6(1) SI 2008/410

- the date of the contract
- the unexpired term together with details of any notice periods
- any provision for compensation payable on early termination of the contract any other provisions that would necessary to enable shareholders to estimate the company's liability in the event of early termination.

EXAMPLE The following is an example of the combined disclosure requirements of the rules in ¶4882 and ¶4884:

Extract: Remuneration Report of Gamma plc

Service contracts

All executive directors appointed since 19X1 have service contracts terminable by the company on two years' notice (prior to this date, notice periods were normally three years), and by the individual directors on one year's notice. These notice periods take into account the international nature of the company's business and the need to remain competitive.

In the event that the contract of Mr A, the company's chairman, is terminated early, he will be entitled to compensation of £50,000.

The unexpired terms of service for all those persons who served as the company's directors during the year are:

Mr A (Chairman)	24 months
Ms B	24 months
Mr C	18 months

Ms D, a non-executive director proposed for re-election at the forthcoming AGM, has no service contract.

8. The company's policy on granting options or awards under employee share schemes and other long-term incentives

The Listing Rules require a statement on the company's policy on the granting of options or awards under its employees' share schemes and other long-term incentive schemes. The statement should also explain and justify any departure from that policy in the period under review as well as any change in policy from the preceding year. 4886 LR 9.8.8(10)

9. Directors' pension entitlements

4888 LR 9.8.8(11), (12) The Listing Rules require the remuneration report to include the following information on directors' pension entitlements.

For money purchase schemes

4889 Details of the contribution or allowance payable or made by the company in respect of each director during the period under review.

For defined benefit schemes

4890 a) details of the amount of the increase during the period under review (excluding inflation), and of the accumulated total amount at the end of the period in respect of the accrued benefit to which each director would be entitled on leaving service or is entitled having left service during the period under review, and
b) either:

(i) the transfer value (less directors' contributions) of the relevant increase in accrued benefit (to be calculated in accordance with Actuarial Guidance Note GN11, but making no deduction for underfunding) as at the end of the period; or

(ii) so much of the following information as is necessary to make a reasonable assessment of the transfer value in respect of each director:
1. age;
2. normal retirement age;
3. the amount of any contributions paid or payable by the director under the terms of the scheme during the period;
4. details of spouse's and dependants' benefits;
5. early retirement rights and options;
6. expectations of pension increases after retirement (whether guaranteed or discretionary);
7. discretionary benefits for which allowance is made in transfer values on leaving;
8. any other relevant information that will significantly affect the value of the benefits.

Voluntary contributions and benefits are not disclosed.

EXAMPLE Mr X has been a director of **M Ltd** for the past 3 years. He joined the company 10 years ago. His basic salary for the current year is £120,000 (previous year £100,000). His maximum pension is 25/50 of his final salary after 25 years.

Calculation of accrued pension:	**Current year**	**Previous year**
10/50 x £120,000	£ 24,000	
9/50 x £100,000		£ 18,000

The difference between the accrued pension at the end of the current and previous years is £6,000. However, the effect of inflation must be excluded in the disclosure of the amount of the increase to which Mr X would be entitled on leaving service.
Assuming the rate of inflation for the current year to be 1%, and applying it to the accrued pension entitlement for the previous year, the result is £180.
Therefore, the increase for the year is £6,000 – £180 = £5,820.

Sch 8 para 13 SI 2008/410 Schedule 8 of the Act requires further disclosure than is set out in the Listing Rules. In particular, it requires the **transfer value of a director's accrued pension** at the beginning and end of the year to be given. Under the Listing Rules either the transfer value of the increase in accrued pension – or sufficient information to enable it to be ascertained – is all that is required.

10. Emoluments waived

4892 LR 9.8.4(5) (6) The Listing Rules require companies to disclose particulars of any arrangement under which directors have waived or agreed to waive any current or future emoluments from the company or any of its subsidiaries.

Details of emoluments waived in respect of future periods must be shown separately from emoluments waived during the current period.

11. Sums paid to third parties in respect of directors' services

The Act requires unquoted companies (but not quoted companies) to disclose, in the aggregate, amounts paid to third parties in respect of directors' services. Quoted companies, however, are obliged to disclose the following information with respect to each director individually for any consideration paid to any third party for making available the services of the director as director of the company or while a director of the company: 4894 Sch 8 para 16 SI 2008/410
- as director of any of its subsidiary undertakings;
- as director of any other undertaking of which he was a director by virtue of the company's nomination (direct or indirect); or
- otherwise in connection with the management of the affairs of the company or any such other undertaking.

MEMO POINTS 1. Third parties do not include:
- the director himself or a person connected with him or a body corporate controlled by him;
- the company or any other undertaking of which he is a director (while director of the company) by virtue of the company's nomination (direct or indirect).

2. "Consideration" includes the estimated money value of any benefits settled otherwise than in cash.

12. Performance graph

The directors' remuneration report is required to include a performance graph showing the total shareholder return for: 4896 Sch 8 para 5(1) SI 2008/410
- a holding of shares of the company's equity share capital whose listing has led to the company's being defined as a quoted company, and
- a hypothetical holding of shares made up of shares of the same kind and number as those by reference to which a broad based equity market index is calculated.

The graph, which is not subject to audit, should take the form of a line graph and should cover **five financial years** (i.e., the current financial year and the four preceding financial years). Where the company has been in existence for less than five years, a shorter period, commencing from the year the company came into existence, may be given. For example, if the current financial year is the company's third, the graph would cover three financial years. Sch 8 para 5(3) SI 2008/410

The total shareholder return (TSR) must be calculated using a fair method that: Sch 8 para 5(4) SI 2008/410

1. starts with the percentage change, over the period, in the market price of the holding
2. assumes that, in relation to reinvestment of income,

a) any benefit in the form of shares of the same kind as those in the holding is added to the holding when that benefit becomes receivable.

b) any benefit in cash, and the value of any benefit not in cash and not falling into (a) above, is used when the benefit becomes receivable to purchase shares of the same kind as the existing holding at market price and that the notional shares so purchased are added to the existing holding at that time.

c) the word "benefit" above includes any benefit (in particular, dividends) receivable in respect of the holding from the company of whose share capital the holding forms part.

3. assumes that, in relation to the funding of liabilities,

a) where the holder has a liability to the company of whose share capital the holding forms part, shares are sold from the holding immediately before liability is due, and in such numbers that, at the time of sale, the market price of the shares sold equals the amount of the liability in respect of the shares in the holding that are not sold.

b) the word "liability" means a liability in respect of any shares in the holding or from the exercise of a right attached to any of those shares.

4. makes provision for any replacement of shares in the holding by shares of a different description.

4897 The following example of a performance graph illustrates the performance of A Ltd measured by TSR relative to an appropriate index over the past five years (Dec 20X1 – Dec 20X6).

The FTSE 100 is considered to be the most appropriate index against which to measure performance, as A Ltd has been a constituent of the FTSE 100 throughout the five-year period and the index is widely used. TSR is the measure of the returns that a company has provided for its shareholders, reflecting share price movements and assuming reinvestment of dividends.

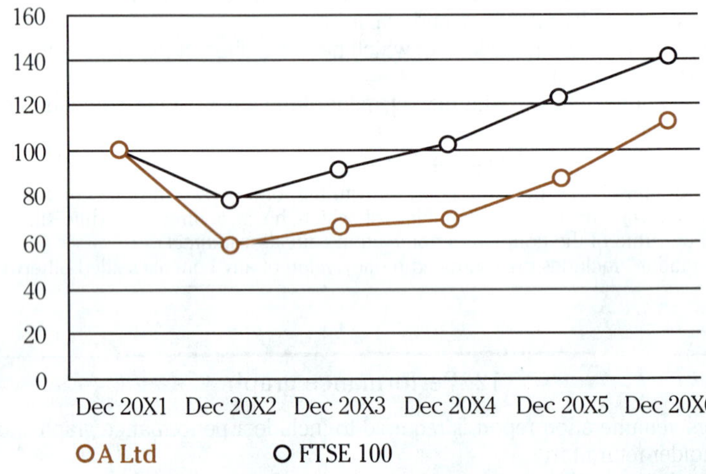

13. Compensation for past directors

4898 Sch 8 para 15 SI 2008/410 Any significant award that has not already been disclosed in the table of individual directors' emoluments in respect of any past director must be separately disclosed and explained. These awards include compensation for loss of office and pensions but exclude any sums shown separately in the remuneration report as compensation for loss of office. Another example may be where a payment is made to a former director arising out of a dispute that was resolved only some time after the person ceased to be a director.

14. Conditions in company and group

4899 Sch 8 para 4 SI 2008/410 The directors' remuneration report must contain a statement of how pay and employment conditions of employees of the company and of other undertakings within the same group as the company were taken into account when determining directors' remuneration for the relevant financial year.

CHAPTER 4

Related party transactions

OUTLINE ¶¶

Introduction

5000 FRS 8 (8) In the absence of information to the contrary, users of financial statements assume that companies go about their business **independently** and without regard to any special interests of their owners, managers and other parties who have involvement with the enterprise. Transactions are presumed to have been undertaken on an arm's length basis, i.e., on terms such as could have been obtained in a transaction with an external party, in which each side bargained knowledgeably and freely, unaffected by any relationship between them.

However, business enterprises – in whatever form they take, such as companies, trusts, partnerships and individuals – can be related to one another in various ways. As these groups increase in both size and diversity, transactions between the related entities within them are not only inevitable, but indeed, commonplace.

To ensure that readers of financial statements understand the degree to which an enterprise is involved in transactions with such related parties, disclosure in the financial statements of these transactions is required by company law and by FRS 8, "Related party disclosures". For listed and AIM companies, additional requirements – set out in the Listing Rules and those of the London Stock Exchange, respectively – apply.

FRS 8 was issued in 1995 and while there have been subsequent amendments, it has become necessary for another, in November 2010. In 2009 the IASB amended its corresponding standard, IAS 24, to simplify the definition of a related party. As UK company law refers to the definition of a related party "as set out in International Accounting Standards", the ASB has now amended FRS 8 to ensure consistency. The amendments apply to periods beginning on or after 1 January 2011. Earlier adoption is permitted.

SECTION 1

Identifying related parties

A. General criteria

5002 According to FRS 8, a related party is a person or entity that is related to the reporting entity. For instance:

a. A person, or a close member of that person's family, is related to a reporting entity if that person:
- has **control or joint control** over the reporting entity,
- has **significant influence** over the reporting entity, or
- is a member of the **key management** personnel of the reporting entity or its parent.

b. An entity is related to a reporting entity if any of the following applies:
- the entity and the reporting entity are **members of the same group** (which means that each parent and each subsidiary are also related),
- one entity is an **associate or joint venture** of the other (or an associate or joint venture of a member of a group of which the other entity is a member),
- both entities are joint ventures of the **same third party**,
- one entity is a joint venture of a **third entity** and the other entity is an associate of that third entity,
- the entity is a **retirement benefit scheme** for the benefit of employees of either the reporting entity or an entity related to it; if the reporting entity is itself such a scheme, the sponsoring employers are also related to the reporting entity,

– the entity is **controlled** – or jointly controlled – by a person described in **a**., above,
– a person who has control or joint **control over the reporting entity** has significant influence over the entity or is a member of the key management personnel of the entity or its parent.

1. Control

"Control" is defined as the ability to direct the financial and operating policies of an entity with a view to gaining economic benefits from its activities. **5004** FRS 8 (2.2)

This definition seems to suggest that control will exist where a company or an individual holds more than 50 percent of the reporting entity's voting rights. In addition, the possibility of economic benefit for the controlling party, through this control, must be present. It is not uncommon, however, for shareholders who hold less than 50 percent of the voting power to actually exercise control over a company's activities. Where this is the case, the control will be recognised.

2. Common control

Common control arises when two entities are subject to common control either by the same individual or from boards of directors having a controlling nucleus of directors in common. (see ¶5013, Scenario 4.) **5006** FRS 8 (13)

Entities under common control are deemed to be related parties because the controlling entity is in a position to compel them to enter into specific transactions and set the particular terms. For either of the controlled parties, the relationship might therefore have a material effect on their operations and results.

3. Influence

Influence is said to exist when one party (A) is able, despite a theoretical lack of control over another party, (B), to exert such power over the financial and operating policies of B that B might not be free to pursue its own separate interests at all times. **5008**

4. Common influence

Where two parties that enter into a transaction are subject to influence from the same source to the extent that one of them subordinates its separate interests in favour of the other, common influence is said to exist. **5010**

On the other hand, the presence of influence alone from a common source is not sufficient to justify the supposition of a related-party relationship; there has to be subordination as well. Thus, two related parties of a third entity are not necessarily related parties if transactions between them have been conducted on a basis consistent with an arm's length transaction. Every case must be judged on the facts and circumstances pertinent to it.

5. Establishing the presence of influence and common influence

Where a relationship between two companies results from the power or right that one is able to exert on the other (i.e., influence), transactions between them have to be disclosed whether or not this power was actually imposed. **5012**

In the case of common influence, transactions between the parties need to be disclosed only where the influence was actually exerted and, as a result, one or both of the transacting parties subordinated their separate interests. Each case must be judged on its own merits. For example, if one company sells an asset to another at a price that differs from the commercial price, this would indicate that subordination has taken place. On the other hand, the mere fact that a transaction has taken place at the commercial rate does not necessarily mean that it should not be disclosed.

5013 The following examples illustrate whether related-party relationships exist.

EXAMPLE Scenario 1

A Ltd has a subsidiary, B Ltd, and an associate, C Ltd.

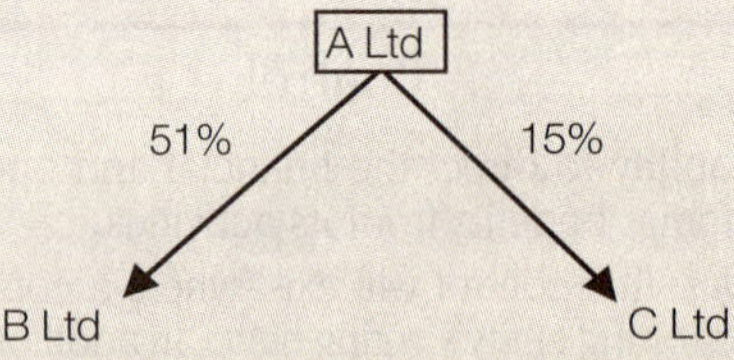

Because C Ltd is subject only to *influence* from A Ltd, while B Ltd is subject to its *control*, the relationship between B Ltd and C Ltd does not normally justify treating them as related parties.

Scenario 2

Mr X sits on the boards of D Ltd and E Ltd.

The mere fact that they have a director in common does not make D Ltd and E Ltd related parties.

Scenario 3

Two companies, F Ltd and G Ltd, are associated companies of the same investor, H Ltd.

Since both companies are subject only to the influence, rather than the control, of H Ltd, the connection is insufficient to regard them as related parties.

Scenario 4

Y Ltd, a manufacturer, purchases raw materials from Z Ltd. The composition of the companies' boards of directors is as follows:

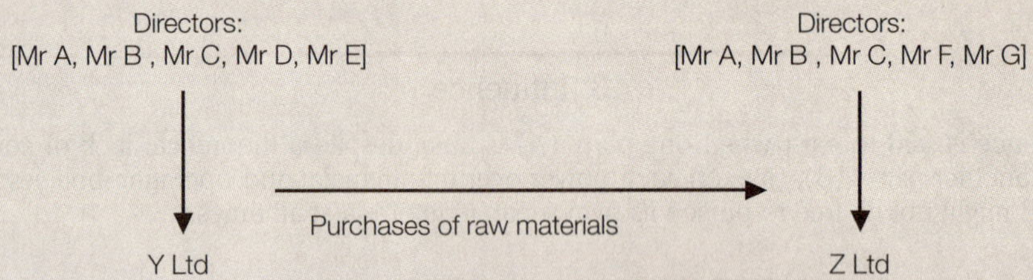

Given that there is a controlling nucleus of directors in common (Messrs A, B and C), Y Ltd and Z Ltd are related parties.

6. Parties that are not related

5015 FRS8(12) In its 2010 amendments to FRS 8, the ASB added a clarification to specify that the following are not regarded as related parties:

– two entities that happen to have a director or other member of key management in common, or where a member of key management of one entity happens to have significant influence over the other entity; and

– two venturers simply because they happen to share joint control over a joint venture.

5016 The following are also not considered related under FRS 8 and fall outside of its scope. (See also ¶5073.)

– providers of finance;

– trade unions;

– public utilities;

– government departments or agencies that do not control, jointly control, or significantly influence the reporting entity simply by virtue of their normal dealings with an entity (even where they may affect the decision-making or the entity's freedom of action);

– a customer, supplier, franchisor, distributor or general agent with whom an entity transacts a significant volume of business, simply by virtue of the resulting economic dependence.

B. Additional criteria for listed companies

The definition of related parties under the Listing Rules is expanded to include: 5020 LR 11.1.4
a) a **substantial shareholder**, which means any person who, within the 12 months preceding the date of the transaction, was entitled to exercise (or control the exercise) of 10 percent or more of the votes able to be cast at general meetings of the company (or its subsidiary, parent or fellow subsidiary),
b) anyone who, during the previous 12 months, was a **director or shadow director** (¶5031) of the company (or subsidiary, parent, or fellow subsidiary),
c) anyone who was an **associate** of the above,
d) a person exercising significant influence.

MEMO POINTS An **associate** of a director or substantial shareholder is:
- that person's spouse, civil partner or child (the "family"),
- the trustees of any trust of which the person (or their family) is a beneficiary,
- any company in whose equity shares the person or their family is able to control 30 percent of the votes at a general meeting or appoint or remove directors holding a majority of voting rights at board meetings.

Where the **substantial shareholder is a company**, its associate means:
a) its subsidiary, parent or fellow subsidiary,
b) any company whose directors are accustomed to act in accordance with the substantial shareholder's or person exercising significant influence's directions or instructions,
c) any company in the capital of which the substantial shareholder or a person exercising significant influence and a company described in (a) or (b) above are able:
- to exercise or control 30 percent of the votes at a general meeting;
- to appoint or remove directors holding a majority of voting rights at board meetings.

SECTION 2

Identifying transactions between related parties

Exactly what constitutes a related party transaction differs under the Companies Act 2006, FRS 8 and the Listing Rules (whether applying to companies listed on the Stock Exchange or the Alternative Investment Market). 5025

I. Under Companies legislation

Company law is concerned primarily with relationships between the reporting entity and its directors (including other persons connected with such directors). FRS 8 is more inclusive and considers the relationships between the reporting entity and other entities. 5026

A. Directors

Directors have a fiduciary duty towards their companies. This means that they are obliged to avoid any circumstances in which their personal interests could conflict with the company's interests. 5027

There are **restrictions on dealings between companies and directors** in terms of which certain transactions have to be approved by shareholders. While under the 1985 Act, a range of transactions were prohibited outright, under the 2006 Act, many of these transactions are no longer prohibited though they do require approval by a company's members.

In respect of any **arrangements or transactions between the company and a third party** in which a director is interested, full disclosure must be made both to the board of directors and in the company's financial statements. The disclosure requirements apply whether or not the transactions are prohibited.

1. Definitions

5030 s 250 CA 2006 For the purposes of the Act, the term "**director**" includes any person who occupies the position of director by whatever name called. From this definition it is clear that it is the person's functions and responsibilities, and not his title, that determines whether or not he is a director.

A person can therefore be a director even if his title does not contain the word "director" and, conversely, someone whose title may contain the word "director" is not necessarily a director for purposes of the Act.

It is also possible that someone may be deemed to be a director even if not validly appointed to the post. This is known as a *de facto* director.

5031 s 251 (1), (2) CA 2006 A **shadow director** is a person in accordance with whose directions or instructions the directors of a company are accustomed to act. However, a person is not deemed to be a shadow director by reason only that the directors act on advice given in a professional capacity. Advisers such as accountants or stockbrokers, who are not involved in the running or management of the company, are not considered shadow directors.

An **alternate director** is someone whose position is determined by the articles of association and who is appointed by a particular director to fulfil all his/her functions – such as voting at board meetings – when he/she is absent. Attendance and voting at board meetings is only permitted when the appointing director is absent. If the alternate director is not already a director, the other directors must approve his appointment. If the director who appointed the alternate director ceases to be a director, the appointment of the alternate ceases simultaneously.

In the interests of clarity and convenience, references to directors will include *de facto*, shadow and alternate directors.

5032 s 252 CA 2006 A **person "connected" with a director** is:

– the director's spouse or civil partner, or any other person that the director lives with in an enduring family relationship,

– the director's children or stepchildren, or any children or stepchildren of a person within the above point (who are not children of stepchildren of the director) who live with the director and are under the age of 18,

– the director's parents,

– a company with which the director is associated,

– a person acting in the capacity of trustee of any trust whose beneficiaries include the director or any of the persons described above (including a trustee of a discretionary trust that includes the persons as potential beneficiaries, but excluding a trustee under an employee's share scheme or a pension scheme), and

– a person acting in the capacity as partner of the director or anyone falling into the categories above.

5033 Sch 1 para (5) CA 2006 A director's interests in shares must be aggregated with those of his connected persons. A person is considered to be **interested in shares** if a company is interested in them and one of the following two conditions are met:

– the person is entitled to exercise or control the exercise of more than 50 percent of that company's voting power at general meetings, or

– that company or its directors are accustomed to act in accordance with his directions or instructions.

A director is said to be **connected** with a company if the director, together with the persons connected with him: 5034 s 254 CA 2006
– is interested in at least 20 per cent of its equity share capital, or
– is entitled to exercise, or control the exercise of, more than 20 per cent of the voting power at any general meeting.

A director of a company is said to control a company if: s 255 CA 2006
a. the director, together with the persons connected with him, is interested in any part of the equity share capital of the company, or is entitled to exercise or control the exercise of any part of the voting power at any general meeting of the company;
b. the director, the persons connected with him and the other directors of the company together are interested in more than 50 percent of the share capital or entitled to exercise or control the exercise of more than 50 percent of the voting power.

MEMO POINTS For the purpose **only** of determining whether a company is connected with or controlled by a director, another company with which the director is connected is not regarded as connected, unless that company is:
– a partner of the director or of a person who is connected with him, or
– a trustee of a trust the beneficiaries of which include a body corporate with which the director is associated.

Companies are considered to be **associated** under the Companies Act 2006 if one is a subsidiary of the other or both are subsidiaries of the same company. Note that while the 1985 Act contemplated the idea of directors being associated with bodies corporate, this term has not been preserved under the new Act. 5035 s 256 CA 2006

The following examples show the operation of these rules and definitions. 5036

EXAMPLE Scenario 1

Mr A owns 19% of the equity share capital of Y Ltd and 21% of Z Ltd. Z Ltd owns 15% of Y Ltd.

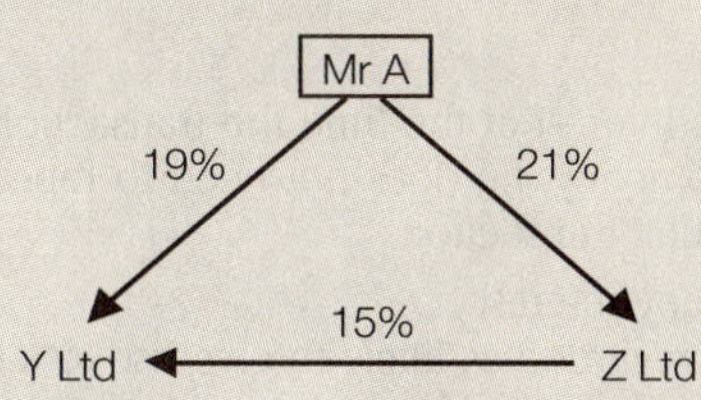

Mr A is connected with Z Ltd because his interest exceeds 20% of the equity share capital.
Before calculating Mr A's effective shareholding in Y Ltd, it must first be determined whether Mr A controls Z Ltd.
Mr A's holding is less than 50% and, because Z Ltd is neither a partner nor a trustee of Mr A, its holding in Y Ltd is not aggregated with Mr A's. Interestingly, though Mr A theoretically has an effective holding of 22.15% in Y Ltd [19% + (21% of 15%)] he is not connected with it.

Scenario 2

Ms B owns 7% of the equity share capital of W Ltd and 60% of X Ltd. X Ltd owns 18% of W Ltd.

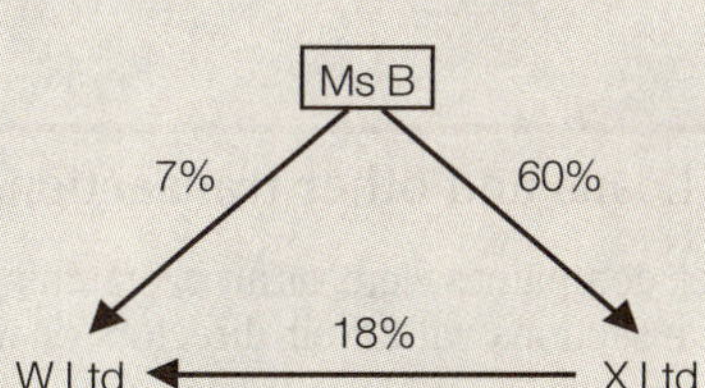

Ms B has an effective holding of 17.8% (7 % + [60 % of 18%]) in W Ltd, yet she is connected with it. The reason is that through her holding in X Ltd (which she controls by virtue of her shareholding being greater than 50%) she is able to control the exercise of the full 18% of X Ltd in W Ltd. This, together with her direct holding of 7%, means that her effective holding is 25%, which makes her connected with W Ltd.

Scenario 3

Mr C owns 5% of the equity share capital of U Ltd and 25% of V Ltd. V Ltd owns 22% of U Ltd.

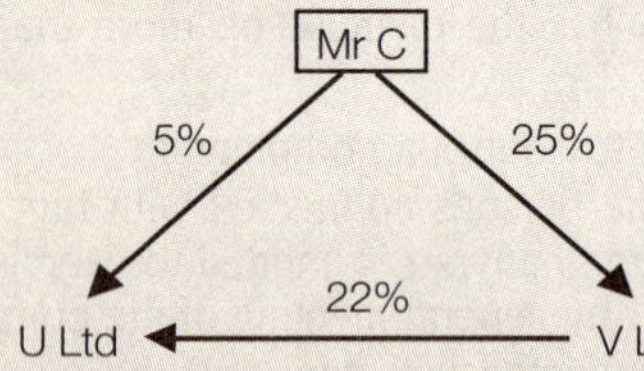

Mr C is connected with V Ltd because he owns more than 20% of the equity shares.
In determining whether he is connected with U Ltd, the interest of V Ltd should be ignored. Mr C is not assumed to be interested in the shares of U Ltd owned by V Ltd because, owning just 25% of V Ltd, he does not control that company or how it votes in U Ltd. Therefore, he is not connected with U Ltd.
The situation would be different if Mr C held more than 50% of the equity shares of V Ltd. In this event he would be able to control the vote of V Ltd in U Ltd and – because V Ltd can exercise more than 20% of the vote in U Ltd – U Ltd would be regarded as being connected with Mr C.

2. Transactions in which directors have a material interest

5040 s 177 – s 185 CA 2006 Under the 2006 Companies Act, directors are required to declare the nature and extent of any interest, direct or indirect, that they have in a proposed, or existing, transaction or arrangement entered into by the company. The declaration should be made as soon as is reasonably practicable and may be made:
- at a meeting of the directors; or
- by notice in writing; or
- by general notice.

If a director has declared his interest at the time the transaction was proposed, and before it was entered into by the company, he does not need to repeat that declaration once the transaction becomes an existing transaction.

A director need not declare any interest:
- that cannot reasonably be regarded as likely to give rise to a conflict of interest;
- that the other directors already know about, or ought reasonably to know about; or
- that concerns the terms of his service contract, considered (or to be considered) by a meeting of directors.

A director may give a general notice of his interests. This is a declaration that a director is interested in another company or connected with another person. If the company then enters into a contract with the company or person named in the general notice, the director does not need to declare any direct or indirect interest that arises as a result. In order to be effective, the general notice must state the nature and extent of the director's interest or connection.

3. Loans and other transactions

5045 Under the 1985 Companies Act, companies were, as an overarching general rule, **not permitted** to enter into the following transactions with their directors or with anyone connected with them:
- loans,
- quasi-loans (i.e., arrangements in terms of which the company pays or agrees to pay sums on behalf of a director on the understanding that the director has an obligation to repay the amount at a later date),
- credit transactions (i.e., leasing, hire-purchase or other deferred payment terms),

- guarantees or provision of security in respect of any of the above transactions, and
- any agreement to enter into any of the above transactions.

These prohibited transactions were commonly referred to as **Section 330 transactions**.

The 2006 Act abolished the prohibition (effective 1 October 2007); however, certain transactions, though now permitted, still require approval by the company's members.

Rules under CA 2006 The following transactions, which require member approval under the Companies Act 2006 – as well as exemptions applying to them – are discussed below. **5051**

Loans In general, all loans to directors (including the provision of a guarantee or security in connection with such loans) must be **approved** by a resolution of the company's members. If the director is also a director of the company's holding company, the transaction must be approved by a resolution of the holding company's members. **5052** s 197 CA 2006

There is an exception in respect of **small loans**, in terms of which member approval is not required for transactions not exceeding S$10,000.

MEMO POINTS The value of a loan is the principal amount of the loan (i.e., without interest). If the value cannot be determined as a specific sum, it is deemed to be in excess of S$50,000.

Quasi-loans A quasi-loan is a transaction where one party (the creditor) pays an amount for another (the borrower), or reimburses expenditure incurred by another party for the borrower; where either: **5053** s 198 – s 200 CA 2006
- the transaction's terms are such that the borrower (or a person on his behalf) will reimburse the creditor, or
- the circumstances surrounding the transaction give rise to a liability on the borrower to reimburse the creditor.

An **example** of a quasi-loan is where a director uses a company credit card or orders goods for himself on the company's corporate account on the understanding that while the company will settle the liability the director will reimburse the company later.

A public company, or a private company associated with a public company, may only enter into a credit transaction or give a guarantee or provide security in connection with a credit transaction entered into by a third party with a director of the company, or its holding company or a person connected with such a director, if the transaction is **approved by a resolution** of the company. As with loans, there is an exemption for small quasi-loans, i.e., those not exceeding S$10,000.

Credit transactions As with quasi-loans, a company, or a private company associated with a public company, may only enter into a credit transaction or give a guarantee or provide security in connection with a credit transaction entered into by another third party with a director of the company, or its holding company or a person connected with such a director, if the transaction is **approved by a resolution** of the company. An exemption in respect of minor transactions exists for transactions not exceeding S$15,000. **5054** s 201 CA 2006

Indirect arrangements A company may not enter into an arrangement as a result of which **another person becomes party to a transaction** that would have required member approval had the company itself entered into it, and where that other person receives a benefit of any kind from the company (or its holding company, subsidiary or fellow subsidiary) unless the arrangement in question has been approved by a resolution of the members of the company. **5055** s 203 CA 2006

General exemptions from members' approval

In addition to the exemptions that apply to the particular transactions discussed above, the following are also exempted: **5056**
- intra-group transactions,
- directors' business expenditure (under S$50,000), and
- directors' expenditure on defending proceedings or in connection with regulatory action/-investigation.

B. Officers other than directors

5057 Although under the Companies Act 1985, there was a requirement to disclose transactions between a company and officers other than directors, there is no such requirement under the Companies Act 2006.

C. Money-lending and banking companies

5060 s 209 (2) CA 2006 Companies legislation defines a money-lending company as "a company whose ordinary business includes the making of loans or quasi-loans, or the giving of guarantees in connection with loans or quasi-loans". Money-lending companies are not necessarily banking companies as defined under the Banking Act 1987, but, for the purposes of these rules, banking companies fall within the definition of money-lending companies.

a. Money-lending companies

5065 In general, transactions requiring approval under the Companies Act 2006 (see ¶5051) – relating to companies in general – relate also to money-lending companies. However, member approval is not required for loans or quasi-loans made by money-lending companies in the ordinary course of business, provided the value of the transaction is not greater, and its terms are not more favourable, than it is reasonable to expect the company would have offered to a person of the same financial standing but unconnected to the company.

This does not prevent a money-lending company from making a home loan to a director of the company or its holding company, or an employee of the company, if such loans are ordinarily made by the company to its employees and the terms of the loan are no more favourable than those on which such loans are ordinarily made.

b. Banking companies

5066 Banking companies are free to ignore any loans made on commercial terms when calculating amounts that can be loaned to directors on beneficial terms.

II. Under FRS 8

A. General rule

5068 FRS 8 (2.6) The notion of related party transactions is wider, and more comprehensive, under FRS 8 than under the Act.

The standard defines a related party transaction as "the transfer of assets or liabilities or the performance of services by, to or for a related party irrespective of whether a price is charged".

Unlike the Act, FRS 8 does not exempt transactions from the requirement to disclose on the grounds of the **size of the consideration** (including where there was **no consideration**), or on the basis that the transaction took place at **arm's length**.

The following are **examples of transactions** that are specified by FRS 8 to require disclosure: **5069**
- purchases or sales of goods (finished and unfinished), property and other assets,
- rendering or receiving of services,
- agency and leasing arrangements,
- transfer of research and development,
- licence agreements,
- provision of finance (e.g., loans and equity contributions – cash or non-cash), guarantees or collateral security,
- management contracts.

Note that this is not an exhaustive list.

In certain cases, the relevant transaction might not involve a consideration and, for this reason, might also not appear in a company's accounting records. Nevertheless, it is the responsibility of the reporting entity to capture this data for disclosure in the financial statements. **5070**

Examples of such transactions are:
- management services provided free of charge by one company to another,
- goods manufactured under a patent granted free of charge by a fellow subsidiary,
- guarantees to third parties in respect of other group companies,
- interest-free loans,
- loans of assets at no charge (including fixed property, vehicles, etc).

B. Scope

The FRS applies to all financial statements that are intended to give a true and fair view of a reporting entity's financial position and profit or loss for a period. However, disclosure is not required by the FRS: **5072**
- in consolidated financial statements of intra-group transactions that have been eliminated on consolidation, FRS 8 (3), (16)
- of transactions entered into between two or more members of a group, provided that any subsidiary undertaking that is a party to the transaction is wholly owned by a member of that group (note, however, that this exemption applies only where all subsidiary undertakings that are party to the transaction are wholly owned, directly or indirectly, by the ultimate controlling entity of the group),
- of pension contributions paid to a pension fund,
- of emoluments in respect of services as an employee (however, the rules on disclosure of directors' emoluments apply, see ¶4800),
- where there is a legal duty of confidentiality (e.g., banks do not have to disclose transactions made in the normal course of business).

In addition, neither the **relationship** nor **transactions** between the reporting entity and the following parties that arise as a result of the **normal roles and functions** of those other parties need be disclosed: **5073** FRS 8 (4)
- providers of finance in the course of their business,
- utility companies,
- government departments and their sponsored bodies,
- customers, suppliers, franchisers, distributors or general agents with whom an entity transacts a significant volume of business.

III. Under the Listing Rules

5075 The Listing Rules apply to companies that have listed equity shares, or listed securities convertible into equity shares.

LR 11.1 (a) The following are **examples** of related party transactions that fall to be disclosed under the Listing Rules:

– a transaction, other than one of a revenue nature in the ordinary course of business, between a company (or any of its subsidiaries) and a related party,

– an arrangement pursuant to which a company (or any of its subsidiaries) and a related party each invests in or provides finance to another undertaking or asset,

– a transaction, other than one of a revenue nature in the ordinary course of business, between a listed company (or any of its subsidiaries) and any person the purpose and effect of which is to benefit a related party.

5076 The Listing Rules **exempt** the following types of related party transactions:

– the issue of new securities for cash made available to all shareholders on equal terms,

– certain employee share schemes,

– granting of credit to the related party on normal commercial terms, to a director for an amount and or terms not more favourable than those offered to employees and by the related party on normal commercial terms and on an unsecured basis,

– the grant of an indemnity to or maintenance of an insurance contract for a director of the company (or any of its subsidiaries),

– certain underwriting and joint investment arrangements,

– small transactions where each of the ratios based on net profits, profits, consideration to assets, consideration to market capitalisation and gross capital is equal to or less than 0.25 percent,

– a transaction with an insignificant subsidiary – where the related party is a related party only by virtue of being a substantial shareholder or director of a subsidiary of the company and which has contributed less than 10 percent of the profits and assets of the listed company in the last three years.

IV. Under the Alternative Investment Market Rules

5080 Alternative Investment Market (AIM) companies are also required to disclose related party transactions in their financial statements. A related party is defined in terms similar to those of the Listing Rules.

V. Materiality

5082 FRS 8, 20 Only material items need be disclosed. Transactions should not be excluded because they might be at arm's length or in the normal course of business. All material related party transactions, whether normal or abnormal, must be disclosed. According to FRS 8, transactions are material when their disclosure "might reasonably be expected to influence decisions made by the users of general purpose financial statements". This definition renders material almost any related party transaction that might be sensitive from the shareholders' point of view, even before the financial amount is taken into account.

However, where the related party is:
– a director, key manager, or other individual in a position to influence, or accountable for stewardship of, the reporting entity, or
– a member of the close family of any individual referred to above, or
– an entity controlled by any individual referred to above,
the materiality of the transaction must be considered not only in terms of its **significance to the reporting entity, but also to the other related party**.

SECTION 3

Information to be disclosed

A. Under Companies legislation

This section deals with information to be disclosed in respect of **directors**. 5085

1. General rule

In the case of a company that does not prepare group accounts, details of: 5087 s 413 CA 2006
– advances and credits granted by the company to its directors, and
– guarantees of any kind entered into by the company on behalf of its directors,
must be shown in the notes to the accounts. In the case of a parent company that prepares group accounts, this information must also be provided in relation to subsidiary undertakings.

The details required of an advance or credit are its amount, an indication of the interest rate, its main conditions and any amounts repaid. In addition, the total amount of advances or credits and the total amounts repaid must be stated.

The details required of a guarantee are:
a. its main terms,
b. the amount of the maximum liability that may be incurred by the company (or its subsidiary),
c. any amount paid and any liability incurred by the company (or its subsidiary) for the purpose of fulfilling the guarantee,
d. the totals of amounts stated in (b) and (c):
– in respect of each of the above transactions, the aggregate amounts outstanding at the end of the financial year made by the company or its subsidiaries, and
– the number of officers for whom transactions in each category were made.

2. Comparative figures

Although FRS 8 is silent on the matter of comparative figures, they are required by the Act in respect of related party transactions. 5088 Sch 1 para 7 (1) SI 2008/410

The following questions can arise where the related parties in the current year are not the same as those in the previous year:
a) Where a party is a related party in the **current year**, but was **not in the previous year**, there are no comparatives to be disclosed because any transactions before the parties were related did not affect the results.
b) Where a party was **related in the previous year**, but **not in the current period**, the comparative figures should be disclosed. If the presence of comparative figures with no

corresponding amount for the current period might cause confusion, an explanation should be given.

MEMO POINTS The amendment to FRS 8, effective for accounting periods beginning on or after 6 April 2008, withdraws the relief for disclosure of transactions with 90 percent subsidiary undertakings. In doing this, the ASB considered how to address the requirement in FRS 28, "Corresponding Amounts", that requires corresponding amounts for all amounts disclosed in the notes to the financial statements. Companies may not have the necessary information to provide corresponding amounts and therefore the amendment provides relief from the requirement in FRS 28 by not requiring, in the first year of adopting the amendment, corresponding amounts where the information cannot be obtained.

B. Under FRS 8

5090 Two separate elements of disclosure can be identified: (1) disclosure of the existence of control, and (2) disclosure of transactions and inter-party balances.

1. Control

5091 FRS 8 (5) Where the reporting company is controlled by another party (¶5004), the following disclosures are required, whether or not any transactions took place between the parties:
- the related party relationship,
- the name of the controlling party, and
- the name of the ultimate controlling party, if appropriate.

Disclosure of the existence of control by a parent company is required even where the reporting entity is a wholly owned subsidiary. The exemption in respect of 90-percent subsidiaries that applies to the disclosure of transactions and balances with other group members does not apply.

The controlling party need not be an individual person or other entity, but may consist of two or more parties acting in concert. Where no ultimate parent company is disclosed because the company is controlled by a trust or other unincorporated entity, it is necessary to consider whether that entity itself is controlled by a person whose identity should be disclosed as the ultimate controlling party.

If the controlling party, or ultimate controlling party, is not known, this fact must be disclosed.

Where the relationship is such that the reporting entity is a **subsidiary**, additional disclosures applicable to subsidiaries are required by Schedule 5 of the Act.

2. Transactions and balances

a. Transactions

5093 FRS 8 (6) (a)-(e) The following details must be disclosed in respect of material transactions (see ¶5082) undertaken by the reporting entity and its related parties. These disclosures are to be made whether or not a price was charged:
- the names of the transacting related parties,
- the relationship between the parties,
- a description of the transactions,
- the amounts involved, and
- any other elements of the transactions necessary for an understanding of the financial statements.

Further disclosures are required concerning the year-end balances, discussed in ¶5095.

The example given by FRS 8 to illustrate the meaning of the phrase "any other elements" is that of a transfer of a major asset at an amount materially different from the price that would have been obtainable on commercial terms.

The Act requires disclosures of certain transactions in which directors are materially interested (¶5040). It does, however, exempt from disclosure those transactions entered into in the normal course of business, and at arm's length (i.e., on terms no less favourable to the reporting entity or its subsidiary than would have been reasonable if the director had not been a director). FRS 8 does not give this exemption and consequently any such transactions remain to be disclosed in the financial statements.

b. Balances

The following information regarding balances between the parties must also be disclosed: **5095**
- the amounts due to or from related parties at the balance sheet date,
- the amount of any provisions for doubtful debts due at the balance sheet date, and
- any amounts written off in the period in respect of debts due to or receivable from related parties.

The requirement to disclose the **balances** is separate from the requirement to disclose **transactions** that take place during a given financial year. If this were not the case, and assuming that there is a material long-term loan in existence, but with no material transactions during the current year, the transaction would not be disclosed. This could potentially be to the detriment of shareholders, potential shareholders and other users.

Aggregation of balances

To reduce the volume of information to be given if each transaction with each related party were disclosed, FRS 8 generally allows aggregation of similar transactions with similar parties. The exception is where the disclosure of particular transactions is required by law or is otherwise necessary for a proper understanding of the financial statements. **5097** FRS 8 (6)

However, aggregation should not be used in such a way that significant transactions are obscured or concealed. Therefore, purchases or sales of goods with group companies should not be aggregated with purchases or sales of fixed assets. FRS 8 (21)

5098

EXAMPLE The following illustrates the disclosure of related party transactions in the notes to the financial statements.

B Ltd
Notes to the financial statements at 30 September 20X2
Related party transactions

During the year, the group purchased goods from, and sold goods to, X Ltd, a company owned by Mr X, a director of the company, as follows:

	20X2 £000	20X1 £000
Sales:		
Services supplied	401	266
Goods sold	58	27
	459	293
Purchases:		
Goods	122	69
Fixed assets	212	204
	334	273

The amounts outstanding at year-end on these purchases and sales are £95,000 and £85,000 respectively (20X1 – £57,000 and £52,000), and are shown separately under creditors and debtors due within one year respectively.

C. Under the Listing Rules

a. Requirements for related party transactions

5100 Chapter 11 of the Listing Rules prescribes that where a listed company (or its subsidiaries) proposes to enter into a transaction with a related party, it must:
- give details to the Company Announcements Officer of the Stock Exchange,
- send a circular to the shareholders with the required information,
- obtain the shareholders' approval for the transaction,
- ensure that the related party does not vote on the relevant resolution,
- take all reasonable steps to ensure that the related party's associates do not vote on the relevant resolution.

b. Modified requirements for smaller related party transactions

5102 For smaller related party transactions, which are those in which each of the following ratios is less than 5 percent but one or more exceeds 0.25 percent:
- gross assets in the transaction: total gross assets of the company,
- profits attributable to assets in the transaction: total profits of the company;
- consideration: market capitalisation of ordinary shares,
- gross capital of business or company being acquired: gross capital of company,

the listed company must:
- inform the FSA in writing of the details of the proposed transaction,
- provide the FSA with written confirmation from an independent adviser acceptable to the FSA that the terms of the proposed transaction with the related party are fair and reasonable as far as the shareholders of the listed company are concerned, and
- undertake in writing to the FSA to include details of the transaction in the next published annual accounts.

MEMO POINTS Small transactions are those where each of the applicable percentage ratios is equal to or less than 0.25 percent. Related party transaction rules do not apply to such transactions.

c. Aggregration of transactions

5105 If a listed company enters into transactions or arrangements with the same related party (and if any of its associates) in any twelve month period and the transactions or arrangements have not been approved by shareholders, the transactions or arrangements must be aggregated. If any percentage ratio (as described above) is 5 percent or more for the aggregated transactions or arrangements, the listed company must treat this as a related party transaction and follow the requirements set out in ¶5100.

If transactions or arrangements that are small transactions are aggregated and for the aggregated small transactions each of the percentage ratios is less than 5 percent, but one or more of the percentage ratios exceeds 0.25 percent, the listed company must follow the steps set out in ¶5102 in respect of the latest small transaction and in respect of the aggregated small transactions.

Chapter 9 of the Listing Rules requires listed companies to disclose particulars of the following in their financial statements:

a. "contracts of significance" subsisting during the year:
- to which the company (or any of its subsidiaries) is a party and in which a director is materially interested,
- between the company (or any of its subsidiaries) and a controlling shareholder,

b. contracts subsisting during the year for the provision of services to the company (or any of its subsidiaries) by a controlling shareholder, unless:
- it is a contract for the provision of services which it is the principal business of the shareholder to provide, and
- it is not a contract of significance.

MEMO POINTS A "contract of significance" is one representing an amount equal to 1 percent of:
- the aggregate of the group's share of capital and reserves (where the transaction concerned is a capital transaction or the granting of credit) or
- total annual purchases, sales, payments or receipts, as the case may be, of the group.

For these purposes, a controlling shareholder is defined as a person (or persons acting jointly) who is able to control:
- the exercise of 30 percent or more of the voting rights of the company, or
- the appointment of directors who are in turn able to exercise a majority of votes at board meetings.

D. Under the London Stock Exchange Rules

For any transaction with a related party where any percentage ratio based on gross assets, profits, turnover, consideration to market capitalisation and gross capital exceeds 5 percent, Alternative Investment Market (AIM) companies are required to issue notification without delay as soon as the terms of a transaction with a related party are agreed, disclosing: 5107
- particulars of the transaction, including the name of any other relevant parties;
- a description of the assets which are the subject of the transaction, or the business carried on by, or using, the assets;
- the profits attributable to those assets;
- the value of those assets if different from the consideration;
- the full consideration and how it is being satisfied;
- the effects on the AIM company;
- details of the service contracts of any proposed directors;
- in the case of a disposal, the application of the sale proceeds;
- in the case of a disposal, if the shares or other securities are to form part of the consideration received, a statement whether such securities are to be sold or retained;
- the name of the related party and the nature and extent of their interest in the transaction;
- a statement that with the exception of any director who is involved in the transaction as a related party, its directors consider, having consulted with its nominated adviser, that the terms of the transaction are fair and reasonable insofar as its shareholders are concerned; and
- any other information necessary to enable investors to evaluate the effect of the transaction upon the AIM company.

AIM companies must also disclose in their published annual accounts any transaction with a related party where any of the class tests exceeds 0.25 percent, specifying the identity of the related party and the consideration for the transaction.

SECTION 4

Comparison with IAS rules

IAS 24, "Related party disclosures", contains similar requirements to those of FRS 8. 5110

Appendix III of FRS 8 states that compliance with the FRS will ensure compliance with IAS 24 in all material respects except for the following:
- FRS 8 provides that particulars need not be given of transactions entered into between two or more members of a group, provided that any subsidiary undertaking which is a

party to the transaction is wholly owned by a member of that group. IAS 24 does not provide relief from a disclosure of transactions entered into between wholly owned subsidiaries; and

– IAS 24 requires disclosure of key management compensation, whereas FRS 8 does not contain such provision.

5115 Other differences are as follows:

Under IAS 24	Under FRS 8
No exemption for pension contributions paid to a pension fund and emoluments in respect of services as an employee.	Exemption for pension contributions paid to a pension fund and emoluments in respect of services as an employee.
Disclosure of related party relationship where control exists – whether or not there have been transactions.	Same as IAS 24 but also disclosure of the ultimate controlling party.
In respect of transactions: – nature of related party relationships – types of transactions – elements of the transactions necessary for an understanding of the financial statements, for example: • an indication of the volume of transactions (by amount or proportion) • outstanding items (amounts or proportions) • pricing policies	*In respect of transactions*: – names of the transacting related parties – relationship between the parties – description of the transactions – amounts involved – elements of the transactions necessary for an understanding of the financial statements, for example: • transfer of asset at terms that differ from commercial terms • balances owing to/from related parties

5116 The differences between UK and International reporting will largely fall away if FRS 8 is superseded by a new standard based on IAS 24. Some of the **differences in disclosure requirements** expected to remain in the future include the following:

Current situation	Future situation
Names of transacting parties.	Not required.
Description of relationship.	Nature of relationship.
Description of transactions.	Information about transactions.
Information on any other elements necessary for an understanding of the financial statements.	Information about the transactions and outstanding balances necessary for an understanding of the potential effect of the relationship on the financial statements.
Amounts due to or from related parties.	Same, and in addition, disclosure of the terms and conditions, the nature of the consideration and details of any guarantees given or received.
Amounts written off in respect of debts due to or from related parties.	Expense recognised in respect of bad or doubtful debts due from related parties.

CHAPTER 5

Corporate governance disclosures

OUTLINE ¶¶

SECTION 1

Introduction

Corporate governance is concerned with the processes by which enterprises are directed and controlled – for the good of companies and their long-term success – by taking into account the **rights and aspirations** of shareholders and other stakeholders. These processes and principles are brought together in the **UK Corporate Governance Code** (formerly called the Combined Code on Corporate Governance – the new title is one of the results of a review in 2009) as a means of laying down rules of best practice for companies listed on the London Stock Exchange. 5200

The Code is overseen by the Financial Reporting Council (FRC) and it covers a wide range of matters including legal, company secretarial, strategic, management, accounting and information systems, as well as investor relations.

A revised Code, issued in May 2010, applies to accounting periods beginning on or after 29 June 2010. In addition, in July 2010 the FRC issued the **UK Stewardship Code**, to deal specifically with the quality of engagement between institutional investors and companies. (¶5295)

A. Scope and objective of corporate governance disclosures

Because some of the issues surrounding corporate governance attracted political and public attention, corporate governance **disclosures** were designed to ensure that interested parties 5201 are enabled to make reliable estimates of the value of companies for the purpose of assessing their exposure to risk before investing in, or withdrawing investments from, listed companies.

The Code **applies to all companies with a Premium Listing** of equity shares – regardless of whether they are incorporated in the UK or not. Private companies are, however, also encouraged to conform but there is no requirement for disclosure of compliance in their accounts.

Corporate governance rules serve another purpose too: to add transparency to the **remuneration and other benefits** that are received by the directors of the company. These issues, however, are dealt with in the chapter on directors' remuneration (¶4800).

5205 The **main areas** with which corporate governance is concerned include:
– **procedures** adopted by the board and its committees to discharge its duties (e.g., membership of the board, frequency of and procedures at board meetings, the role of non-executive directors, constitution and terms of reference of audit and remuneration committees, and the role of the company secretary),
– the board's **accountability** to shareholders and other stakeholders (e.g., annual reporting, use of AGMs and shareholders' voting rights),
– the **manner in which the board controls** the company or group (e.g., management structures, group legal structure, and internal control practices).

5207 The following table gives a short overview of the development of corporate governance:

The history of corporate governance	
1	The report of the Committee on the Financial Aspects of Corporate Governance, referred to as the **Cadbury Report**, was issued in December 1992 to give directors guidance on what was expected of them.
2	Issuance of the **Rutteman Guidance** on **internal financial control** and **going concern**.
3	Because the level of remuneration to directors remained a contentious issue – especially in the case of privatised utilities – a new report known as the **Greenbury Report** was published in July 1995. One of the results was the adoption of **additional disclosure requirements** in the Listing Rules relating to directors' pay packages (see ¶4865).
4	In accordance with the recommendations of the Cadbury Committee, a successor body was established to review progress. This body became known as the Committee on Corporate Governance or the Hampel Committee which, in turn, published its final report (known as the **Hampel Report**) in January 1998. The recommendations contained in it, many of which were derived from the previous reports, are aimed at ensuring a balance between business prosperity on the one hand and accountability on the other.
5	Following discussions with the London Stock Exchange, the Hampel Report became the basis of the **Combined Code**, and has been made part of the **appendix to the Listing Rules**.
6	After publication of the Combined Code, a new working group was set up to consider the guidance necessary to enable directors to report on internal controls. The chairman of this working group was Nigel Turnbull and its final guidance is known as the **Turnbull Report**. In respect of years ending after 23 December 2000, full disclosure in accordance with the Turnbull Report became mandatory.
7	In July 2003 the Financial Reporting Council (FRC) published the new Combined Code, which derives from recommendations made in the **Higgs Review** of the Role and Effectiveness of Non-Executive Directors, and in the **Smith Report** on Audit Committees (both published in January 2003). The new Combined Code supersedes and replaces the 1998 Code and came into effect for listed companies with reporting years beginning on or after 1 November 2003. It comprises main principles, supporting principles and associated code provisions, all aimed at promoting transparency and openness in disclosure.
8	In June 2006 the FRC released an **updated version** of the Code, effective for reporting periods commencing on or after 1 November 2006. It contains a small number of modifications – in general it was felt that the 2003 Code had been well accepted and had had a positive effect on corporate governance.

The history of corporate governance	
9	In 2007 the FRC made a review of the impact and effectiveness of the Code and incorporated changes into a new edition of the Code (the June 2008 edition), which applies to accounting periods beginning on or after 29 June 2008.
10	A review was undertaken at the request of the Government by Sir David Walker on corporate governance in UK banks and other financial industry entities and the findings published in 2009. In May 2010, the FRC issued a **new edition** of the Code, which applies to accounting periods commencing on or after 29 June 2010.
11	The new Code included in Schedule C some engagement principles for institutional investors. This Schedule has now been superseded by the **UK Stewardship Code**, published in July 2010. It aims to enhance the quality of engagement between institutional investors and companies to help improve long-term returns to shareholders and the efficient exercise of governance responsibilities.

Main changes resulting from 2010 revision

The following are the main differences between the 2008 and 2010 editions of the Code: **5208**
– New principles on the **composition and selection of the board**, including the need to appoint members on merit, against objective criteria, and with due regard for the benefits of **diversity**, including gender diversity.
– New principles on the leadership of the **chairman**, the responsibility of the **non-executive directors** to provide constructive challenge, and the time commitment expected of all directors.
– To facilitate improvements in the board's performance and awareness of its strengths and weaknesses, new provision is made for the chairman to hold regular **development reviews** with each director. Board **evaluation reviews** in FTSE 350 companies should be externally facilitated at least every three years.
– To increase accountability to shareholders, all directors of FTSE 350 companies should be subject to **annual re-election** and chairmen are encouraged to report personally on how the principles relating to the leadership and effectiveness of the board have been applied.
– To improve **risk management**, the company's business model should be explained and the board should be responsible for determining the nature and extent of the significant risks it is willing to take.
– New provision is made for **performance-related pay** to be aligned to the **long-term interests** of the company and its risk policies and systems.

B. Exemptions from corporate governance disclosures

Corporate governance disclosures are **required by the Listing Rules**. The following exceptions and partial exemptions apply. **5210**

Corporate governance disclosures are not required of companies that do not have a **premium listing** of equity shares, though other companies may choose to report **voluntarily** in compliance with the Code. **5212**

Corporate entities whose securities are traded on the **Alternative Investment Market** (AIM) are not required to comply with the corporate governance disclosure rules (because the Listing Rules do not apply to them). However, as a practical matter, AIM-traded companies may – in the interests of generating investor confidence – adopt some or all of the guidelines. Should they elect to do so, it is recommended that they explain that the information was provided voluntarily. **5214**

5216 **Certain categories** of listed companies, set out below, **can claim relief** from some of the disclosure requirements. These are not necessarily full exemptions from corporate governance disclosures because some remuneration and/or governance disclosures may still be required to be made.

Where a company is able to avail itself of an exemption, it should clearly disclose the exemption taken and the grounds for taking it. This will avoid misunderstandings among readers who may otherwise believe that some information was simply not provided. Similarly, where companies that are entitled to exemptions from disclosure nevertheless elect to make them, they should indicate this fact.

The following are the categories of listed companies to which **exemptions or partial exemptions** apply.

Specialist debt securities

5218 LR 23.22 Companies whose equity consists solely of specialised debt securities are exempt from the obligations on corporate governance, directors' remuneration and going concern disclosures. For these purposes, specialist debt securities are those that, because of their nature, are traded by a **limited number of investors** who are **particularly knowledgeable** about such companies.

Other debt securities and fixed income shares

5220 LR 9.46-47 Companies with only debt securities or fixed income shares are released from the obligation to comply with the Listing Rule paragraphs on corporate governance and directors' remuneration.

Overseas companies

5222 LR 17.12, 17.14 These companies, if they have a **primary or secondary listing** by the UK Listing Authority, need not make disclosures of corporate governance, going concern, and directors' remuneration. However, companies with a primary listing are still required to disclose the **unexpired term of any service contract** of a director proposed for election or re-election at the next AGM.

Investment companies, investment trusts, and venture capital trusts

5226 LR 21.20 (i), 26.9 (c) These entities, if they do not have executive directors, are exempt from some elements of the narrative statement (¶5245) and the compliance statement (¶5282).

SECTION 2

Disclosure

5235 LR 12.43 The main disclosure requirements of the Listing Rules, which may be given either within the directors' report or as a separate report, are:
- a **narrative statement** explaining how the reporting entity has applied the principles of Section 1 of the Corporate Governance Code
- a **compliance statement** detailing the level of the company's compliance with the Code during the accounting period
- disclosure of **specific information or circumstances** (see table below), if these were applicable during the accounting period.

5237

Specific information or circumstances to be reported	As required by Corporate Governance Code, Section:
The chairman, deputy chairman (if one has been appointed), the chief executive officer, the senior independent director, and the chairmen and members of the nomination, audit and remuneration committees **must be identified**. It should also set out the number of **meetings** of the board and its committees, and individual **attendance** by directors.	A.1.2
The board must identify in the annual report each non-executive director it considers to be **independent**. If there are any relationships or circumstances that may affect (or appear to affect) a director's independence, the directors must state their reasons for determining that the director concerned is nevertheless independent.	A.3.1
The board should state in the annual report how **performance evaluation** of the board, its committees and its individual directors has been conducted.	A.6.1
The names of directors submitted for election or re-election should be accompanied by sufficient **biographical details** to enable shareholders to make an informed decision.	A.7.1
If a company releases an executive director to serve as a **non-executive director elsewhere**, the remuneration report should state whether the director will retain such earnings and the amount concerned.	B.1.4
The directors should explain in the annual report their **responsibility for preparing the accounts**.	C.1.1
The directors should include in the annual report an explanation of the basis on which the company generates or preserves value over the **longer term**.	C.1.2
The directors should report in annual and half-yearly financial statements that the business is a going concern.	C.13
If there is **no internal audit function**, the reasons should be explained in the annual report.	C.3.5
If the board does **not accept the audit committee's recommendation** on matters relating to the appointment, reappointment and removal of auditors, this fact, together with reasons, should be included in the annual report.	C.3.6
If the company's auditor provides non-audit services, the annual report should explain how **objectivity and independence of the auditor** is safeguarded.	C.3.7
The board should report on how they have developed an understanding of the **views of major shareholders**.	D.1.2

No official guidance has been issued on the **specific format** or the **contents** of the narrative and compliance statements. Instead, the London Stock Exchange has left it to directors to use their best judgement in explaining the governance policies adopted by their companies in accordance with their specific circumstances. 5239

A. Narrative Statement

The narrative statement should describe the manner in which the directors have applied the principles of the Code. Generally, it contains what the directors believe to be the most **important features of their governance** so as to enable shareholders to evaluate how the principles have been applied. 5245

In addition, the directors enjoy the **freedom to place the narrative statement** wherever it seems to them most appropriate to do so. Consequently, most companies include it as part of the Directors' Report or disclose it as a separate Corporate Governance Statement.

The following table shows the various matters that are to be covered in the narrative report as well as the paragraph number in this manual where they are discussed.

Subject to be covered	Reference to detailed discussion ¶¶
Directors – in general – responsibilities – remuneration	 ¶5247 ¶5250 ¶4800
Relations with shareholders	¶5255
Going concern	¶5260
Internal control	¶5270
Audit and internal audit – audit committee – reappointment of auditors – responsibilities of auditors	 ¶5276 ¶5279 ¶5808

1. Directors

5247 The Corporate Governance Code adds a number of disclosures to those of the Listing Rules in terms of which the **names** of the following should be disclosed:
– the Chairman, and chief executive officer;
– the non-executive independent directors;
– the balance of the board; and
– the directors submitted for election or re-election.

Directors' responsibilities

5250 A significant number of companies provide a statement of directors' responsibilities in their annual accounts and although it is not a requirement of **company law** or an **accounting standard**, it is required by the Statement of Auditing Standards (SAS) 600, Auditors' Reports on Financial Statements. The **Cadbury Report** also included a recommendation that the directors' reports of listed companies contain a statement of directors' responsibilities. Companies **exempt from an audit** need not comply with this requirement.

The directors' responsibility statement can be either free-standing or included within the directors' report, and should cover the following:
– legal requirement for directors to prepare financial statements for each financial year that give a **true and fair view** of the company's finances at the end of the financial year;
– confirmation that suitable **accounting policies** have been consistently applied;
– confirmation that applicable **accounting standards** have been followed and any material departures have been disclosed in the notes to the financial statements; and
– directors' legal responsibility for maintaining adequate **accounting records**, safeguarding the assets of the company, and the detection of fraud.

Directors' remuneration

5252 The Corporate Governance Code requires a remuneration report (¶4865) from the board of directors that sets out the company's policy on executive remuneration and details of each element of the remuneration package.

2. Relations with shareholders

5255 The directors' report should include details of how the company maintains an ongoing communication with its shareholders. This is illustrated in the example below.

EXAMPLE DIRECTORS' REPORT (extract) 5256

The Group maintains an active dialogue with its shareholders through an organised programme of investor relations. This activity is a key component of our corporate communications programme and is headed by the Director of Investor Relations.

The programme includes formal presentations in both London and Paris of our full-year and interim results, trading statements are produced three times a year, and regular meetings are held between senior managers and institutional investors.

Regular communication with shareholders also takes place through the Annual and Interim reports and by way of the Group's website (www.xxx.co.uk).

The annual general meeting is used as an important opportunity for communication with both institutional and private shareholders, including a short presentation on the business and the latest trading position.

3. Going concern

The Corporate Governance Code requires directors to report "that the business is a going concern, with supporting assumptions or qualifications as necessary." 5260 CC Sec 1, C.1.2; LR 12.43 (v)

The **purpose** of the going concern report is not to guarantee the company's continued success but rather to state whether or not the directors believe it appropriate to continue using the going-concern basis in the preparation of financial statements.

To determine whether or not the going-concern basis is appropriate, the directors must take account of the circumstances prevailing at the date of signing the financial statements. Careful consideration of the following will assist them in reaching a proper determination:

- forecasts and budgets
- borrowing requirements
- liability management
- contingent liabilities
- products and markets
- financial risk management
- other factors
- financial adaptability.

In relation to whether a business is a going concern, there are three possibilities: 5262

1) The company will continue operating for the foreseeable future. The vast majority of companies fall into this category, and they should make their disclosures as shown in the following example. 5264

EXAMPLE DIRECTORS' REPORT (extract)

The directors believe that the company and the consolidated group have adequate resources to continue in operational existence for the foreseeable future. For this reason, they continue to adopt the **going-concern basis** in producing accounts. A statement of the responsibilities of the directors in relation to the accounts appears on page xxx.

2) Factors exist that cast doubt on the company's ability to continue operating. Despite the existence of doubts, the directors may nevertheless be of the opinion that the company's ability to continue operating has not been compromised and that the going concern is still appropriate – for example, where a company is in breach of its loan agreements but negotiations to extend them are in progress. In cases such as these, directors are required to investigate the extent of the problem and then explain not only the circumstances but also how they intend to deal with them. 5265

The disclosure can be made as shown in the following example.

EXAMPLE DIRECTORS' REPORT (extract)

At the balance sheet date, the company is in breach of certain loan covenants and, consequently, the company's bankers could recall their loans at any time. The directors continue to be involved in negotiations with the company's bankers and as yet no demands for repayments have been received. The negotiations are at an early stage and, although the directors are optimistic about the outcome, it is too early to make predictions with any degree of certainty.

In the light of the actions described elsewhere in the Operating and Financial Review, the directors consider it appropriate to adopt the going-concern basis in preparing the financial statements.

5266 **3) The going-concern basis is inappropriate**. Where the directors conclude that the company is not likely to be able to continue in operational existence for the foreseeable future, the financial statements should be prepared on a basis other than the going-concern basis. In addition, this fact must be disclosed.

In light of the seriousness of such a disclosure, directors should seek the counsel of their legal advisors in relation to the precise wording of such a statement.

MEMO POINTS The fact that an entity may make a non-going-concern disclosure in terms of the corporate governance provisions does not affect its obligation to make any such disclosures under the Companies Act and accounting standards (see ¶23).

5268 **Directors of a parent company** are required to make going-concern disclosures in relation to both the parent's financial statements and those of the group as a whole. Such a statement is not necessarily meant to imply that each individual company in the group is a going concern, but rather that the directors' procedures take into account the effect of any individual subsidiaries' difficulties on the group as a whole.

4. Internal control

5270 CC Sec 1, C.2.1 The Corporate Governance Code prescribes that the directors should maintain a sound system of internal control to safeguard both the investment of shareholders and the company's assets. Moreover, they:

> "should, at least annually, conduct a review of the effectiveness of the… system of internal controls and should report to shareholders that they have done so. The review should cover all material controls, including financial, operational and compliance controls and risk management systems."

5272 The Turnbull guidance proposes simple disclosure with the intention of avoiding generic descriptions.

Each element of disclosure requires the board to ensure it has sufficient support for its statements. For instance, the board should disclose that:
- there is an **ongoing process** for identifying, evaluating and managing the significant risks faced by the company,
- this **process has been in place during the year** under review (and up until the date of approval of the annual report),
- the **process is regularly reviewed** by the board and accords with the Turnbull guidance.

The above is the minimum disclosure requirement; additional information can be given, especially if, by doing so, it would facilitate users' understanding of the company's **risk management processes** and system of internal control. As a result, some companies describe their significant risks (and opportunities) and explain how these are managed.

5273 In addition to the above, it should be specifically stated that the **board is responsible for the company's system of internal control** and for reviewing its effectiveness. Finally, it should also be made clear that a system of internal control is designed to manage rather than eliminate the risk of failure to achieve business objectives, and it can provide reasonable – but not absolute – assurance against material misstatement or loss.

The board should summarise the process undertaken to review the effectiveness of the internal control system. In addition, if **any significant problems** have been noted in the annual report (e.g., in the Chairman's statement) the material internal control aspects of these **should be identified**.

A revision made to the Turnbull Guidance in 2005 **expanded** the recommendation to the effect that the board should, in its statement on internal control, "confirm that necessary actions have been or are being taken to remedy any significant failings or weaknesses identified from that review." 5274

As a point of interest, the auditors' review responsibility with respect to this recommendation includes reviewing the documentation prepared by or for the board in connection with these failings or weaknesses, discussing with them the actions they have already taken or still consider necessary, and taking these matters into account during the audit of the financial statements.

EXAMPLE **Specimen disclosure:**

The directors are responsible for the Group's system of internal control and for maintaining and reviewing its effectiveness from both a financial and operational perspective. The system of internal control is designed to manage, rather than eliminate, the risk of failure to achieve business objectives and to provide reasonable but not absolute assurance against material misstatement or loss. The Group's approach to internal control is based on the underlying principle of line management's accountability for control and risk management.

In reviewing the effectiveness of the system of internal control, the Board has taken account of the results of the work carried out to audit and review the activities of the Group.

There is an ongoing process to identify, assess and manage risk, including those risks affecting the Group's reputation. This process is subject to continuous improvement and has been in place throughout the financial year to which these statements apply and up to the date of their approval. The risk review framework has been enhanced at both programme and sector level, and assurance activities more closely coordinated with the risk-management process.

The Board has reviewed the risk-management process and confirms that ongoing processes and systems ensure that the Group continues to be compliant with the current Turnbull Committee Guidance on Internal Control and the Revised Guidance for Directors on the Code issued in October 2005.

5. Audit and internal audit

The directors are required to establish an **Audit Committee**, whose members normally include non-executive directors and the finance director. Brief details of the Audit Committee's terms of reference including accounting issues, financial reporting and internal controls should be given in the directors' report. The Committee should also monitor changes in accounting policy, review internal audit functions, liaise with external auditors and discuss the accounting implications of major transactions. 5276

EXAMPLE DIRECTORS' REPORT (extract)

The Audit Committee is chaired by Mr X and comprises the non-executive Directors Mr J, Ms K and Mr L. It regularly reviews the work of the internal audit department, the financial implications of significant transactions including acquisitions and disposals, and the application of accounting policies in determining the financial statements of the Group. The Audit Committee has responsibility for ensuring that all the financial information laid down in both the Group's published report and accounts and in other public statements is properly supported by detailed working papers.

In addition, the Audit Committee has responsibility for the approval of significant amendments, additions and deletions to the Group's financial control procedures. It also reviews the scope, results and cost of the external audit, and monitors the objectivity of the auditors, taking into account the extent of non-audit services that they provide.

The Board regularly reviews the effectiveness of the Group's systems of internal financial control in consultation with the Audit Committee, Executive Directors and the internal audit department.

Although there is no statutory requirement to this effect, companies often include a statement dealing with the reappointment of the auditors. 5279

EXAMPLE DIRECTORS REPORT (extract)

Auditors – reappointment

Messrs PQR & Co. have indicated their willingness to accept reappointment as auditors of the Company for a further term and a resolution proposing their reappointment will be put to the shareholders at the annual general meeting.

B. Compliance Statement

5282 LR 12.43A (b) The other main disclosure requirement of the Listing Rules is a statement as to whether a company has complied throughout the accounting period with the provisions of the Corporate Governance Code.

Where a company has either not complied with all the provisions, or has complied for only **part of an accounting period**, the compliance statement must specify the Code provisions that were not complied with. In addition, the company **must identify the period** during which the non-compliance continued and give reasons for any such non-compliance.

EXAMPLE REPORT OF THE DIRECTORS (extract)

Compliance with the UK Corporate Governance Code

The directors believe that the Company complied with the provisions of the UK Corporate Governance Code throughout the financial year. The Code requirements on internal control have been met.

5284 The Corporate Governance Code does not specify where the statement of compliance should be located within the annual report. In practice, it generally forms a separate section dealing with corporate governance and is placed either just before the directors' report or within it. Occasionally, it is dealt with or referred to within the Chairman's statement.

5285 The following are the most commonly disclosed **non-compliance issues**:
- identification of a senior independent non-executive director
- executive directors exceeding the recommended one-year service-contract period
- directors' appointments exceeding three years
- composition of the board is such that non-executive directors account for less than one third
- executive directors are on the audit committee
- directors' remuneration is not sufficiently linked to performance
- there is no nominations committee (however, note that this requirement does not apply when the board is small).

C. Examples

5290 Two sample corporate governance disclosures follow. **A Ltd** is a smaller company, while **B Ltd** is a larger company.

5291

A Ltd Corporate Governance Report

The Company recognises the importance of, and is committed to, high standards of corporate governance, and the Directors acknowledge their overall responsibility for the system of internal control and for reviewing its effectiveness. This report sets out how the Company has applied the relevant principles published as the UK Corporate Governance Code.

The Board of Directors

The Board of Directors at the date of this report consists of three executive and one non-executive director (biographical notes are set out on page *xx*).

The Board believes that the composition and breadth of experience of the Board are appropriate for the Company. The Board meets at least twelve times throughout the year and all Directors have full and timely access to information. The Board reserves to itself such key matters to approve or monitor strategic plans, annual operating budget, major capital expenditure, treasury policies and financial performance. It delegates responsibility for the day-to-day operation of the business to the executive directors.

Internal control

A system of internal control cannot provide absolute assurance against material misstatement or loss. The Company's systems are designed to manage rather than eliminate the risk of failure to meet business objectives and can provide the directors only with reasonable assurance that material errors and irregularities are prevented or they are detected on a timely basis and dealt with appropriately.

The Board confirms that there are ongoing procedures in place for identifying, evaluating and managing significant risks faced by the Company and that these have been in place for the year under review and up to the date of approval of this annual report and accounts. The procedures have been reviewed by the Board and accord with the Turnbull guidance for directors in the UK Corporate Governance Code.

The Board has reviewed the major risks affecting the business and the effectiveness of the system of internal control. Because of the size and nature of the business, the executive directors are closely involved in managing the business at a detailed level. This provides for direct monitoring of risks and control processes, conducted within a culture of integrity, quality and high levels of communication. This is supported by reviews of daily, weekly and monthly detailed analyses of the performance of the business and key performance indicators associated with the trading risks facing the company.

Compliance with the UK Corporate Governance Code

The Company has complied with the requirements set out in Section 1 of the UK Corporate Governance Code throughout the accounting period other than as follows:

The Code recommends that there should be a strong independent non-executive element on the Board with non-executive directors comprising not less than one third of the Board and a division of responsibility between the Chairman and the Chief Executive. While the composition of the Board does not meet this recommendation, the Board nevertheless is of the opinion that owing to the size and nature of the Company, its Board is appropriately constituted.

The UK Corporate Governance Code recommends the formation of audit, remuneration and nomination committees. Again, due to the size and nature of the Company and the Board, these committees have not been established. The Board does however adhere to certain principles in establishing levels and forms of remuneration, and these are detailed on page *xx*.

Going concern

The Group continues to trade profitably and to generate a healthy positive operating cash flow, and this is reflected in the current budgets and forecasts. The Directors therefore reasonably expect that the Company has adequate resources to continue in operational existence for the foreseeable future. For this reason, they continue to adopt the going-concern basis in preparing the accounts.

B Ltd Corporate Governance Report

The Group is committed to high standards of corporate governance. The Board is accountable to the Company's shareholders for good governance and this statement describes how the relevant principles of governance are applied to the Company. Throughout the year the Company has been in compliance with the provisions set out in the Corporate Governance Code appended to the Listing Rules of the UK Listing Authority.

The Board currently consists of the Chairman, the Chief Executive, five other Executive Directors and five Non-Executive Directors. Their biographies appear on page *xx*, and reveal a range of business, financial and global experience, all of which is essential to the effective leadership and administration of a multi-national company such as this. The non-executive directors are independent of management.

All directors are equally accountable under the law for the proper stewardship of the Company's affairs. The non-executive directors have a particular responsibility to ensure that the strategies proposed by executive directors are fully discussed and critically examined against the best long-term interests of not only the shareholders, but also employees, customers, suppliers and the various communities within which the company operates. The non-executive directors also test fully the operational performance of the whole Group. The Board has prescribed reserved powers which reinforce its control of the Company. There is a procedure for directors to obtain independent professional advice (at the Company's expense) to enhance the performance of their duties as directors.

All directors have full and timely access to relevant information. The Board meets at least ten times per annum; in addition there is frequent contact between formal meetings in connection with the Company's business.

The role of the non-executive directors is a vital element in corporate accountability. The remits and memberships of the three relevant Board Committees are set out on page *xx*. The Remuneration and Nomination Committee and the Audit Committee are constituted solely of non-executive directors and both report regularly to the Board.

Remuneration and Nomination Committee

The Chairman and Chief Executive attend meetings of the Remuneration and Nomination Committee for appropriate items but are always excluded when their own performance and remuneration are under review. The Chairman from time to time promotes discussion with the executive Directors about non-executive directors' remuneration based on full external comparisons. Any recommendations made are tabled to the full Board. Non-executive directors have the option of taking a portion of their remuneration in the Company's shares.

Details of remuneration policy and practices, together with the remuneration of directors, are given in the Remuneration report on page *xx*.

The Chairman of the Remuneration and Nomination Committee, Mr *X*, acts as the Company's lead non-executive director. In this position he promotes discussion at appropriate times about the Company's chairmanship and succession to it.

The Non-Executive Directors normally meet twice a year with the Chairman and Chief Executive to discuss Board and individual directors' performance and succession plans. At appropriate times the Chairman and the Chief Executive absent themselves so their performance can be assessed. The final discussion is led by the Chairman of the Remuneration and Nomination Committee and there is feedback to individuals.

Appointments to Executive Director are fully discussed by the Chairman and Chief Executive with the Remuneration and Nomination Committee before a proposal is formally made to the Board by the Chairman of that committee. Possible new non-executive directors are suggested by all members of the Board in the light of the Company's business requirements and the need to have a balanced Board. Where it is appropriate, recruitment consultants are used to assist the process. Possible candidates are discussed among all directors before any approach is made to them. All Directors are subject to re-election at least every three years.

Audit and internal control

Following the Turnbull guidance for directors on internal control, the Board confirms that there is a process for identifying, evaluating and managing the significant risks to the achievement of the Group's strategic objectives. This process has been in place throughout the period under review up to the date of approval of this Annual Report. The effectiveness of this process has been reviewed regularly by the Audit Committee who report their findings for consideration by the Board. The processes used by the Audit Committee to review the effectiveness of the system of internal control include:
- discussions with management on risk areas identified by management and/or the audit process
- the review of internal and external audit plans
- the review of significant issues arising from internal and external audits
- the review of significant Group risks reported by the Group Risk Committee.

The audit Committee reports to the Board the results of their review of the risk assessment process to allow the Board to reach a conclusion as to the effectiveness of the system of internal control.

Audit and internal control

Following the Turnbull guidance for directors on internal control, the Board confirms that there is a process for identifying, evaluating and managing the significant risks to the achievement of the Group's strategic objectives. This process has been in place throughout the period under review up to the date of approval of this Annual Report. The effectiveness of this process has been reviewed regularly by the Audit Committee who report their findings for consideration by the Board.

The processes used by the Audit Committee to review the effectiveness of the system of internal control include:

- discussions with management on risk areas identified by management and/or the audit process
- the review of internal and external audit plans
- the review of significant issues arising from internal and external audits
- the review of significant Group risks reported by the Group Risk Committee.

The audit Committee reports to the Board the results of their review of the risk-assessment process to allow the Board to reach a conclusion as to the effectiveness of the system of internal control.

The Group Risk Committee was established during the year to consolidate and prioritise input received from management of the businesses and corporate functions. The chairman of the Group Risk Committee is the Executive Director for Strategy and Group Control. Other members are the heads of major corporate functions and the Chief Internal Auditor. The Group Risk Committee meets on a regular basis to review input for businesses and corporate management and to report its conclusions to the Audit Committee.

The internal audit function reviews internal controls in all key activities of the Group, typically over a three-year cycle. It acts as a service to the businesses by assisting with continuous improvement of controls and procedures. Actions are agreed in response to its recommendations and these are followed up to ensure that satisfactory control is maintained. In addition, quarterly reviews between internal audit management and the senior management of the businesses and major functions are conducted not only to assess their current control status but also to identify and address any areas of concern.

The Board is responsible for the effectiveness of the Group's system of internal controls. The internal control systems are designed to meet the Group's particular needs and the risks to which it is exposed, and by their nature it can provide reasonable but not absolute assurance against misstatement or loss.

The Board regularly reviews the Group's strategic direction and considers the strategy for the individual businesses on a biannual basis. Yearly plans and performance targets for each business are set by the Chief Executive and are reviewed by the Board in the light of the Group's overall objectives.

The processes to identify and manage the key risks to the success of the Group are an integral part of the internal control environment. Such processes, which are reviewed and improved as necessary, include strategic planning, the appointment of senior managers, the regular monitoring of performance, control over capital expenditure and investments and the setting of high standards and targets for safety, health and environmental performance.

Within the financial and overall objectives for the Group, the management of the Group as a whole is delegated to the Chief Executive and the Executive Directors. The conduct of the individual businesses is delegated to the Executive Management team. They are accountable for the conduct and performance of their businesses within the agreed business strategy. They have full authority to act subject to the reserved powers and sanctioning limits laid down by the Board and to Group policies and guidelines.

Businesses are responsible for meeting the defined reporting timetables and compliance with Group accounting manuals, which set out accounting policies, controls and definitions.

The Executive Management team receives a monthly summary of financial results from each business, and the Group's published quarterly financial information is based on a standardised and timely reporting process.

On completion of all major investments, post-event reviews are carried out by the relevant businesses and reviewed by the Executive Management team. This process helps improve the quality of business judgements.

Responsibility for ensuring compliance with selected Group policies and guidelines has been delegated by the Board to nominated senior functional managers. These nominated managers receive annual compliance reports from Chief Executive Officers of businesses and other senior managers. In turn, there is an annual report to the Audit Committee, on behalf of the Board, on the degree of compliance with Group policies and guidelines. Corrections to any weaknesses found are monitored, and controls are developed to match changing circumstances.

Principles of business conduct

The Group's reputation for high ethical standards is central to its business success. A new Code of Business Conduct has been developed to replace the previous Business Ethics Statement and is now being communicated throughout the Group.

Communications with shareholders

The board believes it is important to respond adequately to the queries of both private and institutional shareholders. The Group responds throughout the year to numerous letters from shareholders on a wide range of issues, while at the Annual General Meeting shareholders are offered an opportunity to raise with the board and respective committee chairmen any specific questions they may have. Directors also meet informally with shareholders after the Meeting.

The Group's website contains up-to-date information on Group activities and published financial results. There is a regular dialogue with individual institutional shareholders as well as presentations to analysts after the quarterly results.

Going concern

After making enquiries, the Board feels that the operation of the Group's control procedures gives a reasonable expectation that the Group has adequate resources to continue in operation for the foreseeable future. Accordingly, they continue to adopt the going-concern basis in preparing the Group accounts.

Compliance with UK Corporate Governance Code

The Group was in compliance throughout the year under review with the provisions of Section 1 of the Code.

SECTION 3

The UK Stewardship Code

5295 The underlying intent of the UK Stewardship Code – issued by the FRC in July 2010 – is to enhance the quality of engagement between institutional investors and the companies in which they invest. "Engagement" in this context means pursuing purposeful dialogue on strategy, performance, and the **management of risk**. It also includes dealing with issues that are the subject of votes at general meetings.

The FRC sees the UK Stewardship Code as complementary to the UK Corporate Governance Code for listed companies, as revised in June 2010. Changes were made to that Code to increase the accountability of company boards and encourage them to seek ongoing dialogue with investors. The UK Stewardship Code is intended to incentivise investors to do the same.

Institutional shareholders are not obliged to engage with investor companies – they are free to elect whether to do so – but their choice should be a considered one based on their investment approach. Their managers or agents are responsible for ensuring that they comply with the terms of the mandate as agreed.

Disclosures made by institutions under the Code should assist companies to understand the approach and expectations of their major shareholders.

The FRC recognises that not all parts of the Code will be relevant to all institutional investors. For example, smaller institutions may judge that some elements of the Code's principles and guidance are disproportionate in their case. In these circumstances investors and providers should take advantage of the "comply or explain" approach and set out why they consider this to be the case.

Scope of the Code – who must apply it

5296 The Code is addressed, primarily, to firms that manage assets on behalf of institutional investors, e.g., pension funds, insurance companies, investment trusts and other collective investment vehicles. These firms should disclose on their websites how, and to what extent, they have complied with the Code. Institutions that manage several types of fund need only make one statement.

The responsibility for an effective engagement process does not rest with asset managers alone. The actions of other investors can have a significant beneficial impact on the quality and quantity of engagement with UK companies, and the FRC encourages all institutional investors to report if and how they have applied the Code, on the same basis as asset managers. Pension funds and other owners that do not wish to become directly involved in engagement can contribute by, for instance, mandating their fund managers to do so on their behalf and scrutinising their reports.

Under the UK Stewardship Code, institutional investors are required to: **5297**
- publicly disclose their policy on **discharging their stewardship responsibilities**;
- publicly disclose their policy on managing **conflicts of interest** in relation to stewardship;
- monitor their **investee companies**;
- establish clear guidelines on when and how they will escalate their activities as a method of **protecting and enhancing shareholder value**;
- show willingness to **act collectively** with other investors, where this is appropriate;
- put in place a clear policy on **voting**, and disclosure of voting activity;
- **report** periodically on their stewardship and voting activities.

CHAPTER 6

Preliminary announcements

OUTLINE ¶¶

The preliminary announcement (report) is a statement of annual results issued by companies listed on a regulated market such as the London Stock Exchange. Following the introduction of the EU Transparency Obligations Directive, preliminary announcements are no longer compulsory. Where listed entities **voluntarily elect** to issue these announcements, they must comply with the Listings Rules and apply the principles underpinning preliminary reporting contained in the statement entitled "Preliminary Announcements" (PA), issued by the ASB. Although listed companies must now adopt IFRS there is no equivalent international accounting standard covering preliminary announcements. **5400**

MEMO POINTS "Preliminary announcements" is a reporting statement issued by the ASB promoting the development of best practice in financial narrative reporting. The statement is outside the scope of the Companies Act and accounting standards and although not mandatory, its use is recommended by the FRC, The Hundred Group of Finance Directors and the London Stock Exchange.

The preliminary report requires the same level of detail, scope and content as the **interim report**. Where an entity voluntarily publishes a preliminary report it must comply with the Listings Rules and make the announcement of the financial results and dividend policy without delay, after board approval. **5402**

There is **no mandatory requirement** for this information to be sent to shareholders. In practice only financial analysts and institutional shareholders receive copies. Companies **can elect to distribute** the information to shareholders via press advertisements, pre-registration schemes or by publishing the information on their website. **5404**

However, there is a requirement under the Companies Act for preliminary announcements to be consistent with the audited full year financial statements, and any changes in accounting policy must also be disclosed.

1. Content

A preliminary announcement **must contain** a summarised: **5406**
- narrative commentary;
- profit and loss account, balance sheet and cash flow statement;
- a statement of total recognised gains and losses; plus
- notes to the accounts.

The ASB statement advocates that **supplementary information** is provided for such items as fixed assets or borrowings, plus other significant items contained in the primary financial statements.

5408 PA (25) The information **must be consistent** with that given in the full report and accounts and must not be altered after publication. The preliminary announcement should state the period covered by the report and the date approved by the board of directors. Sufficient supplementary information supporting the trends or significant events included in the preliminary announcement should be disclosed in the notes to the accounts or on the face of the profit and loss account.

Narrative commentary

5410 The information in the commentary should be in line with the figures in the audited or draft financial statements. A balanced narrative should explain the reasons for significant movements in **key indicators and trends** within the business, including the:
- main factors influencing the company's performance in the financial year (seasonal activity); and
- forthcoming events and changes that could have a significant effect on performance.

5412 The commentary **is not intended to be** as detailed as an operating and financial review, but should draw attention to the summarised balance sheet and cash flow statement by highlighting any key changes since the interim report and financial statements. This particularly concerns working capital, liquidity and net debt.

The commentary and notes to the preliminary announcement should cover **significant movements** in the following:
- acquisitions and disposals of major fixed assets or investments during the year;
- changes in contingencies, commitments and off-balance sheet financial instruments;
- material changes in capital structure or financing;
- post balance sheet events;
- the effect of foreign exchange movements during the year; and
- the impact of revised actuarial valuations on pension costs.

5416 **Final interim period** As the preliminary announcement focuses on the results for the year, the results for the period since the interim report will be subsumed within the total and not normally reported to shareholders. It is important that the salient features of this period are referred to in the management commentary. Separate presentation of the final period results is encouraged in so much that it would facilitate an understanding of the current performance.

Profit and loss account

5420 A summary profit and loss must be provided, **based on a standardised format** of general headings, with additional disclosures as required.

PA (36) The profit and loss account should include the following, with separate identification where applicable, **significant amounts** attributable to joint ventures and associates; namely:
- net turnover;
- operating profit or loss;
- interest payable less interest receivable (net);
- profit or loss before taxation and extraordinary items;
- taxation on profits on ordinary activities;
- profit or loss on ordinary activities after tax;
- minority interests;
- extraordinary items;
- profit or loss for the period attributable to shareholders;
- dividends paid or proposed; and
- earnings per share expressed as pence per share.

Additional disclosures Other important profit and loss disclosures are listed below. 5424

1. The **turnover and operating profit** of any acquisitions and discontinued operations should be disclosed separately on the face of the profit and loss account, in accordance with FRS 3 "Reporting financial performance".

2. **Segmental information** classified by turnover (eliminating inter-segment sales) and segmental profit or loss should be provided on the same basis as in the financial statements; namely profit or loss before accounting for interest, tax and minority interests. Segmental information should be disclosed in the notes to the preliminary announcements. PA(38)

3. Sufficient information should be given to enable users to understand any significant changes in the **effective tax rate** from the prior year. It may be necessary to analyse the tax charge into its significant components; namely UK and overseas tax. PA(39)

4. **Exceptional items** should be disclosed in the preliminary announcement, either on the face of the profit and loss account or in a note in accordance with FRS 3.

5. It is a requirement of listed companies to disclose **earnings per share** expressed as pence per share. **Basic** and **diluted** earnings per share should be calculated and disclosed in the same manner as in the financial statements. Entities that choose to present, in their financial statements, additional amounts per share based on another level of earnings, should also present them in their preliminary announcements, in accordance with FRS 3. An example would be where a company reports an earnings per share adjusted for exceptional items or acquisition goodwill. PA(41)

Balance sheet

A summarised balance sheet **should utilise the same classifications** as those used in the annual financial statements; namely: 5430
- fixed assets;
- current assets (stock, debtors, cash at bank and other current assets);
- creditors: amounts due within one year;
- net current assets;
- total assets less current liabilities;
- creditors: amounts falling due after more than one year;
- provisions for liabilities and charges;
- capital and reserves; and
- minority interests.

Statement of total recognised gains and losses

A statement of total recognised gains and losses (STRGL) should be included where material gains or losses, other than profit or loss for the financial year, are recognised in the period. 5434 PA(44)

A reconciliation of movements in shareholders' funds should be included in the preliminary announcement only where movements other than those in the STRGL need to be explained.

Cash flow statement

The cash flow statement as specified in FRS 1 should comprise the **following categories**: 5436
- net cash inflow or outflow from operating activities;
- dividends received from joint ventures and associates;
- returns on investments and servicing of finance;
- taxation;
- capital expenditure and financial investment;
- acquisitions and disposals;
- equity dividends paid;
- management of liquid resources;
- financing; and
- increase (decrease) in cash.

5438 The preliminary report should also **include a reconciliation** of:
- operating profit to operating cash flow; and
- movement of cash in the period to the movement in net debt, including the effects of changes in short and long-term borrowings, cash and other components of net debt, unless disclosed elsewhere in the preliminary announcement.

Dividend policy

5440 The preliminary announcement **must contain details of** any proposed dividend payment or share distribution covering:
- the net dividend per share;
- the payment date; and
- foreign income dividend elections and any income tax treated as payable at the lower rate and not therefore repayable.

If the entity has decided to withhold any dividend or interest payment on listed securities, details must also be given.

Notes to the accounts

5442 **Comparative figures** for the previous full financial year should be provided in the financial statements. The ASB has recommended in its statement that preliminary announcements should also disclose the period covered by the report and the date it was approved by the board of directors.

Omission of information

5444 The UK Listings Authority may authorise the omission of information from the preliminary announcement upon a written application from an individual company. Agreement is forthcoming where it considers this request appropriate, or where disclosure would be against the public interest or detrimental to the company itself.

2. General requirements

Audited reports

5450 The UK Listing Rules require that preliminary announcements be reviewed and agreed by the auditors.

All the figures in the preliminary announcement should agree with the figures in the **audited financial statements** or in the draft financial statements. The audit of the financial statements should be complete or at least at an advanced stage at the date of the preliminary announcement. If the audit report is to be qualified then the details of the qualification must be given. The preliminary announcement **must also include** any significant additional information that will help in the assessment of the financial results.

Under the Companies Act, entities must state whether a company's auditors have produced an audit report on the statutory accounts, on which the non-statutory accounts (preliminary announcements) are based. If the audit report on the full financial statements has yet to be signed this should be noted in the preliminary accounts.

EXAMPLE **Preliminary results for 2010 (based on draft accounts)**

The preliminary results for the year ended 31 December 2010 are unaudited. The financial information disclosed in the announcement does not constitute the company's statutory accounts for the year ended 31 December 2010, which will be finalised on the basis of the financial information set out by the directors in this preliminary announcement and delivered to the Registrar of Companies after the company's AGM in May 2011.

APB Guidance Guidance has been provided by the Audit Practices Board (APB) on auditors' consent to the release of preliminary announcements. The **advice is that** approval be withheld if: 5453
- the statutory numbers have not been given due prominence;
- the pro-forma information has not been reconciled to the statutory numbers; and
- the pro-forma information is misleading in terms of presentation.

The APB Bulletin provides **additional guidance** on dealing with any fundamental uncertainties in a preliminary report. The APB recommends that the content of the preliminary announcement must be agreed by the Board of Directors or authorised by a committee of the board. The Bulletin **further advocates**:
- that auditors should confirm their agreement to the release of the preliminary announcement through a letter to the directors; and
- the procedures to be followed prior to the approval of the preliminary report.

The APB Bulletin advocates that the audit of the statutory accounts must be at an **advanced stage** before the preliminary report is approved by the auditors. For these purposes, the audit is considered to be at an advanced stage where it is deemed that any outstanding issues will result in changes to the preliminary report.

Change of accounting policy

Following a change in accounting policy, the amounts for the **current and prior year** should 5454
be restated on the basis of the new policies, consistent with the annual financial statements. The **cumulative effect of the policy change** on opening reserves (beginning of the financial year) should be disclosed at the foot of the statement of total recognised gains and losses of the year.

Similar disclosures should be made in respect of **other prior year adjustments** arising from PA(18)
the discovery of fundamental errors. A description should be given to help users understand the nature of each change or adjustment.

CHAPTER 7

Interim reports

OUTLINE ¶¶

Interim reports are intended to be a **progress report** on the operating, financing and investing activities of a company that permits users to both monitor the entity's performance since the publication of its last financial statements and assess the impact of recent developments on the company's operating and financial position. 5500

Guidance on the content of an interim report, together with details of the principles underpinning interim reporting, are enshrined in the following standards/statements: 5502
- "Interim reports" issued by the Accounting Standards Board (ASB);
- Financial Services Agency (FSA) Listing Rules incorporating the new Disclosure and Transparency Rules (DTR);
- IAS 34 "Interim financial reporting";
- EU Transparency Directive.

Type of entity	Regulation
Non-listed companies	**Voluntary** – FSA Listing rules + DTR
Listed Companies – preparing IFRS consolidated accounts	**Compulsory** – IAS 34 – FSA Listing rules + DTR

MEMO POINTS The ASB has issued an exposure draft covering interim reports published by **non-listed companies**, which encompass the requirements of the DTR, issued by the FSA. The proposed changes will have the effect of bringing the current statement "Interim Reports" into line with

IAS 34. The DTRs have been developed by the FSA to permit UK implementation of the EU Transparency Directive.

5504 Interim reports are usually prepared (and signed by the directors) for the **first six months** of the financial year. In **exceptional circumstances**, the UK Listing Authority may grant an extension to this time limit. A **copy of the report** should be sent to the Company Announcement Office.

If an entity's accounting reference date (ARD) **is extended beyond 12 months**, a second interim report must be prepared at the old ARD, or at a date within the last 6 months of the accounting period, to cover the period from the end of the interim report to the selected date. **Groups** must prepare interim reports on a consolidated basis. Some companies with significant interests in the USA may following the American practice of quarterly reporting.

Changes to UK GAAP include the requirement for UK listed companies to apply IAS 34, and publish Interim Management Statements (IMS) and a directors' responsibility statement. For listed entities, the **publication deadline** is 60 days after the end of the financial year.

A. Methods of presentation

5514 The **two recognised methods** of presenting interim reports are the discrete and integral methods. Neither method predominates and the degree of content will vary depending on the industry concerned. A number of areas such as taxation, changes in accounting policies and income and expenditure determined annually, require special treatment in the reporting process.

5516 Int Rep (4) The **choice of method depends on** how the entity views the purpose of the interim report, as either part of a larger accounting period (integral method), or a report distinct from the annual reporting cycle requiring a different approach (discrete approach). Although **the ASB recommends** the use of the discrete approach, it recognises that in practice the result is often a combined approach with some items being based on an integral approach (e.g. taxation and discounts).

The style of presentation of the interim report should mirror that of the entity's annual report. The ASB statement incorporates the key principle that the same **recognition and measurement bases** be used for both interim and year end financial statements. This should enable a fair comparison to be made between different reporting periods and is consistent with both the discrete and the integral method.

Discrete method

5518 Under this method the interim period is treated as an accounting period distinct from the annual reporting cycle. This method has the advantage that the report is underpinned by the same accounting policies and principles as the annual financial statements.

For instance, for certain items of revenue and expense that occur on an annual basis (i.e. commissions), it will be necessary to pro-rata the expense or income for the interim period on some selected basis such as time, or benefits received.

The ASB recommends the discrete approach with the **key exceptions** being the treatment of:
- taxation (estimated effective tax rate for the year); and
- expenses and income determined annually (discounts etc).

Integral method

5520 Under the integral method, the interim report is part of the larger annual reporting cycle. Items are recognised in specific interim periods on the basis of the total annual revenue and expenses being estimated and allocated accordingly. The integral method attempts to relate the interim results to the expected results for the financial year.

In addition, **some alterations** to accounting policies **are permissible** in order that the interim report may give a better assessment of the predicted financial year's results and to enable a more equitable match of costs to revenues generated at different times. This smoothing process helps correct distortions, particularly in seasonal industries such as the holiday industry.

B. Content

The interim report required for the purposes of the UK Listing Authority must contain profit and loss information and a narrative commentary. The **majority of entities** also provide, as recommended by the ASB statement, a summarised balance sheet, cash flow statement, and a statement of total recognised gains and losses, in addition to detailed notes to the accounts, and comparative figures for the preceding financial year. The **general content** of the report will not be affected by the choice of either the discrete or integral reporting method. 5524

Narrative commentary

The commentary often **takes the form of** a Chairman's statement, Managing Director's review or OFR and should explain: 5528 Int Rep (34)
- the reasons underpinning the key indicators and trends in the business;
- the stewardship of the business;
- the regulatory environment; and
- the general trading outlook for the future.

The narrative is not expected to be as comprehensive as an OFR although it could mirror it in structure. Sufficient information should be provided to facilitate an informed assessment of an entity's financial position, including financial highlights by business segment.

The **commentary should also indicate** and explain any movements in **key indicators** such as balance sheet and cash flow changes since the last financial statements, and in particular movements in working capital, liquidity, and net debt.

5530

Additional information	
Financial highlights – in narrative or tabular form	– turnover, EPS, operating profit before/after tax, dividend per share, gearing ratio or assets per share
Other narrative disclosures	– material changes in capital structure, post-interim balance sheet events, acquisitions and disposal of significant investments or fixed assets completed or agreed during the relevant accounting period, post acquisition results of an operation relating to the interim period
Nature of seasonal activity	– its relevance and impact on the company's business cycle. The principles adopted should be stated as well as an assessment of any expected changes resulting from the effects of the different seasons

MEMO POINTS The Financial Reporting Council has published guidance on going concern and liquidity risk assessments. The purpose of the new guidance, is to ensure that these assessments are based on a diligent appraisal of the underlying risks and that the disclosures made are supportable under the circumstances prevailing at the date the interim financial statements are approved.

Summary profit and loss account

5536 Int Rep (40) The key profit and loss disclosures, recommended by the ASB, include:
- turnover;
- operating profit or loss;
- interest payable less interest receivable (net);
- profit and loss on ordinary activities, before taxation and extraordinary items;
- taxation;
- tax on profit or loss on ordinary activities after taxation;
- minority interests;
- profit or loss for the period;
- dividends paid and proposed; and
- earnings per share (for listed companies).

In addition, the ASB statement also recommends that entities provide segmental information (¶750), and an analysis of turnover and operating profit **for continued and discontinued operations**. A note is often also provided detailing the calculation of the earnings per share. If any of the required headings are not suited to the company's activities, they can be adjusted as necessary.

Summary balance sheet

5538 Int Rep (52) A summarised balance sheet should be provided in the **same classifications** as those adopted in the annual financial statements. The classifications incorporated in the Companies Act are recommended (see ¶6500).

The **constituent parts** of current assets must be disclosed. Other categories of assets and liabilities in the balance sheet should be expanded upon if this would improve the level of understanding of the accounts. For example, an entity with significant additions to fixed assets in an interim period should disclose this fact, as it would highlight either considerable investment or the replacement of ageing assets.

Summary cash flow statement

5540 Int Rep (53) The purpose of the cash flow statement is to provide information on the level of sources and utilisation of cash, by an entity in the period covered by the interim report, and is an indication of the relationship between profitability and the cash generating ability of the entity.

5542 The **format** for the cash flow statement is presented in FRS 1 "Cash flow statements" and is presented in outline below. The ASB recommend the disclosure of the total amounts only for each category:
- net cash inflow or outflow from operating activities;
- dividends from associates and joint ventures;
- returns on investments and servicing of finance;
- taxation;
- capital expenditure;
- acquisition and disposals;
- equity dividends paid;
- management of liquid resources; and
- financing.

The ASB recommend the inclusion of a reconciliation of operating profit to net cash inflow from operating activities, and also the reconciliation of operating cash flow and net cash (debt). Comparative information for the previous year should also be given. For a sample layout of a cash flow statement and related disclosures, refer to ¶4000.

Net cash flow to movement in net debt (funds)

5544 This disclosure reconciles the cash movement in the period to the movement in net debt after adjusting for cash flows from liquid resources (i.e. term cash deposits) and cash outflows resulting from any movements in debt. Examples include loan notes issued, exchange differences and any loans or finance leases acquired through subsidiary companies.

Analysis of net funds (debt)

Information on movements in net funds or debt (borrowings less cash and other liquid resources) illustrates how a company finances its activities. The information highlights the entity's **liquidity position** and its **solvency profile**, through an analysis of items such as: 5546
- cash at bank and in hand;
- term deposits;
- current investments;
- overdrafts;
- short and long-term debt; and
- current commitments under finance leases.

Statement of total recognised gains and losses

A statement of total recognised gains and losses (STRGL) should be included in the interim report, where material gains and losses other than profit or loss (for the interim period) are recognised in the period. **Examples include** currency translation differences and property revaluations. Alternatively, an entity could also include a note in its interim report to the effect that the group had no recognised gains or losses during the period other than those reflected in the group profit and loss account. 5548 Int Rep (49)

Investment companies that continually revalue their investment portfolios must provide a statement of total recognised gains and losses. 5550

Shareholders' funds

This information provides a reconciliation of the movements in shareholders' funds between the opening and closing periods, after adjusting, for example, for dividends and share issue proceeds. A **reconciliation is only required when** movements other than those in the STRGL need be explained, such as the revaluation of fixed assets. 5554

Notes to the interim financial statements

The scope and content of the notes to the interim report will vary between entity and between industry. 5556

All interim reports should include notes detailing:
- the period covered by the report;
- the date approved by the board of directors; and
- the extent to which the information has been audited or reviewed.

Other **general disclosures** should include a note confirming that the interim statements have been prepared under the historic cost convention, on the basis of accounting policies consistent with those adopted in the full annual accounts for the year ended (e.g. 31 May 2010). The adoption of any new accounting standards should also be disclosed as in scenario 1.

Detailed disclosure requirements are covered in section C.

EXAMPLE **Scenario 1**

ABC Ltd

Notes to the interim report (extract)

The interim accounts for the half-year ended 30 November 2010 have been prepared in accordance with accounting policies consistent with those adopted in the accounts for the year ended 31 May 2010, which were approved by the directors on 15 August 2010. The interim accounts do not constitute statutory accounts and are unaudited, but have been reviewed by the auditors as confirmed in their report.

Scenario 2
XYZ Ltd
Notes to the interim report (extract)
The interim statement does not constitute full accounts as defined by the Companies Act.
The interim accounts, which are unaudited, have been prepared on the basis of accounting policies consistent with those adopted in the company's 2010 annual report and accounts, except for the adoption of FRS 15 "Tangible fixed assets".

Information that may be omitted

5558 Under the UK Listing Rules certain information may be omitted from the interim report, including the net turnover and the profit and loss before tax and extraordinary items.

These omissions **must be authorised by** the UK listings authority. Such authorisation is only likely in those rare cases where the Authority considers disclosures deemed contrary to the public interest or detrimental to the company, although the purpose of such omissions must not be designed to mislead the users of the report.

C. Accounting treatment and disclosures

5562 A number of problem areas inherent in interim reporting require specific accounting and reporting treatments; the main categories are considered below.

Accounting policies

5564 Int Rep (11) The Listing Rules stipulate that accounting policies and the method of presentation used in the interim report should be consistent with those applied in the annual financial statements.

If at the date the interim report is prepared:	Action
– it is known that an **accounting policy** will be **changed** or a new accounting policy, standard or abstract adopted	any adjustments should be incorporated into the interim report – this ensures consistency with the full year's financial results
– there is a change in accounting policy then **additional disclosures** are required, including:	– the current and prior-period results on the basis of the new policies; and – the cumulative effect of the policy change on opening reserves (in the STRGL)
– an **amended or new accounting policy or standard has not been introduced**	– an estimate of its effect or a statement of explanation should be included
– there are **prior period adjustments**	– arising from the discovery of fundamental accounting errors should also be disclosed by way of note detailing the nature and effect of each change or adjustment

Seasonal industries

5570 Int Rep (16) In certain industries there may be a significant continual variation between **income and profit** in the interim period and the full financial year. Seasonal businesses as such may prefer to adopt the **integral approach** to interim reporting, where estimated expenditures can be allocated to the revenues of interim periods.

However, the ASB recommends that **seasonal variations** be dealt with by disclosure rather than by smoothing the results, with a narrative discussion of material items. Even if there is not a regular or predictable seasonal pattern, the view of the ASB is that fluctuating seasonal revenues are generally understood by the market and as such these variations should be reported as they arise.

Taxation

The **general treatment** is to predict the effective rate of tax for the year and apply it to the interim results. Capital allowances, deferred tax, tax jurisdictions and the tax aspects of exceptional items all require specific treatment. **5572** Int Rep (17)

The **interim tax charge** should be based on an estimate of the likely effective tax rate for the year, expressed as a percentage of the anticipated annual results and applied to the estimated interim profit or loss. This approach includes both permanent and timing tax differences and is in common with the principles used to determine the recognition of annually determined income and expenditure. The interim report should provide a brief explanation of the basis for calculating the effective tax rate in the narrative commentary. **5574**

MEMO POINTS 1. Treating the interim date as a year end for tax purposes would require the calculation of the interim tax charge without consideration of **capital allowances** and other adjustments that could influence the tax rate. However, where capital expenditure is actually planned in advance it may be possible to estimate the total capital allowances in calculating the tax rate for the year. Capital expenditure that is not definitely committed should be excluded from the calculation.
2. The **general approach** of making an **estimate of the effective tax rate** for the year should be used where, for example, a company's results in the first half of the year are expected to be completely offset by its result in the second part of the year. Even if the overall result is break-even then there will still be an effective tax rate applied to both profits and losses. A tax credit for losses should only be recognised if there is a reasonable assurance that it will be reversed in the foreseeable future.

EXAMPLE If there was a tax loss brought forward of £60,000; estimated first half-year taxable profits of £100,000; and an expected second half-year tax loss of £40,000; then tax losses of £60,000 would be absorbed in the first half of the year, leaving £40,000 first half-year taxable profits to be set against second half-year taxable losses of £40,000. This would result in a tax charge (using an effective rate of 30%) of £12,000 in the first half of the year (40,000 x 30%) and a tax credit of £12,000 in the second half of the year, resulting in a nil overall tax charge.

3. If the entity's results cover **several tax jurisdictions** then separate tax calculations will be required for jurisdictions deemed material; alternatively a weighted average of all the rates could be used.

Valuations

Changes in **asset values** should be recognised depending on the type of asset and the difficulty of obtaining valuations. **5576** Int Rep (26)

For **properties** that have been revalued it will usually be sufficient to use the most recent valuations. Property valuations brought forward from the previous year-end that have not been revalued, should include a statement to that effect, along with a management commentary on any material price movements since the last valuation. **5577**

Pension costs and any pension asset or liability recognised in the balance sheet should be based on the latest actuarial valuation unless a significant event, such as a change in the actuarial rules or legislation, renders the previous estimate misleading. **5578**

Stock valuations in the interim accounts should be calculated on the same basis as adopted in the statutory financial statements; if this measurement basis differs, this should be disclosed in the notes to the accounts. **5580**

However, if any **diminutions in the value** of stock **result from temporary factors** such as seasonal issues, that are expected to reverse by the year-end, then it would be misleading to adjust the stock figure in the interim accounts. Permanent diminutions in value should be recognised in the interim accounts.

Foreign exchange

The financial statements of a foreign entity should be translated in a manner consistent with the company's accounting policies. If the **closing rate method** is adopted, then the exchange **5584** Int Rep (25) rate at the end of the interim reporting period should be used. If the **temporal method** is preferred then the average exchange rate over the interim period should be adopted.

Income (expenditure) determined annually

5586 The following types of income and expenditure are often determined on an annual basis when the full financial statements are prepared:
- bonuses;

Int Rep (13)
- sales commissions;
- volume discounts; and
- profit sharing commitments.

In these cases it is necessary to establish whether an obligation to transfer economic benefits exists at the date the interim report is prepared. **If such a constructive or contractual obligation exists** then provision should be made in the interim accounts with disclosure by way of note. Some examples are given below.

EXAMPLE

1. A **discretionary one-off bonus** will only be determined (and therefore recognisable) at the financial year end.

2. Conversely, **profit related bonuses** may be decided on the basis of profits earned throughout the financial year. In such a scenario it is possible to recognise a proportion of the bonus based on profits earned in the interim period.

3. Another example is that of a **volume discount on newspaper advertising** based on spend. In this instance the media will typically reimburse the discount, usually calculated as a percentage of the advertising spend i.e. 5%.

Non-recurring items

5588 Non-recurring items include reorganisation costs, major refits, upgrade or repair costs. Under the discrete approach the costs will be allocated to the period in which they are incurred, whereas the integral approach advocates the costs be spread evenly over the accounting period.

Exceptional items

5590 Exceptional items relate to unusual items that rarely extend beyond one year, and include:
- profits and losses on sale or termination of an operation;
- costs of a reorganisation or restructuring of operations;
- redundancy and associated costs; and
- profits or losses on sale of fixed assets.

Exceptional items should be recognised in the profit and loss account of the interim period in which they occur and disclosed separately, after operating profit and before interest where this is permitted by FRS 3. Other exceptional items should be included under the relevant statutory heading and described by way of a note.

EXAMPLE **Astrid Collections Plc**
Interim report 30 June 2010 – Note to the accounts

4 – Exceptional costs
The company has made provision in its interim accounts for the following exceptional costs:
Restructuring costs including redundancy and other costs incurred in connection with the combination of Argonauts Disposal Ltd and our main disposal operations and the formation of a new business venture, totalling £4.6m.
Loss on the sale of Highway Vehicle Management Ltd of £5.6m.
The total exceptional charge is £10.2m which has been provided for in full in the interim accounts.

Acquisitions and discontinued operations

5592 The turnover and operating profit on acquisitions and discontinued operations as stipulated in FRS 3 should be disclosed on the face of the profit and loss account. The disposal of operations should be regarded as discontinued if the sale or termination is completed in the interim period or prior to the earlier of the elapse of three months from the interim period-end or date the directors approve the interim report.

AIM companies

Companies listed on the alternative investment market must prepare a half-year report, covering the six month period from the end of the financial period for which financial information has been disclosed in its admission document and every six months thereafter. These reports must be filed with the Regulatory Information Service, within three months of the end of the reporting period. Companies can be suspended from the AIM if interim statements are published late. 5593

AIM companies are not mandated to apply IAS 34.

Plus-quoted companies

Plus-quoted companies are governed by The Plus Market Rules and are required to issue interim reports for the first half of each financial year, no later than three months after the end of the period. The interim report should contain the following: 5594
- a statement by the Board, including whether the interim report has been audited; and
- the profit and loss account.

The annual financial results must be published within 5 months of the period end and include, along with the information contained in the interim report, a balance sheet, a statement of earnings per share, comparative information and details of dividend payments.

MEMO POINTS PLUS Markets Group, formerly known as OFEX, is a stock exchange based in London, which has been designated a Recognised Investment Exchange by the UK's Financial Services Authority.

Other important disclosures

5595 Int Rep (55)

Type	Required
Comparative figures	Comparative figures for the financial statements should be presented for the **corresponding interim period** and the previous full financial year
EPS	Int. Rep (48) **Listed companies** are required to disclose EPS as pence per share. The basic EPS is derived from the interim results of the period and calculated and disclosed on the same basis as the year-end
Segmental reporting	(See ¶750) Companies should adopt the same **business or geographical segments** adopted in the full annual report and accounts and disclose segmental turnover (highlighting inter-segment sales if material) and segmental profit or loss before interest, tax and minority interests
Shareholder information	A specific note covering: – shareholder concessions; – share dealing services; – share price information; – address of the head office; – details of the company registrars; – announcements and meetings; – dividend payment dates; and – shareholder enquiries
Interim dividend	Details of the **interim dividend (if any) and payment date** should be given. Comparative figures for the proceeding interim period should also be provided
Interest payable or receivable	The **net figure** for interest payable or receivable should be disclosed in the P & L

Int Rep (43)

Type	Required
Associates and joint ventures	**Where material**, the share of the results of associates and joint ventures should be disclosed separately
High growth companies	The **Listing Rules** allow innovative high growth companies and strategic investment companies to obtain a listing on the stock exchange without a three year record. However, these reports must meet additional reporting requirements including the obligation to produce quarterly activity reports, covering financial and non-financial information
Audit requirements	See below

Audit requirements

5608 Although **not a legal requirement**, some interim reports may be audited or subject to a limited review. The Auditors must confirm that they have reviewed the financial information set out in the interim report (which is the responsibility of the directors), in accordance with the Statement of Standards, entitled "Review of interim financial information performed by the independent auditor of the entity" (ISRE 2410), published by the Auditing Practices Board (APB).

5610 **The report should** outline the scope of the audit, review the procedures applied and give an opinion as to whether:
- the interim financial information has been prepared using **accounting policies** consistent with those adopted in the annual financial statements; and
- **material modifications** need be made to the interim financial information presented.

Set out below is the standard wording given in the APB Bulletin, for use where the auditor has undertaken a review in accordance with the recommendations of that bulletin.

EXAMPLE **Independent review report to ABC Plc**

Introduction
We have been instructed by the company to review the financial information set out on pages 5-8 and we have read the other information contained in the interim report for any apparent misstatements or material inconsistencies with the financial information.

Directors' responsibilities
The interim report, including the financial information contained therein, is the responsibility of, and has been approved by, the directors. The Listing Rules require that the accounting policies and presentation applied to the interim figures should be consistent with those applied in preparing the preceding annual accounts except where any changes, and the reasons for them, are disclosed.

Review work performed
We conducted our review in accordance with the guidance issued by the Auditing Standards Board. A review consists principally of making enquiries of management and applying analytical procedures to the financial information and underlying financial data and, based thereon, assessing whether the accounting policies and presentation have been consistently applied unless otherwise disclosed. A review excludes audit procedures such as tests of controls and verification of assets, liabilities and transactions. The audit is substantially less in scope than an audit performed in accordance with Auditing Standards and therefore provides a lower level of assurance than an audit. Accordingly we do not express an audit opinion on the financial information.

Review conclusion
On the basis of our review we are not aware of any material modifications that should be made to the financial information as presented for the six months ended 31 August 2010.
XYZ & Co
Chartered Accountants
Woking
30 October 2010

Quarterly reporting

Entities with shares listed on a regulated exchange must now issue **interim management statements (IMS)**. The disclosure requirements for IMS are limited and should be published in the period one week after the end of the first quarter and 6 weeks before the end of the second quarter. For instance, a company with a March year end should issue the IMS sometime in the period between early July and mid September. 5612

The disclosures required, include an account of the financial position of the entity, details of any material transactions and a general review of how the business has performed.

EXAMPLE **Peartree's nine-month Interim Management Statement**

Strong trading in all business sectors and full-year guidance raised: adjusted EPS now expected to be approximately 15% ahead of last year This is an update on trading in the first nine months of 2010. Demand in some of our markets remained subdued in the third quarter, and the macroeconomic outlook is still uncertain. Even so, Peartree has increased sales by 7% and adjusted operating profit 15% in the first nine months of 2010. All parts of the company continued to perform strongly, with sales growth of 5% in book publishing, 7% in education and 11% at the news services. Our businesses continue to generate significant growth in digital and in developing markets, and to benefit from further efficiency gains. We are also building our position in developing economies and services businesses, reinvesting some of the Interactive Data sale proceeds in the acquisitions of America's Brookwool Institutes, SEBO and Metrostar. The end of the year is a key selling season in education and consumer publishing, and both businesses face tough comparables in the fourth quarter of 2010. However, we are trading ahead of previous guidance and we now expect full year adjusted earnings per share to increase by approximately 15% on the 2009 base of 65.4p. This guidance includes the profit contribution from Interactive Programmes for seven months of 2010 (compared with a full year in 2009) and assumes that the current exchange rate of £1: $1.57 prevails in the fourth quarter (a 5% movement in the average £: $ exchange rate for the full year has an impact of approximately 1.3p on adjusted earnings per share).

Highlights for the first nine months of 2010

In education, we continue to accelerate our transformation from book publisher to the leading global learning technology and services company through organic investment and bolt-on acquisitions. In North America, this strategy enabled us to gain share and grow faster than our market, with sales growth of 5% in the first nine months. Our Higher Education business grew strongly once again. Its market remains healthy (industry sales up 10% in the first eight months) and our leadership in digital learning continues to produce market share gains. More than 3.5m students have enrolled in an on-line course provided by eUniversity in the first nine months, an increase of almost 39% over last year. More than 5.5m college students have registered for our subject-specific digital learning tools (TryOurLabs), an increase of almost 26%. Our Assessment and Information business remained resilient as we won or renewed a number of contracts including a teacher certification contract in Minnesota and student data systems in Texas.

Sales in International Education are up 8% after nine months. We are benefiting from strong demand in developing markets and for assessment services, English Language learning in China and digital, while developed markets and school publishing are generally soft. In the first nine months, TryOurLab registrations outside North America were up almost 32% on the same period last year to more than 432,000. We are continuing to build our business in fast-growing developing economies, taking a strong position in global English teaching through the acquisition of the Brookwool Institute which now has 428 schools in 27 countries.

Book publishing sales are up 5%. Physical retail markets are tough, but are offset by strong publishing and rapid growth in eBook sales (which have increased threefold), plus innovations in digital publishing, with 16,500 eBook titles now available and a number of children's applications for best-selling brands.

Balance sheet At the start of 2010, Peartree had net debt of £1.1bn. Our 2009 net debt/EBITDA ratio was 1.1x and interest cover was 8.8x. 2010 net debt peaked in June at £1.7bn, following the normal seasonal build-up of working capital in the first half of the year. Strong cash generation and the receipt of the proceeds from the sale of Interactive Data (£1.1bn) on 29 July 2010, partially offset by acquisitions (totalling approximately £0.6bn, reflecting only the first tranche payment for SEBO), helped to reduce our net debt at the end of September 2010 to £0.7bn (September 2009: £1.7bn). We will pay £0.25bn of tax on the Interactive Data disposal proceeds in the fourth quarter.

Exchange rates Peartree generates approximately 60% of its sales in the US. Excluding Interactive Data, a 5 cent move in the average £: $ exchange rate for the full year (which in 2009 was £1: $1.57) has an impact of approximately 1.3p on adjusted earnings per share. The average rate during the first nine months of 2010 was £1: $1.53 (compared to £1: $1.54 in the first nine months of 2009), and the closing rate at the end of September was £1: $1.56).

Forward looking statements Except for the historical information contained herein, the matters discussed in this statement include forward-looking statements. In particular, all statements that express forecasts, expectations and projections with respect to future matters, including trends in results of operations, margins, growth rates, overall market trends, the impact of interest or exchange rates, the availability of financing, anticipated costs savings and synergies and the execution of Peartree's strategy, are forward looking statements. By their nature, forward looking statements involve risks and uncertainties because they relate to events and depend on circumstances that will occur in future. There are a number of factors which could cause actual results and developments to differ materially from those expressed or implied by these forward looking statements, including a number of factors outside Peartree's control. These include international, national and local conditions, as well as competition. Any forward looking statements relate only to the date they are made, and Peartree gives no undertaking to update forward-looking statements to reflect any changes in its expectations with regard thereto or any changes to events, conditions or circumstances on which any such statement is based.

Responsibility statements

5614 Under the new DTR rules, the directors must include a responsibility statement, stating that the interim report gives a true and fair view of the company's financial position at that date. The statement should include details of any related party transactions and the name and position of all signatories to the statement.

EXAMPLE **Management's Statement of Responsibility for Financial Reporting – Interim Report of the Kahnray Group**

The consolidated interim financial statements of the Khanray Group have been prepared by the management, which is responsible for the substance and objectivity of the information contained therein. The same applies to the interim Group management report, which is consistent with the consolidated financial statements and is combined with the management report of the Kahnray Group. Our financial reporting complies with the rules issued by the International Accounting Standards Board, as endorsed by the European Union. The Board of Management conducts the business of the Group in the interests of the shareholders and in awareness of its responsibilities toward employees, communities and the environment in all the countries in which we operate.

Directors' responsibilities
Our declared aim is to deploy the resources entrusted to us in order to increase the value of the Khanray Group as a whole. In accordance with the resolution of the Annual Shareholders' Meeting, the Supervisory Board appointed PWCO as the independent auditor of the consolidated financial statements and of the statements' compliance with IFRS. We can confirm that there are no significant related party transactions.

Review work performed
The scope of the auditor's report also includes Khanray's risk management system, audited in light of the UK Law on Corporate Supervision and Transparency. The consolidated financial statements, the combined management report and the auditor's report were discussed in detail, in the presence of the auditor, by the Audit Committee of the Board of Directors.

Review conclusion
The Board of Management (see page xx for more detail)
30 October 2010

D. Comparison between UK GAAP and IAS (IFRS)

5620 The IASB has developed a **mandatory** International Accounting Standard (IAS 34) covering the reporting of interim financial information. The standard stipulates the form and content of interim reports and **must be adopted by all listed companies**.

The accounting standard advocates the publication of a condensed balance sheet, income statement and cash flow statement and an equivalent form of the STRGL. In addition, certain notes to the accounts are required and the format should follow that of the entity's annual report and accounts.

IAS 34 sets out the **minimum content** of an interim report covering disclosures and the recognition and measurement principles that must be applied. In general, these requirements are similar to the requirements of UK GAAP, as are the requirements covering the disclosure of basic and diluted earnings per share, contingencies, taxation and dividends.

Key differences between UK GAAP and IAS 34

5622

UK GAAP	IAS 34
An interim report is a **voluntary statement** of best practice, **except for** listed companies who are now required to report under IFRS	Entities required or electing to publish an interim report in accordance with IASs must apply IAS 34
Comparatives for the **balance sheet** required for the corresponding interim date in the previous financial year. Comparatives from last annual financial statements recommended (Int. Rep. 56)	Full year comparatives for the balance sheet as at the end of the previous financial year must be disclosed (IAS 34. 20a)
Income statement Comparatives for corresponding prior year interim period required. No requirement to supply year to- date information	Data is required for the current interim period and for the current year to date along with comparatives for both (IAS 34.20b)
Content of interim reports (see ¶5524)	Content must include a condensed balance sheet, income statement and cash flow statement as in UK GAAP. Main differences are in the explanatory notes
Notes to the interim reports The Listing Rules require disclosure of: – a group's prospects – the effective tax rate – the date the interim report is approved by the directors	No equivalent requirements under IAS 34
Segmental information required for both geographical and business segments. (Int. Rep. 43) For **seasonal industries** there is no specific requirement under UK GAAP to present additional financial information	Segmental information on revenues and results should be published for the **primary segment**. Highly seasonal industries are expected to publish financial results for the 12 months to date, along with comparatives (IAS 34.21)
Preliminary announcements ASB best practice requires separate presentation of the final interim results, and corresponding amounts	Significant movements in estimates previously published should be discussed in the annual financial statements where a separate final interim report is not published
Effects of **changes in composition of a group** should be outlined. (Int. Rep 39) Analysis also required of continuing and discontinued operations of turnover and operating profit on face of profit and loss account	Effects of changes in composition of a group should be discussed
No **statement of compliance** with Listing Rules required	Where an interim report is prepared in accordance with IAS 34, this act of compliance must be stated
The interim report **must be lodged** with the Regulatory Information Service, and despatched to holders of listed securities or advertised in the national press	No such requirement under IAS 34
Where the interim report **has been audited** the review report must be included in the interim report	No such equivalent requirement under IAS 34

First-time adoption of IFRS

5626 IFRS 1 (20b) An **entity reporting** under international financial reporting standards **must apply** IFRS 1 "First-time adoption of International Financial Reporting Standards", to each interim report that it presents under IAS 34, for the period covered by its first IFRS financial statements. This could result in an extensive interim report being prepared in order to meet the reconciliation requirements of IFRS 1 (outlined below) and the requirements of IAS 34, although the impact of the transition to IFRS in terms of reporting will vary from entity to entity.

The **minimum disclosure requirements** for an interim report prepared under IAS 34 **will not be adequate**, as the financial statements prepared under IFRS could differ significantly from those previously prepared under UK GAAP, in terms of presentation, recognition, measurement and disclosure requirements.

Accounting policies	Key reconciliations
1. **Changes in accounting policy** resulting from transition to IFRS must be reflected in interim financial statements in year of transition	The entity must disclose how the **change to IFRS** has affected its financial performance and cash flows, through reconciliations in the notes to the interim financial statements
2. **Subsequent interim reports** should use the accounting policies adopted in the last annual financial statements, except for changes in accounting policy	The **following reconciliations** are required by IFRS 1 **for the 1st set of IFRS financial statements** and any interim reports covered by this period: **a.** equity reported under UK GAAP to equity stated under IFRS as at: – the date of transition to IFRS; and – end of the period covered by the last financial statements under UK GAAP **b.** a reconciliation of the profit (or loss) stated under UK GAAP in the entity's most recent annual financial statements to the profit (or loss) under IFRS for the corresponding period.
3. **Current changes in accounting policy** should be reflected in the next annual financial statements (IAS 34.28)	The reconciliations set out in 2 above **are also required** where an entity has published an interim financial report for the corresponding amounts in the previous year
4. Where an interim report prepared under IAS 34 **covers part of a period** covered by the **first financial statements under IFRS,** the entity must restate the comparatives	Where **quarterly financial reports** are prepared in accordance with IAS 34, the reconciliations listed in 2 above should be included in the interim financial report

5628 **AIM companies** AIM companies must now report under IFRS.

AIM companies reporting under IFRS for the first time **have a choice of preparing** an interim report under IAS 34 or complying with the minimum disclosures set out in the AIM rules. AIM companies are not subject to the new Disclosure and Transparency Rules (DTR).

CHAPTER 8

Post-balance sheet events

OUTLINE ¶¶

Events that occur between the balance sheet date and the date on which the financial statements are approved by the board of directors, are known as post-balance sheet events. The **two categories** of post-balance sheet events are **adjusting** and **non-adjusting events**, each of which requires a different accounting treatment. **5700** FRS 21 (3)

The **main principle** is that adjusting events require changes to be made to amounts included within the financial statements whereas material non-adjusting events need only be addressed by way of a note to the accounts.

The key reporting standard is FRS 21 "Events after the Balance Sheet Date", which is **mandatory** for all reporting entities **except those** applying the Financial Reporting Standard for Smaller Entities (FRSSE). Events occurring after the date the accounts are signed by the directors are not covered by FRS 21. Listed entities apply IAS 10 'Events after the balance sheet date'. **5702** FRS 21 (8)

1. Adjusting events

Adjusting events are those events that **existed at the balance sheet date**, but for which information only came to light later, thus requiring a revision of the amount recorded in the financial statements. **5706** FRS 21 (8)

Failure to recognise the effect of these adjusting events on the financial statements may raise doubts as to the appropriateness of the going concern assertion.

Statutory events, custom and practice

The statutory requirements **include the following**: **5710** FRS 21 (22)
– a declaration of dividends paid by subsidiaries and associate companies relating to periods prior to the balance sheet date;
– the effects of significant changes in rates of taxation; or
– amounts appropriated to reserves.

Non-statutory events

5712 FRS 21 (9) It is not possible to produce a definitive list of potential non-statutory events. The **following list** gives some possible examples but is not intended to be exhaustive:

1. Valuations that provide evidence of an impairment (¶1550) in value e.g. property or other fixed asset investments.
2. Changes in debtor balances due to a renegotiation of the terms or insolvency of one of the debtors.
3. Discovery of fraud or material errors.
4. Subsequent determination of a purchase price or proceeds of a sale of assets purchased or sold before the year-end.
5. Incorrect (material) estimates of profits on long term contracts (¶2200).
6. Sale proceeds from stock (¶2000) after the balance sheet date differing from net realisable value.
7. Receipt of information regarding rates of taxation.
8. The determination after the balance sheet date of profit-sharing or bonus payments, relating to legal or constructive obligations to make such payments, at the balance sheet date.
9. Insurance or other legal claims not quantified at the balance sheet date. For instance, the settlement of a court case after the balance sheet date that results in the entity effectively having an obligation at the balance sheet date. As a result, any previous provision recognised under FRS 12 should be adjusted or a new provision recognised.
10. Discontinued operations.

5714 **Discontinued operations** A decision to terminate an operation made after the end of the financial period, but before the accounts are signed, will constitute an "adjusting event", even if this indicates that applying the going concern concept to the whole or a significant part of the company is not appropriate. In this instance, **a provision for anticipated losses** arising from the closure should be made, as well as disclosure by way of note and the disclosures required by FRS 3, "Reporting financial performance", given in the profit and loss account and notes thereto.

5716 FRS 12 (75) In accordance with FRS 12 "Provisions, contingent liabilities and contingent assets", **closure** or **reorganisation** provisions may only be included as an adjusting event where the closure was effectively in progress at the end of the year.

Taxation

5720 There are a number of areas where tax problems can arise in relation to post balance sheet events, including directors' emoluments and loan accounts. Directors' emoluments such as bonuses, are often determined after the year-end on the basis of draft final accounts and any provisions made will impact on the corporation tax charge for the financial year. These provisions are classified as adjusting events and are charged to the profit and loss account with the credit to the directors' loan account. A tax obligation (PAYE/NI) could arise at the time the bonus is credited and therefore only the net bonus should be credited.

The picture can be further complicated by other post balance sheet adjustments resulting from, for instance, stock valuation adjustments, provisions for warranty claims, or valuation of long term work in progress.

Disclosures

5722 FRS 21 (17) The **general rule** is that all **adjusting post-balance sheet events** must be reflected in the financial statements. Separate disclosure of adjusting events by way of note is not a specific requirement of the standard.

However, the Companies Act requires that the **directors' report** includes particulars of materially adjusting events affecting the company which have occurred since the year-end, although the Act does not make any distinction between adjusting and non-adjusting events.

Window dressing The reversal in the post-balance sheet period of significant sales recorded prior to the balance sheet date, in order to boost turnover and debtors, is more commonly known as window dressing. This practice is discouraged. 5723

2. Non-adjusting events

Non-adjusting post-balance sheet events are categorised as such, if no evidence of any transaction existed at the balance sheet date but is forthcoming before the accounts are signed. 5730 FRS 21(3b)

However, **if the event is material** then disclosure should be made by way of a note to the accounts, in order to ensure that the financial statements are not misleading.

The **most common types** of disclosed non-adjusting events include the following:
- financial restructuring;
- the management of fixed assets; and
- operational activities.

MEMO POINTS The ASB has issued guidance on the accounting treatment for contingent fee arrangements that are incomplete at the balance sheet date. The resolution of a contingent event in the post-balance sheet period is deemed to have occurred after the balance sheet date and, as such, the accounting treatment adopted at the financial year-end should not be adjusted. The ASB has also confirmed the use of two generally accepted accounting treatments covering costs incurred under contingent fee contracts that straddle a period end. The costs can either be expensed as incurred or recognise as work in progress at the balance sheet date.

Financial restructuring

Financial restructuring includes: 5732
- mergers and acquisitions;
- reconstructions; and
- issues of shares and debentures.

EXAMPLE **X Ltd. Report and accounts**
Non-adjusting event – acquisitions

A company prepared its balance sheet as at 31 December 2010 which was then approved by the board of directors on 31 March 2011. On 20 February 2011 the company announced the acquisition of a 100% stake in BSE Energy, based in Northumberland. As the contract was signed after the financial year-end it is classified as a **non-adjusting event** with the following information being disclosed by way of note.

Notes to the accounts (extract)

The company agreed to pay £200m. As at 31 December 2010 BSE Energy had net debt of £135m and preference shares totalling £65m. The acquisition will be wholly financed from existing internal resources and is conditional upon both groups of shareholders as well as the regulatory authorities approving the deal.

Management of fixed assets

Management of fixed assets includes the: 5734
- purchases and sales of fixed assets and investments;
- fixed assets or stock losses resulting from a catastrophe such as fire or flooding; and
- a post-balance sheet decline in the value of fixed assets or property (verified).

An example of a non-adjusting event is a fall in the market value of investments between the balance sheet date and the date the financial statements are authorised. As the fall in value does not usually reflect conditions that existed at the balance sheet date, the value of the investments is not adjusted, although additional disclosures in the notes may be required.

Operational activities

5736 Operational activities include the following:
- exchange rate fluctuations;
- government action (i.e. nationalisation), strikes or other labour disputes;
- opening or extending new trading activities; and
- the discontinuance of a business not envisaged at the year-end.

EXAMPLE **Exchange rate fluctuations**

Company A has translated the results of its **overseas subsidiary** at the exchange rate prevailing at the balance sheet date. Subsequent to the financial year-end the sterling-zloty exchange rate declined turning a small moderate profit into a loss. Accordingly, the effect of the exchange rate fluctuations should not be adjusted for in the financial statements although they should be referred to in the directors' report as a post-balance sheet event.
If the **fluctuations are so material** that non-disclosure might affect the true and fair view, then their financial effect should be estimated and disclosed by way of note to the financial statements as a non-adjusting post balance sheet event.

5738 **Directors' interests** Any change in directors' interests occurring between the end of the financial period and a date not more than one month prior to the date of the notice of the annual general meeting, at which the financial statements are presented, should be disclosed. Similar rules apply to **major interests** in a company's share capital.

Dividends

5739 FRS 21 (12) Where an entity declares a dividend to holders of equity instruments **after the balance sheet date**, it is not required to recognise those dividends as a liability under FRS 12 at the balance sheet date. This is because the obligation does not meet the criteria of a present obligation in FRS 12. Details must, however, be given in the notes to the accounts. Dividends declared by a subsidiary or associate company after the balance sheet date should also be treated as a non-adjusting event.

Disclosures

5740 FRS 21 (21) Disclosure of post-balance sheet events are required where:
- the event is a **material non-adjusting event** and where non-disclosure would impair the ability of users of financial statements to fully understand the financial position; or
- the **going concern assertion** is brought into question resulting from, for instance, a deterioration in the trading results and financial position of the entity or the withdrawal of credit facilities by the bank.

An entity **should not prepare financial statements** on a going concern basis if it intends to liquidate the entity or cease trading. If the deterioration in operating performance and financial position after the balance sheet date is very severe, and calls into question the going concern assumption, a fundamental change to the basis of accounting is required, rather than adjusting the amounts originally recognised.

MEMO POINTS 1. The standard does not give a measurement or definition of **immateriality** as it is dependent on the size and nature of an item and the particular circumstances in which it arises. The extent to which an item of accounting information is material is determined by the fact that its omission from the financial statements could influence the decision making of its users.
2. The planned **reduction in corporation tax rates** of 1% per annum over a 4-year period to 2014 will have implications for deferred tax calculations and their disclosure. Amendments to tax legislation are usually not reflected in the amounts included in the balance sheet until the law is in force at the relevant balance sheet date. However, FRS 21, "Events after the balance sheet date", requires non-adjusting post-balance sheet events to be disclosed in relation to announced changes in tax rates, where the effect is material and where the changes have not yet been enacted.

5741 The **general rule** is that disclosure of non-adjusting events should be stated by way of a note to the accounts and include the nature of the event and an estimate of the financial effect. If this is not possible then a statement should be added advising that it is not possible to quantify the effect. Where applicable, any taxation implications should be separately disclosed.

EXAMPLE **Infrarail Group Plc**
Annual report and accounts 2010
Notes to the financial statements (extract)

Non-adjusting post-balance sheet events
Non-adjusting post-balance sheet events arising from the actions of the secretary of state for transport, local government and the regions are:

Administration order
The administration order against Infrarail Plc placed it in a position of default in relation to debt of £2,963m included within creditors greater than one year, which immediately became repayable on demand. No adjustment has been made to reflect this and the debt has been classified in the summary group balance sheet consistent with the position as at 30 September 2010.

Channel Tunnel Rail Link Railway derivatives
In 2010 Infrarail Limited entered into a series of interest rate swaps and gilt lock transactions to hedge the financing costs associated with the purchase of section 1 of the CTRL. The bank providing these hedges required certain standard credit protection terms, which subsequently gave it the option to force termination of these hedges should Infrarail be placed in administration. To avoid unnecessary losses and an event of default within Infrarail Limited, the directors pre-emptively instructed the bank to unwind the hedges in an orderly manner. The final termination value of the hedges was a loss of £15.8m

Other non-adjusting post-balance sheet events are:

Infrarail Travel
As disclosed in Note 1, Awayday Ltd, a **joint venture** between Infrarail Travel and First Group, closed its website and ceased commercial operations on 15 November 2010. Investments include a balance of £61,000 in respect of an investment in Awayday Ltd. No provision has been made for additional cost that may be incurred to complete the disposal or closure of the company, including an agreed settlement with the Normanton Group of £1.6m.

Date of authorisation An entity is required to disclose the date the financial statements were authorised for issue and the signatory. If the owners have the power to amend the financial statements after issue, the entity should disclose this fact. 5742

Updating disclosures Where an entity receives information after the balance sheet date concerning events that existed at the balance sheet date, the disclosures should be updated to reflect the new information. This information should be supplied even when it does not affect the amounts recognised in the financial statements. An example would be where evidence comes to light after the balance sheet date, concerning a contingent liability that existed at the balance sheet date. 5743 FRS 21 (19)

Reclassification of non-adjusting events

In **exceptional circumstances** and in accordance with the **prudence concept**, an event previously classified as non-adjusting may need to be redefined as an adjusting event. In this instance full disclosure of the adjustment is required. 5744

An example would be the disposal of a significant fixed asset after the balance sheet date that was not previously envisaged and that would normally have been classified as a non-adjusting event. 5746

However, **if a large loss was incurred** on the disposal of an asset, this might provide evidence of an impairment requiring an adjustment to the value of fixed assets recorded in the balance sheet, as required by FRS 11. It should be noted that the standard itself does not provide any guidance as to the circumstances under which the provision should be applied.

Adjusting events should not be reclassified as non-adjusting events.

Summary

5750

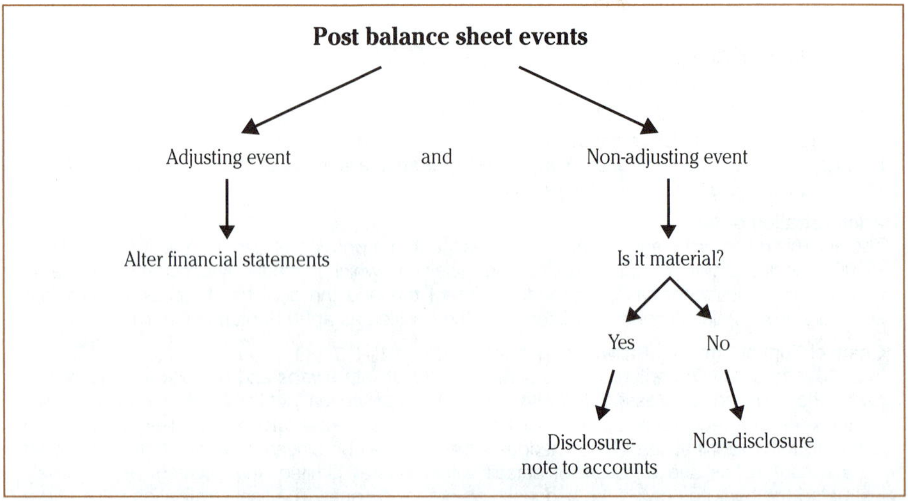

Adjusting events: Conditions exist at the balance sheet date. Separate disclosure by way of note is not specifically required by the standard, although the Companies Act requirements for the directors' report may well require disclosure.

Non-adjusting events: Conditions did not exist at the balance sheet date. Disclosures required in the notes to the accounts for material items.

3. Comparison between UK GAAP and IAS (IFRS)

5754 The relevant international accounting standard is IAS 10 "Contingencies and events occurring after the balance sheet date". The requirements, scope and effective date of IAS 10 are identical to FRS 21. There are no major differences between UK GAAP and IFRS.

First-time adoption

5758 The **general rule** is that an entity should apply IAS 10 in determining whether:
– its opening IFRS balance sheet reflects an event that occurred after the transition date to IFRS; and
– comparative balance sheet amounts in its first IFRS financial statements reflect an event that occurred after the end of the comparative period.

In applying the above rule, certain modifications in IFRS 1 need to be reviewed, to determine whether changes in estimates qualify as adjusting or non-adjusting events at the transition date to IFRSs.

5759 **Adjusting events** Where an entity has made estimates based on accounting policies that are inconsistent with its accounting policies under IFRS, then the entity is required to adjust its opening IFRS balance sheet to account for the differences in accounting policies.

5760 **Non-adjusting events** Estimates made under IFRS must be consistent with estimates made under previous GAAP (based on adoption of similar accounting policies), unless the previous estimates are clearly inaccurate. In this instance, the entity reports any adjustments to estimates in the next reporting period, rather than as an adjusting event resulting from information gleaned about conditions that existed at the date of transition to IFRS.

CHAPTER 9

Auditors' reports

OUTLINE ¶¶

A. Audit reports on Annual Financial Statements

All companies incorporated under the Companies Act are obliged to produce annual financial statements which, together with the reports of the directors and that of the auditors, must be sent to every member, every debenture holder, and every person who is entitled to receive notice of general meetings. In addition, a copy must be lodged with the Registrar of Companies. **5800** s 394 CA 2006

As discussed in the appropriate sections, certain companies are able to claim exemption from the general duty to have their financial statements audited – e.g., dormant companies (see ¶6430) and small companies (see ¶6070) – but this chapter is concerned with entities that are not exempt. While auditors are called upon in the course of their varied engagements to issue many kinds of reports, the majority issued by them are those **addressed to the shareholders** in respect of annual financial statements.

The Act specifies that the accounts should comprise a balance sheet, a profit and loss account and accompanying notes that give a true and fair view (¶2) of the state of affairs of the reporting entity at the end of the financial year and of the profit or loss for the period then ended.

Company law requires the auditors to state explicitly whether, in their opinion, the company's annual accounts have been **prepared in accordance with the Act** and **give a**

true and fair view. In determining whether the financial statements give a true and fair view, the auditor should consider the accounting requirements not only of the Act but also **Financial Reporting Standards** and other pronouncements by the accounting profession – such as UITF abstracts, or industry-specific guidance such as the charities SORP. Where a company fails to comply with any of these, an auditor will have to assess the effect and consider whether the audit opinion on those financial statements should include details of how the company has failed to comply.

5801 In addition, auditors are required to satisfy themselves that proper accounting records have been kept and that the financial statements are in agreement with them. Moreover, they must make certain that any information given in the directors' report is consistent with the books and records of the company.

If any of these requirements are not met, or if the auditors have not been able to obtain all the necessary information and explanations required to enable them to form their opinion, they are obliged to disclose this fact in their report.

With regard to information that is required to be given in the directors' report or elsewhere in the financial statements – e.g., disclosures of directors' emoluments, benefits, loans or transactions required by Schedule 3 of The Small Companies and Groups (Accounts and Directors' Report) Regulations 2008 (SI 2008/409) and Schedule 5 to the Large and Medium-sized Companies and Groups (Accounts and Reports) Regulations 2008 (SI 2008/410) – if the directors fail to provide this information, the auditors should do so.

5802 In the following paragraphs, the various **essential elements of an auditors' report** are discussed. These are:
- a title identifying the persons to whom the report is addressed;
- an introduction identifying the financial statements referred to;
- a headed section dealing with both directors' and auditors' responsibilities;
- a headed section dealing with the basis of the auditors' opinion (scope paragraph);
- a headed section expressing the auditors' opinion;
- the auditors' name and signature;
- the auditors' address; and
- the date of the report.

5803 The coming into force of the **Companies Act 2006** and strong support for a shorter audit report by institutional investors, preparer organisations, public sector bodies and some auditing firms following the Auditing Practices Board's 2007 Discussion Paper "The Auditor's Report: A time for change? " resulted in the revision of ISA 700 in 2009.

In December 2010, the APB issued Bulletin 2010/2 "Compendium of Illustrative Auditor's Reports on United Kingdom Private Sector Financial Statements for periods ended on or after 15 December 2010." This bulletin was in turn revised in February 2011 to reflect an auditor's responsibility to report on reading all financial and non-financial information in the annual report and to identify any material inconsistencies. This additional responsibility is for financial periods ending on or after 23 March 2011. (See ¶5809)

The examples of audit reports given in this chapter are taken from the most recently revised ISA 700, unless otherwise explained.

1. Title

5804 ISA 700 (Revised) (7) ISA 700 (Revised) states that the auditors' report should have an appropriate title and that it may be appropriate to use the term "Independent Auditor" to distinguish the auditors' report from reports that might be issued by others.

2. Addressee

5805 ISA 700 (Revised) (8) The auditors' report should be appropriately addressed. The Companies Act 2006 requires the auditor to report to the company's members because the audit is undertaken on their behalf. Auditors' reports are therefore typically addressed to either the members or shareholders of the company.

> EXAMPLE Sample Title and Address
> INDEPENDENT AUDITORS' REPORT TO THE MEMBERS OF A LIMITED

3. Identification of financial statements

The **auditors' report** should identify the financial statements that have been audited, including the date of and period covered by the financial statements. 5806 ISA 700 (8)

Usually, the financial statements of larger companies contain other financial information (e.g., in the directors' report or the chairman's statement). Auditors have no responsibility for such information beyond being satisfied that it is not inconsistent with the financial statements or otherwise misleading. It is therefore necessary that they **clearly identify** the parts of the financial statements to which their opinion does refer.

> EXAMPLE We have audited the annual financial statements of [*name of entity*] for the year ended [*date*], which comprise the profit and loss account, the balance sheet, the cash flow statement, the statement of total recognised gains and losses, and the related notes 1 to 22. The financial reporting framework that has been applied in their preparation is applicable law and United Kingdom Accounting Standards (United Kingdom Generally Accepted Accounting Practice).

Auditors' reports of entities that do not publish their financial statements on a web site – or publish them in 'PDF' format – may continue to refer to the financial statements by means of page numbers.

> EXAMPLE We have audited the annual financial statements of [*name of entity*] for the year ended [*date*] which comprise the profit and loss account, the balance sheet, the cash flow statement, the statement of total recognised gains and losses, and the related notes set out on pages 28 to 48. The financial reporting framework that has been applied in their preparation is applicable law and United Kingdom Accounting Standards (United Kingdom Generally Accepted Accounting Practice).

It is becoming increasingly common for this introductory paragraph to include wording specifically designed to limit the parties to whom the auditor acknowledges responsibility or duty of care. This development has not taken place under the aegis of the APB but rather as a decision by some members of the profession.

> EXAMPLE **Sample of wording to limit the parties to whom auditors acknowledge responsibility**:
> This report is made solely to the company's members, as a body, in accordance with Sections 495 and 496 of the Companies Act 2006. Our audit work has been undertaken so that we might state to the company's members those matters we are required to state to them in an auditors' report and for no other purpose. To the fullest extent permitted by law, we do not accept or assume responsibility to anyone other than the company and the company's members as a body, for our audit work, for this report, or for the opinions we have formed.

MEMO POINTS If the company is a quoted company, this disclaimer should also include a reference to Section 497 of the Companies Act 2006: "This report is made solely to the company's members, as a body, in accordance with Sections 495, 496 and 497 of the Companies Act 2006".

In the case of small and medium-sized companies that prepare financial statements in accordance with FRSSE, the auditors should refer to this fact in the introductory paragraph of their report. They can also – but need not – draw attention to such a company's exemption from the requirement to present a **cash flow statement**. 5807

> EXAMPLE **Extract from auditors' report of a company that prepares its financial statements in accordance with the FRSSE**
> We have audited the annual financial statements of [*name of entity*] for the year ended [*date*] comprising the profit and loss account, the balance sheet, the statement of total recognised gains and losses and the related notes 1 to 22. The financial reporting framework that has been applied in their preparation is applicable law and the Financial Reporting Standard for Smaller Entities

(Effective April 2008) (United Kingdom Generally Accepted Accounting Practice applicable to Smaller Entities).

4. Respective responsibilities of auditors and directors

5808 ISA 700 (Revised) (11) The report should include a statement that distinguishes between the responsibilities of auditors, and those of directors. The distinction would be clearly expressed by including the following:
- a statement that the preparation of the financial statements is the **responsibility of the directors**,
- a **description** of these responsibilities or a reference to them if they appear elsewhere in the financial statements or accompanying information,
- a statement that the auditors' responsibility is to audit and **express an opinion** on the financial statements in accordance with an applicable legal requirements and International Standards on Auditing (UK and Ireland). The report should also state that those standards require the auditor to comply with the APB's Ethical Standards for auditors,
- the nationality of the accounting standards and the law under which the financial statements have been prepared.

EXAMPLE **Extract from auditors' report**

Respective responsibilities of directors and auditors

As described in the Director's Responsibilities Statement, the company's directors are responsible for the preparation of the financial statements and for being satisfied that they give a true and fair view. Our responsibility is to audit the financial statements in accordance with applicable law and International Standards on Auditing (UK and Ireland). Those standards require us to comply with the Auditing Practices Board's Ethical Standards for Auditors.

5. Scope of the audit of the financial statements

5809 APB Bulletin 2010/2 (2) The auditor's report should either:
- cross refer to a "Statement of the Scope of an Audit" that is maintained on the APB's website; or
- cross refer to a "Statement of the Scope of an Audit" that is included elsewhere in the Annual Report; or
- include a description of the scope of an audit as given in the following example.

EXAMPLE An audit involves obtaining evidence about the amounts and disclosures in the financial statements sufficient to give reasonable assurance that the financial statements are free from material misstatement, whether caused by fraud or error. This includes an assessment of: whether the accounting policies are appropriate to the company's circumstances and have been consistently applied and adequately disclosed; the reasonableness of significant accounting estimates made by the directors; and the overall presentation of the financial statements. **In addition, we read all the financial and non-financial information in the [*describe the annual report*] to identify material inconsistencies with the audited financial statements. If we become aware of any apparent material misstatements or inconsistencies we consider the implications for our report.**

MEMO POINTS The last two sentences (in bold type) were added by a revision to ISA 700 (and also to Bulletin 2010/2) issued in February 2011. Inclusion of these two sentences is mandatory in respect of financial periods ended on or after 23 March 2011 although earlier adoption is permitted.

6. Classification of companies

5810 APB Bulletin 2010/2 (5) Company Law and the Listing Rules classify companies in a number of ways, which affect the content of the auditors report. These differences are shown in the examples provided throughout the chapter.

Small companies

The small companies' regime applies to the accounts of a company for a financial year during which it qualifies as small. An auditor's report in such a case must state that the financial reporting framework applied in their preparation is "applicable law and the Financial Reporting Standard for Smaller Entities". 5811

Publicly traded and non-publicly traded companies

Publicly traded companies are defined as those whose securities are admitted to trading on a regulated market in any member state in the European Union while non-publicly traded companies are those having no such securities. 5812

MEMO POINTS If a publicly traded company governed by the law of a Member State is required to prepare consolidated accounts, these must follow international accounting standards (IAS). The rule does not apply where a publicly traded company is not required to prepare consolidated accounts.

Publicly traded companies are also required to include a Corporate Governance Statement in their annual report. If this statement has not been prepared, the auditors must make a statement to this effect under the heading "Matters on which we are required to report by exception."

Quoted and listed companies

The Companies Act also classifies companies as being either **quoted or unquoted**. For the purposes of the auditor's report the implication of being a quoted company is that a directors' remuneration report is required, and the auditor has to report on certain elements of it. 5813

Similarly, a company that is **listed** on the Official List maintained by the United Kingdom Listing Authority (UKLA) will either have a Premium or a Standard Listing for each listed security. For the purposes of the auditor's report, a standard listing does not give rise to additional requirements over that of a non-traded company (but they must meet the requirements with respect to a corporate governance statement). Audit reports for listed companies are discussed further at ¶5830.

7. Opinion on the financial statements

The opinion paragraph of the auditors' report should clearly state the auditor's opinion as required by the relevant financial reporting framework used to prepare the financial statements including applicable law. 5814 ISA 700 (Revised) (17)-(21)

a. Unqualified opinion

When expressing an unqualified opinion on the financial statements prepared in accordance with a true and fair framework, the opinion paragraph should clearly state that the financial statements give a true and fair view. An unqualified opinion on the financial statements should be expressed only when the auditor concludes that the financial statements have been prepared in accordance with the identified financial reporting framework, including the requirements of applicable law, and that the financial statements give a true and fair view. 5816

EXAMPLE **Extract from auditors' report**

Opinion on financial statements

In our opinion the financial statements:

– give a true and fair view of the state of affairs of the Company at [date], and of the company's profit (loss) for the year then ended;

– the financial statements have been properly prepared in accordance with United Kingdom Generally Accepted Accounting Practice; and
– have been prepared in accordance with the requirements of the Companies Act 2006.

If the company reports under FRSSE, the opinion section will read as follows:

Opinion on financial statements
In our opinion the financial statements:
– give a true and fair view of the state of the company's affairs at [date], and of its profit (loss) for the year then ended;
– have been properly prepared in accordance with United Kingdom Generally Accepted Accounting Practice applicable to Smaller Entities; and
– have been properly prepared in accordance with the requirements of the Companies Act 2006.

5816 s 496 CA 2006 The auditor must state in his report on the company's annual accounts whether in his opinion the information given in the directors' report for the financial year for which the accounts are prepared is consistent with those accounts.

The auditor should address this additional reporting responsibility in a separate section of the auditor's report following the opinion on the financial statements.

EXAMPLE **Extract from auditors' report**

Opinion on other matter prescribed by the Companies Act 2006
In our opinion the information given in the Directors' Report for the financial year for which the financial statements are prepared is consistent with the financial statements.

5817 s 498 CA 2006 A company's auditor, in preparing his report, must carry out such investigations as will enable him to form an opinion as to:
– whether adequate accounting records have been kept by the company and returns adequate for the audit have been received from branches not visited by him; and
– whether the company's individual accounts are in agreement with the accounting records and returns.

If the auditor reaches the opinion that:
– adequate accounting records have not been kept or that returns adequate for the audit have not been received from branches not visited; or
– that the company's individual accounts are not in agreement with the accounting records and returns,

he should report on these matters by exception.

In addition, if the auditor:
– fails to obtain all the information and explanations which, to the best of his knowledge and belief, are necessary for the purposes of his audit; or
– finds that disclosures of directors' remuneration required by company law have not been made,

he should state that fact in his report.

Issues such as the above should be included under a separate heading "Matters on which we are required to report by exception" and should include a suitable conclusion in respect of these matters. Where the auditor has discharged his responsibilities and has nothing to report in respect of them, the conclusion can be expressed as in the following example.

EXAMPLE **Extract from auditors' report**

Matters on which we are required to report by exception.
We have nothing to report in respect of the following matters where the Companies Act 2006 requires us to report to you if, in our opinion:
– adequate accounting returns have not been kept, or returns adequate for our audit have not been received from branches not visited by us;
– the financial statements are not in agreement with the accounting records and returns;
– certain disclosures of directors' remuneration specified by law are not made; or
– we have not received all the information and explanations we require for our audit.

Where auditors wish to emphasise a matter that does not affect their unqualified opinion (for instance, the possible outcome of a lawsuit), this can be expressed as follows: 5818 ISA 700 (Revised) (30)

EXAMPLE In forming our opinion, which is unqualified, we have considered the adequacy of the disclosures made in Note 31 to the financial statements concerning the possible outcome of a lawsuit, in which the company is the defendant, alleging infringement of certain patent rights and claiming royalties and punitive damages. The company has filed a counter action, and preliminary hearings and discovery proceedings on both actions are in progress. The ultimate outcome of the matter cannot at present be determined. No provision for any liability that may result has been made in the financial statements.

b. Other opinions

Where: 5819 ISA (Revised) 700 (57)

– there is a **disagreement** with those charged with governance regarding the acceptability of the accounting policies selected, or the method of their application to the adequacy of financial statement disclosure; or

– there is a **limitation on the scope** of the auditors' work, the effect of which is or may be material to the financial statements,

the auditors cannot express an unqualified opinion.

Their opinion must therefore be expressed in one of the following alternative ways:
- a **qualified** opinion;
- an **adverse** opinion; or
- a **disclaimer** of opinion.

The table below summarises the circumstances giving rise to the various opinions. Each is discussed in detail subsequently. 5820 ISA 700 (Revised) (61), (63)-(64)

	Material	Material and pervasive
Disagreement	Qualified opinion ("Except for…")	Adverse opinion ("In view of the effect of…")
Scope limitation	Qualified opinion ("Except for…")	Disclaimer ("Because of the possible effect…")

Qualified opinion

A qualified opinion should be expressed when the auditor concludes that an unqualified opinion cannot be given but that the effect of any disagreement or limitation on scope is not so material and pervasive as to require an adverse opinion or disclaimer of opinion. A qualified opinion should be expressed as being 'except for' the effects of the matter to which the qualification relates. 5821 ISA 700 (Revised) (61), (64)

A clear description of all the substantive reasons for the qualified opinion should be included in the report and, unless impracticable, a quantification of the possible effects on the financial statements. Ordinarily this information would be set out in a separate paragraph preceding the opinion or disclaimer of opinion and may include a reference to a more extensive discussion, if any, in a note to the financial statements.

EXAMPLE **Extract from auditors' report**

Qualified opinion arising from disagreement about accounting treatment
Included in the debtors shown on the balance sheet is an amount of £XX due from a company that has ceased trading. The company has no security for this debt. In our opinion the company is unlikely to receive any payment and full provision of £XX should have been made. Accordingly, debtors should be reduced by £XX, the deferred tax liability should be reduced by £YY, and profit for the year and retained earnings should be reduced by £ZZ.

Except for the financial effect of not making the provision referred to in the preceding paragraph, in our opinion the financial statements:
- give a true and fair view of the state of the company's affairs as at 31 December 20X9 and of its profit for the year then ended;
- have been properly prepared in accordance with United Kingdom Generally Accepted Accounting Practice; and
- have been prepared in accordance with the requirements of the Companies Act 2006.

Adverse opinion

5822 ISA 700 (Revised) (63)

An adverse opinion should be expressed when the effect of a disagreement is so material and pervasive to the financial statements that the auditor concludes that a qualification of the report is not adequate to disclose the misleading or incomplete nature of the financial statements.

EXAMPLE **Extract from auditors' report**

Basis for adverse opinion on financial statements
As more fully explained in Note [x] to the financial statements, no provision has been made for losses expected to arise on certain long-term contracts currently in progress, as the directors consider that these losses should be off-set against amounts recoverable on other long-term contracts. In our opinion, provision should be made for foreseeable losses on individual contracts as required by Statement of Standard Accounting Practice 9, *Stocks and long-term contracts*. If losses had been so recognised, the effect would have been to reduce the carrying amount of contract work in progress by £X, the deferred tax liability payable by £Y, and the profit for the year and retained earnings at [*date*] by £Z.

Adverse opinion on financial statements
In our opinion, because of the significance of the matter described in the Basis for Adverse Opinion paragraph, the financial statements:
- do not give a true and fair view of the state of the company's affairs as at *[date]* and of its profit (loss) for the year then ended; and
- have not been properly prepared in accordance with United Kingdom Generally Accepted Accounting Practice.

In all other respects, in our opinion the financial statements have been properly prepared in accordance with the Companies Act 2006.

Opinion on other matters prescribed by the Companies Act 2006
Notwithstanding our adverse opinion on the financial statements, in our opinion the information given in the Directors' Report for the financial year for which the financial statements are prepared is consistent with the financial statements.

Matters on which we are required to report by exception
We have nothing to report in respect of the following matters where the Companies Act 2006 requires us to report to you if, in our opinion:
- adequate accounting records have not been kept, or returns adequate for our audit have not been received from branches not visited by us; or
- the financial statements are not in agreement with the accounting records and returns; or
- certain disclosures of directors' remuneration specified by law are not made; or
- we have not received all the information and explanations we require for our audit.

Disclaimer of opinion

5824 ISA 700 (Revised) (62)

A disclaimer of opinion is expressed when the possible effect of a limitation on the scope of the auditors' work is so material and pervasive that the auditors have not been able to obtain sufficient appropriate audit evidence to form an opinion. Their report therefore indicates that the scope of the examination was limited and includes a disclaimer of opinion on the financial statements arising from that limitation.

5825 ISA 700 (Revised) (67)

A limitation on the scope of the auditor's work may sometimes be imposed by an entity (for example, when the terms of the engagement specify that the auditor will not carry out an audit procedure that the auditor believes is necessary). When the limitation in terms of a proposed engagement is such that the auditor believes the need to express a disclaimer of opinion exists, the auditor would ordinarily not accept such a limited engagement as an audit engagement, unless required to do so by statute. Also, a statutory auditor would not accept such an audit engagement when the limitation infringes on the auditor's statutory duties.

A limitation on the scope of the auditor's work may sometimes be imposed by an entity (for example, when the terms of the engagement specify that the auditor will not carry out an audit procedure that the auditor believes is necessary). When the limitation in terms of a proposed engagement is such that the auditor believes the need to express a disclaimer of opinion exists, the auditor would ordinarily not accept such a limited engagement as an audit engagement, unless required to do so by statute. Also, a statutory auditor would not accept such an audit engagement when the limitation infringes on the auditor's statutory duties. **5826** ISA 700 (Revised) (68)-(75)

EXAMPLE **Extract from auditors' report**

Basis of disclaimer of opinion on financial statements
The audit evidence available to us was limited because we were unable to observe the counting of physical stock having a carrying amount of £X and send confirmation letters to trade debtors having a carrying amount of £Y due to limitations placed on the scope of our work by the directors of the company. As a result of this we have been unable to obtain sufficient appropriate audit evidence concerning both stock and trade debtors.

Disclaimer of opinion on financial statements
Because of the significance of the matter described in the Basis for Disclaimer of Opinion on Financial Statements paragraph, we have not been able to obtain sufficient appropriate audit evidence to provide a basis for an audit opinion. Accordingly, we do not express an on the financial statements.

Opinion on other matter prescribed by the Companies Act 2006
Notwithstanding our disclaimer of an opinion on the view given by the financial statements, in our opinion the information given in the Directors' Report for the financial year for which the financial statements are prepared is consistent with the financial statements.

Matters on which we are required to report by exception
Arising from the limitation of our work referred to above:
- we have not obtained all the information and explanations that we considered necessary for the purpose of our audit; and
- we were unable to determine whether proper accounting records have been kept.

We have nothing to report in respect of the following matters where the Companies Act 2006 requires us to report to you if, in our opinion:
- returns adequate for our audit have not been received from branches not visited by us;
- the financial statements are not in agreement with the accounting records and returns; or
- certain disclosures of directors' remuneration specified by law are not made.

8. Dating and signing of auditors' report

Auditors should not express an opinion on financial statements until the statements have been approved by the directors and the auditors have completed an assessment of all the evidence considered necessary for the opinion to be given in the auditors' report. Furthermore, the date of the report should be the date on which the auditors actually sign the report expressing their opinion. Auditors should not backdate an audit report. **5827** ISA 700 (32)-(41)

The report should name the location of the office where the auditor is based and state the name of the auditor.

The report may be signed in the name of the auditors' firm, the personal name of auditor, or both. Where the auditor is an individual, the report is required to be signed by the individual. Where the auditor is a firm, the report is required to be signed by the senior statutory auditor in his or her own name, for and on behalf of the auditor.

9. Changes to wording occasioned by Companies Act 2006

The Auditing Practices Board from time to time issues revisions to ISA 700 and also publishes Bulletins to illustrate the requirements. **5828**

During 2008, the Auditing Practices Board published the following five bulletins that provide guidance on other aspects of the requirements of the Companies Act 2006:
- 2008/3 "The auditors' statement on the summary financial statement in the United Kingdom";
- 2008/4 "The special auditors' report on abbreviated accounts in the United Kingdom";
- 2008/5 "Auditors' reports on revised accounts and reports, in the United Kingdom Companies";
- 2008/6 "The Senior Statutory Auditor under the United Kingdom Companies Act 2006";
- 2008/9 "Miscellaneous reports by auditors required under the United Kingdom Companies Act 2006".

Where the example reports in these bulletins are effective for accounting periods beginning on or after 6 April 2008, examples of the changes required under the Companies Act 2006 in accordance with these five bulletins have been included in this chapter where appropriate.

In September 2008, the Auditing Practices Board issued Bulletin 2008/8 "Auditors' reports for short accounting periods in compliance with the United Kingdom Companies Act 2006". This bulletin provides guidance on the wording of auditor's reports for companies issuing financial statements for periods commencing on or after 6 April 2008 and ending before 5 April 2009.

5829 In respect of periods ended on or after 15 December 2010, the APB issued a compendium of illustrative auditor's reports contained in Bulletin 2010/2, from which the following general example has been taken. A revised version of the Bulletin was issued in February 2011 to reflect the auditor's responsibility to read all financial and non-financial information in the annual report and to identify any material inconsistencies. The added requirement is shown in the "Scope" paragraph in the example below in bold type, and is mandatory in respect of financial periods ended on or after 23 March 2011 although earlier adoption is encouraged. The Bulletin is obtainable on the APB's website (www.frc.org.uk/apb/).

EXAMPLE **Auditors' report on group and parent company financial statements of a non-publicly traded company**

Independent Auditors' Report to the members of XYZ Ltd

We have audited the group and company financial statements of XYZ Ltd for the period ended... which comprise [*state the primary financial statements such as the Group Profit and Loss Account, the Group and Company Balance Sheets, the Group Cash Flow Statement*] and the related notes. The financial reporting framework that has been applied in their preparation is applicable law and United Kingdom Accounting Standards (United Kingdom Generally Accepted Accounting Practice).

Respective responsibilities of directors and auditors

As explained more fully in the Directors' Responsibilities Statement [set out...], the directors are responsible for the preparation of the financial statements and for being satisfied that they give a true and fair view. Our responsibility is to audit and express an opinion on the financial statements in accordance with applicable law and International Standards on Auditing (UK and Ireland). Those standards require us to comply with the Auditing Practices Board's [(APB's)] Ethical Standards for Auditors.

Scope of the audit of the financial statements

Either: A description of the scope of an audit of financial statements is [provided on the APB's website at www.frc.org.uk/apb/scope/private.cfm] / [set out [on page...] of the Annual Report].

Or: An audit involves obtaining evidence about the amounts and disclosures in the financial statements sufficient to give reasonable assurance that the financial statements are free from material misstatement, whether caused by fraud or error. This includes an assessment of: whether the accounting policies are appropriate to the company's circumstances and have been consistently applied and adequately disclosed; the reasonableness of significant accounting estimates made by the directors; and the overall presentation of the financial statements. **In addition, we read all the financial and non-financial information in the [*describe the annual report*] to identify material inconsistencies with the audited financial statements. If we become aware of any apparent material misstatements or inconsistencies we consider the implications for our report.**

Opinion on financial statements
In our opinion the financial statements:
– give a true and fair view of the state of the company's affairs as at... and of the group's profit (loss) for the year then ended;
– have been properly prepared in accordance with United Kingdom Generally Accepted Accounting Practice; and
– have been prepared in accordance with the requirements of the Companies Act 2006.

Opinion on other matter prescribed by the Companies Act 2006
In our opinion the information given in the Directors' Report for the financial year for which the financial statements are prepared is consistent with the financial statements.

Matters on which we are required to report by exception
We have nothing to report in respect of the following matters where the Companies Act 2006 requires us to report to you if, in our opinion:
– adequate accounting records have not been kept, or returns adequate for our audit have not been received from branches not visited by us; or
– the financial statements are not in agreement with the accounting records and returns; or
– certain disclosures of directors' remuneration specified by law are not made; or
– we have not received all the information and explanations we require for our audit.

[Signature]
John Smith (Senior Statutory Auditor)
for and on behalf of ABC LLP, Statutory Auditor
[Address]
[Date]

B. Audit reports on listed companies

The auditors' reports of companies that are listed are subject to **additional requirements**. 5830
These result from the auditors' duty under the **Listing Rules** to review and report on:
– corporate governance statements,
– directors' remuneration reports,
– going-concern statements,
– preliminary announcements,
– interim financial information.
The auditors' report reflects these additional duties in the following way:

EXAMPLE **Extract from auditors' report**

Opinion on other matters prescribed by the Companies Act 2006
In our opinion:
– the part of the Directors' Remuneration Report to be audited has been properly prepared in accordance with the Companies Act 2006;
– the information given in the Directors' Report for the financial year for which the financial statements are prepared is consistent with the financial statements; and
– the information given in the Corporate Governance Statement set out on pages x to y in [*describe document*] at [*include web address*] with respect to internal control and risk management systems in relation to financial reporting processes and about share capital structures is consistent with the financial statements.

Matters on which we are required to report by exception
We have nothing to report in respect of the following matters where the Companies Act 2006 requires us to report to you if, in our opinion:
– adequate accounting returns have not been kept, or returns adequate for our audit have not been received from branches not visited by us;
– the financial statements and the part of the Directors' Remuneration Report to be audited are not in agreement with the accounting records and returns;
– certain disclosures of directors' remuneration specified by law are not made; or
– we have not received all the information and explanations we require for our audit; or
– a Corporate Governance Statement has not been prepared by the company.

1. Corporate governance statements

5831 LR 9.8.10 The Listing Rules of the Financial Services Authority require listed companies to ensure that the auditors review each of the following statements required by the Listing Rules before the annual report is published:
a. the directors' statement in relation to going concern; and
b. the parts of the statement by the directors that relate to the following provisions of the UK Corporate Governance Code:
– C1.1 (The directors should explain their responsibility for preparing the financial statements and there should be a statement about their reporting responsibilities);
– C2.1 (The Board should conduct a review of the effectiveness of the group's system of internal controls); and
– C3.1 to C3.7 (Various matters relating to Audit Committees and Auditors).

5832 If, based on their review, the auditors disagree with the statement by the directors on going concern or conclude that the Corporate Governance Statement does not appropriately reflect the company's compliance with the nine provisions of the Combined Code, the auditors' report that under the heading 'Other matter' in their report. However, the auditors are not required to consider whether the directors' statements on internal control cover all risks and controls, or form an opinion on the effectiveness of the group's corporate governance procedures or its risk and control procedures..

EXAMPLE **Extract from auditors' report**

Opinion

[Normal unqualified opinion]

Other matter

We have reviewed the board's description of its process for reviewing the effectiveness of internal control set out on page x of the annual report. In our opinion the board's comments concerning... do not appropriately reflect our understanding of the process undertaken by the board because...

2. Reports by the board on directors' remuneration

5834 Listing Rule 9.8.11 requires listed companies to ensure that auditors review disclosures concerning: the amount of each element in the remuneration package and information on share options; details of long-term incentive schemes for directors; and money purchase and defined benefit pension schemes. If, in the opinion of the auditors, the listed company has not complied with any of the requirements set out in LR 9.8.11, the listed company must ensure that the auditors' report includes, to the extent possible, a statement giving details of the non-compliance. In relation to the remuneration report, **two issues** can arise.

The **first** is whether the **disclosures are cross-referenced within the financial statements** in such a way as to make it clear that they fall within the scope of the audit. If this is not the case, the auditors are obliged to modify their introductory paragraph so as to specifically include the disclosures within the scope of the report. The modification is shown in italics in the following example.

EXAMPLE **Extract from auditors' report**

We have audited the annual financial statements of [*name of entity*] for the year ended 31 December 20X9, which comprise the profit and loss account, the balance sheet, the cash flow statement, the statement of total recognised gains and losses and the related notes 1 to 22.
In addition, we have audited the information that is specified by the Financial Services Authority to be audited in respect of any directors' remuneration, share options, long-term incentive schemes and pension entitlements set out in the tables headed "Xxxx" and "Yyyy" of the report to shareholders by the board on directors' remuneration.
The financial reporting framework that has been applied in their preparation is applicable law and United Kingdom Accounting Standards (United Kingdom Generally Accepted Accounting Practice).

In extreme cases, where the information may be interspersed with other information and is not capable of being easily cross-referenced, it may be necessary for the auditors to reproduce the detailed disclosures within their own report.

The **second** issue is whether the **information required to be given under the Listing Rules has been adequately disclosed**. If, in the opinion of the auditors, it has not been, they are obliged to note this in their report. Because this note does not, on its own, amount to a qualified audit opinion, it should be dealt with separately: generally, under the heading "other matter" as illustrated below.

EXAMPLE **Extract from auditors' report**

Other matter

The Listing Rules of the Financial Services Authority require us to report any instances when the company has not complied with certain of the disclosure requirements set out in the Rules. In this connection we report that, in our opinion, the company has not complied with the requirements of paragraph... of those rules, because the board's report on directors' remuneration does not disclose...

3. Going concern statements

The financial statements of listed companies are required to include a statement that the business is a going concern. The listed company must ensure that the auditors review this statement before publication. **5836** LR 9.8.6

In the case of a qualified opinion having to be given as a result of non-disclosure of going concern problems, the audit report could take the following form. **5837**

EXAMPLE **Extract from auditors' report**

Qualified opinion arising from omission of information concerning going concern

The company's financing arrangements expire and amounts outstanding are payable on 29 August 20X2. While the directors continue to investigate alternative sources of finance, the company has so far been unable to renegotiate or obtain replacement financing. This situation indicates the existence of a material uncertainty that may cast significant doubt on the company's ability to continue as a going concern and therefore it may be unable to realise its assets and discharge its liabilities in the normal course of business. The financial statement, and the notes thereto, do not disclose this fact.

Except for the omission of the information included in the preceding paragraph, in our opinion the financial statements:

- give a true and fair view of the state of the company's affairs as at 31 December 20X1 and of its profit (loss) for the year then ended;
- have been properly prepared in accordance with United Kingdom Generally Accepted Accounting Practice; and
- have been prepared in accordance with the Companies Act 2006.

4. Preliminary announcements

Preliminary announcements are no longer mandatory for listed companies. However, the Listing Rules specify that a company that prepares a preliminary announcement must publish it as soon as possible after it has been approved by the Board. The preliminary statement must: **5838** LR 9.7.A.1R (1)

- have been agreed with the company's auditors prior to publication (but note that this does not constitute an audit of the announcement);
- show the figures in the form of a table, including the items required for a half-yearly report, consistent with the presentation to be adopted in the annual financial statements;
- give details of the nature of any likely modification that may be contained in the auditors' report; and

– disclose any significant additional information necessary for a proper assessment of the results.

Before agreeing to a preliminary announcement, the auditors assess:
– whether the directors have given adequate prominence to significant additional information concerning going concern; and
– the adequacy of the directors' disclosure, within the announcement, of any likely modification relating to going concern that may be contained in the auditors' report.

MEMO POINTS The Listing Rules do not indicate what form the agreement with the auditor should take, or the extent of work expected of the auditor before the auditor gives its agreement. Guidance for auditors on preliminary announcements is set out in Bulletin 2008/2, "The auditor's association with preliminary announcements made in accordance with the requirements of the UK and Irish Listing Rules", issued by the Auditing Practices Board.

5. Interim financial statements

5840 Interim and other similar reports are not required to be audited. Nevertheless, auditors are frequently asked to **review** these statements before they are sent to members. International Standard on Review Engagements (ISRE) (UK and Ireland) 2410 "Review of Interim Financial Information Performed by the Independent Auditor of the Entity", issued by the Auditing Practices Board, establishes standards and provides guidance on the auditor's professional responsibilities when the auditor undertakes an engagement to review interim financial information of an audit client and on the form and content of the report.

EXAMPLE **Report on review of interim financial information to A Ltd**

Introduction

We have reviewed the accompanying balance sheet of A Ltd as of…, and the related statements of income, changes in equity and cash flows for the three-month period then ended, and a summary of significant accounting policies and other explanatory notes. Management is responsible for the preparation and fair presentation of this interim financial information in accordance with United Kingdom Accounting Standards (United Kingdom Generally Accepted Accounting Practice). Our responsibility is to express a conclusion on this interim financial information based on our review.

Scope of Review

We conducted our review in accordance with International Standard on Review Engagement 2410, "Review of Interim Financial Information Performed by the Independent Auditor of the Entity". A review of interim financial information consists of making inquiries, primarily of persons responsible for financial and accounting matters, and applying analytical and other review procedures. A review is substantially less in scope than an audit conducted in accordance with International Standards on Auditing and consequently does not enable us to obtain assurance that we would become aware of all significant matters that might be identified in an audit. Accordingly, we do not express an audit option.

Conclusion

Based on our review, nothing has come to our attention that causes us to believe that the accompanying interim financial information does not give a true and fair view of the financial position of the entity as at…, and of its financial performance and its cash flows for the three-month period then ended in accordance with United Kingdom Accounting Standards (United Kingdom Generally Accepted Accounting Practice).

[Auditor]
[Date]
[Address]

5841 If a material uncertainty relating to an event or condition comes to the auditor's attention that may cast significant doubt on the entity's ability to continue as a going concern, and adequate disclosure is made in the interim financial information, the auditor modifies his review report by adding an emphasis of matter paragraph. However, if there is not adequate disclosure, the auditor is required to express a qualified or adverse conclusion as appropriate. In these circumstances the report is required to include specific reference to the fact that there is such a material uncertainty.

MEMO POINTS ISRE 2410 includes illustrative examples of reports on reviews of interim financial information.

C. Special reports required by companies' legislation

1. Abbreviated accounts

Certain small and medium-sized companies are entitled to take advantage of various exemptions under the Act and may file abbreviated accounts with the Registrar of Companies (¶6270). These accounts are required to be accompanied by a copy of a special auditors' report in which the auditors must state that, in their opinion: 5845
- the company is entitled to deliver abbreviated accounts; and
- the abbreviated accounts are properly prepared.

If the auditors are not able to report positively in respect of both of the above, the company may not deliver abbreviated accounts to the Registrar.

If the auditors' report on the full financial statements is unqualified, there is no need to reproduce it in full in the special report. Where, however, the auditors' report on the full-form financial statements is qualified, it should be set out in full – together with any further material necessary to understand the qualification – in the special report.

The exact wording of the special report will depend upon whether the company is small or medium-sized.

EXAMPLE **Example of a report on the abbreviated accounts of a small company**

Independent Auditors' Report to B Ltd under Section 449 of the Companies Act 2006

We have examined the abbreviated accounts set out on pages xx to xx, together with the financial statements of the company for the year ended 30 September 20XX prepared under Section 396 of the Companies Act 2006.

Respective responsibilities of directors and auditors

The directors are responsible for preparing the abbreviated accounts in accordance with Section 444 of the Companies Act 2006. It is our responsibility to form an independent opinion as to whether the company is entitled to deliver abbreviated accounts prepared in accordance with Section 444 of the Act to the Registrar of Companies and whether the accounts to be delivered are properly prepared in accordance with that provision and to report our opinion to you.

We conducted our work in accordance with Bulletin 2008/4 issued by the Auditing Practices Board. In accordance with that Bulletin, we have carried out the procedures we consider necessary to confirm, by reference to the financial statements, that the company is entitled to deliver abbreviated accounts and that the abbreviated accounts to be delivered are properly prepared. The scope of our work for the purpose of this report did not include examining or dealing with events after the date of our report on the full financial statements.

Opinion

In our opinion the company is entitled to deliver abbreviated accounts prepared in accordance with Section 444(3) of the Companies Act 2006, and the abbreviated accounts are properly prepared in accordance with the regulations made under that section.

[Signature]

John Smith (Senior Statutory Auditor)

For and on behalf of ABC LLP, Statutory Auditors

[Address]

[Date]

MEMO POINTS In a special report on the abbreviated accounts of a medium-sized company, references to sections 444 and 444(3) of the Companies Act 2006 are replaced by references to sections 445 and 445(3) respectively.

2. Initial accounts

5847 If a public company plans to pay a dividend to shareholders before the end of its **first accounting period**, it must prepare initial accounts in order to determine whether the distribution is legal. These initial accounts must be accompanied by a report from the auditors stating whether they have been properly prepared and give a true and fair view. In order to give an opinion on this, the auditors will have to carry out an audit.

If the opinion given by the auditors is not unqualified, the auditors must also state whether the matter that gave rise to the qualification is material for the purposes of determining the legality of the distribution. The Auditing Practices Board issued Bulletin 2008/9 in October 2008 which provides the following example of an auditor's report on initial accounts when a public company wishes to make a distribution.

EXAMPLE **Example of an unqualified report on the initial accounts of a public company**

Independent Auditors' Report to the Directors of J plc under Section 839(5) of the Companies Act 2006
We have audited the initial accounts of J plc for the period from... to... which comprise the Profit and Loss Account, the Balance Sheet, the Cash Flow Statement, and the related notes. The initial accounts have been prepared in accordance with the accounting policies set out therein.

Respective responsibilities of directors and auditors
As described... the directors are responsible for preparing the initial accounts, which must be properly prepared in accordance with the applicable laws and United Kingdom Accounting Standards (United Kingdom Generally Accepted Accounting Practice).
Our responsibility is to report to you our opinion as to whether the initial accounts have been properly prepared within the meaning of Section 839(4) of the Companies Act 2006.

Opinion
In our opinion the initial accounts for the period from... to... have been properly prepared within the meaning of Section 839(4) of the Companies Act 2006.

[Signed]
John Smith (Senior Statutory Auditor)
For and on behalf of ABC LLP, Statutory Auditor
[Address]
[Date]

5848 Where the auditors' report on the initial accounts is qualified, but the matter is not material for purposes of determining the amounts available for distribution, the opinion paragraph above should be replaced by the following:

EXAMPLE **Example of a qualified opinion on the initial accounts of a public company**

Qualified opinion
Except for the failure to disclose [insert details of circumstances giving rise to qualification of opinion] as required by the Companies Act, in our opinion the initial accounts for the period from... to... have been properly prepared within the meaning of Section 839(4) of the Companies Act 2006.
In our opinion, the matter in respect of which our opinion is qualified is not material for determining by reference to those financial statements whether the distribution of £xxx proposed by the company would contravene Section 831 of the Companies Act 2006.

3. Distributions

5850 s 837 CA 2006 When a company intends to make a distribution, it must first determine the amount that is legally available for the purpose (¶3711). This is usually done by reference to the last annual financial statements before the distribution. If the audit report on those accounts was **qualified**, the company must obtain a further report from the auditors stating whether, in their opinion, the circumstances giving rise to the qualification is material in the determination the legality of the distribution.

This statement may be made either at the time of the audit report – as an addition to the opinion section – or it can be made in a separate report.

EXAMPLE **Example of report given separately from the audit report on the last financial statements**

Independent Auditors' Report to the Members of K Ltd Pursuant to Section 837(4) of the Companies Act 2006
We have audited the financial statements of K Ltd for the year ended... in accordance with International Standards on Auditing (UK and Ireland) issued by the Auditing Practices Board and have expressed a qualified opinion thereon in our report dated...

Respective responsibilities of directors and auditors
The directors are responsible for preparing the financial statements in accordance with the applicable laws and United Kingdom Accounting Standards (United Kingdom Generally Accepted Accounting Practice).
They are also responsible for considering whether the company, subsequent to the balance sheet date, has sufficient distributable profits to make a distribution at the time the distribution if made.
Our responsibility is to report whether, in our opinion, the subject matter of the qualification of our auditors' report on the financial statements for the year ended... is material for determining whether, by reference to those financial statements, the distribution is permitted under section 830 of the Companies Act 2006. We are not required to form an opinion on whether the company has sufficient distributable reserves to make the distribution proposed at the time it is made.

Opinion
In our opinion, the subject matter of the qualification is not material for determining whether, by reference to those financial statements, the distribution of £xx, xxx proposed by the company is permitted under Section 830 of the Companies Act 2006.

Statutory Auditor
[Address]
[Date]

4. Valuation report on non-cash assets

Public companies may not allot shares for a non-cash consideration unless a report on the value of that consideration has been made within six months before the share allotment by an independent person qualified to be auditor of the company. **5851** s 593 CA 2006

The valuer's report must state: s 596 CA 2006
1. the nominal value of the shares to be issued;
2. the amount of any premium payable;
3. the description of the consideration, the method used to value it and the date of valuation;
4. the extent to which the nominal value of the shares and any premium are to be treated as paid up by the consideration and by cash;
5. where another person has performed any part of the valuation:
– that fact;
– the valuer's name;
– a description of their knowledge and experience to carry out the valuation;
– the method of valuation used;
– the date the valuation was carried out;
– that it appears reasonable to accept the valuation of the other person;
6. that whoever made the valuation, the method of valuation was reasonable in all the circumstances;
7. that it appears to the valuer that there has been no material change in the value of the consideration in question since the valuation;
8. that on the basis of the valuation, the value of the consideration, together with any cash, is not less than so much of the aggregate of the nominal value and premium as will be treated as paid up.

MEMO POINTS The provisions of the Companies Act 2006 relating to the valuation report on non-cash assets came into effect on 1 October 2009. APB Bulletin 2008/9 provides an example of the statements that will be required when a private company wishes to allot shares otherwise than for cash under the Companies Act 2006.

EXAMPLE **Independent Auditors' Report to M Ltd for the Purposes of Section 593(1) of the Companies Act 2006**

We report on the value of the consideration for the allotment of 100,000 ordinary shares with a nominal value of £1 each, to be issued at a premium of £10. The whole of the nominal value and share premium is to be treated as fully paid up by the consideration.
The consideration consists of land and buildings as listed in [xxx].

Basis of valuation
The land and buildings were valued at £1,250,000 on the basis of net current replacement cost taking into account their condition and remaining useful life, by XYZ and Co., Chartered Surveyors. We believe that it is reasonable to accept such a valuation.

Opinion
In our opinion, the methods of valuation used in the above valuations were reasonable in all the circumstances and there appears to have been no material change in the value of the consideration since the valuations were made.
On the basis of the valuation, in our opinion, the value of the total consideration is not less than £1,100,000 being the aggregate of the nominal value and premium on shares that are treated as paid up by the consideration.

[Signed]
Registered Auditors
[Address]
[Date]

5. Reports pertaining to private companies

Share capital

5853 Where a private company either intends to:
- give financial assistance for the purchase of its own shares, e.g., by lending money to a potential shareholder (¶3615), or
- purchase or redeem its own shares out of capital, i.e., when there are no other reserves out of which the purchase could be made (¶3661)

it has to comply with a number of conditions. One of these is the requirement that the directors make a declaration that the company's financial position will not be compromised as a result of the proposed transactions. The Companies Act 1985 required the auditors to report on the directors' declaration to the effect that they are not aware of anything that indicates that the opinion expressed therein is unreasonable.

However, under the Companies Act 2006, the report on a private company providing financial assistance for the purchase of its own shares is no longer required as the relevant provisions under the Companies Act were repealed as from 1 October 2008.

The provisions of the Companies Act 2006 relating to a private company wishing to redeem or purchase its own shares out of capital came into effect on 1 October 2009. The Auditing Practices Board issued Bulletin 2008/9 in October 2008, which provides an example of the statements required when a private company redeems or purchases its own shares out of capital under the Companies Act 2006:

EXAMPLE **Report of the independent auditor to the directors of XYZ Limited pursuant to Section 714(6) of the Companies At 2006**
We report on the attached statement of the directors dated..., prepared pursuant to the Companies Act 2006, in connection with the company's proposed [purchase]/[redemption] of... (number) [ordinary]/[preferred] shares by a payment out of capital.

Basis of opinion
We have inquired into the company's state of affairs in order to review the bases for the directors' statement.

Opinion
In our opinion the amount of £xx specified in the directors' statement as the permissible capital payment for the shares to be [purchased]/[redeemed] is properly determined in accordance with sections 710 to 712 of the Companies Act 2006. We are not aware of anything to indicate that the opinion expressed by the directors in their statement as to any of the matters mentioned in section 714(3) of the Companies Act 2006 is unreasonable in all the circumstances.

Re-registration as a public company

If a private company intends to re-register as a public company, it must lodge with the Registrar of Companies various documents, including the company's balance sheet as at a date not more than seven months before the application to re-register. It is usual to submit the balance sheet from the last audited accounts for this purpose but, if more than seven months has elapsed since the last financial year end, a more recent balance sheet is needed. In addition, the following is required from the company's auditors: **5855** s 92 CA 2006
- an unqualified audit report in relation to the balance sheet, and
- a written statement from the auditors that the balance sheet shows, in their opinion, that the company's net assets did not amount to less than the aggregate of its called up share capital and undistributable reserves.

MEMO POINTS The provisions of the Companies Act 2006 relating to re-registration came into effect on 1 October 2009. APB Bulletin 2008/9 provides an example of the statements that are required if a private company wishes to re-register as a public company under the Companies Act 2006.

EXAMPLE **Independent Auditors' Report to A Ltd for the Purpose of Section 92(1) (b) and (c) of the Companies Act 2006**

We have examined the balance sheet and related notes of A Ltd as at 31 December 20X9, which formed part of the financial statements for the year then ended which were audited by us.
Respective responsibilities of directors and auditors
The company's directors are responsible for the preparation of the balance sheet and the related notes.
It is our responsibility to:
- report on whether the balance sheet has been properly prepared in accordance with the Companies Act 2006; and
- form an independent opinion, based on our examination, concerning the relationship between the company's net assets and its called up share capital and undistributed reserves at the balance sheet date.

Opinion concerning proper preparation of balance sheet
In our opinion, the audited balance sheet at 31 December 20X9 has been properly prepared in accordance with the requirements of the Companies Act 2006.

Statement on net assets
In our opinion, at 31 December 20X9 the amount of the company's net assets (within the meaning given to that expression by Section 831(2) of the Companies Act 2006) was not less than the aggregate of its called-up share capital and undistributable reserves.

[Signed]
Statutory Auditor
[Address]
[Date]

6. Summary financial statements

If a listed company sends a summary financial statement to members instead of the full directors' report and annual accounts, it must include a statement of opinion from the auditors as to whether the summary is consistent with the annual accounts and directors' report. APB Bulletin 2008/3, issued in April 2008 and applicable to accounting periods beginning on or after 6 April 2008 clarifies auditors' responsibilities in connection with summary financial statements and provides examples of wording for auditors' statements. **5858**

EXAMPLE **Independent Auditors' Statement To The Shareholders of B Ltd**

We have examined the summary financial statement of B Ltd set out on page xx to xx.

Respective responsibilities of directors and auditors

The directors are responsible for preparing the summarised annual report in accordance with applicable United Kingdom law.

Our responsibility is to report to you our opinion on the consistency of the summary financial statements within the summarised annual report with the full annual financial statements, the Directors' Remuneration Report and the Directors' Report, and its compliance with the relevant requirements of Section 428 of the Companies Act 2006 and the regulations made thereunder. We also read the other information contained in the summarised annual report and consider the implications for our report if we become aware of any apparent misstatements or material inconsistencies with the summary financial statement. The other information comprises only [the Chairman's Statement and the Corporate Governance Statement].

We conducted our work in accordance with Bulletin 2008/3 issued by the Auditing Practices Board. Our report on the company's full annual financial statements describes the basis of our opinions on those financial statements, the Directors' Remuneration Report and the Directors' Report.

Opinion

In our opinion the summary financial statement Is consistent with the full annual financial statements, the Directors' Remuneration Report and the Directors' Report of B Ltd for the year ended... and complies with the applicable requirements of Section 428 of the Companies Act 2006 and the regulations made thereunder.

[Signed]
Statutory Auditor
[Address]
[Date]

7. Revised annual financial statements

5860 s 454 CA 2006 If the directors discover that the annual accounts, or directors' report, contained errors or were otherwise defective, they may, at their option, prepare revised accounts (including reports). If the previous statements have already been presented to the company in general meeting or delivered to the Registrar, the revisions that may be made are confined to correcting instances of non-compliance with the Act (which, in practice, includes compliance with Accounting Standards) and the necessary consequential alterations.

At the directors' discretion, the corrections may be made by replacing the accounts and reports in their entirety, or by issuing a supplementary note.

The provisions of the Act are supplemented by the ability of the Financial Review Panel to require a listed company to revise its financial statements. If such a revision does take place, the directors should follow the provisions of the Act even though the revision may not in reality be voluntary.

The **auditor's opinion** on the view given by the revised accounts is given at the date the original accounts were approved – and the opinion should not be influenced by events after that date. The following examples show how the relevant paragraphs of the auditors' report will be affected.

EXAMPLE **1. Introduction to auditors' report of a company that revised its accounts by replacing them in their entirety:**

We have audited the revised financial statements for B Ltd for the year ended... which comprise the Profit and Loss Account, the Balance Sheet, the Cash Flow Statement and related notes. These revised financial statements have been prepared under the accounting policies set out therein and replace the original financial statements approved by the directors on [date of directors' original approval].

2. Introduction to auditors' report of a company that revised its accounts by a supplementary note:

We have audited the revised financial statements for B Ltd for the year ended... which comprise... The revised financial statements replace the original financial statements approved by the directors on [date] and consist of the attached supplementary note together with the original financial statements that were circulated to members on [date].

3. *Opinion* section of auditors' report on revised accounts:

In our opinion:
– the revised financial statements give a true and fair view, seen as at the date the original financial statements were approved, of the state of the company's affairs as at... and of its profit for the year then ended;
– the revised financial statements have been properly prepared in accordance with United Kingdom Generally Accepted Accounting Practice seen as at the date the original the financial statements were approved;
– the revised financial statements have been properly prepared in accordance with the provisions of the Companies Act 2006 as they have effect under the Companies (Revision of Defective Accounts and Reports) Regulations 2008;
– the original financial statements for the year ended... failed to comply with the requirements of the Companies Act 2006 in the respects identified by the directors in the statement contained in note [x] to these revised financial statements; and
– the information given in the revised Directors' Report is consistent with the revised financial statements.

4. In the case of revision by replacement:

In our opinion the original financial statements for the year ended... failed to comply with the requirements of the Companies Act 2006 in the respects identified by the directors in the statement contained in Note x to these revised financial statements.

5. In the case of revision by supplementary note:

In our opinion the original financial statements for the year ended... failed to comply with the requirements of the Companies Act 2006 in the respects identified by the directors in the supplementary note.

CHAPTER 10

Ratio analysis

OUTLINE ¶¶

Ratio analysis is a technique that allows investors, finance directors and analysts to gain a better understanding of how an organisation has performed by analysing the financial statements. Once the ratios have been calculated, comparisons can be made of the entity's performance versus previous years and other organisations in the same industry and trends can be analysed. With the **exception** of the ratio for earnings per share (EPS), provision of this information in the financial statements is not compulsory. 5900

Five groups of ratios are commonly employed; namely: liquidity, profitability, assets, investments, and debt (gearing) ratios. Within each category, there are a number of standard ratios that are generally calculated. **Individual ratios** should not be considered in isolation and a number of ratios should be calculated and reviewed in unison with the trends determined over time.

There are **a number of limitations** in using ratio analysis: 5902
- financial statements are based partly on estimates (e.g. depreciation, revaluations, accruals, etc.) and should these be materially incorrect then this will impact on the quality of the ratio analysis;
- changes in accounting policies make comparisons over a number of years and with other entities difficult;
- ratios are based on past performance and are no guide to the future; and
- the economic climate must be taken into consideration when interpreting trends.

A. Liquidity ratios

Management monitors liquidity in order to maintain the solvency of the business through managing the working capital that is tied up in debtors, stock and cash. The two principal liquidity ratios are the current ratio and acid test. 5910

Liquidity ratios **give an insight into** an entity's ability to meet its financial obligations as they fall due, through the availability of liquid assets. Liquid assets are current assets that can be converted into cash promptly and include:
- cash;
- short-term investments;
- fixed term deposits; and
- trade debtors.

It is not unusual for a business to be making a profit but at the same time experience liquidity problems. A **common problem** is that of **overtrading**, where most of the profits are used to finance expansion in the form of additional fixed assets, stocks and debtors required to sustain a growing business. This can result in a shortage of cash to meet short-term financial obligations. The liquidity and working capital ratios are useful in detecting early signs of overtrading.

Some assets are more liquid than others. Stocks of **finished goods** might be sold quickly and consumer goods held as stock can also be sold on. Other stocks are not so liquid. **Raw materials and components** in a manufacturing company are required in the production of a finished good before they can be sold on and cash generated. In this case, the degree of liquidity will depend on the speed of the stock turnover and length of the production cycle.

1. Current ratio

5912 The current ratio measures the relationship between an entity's current assets and current liabilities.

EXAMPLE $\frac{\text{Current assets £60,000}}{\text{Current liabilities £20,000}} = 3: 1$

For every £1 of current liabilities the entity has £3 of current assets.

The **ideal current ratio** will depend on the type of industry and a ratio that is acceptable for one industry will not necessarily be suitable for another. For example, fast food outlets typically operate with low current ratios, resulting from minimum levels of current stock and debtor balances and the quick recycling of resources generated from cash (rather than credit) sales.

A **low ratio** could mean that a business is nearing insolvency, although the timing of the liabilities must also be considered. For instance, some liabilities such as finance lease repayments or corporation tax repayments may not be due for a number of months. Alternatively, **a high ratio** could indicate that one or more categories of current assets are too high and therefore not being managed efficiently (i.e. stock levels).

2. Acid test

5916 The acid test ratio ignores the stock component of the current ratio and concentrates on assets which can be turned quickly into cash, should liquidity problems occur. Stock is excluded from this ratio because it may take longer to liquidate, especially if it is of a specialist nature.

EXAMPLE $\frac{\text{Current assets- stock £60,000 – £30,000}}{\text{Current liabilities £20,000}} = 1.5: 1$

5917 Some companies may not be able to convert current assets into cash quickly. Manufacturing companies, for instance, may hold large quantities of raw materials and finished goods could also be warehoused for a considerable time or sold on generous credit terms. Where the stock turnover is slow, stocks are not deemed liquid assets as the cash cycle is relatively long.

Ideally, this ratio should be at least 1 for companies with a slow stock turnover. For companies with a quick stock turnover, a ratio could be less than 1, without necessarily indicating cash flow problems. **Remedial action** includes encouraging debtors to settle more promptly, whilst short-term investments can be sold and converted into cash.

The reverse applies where the ratio is bigger than it should be. This occurs when an entity has over invested its working capital in terms of stocks and debtors and so has more funds tied up in the business than required.

The **minimum safety ratio** will vary from industry to industry. Where this ratio differs markedly from other entities in the same sector, this could indicate a number of problem areas as set out in the table below. 5918

Problem	Underlying causes
A ratio significantly lower than industry average	Entity too dependant on short-term borrowings for daily funding (i.e. high levels of trade creditors, short-term loans and overdrafts)
High acid/current ratios	Indicate an entity is not utilising resources efficiently = low rates of return **Solutions**: Excessive stock levels require better stock control High debtor balances require – better credit control-prompt payment Cash balances should be reinvested

B. Profitability ratios

Profitability ratios help illustrate how effective a company is in utilising the assets at their disposal to generate profits. Investors, banks and other lenders and suppliers will want to know how profitable a company is and that it is generating enough profits to meet its financial commitments. 5920

The key profitability ratios are the gross profit percentage and net profit percentage.

Expressing profit as a percentage of sales indicates how efficiently an organisation is controlling its costs.

1. Gross profit percentage

The gross profit ratio expresses the gross margin as a percentage of total sales. 5922

EXAMPLE $\frac{\text{Gross profit £150,000}}{\text{Total sales £300,000}} \times 100 = 50\ \%.$

For every £100 of sales the company makes a gross profit of £50.

Changes in gross profit margin may result from:
- lower turnover;
- increased cost of raw materials where higher costs have not been passed onto the
- customer;
- increased competition; or
- a change in the product mix, with the entity selling a higher proportion of goods with a lower gross product margin.

2. Net profit percentage

5924 The net profit percentage shows an organisation's net profit as a percentage of total sales.

EXAMPLE $\frac{\text{Net profit £25,000}}{\text{Sales £250,000}} \times 100$ = net profit percentage of 10%.

Changes in the net profit percentage may not be accompanied by a similar change in gross profit percentage. This indicates that an organisation needs to review its expenses, salary costs, etc.

C. Asset ratios

5930 There are a number of ratios that can be used to indicate how efficiently an organisation is using its assets, the most common of which are reviewed below.

1. Sales to fixed assets

5932 The sales to fixed asset ratio indicates how much of each £1 invested in fixed assets generates sales.

For example, an entity with annual sales of £250,000 and a fixed asset net book value of £100,000; the ratio will be 2.5 to 1. Every £1 invested generates £2.50 in sales.

5933 The **higher the ratio** of sales to fixed assets the more efficient the utilisation of the fixed assets. However, **the ratio** should be interpreted with care as it **may be distorted** by the following factors:
– a significant increase in fixed assets will increase the value of fixed assets and result in a short-term lowering of the ratio; or
– alternatively, if there is little or no investment in new fixed assets, this would increase the sales to fixed asset ratios and mask the under investment reflected in the low assets values carried in the balance sheet.

2. Stock turnover

5934 The stock turnover ratio expresses the average number of days' stock is held by the entity.

EXAMPLE $\frac{\text{Average stock £12,000}}{\text{Cost of sales £500,000}} \times 365$ = approximately 9 days

5935 **High levels of stock** result in:
– increased storage, handling, insurance and security costs;
– risk of stock obsolescence with slow moving items; and
– valuable resources being committed.

5936 The shorter the stock turnover period the better as less resources are committed.

The **average length of time** that **stock is retained** will depend on the organisation and industry sector. For example a restaurant would not hold fresh food stocks for very long while a coal based electricity generating company would typically hold a few months stock of coal. Also, some manufacturers operate a "just-in-time" delivery system, with pressure placed on suppliers to hold stocks of spare parts on their behalf (e.g. car manufacturers).

A **low stock turnover** could result from significant quantities of obsolete or damaged stock that cannot be sold, or that stock levels are simply too high. Other reasons include poor stock control and bulk buying to obtain discounts, resulting in excess funds committed to stocks. The idea is that the entity should not burden itself with excessive levels of stock, but should retain sufficient supplies so that sales are not threatened. Good stock control/delivery systems are required to determine and then manage the optimum level of stock.

3. Average trade debtor collection period

The debtor collection period indicates the number of days elapsing between a credit sale and receipt of the cash. 5937

EXAMPLE $\frac{\text{Average trade debtors £50,000}}{\text{Credit sales £750,000}} \times 365 = \text{approx. 24 days}$

The **shorter the collection period**, the better the liquidity and the lower the risk of bad debts. A good credit control system will ensure that the debtor collection period is kept as short as possible and that cash is available to meet creditors as they fall due.

Generally, normal terms of credit are 30 days, so anything in excess of this figure should be investigated. Note that debtors are quoted inclusive of VAT whilst the turnover is stated net.

4. Creditor turnover period

This ratio shows the average number of days an entity takes to pay its suppliers for goods purchased on credit. If a figure for credit sales is not available the annual cost of sales figure can be used. 5938

EXAMPLE $\frac{\text{Average trade creditors £25,000}}{\text{Credit purchases £350,000}} \times 365 = \text{27 days}$

Although some entities view delaying payment as a form of interest free credit, there are costs involved as discounts for prompt payment are often sacrificed and business credit ratings can suffer.

D. Investment ratios

Investors seek returns on investments in the form of dividends and profits on share sales that compensate them for the risk attached to the investment. Investors also require information on share performance to aid them in their decision making process on whether to buy, sell or hold shares. Ratios are often used to assess the return on an investment, the most common of which are set out below. 5940

1. Return on capital employed (ROCE)

The ROCE ratio indicates how well an entity utilises the resources invested in it, by expressing its profit as a percentage of the total capital employed required to generate the profit. 5942

The ROCE measures both profitability and the efficient use of assets in generating sales, as measured by net profit margin and asset turnover. There is often a **trade-off between** these two ratios in different industry sectors. For instance, retailers usually operate on lower profit margins, while capital intensive industries such as building or engineering have higher asset turnovers.

EXAMPLE $\frac{\text{Profit before interest and taxation £15,000}}{\text{Capital employed £150,000}} \times 100 = 10\ \%$.

From the investor's standpoint, the higher the ROCE the more efficient the use of the resources employed by the company.

5943 The **problem** is deciding which definition of "capital employed" to use. Some entities only include shareholders funds (share capital/reserves) while others include shareholders funds and long-term debt including creditors falling due after one year.

Whichever definition is adopted it should be applied consistently.

2. Dividend cover

5944 The dividend cover ratio indicates the proportion of available profits distributed to shareholders retained in the organization. Entities seek to strike a balance between the funding requirements of the organization and the expectations of the investors.

EXAMPLE $\frac{\text{Profit after tax less preference share dividend £25,000}}{\text{Gross dividend on ordinary shares £10,000}}$ = dividend cover 2.5: 1

For every £2.50 profit made, £1 is distributed to the investors by way of a dividend, with the balance retained in the organization.

3. Dividend yield

5946 The dividend yield expresses the shareholder's dividend as a percentage of the market value of a share.

The yield **will be influenced by** the dividend policy adopted by the company and the level of funds retained (reinvested) in the business. From an investor's viewpoint, the dividend yield indicates the return that an investor earns from holding shares in a certain company, so allowing comparison with other forms of investment.

EXAMPLE $\frac{\text{Ordinary dividend per share £0.25p}}{\text{Market price per share £4.00}} \times 100 = 6.25\ \%$

The dividend yield is compared with the market average. **Low dividend yields** will encourage investors to switch their money into other shares so affecting the share price and with it the ability of the entity to attract further investment.

4. Price/earnings

5948 The price/earnings ratio (PER) indicates how cheap or expensive a particular share is and is determined by dividing the market price of a company's ordinary shares by the earnings per share (EPS).

EXAMPLE Price/earnings ratio = $\frac{\text{market price of share 550p}}{\text{Earnings per share 50p}} = 11$

Eleven years earnings of 0.50p per share are being purchased.

The current market price of the share reflects the expectations of the market regarding the future profits of the company and the price/earnings ratio helps elaborate this through comparison with other entities. Companies with higher PER's, all other factors being equal, will be deemed to have the better commercial prospects. On the other hand, an entity may have a low PERs as a result of one poor trading year, or exceptional circumstances that may be short-term in nature.

The PER is therefore highly subjective, as it is primarily dependant on the opinion of investors concerning future profitability.

E. Debt ratios

Debt ratios illustrate how much a company owes in relation to its size and whether the **debt burden** is increasing or decreasing along with the resulting impact on the long-term capital structure of the company. 5950

1. Debt ratio

The debt ratio shows the relationship between a company's total debt and its total assets. Assets consist of fixed and current assets at the balance sheet date and debts consist of all creditors, including those falling due after more than one year. Long-term provisions and liabilities are ignored. 5952

A debt ratio of 50% is generally deemed prudent, although many companies operate with a debt ratio in excess of this. **Examples include** companies that have a dominant market position or companies funding takeovers with high levels of debt.

2. Gearing

The term "gearing" expresses the relationship between a company's borrowings and shareholders funds. Investors and other lenders will be interested in an entity's long-term funding arrangements. 5954

EXAMPLE

$$\frac{\text{Long-term debt}}{\text{Long-term debt + shareholders funds}}$$

$$\frac{£200{,}000}{£500{,}000} = \text{a gearing ratio of 0.4.}$$

For every £100 of equity, £40 represents long-term borrowings (amounts due for repayment after one year).

The **higher the ratio of debt to equity**, the more dependent the organization is on borrowed funds and the greater the risk of defaulting on interest or dividend payments. **Poor gearing ratios** will result in these entities having to pay a premium to attract adequate funding.

There is no generally agreed norm for this ratio and many companies are highly geared. The problem is that these types of companies may have difficulty in raising future funds unless they can increase shareholders' capital either through retained profits or through a share issue.

A **number of questions** should be addressed, such as: 5956

1. Are long-term financial commitments being financed by long-term finance?
2. Do the company's ratios for gearing levels and interest cover (see below) seem reasonable?
3. Have any significant changes in funding been highlighted by the ratios? If so what does this indicate?

3. Interest cover

5958 This ratio indicates how many times interest payments on short-term debt are covered by profit before tax and interest. The **higher the ratio**, the less the likelihood of an entity defaulting on its interest payments and hence the lower the financial risk of investing in the entity. Generally, an interest cover of 3 times is deemed suitable.

EXAMPLE $\frac{\text{Profit before interest and tax £250,000}}{\text{Interest charges £60,000}} = 4.17 \text{ times}$

PART 8

Smaller entities

CHAPTER 1

Small and medium-sized companies

OUTLINE ¶¶

Introduction

In general, the financial statements of small and medium-sized businesses are seldom as complex as those of large companies. Moreover, the types of activities undertaken by smaller enterprises typically do not require the same level of disclosure in order to give users of their financial statements a proper appreciation of their results. **6000**

To recognise these differences, special concessions apply to small and medium-sized companies. These concessions simplify certain disclosure requirements or, in some cases, even remove them entirely. There are also concessions granted to small and medium-sized **groups**.

6001 The type and extent of reporting concessions available depend also on the **purpose** for which the accounts in question are prepared. This is summarised in the table below.

Financial statements for presentation to:	Exemptions available to:
Shareholders (Shorter-form statements)	Small companies
Registrar of Companies (Abbreviated statements)	Small and medium-sized companies

6002 It should be noted that the exemptions are voluntary and that, as a result, some small and medium-sized companies choose to continue preparing their financial statements under the rules applying to larger companies. There can be a number of reasons for this; e.g., if they are part of a group or if, due to anticipated future growth, they do not expect to be able to take advantage of the exemptions in the future. Similarly, while certain medium-sized companies are entitled to prepare abbreviated financial statements, they may prefer to avoid the additional expense of doing so and simply file a conventional set of accounts (such as are given to shareholders) with the Registrar, especially if there are no issues of confidentiality that would otherwise influence this decision.

6005 The various **options available** to small and medium-sized companies are therefore as follows:

Financial statements for presentation to:	Small companies	Medium-sized companies
Shareholders	• **Full** financial statements (i.e., in terms of companies legislation, and all current FRSs); **or** • **Shorter-form** financial statements (i.e., in accordance with FRSSE)	• **Full** financial statements
Registrar of Companies	• **Full** financial statements; **or** • **Abbreviated** financial statements (i.e., in terms of companies legislation) for small companies [1, 2]	• **Full** financial statements; or • **Abbreviated** financial statements (i.e., in terms of companies legislation) for medium-sized companies [2]

Notes:
1. Even if a small company files abbreviated financial statements with the Registrar of Companies, it is still required to provide full or shorter-form financial statements for its members.
2. Abbreviated financial statements for small companies are not the same as those for medium-sized companies.

Small and medium-sized **groups** are discussed in Section 4 (¶6340).

6006 Another concession that applies to small companies is their choice (subject to satisfying certain criteria) as to whether they wish to have their accounts audited. This is discussed in greater detail at ¶6070.

6007 Until 2005, the authority for the various concessions was given by company law on the one hand, and accounting standards on the other. With the publication in April 2005 of the Financial Reporting Standard for Smaller Entities (**FRSSE**), and amendments, which now incorporates the legal provisions, there is for the first time a single source to which smaller enterprises can refer.

6008 Rules and formats under the **Companies Act 2006** make certain changes to those which were effective under the prior act. As these came into effect in respect of financial years beginning on or after 6 April 2008, references in this chapter are to the Companies Act 2006. In response to the new Act, a new version of the FRSSE (effective April 2008) was published. It updates and supersedes the FRSSE (effective January 2007) and should be regarded as standard for financial statements relating to accounting periods beginning on or after 6 April 2008. References to the FRSSE contained in this chapter are therefore to the most recent version of the FRSSE (effective April 2008).

SECTION 1

Qualification criteria

There are **three stages** in establishing whether a company is entitled to the small and medium-sized company exemptions. 6010

Stage 1	Make sure that the company is not **ineligible** by virtue of its **nature** or **activities**
Stage 2	Test whether the company falls within the **size limits**
Stage 3	Test whether the company satisfies the **reference-period conditions**.

1. Nature or activities

For financial years beginning on or after 6 April 2008, the following companies are excluded from the small company criteria: 6015
– a public company;
– a company that is an authorised insurance company, a banking company, an e-money issuer, an ISD investment firm or a UCITS management company or that carries on insurance market activity, or
– a member of an ineligible group.
A group is ineligible if any of its members is:
– a company disqualified as above,
– a person who has permission under Part 4 of the Financial Services and Markets Act 2000 to carry on one or more regulated activities, or
– a body corporate whose shares are admitted to trading on a regulated market in an EEA State.

MEMO POINTS (1) Companies that would otherwise qualify as small but for the fact that they are members of ineligible groups can still take advantage of the exemption from including a **business review** in the directors' report prepared for members and from filing the directors' report at Companies House.
(2) These exclusions do not preclude a company being treated as small or medium-sized if it is a subsidiary of a **large private company** but still meets all the other qualification criteria.

2. Size limits

To be treated as a small or medium-sized company under the Companies Act 2006, a company must meet any two of the following three size criteria: 6017

Criterion	Small company	Medium-sized company
Turnover (adjusted proportionately if the period is not a full year) must not exceed	£ 6,500,000	£ 25,900,000
Gross assets (i.e., total assets before the deduction of liabilities) must not exceed	£ 3,260,000	£ 12,900,000
Average number of employees must not exceed	50	250

Notes:
1. The average number of employees is determined by adding those defined as employed for each month and dividing the total by the number of months in the period.
2. The size limits are subject to periodic review and therefore change from time to time. The amounts shown above came into effect by the Companies Act 2006 (Amendments) (Accounts and Reports) Regulations 2008.

3. Reference period

6020 The final stage in the determination of whether a company will qualify for the relevant exemptions is to make sure that it satisfies the reference-period conditions:

– In respect of its **first financial year**, a company will qualify provided that it satisfies the size conditions in that year.

ss 382 (2), 465 (2) CA 2006 – In respect of **subsequent years**, a company will qualify provided that it satisfies the size conditions in both the year in question and the preceding year.

s 247 (1)(c) CA 2006 – A company that qualifies as small or medium-sized in a particular year will **continue to be treated** as one in the following year, even if it fails to satisfy the size conditions in that year. However, if it does not satisfy the qualifying conditions in the year after that, then, for the third year, it must produce its financial statements in a format appropriate to its size. On the other hand, if the company again satisfies the qualifying conditions in the third year, it may continue to take advantage of the exemptions to which it became entitled in the first year.

6024 EXAMPLE Scenario 1

A Ltd was incorporated on 1 July 20X7. The following details relate to reporting periods ending 31 December 20X7, 20X8, and 20X9. Assume the prevailing size limits applied in each of the three reporting periods.

	20X7	20X8	20X9
Turnover	£ 2,375,000	£ 5,800,000	£ 5,400,000
Gross assets	£ 2,600,000	£ 3,000,000	£ 3,000,000
Average number of employees	55	60	49

In **20X7**, its year of incorporation, A Ltd meets the size criteria of a small company on the basis of its turnover and gross assets. (Because the company was in existence for only six months, the turnover for the period is annualised to £4,750,000. However, this figure remains within the limit.) Note that even though the average number of employees exceeds 50, the company has only to meet two of the three requirements. As 20X7 is its first financial year, the company qualifies as a small company.

In **20X8**, A Ltd exceeds all the size criteria. However, it will still qualify as a small company because, in terms of section 382 (2), it fulfilled the size conditions in the previous financial year, which was its first. As a result, it is permitted to continue to prepare its financial statements as a small company.

In **20X9**, the company again satisfies the size criteria (on the basis of its turnover and number of employees falling below the respective limits). Despite the fact that it did not satisfy the size conditions in 20X8, it nonetheless qualifies as a small company in 20X9 because it had been treated as one in the previous year.

Scenario 2

B Ltd has been in existence for many years. It has consistently met the size requirements applicable to a medium-sized company since inception.

	20X7	20X8	20X9	20Y0
Turnover	£24,000,000	£26,500,000	£26,500,000	£25,100,000
Gross assets	£11,200,000	£13,800,000	£13,700,000	£12,700,000
Average number of employees	220	234	255	248

In 20X7, B Ltd meets all the size criteria that qualify it to be treated as a medium-sized company. And, because it has also fulfilled the size conditions for two consecutive years, it is entitled to the exemptions.

In 20X8, gross assets and turnover exceed the size criteria. However, B Ltd still qualifies as a medium-sized company because it fulfilled the size criteria in the two prior years.

In 20X9, the company once again exceeds the limits applicable to a medium-sized company. It therefore cannot prepare abbreviated financial statements.

In 20Y0, B Ltd meets the size criteria for a medium-sized company. However, for purposes of preparing abbreviated financial statements, it will not qualify as a medium-sized company because, in the previous two consecutive years, it did not qualify. (Note that if it meets the criteria again in 20Y1, it will be able to file abbreviated financial statements again.)

SECTION 2

Small companies

I. Shorter-form statements

When a company adopts the FRSSE it is released from the requirements of the other Financial Reporting Standards. Because adoption of the FRSSE is voluntary, if a company decides against adoption, it therefore in effect elects to remain bound by the requirements of all other accounting standards and UITF abstracts instead. **6030**

Where the FRSSE is adopted, this fact must be disclosed in the financial statements. This can be done in the directors' statement or separately within the notes to the accounts. **6032**

The decision by an eligible entity to adopt the FRSSE can be taken independently of any decision regarding the adoption of other accounting and disclosure exemptions of companies legislation. Furthermore, where an entity elects to adopt the FRSSE it may still on a selective basis comply with the additional requirements of various other Financial Reporting Standards. This should be made clear in the note on accounting policies. **6033**

MEMO POINTS 1. In spite of the relevant dispensation under companies legislation, the adoption of the FRSSE is not permitted by entities that were required to prepare their accounts in accordance with SORPs in existence at the time that the FRSSE was first issued (November 1997). The provisions of those SORPs should therefore continue to be followed. In respect of later SORPs, these may contain relevant guidance not only in relation to the FRSSE, but indeed whether it would be appropriate for the entities concerned to apply the FRSSE at all.
2. Effective 1 January 2005, when the EU Regulation on international accounting standards came into effect, UK companies not required to apply international standards were given the choice of whether to prepare their financial statements using IAS or UK accounting standards. Companies that meet the criteria for the FRSSE will be able to continue using it after 2005.

Revisions to Reporting Standards Both the FRSSE and other Financial Reporting Standards are updated periodically. There may be times, therefore, that a new FRS is implemented before the FRSSE has been revised to reflect a similar change applicable to smaller entities. In such cases, entities adopting the FRSSE are permitted to continue to apply its provisions even though they may be out of line with the provisions of the new standard. However, this is consistent with the general rule that when a company adopts FRSSE it is no longer obliged to follow other FRSs. **6036**

A. General accounting rules

1. True and fair view

The financial statements should present a true and fair view of the results for the period and of the state of affairs at the end of the period. To this end, the **substance** of any arrangement or transaction, or any series of such, into which the entity has entered should be considered. **6040** FRSSE 2.2

Departures from true and fair view

6041 FRSSE 2.3 If there are circumstances in which compliance with any of the provisions of the FRSSE or of the Act does not give a true and fair view, the directors are obliged to **depart** from the relevant provision to the extent necessary to give a true and fair view (this is the so-called **true and fair override**). In this event, the following should be disclosed in the notes:
– a statement that there has been a departure from the requirements of the FRSSE or Companies Act and that the departure is necessary to give a true and fair view;
– a statement of the treatment that the FRSSE or Companies Act would normally require and a description of the treatment adopted;
– a statement of the reasons why the treatment prescribed would not give a true and fair view; and
– a description of how the position shown in the financial statements is different as a result of the departure.

6043 FRSSE 2.4 Where a departure continues in **subsequent financial statements**, the disclosures should be made in all subsequent statements and should include corresponding amounts for the previous period.

6044 FRSSE 2.5 If any **doubt exists** as to whether applying the FRSSE would be sufficient to give a true and fair view, adequate explanation should be given in the notes to the accounts of the arrangement or transaction.

2. Accounting principles, estimation techniques, and accounting policies

6046 FRSSE 2.6 The financial statements should **state** that they have been "prepared in accordance with the Financial Reporting Standard for Smaller Entities (effective April 2008)". This statement may be included with the note of accounting policies or given on the balance sheet. If abbreviated accounts are also being prepared, the statement should be included with the note of accounting policies so that it is reproduced in the abbreviated accounts.

6048 FRSSE 2.9 Accounting policies and estimation techniques should be consistent with the requirements of both the FRSSE and companies legislation. Where this permits a choice, an entity should select the policies and techniques most **appropriate to its particular circumstances** for the purpose of giving a true and fair view, taking account of the objectives of relevance, reliability, comparability and understandability (¶27).

6050 FRSSE 2.10 Accounting policies should be **applied consistently** and **reviewed regularly** to ensure that they continue to give a true and fair view. However, in deciding whether a new policy is more appropriate than an existing policy, consideration should be given to the effect on comparability. Where a change in accounting policy is made, the amounts for the current and corresponding periods should be restated on the basis of the new policies.

6052 FRSSE 2.7 Financial statements should include:
– a description of each material accounting policy followed;
– details of any changes to the accounting policies previously followed, including a brief explanation of why each new accounting policy is more appropriate, and an indication of the effect of the change on the current period's results, and
– if material, the effect of a change to an estimation technique, a description of the change, and where practicable, the effect on the current period's results.

3. Going concern

6055 FRSSE 2.12 The company should be **presumed to be operating** as a going concern. In preparing financial statements, the directors should assess whether there are significant doubts about the entity's ability to continue as a going concern. Any material uncertainties should be disclosed. Where the period considered by the directors in making this assessment has been limited to a period of less than one year from the date of approval of the financial statements, that fact should be stated.

Financial statements should be prepared on the going concern basis unless the directors determine after the balance sheet date either that they intend to liquidate the entity or to cease trading, or that they have no realistic alternative but to do so. 6056

4. Prudence

The amount of any item should be determined on a prudent basis. Prudence is the inclusion of a degree of caution in the exercise of the judgements needed in making the estimates required under conditions of uncertainty, such that gains and assets are not overstated and liabilities are not understated. It is not appropriate to use prudence as a reason to knowingly understate assets or gains, or overstate liabilities or losses. 6058 FRSSE 2.13

5. Accruals

Except for cash flow information, financial statements are required to be prepared on the accruals basis of accounting. Therefore, all income and expenditures – whether or not actually received or paid at the end of the financial year – are brought into account. 6060 FRSSE 2.14

6. Prior period adjustments

Prior period adjustments should be accounted for by **restating** the comparative figures for the preceding period in the primary statements and the notes, and **adjusting** the opening balance of reserves to take account of the cumulative effect. The cumulative effect of the adjustments should also be noted at the foot of the statement of total recognised gains and losses (STRGL) (if it is necessary to present one, see ¶6101) in respect of the current period. The effect of prior period adjustments on the results for the preceding period should be disclosed where it is practicable to do so. 6062 FRSSE 2.15

7. Approval and signing of accounts

A company's annual accounts must be approved by the board of directors and signed on its behalf, on the face of the balance sheet, by one of their number. The date on which the financial statements are approved by the board must be disclosed. In addition, the balance sheet must clearly show by way of a prominent statement that the accounts have been prepared in accordance with the special company law provisions relating to small companies. (Note that this statement is separate from the requirement discussed in ¶6032 to disclose whether the company has adopted the FRSSE.) 6063 FRSSE 2.30 - 2.36

Every copy of the balance sheet which is published by or on behalf of the board must state the name of the director who signed it on behalf of the board.

The financial statements of the balance sheet delivered to the **Registrar** must, in addition to having been signed, also prominently state the company's registration number, the name of the director who signed on behalf of the board and the registered auditors as appropriate.

8. Report of the directors

The following disclosures are required to be made within the directors' report: 6066 FRSSE 18.1 - 18.15
- the principal activities of the company,
- details of the company's directors,

– political donations and expenditure and charitable donations (where the aggregate of each exceeds £2,000),
– acquisitions by the company of its own shares,
– employment of disabled persons (where the average number of employees exceeds 250),
– a statement that there is no relevant audit information of which the company's auditors are unaware and that the directors have taken the necessary steps to make themselves aware of any such information and to have established that it had been made available to the auditors.

The report must be approved by the board and signed, stating the name of the person who signed it.

9. Audit

Exemptions from audit

6070 s 477 CA 2006 Small companies can elect not to have their accounts audited if they qualify to be treated as a small company as set out in ¶6017, and they meet the following conditions:
– annual turnover does not exceed £6.5 million;
– balance sheet total does not exceed £3.26 million.

s 478 CA 2006 A company is not entitled to the exemption from audit if at any time during the financial year it was:
– a public company;
– a company that is an authorised insurance company, a banking company, an e-money issuer, an ISD investment firm or a UCITS management company;
– a company that carries on insurance market activity; or
– a special register body or an employers' association.

Under the Companies Act 2006, a company is not entitled to exemption from audit if it was at any time during the year a group company, unless the group qualifies as a small group.

6071 FRSSE 2.37 **Where** a company meets these conditions, and has **elected accordingly** (i.e., not to be audited), its balance sheet must contain a statement by the directors to the effect that:
– for the year in question, the company was entitled to exemption under the Companies Act 2006;
– no member or members eligible to do so have deposited a notice requesting an audit within one month before the end of the financial year; and
– the directors acknowledge their responsibility for ensuring that the company keeps accounting records consistent with its duty to do so and for preparing accounts that give a true and fair view of the state of affairs of the company as at the end of the financial year and of its profit or loss for the year.

6072 FRSSE 2.37 The Act provides a safeguard to protect the **interests of external shareholders**. Where holders of at least 10 percent of the share capital of a company so require, an audit of the accounts will be mandatory.

6073 FRSSE 2.38 Where the company has taken advantage of the exemption from audit because the **company is dormant**, and the company, during the financial year, has acted as an agent for any person, that fact must be stated.

6074 FRSSE 2.39 Where exemption from audit is not available, or the directors have not taken advantage of the exemption, and the company has entered into a liability limitation agreement with its auditors, the notes to the accounts must disclose the principal terms of the agreement and either the date of the resolution:
– approving the agreement or the agreement's principal terms, or
– waiving the need for such approval.

Report of the auditors

If a small company following the FRSSE is not exempt from the requirements to be audited, there will be no effect on the auditor's report other than a slight modification to its wording. However, in certain cases, it is possible that these accounts might not give a **true and fair view** of the company's affairs. If this should be the case, the auditors are obliged to qualify their opinion accordingly. 6075

B. Profit and loss account

1. Format

The format of the profit and loss account must comply **with one of the following formats**, with items listed in the order – and under the headings – shown in ¶6077 and ¶6079. 6076 FRSSE 2.28 – 2.29

Small companies are required to retain the same format in preparing their accounts for subsequent financial years of the company unless in their opinion there are special reasons for a change. Particulars must be disclosed of any change in the profit and loss account format, together with the reasons for the change. Where compliance with the provisions of companies legislation as to the matters to be included in a company's individual accounts or in notes to those accounts would not be sufficient to give a true and fair view, the necessary additional information must be given in the accounts or in a note. FRSSE 2.17 – 2.18

6077

Profit and loss account (Format 1)
1. Turnover
2. Cost of sales*
3. Gross profit or loss
4. Distribution costs
5. Administrative expenses
6. Other operating income
7. Income from shares in group undertakings
8. Income from participating interests
9. Income from other fixed asset investments
10. Other interest receivable and similar income
11. Amounts written off investments
12. Interest payable and similar charges
12a. Profit or loss on ordinary activities before taxation
13. Tax on profit or loss on ordinary activities
14. Profit or loss on ordinary activities after taxation**
19. Other taxes not shown under the above items
20. Profit or loss for the financial year
* This figure must include provisions for depreciation and write-downs of tangible and intangible fixed assets, and must also be separately disclosed in a note to the accounts. ** Extraordinary items, which are extremely rare, would be shown separately after the profit or loss on ordinary activities after taxation.

6079

Profit and loss account (Format 2)		
1. Turnover		
2. Change in stocks of finished goods and in work in progress		
3. Own work capitalised		
4. Other operating income		
5.	A.	Raw materials and consumables
	B.	Other external charges
6. Staff costs:		
	A.	Wages and salaries
	B.	Social security costs
	C.	Other pension costs
7.	A.	Depreciation and other amounts written off tangible and intangible fixed assets
	B.	Exceptional amounts written off current assets
8. Other operating charges		
9. Income from shares in group undertakings		
10. Income from participating interests		
11. Income from other fixed asset investments		
12. Other interest receivable and similar income		
13. Amounts written off investments		
14. Interest payable and similar charges		
14A. Profit or loss on ordinary activities before taxation		
15. Tax on profit or loss on ordinary activities		
16. Profit or loss on ordinary activities after taxation*		
21. Other taxes not shown under the above items		
22. Profit or loss for the financial year		
* Extraordinary items, which are extremely rare, would be shown separately after the profit or loss on ordinary activities after taxation.		

2. Specific treatment

6084 FRSSE 3.1 All **gains and losses** recognised in the financial statements for the period must be included in the profit and loss account or the STRGL. Only profits that are realised at the balance sheet date should be included in the profit and loss account. All **liabilities** that have arisen in respect of the period (or in respect of a previous period) are to be taken into account (including any that may have become apparent between the balance sheet date and the date on which it is signed).

6085 FRSSE 3.2 Gains and losses may be **excluded** from the profit and loss account only if they are specifically permitted or required to be **taken directly to reserves** by the FRSSE or by company law.

6086 FRSSE 3.3 Where an amount relating to any **preceding financial year** is included in the profit and loss account, the effect of its inclusion must be stated.

6087 FRSSE 3.4 If the company has supplied **markets outside the UK** during the financial year, it must disclose separately the percentage of turnover that is attributable to those markets. In analysing the source of turnover, account must be taken of the manner in which the company's activities are organised.

a. Exceptional items

All exceptional items must be taken into account in arriving at the profit or loss on ordinary activities and included under the **statutory format headings** to which they relate. However, the following are **exceptions** because they are required to be shown separately in the profit and loss account: **6089** FRSSE 3.5 - 3.6
- profits or losses on the sale or termination of an operation,
- costs of a fundamental reorganisation or restructuring having a material effect on the nature and focus of the reporting entity's operations, and
- profits or losses on the disposal of fixed assets.

The **amount** of each exceptional item, either individually or as an aggregate of items of a similar type, should be disclosed separately by way of a note - or on the face of the profit and loss account if that degree of prominence is necessary in order to give **a true and fair view**. A **description** of each exceptional item should be given to enable its nature to be understood.

b. Revenue recognition

As a general rule, revenue is recognised by a seller when it obtains **the right to consideration** in exchange for its performance. (Typically, at the same time it would recognise a new asset, i.e., a debtor.) **6091** FRSSE 4.1

If a seller receives **payment in advance** of performance, the amount should be recognised, and accounted for, as a liability. Later, when the seller, by its performance, obtains the right to consideration, the liability should be reduced (in part or in full, as the case may be) and the amount transferred to revenue. In cases where a seller has partially performed its contractual obligations, it should recognise revenue to the extent that it has obtained the right to consideration. **6092** FRSSE 4.2

Revenue must be measured at the **fair value** of the right to consideration, which is normally the price specified in the contractual arrangement, net of discounts, value added tax and similar sales taxes. However, where the effect of the time value of money is material, the present value of the amounts expected to be received should be used. (The unwinding of the discount should be credited to finance income as this represents a gain from a financing transaction.) **6093** FRSSE 4.4 - 4.5 FRSSE 4.4

c. Turnover

Turnover is the revenue arising from transactions under which a seller supplies goods or services to customers in the ordinary course of its business. Sellers may, of course, enter into other transactions (e.g., the sale of fixed assets) that do not give rise to turnover. **6095** FRSSE 4.8 - 4.9

d. Profit or loss on disposal

The profit or loss on the disposal of an asset should be accounted for in the profit and loss account of the period in which the disposal occurs. It is **computed** as the difference between the net **sale proceeds** and the net **carrying amount**, whether carried at historical cost (less any provisions made) or at a valuation. Profit or loss on disposal of **a previously acquired business** should include the attributable amount of purchased goodwill where it has previously been eliminated against reserves as a matter of accounting policy and has not previously been charged in the profit and loss account. **6097** FRSSE 3.7

e. Auditors' remuneration

6099 FRSSE 3.8 Amounts paid to auditors by way of remuneration, including expenses, must be disclosed in the notes to the accounts. The nature and value of benefits in kind, if any, must also be given.

C. STRGL

6101 FRSSE 5.1 If the only recognised gains and losses are included in the profit and loss account, no separate statement to this effect needs to be made. In other cases, a **primary statement** should be presented, i.e., with the **same prominence** as the profit and loss account, showing the total of recognised gains and losses (see ¶4307).

D. Balance sheet

1. Format

6105 The FRSSE adopts the balance sheet formats of SI 2008 No. 409 ("The Small Companies and Groups (Accounts and Directors' Report) Regulations 2008"). These are a simplification of those in SI 2008 No. 410 ("The Large and Medium-Sized Companies and Groups (Accounts and Directors' Report) Regulations 2008"), which are prescribed for companies that do not qualify as **small** companies.

The following table compares the requirements of the two Schedules under Format 1.

Items in coloured print under SI 2008 No. 409 may be combined under the item shown opposite under SI 2008 No. 410 also in coloured print. The items in black print are the same under both Schedules.

Format per SI 2008 No. 410		Format per SI 2008 No. 409	
A	Called up share capital not paid	A	Called up share capital not paid
B	Fixed assets	B	Fixed assets
B-I	Intangible assets	B-I	Intangible assets
	3. Goodwill		1. Goodwill
	1. Development costs		2. Other intangible assets
	2. Concessions, patents, licences…etc		
	4. Payments on account		
B-II	Tangible assets	B-II	Tangible assets
	1. Land and buildings		1. Land and buildings
	2. Plant and machinery		2. Plant and machinery, etc
	3. Fixtures, fittings…		
	4. Payments on account and assets in the course of construction		

Items in coloured print under SI 2008 No. 409 may be combined under the item shown opposite under SI 2008 No. 410 also in coloured print. The items in black print are the same under both Schedules.

	Format per SI 2008 No. 410		Format per SI 2008 No. 409
B-III	Investments	B-III	Investments
	1. Shares in group undertakings 3. Participating interests		1. Shares in group undertakings and participating interests
	2. Loans to group undertakings 4. Loans to undertakings, etc		2. Loans to group undertakings and undertakings in which the company has a participating interest
	5. Other investments other than loans		3. Other investments other than loans
	6. Other loans 7. Own shares		4. Other investments
C	Current assets	C	Current assets
C-I	Stocks	C-I	Stocks
	1. Raw materials, etc. 2. Work in progress 3. Finished goods/goods for resale		1. Stocks
	4. Payments on account		2. Payments on account
C-II	Debtors	C-II	Debtors
	1. Trade debtors		1. Trade debtors (See Note 1)
	2. Amounts owed by group undertakings 3. Amounts owed by undertakings in which the company has a participating interest		2. Amounts owed by group undertakings and undertakings in which the company has a participating interest
	4. Other debtors		3. Other debtors
	5. Called up share capital not paid		
	6. Prepayments and accrued income		
C-III	Investments	C-III	Investments
	1. Shares in group undertakings		1. Shares in group undertakings
	2. Own shares 3. Other investments		2. Other investments
C-IV	Cash at bank and in hand	C-IV	Cash at bank and in hand
D	Prepayments and accrued income	D	Prepayments and accrued income
E	Creditors: amounts…within one year	E	Creditors: amounts…within one year
	2. Bank loans and overdrafts		1. Bank loans and overdrafts
	4. Trade creditors		2. Trade creditors
	6. Amounts owed to group undertakings 7. Amounts owed to undertakings in which the company has a participating interest		3. Amounts owed to group undertakings and undertakings in which the company has a participating interest
	1. Debenture loans		4. Other creditors

Items in coloured print under SI 2008 No. 409 may be combined under the item shown opposite under SI 2008 No. 410 also in coloured print. The items in black print are the same under both Schedules.

Format per SI 2008 No. 410		Format per SI 2008 No. 409	
	3. Payments received on account 5. Bills of exchange payable 8. Other creditors including taxation and social security 9. Accruals and deferred income		
F	Net current assets (liabilities)	F	Net current assets (liabilities)
G	Total assets less current liabilities	G	Total assets less current liabilities
H	Creditors amounts…after one year 2. Bank loans and overdrafts 4. Trade creditors 6. Amounts owed to group undertakings 7. Amounts owed to undertakings in which the company has a participating interest 1. Debenture loans 3. Payments received on account 5. Bills of exchange payable 8. Other creditors including taxation and social security 9. Accruals and deferred income	H	Creditors: amounts…after one year 1. Bank loans and overdrafts 2. Trade creditors 3. Amounts owed to group undertakings and undertakings in which the company has a participating interest 4. Other creditors
I	Provision for liabilities and charges 1. Pensions and similar obligations 2. Taxation, etc 3. Other provisions	I	Provisions for liabilities and charges (Items 1-3 need not be shown)
J	Accruals and deferred income	J	Accruals and deferred income
K	Capital and reserves	K	Capital and reserves
K-I	Called up share capital	K-I	Called up share capital
K-II	Share premium account	K-II	Share premium account
K-III	Revaluation reserve	K-III	Revaluation reserve
K-IV	Other reserves 1. Capital redemption reserve 2. Reserve for own shares 3. Reserves provided for by articles 4. Other reserves	K-IV	Other reserves (Items 1-4 need not be shown)
K-V	Profit and loss account	K-V	Profit and loss account

Note 1 – a small company need not show amounts falling due after more than one year separately for each item included under debtors if it discloses the aggregate amount of debtors falling due after more than one year in the notes.

2. Fixed assets and goodwill

a. Disclosure

In respect of all fixed assets and goodwill, the cost or valuation at the beginning and the end of the year, together with the effect of any of the following during the year must be shown: **6107** FRSSE 6.1 - 6.2
- revaluations,
- acquisitions,
- disposals, and
- transfers.

In respect of provisions for **depreciation** or diminutions in value, the cumulative amount of such provisions as at the beginning and end of the year must be shown, as well as the effects of the amount of any provisions or other adjustments made during the year.

b. Research and development

The **cost** of **fixed assets acquired or constructed** in order to **provide facilities** for research and development activities over a number of accounting periods should be capitalised but written off over their useful lives through the profit and loss account. **6109** FRSSE 6.3 - 6.10

Expenditure on pure and applied research should be charged to the profit and loss account in the year incurred.

Expenditure on **development** should generally be written off **in the year incurred**. Where the development expenditure may be **deferred** to future periods (to the extent that its recovery is assured), it should be amortised commencing with commercial production or application of the relevant product, service, process or system. Deferral is appropriate when: **6110**
a) there is a **clearly defined project**; and
b) the related expenditure is **separately identifiable**; and
- the outcome of such a project has been assessed with reasonable certainty as to its technical feasibility and its ultimate commercial viability; and
- the aggregate of the deferred development costs, any further development costs, and related production, selling and administration costs is reasonably expected to be exceeded by related future sales or other revenues; and
- adequate resources already exist or are reasonably expected to be available to enable the project to be completed and to provide any consequential increases in working capital.

If a policy of **deferral** is adopted, it must be applied to all development projects.

At the end of each accounting period, deferred development expenditure for each product should be **reviewed**. If the circumstances that originally justified the deferral of expenditure no longer apply, or are considered doubtful, the expenditure should be written off.

The amount of deferred development expenditure carried forward at the beginning and end of the period should be **disclosed under intangible assets** in the balance sheet or in the notes to the balance sheet. Disclosure must also be made of the **reason for capitalising** these costs as well as the **period** over which they are being depreciated.

Where development costs are not treated as a realised loss or realised revenue loss this must be stated together with an explanation of the circumstances relied upon by the directors to justify this decision.

c. Other intangible assets and goodwill

Internally generated goodwill and intangible assets should not be capitalised, while **purchased** positive goodwill and intangible assets should be. **6112** FRSSE 6.11 - 6.16

Intangible **assets purchased with a business** should be recognised separately from the purchased goodwill if their value can be measured reliably.

Capitalised goodwill and intangible assets should be **depreciated** on a straight-line (or more appropriate) basis over their useful economic lives, which in any event may not exceed 20 years. The period chosen, and the reason for choosing it, must be shown by way of a note.

The **residual value** assigned to goodwill should be zero. A residual value exceeding this may be assigned to an intangible asset only when this value can be established reliably – e.g., if it has been agreed contractually.

At the end of each accounting period, useful economic lives should be reviewed and, if necessary, **revised** but by no more than 20 years from the date of acquisition. At the date of revision, the carrying amount should be depreciated over the **revised estimate** of the intangible asset's remaining useful economic life. Goodwill and intangible assets are not revalued.

6113 FRSSE 6.17 If an acquisition appears to give rise to **negative goodwill**, fair value should be checked to ensure that the assets acquired have not been overstated and liabilities have not been understated. The negative goodwill up to the fair value of the non-monetary assets acquired should be released to the profit and loss account over the lives of those assets. Any additional negative goodwill should be recognised in the profit and loss account over the period expected to benefit from it. Both the amount of negative goodwill on the balance sheet and the period over which it is to be written back must be disclosed.

There are **no specific rules** on how negative goodwill should be **disclosed** in the balance sheet.

d. Tangible fixed assets – other than investment properties

6116 FRSSE 6.19 Tangible fixed assets should **initially be measured** at cost, then written down to recoverable amount if necessary (see ¶6138). The initial carrying amount of a tangible fixed asset received as a **gift or donation** by a charity should be its current value – i.e., the lower of **replacement cost and recoverable amount** – at the date received. If no record of the purchase price or production cost of an asset can be found (or if it cannot be obtained without unreasonable expense or delay), the value ascribed shall be the earliest available record of its value. Where the value is determined under these circumstances, particulars must be given.

6117 FRSSE 6.20 Only those **costs** that are **directly attributable** to bringing the tangible fixed asset into working condition should be included in its measurement. In the case of entities that have adopted the **accounting policy of capitalising finance costs**, only those that are directly attributable to the construction of tangible fixed assets should be capitalised. The total amount of finance costs capitalised during a period should not exceed the total amount of finance costs incurred during the same period. The notes should disclose the fact that finance costs have been included in determining the cost of the asset, as well as the amount concerned.

FRSSE 6.21 Capitalisation of directly attributable costs, including finance costs, should be **suspended** during extended periods in which active development is interrupted. Capitalisation should cease when substantially all the activities that are necessary to get the tangible fixed asset ready for use are complete, even if the asset has not yet been brought into use.

6119 FRSSE 6.22 **Subsequent** expenditure should be **capitalised** if:
- it enhances the economic benefits of a tangible fixed asset – i.e., if it is an **improvement**, or
- it **replaces or restores** a component that had been separately depreciated over its useful economic life.

In all other cases, it should be charged to the profit and loss account.

Revaluations

6121 FRSSE 6.23 - 6.24 Where an entity adopts an **accounting policy of revaluing** tangible fixed assets, the asset's carrying amount at the balance sheet date should be its **market value** (or the best estimate thereof) at the time. Where, in the directors' opinion, market value is not an appropriate basis, **current value** – i.e., the lower of replacement cost and recoverable amount – may be used instead. Where a tangible fixed asset is revalued, all tangible fixed assets of the same class should be revalued. However, a policy of revaluation does not have to be applied to all classes of tangible fixed assets.

It may be possible to establish with reasonable reliability the values of certain tangible fixed assets, other than properties, by reference to active second-hand markets or appropriate publicly available indices. In respect of other tangible fixed assets for which values are not easily determinable, including properties, an experienced valuer should **perform a valuation** at least every five years. It should be updated by an experienced valuer in the intervening years if it is likely that there has been a material change in value.

Revaluation losses caused only by changing market prices should be recognised in the STRGL until the carrying amount of the asset reaches its depreciated historical cost. Other revaluation losses should be recognised in the profit and loss account. 6123 FRSSE 6.25

Revaluation gains should be recognised in the statement of total recognised gains and losses, except to the extent (after adjusting for subsequent depreciation) that they reverse revaluation losses on the same asset that were previously recognised in the profit and loss account. These should be recognised in the profit and loss account. The adjustment for subsequent depreciation is aimed at achieving the same effect as would have prevailed if the original downward revaluation had not occurred. 6125 FRSSE 6.26

Where tangible fixed assets have been **revalued, disclosure** must be made of: 6126 FRSSE 6.27 - 6.29
- the aggregate historical cost amount that would have been included if the assets not been revalued, or
- the differences between those amounts and the amounts actually shown.

If, however, tangible fixed assets are constantly being replaced and, neither their value nor their degree of variation is material, they may be included at a fixed quantity and value.

The **year in which** assets have been **revalued** should be disclosed. Where the revaluation took place in the current year, the basis of the valuation should be disclosed together with the names of the persons performing the valuation or particulars of their qualifications. 6128

e. Depreciation – other than relating to investment properties

A tangible fixed asset's cost (or revalued amount) less its estimated residual value should be depreciated on a **systematic basis** over its **useful economic life**. The depreciation method used should fairly reflect the pattern in which the asset's economic benefits are consumed. The depreciation charge for each period should be recognised as an expense in the profit and loss account unless it is permitted to be included in the carrying amount of another asset. 6130 FRSSE 6.38 - 6.40

In the case of a tangible fixed asset consisting **of two or more** major **components**, with substantially different useful economic lives, depreciation on the individual components should be accounted for separately.

The useful economic lives and residual values of tangible fixed assets should be reviewed regularly and revised if necessary. The carrying amount of the tangible fixed asset at the date of revision, less the revised residual value, should be depreciated over the revised remaining useful economic life.

A **change in the method of providing depreciation** is permissible only on the grounds that the new method will render fairer presentation. Such a change does not constitute a change of accounting policy; the carrying amount of the tangible fixed asset is depreciated using the revised method over the remaining useful economic life, beginning in the period in which the change is made. 6132 FRSSE 6.41

The following should be **disclosed** in the financial statements for **land and buildings**, and for the **aggregate of other tangible fixed assets**: 6133 FRSSE 6.42 - 6.43
- the depreciation methods used;
- the useful economic lives or the depreciation rates used; and
- where material, the financial effect of a change during the period in either the estimate of useful economic lives or the estimate of residual values.

Where there has been a change in the depreciation method used, the effect, if material, should be disclosed in the period of change together with a brief explanation of the reason.

MEMO POINTS Generally, **land** is regarded as having an unlimited life and therefore is not depreciated.

f. Write-downs to recoverable amount – except investment properties and financial instruments

6138 FRSSE 6.44 - 6.48 Fixed assets and goodwill should be carried in the balance sheet at a value no higher than their recoverable amounts.

6139 If the net book amount of a fixed asset or goodwill is considered not to be recoverable in full at the balance sheet date, the net book amount should be **written down** to the estimated recoverable amount. This revised amount is then written off over the remaining useful economic life of the asset.

6140 If the recoverable amount of a **tangible fixed asset** or investment subsequently increases as a result of a change in economic conditions or in the expected use of the asset, the net book amount should be **written back** to the lower of:
– recoverable amount; and
– the amount at which the asset would have been recorded had the original write-down not taken place.

If the recoverable amount of an **intangible asset or capitalised goodwill** subsequently increases, the net book amount should be written back only if the original write-down was the result of an external event and subsequent external events **clearly and demonstrably reverse the effects** of that event in a way that was not foreseen when the original write-down was calculated.

6141 Write-downs, and any reversals, to recoverable amount should be taken to the profit and loss account in the period concerned. However, write-downs of revalued tangible fixed assets that reverse previous revaluation gains simply as a result of changing market prices should instead be recognised in the **statement of total recognised gains and losses**, to the extent that the carrying amount of the asset is greater than its depreciated historical cost. Any amounts not shown in the profit and loss account must be disclosed in a note to the accounts.

6142 FRSSE 6.49 If fixed assets are not actually revalued in the balance sheet but their value has been considered by the directors, a note to the accounts should be given to reflect that:
– the directors have considered the value of fixed assets, without actually revaluing those assets;
– the directors are satisfied that the aggregate value of those assets at no time was less than the aggregate amount at which they are stated; and
– the assets affected are accordingly stated in the accounts on the basis that a revaluation of the company's fixed assets took place at that time.

MEMO POINTS It is worth noting that **compared to FRS 15**:
– there is no specific requirement for an annual impairment review where depreciation is immaterial or where the remaining useful life of the asset exceeds 50 years;
– residual values and estimates of useful economic lives are required "regularly" rather than annually;
– there is no reference to:
  – start-up or commissioning period for tangible fixed assets,
  – when capitalisation of finance charges should begin,
  – construction of fixed assets in parts,
  – accounting for major inspections or overhauls of tangible fixed assets,
  – renewals accounting.

g. Investments

Investment properties

6145 FRSSE 6.50 - 6.53 Investment properties should **not** be **subject to** periodic **depreciation** charges unless they are held on lease and the lease has an unexpired term of less than 20 years.

Investment properties should be disclosed in the balance sheet at their **open market value**. The carrying value should be stated prominently on the face of the balance sheet or in the notes. 6146

Changes in market value should be taken to the STRGL and not the profit and loss account. Where a deficit, or its reversal, on an individual property is expected to be permanent, it should be taken to the profit and loss account. 6147

The names of the persons undertaking the valuations or particulars of their qualifications, together with their bases of valuation and, if relevant, the fact that they are an employee or officer of the company or group, should be disclosed. 6148

Other investments

Initially, fixed asset investments should be **measured at cost**. Alternatively, they may be measured at a market value determined as at the date of their last valuation or on any other value determined by the directors to be appropriate. In this event, the method of valuation adopted and the reasons for adopting it should be disclosed by way of a note to the accounts. Gains and losses must be recognised in the profit and loss account or STRGL using the same basis applied to tangible fixed assets. 6150 FRSSE 6.30

Where fixed asset investments have been revalued, either the **comparable amounts** determined under the historical cost accounting rules (i.e., the aggregate historical cost amount that would have been included had the assets not been revalued, reflecting any write-downs to recoverable amount that would have been necessary) or the differences between those amounts and the corresponding amounts actually shown in the balance sheet should be shown separately in the balance sheet or in a note to the accounts. 6151 FRSSE 6.31

The aggregate amount of listed investments included under each item of investments shown in the balance sheet should be disclosed as follows: 6152 FRSSE 6.32
- the aggregate market value of the listed investments if this differs from the amount at which they are shown in the balance sheet; and
- both the market value and the stock exchange value, of which the market value is taken as being higher than the stock exchange value.

If a company has at the end of the financial year a significant holding in an undertaking that is not a subsidiary and the holding represents either 20 percent or more of the nominal value of any class of shares in the undertaking, or more than 20 percent of the book value of the investing company's total assets, it must disclose the following: 6153 FRSSE 6.33
- the name of the undertaking;
- if incorporated outside Great Britain, the country in which it is incorporated;
- if unincorporated, the address of its principal place of business;
- the identity and proportion of the nominal value of each class of shares held;
- the aggregate amount of the capital and reserves of the undertaking as at the end of the most recent financial year ending with or before that of the investing company; and
- its profit or loss for that year.

h. Revaluation reserve

Any losses or gains arising on the revaluation of assets that have been recognised in the STRGL should be debited or credited to a separate revaluation reserve. 6155 FRSSE 6.34 – 6.36

Amounts may be transferred from the revaluation reserve to the profit and loss account as and when they are realised. In the case of tangible fixed assets, this will normally result in an annual transfer from the revaluation reserve to the profit and loss account over the useful economic life of the asset (i.e., in line with the depreciation charge). Realisation may also occur on disposal of the asset.

The tax treatment of amounts credited or debited to the revaluation reserve must be disclosed by way of a note.

i. Government grants

6157 FRSSE 6.54 - 6.57 Government grants should be recognised in the profit and loss account so as to **match** them with the expenditure towards which they are intended to contribute. Even though a grant may have been received as a contribution towards expenditure on a fixed asset, company law does not allow the cost of the asset to be reduced – the grant, therefore, should be treated as **deferred income**.

6158 A government grant should not be recognised in the profit and loss account until the **conditions for its receipt** have been complied with and there is reasonable assurance that the grant will be received.

Potential liabilities to repay grants should be provided for only to the extent that **repayment is probable**. The repayment of a government grant should be set off against any unamortised deferred income relating to the grant. Any excess should be charged immediately to the profit and loss account.

6159 The following information should be **disclosed** in the financial statements:
- the effects of government grants on the results for the period and/or the financial position of the entity; and
- where the results of the period are affected materially by the receipt of forms of government assistance other than grants, the nature of that assistance and, to the extent possible, an estimate of the effects.

3. Leases

6162 Hire purchase contracts that are of a financing nature should be accounted for on the same basis as **finance leases**. Other hire purchase contracts should be accounted for in the same way as **operating leases**.

a. Accounting by lessees

6164 FRSSE 7.2 - 7.3 A finance lease should be recorded in the balance sheet of a lessee both as an **asset** and as an **obligation** to pay future rentals. In other words, at inception, the fair value of the asset should be recorded both as an asset and a liability. This represents a difference to SSAP 21, which requires the value of the asset and liability to be recorded initially at the present value of the minimum lease payments. However, where the **fair value** of the asset does not give a realistic estimate of the cost of the asset and the value of the obligation entered into, a more reliable estimate should be made. For example, if the lessee has benefited from grants and capital allowances such that the minimum lease payments can be adjusted to an amount less than the fair value of the asset, discounting the lease payments at the interest rate implicit in the lease would provide a more suitable estimate. A negative finance charge should not be shown.

6166 FRSSE 7.4 The **total finance charge** under a finance lease should be allocated to accounting periods during the lease term so as to produce a constant periodic rate of charge on the remaining balance. The straight-line method may provide such a reasonable approximation.

6167 FRSSE 7.5 - 7.7 The **rental under an operating lease** should be charged on a straight-line basis over the lease term even if the payments are not made on that basis, unless another basis is more appropriate.

Incentives to sign a lease, in whatever form they may take, should be spread over the lease term on a straight-line basis. If these are shorter than the full lease term, they should be spread over the period to the review date on which the rent is first expected to be adjusted to the prevailing market rate.

An asset leased under a finance lease should be **depreciated** over the shorter of the lease term and its useful life. However, in the case of a hire purchase contract that has the characteristics of a finance lease, the asset should be depreciated over its useful life.

b. Accounting by lessors

The amount due from a lessee under a finance lease should be recorded in the lessor's balance sheet as a debtor at the amount of the **net investment** (i.e., after providing for items such as bad and doubtful rentals receivable) in the lease. **6170** FRSSE 7.8 - 7.11

The **total gross earnings** under finance leases should be recognised on a systematic and rational basis – such as a constant periodic rate of return on the lessor's net investment.

Rental income from an operating lease should be recognised on a straight-line basis over the period of the lease, even if the payments are not made on that basis, unless another basis is more representative of the time pattern in which the benefit from the leased asset is receivable. **6171**

An asset held for use in operating leases by a lessor should be recorded as a fixed asset and depreciated over its useful life.

A lessor that is a manufacturer or dealer should not recognise a selling profit under an **operating lease**. Under a **finance lease**, the selling profit should be restricted to the excess of the fair value of the asset over the cost to the manufacturer/dealer less any grants towards the purchase, construction or use of the asset. **6172**

c. Sale and leaseback transactions

In a sale and leaseback transaction that results in a **finance lease**, any apparent profit or loss (i.e., the difference between the sale price and the previous carrying value) should be **deferred and amortised** in the financial statements of the seller/lessee over the shorter of the lease term and the useful life of the asset. **6175** FRSSE 7.13 - 7.14

In the case of an **operating lease**, any profit or loss should be **recognised immediately** provided it is clear that the transaction is established at fair value. However, if the sale price is not at fair value, two possibilities exist: **6176**

- if the sale price is **below fair value**, any profit or loss should be recognised immediately, except that if the apparent loss is compensated for by future rentals at below market price it should to that extent be deferred and amortised over the remainder of the lease term (or, if shorter, the period during which the reduced rentals are chargeable);
- if the sale price is **above fair value**, the excess over fair value should be deferred and amortised over the shorter of the remainder of the lease term and the period to the next rent review (if any).

Disclosure by lessees

Disclosure should include the following: **6178** FRSSE 7.16

- the gross amounts of **assets held under finance leases** together with the related accumulated depreciation and analysed into "land and buildings" and "other fixed assets" in aggregate; or, alternatively, leased assets may be aggregated with owned fixed assets provided that there is separate disclosure of the net amount of assets held under finance leases and the amount of depreciation for the period attributable to them;
- the amounts of **obligations related to finance leases** (net of finance charges allocated to future periods). These should be disclosed separately from other obligations and liabilities, either on the face of the balance sheet or in the notes to the accounts;
- the amount of any commitments existing at the balance sheet date in respect of finance leases entered into but whose inception occurs after the year end;
- the amount of **commitments in respect of operating leases** for the next year, analysed into those in which the commitment expires within that year, those expiring in two to five years, and those expiring more than five years after the balance sheet date. There is no requirement, as there is under SSAP 21, to analyse these commitments into those relating to land and buildings, and all other operating leases.

Disclosure by lessors

6180 FRSSE 7.18 Disclosure should include the following:
- the gross amounts of assets held for use in operating leases and the related accumulated depreciation;
- the cost of assets acquired, whether by purchase or finance lease, for the purpose of letting under finance leases;
- the net investment in finance leases and in hire purchase contracts at balance sheet date.

4. Current assets

a. Stocks and long-term contracts

6185 FRSSE 8.1 – 8.5 Stocks are stated in the financial statements at the lower of cost and net realisable value. This amount must be given in respect of **separate** items of stock or of **groups** of similar items.

If there is **no record** of the purchase price or production cost of stock, the earliest available record of its value must be used (and this fact disclosed in the first year it applies).

Finance costs (such as interest) that are directly attributable to the acquisition, construction or production of stock may be included as part of the cost. By way of note, the fact that finance costs are included in determining the cost of the asset, and the amount, must be disclosed.

Where **stocks are constantly being replaced** and their value is not material to assessing the company's state of affairs and their quantity, value and composition are not subject to material variation, they may be included at a fixed quantity and value.

Distribution costs may not be included in the production costs of stocks.

6187 FRSSE 8.6 – 8.7 Long-term contracts should be assessed on a contract-by-contract basis and reflected in the profit and loss account by recording turnover and related costs as contract activity progresses. Turnover is ascertained in a manner appropriate to the stage of completion of the contract, the business, and the industry in which it operates.

Where it is considered that the outcome of a long-term contract can be assessed with reasonable certainty, attributable profit should be calculated on a prudent basis and recognised in the profit and loss account as the difference between turnover and related costs for that contract.

6189 FRSSE 8.8 Long-term contracts should be **disclosed** in the balance sheet as follows:
- the amount by which recorded turnover is in excess of payments on account should be classified as "amounts recoverable on contracts" and disclosed separately within **debtors**,
- the balance of payments on account (in excess of the amounts matched with turnover and offset against long-term contract balances) should be classified as "payments on account" and disclosed separately within **creditors**,
- the amount of long-term contracts, at cost, net of amounts transferred to cost of sales, after deducting foreseeable losses and payments on account not matched with turnover, should be classified as "long-term contract balances" and disclosed separately within **stocks** in the balance sheet, with the following balances shown in the notes:
- net cost less foreseeable losses, and
- applicable payments on account,
- the amount by which the provision or accrual for foreseeable losses exceeds the costs incurred (after transfers to cost of sales) should be included within "provisions for liabilities and charges" or "creditors".

Consignment stock

6190 FRSSE 8.9 Where consignment stock is in substance an asset of the dealer, it should be recognised as such on the dealer's balance sheet, together with a corresponding liability to the manufacturer. Any deposit should be deducted from the liability and the excess classified as a trade creditor.

Where stock is not in substance an asset of the dealer, the stock should not be included on the dealer's balance sheet until title has transferred. Any deposit should be included under "other debtors".

b. Debt factoring

Where all significant **benefits** (i.e., the future cash flows) and all significant **risks** (i.e., slow payment risk and the risk of bad debts) relating to the factored debts have been **transferred** to the factor, the debts should be removed from the entity's balance sheet and no liability should be shown in respect of the proceeds received from the factor. A profit or loss, calculated as the difference between the carrying amount of the debts and the proceeds received, should be recognised. **6192** FRSSE 8.10 - 8.12

Where the entity has **retained significant benefits and risks** relating to factored debts, but all of the following conditions are met: **6193**

- there is no doubt that the entity's exposure to loss is limited to a fixed monetary amount,
- amounts received from the factor are secured only on the debts factored,
- the debts factored are capable of being separately identified,
- the factor has no recourse to other debts or assets,
- the entity has no right to reacquire the debts in the future, and
- the factor has no right to return the debts even in the event of the cessation of the factoring agreement,

the factored debts should be shown **gross** (after providing for bad debts, credit protection charges and any accrued interest) separately on the face of the balance sheet. Any amounts received from the factor in respect of those debts, to the extent that they are not returnable, should be shown as deductions against the debts on the face of the balance sheet (i.e. – a **linked presentation**).

The financial statements should include a note stating that the entity is not required to support bad debts in respect of factored debts and that the factors have stated in writing that they will not seek recourse other than out of factored debts. The **interest element** of the factor's charges should be recognised as it accrues and included in the profit and loss account with other interest charges. **6194**

In all other cases, a **separate presentation** should be adopted (i.e. – the gross amount of the debts should be shown on the balance sheet of the entity within assets, and a corresponding liability in respect of the proceeds received from the factor should be shown within liabilities). The interest element of the factor's charges and other factoring costs should be recognised as it accrues and included in the profit and loss account with other interest charges. **6195**

c. Current asset investments

Current asset investments must initially be stated in the financial statements at the lower of cost and net realisable value. They may alternatively be measured at their current cost. Gains and losses must be recognised, in the profit and loss account or STRGL, using the same basis applied to tangible fixed assets (¶6123 and ¶6125). **6198** FRSSE 8.13 - 8.14

If listed shares are held as a current asset investment, the following disclosure requirements apply: **6199**

- the aggregate market value (where it differs from their balance sheet amount), and
- both the market value and the stock exchange value of any investments, of which the market value is taken as being higher than the stock exchange value.

d. Start-up costs and pre-contract costs

6202 FRSSE 8.15 Start-up costs should be accounted for on a basis consistent with the accounting treatment of similar costs incurred as part of the entity's ongoing activities. Where no such similar costs are incurred, start-up costs that do not meet the criteria for recognition as assets under any other specific requirement of the FRSSE should be recognised as an expense when they are incurred. They should not be carried forward as an asset.

6203 FRSSE 8.16 **Pre-contract** costs shall be expensed as incurred, except that directly attributable costs shall be recognised as an asset when it is virtually certain that a contract will be obtained and the contract is expected to result in future net cash inflows with a present value no less than all amounts recognised as an asset. Costs incurred before the asset recognition criteria are met shall not be recognised as an asset.

5. Taxation

6205 FRSSE 9.1 - 9.3 Tax, both current and deferred, should be **recognised in the profit and loss account**, except to the extent that any part of it is attributable to a gain or loss that has been recognised directly in the **statement of total recognised gains and losses** (STRGL). In that event, the relevant tax should be recognised directly there as well.

The material components of the tax charge or credit for the period, as well as those of the deferred tax balance, should be disclosed separately.

Any special circumstances that affect the overall tax charge or credit for the period – or future periods – should be disclosed, and their individual effects quantified, by way of a note. The effects of a fundamental change in the basis of taxation should be included in the tax charge or credit for the period and separately disclosed on the face of the profit and loss account.

6207 FRSSE 9.4 - 9.12 While deferred tax should be recognised in respect of all **timing differences** that have **originated but not reversed** by the balance sheet date, in the following instances it should not be recognised:
- in respect of **permanent differences**,
- on **revaluation gains and losses** unless, by the balance sheet date, the entity has entered into a binding agreement to sell the asset and has revalued it to selling price, and
- in respect of taxable gains on revaluations or sales if it is more likely than not that the gain will be rolled over into a replacement asset.

Unrelieved tax losses and other deferred tax assets should be recognised only to the extent that it is more likely than not that they will be recovered against the reversal of deferred tax liabilities or other future taxable profits.

MEMO POINTS The existence of unrelieved tax losses serves as strong evidence that there may not be other future taxable profits against which the losses will be relieved.

Deferred tax should **be recognised** when **tax allowances** relating to the cost of a fixed asset are received either before or after the related depreciation is recognised. Only when all the conditions for retaining the tax allowances have been met should the deferred tax be reversed.

Deferred tax should be measured at the **average tax rates** expected to apply when the timing differences are due to reverse, based on tax rates and laws enacted by the balance sheet date.

6209 The discounting of deferred tax assets and liabilities is not required. However, if an entity adopts a policy of discounting, all deferred tax balances that have been measured without discounting, and for which the impact of discounting is material, should be discounted. Where discounting is used, the unwinding of the discount should be shown as a component of the tax charge and disclosed separately.

The following should be **disclosed** in respect of deferred tax: 6211
- the balance at the end of the period and its material components,
- any movement between the opening and closing net deferred tax balances,
- the material components of this movement,
- in cases where assets have been revalued (or their market values have been disclosed in a note) the amount of tax that would be payable or recoverable if the assets were sold at the values shown.

Tax on dividends

Both incoming and outgoing dividends (and similar amounts receivable and payable) should be recognised net of any withholding tax but excluding other taxes, such as attributable tax credits. Withholding tax suffered should be shown as part of the tax charge. 6214 FRSSE 9.13

Value added tax (VAT)

Turnover shown in the profit and loss account excludes either VAT on taxable outputs or VAT imputed under the flat rate VAT scheme. **Irrecoverable VAT** allocable to fixed assets and to other items disclosed separately in the financial statements should be included in their cost where practicable and material. 6216 FRSSE 9.15

6. Retirement benefits

a. Defined contribution schemes

The **cost** of a defined contribution scheme is equal to the contributions payable to the scheme for the accounting period. The cost should be **recognised** within operating profit in the profit and loss account. 6220 FRSSE 10.1 – 10.4

Disclosure must be made of pension commitments – whether included under any provision shown in the balance sheet or not. Where any such commitment relates to pensions payable to past directors of the company, separate particulars must be given of that commitment. 6221

The following **disclosures** should be made: 6222
- the nature of the scheme (i.e., defined contribution);
- the cost for the period; and
- any outstanding or prepaid contributions at the balance sheet date.

b. Defined benefit schemes

Because **defined benefit schemes** have limited applicability to smaller entities (very few participate in them), the accounting requirements relating to such schemes are not contained in the FRSSE itself but set out in Appendix II. They are based on FRS 17, "Retirement benefits". 6225

7. Provisions, contingent liabilities and contingent assets

The requirements under this heading do not apply to leases, deferred tax, and retirement benefits for which there are specific requirements (dealt with above in ¶6162, ¶6207, and ¶6220 respectively). 6228

A provision should be recognised only where it is more likely than not that a present obligation exists as a result of a past event, and that it will require a transfer of economic benefits in settlement that can be estimated reliably. The amount recognised as a provision should be the best estimate of the **expenditure required to settle the obligation** at the balance 6230 FRSSE 11.2

sheet date. Where the effect of the time value of money is material, the amount of a provision should be the present value of the expenditures expected to be required to settle the obligation. Where discounting is used, the unwinding of the discount should be shown as "other finance costs" adjacent to interest.

6232 FRSSE 11.3 - 11.5 Where some or all of the expenditure required to settle a provision may be **reimbursed by another party** (for instance, resulting from an insurance claim), the reimbursement should be recognised as a separate asset only if it is virtually certain to be received. In the profit and loss account, the expense relating to the provision may be presented net of the recovery. Gains from the expected disposal of assets should be excluded from the measurement of a provision.

Provisions should be **reviewed** at each balance sheet date and adjusted to reflect the current best estimate. They should be used only in respect of expenditures for which the provision was **originally recognised**.

6233 FRSSE 11.6 For each class of provision the following must be disclosed:
- the amount of the provision at the beginning and the end of the financial year;
- amounts transferred to or from the provision during the year;
- the source and application of the amounts transferred; and
- particulars of each material provision included under "other provisions" in the company's balance sheet in any case where the amount of that provision is material.

MEMO POINTS The above disclosures are not required where the movement consists of the application of a provision for the purpose for which it was established.

6235 FRSSE 11.7 - 11.11 Contingent liabilities and contingent assets should not be recognised in the accounts but the following should (unless, in the case of contingent liabilities, where their existence is remote) be disclosed in the notes:
- a brief description of the nature of the contingent item;
- where practicable, an estimate of its financial effect;
- its legal nature.

6236 Where any valuable security has been provided by the company in connection with a contingent liability, details must be disclosed.

Where practicable, the aggregate amount, or estimated amount, of contracts for capital expenditure not provided for must be disclosed. Details of any other financial commitments not provided for, which are relevant to assessing the company's state of affairs, must also be disclosed.

Particulars must be given of any charge on the assets of the company to secure the liabilities of any other person, including where practicable, the amount secured.

8. Financial instruments

6238 FRSSE 12.1 - 12.6 A financial instrument – or any of its components – must be classified as a financial liability, a financial asset or an equity instrument in accordance with the **substance of the contractual arrangement** rather than its legal form. Some financial instruments take the legal form of equity but are liabilities in substance. Others combine features associated with equity instruments and features associated with financial liabilities; they must, however, be classified according to the substance of the contract. For instance, a preference share that provides for mandatory redemption by the issuer for a fixed or determinable amount at a fixed or determinable future date, or gives the holder the right to require the issuer to redeem the instrument at or after a particular date for a fixed or determinable amount, is a financial liability.

6239 All **finance costs** should be charged in the profit and loss account. The finance costs of borrowings should be allocated to periods over the term of the borrowings at a constant rate on the carrying amount.

Where an **arrangement fee** is such that it represents a significant additional cost of finance when compared with the interest payable on the instrument, the same treatment should be followed. However, if the arrangement fee is not material, it should be charged to the profit and loss account at once.

Any convertible debt issued should be disclosed separately from other liabilities.

Initially, borrowings should be **stated in the balance sheet** at the fair value of consideration received. The carrying amount of borrowings should be increased by the finance cost in respect of the reporting period and reduced by payments made in respect of the borrowings in that period.

Dividends relating to a financial instrument or a component that is a financial liability must be recognised as **expense**. Distributions to holders of an equity instrument should be debited by the entity directly to equity, net of any related income tax benefit. If an entity declares dividends after the balance sheet date, the dividends are not recognised as a liability at the balance sheet date.

The following is the required **disclosure of dividends** in the notes: **6240** FRSSE 12.7 - 12.8
- the aggregate amount of dividends **paid** in the financial year (other than those for which a liability existed at the immediately preceding balance sheet date);
- the aggregate amount of dividends **liable to be paid** at the balance sheet date;
- the aggregate amount of dividends that are **proposed** before the date of approval of the accounts, and not otherwise disclosed above; and
- any fixed cumulative dividends on the company's shares that are **in arrears** (i.e., the amount of the arrears and the period for which each class of dividends is in arrears).

9. Share capital

The following must be disclosed with respect to the company's share capital: **6242** FRSSE 12.9 - 12.12
- the number and aggregate nominal value of shares of each class allotted;
- for any part of the allotted share capital that consists of redeemable shares:
  a) the earliest and latest dates on which the company has the power to redeem those shares,
  b) whether those shares must be redeemed in any event or are liable to be redeemed at the option of either the company or the shareholder, and
  c) any premium payable on redemption;
- in respect of shares allotted during the period:
  a) the classes of shares allotted; and
  b) for each class, the number allotted, their aggregate nominal value, and the consideration received;
- the amount of allotted share capital and of called up share capital that has been paid up;
- the number, description and amount of shares in the company held by any of its subsidiaries.

10. Share-based payments

If a company undertakes a share-based transaction – i.e., one in which it acquires goods or services and incurs a liability to be settled either by its own shares ("equity-settled") or by a cash payment based on the value of its equity instruments ("cash-settled"), it must account for the transaction accordingly. **6243** FRSSE 12.13

If a **cash-settled** share-based transaction:
- the goods or services should be treated as assets or expenses – as the circumstances dictate;
- the corresponding liability must reflect the best estimate of the expenditure required to settle the liability at balance sheet date;
- at each subsequent balance sheet date and at the date of settlement the liability must be remeasured;

– a description of the principal terms and conditions relating to the transaction – including its current and potential financial effect – must be disclosed by way of a note.

If an **equity-settled** share-based transaction, disclosure in the notes of:
– the principal terms and conditions – including the number of shares and the number of employees and others potentially involved;
– the grant date;
– any performance conditions, and the period over which these apply;
– any option exercise prices, if applicable.

6244 FRSSE 12.14 Where the **other transacting party has the choice** of whether the entity settles in cash or equity, the transaction should be treated as a cash-settled transaction. However, if the obligation is eventually settled by the issue of equity, the previously recognised liability should be treated as the proceeds of the issue of that equity.

FRSSE 12.15 Where the **entity itself has the choice** as to method of settlement, the transaction should be treated as either cash-settled or equity-settled as is felt appropriate.

11. Foreign currency translation

a. Transactions in foreign currencies

6245 FRSSE 13.1 – 13.6 If any sums that were originally denominated in foreign currencies have been brought into account in the balance sheet or profit and loss account, the basis on which they were translated into local currency must be disclosed.

6246 Assets, liabilities, revenues and costs arising from transactions in foreign currencies should be translated into local currency at the exchange rate prevailing at the time of the transaction. An **average rate** may be used if the rates do not fluctuate significantly. However, where the transaction is to be settled at a **contracted rate**, that rate should be used and where a trading transaction is covered by a related or matching forward contract, the rate of exchange specified therein may be used.

6247 Once translated and recorded, no subsequent translations should be made in respect of non-monetary assets. However, for monetary assets and liabilities denominated in a foreign currency, they should each year be translated at each balance sheet date using the **closing rate** or, where appropriate, rates of exchange fixed under the terms of the relevant transactions. Where there are related or matching forward contracts in respect of trading transactions, the rates of exchange specified in those contracts may be used.

All exchange gains or losses on settled transactions and unsettled monetary items should be reported as part of the profit or loss for the year from ordinary activities.

6248 Subject to the conditions below, where a company has used foreign currency borrowings to finance – or to provide a hedge against – its foreign equity investments, the investments may be denominated in the foreign currency and the carrying amount translated at the end of each accounting period at **closing rates**. Where investments are treated in this way, any **exchange differences** arising should be **taken to reserves** and the exchange gains or losses on the foreign currency borrowings should then be offset, as a reserve movement, against these exchange differences. The conditions that must apply are as follows:
– in any accounting period, exchange gains or losses on the borrowings may be offset only to the extent of exchange differences arising on the equity investments,
– the foreign currency borrowings in respect of which the exchange gains or losses are used in the offset process should not exceed, in the aggregate, the total amount of cash that the investments are expected to generate, whether from profits or otherwise, and
– the accounting treatment adopted should be applied consistently from period to period.

b. Incorporating accounts of foreign entities

When preparing accounts for a company and its foreign entities (including the results of associated companies or foreign branches) the closing rate/net investment method of translating the local currency financial statements should normally be used. **6250** FRSSE 13.7 -13.12

Exchange differences arising from the retranslation of the opening net investment in a foreign entity at the closing rate should be recorded as a movement on reserves.

The profit and loss account of a foreign entity accounted for under the closing rate/net investment method should be translated at the closing rate or at an average rate for the period. Where an average rate is used, the difference between the profit and loss account – translated at an average rate and at the closing rate – should be recorded as a movement on reserves. The average rate used should be calculated by the method considered most appropriate.

Where the trade of the foreign entity is more dependent on the economic environment of the investing company's currency than that of its own reporting currency, the transactions of the foreign operation should be reported as if they had been entered into by the investing company itself in its own currency. **6251**

Unless there have been changes in financial and operational relationships between an investing company and its foreign entities, the method used for translating the financial statements should be applied consistently from period to period.

Subject to the following conditions, where foreign currency borrowings have been used to finance – or provide a hedge against – group equity investments in foreign entities, exchange gains or losses on the borrowings (which otherwise would have been taken to the profit and loss account) may be offset as reserve movements against exchange differences arising on the retranslation of the net investments. The conditions that must apply are: **6252**
- the relationships between the investing company and the foreign entities concerned justify the use of the closing rate method for consolidation purposes,
- in any accounting period, the exchange gains and losses arising on foreign currency borrowings are offset only to the extent of the exchange differences arising on the net investments in foreign entities,
- the foreign currency borrowings whose exchange gains or losses are used in the offset process should not exceed the total amount of cash that the net investments are expected to generate, whether from profits or otherwise, and
- the accounting treatment is applied consistently from period to period.

12. Post balance sheet events

An entity must adjust the amounts recognised in its financial statements to reflect **adjusting events** after the balance sheet date but must not make adjustments to reflect non-adjusting events after the balance sheet date. However, if non-adjusting events after the balance sheet date are **material**, non-disclosure could adversely affect users. Some form of disclosure is therefore necessary, and the FRSSE requires details of the **nature** of the event, and an **estimate** of its financial effect (or a statement that such an estimate cannot be made, if applicable) to be given. The date on which the financial statements are approved for issue and the names of those who gave that approval should be disclosed. **6255** FRSSE 14.1 - 14.4

13. Related party transactions

If a reporting entity enters into a transaction with, or on behalf of, a related party (whether or not a price is charged) and the **transaction is material** to the reporting entity, it should be disclosed in the financial statements. The **following details** must be given: **6258** FRSSE 15.1
- the names of the transacting related parties;
- details of the relationship between the parties;

– a description of the transactions;
– the amounts involved;
– any other elements of the transactions necessary for an understanding of the financial statements;
– the balances due to or from related parties at the balance sheet date including, where necessary, provisions for doubtful debts due;
– amounts in respect of debts due to or from related parties that were written off during the period.

Transactions with related parties may be **disclosed on an aggregated basis** unless separate disclosure of an individual transaction (or series of individual but connected transactions) is required by law or is necessary for a proper appreciation of the effect on the financial statements of the reporting entity.

Personal guarantees given by directors in respect of borrowings by the reporting entity should be disclosed in the notes.

6259 FRSSE 15.3 - 15.5 Separate disclosure is required for amounts included in the profit and loss account under **"Investment income"** and **"Other interest receivable and similar income"** that were received, or are receivable from, group undertakings. Similarly, amounts included under **"Interest payable and similar charges"** paid (or payable) to group undertakings should be shown separately.

Commitments undertaken for the benefit of a parent undertaking or fellow subsidiary, or a subsidiary undertaking of the company, must be shown separately from those commitments in respect of **pensions** or **provisions** and also from each other.

6260 FRSSE 15.7 **Disclosure is not required** of:
– pension contributions paid to a pension fund;
– emoluments for services as an employee of the reporting entity;
– transactions with the following if the transaction occurs simply as a result of their role as providers of finance in the course of their business in that regard:
  – utility companies;
  – government departments and their sponsored bodies; or
  – a customer, supplier, franchiser, distributor or general agent.

6262 FRSSE 15.8 When the reporting entity is **controlled by** another party, there should be disclosure of the related party relationship and the name of that party and, if different, that of the ultimate controlling party. If the controlling party or ultimate controlling party of the reporting entity is not known, that fact should be disclosed. This information should be disclosed irrespective of whether any transactions have taken place between the controlling parties and the reporting entity.

14. Holding companies and subsidiaries

6265 FRSSE 15.9 - 15.16 If a company is a subsidiary of another company, it must state the name of its **ultimate parent** and its country of incorporation (if outside Great Britain).

If, at the end of the financial year, a company has subsidiary undertakings, it must state the name of each subsidiary and – if it is incorporated outside Great Britain – the country in which it is incorporated (if it is unincorporated, the address of its principal place of business must be given). In addition, the reason why the company is not required to prepare group accounts must be stated.

E. Cash flow statement

6268 Small companies are not required to provide a cash flow statement although the Board **encourages** doing so, using the indirect method, as shown by the following steps.

Step 1 – The indirect method starts with operating profit (i.e., normally profit before income from shares in group undertakings) and adjusts it for non-cash charges and credits to reconcile it with cash generated from operations. Other sources and applications of cash are shown to arrive at total cash generated (or used) during the period.

Step 2 – Cash is taken as "cash at bank and in hand" less overdrafts repayable on demand, which should be reconciled to the balance sheet.

Step 3 – Cash flows are shown net of any attributable VAT or other sales tax unless the tax is irrecoverable by the reporting entity.

Step 4 – It is recommended that material transactions not resulting in movements of cash of the reporting entity are disclosed by way of note, if disclosure is necessary for an understanding of the underlying transactions.

II. Abbreviated accounts

In general, small companies deliver their accounts to the Registrar of Companies in the same format as those presented to shareholders. Small and medium-sized companies may take advantage of the exemptions offered under the Act to file abbreviated accounts. This entails the preparation of a separate set of accounts solely for this purpose, with levels of disclosure that differ according to whether the company is small or medium-sized. These disclosures are even less onerous than those required for shorter-form accounts prepared for shareholders. **6270**

Small companies do not necessarily avail themselves of the exemption – especially in light of the fact that small companies are able to prepare shorter-form accounts for members and usually have no objection to filing those with the Registrar as well. Abbreviated accounts are often filed for reasons of business confidentiality. **6271**

Abbreviated accounts must be accompanied by a **special auditors' report** (¶5845), unless the company qualifies for and has taken advantage of the exemption not to appoint auditors. **6272**

Abbreviated accounts are not required to give a **true and fair view** (¶2) or comply with the disclosure requirements of the accounting standards, including the FRSSE. The disclosure requirements are governed solely by the Companies Act.

Under the Companies Act 2006, a parent company that is subject to the **small** companies regime may prepare group accounts if it opts to do so. Although under the Companies Act 1985, an exemption from preparation of group accounts for a parent of a **medium**-sized group was given, that exemption is abolished under the Companies Act 2006. **6273** s 398 CA 2006

The statutory framework governing the form and content of abbreviated accounts is contained in the Companies Act 2006 under Schedule 4 of SI 2008 No. 409. A number of exemptions from the disclosure requirements of Schedule 2 (information about related undertakings) and Schedule 3 (information about directors' benefits: remuneration) are available.

The following table summarises the requirements concerning abbreviated accounts for small companies: **6275** s 444(5) CA 2006

Element of financial statements	Details of disclosure
Profit and loss account	Not required
Balance Sheet	Abbreviated balance sheet – Schedule 4 format (¶6278) Debtors and Creditors falling due after more than one year to be disclosed in the notes
Directors' report	Not required
Directors' statement (on face of balance sheet)	As required by s 414 (3) CA 2006 – see ¶6285

Element of financial statements	Details of disclosure
Cash flow statement	Voluntary disclosure encouraged
Notes to the accounts	Limited disclosures – Schedules 2, 3 and 4
Auditors' report	Special report required – unless company is exempt from requirement to appoint auditor. See ¶6070

1. Balance sheet

6278 SI 2008/409 A choice of two **abbreviated balance sheet formats** is permitted by Schedule 4 of SI 2008 No. 409 for a small company (see table below). These formats are adapted from the formats for large and medium-sized companies by aggregating the balance sheet headings to which an arabic number is assigned under SI 2008 No. 410. In other words, only **totals** for those balance sheet headings to which a roman numeral is assigned in Schedule 4 are required to be shown. Note that the above principle applies equally to Format 1 and Format 2.

6279 s 450(1)(2) CA 2006 The abbreviated balance sheet must be **signed on behalf of the board** of directors by a director of the company.

6281

The following table shows the requirements under Format 1.		
A	Called up share capital not paid	
B	Fixed assets	
	I	Intangible assets
	II	Tangible investments
	III	Investments
C	Current assets	
	I	Stocks
	II	Debtors [see Note 1]
	III	Investments
	IV	Cash at bank and in hand
D	Prepayments and accrued income	
E	Creditors: amounts falling due within one year.	
F	Net current assets (liabilities)	
G	Total assets less current liabilities	
H	Creditors: amounts due after more than one year	
I	Provisions for liabilities and charges	
J	Accruals and deferred income	
K	Capital and reserves	
	I	Called up share capital
	II	Share premium account
	III	Revaluation reserve
	IV	Other reserves
	V	Profit and loss account
Note 1: The aggregate amount falling due after more than one year must be shown separately, unless it is disclosed in the notes to the financial statements.		

2. Directors' statement

Abbreviated accounts must contain a statement in a prominent position on the balance sheet, above the signature of the director, that the accounts have been prepared in accordance with the special provisions relating to small companies. 6285 s 450(3) CA 2006

EXAMPLE **Extract from directors' report**
The directors' report has been prepared in accordance with the special provisions applicable to companies entitled to the small companies exemption.

Accounts that are subject to audit exemption are also required to attach similar statements. Where advantage is taken of the audit exemption, the directors must ensure that there is a statement on the **balance sheet** confirming: 6286 s 475(3) CA 2006
- the company's entitlement to an audit exemption;
- that the members have not required the company to obtain an audit;
- their duty to keep accounting records and prepare accounts in accordance with companies legislation.

EXAMPLE For the year ending [*date*] the company was entitled to exemption under section 477 of the Companies Act 2006 relating to small companies.
The members have not required the company to obtain an audit in accordance with section 476 of the Companies Act 2006.
The directors acknowledge their responsibilities for complying with the requirements of the Act with respect to accounting records and the preparation of accounts.
These accounts have been prepared in accordance with the provisions applicable to companies subject to the small companies regime.

3. Notes to the accounts

The notes to the abbreviated accounts must contain the disclosure requirements listed in Schedules 2, 3 and 4 – as detailed below. 6288

a. Accounting policies

The accounting policies adopted in determining the amounts to be included in respect of items shown in the balance sheet and in determining the profit and loss of the small company must be disclosed in a note to the abbreviated financial statements. 6290 Sch 4 para 3 SI 2008/409

Most of the **disclosures required by the FRSSE** do not apply to small companies filing abbreviated accounts. However, where assets, liabilities, income or expenses have been measured in accordance with the requirements of the FRSSE, this fact should be disclosed in the note to the accounts, usually within the accounting policies.

EXAMPLE The full financial statements from which these abbreviated financial statements have been extracted have been prepared in accordance with the Financial Reporting Standard for Smaller Entities (effective April 2008) under the historical cost convention.

b. Share capital

The following information must be given regarding the small company's share capital: 6293 Sch 4 para 4 SI 2008/409
- the number and aggregate nominal value of shares of each class allotted,
- share allotments during the year including the type of shares allotted; their number and aggregate nominal value; the reasons for the allotment; and the consideration received by the company, and
- for redeemable shares, the earliest and latest redemption dates, redemption premiums and details of options held.

c. Fixed assets

6295 For tangible assets, intangible assets and investments classified under the general term "fixed assets" in the balance sheet, the following information must be given:

Sch 4 para 6 SI 2008/409

1. The cost or valuation at the beginning and end of the financial year.
2. The impact of any of the following movements during the financial year:
– revaluations;
– acquisitions;
– disposals; or
– transfers.
3. In respect of provisions for depreciation or diminution in value:
– the cumulative amount of such provisions as at the beginning and end of the year;
– the total provision provided during the year;
– the amount of any adjustments to the provision on disposal of a fixed asset; or
– the amount of any other adjustments to the provisions during the year.

d. Creditors

6298 For all items shown under creditors the following **aggregate figures** must be stated:

Sch 4 para 8 (1) SI 2008/409

– creditors payable **otherwise than in instalments** and falling due for payment more than five years after the balance sheet date.

– any creditors payable **by instalments** and the amount of any instalments that fall due more than five years after the balance sheet date.

Sch 4 para 8 (2) SI 2008/409

In respect of each item shown under creditors in a small company's abbreviated balance sheet, the aggregate of any debts included under that item for which the company has given any security must be disclosed.

If any fixed cumulative dividends of a small company are in arrears, the following must be shown:

– the amount of the arrears;

– the period for which the dividend or (if there is more than one class of share) for each class is in arrears.

e. Foreign currencies

6301 Where sums originally denominated in foreign currencies have been brought into the balance sheet or profit and loss account, the basis on which those sums were converted into sterling should be stated.

Sch 4 para 9 SI 2008/409

f. Comparative figures

6305 Comparative figures must be stated for items appearing in the notes to the financial statements. Where corresponding amounts in respect of the preceding year are not comparable, they should be adjusted and particulars and the reasons for it must be given. Comparative figures are not required for:

Sch 1 para 7 SI 2008/409

– directors' loans,
– shareholdings in other undertakings,
– accounting treatment of acquisitions, and
– fixed assets.

g. Subsidiaries and other investments

Disclosures are limited to the following: **6308** Sch 2 paras 1-3 SI 2008/409
(a) subsidiary undertakings
- details of subsidiary undertakings;
- shareholdings in subsidiary undertakings; and
- financial information about subsidiary undertakings.

(b) other investments:
- significant holdings in undertakings other than subsidiary undertakings; Sch 2 paras 5-10 SI 2008/409
- membership of certain partnerships and unlimited partnerships;
- a parent undertaking drawing up financial statements for a larger group; and
- identification of the ultimate parent company.

Under the provisions of the Companies Act 2006, the requirement to disclose information about related undertakings in the notes to a company's annual accounts applies irrespective of whether the company has to produce group accounts.

h. Loans and transactions involving directors and officers

The small company preparing abbreviated financial statements has to provide the disclosures required by companies legislation that deal with loans, quasi-loans and other dealings in favour of directors and particulars of transactions, arrangements and agreements with officers. **6311** s 413 CA 2006

i. Auditors' reports

Normally, abbreviated accounts filed with the Registrar of Companies must be accompanied by a copy of a special report from the auditors, stating that in their opinion: **6314** s 247B(2) CA 2006
- the company is entitled to deliver abbreviated financial statements in accordance with the relevant provisions, and
- the abbreviated financial statements have been properly prepared in accordance with the said provisions.

The special auditors' report on the abbreviated accounts should be dated on, or as soon as possible after, the date of the full audit report. This report is not required where a company is entitled to and has taken advantage of the exemption from appointing auditors. **6315**

EXAMPLE **Special Auditors' Report**

In our opinion the company is entitled to deliver abbreviated financial statements prepared in accordance with Section 444 (3) of the Companies Act 2006, and the abbreviated financial statements on pages xx to xx have been properly prepared in accordance with those provisions.

Where a small company files abbreviated accounts, it is not obliged to file a copy of the complete audit report with the Registrar of Companies, unless the **full audit report**: **6316** s 449(3)(a), (b) CA 2006
- was **qualified**, in which case the special auditors' report must set out that report in full together with any further information necessary to understand the qualification, and;
- **contains a statement** that:
  - the accounts, records or returns are inadequate or that the accounts do not agree with the records and returns, or
  - the auditors have failed to obtain the necessary information and explanations.

Where the full audit report is **unqualified**, but contains an **explanatory paragraph** regarding a fundamental uncertainty, such as the going concern basis, the special auditors' report should also include the explanatory paragraph, under a section entitled "other information". The auditor should also include any further information necessary for a proper understanding of the report. **6318**

SECTION 3

Medium-sized companies

6325 s 455(3) CA 2006 Medium-sized companies enjoy no concessions in respect of financial statements prepared for shareholders. Even where they prepare abbreviated accounts (for the Registrar), the concessions that are available relate principally to the profit and loss account, leaving the normal requirements in respect of the directors' report, balance sheet and notes to the financial statements fundamentally intact.

MEMO POINTS Under the Companies Act 2006, the Secretary of State is given the power to make regulations concerning abbreviated accounts for medium-sized companies.

Profit and loss account

6326 s 455(3)(a) CA 2006 Limited exemptions permit the following items in the profit and loss account items to be aggregated and shown as one item under "Gross profit or loss":

Format 1 and 3:	Format 2 and 4:
– Turnover, – cost of sales, – gross profit or loss, and – other operating income	– Turnover, – the change in stocks of finished goods and in work in progress – own work capitalised, – other operating income, – raw materials and consumables, and – other external charges

Notes to the accounts

6328 s 445(3)(b) CA 2006 Under the dispensation for medium-sized companies preparing abbreviated financial statements, the notes to the financial statements may omit the **segmental analysis** of turnover that would otherwise be required by paragraph 55 of Schedule 4 / by paragraph 68 of Schedule 1 to SI 2008 No. 410 ("The Large and Medium-sized Companies and Groups (Accounts and Reports) Regulations 2008").

6330 Because the concessions applicable to medium-sized companies are limited, the cost of preparing abbreviated accounts might seem to outweigh the possible benefits of confidentiality. Where, however, the directors are of the opinion that publishing certain sensitive information may be detrimental to the company's business (e.g., under FRS 8), they will choose the option of filing abbreviated statements. In this event, as with small companies, the statements must contain a declaration – occupying a prominent position on the balance sheet – that they have been prepared in accordance with the special provisions relating to medium-sized companies.

Auditors' report

6332 s 449 CA 2006 The rules relating to the auditors' report on abbreviated financial statements filed by a medium-sized company are the same as those for small companies, and are discussed at ¶6075.

SECTION 4

Parents of a group

6340 s 383(1), s 466(1) CA 2006 A company that qualifies as a small or a medium-sized company can be the parent company of a group. However, the parent company will not be entitled to qualify for the exemptions in respect of a particular financial year, unless the group, during the year in question, qualifies as

- a small group, where the parent is a small company, or
- a medium-sized group, where the parent is a medium-sized company.

For the purposes of preparing **abbreviated financial statements**, a parent company may not be treated as either a small or medium-sized company in a specific year unless the group it heads **also qualifies** as a small or medium-sized group. Therefore, if the parent is a small company, it may file abbreviated financial statements if it is also the parent of a **small group**. Furthermore, if the small company is the parent of a medium-sized group, it may file abbreviated financial statements applicable to a medium-sized company only. **6342** s 383(1), s 466(1) CA 2006

MEMO POINTS It should be noted that these exemptions apply to the individual company accounts of the parent where it is eligible for – and has taken advantage of – the exemption not to prepare group accounts. There is no provision for small and medium-sized groups to file abbreviated group accounts.

The rules for the parent company's individual accounts are summarised in the following table: **6344**

Exemptions based on size of company and group	Parent company is a small company	Parent company is a medium-sized company
Group is a small group	May file abbreviated accounts and prepare shorter-form accounts for shareholders	
Group is a medium-sized group	May file abbreviated accounts as a medium-sized company (i.e., exemptions are less extensive than for small companies).	May file abbreviated accounts as a medium-sized company
Group is neither small nor medium-sized	May not file shorter-form accounts	

Size limits

Under the Companies Act 2006 a group may be entitled to be treated as small or medium-sized in respect of a financial year if it satisfies any two of the following three conditions: **6346**

	Small group		Medium-sized group	
Aggregate[1] turnover	Net[2]	£ 6,500,000	Net[2]	£ 25,900,000
	Gross[3]	£ 7,800,000	Gross[3]	£ 31,100,000
Aggregate[1] balance sheet total	Net[2]	£ 3,260,000	Net[2]	£ 12,900,000
	Gross[3]	£ 3,900,000	Gross[3]	£ 15,500,000
Average number of employees		50		250

Notes:
1. Aggregate figures are the sum of the relevant figures for each member of the group.
2. Net figures are stated after set-off and elimination of intra-group turnover, balances and profits/losses.
3. Gross figures are stated before set-off and elimination of intra-group turnover, balances and profits/losses.

The size limits are subject to periodic review and therefore change from time to time. The amounts shown above came into effect by the Companies Act 2006 (Amendments) (Accounts and Reports) Regulations 2008.

MEMO POINTS The criteria do not have to be satisfied on the same basis (i.e., gross or net) from year to year. In addition, in any one year, it is permitted to use gross, net, or a combination of the two, in determining eligibility for the exemptions.

Reference period

In addition to satisfying the basic size tests referred to above, groups must also satisfy the following criteria before they qualify for the relevant exemptions: **6349**

– In respect of the parent company's **first financial year**, the group will qualify provided that it satisfies the size conditions in that year.
– In respect of **subsequent years**, the group will qualify provided that it satisfies the size conditions both in the year in question and the preceding year.
– A group that qualifies as small or medium-sized in one year will **continue to be treated** as so qualifying in the following year, even if it fails to satisfy the size conditions in the following year. However, if it does not satisfy the qualifying conditions in the year after that, then, for the **third year**, the group's financial statements must be prepared in a format appropriate to its size. On the other hand, if the group is able to satisfy the qualifying conditions in this third year, it may continue to take advantage of the exemptions.

6351 s 383(7) CA 2006 The financial years of a parent and its subsidiaries are not necessarily the same. Where this situation exists, the financial statements of the subsidiary to be used are the **most recent** available, as long as they **predate** the financial statements of the parent. However, if the subsidiary's figures cannot be ascertained without disproportionate expense or undue delay, the latest available figures may be used.

Consolidated financial statements

6355 s 399 CA 2006 As a general rule, parent companies are required to prepare consolidated financial statements under both the Companies Act and the accounting standards (in particular, FRS 2, "Accounting for subsidiary undertakings"). However, there are specific exemptions from this general requirement, namely that a parent company does not have to prepare consolidated financial statements if the group:
– qualifies as a small group, and
– is not an ineligible group.

A small company is not entitled to the exemptions with respect to abbreviated or shorter-form financial statements if it is, or was at any time during the financial year, a **member of an ineligible group**. Similarly, the company is not entitled to the exemption from preparing consolidated financial statements if, at the year end, it is a **parent of an ineligible group**.

6356 s 398 CA 2006 If at the end of a financial year a company subject to the small companies' regime is a parent company, the directors, as well as preparing individual accounts for the year, may prepare group accounts for the year but are not obliged to do so.

MEMO POINTS The exemption points given by s 248 of the Companies Act 1985 from the preparation of group accounts by parent companies heading medium-sized groups was abolished by the Companies Act 2006.

6357

EXAMPLE Consider the following group of companies:

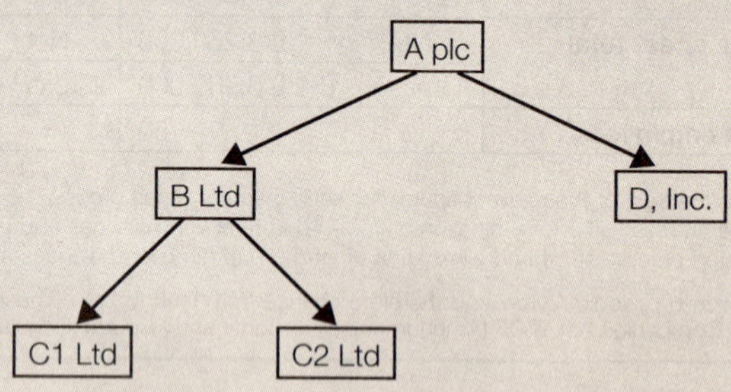

A plc	Public holding company
B Ltd	Small private company, wholly owned by A Ltd; has two subsidiaries
C1 Ltd and C2 Ltd	Wholly owned by B Ltd
D, Inc.	Incorporated in the USA and 85% owned by A Ltd

B Ltd is not entitled to the exemptions relating to abbreviated financial statements as it is a member of an ineligible group (A plc is a public company).

Where a small reporting company prepares consolidated financial statements, it should follow the accounting practices and disclosure requirements set out in FRSs 2, 6, 7 and, as they apply in respect of consolidated financial statements, FRSs 5, 9, 10 and 11. **6359** FRSSE 16.1

Where a small company has prepared individual accounts in accordance with the legal requirements reflected in the FRSSE and is preparing group accounts in respect of the same year: **6360**
- it is bound by the legal requirements reflected in the FRSSE and companies legislation;
- it must modify the balance sheet format (set out in ¶6105) in respect of item **B-III Investments** so as to contain:

1. Shares in group undertakings
2. Interests in associated undertakings
3. Other participating interests
4. Loans to group undertakings and undertakings in which a participating interest is held
5. Other investments other than loans
6. Others; and the balance sheet must state in a prominent position that they are prepared in accordance with the special regulations relating to small companies.

Under the Companies Act 2006, the requirement to disclose information about related undertakings in the notes to a company's annual accounts applies whether or not the company has to produce group accounts, unless certain grounds for exemption are met. These grounds are applicable if the directors consider that disclosing information about a related undertaking would be seriously prejudicial to the business of: **6362** s 409 CA 2006
- that undertaking,
- the company,
- any of the company's subsidiary undertakings, or
- any other undertaking which is included in the consolidation.

A parent undertaking making use of an exemption from preparing consolidated accounts should make a statement that its financial statements present information about it as an individual undertaking and not as a group. The statement should also give the grounds on which the parent undertaking is exempt from preparing consolidated financial statements. FRS 2(22)

A small parent company of a small group that has prepared shorter-form financial statements but is exempt from preparing consolidated financial statements may decide in favour of preparing consolidated financial statements all the same. In this case, it may adopt the **shorter format as modified for consolidated financial statements**. This modification consists of the standard exemptions available to small companies but requires the information in the balance sheet formats under Item B III to be expanded by requiring each of the following to be disclosed separately: **6364** FRSSE 16.4
- shares in group undertakings FRSSE 16.6
- interests in associated undertakings
- other participating interests
- loans to group undertakings and undertakings in which a participating interest is held
- other investments other than loans
- others.

Similarly, these small companies are also entitled to take advantage of the FRSSE provisions, in terms of which consolidated financial statements prepared in accordance with the accounting practices and disclosure requirements set out in FRSs 2, 6, 7 and – as they apply in respect of consolidated financial statements – FRSs 5, 9, 10 and 11. Where the reporting entity is part of a group that prepares publicly available consolidated financial statements, it is entitled to the exemptions given in FRS 8 paragraph 3(a)-(c).

There is no provision, however, for a small parent company that voluntarily prepares consolidated accounts to file abbreviated accounts.

SECTION 5

Appendices

1. Illustrative financial statements

6370 In the following set of financial statements, S Ltd is the parent company of a small group that has taken advantage of the exemption in respect of producing group accounts. It has chosen to file abbreviated financial statements with the Registrar of Companies.

S Ltd
Abbreviated Accounts
30 April 2X09

INDEPENDENT AUDITORS' REPORT TO S LTD UNDER SECTION 449 OF THE COMPANIES ACT 2006

We have examined the abbreviated accounts set out on pages xx to xx, together with the financial statements of S Ltd for the year ended 30 April 2X09, prepared under section 396 of the Companies Act 2006.

Respective responsibilities of directors and auditors

The directors are responsible for preparing the abbreviated accounts in accordance with section 444 of the Companies Act 2006. It is our responsibility to form an independent opinion as to whether the company is entitled to deliver abbreviated accounts to the Registrar of Companies and whether the abbreviated accounts have been properly prepared in accordance with the regulations made under that section and to report our opinion to you.

We conducted our work in accordance with Bulletin 2008/4 issued by the Auditing Practices Board. In accordance with that Bulletin we have carried out the procedures we consider necessary to confirm, by reference to the financial statements, that the company is entitled to deliver abbreviated accounts and that the abbreviated accounts are properly prepared. [See *Memo Point 3*, below]

Opinion

In our opinion the company is entitled to deliver abbreviated accounts prepared in accordance with section 444(3) of the Companies Act 2006, and the abbreviated accounts have been properly prepared in accordance with the regulations made under that section.

Other information

[*This section would be used only if other information needs to be given, e.g. any qualification the auditors deem necessary in particular circumstances.*]

...

[Signature]

A.N. Other (senior statutory auditor).

for and on behalf of: **XYZ LLP, Statutory Auditors**

[Address] [Date]

MEMO POINTS 1. In the above, it is assumed that the company has taken advantage of sections 444 (3). This reference should be included or amended as appropriate.
2. The wording for a Special Auditors' Report for a medium-sized company is essentially the same as the above except that reference is made to section 445 of the Act (directors' and auditors' responsibilities, declaration and opinion) and the abbreviated accounts have been prepared in accordance with section 445 (3) of the Act.
3. The auditor dates the special report with the date on which it is signed. The auditor does not sign the special report until the directors have approved and signed the abbreviated accounts. Therefore, if the special report is dated after the signing of the auditor's report on the full annual accounts, add appropriate wording such as "The scope of our work for the purposes of this report

does not include examining events occurring after the date of our auditor's report on the full financial statements."

S Ltd
Abbreviated Balance Sheet
30 April 2X09

	Notes	2X09	2X08
Fixed assets	2	£	£
Intangible assets		xxx	xxx
Tangible assets		xx, xxx	xx, xxx
Investments		x, xxx	x, xxx
		xx, xxx	xx, xxx
Current assets			
Stocks		xxx	xxx
Debtors	4	xxx	xxx
Cash at bank and in hand		x, xxx	x, xxx
Creditors: amounts falling due within one year	5	xxx	xxx
Net current assets		xx, xxx	xx, xxx
Total assets less current liabilities		**xx, xxx**	**xx, xxx**
Creditors: due after more than one year	5	xxx	xxx
Provisions for liabilities and charges		x, xxx	x, xxx
Net assets		xx, xxx	xx, xxx
Capital and reserves			
Share capital	6	xx, xxx	xx, xxx
Profit and loss account		xxx	xxx
Shareholders' funds		xx, xxx	xx, xxx

Directors' statement

These abbreviated accounts have been prepared in accordance with the special provisions relating to small companies contained in Part 15 of the Companies Act 2006, and are signed on behalf of the Board of Directors.

[Name]
Director
[Date]

MEMO POINTS Where a company with an accounting period starting on or after 6 April 2008 has taken advantage of the exemption from audit, it must include the following statement on the balance sheet:
For the year ending... [date] the company was entitled to exemption from audit under section 477 of the Companies Act 2006 relating to small companies.
Director's responsibilities:
– The members have not required the company to obtain an audit of its accounts for the year in question in accordance with section 476,
– The directors acknowledge their responsibilities for complying with the requirements of the Act with respect to accounting records and the preparation of accounts.

These accounts have been prepared in accordance with the provisions applicable to companies subject to the small companies regime.
(Source: Companies House website)

S Ltd
Notes to the accounts at 30 April 2X09

1. Accounting policies

Basis of accounting

The accounts have been prepared under the historical cost convention and in accordance with the Financial Reporting Standard for Smaller Entities (effective April 2008). The company and its subsidiaries comprise a small group. The company has therefore claimed the exemption provided by section 398 of the Companies Act 2006 not to prepare group accounts.

Turnover

Turnover comprises invoiced sales net of returns, trade discounts and VAT.

Goodwill

Goodwill arising on acquisition is capitalised and amortised over the useful economic life of the asset, subject to a maximum of 20 years.

Tangible fixed assets

The following depreciation rates are applied in order to write off each asset over its estimated useful life:

– Freehold land and buildings	2% on cost or revalued amounts
– Plant and machinery	20% on cost
– Fixtures/fittings	10% on cost
– Motor vehicles	25% on cost

Stocks

Stocks and work in progress are valued at the lower of cost or net realisable value, after allowing for slow-moving and obsolete items. The cost of stock comprises all direct expenditure and a proportion of fixed and variable overheads.

Research and development

Research and development expenditure is written off in the year it was incurred. Development expenditure is also written off, except where the directors are confident of the technical, commercial and financial viability of individual research projects. In these cases the development expenditure is deferred – to be amortised over the period during which the group is expected to benefit from the research.

Government grants

Government grants relating to expenditure on tangible fixed assets are treated as deferred income and released to the profit and loss account over the expected useful lives of the assets. Revenue related grants are credited to the profit and loss account as the expenditure is incurred.

Foreign currencies

Assets and liabilities in foreign currencies are translated into sterling at the rates of exchange ruling at the balance sheet date. Foreign currency transactions are translated into sterling at the rate of exchange ruling at the transaction date. Exchange gains and losses are taken to the profit and loss account or reserves as appropriate.

Pension costs

Contributions to the company's defined contribution pension scheme are charged to the profit and loss account for the year in which they are payable to the scheme. Differences between contributions payable and contributions actually paid in the year are shown as either accruals or prepayments at the year end.

Taxation

Corporation tax payable is provided for on taxable profits at the current rate.

2. Fixed Assets

	£
Cost or valuation	
1 May 2X08	xx, xxx
Additions	x, xxx
Disposals	
30 April 2X09	xx, xxx
Depreciation	
1 May 2X08	x, xxx
Disposals	x, xxx
Charge for the year	x, xxx
30 April 2X09	x, xxx
Net book value	
30 April 2X09	xx, xxx
30 April 2X08	xx, xxx

3. Subsidiary undertakings

As at 30 April 2X09 investments consist of an investment in a subsidiary undertaking totalling £xxx, which represents the acquisition cost of 100 percent of the ordinary share capital of M Ltd, which specialises in importing and distributing music. At 30 April 2X09 the aggregate share capital and reserves of M Limited totalled £xx, xxx and its profit for the year was £x, xxx.

4. Debtors

Debtors include an amount of £x, xxx (2X08: £x, xxx) falling due after more than one year.

5. Creditors

		2X09	20X8
		£	£
Bank loan	– due within 5 years	xxx	xxx
	– due after 5 years	xxx	xxx
		xxx	xxx
Bank overdraft		xxx	xxx
		xxx	xxx

6. Share capital

	2X09	2X08
	£	£
50,000 ordinary shares of £1 each		
Allotted, called up and fully paid		
30,000 ordinary shares of £1 each	xx, xxx	xx, xxx

7. Transaction with directors

Loan to director

During the course of the financial year Mr C was granted a short-term advance of £x, xxx, which is repayable on 1 January 2X11. Interest is charged at 6% per annum, payable at the end of the financial year.

2. Decision Table

6375 Choice of financial statements for shareholders and for filing

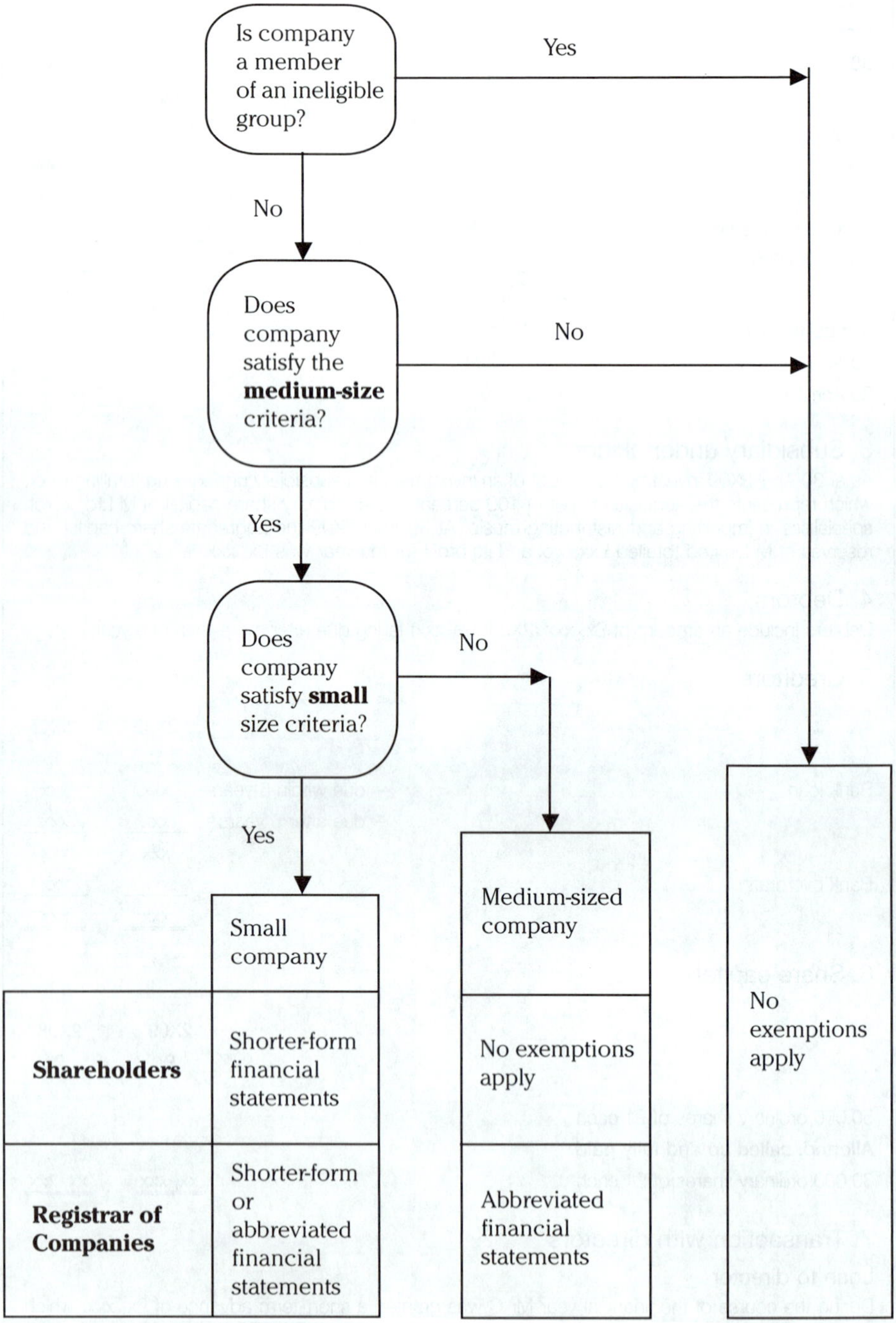

CHAPTER 2

Dormant companies

OUTLINE ¶¶

A dormant company is defined as an entity that has **no significant accounting transactions** during the accounting period. Dormant companies are not exempt from the normal requirements to prepare, issue, and file financial statements. The form and content of dormant accounts should be prepared in accordance with the Small Companies' Accounting Regulations, although in the absence of any significant accounting transactions the content of dormant company accounts will inevitably be brief. Although dormant companies are permitted to be prepared under FRSSE, there would generally be no advantage to doing so. 6400

The directors can decide to keep a company dormant for a number of reasons – e.g. to protect a company name, to hold an asset or intellectual property, or as a flat management company set up as a vehicle to own the head lease or freehold of a property. The directors must ensure that, to retain the company's dormant status, no significant expenses are incurred, as these would compromise the claim for dormancy.

Agency, non-trading, and **nominee** companies are other types of entities that may claim dormant status. 6402

SECTION 1

Dormancy

Companies can be dormant from **date of inception** or they can qualify **subsequently** if they meet certain criteria. 6404

The main benefit of dormant status is that an entity qualifies for **exemption from audit** providing certain criteria are met, although the benefits of dormant status have been considerably ameliorated by the introduction of exemptions from audit now available to small companies.

A dormant company remains obligated to prepare accounts albeit that it has had no financial activity and can show no financial results. Accounts must be filed even if the company has been dormant for a number of years or where it has never traded.

Sample dormant company accounts are provided at the end of this section.

a. Criteria for claiming dormant status

6410 A company can be **classified** as dormant only if it has no significant accounting transactions in the financial period.

The Companies Act requires an entity's accounting records to contain entries regarding all:
- monies received or expended;
- assets and liabilities; and
- stocks purchased or sold.

The existence of these transactions would prevent a company claiming dormant status. However, such a company might still be able to avoid the audit requirement if it fulfils the requirements to be considered a small company (¶6017).

6412 When planning to make a company dormant, care must be taken to ensure that the company's **dormant status is not compromised** by incidental transactions such as:
- bank charges;
- interest received on bank and other balances;
- movement on inter-company accounts;
- sundry expenses; and
- write offs.

6414 The audit concept of **materiality** does not apply in the consideration of whether a company is dormant or not as it is the presence of a transaction, without regard to its monetary value, that affects the dormant classification. The exception to this rule are the transactions deemed insignificant, below.

Insignificant transactions

6416 The following transactions are deemed immaterial and **will not affect** a claim for dormant status:
a. The payment of a fee to the registrar of companies in relation to:
- a change of name;
- re-registration of the company;
- registration of the annual return; or
- a penalty for failing to deliver financial statements within the statutory time limits.

b. A transaction generated by a subscriber to the company's Memorandum of Association acquiring shares in the company as a result of an obligation under the memorandum.

MEMO POINTS 1. In some cases a dormant company can submit **Form DCA** (Dormant Company Accounts) to Companies House, although this is **not suitable for all dormant companies**. The form has been designed for those companies seeking only to issue shares to subscribers to the Memorandum of Association. The form cannot be used for recording other transactions.
2. If a company has been dormant since incorporation, Form DCA can be used where any fees or penalties are paid by a third party without any right of reimbursement. Also, the form is not suitable for companies who have become dormant in the current financial year but who have residual balances on the balance sheet relating to earlier periods. In practice, therefore, Form DCA is suitable only for companies that have been dormant since incorporation, their only transaction being to issue shares to the initial subscribers. The completion of this form does not eliminate the need to prepare accounts for shareholders.

6418 A company wishing to remain dormant is **not permitted any paid employees** because the related transactions would have to be recorded in the company's accounting records and have the effect of setting aside the dormant status. Nevertheless, dormant companies are required to have at least one director, if private, or two directors, if public, as well as a company secretary.

b. Preparing and filing dormant accounts and other directors' responsibilities

6420 A dormant company is not exempt from **preparing, filing, and issuing financial statements**, although it can be eligible for certain other exemptions.

The **directors and company secretary** for a dormant company have the same responsibilities as those of a trading company – namely to manage the company on behalf of the shareholders or members and to ensure all the required returns, accounts and other documents reach Companies House by due date. If accounts are filed late the company will be penalised as there is no special treatment for dormant companies. 6422

Typically, **a dormant set of accounts** will include a balance sheet and related accounting policies and notes, although they will inevitably be relatively brief. However, in respect of the first year in which a company is dormant (i.e., where it had traded in the previous financial year), a profit and loss account showing the comparative figures is required. A Statement of Gains and Losses under FRS 3 "Reporting Financial Performance" may also be required to show the comparative figures for the previous year. 6424

Filing time limits

Dormant companies are required to file a **balance sheet and any relevant notes** to the accounts that must comply with the statutory requirements of the Companies Act. Annual accounts must be delivered to Companies House in accordance with the normal rules: within ten months of a company's accounting reference date (ARD) for a private company and seven months for a public company (see ¶9354). 6426

---

c. Audit exemption

One of the most important implications for dormant companies is that the majority of them are exempt from the obligation to have their financial statements audited. 6430

Certain entities enjoy automatic exemption, but others also qualify for this status if they meet additional criteria.

A dormant company is **automatically exempt** if it has been dormant since formation. 6432

It may also **claim exemption** in respect of a particular financial year if it has been dormant since the end of the previous financial year and it meets the following conditions:

a. it is entitled to prepare its accounts as a **small company** (see ¶6436), or it would have been entitled to do so but for the fact that it was a public company or a member of an ineligible group; and

b. it is not required to prepare group financial statements for the year.

MEMO POINTS Note that there is a specific exclusion in respect of a company that at any time during the financial year was a banking company, an authorised insurance company or an authorised person under Part 4 of the Financial Services and Markets Act 2000. Such a company is never exempted from the audit requirement.

Any member, or group of members, holding not less than 10 percent of the company's issued share capital may require the company to be audited notwithstanding any exemption it would otherwise enjoy. Thus, even if a company would be automatically exempt, this exemption would fall away if the requisite number of shareholders wished it. They would achieve their objective by lodging a notice during the financial year in question but not later than one month before the end of the year. 6434

A further condition for the exemption is that the balance sheet must contain a **signed statement by the directors** that: 6435

– the company was entitled to exemption from audit under section 480 of the Companies Act 2006;

– no members have required the company to obtain an audit;

– the directors acknowledge their responsibilities for complying with the requirements of the Act relating to accounting records and the preparation of accounts.

6436 The **qualifying criteria for small companies** (dealt with in detail in ¶6017) are that at least two of the following conditions must be met:
- the annual turnover is £6.5m or less;
- the balance sheet total is £3.26m or less; and
- the average number of employees is 50 or less.

6438 Where a company **has not been dormant since formation** but subsequently seeks dormant status, it must pass the test that it was permitted to prepare small company financial statements for the previous financial year. The following examples illustrate how the test is applied.

EXAMPLE **Small company seeking dormant status**

1. If Company A was a small company with a December year end, and it became dormant during 20X1, it could elect to **dispense with an audit** in 20X2.
2. If Company B first met the criteria for classification as a small company in 20X1, it would become entitled to prepare small company financial statements in respect of 20X2. This results from the requirement to meet the small company criteria **two years in succession**. The company may dispense with the audit in 20X3.
3. If Company C was not a small company in 20X1, the **earliest date** at which it could elect to dispense with the audit would be 20X4 because it would not be able to prepare small company accounts until 20X3.

Companies not meeting small company criteria

6440 **Public company and ineligible groups** There is a relaxation of the normal "small company" rules in respect of dormant public companies and members of ineligible groups that are dormant. As long as these companies meet the size criteria to be a small company, their status as a public company or their membership of an ineligible group does not stop them taking advantage of the audit exemption available to other dormant companies.

6442 Where a dormant company files **abbreviated accounts** (¶6270) with the Registrar of Companies, it is exempt from the requirement that they be accompanied by a copy of a special auditors' report (¶5800).

Accounts to be filed when audit exemption is claimed

6444 Dormant companies that are **eligible and wish to claim audit exemption** can be distinguished as follows:
a. Private companies need only prepare and deliver to Companies House an abbreviated balance sheet and notes. A profit and loss account and directors' report are not required for filing at Companies House but a directors' report and, where a company traded in the previous financial year, a profit and loss account must be supplied to members.
b. Dormant public companies must prepare and file with Companies House:
- a balance sheet;
- directors' report;
- notes to the accounts; and
- if the company traded in the previous financial year, a profit and loss account.

6446 Where a dormant company's accounts are not audited, then the balance sheet delivered to the Registrar of Companies must also contain **a statement by the directors**, in a position above the signature or signatures of the director(s), stating that:
1. the company was dormant throughout the financial year and so entitled to claim exemption from audit under the Companies Act;
2. the **members have not requested** the company have its accounts for the respective financial period audited; and
3. the directors recognise their responsibilities for ensuring the company keeps **adequate accounting records** (under section 221) and for preparing accounts that give a true and fair view of the company at the end of the financial period in accordance with the requirements of the Companies Act.

An example of a directors' statement is given in the sample accounts for a dormant company (see ¶6454).

MEMO POINTS The director's statement replaces, on the grounds of dormancy, the requirement to pass a special resolution to claim exemption from appointing auditors.

d. Ending of dormant status

In general a company may **forfeit its dormant status** either by resuming trading, engaging in "significant transactions" or failing to continue to satisfy the conditions required for any of the exemptions. 6450

Where the company ceases to fulfil the conditions required for dormant status, the consequence is that audit exemptions will also cease and the entity will no longer be exempt from the obligation to appoint auditors for the financial year in which it lost its dormant status. However, the company may remain exempt from audit if it nevertheless satisfies the audit exemption criteria for small companies.

When a company loses its dormant status it is not required to notify the Registrar of the fact.

Appointment of auditors

Where a **company ceases to be dormant**, it is the directors' responsibility to appoint auditors (unless exemption from audit can be claimed on the grounds of being a small company). 6452

The directors are required under the Act to appoint the auditors either:
a. at any time before the next meeting of the company at which accounts are to be laid, or
b. where the company is a private company that has dispensed with the requirement to lay accounts in general meeting:
– at any time before the end of the period of 28 days beginning with the day on which copies of the company's annual financial statements are next sent to members; or
– at the beginning of the general meeting if notice has been given by any member or director requiring the laying of accounts.

e. Sample accounts

The following sample accounts illustrate the accounts of a company that was dormant throughout the financial year and which was exempt from the provisions relating to the audit of accounts. 6454

Registered number:
01568974834
England and Wales

Dormant Limited
Annual Report and Unaudited Accounts
Year ended 31 December 20X4

Report of the directors

(Not required in abbreviated accounts)

The directors present their annual report with the unaudited accounts of the company for the year ended 31 December 20X4. The company is dormant and has not traded during the year. The company has, however, **acted as an agent** during the year.

Mr A, Mr B, and Mr C were directors of the company throughout the accounting period. Their interests in the parent company, X Ltd, are disclosed in the report and accounts of that company.

Signed on behalf of the board of directors by

Mr A
Director/Secretary

Approved by the board on [date]

Profit and loss account for the year ended 31 December 20X4

The company has not traded during the year or the preceding financial year. During these years, the company received no income and incurred no expenditure and made neither a profit nor a loss. There were no other gains or losses in the year.

Balance Sheet at 31 December 20X4

	20X4	20X3
	£	£
CURRENT ASSETS		
Debtors		
Amounts due by group undertakings – parent company	xxx	xxx
Total assets less current liabilities	xxx	xxx
	xxx	xxx
CAPITAL AND RESERVES		
Called up share capital		
Allotted and fully paid		
xxx shares of £1	xxx	xxx
SHAREHOLDERS' FUNDS	xxx	xxx

For the financial year ended 31 December 20X4, the company was entitled to exemption from audit under section 480 of the Companies Act 2006 relating to dormant companies. Members have not required the company to obtain an audit of its accounts under section 476. The directors acknowledge their responsibilities under the Act in respect of maintaining accounting records and the preparation of accounts.

Signed on behalf of the board of directors by

Mr A
Director

Approved by the board on [date]

Notes to the accounts

Agency arrangements (disclosed to third parties) The company was dormant and has not traded during the financial year. It has, however, acted in certain transactions as an agent for the parent company.

SECTION 2

Special companies that may claim dormant status

1. Agency companies

6460 A dormant company may **act as an agent** and allow its name to be used by another trading company. The trading company acting as the principal is frequently another company in the same group.

Type of agency agreement

6462 The precise details of the agreement between an agency company and its principal company determine whether the agency is dormant or not. One of the most significant details in this respect is the **type** of agency agreement and whether it is disclosed or undisclosed.

Disclosed agency agreement A disclosed agency arrangement is one in which the parties transacting with the agent are made aware of the identity of the principal and the fact that the company is acting as agent for that principal. Where the agency agreement is disclosed to a **third party**, the agent will be able to claim **dormant status**, subject to the relevant disclosure requirements. 6464

Where the agent contracts on behalf of a principal whose existence is disclosed to all parties in the documentation, it is the principal who becomes a party to the contract. In this instance, the transactions are shown in the principal's accounts. The agent is not directly liable under the contract and therefore records nothing in its books of account. As a result, the agent has no significant transactions (¶6416) arising from the agency which could prevent it being regarded as a dormant company.

One potential problem area is that of agency fees. If the agency does not earn any fees or commission, there will not be any significant accounting transactions, thus allowing dormant status to be claimed. It must be made clear in the terms of trade underpinning each agreement that the company enters into that the agent is acting only in the **capacity of an agent** and not as the principal.

An **example of a disclosed agency agreement** might be a travel agent tied to a particular travel operator, who states on its booking forms, or in its terms and conditions of business, that the contractual relationship is a direct one between the travel operator and the customer. 6466

Undisclosed agency agreement An agent acting for an undisclosed principal is deemed to be contracting on its own behalf and is liable on any contracts so entered into. As a result, the agency will have to account for any transactions in its accounting records and will not then qualify as a dormant company. 6468

An **example of an undisclosed agency agreement** is where a company leasing equipment to customers may enter into an arrangement with a finance company, who assumes the legal rights and obligations of the lease agreement. However, the documentation may also indicate that the company has entered into a direct contract with the customer and not the financier.

Another **example** is where a subsidiary transfers its business to a parent company but effectively continues to act as an agency for trading purposes.

Disclosure requirements Where the agency does not disclose the principal, it will have to account for any transactions entered into with the principal as its own transactions through its profit and loss account. Any debtor or creditor balances with customers and the principal will also have to be reported in the balance sheet. 6470

The **profit and loss account disclosures** will depend on the terms of the agency agreement. For instance, if the principal invoices the agent for goods that the agent sells to third parties and invoices, then the gross trading figure should be recorded in the profit and loss account. Where no trading is shown through the profit and loss account, transactions are conducted through an **inter-company account** with its principal. 6472

When **claiming exemption from audit** on the grounds of being dormant under section 285 of the Companies Act 2006, any company that has acted as an agent for any person in the financial year must state this fact in their accounts. This disclosure will not jeopardise any claim for dormancy. 6474

2. Non-trading companies

The fact that a company might not currently be trading does not necessarily mean that it is dormant. For example, **incidental transactions** such as various non-trading expenses or sundry other activity in accounts (see ¶6412 for a more complete listing) can compromise a dormant company's status. Nevertheless, such non-trading companies may still be able to claim dormant status where either of the following apply: 6476

– the accounting transactions are deemed insignificant and can be disregarded for the purpose of claiming dormant status; or
– it may be able to claim exemption under the rules for exemption from audit.

Non-trading companies with significant accounting transactions passing through its books **will not qualify as dormant in a legal sense**, and will not be able to take advantage of the dormant company audit exemption.

3. Nominee companies

6480 Generally, a nominee company is one that has been nominated by another to hold shares on its behalf. Such a company does not receive an income or incur costs that need be shown in the profit and loss account. Neither is it permitted to hold assets or liabilities in its own name.

As such, it can be likened to a non-trading company. However, in its ordinary course of business, it acquires, disposes of, or transfers investments on behalf of the beneficial owners. Even though the nominee company does not have a **beneficial interest** in the transactions it records in its books, these activities can be construed as significant accounting transactions and would preclude dormant status.

PART 9

Group accounts

CHAPTER 1

General requirements

OUTLINE ¶¶

A group comprises a parent and its subsidiary undertakings structured for a variety of legal, tax and strategic objectives. A group company is defined as a holding company or subsidiary undertaking, whilst an undertaking is defined in the Companies Act and FRS 2 "Accounting for subsidiary undertakings" as a body corporate or partnership, or an unincorporated association carrying on a "trade" or "business" with or without a view to a profit. 6500

Under the Companies Act, a group is not recognised as a separate legal person, but rather as a concept for enabling one or more individual companies to report as a single entity, for the purposes of providing financial information. **Each individual undertaking** comprising a group, has its own obligation to maintain accounting records and produce individual financial statements.

Group accounts consist of the financial statements of the individual companies in the group, which are added together, before a number of consolidation adjustments are made. Group accounts must also be accompanied by a group directors' report (see ¶4500). 6501

A group is effectively treated as if it is a separate company, with one group of shareholders. The group financial statements as such, represent the balances and profits (or losses) resulting from transactions with external third parties after eliminating all inter-company transactions.

This chapter covers **the rules** regulating the requirement **to prepare group accounts**, the exemptions available to parent undertakings, the criteria for determining whether a **parent and subsidiary relationship** actually exists and the circumstances that permit individual subsidiary undertakings exemption or exclusion from consolidation. 6502

The **form and content** of consolidated accounts is covered in ¶6700.

MEMO POINTS 1. Under the Companies Act 2006, the Secretary of State has the power (through drafting new regulations) to adjust the formats of the financial statements. **As at April 2009**, two

sets of regulations have been issued: one set specific to small companies (see ¶6000) and the other to large and medium-sized companies (see ¶552). These regulations effectively restate the provisions of the 1985 Act.
2. The terms "Consolidated accounts" and "Group accounts" are synonymous.
3. Each individual undertaking forming part of a group is responsible for its own tax affairs as they are dealt with as separate entities under the UK tax system. There is, however, a system of Group Loss Relief for UK Corporation Tax purposes, governed by a different set of criteria. Group aspects of taxation are covered in ¶9000.
4. As with individual accounts, non-listed companies can elect to prepare group accounts in accordance with the Companies Act or under international accounting standards.
5. The ASB has published amended versions of FRS 2 and FRS 6 "Mergers and Acquisitions", that reflects changes introduced in the Companies Act 2006. The amendments do not alter the existing requirements of FRS 2 and FRS 6, but update the references to correspond with the Companies Act 2006 and the Large and Medium-sized Companies (and Reports) Regulations 2008.
6. The IASB issued ED 10 "Consolidated Financial Statements" in December 2008 with the aim of improving the disclosures requirements for consolidated (and unconsolidated) financial statements, and applies to entities that fall within the scope of IAS 27 "Consolidated and Separate Financial Statements" and SIC-12 "Consolidation – Special Purpose Entities".

A. Overview

6504 The Companies Act requires **a company that is a parent undertaking** at the end of the financial year, to produce group consolidated accounts in addition to individual accounts for the parent undertaking. **Consolidation** refers to the process of adjusting and combining the individual financial information of a parent undertaking and its subsidiary undertakings, within consolidated financial statements.

All parent companies are required to prepare group accounts, including entities that prepare financial statements intended to give a true and fair view and which have subsidiary undertakings, including charitable trusts and pension funds, that undertake trading activities or that control resources through subsidiary undertakings.

6505 **The test of whether group accounts should be prepared** is based on the situation pertaining at the end of the financial year. For instance, where a parent company has subsidiary undertakings throughout most of the accounting period, but not at the financial year-end, there is no duty to prepare group accounts. However, a company which on the last day of its financial year acquires a subsidiary undertaking, is obliged to prepare group accounts for the year, unless it is entitled to one of the exemptions outlined in ¶6570.

6508 **General framework requirements** There are a number of general requirements that are applicable to the preparation of group accounts.
1. **Group accounts should comprise** a consolidated balance sheet and profit and loss account covering the parent company and its subsidiary undertakings.
2. The group accounts must comply with the Companies Act provisions as to the **form and content** of the consolidated financial statements.
3. The group accounts must apply the usual **true and fair view concept**. If compliance with the provisions of the Companies Act is insufficient to meet this requirement, additional information must be given in the notes to the financial statements.
4. All companies within the reporting group must use **uniform accounting policies**. If this does not apply, consolidating adjustments should be made to the subsidiaries' financial statements prior to consolidation.
5. All **companies within the group** should have the same financial period except in the year of acquisition, and the same financial year-end date. The **exceptions are as follows**:
– where a subsidiary does not prepare co-terminus financial statements, for instance **due to legal reasons**, interim financial statements for the subsidiary company should be used, made up to the same date as the parent company's year end.

– **where this is not possible**, the financial statements of the subsidiary may be drawn up to a date not more than 3 months preceding the group's year end.

B. Identifying the parent-subsidiary relationship

Whether a parent-subsidiary relationship exists is determined by **the degree of control** exercised by the parent over the "subsidiary". The principal test is therefore one of control, whereas previously, the emphasis of a parent and subsidiary relationship was primarily based on share ownership. This **change in emphasis** has reduced the opportunities for structuring groups in ways that enabled certain ventures or enterprises to be excluded from consolidation. "Control" may take a number of forms as discussed below. 6512 FRS 2 (14)
The term "subsidiary company" has now been replaced by "subsidiary undertaking" as it covers a greater range of entities such as charitable trusts and pension funds, that undertake trading activities or that control resources through subsidiary undertakings.
Unincorporated undertakings are also subject to the requirements for inclusion in group financial statements.

1. Evidence of a parent-subsidiary relationship

Both the Companies Act 2006 and FRS 2 stipulate that **an undertaking is a parent undertaking** of another subsidiary where one or more of the following aspects of control apply, as set out in the table below. 6514 FRS 2 (14)

Control category	Parent company – basis of control
a. Voting rights (ownership – s1159 CA 2006)	It holds a majority of **voting rights** in the subsidiary undertaking subject to a number of general rules)
b. Member of the undertaking	It has the **right to appoint or remove directors** holding a majority of the voting rights at meetings of the board on all, or substantially all, matters
c. Dominant influence	It has the right to exercise dominant influence over the undertaking: **a.** by virtue of **provisions** contained in the undertaking's Memorandum and Articles of Association; or **b.** by virtue of a **control contract** (in writing, authorised by the Memorandum and Articles of the controlled undertaking and permitted by the law under which the undertaking is established); or **c.** It is a **member** of the undertaking and controls alone, pursuant to an agreement with other shareholders or members, a **majority of the voting rights** in the undertaking. There is no longer any reference to participating interest.

MEMO POINTS 1. A parent undertaking will be treated as the parent of any subsidiary undertakings and its immediate subsidiary undertakings.
2. Shares held by another on behalf of the parent company are treated as direct holdings of the parent in the undertaking.

a. Voting rights

"Voting rights" is taken to mean the rights conferred on shareholders in respect of their shares, or if the undertaking does not have a share capital, on its members, to vote at general meeting. Where an undertaking **does not conduct general meetings** at which matters are 6515 decided by the exercise of voting rights, references to "a majority of voting rights" mean having the right to direct its overall policy or to alter the terms of its constitution.

General rules

6516 The general rules which should be applied in determining whether **an undertaking holds a "right"** in another undertaking are as follows:
1. Rights that are exercisable in **certain circumstances** can only be taken into account if:
– these circumstances have arisen and continue to arise; or
– these events are within the control of the persons owning the rights;
2. Rights normally exercisable, but **temporarily incapable of being exercised**, must continue to be taken into account;
3. Rights held by a person in a **fiduciary capacity** are to be disregarded;
4. Rights **held by a nominee** for another are to be treated as held for the other;
5. Rights **attached to shares held** by way of security are to be treated as held by the person holding the security:
– where the rights are exercisable only in accordance with that person's instructions, disregarding any right to exercise them in order to preserve the value of, or realise, the security; and
– with regard to shares held in connection with the granting of loans as part of normal business activities, where the rights are exercisable only in that person's interests, disregarding any right to exercise them in order to preserve the value of, or realise, the security.

b. Member of an undertaking

6518 An undertaking shall be treated **as a member of another undertaking** if:
– any of the first undertaking's subsidiary undertakings is a member of the second undertaking; or
– a person acting on behalf of the first undertaking or any of its subsidiary undertakings holds any shares in the second undertaking.

These provisions confirm, that any shares held by another on behalf of the parent undertaking, are effectively **direct holdings** of the parent undertaking.

c. Dominant influence

6520 The term "dominant influence" **is defined as**, the influence that can be exercised to achieve the operating and financial policies desired by the holder of the influence, notwithstanding the legal rights or interests of any other party.

The recognition by the Companies Act of dominant influence, as the key factor that impacts on the obligation to prepare group accounts, supports the emphasis placed on *de facto* control, rather than legal ownership, as the basis for consolidation.

6522 As there is no definition of "**operating and financial policies**" in the Companies Act or in FRS 2, it is commonly interpreted as being the high level strategic decisions taken by an undertaking.

Examples include the indentifying the following:
– the markets an undertaking should target for expansion;
– sources of finance and optimal gearing structure; and
– determining dividend policy.

Right to exercise dominant influence

6524 FRS 2 (7a) FRS 2 (7b) The right to exercise dominant influence refers to the right of the holder to give directions, concerning the operating and financial policies of another undertaking. The **following guidance** can be used to assess whether there is actual exercise of dominant influence:

1. The **individual circumstances of each case** should be considered, including the effect of any formal or informal agreements between the undertakings.
2. A **power of veto**, or any other reserve power that has the necessary effect in practice, can allow an undertaking to exercise dominant influence over another. However, the legal holder of such power, may be able to exercise dominant influence over an undertaking only if the powers are held in conjunction with other rights or powers, or if they relate to the day-to-day activities of that undertaking and no similar veto is held by other, albeit unconnected, parties.
3. The influence may actually be exercised in an **interventionist or non-interventionist manner**. For instance, this influence could take the form of setting outline performance targets to be achieved without being involved on a regular or continuous basis. Dominant influence could also be exercised through "intervention" only on critical matters.
4. **Commercial relationships** such as that of supplier, customer or lender do not of themselves constitute dominant influence.
5. On **evidence that one undertaking** has exercised dominant influence over another, it is assumed that the influence of the dominant undertaking continues, until there is evidence to the contrary. However, for consolidated financial statement purposes, the relationship between the undertakings should be examined each year to assess any evidence of a change in status.

2. Problems with identifying subsidiary-parent relationships

There are a number of possible **problem areas in trying to identify** whether a parent-subsidiary relationship exists, including where: 6530
- there is more than one parent undertaking;
- entities are managed on a unified basis;
- control is exercised by a third party;
- the status of quasi-subsidiaries needs to be determined; and
- others (e.g. venture capital companies and limited partnerships).

Each of these is discussed below.

More than one parent undertaking

The criteria for identifying whether a parent and subsidiary relationship exists includes **some tests based on ownership** (e.g. voting rights), as well as other **tests based on control** (e.g. dominant influence). As a consequence, more than one undertaking may qualify as the parent of a particular subsidiary undertaking, such as where: 6532 FRS 2 (14)
- undertaking A holds the majority of voting rights in undertaking X; or
- undertaking B holds the remaining minority of voting rights in undertaking X, but actually exercises dominant influence over undertaking X.

In the above circumstances, both undertakings A and B would technically qualify as the parent of undertaking X. However, in this scenario, FRS 2 does not provide any guidance on what is an appropriate course of action in terms of consolidation. 6534

In practice, it will be necessary for each of the "parents" to carefully consider whether, despite its own shareholdings or its rights of control, the rights of the other parent effectively stop it exercising its own theoretical rights and if so to exclude the undertaking from its own group accounts on the grounds of severe long-term restrictions hindering the exercise of its rights.

MEMO POINTS The **scope of the term "undertaking"** is more inclusive than the term "company" and is defined as a body corporate, partnership, or unincorporated association carrying on trade or business.

Specific guidance is given in the Companies Act on the following:
1. For **group financial statements**, references to shares in an undertaking with a structure that has capital but no share capital, should be interpreted as the rights to share in the capital of the undertaking, as it is structured.

2. Where the **undertaking does not have any capital**, the interests of the parent company relate to any right to share in the profits or liability to contribute to the losses of the undertaking, or any potential obligation to contribute to the debts or expenses of the undertaking, in the event of winding up.

Entities managed on a unified basis

6535 FRS 2 (12) Where two or more undertakings are managed on a unified basis, because the whole of the operations of the undertakings are integrated and they are managed as a single unit, a parent-subsidiary relationship will not exist.

However, unified management does not arise solely because one undertaking manages another, as this may not meet the condition that the operations of the undertakings are integrated. The **test for management on a unified basis** should be considered in conjunction with the test on existence of dominant influence.

Control exercised by a third party

6539 FRS 2 (6) Control **is defined** as the ability of an undertaking to direct the operating and financial policies of another undertaking, with a view to gaining economic benefit from its activities. Situations may arise where control flows from a common third party, which brings into question whether a parent-subsidiary relationship exists.

6540 **Benefits of control enjoyed by other parties** In certain cases, one party exercises control over an entity, but another party obtains the benefits from the entity. This gives rise to the question whether a parent and subsidiary relationship exists.

FRS 5 (D1) **A practical example** of this **is the securitisation industry**. Securitisation is the means by which the providers of finance fund a specific block of assets rather than the general business of the company. The assets that have been most commonly securitised in the United Kingdom are:
- household mortgages;
- trade debtors; and
- credit card balances.

The assets to be securitised are transferred by a company (the "originator") to a special purpose vehicle (the "issuer") in return for an immediate cash payment. Additional deferred consideration may also be payable.

6541 The major **financial and operating policies of the issuer** are usually predetermined by agreements that constitute the securitisation, so that neither the owner of its share capital nor the originator, has any significant discretion over how it is run. The originator is granted rights to surplus income, and where relevant, capital profits, from the assets. The mechanisms used to achieve this include:
- servicing or other fees;
- deferred sale consideration; or
- "super interest" on amounts owed to the originator and dividend payments. The originator is usually protected from losses beyond a certain limited amount and transfers risk to the issuer.

6542 **Under these circumstances**, the originator does not enjoy an ownership interest in the issuer nor does it exercise dominant influence over it. Hence, it is not a parent undertaking within the rules of either the Companies Act or FRS 2, but could fall within the definition of a quasi-subsidiary under FRS 5, as discussed below.

The status of quasi-subsidiaries

6543 A quasi-subsidiary of a reporting entity **is defined as** a company, trust, partnership or other vehicle that, though not fulfilling the definition of a subsidiary, is directly or indirectly controlled by the reporting entity and gives rise to benefits for that entity, that are in substance no different from those that would arise were the entity a subsidiary.

The **ability to direct** the financial and operating policies of that entity with a view to gaining economic benefit from its activities, and the ability to prevent others from so doing, is evidence of control, as is the ability to prevent others from enjoying the benefits arising from the vehicle's net assets.

The definition of a subsidiary undertaking is based on the concept of control. However, it was nevertheless still possible to **design organisational structures** where some entities, though controlled by the reporting entity, could avoid consolidation. This was achieved by placing assets and liabilities in an entity, or "vehicle", generally called a "controlled non-subsidiary", that fell beyond the reach of the legal definition of subsidiary undertaking. 6544

With these organisational structures, the commercial effect of the transactions from the perspective of the reporting entity, would be no different from that which would result were the "vehicle" actually a subsidiary. The reporting entity would still benefit from the overall contribution of the "vehicle".

FRS 5 seeks to ensure that such "vehicles" are consolidated by introducing the concept of a quasi-subsidiary.

Evidence of **which party gains the benefit** from the net assets of any entity depends on which party is exposed to the risks inherent in them. Where the financial and operating policies of a "vehicle" are in substance predetermined, contractually or otherwise, then the party possessing control will be the one that gains the benefits arising from the net assets of the entity. 6545 FRS 5 (32)

Exclusion Under FRS 5, quasi-subsidiaries should be included in the consolidated accounts as if they were legal subsidiaries. The **only circumstance** in which it is appropriate to exclude a quasi-subsidiary from consolidation, is where the interest in the quasi-subsidiary is held exclusively with a view to subsequent resale and the subsidiary has not previously been included in the reporting entity's consolidated financial statements. The general conditions for exclusion from consolidation are addressed in ¶6570. 6546 FRS 5 (35)

Venture capital companies

In the venture capital and investment trust industry, the business of the investor is to provide capital to other entities, often accompanied by advice and guidance. The stake taken by the investor and the rights attributable to that stake, vary according to circumstances. 6550 FRS 9 (50)

When considering investments made by venture capital companies, care must be taken to **distinguish between those investments** described as short/term "trade investments", which are bought with the intention of being sold for a quick profit and where the investors' relationship to its investment tends to be that of a portfolio investor, and those which are part of the venture capitalist's long term strategic investment policy.

A stake in trade investments should be accounted for as an investment according to the method of accounting applied to other investments within that investment portfolio, rather than as an associate or joint venture or subsidiary, even where the investor has significant influence or joint control. 6552

Outside their "trade investment" portfolio, venture capital funds and investment trusts may hold **investments that qualify as** associates, joint ventures or subsidiary undertakings. Such investments should be included using the equity method or gross equity method, or treated as a subsidiary as appropriate.

Limited partnerships

The topic of limited partnerships is discussed in greater detail in ¶7600 **except the requirements** that effect group accounts, which are outlined below. 6553

With a limited partnership, one or more of the partners has limited liability for the firm's debts. However, **there must be at least one general partner** whose liability is unlimited. A body corporate may be a limited partner. A limited partner may not bind the partnership contractually, nor take part in its management which gives rise to the following scenarios as set out in the table below.

Scenario	
A **limited partner** holds the majority of the equity interest	Limited partners do not take part in the management of the business
A **general partner holds a minority interest** but exercises dominant influence	If the general partner is a company or an undertaking that prepares true and fair financial statements, this would make them parent undertakings (under both the Companies Act and FRS 2) and the limited partnership would be a subsidiary undertaking
Where a **general partner** has **no equity interest**, but exercises a dominant interest	The lack of equity interest may make it harder to demonstrate that a parent-subsidiary undertaking relationship exists

C. Exemptions from obligation to prepare group accounts

6556 Under the Companies Act, consolidated accounts **are not required** for a financial year, **where**:
- the parent is itself a subsidiary undertaking included in the accounts of a larger group;
- the group headed by that company qualifies as small and is not an ineligible group; or
- all subsidiary companies within the group are excluded from consolidation.

Parent undertakings that are exempt from the requirement to prepare group accounts may still elect to do so voluntarily.

Parents included in the accounts of a larger group

6558 FRS 2 (21) A company **is exempt from** the requirement to prepare group accounts, if it is itself a subsidiary undertaking that is included in the accounts of a larger group.

The **exemption is only available where**:

1. The company claiming the exemption is a wholly owned subsidiary of that immediate parent undertaking; or
2. The parent undertaking holds more than 50% of the shares in the company claiming the exemption and a notice requesting the preparation of group accounts has not been served on the company by shareholders, holding in aggregate:
- more than half of the remaining shares of the company; or
- 5% of the total shares of the company.

Such **notice must be served** no later than six months after the end of the financial year to which it relates.

MEMO POINTS In determining whether shares are **majority owned**, the following must be attributed to the parent undertaking:
- shares held by a wholly-owned subsidiary of the parent company; or
- held on behalf of the parent undertaking or a wholly-owned subsidiary.

3. The **company claiming the exemption** does not have any of its securities listed on a stock exchange in any European Union member state. This requirement is extended under FRS 2 to cover any parent undertaking, that is not in itself a wholly-owned subsidiary and its immediate parent is established under the law of a EEA member state.

The **consolidated financial statements** must also be: 6560 FRS 2 (21b) s 400 CA 2006
– prepared to the same date, or an earlier date, in the same financial year, as the company claiming the exemption;
– drawn up and audited in accordance with the law based on the European Union 7th Directive or IFRS; and
– submitted, together with the auditor's report, to the UK Registrar of Companies, within the required filing deadline, together with the company's individual accounts. The name of the parent undertaking that prepares group accounts, its country of incorporation or if unincorporated, the address of its principal place of business, should also be included.

MEMO POINTS 1. UITF 43 "The interpretation of equivalence for the purposes of the Companies Act" issued in October 2006, contains guidance on determining whether the group accounts of a **non-EEA parent company**, satisfy the criteria for "equivalence" under the EEC 7th Directive. Entities adopting the FRSSE are exempt from this abstract as are banks and insurance companies and entities operating in specialist industries.
2. **Intermediate parents** may now be exempt from preparing consolidated accounts, where the parent is not established under the law of an EEA state. "Equivalence" does not mean compliance with every aspect of the EU 7th Directive, as a qualitative rather than quantitative approach has been championed.

Small groups

A parent company **need not prepare group accounts** for a financial year in which the group headed by that company qualifies as small or medium-sized (¶6000) and is not an ineligible group. A group meeting the size criteria may still be deemed ineligible under certain conditions (see ¶6010). 6562 FRS 2 (21a)

MEMO POINTS 1. Under the **Companies Act 2006**, the exemption from the preparation of group accounts by parent companies heading medium-sized groups has been withdrawn (from 6 April 2008). All parent companies, except for those heading small groups, are required to prepare group accounts.
2. The **thresholds for qualifying as small** (under CA 2006) are as follows: s 399 CA 2006
– Aggregate turnover (net) – less than £6.5m (Gross: £7.8m);
– Aggregate balance sheet total (net) – less than £3.26m (Gross: £3.9m);
– Aggregate no: of employees (net) – less than 50.
The net amounts apply after all consolidation adjustments have been made (e.g. elimination of intra-group sales and balances). The gross amount is useful guide by which a parent can see if its meets the small company criteria without performing a partial consolidation.

The exemption from small group is not available if any of its members are: 6563
– a public company;
– a corporate entity with securities listed on an EEA exchange; or
– insurance companies, banks, and investment firms.

The Charity SORP is more restrictive and allows exemption on grounds of size, only if the group's gross income does not exceed the **audit threshold** under the Charities Act 2006 (see ¶9744) Under FRS 2, a "not for profit" organisation is not allowed to exclude from consolidation, a subsidiary undertaking that trades commercially. 6564

All subsidiaries are excluded from consolidation

Both the Companies Act and FRS 2 permit a parent company exemption from preparing group accounts, where all the subsidiary undertakings comprising the group are individually excluded from consolidation. Where this is the case, a number of disclosures are required in the accounts of the parent undertaking (see ¶6588). 6566 FRS 2 (21d) s 402CA 2006

D. Exclusion of an individual subsidiary undertaking from consolidation

6570 s 405 CA 2006 The **general rule is** all confirmed subsidiary undertakings of a parent undertaking must be included in the group's consolidated accounts, subject to the exemptions discussed in section C.

However, there are a number of instances where an individual subsidiary undertaking need not be included in the consolidated accounts; namely as a result of:
- immateriality:
- undue expense and delay;
- severe long-term restrictions; or
- it is a subsidiary undertaking held for subsequent resale.

Where subsidiary undertakings are excluded, **certain disclosures** are required in the parent undertakings accounts.

1. Immateriality

6572 A subsidiary undertaking may be excluded from consolidation if its inclusion is not material for the purpose of giving a true and fair view. **Two or more subsidiary undertakings** may be excluded if they are not material in aggregate.

2. Undue expense and delay

6574 FRS 2 (24) In terms of the Companies Act, a subsidiary undertaking may be excluded from consolidation, where the required information is only available at disproportionate expense or with undue delay. However, guidance on how "disproportionate undue expense and delay" should be determined is not given in the Act.

In addition, this **exemption is only permitted** where the subsidiaries are immaterial, individually or collectively relative to the size of the group.

3. Severe long-term restrictions

6576 FRS 2 (25) Under the Companies Act 2006, a subsidiary undertaking may be excluded from consolidation if there are "severe long-term restrictions", that greatly impede the ability of a parent company to exercise its rights or control over the assets or management of that subsidiary. **The rights affected include**:
- voting rights attached to shares;
- the right to appoint or remove the board of directors; and
- the right to exercise dominant influence.

FRS 2 is more equivocal on this issue and **advocates exclusion**, where it can be justified, on the grounds that the long term restrictions effectively mean that the parent company is not able to control the subsidiary.

There is **no formal definition** of what constitutes long term. In practice, a judgement will have to be made at each year end as to whether the severe restrictions will persist for the foreseeable future. If so, the restriction should be regarded as long term and the exclusion from consolidation should continue.

6577 A subsidiary undertaking **should not be excluded** merely because the restrictions are threatened or the other party has the power to impose them, unless such threats or the existence of such powers has in practice, a severe and restrictive long-term impact on the rights of the parent undertaking.

Examples of types of "severe long-term restrictions" include: 6578
– a subsidiary undertaking subject to UK insolvency proceedings; and
– the existence of restrictions on cash flows from a subsidiary undertaking (e.g. an overseas subsidiary which is not permitted to remit dividends to its parent).

However, **both scenarios may not automatically justify** the exclusion of the subsidiary undertaking from the group consolidation. For instance, a receivership or administration order may not necessarily mean severe long-term restrictions, as the subsidiary could subsequently trade its way out of receivership or administration.

Where **severe restrictions** exist, but the directors of the parent do not believe they are long term, the appropriate treatment is to make full disclosures of the facts in the notes to the financial statements, rather than opt for non-consolidation.

Accounting treatment

Where restrictions have been imposed **after control has been acquired**, the following accounting treatment is required: 6580 FRS 2 (27)

1. The subsidiary should be consolidated up to the date the restrictions came into force.
2. The subsidiary should cease to be consolidated at the date restrictions were imposed, and should be transferred to fixed asset investments at a valuation derived using the equity method.

Once the restrictions come into effect, the ongoing accounting treatment will be dependent upon the level of influence retained by the parent. 6581

Issue	Accounting treatment
Where **significant influence is not retained** during the period of restriction	– the subsidiary should continue to be classified as a fixed asset at the initial valuation, subject to impairment which should be charged to the consolidated profit and loss account. No further accrual should be made for the profits or losses of that subsidiary.
Where **significant influence is retained** during the period of restrictions	– the subsidiary should be accounted for as an associate under the equity method
The **carrying amount** of subsidiary undertakings subject to severe long-term restriction	– should be reviewed each year and where appropriate written down for any **diminution in value**. In assessing diminution in value, each subsidiary undertaking should be considered individually.
Any **intra-group amounts** due from subsidiary undertakings excluded on these grounds	– should also be reviewed and written down if required
Similarly, any **amounts previously charged** for diminution in value	– should be written back as a result of the restrictions ceasing, should be separately disclosed

On **termination of the restrictions**, and where significant influence has been retained, the unrecognised profit and loss that has accrued during the period of restrictions relating to that subsidiary, should be recognised in and disclosed separately in the consolidated profit and loss account. 6582 FRS 2 (28)

4. Held for subsequent resale

A subsidiary undertaking **may be excluded** from consolidation, where the interest of the parent company is held exclusively with a view to subsequent resale and the undertaking has not previously been included in the parent company's group accounts. 6583

Mandatory exclusion FRS 2 makes exclusion of the subsidiary undertaking from consolidation mandatory rather than optional where the following conditions are satisfied: 6584

1. A purchaser has been identified or is being sought, and there is reasonable expectation that the undertaking will be disposed of within approximately one year of its acquisition date; or FRS 2 (25b), (11)

2. The interest that was acquired as a result of the enforcement of the security, unless the interest has become part of the continuing activities of the group, or the holder acts as if it intends the interest to become so.

6584-1 FRS 2 (78d) The **first of these two circumstances** depends on the immediate intention to dispose of the subsidiary and the expectation of a sale within approximately one year. An interest for which a sale is not completed within a year of its acquisition may still fulfil the condition for mandatory exclusion if, at the balance sheet date the terms of the sale have been agreed and the process of disposing of that interest is substantially complete.

Where this condition is not met but directors have purchased the subsidiary with a view to resale, they still have the option of excluding it from consolidation.

6584-2 These **exclusions apply only** to those undertakings, that have never formed a continuing part of group activities and have not previously been included in the consolidated financial statements, prepared by the parent undertaking. **For example**, a parent undertaking with a subsidiary undertaking that has been part of the group for several years, could not now be excluded from consolidation on the grounds that the parent has decided to dispose of the subsidiary.

6585 **Accounting treatment** Subsidiary undertakings held exclusively for resale, should be excluded from consolidation and the temporary nature of the parent undertaking's interest recognised, by carrying it as a current asset (or fixed asset investment) at the lower of cost and net realisable value.

E. Disclosures

1. Exempt groups

6588 FRS 2 (22) **Parent undertakings – individual financial statements** A parent undertaking that takes advantage of one of the exemptions from preparing group financial statements, must disclose this fact in its individual financial statements at the end of the financial year, and the reasons for so doing. **Where exemption is based on** all subsidiaries being excluded from consolidation, the following information is required:
- the reasons for excluding the various subsidiaries from consolidation; and
- if they are incorporated, the address of their principle place of business or country of incorporation if not the UK.

6589 **Intermediate parents** A **parent undertaking may be exempt** from the duty to prepare group accounts by virtue of it being an intermediate parent. The intermediate parent is required to disclosure in its individual financial statements, that it is exempt from the obligation to prepare group accounts and give the name and details of incorporation of the ultimate parent undertaking.

6590 For **subsidiary undertakings** the following information should be given in their financial statements, in respect of the parent undertaking of:
- the largest group of undertakings for which group accounts are drawn up and of which the company is a member; and
- the smallest group of undertakings.

The disclosures relating to the name and incorporation of the parent company should also be given.

2. Where individual subsidiaries are excluded

Consolidated accounts

An **individual subsidiary undertaking** may be excluded from the group financial statements for various reasons as outlined in ¶6570 above. The following information regarding the subsidiary undertaking should be given in the notes to the consolidated financial statements: 6591

1. The **name of the subsidiary and the reasons** for its exclusion from consolidation;
2. The **aggregate amount** of its capital and reserves as at the end of its relevant financial year and its profit and loss for that year. This information need not be given if:
a. the group's investment in the undertaking is included in the financial statements by way of the equity method of valuation; or
b. the subsidiary is not required to deliver a copy balance sheet and does not otherwise publish that balance sheet in GB or elsewhere, and the holding of the group is less than 50% of the nominal value of the shares in the undertaking; or
c. the information is not material.
3. Details of the **balances between** the excluded subsidiary undertakings and the rest of the group;
4. The **nature and extent of transactions** of the excluded subsidiary undertakings with the rest of the group;
5. For an excluded subsidiary undertaking **carried other than by the equity method**, any amounts included in the consolidated financial statements in respect of:
– dividends received and receivable from the undertaking;
– any write down in the period in respect of the investment in that undertaking or amounts due from that undertaking; and
– for subsidiary undertakings excluded because of different activities the separate financial statements of those undertakings.

MEMO POINTS The disclosures required are contained in Sch. 4 Large and Medium-sized Companies and Groups (Accounts and Reports) Regulations 2008 (SI2008/410).

The information may be **presented on an aggregate basis**, for sub-units of subsidiary undertakings that fall within one of the afore-mentioned grounds for exclusion. However, separate disclosure is required for any individual excluded subsidiary undertaking, including its subsidiaries, that alone accounts for more than 20% of any one or more of the group's operating profits, turnover or net assets. The group amounts should be measured by including all excluded undertakings. 6591-1

There may be circumstances where in the opinion of the directors of the parent undertaking, the above mentioned disclosures are likely to be **seriously prejudicial** to the business of the parent or group. In such cases, where the prejudicial impact can be shown, application may be made to the Secretary of State for exemption from the specified disclosures. The **following conditions** relate to the subsidiary undertaking in question; namely: 6591-2
– that it is established under a law of a country outside the United Kingdom; or
– it carries on business outside the United Kingdom.

3. Omission of parent company profit and loss account from consolidation

Where a parent company is required to prepare group financial statements, **its individual profit and loss account** may be omitted from the group financial statements provided that: 6593
– the notes to the parent company's individual balance sheet show the parent's profit and loss for the financial year;
– there is disclosure in the group financial statements that the exemption applies; and
– the parent's individual profit and loss is nevertheless prepared, approved by the board and signed by a director in accordance with the general rules for approving and signing financial statements.

Under these circumstances, the parent company's individual profit and loss account need not contain the information required by the Companies Act, namely regarding **supplementary information** to the profit and loss account, such as:
- interest and similar charges;
- particulars of taxation;
- turnover details; and
- particulars of staff.

F. Comparison between UK GAAP and IAS (IFRS)

6594 The **general requirement** to prepare group accounts is included in IAS 27 "Consolidated and separate financial statements", which includes a definition of control that in turn helps determine which entities should be consolidated.

MEMO POINTS IAS 27 is supported by a number of interpretations from the Standing Interpretations Committee (SIC), which give guidance on the application of IAS 27; namely: SIC 12 "Consolidation-Special Purpose Entities" and SIC 33 "Consolidation and Equity Method-Potential Voting Rights and Allocation of Ownership Interests".

Overview of IAS 27

6595 1. A parent company is required to present consolidated financial statements including investments in subsidiaries.
2. An entity (including an unincorporated entity) is classified as a subsidiary, when it is controlled by another entity.
3. Control is defined as the power to direct the operating and financial policies of the subsidiary.
4. Parents that are subsidiaries of another entity can claim exemption from preparing consolidated financial statements, where certain criteria are met.
5. IAS 27 sets out the consolidation procedures that must be followed.
6. The treatment of minority interest in subsidiaries' net assets are presented separately, in the consolidated balance sheet within equity. Minority interests in a subsidiary's profit and loss account is shown separately from the parent shareholder's interest.
7. In addition to subsidiaries, IAS 27 also covers the accounting treatment for jointly controlled entities (JCE's) and associates where a company elects or is required by local law, to present separate financial statements.

6596 **Proposed amendments to IAS 27** The IASB issued a revised review of IAS 27 in May 2008 as part of a joint convergence project with the FASB. The **key changes** are expected to be as follows:
1. **Minority interests** should be referred to as 'non-controlling interests (NCIs)'.
2. **Any change in the controlling interest** of a parent in a subsidiary, that does not result in a loss of control (through selling shares to the minority), should be recorded as a transaction with equity shareholders. As such, no gain or loss on the sale transactions should be recorded in the profit and loss account.
IAS 27 permits gains or losses on disposals to be taken to the income account. The **gain or loss is measured by** comparing the fair value of the consideration at the date of disposal, plus the fair value of the investment retained, with the book value of the subsidiary's net assets. In addition:
a. Any remaining non-controlling interest should be recorded at fair value and then accounted for under IAS 39 in the consolidated financial statements.
b. Any remaining interest held by the parent would be accounted for as an associate or joint venture under IAS 28 or IAS 31.
3. **Losses applicable** to NCI's should be allocated directly to the NCI. Currently, losses under IAS 27 are not allocated to minorities.

Key differences between UK GAAP and IAS (IFRS)

6597

Issue	IAS (IFRS)	UK GAAP
Treatment of Investments in an investor's individual financial statements	Gives guidance on treatment of investments	Not covered
Exemption from preparing consolidated financial statements	Exemption criteria wider than UK GAAP. Does not specify that the parent must be located in a particular country for exemption to apply. Ultimate parent must produce IFRS consolidated statements	Requirement for immediate parent to be established under law of EC member state has been amended
Exclusion of subsidiaries – long-term restrictions on transfer of funds	Restriction removed from IAS 27	Rule still applies
Consolidation procedures	Similar to FRS 2, except that the cumulative Forex differences are taken to equity in accordance with IAS 21	No such requirement
Control – direct operating and financial policies	1. Based on legal control – i.e. voting rights etc. 2. Where control is temporary the entity is exempt from consolidation.	1. Based on the ability to direct operating and financial policies to maximise own benefit. 2. No such requirement

Non current assets held for resale

The IASB has also **revised its requirements** through the issue of IFRS 5 "Non-current Assets Held for Sale and Discontinued Operations". The revised standard is applicable to accounting periods beginning on or after 1 July 2009. 6598

Newly acquired subsidiaries held for resale should be:
- recorded at lower of carrying value and fair value less costs to sell; and
- recorded in the balance sheet with the underlying assets and liabilities shown separately.

The IASB has published an amendment to IFRS 5, requiring an entity to classify an interest in an associate or jointly controlled entity as held for sale, when it is committed to selling that interest. The same applies where an entity plans a part disposal that will result in the loss of significant influence. The amendment forms part of the project entitled "Improvements to IFRSs", set out in ED/2009/11 and becomes effective from January 2011, although earlier adoption is permitted. 6599

CHAPTER 2

Form and content of group accounts

OUTLINE ¶¶

The **Companies Act requires** group accounts in the form of consolidated accounts, consisting of a consolidated balance sheet and profit and loss account, that meet the true and fair criteria from the perspective of the members of the parent company. In addition, the accounting standards also require the preparation of a consolidated cash flow statement and consolidated statement of total recognised gains and losses (STRGL). **6700** FRS 1 (b) FRS 3 (27)

The consolidated balance sheet and profit and loss account must incorporate in full, the information contained in the individual accounts of the undertakings included in the consolidation as if it were a single company (aggregation). This requirement is subject to the adjustments required by the legislation and generally accepted accounting principles or practice.

The **adjustments required** relate to:
- the elimination of group transactions;
- uniform bases for valuing assets and liabilities in the subsidiaries and group accounts;
- acquisition and merger accounting;
- minority interests; and
- the adoption of uniform accounting policies and accounting reference dates.

MEMO POINTS Consolidated accounts must be prepared under Section 404 Companies Act 2006 (SI 2008/410) or under IFRS (IAS 1). The group accounts for small companies are governed by Schedule 6 to SI 2008/409.

A. Accounting policies

The **general rule** is that all group companies should use uniform accounting policies. For practical purposes it is more efficient to apply the same accounting policies at the individual entity level and for the group accounts. This is likely to minimise the volume of **consolidation adjustments**. **6704**

However, a departure from the requirements of the Companies Act in the preparation of group accounts is permitted under certain conditions, as discussed below.

6706 **Reasons for not adopting uniform accounting policies** A departure from the requirements of the Companies Act in the preparation of group accounts **is permitted**:
- where the directors decide that there are **special reasons** for any subsidiary undertaking departing from the group accounting policies; or
- on grounds of materiality.

Valid reasons for not adopting uniform accounting policies in the preparation of individual financial statements for each group undertaking, include the following:

1. To ensure maximum tax efficiency, it may be necessary to allow certain companies to pursue policies which do not accord with the group accounting policies; or

2. The group policies may not be compatible with the legislation or the generally accepted accounting principles of any other countries in which a subsidiary might operate.

6708 **Disclosures required** Where uniform accounting policies are not adopted, disclosures to this effect are required by way of a note to the consolidated financial statements. The note should explain the actual accounting policy adopted, the reasons and the effect on the financial statements of such a departure. Furthermore, any difference between a parent's individual accounts for a financial year and its group accounts should be disclosed and explained in the notes to the group accounts.

B. Accounting periods and dates

6714 FRS 2 (42) The **general rule** is that the financial statements for all subsidiary undertakings included in the consolidated financial statements, should be prepared to the same accounting period as that of the parent undertaking (co-terminous). This is a requirement of the Companies Act, **unless in the opinion of the directors** other considerations are paramount.

6716 **Non co-terminous year-ends** might be justifiable between certain group undertakings for the reasons set out in the table.

Scenarios	Justification
1. Legislation in different countries	Different legislation may compel, or make it more practical, to prepare financial statement of an individual group undertaking to a particular date
2. Different annual trading cycles	The decisions regarding the year ends of the various undertakings within a group may be driven by the respective annual trading cycles of the industries in which they operate. For example, some group undertakings may be geared to peak business activities in the summer months and others in the winter months.
3. Tax planning considerations	Tax planning issues for various group undertakings
4. Undertakings in other countries	Overseas subsidiaries – difficulties in meeting a group reporting timetable. Undertakings may decide to close their accounts ahead of the parent undertaking to allow time for preparation of reporting packs/consolidation information.

6718 **Remedies** FRS 2 reinforces the Companies Act preference for co-terminous year ends within a group and endorses the alternatives available where the ideal situation does not prevail. The **preferred remedy** is to use specially prepared co-terminous interim accounts for the subsidiary undertaking. Only **where this is not practical**, should the parent undertaking resort to the latest statutory accounts of the subsidiary undertaking, provided that the year end is no more than three months before that of the parent undertaking.

EXAMPLE Easter Bunnies Limited last financial year ended on 30 April 2009 whereas its two subsidiary companies Wacky Toys Limited and Easter Chicks Limited prepared their last statutory accounts to 31 January 2009 and 31 December 2008 respectively.
Under FRS 2, both subsidiaries should ideally produce interim accounts made up to 30 April 2009. If in the case of Wacky Toys Limited this is not a practicable alternative, the directors of the parent could consider using the accounts of Wacky Toys at 31 January 2009, with appropriate **consolidation adjustments**, as the gap falls within the 3 month period allowed.
However, this option is not available in the case of Easter Chicks Limited, as the gap between its own year end and that of the group (four months) exceeds the three month limit allowed under the Act and FRS 2 and therefore, interim accounts will have to be prepared.

Where the recent financial statements of a subsidiary undertaking are included in the consolidation, then any changes that have taken place in the intervening period, that would **materially impact on the true and fair view** given by the group financial statements, should be reflected in the consolidated financial statements. 6720 FRS 2 (43)

Disclosures

For each **material subsidiary** undertaking that is included in the group's financial statements, on the basis of information prepared to a different date or for a different accounting period from that of the parent undertaking of the group, the following information must be provided; namely: 6724 FRS 2 (44)
- the name of the subsidiary undertaking;
- the accounting date or period of the subsidiary undertaking; and
- the reason for using a different accounting date or period for the subsidiary undertaking.

C. Elimination of intra-group transactions

In preparing group accounts, the following material inter-group transactions between undertakings included in the consolidation, should be eliminated: 6730

1. **Sales or other types of transactions** between group undertakings that may materially inflate the figures relating to group turnover and group cost of sales, as well as distort the gross margin.
2. Intra-group **debtor and creditor balances**.
3. **Dividends**.
4. **Unrealised profits and losses** included in book values of assets (e.g. stock, fixed assets) transferred between group undertakings, and which at the year end remain within the group, so distorting the true profit of the group (see ¶6732).
5. Where the **acquisition method** of accounting is used to consolidate a subsidiary undertaking, the identifiable assets and liabilities acquired must be included in the consolidation at fair values as at the acquisition date. Where the **merger method** is used, the assets and liabilities of the acquired undertaking must be consolidated at their balance sheet values at the acquisition date.

1. Treatment of unrealised profits/losses

Most consolidation adjustments are relatively straight forward. However, **problems can arise** in trying to measure unrealised profits (or losses), such as the unrealised profit included in intra-group sales retained in closing stock. This problem can be further exacerbated where the intra-group items form part of, or are an ingredient in, one or several other products. 6732

In practice, one might be able to take advantage of **the concession** afforded by the Companies Act, where the need to eliminate unrealised profits or losses is removed, if the amounts concerned are not material for the purposes of giving a true and fair view.

Where unrealised profits or losses **are deemed material**, a number of rules should be observed as set out under the specific headings below.

Unrealised profits reflected in book value of assets

6733 Any unrealised profit reflected in the book value of assets should be eliminated in full. For example, if an engineering company supplies a fellow subsidiary in the manufacturing trade with an item of plant, the intra-group profit element included in fixed assets should be eliminated, along with the depreciation charge.

Allocation of unrealised profits

6734 The unrealised profits or losses should be set off against the interests held by the group and the minority interest, in proportion to their holdings in the undertaking whose individual financial statements contain the eliminated profits or losses. The minority interests must be allocated their share of unrealised profits or losses.

Transfer of fixed assets

6735 There are occasions when group undertakings are likely to transfer fixed assets between each other. Under these circumstances, the **"group entity" principle** must be maintained and the fixed asset carried in the consolidated financial statements at cost to the group, whilst any depreciation charge must be based on the cost to the group. As a consequence, **two consolidation adjustments** will be necessary; namely:

1. The removal of any unrealised profit from the carrying value of the fixed asset in the consolidated balance sheet; and

2. An adjustment to ensure that the current year charge and opening and closing balances on the depreciation provision are based on cost to the group. **Gains and losses** on realisations of fixed assets would also have to be eliminated.

The **consequence of transferring fixed assets** around the group at above or below the cost to the vendor company is particularly complex. The consolidation adjustments referred to above will need to be made each year, and those in respect of depreciation changed each year, until the asset is finally scrapped or sold.

Constructed assets

6736 Construction or contracting companies that are members of a group, may construct assets such as an investment property or new factory, for other members of the same group. There are two possible scenarios, as follows:

1. The asset is **classified as a fixed asset** and therefore any unrealised profit must be eliminated as outlined above; or

2. The asset is to be **sold on to a third party**, for which a contract of sale exists. The asset is likely to be shown in the consolidated balance sheet as a current asset. However, in such cases, the **unrealised profit arising** on the initial intra-group sale need not be eliminated provided that the profit arising on that sale is materially the same as that which would have arisen in the books of the purchasing company (for long term contracts under SSAP 9), had it acquired the asset from its fellow group company at cost.

6737 **Interest** The question that arises is whether the interest on borrowed funds as part of the cost of construction, should be eliminated on consolidation. The treatment to be adopted depends on whether the interest:

– represents interest paid on monies borrowed externally, including by another group company to finance the project; or

– is merely a notional charge.

Where the interest is clearly **a cost to the group**, the interest should not be eliminated. However, where the interest is a notional intra-group charge, it should be eliminated.

Subsidiaries held for resale or that have long-term restrictions

In general, profits and losses on transactions with undertakings excluded from consolidation, because they are held with a view to subsequent resale or because of severe long-term restrictions need not be eliminated, **except where significant influence** is retained and the subsidiary undertaking is classified as an associate undertaking. 6739

For more detail on subsidiaries excluded from consolidation see ¶6500.

The following scenarios can arise in practice: 6740

a. A **parent undertaking** sells an asset to partly held subsidiary undertaking at a profit. The asset including unrealised profit is held by the subsidiary undertaking at the end of the financial year;

b. A **partly held subsidiary undertaking** sells an asset at a profit to the parent undertaking. The asset including unrealised profit is held by the parent undertaking at the end of the financial year; or

c. A **partly held subsidiary undertaking** sells an asset to a fellow partly held subsidiary undertaking at a profit. The asset whose "cost" includes an element of unrealised profit is held at end of financial year by the subsidiary that purchased the asset.

EXAMPLE **Consolidated financial statements**

Scenario A

Sale by group company to a partly held subsidiary

The **parent company** has a 75% interest in a **subsidiary company**

During the financial year, the parent company sold goods to the subsidiary company for £100,000. The cost of these goods was £60,000. All of the goods were still in stock at the end of the financial year.

Accounting treatment

Compute unrealised profit in stock: £100,000 – £60,000 = £40,000;

1. Eliminate the full £40,000 from group stock and group operating profit;

2. The consolidating "journal entry" representing the elimination of unrealised profit in closing stocks, is as follows:

Debit	Group operating profit	£40,000	
Credit	Group stock (Balance sheet)		£40,000

Under this scenario, there is **no elimination** of the unrealised profit **against the minority interest**. The full debit is made against group profits on the grounds that the stock is still sitting in the partly held subsidiary undertaking and hence should not impact upon the minority interest.

Scenario B

Sale by a partly held subsidiary to the parent

The Parent company has a 75% interest in one of its subsidiaries.

During the financial year, the subsidiary company sold goods to the parent company for £100,000. The cost of these goods was £60,000, all of which were still in stock at the end of the financial year.

The **accounting treatment** is to eliminate £100,000 from group turnover and £60,000 from group cost of sales, thereby reducing group operating profit by £40,000. The effect of this would be to reduce the profit attributable to minority interests by 25% of £40,000 = £10,000.

2. Treatment of deferred tax

UK **corporation tax** is charged on the profit of individual companies rather than on groups. The impact of this, is that the eliminations required by the Companies Act and FRS 2 may in themselves cause timing differences, as far as the group is concerned. 6742

If an element of profit, or expense has been eliminated on consolidation but has been taken into account in arriving at the individual company's taxable profits, a **timing difference** arises, between when the item is recognised for tax purposes and when it is reflected in the group accounts, will arise that did not exist at the entity level. This is because **material eliminations** are likely to cause misalignment, between the income recognised for consolidated financial accounts purposes and the income recognised for taxation purposes. As a consequence, if a liability or asset is likely to crystallise in the foreseeable future, a consolidation adjustment will be required to the amount set aside for deferred taxation in the consolidated financial statements, in respect of these additional timing differences. The treatment of deferred taxation is covered in more detail in ¶9000.

D. Minority interests (Non-controlling)

6750 FRS 2 (13) Minority interests **are defined** as subsidiary profits or losses, and capital and reserves owned by external shareholders. The process of consolidation involves the aggregation of the assets and liabilities of the individual group undertakings and **where the group does not own** all the share capital of a subsidiary, an adjustment is required to account for the interests of other external (non-group) shareholders.

Under IFRS, minority interests are known as non-controlling interests.

Despite the title "Minority interests", **there is in principle no upper limit** to the proportion of shares in a subsidiary undertaking which may be held as a minority interest. This is because the parent-subsidiary relationship is established on the basis of control rather than on majority shareholding (equity ownership).

6751 FRS 2 (34) A company **is deemed to be a subsidiary where** the parent exercises dominant influence. For example, a parent company could own only 45% of the equity but still exercise dominant influence, in which case the group should consolidate 100% of the assets and liabilities of the subsidiary but also show minority interests of 55%. The basis of the parent company's dominant influence must be disclosed.

6752 FRS 4 (49) An **exception to this rule** is that, shares issued by subsidiaries to external shareholders should be accounted for in the consolidated financial statements as liabilities and not minority interests, where the group has an obligation to transfer economic benefits in relation to the shares. In this situation, the substance of the transaction prevails over the legal form.

1. Classification

6754 FRS 4 (50) Minority interests **should be analysed between** equity and non-equity minority interests; this analysis is given on the face of the balance sheet. Where the minority interests **are immaterial**, an indication should still be given on the face of the balance sheet with further details provided in the notes.

Equity interests

6755 Equity shares can confer unrestricted rights to shareholders to participate in the distribution of profit in the form of dividends or in the event of a company being wound up. The **most common form** is ordinary shares.

Equity minority interests represent the net proceeds on the issue of the equity shares (proceeds less issue costs), plus the equity minority shareholders' percentage interest in the other reserves (i.e. revaluation reserve).

The calculation of equity interests is illustrated in ¶6762.

Non-equity interests

6756 Non-equity interests **represent shares** with any of the following characteristics:
– where rights to receive payments (e.g. dividends or on redemption) are restricted to a certain amount that is independent of the company's assets or profits, or the dividends on any class of equity share;
FRS 4 (12) – where rights to participate in a surplus where a company is wound up are restricted to a certain amount, irrespective of the company's profits or assets; or

– where the shares are redeemable according to the terms of issue or at the bequest of the holder or any other party.

Preference shares are an example of non-equity interests.

Where there are non-equity minority interests a description should be given of any rights of holders of the shares against other group companies.

The following **amounts should to be attributed to** the non-equity interests:
– the nominal value (less issue costs, dividends paid); plus
– the premium received; plus
– an accrual reflecting the additional premium payable on redemption.

Through the **consolidation process**, the non-equity minority interests will be apportioned part of the group's reserves, in addition to the nominal value of the non-equity shares. The group's reserves will be reduced over the term to redemption of the non-equity interests.

EXAMPLE A subsidiary company's **only minority interest is** a redeemable preference share of £200,000 issued to an external shareholder at a premium of £20,000, with a redemption premium of £30,000 payable in ten years time. Issue costs are immaterial.

Year 1
Initial investment £200,000 + £20,000 premium = £220,000.
Plus the accrual expected to produce a constant return over the term of the investment of £30,000/10 = £3000. Total investment £223,000.

End of the term (10 years):
The non-equity interest equals £250,000 (£220,000 + the £30,000 representing the redemption premium).
This accounting treatment fully reflects the entitlements of the minority interests as it presents a larger figure for non-equity minority interests and a smaller figure for shareholders' funds.

Special classifications

In some specific cases minority interests must be shown in another position in the balance sheet in order to give a true and fair view. 6757

Stapled shares Shareholders in the parent company may have been issued with shares in a subsidiary that have been "stapled" or grouped with their shares in the parent company. This method of issuing shares is sometimes used where the subsidiary is resident overseas for tax reasons, to ensure that the distributions from it are not subject to UK ACT rules. 6758

Depending on the rights attached to these shares and the circumstances of the share issue (substance of the transaction) it may be more appropriate to classify them as shareholders funds than to minority interests.

Directors' interests 6759

Share issues	Accounting treatment
Directors' nominee shareholdings acquired – as required under articles of association	Shareholdings generally small and do not constitute a minority interest as they are normally held on the parent company's behalf
Where directors have a beneficial interest in the company's shares	Substance of transaction must be considered Does the shareholding constitute a minority interest? If not additional disclosures probably required covering related party transactions.

2. Calculation of minority interests

The first step in calculating the minority interests is to review the group structure, in order to determine which entities are subsidiaries of the parent. This can result in a mixture of direct and indirect holdings. 6760

Direct holdings

6762 The **simple scenario** involves a direct holding in equity shares owned by the parent company. The minority interests in a subsidiary's profit for the year, is calculated by taking the profit after taxation and calculating the proportion of the profit attributable to the minority. The value of the minority interests in the balance sheet at the end of the financial year represents the minority interest in the capital and reserves of the subsidiary.

EXAMPLE **Profit and loss**

A parent company (S) **owns 75%** of a subsidiary's (T) ordinary share capital. The subsidiary's profit and loss account is as follows:

	£'000
Operating profit	1750
Non-operating exceptional item	250
Profit on ordinary activities before taxation	2,000
Tax on ordinary activities	(245)
Profit on ordinary activities after tax	1755
Minority interests (25 % × £1755)	**(438.7)**
Retained profit for the year	1,316.3

Balance sheet calculation

		£'000
Net assets		3605
Equity share capital		250
Share premium		500
Revaluation reserve		300
Profit and loss account	800	
Retained profits	1755	2555
Equity shareholders funds		3605
Minority interests = £3605 × 25% =		**901**

Indirect holdings

6764 Where a parent holds an indirect interest in a subsidiary, the calculation of minorities will be more complicated.

Having determined which undertakings are subsidiaries to be consolidated, one of **two methods** can be adopted to calculate the indirect minority interests in the balance sheet. Both methods will produce the same result **except where goodwill** has been capitalised, in which case the first method should be used.

6766 Under **Method A** the parent company's indirect holdings in its subsidiaries are calculated from the perspective of the parent company.

EXAMPLE **Minority interests in a group – Method A**

Summarised balance sheets – Companies A, B, and C
Company A has a 75% holding in B; MI 25%.

	A 000's	B 000's	C 000's
Investment in subsidiaries	60	30	-
Net assets	140	120	175
	200	150	175
Equity share capital	100	50	100
Profit and loss account	100	100	75
	200	150	175

Minority interest in group

	£
Minorities' share of net assets of company B × direct minority interest	
£120,000 × 25%	30,000
Minorities' share of net assets of company C × indirect minority interest	
£175,000 × 45% (100 – (40 % × 75% + 25%))	78,750
Total minority interest	**108,750**

Method B of calculating minority interests involves the consolidation of the minority interests of Company C with those of Company B, before consolidating Company B with the parent company. The minority interests are as calculated in method A. 6768

Company A has a direct holding in C which forms part of the minority interests from the perspective of Company B.

EXAMPLE **Minority interest in group – Method B**

Based on summarised balance sheet given in the above example.

Stage 1. Company C consolidated into Company B

Equity share capital of Company C (£100,000 × 60%)	60,000
Company C reserves (£75,000 × 60%)	45,000
Minority interest in Group B	**105,000**

Stage 2. Group B consolidated into Company A (parent)

Equity share capital of Company B (£50,000 × 25%)	12,500
Company B reserves (£100,000 × 25%)	25,000
Company C reserves (£100,000 – £60,000 × 25%) (Note 1).	10,000
Adjustment to eliminate 25% of Company C owned directly by Company A (Note 2)	
Equity share capital of C (£100,000 × 25%)	– 25,000
Reserves of C (£75,000 × 25%)	– 18,750
Minority interest in Group A	**108,750**

Notes. 1 The minority in Group B take their proportion of the reserves of Company C that have already been consolidated with Company A's reserves.
2. The adjustment is required as the 60% minority interest in Company C consolidated into Company B includes the 25% held by Company A.

3. Accounting treatment

The requirement under the Companies Act and FRS 2 for full consolidation means that the statutory headings in the consolidated profit and loss account must include the total amount for each item of income and expenditure relating to the subsidiary. A **number of problem areas can arise** in accounting for minority interests including: 6770

- the accounting for loss making subsidiaries;
- allocation of dividends; and
- the treatment of goodwill on acquisition.

Where the **acquisition method** (¶6820) of accounting is used to consolidate a subsidiary undertaking, the assets and liabilities of the acquired undertaking should be consolidated at their fair values at the acquisition date.

Where **merger accounting** (¶7000) is used, the assets and liabilities of the acquired entity should be consolidated at the values stated in the financial statements of the acquired company, subject to any adjustments required or permitted by the Companies Act. 6771

Irrespective of which treatment is adopted, the assets and liabilities attributable to the minority interests should be included on the same basis (i.e. accounting policies), as those attributable to the interests held by the parent and its other subsidiary undertakings.

FRS 2 (37) The **general rule** is that **profits or losses arising** in a subsidiary undertaking should be apportioned between the controlling and minority interests, in proportion to their respective interests held over the period in which the profits or losses arose.

6772 **Where subsidiaries are profit making**, the share attributable to the minority interests should be deducted from the consolidated profit and loss account, so reducing the group's profit attributable to shareholders' funds (see ¶6762). Where the **subsidiaries are loss making**, the minority interests are added to the consolidated profit and loss account, so reducing the loss transferred to shareholders' funds.

Accounting for minorities on acquisition

6774 **Direct subsidiary** When a company acquires a subsidiary it is required to apportion to the minority interests its share of the total net assets of that subsidiary. In the consolidated balance sheet, the relevant percentage of the share capital and reserves are allocated to the minority interest.

However, there is **no allocation of goodwill** to the minority interests.

EXAMPLE **Company X acquires company Y at the end of year 1. The year-end summarised balance sheets show:**

Summarised balance sheets – pre-acquisition	**X**	**Y**
Net assets	750	200
Equity share capital	300	120
Share premium account	100	-
Profit and loss reserve	350	80
Equity shareholders' funds	**750**	**200**

To help fund the acquisition company X issues 10,000 £1 equity shares to the shareholders of company Y, to acquire 80% of its issued share capital. At the acquisition date the fair value of the consideration for company Y is valued at £200,000 and the fair value of the net assets at £250,000.

The balance sheets for the two companies **after the acquisition** will be as follows:

Summarised balance sheets £'000 – post acquisition

	X	**Y**
Investment in subsidiary	200	
Other net assets	750	200
Fair value adjustment	-	50
	950	**250**
Equity share capital	310	120
Share premium	290	
Profit and loss account	350	80
Revaluation reserve		50
Equity shareholders' funds	**950**	**250**

Cost of control account

	£'000		**£'000**
Investment	200	Equity share capital (£120,000 × 80%)	96
		P/L reserve (£80,000 × 80%)	64
		Revaluation reserve (£50,000 × 80%)	40
			200
	200		**200**

Minority interests account

	£'000		**£'000**
Balance	50	Equity share capital (£120,000 × 20%)	24
		P/L reserve (£80,000 × 20%)	16
		Revaluation reserve (£50,000 × 20%)	10
	50		50

Group consolidated balance sheet

	£'000
Net assets (£750,000 + £250,000 (fair value))	**1000**
Equity share capital	310
Share premium	290
Profit and loss account	350
Minority interests	50
Shareholders' funds	**1000**

Indirect subsidiaries Where a subsidiary (A) acquires a controlling interest in another sub-subsidiary (B), **any goodwill arising on this acquisition** should be accounted for in company A's consolidated financial statements. This in turn will effect the calculation of minority interests in A recognised in the consolidated financial statements of the ultimate parent company P. 6775 FRS 2 (82)

Goodwill arising on acquisition **should only be recognised** with respect to the part of the subsidiary undertakings, that is attributable to the interest held by the parent and its other subsidiary undertakings.

EXAMPLE A parent company X has an 80% holding in a subsidiary company Y. Company Y later acquires a 100% holding in company Z on which goodwill of £100,000 arises.

Problem
How should this goodwill be accounted for in the consolidated financial statements of company X (parent)?
Should it be carried at 100% of the goodwill with the minority interest allocated 20% or should the goodwill be carried at 80% with no recognition for the minority?

Solution
Company Y should prepare consolidated financial statements and include 100% of the goodwill.
Company X consolidated financial statements should also carry goodwill of 100% with a minority interest of 20%.

Reasoning:
The capital and reserves attributable to the shares in the subsidiary undertakings includes the goodwill of £100,000 arising on the acquisition of company Z by company Y. This would be included in the financial statements of the parent company X.
The rule that **no goodwill be attributable** to the minority interests **applies only to** direct acquisitions by a parent of a part interest in a subsidiary, because the minority is often not a party to the transaction.

Loss making subsidiaries

Where the subsidiary has net assets the minority interests will be a credit and where the subsidiary has net liabilities the minority interests will be a debit balance. 6778

Debit minority interests require special consideration. The group should make a provision where it has a commercial or legal (formal or implied) obligation to provide finance, that may not be recoverable due to the losses attributable to the minority interests. An example would be a letter issued by the parent company confirming that it will make good any losses in its subsidiary. 6779

Provisions **should be extended to cover** not just debit balances but **the minority's share of any liability** guaranteed by the group. The group must show any guaranteed obligations that it has in respect of a minority as a liability and not as minority interests.

Any provision in respect of minority debit balances should be set against the minority interests shown in the profit and loss account and in the balance sheet.

The minority's interest shares of any losses **should be treated in the following sequence** in the consolidated balance sheet: 6780
- first set against the minority's share of the subsidiary's reserves;

– then set against the minority's share of the subsidiary's capital; and
– finally, recognise as a debit balance in the consolidated balance sheet where the group does not have a legal obligation in terms of the losses attributable to the minority interest.

This **process is reversed** if and when profits attributable to the minority interests are offset against the earlier losses.

Allocation of dividends paid by a subsidiary

6782 The group profit and loss account should only reflect the dividends paid by the parent company to its own shareholders. **If a subsidiary has paid a dividend** during the year, any part paid to the parent company should be cancelled out on consolidation, because the parent will already have accounted for a dividend receivable in its own individual accounts. An adjustment will be required for any dividend paid to minority interests.

EXAMPLE A Ltd is the parent company of company B holding 70% of its share capital. The results of the two companies for the year ending 31 December 2010 are as follows:

	A Ltd 000's	B Ltd 000's
Operating profit	500	270
Income from holdings in group companies	70	-
Interest payable	(120)	(75)
Profit on ordinary activities before taxation	450	195
Taxation	(135)	(45)
Profit on ordinary activities after tax	315	150
Dividend paid	(150)	(100)
Retained profit for the year	165	50

The dividend remitted by B Ltd will cancel the dividend received shown in the financial statements of A Ltd (£70,000). The balance of £30,000 represents the dividend payable to the minority interests and must be removed from the consolidated profit and loss account and dealt with in the consolidated balance sheet under movements on the minority interest account.

The group consolidated profit and loss account:

	A Ltd 000's	B Ltd 000's	Group 000's
Operating profit	500	270	770
Income from holdings in group companies	70	-	-
Interest payable	(120)	(75)	**(195)**
Profit on ordinary activities before taxation	450	195	**575**
Taxation	(135)	(45)	**(180)**
Profit on ordinary activities after tax	315	150	**395**
Minority interests (150 × 30%)			**(45)**
Profit for the year attributable to the group			**350**
Dividend paid	(150)	(100)	**(150)**
Retained profit for the year	165	50	**200**

The **retained profit for the group** of £200,000 represents £165,000 for A Ltd and £35,000 for B Ltd (£50,000 × 70%). The group cash flow statement should show dividends paid to minority interests as a separate heading under "returns on investments and servicing of finance".

4. Disclosure requirements

6783 A minority interest should be disclosed from the date of acquisition. The key disclosure requirements are outlined below.

Consolidated profit and loss account

6784 FRS 2 (36) The Companies Act incorporates the requirement of the EC 7th Directive that minority interests be shown as a separate item in the consolidated profit and loss account formats.

The Companies Act requires minority interests headings within the consolidated profit and loss account, in respect of profits and losses on ordinary activities, excluding extraordinary activities and the minority's share of any extraordinary items. In Formats 1 and 2, this heading should be included after "profit or loss on ordinary activities after taxation." In Format 3 and Format 4, minority interests should be included either under "charges" or "income".

The **minority interests** in the P & L **should be analysed between** equity and non-equity minority interests. Where there are non-equity minority interests a description should be given of any rights of holders of the shares against other group companies.

EXAMPLE **Based on Format 1**

Group profit and loss account
ABC Ltd – Report and Financial Statements – 31 December 2010

	2010	2009
Profit on ordinary activities before tax	250.0	210.0
Taxation	(55,8)	(46.2)
Profit on ordinary activities after tax	194.2	163.8
Minority interests		
- Equity	**(5.0)**	**(5.0)**
- Non-equity	**(20.0)**	**(20.0)**
	(25.0)	**(25.0)**
Dividend on preference shares	(0.5)	(0.5)
Profit attributable to ordinary shareholders	**168.7**	**138.3**

Note- Minority interests
The capital outstanding and dividends payable are classified as non-equity minority interests in both the balance sheet and profit and loss account, where the issues do not represent a contingent obligation on the part of the parent company or another group company that guarantees the issue.

Consolidated balance sheet

The capital and reserves attributable to shares in subsidiary undertakings of the parent company, held by interests other than the parent company and its subsidiary undertakings, should be shown under a separate heading of "Minority Interest". These disclosures are required either after "Provisions for liabilities and charges", or after "Share capital and reserves" in Format 1 and between "Capital and Reserves" and "Provisions for Liabilities and Charges" in Format 2. In some **specific cases** (e.g. stapled shares, directors' interests) minority interests must be shown in another position in the balance sheet. 6786 FRS 2 (35)

EXAMPLE **Based on Format 2**

Balance sheet (extract)
ABC Ltd – Report and Financial Statements – 31 December 2010

Capital and reserves	**2010**	**2009**
Equity share capital	150.2	150.2
Non-equity share capital	5.0	5.0
Called-up share capital	**155.2**	**155.2**
Share premium account	350.0	350.0
Revaluation reserve	227.0	163.0
Profit and loss account	135.7	248.7
Shareholders funds	**867.9**	**916.9**
Minority interests		
– equity	38.6	28.5
– non-equity	150.0	175.0
	188.6	**203.5**
Provision for liabilities and charges	30.0	9.0
Creditors – due within a year	330.0	185.0
Creditors – due after one year	275.0	220.0
	635.0	**414.0**

Notes to the accounts

6787 Disclosures are required for any **non-equity minority interests** including details of the external shareholder rights against other group companies. Where convertible securities are involved, consideration should be given to both the carrying amount when assessing materiality and also the rights and implications on conversion.

FRS 3 (20) The following disclosures in relation to the effect on minority interests are required of:
- profits or losses on the sale or termination of an operation or disposal of a fixed asset;
- costs of a fundamental reorganisation or restructuring; and
- profits or losses on the disposal of fixed assets.

5. Comparison between UK GAAP and IFRS

6788

	UK GAAP	IFRS
Presentation	Companies Act FRS 2 (see disclosures)	1. Consolidated financial statements – Minority Interests (MI) – in accordance with IAS "Presentation of financial statements" and IAS 27 "Consolidated and separate financial statements" 2. In the consolidated balance sheet the MI in consolidated subsidiaries' net assets are presented within equity, distinct from parent's shareholders' equity (IAS 27 para 33).
Treatment of losses	Provision made where group has formal obligation to cover the losses attributable to the minority interest	Losses applicable to the minority in excess of the minority's interests in the subsidiary's equity – allocated against majority interest, except where the minority has a binding obligation to cover the losses (IAS 27 para 35)
Distinction drawn between equity and financial liabilities	FRS 25	No distinction Certain preference shares (e.g. redeemable shares) – should be treated as liabilities under IAS 32. MI also classified as a liability if group has an obligation to deliver cash or another financial asset in respect of the financial instrument

E. Segmental information

6790 Segmental reporting is considered in greater detail in ¶750, except for the two areas discussed below that are particularly relevant to group accounts.

6792 **Segmentation rather than exclusion** Where subsidiary undertakings engage in different activities or are subject to certain restrictions, but are still consolidated, then additional information should be given regarding the assets, liabilities and turnover and results attributable to such undertakings. The reason being that the financial implications of including them within the consolidated accounts can be fully appreciated.

Minority interests Users of consolidated financial statements may be interested in assessing the impact of minority interests, in certain parts of the group, on the expected returns to investors in the parent undertaking. To this end it would be useful to include information showing the amounts attributable to minority interests for different group segments. **6794** FRS 2 (94)

CHAPTER 3

Business combinations

OUTLINE

¶¶

A business combination **is defined as** the fusion of separate entities into one economic unit, as the result of one company uniting with (a merger), or obtaining control over the net assets and operations of another (acquisition). 6800 FRS 6 (4a)

A business combination **is accounted for as an acquisition or merger** depending on the substance of the underlying transaction. The majority of business combinations are accounted for as acquisitions, with the possible exception of some group reconstructions, because the criteria for recognition as a merger are strict.

Where the acquisition takes the form of a **reverse takeover** (i.e. the acquirer is a smaller entity than the acquired entity), the determination of whether acquisition accounting is appropriate is based on the same criteria applied to other business combinations.

The rules governing merger and acquisition accounting are contained in the Companies Act, FRS 2 "Accounting for subsidiaries undertakings", FRS 6 "Acquisitions and mergers", FRS 7 "Fair values in acquisition accounting" and FRS 10 "Goodwill and intangible assets". A financial reporting exposure draft (FRED 36 "Business Combinations") has also been issued.

Reporting entities **applying the FRSSE** are exempt from the requirements of these standards, unless preparing consolidated financial statements, in which case they should apply the FRS's to such statements as required by the FRSSE. There are also a number of **key differences** between UK GAAP and IFRS.

MEMO POINTS The ASB has published an amended version of FRS 6 that reflects changes in the Companies Act 2006. The amendments do not alter the existing requirements of FRS 6 but update the references to correspond with the Companies Act 2006 and the Large and Medium-sized Companies and Groups (Accounts and Reports) Regulations 2008.

6802 An overview of the **principal differences** between acquisition and merger accounting are given in the table below.

	Acquisition accounting	Merger accounting
Consolidated financial statements	Only reflect the acquired company's results from the acquisition date	Results of combined entity incorporated in the consolidated financial statements as if entities had always been combined
Valuation of assets and liabilities	Requires restatement at cost (fair value)	Not restated at fair value – instead book values at merger date used
Goodwill	Goodwill recognised	Does not arise

SECTION 1

Acquisition accounting

6820 FRS 6 (2) In an acquisition, **the shareholders of the acquired entity** typically sell their shareholdings for either:
- cash;
- other non-equity consideration; or
- equity shares in the new parent entity or a combination thereof.

In many cases, the shareholders of the acquired entity do not retain a continuing interest in the shares of the combined entity and even where they do, it is unlikely to be on equal terms with the shareholders of the acquiring entity. One party, usually the shareholders of the acquirer, is likely to have a greater degree of influence.

6821 FRS 6 (20) **The objective of acquisition accounting** is to reflect the cost of the acquisition in the consolidated balance sheet. On acquisition of a subsidiary, the purchase consideration is allocated to the fair values of the identifiable assets and liabilities (net assets) of the acquired entity, with the residue classified as goodwill.

As it is **not always possible to determine accurately the fair values** at the acquisition date, adjustments to the provisional estimates, including goodwill, can be made within the following 12 months, as more information becomes available.

MEMO POINTS **Fair value is defined** as the amount at which an asset or liability could be exchanged in an arm's length transaction between willing parties, other than in a forced sale or liquidation. Assets and liabilities are classified as identifiable when they can be disposed of or discharged separately, without disposing of an entire business or undertaking.

6822 The **general principles** of accounting for a business combination (including reverse takeovers) under the acquisition method of accounting, and the recognition and measurement principles underpinning the fair value of individual acquired assets and liabilities, are set out below.

A. Accounting treatment

1. Determining the cost of acquisition

The cost of acquisition (purchase consideration) may take some or all of the following forms as set out in the table below. 6836 FRS 7 (76)

1.	The **total cash paid** and the fair value of **other monetary considerations** given by the acquirer including the assumption of liabilities.
2.	**Capital instruments** issued by the acquirer such as shares, debentures, loans, debt instruments, share warrants and other options.
3.	**Non-monetary assets** such as the securities of another entity.
4.	**Acquisition expenses** (e.g. fees).
5.	**Contingent consideration**. Where a **purchase consideration is dependent on** one or more **future events**, the acquisition cost should include an estimate of the fair value of any future payments. The acquisition cost should then be adjusted when revised estimates have been prepared, with corresponding adjustments made to goodwill until such time as a final purchase price is determined.
6.	**Piecemeal acquisition** Where a subsidiary is acquired in stages (piecemeal acquisition), the cost of acquisition is the total costs of the interest acquired, as at each transaction date (¶6964).

Cash and other monetary considerations

Where the **purchase consideration** is in the form of cash or other monetary considerations, the fair value attributable to them is the amount paid or due to be paid. 6839

In situations **where the cash payable is deferred**, fair values are determined by discounting to the present value, the cash value to be paid at a future date.

The appropriate discount rate is the interest rate which the acquiring company would have to pay, if it were to borrow an amount equivalent to the deferred cash consideration.

Capital instruments

It is often the case, that **part of the acquisition consideration** given by the purchaser will be capital instruments in the acquiring company. Therefore, for the purposes of calculating the purchase consideration, it will be necessary to determine the fair value of those instruments at the date they were issued. 6840

Where an entity issues capital instruments to raise the cash required to fund an acquisition, the fair value of the instruments issued is not the relevant factor in determining the fair value of the consideration paid, but the cash that is subsequently paid to the vendor.

The fair values of shares and other securities or capital instruments issued by the acquirer, **where quoted** on a readily available market, will be the market price at the acquisition date. The relevant date for valuation purposes where control is transferred through a public offer, or where there are a number of revised offers, is when the successful offer becomes unconditional. 6842

Where securities issued by the acquiring entity **are not quoted**, the fair value is estimated after considering the following: 6843

- the fair value of similar quoted securities; FRS 7 (79)
- any cash alternative to the issue of securities;
- the present value of the future cash flows of the instrument issued; and
- the value of any underlying security incorporating an option to convert.

Non-monetary assets

6844 Where the purchase price is settled in the form of non-cash assets, the fair values should be determined with reference to:
- market prices;
- estimated realisable values;
- independent valuations; or
- other available evidence.

Acquisition expenses

6845 The acquisition process will usually involve expenditure on professional fees paid to:
- merchant banks;
FRS 7 (85)
- accountants;
- legal advisers; or
- valuers and other consultants.

The **general rule** is that these incremental costs incurred directly in making the acquisition should be included in the cost of acquisition.

However, it should be noted that the **expenses of issuing shares or other capital instruments** that qualify as issue costs, should not be added to the cost of acquisition, but accounted for as a reduction in the proceeds of a capital instrument.

Contingent consideration

6850 FRS 7 (81) The **acquisition terms** may stipulate that all or part of the purchase consideration in whatever form, be payable at a later date, perhaps based on some performance criteria. The **fair value of such agreements are often difficult to determine** at the acquisition date, and as such a reasonable estimate of future considerations should be included in the acquisition price.

An example is as "earn-out", where the purchase consideration includes an initial payment, with future payments based on a multiple of future profits (performance based) of the acquired entity. Other examples include consideration in the form of:
- an issue of shares;
- options to settle the consideration partly in shares, partly in cash; or
- other forms of consideration such as non-competition payments or loyalty bonuses.

Initial estimates of the contingent consideration should be revised as more information becomes available and adjustments made to the goodwill recognised, be it positive or negative.

6852 **Issue of shares** Where contingent consideration is to be satisfied by the issue of shares, there is no obligation to transfer economic benefits. The purchase consideration is reported as part of shareholders' funds, as shares yet to be issued. This is effectively a "holding account" until it is known exactly how many shares are to be issued. Appropriate transfers would then be necessary from this "holding account" to the called-up share capital and share premium accounts.

6854 FRS 7 (83) **Option to settle the consideration partly in shares, partly in cash** There may be agreements, where the acquiring undertaking has the option to satisfy part of the purchase consideration through a share issue and partly in cash. In these cases, this element of the future consideration is not a liability because no obligation to transfer economic benefits has arisen. Consequently, the expected future consideration would be accounted for as a credit to shareholders' funds, until an irrevocable decision regarding the form of the consideration has been taken.

However, in those cases the **where the vendor has the right** to demand cash or shares, the expected future consideration is regarded as an obligation to the vendor and would be accounted for as a liability until the shares are issued or the cash is paid.

6856 FRS 7 (84) **Other forms of consideration** Acquisition agreements may require payments such as **non-competition payments** or **loyalty bonuses** to vendors, who continue to work for the acquired undertaking. In such circumstances, it is necessary to determine whether the substance of the agreement is payment for the business acquired, or an expense, such as compensation for services or profit sharing. In the first case, the expected payments would be accounted for as contingent purchase consideration; in the latter case, the payments would be treated as expenses of the period to which they relate (see ¶6944).

2. Specifically excluded acquisition costs

Post-acquisition costs All post-acquisition costs must be excluded from the fair value exercise. Examples include: 6860
- structural/organisational changes made by the acquirer;
- impairment, or other changes resulting from post-acquisition events;
- internal costs and other expenses not directly attributable to the acquisition; or
- provisions or accruals for future operating losses or for reorganisation and expected integration costs resulting from the acquisition, relating to the acquired entity or acquirer at the acquisition date.

If the acquirer subsequently decides to **close a factory** belonging to the acquired entity, this is deemed a post-acquisition event. Similarly, where the acquirer reorganises or restructures the factory to integrate the operation or to improve its efficiency, this is also considered a post-acquisition event.

Pre-acquisition costs Costs that would have been incurred irrespective of the acquisition and other pre-acquisition costs should be expensed in the profit and loss account. Examples include the following: 6861 FRS 7 (40)
- costs of running an acquisitions department;
- expenses incurred in raising acquisition finance (e.g. shares issue); or
- certain provisions for future costs.

Provisions for future costs Where provisions for future costs were made by an acquired entity shortly before an acquisition took place, for example, during the negotiations for sale, it would be necessary to determine whether actual obligations had been incurred by the acquired entity before the acquisition. 6862

If the **acquired entity was committed** to the expenditure irrespective of whether the acquisition was completed or not, it would have incurred a liability at the acquisition date, and any associated provisions would be permissible. For instance, where the acquiring entity was contractually committed to a closure or restructuring plan, prior to completion of the acquisition and was unable to withdraw without due cost, then these types of provisions would be permissible.

Also, **if the obligations were incurred** by the acquired entity **due to influence** from the acquirer, one must determine whether control of the acquired entity had passed to the acquirer at an earlier date. If this were the case, the issue would be whether the acquisition date pre-dated such commitments.

3. Measuring the fair value of acquired assets and liabilities

The general principles governing the initial investigation period, the recognition and valuation of acquired assets and liabilities and the rules for determining the fair value of specific types of assets and liabilities are set out below. 6864

a. Recognition and measurement principles

The **identifiable assets and liabilities** of the acquired entity are recognised at their fair values as at the acquisition date, in accordance with the acquiring undertaking's accounting policies for similar assets and liabilities. The difference between the fair value of these assets and liabilities and the acquisition cost is accounted for as goodwill. 6866 FRS 7 (5)

The identifiable assets and liabilities **acquired by the purchasing entity** represent rights to future economic benefits and obligations to transfer economic benefits, including contingent rights and obligations, of the acquired entity existing at the acquisition date.

Investigation period

6867 FRS 7 (23) Usually the **acquisition transaction does not in itself** determine the values attributed to each asset and liability. For this reason, the Companies Act and the accounting standards require a fair value exercise to determine the initial carrying amounts of individual assets and liabilities on acquisition.

The standard sets out the **general rules** for the investigation period, which can last up to 12 months, during which determination of the fair values should take place; namely:
– the **recognition and measurement** of acquired assets and liabilities should be completed by the date of approval by the directors of the first post-acquisition financial statements; or
– **where this is not possible**, provisional valuations should be prepared and adjusted where necessary in the next financial statements, with corresponding adjustments to purchased goodwill being made at that time.

Thereafter, **any further adjustments** to the provisional valuation, except the correction of fundamental errors which are accounted for as prior-period adjustments, should be recognised in the profit and loss account.

Valuation of acquired assets and liabilities

6870 FRS 7 (42) Fair values should be based on the value at which an asset could be exchanged in an arm's length transaction (market price). The fair value of monetary items should also take into account amounts expected to be received or paid and their timing. Where the replacement cost is **not fully recoverable** then fair value should be based on recoverable amount.

6874 Where **similar assets are bought and sold** on a readily accessible market the market price will represent fair value. Where quoted market prices are not available, they should be estimated by:
– obtaining independent valuations;
– discounting estimated future cash flows to their present values; or
– with reference to subsequent sales of acquired assets.

Impaired assets

6878 FRS 7 (47) Where the **replacement cost** of an acquired asset **is not fully recoverable**, due for example, to reasons of obsolescence, under-utilisation or non-profitability, the fair value is the estimated recoverable amount. The recoverable amount valuation should reflect the condition of the asset on acquisition, but not any impairment resulting from subsequent events.

6880 In some instances, the recoverable amount can be determined only by considering a **group of jointly used assets** (income generating units) as a whole, rather than by attempting to determine the recoverable amount of each identifiable asset in that group. Aggregation can facilitate the allocation of cash flows to the assets that help to generate them.

6881 Any **losses arising on the disposal** of acquired assets (e.g. as part of a post-acquisition reorganisation) that were not impaired at the acquisition date, do not affect the fair values at the acquisition date. These losses could arise from the re-organisation of the enlarged group post-acquisition and should be treated as post-acquisition losses.

Assets and liabilities not previously recognised

6883 FRS 7 (35) The identifiable assets and liabilities may include **items not previously recognised** in the financial statements of the acquired entity (pre-acquisition), because other accounting standards prohibited their inclusion. An example is a contingent asset valued on acquisition but not recognised in the financial statements, because FRS 12 "Provisions, contingent liabilities and contingent assets" prohibits recognition until realisation is all but certain.

However, when an entity is acquired, it is necessary to identify all assets and liabilities acquired, where they can be properly valued. Otherwise, the reporting of post-acquisition performance will be distorted by changes in assets and liabilities not being recognised in the correct accounting period. The accounting practice of **deferring recognition** of contingent assets does not apply, as recognition of the asset represents the expectation by the acquirer that the acquisition costs will be recovered at some stage. However, provisions should be made for any expected losses.

Furthermore, particular **contingent assets and liabilities may crystallise** as a result of the acquisition. Provided that the underlying contingency was in existence before the acquisition, it would be appropriate to recognise them. For example, where the acquired entity entered into contracts containing restrictive clauses that later trigger obligations in the event of a change of ownership. **6884** FRS 7 (37)

MEMO POINTS The ASB has issued FRED 39 which contains revisions to FRS 12 thereby bringing UK GAAP more into line with IFRS. The FRED dispenses with the terms "Contingent assets and liabilities" and forms part of an ongoing project on business combinations. It is not certain if the proposed changes will be incorporated into UK GAAP or when, as the ASB has postponed a firm decision on implementation, pending completion of its convergence programme with IFRS. The ASB also advises that some proposals set out in the FRED may conflict with existing legal requirements, although it is hoped these issues can be resolved with the help of the Department of Business, Innovation and Skills (BIS). The ASB is currently reviewing the feedback comments received for FRED 39.

b. Identifiable individual assets and liabilities

The table below outlines the **valuation bases** for determining the fair value of acquired assets and liabilities. **6890**

Category	Basis for determining fair value
Tangible fixed assets	Lower of recoverable amount or depreciated replacement cost (DRC) reflecting: – the market value for similar assets readily available or – DRC for specialised assets
Intangible fixed assets	Replacement cost (estimated market value)
Stock and work-in-progress	1. Stocks for which an active market exists – use market price 2. Other stocks: use lower of replacement cost or net realisable value 3. Long-term maturing stocks: use historic cost or market value if traded regularly
Long-term contracts	Based on acquirer's accounting policy
Monetary assets and liabilities	Quoted investments: use market price Other monetary items: expected values to be received or paid on settlement.
Non-monetary assets	Market value
Contingent assets and liabilities	Values based on reasonable estimates
Business held exclusively For resale	Estimate of expected net sale proceeds. Special rules (¶6915) apply based on time-scale for sale of investment or part-disposal.
Pension and other retirement benefits following acquisition	Funded scheme: Only recognition of surpluses and liabilities expected to be realised. Unfunded scheme: recognition of valuation of accrued obligations as liabilities.
Deferred tax assets and liabilities	Must satisfy the recognition criteria in FRS 19. Tax losses of the acquired entity recognised as an asset if it can be recovered.

Tangible fixed assets

6892 FRS 7 (9) The fair value of tangible fixed assets should not exceed the recoverable amount of the asset and be based on:

a. **market value** where assets are similar and reliable values are obtainable (e.g. quoted investments and certain types of property); or

b. **depreciated replacement cost (DRC)**. For many types of fixed asset, such as plant and machinery and specialist property, the fair value equals the DRC reduced by depreciation to reflect the age and condition of the asset. The DRC should not exceed the recoverable amount of an asset at the acquisition date and should reflect the acquired undertaking's normal buying process and sources of supply.

For certain assets **where it is difficult to determine the DRC**, the asset's historical cost updated with the aid of price indices, may be the most reliable method of estimating replacement cost. In situations where prices have not changed greatly, it would be acceptable to use a carrying value based on historical cost.

The topic of valuation of tangible fixed assets is dealt with in greater detail in ¶1226.

6893 **Depreciation rates** adopted should, in determining the DRC, reflect the estimated asset lives and residual amounts used by the acquirer for similar assets.

Stocks and work-in-progress

6894 FRS 7 (11) Stocks purchased in a **readily active market** and **work-in-progress**, including commodity stocks that are traded by the acquired entity, should be valued at current market prices.

6896 **Where there is no ready market**, work-in-progress should be valued at the lower of replacement cost and net realisable value. Account should be taken of the manner in which the acquired business purchased or manufactured the stocks; namely for:

– a business buying its stocks in wholesale markets, the replacement cost should be the actual cost; whilst

– the replacement cost of finished goods of a manufacturer should be the current manufacturing cost and not the cost of buying in supplies from another manufacturer.

6898 Where stock is held during **the period up to the acquisition date**, it would be valid to take account of the impact of input price changes during the holding period. However, no addition should be made for any unrealised profit that normally would not be recognised in the acquired undertaking until the stocks are sold.

6899 **Long-term maturing stocks** Replacement costs should be based on market values if stocks are regularly traded in the market. Where similar market transactions do not exist because there is no active market or trading is very thin, use of replacement cost will be difficult. Instead the historical cost of bringing the stock to its present location and condition may be appropriate.

6900 FRS 7 (57) **Slow moving or obsolete stock** Care needs to be exercised in reaching a judgement about the fair value of slow moving or redundant stocks. Any **material write-down** in the carrying value of stock in the acquired entity at the acquisition date must be justified by circumstances prevailing at that time.

Where **exceptional profits** appear to have been earned on the realisation of stocks after the date of acquisition, it will be necessary to re-examine the fair values determined on acquisition. If necessary, these values will have to be adjusted with a corresponding adjustment to goodwill. If, alternatively, the profit is attributable to post acquisition events, it should be disclosed as an exceptional item.

Long-term contracts

6904 SSAP 9 "Stocks and long-term contracts" (see ¶2200) requires **turnover and cost of sales to be recognised as** the contract progresses, and attributable profit recognised in a prudent manner. As such no adjustments to book values are required other than adjustments that would normally result from assessing the outcome of the contract under SSAP 9, or that result from a change to the acquirer's accounting policies.

Onerous contracts Identifiable liabilities include onerous contracts and commitments existing in existence at the acquisition date, irrespective of whether the corresponding obligations were recognised as liabilities in the financial statements of the acquired entity. When an acquisition is made, provisions for liabilities may be recognised when performing the fair value exercise, only if such commitments were made by the acquired undertaking before the date of acquisition. **6905** FRS 7 (38)

Monetary assets and liabilities

The majority of **short-term** monetary assets and liabilities, such as trade debtors and creditors, will be recognised at values expected to be received or paid on settlement. However, the fair values of certain **long-term** monetary items may differ from their book values. An example is where an acquired entity carries material levels of long-term debt at fixed rates that are different from current interest rates on borrowing. The fair values will be greater or lower than the book value depending on the direction of changes in interest rates since the debt was issued. **6906** FRS 7 (60)

The following conditions apply:

a. **Monetary items** must be stated at fair values where they differ materially from book values.

b. **Quoted investments** should be valued at market price, adjusted to reflect unusual price fluctuations or size of holding such as the higher value attached to substantial voting blocks or difficulties in disposing of small shareholdings.

c. For **other monetary items**, the fair values may be calculated after considering the current terms on which a similar monetary asset or liability could be acquired or incurred.

Discounting to present values Another method would be to discount to present values of the total amounts expected to be received or paid. The interest rates selected would need to reflect the current lending rates applicable to a similar credit period, the credit rating of the acquirer and the precise nature of the security involved. **6907**

Differences between fair values determined by discounting and the actual amounts subsequently received or paid represent premiums or discounts on acquisition, that should be treated in the financial statements of the acquired group as interest income or expenses. The amounts are then allocated to accounting periods over the term of the monetary item at a constant rate based on their carrying amounts.

Debt instruments Where debt instruments issued by the acquired company are quoted, market values at the acquisition date should be used instead of present values. Any pre-acquisition risk that the debt would not be repaid, which was reflected in the market value, would not be adjusted as part of the fair value exercise, if the debt is expected to be paid in full. **6909**

Non-monetary assets

The **general rule** is that the fair values of non-monetary assets should be measured at their market value (see also ¶6844). **6910** FRS 7 (45)

Where this is not possible, the fair values should be based on replacement cost, but this should not exceed their recoverable amount as at the date of acquisition.

The **replacement cost** is the cost to the acquired entity of replacing the asset through its normal buying process and sources of supply. Although replacement cost takes into account the effects of input price changes during the period stocks are held.

The **recoverable amount** is the greater of the net realisable value of an asset or the value in use and reflects the condition of the assets on acquisition but nor any impairments resulting from subsequent events.

Contingent assets and liabilities

6912 The value assigned to a contingent asset or liability should reflect the best estimates of the expected outcome (see also ¶6883-4).

FRS 7 (35) An acquired undertaking may have contingent assets and liabilities, that **would not normally be recognised** in its financial statements **if no acquisition was involved**, because other accounting standards preclude their immediate recognition. For example, the acquired undertaking may have previously entered into a contract that contains a clause under which obligations are triggered in the event of a change in ownership. Such contingent assets and liabilities should be recognised, if the underlying contingency was in existence before the acquisition and can be reliably valued.

This accounting treatment is required, **otherwise the possibility of changes** in assets and liabilities not being recognised in the correct period, would distort the reporting of post-acquisition performance.

The **usual accounting practice of deferring recognition** of contingent assets, does not apply, because the recognition of an acquired asset represents the expectation that amounts expended on its acquisition will be recovered; it does not anticipate a future gain. The **recoverable amount** of such assets should however be reviewed to ensure that provision is made for any probable losses.

MEMO POINTS In 2008 the ASB issued "Improvements to Financial Reporting Standards", which included an amendment to FRS 7 regarding contingent consideration.

Business sold or held exclusively for resale (Investments)

6915 FRS 7 (16) (65)-(69) **Sale within one year of acquisition** If a separate business within the acquired entity is sold as a single unit within the first year following acquisition, the investment should be consolidated and treated as a single asset for the purpose of determining fair values, rather than assigning fair values to individual assets and liabilities. The goodwill should be apportioned between the part of the business retained and the part disposed of.

Where the adjustment for goodwill is material, the net proceeds should be discounted to determine their present value at the acquisition date, after allowing for the distribution of profits from the business. The **operational results** during the holding period are excluded from the profit and loss account of the acquiring group.

For this accounting treatment to apply the assets and liabilities should be clearly distinguishable from the other parts of the business.

6916 **Sale not completed by the time the first post-acquisition financial statements are approved** If the sale has not been completed by the date the first post-acquisition financial statements are agreed, the fair value of the business should be based on the estimated sale proceeds, providing:
- a purchaser has been identified; and
- the disposal is expected to be completed with one year of the acquisition date.

6917 **Post-acquisition profit or loss** There are a **number of circumstances** where the acquirer should estimate separately, the fair value of the underlying assets/liabilities of the business, at the acquisition date of a business held for resale and to record a post-acquisition profit or loss on disposal; namely:
- where the acquirer has markedly changed the acquired business before disposal;
- specific post-acquisition events occur during the holding period that materially affect the fair values of the business, compared to the estimates; or
- the disposal is quickly concluded at a reduced price.

Pensions and other post-retirement benefits following acquisition

6920 Accounting for an acquisition requires recognition in the acquirer's group accounts of all assets and liabilities of the acquired entity, identified at the acquisition date. However, a **pension asset** should only be recognised insofar as the acquiring or acquired entity is able to benefit from the surplus. A distinction is drawn between **funded and unfunded** pension schemes.

Any **changes in pension or other post-retirement arrangements** following an acquisition should be accounted for as post-acquisition items. Such an example is the cost of improving benefits to existing members of an acquired scheme in order to harmonise remuneration packages across the enlarged group.

Pensions are treated in greater detail in Part 10 Chapter 4.

Funded defined benefit scheme Where **an acquired company has a pension asset or liability** in its own balance sheet, then that asset or liability should be recognised in the consolidated financial statements of the acquiring company. Where possible, the same actuarial basis used to value the subsidiary's pension asset/liabilities should be adopted by the acquiring company. **6922** FRS 7 (19)

Where an acquired company has a defined benefit scheme **but has yet to recognise** a pension asset or liability, a valuation of the fund is required.

Any **deficiency or surplus** expected to be realised, should be recognised as assets or liabilities of the acquired undertaking.

The **fair value of a pension asset** in a funded defined benefit scheme refers to the extent it can be recovered through reduced contributions or through refunds from the scheme, and not simply the actuarial surplus in the fund.

The **valuation of a pension fund surplus** depends on **several assumptions** such as:
- the level of interest rates;
- level of inflation;
- investment returns;
- the estimated turnover of staff; or
- future salary increases.

The acquiring undertaking should apply its own judgement, in determining the impact on the valuation of the pension fund, if any, of these assumptions.

Unfunded schemes For unfunded schemes, the fair value of accrued obligations should be recognised as liabilities of the acquiring company. **6924** FRS 7 (19)

Deferred tax

Deferred tax **on adjustments** to recorded values of assets and liabilities at their fair value should be recognised in accordance with the principles of FRS 19 "Deferred Tax". **6925** FRS 7 (21) (74)

The existing deferred tax assets of the acquired entity should be included in the fair value exercise.

Where a deferred tax asset arises in the financial statements of the acquirer or another of its group entities as a result of the acquisition, that asset should be taken as a credit to the tax charge of the group in the post-acquisition period. This means that the enlarged group's deferred tax provision will be calculated as a single amount at the end of the accounting period, based on assumptions applicable to the group.

For example, deferred tax assets not considered recoverable prior to acquisition by the acquired entity, such as unrelieved tax losses, may become so post-acquisition by satisfying the recognition criteria set out in FRS 19.

Furthermore, **if the losses had arisen in the acquired entity**, they would be regarded as contingent assets that had crystallised as a result of the acquisition, and would be recognised as assets in the fair value exercise. **If the losses had arisen in the acquiring group**, they would not be assets of the acquired group and hence would not be recognised.

If the **criteria for recognition of tax losses** in group financial statements are not met, within the period allowed for completing the fair value exercise, then any benefits should be recognised in post-acquisition periods if the criteria are subsequently met. In these periods, any **special circumstances** that impact on the tax charge or credit for that period, or may affect **6926** FRS 7 (75) those of future periods, should be disclosed in a note to the consolidated profit and account and their individual effects quantified.

Adjustments to the value of assets and liabilities of the acquired entity at their fair values are treated in the same way, as they would if they were timing differences arising in the entity's own accounts. For instance, a **non-monetary asset** (e.g. building) would be valued on acquisition at its market value. Any tax payable if the building was subsequently sold at its market value would only have to be provided for, if before the acquisition date, the acquired entity entered into a binding agreement to sell the asset and rollover relief was not available.

B. Date control is transferred

6942 FRS 2 (45) An entity should be **accounted for as a subsidiary**, from the date on which control of that undertaking passes to its new parent undertaking. Control is defined as "the ability of an undertaking to direct the financial and operating policies of another undertaking with a view to gaining economic benefits from its activities".

The date on which the consideration for the **transfer of control is paid** is often an important indication of the date on which the subsidiary undertaking is acquired or disposed of.

However, the **complexity of some acquisition agreements** may mean that the terms of each agreement need to be reviewed carefully, in order to determine when control actually passes. This is because the date on which the consideration is paid may not constitute conclusive evidence of the date of the actual transfer of control.

In addition, the determination of the point control passes to the acquirer may be further complicated when **different forms of purchase consideration** are utilised.

Correspondingly, the date for accounting for an undertaking that **ceases to be a subsidiary** is the date on which its former parent undertaking relinquishes control over that undertaking.

1. Different forms of purchase consideration

6943 FRS 2 (85) The purchase consideration for a subsidiary can take a number of forms as set out below.

6944 **Consideration paid in instalments** Some acquisition agreements involve what is known as "**deferred consideration**", whereby part of the consideration is paid to the acquiring undertaking at the time the agreement is signed, with further instalments payable on future specified dates.

Other agreements involve "**contingent consideration**" where the profile of payments made to the acquiring undertaking depends on the outcome of future events, such as the profit performance of the acquired undertaking.

The payment of consideration by instalments or the existence of contingent or deferred consideration clauses in the purchase and sale agreement, does not necessarily delay the passing of control to the acquirer and **the relevant date will be** when actual ownership of the shares in the acquired company passes to the acquirer.

However, **this may not apply in all cases** and the relevant facts need to be assessed on a case by case basis, in order to determine when control actually passes to the acquiring undertaking. **For example**, where the deferred or contingent payments represent all of the acquired undertaking's profits up to a certain date, this suggests that control does not pass on the signing of the purchase and sale agreement, but at a later date when the acquirer becomes entitled to the profits of the acquired company.

Other forms of purchase consideration 1. Where control is transferred by public offer, the date control is transferred is the date the offer becomes unconditional, usually as a result of a sufficient number of acceptances being received. 6945 FRS 2 (85)
2. For **private treaties**, the date control is transferred is generally the date an unconditional offer is accepted.
3. **Other share issues or cancellation**. Where an undertaking become a subsidiary undertaking as a result of the issue or cancellation of shares, the date control is transferred is the date of issue or cancellation. **Examples include** the issue of new shares to minority shareholders or the repurchase by a company of the shares held by certain existing shareholders, the result of which is that one of the remaining shareholders now has a controlling interest in the company.

2. An undertaking ceases to be a subsidiary

A subsidiary undertaking **ceases to be part of the group** in the following scenarios: 6952 FRS 2 (86)
1. The **parent undertaking loses control** of its subsidiary undertaking because of:
– changes in the rights it holds, or those held by another party, in the subsidiary undertaking; or
– changes in the arrangement that gave it control without there being any change in the former parent undertaking's holding in its former subsidiary undertaking (e.g. a change in voting rights or the way these are allocated).
2. The **parent sells all or reduces its shareholding** in the subsidiary undertaking. This may result from a direct disposal of part of the interest it holds or from a deemed disposal. Any reduction in the group's proportional interest other than by a direct disposal is a deemed disposal.

The **accounting consequences** of an entity ceasing to be a subsidiary undertaking of its parent are discussed in ¶7100.

3. Increasing a shareholding

a. Categories of interest in shares

A **change in the level of investment** will require a change in accounting treatment for that investment. 6960

The following table outlines the most common levels of investment.

FRS 9 (b) (d)

Nature of relationship	Arrangement/undertaking	Accounting treatment
Minimal or no influence	Simple or trade investment	Fixed asset investment (passive investment)
Participation in arrangement to carry on own businesses	Joint arrangement not an entity (JANE)	Own accounting for assets, liabilities, cash flows etc.
Participating interest with significant influence over operating and financial policies	Associated undertaking	Equity accounting
Long-term interest with contractual joint control	Joint venture	Gross equity accounting
Control of investee undertaking	Subsidiary	Consolidation

In addition to the change in the accounting treatment adopted for different levels of influence, there are **further considerations** such as: 6962
– the recognition and measurement of fair value adjustments;
– the calculation of any goodwill; and
– the measurement of minority interests.

b. Piecemeal acquisition of a subsidiary

6964 FRS 2 (50) (88) A group's interest in an undertaking may be **acquired in stages**, until full control over the operating and financial policies of an entity is eventually achieved and it becomes a subsidiary undertaking. This is known as a piecemeal acquisition. In such circumstances, FRS 2 reinforces the provisions of the Companies Act, in requiring that the identifiable assets and liabilities of the subsidiary undertaking be included in the consolidated financial statements at their fair value, at the **date control passes** to the acquirer.

FRS 2 (89) The piecemeal acquisition of share acquisition provides **a practical means of applying acquisition accounting**, because once the investee company becomes a subsidiary, it does not require retrospective fair value exercises to be carried out on the identifiable assets and liabilities of acquired undertakings, at the date the previous non-controlling interests were acquired.

However, this approach may, **in certain circumstances** (e.g. when initial purchases result in the investee company becoming an associate of the investor), create a misleading impression of the value of goodwill, in which case goodwill should be based on the difference between the cost of each tranche and the fair values attributable to the interest acquired at that time.

Trade investment becomes a subsidiary undertaking

6966 There may be situations where an undertaking has bought one or more **tranches of shares** in another undertaking, with the initial intention of holding it as a fixed asset trade investment, but subsequently increased its shareholding, in order to secure a long-term controlling interest.

The accounting treatment is as follows:

1. The **identifiable assets and liabilities** of the acquired undertaking should be included in the consolidated balance sheet, at fair value only from the date of acquisition; namely the date it becomes a subsidiary.
2. **Goodwill is based on** the fair values of the underlying assets and liabilities and determined only at the date control passes to the acquirer.
3. When the trade investment becomes a subsidiary company, the **fair values of net assets** at the dates the earlier purchases of shares were made are not considered in calculating goodwill.
4. The assets and liabilities attributable to the **minority interest** should be included on the same basis, as those attributable to the interests held by the parent.
5. The **profits from the subsidiary** undertaking are only included in the consolidated profit and loss account from the date the increased holding in the original trade investment qualified as a subsidiary undertaking.

The accounting treatment is illustrated in the following example.

EXAMPLE **Fixed asset investment becomes a subsidiary undertaking**

Piecemeal acquisition

Andrew Smith Limited has the following record of **acquisitions of shares** in Boscombe Industries Limited, which has an issued share capital of 1,000,000 ordinary shares:

1. 31 December 2003: 100,000 shares were purchased for a consideration of £500,000 when the fair value of Boscombe Industries Limited's identifiable net assets was £5,000,000 (Cum. shareholding 10%);
2. 31 December 2004: 75,000 shares were purchased for a consideration of £1,000,000 when the fair value of Boscombe Industries Limited's identifiable net assets was £6,000,000 (Cum. shareholding 17.5%);
3. 31 December 2010: 350,000 shares were purchased for a consideration of £6,000,000 when the fair value of Boscombe Industries Limited's identifiable net assets was £10,000,000 (Cum. shareholding 52.5%).

Under the above scenario, the initial acquisitions of 10% and 7.5% on 31 December 2003 and 31 December 2004 would not qualify, both individually and in aggregate, as **participating interests**; they should initially be treated as fixed asset "trade" investments.

Following the acquisition of a further 350,000 shares in Boscombe Industries Limited on 31 December 2010, Andrew Smith Limited's holding totalled 52.5% at which point control passed to the purchaser. Boscombe Industries Limited became a subsidiary of Andrew Smith.

Only its **profits from that date onward** will be consolidated in the consolidated accounts of Andrew Smith Limited.

Calculation of goodwill

The goodwill arising when Andrew Smith Limited first consolidates Boscombe Industries Limited into its group accounts as at 31 December 2010, should be calculated as follows:

Fair value of identifiable net asset of Boscombe Limited:		
£10,000,000 x 52.5%		£5,250,000
Cost of acquisition in stages:		
31 December 2003	£500,000	
31 December 2004	£1,000,000	
31 December 2010	£6,000,000	
		£7,500,000
Goodwill arising on a acquisition of a subsidiary		£2,250,000

Associated undertaking or joint venture becomes a subsidiary undertaking

The situation may arise where an investment, prior to becoming a subsidiary undertaking, was previously accounted for as an associate or joint venture (see ¶7300). If further acquisitions of shares in the associate result in the investor acquiring control of the investee, the investment becomes a subsidiary undertaking subject to consolidation accounting. 6970 FRS 2 (51) FRS 2 (89)

Further share purchases resulting in a reclassification For further purchases of shares in an associate or joint venture, that lead to a reclassification of the investment as a subsidiary company, **two key issues arise**: 6972

1. **Profits of the associate** previously included in the investor's profit and loss account would be part of the net assets at the date it becomes a subsidiary. As a result, the group's share of profits or losses and reserve movements of the associate or joint venture would be reclassified as goodwill.
2. The **aggregate cost of the shares** in the subsidiary undertaking, will be a combination of old and new purchases, although under the Companies Act the fair value of the net assets is calculated at the date the investment becomes a subsidiary undertaking.

In this situation, compliance with the requirements of the Companies Act would be misleading. The remedy is to invoke the "**true and fair view override**" clause and calculate goodwill on each "tranche" of shares purchased (piecemeal basis). The cost of each "tranche" of shares purchased, should be matched with the fair values of the proportion of net assets acquired. This process is illustrated in the example below.

The subsidiary's net assets will be included in the consolidated balance sheet at fair value at the acquisition date.

EXAMPLE **Associate (or joint venture) becomes an associate undertaking**

Accounting treatment

Tremkost Limited has the following track record of acquisitions of shares in Visco Limited, which has an issued capital of 1,000,000 ordinary shares. Tremkost Limited has always believed that Visco Limited represented a good strategic fit for its own activities and the objective of its investments in Visco Limited have been to initially exercise significant influence and ultimately gain control.

1. 31 December 2006: 200,000 Visco Limited shares were purchased by Tremkost for a consideration of £1,600,000 when the fair value of Visco Limited's identifiable net assets was £7,000,000;
2. 31 December 2007: 150,000 Visco Limited shares were purchased by Tremkost for a consideration of £1,500,000 when the fair value of Visco Limited's identifiable net assets was £8,000,000;
3. 31 December 2010: 250,000 Visco Limited shares were purchased by Tremkost for a consideration of £3,500,000 when the fair value of Visco Limited's identifiable net assets was £10,000,000.

The 2006 and 2007 acquisitions could qualify Visco Limited as an associate of Tremkost Limited and therefore, subject to equity accounting. In terms of FRS 9 this would entail the following general approach:
a. The investment is brought into the investor undertaking's financial statements initially at cost, plus any goodwill arising;
b. The carrying amount of the investment is adjusted in each period by:
- the investor undertaking's share of results of the associated undertaking;
- any amortisation or write off for goodwill;
- the investor undertaking's share of any gains or losses; and
- any other changes in the associated undertaking's net assets;

The **investor undertaking's share of the** associated undertaking's results is recognised in the investor's profit and loss account.

Multi-stage approach
The accounting treatment applying the multi-stage approach would be as follows:

1. On acquisition of associated undertaking (200,000 shares) – 31 December 2006.

Fair value of identifiable net assets of Visco Limited:	
£7,000,000 x 20%	£1,400,000
Cost of acquisition	£1.600,000
Goodwill	£200,000

2. Immediately prior to acquisition of 150,000 shares – 31 December 2007

Fair value of identifiable net assets of Visco Limited as at 31 December 2007	£8,000,000
Fair value of identifiable net assets of Visco Limited as at 31 December 2006	£7,000,000
Increase in profit and loss account	£1,000,000
Equity accounted: £1000,000 x 20%	£200,000

3. On acquisition of £150,000 shares – 31 December 2007

Fair value of identifiable net assets of Visco Limited:	
£8,000,000 x 15%	£1,200,000
Cost of acquisition	£1,500,000
Goodwill	£300,000

Value of investment in Visco included in the consolidated accounts of Tremkost:
Cost [£1,600,000 + £1,500,000] + goodwill* [£200,000 + £300,000] + Attributable post-acquisition profits of Visco [£200,000] = £3,800,000.
* In this example no amortisation has been provided on goodwill.

4. Immediately prior to acquisition 250,000 shares – December 2010

Fair value of identifiable net assets of Visco Limited as at 31 December 2010	£10,000,000
Fair value of identifiable net assets of Visco Limited as at 31 December 2008	£8,000,000
Increase in profit and loss account	£2,000,000
Equity accounted: £2,000,000 x 35%	£700,000

Value of investment in Visco included in the consolidated accounts of Tremkost:
£3,800,000 as at stage 3 above plus equity accounted profits of Visco for the year, £700,000 = 4,500,000

5. On acquisition of third batch of 250,000 shares – 31 December 2010

Fair value of identifiable net assets of Daphne Limited:	
£10,000,000 x 25%	£2,500,000
Cost of acquisition	£3,500,000
Goodwill	£1,000,000

6. Summary

Goodwill:	31 December 2006	£200,000
	31 December 2007	£300,000
	31 December 2010	£1,000,000
Total goodwill		**£1,500,000**
Profits equity accounted	31 December 2007	£200,000
	31 December 2010	£700,000
Total recognised profits		£900,000

The investment in Visco would now no longer appear as a separate item in the consolidated balance sheet of Tremkost.

Parent undertaking increases stake in a subsidiary undertaking

A group **may increase its stake** in an undertaking that is already a subsidiary undertaking, in which case the identifiable assets and liabilities of the subsidiary undertaking should be revalued to fair value and any goodwill arising on the increase in interest, should be calculated by reference to those fair values. 6974 FRS 2 (51) FRS 2 (90)

This **revaluation is not required, where** the difference between the fair values and the carrying amounts of the share of identifiable net assets, attributable to the increased stake, is not material. It should be noted that this exercise does not result in any change to the goodwill calculated when the entity first became a subsidiary of the parent.

C. Treatment of post-acquisition dividends

Where **a recently acquired subsidiary undertaking** pays a dividend shortly after the date of acquisition, a question arises as to how the dividend should be treated, in the individual financial statements of the recipient and the group financial statements 6978

Where a dividend is paid to an acquirer out of **pre-combination profits**, it need not be applied as a reduction in the carrying value of the investment in the subsidiary undertaking but can be treated as a realised profit by the parent undertaking. On **consolidation**, a dividend so treated will be eliminated. FRS 6 (Appendix 1.15)

However, where the payment of a such a dividend by a subsidiary results in the **permanent diminution in value** of that subsidiary, a different accounting treatment is required. For example when, following the acquisition, the assets and trade of the subsidiary were transferred up to the parent and the subsidiary became dormant, then the dividend received should be used to reduce the carrying value of the investment to its new lower value.

When this **accounting treatment is adopted**, consideration should be given as to whether this dividend, in practice, represents a return to the parent of part of the purchase consideration and also whether any associated goodwill arising on consolidation, should be reduced.

D. Disclosure requirements

Mandatory disclosures

The key disclosure requirements in consolidated financial statements covering business combinations accounted for using acquisition or merger accounting are found in SI 2008/410 Schedule 6. 6984

The following disclosures **must be made by** the acquiring entity, or in the case of a merger, the entity issuing the shares:
- the names of the combining entities;
- the method used to account for the business combination (acquisition or merger); and
- the date of the acquisition or merger.

Additional disclosures for material acquisitions

The disclosures set out in the table below must be made in the financial statements for **each material (substantial) acquisition)** and for all other acquisitions, if material when aggregated, unless exempted (as specified below). The test of materiality, is whether the information relating to the acquisition might reasonably be expected to influence decisions made by investors and other stakeholders. 6986 FRS 6 (23)-(27), (35)

Disclosure requirements – individual material acquisitions	
1	**Purchase consideration** **a.** The **composition and fair value** of the consideration given by the acquiring company and its subsidiary undertakings **b.** The nature of any **deferred or contingent purchase consideration** and the range of possible outcomes and principle factors that impact on the outcome **c.** Where the **fair values** of the acquired entity's assets or liabilities or **purchase consideration** can only be determined provisionally at the end of the accounting period in which the acquisition took place, this fact should be stated and the reasons given. Any subsequent adjustments relating to these values, with corresponding adjustments to goodwill, should be disclosed and explained in the relevant financial year.
2	**Assets and liabilities acquired** A table showing, for **each class of** assets and liabilities of the acquired entity: **a.** The book values, as recorded in the acquired entity's books immediately before the acquisition and before any fair value adjustments **b.** The fair value adjustments, giving the reasons therefore, analysed into: – revaluations; – adjustments to achieve consistency of accounting policies; and – any other significant adjustments **c.** The fair values at date of acquisition **d.** A statement of the amount of purchased goodwill or negative goodwill arising on consolidation.
3	**Pre-acquisition results** The **profit after taxation and minority interests** of the acquired entity should be given for: **a.** the period from the beginning of the acquired entity's financial year to the date of acquisition, giving the date on which this period began; and **b.** the previous financial year. This information is only required either individually or in aggregate for material acquisitions.
4	**Post-acquisition results**. The post-acquisition results of each acquired entity should be shown as a component of continuing operations in the consolidated profit and loss account, except discontinued operations in the same period. In addition, where the acquisition of an entity has a material impact on a major business segment, this should be disclosed. **Where it is not practical** to determine the post-acquisition results of an operation to the end of the period in which the acquisition took place, then an indication should be given of the contribution of the acquired entity to turnover and operating profit of continuing operations.
5	**Exceptional profits or losses** Examples of exceptional profits or losses arising from the use of fair values recognised on acquisition referred to in 3b above, are: – disposal of stocks at abnormal trading margins after acquisition; – release of provisions in respect of an acquired long-term contract that the acquiring entity is able to make profitable; and – realisation of contingent assets or liabilities at amounts materially different from their attributed fair values.
6	**Costs of reorganising or restructuring** The costs of reorganising, restructuring and integrating an acquired entity may extend over more than one accounting period. For major acquisitions, management may wish to disclose in the notes to the consolidated financial statements, the nature and value of the costs expected to be incurred in relation to the acquisition. The notes should also state the extent to which these costs have been charged to the profit and loss account. If part of these costs relate to asset write downs, beyond any impairment recognised in adjusting to fair values on acquisition, it may be useful to distinguish these from cash expenditure (FRS 6 (31)).

6994 **Substantial acquisitions – pre-acquisition results** For substantial acquisitions, the following additional information should be disclosed in the consolidated financial statements of the combined entity, for the period in which the acquisition took place.

1. The **summarised profit and loss account** and **statement of total recognised gains and losses** of the acquired entity, from the start of its financial year to the effective acquisition date. The summarised profit and loss account should show as a minimum:
- profit after taxation;
- the turnover;
- operating profit and any exceptional items falling within para. 20 FRS 3;

– taxation; and
– minority interests

2. The **profit after tax** and **minority interests** for the acquired entity's previous financial year.

The disclosures set out above are required for entities that meet the following conditions: FRS 6 (36)

Type of entity	Disclosures
Listed companies	When the combination is a **Class 1 transaction** in terms of the Listing Rules
Other entities	Additional disclosures are required where either: **a.** the **net assets or operating profits** of the acquired entity exceed 15% of those of the acquiring entity; or **b.** the **fair value of the consideration** exceeds 15% of the net assets of the acquiring entity
Other exceptional cases	Where the acquisition is of **such significance** that the additional disclosures are necessary to ensure a true and fair view is given by the group financial statements

MEMO POINTS 1. **Class 1 transactions** are defined as those where the ratio, of the assets of the target company to those of the offeror, exceeds 15%.
2. In respect of "**other entities**" the **net assets and profits** should be those shown in the financial statements of the acquiring entity, for the last financial year before the date of the acquisition. Net assets should also include an adjustment for any purchased goodwill that has been eliminated against reserves, as a matter of accounting policy, rather than charged to the profit and loss account.

Consolidated cash flow statement

The consolidated cash flow statement should show the amounts of cash and cash equivalents paid for each acquisition, net of any cash or cash equivalents transferred as part of each acquisition. In addition, the notes to the cash flow statement should also provide a summary of the cash flow effects resulting from the acquisitions, including how much of the consideration comprised cash and cash equivalents. This accounting treatment meets the requirements of FRS 1 "Cash flow statements", although it should be noted that FRS 1 (revised) no longer makes references to cash equivalents. **6996** FRS 6 (34) FRS 1 (45)

The **notes to the cash flow statement** should also, where practicable, contain information on any material effects that the cash flows of the acquired undertakings had on each of the standard headings in the consolidated cash flow statement. This information could be given by dividing cash flows between continuing and discontinued operations and acquisitions and need be given only for the period in which the acquisition occurs.

E. FRED 36 – Proposals

FRED 36 "Business Combinations" **is based on** the exposure draft of proposed amendments to IFRS 3 "Business Combinations" and the exposure draft of proposed amendments to IAS 27 "Consolidation and Separate Financial Statements", issued by the IASB and developed jointly with the Financial Accounting Standards Board (FASB). **6997**

The deliberations **have focused on** reconsidering the guidance for applying the acquisition method of accounting to a business combination and in particular the method the acquirer uses to recognise and measure the acquired business.

The ASB has canvassed views, on whether the UK standard that evolves from FRED 36 should be based entirely on the IFRS standard, or amended for cost-benefit reasons and an option inserted permitting amortisation of goodwill.

In addition, the ASB has also listed a **number of options** for implementing the proposals set out by the IASB, ranging from simultaneous implementation to advocating a delay in order to consider the impact of the IASB's proposals. The feedback from respondents is currently being analysed and a new standard is expected in 2011.

At present **only the acquisition method** is permitted under IFRS, whereas the UK also permits the use of merger accounting. In addition, the objective of acquisition accounting under current UK GAAP, is to reflect the cost of the acquisition. If part of the acquisition cost is not supported by identifiable assets and liabilities (measured at fair value), this represents goodwill, which is reported separately in the financial statements.

FRED 36 **adopts a different perspective** and requires that the acquirer reflects in the financial statements, the fair value of the acquired business as a whole, at the acquisition date. This requirement applies even if the acquisition is less than 100% of the equity at the acquisition date or where the business combination is completed in stages (piecemeal acquisitions).

Other principal differences between current UK GAAP and the FRED are set out in the following table:

Accounting Issue	Current UK GAAP	FRED (IFRS)
Method of accounting	Both acquisition accounting and merger accounting permitted	Acquisition accounting advocated Some provisions in FRS 6 concerning accounting for group reconstructions may be retained.
Acquisition costs	Accounted for as part of cost of investment	Account for separately from the cost of the investment – costs deemed not part of fair value exchange between buyer and seller
Goodwill on acquisition	Goodwill arising on consolidation only recognised where it relates to that part of the subsidiary undertaking attributable to the interest held by the parent	1. Goodwill should be recognised in full even where less than 100% of the equity is acquired. 2. Where ownership less than 100% – goodwill allocated to non-controlling (minority) interests (NCI's).
Goodwill – subsequent measurement	Capitalised as intangible fixed asset and charged to P & L amortised systematically over time (see ¶1060). FRS 10 contains a rebuttable presumption that goodwill has a UEL of 20 years or less.	After initial recognition – goodwill measured at cost less impairment; amortisation is not permitted. Goodwill should be subject to an annual impairment test.
Negative goodwill	FRS 10 rules – see ¶1063	A gain should reduce any existing goodwill to zero. Thereafter, any excess should be recognised as a gain on acquisition.
Non-controlling interests (Minority interests)	Accounting based on "parent entity concept" – consolidate in full the assets and liabilities of an entity even when it is not wholly owned. NCI's and transactions with NCI's are identified separately in the financial statements.	1. Treat group as a single economic entity with transactions between group and NCI's shown in equity – and not the P & L. 2. Outside equity interest in a subsidiary should be treated as part of the overall ownership interest in the group – as such transactions with NCI's do not give rise to gains or losses. 3. Changes in a parent's ownership interest that does not result in a change of control should be recognised as changes in equity.
Fair value hierarchy	FRS 7 specifies methods of determining fair value if identifiable assets and liabilities at acquisition – see ¶6864.	Guidance in FRED could result in different values being attributed to specialised tangible fixed assets, stocks, and WIP.

MEMO POINTS The ASB has postponed a decision on implementing FRED 36 pending completion of its convergence programme with IFRS.

SECTION 2

Merger accounting

A "true" merger is defined as a business combination that creates a new reporting entity, formed from two or more combining parties, whose shareholders join together to share the risks and benefits of the combined entity. The results of the merging entities are combined as if they had always been part of the same reporting entity, even where the merger is completed part way through a financial year. 7000 FRS 6 (41) (44)

The **rationale for merger accounting** is that no one party to the combination gains control over the other, or is otherwise seen to be dominant, as a result of either shareholders' rights in the combined entity, or through directoral influence.

For both "true" mergers and group reorganisations, merger accounting **can only be applied** when strict criteria are met. **Goodwill** does not arise in merger accounting as the assets and liabilities need not be adjusted to reflect their fair values at the merger date. However, **merger relief is available where** a difference arises between the consideration received and the identifiable assets and liabilities.

MEMO POINTS 1. In March 2008, the OFT issued revised merger control guidance. This includes advice on determining when an acquiring company is deemed to materially influence the target company, and the adoption of a pre-notification merger notice procedure. The OFT is currently finalising its guidance on these issues. 2. Merger relief and group reconstruction relief are contained in s611 and s612 Companies Act 2006.

1. Criteria for a "true" merger

Before a business combination can be accounted for as a merger, a number of criteria must be met under both the Companies Act and FRS 6. **Failure to meet any of these criteria** will mean that a merger has not taken place and that acquisition accounting should be applied. 7002 FRS 6 (54)

a. Key criteria

Shares acquired At least 90% of the nominal value of the **relevant equity shares with unrestricted rights**, in the undertaking acquired, must be held by or on behalf of the parent. Furthermore, the shares acquired must have been attained, pursuant to an agreement allowing the **issue of equity shares** by the parent company or one or more of its subsidiary undertakings. 7003

MEMO POINTS 1. The reference to "**relevant shares**" in an undertaking acquired, relates to those shares carrying unrestricted rights to participate both in distributions and in the assets of the undertaking upon liquidation.
2. **Equity share capital** means, in relation to a company, its issued share capital excluding any part of that capital which, neither in respect of dividends or capital, carries a right to participate (beyond a specified amount) in any distribution.

The **fair value of any consideration** (other than the issue of equity shares) given pursuant to the arrangement by the parent company or subsidiary, must not exceed 10% of the nominal value of the equity shares issued. 7004

7005 FRS 6 (55) **Substance and form of the transaction** The substance and not just the form of the merger arrangements must be analysed, including any related arrangements that are connected to the business combination, such as:
- the method by which the combination was achieved;
- the plans for the combined entity's future operations (e.g. whether any closures or disposal will impact more on one party than the other); and
- the proposed corporate image (e.g. name, logo and location of the headquarters) and principal operations.

b. Additional criteria

7006 Other information relevant to the combination must be taken into account, such as:
- the management structure and personnel;
- relative size of the parties to the combination;
- details of any non-equity consideration given;
- post merger performance arrangements;
- divestment; and
- combinations achieved by using a new parent company.

Each of these subject areas is considered below.

Management structure and personal

7007 FRS 6 (63) (65) **All the parties** to the combination, as represented by the board of directors or their appointees, must participate in establishing the management structure for the combined entity and selecting the management personnel.

Such decisions must be made on the basis of consensus between the parties to the combination, rather than purely by exercise of the respective voting rights.

Where **one party clearly dominates** the process of setting up the management structure and selection of management personnel, this would indicate that the combination is not a genuine pooling of interests. However, all the parties may agree that the management team of the combined entity should come from only one of the parties. In order for merger accounting to apply in this situation, it must be clear that all the parties to the merger genuinely participated in the decision making process that led to this structure.

7008 In addition to the **formal management structure** of the combined entity, the following must also be considered:

FRS 6 (64)
- the identity of all the persons involved in the main financial and operating decisions; and
- the way in which the decision making process is expected to operate in practice.

Relative sizes of the combining parties

7009 FRS 6 (8) (67) The relative sizes of the combining entities **must not be so disparate** that one party dominates the combined entity by virtue of its relative size. Where one party is substantially larger than the others, it will be presumed that the larger party can or will dominate the combined enterprise.

FRS 6 (59) (68) The **guidance on relative size**, is that a party would be presumed to dominate if it is 50% larger than each of the other parties to the combination. This is judged by reference to ownership interests; namely, by considering the proportion of equity of the combined entity attributable to the shareholders of each of the combining parties.

However, **this presumption may be rebutted**, if it can be clearly demonstrated that there is no such dominance. Factors that may indicate that a party to the combination has more influence, or less influence, than is indicated by it relative size, are as follows:
- voting or share agreements; or
- blocking powers or other arrangements.

Circumstances that rebut the presumption of dominant influence based on relative size should be disclosed and explained.

Where a party to the combination is a **company without a share capital**, the conditions applying to equity shares should be interpreted as applying to those elements of its capital structure that allocate rights to profits and control.

Non-equity consideration

There may be combinations where the equity shareholders of the combining entities receive some consideration in a form other than equity shares (e.g. in cash, loan stock, or preference shares). This category also includes equity shares carrying substantially reduced voting or distribution rights. **7010** FRS 6 (9) (69)

The rules governing non-equity consideration **are as follows**: **7011**

1. The **fair value** of any consideration other than equity shares must not exceed 10% of the nominal value of the equity shares issued (see ¶7003).

2. Any **non-equity consideration** (or equity shares carrying substantially reduced voting or distribution rights), must represent only an immaterial proportion of the fair value of the consideration received by that party. In addition, where one party to the combination acquired equity shares in another of the combining parties for up to two years prior to the merger, the consideration for this acquisition must be taken into account, when determining whether this criterion has been met.

Consideration in form of cash Equity shareholders will be deemed to have disposed of their shareholdings for cash, where any arrangement is made as part of the merger, to exchange or redeem the shares received in the combination for cash or other non-equity consideration. Cash received by the shareholders should be regarded as the consideration for the sale of their original shares when determining whether the criteria for non-equity consideration have been met. **7012** FRS 6 (71)

Normal market selling transactions, or privately arranged sale, entered into by a shareholder and not made in conjunction with the combination will not prevent the criterion being met.

Consideration in form of shares with rights In general, where a material part of the consideration offered by the issuing entity to the equity shareholders in the other parties, is in the form of shares with substantially reduced rights, the combination will fail to meet the merger criteria. In determining whether **equity shares with reduced rights** have been issued, the voting rights, as well as the rights to distributions, would need to be taken into account. **7014** FRS 6 (72)

However, some of the adjustments attaching to the shares held by the non-issuing entities' shareholders could be deemed compatible with the combination being a merger. This is because business combinations result from a negotiating process where **different pre-existing rights** have to be reconciled. Whether any changes in the rights of one group of shareholders is sufficient to prevent a particular business combination being treated as a merger, will depend on the facts of each individual case. **7015**

Factors for consideration include:
- the original rights of the shareholders;
- the overall arrangement negotiated;
- time limits; and
- whether any new restrictions apply equally to all classes of shareholders.

Post-merger performance arrangements

There may be business combinations, where the share of the equity in the combined entity allocated to one of the parties, depends on the post-combination performance of only a part of the combined entity. This runs counter to the concept of a merger, whereby the participants enter into a mutual sharing of the risks and rewards of the combined entity, including the pooled future results. As such, equity shareholders of any combining entities may not retain a material interest in the future performance of only part of the combined entity. **7020** FRS 6 (11), (75)

FRS 6 (76) Similarly, "**earn-outs**" or similar **performance related schemes** included in the arrangements to achieve a combination, would run counter to this criterion and thereby preclude the use of merger accounting for the combination.

7021 If there is a **material minority** of shareholders in one of the combining parties that have not accepted the terms of the combination offer, the arrangement will not qualify as a merger.

FRS 6 (77) However, **the merger approach** would not necessarily be invalidated by an arrangement, in which the allocation of consideration between the shareholders of the combining parties depended on the future determination of the value of a specific asset or liability contributed by one of the parties. **An example** would be the eventual outcome of a claim against one of the parties, or the eventual sales value of a specific asset owned by one of the parties.

Divestment

7022 FRS 6 (58) There may be instances where one of the parties to a business combination is the product of recent divestment by a larger entity. In these circumstances, merger accounting would not be appropriate for the combination, because the divested business will not have been independent for a sufficient time to establish itself as being a party separate from its previous owner. Once the divested business has established a track record of its own it can be considered as a party to a merger.

Combinations achieved by using a new parent company

7024 FRS 6 (14) One of the ways of creating a merger is to use a newly formed parent company to hold the shares of each of the other parties to the combination. In such circumstances, the accounting treatment depends on the **substance of the business combination** under consideration; namely, whether the combination of the entities involved, other than the new parent company, would have been an acquisition or merger.

Two different scenarios are envisaged:

1. A **genuine merger** exists between the parties to the combination. In such circumstances, the new parent and the other parties should be combined by using merger accounting; or

2. **Where one party can be identified** as the acquirer. In these circumstances, the acquirer and the new parent company should first be combined using merger accounting. Then the other parties to the combination should be treated as acquired by the new parent company by using the acquisition method of accounting.

2. Accounting treatment

7030 FRS 6 (41) When considering a business combination it is important to understand how merger relief can affect the accounting treatment. Merger relief can take one of two forms; namely: merger relief or group reconstruction relief and is given under section 611 and 612 of the Companies Act 2006.

Merger relief means that a company need not recognise a share premium paid on acquisition of another company, and its application is compulsory when certain criteria have been met. Merger relief applies to business combinations accounting for as mergers and some acquisitions accounted for using acquisition accounting techniques. Merger relief can be claimed where a group wishes to distribute pre-acquisition profits that would otherwise be retained in the subsidiary acquired.

With **group reconstruction relief** the minimum share premium must be recorded in the share premium account. This relief could be utilised in certain situations where assets are transferred within a group involving wholly-owned subsidiaries. The rules for calculating the minimum share premium are complex and are reviewed in outline in paragraphs ¶7040-7054.

Merger relief

The **merger accounting approach** to business combinations is outlined in the table below. 7030 s 612 CA 2006

Accounting Issue	Current UK GAAP
Merger expenses	Merger expenses should be charged to the profit and loss account of the combined entity at the effective date of the mergers, as a reorganisation or restructuring expense in accordance with FRS 3 "Reporting Financial Performance".
Valuation of assets and liabilities	The assets and liabilities of the acquired undertaking are included in the group financial statements at book value (nominal value), subject to the adjustments authorised or required by the Companies Act, or that arise from the adoption by the subsidiary of group accounting policies different from those previously followed.
Pre-acquisition profits and cash flows	The results and the cash flows of the acquired undertaking, should be included in the group financial statements for the entire financial year in which the combination occurred, including the period before the merger, adjusted so as to achieve uniformity of accounting policies.
Adjustment to consolidated reserves	The nominal value of the issued share capital of the acquired undertaking, held by the parent undertaking and its subsidiary undertakings, is set off against the aggregate of: – the nominal value of qualifying shares issued by the parent undertaking or its subsidiary undertakings as part of the purchase consideration; and – the fair value of any other consideration for the acquisition of shares in the acquired undertaking, determined as at the date those shares were acquired.

Share premium Merger relief means that an entity does not have to recognise a share premium arising on the acquisition of another company, providing **certain criteria** are met. A share premium represents **a difference** between the nominal value of shares issued, plus the fair value of other forms of consideration and the aggregate value of the nominal shares received in exchange and normally treated as a movement on consolidated reserves. Any share premium accounts and capital redemption reserves of the new subsidiary undertaking are not preserved in the consolidated financial statements. 7032

Relief from recording a share premium account – criteria. 7033

Merger Relief – is only available where all of the following conditions are met; namely:
- the equity shares are issued as part of the acquisition agreement;
- the issuer increases its equity holding in another entity to 90% or over (in aggregate); and
- the consideration for the shares allocated represents either the issue or transfer of equity shares in the acquired company to the issuing company, or the cancellation of those equity shares in the acquired company that the issuing company does not currently own.

Where the acquired entity has **more than one class of equity share**, the criteria must be satisfied for all classes of equity share and the shares acquired must not have been transferred from a wholly-owned entity already claiming merger relief.

EXAMPLE 1. Company M issues equity shares and acquires 95% of Company P's equity shares in a straight share-for-share exchange. This transaction meets the qualifying criteria for merger relief.
2. Company S owns 65% of Company T's equity shares. The shareholders of T agree to cancel the remaining 35% of shares which S does not hold in exchange for shares in Company S. Company S is entitled to merger relief as the cancellation of shares by T takes its holding over the threshold of

90%. The consideration for the allotment of shares by Company S is the cancellation of the shares by T.

7034 This relief **applies to**:
– the entity issuing the shares;
– equity shares issued to acquire other equity shares, including part consideration where all the conditions set out above have been met; or
– the acquisition of non-equity shares in another entity, in which case the relief covers both equity and non-equity shares issued.

3. Group reconstructions

7040 FRS 6 (2), (78) Merger relief provisions as outlined above are not available for group reconstructions. A group reconstruction **is represented by** any of the following arrangements:
– the transfer of a shareholding in a subsidiary undertaking from one group company to another;
– the addition of a new parent company to a group;
– the transfer of shares in one or more subsidiary undertakings of a group to a new company that is not a group company but whose shareholders are the same as those of the group's parent;
– the combination into a group of two or more companies that before the combination had the same shareholders; or
– the splitting off of one or more subsidiary undertakings, as in some de-mergers, where a separate group is formed.

7041 Group reconstructions often include the transfer of various combinations of assets as well as non-share considerations such as intra-group debt. **The objective** of accounting for a group reconstruction as a merger **is to avoid**:
– the recognition of unrealised gains or losses arising from the fair value of a share consideration; and
– the fair valuation of transferred assets and liabilities and recognition of goodwill.

This is achieved by applying a **special relief** available under the Companies Act (s 611 CA 2006).

Criteria for adopting merger accounting

7042 FRS 6 (13) Group reconstructions may be accounted for by using merger accounting, provided:
– the use of merger accounting is not prohibited by companies legislation;
– the ultimate shareholders remain the same;
– the rights of each such shareholder, relative to the others, are unchanged; and
– the transfer does not alter the minority's interest in the net assets of the group, such as the transfer of a subsidiary undertaking within a sub-group that has an existing minority shareholder.

MEMO POINTS In terms of **minority interests**, merger accounting **will not apply where**:
1. A subsidiary undertaking that is transferred out of, or into, a sub-group that has a minority shareholder would require the use of acquisition accounting; or
2. A minority has effectively acquired, or disposed of, rights to part of the net assets of the group.
In both these scenarios, acquisition accounting should be applied to the group reorganisation.

Group reconstruction relief

7044 s 611CA 2006 Shares issued as part of the group reconstruction arrangement at a premium, would, were it not for the provisions of the Companies Act, normally be transferred in full to the share premium account. However, the Act allows the issuing company to restrict the amount of share premium arising to the "**minimum premium value**", which is defined as the amount by which the base value of the consideration for the shares allotted, exceeds the aggregate nominal value of those shares. Shares consideration in excess of the minimum premium value is not transferred to a share premium account.

MEMO POINTS 1. The **base value of the consideration for the shares allotted**, is the amount by which the base value of the assets transferred exceeds the base value of any liabilities of the transfer or company, assumed by the issuing company as part of the consideration for the assets transferred.
2. The **base value of the assets transferred is the lower of**:
– the carrying amount of the assets transferred as recorded in the accounting records of the transferor company immediately before the transfer; and
– the cost of the assets transferred.
3. The **base value of liabilities assumed** is the amount at which they are stated in the transferor company's accounting records immediately before the transfer.

EXAMPLE **Calculation of minimum premium amount**

1. Carrying amount of assets transferred, as per accounting records of transferor, immediately prior to transfer	5,000
2. Cost of assets transferred	9,000
Base value of assets transferred, being lower of (1) and (2) above	5,000
Less: Base value of liabilities assumed	– 4,500
Base value of consideration for shares allotted	500
Less: Aggregate nominal value of shares allotted	– 400
Minimum premium amount	100

Criteria The Companies Act sets out the criteria **that must be satisfied** for a combination to be eligible for group reconstruction relief; namely where the company issuing the shares: 7046
– is a wholly owned subsidiary of a parent company, and allots shares to its parent company or any fellow subsidiary of the issuing company; and
– in exchange, receives assets other than cash, from the parent company or any fellow subsidiary of the issuing company.
Use of the relief is not compulsory and only applies to the transfer of "non-cash" assets. If the assets transferred include an element of cash, the issuing company must determine how many allotted shares this represents and the relevant share premium recognised for these shares.

Options Where the criteria are fulfilled, **three accounting options** are available. 7047
1. Assets can be transferred within a wholly owned group at nominal (book) value, so avoiding the recognition of unrealised gains or losses.
2. Assets can be revalued at fair value, with the additional premium recognised as a share premium or other reserve such as the merger reserve.
3. The investment can be recorded at its previous carrying value in the transferor company (nominal value of shares issued) and the shares then subsequently revalued, with any increase credited to the revaluation reserve.

Where fair value is used, the additional credit arising is taken not to a share premium account but to another reserve, usually referred to as either a merger reserve or merger relief reserve. 7054

EXAMPLE Tate Haulage Limited owns 100 per cent of Dingle Limited and Woolpack Limited, which both have an issued share capital of £100,000 comprising 100,000 ordinary shares of £1 each. Tate Haulage decides that it would like to convert the current horizontal group structure into a vertical structure. The intended outcome is for Tate Haulage Limited to wholly own Dingle Limited which will in turn wholly own Woolpack Limited.
Dingle Limited is to **issue 40,000 shares** to Tate Haulage Limited in **consideration for the transfer** of its holding of shares in Woolpack Limited to Dingle Limited.
Tate Haulage Limited's investment in Woolpack Limited is carried in its balance sheet at its original cost of £45,000. Relevant details relating to Woolpack Limited are as follows:

Woolpack Limited	Original cost	Carrying value	Fair value
Assets transferred	£100,000	£170,000	£250,000
Liabilities assumed	£55,000	£55,000	£55,000
Net	£45,000	£115,000	£195,000

Accounting treatment	
Tate Haulage Limited	**£**
1. Carrying amount of assets in Woolpack Limited transferred, as per accounting records of transferor, immediately prior to transfer	170,000
2. Cost of assets of Woolpack Limited transferred	100,000
Base value of assets transferred, being lower of (1) and (2) above	100,000
Less: Base value of liabilities assumed	– 55,000
Base value of consideration for shares allotted	45,000
Less: Aggregate nominal value of shares allotted	-40,000
Minimum premium amount	5,000

Dingle Limited	£ Dr.	£ Cr.
a. Minimum premium amount Accounting for the investment in Woolpack Limited at **base value**		
Investment in subsidiary undertaking	45,000	
Share capital		40,000
Share premium account		5,000
Or an optional alternative treatment		
b. Recorded at fair value Accounting for the investment in Woolpack Limited at **fair value of net assets** and creation of merger relief reserve.		
Investment in subsidiary undertaking	195,000	
Share capital		40,000
Share premium account		5,000
Merger reserve		150,000

4. Disclosure requirements

7060 FRS 6 (21) For each business combination accounted for as a merger, the following information should be disclosed in the financial statements of the combined entity for the period in which the merger took place.

An **analysis of the principal components** should be given as follows:

1. The current (and previous) year's **profit and loss account** (e.g. turnover, operating profit and exceptional items, split between continuing operations, discontinued operations and acquisitions; profit before taxation; taxation and minority interests; and extraordinary items) split into:

– amounts relating to the merged entity for the period after the date of the merger; and

– for each party to the merger, amounts relating to that party for the period up to the date of the merger;

2. A breakdown of the principal components of the current and previous period's **STRGL**, divided into:
– amounts relating to the merged entity for the period after the date of the merger;
– for each party to the merger, amounts relating to that party for the period up to the date of the merger.

Additional information 7062

1. The composition and fair value of the consideration given by the issuing company and its subsidiary undertakings.

2. The aggregate book value of the net assets of each party to the merger at the date of the merger.

3. The nature and amount of significant accounting adjustments made to the net assets of any party to the merger designed to achieve consistency of accounting policies, and an explanation of any other significant adjustments made to the net assets of any party to the merger, as a consequence of the merger.

4. A statement of adjustments to consolidated reserves resulting from the merger.

5. Corresponding figures (Comparatives) should be restated, by including the results for all the combining entities and their balance sheets, for the previous period, adjusted where necessary to achieve uniformity of accounting policies.

SECTION 3

Comparison between UK GAAP and IAS (IFRS)

IFRS 3 "Business Combinations" **applies to all** business combinations, except arrangements, that simply comprise group reorganisations or where entities combine to form a joint venture. An important exemption is available for entities adopting IFRS for the first time (see below). 7070

Companies planning an acquisition must be aware of the implications of the new standard, as the acquirer will need to know whether the deal will enhance or reduce earnings per share (EPS). **Listed companies** will be required to explain the rationale for such acquisitions and the expected impact on earnings. A revised version of IFRS 3 was issued in 2008, extending the acquisition model of accounting and covering more transactions, including mutual entities for the first time. Common control transactions and joint ventures are not covered by the standard.

MEMO POINTS The Accounting Standards Board (ASB) has published its initial conclusions on the consultation document "Policy Proposal: the Future of UK GAAP" and has amended a number of its original proposals. One such change is the requirement for reduced disclosure requirements for subsidiaries, thereby lessening the burden on those entities that prepare accounts under both IFRS and IFRS for SMEs. The ASB now plans to develop an ED for public comment.

Principal changes introduced by IFRS 3

The principal changes introduced by IFRS 3 **are as follows**: 7071

1. **All business combinations** should be accounted for as acquisitions because merger accounting is now prohibited.

2. **Goodwill and intangible assets** with indefinite lives can no longer be amortised but instead are subject to an annual impairment test or more frequently where impairment is suspected.

3. **Impairments** should be taken to the profit and loss account.

4. **Restructuring costs** should generally be charged against income.

5. **Contingent liabilities** should be recognised at fair values.

6. **Detailed disclosures** on transactions (business combinations) and impairment testing are required.

7. "**Negative goodwill**" is no longer recognised as such and should now be recorded in the profit and loss account in the year of transition.

7072 The IASB has completed its harmonisation project on business combinations, between IFRS and US GAAP. The revised IFRS and an amended version of IAS 27 "Consolidated and Separate Financial Statements" came into effect in July 2008. The new standards bring US GAAP more into line with IFRS, with some minor changes to IFRS and IAS 27 as follows:

1. In **staged acquisitions**, it is no longer a requirement that each asset or liability be valued at fair value.

2. More choice is permitted in terms of the **valuation method** used.

3. **Acquisition costs** must be accounted for separately from the business combination as expenses (as opposed to goodwill). The transaction costs must now be disclosed.

4. Business combinations involving **mutual entities** are covered by IFRS 3 for the first time.

5. **Purchase consideration** now includes the fair value of all interests that the acquirer may have previously held in the business, including interests in joint ventures or associates. On acquisition these stakes are deemed to have been sold for an interest in the new entity, with any gain or loss on disposal recorded.

6. The rules for **contingent consideration** have also changed. Contingent consideration should now be recorded at fair value.

Key differences

7073 There are also a **number of significant differences** between IFRS 3 and UK GAAP. Under UK GAAP:
– merger accounting is permitted under certain circumstances (see ¶7002);
– there is a "rebuttable presumption" under FRS 10, that the useful economic life of goodwill should not exceed 20 years;
– the rules identifying intangible assets are not as strict as the requirements of IFRS 3; and
– "negative goodwill", exceeding the aggregate fair value of non-monetary assets acquired, can be carried in the balance sheet and subsequently released to the profit and loss account.

The **treatment of goodwill and intangible assets** between IAS and UK GAAP is inconsistent, because under IAS 38, intangible assets with finite lives are amortised, whilst goodwill is not. However, under FRS 10 the accounting treatment of goodwill and intangible assets has been aligned.

CHAPTER 4

Disposals

OUTLINE ¶¶

1. Accounting treatment

The **sale or reduction of interests** by a parent undertaking in a subsidiary undertaking will take the form of one of the scenarios set out in the table below. 7100 FRS 2 (47)

Degree of control disposed of	Reduction of parent company interest in a subsidiary undertaking
Complete disposal	The parent undertaking **retains no interest** in the subsidiary undertaking
Partial reduction in holding	The parent undertaking **reduces its interest partially**, but not enough to undermine its control and so retains its parent status. However, a minority interest is created or an existing minority interest is increased
Significant reduction in holding	The parent undertaking **reduces its interests** in the subsidiary, to the extent that it ceases to be a subsidiary and becomes an associated undertaking (¶7300)
Considerable reduction in holding	The parent undertaking **divests its controlling interest** in the subsidiary, but holds on to a small interest-accounted for as a fixed asset investment (¶1750)

a. Complete disposal of a subsidiary

An undertaking **may cease to be a subsidiary** as a result of the sale of a holding for cash or where the parent loses control over voting rights. 7102

Sale of shares for cash

7104

EXAMPLE Robust Technical Services Limited acquired and then later disposed of shares in Shillelagh Limited, which has an issued share capital of 1,000,000 ordinary shares, as follows:
A. 31 December 2002: **Acquired 1,000,000 shares** for a consideration of £9,000,000 when the fair value of Shillelagh Limited's identifiable net assets was £6,000,000

B. 31 December 2010: **Disposed of 1,000,000 shares** for proceeds of £14,000,000 when the fair value of Shillelagh Limited's identifiable net assets was £7,000,000, its post-tax profits for the year being £1,000,000.

A. On initial acquisition of 100% of subsidiary undertaking in 2002

The **parent company** Robust Technical Services Limited accounts for its investment in the subsidiary undertaking, Shillelagh Limited, at the acquisition cost of £9,000,000. On consolidation goodwill would be determined as follows:

	£
Purchase consideration paid	9,000,000
Fair value of identifiable net assets acquired	6,000,000
Goodwill arising on consolidation	**3,000,000**

B. On subsequent disposal of 100% of subsidiary undertaking – 31 December 2010
Parent company

	£	£
Proceeds received on disposal of entire holding		14,000,000
Less: Original purchase consideration paid		9,000,000
Gain arising on disposal of subsidiary undertaking		**5,000,000**
Consolidation entries		
1. Set-off of investment in subsidiary undertaking against identifiable net assets on consolidation		
Net assets of Shillelagh Limited	6,000,000	
Goodwill on consolidation	3,000,000	
Investment in Shillelagh Limited		9,000,000
2. Post-acquisition profits of a subsidiary		
Net assets of Shillelagh Limited	1,000,000	
Profit and loss account		1,000,000
3. Determination of gain arising on disposal of subsidiary undertaking		
Proceeds of disposal of shares in Shillelagh Limited	14,000,000	
Net assets of Shillelagh Limited		7,000,000
Goodwill on consolidation		3,000,000
Gain on disposal of Shillelagh Limited		4,000,000

C. Reconciliation to gain shown in accounting records of parent undertaking

Net gain on disposal of subsidiary per group financial statements	4,000,000
Post-acquisition/pre-disposal profits of Shillelagh included in the consolidated profit and loss account of Robust Technical Services Limited	1,000,000
Net gain as per parent undertaking accounting records	**5,000,000**

7106

Issue	Accounting treatment
In the accounting records of the parent undertaking that disposes of the subsidiary undertaking	Any proceeds of the sale should be credited against the carrying value of the investment. This will determine the gain or loss generated from the sale of the subsidiary undertaking.
In the consolidated financial statements	1. The **proceeds of the disposal** should be set off against the carrying amount of the identifiable net assets of the subsidiary, attributable to the group's interest at the date of disposal, together with any goodwill arising on the original acquisition of the subsidiary undertaking. 2. The **gain or loss** should be shown as an exceptional item after operating profit and before interest in the consolidated profit and loss account. 3. The consolidated financial statements should include the results of that subsidiary undertaking, up to the date that it ceases to be a subsidiary.
Where any of the subsidiary's assets have been revalued	The relevant balance on the group revaluation reserve should be transferred, at the disposal date, to the profit and loss account reserve.

Goodwill There may be goodwill **related to the shares** that have been sold, that has not previously been either written off through the profit and loss account or attributed to prior period amortisation or impairment. Such goodwill should be added to the carrying amount of the net assets of the subsidiary for the purpose of the calculation of the gain or loss on disposal. 7109 FRS 2 (47)

Change in voting rights

The parent undertaking may lose control over the subsidiary, because of changes in the voting rights it holds or in those held by another party in that subsidiary. **Control may pass** where there is a change: 7110
- in voting rights given to different classes of shares issued by the subsidiary; or
- the method for allocating rights between different classes of shares.

Deemed disposals

The **parent may forfeit control** without actually disposing of any of its shares (referred to as a deemed disposal), as the group's interest in a subsidiary undertaking is reduced, because: 7112
- the parent undertaking and its group do not take up their full allocation of rights in a rights issue;
- the parent undertaking and its group do not take up their full share of scrip dividends while other equity holders in that subsidiary undertaking take up some, or all, of their share;
- another party has exercised options or warrants it holds; or
- the subsidiary undertaking has issued shares to parties other than the parent undertaking and its group.

Demergers

Under a demerger, an undertaking ceases to be a subsidiary undertaking, as all or a majority of the shares in the subsidiary undertaking are re-distributed "in-specie" to members of the parent. 7120

Any **shareholding retained by the parent** will represent either an associate undertaking (equity method) or a trade investment accounted for on a cost basis.

---

b. Partial disposal of an interest in a subsidiary

A group reduces its interest in a subsidiary

A parent undertaking may dispose of part of its interest in a subsidiary undertaking **but retain sufficient interest** for the investment to remain a subsidiary undertaking. The accounting treatment in this case is similar to that applicable to a subsidiary leaving the group (see ¶7106). **Any gain or loss arising** should be calculated as **the difference between**: 7128 FRS 2 (52)
- the carrying amount of the net assets of that subsidiary undertaking attributable to the group's interest before the reduction; and
- the carrying amount attributable to the group's interest after the reduction, together with any proceeds received.

The **net assets compared** should include any related goodwill not previously written off through the profit and loss account.

Treatment of minority interests The minority interest should be introduced, or if already in existence, increased by the carrying amount of the net identifiable assets now attributable to the minority interest, as a result of the decrease in the group's interest. 7130

In the accounting records of the parent undertaking disposing of part of its interest in a subsidiary undertaking, the relevant portion of the **carrying value of the investment** should be transferred to a disposals account. The proceeds from the sale of the shares should be credited to the disposals account and the gain or loss determined.

7132 **Consolidated balance sheet** Although the status of the investment is unaltered as it remains a subsidiary undertaking, **adjustments should be made** to any goodwill and interests held by minority interests.

Although there is no change in the carrying amount of the net assets of the subsidiary undertaking included in the consolidation, the percentage attributable to the **minority interests** increases accordingly to the level of their holding at the end of the financial year. **Goodwill** that arose on acquisition of the group's interest should not be attributed to the minority interests. However, goodwill originally recognised on acquisition should be adjusted to reflect the percentage holding disposed of.

In the **consolidated profit and loss account**, the minority share of profits is increased according to the additional level of interest held by the minority shareholders.

Significant reduction – investment becomes an associate

7133 A parent undertaking may dispose of part of its interest in a subsidiary undertaking **but retain sufficient interest** for the investment to be classified as an associated undertaking.

7134 In the **accounting records of the parent undertaking**, disposing of its controlling interest in the subsidiary undertaking, the relevant portion of the carrying value of the investment should be debited to a disposals account.

The proceeds from the sale of the shares should be credited to the disposals account and the gain or loss determined. The **residual carrying value** of the shares should then be transferred and reclassified as an "investment in an associated undertaking".

7135 **Consolidation process** The consolidation process will need to reflect the **change in status** of the investment to an associated undertaking during the accounting period, as follows:

a. The **subsidiary undertaking** should be accounted for and consolidated up to the date of disposal of the controlling interest;

b. A **gain or loss on disposal** should be calculated in the same way as for a partial disposal and recognised in the consolidated profit and loss account;

c. The **investment in the associate** should be shown as a one line item within Fixed Asset Investments, valued at the investing company's share of the net assets of the associate; and

d. The **parent company's share** of net profits or losses and changes in net investment in the associated undertaking, should be accounted for under the equity method (see ¶7460).

EXAMPLE Pike Limited acquired and disposed of shares in Salmon Limited, which has an issued share capital of 1,000,000 ordinary shares:
A. 31 December 2009: **Acquired 1,000,000 shares** for a consideration of £9,000,000 when the fair value of Salmon Limited's identifiable net assets was £6,000,000.
B. 31 December 2010: **Disposed of 800,000 shares** for proceeds of £14,000,000 when the fair value of Salmon Limited's identifiable net assets was £7,000,000, including £1,000,000 post-acquisition profits.
C. The residual investment held by Pike in Salmon satisfies the criteria to be treated as an associate.

A. On initial acquisition of 100 per cent of subsidiary undertaking – Dec. 2009

In the accounting records of the parent company Pike Limited, its investment in subsidiary undertaking, Salmon Limited would be carried at the acquisition cost of £9,000,000.
On consolidation, **goodwill would be determined** as follows:

Reconciliation	£
Purchase consideration paid	9,000,000
Fair value of identifiable net assets acquired	6,000,000
Goodwill arising on consolidation	**3,000,000**

B. On subsequent disposal of 80% of subsidiary undertaking – 31 December 2010

In the accounting records of Pike Limited, the disposal of Salmon Limited would be dealt with as follows:

	£
Investment in subsidiary undertaking, at cost	9,000,000
Less: Transferred to disposals account – 80%	7,200,000
Investment in associated undertaking, at cost	**1,800,000**

	£
Proceeds received on disposal of 80% of Salmon Limited	14,000,000
Less: Purchase consideration paid – 80% of £9,000,000	7,200,000
Gain arising on disposal of shares in subsidiary undertaking	**6,800,000**

Consolidated financial statements
On consolidation, the **realisation of 80%** of Salmon Limited would be dealt with as follows:

Exceptional item	£	£
Proceeds received on disposal of 80% of holding		14,000,000
Less: Fair value of identifiable net assets disposed (80 % of £7,000,000)	5,600,000	
Goodwill arising on acquisition (80 % of £3,000,000)	2,400,000	8,000,000
Net gain on disposal of 80% of subsidiary undertaking		**6,000,000**

Reconciliation to gain shown in accounting records of parent undertaking

Net gain on disposal of 80% of shares in subsidiary	6,000,000
Increase in identifiable net assets included in profit and loss account – relating to the 80% shareholding sold	800,000
Net gain as per parent undertaking accounting records	**6,800,000**

Goodwill

Goodwill on acquisition of subsidiary undertaking	3,000,000
Less: Transferred on disposal of 80% of subsidiary undertaking	2,400,000
Balance of goodwill transferred to the carrying value of the associate	**600,000**

Investment in associated undertaking

Net assets £7,000,000 × 20%	**1,400,000**
Goodwill arising at the date of original purchase (not yet amortised)	600,000
Carrying value of associate	2,000,000

Reconciliation
Reconciliation to net assets shown on records of parent undertaking

Cost per accounting records of parent undertaking, £9,000,000 × 20%	1,800,000
Add: Post-acquisition profits attributable to remaining shares in Salmon held by Pike (equity accounted) £1,000,000 x 20%	200,000
Carrying value per consolidated financial statements	**2,000,000**

Consolidation entries
The consolidation entries would be as follows

1. Set off of investment in subsidiary undertaking on consolidation

	£	£
Net assets of Salmon Limited	6,000,000	
Goodwill on consolidation	3,000,000	
Investment in Salmon Limited		9,000,000

2. Post-acquisition profits of subsidiary undertaking

Net assets of Salmon Limited	1,000,000	
Profit and loss account		1,000,000

3. Determination of gain arising on disposal of subsidiary undertaking

Proceeds of disposal of shares in Salmon Limited	14,000,000	
Net assets of Salmon Limited		5,600,000
Goodwill on consolidation		2,400,000
Gain on disposal of Salmon Limited		6,000,000

Investment in subsidiary undertaking becomes a fixed asset investment

7140 A parent undertaking **may dispose of part of its interest** in a subsidiary undertaking but retain sufficient interest for the investment to be classified as a trade investment.

7142 **Parent undertaking** In the accounting records of the parent undertaking disposing of its controlling interest in the subsidiary undertaking, the relevant portion of the carrying value of the investment should be transferred to a disposals account.

The **proceeds from the sale** of the shares should be credited to the disposals account and the gain or loss determined. The residual carrying value of the shares should be accounted for as a trade investment.

Consolidated financial statements	Accounting treatment
1. Proceeds of the shares disposed	1. Proceeds should be set off against the carrying amount of the identifiable net assets of the subsidiary attributable to the group's interest at the date of disposal, together with any relevant part of goodwill arising on the original acquisition of the subsidiary undertaking. 2. The net gain or loss should be shown as an exceptional item after operating profit and before interest in the consolidated profit and loss account.
2. Results of the subsidiary undertaking	Results attributable to the group up till the date of disposal must be recognised in the profit and loss account
3. Disposal reducing investment from subsidiary to that of a fixed asset investment	Only dividends received or receivable would be recognised
4. Carrying value of investment	The investment should be carried at the same amount it is shown in the balance sheet of the parent undertaking

EXAMPLE **Considerable disposal of an investment in a subsidiary – becomes a trade investment**

Evergreen Limited has recently made both an acquisition and disposals of shares in Sole Limited, which has an issued share capital of 1,000,000 ordinary shares:

A. 31 December 2008: **Acquired 1,000,000 shares** for a consideration of £9,000,000 when the fair value of Sole Limited's identifiable net assets was £6,000,000.

B. 31 December 2010: **Disposed of 900,000 shares** for £16,000,000 when the fair value of Sole Limited's identifiable net assets was £7,000,000, its profit for the year being £1,000,000.

A. Original acquisition of shares

In the accounting records of the parent company Evergreen Limited, the investment in its subsidiary undertaking, Sole Limited, would be carried at the cost of acquisition of £9,000,000

On consolidation goodwill would be determined as follows:

No provision for amortisation of goodwill has been made.

	£
Purchase consideration paid	9,000,000
Fair value of identifiable net assets acquired	6,000,000
Goodwill arising on consolidation	3,000,000

B. Subsequent disposal of 90% of subsidiary undertaking – 31 December 2010

In the accounting records of the parent company Evergreen Limited, the disposal of Sole Limited would be dealt with as follows:

	£
1. Investment in subsidiary undertaking, at cost	9,000,000
Less: Transferred to disposals account – 90%	8,100,000
Trade investment, at cost, included in fixed asset investments	**900,000**

2. Exceptional item

	£
Proceeds received on disposal of 90% of Sole Limited	16,000,000
Less: Purchase consideration paid – 90% of £9,000,000	8,100,000
Gain arising on disposal of shares in subsidiary undertaking	**7,900,000**

Consolidation
On consolidation, the realisation of 90% of Sole Limited would be dealt with as follows:

1. Exceptional item	£	£
Proceeds received on disposal of 90% of holding		16,000.000
Less: Fair value of identifiable net assets of Sole at date of disposal*	7,000,000	
Goodwill arising on acquisition of Sole not amortised at date of disposal*	3,000,000	(10,000,000)
Residual value of trade interest remaining in books of Evergreen.		900,000
Net gain on disposal of 90 per cent of subsidiary undertaking		**6,900,000**

* Although only a 90% holding has been sold as far as the group accounts are concerned, the entire subsidiary is de-consolidated and replaced with a trade investment at cost, a treatment which does not permit the inclusion of any goodwill.

2. Reconciliation to gain shown in accounting records of parent undertaking

Net gain on disposal of 90 per cent of shares in the subsidiary	6,900,000
Post-acquisition profits of Sole consolidated in the Evergreen group accounts	1,000,000
Net gain as per parent undertaking accounting records	7,900,000

3. Fixed assets: Trade investment
Instead of consolidating the assets and liabilities of Sole, the group accounts will show (as will the parent undertaking's own accounts) a trade investment in Sole at cost.

At cost, £9,000,00 x 10 per cent	900,000

Consolidation entries
As Sole Limited is not a subsidiary of Evergreen at the period end it will not be included in the consolidation of the balance sheet.
The profit and loss account of Sole will be consolidated up to the date of the 90% disposal; namely, the date it ceases to be a subsidiary. In this instance, the group profits of Evergreen will include £1,000,000 of the profits relating to Sole.

2. Disclosure requirements

Companies Act requirements

The Companies Act stipulates, that if during the financial year, there has been a disposal of an undertaking or group, **which significantly impacts on** the figures shown in the group financial statements, the notes to these financial statements should include the **following information**: 7170
- the name of that subsidiary undertaking, or parent of the group disposed of;
- the extent to which the profit or loss of the group is attributable to the disposed subsidiary undertaking or group; and
- comparative figures in respect of the proceeding year must be provided. Where the preceding year figure is not comparable, it should be adjusted and shown on a comparable basis. In addition, the notes should also give the particulars of the adjustment and the reasons for it.

7172 **Exemptions** Exemption from the above mentioned disclosure requirements may be available provided the **following conditions are met**:
- where in the opinion of the directors of the parent company, the disclosures would be seriously prejudicial to the business of the parent company or any of its subsidiary undertakings;
- the Secretary of State agrees that the information should not be disclosed; and
- where the undertaking involved is established under the law of a country outside of the United Kingdom or carries on business outside the United Kingdom.

Additional disclosure requirements

7174 FRS 2 (48) The consolidated financial statements should provide the following financial information **for any material undertaking**, that has ceased to be a subsidiary undertaking during the financial period; namely:
- the name of the undertaking;
- any ownership interests retained; and
- where it has ceased to be a subsidiary undertaking, without disposing of at least the interest held by the group, the circumstances should be explained.

7176 The **notes to the cash flow statement** should provide:
- a summary of the cash flows resulting from the disposal of subsidiary undertakings, indicating how much of the consideration comprised cash; and
- details of any material effects that the cash flows of the disposed undertakings had on the consolidated cash flow position. This information for example, could be given for continuing and discontinued operations and acquisitions.

CHAPTER 5

Associates and joint arrangements

OUTLINE ¶¶

There are a **number of criteria** for determining whether an investment should be classified as an associate, a joint venture, a joint arrangement that is not an entity (JANEs) or a joint venture in form but not substance. **7300**

The accounting rules for associates and joint arrangements apply to all companies regardless of size. The key reporting standard is FRS 9 "Associates and joint ventures".

Entities **applying the FRSSE** are exempt from applying FRS 9, unless preparing consolidated financial statements. In this case, the entity should apply the reporting standard to such statements as required by the FRSSE. In addition to the statutory disclosure requirements for associates and joint arrangements, **additional disclosures** are triggered at particular thresholds.

The **key differences** between UK GAAP and IAS (IFRS) comprising IAS 28 "Accounting for investments in associates" and IAS 31 "Financial reporting of interests in joint ventures", are also covered.

SECTION 1

Classification

Determining the relationship

7304 The **principal methods** by which entities can further their economic activities through investments in other entities is tabulated below, starting with the highest level of involvement: namely, a parent/subsidiary relationship through to associate investments, joint arrangements or simple trade investments.

7305 The **primary difference** between an associate or joint arrangement and a subsidiary interest, is the degree of investor control. Initially, on acquiring an investment, which is of the nature of an associate or joint venture, an assessment of its status should be made.

1. The **first stage** is to assess the relationship between the investor and the investee and to determine the actual interests owned by the investor and the attached voting rights (participating interest).

2. The **second stage involves assessing** the degree of the reporting entity's direct involvement in the management and operations of the investee (significant influence – see ¶7338) and the long-term intentions of the investor. An investor may have overall control, in which case a parent/subsidiary relationship exists. However, if its influence over the investee is not so dominant, then an associate or joint venture relationship may exist.

7306 Once an investee has qualified as an associate or joint venture, **minor or temporary changes in the relationship** between investor and investee should not affect its status.

7308

Entity/arrangement	Nature of relationship	Description of the defining relationship	Investor's treatment of the investment in the consolidated financial statements
Subsidiary	Investor controls the investee	Has the ability to direct and control operational and financial policy	Consolidate assets, liabilities, results and cash flows of its subsidiaries
Associate	Investor holds a participating interest and exercises significant influence but does not control its investee	A substantial minority shareholding enabling the investor to be actively involved in policy	Net equity method (¶7366)
Joint venture	Investors hold long-term interest and shares control under a contractual arrangement	A contractual relationship under which two or more investors control a venture as a separate venture in its own right	Gross equity method (¶7438)
Joint arrangements that are not an entity (JANE)	Entities participate in an arrangement to carry on part of their own trades or business.	Does not carry on a trade of its own. Investor extends its own trade through the joint arrangement.	Each investor accounts directly for its own share of the assets, liabilities, results and cash flows, and its shared items as set out in contractual agreement
Simple investment (¶1750)	Passive	The investor's interest does not qualify the investee as an associate, a joint venture or a subsidiary. The interest involves limited influence.	Investors include their interest as investments at cost or valuation

SECTION 2

Associate companies

A. Determining associate status

An associate undertaking is defined in the Companies Act, as an entity other than a subsidiary or joint venture, in which another entity (the investor): 7320 FRS 9 (14)
- has a **participating interest**; and
- over whose operating and financial policies the investor exercises **significant influence**.

MEMO POINTS An undertaking **is defined in FRS 9** as a body corporate, partnership or unincorporated association carrying on a trade, with or without a view to profit. This extends the definition of an associate to include non-profit making organisations or unincorporated associations. The definition of an associate is contained in the Companies Act 1985, para 20(1), Sch 4A and replicated in para. 19, Sch 6 of the Large and Medium-sized Companies and Groups (Accounts and Reports) Regulations 2008 (SI 2008/410) and para. 19, Sch 6 SI 2008/409 (Small companies and groups).

Participating interest

A holding of 20% or more of the shares (but less than 50%) of an entity is deemed to be a participating interest. This **presumption is rebutted if** the interest is neither long-term nor beneficial to the investor. 7326 FRS 9 (4)

A **combination of direct and indirect holdings** through a group structure may also give rise to a participating interest (see ¶7490).

Even if an investor holds less than 20% of the share capital in an entity, it can still be classified as an associate, if the investor can exercise significant influence (¶7338) or it enjoys equivalent rights.

A **stricter qualifying regime** has been introduced under FRS 9, in which the investor must also show that its investment qualifies as an associate, because it is retained: 7327
- on a **long-term basis** without a view to resale; and
- it contributes to the investor's activities through the **exercise of control** or **significant influence**, arising from that interest.

MEMO POINTS An interest is held on a **long-term basis**, when it is not expected to be disposed of within one year of the acquisition date and where it is intended that the acquisition will become part of the continuing activities of the group.

Equivalent rights A participating interest in the shares of another entity could take the form of equivalent rights; namely: 7330
- an option to acquire shares; or
- an interest convertible into a shareholding (i.e. a type of management contract).

"Equivalent rights" refers to any **conversion rights or options** held by investors, which if taken up would mean the 20% threshold being breached. However, this does not mean an associate relationship automatically comes into existence when the options can be exercised.

Where the 20% rule is rebutted (i.e. where it can be demonstrated, that irrespective of the level of shareholding, an associate relationship does not exist), then the equivalent rights (in the form of "interests" or shares) need not be taken into account.

Management contracts Participating interests could also take the form of control exercised through a management contract, with a performance based fee, in which the recipient 7334 is deemed to be more than a manager. In another scenario, an investor could be deemed to hold a participating interest, even if his equity holding is less than 20%. This type of investment is common in internet companies.

Significant interest

7338 The Companies Act dictates that for an investment to be classified as an associate, its investor must exercise significant influence over the investee's operating and financial policies, based on the voting rights controlled. Once significant influence has been established, it should be regarded as continuing to do so until an event or transaction alters this state of affairs.

The **requirements of FRS 9 are more stringent** and state that significant interest should be determined with reference to the degree of direct control and the level of active participation exercised by the investor.

7339 **Direct control** Direct involvement in the entity's operating and financial policies is taken to mean, that over a period of time, the associate will generally implement policies that are consistent with the strategy of the investor. If an associate persistently implements policies that are inconsistent with its investor's strategy, that investor would not be exercising significant influence over the management of the entity.

FRS 9 (16) The investor's direct involvement in its associate is **commonly achieved through**:
- nomination to the board of directors, or its equivalent; or
- an arrangement that allows the investor to actively participate in policy making decisions.

7340 FRS 9 (14) **Level of active participation** Significant interest is present where the investor influences the direction of its associate through **active participation in policy decisions**, including strategic issues such as:
- the expansion or contraction of the business;
- participation in other entities;
- changing its products, markets and activities; and
- determining the balance between dividend and reinvestment.

7348 **Voting rights** Where an undertaking holds a participating influence (of 20% or more of the voting rights in another undertaking), it shall be presumed to exercise significant influence over that entity, unless the contrary can be shown. Any shares held by a parent and its subsidiaries in that entity should be aggregated for this purpose. **Rights held by other associates** of the investor should be excluded.

MEMO POINTS Voting rights effectively mean those rights conferred on shareholders in respect of their shares or in the case of an undertaking not having a share capital, on members who can vote at general meetings on substantially all matters.

FRS 9 (17) In practice, **it can be difficult to determine** whether the relationship constitutes that of an associate. When assessing whether significant influence exists, the distribution of the remaining voting rights must be considered as other large shareholders may prevent a 20% shareholder from exercising any real influence. This is illustrated in the following example.

EXAMPLE **Scenario A**

Brown plc – Annual Report & Accounts 2010

Brown plc has a 22.5% interest in ABC plc. There are two other shareholders, Smith who holds 30% and Jones who has 47.5% of the shares. Brown is entitled to nominate two directors to the board which has 10 members in total. Smith nominates three directors and Jones, five. The Chairman of the board is a nominee of Jones and he has the casting vote.

Although it might initially appear that Brown's relationship with ABC is that of an investment in an associate (as it exceeds the 20% threshold), the much stronger position of Jones, in particular, will in practice prevent Brown exercising any significant influence. Therefore, Brown should not classify ABC as an associate.

Scenario B

Likewise, if an individual holds **less than 20% of the voting rights**, he can still be deemed to exercise significant influence and the holding can still be accounted for as an associate.

Williams Plc has recently acquired 18% of the share capital of XYZ plc from the last remaining, founding shareholders. The remainder of the shares are widely held between employees, ex-employees and the distant family of the founding members. No other shareholder has more than 2% of the votes. Williams has, at the first annual general meeting since it acquired the shares, managed to secure five out of nine places on the board of directors for its nominees.

Given the disposition of the other shareholders and Williams' ability to secure a majority of board directors, there is clear evidence that it has significant influence and despite its shareholding falling below the 20% threshold, it should account for its investment as an associate.

Subsequent re-classifcation The actual relationship might develop differently from that assumed from the arrangements on acquisition. There may be instances where the **information available to the investor** is extremely limited. In this case, the investor's relationship with its investee will need to be reassessed as post-acquisition evidence emerges, as there may be doubts as to whether the investor's influence is significant or whether it jointly controls its investment. In such circumstances, it may be necessary to modify the treatment originally adopted in the financial statements. For more detail on this topic see ¶7474. 7352

EXAMPLE Group A held a 25% investment in a company at the beginning of the financial year, having accounted for it as an associate in the consolidated financial statements. However, another investor subsequently acquired a 60% shareholding in the associate. Group A subsequently concluded, that it no longer exercised significant influence over the associate and downgraded it to a trade investment.

B. Accounting for associates

The treatment of an investment in an associate will depend upon whether or not the investor is preparing consolidated group accounts. 7360

1. Individual company financial statements

Where an investor prepares consolidated financial statements the interest in an associate should be accounted for using the equity method. In the investor's individual financial statements, the interest in an associate should be shown as a **fixed asset investment** and shown either at cost, less any amounts written off, or at valuation. Any goodwill arising should be separately identified. 7362 FRS 9 (26)

Where an **investor does not prepare** consolidated financial statements, it should prepare a set of individual financial statements including the relevant amounts for its associates (and joint arrangements), or disclose the relevant amounts in the notes to its own financial statements. Investing entities **that are exempt** from preparing consolidated financial statements, or who would be exempt if they had subsidiaries, are exempt from this requirement. FRS 9 (48)

2. Consolidated financial statements

The Companies Act requires that associated undertakings be included in group accounts using the equity method of accounting (with detailed guidance set out in FRS 9), except where the amounts involved are not material. 7366

FRS 9 (4) The equity method **is defined** as a method of accounting, that brings an investment into its investor's financial statements initially at cost, with any goodwill identified separately. The ongoing process is as follows:

1. The **carrying amount** of the investment must be adjusted in each accounting period for the investor's share of the results of its investee, less:
– any amortisation or write-off for goodwill;
– the investor's share of any gains or losses; and
– any other changes in the investee's net assets including distributions to owners, such as dividends.

2. The **investor's share** of its investee's results is recognised in the profit and loss account.

3. The **investor's cash flow statement** includes the cash flows between the investor and its investee such as dividends or loans.

7368 The **objective of the equity method** is to reflect the actual relationship between the investor and the associate in the:
– profit and loss account, by reporting profits or losses attributable to the investor rather than dividends; and
– balance sheet, by including information based on net assets of the investee, rather than the cost or market value of the investment in shares.

Profit and loss account

7374 FRS 9 (27) The information detailed in the table below should, where appropriate, be included in the investor's consolidated profit and loss account. A sample profit and loss account based on the equity method is also given below.

Consolidated profit and loss account	Investor's share in the results of the associates
Turnover	**1**. A total combining the investor's share of its **associates' turnover** with group turnover may be shown as a memorandum item in the profit and loss account. **2**. The investor's share of its associates' turnover should be clearly distinguished from group turnover.
Operating results – investors share of	The investor's share of the **operating results** of the associate(s) should be included immediately after the group operating result, but after the investor's share of the results of any joint ventures
Goodwill write-off or amortisation	Such items arising on the **acquisition of associates** should be charged immediately after the associates' operating results and disclosed
Exceptional items	Any **exceptional items** included after operating profit in the associates' own financial statements, or interest should be shown separately from the amounts for the group. Examples include profits or losses on sale or termination of an operation, costs of reorganisation or restructuring or profits or losses on disposal of fixed assets.
Profit before tax	1. The investor's share of the relevant **figures for associates** should be included within the amounts for the group (including minority interests in subsidiaries held by associates). 2. For items below this level, such as interest and taxation, the amounts relating to associates should be separately disclosed.
Segmental analysis	**Turnover and operating profit**, if given, should clearly distinguish between that of the group and that of any associate companies

More detail on the disclosure requirements outlined in the table above is given in Section 5.

EXAMPLE Equity method of accounting FRS 9 (Appendix IV)

Consolidated profit and loss account
Year to 31 December 2010

	£m	£m
Turnover: group and share of associates	400	
Less: share of associates' turnover	(200)	
Group turnover		200
Cost of sales		(120)
Gross profit		80
Administrative expenses		(40)
Group operating profit		40
Share of operating profit in:		
Joint ventures	30	
Associates	24	
Amortisation of goodwill on associates	(7)	
Exceptional items-reorganisation costs of associate	(4)	
		43
		83
Interest receivable (group)		6
Interest payable:		
Group	(26)	
Joint ventures	(10)	
Associates	(12)	
		(48)
Profit on ordinary activities before tax		41
Tax on profit on ordinary activities		(12)
Profit on ordinary activities after tax		29
Minority interests		(6)
Profit on ordinary activities after tax and minority interests		23
Equity dividends		(10)
Retained profit for group and its share of associates and joint ventures		13
* Tax relates to the following:		
Parent and subsidiaries	(5)	
Joint ventures	(5)	
Associates	(2)	

Dividends and retained profit or loss The group's share of dividends paid by associates should contra the dividends received, accounted for in the investor's consolidated accounts, with neither payments or receipts included in the group profit and loss account. 7376

Elimination of profit and losses on associate transactions The investor's share of any profit or loss on transactions between an investor and an associate, should be eliminated from the consolidated accounts. Balances between the group and its subsidiaries and associates are not eliminated, so any **unsettled trading balances** should be shown as current assets or liabilities in the consolidated balance sheet. 7378

The amounts shown for "Associates" are subdivisions of the item for which the statutory prescribed heading is "Income from interests in associated undertakings". The subdivisions may also be shown in a note rather than on the face of the profit and loss account. FRS 9 (Appendix IV)

EXAMPLE **Notes to the accounts**
Investor's share of operating results of an associate

Y. Ltd has a share capital of 10,000 ordinary shares of £1, each carrying one vote. Z. Ltd holds 2,000 of Y's shares and is represented on the board of Y. Ltd.
Z. Ltd accounts for Y. Ltd as an associate in its group accounts. Both companies have a financial year-end of 31 December 20XX and Y's profit and loss for the year was £120,000. The consolidated profit and loss account for Z. Ltd includes £24,000 in respect of Y's operating profit (£120,000 x 20%).

Balance sheet

7384 FRS 9 (29) **At the date of acquisition**, the investment in an associate should be shown as the aggregate of the investor's share of the associates' net assets, plus any goodwill arising on the acquisition.

In subsequent years, the carrying value of the associate in the consolidated balance sheet is adjusted in each period in respect of the investor's share:
- of the results of its associate less any amortisation or write-off for goodwill;
- of any relevant gains or losses; and
- any other changes in the investee's net assets including distributions to its owners (e.g. dividends).

In this way, the carrying value is maintained at the investor's share of the associates' net assets plus the unamortised goodwill.

Although **goodwill arising** on an investor's acquisition of an associate, less amortisation or write-offs should be included in the carrying amount of the associate, it should be separately disclosed.

7386 **Where an associate itself has associates** (or subsidiaries), that generate goodwill in its own consolidated accounts, this goodwill should be excluded from the fair value of the associate's net assets used to calculate the goodwill arising on the acquisition of the associate. However, **separate disclosure** is not required for the components of goodwill arising from an acquisition and in particular any goodwill arising on past acquisitions made by the associate itself.

7388 **Loans to associates** that constitute part of their long-term funding should be included in the carrying value of the associate within fixed asset investments, although the loans should still be separately disclosed. Where a loan is short-term in nature, it can be included in debtors.

Any **dividends remitted** by the associate effectively converts part of the investment into cash (or if not yet paid, debtors) and therefore, should be excluded from the carrying value of the associate in the balance sheet.

FRS 9 (Appendix IV) The following balance sheet reflects the normal presentation using the equity method.

EXAMPLE Consolidated balance sheet
As at 31 December 2010

	£m	£m	£m
Fixed assets			
Tangible assets		480	
Investments			
Investments in joint ventures			
Share of gross assets	130		
Share of gross liabilities	(80)		
Goodwill re associates		50	
Investments in associates (See 1)		20	
			550
Current assets			
Stock		15	
Debtors		75	
Cash at bank and in hand		10	
		100	
Creditors		(50)	
Net current assets			50
Total assets less current liabilities			600
Creditors (due after more than one year)			(250)
Provision for liabilities and charges			(10)
Equity minority interests			(40)
			300
Capital and reserves			
Called up share capital			50
Share premium account			150
Profit and loss account			100
Shareholders' funds (all equity)			**300**

Notes to the consolidated balance sheet
1. Investments in associates:

	£m
Share of net assets	10
Loans to associates	5
Goodwill arising on acquisition (less amortisation)	5
Total	**20**

Accounting for acquisition of an associate On purchase of an associate, the fair values (less goodwill) of the underlying net assets and liabilities should be identified, using the accounting policies adopted by the investor. The difference between the investor's share of the fair values and the consideration paid is attributed to goodwill on acquisition. For more information on the fair values see ¶6864. 7392

Associate with subsidiaries Where an associate itself **has subsidiary undertakings**, the amounts to be included in the investor's accounts are the consolidated figures for the associated undertaking and its subsidiaries. **Annual changes in value of the associate** will reflect: 7394
– the share of profits or losses of the associate and the proportion of any other gains or losses as reflected in the STRGL, less any dividends remitted to the group by the associate; and
– any amortisation of goodwill.

Investor's consolidated cash flow statement

The requirements of FRS 9 covering the investor's consolidated cash flow statement are as follows: 7400 FRS 9 (30)
1. Only actual cash flows **between associates and the group** should be included in the consolidated cash flow statement.
2. The consolidated cash flow statement (¶4180) **should include dividends received** from associates, as a separate item between operating activities and returns on investments and servicing of finance.
3. Any **other cash flows** between the investor and its associates such as loans, should be included under the appropriate cash flow heading for the activity giving rise to the cash flow.

The **following items should be excluded** from the consolidated cash flow statement:
– amortisation of goodwill on acquisition of an associate; and
– the group share of any items included on an equity basis such as operating profit, exceptional items, interest payable, and tax.

EXAMPLE **Consolidated cash flow statement**
As at 31 December 2010

	£ m	Notes
Cash flow from operating activities	120	1
Dividends received from associates	27	2
Returns on investments and servicing of finance	(15)	3
Taxation	(8)	4
Capital expenditure	(63)	5
Acquisitions and disposals	50	6
Equity dividends paid	(17)	
Management of liquid resources	11	
Financing	(40)	7
Increase in cash in the period	**65**	

Notes.
1. Group only, excluding associates
2. Could include joint ventures
3. Includes interest on loans to associate
4. Excludes associate
5. Includes loans advanced to/ repaid from associate
6. Includes purchase or sale of shares in associate
7. Finance raised to fund share purchases in associates

STRGL

7402 FRS 9 (28) In the consolidated STRGL, the investor's share of the total recognised gains and losses of its associates should be included (shown separately under each heading), if the amounts included are material, either in the statement itself or in a note that is referred to in the statement.

EXAMPLE **Statement of total recognised gains and losses**
Year to 31 December 2010

	2010 £'000	2009 £'000
Profit/ (loss) for year – Group	480.3	425.6
Joint ventures – revaluation losses	(10.2)	-
Associates	**25.6**	**11.2**
Exchange adjustments	(2.6)	(3.2)
Total recognised gains and losses for the year	**493.1**	**433.6**

SECTION 3

Joint arrangements

7404 "Joint arrangements" is **an umbrella term** covering joint ventures, joint arrangements that are not entities and arrangements that are joint ventures in form but not substance. The different types of joint arrangement and the respective accounting treatments are set out below.

Joint arrangements **are governed by** a formal agreement and comprise two or more investors, even though they are no more than agents for the principle investors. The **level of detail required** of investors in joint ventures, in their consolidated financial statements, is greater than for investments in associates; so investors must take considerable care to correctly categorise their investments.

The **general criteria** for determining the exact nature of a joint arrangement is outlined below, although in reality it can be difficult distinguishing a joint venture from other types of joint arrangement. In addition, the nature of the joint arrangement may change over time.

FRS 9 makes a **clear distinction** between joint ventures which are equity accounted and other joint arrangements which are not.

Types of joint arrangement

7406 There are in essence, three types of joint arrangement, each of which has a separate accounting treatment.

1. A joint arrangement that has **its own trade or business** is potentially a joint venture.
2. A joint arrangement that is not an entity (JANE) is a joint activity entered into by two or more investors, **that does not represent an extension of** their own trade or business.
3. A structure with the **form, but not substance** of a joint venture.

A. Joint ventures

7410 FRS 9 (4) FRS 9 **defines a joint venture** as an entity in which the reporting undertaking holds an interest:
– on a long-term basis; and
– is jointly controlled by the reporting entity and one or more other venturers under a contractual arrangement.

MEMO POINTS The Companies Act defines a joint venture, as an undertaking managed jointly with one or more undertakings that are not included in the consolidation. The legal references for joint ventures are para. 18 Sch 6 SI 2008/409 (small companies and groups) and para. 18 Sch 6 SI 2008/410 (large and medium-sized companies and groups).

The **simplest form** of joint venture involves two investors each with an equal share of control and ownership. As the number of investors increases, so the ability of each to participate in the process of joint control will diminish. 7412

An entity is a joint venture only with respect to an investor that shares control in it. This must be distinguished from an investor, who has an interest in an entity that is a joint venture for some of its other investors. **Where an investor does not share control** of the entity, it is merely an investment and should be accounted for as such. FRS 9 (10)

1. Long term interest

A long-term interest **is defined** as an interest held other than exclusively for subsequent resale, and where the business is reasonably expected to be retained for more than one year from the date of its acquisition. 7414

A long-term interest **can also be** an investment acquired as a result of the enforcement of a security, in which the interest has become part of the continuing activities of the group or the holder acts as if it intends the interest to become so.

Joint control

A reporting entity jointly controls a venture with one or more other entities, if no one particular entity alone can assume overall control of that entity. Decisions on financial and operating policy essential to the activities, economic performance and financial position of the venture require the consent of each venturer. 7416 FRS 9 (4)

Joint venture agreement

The investors usually **exercise joint control** through a joint venture agreement with each participant. Each conducts its part of the contractual arrangement with a view to its own benefit. Each venturer that shares control should play an active role in setting the operating and financial policies of the joint venture, at least in terms of general strategy. This does not preclude one investor managing the joint venture under a separate agreement, provided that the **principal operating and financial policies** are collectively agreed by all the venturers, each of whom has the resources to ensure compliance. 7418 FRS 9 (11)

The requirement for each venturer's consent to strategic decisions does not have to be set out in the joint venture agreement, provided that the joint venture works in practice on the basis of securing such consent.

A joint venture agreement **can override the rights** normally conferred by ownership interests. There is also usually a procedure for settling disputes between venturers and, possibly for terminating the joint venture, after a predetermined period of time or on completion of a particular task. 7420

Unequal shareholdings It is possible to have a joint venture between investors where the venturers do not possess equal shares in the entity, for instance where the investor's holdings are split: 20: 35: 30: 15 or 30: 35: 35. As long as joint control is applied with all parties having the power of veto, then the actual percentage holding does not preclude the investment's classification as a joint venture. 7421

Powers of veto The requirement in the definition for consent to strategic decisions of joint control, effectively gives each venturer a veto on such decisions. This veto distinguishes a joint venture from a minority holder of the shares in a joint stock company, because the latter, having no veto, is subject to majority rule, except for the limited statutory protection for the minority. 7422 FRS 9 (12)

Subsidiary interests An investor may qualify as the parent of an entity, under the definition of a subsidiary in FRS 2 "Accounting for subsidiaries", by holding a majority of the 7424 FRS 9 (11) voting rights in that entity. However, contractual arrangements with the other shareholders could in practice mean the shareholders share control over their investment.

For example, a company may control over 50% of the entity's voting rights, but the joint venture agreement might significantly restrict this control, as it may require unanimous agreement before it can commit to the following strategic decisions:
- commit capital expenditure;
- alter operating or financial policies; or
- pay a dividend.

In such a case, the **interests of the minority shareholders** amount to severe long-term restrictions, that would substantially hinder the exercise of the rights of the parent undertaking over the assets or management of the subsidiary undertaking. The subsidiary therefore, should not be consolidated but should instead be treated as a joint venture according to the requirements of FRS 9.

2. Accounting treatment

7436 FRS 9 (20) The **general rule** is that a reporting entity that prepares consolidated financial statements should include its joint ventures in those statements using the **gross equity method** in all its primary statements. The accounting treatment is similar to that adopted by the equity method, except that the gross equity basis incorporates additional information on the face of the primary statements.

7438 **Individual financial statements** As with the equity method, in the investor's own financial statements, the joint ventures should be treated as fixed asset investments at cost less any amounts written off, or at a valuation.

FRS 9 (21)

Accounting for joint ventures – gross equity basis	
Consolidated financial statements	**Investor's share in the results of the joint venture**
Profit and loss account	The investor's share of its joint ventures: 1. **Turnover** should also be shown separately as a memorandum item (as well as in the segmental analysis) and not as part of group turnover. 2. **Operating results** should be shown after group operating result. 3. **Separate disclosable items** (under FRS 3) – exceptional items – interest – taxation 4. **Goodwill** charged on investments in joint ventures should also be disclosed.
Balance sheet	1. The investor's share of the **gross assets and liabilities** underlying the net amount included for joint ventures should each be shown under the caption "investment in joint ventures", which in turn comes under fixed assets. 2. Any goodwill on acquisition less amounts amortised or written-off should be included in carrying value but disclosed separately.
STRGL	**Share of joint venture** items should be disclosed separately if material, under each heading in the statement or in the notes to the accounts
Cash flow statements	**Dividends received** should be shown separately between operating activities and returns on investments. **Other cash flows** between investor and investee to be shown under the appropriate cash flow heading i.e. interest on loans. No other associate cash flows should be included.

More detail on the disclosure requirements outlined in the table above is given in ¶7494.

Supplementary information

The provision of supplementary information is **subject to the following guidance**: 7440 FRS 9 (22)

a. Except for items below profit before tax in the profit and loss account, any supplementary information given for joint ventures, either in the balance sheet or in the profit and loss account, must be shown separately from amounts for the group and must not be included in the group totals.

b. Because an investor's joint control of its joint venture is a more direct form of influence than the **significant influence** exercised over associates, a reporting entity that conducts a major part of its business through joint ventures should give more detailed supplementary information about them.

One option for including supplementary information on joint ventures is to use the columnar presentation, based on the gross equity method shown in the following examples of a consolidated profit and loss account and balance sheet.

Alternatively, the subdivisions may also be shown in the notes to the accounts rather than on the face of the profit and loss account.

EXAMPLE **Gross equity method**
Consolidated profit and loss account
For the year to 31 December 2010

	£m	£m Group	£m Interests in joint ventures	£m Total
Turnover		**200**	**120**	**320**
Cost of sales		(120)	(85)	(205)
Gross profit		80	35	115
Administrative expenses		(40)	(5)	(45)
Operating profit		**40**	**30**	**70**
Share of operating profit in:				
Joint ventures		30		
Associates		24		
Total operating profit in: group and share of joint ventures and associates		**94**		
Interest receivable (group)		6		
Interest payable:				
Group	(26)			
Joint ventures	(10)			
Associates	(12)			
		(48)		
Profit on ordinary activities before tax		**52**		
Tax on profit on ordinary activities *		**(12)**		
Profit on ordinary activities after tax		**40**		
Minority interests		(6)		
Profit on ordinary activities after taxation and minority interest		**34**		
Equity dividend		(10)		
Retained profit for group and its share of associates and joint ventures		**24**		
* Tax relates to the following:				
Parent and subsidiaries		(5)		
Joint ventures		(5)		
Associates		(2)		

Consolidated balance sheet
For the year to 31 December 20X9

	£m Group	£m Interests in joint ventures	£m Total
Fixed assets			
Tangible assets	480	100	580
Investments			
Investments in joint ventures	50	(50)	
Investments in associates	20		20
	550		600
Current assets			
Stock	15	5	20
Debtors	75	23	98
Cash at bank and in hand	10	2	12
	100	30	130
Creditors	(50)	(20)	(70)
Net current assets	50	10	60
Total assets less current liabilities	600	120	670
Creditors (due after more than one year)	(250)	(70)	(320)
Provision for liabilities and charges	(10)		(10)
Net assets	340		340
Equity minority interests	(40)		
Total net assets	**300**		
Capital and reserves			
Called up share capital	50		
Share premium account	150		
Profit and loss account	100		
Shareholders' funds (all equity)	**300**		

B. Joint arrangements that are not entities (JANEs)

7444 FRS 9 (4) A reporting entity may enter a variety of commercial arrangements, some of which result in the creation of entities. Where a joint arrangement is set up to carry out a **specific project** with no planned activity after its completion, this usually implies there is no separate trade or business and, therefore, cannot be classified as a joint venture under FRS 9. Even if the participants have a **long-term interest** and have **joint control** within an arrangement, this would not necessarily represent a joint venture, unless it constitutes a legal entity.

A JANE represents a **contractual arrangement** under which the constituent parties engage in joint business activities. A JANE **does not carry on a trade or business of its own** and is simply an extension of the separate businesses of its investors.

A contractual agreement where all significant matters of operating and financial policy are predetermined, does not in itself, create a legal entity as the policies are those of its participants and not those of a separate undertaking.

7445 FRS 9 (8) **Criteria** In practice, a joint arrangement **is not an entity (JANE) if**:
– its activities do not amount to its carrying on a trade or business of its own;
– it is no more than a cost or risk sharing device for carrying out a process in the participants' trades or businesses;

– the participants derive their benefit from products or services taken in kind rather than by receiving a share in the results of trading; or
– each participant's share of the output or result of the joint activity is determined by its supply of key inputs to the process producing that output or result.

Although a JANE **may give the legal appearance** of a joint venture, in substance the arrangement may not amount to an entity, as there may be little commonality of interest between the partners. 7446 FRS 9 (9)

Examples of joint arrangements include:
– joint marketing;
– joint distribution; and
– shared production facilities.

EXAMPLE **Scenario A – Joint marketing**
A typical example is a joint marketing or distribution network or a shared production facility. Therefore, a joint arrangement carrying out a single project as, for example, often occurs in the construction industry, is unlikely to meet the criteria of carrying on a trade or business of its own. Instead this is likely to be a facility or agent in its participants' trades or businesses and a cost or risk-sharing device.

Scenario B – Joint distribution
In another example, the investor's reward may involve taking products or services in kind. A joint arrangement may be formed to cover a research project where the investor's gain from the benefits of the research undertaken without being charged for its use by the research institution, such as a university, in return for funding.

Scenario C – Shared production facilities
Investing entities may share in the profits of any joint arrangements, determined by their supply of inputs to the venture. This arrangement can only apply where it is possible to segregate clearly the activities of the joint arrangement. This type of agreement is similar to the type of joint arrangement that has the form but not the substance of a joint venture (see ¶7454).

Joint arrangements that appear to be **no more than agents** for the interest of the respective ventures should be accounted for as a JANE.

Accounting treatment

The **general rule** is that participants in a JANE should account for their own assets, liabilities and cash flows, measured according to the terms of the agreement governing the arrangement. Some assets, liabilities and cash flows may be wholly attributable to one participant or shared in which case, they must be accounted for proportionally in the individual entity accounts of the participants. 7450 FRS 9 (18)

EXAMPLE **Accounting for joint arrangements that are not entities**

Scenario A
Two construction companies, X and Y, set up two joint ventures to build a hospital and access roads. **Joint venture 1 (JV1)** is recognised as an entity under FRS 9 as it will build and maintain the hospital for 30 years under a PFI contract. **Joint venture 2 (JV2)** is accounted for as a JANE as it will construct the access roads (but will not maintain them), under a separate contract with JV1.
The **accounting treatment** of Joint venture 1 – both company X and Y should account for the joint interest under the gross equity method, after eliminating their respective share of unrealised profit Joint venture 2 should be accounted for as a JANE, as follows:

Separate assets, liabilities, cash flows: Construction equipment, materials, resources
Shared assets, liabilities, cash flows: Construction equipment, project management expenses, maintenance expenses.

Scenario B
Aircraft production consortium
Three aerospace companies, A, B and C, jointly manufacture commercial passenger aircraft for sale and share the revenue in agreed proportions. Company A manufactures the fuselage, B the wings and C the engines. The sales revenue is handled by a **jointly owned company**.
Separate assets, liabilities and cash flows: manufacturing facilities, supplies and stocks of unused and partly finished goods, labour costs.
Shared items: revenue from sales, expenses of jointly owned company.

Changing nature of a joint arrangement

7452 The nature of a joint arrangement may change over time and should be reflected in the accounting treatment. For example, a pipeline operated as a joint arrangement that initially provided a service only, directly to the participants, may develop into a pipeline business providing services to others (i.e. joint venture), in which access to the pipeline is sold on the open market. The stocks of oil running through the pipeline are separate assets. In this scenario, the pipeline itself is a shared asset, along with any revenue from third party sales; shared liabilities include running and financing costs.

C. Joint venture in form not substance

7454 FRS 9 (25) There may be circumstances where a reporting entity operates through a structure that has the appearance of a joint venture, in so much that the participants hold a long-term interest in an entity and exercise joint management. However, a joint venture does not exist where there is an extremely **limited commonality of interest** between the venturers, each of which, in effect, operates its own business independently of the others within that structure.

This **form of joint venture** differs from a JANE in that there are no shared assets, liabilities or cash flows.

7456 **Accounting treatment** The nature of such a structure, means that the framework entity acts merely as an agent for the venturers, with each venturer able to identify and control its share of the assets, liabilities and cash flows within that framework. Therefore, in order to **reflect the substance** of its operations, **each venturer should account directly** for its share of the assets, liabilities and cash flows arising within the entity, as predetermined by the agreement governing the venture.

Some **special purpose vehicles** operate in this manner. An example is an arrangement whereby mortgages or loans are secured through a special venture. Each of the participants in the arrangement is able to segregate the assets that each has contributed to the venture, as well as any associated benefits and risks. **Where such an arrangement exists** and is conducted through the medium of a limited company, the undertaking will only be a joint arrangement if it acts as an agent for its principals. The accounting treatment required for arrangements that resemble joint ventures in form not substance, is the same as that outlined for JANEs.

EXAMPLE Four investors form a company X, to supply IT services to a customer. Two investors supply the hardware and the other two the software which are then sold on to the customer. The sole purpose of the arrangement is to meet the customer's requirement for a single source supplier. Each investor is only entitled to the profits from the venture which are generated from the sale of items that they supplied to company X. The determination of the profit and the treatment of company X's own operating costs, are set out in a shareholders' agreement entered into by each of the venturers.

SECTION 4

Principles and rules of equity accounting

7460 FRS 9 (31) When calculating the values to be included in the investor's consolidated financial accounts, using the equity method for associates and the gross equity method for joint arrangements, the same **accounting principles and policies** used in the consolidation of subsidiaries by the investor, should be applied.

Fair values and goodwill

1. **On acquisition**, fair values should be attributed to the associates' underlying assets and liabilities, which provides the basis for subsequent amortisation. **7462** FRS 9 (31)

2. Both the **consideration paid** for the acquisition and the goodwill arising should be calculated in the same way as on the acquisition of a subsidiary.

3. The associates' assets used in calculating the goodwill arising on its acquisition **should not include** any goodwill carried in the balance sheet of the associate.

4. Subject to the presentation requirement in FRS 9, **the goodwill balance** should be treated in accordance with the provisions of FRS 10 "Goodwill and Intangible Assets" (¶1000).

5. Where there has been **impairment in any goodwill attributable** to an associate or joint venture, the goodwill should be written down and the amount written off in the accounting period should be separately disclosed. FRS 9 (38)

6. Thereafter, **any impairment in the underlying net assets** of an associate or joint venture, would normally be reflected at the level of the entity itself and no further provision against the investor's share of these net assets, would usually be necessary. Fair value is discussed in greater detail in ¶6864.

Period-end

Where the period-end of an associate or joint venture **differs from that of the investor**, the entity should be included on the basis of financial statements prepared to the investor's year end. **Where this is not practicable**, the entity should be included on the basis of financial statements, prepared for a period ending not more than three months before the investor's period end. **7464** FRS 9 (31d)

Price sensitive information **In certain cases**, the publication of the financial statements might release restricted, price-sensitive information relating to the associate or joint venture. In these circumstances, financial statements prepared for a period that ended not more than six months before the investor's period-end may be used. **Any changes after the period end** of the associate or joint venture and before that of its investor that would materially affect the view given by the investor's financial statements, should be disclosed. **7465**

Rules governing the provision of information may restrict the extent to which the financial statements of an investor may include information about its associates and joint ventures, unless such information is available to other interested parties at the same time. An investor should be aware of any regulations (and how to satisfy them) on the publishing of information about its associates and joint ventures.

Inter group transactions

Where **profits and losses resulting from** transactions between the investor and its associate or joint venture are included in the carrying amount of assets in either entity, the part relating to the investor's share should be eliminated. This required adjustment **applies only** in the investor's consolidated financial statements, to transfers of assets or liabilities to set up a joint venture or to acquire an initial stake in an associate. **7466** FRS 9 (31b)

EXAMPLE A sale made from **an associate to an investor** will result in an asset that appears in the consolidated balance sheet, whilst any profit will be included in the associate's profit and loss account. The **double entry on consolidation** is as follows:

dr Share of associate/joint venture profit
cr Stocks or other asset – with the investor's share of the unrealised profit or loss.

If a sale is made from **an investor to an associate**, the asset will appear within net assets of the investee and the profit will be included within the group's profit or loss. The entries needed to account for the investor's share of the unrealised profit or loss are as follows:

dr Consolidated profit and loss account
cr Share of associate net assets or joint venture gross assets.

An example of a transaction requiring this treatment would be where assets representing an investor's contribution to a joint venture are transferred at a gain.

Where associates and joint ventures are **not part of the investor's group**, balances between the investor and its associates or joint ventures are not eliminated and therefore unsettled normal trading transactions should be included as current assets or liabilities.

Beginning or cessation of relationship

7468 FRS 9 (40) The **general rules** for determining when an associate or joint venture relationship begins or ends are as follows:

a. An investment **becomes an associate**, on the date which the investor meets the two essential requirements for defining an associated undertaking; namely that the investor holds a participating interest and exercises significant influence. An investment ceases to be an associate on the date it no longer fulfils either of the above elements.

b. An investment **becomes a joint venture** on the date the investor begins to control an entity jointly with other venturers, provided that it has a long-term interest. An investment ceases to be a joint venture on the date which the investor no longer enjoys joint control.

7470 **Disposal of interest** When an interest in an associate or joint venture is disposed of, the profit or loss arising on disposal should be calculated, after taking into account any related goodwill that has not previously been written off.

7471 FRS 9 (41) **Piecemeal disposals** Where an investment in an associate or joint venture is disposed (or acquired) of in stages, processes similar to those set out for subsidiaries in FRS 2 "Subsidiary undertakings" should be followed (see also ¶7100).

UITF 31 (11) *MEMO POINTS* UITF 31 "Exchanges of businesses or other non-monetary assets for an interest in a subsidiary, joint venture or associate", covers the treatment in consolidated financial statements of transactions where an entity (A) exchanges a business or other non-monetary asset for an interest in another entity (B), which then becomes an associate, joint venture or subsidiary.
The abstract discusses whether businesses acquired in this manner should be accounted for at **fair value** at the transaction date or at book values, and how any gain or loss arising on the transaction should be reported.
1. **If accounted for at fair value**, then any difference between these values and book values should be attributed to goodwill.
2. **If the fair value of the consideration** is less than the book value of the part of the business or non-monetary assets exchanged by company A, then A should recognise a loss, as an impairment in accordance with FRS 11. Any loss in excess of the impairment loss, should be reflected in the profit and loss account.
3. **Any gain arising** on the exchange that is not realised should be reported in the STRGL.

Options, convertibles or non-equity shares

7472 FRS 9 (33) The investor may hold options, convertibles or non-equity shares in its associates. **The conditions attached** to such holdings should be considered, along with any costs relating to the exercise of options or exchanging the convertibles, or future payments in relation to the non-equity shares. Care should be taken not to count any interest twice.

Retained interest

7474 FRS 9 (42) There may be instances where an entity ceases to be either an associate or joint venture, but the investor nevertheless retains an interest in the investee. Then the **initial carrying amount** of any interest retained in the entity, is based on the percentage retained of the final carrying amount for the former associate or joint venture, at the date the entity ceased to qualify as such (including the investor's share of associates profits or losses up to that sale date).

The initial carrying amount **should include** any related goodwill in terms of FRS 10, "Goodwill and Intangible Assets" and if calculated on this basis, then the carrying amount should be reviewed and written down, to its recoverable amount.

Former associates or joint ventures **When an entity ceases** to be either an associate or joint venture, the investor may retain all or some of its interest in that entity as a simple investment. 7475 FRS 9 (43)

The initial carrying amount of any **interest retained** in a former associate or joint venture is a surrogate cost derived from the former carrying amount rather than any consideration paid. In applying the requirement to review and write down that initial amount, to its recoverable amount, it should be noted that the recoverable amount could be affected by the amount that has been paid in dividends or through other distributions to owners.

An interest in another entity that ceases to be a joint venture may still qualify as an associate. Once an interest qualifies as long-term it should continue to be treated as long-term, irrespective of whether the investor intends to keep its interest or dispose of it.

An **investment may be increased** so that it becomes an associate where: 7476
- the group acquires a further shareholding that takes it over the 20% barrier; or
- the group acquires significant influence.

In the former case, the consideration paid by the investor plus cost of additional shareholdings should be compared with the fair value of the underlying net assets and liabilities of the associate, at the date the shareholding exceeded 20%.

In the latter case, the relevant valuation date is when significant interest influence was acquired, with the differences between the price paid and the fair value of underlying assets and liabilities representing goodwill.

Subsidiary that becomes an associate A parent company could dispose of part of its shareholding in a subsidiary but retain an investment exceeding 20% plus significant influence; the subsidiary then becomes an associate. 7478

The **accounting treatment** is as follows:
- the subsidiary's results are consolidated up to the date it ceased to be a subsidiary;
- the profit or loss on disposal is calculated by comparing the sale proceeds with the group's share of the subsidiary's net assets at the disposal date;
- the results of the associate are included in group accounts on an equity basis from the date the former subsidiary became an associate; and
- in the group balance sheet, the investment in the associate is shown at cost, plus share of associate's retained profit or loss since acquisition (less goodwill written-off).

Treatment of losses and interests in net liabilities

The investor should record changes in the carrying amount for each associate and joint venture, even if application of the equity method or gross equity method results in an interest in net liabilities rather than net assets. 7480 FRS 9 (44)

The **only exception**, is where there is sufficient evidence that an event has irrevocably changed the relationship between the investor and its investee, in that the investor downgrades its investment in an associate or joint venture to that of a passive investment.

Evidence that the necessary irrevocable change has taken place, includes a public statement from the investor that it is withdrawing, or confirmation that the direction of the operating and financing policies of the investee is to become the responsibility of the investee's creditors (e.g. bankers), rather than its equity shareholders.

Where an interest in net liabilities arises, the amount recorded should be shown as a provision or liability.

Non-corporate associates and joint ventures

There may be situations where an investor has an interest in a non-corporate associate or joint venture. In such instances, the investor should ensure that **all its liabilities** with respect to that entity are reflected appropriately in its financial statements. 7482 FRS 9 (46)

Where an investor has an interest in an **unincorporated entity**, a liability could arise, for example, as a result of joint and several liability in a partnership, that exceeds the amount resulting from only taking into account the investor's share of net assets. In these circumstances it may be necessary either to include an additional amount for that liability or to report it as a contingent liability.

Investment funds

7484 FRS 9 (49) **Venture capital companies** have successfully argued that equity accounting is inappropriate for them in determining the valuation of investment funds. As such, investment funds can now account for investments that might otherwise be regarded as associates or joint ventures using the same accounting policies as those applied to other investments in its portfolio. This rule now applies even if the investor exercises significant influence or joint control.

The rationale is that the investments must be held as part of a basket of investments with a marketable value, rather than as medium through which the investor carries out its business. Investments of this type are now excluded from the requirements of FRS 9.

Where the investor still exercises **significant influence** over financial and operating policies of the various investments, as is often the case in the venture capital industry, then the reasons and effect of invoking the **exemption clause** in FRS 9 must be given.

Group interests

7486 FRS 9 (32) Where the **investee is a group**, the investor's share is the aggregate of the parent's interest and the interests of its subsidiaries in the investee. The group's aggregate interest in that entity provides the basis of its entitlement to dividends and other distributions.

7488 **Percentage shareholding** The most straightforward example is where the investors hold only an interest in the equity share capital of an associate or joint venture. In this case the number of shares held is divided by the total number of shares in issue to ascertain the percentage shareholding.

Complications arise when the investor holds **different types of shares** or where the entitlements to dividends and other distributions are different. In this case the actual rights and substance attached to each class of share must be considered in order to determine the appropriate percentage held, and the level of group interest.

EXAMPLE A group owns 30% of the **equity shares in an associate** that has remitted £75,000 in dividends, and all 200,000 of the 4% cumulative preference shares in issue. The **investor's (the group) share of net assets** is determined by adding together its entitlement to dividends on the preference shares with the dividends from the equity shareholding.
In this instance the total dividends were:

Equity dividends.	£75,000 x 30% = £22,500
Preference dividends	£200,000 x 4% = £8,000 Preference dividends.

Whether the 30% equity shareholding in addition to the preference shares could be deemed to be a **participating interest**, depends on the substance of the specific rights attached to the preference shares.

7489 **Economic interest** Although entities X and Y may have an equal shareholding in a joint venture 50: 50, they may have an agreement whereby one company is entitled to a greater share of the profits, say 55: 45. In this instance it would be more appropriate to equity account for the economic interest rather than the equity shareholding.

7490 **Calculating group interests** An associate may itself have subsidiaries, associates or joint ventures. These are known as **direct interests**.

1. In such cases, the results and net assets to be taken into account by the equity method are those reported in the investee's consolidated financial statements. This includes the investor's share of the results and net assets of its associates and joint ventures, after any adjustment necessary to support the investor's accounting policies.

2. Where an investing group holds an **indirect interest** in an associate or joint venture through a subsidiary undertaking, or another associate or joint venture, then the investor's

share of the results and net assets should be based on the aggregate holdings of the investor and its subsidiaries. Interests held by associates and joint ventures of the group should be disregarded, as the parent has little or no control over these shareholdings.

The **following example** illustrates how Company A calculates both its direct and indirect holdings in company D. 7492

EXAMPLE **Calculating Company A's direct and indirect interests in Company D.**

Classification	Share	Note
Direct holding in D	25%	
Indirect holding in D via B	20%	1
Indirect holding in D via C	0%	2
Total share	45%	

1. A holds a controlling interest in B and is therefore able to control all of B's 20% stake in D, which should be aggregated in full.
2. A does not hold a controlling interest in C and is not able to control any of C's 25% stake in D, which is disregarded in determining whether D is an associate of A.

Accounting treatment
A's consolidated statements:
The share of the associate's results (operating profit to tax line) and net assets:
- 45% share of D
- 20% share of C (to include C's 25% share of D).

Minority interests
The share of the associate results attributable to minority interests.
- 6% share of D (equal to the minority interest in B (20 % –14 % (70 % x 20% = 14 %)).

SECTION 5

Disclosures

The **general disclosures** for associates and joint ventures are contained in the Companies Act, FRS 9, and SSAP 25 "Segmental Reporting". 7494

The general disclosures required for both the equity and the gross equity method must be given separately. Certain information is required to be given on the face of the primary financial statements for all associates and joint ventures, with other supplementary information given by way of note. The **level of disclosure** is also dependent upon the extent of the investor's interest in the associate or joint venture. FRS 9 (57)

1. Companies Act disclosures

Associates and joint ventures (arrangements)

The Companies Act requires the following disclosures where, at the end of a financial year, a company has a significant holding in an undertaking which is not a subsidiary of the company: 7496
- the name of the undertaking;
- if the undertaking is incorporated outside the UK, the country in which it was incorporated;
- the identity of each class of shares held separately in the undertaking by the parent and other group companies;

– the proportion of the nominal value of the shares of that class represented by those shares, separately for parent and other group companies;
– the aggregate amount of the capital and reserves of the undertaking as at the end of its relevant financial year; and
– the profit and loss for that year.

If the holding is less than 50% and the undertaking is not required to deliver or publish financial statements, then the disclosures required by the Companies Act do not apply.

Joint ventures

7498 Where a joint venture is dealt with in consolidated financial statements by use of the **proportional consolidation method**, the following disclosures are required in respect of the undertaking:
– its name;
– the address of the principle place of business;
– the factors on which the joint management is based; and
– the proportion of the capital of the joint venture held by undertakings included in the consolidation.

Where the financial year of the joint venture did not end with that of the company, the date of its most recent year-end must be disclosed.

Where an undertaking included in the consolidation **manages another undertaking jointly** with one or more other entities, which are not included in the consolidation, then the other undertaking ("the joint venture") may be dealt with in the group accounts by the proportional consolidation method, **provided it is not**:
– a body corporate; or
– a subsidiary undertaking of the parent company.

Although, the use of proportional consolidation is permitted by the Companies Act it does not fit with the requirements of FRS 9; as such this method is not greatly used.

Disclosure exemptions

7504 There are a number of available reliefs from the disclosure requirements of the Companies Acts, such as prejudicial or excessive information.

7506 There may be circumstances where in the opinion of the directors, the disclosures required would be **seriously prejudicial** to the business of that entity, or any of its subsidiary undertakings. The fact of the non-disclosure must be stated.

In these cases, the Secretary of State may approve non-disclosure if the undertaking:
– is established under the law of a country outside the United Kingdom; or
– carries on business outside the United Kingdom.

7508 **Excessive information** The directors of the company may be of the opinion, that the number of entities requiring disclosure is such, that compliance with the provision would result in information of excessive length being given.

In such a case, the information need only be given for those undertakings:
– whose results or financial position, in the opinion of the directors, principally affected the figures shown in the company's annual financial statements; or
– they are excluded from consolidation under Section 229 (3) of the Companies Act 1985.

Where advantage is taken of the above relief from disclosure:
– a statement that the information is given only regarding significant undertakings must be given in the notes accompanying the company's annual financial statements; and
– detailed information not disclosed in the notes to the financial statements, must be annexed to the company's next annual return. This provision is reinforced with a penalty regime.

2. FRS 9 disclosures

FRS 9 disclosures supplement those required by the Act. There are however, **no exemptions** from the detailed disclosure requirements under FRS 9 for associated undertakings, preparing either shorter-form accounts or abbreviated accounts for small or medium-sized companies. 7510

Principal investments

The names of the principal associates and joint ventures should be disclosed in the financial statements of the investing group, showing: 7512 FRS 9 (52)
- for each class of issued shares the proportion held by the investing group, indicating any special rights or constraints attaching to them;
- the accounting period or date of the financial statements, where these differ from those of the investing group; and
- an indication of the type of its business.

EXAMPLE **Notes to the accounts**
Principle associates and joint ventures as at 31 December 2010

Company	Country of incorporation	Group equity holding %	Total issued capital £m
Hamish Kilpatrick	Scotland	35.6	1.5
BICC Finance	Holland	46.5	2.0
Capital Projects	England	25.6	8.5
Metrorail	England	50.0	15.2
Environmental Services ltd	England	50.0	7.6

Associates or joint ventures whose results did not, in the opinion of the Directors, materially affect the results or the assets of the Group are not shown.

Contingent liabilities and commitments Any information relating to the financial statements of associates and joint ventures, that should have been noted had the investor's accounting policies been applied, and that are material to understanding the effect on the investor of its investments should be disclosed, in particular the **investor's share of**: 7514 FRS 9 (53)
- contingent liabilities incurred jointly with other venturers; or
- the capital commitments of the associates and joint ventures themselves.

Restrictions on distributable reserves There may be circumstances where there are significant statutory, contractual or exchange control restrictions on the ability of an associate or joint venture to distribute its reserves, other than those shown as non-distributable. In such cases, the extent of the restrictions should be indicated. 7516 FRS 9 (54)

Balances between investor, associate and joint venture The amounts owing and owed between an investor and its associates or its joint ventures, should be analysed into amounts relating to loans and trading balances. 7518 FRS 9 (55)

Rebuttal of the twenty percent rule There may be instances where the 20% rule that implies that the investor has a participating interest or exercises significant influence over its investee (through either share ownership or voting rights), is rebutted. In such instances, a note should explain why the facts rebut the assumption. 7520 FRS 9 (56)

An investor not preparing consolidated financial statements If the investor does not prepare consolidated financial statements, it should present the relevant figures for associates and joint ventures, as appropriate, by either: 7522 FRS 9 (48)
- preparing a separate set of financial statements; or

– by showing the relevant amounts, together with the effects of including them in the entity's own financial statements, as additional information to its own financial statements.

Threshold disclosures

7524 FRS 9 (57) The **general rule** is that disclosures required for all associates and joint ventures should be supplemented if **certain thresholds** are exceeded. The thresholds are applied by comparing the investor's share, for either its associates or joint ventures in aggregate or its individual associates or joint ventures, with the corresponding amounts for the investor group (excluding amounts included under the equity method for associates and the gross equity method for joint ventures) of:
- gross assets;
- gross liabilities;
- turnover; and
- operating results (on a three year average).

If any of the relevant amounts for the investor's share exceed the specified proportion of the same amounts for the investor group, the threshold has been exceeded and the additional disclosures outlined below, should be made.

Where the **investor's share** in any **individual associate or joint venture exceeds** a 25% threshold with respect to the investor group, the associate or joint venture should be disclosed in a note to the accounts, along with its share of the relevant categories as listed in the table below.

Disclosures Associates and joint ventures	Aggregate disclosure 15 per cent threshold	Aggregate disclosure 25 per cent threshold
Name		Yes
Share of:		
Turnover	**Yes** (Associates only)	**Yes**
Profit before tax		**Yes**
Taxation		**Yes**
Profit after tax		**Yes**
Fixed assets	**Yes**	**Yes**
Current assets	**Yes**	**Yes**
Liabilities within one year	**Yes**	**Yes**
Liabilities due after one year or more	**Yes**	**Yes**

7525 If **one individual associate or joint venture** accounts for primarily all of the amounts included for that class of investment, only the aggregate, not the individual information need be given, provided that this is explained and the associate or joint venture identified, as illustrated in the following example.

In addition to the disclosures required, as outlined in the table above, **further information should be given** where necessary to aid comprehension of the nature of the amounts disclosed. In deciding the most relevant balance sheet headings to use in the analysis, regard should be given to:
- the nature of the business; and
- provide an indication of the size and maturity profile of the liabilities held.

EXAMPLE **Notes to the accounts – Joint ventures**

The group has investments in joint ventures established to provide long-term services to the government as part of the Private Finance Initiative (PFI). The aggregate share of the net assets of all joint ventures are noted below.

Share of joint venture balance sheets (extract)

	£ 2010	£ 2009
Fixed assets	115,367	99,655
Current assets	11,286	8,756
Liabilities due within one year	(6,789)	(5,897)
Liabilities due after one year	(98,756)	(82,633)
Net assets	**21,108**	**19,881**
Net loans to joint ventures	2,010	1,655
Total investment in joint ventures	**23,118**	**21,536**

Included within the aggregated figures above is the Group's share of AMC Group Ltd, the details of which are separately shown below.

Group's share of AMC Group's:

Profit and loss account	£ 2010	£ 2009
Turnover	**9,578**	**8,569**
Operating profit	5,456	4,689
Interest	(4,568)	(3,897)
Profit before tax	888	792
Tax	(267)	(253)
Profit after tax	**621**	**539**
Balance sheet		
Fixed assets	77,850	79,865
Current assets	8,622	7,387
Liabilities due within one year	(5,895)	(2,758)
Liabilities due after one year	(70570)	(75,384)
Net assets	**10,007**	**9,110**

Additional information.
The group has a contingent commitment to invest a further £4.25m in AMC.
The Group also has investments in other joint ventures with the government as follows:
a. £2.5m in equity in Chertsey Healthcare (Ltd) in which it has a 35% interest.
b. £6.5m in equity in Woodford Healthcare Ltd in which it holds a 45% stake.
All joint venture borrowings are without recourse to the Group.

3. SSAP 25 disclosures

If an associate accounts for at least 20% of the total results or net assets of the reporting entity (investor), the following disclosures are required under SSAP 25 "Segmental Reporting"; namely, the entity's share of associates' results before tax, minority interests and extraordinary results and net assets. 7526

SECTION 6

Comparison between UK GAAP and IAS (IFRS)

The two international accounting standards dealing with associates and joint arrangements are IAS 28 "Accounting for Investments in Associates" and IAS 31 "Financial Reporting of Interest in Joint Ventures". There are at present no plans for full UK convergence with IFRS. 7530

1. Associates

The requirements of FRS 9 and IAS 28 are broadly similar for associates, both requiring the use of the equity method in the investor's consolidated statements. However, **the criteria** 7532

for classifying associates in FRS 9 are considered more restrictive than those in IAS 28. Some investments classified under IAS 28 as associates may not be associates under FRS 9.

Key differences

7533 The principal differences are as follows:
1. The **emphasis in the FRS** is on both the existence of and the exercise of significant influence, whereas IAS 28 focuses only on the existence of significant influence, which it defines as the "power to participate in the financial and operating policies of the investee". This definition implies that the investee has ability to influence the investee without necessarily doing so.
2. IAS 28 contains the **rebuttable presumption of significant influence** where an investor holds, either directly or through subsidiaries, 20% or more of the voting power of the investee. This presumption is mirrored in the companies legislation, although the FRS moves away from this threshold noting that it suggests, but does not ensure, that the investor exercises significant influence over that entity. The presumption of the exercise of significant influence at the 20% threshold is rebutted, if the investor does not meet the criteria for the exercise of significant influence.
3. IAS 28 **excludes from equity accounting**, any associate that is acquired and held exclusively with a view to its subsequent disposal in the near future or which operates under long term restrictions, that significantly impair its ability to transfer funds to the investor.
4. IAS 28 stipulates that an associate be included in its investor's individual financial statements using the **equity method** or at cost or revalued amount. This includes investors that do not have subsidiaries but do have associates. In this respect IAS 28 is more comprehensive than FRS 9. Under the equity method, investments in associates are classified as non-current assets and disclosed separately on the face of the balance sheet. The FRS requires an associate to be carried at cost or valuation in its investor's individual financial statements.
5. Under IAS 28, the **consolidated income statement should reflect** its share of the results of the operations of the investee. The treatment in the FRS is different in that the investor's share of its associates' operating results should be brought into its consolidated profit and loss account immediately after group operating profit, after its share of the operating results of its joint ventures, if appropriate.
6. The **additional disclosures** required at the 15 and 25% thresholds by the FRS are not required by the IAS.
7. Under IAS 28 **any losses incurred** by the associate are recognised, only to the point the investor's interest is reduced to nil. A liability on an investment in a subsidiary is only recognised if the investor has incurred obligations on behalf of the associate.
8. IAS 28 **exempts** venture capital organisations, mutual funds, unit trusts and other similar entities from the need to apply equity accounting to investments over which they exercise significant influence, and which were initially accounted for at fair value or classified as "Held For Trading" in accordance with IAS 39.

MEMO POINTS In October 2010 the ASB issued a proposal to introduce an IFRS framework for medium-sized entities (FRSME), not covered by the FRSSE or full IFRS (Listed companies). The intention is that the new framework will replace the FRSSE from 1 July 2013 and is based on the IFRS for SMEs. FRS 9 requires that associates be accounted for using the equity method and joint ventures by the gross equity method. The FRSME has three options; namely: The cost model, the equity method and the fair value model.

7534 **First-time adoption** Where entities are classified as associates under IFRS, but not UK GAAP, an entity adopting IFRS for the first time, has the option of applying the business combinations exemption contained in IFRS 1. This stipulates how to determine goodwill without having to undertake a retrospective fair value exercise.

2. Joint ventures

7535 IAS 31 defines a joint venture in similar terms to those used in FRS 9, and identifies three general categories of joint venture as follows:
– jointly controlled operations;

- jointly controlled assets; and
- jointly controlled liabilities (JCE's).

The **key difference** is that, the IAS states that it is **the contractual relationship** between the entities that determines whether it represents a joint venture or associate. If a contractual relationship doesn't exist then neither can the joint venture. The contract itself plus the minutes of meetings between the ventures should be taken into consideration, in determining the exact relationship.

The **contract should cover** the joint ventures:
- activity;
- timescale;
- reporting obligations;
- appointments to the board and voting rights;
- capital contributions by the ventures; and
- details of sharing the income, expenses and profits of the venture.

Furthermore, FRS 9 requires that an entity must exist before a joint venture accounting can be adopted. This requirement does not exist in the IAS.

Proportional consolidation IAS 31 prefers, whereas FRS 9 strictly prohibits, the use of line-by-line proportionate consolidation, which involves the investor including its share of assets and liabilities of a joint venture in its financial statements. IAS 31 also sets out the rules covering transactions between a venturer and a joint venture. **7536**

IAS 31 **allows as an alternative**, the use of the equity method for reporting interests in joint ventures which are entities. FRS 9 requires the use of the gross equity method for joint ventures.

Threshold based disclosures The additional disclosures required at the 15 and 25% thresholds by the FRS are not required by the IAS. **7539**

Jointly controlled entities 1. JCE's that do not carry on their own business are accounted for as JANEs. There is no such distinction in IAS 31. **7540**

2. IAS 31 applies to parties to a joint venture that do not have any subsidiaries, but do have investments in JCE's. This is wider than the requirements of FRS 9.

3. IAS 31 **exempts** venture capital organisations, mutual funds, unit trusts and other similar entities, from the need to proportionately consolidate or equity account investments over which they exercise joint control, and which were initially accounted for at fair value or classified as "Held For Trading" in accordance with IAS 39.

MEMO POINTS The IASB has issued an exposure draft (ED 9 Joint arrangements) proposing amendments to IAS 31; this ED forms part of a convergence programme between the IASB and the US Financial Accounting Standards Board (FASB) and is designed to provide investors with more information about operations an entity conducts through joint arrangements.

CHAPTER 6

Partnerships

OUTLINE ¶¶

A partnership **is defined** as the relationship between persons carrying on a business with a view to profit. Partnerships range from an informal grouping between two people to professional practices comprising several hundred partners, usually bound by a written partnership agreement that sets out how the partnership will operate and the profits or losses allocated. 7600

Partnerships can be structured in a number of ways as summarised below. The most common forms are qualifying partnerships and limited liability partnerships (LLP's). An overview of the legal and administrative requirements are covered in the tables below. Limited companies have been included for comparative purposes.

7602

Types of partnership – legal framework					
	Unlimited partnerships	**Limited partnerships**	**Limited liability partnerships**	**Limited company**	**Qualifying partnerships**
Legal framework	Partnership Act 1890	Limited Partnerships Act 1907 The Legislative Reform (Limited Partnerships) Order 2009	**1.** Limited Liability Partnership Act 2000 **2.** Limited Liability Partnership Regulations (LLP) SI 2001/ 2008/2009 **3.** LLP SORP 2006 (Revised 2010)	Companies Acts 1985 (as amended), 2006	**1.** The Partnerships and Unlimited Companies Regulations 1993 (SI 1993/1820) **2.** Part VII CA 1985 (amended 2006)

Types of partnership – legal framework					
	Unlimited partnerships	**Limited partnerships**	**Limited liability partnerships**	**Limited company**	**Qualifying partnerships**
Legal status	No separate legal status		Separate legal entity – independent of members	Separate legal entity – independent of members	
Liability of members	Unlimited	Must have 1 general partner with unlimited liability	Liability of individual members limited	Liability of members limited to investment in company shares	
Constitutional basis	Partnership agreement preferable- default provisions available		Members' agreement preferable –default provisions available	Memorandum and articles of association –mandatory	

7604

Types of partnership – administrative framework					
	Unlimited partnerships	**Limited partnerships**	**Limited liability partnerships**	**Limited company**	**Qualifying partnerships**
Contracts	Signed by partners in own name	General partner can sign contracts	Partnership may contract, sue and be counter sued in own name	Company may contract, sue and be counter sued in own name	
Ownership of assets	Partnership Assets owned independently by specific partners		Can legally own assets in own name	Can legally own assets in own name	
Management of business	All partners can participate in management and sign legally binding contracts	A limited partner should not take part in management of business- otherwise liable for partnership debts	All members can take part in management of the business	Directors act on behalf of company	
Taxation	Partners – assessed to income tax		Partners – assessed to income tax	Corporation tax	
Audit	No statutory requirement		Mandatory- unless audit exemption apply.	Mandatory- unless audit exemption apply	Mandatory- unless audit exemption apply
Filing of accounts	No statutory requirement		Mandatory- within 9 months of financial year end	Mandatory- within 9 months of financial year end	Mandatory- within 9 months of financial year end

MEMO POINTS 1. The Department for Business, Innovation and Skills (formerly the Department for Enterprise and Regulatory Reform (BERR)), has published a **consultation document** covering the application of the new Companies Act (2006). The document sets out in detail which provisions are expected to apply to LLPs, including filing periods and late filing penalties.
2. The BIS also intends to **exempt LLPs from a number of provisions** contained in the new Companies Act, because there is no distinction between those who manage the business and the owners. These provisions include the statutory duties of directors and derivative actions.
3. The provisions relating to **overseas companies** (except trading disclosures) **and directors' duties** contained in the Companies Act 2006 will not apply to LLPs. The current system of incorporation will also be retained but modified to comply with the requirements of the Companies Act.

A. Qualifying partnerships

A qualifying partnership including a limited partnership, **is defined as such** under the Qualifying Undertaking Regulations, if all of the members are either: 7606
- a limited company;
- an unlimited company (or a Scottish firm), each of whose members is a limited company.

Qualifying partnerships are required to prepare financial statements which must be filed with the Registrar of Companies, although **many partnerships avoid these requirements by** taking advantage of the exemptions available under the Qualifying Regulations (¶7610).

MEMO POINTS The Department for Business, Innovation and Skills (BIS) has issued a regulation correcting a technical defect in the Partnerships (Accounts) Regulations 2008, relating to the preparation and publication of annual accounts by certain types of partnerships, including limited partnerships incorporated under the Limited Partnerships Act 1907. The new regulation incorporates a revised definition of a "qualifying partnership" and is effective for accounting periods beginning on or after 6 April 2011.

"Indirect members" The **definition** of members of a qualifying partnership **is extended to include** the following indirect members: 7608
- an unlimited company (or Scottish firm), whose members are themselves limited companies; or
- a member of another partnership each of whose members is a limited company.

The **obligation to file, publish and deliver** financial statements for the partnership is extended to indirect members that have an interest in the partnership through an unlimited company.

EXAMPLE **Qualifying partnership**
The partnership has two members, Smith and Jones. Jones is unlimited but has two members who are limited. Therefore, the partnership is a qualifying partnership. If either A. or B. were unlimited then the partnership would not be a qualifying partnership, as all members must be limited companies.

Exemptions

The Regulations governing the preparation, delivery and publication of financial statements offer a **key exemption** to qualifying partnerships. Where at **least one member** of the partnership is a resident of an EU member state and consolidates or equity accounts for the qualifying partnership, then there is no requirement to prepare financial statements for the partnership. 7610

Where **advantage of the above exemption** is taken (under Regulation 7), then any member of the qualifying partnership which is also a limited company, must disclose the name of one member or parent undertaking in whose group financial statements it has been consolidated. 7611

It is quite common for this exemption to be applied, because even though the majority of partnerships consist of a small number of partners, there is usually one partner with sufficient interest or control who can consolidate or equity account for their interest.

Where the partnership is structured so that no one member exercises significant influence, and group accounts are not prepared, the exemption under Regulation 7 is not available.

EXAMPLE **ABC Group Ltd**
Financial statements – period ending 31 December 2010
Note 15 Qualifying partnerships

The group holds a 40% interest in the joint venture partnership Thameside Smithson, which has been included in these financial statements on a consolidated basis (equity accounting). As such, advantage has been taken of the exemptions permissible under Regulation 7 of the Partnerships and Unlimited Companies (Accounts) Regulations 1993.

Reporting requirements

7614 Partnerships **not entitled to the exemptions** available under Regulation 7 are required to prepare and deliver financial statements, including a directors' report to the Registrar of Companies. The financial statements must state that they have been prepared under the Regulations and must also be audited.

7616 **Requirements for limited companies** **Each limited company** that is a member of a qualifying partnership at the end of the financial year must:

1. Attach a copy of the partnership financial statements to its own annual financial statements delivered to the Registrar. This requirement is subject to the exemptions set out in ¶7610 above.

2. Give to any person on request:

i. the name of each member required to deliver to the Registrar, a copy of the partnerships latest financial statements; and

ii. the name of each member incorporated outside the UK but within the EU, required to publish partnership financial statements in accordance with the EU 4th and 7th Directives.

7620 **Publication requirements** Subject to the exemptions discussed in ¶7610, there are a **number of additional** publication requirements relevant to a qualifying partnership, whose head office is in the UK and where each of the members is:
– an entity similar to a limited company which is incorporated outside the UK;
– an entity similar to a limited company or partnership, which is incorporated outside the UK and whose members are undertakings similar to a limited company also incorporated outside the UK.

The **following requirements** apply only to those qualifying partnerships, whose head office is in the UK but whose members are incorporated outside the UK, who would not be covered by the requirements set out in ¶7616 above and would not otherwise be required to publish financial statements in the EU.

7622

Requirements for members of a qualifying partnership (where exemptions not applicable)
1. The members of the qualifying partnership should make available at the head office of the partnership, a copy of the latest financial statements for inspection by any person, without charge during office hours. 2. Copies should be supplied to a person upon request. A small administrative charge can be levied.

Penalties

7624 **All members** (or directors of such members) of a partnership at the end of the financial year could be liable on summary conviction to a fine if:

– audited financial statements are not filed with the Registrar of Companies within 10 months of the end of the balance sheet date; or
– the said financial statements do not comply with the Regulations governing delivery and publication.

Disclosures

The following disclosures **are required** in the notes to the financial statements of a company or group, that is a member of a qualifying partnership: 7625
– the name of the entity;
– the address of the registered office or head office;
– a statement that the latest financial statements for the partnership have been appended to the company's financial statements filed with the Registrar; or
– the name of another one entity in which the partnership accounts have been dealt with on a consolidated basis.

The last two disclosures outlined above are not required where advantage has been taken of the exemption in Regulation 7 (see ¶7610).

EXAMPLE **ABC Ltd**
Report and accounts
Note 25. Qualifying partnerships

ABC Ltd owns a 35% stake in the partnership Clowes/Johnstone, which is governed under English Law. The registered office is: 25 Park Avenue, Bankside, London.
A copy of the financial statements for the partnership will be appended to these financial statements to be filed with the Registrar of Companies.

Limited partnerships

A limited partnership (LP) is formed and registered under the Limited Partnerships Act 1907, and **should not be confused** with an LLP. An LP may be a qualifying partnership. Limited partnerships are form of partnership used only rarely in the UK and are useful where one partner wishes to invest in the partnership, without being heavily involved in its day to day activities. 7626

A limited partner contributes a fixed amount of capital. Every LP **must contain at least** one general partner with unlimited liability and one limited partner. A limited partner may not take part in the management of the business or bind the company contractually with third parties. **Where a limited partner does participate** in the management of the business they will, as with the general partners, be liable for the debts and obligations incurred by the business.

The **group aspects** of limited partnerships are covered in the chapter outlining the general requirements of group accounts (see ¶6553).

MEMO POINTS 1. The Government has temporarily shelved a number of planned reforms to partnership law, except for a small number of changes to the registration requirements for limited partnerships. Revisions to the Limited Partnerships Act 1907 affect new registration applications to Companies House.
2. The **principal changes** include the requirement for the name of the partnership to end in LP or Limited Partnership and the need to inform Companies House of any capital contributed by the partners. Other regulations relate to the information that must be supplied on the registration forms. In addition, a certificate of registration will now be issued to Companies House to limited partnerships, confirming when the partnership came into existence.
3. The Legislative Reform (Limited Partnerships) Order 2009 states that a limited partnership is formed on the date it is registered and that the certificate issued by the Registrar is proof of such. All new limited partnerships should include the initial "lp" after their names. in order to clarify their status.

B. Limited Liability Partnerships

7630 Limited Liability Partnerships (LLP) **are defined** as a separate legal entity that combines the benefit of the protection of limited liability for its members, with the flexibility to organise internal structures along the lines of traditional partnerships.

An LLP **should not be confused** with limited partnerships under which at least one partner must have unlimited liability. The liability of the partners in an LLP is limited to the capital they have contributed to the partnership.

The **regulatory requirements** in terms of the filing and audit of financial statements for LLP's are more stringent than for limited partnerships (but similar to limited companies), due to the limited liability of the members. Examples include the professions with member firms (e.g. accountancy or legal). Appropriate **legal and tax advice** should be sought by entities thinking of adopting this type of structure.

SORP (1) The **regulatory framework** is set out in the table in the introduction (¶7602). Regulations issued under the new Companies Act will be phased in over the next 18 months.

MEMO POINTS The Consultative Committee of Accountancy Bodies (CCAB) has issued a revised Statement of Recommended Practice (SORP) for Limited Liability Partnerships (LLPs), incorporating amendments to FRS 25 "Financial instruments: Presentation". The changes concern the treatment of "puttable" instruments and obligations arising on liquidation. The new SORP applies to accounting periods beginning on or after 1 January 2010.

7631 The **purpose** of the LLP SORP is to complement and not replace the reporting requirements under the accounting standards, UITF Abstracts and LLP Regulations. Where **conflicts arise**, the LLP Regulations and accounting standards take precedence. There is no strict legal requirement to comply with the SORP, although non-compliance must be disclosed in accordance with FRS 18 "Accounting Policies".

An LLP entitled to the **exemptions available** to small companies may prepare its financial statements in accordance with the FRSSE.

1. Legal framework

7632 An LLP is a legal entity created under the Limited Liability Partnership Act 2000, and is more similar to a limited company than a partnership. A new or existing firm of two or more persons can incorporate as an LLP, which can own assets and enter into contracts in its own name. **Contractual claims** against third parties will be against the LLP and not against the members themselves. An LLP must register at Companies House.

MEMO POINTS 1. The following regulations have been issued regarding the **accountancy provisions** of the Companies Act 2006, applicable to LLP's; namely:
– The Limited Liability Partnerships (Accounts and audit) (Application of the Companies Act 2006) Regulations 2008 (SI 2008/1911);
– The Large and Medium-sized Limited Liability Partnerships (Accounts) Regulations 2008 (SI 2008/1912);
– The Small Limited Liability Partnerships (Accounts) Regulations 2008 (SI 2008/1912).
These regulations came into force on 1 October 2008.
2. The Department for Business Innovation and Skills has published a final version of the LLP (Application of the Companies Act 2006) Regulations 2009, designed to implement the remaining provisions of the CA 2006. These regulations cover a range of matters, including LLP names and trading disclosures, annual returns, accounts audit, company reorganisation and fraudulent trading. The amendments covering overseas LLPs have not been included. These regulations apply from 1 October 2009. More information on these topics can be found in Company Law Memo.
3. The requirements of the Companies Act 2006 and subsequent regulations do not cover, in relation to LLPs, narrative reporting and summary (interim) financial statements.

Exemptions

1. The Companies Act exemptions **available to small and medium-sized companies** are also available to small and medium-sized LLPs. 7634 SORP (21)

2. The **thresholds** for qualifying as a small or medium-sized LLPs are the same as for small and medium-sized companies.

3. An LLP can file **abbreviated accounts** with the Registrar of Companies (where the LLP is not audit exempt).

4. A **small LLP** can prepare accounts for its members using the disclosure exemptions contained in the Companies Act.

5. The exemption from preparing consolidated accounts is also available to **small and medium-sized groups** headed by an LLP.

"Designated members"

An LLP **must have at least two** "designated members" who should be named on the incorporation document when the company is formed. Where all members are "designated" members this must also be stated. 7635

"Designated members" and other members have the same rights and responsibilities towards the LLP, **but in addition** have the following responsibilities:
- the appointment of auditors when applicable;
- signing the accounts on behalf of the members;
- filing accounts with the Registrar;
- notifying the Registrar of changes in membership, name of LLP or address of registered office;
- preparation, approval and delivery of the annual return to the Registrar; and
- representing the LLP in the event of dissolution or a winding up.

"Designated members" take on the legal administration of the LLP that in a limited company would be dealt with by the Company Secretary or directors.

Where directors **change their status** from "non-designated" to "designated" and vice versa, this should be reported to the Registrar. Changes in membership such as appointments or terminations must also be notified to the Registrar within 14 days.

Audit requirements

LLP's **are subject to** the same audit requirements as private limited companies. A small LLP will qualify for exemption from audit if the annual turnover does not exceed the small company thresholds. 7636

Auditors are appointed annually and only by a designated member.

The **first auditor appointed** by the LLP must be in place before the end of the financial year for which they have been appointed. **In subsequent years**, the auditor must be re-appointed or a new appointment made within two months of the approval of the preceding years financial statements.

2. Preparation of financial statements

The **key requirements** covering the preparation of financial statements for LLP's are covered below. 7640

Accounting records

The requirement for LLP's to keep accounting records is the same as for other types of entity. 7641 SORP (25)

Depending on whether the LLP is entitled to the exemptions for small and medium-sized companies, the **financial accounts should comprise**:
- a profit and loss account (or consolidated profit and loss);

– a balance sheet duly signed by a designated member;
– a cash flow statement;
– a STRGL;
– notes to the accounts; and
– a statement of members' responsibilities in relation to the production of financial statements;
– an auditor's report on the financial statements; and
– a Members' Report.

Formats

7642 LLP's **must prepare** financial statements that comply with the Companies Act and that give a true and fair view. The provisions for small and medium-sized companies contained in the Companies Act are applicable to small and medium-sized LLP's.

The **one exception** in the **profit and loss account** is the heading "Profit or loss for the financial year", which is replaced by "Profit or loss for the financial year before members remuneration and profit shares", as illustrated below.

EXAMPLE **Profit and loss account**
As per Companies Act – Format 1

Profit or loss for the financial year before members' remuneration and profit shares	X
Members' salaried remuneration	(X)
Profit or loss for the financial year available for division among members	X

7643 Part VII SI 2001/1090 **Balance sheet** The balance sheet **must follow** the Schedule 8 formats for limited companies contained in the Companies Act, with one exception. The part "Capital and reserves" (Item K) should be replaced by two new headings specific to LLPs, which should also be shown separately on the face of the balance sheet; namely:
– Loans and other debts due to members; and
– Members' other interests including:
i. Members' capital;
ii. Revaluation reserve;
iii. Other reserves.

Disclosures are required for the **aggregate movements** on the above including:
– capital contributed by the members of the LLP;
– money advanced to the LLP by members in the form of loans;
– monies owed to members in terms of profits;
– other amounts contributed to the LLP by the members; and
– aggregate amounts contributed or withdrawn by members.

7644 **Cash flow statement** The **following adjustments** to the statutory cash flow format are required.

1. Loans and other debts due to members should not be accounted for in net debt but re-designated as members' capital. This is because these loans and debts, although legally liabilities of the LLP, do not form part of the external financing of the LLP.

SORP (67) 2. The heading "Transactions with members and former members" should substitute the heading "Equity dividends paid", with the following disclosures required:
– payments to members;
– members' contributions; and
– retirement benefits paid to former members.

Annual report

7645 The **content** of the annual report for LLP's is principally governed by the SORP.

The annual report prepared by an LLP **should contain** the following:
– financial statements, as required for limited companies in compliance with company law and accounting standards, subject to exemptions for small and medium-sized entities;

- a statement of members' responsibilities;
- an auditor's report on the financial statements where required by LLP Regulations; and SORP (24)
- a Members' report.

Members' report

The SORP recommends that LLP's produce a Members' report consisting of the following: 7646
- the principal activities of the LLP and its subsidiary undertakings, outlining significant changes during the year; SORP (62)
- details of branches located overseas;
- the identity of "designated members" during the year; and
- the policy on members' drawings and the subscription and repayment of capital.

3. Accounting treatment

Members' interests

Members' interests in an LLP previously classified as capital should now be treated as debt due to members. The **exception** is where the LLP has a discretionary right to avoid distributing cash or other assets to the member. 7652 SORP (44)

The **key elements** of members' interests and the required accounting treatment are set out in the table below.

Category	Accounting treatment
Allocated profits	When profits are allocated they become a "debt due to the members". This requires a transfer from "Members' other interests" to "Loans and other debts due to members". **Profit sharing**: Where an LLP has no discretion on distribution of profits, the members' profit shares should be accounted for as an expense in the profit or loss account.
Unallocated profits	Unattributed profits should be shown under "Other reserves" on the balance sheet subsequent to their being allocated
Unallocated losses	Unallocated losses should be deducted from "Other reserves"
Debts due to members	1. The capital in an LLP can be reduced by agreement of members by repayment or conversion to debt. 2. Unless otherwise agreed by the members, debts due to members rank *pari passu* with ordinary creditors in event of a winding-up.

MEMO POINTS **The original SORP remains largely intact**, although the provisions of FRS 25 "Financial Instruments: Disclosure and Presentation" and UITF 39 "Members' Shares in Co-operative Entities and Similar Instruments" influence the presentation of members' interests. Where the LLP does not have the right to withhold payments, then amounts contributed by members to the LLP will be recorded as debt rather than equity. In addition, members' remuneration will be charged to the profit and loss account, rather than treated as an appropriation of profit and any liability for post-retirement payments to members is to be accrued as the rights to the payments accrue.

Interest paid to members on capital

The members' agreement could include a provision for interest to be paid to members on capital invested in the business. A note to the statutory formats for LLPs stipulates, that interest payable to members should not be treated as an expense under the heading "interest payable". 7654

However, interest due on balances with members classified as debt due to members could be treated as an expense and charged to the profit and loss account.

Retirement benefits

7656 SORP (68) LLPs are required to make provisions for post-retirement obligations for their **members** and former members, such as the rights to a share in future profits. The position in respect of **employees** is relatively straight-forward compared with members both past and present. The retirement benefits provided for employees of the LLP are accounted for under the requirements of FRS 17 "Retirement benefits" (see ¶8400), including salaries and benefits awarded to members under membership contracts. A distinction should also be drawn between profit dependent and pre-determined benefits.

The SORP **also advises** the following with respect to retirement benefits; namely that:

1. **Current and past members** are beyond the scope of FRS 17, except when the members are also employees and have related pension entitlements.
2. A liability for the **pension commitments** of non-salaried current members should not be recognised.
3. For **former members, pension provisions** should be made in the financial statements at the date of the members' retirement. The provision should represent the estimated present value of the future payment liabilities.
4. Details should be disclosed in the notes to the financial statements of investments in assets used to fund the **post-retirement benefits**.

7658 **Profit dependent obligations** The LLP **is required to** calculate the value of its retirement benefits provision based on estimates of future profits. If the number of claimants is high or the amounts material, actuarial advice should be sought in calculating the liability. Profit-dependent obligations to former members should be recognised as liabilities in the balance sheet. The requirements of the SORP are as follows:

1. **Retirement provisions** should be recalculated annually to take account of changes:
   - in the number of former members;
   - financial projections; and
   - actuarial assumptions.
2. Any **changes in the level of the liability** should be recorded in the profit and loss account within operating profit and shown separately where material.
3. Where the **liability has been discounted**, the unwinding of the discount should be shown next to the interest line in the profit and loss account.
4. **Settlement and curtailment gains and losses** should be recognised immediately in the profit and loss account.
5. The LLP's **accounting policy note** should detail the policy concerning retirement provisions, stating:
   - the basis for recognition of the liability in the profit and loss account or STRGL; and
   - the actuarial assumptions used to calculate the liability.
6. An **indication should be given** in the notes to the accounts of the expected timing and value of future retirement benefits.
7. When a **member retires**, a transfer should be made to creditors to "Members' interests", from the general reserve or other special reserve specifically designed for this purpose. The provision should be further divided into:
   - Creditors: due falling due within one year;
   - Creditors: due after more than one year; and
   - Provisions for liabilities and charges.

Provisions

7662 SORP (113) Partnership accounting must take account of the fact that partnerships may have different **partnership personnel or profit sharing agreements** in the same year and/or in successive years. Major liabilities are often provided for by spreading them over several years in order to match cash flows.

An LLP may also enter into a guarantee or indemnity in relation to personal borrowings of members. Such guarantees must be provided for where it is probable that the guarantee or indemnity will be called. This is the **principle of "constructive liability"** as defined in FRS 12 "Provisions, Contingent Liabilities and Contingent Assets". If it is unlikely that the guarantee or indemnity will be exercised, its existence should be disclosed in a note to the accounts.

Related parties

The requirements of FRS 8 "Related Party Transactions" including the definitions apply to LLP's. This means that an LLP controlled by another LLP, partnership, or company will be a related party of that other entity. **7664**

Other important considerations are as follows:

1. **Previous partners** of LLP's are deemed to be related parties.

2. The **name of the controlling party** should be disclosed in accordance with FRS 8. This includes an individual or entity that has the ability to direct the financial or operating policies of the LLP, even where not entitled to the majority of the profits or where members act in concert to control the LLP. SORP (121)

3. **Not all members of an LLP** are related parties under FRS 8. The **test** is the level of involvement by the individual member in the LLP. In smaller LLP's, it is probable that all members play a significant role in the running of the partnership and so would qualify as related parties. In larger LLPs there is probably a greater segregation of duties and level of involvement. Certain members therefore, may not be considered related parties compared to key individuals involved in the management of the business (i.e. "Designated members").

4. **Where members of an LLP** are members of **another LLP or partnership**, it does not automatically mean that the businesses are related parties; this must be determined on the basis of common control.

Stocks and long-term contracts

The cost of members' time, such as salaried remuneration and accompanying overheads normally expensed in the profit and loss account, should be accounted for under SSAP 9 "Stocks and Long-term Contracts". Even when the time cost is not included in the cost of stock, the related overheads should be. Long-term contracts should be accounted for in accordance with SSAP 9, FRS 5 and Application Note G – Revenue recognition. **7666** SORP (93)

Taxation

An LLP may have **subsidiary undertakings** that are companies as opposed to partnerships or other LLPs. If consolidated accounts are prepared, the tax liabilities of such entities should be accounted for in the profit and loss account under the relevant heading, with any related liability recorded as a creditor in the balance sheet. **7668** SORP (88)

Where tax is a **personal liability** of the members levied on their remuneration, it is accounted for under "Members' interests" in the balance sheet; separate disclosure of these amounts is not required.

Business combinations

An LLP **may have subsidiary companies**. Therefore, the LLP should follow the normal rules in company law and the accounting standards, modified where necessary to comply with LLP Regulations. The accounting treatment for business combinations which include one or a number of LLPs, should **consider the substance** of the combination. **7670** SORP (95)

The application of UK GAAP concerning mergers and acquisitions and group reconstructions, should be reviewed in context of both consolidated financial statements and the entity's accounts of the LLP.

A business combination **involving two or more LLPs** gives rise to the following scenarios:
- a new LLP is formed;
- a larger combined LLP results; or
- an LLP becomes a member of another LLP.

SORP (98) The required accounting treatment may apply to both the financial statements of the individual LLP, and where appropriate, the consolidated financial statements. The first step is therefore, to determine whether the new business combination is:
- an acquisition;
- merger; or
- the granting of membership to one or more individuals.

7671 SORP (99) **Acquisition accounting** Acquisition accounting **applies where** the conditions for merger accounting set out in FRS 6 are not met. Under acquisition accounting, the fair value of the purchase consideration should be assessed in accordance with the principles of FRS 7 "Fair values in acquisition accounting".

For instance, the **profit sharing** for new members in an enlarged LLP could contain a portion of remuneration that represents consideration for the business acquired, as opposed to being just part of the future remuneration of members. An example would be where members of the entity acquired were awarded an increased profit share arrangement for a limited time after the acquisition.

The situation could also arise where, for example, the consideration paid for the acquisition is in the form of a profit share, under which it is difficult to separate the exact portion forming part of the future members' remuneration from the purchase consideration.

SORP (101) Where **it is not possible to assess** the fair value of the **consideration paid** for the acquired entity in accordance with the principles of FRS 7, the best estimate of its value should be obtained by valuing the entity acquired.

In situations where the **fair value of stocks** and work-in-progress **cannot be derived** from the market value because it is not practical then current cost should be used.

7672 SORP (103) FRS 6 (68) **Merger accounting** Merger accounting is required when all the **criteria specified** in FRS 6 (see also ¶7000) indicate that a merger, as opposed to an acquisition, has taken place. One problem area for LLP's might be the application of the size criteria in FRS 6.

As such, **suitable alternatives** for establishing relative sizes should be considered such as:
- respective revenues;
- profits;
- number of employees; or
- relative voting rights.

In addition, the **nature of the business combination** should be reviewed to determine whether circumstances indicate that the size criteria should be rebutted.

7673 **Group reconstructions** A group reconstruction applies where the **assets, liabilities and business** of a partnership have been transferred into an LLP, incorporated specifically for that purpose. Entities both new and existing, including partnerships, may choose to incorporate as LLPs. Where there is **a transfer of an existing entity** to an LLP, it should be accounted for as a group reconstruction where the conditions of FRS 6 are met. Where the requirements of FRS 6 have not been met, this accounting treatment does not apply.

4. Disclosure requirements

Members' remuneration

The LLP Regulations require an amendment to the statutory profit and loss formats as illustrated in ¶7642 above. The **revised formats** allow for the disclosure of all amounts earned by partners either in the form of salaries, interest on capital or share of profits. These amounts are treated as appropriations of profit rather than as charges in arriving at the profit for the period. The precise nature of the salaried remuneration will depend on each member's contract. **7676** SORP (31)

The SORP requires that **salaried remuneration** should be shown separately on the face of the profit and loss account. This figure should be further analysed in the notes to the financial statements, with details of amounts paid under employment contracts and other sums.

Furthermore, the **treatment of each element** of remuneration should be disclosed by way of note.

Headings	Disclosure required under:	Formula
Members' remuneration	LLP Regulations	
Average number of members in financial year	Required by the LLP Regulations	Divide the aggregate number of members of the LLP for each month by number of months. (LLP SORP 41)
Average members' remuneration	Disclosure voluntary – as not required by the SORP or LLP Regulations	Divide the "Profit before members' remuneration and profit shares" by the average number of members of the LLP
Highest paid member	1. Disclosure of profit (including remuneration) attributable to members with largest entitlement to profit (including remuneration), where the profits of the LLP before members' remuneration and profit shares exceed £200,000. 2. No requirement to reveal identity of highest paid member. (LLP SORP 40)	N/A

Members' interests

A **distinction is made** between "Loans and other debts due to members" and "Members' other interests" and both are disclosed separately on the face of the balance sheet. **7678**

The **key disclosures** required are as follows: SORP (48)
- the amount brought forward from the previous year;
- the movement in the year arising from the profit or loss for the financial year, available for distribution to members;
- amount allocated to members during the year; and
- the year-end balance carried forward.

The SORP provides an **agreed format** for these disclosures (see table below), but encourages further disclosures where this would aid better understanding of the financial statements.

Members' Other Interests						
Category	Members' capital (class as equity)	Revaluation reserve	Other reserves	Total	Loans and other debts due to members less amounts due from members in debtors	Total
Amounts due to members					X	
Amounts due from members	X	X	X	X	(X)	
Members' interests: Balance at date					X	
Remuneration of salaried members, including employment and retirement benefit costs)					X	X
Profit (loss) for the financial year available for division among members			X	X		X
Members' interests after profit (loss) for the year	X	X	X	X	X	X
Allocated profits			(X)	(X)	X	
Surplus arising on revaluation of fixed assets		X		X		X
Introduced by members	X			X	X	X
Repayments of capital	(X)			(X)		(X)
Repayment of debt					(X)	(X)
Drawings					(X)	(X)
Other movements	X	X	X	X	X	X
Amounts due to members					X	
Amounts due form members					(X)	
Members' interest as at 31.12.2010	X	X	X	X	X	X

Creditor protection

7680 LLPs do not have a fixed capital available for the protection of creditors. Therefore, in order to obtain credit, some LLP's subordinate debt due to members to other creditors in the event of a winding up.

The **following disclosures** on creditor protection are required:
– explanation of where "Loans and other debts due to members" rank in relation to unsecured creditors in winding-up proceedings;
– details of any legally enforceable creditor protection measure; and
– disclosure where applicable, of the fact that no such protection is available.

Loans and debts

The LLP Regulations **also require** additional disclosures: 7682
- the total of loans and debt due to members after more than one year;
- the aggregate amount of money advanced by members through loans;
- the aggregate amount of money owed to members for profits and other amounts; and
- debts owed by members to the LLP.

PART 10

Miscellaneous

CHAPTER 1

Overseas Companies

OUTLINE ¶¶

An overseas company is defined as a limited company that is incorporated overseas, but conducts commercial activity in the United Kingdom through a business establishment. Overseas companies are subject to **a different registration regime** from companies incorporated in the UK and registration is not required when there is no actual physical business location. A **single registration and filing regime** will now apply to all overseas companies, following a recent reorganisation of the registration process, which replaced the former "branch" or "place of business" schemes. 7700

UK company law and the EC 11th Directive govern the requirements relating to overseas companies, including the preparation and filing of financial statements; there are no equivalent requirements under IAS (IFRS). There are in excess of 9,000 overseas companies currently registered with Companies House.

MEMO POINTS 1. The terms "financial statements" and "accounts" are interchangeable as are "oversea" and "overseas".
2. The UK comprises England, Scotland, Wales and Northern Ireland. The Channel Islands and Isle of Man are not deemed part of the UK, but Gibraltar is, for the purposes of overseas companies legislation. Under the Companies Act 2006, "GB" has been replaced by "UK", as the act now covers Northern Ireland.
3. The requirements of the Listings Rules and Disclosure and Transparency Rules applicable to overseas companies are beyond the scope of this book.
4. Separate rules exist for credit and other financial institutions that have established an establishment in the UK.
5. More detail on Company Secretarial matters relating to overseas companies can be found in the *Company Law Memo*.

SECTION 1

Registration

A single registration and filing regime will now apply to all overseas companies establishing a business operation in the United Kingdom. Regulations issued under the Companies Act 7702

2006 simplified the registration process and came into force on 1 October 2009. Overseas companies registered before this date under the old **branch or place of business schemes**, will now also be referred to as "establishments", along with all new registrations.

MEMO POINTS 1. The relevant legislation covering the registration of overseas companies is as follows:
– Part 34 Companies Act 2006 (sections 1044-1059);
– The Overseas Companies Regulations 2009; and
– The Overseas Companies (Company Contracts and Registration of Charges) Regulations 2009.
2. Overseas companies that registered as a branch or "place of business" before 1 October 2009 were required to submit a transitional return (form OS TN01) by 31 March 2010.

Establishing a business presence

7704 An overseas company should register at Companies House when it establishes a physical business presence in the UK; namely where:
– it represents a location where there is a physical or visible indication that a company is present and can be contacted;
– it frequently conducts business from a particular location in the UK, even where there is no physical sign of the company's connection to this site;
– the company directors are present at the representative office; or
– there is a share transfer or share registration office.

7707 A business presence is **not established simply by**:
– conducting business through an agent (Re Lloyd Generale-Italiano (1985));
– conducting business from a temporary location, such as a hotel (Deverall v Grant Advertising Inc. (1954));
– owning a resident subsidiary company (Deverall v Grant Advertising Inc. (1954)); or
– operating a property holding company with investments in the UK (Companies House guidance notes).

MEMO POINTS 1. The **tax implications** of setting up a business establishment in the UK must be considered and specialist advice should be obtained.
2. **Guidance notes** on setting up a business establishment are available from Companies House.
3. A **summary** of the old registration structure (pre-1 October 2009) for overseas companies establishing a place of business or branch in the United Kingdom is given in the table below.

Degree of business presence in Great Britain	Registration requirements
Ancillary business activity A "**place of business**" is established if the business has a physical or visible connection with premises (e.g. a sign outside an office), or if business is regularly carried out at particular premises. A place of business is a less significant presence than a branch. A place of business is not established if the business is carried out through a subcontractor or independent agent, nor is it established if the premises are used only occasionally (e.g. a hotel used by a director on his visits).	Place of business scheme
Central to business activity of parent company Similar in operational terms to a subsidiary, although not a separate body corporate A "**branch**" is an establishment which allows business to be conducted through local representatives rather than an overseas office. The organisation must appear to be permanent and must be capable of dealing with business by itself (e.g. through appropriate management and a physical presence).	Branch registration scheme

1. Initial registration

Documentation

An overseas company that has established a presence in the UK **must deliver** to the Registrar of Companies, **within one month** of opening, a completed company registration form OS IN01, containing information about the parent company and the UK operation, including: 7726
- corporate name, plus UK name where different;
- country of incorporation;
- type of company: public or private;
- a list of directors;
- whether company is subject of winding up or insolvency proceedings; and
- the registration fee.

The **following information** is also required concerning the establishment: 7727
- the location;
- date opened;
- details of business activity;
- details of persons resident in UK acting on behalf of the company (directors, secretaries) and the extent of their responsibilities; and
- name of business if different from name of the parent company.

In addition, overseas companies not registered in the EU must give details of the parent company's accounting reference date and filing deadlines in its country of incorporation.

Registrations should be submitted to the Registrar covering the locality of the establishment (i.e. England and Wales, Scotland or Northern Ireland). Constitutional documents and accounts submitted must be in their original language, except where this is not English, in which case certified translations should also be provided. The current registration fee is £20. 7728

Additional documentation required on initial registration If the company is registering its first UK establishment then it must also deliver the following documents to Companies House on registration: 7729
- a certified copy of the constitutional documents (charter, statute, operating agreement); and
- a copy of the latest set of the parent's audited accounts prepared under its national law, plus a certified English translation.

Multiple establishments Where individual business establishments (in UK) are linked together under a **uniform management structure**, all locations can be treated as the same establishment for registration purposes. The test is whether each establishment has its own separate management structure with distinct reporting lines to the parent company. If so, then each unit must register in its own right. 7730

Each time an overseas company opens a UK establishment (from 1 October 2009), it will have to file a return with Companies House, detailing the activities of the company and how the accounting requirements will be met. A certified copy of the company's constitution must also be filed. The deadline for registrations remains one month. If the overseas company has already filed this information in relation to another establishment, then it can refer to that return (by quoting the registration number) and avoid duplicating certain information. 7731

Amendments to original registration

Once an overseas company has been registered in the UK there are ongoing disclosure requirements covering changes to registered details, trading disclosures, accounts, charges, insolvency and cessation of business. 7732

Amendments must be notified to Companies House, within 21 days of any changes to the original information files. Fines will be levied on overseas companies and their officers, if they fail to update their registration details, within the statutory time limits.

These requirements are listed in the table below.

Amendments to registration details	Form
Company details – legal form, accounting requirements, head office address, share capital and governing law.	OS CH02
Changes to business activity of UK establishment	OS CH01
Changes to the constitutional documents of an overseas company	OS CC01
Change of name of overseas company or UK establishment	OS NM01
Directors or secretary or of their particulars (e.g. appointment, termination)	OS AP01-AP04 + OS CH03-CH06 + OS TM01-03
Appointment of person(s) authorised to represent the business establishment, or changes to their particulars.	OS AP05-7 + OS CH 07
Change of UK establishment for which the constitutional documents and accounts of the overseas company are registered.	OS CC02

7736 **Closure of a branch** Overseas companies with an establishment in the UK have to notify Companies House, if the establishment is closed or moves to another part of the UK. Notification is made on form OSDS01 (Reg.77 SI 2009/1801)

7737 **Insolvency** An overseas company that is subsequently wound up, must file certain documents with Companies House in respect of each UK establishment, including details of winding up/insolvency proceedings.

Where an overseas company is wound up or enters other insolvency proceedings after it has registered its UK establishment, it must comply with all filing requirements within 14 days of the commencement of the winding up. Failure to file the required forms renders the defaulting company, officer or liquidator liable to a fine. More information on this topic, with details of all the requisite forms, can be found in the *Company Law Memo*.

2. Filing of financial statements

7738 In general, **all overseas companies** must file a copy of the financial statements of the "parent" with the Registrar of Companies, for each accounting period.

In determining the appropriate filing deadlines, the Companies Act requires a **distinction be drawn** between overseas companies that are required by the law of the country of the parent company to prepare, have audited and publicly disclose financial statements (¶7750), and those entities that do not (¶7756).

7742 **Content of financial statements** The financial statements of an overseas company should for filing purposes **consist of the following**:
– the individual financial statements of the parent prepared in accordance with the requirements of the country in which the parent has its head office;
– the consolidated financial statements where appropriate;
– the directors' report;
– the auditor's report on the financial statements; and
– where applicable, the auditor's report on the directors' report.

7744 **Accounting Reference Period (ARP)** A company **incorporated outside the EC** must notify the Registrar of Companies on registration of its accounting reference period (ARP) and the date by which it must file its financial statements in the country of incorporation. The ARP must be the same as that adopted in its own country.

The rules concerning a company's accounting reference period (ARP) are similar to those in respect of UK incorporated companies (and EU companies), except for the following:
- the date of incorporation is taken as the date the company first established a business presence in the UK; and
- the restriction that the ARP may not be extended twice within five years does not apply to overseas companies.

The Accounting Reference Date (ARD) is the date in each year to which the accounts of are made up. The first accounting reference period (ARP) must run from the date of incorporation in the UK and end on the first anniversary of the ARD. Accounts may be made up to a date within seven days either side of that date if convenient. Subsequent ARPs run from the day following the end of the previous ARP to the next ARD or date within seven days either side of this. **7745**

A branch may **lengthen or shorten** its current and future ARDs by completing the prescribed form and submitting it to the Registrar of Companies. There are no restrictions on how often an ARP may be extended, although it cannot be extended beyond 18 months.

Companies required by law to file accounts in country of incorporation

Filing deadlines After the **initial process of registration**, financial statements prepared for future financial periods must be delivered to the Registrar of Companies, within **three months of the filing date**, in accordance with the law of the country of incorporation. The accounting documents required include the accounts, plus if prepared, a directors' report and audit report. **7750**

In addition to the financial statements, the establishment must also deliver a statement containing details of the following:
- the legislation under which the accounts have been prepared;
- whether the accounts have been prepared in accordance with Generally Accepted Accounting Principles (GAAP); and
- confirmation of whether the accounts have been audited or not, in accordance with Generally Accepted Auditing Standards (GAAS).

The **general rule** is that separate financial statements should be filed for each establishment, except where a principle establishment has been nominated to file financial statements. Where the separate entity financial statements have been consolidated, this fact should be specified in the financial statements of the principle establishment. **7752**

The Secretary of State can **extend a company's filing deadline** if an application for extension is received by him before the expiry of the filing deadline.

Where the law of the country of incorporation allows the disclosure of financial statements in **modified or abbreviated form**, the overseas company may file these with the Registrar of Companies.

Failure to submit the required accounting documents to Companies House will leave the company and its officers liable to penalties, similar to those for UK companies.

Companies not required by law to file accounts in country of incorporation

The financial statements prepared under the laws of a **non-EC country** are only acceptable for filing purposes in the UK, where the law of the country of incorporation also requires the audit and public disclosure of those financial statements. **7756**

Where the **parent company is not required** to prepare and file audited financial statements under recognised accounting principles, in its country of incorporation, then the overseas company must prepare and file financial statements, at Companies House, covering its UK operations. The content of the accounts must meet the requirements contained in the **Overseas Companies Regulations 2009**, or be in accordance with international accounting standards (IFRS). The financial statements must be approved by the board of directors and signed on behalf of the board by a director and delivered to Companies House, within 13 months of the end of the relevant accounting period. A certified translation of the financial statements is required where they are not published in English.

MEMO POINTS Copies of the Overseas Companies Regulations 2009 are available from the Companies House website.

SECTION 2

Special issues

Credit or financial institutions

7788 A credit or financial institution that establishes a business presence in the UK is subject to the registration requirements for overseas companies. **The general requirement is** that credit and financial institutions must file financial statements in the UK, where they are required to do so in the country of incorporation of the parent company.

However, **where audited financial statements** have to be prepared but not filed in the country of incorporation, the institution does not have to file the financial statements in the UK, although a copy must be made available for public inspection at each establishment operating in the UK.

Where the financial or credit institution **is not required** under the law of the country of its parent company, to prepare audited accounts and to file them, it is required to prepare accounts for filing at Companies House.

MEMO POINTS The detailed accounting requirements for credit and financial institutions relating to overseas companies are beyond the scope of this book.

Listed overseas companies

7790 LR 17.46 **Additional requirements** are required for listed companies. An overseas company with securities listed in the UK must comply with the **Listings Rules** and Disclosure and Transparency Rules (DTR) and circulate annual financial statements to all shareholders.

An overseas company with a full UK listing on the London Stock Exchange or the Plus-listed market is required to publish annual financial statements and half-yearly interim reports, that comply with the requirements of the DTR rules.

Financial statements prepared under foreign accounting standards may be accepted by the UK Listing Authority, if the said standards meet internationally recognised standards. Depending on the requirements imposed by the Listings Authority, the overseas company may not be able to take advantage of some of the disclosure exemptions normally available to overseas companies.

Financial statements **prepared under the laws of a non-EC country** which do not incorporate the principle of a "true and fair view", must submit for review, the standards under which they are drawn up.

An overseas company with a registered office in a non-EEA state, whose laws are deemed the equivalent by the FSA, are exempted from the requirements of the DTR rules, covering annual financial reporting and interim financial reporting.

MEMO POINTS Overseas companies should refer to DTR 4 (Periodic financial reporting), DTR 5 (Vote holder and issue notification notes) and DTR 6 (Access to information).

AIM-listed companies

EEA companies listed on the alternative investment market (AIM) are required to publish annual and interim financial statements prepared under IFRS. If at the year-end such a company is not a parent company, it can elect to prepare its financial statements under IFRS or the accounting regulations and legislation of its country of incorporation. Overseas companies registered in non- EEA countries must prepare accounts under IFRS or US, Canadian, Australian or Japanese GAAP. **7791**

CHAPTER 2

Government grants

OUTLINE ¶¶

Government grants are broadly defined as, assistance in the form of cash to a company, in return for past or future compliance with certain conditions relating to the operations of the enterprise. Government assistance may also take the form of subsidised loans or non-cash loans such as guarantees, consultancy, or leasing of government property. **7900** SSAP 4 (22)

The **classification of** government grants as either revenue, capital or non-cash grants, will determine its recognition and accounting treatment. **Capital grants** are generally specific and fund purchases of fixed assets for continuing use in the business. **Revenue grants** on the other hand, can be general (discretionary) or awarded for a specific project. Government grants are generally provided to persuade or assist companies in pursuing courses of action that are deemed socially or economically desirable. The **range of grants** is often flexible and diverse, reflecting changes in the priorities and direction of government policy. **7902**

SSAP 4, "Accounting for government grants", contains the **general principles** that should be applied to different types of government grants. The Companies Act does not deal explicitly with the issue of government grants, although some of its provisions do affect how they are recorded in the financial statements. **7904**

Reporting entities applying the Financial Reporting Standard for Smaller Entities (FRSSE) **are exempt** from applying SSAP 4. Charities are subject to the additional requirements of the SORP "Accounting for Charities", especially with regard to non-cash grants. Higher and further education institutions are covered by the HEFE SORP (see ¶9850).

The relevant international accounting standard is IAS 20 "Accounting for Government Grants".

Definition of government

In respect of government grants, the term "government" is defined as the various tiers of local, regional, and national government, as well as: **7910**
- government agencies and quangos; SSAP 4 (21)
- the European Commission and other EC agencies; and
- other international agencies and bodies.

Government grants **can be awarded** for the following reasons: **7912**
- research and development;
- technical support;
- acquisition of fixed assets;

– reimbursement of costs already incurred;
– financing the activities of a company over a specified period of time; or
– compensation to a company for loss of income.

A. Accounting treatment

7916 The **main accounting issue** is how to treat revenue or capital grant income.

SSAP 4 (4) The accounting treatment adopted for both capital and revenue grants is determined by the application of the matching and prudence concepts. Under the matching principle, **capital grants** intended to subsidise the cost of fixed assets are credited to revenue over the life of the assets involved, whilst **revenue grants** (including discretionary grants) are matched to related expenditure.

1. Recognition in the profit and loss account

7922 The **key principles** are that **revenue grants** should be recognised in the profit and loss account over the same period as the related expenditure, be it revenue expenditure or amortisation of capital expenditure. The **grants should only be recorded** as income, when the conditions that give rise to the grant have been met and there is a reasonable assurance that the grant will be received.

7924 SSAP 4 (8) The **terms and conditions** attached to each grant will vary. The determination of the relationship between grants received and related expenditure is simple, where the grant is a straightforward contribution towards agreed expenditures.

The following **general rules** should be applied:

a. Grants received in respect of expenditure which has already been incurred, should be recorded as income earned and taken immediately to the profit and loss account.

b. If the grant has been received but the expenditure has not been incurred, then it will be necessary to defer a part of the grant in deferred income.

For this purpose, expenditure incurred includes the amortisation of capital expenditure, whilst the unamortised element of the capital expenditure should be regarded as not having been incurred.

Difficulties in matching grant income and expenditures

7928 There may be difficulties in matching the grant to the related expenditure, especially when the reason for the grant is not clear, as illustrated in the following scenarios.

7930 SSAP 4 (9) **a. Where the terms of the grant** do not specify precisely the expenditure it is intended to meet. Examples include grants for capital expenditure that are linked to research and development targets or the general costs of relocating production facilities to government sponsored enterprise zones. In these instances, it is appropriate to consider the circumstances that give rise to the payment of instalments of the grant in determining its recognition.

b. The award of a grant may also **rely on more than one criterion** being met or not tied to any particular expenditure. For instance, a grant may be linked to both capital expenditure and the number of jobs created in a certain time period or by project, or the grant awarded may form part of a package of government assistance with different costs and terms, each requiring a different treatment.

SSAP 4 (11) **c.** The grant might be paid on the **achievement of a non-financial objective**. In these circumstances, the grant should be matched with the identifiable costs of creating and maintaining the jobs for an agreed time period. The costs in these instances may be higher at the start of the project, therefore a higher proportion of the grant should be recognised in the earliest periods.

There are a **number of rules** that cover the **matching process**: 7932
a. If an instalment payment of the grant is dependent on evidence of expenditure being produced, then the income should be treated in the same accounting period as the expenditure incurred.
b. If the grant payment is dependent on another basis, such as the number of jobs created, then income should be matched to the projected costs of reaching that objective.
c. If a grant is designed to reimburse a company for a range of separate expenditures, it should be allocated to each form of expenditure in proportion to the total cost of that type of expenditure, as illustrated in the following example.

EXAMPLE **Capital and revenue grant combined**

A company was awarded a **mixed grant** of £60,000 upfront towards the cost of a project lasting two years to develop new accountancy software. The **revenue portion** of the grant totalled £40k and the **fixed asset** element £20k. Total project costs of £100,000 are to be split evenly over the two years of the project.
The grant is to be apportioned over the life of the project against the following costs:

	Total Cost		Total Grant
– Fixed assets	£20,000	100%	£20,000
– Staff costs	£30,000	50%	£15,000
– Materials	£50,000	50%	£25,000
	£100,000		**£60,000**

Year 1.
At the end of the financial year 2010, fixed assets costs of £20,000 were matched by a capital grant. Staff and material costs of £30,000 were incurred, 50% of which were met by a revenue grant. Additional costs of £50,000 are expected in 2010, 50% of which will be met by a revenue grant of £25,000 carried forward.

Discretionary grants

The government may authorise discretionary grants to be awarded as a **revenue contribution** to certain costs, such as training or the provision of working capital. However, where the relationship between the grant and related expenditure is not clearly defined, a number of accounting treatments are possible. 7934

Depending on the **precise terms** under which a government grant relating to training costs was awarded, it could be treated in the following manner, namely: 7936
– matched directly against training costs;
– deferred and matched with salary costs over the period staff are expected to benefit from the training (i.e. duration of the project);
– simply matched against total project costs; or
– recognised as income when received.

Summary

7938

Purpose of the grant	Recognition in the profit and loss account
Reimburse related expenditure	Recognise in the profit and loss in same period
Immediate financial assistance	Recognise income in period as cash received
Compensation for loss of revenue	Recognise income when cash received
Finance general activities of the enterprise	Recognise income when cash received
Contribution to the purchase of fixed assets (capital grants)	Income recognised over the useful economic life of the asset

2. Recognition in the balance sheet

7944 SSAP 4 (15) In some instances, all or part of the grant may not be immediately recognised in the profit and loss account, in which case it should be classified as deferred income in the balance sheet.

a. Capital grants

7946 Where a capital grant is made towards the cost of fixed assets, there are theoretically **two possible treatments**, namely:

a. The fixed asset is initially recorded at cost and depreciated over its useful economic life. The grant should be treated as **deferred income** and credited to the profit and loss account in instalments over the same period, and on the same basis as the depreciation charge.

b. The grant is deducted from the purchase price or production cost of the relevant asset, reducing the annual depreciation charge accordingly. This is known as the "**netting method**".

Whilst both methods are permitted under SSAP 4, the deferred income method is generally adopted.

Deferred income method

7948 Capital grants should be recorded as deferred income and credited to the profit and loss account over the estimated useful life of the asset.

EXAMPLE A company purchased a fixed asset at the start of 2009 at a cost of £250,000. The asset is deemed to have a useful economic life of 10 years, and is depreciated on a straight-line basis. The company has been awarded a grant of £75,000 towards the cost of the asset. The net charge represents the depreciation charge of £25,000 less the grant income of £7,500.

Year	Asset book value £	Deferred income £	Depreciation £	Grant income £	Net Charge (P & L) £
2009	225,000	67,500	25,000	(7,500)	17,500
2010	200,000	60,000	25,000	(7,500)	17,500
2011	175,000	52,500	25,000	(7,500)	17,500
2012	150,000	45,000	25,000	(7,500)	17,500
2013	125,000	37,500	25,000	(7,500)	17,500
2014	100,000	30,000	25,000	(7,500)	17,500
2015	75,000	22,500	25,000	(7,500)	17,500
2016	50,000	15,000	25,000	(7,500)	17,500
2017	25,000	7,500	25,000	(7,500)	17,500
2018	0	0	25,000	(7,500)	17,500
			250,000	**(75,000)**	**175,000**

Netting method

7952 SSAP 4 (25) Grants may be given as a contribution to assets, which are not depreciated on the basis that they do not have a finite life. Such a policy of non-depreciation is used by the utility companies concerning **infrastructure assets** (¶1472). Grants awarded to cover part of the infrastructure costs are not carried indefinitely in the balance sheet as deferred income but "netted-off" against the expenditure concerned, even though this represents a departure from the Companies Acts.

EXAMPLE Alpha Plc
Annual report and accounts
Non-depreciating assets
Accounting policies (extract)

1. Basis of policy
The financial statements have been prepared under the historical cost convention and, except for the treatment of certain grants, comply with both the Accounting Standards and the Companies Act. A departure from the requirements of the Act is given in the policy note on grants below.

15. Grants
Grants and contributions received in respect of **new infrastructure assets** are treated as **deferred income** and are recognised in the profit and loss account over the useful economic life of those assets. Grants and contributions relating to infrastructure assets have been deducted from the original cost of the fixed assets, contrary to the requirements of Companies Act, which requires assets to be shown at their purchase price or production cost and grants presented as deferred income.
The departure from the requirements of the Act is, in the opinion of the Directors, necessary to give a **true and fair view** as, while a provision is made for the depreciation of infrastructure assets, these assets do not have determinable finite lives and therefore, no basis exists by which to recognise the grants as deferred income. The effect of this departure from the Act is that the cost of fixed assets is £35.7m lower than it would otherwise have been (2009 £21.6M).
Those grants relating specifically to maintaining the operating capability of the infrastructure network, are taken into account in determining the depreciation charged for infrastructure assets.

b. Non-cash grants

Grants can sometimes be given in the form of non-cash assets. For instance, in local enterprise zones, a local authority may lease a factory or land to a company at a peppercorn rent. These assets should be accounted for in the balance sheet at fair value, with the "grant" recorded as deferred income and taken to income over the same period as the useful economic life of the asset. **7956** SSAP 4 (16)

Government assistance in the form of consultancy or advice is now a more popular form of government aid, although it is unlikely that the benefits associated with the non-financial assistance can be quantified for inclusion in the financial statements.

3. Post-income recognition issues

There are a number of post-grant income recognition issues including repayment of grants, asset disposal, taxation and impairment, which are discussed below. **7960**

Repayment of grants

Grant covenants There are usually conditions attached to the receipt of a government grant, in order to ensure that the grants are utilised for the purpose for which they were awarded. The criteria may relate to a specific period of time, such as the retention of an asset for a contracted period, or to a particular event. **7964**

Failure to comply with the grant covenants may mean that the grant has to be repaid. If a breach of the terms of the grant is expected to occur, then provision should be made for the repayment of grants already accrued as required by FRS 12 "Provisions, Contingent Liabilities and Contingent Assets", unless the possibility of repayment is remote. For disclosure requirements relating to contingent liabilities arising on grants, see ¶7990. SSAP 4 (27)

Full or partial repayment Where a company is required to repay a government grant, either in full or part, the amount to be repaid, after allowing for any excess deferred income relating to the grant, should be charged to the profit and loss account as it becomes payable. This treatment is also in accordance with FRS 3 "Reporting financial performance". **7966** SSAP 4 (14)

The **qualifying conditions** that must be complied with are not always linked to the financial period that benefits from the grant income. Certain types of grant may be repayable if assets cease to be used for a qualifying purpose within an agreed time period. **7968**

Asset disposal

In a situation where the company disposes of an asset on which a **deferred income balance** remains, and where the grant has to be repaid, this should be accounted for by first reducing **7970** the balance on the deferred income account, with any additional charge being direct to the profit and loss account.

Where the grant itself does not need to be repaid, then the balance on the deferred income account should be considered in calculating the profit or loss on disposal.

EXAMPLE A company sells an asset originally purchased for £45,000, on which depreciation of £30,000 has been charged. A government grant for £22,500 was awarded to help fund the purchase, which is being released to the profit and loss account over the useful economic life of the asset (15 years).
The asset was subsequently sold for £8,000 after year 10 and the company was not required to repay the outstanding grant.

The profit or loss on disposal can be calculated as follows:

	£	
Cost	45,000	
Accumulated depreciation	(30,000)	(£45,000/15 × 10 yrs)
Net book value	**15,000**	
Less deferred income remaining	(7,500)	(£22,500/15 × 5 yrs)
Net amount transferred to P & L	**7,500**	
Sale proceeds	8,000	
Profit	**500**	

Taxation

7974 SSAP 4 (7) The accounting treatment for taxation purposes will vary according to the terms attached to each grant and the statute or regulation under which it was made. Some grants will be tax-free (capital) whilst others are taxed as income upon receipt.

7976 The **tax treatment** of an item does not necessarily determine its accounting treatment and a grant may be taxed in a different period, from that in which it is recognised in the profit and loss account. Any **timing differences** that may arise between the tax charge and the recognition of the corresponding credit in the profit and loss account, should be dealt with in accordance with FRS 19 "Deferred tax" (¶9000).

7978 SSAP 21 (41) **Leased assets** Tax-free grants that are available to lessors to be set against the purchase price of the assets should be spread over the period of the lease. The grant should be treated as non-taxable income. Grants relating to leased assets should be accounted for in the financial statements of the lessor in accordance with SSAP 21 "Accounting for leases and hire purchase contracts" (¶3400).

Impairment

7980 Where an asset funded through a government grant has become impaired, then the release of the grant to the profit and loss account should match the impairment write-down.

Monitoring the dispensing of grant funding

7981 The ICAEW has issued a "Framework document for accountants' reports on grant claims" (AF01/10), setting out best practice principles for grant-paying bodies, in terms of securing assurance on how grant funding is dispensed. It is hoped that this guidance will help streamline the process for monitoring grant funding and make it more efficient and cost effective, as well as reduce the regulatory burden. The framework document sets out the scope and form of the accountant's report in relation to the level of assurance required, as well as the responsibilities of the funding body and grant recipient in the grant-funding process.

B. Disclosures

There are a number of disclosures required in the financial statements relating to government grants, which are set out briefly below. 7982

Balance sheet The Companies Act balance sheet formats require that accruals and deferred income be shown under the heading "Creditors" or separately as "Accruals and deferred income". Where the deferred income will be released to profit and loss account over several years, the balance at the year-end should be split between creditors due within one year and due after more than one year as appropriate. 7984

EXAMPLE **ABC Ltd. - Annual report and accounts**
Notes to the accounts
Creditors: amounts falling due within one year

	2010	**2009**
	£m	**£m**
Trade creditors	478.2	378.5
Amounts owed to subsidiary undertakings	15.2	12.3
Taxation	25.3	13.6
Dividends	–	5.0
Accruals and deferred income	**245.7**	**137.6**
	764.4	**547.0**

Notes to the accounts The **following information should be disclosed** in the financial statements in respect of government grants: 7986
- the accounting policy adopted;
- type and value of government grants reflected in the financial statements;
- the effects of government grants on the results for the period and/or the financial position of the company; SSAP 4 (28)
- where the results for the period are materially affected by the receipt of government assistance, the nature of that assistance and its impact on the financial statements; and
- where appropriate, the balance on deferred grants should be analysed between its major components, such as building grants or plant and machinery.

Details should also be given of material revenue grants deducted from the cost of an asset as opposed to being treated as deferred income.

The **accounting policy** selected and the periods over which the grants are credited to the profit and loss should be disclosed, where practical. This may not be the situation, if a large number of different types of grant are given. If this is the case, a broad indication of future periods expected to benefit from the grants already received and recognised in the profit and loss account should also, where practical, be disclosed. 7988 SSAP 4 (17)

Where there is some doubt over how the grant is to be recognised in the accounts, and it is a material sum, the entity should disclose the accounting treatment adopted.

The first part of the following example is of a general accounting policy note for government grants. The second part illustrates the accounting treatment for the two elements of the grant; namely a deferred grant and a grant related to the upgrading of the rail network.

EXAMPLE **Railnet Group PLC**
Notes to the accounts
Accounting policies (extract)

2. Grants
Capital grants and other contributions received towards the cost of tangible fixed assets are included in creditors as deferred income and credited to the profit and loss account over the life of the asset. **Revenue grants** are credited to the profit and loss account so as to match them with the expenditure to which they relate.

5. Turnover

	2010 £m	2009 £m
Passenger revenue	742	1024
Revenue grant	**635**	
Freight revenue	26	17
Property rental income	15	13
Other income	21	20
Total	**1439**	**1074**

Revenue grants comprise the following:
– **Deferred income grant**. The Government agreed to release revenues due for settlement in 20X9. The first payment of £215m was received on 30.8.2010.
– **Network grant**. The grant replaces the loss of track access charges forfeited in line with the upgrading of the network and the disruption caused to the train operating companies.

In accordance with SSAP 4, and on the basis that the Directors at the time of the interim statements had reasonable assurance that future payments will be received from the Government, the grants due in respect of services provided in the year have been credited to revenue and amount to £420m.

7990 **Contingent liabilities** Where the possibility exists of **repayment of a government grant**, a contingent liability should be created, and the following information disclosed:
– the amount or estimated liability;
SSAP 4 (35) – the legal nature of the liability; and
– whether any security has been provided by the company in connection with the liability and if so, what security.

7992 **Accountant's report** The ICAEW has issued a "**Framework document for accountants' reports on grant claims**" (AF01/10), setting out best practice principles for grant-paying bodies, in terms of securing assurance on how grant funding is dispensed. It is hoped that this guidance will help streamline the process for monitoring grant funding and make it more efficient and cost effective, as well as reduce the regulatory burden. The framework document sets out the scope and form of the accountant's report in relation to the level of assurance required, as well as the responsibilities of the funding body and grant recipient in the grant-funding process.

C. Comparison between UK GAAP and IFRS

7994 The equivalent international standard to SSAP 4 is IAS 20 "Accounting for Government Grants and Government Assistance". Under IAS 20, grants received to cover the purchase of fixed assets can be treated as either deferred income or deducted from the cost of the asset.

There are no specific **transition requirements** concerning government grants under IFRS 1, as a first-time adopter must apply IAS 20 retrospectively in full.

7995 The following topics are not covered by IAS 20:
– Government assistance in the form of tax benefits;
– Government participation in ownership of an entity; and
– Government grants covered by IAS 41.

Key requirements of IAS 20

7996 1. IAS 20 **requires that all forms of government grants**, including non-monetary grants at fair value, should not be recognised in the financial statements unless it is reasonably certain that:
– the entity will comply with all conditions attached to the grant; and
– the grants will be received.

2. Government grants **should be recognised** as income over the periods expected to benefit from them, having been matched with related costs.

3. **Asset related** government grants should be accounted for as deferred income or deducted from the cost of the asset.

4. The **following disclosures** are required:
- the accounting policy adopted;
- type and total of government grants reflected in the financial statements; and
- details of any conditions yet to be met or other contingencies attached to the award of the grant.

Proposed amendments to IAS 20

The IASB is also **proposing the following amendments** to IAS 20 based on IAS 41, namely: 7997

a. A distinction should be drawn between conditional and unconditional grants.

b. An entity should recognise a government grant as an asset (not necessarily income) at the earlier of:

i. obtaining an unconditional right to receive the grant; or

ii. actually receiving the grant.

c. Introduce the requirement for companies receiving government grants related to the acquisition of assets to test these assets for impairment on initial recognition.

CHAPTER 3

Foreign currency transactions

OUTLINE ¶¶

This chapter reviews the accounting treatment and disclosures required for foreign currency transactions, covering individual companies and the preparation of consolidated financial statements, including foreign branches. Exchange rate gains and losses, the hedging of foreign currency transactions and the financing of foreign equity investments from foreign currency borrowings are also covered. **8000**

A company can **directly enter** into foreign currency transactions before translating them into the presentation currency used in its financial statements (Individual company stage). **8002** SSAP 20 (1)
Alternatively, a company can conduct currency operations through ownership or control

of a foreign enterprise, whose financial statements are then translated into the currency of the investing company for consolidation.

For the purposes of this chapter, a **foreign enterprise is defined** as a company or branch, whose operations are based in a country other than that of the investing company or whose assets and liabilities, are mainly denominated in a currency other than the reporting currency of the investing company.

8003 **Accounting framework** The accounting framework covering foreign currency transactions is now governed by **three different sets of standards**, depending on the size of the entity, the accounting policies adopted and whether the entity is listed. In general, most small and medium sized companies continue to adopt UK GAAP, whilst listed companies must adopt international accounting standards (IFRS).

Entity	Standards
Entities applying the FRSSE	Exempt from applying standards listed below
Companies applying historical cost accounting	SSAP 20 "Foreign currency transactions" and UITF 9 "Accounting for operations in hyperinflationary economies"
Companies applying fair value accounting	FRS 23 "The effects of changes in foreign exchange rates" and FRS 24 "Financial Reporting in Hyperinflationary Economies" + FRS 26 "Financial instruments: measurement and the disclosure requirements of FRS 29 "Financial instruments: disclosures" (¶3400)
Listed companies (IFRS) (see note 1. below)	IAS 21 "Accounting for the effects of changes in foreign exchange rates" and IAS 29 "Financial reporting in hyperinflationary economies"

MEMO POINTS 1. The ASB has issued a draft accounting standard for medium sized companies (FRSME), based on international accounting standards, that will come into force in 2013.
2. FRS 23 and FRS 24 only apply to those entities which have adopted FRS 26, which covers the accounting treatment of all financial instruments, including those involving foreign exchange. FRS 26 is mandatory for the small number of companies who have opted to apply fair value accounting. Most companies will probably continue to adopt SSAP 20 for the foreseeable future.

SECTION 1

Definitions of currency

8004
SSAP 20 (39)
All these **terms/definitions** are regarded as being interchangeable.

Definitions	
"Local currency"	Defined in the accounting standard as the currency of the primary economic area in which the enterprise operates and generates cash flows
"Functional currency"	The term is used more widely in FRS 13 "Derivatives and other financial instruments" and in US GAAP, and in practice is equivalent in meaning to "local currency"
"Reporting currency"	Used in the international accounting standards to describe the currency in which the financial statements are actually prepared. This term is not defined in the UK accounting standard.

MEMO POINTS Under UK company law, there is no requirement for a company to prepare the financial statements it files with the Registrar of Companies in sterling. Other currencies, such as

US Dollars or the Euro may be used. A company may elect to do this, for example, where most of its transactions are denominated in a currency other than sterling. In such cases the functional or reporting currency would be different from the local currency.

Translation process

Translation is the process by which the transactions, balances and indeed complete financial statements denominated in one currency, are converted into the local currency of the individual or parent company. Translation should be distinguished from currency conversion which represents the physical exchange of currency. 8010

The **purpose of the translation** of foreign currency transactions and financial statements is to: 8012

- reflect the transactions and balances in a foreign currency in the company's reporting currency; and SSAP 20 (2)
- highlight the effects of exchange rate changes on a company's profits, cash flow and its equity.

Exchange gains and losses arise primarily on the translation of monetary assets and liabilities and are recorded separately from the original transaction. This is because these transactions result from an event that is unrelated to the original purchase or sale transaction; namely exchange rate movements.

Translation rates

8014

Translation rates for recording transactions in foreign currencies	Description
Historical rate	The exchange rate ruling on the transaction date
Average rate	An approximation of the actual exchange rates prevailing over a given time period (i.e. month, quarter)
Contract rate	Where a trading transaction is covered by a related or matching forward contract, the rate of exchange specified in the contract should be used
Closing rate	The exchange rate ruling at the balance sheet date

SECTION 2

Accounting treatment under SSAP 20

The first stage is the preparation of the financial statements for an **individual company**, including those that are part of a group, prior to the preparation of the consolidated financial statements. 8018

A. The individual company stage

This section covers the procedures to be followed by an individual company accounting for foreign currency transactions. This involves the initial recording of the individual transactions concluded during the financial year, where a distinction first needs to be drawn between non-monetary assets and monetary assets and liabilities. 8020 SSAP 20 (45)

The accounting treatment for **exchange rate gains and losses** arising on unsettled transactions giving rise to monetary assets and liabilities at the balance sheet date is also discussed.

Individual companies Translation date	Non-monetary assets e.g. Stocks, properties, plant and machinery	Monetary assets & liabilities e.g. Cash and bank balances, foreign currency loans, debtors and creditors
Transactions during the financial year	All companies have a choice between: 1. Historical rate 2. Contract rate 3. Average rate **Exemption**: applies to foreign equity investments (¶8220)	When initially recording the transaction companies have a choice between: 1. Historical rate 2. Contract rate 3. Average rate Exchange gains or losses **on settled transactions** are recognised in the profit and loss account (on settlement date)
Balance sheet date	No re-translation	**Unsettled transactions are re-translated using**: 1. Short-term – closing rate (¶8050) 2. Long-term – closing rate (¶8054) (Use of average rate permitted) Exchange gains or losses recognised in the profit and loss account.

1. Transaction recording during the financial year (settled)

8024 SSAP 20 (46) The accounting process is straightforward for companies undertaking a **one-off or small number of individual transactions** in a foreign currency. Irrespective of whether the transaction relates to a non-monetary asset or a monetary asset and liability, it **should be translated at** the historical rate prevailing on the transaction date or a contracted rate where applicable.

For **larger non-listed companies**, the translation process is the same, except greater use is usually made of the average rate of exchange for a given time period (e.g. month, quarter), which may be used as an approximation if rates do not fluctuate greatly.

Where a trading transaction is covered by a related or matching forward contract, the rate of exchange specified in the contract may be used.

Non-monetary assets

8028 SSAP 20 (47) Once a **non-monetary asset** denominated in a foreign currency has been recorded in the balance sheet, its value is set. The transaction is not re-translated and as such no subsequent gains or losses on translation are generated.

However, where for example, the purchase of a non-monetary asset is settled at a date subsequent to that on which the transaction was initially recorded, the actual amount paid in sterling may differ from the amount recorded in the company's ledgers. This difference is treated as a foreign currency gain or loss.

The **one exception to this rule** applies to foreign equity investments hedged by foreign currency borrowings, where the net realisable value of equity investments should, where certain conditions are satisfied, be re-translated at the closing rate at the end of the period. The conditions to be met are specified in ¶8220.

Monetary assets and liabilities

A **settled transaction** is defined as one that is completed by the balance sheet date. Where settled transactions generate exchange gains or losses, the effects of fluctuating exchange rates on settled transactions are automatically reflected in the cash flows of an individual company's operations, as the movement in the exchange rate either increases or decreases the local currency equivalent paid or received in cash settlements. 8032

All exchange gains or losses on settled transactions should be reported as part of the profit or loss for the year from ordinary activities. The distinction between trading and non-trading transactions is primarily an issue of disclosure, as the accounting treatment is the same. A distinction would normally only be made for material trading or non-trading activities. SSAP 20 (49)

Trading activities **Exchange gains and losses** arising from normal trading operations should be recognised in the profit and loss account in arriving at the profit or loss on ordinary activities. In practice they are included under "other operating income or charges". This accounting treatment should be adopted for all exchange rate differences arising from monetary items. 8034 SSAP 20 (8)

EXAMPLE **Treatment of an exchange loss on trading activity.**

In June 2010, a British company purchased for immediate delivery, plant and equipment from a Dutch company for €255,000. The sterling exchange rate was £1 = €1.20. The company's financial year-end was October 2010.
The purchase price was due for settlement two months hence and was recorded as a liability in the accounts at £212,500 (€255,000/1.20). In August 2010, the Euro exchange rate had moved to £1 = €1.10 resulting in a liability of £231,818 and an exchange loss of £19,318, which was recorded in the profit or loss account under other operating charges.

Non-trading activities Exchange rate gains and losses from non-trading activities, such as finance arrangements, will usually be included for the purposes of the year-end financial statements, within "Other interest receivable and similar income" or "Interest payable and other charges". **Exchange gains or losses on extraordinary items**, in the unlikely event that there should be such an item, should be accounted for as part of that item. 8036

2. Unsettled transactions at the balance sheet date

Unsettled transactions are monetary transactions outstanding at the balance sheet date, and can be **classified as short or long-term**. The accounting treatment for exchange gains and losses arising on unsettled (unrealised) transactions is the same as for settled transactions (translated at the closing rate). An average rate may only be used where this provides a close approximation to the closing rate. 8040

Special attention should be paid to the treatment of **unrealised exchange rate gains** on long-term monetary items.

Where there is **a related or matching forward contract** in respect of the underlying transaction, giving rise to the balance, the rate specified in the contract may be used instead of the closing rate. 8042

Also, it is necessary to consider in terms of **prudence**, whether the exchange gain (or the amount by which such a gain exceeds past exchange losses on the same items), recognised in the profit and loss account should be restricted, where there are doubts over the convertibility or marketability of the currency concerned.

Short-term monetary items

Short-term monetary assets and liabilities are items that are realised within one year of the balance sheet date. 8050

Where the **exchange rate differences relate** to short-term monetary items they will be reported in arriving at the profit and loss for the year from ordinary activities, even though the cash has not been physically realised at that instant. SSAP 20 (8)

The **following examples** illustrate the accounting treatment for unrealised exchange rate gains and losses on short-term monetary items calculated at the balance sheet date.

EXAMPLE **Scenario 1**

Unsettled short-term monetary item
Exchange gains or losses
In March 2010, a UK company brought telecommunications equipment from a company in the US for $550,000, due for settlement on 30 June 2010. The $/£ exchange rate on the date of delivery was $1.65 = £1 and the asset and liability initially therefore recorded in the company's books at £333,333. The balance sheet date was 30 May 2010.

At the **balance sheet date** of 30 May 2010, the **creditor** was still outstanding. No further translation of the rate at which the purchased equipment was recorded is necessary. The creditor however, should be re-translated at the rate of exchange at the balance sheet date; namely £1 = $1.52 = £361,842. The **loss on exchange** of £28,509 (£361,842 – 333,333) should be taken to the profit and loss account.

Similarly, if the rate of exchange at the balance sheet date was £1 = $1.75, the creditor balance would be re-translated at £314,286 resulting in the recognition of an unrealised exchange rate gain of £19,047.

Scenario 2
Unsettled short-term monetary item
Exchange gain
Portland Stone Ltd., purchases some goods from Voller AG in Germany on 30 September 2010 for €40,000 due for settlement in equal instalments on 30 November 2010 and 31 January 2011. The balance sheet date is 31 December 2010. The exchange rate moved as follows:

	£ = €
30 September	1 = 1.50
30 November	1 = 1.60
31 December	**1 = 1.70**
31 January	1 = 1.80

The accounting treatment for the following entries is as follows:

A. 30 September 2010 – equipment ordered/purchased
Purchase price (€40,000/ 1.50)

Debit:	Purchases (historical rate)	£26,667	
Credit:	Trade creditors		£26,667

B. 30 November 2010 – (First instalment)
The first instalment of €20,000 (£13,333) falls due. This will now cost €20,000 at €1.60/£1 = £12,500 as the exchange rate has moved from €1.50 to €1.60 to the £. The company has made an exchange gain of £833 (£13,333 – £12,500).

Debit:	Trade creditors	£13,333	
Credit:	Exchange gains: P & L account		£833
	Cash		£12,500

C. 31 December 2010 – the balance sheet date.
The outstanding liability at the year-end will be recalculated using the rate applicable on that date €20,000 at €1,70/£1 = £11,764.
A further exchange gain of £736 has been made and should be accounted for as follows:

Debit: Trade creditors	£736	(closing rate)
Credit: Exchange gains: Profit & loss account		£736

At the year end the remaining creditor of €20,000 is now stated at £12,597 [£13,333 – £736]. The **total exchange gain** of £1,569 (£736 + £833) will be included in the operating profit for the year 2010.

D. 31 January 2011 – (the second instalment)
Portland Stone Ltd. must settle the second instalment of €20,000 at a cost of £11,111 (€20,000/ €1.80). As the £ has strengthened further against the Euro, an additional exchange gain has materialised.

Debit: Trade creditors	£12,597	
Credit: Exchange gains		£1,486
Credit: Cash		£11,111

Reconciliation

	£	
Total cash paid (1st + 2nd instalments) =	23,611	(£12,500 + 11,111)
Trade Creditor initially recorded in the accounts	26,667	
Total exchange gain	**3,056**	(£833 + £736 + £1,487)

Long-term monetary items

Long-term monetary items are items realised more than one year after the balance sheet date. **8054**

Exchange rate gains and losses **arising from the re-translation of** long-term monetary items should be recognised in the profit and loss account, even though they may not be reflected in cash flows for some considerable time.

Predicting the exchange rate at which long-term monetary assets or liabilities mature is a subjective process. However, it is necessary, when stating the liability or asset in the reporting currency, to make the best assessment in the light of the information available. In general, **translation at the closing rate** will provide the best estimate, particularly where the currency concerned is traded on the spot and forward exchange markets (¶8310). There is an important exception to this rule (see ¶8057). **8055**

When dealing with long-term monetary items, **additional factors** must be considered. A **possible conflict may arise** between the requirements of the Companies Act, that only profits realised at the balance sheet date be included in the profit and loss account and SSAP 20, where unrealised gains on long-term monetary items should be recognised in the profit and loss account. The problem is that recognising losses whilst deferring gains, would be inconsistent, as it does not allow for any favourable movements in exchange rates. **8056**

The requirement to give a true and fair view provides the basis for the departure from the Companies Act. Disclosure of this departure and the reasons for it is required in the notes to the accounts. Two such examples are given below. SSAP 20 (10)

EXAMPLE **Departure from the Companies Act**
Nightingale Services - Annual report and accounts 2010

Notes to the accounts
Accounting policies (extract)

Foreign currencies - long-term monetary items

All **transactions** denominated in foreign currencies are translated into sterling at the actual rate of exchange ruling on the date of the transaction.
Assets and liabilities in foreign currencies including **long-term liabilities** are translated into sterling at the rates of exchange prevailing at the balance sheet date.
All **exchange differences** are processed through the profit and loss account. This treatment is required by SSAP 20 "Foreign currency transactions" in order to give a true and fair view of the company's results. **Compliance with SSAP 20** overrides the Companies Act 1985, which states that only realised profits at the balance sheet date should be included in the profit and loss account. The effect of currency revaluation is disclosed in note 5

5. Operating costs (extract)	**2010**	**20X9**
Foreign currency (gains)/ losses	(£1.4m)	(£0.8m)

EXAMPLE **Departure from the Companies Act.**
ABC Ltd. Annual report and accounts 2010

Notes to the accounts (extract)

Foreign currency - unrealised exchange gains

The profit and loss account includes **unrealised exchange gains** of £27,875 (2009 – £45,346) arising from unsettled long-term monetary items. The directors consider this **departure from the statutory requirements** of the Companies Act to include only realised profits in the profit and loss account, necessary in order for the financial statements to provide a true and fair view.

Exception There is one exception to the general rule that long-term monetary items should be translated at the closing rate; namely that an exchange gain (including gains that exceed past exchange losses on the same items) recorded in the profit and loss account should be restricted, where there is uncertainty as to the convertibility or marketability of the currency involved. **8057** SSAP 20 (50)

EXAMPLE **Taschen Rechners Ltd. – Annual Report and Accounts – 2010**
Notes to the accounts (extract)

Taschen Rechners Ltd. has doubts over the **convertibility** of a long-term monetary loan of £3m made to an overseas supplier, on which foreign exchange control restrictions have been imposed prior to repayment. Given the current circumstances, the realisable value of the loan has been assessed and the exchange gains that would arise on re-translation should be withheld.

B. Consolidated financial statements

8060 The **consolidation process** involves the preparation of group accounts for a company and its foreign enterprises including overseas branches. The accounting treatment for consolidating branch accounts and the **choice of translation methods** and allocation of any resulting exchange gains or losses are also considered.

1. Translation methods

8064 SSAP 20 (13) When preparing consolidated financial accounts the financial statements of any overseas operations must be translated into the reporting currency of the parent company, using a recognised translation method.

8066 SSAP 20 (17) There are three methods that could be applied; namely the **closing rate, average rate** and the **temporal method**.

The **method used** for translating financial statements for consolidation purposes **depends on** the financial and other operational relationships, that exist between an investing company and its foreign entities. However, **once a method is adopted** it should be applied consistently from period to period.

8070 In the **majority of circumstances** the closing rate or average rate method is used. In general when the closing rate is used, the currency of the country in which the foreign company operates will be its reporting currency. The temporal method is adopted, primarily where the foreign enterprise trades as a direct extension of the investing company and not as a separate entity and the reporting currency of the investing company will usually be the local currency.

Translation method	Relationship with foreign enterprise	Treatment of gains or losses on retranslation of opening net investment
Closing rate method	Independent of parent company (i.e. subsidiary, associate)	Reserves
Average rate method	As above	Reserves
Temporal method (historical rate)	Extension of parent company (i.e. branch)	Profit and loss account

a. Closing rate method

8074 The closing rate method is also known as the net investment method and it is based on the assumption that a foreign entity operates as a largely independent entity.

8076 SSAP 20 (15) This method recognises that the investment in an overseas company is its net worth, rather than a direct investment in the individual assets and liabilities of the company. Where the **net current assets** and **fixed assets** of the foreign enterprise are primarily financed through borrowings in the local currency, the daily operations of the foreign company will not be fully dependent on parent company finance. In this instance, the foreign enterprise will be managed normally with the aim of providing a stream of dividends to the parent company and as such, use of the closing rate method is more appropriate. The **net investment** in a foreign enterprise owned by the parent company represents its equity stake. The closing rate is more likely to help achieve the objective of translation; namely to reflect the financial results and relationships, as measured in the foreign currency financial statements prior to translation.

Equity investments in foreign enterprises normally take the form of: 8077 SSAP 20 (20)
- share purchases;
- long-term loans; and
- inter-company deferred trading balances (¶8176).

Translation process

8080 SSAP 20 (17)

	Treatment
Profit and loss account	The values in P & L of the foreign entity should be translated at the closing rate for the accounting period.
Balance sheet	The assets and liabilities in the balance sheet of a foreign enterprise should be translated into the reporting currency of the parent company, using the closing rate of exchange ruling at the balance sheet date.
Exchange rate differences	Can arise under the closing rate, if the exchange rate used for translating the balance sheet differs from the rate in force at the previous balance sheet date or at the date of any future capital injection or reduction. Exchange rate gains or losses are taken to reserves.

In the following example, the profit and loss account items of Company B are translated into the currency of the parent company. A similar process is adopted for the assets and liabilities in the balance sheet. **A reconciliation between** the Parent Company and the consolidated profit and loss accounts is also included. 8082

EXAMPLE **Closing rate method – translation process**

Company A purchased 100% of the share capital of Company B, a US subsidiary on 30 September 2010, when the exchange rate was £ = $1.48. The net assets of Company B on this date were £87,330 and Company A paid £117,112 including goodwill of £29,782. Company A used the **closing rate** method for the balance sheet, with the average exchange rate being used for the translation of the profit and loss account.
During 2010, the **average exchange rate** was £1 = $1.50, whilst the closing rate was £1 = $1.47 at the end of 2010 and £1 = $1.52 at the end of 2009. Goodwill will be amortised over a period of 15 years, with a full year's charge in the year of acquisition.

Profit and loss account 2010

	A £	B $	@ $1.50 B in £	Total £
Turnover	845,313	355,750	237,167	1,082,480
Cost of sales	557,000	200,800	133,867	690,867
Gross profit	**288,313**	**154,950**	**103,300**	**391,613**
Overheads	202,800	92,400	61,600	266,707
Profit before tax	**85,513**	**62,550**	**41,700**	**124,906**
Taxation	45,000	21,700	14,467	59,467
Profit after tax	**40,513**	**40,850**	**27,233**	**65,289**
Dividends	25,000	4,000	2,667	27,667
Retained profit	**15,363**	**36,850**	**24,566**	**37,622**
Profit b/f	244,152	65,243	43,495	-
Profit c/f	**259,515**	**102,093**	**68,061**	-

MEMO POINTS 1. Total overheads include goodwill amortisation of $2,307.
2. The total column comprises Company A plus Company B translated at the average rate (including goodwill of $2,307).

Balance sheet 2010

	A	B	B @ $1.47	Total
	£	&	£	£
Tangible fixed assets	348,241	136,000	92,517	440,758
Investments	87,330			-
Goodwill				25,168
	435,571	**136,000**	**92,517**	**465,926**
Current assets	167,694	70,623	48,042	215,736
Current liabilities	116,050	43,760	29,768	145,818
Net current assets	**51,644**	**26,863**	**18,274**	**69,918**
Long-term liabilities	27,700	15,770	10,727	38,427
	459,515	**147,093**	**100,064**	**497,417**
Share capital	200,000	45,000	-	200,000
Profit and loss account	259,515	102,093	-	297,417
	459,515	**147,093**		**497,417**

MEMO POINTS 1. The investment in Company B is replaced by the goodwill arising in consolidation.
2. The share capital is that of Company A.
3. The goodwill on consolidation is $34,615/15 years = $2,307 p.a (x 2 yrs. = $4,614)
A higher goodwill charge was taken in years 1 & 2. $29,782 – $2,307 x 2 = $25,168).
Under FRS 10 "Goodwill and intangible assets" purchased goodwill must be capitalised.

Reconciliation – Calculation of consolidated profit and loss account
1. The balance b/fwd. at beginning of 2010.

	£	£
A Ltd. from profit & loss account		244,152
B Ltd – the increase in profit/loss reserve from acquisition to beginning of 2010		
Beginning of 2010 – Profit & loss $65,243/ £1 = $1.47	44,382	
On acquisition of 30 September 2010 – Net assets of £87,330 less share capital £45,000 = £42,330/ $1.48 =	28,601	
		15,781
B Ltd – The change in shares from acquisition to the beginning of 2010 = $45,000/ 1.52 = £29,605 – $45,000/1.48 = £30,405		(800)
Goodwill amortisation		(2,307)
		256,826

2. Movements during 2010

A Ltd – retained profit from profit/loss account	15,363
B Ltd – Retained profit of $36,850 translated at Average rate of $1.50	24,566
Goodwill amortisation	(2,307)
Exchange differences on translated **retained profit** at the year-end rate of $1.47 in the balance sheet & $1.50 in the Profit and loss account. $36,850/$1.50/47 = £25,068-£24,566	502
Exchange differences on translation of **opening net assets** for B Ltd at the year-end rate of $1.47 in 20X9 & $1.52 for the previous year $110,242/ 1.47 – $110,242/ 1.52	2,467

Opening net assets derived for B Ltd as follows:

– Closing net assets	$147,093
– Less retained profit 2010	($36,850)
	$110,243
Balance sheet – profit and loss account 2010	**297,417**

A **criticism of the closing rate method** is that where it is only applied to some assets this leads to a mixture of items stated at historical rate and others at the closing rate. 8084

---

b. Average rate method

SSAP 20 recognises that the use of the average rate may more fairly reflect the profit and losses, of a foreign entity, than the closing rate as they arise throughout an accounting period. It therefore permits the use of this method as an **alternative to the closing rate**, for the translation of profit and loss account items. If the subsidiary's profit and loss account is translated at an average rate, this should be determined over the accounting period of the individual company and not the group. 8086 SSAP 20 (17)

The average rate method can also be used **by individual companies** with high volumes of foreign currency transactions during the year.

Calculating the average rate

There is no one particular method of calculating the average rate as this will vary from group to group, and between individual companies within a group. For instance, the average rate could be **calculated weekly, monthly or quarterly**. If monthly, the rate could be the closing rate on either the last day or the middle day of each month. A system of weights could also be applied. 8088 SSAP 20 (18)

Whichever method is applied it should be used consistently.

The **average rate is** in practice **determined by**:
- the nature and size of a company's accounting systems;
- the materiality of the transactions;
- the period to which the rate should apply;
- the volume of transactions; and
- the frequency of transactions.

Exchange gains or losses

Where the average rate is used for profit and loss account items any differences between the **average rate** and the **closing rate** should be accounted for in reserves. 8092

If exchange differences arising from the re-translation of a company's net investment in its foreign enterprise, were included in the profit and loss account, the results from the trading operations, as shown in the local currency financial statements would be distorted. Any such **differences may arise from** factors unrelated to the trading performance of the foreign enterprise and, therefore, it would not be prudent to regard them as profits or losses. SSAP 20 (19)

Translation differences arising on the re-translation of the opening net investment in a foreign enterprise should therefore be processed directly through reserves.

---

c. Temporal method

Use of the temporal method is recommended in the situations outlined in ¶8064. 8094

Under the temporal method, foreign currency transactions are translated at the exchange rate ruling on the transaction date (historical or contract rate). The **mechanics of the temporal method** are similar to the procedures adopted, in the preparation of individual company financial statements. **The problem is that** applying this method requires detailed additional record keeping and it is more complicated to use than the closing rate method.

Under the temporal method, all the transactions and balances of the foreign enterprise are accounted for, as if they had been entered into by the investing company in its own currency. 8096 SSAP 20 (22)

Any **exchange rate gain or loss** is taken to the profit and loss account. This contrasts with the closing rate or net investment method where exchange rate differences are taken to reserves.

Application

8100 SSAP 20 (22) Application of the temporal method **may be more appropriate**, where the activities of a foreign enterprise are closely linked with those of the investing company and it is more dependent upon the economic environment of that entity than its own reporting currency.

8102 The **factors that should be considered** in adopting the temporal method include determining:

SSAP 20 (23) a. The currency in which the majority of trading transactions are denominated, such as the invoicing and payment of expenses, or whether the transactions are predominately based in the currency of the investing company;
b. The principal currency to which the financial structure of the foreign entity is exposed;
c. The extent to which the cash flows of the enterprise have a direct impact upon those of the investing company, such as the frequency of cash movements between the group companies or just periodic remittances such as dividends; and
d. The extent to which the operations of the foreign entity directly depend upon the investing company; namely, is the management locally or head office based.

8104 The **temporal method can be used where** the overseas entity:
SSAP 20 (24) – acts as a selling agency receiving stocks from and remitting the proceeds to the investing company;
– produces raw materials, parts or sub-assemblies for shipment to the investing company for inclusion in its own products; or
– is located overseas for tax, exchange control or other reasons that support the raising of finance for other companies in the group.

Translation process

8106

Classification	Treatment
Non-monetary items (stock, fixed assets)	Initially measured at historical cost, translated at the rate ruling on the transaction date and not re-translated at the balance sheet date
Monetary items (debtors, creditors, loans)	Both short and long-term are translated using the closing rate at the balance sheet date
Profit and loss account items (sales, expenses)	Translated at the historic rate. An average rate may also be used except for depreciation and stock. 1.Depreciation should be translated at same rate as for fixed assets. 2. Dividends proposed are translated at the closing rate and dividends paid at the payment date.
Exchange gains and losses on the net monetary assets or liabilities	Should be taken to profit and loss account for the year from operating activities

This example follows on from the one used for the closing rate method with the following **additional assumptions**. All fixed assets where acquired when the exchange rate was \$1 = €1.45. Depreciation totals 40% of the overheads excluding goodwill amortisation and opening and closing stocks were purchased when the exchange rates were €1.49 and €1.52 respectively.

EXAMPLE **Profit and loss account**

	A		B		Ex. Rate	B		Total
	£	£				£	£	£
Turnover		845,313		355,750	1.5		237,167	1,082,480
Opening stock	98,650		16,500		1.49	11,073		
Purchases	547,500		200,000		1.5	133,333		
Closing stock	(89,150)		(15,700)		1.5	(10,466)		
Cost of sales		(557,000)		(200,800)			(133,940)	690,940
Gross profit		**288,313**		154,950			**103,227**	**391,540**
Depreciation		(81,120)						(81,120)
Goodwill amortisation		(2307)						(2,307)
Other overheads		(121,680)		(92,400)	1.5		(61,600)	(183,280)
Profit before tax		**83,206**		62,550			**41,627**	**124,833**
Taxation		(45,150)		(21,700)	1.5		(14,467)	(59,617)
Profit after tax		**38,056**		40,850			**27,160**	**65,216**
Dividends		(25,000)		(4,000)	1.5		(2,667)	(27,667)
Retained profit		**13,056**		36,850			**24,493**	**37,549**

Balance sheet

	A	B	Ex. Rate	B	Total
	£	e	e/£.	£	£
Tangible fixed assets	348,241	136,000	1.45	93,793	**442,034**
Investments	87,330				-
Goodwill					25,168
	435,571	**136,000**		**93,793**	467,202
Stocks	89,150	15,700	1.52	10,329	99,479
Other current assets	78,544	54,923	1.52	36,133	114,677
Current liabilities	(116,050)	(43,760)	1.52	(28,789)	(147,471)
Net current assets	**51,644**	**26,863**		**15,041**	**66,685**
Long-term liabilities	(27,700)	(15,770)	1.52	(10,375)	(38,075)
	459,515	**147,093**		**4,666**	**495,812**
Share capital	200,000	45,000			200,000
Profit and loss account	259,515	102,093			295,812
	459,515	**147,093**			**495,812**

MEMO POINTS Exchange rate differences on monetary assets and liabilities taken to consolidated profit and loss account.

d. Change of method

A company can **in certain circumstances** change the method used for translating the financial statements of a foreign enterprise, from the temporal to the closing rate and vice-versa. Circumstances where this might happen, include **changes to the operational or financial relationships** that exist between a parent and its foreign subsidiary, that render the initial basis inappropriate. A change of method does not constitute a change in accounting policy. No guidance is given in SSAP 20 on this topic but the following is regarded as an appropriate accounting treatment. 8108

Closing rate to the temporal method

8110 This practice **might be adopted where** the operations of the foreign subsidiary have become significantly dependent on the parents reporting currency. The translated values for non-monetary assets at the end of the prior year-end, form the accounting basis for those assets in the period of change and subsequent periods.

There is no requirement to restate non-monetary assets at rates applicable when those assets were originally acquired by the foreign enterprise. Any **cumulative exchange adjustments** for prior periods already taken to reserves, remain there and are not reflected in the profit and loss account in the period of change.

2. Foreign enterprises

8114 The accounting treatment for foreign currency transactions involving foreign branches, associates and joint ventures are outlined in this section.

Foreign branches

8116 SSAP 20 (37) A foreign branch is either a legally constituted enterprise located overseas or a group of assets and liabilities which are accounted for in foreign currencies. This **broad definition** allows, a company owning for instance, a fleet of aircraft or ships to account for each as a separate branch.

Where a UK company undertakes foreign operations through the legal form of an overseas branch, **the translation method adopted will either be** the closing rate or temporal method, depending on the type of operation or activities involved; each branch should be assessed individually.

8118 SSAP 20 (25) The **closing rate method should be used where** the foreign branch operates as a separate business complete with local finance, or as the owner of international assets that earn revenues in a foreign currency and are financed by **borrowings in the same currency**. This rule applies to both the financial statements of individual companies as well as to consolidated financial statements.

EXAMPLE A **branch** operating in Florida has borrowed dollars to finance the construction of a marina on the Florida coastline, generating revenues and expenses in dollars. In this instance the branch clearly operates as a separate distinct business complete with local finance. The **net investment** in the US branch can be accounted for through a Head Office Account, with the closing rate method used to translate transactions. Any **exchange differences** should be taken to reserves.

8120 The **temporal method should be used** when the foreign branch simply operates as an extension of the company's trade and its cash flows directly impact on the parent company's cash flows. If in the above example, the finance for the construction of the marina was raised in sterling, it could be argued that the project is merely an extension of the company's trade, in which case the temporal method would be more suitable.

8122 **Translation process** The translation process is essentially the same irrespective of the translation method adopted and **involves the following stages**:
1. The branch trial balance should be translated into sterling using the closing rate or temporal method as appropriate.
2. Include any year-end adjustments for depreciation, closing stocks, accruals in the foreign currency concerned and then translate values into sterling using the translation method selected.
3. Treat the difference on the branch sterling trial balance as the profit and loss on exchange.
4. The profit or loss on exchange is shown as follows:
- as a movement on reserves if the closing rate used (see example below); or
- in the profit and loss account if the temporal method is used.

5. Combine the sterling branch results with other group companies in the consolidation process.

EXAMPLE **Consolidation process – Closing rate method**

Bliss Ltd operates a branch in Krakow. At 1 January 2010 the exchange rate was £1 = 8 zloty. The summarised branch balance sheet was as follows:

1. Trial balance as at 31 December 2010 (exchange rate 8 zl = £1)

	Zloty	**Exchange rate**	**£**
Fixed assets	850,000	8	106,250
Net current assets	350,000	8	43,750
	1,200,000		**150,000**
Head office current account	1,200,000		

2. The **summarised branch Profit and Loss account ended 31 December 2010** (including year-end adjustments) was as follows:

	Zloty	**Exchange rate** (closing rate)	**£**
Sales	1,500,000	6	250,000
Less cost of sales	650,000	6	108,333
Gross profit	**850,000**		**141,667**
Salaries	250,000	6	41,667
General expenses	150,000	6	25,000
Depreciation	150,000	6	25,000
Net profit	**300,000**	**6**	**50,000**

3. Closing balance sheet: Dec. 2010 – exchange rate 6 zloty = £1.

	Zloty	**Exchange rate**	**£**
Fixed assets (less depreciation)	700,000	6	116,667
Net current assets	800,000	6	133,333
	1,500,000		**250,000**
Head office current account			
Opening balance –Jan. 2010	1,200,000	8	150,000
Profit for the year	300,000	balancing figure	100,000
Closing balance –December 2010	**1,500,000**		**250,000**

4. Treatment of profit or loss on exchange

The **profits or losses on currency translation** are attributable to the current year, the opening balance on the head office current account is translated at the opening rate. The profit for the current financial year of £100,000, which is included in the sterling balance sheet represents the balancing figure, and includes an exchange gain of £50,000.

In the **consolidated accounts**, the translated results of the branch are added to those of the parent company. The exchange gain will be shown as a movement on reserves, as follows:

	£
Opening capital (net investment)	**150,000**
Profit for the year – to 31 Dec. 2010	50,000
Movement on reserves – foreign exchange gains	50,000
Closing capital	**250,000**

Where the **temporal method** is adopted the exchange gain of £50,000 would be included in the profit and loss account for the year ended December 2010.

Foreign associates and joint ventures

8124 The provisions in the accounting standard covering consolidated statements cover the incorporation of the results of overseas associates and joint ventures, through the adoption of the closing rate method. However, where the investing company does not exercise **significant influence** (¶7300) over an associate or joint venture, use of the temporal method may be more appropriate.

3. Treatment of exchange gains or losses

8130 There are a number of other important accounting issues related to the treatment of exchange gains or losses, generated by foreign currency transactions for both **individual companies** and in the **consolidation process**. The topics covered include the accounting treatment of foreign currency exchange gains or losses arising from:
- taxation;
- dividends;
- intra-group trading;
- intra-group loans;
- goodwill arising on translation; and
- the issue of hyperinflation.

Taxation

8132 The gains or losses arising on the translation of financial statements of overseas subsidiaries and associates do not create timing differences for tax purposes. However, gains or losses arising on translation of an entity's overseas assets and liabilities could give rise to timing differences. In addition, exchange gains arising on foreign currency borrowings used by a company to finance or hedge its investment in a foreign enterprise, may be taxable. Determining whether exchange gains or losses are taxable as they arise for accounting purposes or are taxable when the gain or loss is crystalised at a later date, will depend on the election made under the appropriate tax legislation.

The tax rules regarding treatment of exchange gains or losses are highly complex and **specialist tax advice should be sought**

The **circumstances where** a **tax charge** could arise are where:
a. a matching election for tax purposes is not made;
b. the foreign investment and borrowings are located in different companies in a group, and where a matching election is not available; or
c. the offset restriction applies to a matching election under which exchange gains or losses should be reported in the profit and loss account.

MEMO POINTS **Special taxation rules** apply to currency contracts which are beyond the scope of this book.

8134 **Exchange gains and losses** should be accounted for by using either the method of matching assets with liabilities or by deferring the recognition of unrealised exchange gains.

8136 **Matching election** The matching rules allow a company, in certain circumstances, to match by election a liability to particular types of asset. When a matching election is made, exchange gains and losses on the liability or currency contract are held over and matched with the asset when it is disposed of. It is at this point, the **aggregate exchange rate gain or loss** is brought into the accounts as a chargeable gain or loss. A matching election is voluntary and may only be made where the foreign investment and the related currency borrowings are held with the same company.

The **currency in which a given liability is denominated** need not be the same currency as that of the underlying asset; although it much be such that it could reasonably be expected to eliminate the currency risk of holding the asset. For instance, many Caribbean countries peg their currencies to the US dollar, so an asset purchased with Barbadian dollars for example, could be matched to a US dollar loan.

The **matching rules permit** a company to eliminate a mismatch that might occur when a company hedges its balance sheet transaction exposure. Where an election for matching is not permitted or made, then the resulting gains and losses should be reported in the STRGL. 8138

EXAMPLE **Matching election**

Beta Ltd, a UK company, raised a $500,000 in June 2010 to finance the purchase of a controlling stake in a US company. The financial year end is August, UK tax rates are 31% and the relevant exchange rates are:
- August 2010 £1 = $1.50
- August 2009 £1 = $1.60

What are the tax consequences of making or not making a matching election, given that the company adopts the **offset procedure** under SSAP 20 taking any exchange difference on the $borrowing to reserves?
- August 2010 – $500,000/ 1.5 = £333,333
- August 2009 – $500,000/ 1.6 = £312,500

Exchange gain on loan **£20,833**

Matching election requested
If the company makes a matching election there will be no tax consequences, as the sterling value of the liability (loan) at the year end matches fully the sterling value of the asset. The exchange gain of £20,833 matches the exchange loss on the asset taken to reserves.

No matching election requested
The company will have the following tax liability.
£20,833 x 31% = £6,458
£20,833 – £6,458 = £14,375 represents the net exchange gain on the borrowing against the exchange loss of £20,833 carried in reserves. Disclosure is required of both the exchange gain and related tax charge.

Reserves The **tax effects of an exchange gain or loss** already posted to reserves under the offset procedure should continue to be recognised in reserves, in accordance with UITF 19, and SSAP 20, and be reported in the STRGL. 8139

UITF 19 "Tax on gains and losses on foreign currency borrowings that hedge an investment in a foreign enterprise", states that where exchange differences on foreign currency borrowings have been used to finance, or provide a hedge against equity investments in foreign enterprises, these should be taken to reserves and reported in the STRGL, as should the **associated tax charges or credits**. This treatment is in accordance with SSAP 20 (paragraphs 51, 57 and 58) and FRS 3 "Reporting financial performance".

The restriction on the amount of the gains or losses arising on the borrowings that should be dealt with in the STRGL, should, apply after taking account of tax charges or credits attributable to the borrowings. Consideration should also be given to the total cash, the related investments are expected to generate and the exposure created by the borrowings in after-tax terms.

Deferral In recognition of cashflow difficulties that can arise by taxing unrealised gains, companies can defer (for tax purposes) the **recognition of unrealised exchange gains** on long-term capital assets and liabilities; this concession does not extent to currency contracts. 8140

A deferred gain is treated as being realised when the company ceases to hold the asset or carry the liability.

Foreign currency financial statements

The Registrar of Companies will accept annual financial statements denominated in foreign currencies, provided the currency is legal and the sterling exchange rate is disclosed in the notes to the accounts. This requirement is supported by SSAP 20, which permits the preparation of financial statements in a foreign currency if that currency is the "**local currency**" of that company. 8144

8146 **The Euro** Companies with cross-border operations based in the European Union or who have significant trading exposure to the European Union may be required to adapt their accounting practices and operations to accommodate the Euro.

The accounting treatment for **costs incurred in introducing the Euro** (e.g. modifying existing assets) is dealt with in detail in UITF 21 "Accounting for the Euro" and through the disclosure requirements of FRS 3.

8148 UITF 21 (11) Under the closing rate/ net investment method, the amounts in the balance sheet of a foreign entity are translated into the reporting currency at the exchange rate ruling at the balance sheet date. **Translation differences** arise where the closing rate differs from the exchange rate ruling at the previous balance sheet date or after a subsequent injection of capital, and are taken to reserves and reported in the STRGL.

8150 UITF 21 (19) FRS 3 advises that the same **exchange gains or losses should not be recognised twice**. The exchange differences already reported in the STRGL should remain there and not be reported in the profit and loss account when the cumulative differences subsequently become permanent.

Where gains and losses on **financial instruments** used as anticipatory hedges are deferred and later matched with related income or expenses, the introduction of the Euro should not alter this treatment of deferral and matching.

Multi-currency share capital

8156 A UK company can issue shares in a currency other than sterling. The accounting treatment and reporting requirements for foreign currency share capital are not covered in SSAP 20. Multi-currency share capital can either be:
- recorded initially at the historical rate when issued; or
- the shares could be re-translated at the end of each financial year using the closing rate, with any exchange differences taken to reserves.

Inter-company dividends

8160 The accounting treatment of dividends will depend on whether the temporal or closing rate method of translation is used. An **exchange rate gain or loss** will arise if the rate of exchange changes between the date the dividend is declared and the date paid, which is reported in the parent's profit and loss account as an inter-company transaction.

8162 Under the **temporal method** the dividend payment should be translated at the exchange rate ruling on the date the dividend is declared; therefore an exchange rate difference will not arise. The payment and receipt of the dividend will be eliminated on consolidation.

8163 Under the **closing rate method** it is usual that the dividend, declared and accounted for by the foreign subsidiary, will be translated at the closing rate or at an average rate. In the **consolidated accounts**, an exchange rate difference will be generated where the rate used to account for the dividend in the overseas subsidiaries, differs from the rate used to translate and record the dividend in the parent's profit and loss account.

8164 The following examples illustrate the **treatment of exchange gains or losses** arising from the translation of an interim dividend using the average rate, which are posted to the profit and loss account and the final dividend using the closing rate method, which are taken to reserves.

EXAMPLE **Interim dividend – treatment of exchange gains or losses arising.**

Average rate method

A **foreign subsidiary** declared an interim dividend of €75,000 on 30 September 2009, payable on 30 October 2009, with the final dividend payable on 30 April 2010.
The **parent company** prepares final consolidated accounts for the period ending 31 March 2010 and uses the average rate for translating the results of the foreign subsidiary.

The relevant **exchange rates** are as follows:

- interim dividend 30 Sept. £1 = €1.50
- payment date 30 October £1 = €1.55
- **Average rate** for the year £1 = €1.53
- year-end rate 31 March £1 = €1.60

The **interim dividend** will be recorded as follows:

	£	
1. **Subsidiary's** profit and loss account: €75,000		
2. **Parent company** profit and loss account.		
– initially recorded at rate ruling on date dividend declared-30 Sept. 2009 £1 = €1.50	50,000	(historical rate)
– Interim dividend paid 30 October 2009. Rate £1 = €1.55	48,387	(historical rate)
– Exchange loss recorded in the profit and loss account	**(1,613)**	

3. Consolidation

Translation of dividend paid by subsidiary at average rate of £1.53 to 1 Euro = £49,020

Parent company P & L – Dividend received	50,000
Subsidiary P & L – Dividend paid	49,020
Exchange gain	**980**

4. Summary

The total exchange difference in the consolidated financial statements is a **loss of £633** (posted to the profit and loss account), being the difference between the loss of £1,613 in the parent company's financial statements less the gain of £980 arising on consolidation, on the cancellation of the inter-company dividends.

Interim dividend outstanding at the year-end

An exchange rate difference can also arise where the interim dividend remains outstanding at the year-end rate. If this were the case and based on the details given in the example above, the **parent company** should account for the dividend as follows:

	£
– 30 Sept. 2009 £1 = €1.50 =	50,000
– Year-end receivable €75,000 £1 = €1.60	(46,875)
Exchange gains/(loss)	**(3,125)**

The **dividend declared but not paid** should be recorded at the transaction rate and the year-end debtor at the closing rate. The subsidiary should record the year end creditor of €75,000 at the closing rate.
The difference (i.e. £3,125) should be recorded in the consolidated accounts, when the dividends are eliminated on consolidation.

EXAMPLE **Final dividend – treatment of exchange gain/loss**

Closing rate method

As an extension of the above example, the foreign subsidiary declares a final dividend €125,000 for the year ending 31 March 2010, with payment of the final dividend on 30 April 2010. The exchange rate ruling at the date of the final dividend was £1 = €1.60 and at the payment date £1 = €1.65
In the consolidated accounts the dividend should be translated at an average rate of €1.53 = £1.

1. Subsidiary (foreign) company – translated financial statements
The total dividend payable will be recorded in the balance sheet of the subsidiary company under the net investment method at the closing rate, with any exchange difference taken to **reserves**.

	£
Profit and loss account €125,000/ £1 = €1.53 =	81,699

2. Parent company's profit and loss account
The dividend receivable will be translated at the closing rate in both the profit and loss account and the balance sheet.

Dividend receivable €125,000/ £1 = €1.65 £75,758

3. Consolidation

The inter-company accounts will cancel one another out on consolidation, but the dividends will generate exchange rate differences in the profit and loss account that will remain on consolidation.

	£	
Parent company – dividend receivable	£75,758	(€1.65)
Foreign subsidiary – dividend payable	£81,699	
Exchange loss	**(5,941)**	

When the final dividend is paid, in this case 30 April 2010, a further exchange loss of £2,367 will arise. €125,000/ 1.65 = £75,758 – €125,000/ €1.60 = £78,125.

8166 **Dividend declared but still outstanding at year-end** Where a dividend has been declared but is still outstanding at the end of the financial year, the following accounting treatment is necessary.

For the **purposes of consolidation**, the dividend payable in the subsidiary's profit and loss account, will be translated at the exchange rate prevailing on the transaction date, with the year-end debtor posted at the closing rate. Any resulting exchange difference should be taken to reserves using the closing rate method.

The parent company **should account for the dividend receivable** at the closing rate in both the profit and loss account and in the balance sheet. The inter-company accounts will cancel each other out on consolidation. However, the dividends will not cancel each other out in the consolidated profit and loss account with the difference accounted for as an exchange loss.

Intra-group trading

8170 SSAP 20 (12) **Transactions between group companies** Exchange rate differences will arise on transactions between group companies located in different countries, which will not be eliminated on consolidation. Where transactions are recorded in the local currency of the subsidiary concerned, the exchange difference should be reported in the profit and loss account of the enterprise, in the same way as transactions with third parties.

8172 The same **accounting principle** applies to an unsettled inter-company account comprising non-trading transactions, such as where the parent finances the purchase of fixed assets by a foreign subsidiary via the mechanism of the inter-company account.

On consolidation, the net exchange rate gain or loss will have been reflected in the group cash flow, and should be included in the consolidated accounts to reflect the currency risk attached to transactions with overseas companies, albeit group companies. This is illustrated in the example below. Where the **same exchange rate is used by both companies**, one recording a gain and the other a loss, any exchange rate differences will cancel each other out on consolidation.

EXAMPLE A **UK Company** with a wholly-owned subsidiary in Poland, who purchased plant and raw materials from the UK parent, had the following transactions during the year. The financial year-end is 30 November 2010.

Polish subsidiary

Transaction 1

Purchased plant at £275,000 on 31 July 2010	£1 = Zlty 6.0
Paid for plant – 30 September 2010	£1 = Zlty 6.10

Transaction 2

Purchased raw materials at £400,000 – 20 Oct. 2010	£1 = Ztly 6.25
Balance of £400,000 30 November 2010	£1 = Ztly 6.20
Average rate for the year	£1 = Ztly 6.15

The **exchange rate** differences will be recorded in the **profit and loss account** of the Polish subsidiary for the year ending 2010.

Transaction 1	Zlty
Plant costing £275,000 @ 6.0	1,650,000
Paid for plant @ 6.10	1,677,500
Exchange loss	**(27,500)**
Transaction 2	
Raw materials at £400,000 @ 6.25	2,500,000
Outstanding £400,000 at the year-end @ 6.20	2,480,000
Exchange gain	**20,000**

Accounting treatment

The net loss recorded in the profit and loss account was 7,500 zloty. The inter-company creditor of Zl. 2,480,000 in the Polish subsidiary's balance sheet, will be translated into sterling at the closing rate (£400,000). The net exchange loss of Zloty 7,500 should be translated at the average rate or the closing rate. The sterling exchange losses will not be eliminated on consolidation and will be reported as part of the consolidated results of the group.

Transfer of assets The **general rule** is **intra-group profits** arising on the transfer of assets between group companies should be eliminated in full on consolidation, as this does not represent profit generated by the group, where the assets are still held by the company at the balance sheet date. 8174

SSAP 20 **does not offer any guidance on** the exchange rate to be used in eliminating profit, although the average rate for translating the results of foreign operations under the net investment/closing rate method would be appropriate.

Long-term sterling loans and deferred trading balances

A parent company can decide to finance an overseas entity through equity or monetary items such as long-term loans and deferred trading balances. The **choice of financing** will depend on a number of factors including taxation. 8176

Equity finance Where financing is intended to be permanent, any such loans or deferred trading balances should be treated as part of the investing company's net investment in the foreign enterprise. Any **exchange rate differences** arising on such loans and inter-company balances should be dealt with as an adjustment to reserves. 8178 SSAP 20 (20)

The inclusion of long-term loans and deferred trading balances as part of the net investment in an overseas subsidiary is only permitted, when the parent company considers the investment to be as permanent as there is no foreseeable intention to repay such balances. **Short-term loans** that are continuously rolled over may also be regarded as permanent. 8179

The same principle also applies to inter-company balances generated through **normal trading transactions**, where settlement in cash is not envisaged for some considerable time. In these situations the trading balances should be treated as part of the equity stake in the overseas enterprise. 8180

Monetary items There are a number of accounting implications where a parent company provides loans to a foreign subsidiary or vice versa. The **accounting treatment** should reflect the substance of the loan. 8182

Intra-group loans made by the parent company to an overseas group company and denominated in the parent company's functional currency, should initially be recorded by the borrower at the exchange rate ruling on the transaction date. At the balance sheet date thereafter, until it is repaid, the loan should be re-translated into sterling at the closing rate with any exchange differences reported in the consolidated profit and loss account.

On consolidation, the **intra-group loan accounts** will cancel each other out, whilst the exchange difference accounted for in the borrowers profit and loss account, will show through in the consolidated profit and loss account (or reserves if deemed an equity stake). 8184

EXAMPLE **Monetary item**

Parent company's sterling loan to an overseas subsidiary.

A UK parent company has an outstanding loan of £650,000 with a Swedish subsidiary as at 31 December 2010 The relevant exchange rates are:
Opening rate Jan. 2010 £1 = Kr 11
Closing rate Dec. 2010 £1 = Kr 10
In the **financial statements** of both the parent and the subsidiary, the following exchange differences arise if the closing rate is used (balance sheet date).

Parent company

There is **no exchange rate difference** as the loan balance is denominated in sterling.

Swedish subsidiary

Jan. 2010 – Loan balance of £650,000 x 11 Kr = Kr 7,150,000
Dec. 2010- Loan balance of £650,000 x 10 Kr = Kr 6,500,000

Exchange gain **Kr 650,000**

Exchange gain translated at the closing rate @ 10 Kr = £65,000.

Accounting treatment.

Debit: Inter-group loan a/c	Kr 650,000	
Credit: Profit and loss account		Kr 650,000

The **rational** for taking the exchange rate gain to the profit and loss account is that the loan was provided in the reporting currency of the parent company, whilst the exchange rate risk was borne by the subsidiary company.
On **consolidation**, the exchange gain in the subsidiary profit and loss account will be translated into sterling at the closing rate, and should be included in the consolidated profit and loss account. Where the loan is regarded as **long-term** and part of the **equity stake** in the foreign enterprise, the exchange gain should instead be taken to the reserves in the consolidated financial statements. There will be a corresponding exchange rate loss included in reserves that will arise from the re-translation of the net assets of the Swedish subsidiary; there is no impact on group cash flows.

8186 **Long-term loan by parent company to a foreign subsidiary** The accounting treatment for a long-term loan by a parent company to a foreign subsidiary in its local currency, is different from that of a sterling loan from the parent company to the foreign subsidiary. In the **consolidated financial statements**, the long-term loan will form part of the net investment in the foreign subsidiary and the related exchange gains or losses will be accounted for in reserves using the closing rate method.

8188 In the **parent company's financial statements**, the following accounting treatment is required for long-term loans to a foreign subsidiary:
a. If the long-term loan is accounted for in the financial statements of the parent company as a **monetary item**, any exchange differences should be charged to the profit and loss account.
b. Where the long-term loan can be considered a **permanent investment on consolidation** it should not be re-translated in the parent company's books, but retained at the historical rate of exchange. As such no exchange differences arise so reflecting the substance of the loan.
c. Where the long-term loan is **financed by foreign borrowings** by the parent company, the loan should be re-translated to offset currency differences.

8190 **Loans from foreign subsidiaries** Where a parent company receives a currency loan from its foreign subsidiary that it converted into sterling, the accounting treatment of foreign exchange differences in the consolidated financial statements will reflect the treatment in the parent company's financial statements.

8191 SSAP 20 (51) **These types of loan are** sometimes regarded as **hedging transactions** as they reduce the net foreign currency investment in the foreign subsidiary. Where the loan is accounted for in the parent's financial statements, as a hedge against the equity investment under the SSAP 20 offset rules (see ¶8226), any exchange differences on the borrowings should be accounted for in reserves. This will offset any exchange differences on the investment being hedged. A similar treatment applies to the consolidated accounts.

MEMO POINTS The issue of loan repayments is covered in ¶8240.

Goodwill on consolidation

Goodwill may arise on consolidation where a company **acquires the equity share capital** of an overseas subsidiary. If the foreign investment is accounted for using the closing rate method, the issue is whether the goodwill calculated at acquisition should be re-translated at the end of each financial year. 8194

Following the publication of FRS 10 "Goodwill and intangible assets", goodwill should be **capitalised as an intangible asset** and amortised through the profit and loss account over its useful economic life. FRS 11 "Impairment of fixed assets and goodwill" requires capitalised goodwill to be attributed to income generating units in order to facilitate annual impairment reviews. The combination of FRS 10 and FRS 11 support the notion that goodwill should be regarded as part of the net assets in the foreign investment. 8196

Where goodwill arising on consolidation is **not translated but regarded as a currency asset**, any exchange differences arising on foreign currency borrowings, used to either finance or provide a hedge against an investment in a foreign subsidiary would be taken to the profit and loss account. **Exchange differences on the currency borrowings are** however, available for offset against the exchange difference arising on re-translated goodwill, which is added to the opening net investment and taken to consolidated reserves. 8198

EXAMPLE **Neckerman Holdings – Financial Statements 30 June 2010**

Accounting policies (extract)

16. Foreign exchange

Foreign currency assets and liabilities of Group companies are translated into sterling using the closing rate of exchange at the balance sheet date. The trading results of overseas subsidiaries and associated undertakings are translated at average rates of exchange ruling during the year, with any exchange rate differences taken to reserves.
The exchange difference arising on the **restatement of the opening net investment**, including goodwill, to overseas subsidiary and associated undertakings, and of matching foreign currency loans and foreign currency swap facilities, are dealt with as adjustments to other reserves. All other exchange differences are taken to the profit and loss account.

Notes to the financial statements

25. Other reserves	**Group £'000**
As at 30 June 2009	(115,675)
Goodwill written off in year (note 34)	**(18,100)**
Goodwill of associates transferred to profit & loss	**15,600**
Exchange adjustments:	
– goodwill	4,300
– hedging arrangements	(7,350)
As at 30 June 2010	(121,225)

34. Goodwill	**Cost of goodwill eliminated £'000**	**Exchange Adjustment £'000**	**Total £'000**
Eliminated to 30 June 2009	239,600	11,235	250,835
Acquisitions during year			
– Associated undertakings	15,800		15,800
– Other businesses acquired	2,300		2,300
	18,100		**18,100**
Transferred to P & L a/c	(15,600)		(15,600)
Exchange adjustments		(4,300)	(4,300)
Eliminated to 30 June 2010	**242,100**	**6,935**	**249,035**

For a more detailed treatment of goodwill in relation to intangible fixed assets see ¶1000.

Hyperinflation

8200 SSAP 20 (26) The **historical cost** accounts of a foreign enterprises operating in a country suffering from high inflation, will probably be misleading when translated into the **local currency** of the parent company. In this instance, the local currency financial statements of the foreign enterprise should be adjusted prior to inflation, in order to reflect current price levels, as assets acquired in a foreign currency would be worth less in sterling terms, if the local currency has weakened against sterling.

MEMO POINTS The IASB has issued an exposure draft (ED) entitled "Severe hyperinflation", as a proposed amendment to IFRS 1, "First-time adoption of international accounting standards". The ED provides guidance on how to present financial statements for a period during which the entity could not comply with IFRS, because its functional currency was subject to severe hyperinflation. The ED is open for public comment until 30 November 2010.

8202 SSAP 20 does not provide a definition of hyperinflation. The subject has since been addressed by UITF 9 "Accounting for operations in hyperinflationary economies", which **requires adjustments to be made** to financial statements in the following circumstances, where:
- the distortions resulting from hyperinflation effect the true and fair view of financial statements;
- the cumulative inflation rate is approximately 100% over a three-year period; and
- the investing company's operations in hyperinflationary economies are material.

8204 **Other factors** that indicate hyperinflation, are where the general population prefers to maintain its wealth in non-monetary assets or in a stable foreign currency and where interest rates, wages and general prices are linked to a price index.

UITF 9 (6) The assessment of cumulative inflation rates should be determined following one of the **two alternative methods**, suggested in UTF 9 as being consistent with SSAP 20 as follows:
a. adjust the local currency to reflect current price levels prior to the translation process for incorporation in the group accounts, taking net monetary gains and losses to the profit and loss account.
b. use of a third (stable) currency for measuring the results of the foreign operations.

Where the financial statements **are initially prepared in the local currency** they must be translated into the stable currency by use of the temporal method, before conversion to sterling for incorporation in the group accounts. In some Latin America economies, the dollar is the predominant business currency or "local currency".

Where neither of these methods is appropriate, UITF 9 states that companies are permitted to use other methods, as long as they disclose:
- the reasons why neither of the normal methods are inappropriate; and
- the accounting policy that has been adopted to eradicate the distortions of hyperinflation.

Where these overseas operations are material in terms of group results or net assets, disclosure of the method for eliminating the distorting effects of inflation is required.

EXAMPLE **Winwood Holdings Plc – Annual report and accounts**

Accounting policies (extract)
Foreign currency translation

The accounts of overseas subsidiaries and associated undertakings are translated into sterling on the following basis:
a. **Assets and liabilities** at the rate of exchange ruling at the year end date, except for tangible fixed assets of undertakings operating in countries where hyperinflation exists which are translated at historical rates of exchange.
b. **Profit and loss account** items translated at the average rate of exchange for the financial year. An inflation adjustment is charged in arriving at the local currency profits of undertakings operating in hyperinflation countries, before they are translated to reflect the impact of the hyperinflation on the undertakings working capital requirements.

8206 **The FRSSE** does not cover the topic of hyperinflation. In the unlikely event that a small company were to have operations in a hyperinflationary economy compliance with the methods advocated in UITF 9, would be appropriate.

Economies that cease to be hyperinflationary Where an economy ceases to be hyperinflationary and the entity no longer prepares financial statements in accordance with this standard, it should use the amounts expressed in the measurement currency as the basis for the carrying amounts in subsequent financial statements. 8207

SECTION 3

Foreign equity investments financed by foreign borrowings

Specific criteria apply to the treatment of foreign equity investments financed from foreign borrowings, in the financial statements of **individual companies** and **groups**. The subject of financing a foreign equity investment as a hedge against a particular currency risk is dealt with in section 4. 8220

1. Individual company financial statements

The **rule that non-monetary items** (¶8020) must be carried at historical cost and not retranslated at the closing rate, does not apply where foreign equity investments are financed through foreign currency borrowings. **In these circumstances**, an individual company may record its foreign equity investments in the relevant foreign currencies and translate the carrying amounts at the end of each financial year at the closing rates of exchange. 8224

Offset method

Exchange gains or losses on **equity investments** financed through foreign borrowings, should be taken to reserves (and not the profit or loss account), as should any exchange differences on the related foreign borrowings. This is often known as the "offset method". 8226

The offset method is **generally applied to** individual investments or borrowings, except where an investment or a number of investments have been financed by a particular loan. This means that the offset method **can also be applied** where investments are managed on a pool basis and financed by a basket of different currency loans. 8228

The **criteria that must be applied** for offset to apply to individual companies are principally the same as that to be applied to groups preparing consolidated financial statements. 8230

1. Any exchange gains or losses in any accounting period, that arise on borrowings, may be **offset only to the extent** of the total exchange differences on the equity investments. SSAP 20 (51)
2. The foreign currency borrowings whose gains and losses are used in the offset process, **should not exceed**, in aggregate, the total net realisable value of the investments.
3. There must be **consistent application** of the accounting treatment adopted over time.

Only that part of total exchange gains or losses that are matched by the opposite movement in the value of the investment can be taken to reserves for offset purposes. Any excess gains or losses should be taken to the profit and loss account in the period concerned.

The **examples** below illustrate how exchange rate gains and losses on foreign currency investments and borrowings can be offset against each other and the treatment of any surpluses.

EXAMPLE **Exchange gain (loss) on equity investments**

A UK company has prepared its financial statements to August 20X8. In March 20X9 the company raised a **dollar loan of $2m** to finance two equity investments; one in Italy costing €1million and one in Switzerland costing SFR 2,5million.

The relevant exchange rates are as follows:

March 2010 £1 = US$1.50 = E 1.60 = SFR 2.0
August 2009 £1 = US$1.55 = E 1.58 = SFR 2.2

	Exchange Difference £	P & L Account £	Reserves £
A. Exchange differences on investments.			
Italian company			
March 2010 €1,000,000/ 1.60	625,000		
August 2009 €1,000,000/ 1.58	632,911		
Exchange gain	**7,911**		
Swiss company			
March 2010 SFR 2,500,000/2.0	1,250,000		
August 2009 SFR 2,500,000/2.2	1,136,363		
Exchange loss	**(113,637)**		
Net exchange gain (loss) equity investments	**(105,726)**		**(105,726)**
B. Exchange difference on $borrowings			
March 2010 $2m/£1.50	1,333,333		
August 2009 $2m/ 1.55	1,290,032		
Exchange gain	**43,301**		**43,301**

The exchange rate gain of £43,301 on the dollar loan can be used to partially offset the exchange loss of £105,726 incurred on the foreign currency investments.
If there had been an exchange rate loss on the dollar loan this would have been taken to the profit and loss account.

EXAMPLE If in the above example, the UK parent company suffered a net exchange loss on investments of £35,000, which was exceeded by the net exchange gains on the foreign currency borrowings of £43,301, the offset procedure would be applicable as follows:

	Total	Offset loss on Investments in reserves	Difference to P & L
Exchange gain on borrowings	£43,301	£35,000	£8,301

8234 **Consistency** A company should not change its accounting treatment simply to accommodate movements in exchange rates, but should adopt a consistent policy as stipulated in FRS 18 "Accounting policies".

Where a company **uses the offset process** to match exchange losses on borrowings to gains on the underlying investment, it should continue to adopt this policy in subsequent periods, even if the opposite situation as regards movements on exchange rates should apply and exchange gains realised on the currency loan. These gains should be taken to reserves and not the profit or loss account.

Pre – arranged loans

8236 The **offset method can also be applied where** borrowings have been arranged prior to the purchase of a foreign enterprise. The period covered by the borrowings will then differ from that covered by the investment. However, only the exchange differences arising on the borrowings which were generated during the period the currency hedge was in place, can be offset against the exchange differences on the investments. Any **exchange differences** arising on the borrowing prior to the date the investment is made, should be taken to the profit and loss account.

Intermediate holding companies

A parent company may hold an investment in an overseas intermediate holding company that in turn holds a number of investments in other overseas subsidiaries. The **general rule** is that if the UK parent company has incurred foreign currency borrowings to finance or hedge its investment, then the offset procedures stipulated in SSAP 20 can be applied. **8238**

An investment in an intermediate holding company could represent a **multi-currency asset**, whose value is susceptible to fluctuations in the local currencies of the subsidiary companies. The **exchange differences** can, therefore, be offset against the differences on each element of the multi-currency asset.

Repayment of loan or sale of foreign equity investment

The **consistency principle** should be applied where a currency loan is repaid or the investment in the foreign enterprise is sold. In both situations the offset procedure should be applied up to the repayment or sale date. **8240**

For instance, a company adopting an accounting policy of matching in reserves, exchange differences on borrowings with exchange differences on equity investments in reserves, should continue this policy up to the date of sale or loan repayment. Where the "offset" is limited, the balance should be taken to the profit and loss account.

Where the foreign enterprise is sold but the **loan remains outstanding**, the parent company must apply the offset procedure up to the date of sale; the loan ceases to be a hedge and any **exchange gains or losses** arising thereafter should be accounted for in the profit and loss account. **8242**

Valuation of a foreign equity investment

The **carrying value** of an investment (individual company's accounts) in a foreign equity investment **is normally based on** historical cost less any provisions (or recoverable amount if impaired). **8246**

Alternatively, a foreign equity investment may be **carried at a valuation**, such as net asset value or the directors' valuation based on an estimate of the market value or cost plus retained post-acquisition profits, could be used. A valuation based on **net asset values** may be appropriate where a subsidiary company was acquired a considerable time before or was set up by the parent company.

Whichever **valuation policy is adopted** must be **applied consistently** from year to year. Any change in accounting policy must be justified on the grounds that it provides a more accurate representation of the reporting entity's financial position. **8248** FRS 3 (62)

Where the foreign equity investment is carried at a valuation, it will be necessary to separately account for the effects of exchange rate movements on the opening value of the investment and the effect of any revaluation of the foreign currency carrying value. **8250**

Currency borrowing restrictions

The **general rule** is that the sum borrowed should not exceed the total amount of cash that the business is expected to generate. SSAP 20 does not give guidance on how cash generation is to be measured or the relevant time period for making profits. In practice, it may be difficult to calculate the cash generated by a particular foreign investment over time, given the number of variables that must be factored into the estimate. A number of restrictions apply. **8254**

For a more detailed review of impairment reviews and permanent diminutions in the value of fixed asset investments see ¶1550.

Restrictions

Problems may occur when the borrowing is related to a foreign enterprise that is either unprofitable or earns negligible profits to meet the loan repayments. If this is the case, the **8256**

expected cash generation will be reflected in the **net realisable value (NRV)** of the investment as stated at the balance sheet date. Where the book value of the investment exceeds the NRV, the borrowing used for offset should be reduced accordingly.

Restrictions may also apply where a foreign investment is subject to exchange control restrictions that limit the finance repatriated for repayment of the initial borrowings. This is illustrated in the following example.

EXAMPLE **Borrowing restriction – Exchange controls.**

A UK company arranged a loan to finance an investment in South Africa, totalling 2m rand. The **initial equity investment** totalled 2m rand whilst the total cash expected to be generated over the life of the investment has since been revised downwards to be approx. 1.8m rand. The financial year end was March 2010.

The relevant exchange rates are as follows:

March 2009 £1 = Rand 16.0
March 2010 £1 = Rand 14.0

In this example there is an **exchange loss** of £17,000 on the currency loan that can be partially offset in reserves against the exchange gain of £50,000 arising on the investment. The **excess** exchange loss of £5,556 must be taken to the profit and loss account.

	Difference	P & L Account	Reserves
	£	£	£
Net realisable value of investment			
March 2009 1.8m/ 16	112,500		
March 2010 1.8m/14	112,857		
Exchange gain	**357**		**357**
Exchange differences			
On loan			
March 2009 2m/16	125,000		
March 2010 2m/14	142,857		
Exchange loss	**(17,857)**	**(17,500)**	**(357)**

In addition the company will also have to write down the initial value of the investment to its net realisable value of 1.8m rand.

2. Consolidated financial statements

8270 Group companies may finance investments in foreign entities **through currency borrowings**, or use these borrowings to provide a hedge against exchange risks associated with similar existing investments.

Any increase or decrease in the level of outstanding borrowings arising from exchange rate movements, will probably be covered by changes in the carrying amount of the net assets underpinning the net investment, which would be reflected in reserves. The group is therefore, protected against movements in the exchange rate, and as such it would not be prudent to record an accounting profit or loss when exchange rates fluctuate.

Offset method

8272 SSAP 20 (31) Exchange differences on currency borrowings can be offset as a movement on **consolidated reserves**, against exchange differences that arise when the opening net investment in a foreign investment is re-translated for consolidation purposes. Although use of the offset method in the consolidation process is optional, certain criteria must still be met.

8274 **Criteria** The offset criteria requirements are principally the same as those demanded for individual companies (¶8226), with an **additional requirement** that the relationship between the investing company and the foreign enterprise should justify the use of the **closing rate method** for the purpose of consolidation.

A company could meet the criteria for offset but still opt not to adopt it, as it must be consistently applied in subsequent years. This may mean forsaking the opportunity to take any larger exchange gains that may arise to the profit and loss account.

Consolidation process Despite the **similar criteria** that apply to the use of the offset method in both individual company financial statements and on consolidation, it will usually be necessary to reverse the entries made at the entity level and recalculate the adjustments on a consolidation basis. This **process is required** at the **entity level** because: 8276

a. The **offset applies to** all foreign equity investments, whereas on consolidation, foreign enterprises accounted for under the temporal method, are excluded. Exchange differences on foreign borrowings taken to reserves in the individual company financial statements should be reversed and recalculated for the consolidated results for the year.

b. The **exchange difference arising each year** on the carrying value of the investment translated at the closing rate is used for offset purposes, whereas on consolidation the exchange difference on retranslation of the opening investment is used.

Where the offset procedure is not applied the following process should be adopted:

- any exchange differences on the net equity investment should be taken to reserves; whilst
- those generated by the borrowings used to finance the investment are taken to the profit and loss account.

Restrictions The offset rules **cannot be applied** to a foreign investment accounted for under the **temporal method** on consolidation, where all exchange gains or losses on foreign borrowings must be taken to the profit and loss account. Even where the offset procedure does apply there are still restrictions. 8278

Exchange rate gains on borrowings can only partially be taken to reserves, to offset any exchange losses on foreign equity investments, with the balance taken to the profit and loss account as it is regarded as speculative. This is illustrated in the following example.

EXAMPLE **Exchange gain (loss) on borrowings**

A UK company has prepared its consolidated financial statements to August 2010. In March 2010 the company raised a **dollar loan of $2m** to finance two equity investments; one in Italy costing € 1m and one in Switzerland costing SFR 2,5m.

The relevant exchange rates are as follows:
March 2010 £1 = US$1.50 = € 1.60 = SFR 2.0
August 2009 £1 = US$1.55 = € 1.50 = SFR 2.2

	Exchange Difference £	P & L Account £	Reserves £
A. Exchange differences			
On investments.			
Italian company			
March 2010 1,000,000/ 1.60	625,000		
August 2010 1,000,000/ 1.50	666,666		
Exchange gain	**41,666**		
Swiss company			
March 2010 SFR 2,500,000/2.0	1,250,000		
August 2010 SFR 2,500,000/2.1	1,190,476		
Exchange loss	**(59,524)**		
Net exchange gain (loss) equity investments	**(17,858)**		**(17,858)**

B. Exchange difference $borrowings

March 2010 $2m/ 1.50	1,333,333		
August 2010 $2m/ 1.55	1,290,032		
Exchange gain	**43,301**	**25,443**	**17,858**

In this example the exchange rate gain on the dollar loan of £43,301, can be used to **offset** the exchange loss of £17,858 incurred on the foreign currency investments. The difference of £25,443 is considered speculative and is taken to the **consolidated profit and loss account**.
If there had been an exchange rate loss on the dollar loan this would also have been taken to the profit and loss account.

8280 **Exception** The **entries for individual companies** should be reversed on consolidation where the foreign entity takes a legal form other than that a subsidiary or an associate. In these instances, the same **offset procedure** applied in the individual company financial statements may be used in the consolidated accounts. This rationale is that a genuine currency hedge at the entity level does not cease to exist at the consolidated level.

SECTION 4

Hedging foreign currency transactions

8300 Hedging is a generic term given to a range of **financial instruments** used by companies to reduce the risks associated with movements in currency exchange rates. In the context of foreign exchange transactions, the most common hedging instruments (also known as "derivative products") are forward exchange contracts and currency options.

8302 The **purpose of hedging** is to reduce or eliminate some of the risk which is inherent in most financial instruments. The issue of currency risk, as well as market (or price) risk and interest rate risk are covered in the chapter on financial derivatives (¶3400).

8304 The **benefit of hedging** must be offset against the cost of holding the financial instrument. When a company has identified a position that is exposed to risk or loss as a result of possible adverse price changes in foreign exchange markets, it can use a "hedge" to mitigate the risk of loss of holding particular currencies. A hedge is arranged by taking a second position that is exposed to a price risk, that moves inversely and is highly co-related with the effects of price risks attached to an existing position.

8306 A **hedge instrument can be designed** to match a particular exposure (i.e. price risk) or form part of a general portfolio of financial instruments, designed to protect a company's position in the foreign exchange markets. It is not currently a requirement that specific hedge instruments be matched with individual items being hedged, although as different assets and liabilities have different exposures to potential gains or losses, the item constituting a group of financial instruments must be similar in content to the particular risk component being insured. It is likely that a new standard addressing hedging will require hedge items to be taken out to match specific contracts, for hedge accounting to be allowed.

Determination of spot and forward exchange rates

8310 A currency exchange rate is determined by the number of units of one currency that may be purchased or sold for one unit of another currency. **Movements in exchange rates** reflect the relative strength of currencies. For example, if the $/£ exchange rate moves from US$1.56/£ to US$1.63/£, sterling will have strengthened against the dollar, as each pound will now buy more dollars. Exchange rates are quoted "**spot" and "forward**", and at offer and bid prices.

Definitions	
"Spot rate"	The exchange rate for immediate delivery
"Forward rate"	The exchange rate quoted today for delivery at some agreed future date. It should be noted that on any one given day there will be several forward rates quoted by a bank – each for a different future transaction date. These rates will change from day to day and sometimes during the course of a single day.
"Offer price"	The price at which the "market-maker" offers the currency for sale
"Bid price"	The price at which the "market-maker" offers to purchase the currency

EXAMPLE **Spot rates**
The **$/£ spot rate** may be quoted as follows:
1.475 – 1.485.

The lower figure represents the "**offer price**" and the higher figure the "**bid price**"
Company A sells $147,500 to the bank at the current offer rate of £1.475 = $1.485, thus receiving £99,327 from the bank.
Company B then decides to buy the same amount of dollars from the bank at their offer price of $1.485 to £1. The sum of £100,000 is paid by B to the bank.
The **difference** represents the bank's profit [£100,000 – £99,327 = £673] resulting from the spread in rates between the bid and offer price.

The spread between the offer and bid prices reflects the stability of the market at the time of the transaction and the depth of the market, as determined by the volume of transactions. **When currency movements are volatile**, the spread between the bid and offer prices will be wider than when exchange rates are more stable.

1. Forward exchange contracts

A forward exchange contract is a **form of legal agreement** under which a company agrees to buy or sell an agreed sum of foreign currency at a specific rate of exchange, for delivery and settlement at a specified future date. Forward exchange contracts are normally obtained from one of the big commercial banks and are available in all major currencies. 8312

Whilst some dealers speculate in currency markets using forward contracts, in the commercial and industrial world, the need to take out a forward exchange contract normally arises, because there is a **commercial or trading contract** anticipated by a company, that will be denominated in a currency other than that in which the company normally operates.

A typical situation in which a company [the contractor] might consider taking out a forward exchange contract is illustrated below.

EXAMPLE Company X agreed on 15 October 2010, to purchase some new plant and equipment from the USA at a fixed price of $1,600,000 payable of 1 January 2011. The company does not normally trade in US dollars and so will have to buy dollars from the bank to settle the transaction. In recent months the exchange rate has moved from between $1.575 and $1.63 to £1. The current exchange rate is $1.62: £1. Whilst the pound is currently quite strong, Company X does not want to be exposed to the potential risk of the exchange rate falling to the previous level again so takes out a forward contract to buy $1,600,000 on 1 January 2011 at today's forward rate of £1.60 to £1.
Company X has therefore effectively guaranteed the sterling price of the new plant and equipment at £1,000.000 and has eliminated the risk that in sterling terms the price might go up should the pound weaken against the dollar.

The **key features** of a forward exchange contract are that: 8314
- the exchange (contract) rate is agreed when the contract is arranged;
- the currencies are exchanged in the future on a specified date at the rate agreed today; and
- the contract must be completed.

Forward exchange contracts **are utilised principally by companies** wishing to protect existing currency positions against exchange losses (or gains) on both existing and anticipated transactions. Forward foreign exchange contracts are traded on an **over the counter market** 8315

(OTC), which can be defined as a purchase of securities from, or sale of securities to, a dealer other than those on a recognised stock exchange.

8316 Apart from eliminating the exposure of the contractor to movement in exchange rates, the **other advantages of forward exchange contracts are** that there is usually:
- no deposit to pay;
- settlement is on the maturity date; and
- they can be tailored to meet the specific requirements of the company, including the amount, currency and maturity date, which are typically agreed for any time period up to a year.

8318 The **disadvantage** is that the company forfeits the right to benefit from any favourable movements in the exchange rate. The decision as to whether to take out a forward contract will therefore depend, upon how risk averse the contractor is and their perception of which way exchange rates will move between the current date and the date on which the underlying trading contract will crystallise.

The **contracts normally mature** on standard month end dates; where this is not the case the costs of arranging the contract are higher. The market for forward exchange contracts in excess of one year is generally small as is the market for the currencies of less developed countries.

Mechanics of forward exchange rates

8320 One of the parties to the contracts assumes a **long-position** by agreeing to buy the specified currency at an agreed future date at the forward rate. The other party assumes a **short position** and contracts to sell the currency on the same date at the same forward rate. The forward rate is quoted at a **premium or discount to the spot rate** based on:
- current market conditions;
- the interest rate differentials between the relevant currencies; and
- the duration of the forward contract.

The **following example** illustrates how the forward exchange contract rate is theoretically calculated.

EXAMPLE **Calculation of the forward exchange rate**

A UK company borrows £2m for one year which it decides to convert into Norwegian kroner at the spot rate to finance an investment. The Company takes out a forward exchange contract for one year to sell the kroners and interest for sterling.

UK interest rates	5%
Norwegian interest rates	4%
Spot rate at 30 June 2010	£1 = Nk 7
One year forward rate (see calculation below).	£1 = NK 6.9

	£
Sterling borrowings £2m	**2,000,000**
Interest 5% for one year	100,000
Total payable on 30 June 2011	2,100,000
Kroner borrowings	
£2m @ 7kr	**14,000,000**
Interest 4%	560,000
Total payable	14,560,000

Calculation of the forward rate

Ignoring transaction costs, the one year forward rate at the start of the contract can be determined arithmetically, by applying the interest rate differential ruling between the two currencies to the spot rate as follows:

Forward rate = 7kr x 1.04/1.05 = 6.933.

On 30 June 2011, when the contract matures the Kroners will be converted into sterling as follows: Kr 14,560/6.933 = £2,100,100.
In reality, other factors will also be incorporated into the forward rate such as the time period or size of contract to reflect other risk elements.

Accounting treatment

The subject of forward exchange currency contracts is dealt with only briefly in SSAP 20. 8324

The specific accounting treatment of forward exchange contracts will depend on whether the contract is for speculative or for hedging purposes.

The **general principle** is that forward exchange contracts are treated as a single transaction; namely a commitment to buy or sell the currency necessary to settle a foreign currency payable or receivable, as part of the purchase or sale transaction. The transaction is recorded under the rate specified in the contract.

Under existing rules there are no accounting entries made in respect of the contract itself until it crystallises. It is simply a question of disclosing the future commitment in the notes to the financial statements.

However, the **terms of a forward contract** may, as discussed below, influence the value at which a transaction hedged by the forward contract is recorded. The accounting treatment for a number of typical situations where a company enters into a forward exchange contract are outlined in examples that follow.

Forward Contracts taken out at the transaction date Under SSAP 20, the contract rate 8326
can be used to translate monetary assets and liabilities denominated in a foreign currency, where they are covered by a matching or related forward exchange rate contract. The adoption of the contract rate recognises the purpose of the contract is to hedge any exchange risk and that no economic gain or loss will materialise. The **premium** or **discount** on a forward contract is recognised in the profit and loss account when the contract is taken out.

EXAMPLE A British company prepares its financial statements to 31 Sept. 2010. In June 2010, the company sells merchandise to a company in Hong Kong for HK$300,000. The Hong Kong company is due to settle the account in December 2010.

When the transaction was signed the £/HK$ rate was HK 1.3, and at the balance sheet date the rate had moved to 1 = 3.2. The UK company has however arranged a forward exchange contract to sell the HK$300,000 it is to receive in December 2010 on the same day as they are due. The exchange rate specified in the forward contract was £1 = HK 2.8.

June 2010	HK$300,000/ 3 =	£100,000	
Sept. 2010	HK$300,000/ 3.2 =	£93,750	(balance sheet date)
Dec. 2010	HK$300,000/ 2.8 =	£107,143	

SSAP 20

The UK company should account for the sale as follows:

The **sale and debtor** to be recorded at the contract rate of £1 = HK$2.8 as £107,143

In December 2010, HK$300,000 will be due from the debtor, which is sold for £107,143.

The contract rate is used because the British company knows the rate it will be applying at the date the payment is received. This is consistent with the provisions of SSAP 20.

No aggregate exchange gain/loss arises.

Hedging a foreign currency obligation Companies may use forward foreign exchange 8330
contracts to hedge future transactions, such as a foreign currency payable or receivable or a commitment such as an agreement to buy or sell goods to a foreign company at some time in the future. The **correct accounting treatment** is to defer any gain or loss arising on the forward contract, until the actual date the obligation is fulfilled, as both the transaction and the forward contract arranged to hedge it are future commitments.

EXAMPLE A UK Company with a financial year ending on 31 December 2009, contracts on 30 September 2009 to buy from a Canadian supplier, equipment worth $400,000. The equipment is due for delivery on 31 March 2010 and due for settlement on 30th June 2010.

The UK Company wishes to hedge the commitment to pay $400,000 on 30th June 2010 at a forward rate of £1 = C$2.

Under SSAP 20, the transaction should be recorded at the forward contract rate: namely the asset and the liability to the creditor should be recorded at £200,000 (£1 = C$2).

It is **important to note** that no accounting entries are required at the 31 December 2009 year-end; the company will record the asset and the future liability in its balance sheet.

Where the forward exchange contract is of a speculative nature, then it may generate a profit or loss, depending on the movement in the exchange rate during the period to maturity. At the end of the financial year the profit and loss on any outstanding contracts should be determined. There are **two generally accepted methods**:
1. Compare the forward rate specified in the contract with the actual forward rate to maturity at the end of the financial year; and
2. Compare the "spot rate" at the date the contract is agreed with the spot rate at the balance sheet date. The contracted forward discount or premium should be amortised over the period of the contract.

The "spot rate" is the exchange rate for immediate delivery.

EXAMPLE A company took out a forward exchange contract on 1 July 2010 to sell €2,500,00, 153 days forward at £1: €1.50. On 30 November 2010, the company must supply €2,500,000 in exchange for £1,666,667.
The financial year end was 31 October 2010 and the 30 day forward rate £1 = €1.52 (£1,644,736).

Method	**£**
Contracted price for delivery of €2,500,000 on 30 November 2010	1,666,667
Cost of €2,500,000 at 31 October 2010 -30 day forward rate at £1 = €1.52	1,644,736
Profit earned to 30 November 2010	**21,931**

8332 **Hedging net investments in foreign enterprises** A parent company may decide to hedge against the effects of movements in exchange rates on a net investment in a foreign subsidiary. This can be achieved by arranging a foreign currency borrowing to hedge a foreign equity investment.

The accounting treatment is to take **any exchange differences** arising on a **forward contract** to reserves, to match the movement in the net investment being hedged. This is consistent with the treatment of exchange differences on borrowings taken out as a hedge. The **premium charged on the forward contract** should be posted to the profit and loss account.

MEMO POINTS UITF 46 "Hedging net investments in foreign enterprises" was issued in December 2008 and implements the IFRIC's interpretation 16 in the UK. The Abstract is applicable to companies applying FRS 23 and FRS 26 (see ¶8381).

2. Foreign currency options

8340 A foreign currency option is a **right but not an obligation**, to buy or sell an amount of currency at a fixed price. The right to buy is known as a "call option" and the right to sell a "put option"; the agreed price is known as the "strike" or "exercise price".

8342 An **important difference** between a foreign currency option and a forward currency contract, is that the buyer of the currency is able to take advantage of any favourable currency movements, in that it will not exercise the options unless the exchange rates have moved to its advantage. Accounting for options is not dealt with by SSAP 20.

8343 In return for the right to place a call or put option with an option seller (i.e. bank) a company will have to pay a commission or non-refundable option premium, which represents the market value of the option. An **option consists of two parts**; namely its intrinsic value and its time value.

8344 The **intrinsic value** represents the benefit to the holder of the option if exercised immediately and for a call option, it equals the excess of market price of the underlying option over the options strike price.

8346 The **time value** represents the difference between the price of the option (premium) and the intrinsic value and dependent on:
– the time remaining to maturity of the option;

– the value placed on the possible increase in the option's intrinsic value prior to the maturity date, as a result of the volatility of the underlying financial item; as well as
– reflecting the income foregone by not holding the underlying item.

Exercising the option If the spot exchange rate is lower than the strike rate, the option holder will not exercise the option as it is said to be "**out of the money**". If the opposite is the case, the option will be exercised as it is aid to be "**in the money**". Where the strike rate is equal to the spot rate the option is considered to be "at the rate". 8348

Disclosure requirements

Where the monies involved in the forward contracts **are material** the method adopted should be detailed in the accounting policies note. The particulars of significant forward contracts with should be disclosed in order to comply with the Companies Act requirements. Whether a contract is a matched/hedge type or open speculative type it still represents a discussable commitment for the purposes of the Act. 8350

SECTION 5

Disclosure framework

The **reporting framework** relating to the disclosure of foreign currency transactions for both individual companies and consolidated accounts is dictated by the disclosure requirements of the Companies Act, SSAP 20, UITF 9, UITF 19 and the Operating and Financial Review/Business Review. The FRSSE does not contain any of the disclosure requirements of SSAP 20. The disclosure requirements for the new rules included in FRS 23 are covered in ¶8385 and for FRS 24 in ¶8387. 8360

Companies Act requirements

The disclosure requirements of the Companies Act are limited. The Act does not include any provisions that deal with the translation of either foreign currency transactions or foreign currency financial statements. The **information that must be disclosed** in the notes to the accounts, is the basis or accounting policy adopted for the translation process and details of any material financial obligations, to the extent that they are relevant to a proper understanding of the company's financial position, such as any amounts due under existing forward exchange contracts. 8362

EXAMPLE **Bonington Group plc – Annual report and accounts 31 December 2010**

Accounting Policies (extract)

A. Basis adopted for foreign currency translation
Assets and liabilities denominated in foreign currencies are principally translated into sterling at the rates ruling at the end of the financial year, **except when covered by** an **open foreign exchange contract**, in which case the rate of exchange specified in the contract is used.

B. Treatment of exchange differences arising from the translation of both the opening balance sheets of overseas subsidiary undertakings (date of control in case of acquisition during the year) and foreign currency borrowings used to finance or hedge long-term foreign investments are taken directly to reserves. All other profits and losses on exchange are credited or charged to operating profit.
The **results of specific overseas undertakings** are translated into sterling at average rates. The exchange differences arising as a result of re-stating net assets to closing rates are dealt with as movements on reserves.

SSAP 20

8364 The disclosure requirements under SSAP 20 are as follows:
SSAP 20 (59) a. The method of translating the financial statements of foreign enterprises.
b. The accounting treatment or exchange differences.
c. The net amounts of exchange of exchange gains or losses on financial currency borrowings, less deposits, showing separately:
– any amounts offset against reserves (net movement), including as a hedge or finance for foreign equity investments; and
– the net amount charged or credited to the profit and loss account.
d. For all companies or groups of companies the **net movement on reserve** arising from exchange differences.
An example of exchange differences offset against reserves is shown in the example below.

8366

EXAMPLE **Polonia Ltd Annual Report and Accounts – 2010**
Notes to the accounts (extract)
Other reserves

	Group £m	Subsidiaries £m	Parent £m
Reserves b/fwd.	**xxx**	**xxx**	**xxx**
Movements during the year			
Profit for the year	xxx	xxx	xxx
Dividends			
Net exchange gains on currency loans	xxx		xxx
Exchange differences on translation of net investments in overseas subsidiaries	(xxx)	(xx)	(xxx)
Total	xxx	xxx	xxx

In the Group accounts £0.7m of net exchange gains on foreign currency loans have been **offset in reserves** against exchange losses on net investment in overseas subsidiaries.

UITF 19

8368 UITF 19 requires the disclosure of the tax charges or credits relating to exchange gains or losses taken to the STRGL, in addition to the gross amount of the exchange differences.

Operating and financial review (Business review)

8370 The disclosure requirements of the Operating and Financial review (OFR) (see ¶4700) covering foreign currency transactions include **details of the following**:
– the currency profile of any borrowings;
– the use of financial instruments for hedging purposes; and
– exposure to exchange rate fluctuations and possible impact on reported results.

8372 The **financial review section** of the OFR should include a discussion on the management of exchange rate risk and the extent to which foreign currency net investments are hedged by currency borrowings and other hedging instruments.

EXAMPLE **Standard Airways Plc**
Annual report and accounts: June 20XX
Operating and financial review (extract)

Currency exposure

The Group engages in business activity in approximately 65 countries accounting for some 65% of Group revenues and expenses. The Group generates a surplus in the majority of these currencies. The principal exceptions are the US dollar in which the Group has its deficit arising from capital expenditure and expenditure on fuel, and sterling covering central overhead and management costs.

Risk However, the Group is **exposed to a broad spread of currencies** through businesses linked to the dollar and sterling, which provides a measure of protection against exchange rate fluctuations.
It should be noted that there would be an adverse effect on the Group's result were sterling to weaken against the US dollar but strengthen against either the Euro or the Yen, with the reverse producing a beneficial effect.
The Group actively **seeks to limit** its foreign currency exposure arising from transactions in various currencies, through a policy of matching receipts and payments in each currency. Currency surpluses are sold spot or forward for dollars or sterling.
In addition to the primary effects outlined above, exchange rate movements can effect demand for some of our services, although it is not possible to quantify the effect at this stage.

SECTION 6

Non-listed companies adopting fair value accounting

This section outlines the reporting requirements contained in FRS 23 "The Effects Of Changes In Foreign Exchange Rates" and FRS 24 "Financial Reporting In Hyperinflationary Economies". **8381**

1. FRS 23

FRS 23 covers the presentation of an entity's financial statements in a foreign currency and **applies to** unlisted entities that choose to adopt accounting policies consistent with the fair value measurement rules contained in the Companies Act, and hence, FRS 26 "Financial Instruments: Measurement". **8382**

FRS 23 **does not apply to** financial statements **where FRS 26 has not been applied** as SSAP 20 remains in force, as well as to entities that apply the FRSSE. FRS 23 is based on IAS 21.

FRS 23 **should be applied**: FRS 23 (3)
- when accounting for transactions and balances in foreign currencies, except derivative transactions and balances falling within the scope of FRS 26;
- in translating the results of the foreign operation included in the entity's financial statements, by way of consolidation, or by the equity method; and
- in translating an entity's results into a "presentation currency".

MEMO POINTS The **"presentation currency"** is defined as the currency in which the financial statements are presented. The **"functional currency"** (local currency), is defined as the currency of the primary economic environment in which an entity operates. Once determined, the functional currency is not changed unless the underlying transactions, events and conditions that determine this choice also change.

The approach adopted by FRS 23

Each entity, whether stand-alone, an entity with foreign operations (such as a parent) or a foreign operation itself (such as a subsidiary or branch), **must determine its functional currency**, before translating foreign currency items into the functional currency. **8383** FRS 23 (17)

Reporting entities often comprise a number of individual entities, such as a group containing a parent and a number of subsidiaries. Different types of entity, irrespective of whether they are members of a group, may also have interests in associates, joint arrangements or branches. The **results of each individual entity** within the reporting group entity must then be translated into the presentation currency of this reporting entity.

Stand-alone entities preparing financial statements or an entity with investments in subsidiaries, associates or joint ventures, are permitted to present their financial statements in any FRS 23 (19) currency. Where the presentation currency and functional currency differ, the results must be translated into the presentation currency, in accordance with certain rules (see ¶8383-6).

8383-1 **Initial recognition** A foreign currency transaction is defined as one that is denominated or requires settlement in a foreign currency, such as when an entity:

FRS 23 (20)
- buys or sells goods or services priced in a foreign currency;
- borrows or lends funds denominated in a foreign currency; or
- acquires or disposes of assets or incurs or settles liabilities denominated in a foreign currency.

On initial recognition, a foreign currency transaction shall be recorded in the functional currency, using the "spot rate" between the functional currency and the relevant foreign currency, at the transaction date. The **transaction date** is defined as the date the transaction first qualifies for recognition as such, under financial reporting standards. Where exchange rates do not vary greatly, an average rate over a week or month is often used for transactions in the same accounting period.

8383-2 **Reporting at subsequent balance sheet dates** The accounting treatment for translating transactions at the balance sheet date is set out in the table below:

FRS 23 (23)

	Accounting treatment- balance sheet date
Monetary items	Use closing rate
Non-monetary items-historical cost	Use exchange rate on day of transaction
Non-monetary items-fair value	Use exchange rate at date fair value was determined

The **carrying amount** of an item is determined with reference to the relevant accounting standards. For example, transactions involving property, plant and equipment are translated into the functional currency in accordance with the requirements of FRS 15 "Tangible fixed assets".

Where **non-monetary assets such as stocks** are measured in a foreign currency, the carrying amount is determined by comparing:
- the cost or carrying amount, translated at the exchange rate prevailing on the transaction date; and
- the net realisable value or recoverable amount, as appropriate at the exchange rate at the date the value was determined. (e.g. the closing rate at the balance sheet date).

8383-3 **Recognition of exchange differences** An overview of the accounting treatment for exchange differences arising on **specific transactions** is given in the table below.

FRS 23 (27) – (33)

Exchange differences arising on:	Accounting treatment
Settlement of (or translation of) monetary items at rates different from those used on initial recognition	Recognise in the STRGL in period they arise, **except for** the conditions set out in FRS 23 (32) (see ¶8383-7). For transactions **settled in a subsequent accounting period**, the exchange difference is allocated to each period, up to the settlement date, as determined by the movement in exchange rates in each period.
Monetary items that form part of a reporting entity's net investment in a foreign operation	1. Report in profit or loss on the separate financial statements of the foreign operation, as appropriate. 2. In the consolidated financial statements of the reporting entity (where the foreign operation is a subsidiary), exchange differences are recognised initially in the STRGL and recognised in the profit or loss account when the net investment is disposed of (see ¶8383-8).
Gains or losses on non-monetary items	Where recognised in STRGL – exchange differences also recorded there. Where recognised in the profit or loss account – exchange differences are also recognised there.

Change in functional currency The functional currency of the entity mirrors the underlying transactions, events and conditions relevant to the entity. **Once determined**, the functional currency can only be changed if there is a change to the underlying transaction etc. For example, a change in the currency that influences sale prices could lead to a change in the entity's functional currency. **8383-4**

The **accounting treatment** for a change in functional currency is as follows:

1. The entity should translate all items into the new functional currency using the exchange rate at the date of change.

2. The resulting translated amounts for non-monetary items are translated at their historical cost. FRS 23 (37)

3. Exchange differences arising from the translation of a foreign operation previously recognised through the STRGL, are not recognised in the profit or loss account, until the disposal of the operation (see ¶8383-3).

Where the presentation currency differs from the functional currency An entity is **free to present** its financial statements in any currency, but where this differs from the entity's functional currency, it is required to translate its results into the presentation currency of the reporting entity. **For example**, a group could contain individual entities who use different functional currencies, but whose consolidated accounts must be presented in a common currency. **8383-5**

The results of an entity whose functional currency is that of a **non-hyperinflationary economy** and that differs from its presentation currency, should be translated into the latter currency using the following procedures as outlined below. FRS 23 (39)

Non-hyperinflationary economy	Accounting treatment/accounting treatment
1. Assets and liabilities (for each balance sheet inc. comparatives)	Translate at closing rate at balance sheet date
2. Income and expenses (for each income statement inc. comparatives)	Translate at exchange rates prevailing at the transaction date
3. Exchange differences	Recognise resulting exchange differences (from 1 and 2 above) through the STRGL

Where exchange differences relate to a foreign operation that is **consolidated but not wholly-owned**, accumulated exchange differences arising from transactions attributable to **minority interests** are allocated to minority interests in the consolidated balance sheet. **8383-6**

If the functional currency of an entity **is that of a hyperinflationary economy**, the entity is required to restate its financial statements in accordance with FRS 24, before applying the translation method set out in the table below, except for comparative amounts that are translated into a currency of a non hyper-inflationary economy. FRS 23 (42)

The results of an entity whose functional currency is that of a hyperinflationary economy that differs from its presentation currency should be translated into the latter currency.

Hyper-inflationary economy	Translation method
All amounts (i.e. assets, liabilities, income and expenses, amounts recognised through the STRGL, comparatives)	Translate at closing rate at date of most recent balance sheet, except where amounts are translated into the currency of a non hyperinflationary economy, the comparatives shall be those presented as current year amounts in the prior-year financial statements (i.e. not adjusted for subsequent changes in price level or exchange rates)

When the economy is **no longer hyperinflationary** and the entity ceases to restate its financial statements in accordance with FRS 24, it should use the amounts restated to the price level at the date the entity ceased restating its financial statements, as the historical costs for translation into the presentation currency.

8383-7 **Translation of a foreign operation** Where the results of a foreign entity are translated into a presentation currency for inclusion in the consolidated financial statements of the reporting entity, this should follow normal consolidation procedures, such as the elimination of intra-group balances and transactions of a subsidiary.

FRS 23 (45)

Accounting problem	Accounting treatment – consolidated financial statements of reporting entity
Intra-group monetary assets (or liabilities) cannot be eliminated against the corresponding intra-group liability (or asset), without producing currency fluctuations in the consolidated financial statements	**Exchange differences** – recognise in the STRGL whatever the currency of the loan. Inter-company loans from part of the net investment in a group
Financial statements – reporting date of foreign operation differs from reporting entity	Foreign operation **usually prepare** additional financial statements as of same date as those of the reporting entity. FRS 2 permits reporting dates to be different provided: – this is no longer than three months before the period-end of the parent entity in the reporting group; and – adjustments are made for significant changes in exchange rates up to the balance sheet date of the reporting entity.
Goodwill arising on acquisition of a foreign operation	Treat as assets and liabilities of the foreign operation and express in the functional currency of the foreign operation and translated at the closing rate
Fair value adjustments to carrying amounts of assets and liabilities arising on the acquisition of the foreign operation	As above

MEMO POINTS The ASB has issued a limited amendment to FRS 23 to mirror recent changes to IAS 21. These changes are reflected in the table above.

8383-8 **Disposal of a foreign operation** The cumulative amount of the relevant exchange differences recognised through the STRGL, shall be reversed out of the STRGL and recognised in the profit or loss account when the gain or loss on disposal is recognised.

FRS 23 (48)

FRS 23 (59a)

However, when FRS 23 is **adopted for the first-time**, an entity **need** not **comply** with the requirement to recognise cumulative translation differences, that exist at the effective date. If an entity **uses this exemption**:
– the cumulative exchange differences for all foreign operations are deemed to be zero at the effective date; and
– the gain or loss on a subsequent disposal of any foreign operation, should exclude exchange differences arising before the effective date and include translation differences that arise subsequent to this date.

8383-9 **Taxation** Gains or losses on foreign currency transactions and exchange differences that arise on the translation of an entity's results into a different currency may have tax effects. The relevant accounting standards are FRS 16 "Current tax" and FRS 19 "Deferred tax".

Key differences between FRS 23 and SSAP 20

8384 The main differences between FRS 23 and SSAP 20 are set out in the table below.

FRS 23 (N21)

Principal topic	Sub topic	SSAP 20	FRS 23
Preparing individual entity financial statements	1. Presentation currency	Entity must determine its local (functional) currency for measuring its results	Same requirement but uses term functional currency. Also covers the presentation currency – SSAP 20 does not. Also permits free choice of functional currency and specifies the method to be used to translate the results into the presentation currency if functional and presentation currency differ.
	2. Use of contracted rates of exchange	Permits use of contract rate	Requires transaction to be measured on initial recognition at the spot rate. Monetary items then retranslated at the closing rate.
	3. Monetary items forming part of a net investment in a foreign operation	Exchange differences on net investment in a foreign operation should be recognised in STRGL of the entity's individual financial statements	Some exchange differences (i.e. arising on monetary items) to be recognised in the individual entity's P & L
	4. Exchange gains on long-term monetary items	Exchange gains and losses on monetary items are recognised immediately in the P & L.	
		SSAP 20 also permits the recognition of exchange gains to be deferred where doubts as to the convertibility exist.	Deferring recognition of such gains is not permitted
Preparing consolidated financial statements	1. Net investment or temporal method	Choice of method permitted	Only permits use of the net investment method
	2. Exchange rate used for P & L items under the net investment method	P & L of the foreign operation is translated at the closing rate or average rate (net investment)	Requires the exchange rate at the transaction date to be used
	3. Translation of goodwill and fair value adjustments to carrying amounts of assets and liabilities of foreign operations	Standard does not specifically address this issue	Adjustments should be treated as assets and liabilities of the foreign operation and translated at closing rate
Disposal of foreign operations		Not explicitly dealt with in SSAP 20. No adjustment made to cumulative exchange differences recognised previously in the STRGL.	The cumulative amount of exchange differences should be reversed out of the STRGL and recognised in the P & L

Principal topic	Sub topic	SSAP 20	FRS 23
Hedge accounting		Sets out the requirements to be followed in accounting for net investments in foreign operations	Does not contain equivalent requirements; instead they are set out in FRS 26-see ¶8384-1 below
Disclosure requirements			Requirements differ from SSAP 20. See ¶8385 below

Disclosure requirements

8385 FRS 23 (52) - (57) The key disclosures required under FRS 23 **are as follows**:

1. The total of the exchange differences recognised in the profit and loss account, minus those arising on financial instruments measured at fair value through profit or loss in accordance with FRS 26.
2. The net exchange differences recognised through the STRG, including a reconciliation of such exchange differences at the beginning and end of the financial period.
3. Details of the functional currency where it differs from the presentation currency, including reasons for the use of a different presentation currency.
4. Where the functional currency of either the reporting entity or significant foreign operation changes, the reason for the change should be disclosed.
5. Where an entity adopts a currency in its financial statements that differs from either its functional currency or its presentation currency, it should:

– disclose the currency in which the supplementary information is presented; and
– disclose the entity's functional currency and translation method used to determine the supplementary information.

Key differences between FRS 26 and SSAP 20

8386 FRS 23 (N31) **Hedge accounting** The net investment hedging provisions in SSAP 20 **apply only to** individual and consolidated financial statements; under FRS 26, they apply only to the latter. The **requirements of FRS 26 are also different** from SSAP 20 in the following areas:

a. In order to use hedge accounting in the individual financial statements to account for the hedge of a net investment in a foreign operation, the hedge must qualify as a fair value hedge of the associated foreign exchange risk. Under FRS 26, gains and losses arising on the hedge instrument and hedged item in a **net investment hedge** are recognised in the STRGL, whereas the gains and losses arising on a hedging instrument and hedged item in a **fair value hedge** are accounted for in the profit and loss account.

b. FRS 26 is **more restrictive** than SSAP 20 on what qualifies for hedge accounting.

c. FRS 26 requires entities to recognise **gains and losses on any ineffective element** of a hedge immediately in the profit and loss account. SSAP 20 does not require this.

d. Both standards require **gains and losses on a net investment hedge** to be recognised in the in the STRGL (consolidated statements). FRS 26 however, requires those gains and losses to be recycled to the profit and loss account on disposal of the foreign operation. SSAP 20 does not require this.

2. FRS 24

8388 The **criteria for adopting FRS 24** is the same as that applies to FRS 23 as outlined in ¶8382 above.

FRS 24 is in the main identical to IAS 29 "Financial reporting in hyperinflationary economies".

The restatement of financial statements based on FRS 24, may generate differences between the carrying amount of individual assets and liabilities in the balance sheet and their tax bases. These **timing differences** should be accounted for in accordance with FRS 19 "Deferred Tax".

Key differences between FRS 24 and UITF 9

The key differences between FRS 24 and UITF 9 **are as follows**: 8389

1. The scope of FRS 24 is wider than UITF 9, which only applies to group financial statements.
2. FRS 24 also deals with the accounting treatment in individual financial statements, for entities whose functional currency is that of a hyperinflationary economy.
3. UITF 9 is less prescriptive than IAS 29, as to the method used to eliminate distortions resulting from hyperinflation.
4. The disclosure requirements in FRS 24 are more extensive than in UITF 9.

Additional disclosures A number of important disclosures are required by FRS 24 in order to clarify the basis for dealing with the effects of inflation in the financial statements and the resulting amounts; namely: 8390

- where financial statements and comparatives have been restated to reflect changes in the general purchasing power of the functional currency and reflected in the presentation currency at the balance sheet date;
- whether financial statements are based on historical cost or a current cost approach; and
- the identity and level of price index at the balance sheet date and the movement in the index over the current and previous accounting period.

SECTION 7

Comparison between UK GAAP and IAS (IFRS)

Compliance with the requirements of SSAP 20 **will generally ensure compliance with** IAS 21 "Accounting for the effects of changes in foreign exchange rates", although there are a small number of differences. Both standards require the use of closing rates to report foreign currency monetary assets and liabilities at the balance sheet date and the recognition of any exchange differences as income or expenses. Both standards also require the use of closing rates to translate the foreign currency financial statements of independent foreign entities on consolidation. 8391

The issue of **hyperinflation** is treated in IAS 29 "Financial reporting in hyperinflationary economies".

Additional guidance on aspects of foreign currency transactions is given in SIC-7 "Introduction of the Euro".

Overview of IAS 21

IAS 21 contains the requirements covering the initial recognition, subsequent measurement and disclosure of foreign currency transactions. 8392

MEMO POINTS The issue of foreign currency derivatives is dealt with in IAS 39 "Financial instruments: recognition and measurement" as is hedge accounting.

Initial recognition The key requirements of IAS 21 relating to the initial recognition of foreign currency transactions as follows: 8392-1

1. Each entity must determine its **functional currency** and measure its results in that currency whether it is:
- a single entity;
- an entity with foreign operations; or
- a foreign subsidiary or branch.

2. Reporting entities can comprise a number of individual entities, who in turn may have overseas branches or investments in associates and joint ventures. The results of each individual entity included within a reporting entity, must be translated into a **presentation currency**. An entity may publish its financial statements in any currency (the "presentation currency"), but must disclose the reasons for so doing.
3. **Foreign currency transactions** should be translated at the exchange rate used at the transaction date (or average rate where appropriate).

8392-2 **Subsequent balance sheet dates** The key requirements of IAS 21 relating to the reporting of foreign currency transactions at subsequent balance sheet dates are as follows:
1. **Monetary assets and liabilities** denominated in foreign currencies must be re-translated at the closing rate (period end).
2. **Non-monetary assets and liabilities** denominated in foreign currencies at historical cost, are reported using the exchange rate at the transaction date.
3. Non-monetary assets and liabilities **carried at fair value** and denominated in a foreign currency, reported at exchange rates used to determine the fair values.
4. Where the monetary and non-monetary assets and liabilities of a foreign entity, are translated into **a different presentation currency**, the closing rate should be used. The profit and loss account should be translated at historical (average) rate with any exchange differences classified as equity.
5. Any **cumulative translation difference** arising on the disposal of a foreign entity should be included in the gain or loss on disposal in the income statement.
6. IAS 21 includes specific rules covering **goodwill and fair value adjustments** arising on the carrying value of assets and liabilities, comprising the acquisition of a foreign entity, to be translated at the closing rate.

Consolidated financial statements

8394 The incorporation of the results of a foreign operation by the parent company follows normal consolidation practice, such as the elimination of intra-group balances and intra-group transactions with subsidiaries.

The **exception** is the treatment of intra-group monetary assets or liabilities, which cannot be eliminated against the matching intra-group liability or asset, without showing the results of the currency fluctuations in the consolidated profit and loss account. **Where the differences arise from a** monetary item, that is part of the reporting entity's net foreign currency investment, it should be accounted of in equity.

Key differences

8396 The key differences between UK GAAP and IAS 21 are outlined in the table below.

Topic	UK GAAP	IAS 21
Matching forward contracts	Use of contract rate permitted to record the transaction and any resulting liability, both initially and at subsequent balance sheet dates (SSAP 20.46)	Use of contract rate not permitted. The forward contract is measured initially at cost and at fair value at subsequent balance sheet dates. The difference in approach affects the timing of gains or losses and their classification in the income statement.
Disposal of a foreign entity	Exchange differences arising on disposal are not recycled through the income statement	The cumulative amount of any related but deferred exchange differences, should be recognised as income or expenses in same period as gain or loss on disposal is recognised

Topic	UK GAAP	IAS 21
Average rate	SSAP 20 permits the use of either the closing rate or average rate to translate income and expenses	Use of closing rate for translating a foreign entity's profit and loss account when applying the net investment method not permitted
Exchange differences		Differences arising on settlement of monetary items are recognised as income or expenses in period they arise
Exchange differences on monetary items – forming part of reporting entity's net investment in a foreign operation	SSAP 20 requires exchange differences to be taken to STRGL in both individual and consolidated financial statements	1. In entity's individual financial statements or those of foreign operation if appropriate- exchange differences are included in income statement (IAS 21.28). 2. Recognise as a separate component of equity in reporting entity's consolidated accounts. Then recognised in profit and loss account if and when net investment is disposed of (see disposals above).
Additional disclosures required by UK GAAP and IAS 21	1. Method used to translate the financial statements of foreign enterprises and treatment of foreign exchange differences (SSAP 20.59). 2. Net amount of exchange gains or losses on foreign currency borrowings less deposits.	1. Details of exchange differences included in the income statement (IAS 21.52a). 2. Reconciliation of exchange differences included in equity at beginning and end of financial period (IAS 21. 52b). 3. Nature of and reasons for change in classification of a foreign entity (IAS 21.54).

Comparison between FRS 23 and IAS 21

The text of IAS 21 "Accounting for the effects of changes in foreign exchange rates", contains references to other IAS standards. These have been amended to enable the standard to be applied in a UK context. **8397**

The **transitional provisions** set out in IFRS 1 "First-Time Adoption of International Accounting Standards" to be applied by an entity using IFRS for the first time, have been incorporated into FRS 23 (paragraph 59A) (see ¶8383-7). FRS 23 is in all other respects identical to IAS 21.

MEMO POINTS The ASB has issued a "Notice to Constituents", advising of a draft technical correction to IAS 21 issued by the IASB. This requires a different technical treatment for exchange differences arising on intra-group loans denominated in a currency other than the functional currency of parties to the loan. The proposals have implications for FRS 23 which is based on IAS 21. The "notice" effectively represents a parallel amendment to FRS 23.

First-time adoption

An **exemption** is included in IFRS 1, permitting the cumulative translation difference on the re-translation of a subsidiary's net assets to be set to zero, at the transition date to IFRS. This means that translation differences do not have to be separately disclosed and recycled in the income statement if the subsidiary is disposed of. However, translation differences arising after the transition date must be disclosed. **8398**

The **rules in IAS 21** covering re-translation of goodwill and fair value adjustments do not have to be applied retrospectively to business combinations, created before the transition date to IFRS.

Hyperinflation

8399 IAS 21 (27) Guidance is supplied in IAS 29 concerning the **characteristics for an economic environment** experiencing hyperinflation; as follows:
- the general population prefers to hold wealth in non-monetary assets or in another stable currency as opposed to the local currency;
- local prices are quoted in both the native and the stable currency;
- sales and purchases on credit are arranged at prices that compensate for any expected loss of purchasing power;
- interest rates, wages and prices are linked to a price index; and
- the cumulative inflation rate over three years is close to 100%.

SSAP 20 does not provide a definition of hyperinflation (¶8202) and the guidance provided in UITF 9, relates to the **adjustments required** to financial statements by entities operating in hyper-inflation environments.

MEMO POINTS The IASB has issued an exposure draft (ED) entitled "Severe hyperinflation", as a proposed amendment to IFRS 1, "First-time adoption of international accounting standards". The ED provides guidance on how to present financial statements for a period during which the entity could not comply with IFRS, because its functional currency was subject to severe hyperinflation. The period for public comment expired on 30 November 2010.

CHAPTER 4

Pensions and retirement benefits

OUTLINE ¶¶

SECTION 1

Introduction

Retirement benefits include all types of remuneration received (typically a pension) in return for the services rendered by the employee. Because of the nature of these benefits, uncertainties relating to valuation and timing in turn affect the accounting treatment. 8400

There are two main types of occupational pension schemes provided by employers: 8401
1. **Defined benefit scheme** (also known as a "final salary scheme") – in which the employer guarantees a pension based on a specific fraction of the employee's salary in turn based on the number of years of service. The employer bears the risk of making up any shortfall in

the fund when the benefits are paid out. This type of pension is being phased out by many employers.

2. **Defined contribution scheme** (otherwise known as a "money purchase scheme") – in which the benefits under the scheme ultimately depend on the fund amount that has accumulated, and the level of contributions paid into it. Consequently, there is no set promise or guarantee about the level of benefits that the employee will receive on retirement. Hence the employee bears the risk of the benefits being inadequate.

8402 Accounting for defined benefits schemes underwent radical change, following a long transition period, with the implementation of FRS 17, while the concept of matching continues to dictate the accounting treatment of defined contribution schemes.

This chapter considers the accounting requirements for both types of pension schemes, in addition to other retirement benefits.

Key definitions

8403 **Retirement benefits** All forms of consideration payable by an employer after the completion of the employment and in exchange for services of the employee, excluding:
- termination payments paid before the normal retirement date; or
- voluntary redundancy paid in respect of the right to future pension benefits.

Examples of retirement benefits include:
- pensions;
- healthcare; and
- continuing use of a car during retirement.

8404 **Pension** A regular payment made to an employee above a specified age, after employment has ceased, as a result of arrangements made by the employer.

8405 FRS 17 (1) **Defined contribution scheme** A pension or other retirement benefit scheme into which an employer pays regular contributions, either fixed as an amount, or as a percentage of pay.

MEMO POINTS Where death-in-service benefits are provided by a defined contribution scheme, these do not change its classification for accounting purposes.

8406 FRS 17 (1) **Defined benefit scheme** A pension scheme **that is not** a defined contribution scheme, which broadly means the scheme rules specify the benefits to be paid, requiring it to be financed accordingly. Actuarial methods are used to determine the amounts that are to be recognised for accounting purposes, because there is great uncertainty as to the ultimate cost of the scheme.

Where a scheme has **features of both** defined contribution and defined benefit schemes, and the employer has a potential liability to pay further contributions, it should be accounted for as a defined benefit scheme.

Future changes

8407 Accounting thinking around the disclosure of pension plans has changed since FRS 17 was developed in the UK, and IAS 19 internationally. It is now felt that existing standards do not always achieve the objective that a company's financial statements should provide full and transparent information on the company's exposure to pensions, including any deficit.

To address these concerns, the ASB in January 2008 published a Discussion Paper, "The Financial Reporting of Pensions." It seeks to establish standards for future practice, necessitating some fundamental differences in the treatment of pensions in the financial statements.

Similarly, the IASB has been considering its project on employee benefits and, in April 2010 published an Exposure Draft "Defined Benefit Plans". The current IASB project plan envisages an IFRS of improvements to IAS 19 by mid-2011.

These issues are discussed more fully at ¶8521.

SECTION 2

Defined benefit schemes

Introduction

In this type of scheme, the **benefits** are determined by the scheme rules, and the fund must be sufficiently financed so that the necessary benefits can be paid as promised. There are two main types of scheme: 8410

1. **Funded schemes**, where the scheme assets are held apart from the company, in a separate legal vehicle. These assets are ringfenced for the purposes of pension provision, and the scheme is usually managed by independent trustees.
2. **Unfunded schemes**, where the employer manages the assets that have been set aside to fund future employee benefits. The assets are not ringfenced for this purpose. In effect, the employer is meeting the cost of the pension benefits from its own resources.

When **accounting for the cost** of providing a defined benefit scheme, the employer looks through the pension structure, to consider the underlying assets and liabilities within the scheme itself. The same accounting principles apply to both funded and unfunded schemes.

Implementation of FRS 17

As FRS 17 required such a radical evolution to pensions accounting, there has been a **slow transition** between the original rules as set out in SSAP 24, and the significant changes which are being fully implemented for accounting periods beginning on or after 1 January 2005. 8413

MEMO POINTS FRS 17 also replaces UITF 6 and UITF 18.

A **new requirement** under FRS 17 is the inclusion of the actuarially assessed pension asset or liability in the employer's own balance sheet, which comes into effect in the first financial year beginning on or after 1 January 2005. 8416

The requirements of FRS 17 are onerous and **annual actuarial advice** (a full valuation every three years with annual updates) is an essential requirement of compliance with its rules. This obviously has cost implications for the employer when preparing the accounts. In addition, the production of actuarially based information can also take some time and therefore employers should plan well ahead in order to ensure that they are able to publish their accounts within applicable deadlines. 8420

MEMO POINTS 1. Often a pension scheme will have a **different year end** to the employer, and so the actuary may need to update a valuation to the employer's year end.
2. Two full **actuarial valuations** may be required on a triennial basis, because different assumptions may be used depending on whether the valuation is prepared for the purposes of inclusion in the accounts, or for the trustees making future funding and investment decisions.

A. Comparison of FRS 17 and SSAP 24

Although the provisions of SSAP 24 have been superseded by those of FRS 17 in respect of periods beginning on or after 1 January 2005, the comparison below has been retained for the convenience of readers who may find the comparison useful. 8425

The **major differences** between the treatment of defined benefit pension schemes by FRS 17 and SSAP 24 are summarised in the following table.

	FRS 17	SSAP 24
Recognition of surplus or deficit	Immediately	Usually spread forward
Balance sheet entry	Difference between the value of scheme assets and scheme liabilities	Difference between recognised cost and contributions paid
Level of analysis for profit and loss entries	Detailed	Basic
Interest cost	Required	Optional
Level of disclosure	Detailed	Basic
Use of the STRGL	Required	Not required
Actuarial method	Projected unit method	Actuary's discretion

B. FRS 17 Requirements

1. General

8430 FRS 17 (1) The **objectives** of FRS 17 are as follows:
- assets and liabilities arising from the employer's retirement benefit obligations are to be reflected at fair value;
- operating costs of providing retirement benefits are to be recognised in the accounting periods in which the benefits are earned by the employees;
- related financing costs and other changes in the value of assets and liabilities are to be recognised in the accounting period in which they arise; and
- there is to be adequate disclosure in respect of the above.

8432 FRS 17 (4) The standard applies to all types of retirement benefits including post-retirement healthcare costs, arising from schemes both in the UK and overseas.

FRS 3 (29) When the standard is **first applied in full**, a prior period adjustment will need to be made to reflect the restatement of reserves in respect of the defined benefit pension asset or liability (¶488).

Dividends

8434 TECH 3/02 In determining the **profits available for distribution** for the payment of an interim dividend, directors should take account of FRS 17's effects. It is thought by the ASB that it would be unusual for the adoption of FRS 17 to affect any intended distribution.

8436 TECH 50/04 **Guidance** has been issued by the ICAEW in this regard, however, which broadly indicates the following:
- a cumulative net debit in reserves should be treated as a realised loss; and
- a cumulative net credit in reserves should be treated as an unrealised profit, except to the extent that it represents agreed refunds.

An unrealised credit will then become realised when it offsets subsequent net debits relating to the pension scheme in the reserves.

Multi-employer schemes

8438 FRS 17 (9) Each employer covered by the scheme should **normally account** for it on a fair and reasonable basis, and pro rate the components required for the accounts (as detailed in the remainder of this section).

There is an **exception** when the employer is liable only for amounts in respect of the current period, and the employer contributions are not affected by any surplus or deficit of the scheme relating to past service of the members. In this case the contributions should be accounted for as if the scheme were a defined contribution scheme (¶8600). This treatment also removes the problem relating to distributable reserves.

It is also possible that the employer is **unable to identify** its share of the underlying assets and liabilities in a multi-employer scheme. Again the employer would account for the scheme as if it were a defined contribution scheme with the following additional disclosures: **8440**
- the fact that the scheme is a defined benefit scheme;
- the reason that the employer does not have sufficient information to account for the scheme as a defined benefit scheme;
- any available information about that surplus or deficit – and the basis used in its determination; and
- any implications for the employer.

In this case, the **consolidated accounts** (¶6500) themselves will still reflect the pension scheme as a defined benefit scheme, requiring a consolidation adjustment to remove each individual company's pension accounting entries.

2. Measurement

The **accounting entries** rely to a large extent on the calculations performed, and the information supplied, by the scheme's actuary. The **persons** who remain ultimately **responsible**, for both the actuarial assumptions and related accounting adjustments, are the **directors**. In addition, they will need to provide some estimates based on their knowledge of the business. **8442**

Pension scheme assets

These assets, net of all liabilities (except the liability to pay future pensions), should be measured at their fair value at the balance sheet date. **8444** FRS 17 (14)

Generally, fair value is the amount at which an asset or liability could be exchanged in an arm's length transaction between informed and willing parties in an unforced sale. The table provides a definition of fair value for certain common assets.

Type of asset	Definition of fair value
Quoted securities	Current bid price
Unquoted securities	Estimate
Unitised securities (such as unit trusts)	Current bid price/Average of bid and offer prices[1]
Property	Open market value or RICS approved valuation
Insurance policies	Best approximation

Note:
1. An amendment to FRS 17, published December 2006 in respect of **quoted securities**, replaced "mid-market value" with "current bid price" but omitted to do the same in respect of **unitised securities**. This has now been corrected by "Improvements to Financial Reporting Standards" issued in December 2008, effective for periods on or after 1 January 2009. If an entity applies this amendment for an earlier period, it must disclose that it has done so.

The estimate of fair value for **unquoted securities** is necessarily subjective, although the problem is diminished for most pension schemes as it is likely that this type of investment will form only a small part of the scheme's overall investment portfolio.

Insurance policies which exactly match the amount and timing of some scheme liabilities (i.e., the benefits payable under the scheme) should be measured at the same amount as those liabilities.

Liabilities to pay future benefits

These pension scheme liabilities should also be measured at an estimate of fair value. Scheme liabilities are **defined** as: **8446** FRS 17 (20)
- benefits to members stated under the scheme terms; and

– other benefits where the employer has created a valid expectation amongst the scheme members that such benefits will arise.

As there are many long-term uncertainties impacting on the scheme liabilities (such as employee turnover, salary rates, and inflation), an actuarial calculation of the fair value is required.

8447 On 8 July 2010 the Minister for Pensions stated that the Government intended to use the Consumer Prices Index (CPI) instead of the Retail Prices Index (RPI) as the inflation measure for determining the minimum pension increases to be applied to the statutory index-linked features of retirement benefits. As a consequence, because annual CPI increases have in general been lower than RPI increases, this change has the potential to cause a **reduction in pension scheme liabilities**.

UITF Abstract 48, issued in December 2010, considers three issues:
– whether there is an reduction in scheme liabilities;
– how the effect should be presented;
– when the effect should be recognised – i.e., in which accounting period.

8448 In short, **whether there has been a reduction** will depend on facts and circumstances.

As to **how the effect should be presented**, the UITF consensus is as follows:
– if there is an obligation to pay benefit increases based on RPI, this is regarded as a change in benefit and is recognised in the profit and loss account;
– if there is no obligation to pay benefit increases based on RPI then a change to CPI is a change in an assumption and is part of actuarial gains and losses (see also ¶8486), which are recognised in the STRGL.

Entities must provide **disclosures** that explain the effect of changes in scheme liabilities arising from the replacement of RPI with CPI.

The question of **when to recognise** a reduction in scheme liabilities – as a result of whether there is an obligation to pay increased benefits based on RPI – is as follows:
– where there is such an obligation, the past service cost should be recognised in the accounting period when any necessary consultations have been concluded or employees' valid expectations have been changed;
– where there is no such obligation, the entity should use financial assumptions to measure scheme liabilities that reflect market expectations at the balance sheet date.

Actuarial considerations

8448 FRS 17 (23) The **overriding principle** is that the assumptions used to measure the liabilities of the scheme should be mutually compatible, and lead to the best estimate of the cashflows that will arise in future. The actuarial assumptions relating to future economic conditions take account of market expectations at the balance sheet date.

8450 The **assumptions** should also take into account any future events, and any commitments made by the employer which have been communicated to the members of the pension scheme, such as expected:
– early retirement;
– salary increases; and
– cost of living increases.

A **future event** in this context would not include redundancies, which are dealt with separately and are not to be anticipated. Similarly any curtailment, where the scheme is terminated or the scheme terms amended, should not be anticipated before the final decision to take action has been made (and indeed communicated to the members).

8452 FRS 17 (23) The **method** to be used by the actuary in his calculations is the projected unit method, which takes account of future increases in salaries, and considers that the cost of providing benefits becomes more expensive as an individual approaches retirement. The time value of money is accounted for on the basis that the age profile of the employees will remain consistent.

The pension benefits are normally allocated to periods of employee service in accordance with the scheme rules. An exception arises when the rules attribute a disproportionate share of the total benefits to later years of service, when a straight-line allocation should be used instead. FRS 17 (22)

In order to obtain the **present value** of the scheme liability, it must be discounted to reflect the time value of money. The rate of discount is prescribed as the current rate of return on a high quality corporate bond, which should mirror the currency and term of the scheme liabilities (such as an AA status bond). For **overseas schemes**, the discount rate should be based on government bonds with a small premium over the risk-free rate. **8454** FRS 17 (32)

Actuarial information will be required on an annual basis due to the information required for appropriate disclosure in the accounts, although a **full valuation** will only need to be undertaken every three years. In the intervening years, the actuary will need to update the valuation to take account of current conditions at each balance sheet date, such as: **8456** FRS 17 (35)
- fair value of scheme assets; and
- changes in financial assumptions.

3. Recognition

Scheme surplus

A scheme surplus is the excess of the value of the scheme assets over the present value of the scheme liabilities. An **asset** should be recognised in the employer's balance sheet in relation to the scheme surplus where it can be recovered through: **8460** FRS 17 (37), (41), (42)
- reduced future contributions by the employer; or
- a refund from the scheme.

In determining the amount of the asset, the actuarial assumptions used for accounting purposes should be used. No growth in the number of active members should be assumed, although a declining membership can be reflected.

Where part of the surplus will be used to **improve the benefits** available to members (such as spousal benefits), this part should not be recognised as an asset. This includes situations where the past actions of the employer have created an expectation amongst the scheme members that the surplus will be used to improve benefits. A **refund of contributions** should be recognised only if the amount has been agreed with the pension scheme trustees at the balance sheet date.

Scheme deficit

A scheme deficit is the shortfall of the value of the scheme assets compared to the present value of the scheme liabilities. A **liability** should be recognised to the extent that it represents an obligation of the employer. Where employees can be required to pay additional contributions, the liability should only recognise the net amount payable by the employer. **8462** FRS 17 (37)

For an **unfunded scheme**, the employer's liability is the obligation to pay future retirement benefits, and only this amount is recognised on the balance sheet. **8464**

Effect on performance statements

A simple example will show the **movement** in the performance statements dictated by the scheme surplus or deficit. **8465**

EXAMPLE A Ltd's pension scheme had a surplus of £20m at the beginning of the year. The charge to the profit and loss account is £15m, and the contribution paid is £10m. The surplus at the end of the year is £12m.

The following entries are made in A Ltd's accounts:

	Dr £	Cr £	Pension surplus asset £
Brought forward			20m
Dr pension charge in P & L	15m		
Cr pension surplus asset		15m	(15m)
Dr pension surplus asset	10m		10m
Cr bank		10m	
Dr actuarial loss in STRGL	3m		
Cr pension surplus asset		3m	(3m)
Closing pension asset			12m

4. Balance sheet presentation

8466 FRS 17 (47) **Contributions payable** to the pension scheme but unpaid at the balance sheet date should be disclosed in "creditors: amounts due within one year".

8468 The presentation of the pension scheme **surplus or deficit** in the balance sheet depends on the format of the balance sheet adopted (¶984). In any event, the amount of the surplus or deficit should be stated net of deferred tax (¶9060), on the face of the balance sheet.

Format 1 balance sheet

8470 FRS 17 (47), (49) The scheme **surplus or deficit** should be reflected directly on the balance sheet of the employer, in a separate caption, after accruals and deferred income. It is likely that the employer will opt to also include a new subtotal on the face of the balance sheet and make the disclosure as follows:

Net assets excluding pension assets and liabilities	X
Pension asset/(liability)	X/(X)
Net assets including pension assets and liabilities	X

Format 2 balance sheet

8472 The scheme **surplus** should be reflected directly on the balance sheet of the employer, in a separate caption, with an optional new subtotal, as follows:

Assets excluding pension asset	X
Pension asset	X
Assets including pension asset	X

Similarly, the scheme **deficit** should be reflected as follows:

Liabilities excluding pension liability	X
Pension liability	X
Liabilities including pension liability	X

8474 FRS 17 (47) If the company has **more than one pension scheme**, the assets and liabilities for all those schemes should not be netted off, but should be shown separately on the face of the balance sheet.

5. Presentation in the performance statements

8476 FRS 17 (50) There are a number of **different elements** which must be disclosed in the performance statements, which relate to the movement in the scheme asset or liability in each accounting

period. The calculation of these components is performed by the scheme actuary. The elements are **classified** as either:
- periodic costs, which will be relevant to every accounting period; or
- non-periodic costs, which will arise from one-off transactions only.

Once these basic aspects have been dealt with, the following issues must also be considered:
- restricted scheme surpluses (¶8494);
- increase to scheme surpluses (¶8496);
- current tax (¶8498); and
- deferred tax (¶8500).

a. Periodic costs

The following table explains the various components that make up periodic costs. **8478**

Component	Explanation	Recognised in	¶¶
Current service cost	Increase in the present value of the scheme liabilities expected to arise from employee service in the current period.	P & L – operating profit [1]	¶8480
Interest cost	Expected increase in the present value of scheme liabilities during the accounting period because the benefits are one period closer to settlement.	P & L – other finance costs/income	¶8482
Expected return on assets	An estimate of the long-term expected return on the scheme assets.	P & L – other finance costs/income	¶8484
Actuarial gains and losses	Gains or losses arising from: – changes in actuarial assumptions; or – discrepancies between past assumptions and reality.	STRGL	¶8486

Note:
1. If capitalised, current service cost should be included in the cost of the asset on the balance sheet.

Current service cost

This cost is **based** on the most recent actuarial valuation at the beginning of the period, with the financial assumptions updated to reflect conditions at that date. The amount should be **stated** net of any employee contributions, in the same statutory accounts heading as other salary costs. **8480** FRS 17 (51)

Interest cost

This cost is **calculated** by applying the discount rate to the present value of the scheme liabilities at the beginning of the accounting period. The interest cost should be netted off against the expected return on assets, and shown in "other finance costs (or income)" adjacent to interest. **8482** FRS 17 (53), (56)

MEMO POINTS "Other finance costs (or income)" is a new format heading, separate from "interest payable and similar charges".

EXAMPLE A Ltd has a defined benefit scheme with the following liabilities at the beginning of each year:

	20X7	20X6
	£m	£m
Pension scheme liabilities	4	3

The discount rate at the beginning of the year is 8.0% and 9.0% for 20X6 and 20X5 respectively. The computed interest cost will be:

	20X7	20X6
	£m	£m
Interest cost: (£4m @ 8%: £3m @ 9%)	0.32	0.27

Expected return on assets

8484 FRS 17 (54) This amount is credited to the profit and loss account, by offset against the interest cost. The expected return should be stable, although ultimately subjective. The following table summarises the **required calculations**, which are based on amounts applying at the beginning of the accounting period.

Type of asset	Calculation
Quoted government or corporate bonds	Current redemption yield x market value of bonds
Other assets including equities	Expected long-term rate x fair value

This is an area that requires careful judgement by the directors, based on advice from the actuary.

Actuarial gains and losses

8486 FRS 17 (57) The **main instances** where such a gain or loss may arise are:
- differences between the actual and expected return on scheme assets;
- differences between the actual and expected change in liabilities in the period;
- the effect of changes in the actuarial assumptions concerning liabilities; and
- where a pension surplus has not been previously recognised as an asset in the company balance sheet.

All actuarial gains and losses are to be **included** within the STRGL only.

b. Non-periodic costs

8488 The following table explains the various components which make up non-periodic costs.

Component	Explanation	Recognised in	¶¶
Past service costs	Employees become entitled to improved benefits, and previous years of service count towards these improved benefits. For example, the employer may make a commitment to grant earlier retirement with extra years added on to the length of service.	P & L – operating profit[1]	¶8490
Gains and losses on settlements and curtailments	Settlements and curtailment are one-off events which are unlikely to have been included in the actuarial assumptions.	P & L – operating profit, unless exceptional item	¶8492

1. If capitalised, current service cost should be included in the cost of the asset on the balance sheet.

Past service costs

8490 FRS 17 (60) These costs should be **recognised** on a straight-line basis over the period when members become entitled to the improved benefits. Often the entitlement arises immediately, in which case the past service cost should be recognised in the current accounting period when the decision to improve the benefits is made.

Past service costs should **normally** be included within the same statutory accounts heading as other salary costs.

An **exception** arises when part of the scheme surplus is not recognised as an asset in the accounts. In this situation, the past service costs may be extinguished by the unrecognised surplus, in which case there will be no entries in the accounts relating to the costs, although disclosure is required (¶8512).

Gains and losses on settlements and curtailments

The following table gives details of when these events might arise: **8492** FRS 17 (1), (64)

Event	Explanation	Examples
Settlement	An irrevocable action which relieves the employer of the responsibility to provide a pension in the future.	– lump sum cash payment in exchange for members' rights to pension benefits; – purchase of an irrevocable annuity contract to cover all accrued benefits.
Curtailment	An event which leads to a reduction in the expected future years of service, or reduction in the defined benefits relating to future service for some employees.	– early termination of employee services, such as the closure of an operation; – amendments to the terms of the scheme, such that the future service of the employees leads to reduced benefits.

The **accounting treatment** for both these types of events depends on whether a loss or gain (basically the movement in the scheme surplus or deficit) results from the decision to settle or curtail.

1. **Losses** should be recognised in the profit and loss account (within operating profit unless the item is exceptional) measured at the date when the employer is demonstrably committed to the transaction. An **exception** arises when part of the scheme surplus is not recognised as an asset in the accounts. In this situation, the loss may be extinguished by the unrecognised surplus and so there will be no entries in the accounts relating to the loss, although disclosure of the extinguished amounts is required (¶8512).

2. **Gains** should be recognised only when all involved parties are irrevocably committed to the transaction giving rise to the gain, and included in the profit and loss account (again within operating profit unless the item is exceptional).

---

c. Other issues

Restriction of surpluses

A scheme surplus will not always be recognised as an asset, as discussed at ¶8460. When part of the surplus **becomes irrecoverable**, the accounting process should follow these steps: **8494** FRS 17 (67)

1. The normal entries should be made, which will result in the full surplus being shown as an asset in the accounts.

2. The following adjustment is then made to reduce the asset to its recoverable amount:

a. the unrecognised surplus is used to extinguish the following costs which would otherwise be charged in the profit and loss account in the period, and this has the effect of increasing the balance sheet asset:

- past service costs;
- losses on settlements; and
- losses on curtailments;

b. a debit entry is made in the profit and loss account to reduce the expected return on assets to no more than the total of all the cost elements of the pension i.e., current service cost, interest cost, past service costs, and settlement and curtailment losses not covered by an unrecognised surplus; and

c. the balance of the unrecognised surplus is reflected as an actuarial loss in the STRGL.

EXAMPLE C Ltd has a defined benefit pension scheme with a surplus of £20m, although only £15m is to be recognised as an asset in the company's accounts.
The movement in the surplus in the year, before taking account of the unrecognised surplus of £5m, is as follows:

	£m
Surplus in scheme at beginning of the year	14
Movement in year:	
Current service cost	(4)
Contributions	2
Past service costs	(2)
Expected return on assets	13
Interest cost	(4)
Actuarial gain	1
Surplus in scheme at end of the year	20

The asset relating to the scheme surplus then needs to be reduced to £15m, and the following steps must be taken:

1. The past service costs of £2m are extinguished by part of the unrecognised surplus. The journal required would be:

	Dr	Cr
Dr recoverable surplus (asset)	£2m	
Cr past service costs (P & L)		£2m

2. The limit of the credit to the profit and loss account is £1m (being the £15m recoverable surplus less the opening balance of £14m).
The total profit and loss items excluding the expected return on assets are:

	£m
Current service cost	4
Past service cost (after step 1)	0
Interest cost	4
Total	8

The expected return on assets cannot exceed £9m, calculated as:

	£m
Total costs in profit and loss account	8
Overall increase in recognised surplus in the year	1
Total	9

3. The expected return on assets is reduced from £13m to £9m by the following journal:

	Dr	Cr
Dr expected return on assets (P & L)	£4m	
Cr recoverable surplus (asset)		£4m

4. The remaining £3m adjustment required is debited against the actuarial gain to create a £2m actuarial loss:

	Dr	Cr
Dr actuarial gain (STRGL)	£3m	
Cr recoverable surplus (asset)		£3m

So the asset has now been reduced to £15m, and the amended movement to the surplus is as follows:

	£m
Surplus in scheme at beginning of the year	14
Movement in year:	
Current service cost	(4)
Contributions	2
Past service costs	0
Expected return on assets	9
Interest cost	(4)
Actuarial loss	(2)
Surplus in scheme at end of the year	15

Increase to surplus

Occasionally a situation will arise where a surplus **previously not recognised** is now deemed to be recoverable in the current accounting period, and this should be included in the accounts as follows: 8496 FRS 17 (67)-(68)

1. If a **refund is received** in respect of a surplus which has not previously been recognised, the refund should be shown as other financial income and separately disclosed in the notes to the financial statements. If the surplus has already been recognised as an asset in the accounts, the receipt of the cash refund will be a pure balance sheet entry.
2. If an **increase in the active membership** results in the recoverable surplus, it should be treated as an operating gain. This might arise as a result of an acquisition of a business.

Current tax

Tax **relief on pension contributions** should be regarded as relating to the items reported in the profit and loss account first, before the actuarial losses reported in the STRGL. Any **excess** tax relief should normally be allocated to the profit and loss account. 8498 FRS 17 (71)

EXAMPLE B Ltd pays corporate tax at the rate of 30% and makes a contribution of £100,000 to its defined benefit scheme in the year, resulting in related tax relief of £30,000. The pension charges in the performance statements are as follows:

	£
Profit and loss account charge	45,000
STRGL- loss	25,000
Total	70,000

The related tax entries would be:

	Pension charge £	Current tax entry £	Net charge after tax relief £
Profit and loss account	45,000	(13,500)	31,500
STRGL	25,000	(7,500)	17,500
Total	70,000	(21,000)	49,000
Excess tax relief		(9,000)	
Total tax relief		(30,000)	

The excess tax relief of £9,000 should be included as a credit to the profit and loss account unless it clearly relates to an item in the STRGL.
The total profit and loss tax credit entry will therefore be £22,500.

Deferred tax

Full **provision** should be made in respect of deferred tax on the pension scheme deficit or surplus, using the appropriate tax rates. The related deferred tax balance is netted against the pension asset or liability. The presentation of the pension related deferred tax charge/credit should follow the usual rules (¶9122), and be allocated to the profit and loss account, unless it relates to items included in the STRGL. 8500 FRS 19 (34)

EXAMPLE Continuing the example in ¶8498, the movement on the pension scheme asset can be analysed as follows:

	£
Profit and loss account charge	(45,000)
Loss in STRGL	(25,000)
Contribution	100,000
Overall movement in scheme asset	30,000

The overall movement results in a deferred tax charge of £9,000, assuming a tax rate of 30%.

1. **One possible option** is to pro rate the deferred tax charge and show it in the performance statements as follows:

	Pension charge £	Deferred tax charge £
Profit and loss account (45,000/70,000 x £9,000)	45,000	5,786
STRGL (25,000/70,000 x £9,000)	25,000	3,214
Total	70,000	9,000

2. **Alternatively**, the charge can be allocated to the profit and loss account to counteract the effect of the excess current tax relief, as follows:

	Pension charge £	Current tax £	Deferred tax £	Total tax charge £
Profit and loss account	40,000	(22,500)	9,000	(13,500)
STRGL	30,000	(7,500)	0	(7,500)
Total	70,000	(30,000)	9,000	(21,000)

Recognising the deferred tax charge in the profit and loss account gives an overall tax entry which is 30% of the pension charge of £45,000, reflecting the correlation between the overall tax charge of £21,000 and pension charge of £70,000.

6. Disclosure

8505 FRS 17(75) The following disclosures should be made in respect of a **defined contribution scheme**:
- the nature of the scheme (i.e., defined contribution);
- the cost for the period; and
- any outstanding or prepaid contributions at balance sheet date.

8506 FRS 17 (76) According to FRS 17 (as amended in December 2006), employers are obliged to disclose, in respect of their **defined benefit schemes**, information that enables users of financial statements to evaluate the nature of the schemes as well as the financial effects of changes in those schemes during the period. The amendments to FRS 17 are effective for years beginning on or after 6 April 2007. The prior rules form the basis of the remainder of this section. The changes required in subsequent years are summarised from ¶8516.

8507 The following disclosures should be made:
- information that will enable users to evaluate the nature of a company's participation in defined benefit schemes and the financial effects of changes in those schemes;
- the principal actuarial assumptions used as at the balance sheet date. Previously, only information regarding the main financial assumptions was required. The most significant change this is likely to bring is the requirement to disclose mortality rates (where this is considered to be a material assumption);
- the contribution made in respect of the current accounting period, and any agreed contribution rates for future years;
- an analysis of the opening and closing scheme liabilities and scheme assets showing separately the movements in scheme assets and scheme liabilities.
- an analysis of scheme liabilities into amounts arising from schemes that are (1) wholly or partly funded and (2) wholly unfunded; and
- information about contingent liabilities arising from retirement benefit obligations as well as the nature of contingent assets, where an inflow of the economic benefits is probable. In addition, in accordance with the provisions of FRS 12, "Provisions, contingent liabilities and contingent assets", companies should in any event disclose contingent assets and contingent liabilities, including guarantees, arising from retirement benefit obligations.

Assumptions

Each of the main financial assumptions used at the **balance sheet date** should be disclosed as separate figures, and not combined or netted off. The **main** assumptions would include: 8509 FRS 17 (78)
- inflation assumption;
- the rate of increase in salaries;
- the rate of increase for pensions in payment and deferred pensions; and
- the rate used to discount scheme liabilities.

MEMO POINTS Before the December 2006 amendment to FRS 17, it had been a requirement that the assumptions **both at the beginning and end of the year** had to be given; now only the assumptions used at the balance sheet date are required. The result is that entities are no longer effectively required to disclose assumptions for a three-year period.

Components of the pension cost

1. The following amounts, which are included in **operating profit**, should be disclosed in the notes to the financial statements: 8512 FRS 17 (82)
- the current service cost;
- any past service costs;
- any previously unrecognised surplus deducted from past service costs;
- gains and losses on any settlements or curtailments; and
- any previously recognised surplus deducted from the settlement or curtailment losses.

2. Any gains and losses on **settlements or curtailments** (and any previously unrecognised surplus deducted from the losses) included within a separate item after operating profit should be disclosed in a note.
3. The following amounts included as **other finance costs or income**:
- interest cost; and
- expected return on assets in the scheme.

4. The following amounts included within the **STRGL**:
- difference between the expected and actual return on assets;
- experience gains and losses arising on the scheme liabilities; and
- effects of changes in the demographic and financial assumptions underlying the present value of the scheme liabilities.

History of amounts recognised in the STRGL

For the **accounting period and previous four periods** (this disclosure is not required to be created retrospectively and will be built up over time): 8513 FRS 17 (86)
- the difference between the expected and actual return on assets expressed both as an amount and as a percentage of the scheme assets at the balance sheet date;
- the experience gains and losses arising on the scheme liabilities expressed both as an amount and as a percentage of the present value of the scheme liabilities at the balance sheet date; and
- the total actuarial gain or loss expressed both as an amount and as a percentage of the present value of the scheme liabilities at the balance sheet date.

Reconciliation to the balance sheet

1. The fair value of the scheme assets, the present value of the scheme liabilities based on the accounting assumptions, and the resulting surplus or deficit. 8514 FRS 17 (88)
2. An explanation of any difference between the asset or liability on the balance sheet and the surplus and deficit of the scheme. Examples of such differences would be deferred tax and any restriction in the recognition of the surplus.
3. An analysis of the movements in the surplus or deficit in the scheme during the period.

Analysis of reserves

The analysis of reserves in the notes to the financial statements should **distinguish** the amount relating to the defined benefit asset or liability net of the related deferred tax. 8515 FRS 17 (90)

EXAMPLE **Balance sheet presentation**

	20X7	20X6
	£m	£m
Net assets excluding pension asset	800	700
Pension asset	380	335
Net assets including pension asset	1,180	1,035

Reserves note

Profit and loss reserve excluding pension asset	500	400
Pension reserve	380	335
Profit and loss reserve	880	735

Pension cost note

Composition of the scheme

The group operates a defined benefit scheme in the UK. A full actuarial valuation was carried out at 31 December 20X6 and updated to 31 December 20X7 by a qualified independent actuary. The major assumptions used by the actuary were:

	At 31.12.20X7	At 31.12.20X6	At 31.12.20X5
Rate of increase in salaries	5.0%	4.0%	5.5%
Rate of increase in pensions in payment	2.5%	2.0%	3.0%
Discount rate	6.5%	4.5%	7.0%
Inflation assumption	3.0%	2.5%	4.0%

The assets in the scheme and the expected rate of return were:

	Long-term rate of return expected at 31.12.20X7	Value at 31.12.20X7 £m	Long-term rate of return expected at 31.12.20X6	Value at 31.12.20X6 £m	Long-term rate of return expected at 31.12.20X5	Value at 31.12.20X5 £m
Equities	6.9%	1,235	7.3%	1,116	8.0%	721
Bonds	6.0%	357	5.5%	298	6.0%	192
Property	4.5%	94	6.0%	74	6.1%	49
Total market value of assets		1,686		1,488		962
Present value of scheme liabilities		(1,143)		(1,009)		
Surplus in scheme		543		479		
Related deferred tax liability		(163)		(144)		
Net pension asset		380		335		

Analysis of the amount charged to operating profit

	20X7	20X6
	£m	£m
Current service cost	42	34
Past service cost	15	12
Total operating charge	57	46

Analysis of the amount credited to other finance income

	20X7	20X6
	£m	£m
Expected return on pension scheme assets	81	73
Interest on pension scheme liabilities	(48)	(53)
Net return	33	20

Analysis of the amount recognised in STRGL

	20X7	20X6
	£m	£m
Actual return less expected return on pension scheme assets	324	480
Experience gains and losses arising on the scheme liabilities	(45)	(58)
Changes in assumptions underlying the present value of the scheme liabilities	(206)	(146)
Actuarial gain recognised in STRGL	73	276

Movement in surplus during the year

	20X7	20X6
	£m	£m
Surplus in scheme at beginning of the year	479	204
Movement in year:		
Current service cost	(42)	(34)
Contributions	15	25
Past service costs	(15)	(12)
Other finance income	33	20
Actuarial gain	73	276
Surplus in scheme at end of the year	543	479

The full actuarial valuation at 31 December 20X6 showed an increase in the surplus from £204m to £479m. Improvements in benefits costing £15m were made in 20X7 and contributions reduced to £15m (4% of pensionable pay). It has been agreed with the pension trustees that contributions for the next three years will remain at that level.

History of experience gains and losses

	20X7	20X6	20X5	20X4	20X3
Difference between the expected and actual return on scheme assets:					
– amount (£m)	324	480	138	(6)	(94)
– percentage of scheme assets	25%	32%	14%	(1%)	16%
Experience gains and losses on scheme liabilities:					
– amount (£m)	(45)	(58)	(6)	34	25
– percentage of scheme assets	(5%)	(6%)	(1%)	5%	2%
Total amount recognised in statement of total recognised gains and losses:					
– amount (£m)	73	276	91	1	66
– percentage of scheme assets	6%	27%	12%	0%	5%

7. The December 2006 amendment

In December 2006, arising out of concerns that financial statements were not giving as clear a picture as possible about the risks and rewards of defined benefit schemes, the ASB published an amendment to FRS 17. As of 6 April 2007, certain additional disclosures were mandated while others, previously required, were dispensed with. 8516

Although the changes have been incorporated into the preceding text, they are repeated here for ease of comparison.

The significant **additional disclosures** include: 8517

– Information to enable users to evaluate the nature of a company's participation in defined benefit schemes and the financial effects of changes in those schemes. Previously, FRS 17 required only the nature of schemes to be disclosed.

– The principal actuarial assumptions used as at the balance sheet date. Previously, only information regarding the main financial assumptions was required. The most significant change this is likely to bring is the requirement to disclose mortality rates – where it is considered to be a material assumption.

– An analysis of the opening and closing scheme liabilities and scheme assets showing separately the movements in scheme assets and scheme liabilities.
– An analysis of scheme liabilities into amounts arising from schemes that are funded and those that are not.
– Information about contingent liabilities arising from retirement benefit obligations as well as the nature of contingent assets, where an inflow of the economic benefits is probable.

8518 The following disclosures are **no longer required**:
– The date of the most recent full actuarial evaluation and whether the actuary is an employee or officer of the company.
– The effects of changes in the demographic and financial assumptions underlying the present value of the scheme liabilities.
– The financial assumptions at the beginning of the period (previously, both those at the beginning and end of the year had to be given; now only the assumptions used at the balance sheet date are required. Consequently, an entity is no longer required to disclose assumptions for a three-year period).
– An analysis of reserves in the notes to the financial statements distinguishing the amount relating to the defined benefit asset or liability net of any related deferred tax.
– For closed schemes and those in which the age profile of the active membership is rising significantly, the fact that under the projected unit method the current service cost will increase, as members of the scheme approach retirement.
– The fair value of the assets held by the pension scheme at the beginning and end of the period analysed into classes of assets and disclosed together with the expected rate of return assumed for each class.
– The difference between the expected and actual return on assets in respect of the current period and previous four periods. Instead, the present value of the defined benefit obligation; the fair value of the scheme assets and surplus or deficit arising in the scheme; and experience adjustments arising on the assets and liabilities of the scheme expressed either as an amount or a percentage of the scheme assets at the balance sheet date should be given.

8519 At the same time as the amendment to FRS 17 was issued, the APB also published a Reporting Statement (RS), "**Retirement benefits**", intended as a formulation of **best practice**. As such, it does not have mandatory force. However, it sets out the following six principles to be considered when providing disclosures for defined benefit schemes:
– the relationship between the entity and trustees (managers) of the defined benefit scheme;
– the principal assumptions used to measure scheme liabilities;
– the sensitivity of scheme liabilities to changes in the principal assumptions used to measure the scheme liabilities;
– how the liabilities arising from defined benefit schemes are measured;
– the future funding requirements to the defined benefit scheme; and
– the nature and extent of the risks arising from the assets held by the defined benefit scheme.

8. Current developments

8521 For the past few years it has been felt by both the ASB and the IASB that pension accounting is in need of an overhaul. The ASB's 2008 **discussion paper**, "The Financial Reporting of Pensions", contained proposals for fuller and more transparent disclosure of pensions in the financial statements – specifically, the way in which pension fund assets and liabilities are calculated and reported.

The recent financial crisis has refocused attention on the need to provide users of financial statements with an understanding of the risks an entity is exposed to. For instance, since 2005, pensions have been affected by an increase in the number of defined benefit schemes that are closing to both new entrants and future accruals. The main focus for many entities is now on **funding** pension plans and managing the **risk**.

The main issues raised in the discussion paper were:

1. **Changes in pension assets and liabilities** should be reported in the period in which they arise, rather than being spread forward. Financial statements should reflect the actual return on assets, rather than the expected value as is currently required. Both would reflect the underlying economic reality rather than allowing smoothing mechanisms.
2. In **measuring liabilities**, a risk-free rate (instead of the high-quality corporate bond rate required by current accounting standards) should be used. A reduced discount rate would increase the size of liabilities.
3. Whether the liability should include the **effect of future increases in salaries** (as under current standards) or if this measure should be changed to reflect the employer's discretion over salary increases. Such a change would reduce the size of liabilities.
4. Where an employer controls a pension plan, whether it should be **consolidated** in the employer's financial statements. Current requirements provide an exemption.
5. The question of **financial reporting by pension plans** to their members (i.e., as a separate issue to financial **reporting by the employer**). The discussion paper recommends that pension plans should be required to include the liability to pay future benefits. At present, if a liability is reported, it tends to be the amount required by regulations rather than an amount that measures the true economic burden.

In November 2009, having received feedback and redeliberated the issues raised, the ASB issued a report containing its recommendations. **8522**

In general, the report affirmed the views set out in the discussion paper, acknowledging that a number of them cover difficult issues and are controversial. On the measurement of liabilities, its view is that the discount rate used should reflect the time value of money - and should for this reason be a risk-free rate. The ASB has reiterated that it is not possible to make a reliable estimate of the risk arising from the size and variability of the liability to pay pension benefits. Users of financial statements are probably better served by disclosures regarding the risk rather than through adjustment of the underlying liability. In addition, the spread between AA corporate bonds and gilt yields has had the effect of reducing the liability for pensions in financial statements.

One of the objectives of the report was to provide the IASB with views it could consider in developing a future financial reporting standard on pensions.

In April 2010 the IASB published an Exposure Draft, "Defined Benefit Plans". Its proposals, which are not necessarily the same as the ASB has put forward, are aimed at making it easier for users of financial statements to understand how defined benefit plans affect an entity's financial position, financial performance, and cash flows. The ASB has given broad support to many of the proposals in the exposure draft. **8523**

The IASB's plan is to issue improvements to IAS 19 in 2011.

C. SSAP 24 Requirements

While the **application** of SSAP 24 has all but ceased (as FRS 17 is mandatory for accounting periods beginning on or after 1 January 2005), some employers may still need to refer to it. For the purposes of completeness, therefore, this section is being retained. **8524** SSAP 24 (16), (77)

The **objective** of SSAP 24 was to match the expected cost to the employer of providing pensions with the benefit of employee services which the employer enjoys. Its **scope** includes all pensions schemes provided by UK companies that report under UK GAAP, although there is additional flexibility in the reporting of foreign schemes (¶8558). **8525**

1. Measurement

8526 SSAP 24 (20), (21) There are two elements of **pension cost** to be accounted for in the financial statements:
1. **Regular** cost, being the amount that should be contributed to the scheme to provide the eventual pensions in respect of future service, based on current actuarial calculations. The regular cost is usually expressed as a percentage of pensionable earnings.
2. **Variations** from regular cost, which can arise due to the unpredictability of such factors as investment growth, years of service and levels of final salary.

8527 SSAP 24 (79) The **acceptable actuarial methods** are to be determined at the actuary's discretion so that the assumptions and methods, taken as a whole, should be compatible. The exact method is not dictated by the standard, although the result should be a regular pension cost which is a substantially level proportion of the current and expected future pensionable payroll. The method anticipates the final salary on which the pension benefits will be based.

The actuary should take the **following factors** into account:
- future rates of inflation;
- pay increases;
- increases to pensions;
- earnings on investments;
- number of new joiners;
- age profile of the employees; and
- death and leavers.

2. Recognition

Regular cost

8528 SSAP 24 (20) This cost should usually be taken to the profit and loss account as an application of the matching concept.

Variations from regular cost

8530 SSAP 24 (80) The **general rule** is that the variation should be spread forward and amortised over the expected remaining service lives of the employees, with the resulting charge included in the profit and loss account.

It should be noted that the recognition of the pension charge in the profit and loss account will not always **match** the cash flow of the pension contribution payments. For example, the directors may decide to correct an experience deficit by way of a single immediate top-up payment. This payment will be spread forward, and a prepayment will be shown in the balance sheet that will gradually reduce over the expected service lives of the employees.

Exceptions to the general rule are given in ¶8540.

MEMO POINTS The **expected remaining lives** of current employees is often calculated using the average remaining service life, which is a weighted average of the expected future service of the current members of the scheme up to their normal retirement dates, or expected dates of earlier withdrawal or death in service.

8532 UITF 18 **Examples** of variations are:
- experience surpluses or deficits which arise when the actuarial assumptions are not borne out in practice;
- pension increases for which provision has not been made; and
- changes in the tax system, such as the withdrawal of dividend tax credit refunds to pension schemes following the 1997 Budget.

Spreading forward

8534 The variation cost is **often** recognised on a straight-line basis, as shown in the following example.

EXAMPLE There is a £600,000 deficit on A Ltd's defined benefit pension scheme. The average remaining service life of the employees is six years. The standard level of pension contribution is 6% of payroll costs, which are expected to increase by 2% per annum. A Ltd is paying three equal contributions over the next three years to resolve the deficit and will then continue to pay the regular contribution in subsequent years.
The expected payroll costs over the next six years are:

Year	Payroll costs	Regular cost at 6%
	£	£
1	3,000,000	180,000
2	3,060,000	183,600
3	3,121,200	187,272
4	3,183,624	191,017
5	3,247,296	194,838
6	3,312,242	198,735

The contributions in years 1 to 3 are calculated as follows:

Total regular cost for years 1 to 3	£550,872	(£180,000 + £183,600 + £187,272)
Total deficit	£600,000	
Total cost over years 1 to 3	£1,150,872	
Cost for each year	£383,624	(£1,150,872/3)

The entries in the financial statements would be:

Year	Regular cost	Variation cost	Total cost – P & L charge	Payments	Asset
	£	£	£	£	£
1	180,000	100,000	280,000	383,624	103,624
2	183,600	100,000	283,600	383,624	203,648
3	187,272	100,000	287,272	383,624	300,000
4	191,017	100,000	291,017	191,017	200,000
5	194,838	100,000	294,838	194,838	100,000
6	198,735	100,000	298,735	198,735	0

The asset amount will appear in the balance sheet as a prepayment and is the cumulative payment in excess of the total cost.
If a pension surplus existed instead, and A Ltd took a contribution holiday, a balance sheet liability would be created in Year 1 as payments would be less than the total cost.

To take account of the **time value of money** the amounts calculated by the actuary are discounted to give present values, and some employers choose to recognise interest in respect of the surplus or deficit. The interest should be presented as part of the pension cost. **8536**

EXAMPLE Continuing the example at ¶8534 but now recognising interest on the deficit at 5%:

Year	Deficit (note 1)	Regular cost	Payments	Balance before interest (note 2)	Interest charge (note 3)	Variation cost	Total P & L charge (note 4)
	£	£	£	£	£	£	£
1	600,000	180,000	383,624	396,376	19,819	100,000	299,819
2	416,195	183,600	383,624	216,171	10,809	100,000	294,409
3	226,980	187,272	383,624	30,628	1,531	100,000	288,803
4	32,159	191,017	191,017	32,159	1,608	100,000	292,625
5	33,767	194,838	194,838	33,767	1,688	100,000	296,526
6	35,455	198,735	198,735	35,455	1,773	100,000	300.508
Total		1,135,462			37,228	600,000	1,772,690

Notes:
1. The deficit balance is increased by the regular cost and interest charge, and decreased by the payments.
2. The balance before interest is calculated as the sum of the deficit and regular cost less the payments.
3. Interest is calculated at 5% of the balance.

4. The total profit and loss account charge is the sum of the regular cost, interest charge and variation cost.

8538 Each actuarial valuation calculates a variation from regular cost, which is usually spread over a period exceeding three years. As actuarial valuations are performed triennially, it is common for **several variations to coexist**, each amortising over different periods.

There are two possible accounting solutions to this scenario:

1. Each variation is amortised on its own basis, which can become complex after multiple valuations, as each will require its own separate disclosure.
2. The surplus or deficit at the latest valuation date is assessed and combined with all unamortised variations. The aggregate balance is then spread over the expected remaining service lives of the current employees.

The **simpler** second method is shown in the following example.

EXAMPLE At 31 December 20X2, there is a £600,000 deficit on B Ltd's defined benefit pension scheme. The average remaining service life of the employees is six years, and so the annual charge in respect of the deficit is £100,000 (on a straight-line basis).
The standard level of pension contribution is £240,000. B Ltd is paying an extra £150,000 over each of the next four years to resolve the deficiency and will then continue to pay the regular contribution in subsequent years.
After three years, a new valuation identifies a deficit of £200,000 (we should have expected a deficit of only £150,000, being the £600,000 less the three special payments of £150,000 in 20X2 to 20X4). B Ltd decides to pay an extra £50,000 in 20X6 in respect of the increase to the deficit. The cumulative deficit balance as at 31 December 20X5 is calculated as:

	£
Original deficit identified in 20X2	600,000
Variation of £100,000 per year recognised in years 20X2 to 20X4	(300,000)
	300,000
Increase from expected deficit (£200,000 less £150,000) in 20X5	50,000
Accounting deficit balance as at 31 December 20X5	350,000

The accounting deficit of £350,000 spread over six years gives an annual cost of £58,333.

Year	Deficit balance	Regular cost	Variation cost	Payments	Balance sheet
	£	£	£	£	£
20X2	600,000	240,000	100,000	390,000	50,000
20X3	500,000	240,000	100,000	390,000	100,000
20X4	400,000	240,000	100,000	390,000	150,000
20X5	350,000	240,000	58,334	390,000	241,666
20X6	291,666	240,000	58,333	290,000	233,333
20X7	233,333	240,000	58,333	240,000	175,000
20X8	175,000	240,000	58,333	240,000	116,667
20X9	116,666	240,000	58,334	240,000	58,333
2X10	58,333	240,000	58,333	240,000	0

Exceptions

8540 The following table provides a summary of the situations when a resulting variation to the regular cost **should not be spread forward**, but recognised in a different way:

Situation giving rise to the variation	¶¶	Spreading allowed
Significant reduction in number of employees.	¶8542	No
Material deficiency due to a major event not factored into the actuarial calculations and requiring significant additional contributions.	¶8544	Optional over shorter period
Taxed refund of surplus to employer.	¶8546	Optional
Capital cost of ex gratia pension, not covered by surplus and not in actuarial assumptions.	¶8548	No

Where the variation relates to a surplus or deficiency as result of a **significant reduction in the number of employees** covered by the scheme, two special rules apply: **8542** SSAP 24 (81)
1. Where the reduction relates to the sale or termination of an operation, the associated pension cost or credit should be recognised immediately as an exceptional item. FRS 3 (18)
2. Otherwise, the reduction should be recognised as it occurs. For example, the effects of a contribution holiday of three years should be spread over the next three years.

Where the variation relates to a **material deficiency**, and both conditions below are met, then prudence dictates that the deficit is recognised over a shorter period than the expected service lives of the current employees: **8544** SSAP 24 (82)
- a major event or transaction has occurred, which has not been allowed for in the actuarial assumptions (such as the liquidation of a company which the scheme has invested in); and
- significant additional contributions have been paid.

If a **taxed refund** is received by the scheme, it can either be accounted for in the period in which it is received, or spread forward over the expected remaining service lives of the current employees. **8546** SSAP 24 (83)

The capital cost of an **ex gratia pension** should be recognised in the accounting period when the pension is granted, unless the cost is covered by a scheme surplus. **8548** SSAP 24 (84)

EXAMPLE D Ltd's pension scheme has a surplus of £1m. The company has decided to make a one-off ex gratia payment from the pension scheme which will cost £800,000. The remaining service lives of employees in the scheme is ten years.

	£
Surplus	1,000,000
Amount used for ex gratia	(800,000)
Unutilised surplus	200,000

If instead, the surplus had been passed onto the company in the form of reduced contributions, the variation of £200,000 would have been spread forward over ten years.
Alternatively, if the ex gratia pension had exceeded the surplus, any shortfall would have been taken direct to the profit and loss account. If there had been no surplus at all, the £800,000 payment would have been included within the current profit and loss account as a pension cost.

If the **employer pays** the ex gratia **direct**, and makes no claim on the pension fund, then the full cost should be recognised in the profit and loss account even when there is a scheme surplus. **8550**

Similarly **discretionary increases** to pensions should be recognised in the accounting period when the increase is granted unless both conditions below apply: **8552** SSAP 24 (85)
- the increase is included in the actuarial assumptions; and
- the increase is covered by the scheme surplus.

Special situations

It is possible for a **negative pension cost** to arise, if the surplus is so large that the variation credit exceeds the regular cost. It is acceptable to record this income assuming there will be a future economic benefit to the company. **8554**

For **group schemes**, the actuarial valuation will take account of the group's characteristics and compute a global actuarial liability for the whole group. A subsidiary's accounts must contain sufficient disclosure to demonstrate how the pension liability has been calculated, indicating whether the contributions are based on pension costs across the group as a whole. **8556** SSAP 24 (90)

If pensions are provided in respect of **foreign operations**, the related pension cost should reflect the UK accounting and an adjustment on consolidation may be necessary. Where the nature of the foreign pension commitment is very different to the usual circumstances found in the UK, no accounting adjustment may be appropriate, although sufficient disclosure should be made of the amount charged in the profit and loss account and the basis of the pension charge. **8558** SSAP 24 (91)

3. Presentation in the accounts

8565 SSAP 24 (86) The cumulative pension cost chargeable in the profit and loss account may have been **overpaid or underpaid** at the balance sheet date. Overpaid contributions will be shown in the balance sheet as a prepayment. Underpaid contributions are shown as a net pension provision.

8567 The pension cost in the profit and loss account is usually shown as part of the operating profit. The following **components of the cost** should be detailed in the notes to the accounts:
- regular cost; and
- variation from regular cost.

4. Disclosure

8570 SSAP 24 (87) The following disclosures are required:
1. The nature of the scheme (i.e. that it is a defined benefit scheme).
2. Whether it is funded or unfunded (¶8410).
3. The accounting policy, and if different, the funding policy.
4. Whether the pension cost is assessed in accordance with the advice of a professionally qualified actuary and, if so, the date of the most recent formal actuarial valuation. If the actuary is an employee or officer of the reporting company (or group), this must also be stated.
5. The pension cost charge for the period together with explanations of significant changes in the charge compared to the previous period.
6. Any provisions or prepayments in the balance sheet resulting from a difference in the amounts paid and recognised as the pension cost.
7. The amount of any deficiency which exists, calculated on a current funding level basis, and the action that will be taken to deal with the deficiency.
8. An outline of the results of the most recent formal actuarial valuation or later formal review of the scheme on an ongoing basis, to include the following:
- the actuarial method used, and a brief description of the main actuarial assumptions;
- the market value of scheme assets at the date of the valuation or review;
- the level of funding expressed in percentage terms; and
- comments on any material actuarial surplus or deficiency.
9. Any commitment to make additional payments over a limited number of years.
10. The accounting treatment adopted in respect of a refund where a related credit appears in the financial statements.
11. Details of the expected effects on future costs of any material changes in the company (or group's) pension arrangements.

MEMO POINTS With regards to **7.** above, a current funding level valuation is based on the rights that have already accrued to the members, and ignores any future salary changes. This information would be provided by the actuary.

Accounting periods ending on or after 22 June 2002

8572 In order to effect a smooth transition to FRS 17, the following disclosures are also required for accounting periods ending on or after 22 June 2002, in addition to the disclosures stated at ¶8570. Although **balance sheet disclosures** must be given for both the opening and closing balance sheets, no comparatives are required for the performance statements.
1. The fair value (¶8444) of the following classes of asset held by the scheme at the end of the period, together with the expected rate of return for the current period and next period:
- equities;
- bonds; and
- other assets.

2. The fair value of scheme assets, the present value of scheme liabilities (based on the accounting assumptions), the resulting surplus or deficit, together with an analysis of the movements during the period.
3. The analysis of reserves should identify the amount relating to the defined benefit asset or liability, net of deferred tax (¶8500).
4. **Profit and loss disclosures**:
a. the following amounts, which will be included within operating profit (or capitalised as part of employee remuneration in the cost of an asset) (¶8478):
- current service;
- any past service costs;
- any previously unrecognised surplus deducted from past service costs;
- gains and losses on any settlements and curtailments; and
- any previously unrecognised surplus deducted from settlement or curtailment losses;

b. any gains and losses on settlements and curtailments (and any previously unrecognised surplus deducted from the losses) to be included within a separate item after operating profit; and
c. interest cost and, separately, expected return on assets in the scheme, to be included as other finance costs or income.
5. **STRGL** disclosures:
- difference between the expected and actual return on assets;
- experience gains and losses arising on scheme liabilities; and
- effects of changes in the demographic and financial assumptions underlying the present value of scheme liabilities.

6. History of amounts recognised in the STRGL (initially for the current accounting period only):
- difference between the expected and actual return on assets expressed as an amount and as a percentage of the scheme assets at the balance sheet date;
- experience gains and losses arising on the scheme liabilities expressed as an amount and as a percentage of the present value of the scheme liabilities at the balance sheet date; and
- total actuarial gain or loss expressed as an amount and as a percentage of the present value of the scheme liabilities at the balance sheet date.

MEMO POINTS In each subsequent year, the STRGL history described in **6**. above will be expanded until the fifth year of applying FRS 17 when the information for the current period plus the four preceding periods is disclosed. FRS 17 (94)

This **example** gives the disclosures for a typical stand-alone company preparing financial statements for a year end after 22 June 2002, following the rules in ¶8572. **8574**

EXAMPLE For accounting period ending on 31 March 20X4

Accounting policy

The company operates a pension scheme providing benefits based on final pensionable pay. The assets of the scheme are held separately from those of the company.
Contributions to the scheme are charged to the profit and loss account so as to spread the cost of pensions over employees' working lives. The contributions are determined by a qualified actuary on the basis of triennial valuations.

Balance sheet presentation

Debtors

	20X4	20X3
	£	£
Prepayments and accrued income	135,500	172,834

Prepayments and accrued income include £45,000 (20X3 £42,000) in respect of the pension scheme.

Notes to the accounts

The pension charge for the year has been determined using the projected unit basis. The results of the most recent valuation at 31 March 20X3 were:

Market value of assets	£1,000,641
Value of accrued liabilities	£850,781
Funding level	102%

The assumptions which have the most significant effect on the results of the valuation are those relating to the rate of return on investments and the rates of increase in salaries and pensions as follows:

Investment return	6.0%
General long-term pay increases	3.2%
Pension increases	2.3%

The pension charge for the period was £57,099 (20X3 £50,000). This included £24,000 (20X3 £20,000) in respect of the amortisation of past service liabilities that are being recognised over ten years, the average remaining lives of employees.

FRS 17
Whilst the financial statements continue to include a pension charge and pension prepayment calculated under the principles of SSAP 24, the new standard requires certain additional disclosures. The actuarial valuation was updated by the Scheme Actuary to 31 March 20X4.
The main assumptions used by the independent qualified actuary in updating the last valuations of the scheme for FRS 17 purposes were:

	20X4	**20X3**
Inflation	2.7%	2.9%
Rate of general long-term increase in salaries	3.4%	3.6%
Rate of increase to pensions in payment	2.5%	2.7%
Discount rate for scheme liabilities	5.4%	5.9%

The market value of the scheme assets, the present value of the liabilities and the resulting surplus together with the expected rates of return on the assets were as follows:

	Long-term rate of return expected at 31.03.20X4	Value at 31.03.20X4 £	Long-term rate of return expected at 31.03.20X3	Value at 31.03.20X3 £
Bonds	5.0%	1,005,996	5.3%	960,567
Other assets	4.2%	46,778	4.7%	40,074
Total market value of assets		1,052,774		1,000,641
Present value of scheme liabilities		(954,367)		(903,897)
Surplus in scheme		98,407		96,744
Related deferred tax liability		(29,522)		(29,023)
Net pension asset		68,885		67,721

If the company had adopted FRS 17, the financial statements would have reflected the following amounts during the year:

	20X4 £
Amounts charged to operating profit	
Current service cost	68,246
Past service costs	13,589
Total operating charge	81,835
Amounts included as other finance income	
Expected return on pension scheme assets	49,589
Interest on pension scheme liabilities	(43,728)
Net return	5,861
Amounts recognised in the STRGL	
Actual return in excess of expected return on pension scheme assets	32,489
Experience gains arising on the scheme liabilities	12,432
Changes in assumptions underlying the present value of the scheme liabilities	(27,284)
Actuarial gain recognised in the STRGL	17,637

Analysis of movement in surplus during the year	
Surplus in scheme at beginning of the year	96,744
Current service cost	(68,246)
Contributions	60,000
Past service costs	(13,589)
Other finance income	5,861
Actuarial gain	17,637
Surplus in scheme at end of the year	98,407

History of experience gains and losses	
Difference between expected and actual return on scheme assets	
– amount	32,489
– percentage of scheme assets	3.1%
Experience gains on scheme liabilities	
– amount	12,432
– percentage of present value of the scheme liabilities	1.3%
Total amount recognised in STRGL	
– amount	17,637
– percentage of the present value of the scheme liabilities	1.8%

If the above amounts had been recognised in the financial statements, the company's net assets and profit and loss reserve at 31 March would be as follows:

Company net assets and reserves reconciliation

	20X4 £	20X3 £
Net assets as reported	1,823,091	1,567,341
Benefit of including net pension assets	68,885	67,721
Less SSAP 24 pension prepayment net of deferred tax	(31,500)	(29,400)
Net assets restated for FRS 17	1,860,476	1,605,662
Profit and loss account reserve as reported	1,244,142	1,038,392
Benefit of including net pension asset	68,885	67,721
Less SSAP 24 pension prepayment net of deferred tax	(31,500)	(29,400)
Profit and loss account reserve restated for FRS 17	1,281,527	1,076,713

Multiple schemes

Where there are multiple schemes, disclosure should be made on a combined basis, unless this impedes the proper understanding of the accounts. A deficiency in one scheme should not be set off against a surplus in another. **8576** SSAP 24 (89)

Commitments

Commitments that have **not been provided for** in the accounts should be disclosed. **8578**

Group schemes

A subsidiary company which is a member of a **group scheme** should disclose this fact, and the nature of the scheme. The subsidiary does not need to disclose the items at **7**. and **8**. of ¶8570 if the holding company is registered in the UK or Republic of Ireland, but should state the name of the holding company in whose financial statements the relevant particulars are disclosed. **8580** SSAP 24 (90)

SECTION 3

Schemes other than defined benefit schemes

A. Defined contribution schemes

8600 Under this type of scheme, the employer does not guarantee a level of pension benefit and so there is **no obligation** to pay extra contributions into the fund. The benefits are based on the amount of contributions paid into the scheme as amplified by investment return on those contributions. These funds may also provide death-in-service benefits.

8602 SSAP 24 (78) FRS 17 (7) The **charge against profits** should be the amount of the employer's contributions payable to the pension scheme in respect of the accounting period. A balance sheet asset or liability may result from the application of the normal matching concept, if payments do not equal the contributions falling due.

8604 SSAP 24 (87) FRS 17 (75) The following **disclosures** should be made:
- the nature of the scheme;
- accounting policy;
- the pension cost charge for the period;
- any outstanding or prepaid contributions at the balance sheet date.

EXAMPLE D Ltd operates a defined contribution pension scheme. The assets of the scheme are held separately from those of the company in an independently administered fund. The pension cost charge represents contributions payable by the company and amounted to £500,000 (20X4 £450,000). Contributions totalling £40,000 (20X4 £37,000) were payable to the fund at the year end and are included in creditors.

8606 FRS 17 (7) The cost relating to a defined contribution scheme should be **recognised** within operating profit in the profit and loss account.

B. Other retirement benefits

8610 Other retirement benefits, such as continuing medical cover, are often provided to employees who have retired. The related cost of these benefits should be **measured and recognised** in accordance with the rules for defined benefit schemes.

8612 FRS 17 (30) Estimating the **future changes** in the cost of retirement healthcare is particularly difficult due to:
- advances in medical skills and technologies;
- the rise in the expectations of patients; and
- the reduction in future benefits in light of the above.

It is **not appropriate** to anticipate the reduction of any benefits or assume that the employer may curtail the scheme at some time in the future. An actuary will need to be appointed by the scheme managers to enable the cost of providing the benefit offered under the scheme to be estimated, and to enable the appropriate accounting entries to be made.

Death-in-service and incapacity benefits

8614 FRS 17 (73) UITF 35 The **expected cost** of these benefits should be recognised in the profit and loss account as part of the operating profit. The cost will depend on whether the benefits are insured.

Type of scheme	Applicable cost	Accounting treatment
Insured	Insurance premium	Profit and loss charge
Not insured	Estimated expected cost	Profit and loss charge
	Difference between actual and expected cost	Gain or loss in STRGL

The difference between the expected cost and the actual cost should be treated as an actuarial gain or loss. In practice such a difference is usually insured against, and is therefore unlikely to arise.

Uninsured benefits should be measured using the projected unit method (¶8452).

Disclosure **Prior to the implementation of FRS 17**, the following disclosures should be made: **8616** UITF 6
- accounting treatment and assumptions made in the measurement of benefits;
- nature of the benefits; and
- amount charged to the profit and loss account.

When FRS 17 is adopted, the disclosure should follow the rules for defined benefit schemes as set out at ¶8505.

SECTION 4

Comparison with International Financial Reporting Standards

The requirements for retirement benefit costs are included in IAS 19 "Employee Benefits." **8630**
This standard is **broadly similar** to FRS 17, but there are some notable differences, which are summarised in the table below. The 2006 amendments to FRS 17 had the effect of replacing the former disclosure requirements with those of IAS 19. The fundamental premise behind IAS 19's treatment of post-employment benefits is to recognise the cost of providing benefits as an expense in the period in which the employee earns those benefits.

MEMO POINTS **IAS 19 also deals** with the following topics, for which there are no current specific UK accounting standards:
- termination benefits; and
- other long-term employee benefits, such as sabbaticals and disability benefits.

Type of scheme	Area	IAS 19 requirement	IAS reference
Defined contribution	Balance sheet creditor	Where due after more than one year, the liability should be discounted to reflect the time value of money.	IAS 19 (45)
Defined benefit	Actuarial gains and losses	Either a 10% corridor is recognised in the income statement or the full amount is recognised in a statement of recognised income and expense (¶8632).	IAS 19 (92)
	Profit and loss components of the pension expense (¶8476)	Single net presentation in the income statement.	IAS 19 (61)
	Balance sheet presentation (¶8468)	No separate caption required on face of balance sheet.	IAS 19 (54)
	Use of a qualified actuary to measure all retirement benefits	Recommended, not mandatory.	IAS 19 (57)

8632 IAS 19 (92) If the **actuarial gains and losses** exceed 10 percent of the greater of the gross assets or gross liabilities of the scheme, the IAS requires recognition of the excess in the income statement. There is an option to spread forward the excess over the average remaining working lives of the members of the scheme. The 10 percent "corridor" itself does not need to be recognised in the financial statements.

Profit volatility is a common problem for both accounting regimes, because of a balance sheet approach to accounting for pensions. The ASB has attempted to reduce this volatile effect by requiring actuarial gains and losses to be presented in the STRGL, rather than the profit and loss account.

Alignment with FRS 17

8634 For accounting periods beginning on or after 1 January 2005, the following **amendments** apply, representing an alignment with FRS 17:

1. An additional option for the recognition of **actuarial gains and losses**, so that they can be fully recognised in the period when they occur in a statement of recognised income and expense (thus avoiding the profit and loss account). The full pension scheme surplus or deficit is included on the employer's balance sheet. This option needs to be consistently applied for all the employer's defined benefit schemes.
2. Qualifying members of a group should be able to treat a **group defined benefit scheme** as a multi-employer scheme, and therefore account for it as a defined contribution scheme. Members which do not qualify should continue to account for the scheme on a reasonable allocation basis.

MEMO POINTS For these purposes, a **qualifying member** is either:
- a parent which files consolidated accounts, which are publicly available and comply with International Financial Reporting Standards; or
- a wholly owned subsidiary of such a parent.

3. An alignment of **disclosure requirements**, including the following:

a. information about scheme assets;
- percentage of total asset fair value that the major classes of assets represent;
- expected rate of return for each class of asset; and
- a narrative description of how each expected rate of return was calculated;

b. information detailing the sensitivity of defined benefit schemes to changes in healthcare costs;
c. information about contributions to the scheme, and the nature of the scheme; and
d. five-year histories of the following:
- scheme assets;
- scheme liabilities;
- scheme deficit/surplus; and
- experience adjustments.

8635 As discussed in ¶8521, proposals for improvements to pension fund accounting are ongoing. The IASB plans to finalise amendments to IAS 19 during 2011. The ASB is in broad agreement with its proposals.

CHAPTER 5

Secretarial issues

OUTLINE ¶¶

Company law prescribes corporate responsibility for both financial management and administration, the latter duties traditionally being undertaken by the company secretary. This chapter contains advice on these **administrative and secretarial matters**, with special emphasis on the areas in which the Companies Act 2006 implements significant changes. Although these matters are dealt with throughout this volume under the relevant headings, the main points are summarised in this chapter to provide an overview for ease of reference. **8700**

A. The company secretary

Since April 2008, **private companies** have been freed from the obligation to appoint a company secretary. The rule did not change, however, for **public companies**, which must not only appoint a secretary but also ensure that the person appointed has the necessary knowledge and experience to perform the role properly. **8702**

Though the post of company secretary in a private company may have ceased to be a legal requirement, the tasks formerly performed by a **person in the role** still need to be undertaken by a director or other person authorised by the board.

MEMO POINTS A private company's articles may well require it to have a secretary, in which case it must still comply with this requirement. However, if the articles merely refer to the office of secretary without actually obliging the company to have one, no obligation is implied as a result.

In general, anyone – including another company – may act as company secretary. **Exceptions** are the company's auditor and any person disqualified from acting as a director. Where there is a company secretary, the individual concerned need not be an employee of the company but equally someone appointed from outside. **8703**

Although a rarity in practice, **more than one** secretary or **joint** secretaries can be appointed, with their details being recorded separately. In practice, however, since there are no prescribed duties (see ¶8707) of a secretary, there is nothing to prevent a company from appointing one company secretary (whose name appears on the register) even if the duties are performed by another person (or persons) under the secretary's supervision.

8704 A secretary is regarded as an **officer** of the company – with the duties of care such a position entails. A company secretary therefore acts as a company's **agent** and has implied authority to sign routine administrative papers but not more onerous documents, such as loan contracts or similar.

A secretary cannot sign a document in the dual capacity of director and secretary. In such a case, another director must sign it as director.

First secretarial appointment

8705 The name of a company's first secretary should be submitted to Companies House with the documents pertaining to the registration of a new company. This rule does not apply in respect of private companies that choose to have a secretary.

Changes to secretarial appointment

8706 As a general rule, changes to secretarial appointments occur when a secretary **resigns** or is **dismissed**. If a company desires to dismiss its secretary, it does so by way of a directors' resolution and also in accordance with any relevant employment or other contract. (The model articles do not set out a procedure for **removing** secretaries nor do they provide for the office of secretary to be **automatically vacated** upon the happening of a specific event.)

Less commonly, a secretary could become disqualified on grounds such as:
- bankruptcy,
- breach of an administration order,
- breach of company filing requirements,
- wrongful trading, or
- fraud.

Companies House must be kept notified of any changes (including changes to the registered details of the incumbent secretary), on the appropriate form and within 14 days.

Duties of secretary

8707 While there is no formal list of duties applicable to the post of company secretary, the following tasks usually fall to the secretary (or the person/s who will fulfil the role in a private company that does not have an official secretary).

Regular duties	Occasional duties
– Sending out notice of meetings – Sending accounts to members – Attending to dividend payments – Filing accounts and annual return with Companies House – Keeping statutory books up to date	– Sending copies of written resolutions to auditor – Making sure the company acts within its powers and generally keeps within the law – Filing details with Companies House of changes that have to be filed (e.g., changes to articles, changes to auditors, changes to registered office, etc) – Preparing and filing minutes of general meetings – Making sure board meetings are carried out correctly and minuted – Dealing with share transfers

Note that this list is illustrative rather than exhaustive.

B. Accounting records and statutory books

8710 All companies are obliged to keep proper books and records both to serve as evidence of incorporation as well as to enable them to report annually to their shareholders on the financial position and results of operations.

Accounting records

The accounting records must be **retained** for six years (if a public company) or three years (if a private company) from the date on which they are made. 8711

A company's accounting records must provide the following information: 8712
- amounts of money received and expended on a day-to-day basis, together with explanations of the amounts it received and expended;
- a record of the assets and liabilities;
- where the company deals in goods, statements of stocks the company held at the financial year end, together with supporting statements of stock takes and, except in the case of retailers, details of all goods sold and purchased by the company, in sufficient detail to enable the goods and the buyers and sellers to be identified.

Accounting records should be held at the registered office (see ¶8725) or any other place as deemed appropriate by the directors, and must be open for inspection at all times by the officers of the company. Consequently, the records need to be kept up to date. The term "officers" includes directors, managers and the company secretary. 8713

Statutory books and records

Companies are required to keep certain statutory books and records. These can be kept in paper or electronic form and consist of the following: 8714

Register of directors and secretaries, including names and addresses. Note that for directors, their date of birth, occupation and nationality must also be given. Under the 2006 Companies Act, directors need not provide their residential addresses for public disclosure (though the addresses will still be held on file). After April 2008, the requirement for a register of secretaries falls away for private companies choosing not to have a company secretary.

Register of members, including past members. The information required in respect of members is full name and address, date of becoming a member, number of shares held, date of ceasing to be a member, and dates of share transfers. The details of past members need to be maintained on file for 10 years. This retention period was reduced from 20 to 10 years in 2008. As a transitional measure, copies of details removed after 10 years must be kept until 6 April 2018 or 20 years after the membership in question ended (whichever expires first).

Register of persons interested in 3 percent or more of the company's voting shares (public companies only – where that information has been disclosed).

Directors' service contracts, which must be available for inspection by all shareholders. A copy needs to be kept for one year after termination/expiry. However, for contracts entered into before 1 October 2007, there is no requirement to keep a copy for one year after it has ended. In addition, such contracts – if they were short-term contracts (i.e., with less than 12 months to run or that can be terminated within 12 months without compensation) – do not have to be made available for inspection.

Register of charges, containing all mortgages and charges, and detailing all fixed and floating charges, a description of the property subject to the charge, the amount of the charge and the persons entitled to it.

Minute books, containing records of all members' and directors' (board) meetings. The Companies Act 2006, unlike its predecessor, specifies a retention period for minutes of 10 years. This change became effective on 1 October 2007. Therefore, any meeting or resolutions held after that date will need to be kept for 10 years; earlier resolutions do not fall under this rule.

MEMO POINTS 1. Many companies, especially larger ones, keep **non-statutory registers** of share applications and allotments, share transfers, debenture holders, etc.
2. Note that the requirement for the **Register of directors' interests** fell away effective April 2007.

C. Company name

8715 The choice of a company's name is one that needs to be made with a great deal of care as it can affect the way the company is perceived by its customers, the business community, and the general public. Often companies use their **official company name** (i.e., the one registered at Companies House) as their **trading name**, but they are not obliged to. The name under which it trades can also be referred to as its **business** name.

8716 Company law imposes requirements on the use of both types of name – to avoid confusion and to ensure that those with whom the company transacts can be fully aware of the company's registered name, its registered numbers, and the location of its registered office. This precludes a company from "disappearing" behind different names.

8717 No company name should be the **same as** – or very similar to – an existing company's name. In addition, **certain words** and phrases are **not permitted** to be used, while others may be used only with the express **permission** of the Secretary of State – for instance where the name seems to imply national or international pre-eminence (e.g., words such as British, Scottish, Welsh, etc) or business pre-eminence or representative or authoritative status (e.g., words such as Council, Federation, Institution, etc). Full details are available on the Companies House website.

8718 A private limited company must end its name with the word "limited" or the abbreviation "ltd", and a public company must end its name with "public limited company" or "plc". By the same token, an unlimited company is not allowed to use the word "limited" (or any abbreviation thereof) in its name.

8720 Companies are permitted to **change their name** for any reason. This is done by way of a special resolution and registration of the change at Companies House.

Display of company name

8721 A company's name must, in addition to being displayed outside every one of its **offices** and **places of business**, be included in the following **documents** (paper and electronic):
- the memorandum,
- business letters,
- order forms,
- notices and official publications,
- orders for goods or services,
- invoices and receipts,
- cheques, promissory notes and other financial documents,
- applications for licences to carry on a trade or activity,
- websites,
- all other business documents and correspondence.

D. Registered office

8725 All companies are obliged to have an effective registered office at all times. A registered office must be situated in the country of incorporation and staffed in such a way that correspondence and other matters can be dealt with directly.

8726 Changes to the registered office should be determined by a special resolution of the company and communicated to Companies House within 15 days. The change takes effect only when the form is registered by Companies House.

The registered office is the address at which legal notices can be served. It is also the address at which the statutory books and records must be kept. This will allow for the inspection of records by interested parties. 8727

E. Corporate constitution

The terms governing how a company is run are contained in its constitution. The constitution comprises the **articles** and any decisions or agreements that affect them. The articles, which companies can tailor to their specific needs, deal with managerial and administrative matters. The nature of the constitution changed on 1 October 2009, when the relevant provisions of the new Companies Act came into force. Previously, the **memorandum** used to form part of the constitution, and it contained information about a company's powers, rights and liabilities, as well as basic information such as its name and the details of its subscribers. After this date, the memorandum will be preserved, but only as a record of historical information. 8730

MEMO POINTS Companies incorporated before 1 October 2009 are now **deemed** to have various provisions included in their articles that used to be in their memoranda. Companies incorporated after that date may **elect** to include these provisions.

Other changes effective from October 2009 are: 8732
– a new Model Articles to become the default articles for newly incorporated companies (replacing Table A, which was the default set of articles for companies incorporated before 1 October 2009);
– new companies will no longer require an objects clause, while existing ones will be free to abolish theirs;
– authorised share capital no longer to exist and companies will no longer include it in their formation documents.

New Model Articles/Table A

New Model Articles have replaced Table A as the default articles for all new companies incorporated on or **after 1 October 2009**. There are different new model articles for private companies limited by shares, public companies, and private companies limited by guarantee. 8733

A transitional version of Table A applied to companies incorporated **after October 2007**. This avoided conflict with the parts of the Companies Act 2006 that had come into effect by that date and the remaining provisions of the 1985 Act.

Note that companies are not obliged to use Model Articles, but can write their own. It is only when they do not register their own articles of association that the Model Articles apply by default.

MEMO POINTS (1) The new Model Articles do not affect existing companies unless they choose to adopt them. Existing companies can choose to amend their existing articles of association, by special resolution, to bring them in line with changes in the law as expressed in the new model articles.
(2) For readers interested in a detailed comparison of Table A and the Model Articles, please refer to our sister Memo publication, *Company Law 2011*.

Alterations to the articles

In general, a company has the power, subject to certain constraints, to change its articles. This is formally achieved by special resolution, which must be filed at Companies House within 15 days of being passed. The Registrar will then publish a notice of the change in the *Gazette*. Once the amendment is registered, it must be reflected in all copies of the articles. 8734

Other documents

8735 Other documents included within the definition of the company's constitution include essentially any resolutions or agreements that need to be filed at Companies House, for example:
- special resolutions;
- unanimous shareholder resolutions or agreements that – had they not been taken unanimously – would need to be in the form of a special resolution;
- unanimous class resolutions or agreements that – had they not been taken unanimously – would need to be passed by a particular majority of the class;
- resolutions or agreements that bind all members of a class, even though they were not agreed to unanimously; and
- other resolutions or agreements that are required to be filed at Companies House.

F. Annual return

8740 All companies are required to file an annual return. Its purpose is to provide Companies House with a summary of specified information about the company at a particular point in time. Companies House generates a computerised and individualised pro-forma return (known as a "shuttle"), which is sent to the registered office for further completion.

8741 The annual return must be lodged in the **prescribed form** and **on time**, which is the anniversary of:
- the company's incorporation; or
- the date of the filing of the previous return.

Failure to do so will render the company, its directors, its secretary (in the case of a public company, or a private company that chooses to appoint one) and any other officer liable to a fine.

8742 The annual return form must state the:
- **date** to which it is made up;
- company's registered **name** and **number**;
- address of the company's **registered office**;
- **type** of company (e.g., public or private), and a description of its principal **business activity**;
- name and address of the company **secretary**;
- details of company's **directors**, including their full name, address, nationality, date of birth, and business occupation;
- locations of the register of members and the register of debenture holders (if not kept at the registered office);
- details of the company's issued share capital and each class of shares;
- **names of members and their holdings** at the return date, the names of persons who have ceased to be members since the last return date and the number of shares transferred since that date by each member or past member together with the date of registration of the transfers. A complete list of shareholders is required in the first annual return and, subsequently, every third year. In the intervening years, a **list of changes in membership and holdings** is sufficient.

MEMO POINTS For return dates on or after 1 October 2009, **service addresses** for directors and secretaries must be given. A service address can be the company's registered office address but in any event must be a place where documents can be delivered and their delivery acknowledged.

8743 All documents must comply with certain **document quality requirements** to enable Companies House to scan them and produce electronic versions. As a result, the Registrar may reject documents that cannot be reproduced electronically and require the company to submit documents that do comply within 14 days. If a suitable replacement is not delivered on time, the original submission cannot be treated as having been received on time.

G. Preparing and approving financial statements

The directors have a duty to prepare individual financial statements every financial year in accordance with UK or International GAAP as appropriate. Although this topic is covered in detail from ¶9300, the implications of the new Companies Act on the secretarial and administrative function are covered briefly here. 8746

The board of directors must approve the company's financial statements, which are required to be signed on the board's behalf by a director signing the company's balance sheet. While there is no legal requirement for the consolidated balance sheet to be signed in the same way, such treatment would represent good practice. 8747

If a company is a **parent** company as at the year end, it must prepare consolidated financial statements. As with individual financial statements, these may be prepared in accordance with either UK or International GAAP. 8748

The financial statements must be sent to all members. Before October 2007, the circulation **deadline** was 21 days before the AGM, but under the Companies Act 2006 this has changed and is now the earlier of: 8749
- the date on which the statements are filed at Companies House; and
- the last date by which the statements have to be filed at Companies House.

It is no longer necessary for private companies to hold an AGM or to lay the accounts before members. If, however, a private company chooses to hold an AGM and lay the accounts before members, the members are regarded as only receiving, and not approving, such accounts. Public companies, on the other hand, are still obliged to lay their accounts before their members at a general meeting (usually the AGM). 8750

Filing with the Registrar

In addition to their responsibility for distributing accounts to members, the company's directors also have a duty to send a copy of the company's financial statements and reports to the Registrar. The financial statements and reports must consist of the following: 8752
- the company's individual financial statements;
- any consolidated financial statements (if applicable);
- the directors' report;
- in the case of a quoted company, the directors' remuneration report;
- the auditors' report on those financial statements and that directors' report and, in the case of a quoted company, on the auditable part of the directors' remuneration report.

The usual period allowed for filing is the number of months shown in the table below after the end of the relevant accounting reference period: 8753

	Private companies	Public companies
Financial years beginning before 6 April 2008	10 months	7 months
Financial years beginning after 6 April 2008	9 months	6 months

If a company's first accounting reference period exceeds twelve months, the period allowed is the later to expire of (a) or (b):

	Private companies	Public companies
(a)	21 months from incorporation	18 months from incorporation
(b)	3 months from the end of the accounting reference period	3 months from the end of the accounting reference period

See also ¶9350.

Filing exemption for unlimited companies

8755 The directors of an unlimited company do not have to file financial statements with the Registrar – but only if the company was not one of the following at any time during the relevant accounting reference period:
- a **subsidiary** or a **parent** of a limited company;
- **subject to rights exercisable** by two or more limited entities which, if exercised by one of them, would have made the company its subsidiary;
- a **banking or insurance company** or the parent company of a banking or insurance group;
- a **qualifying company** under SI 1993/1820, "Partnerships and Unlimited Companies (Accounts) Regulations 1993" (an unlimited company is considered a qualifying company if each of its members is a limited company, or is another unlimited company or Scottish firm, each of whose members is a limited company);
- a company carrying on a business as the **promoter of a trading stamp scheme** (under the Trading Stamps Act 1964).

H. Meetings and resolutions

8760 One of the biggest changes introduced by the 2006 Act is the new **written resolution procedure** available to private companies, whereby they can opt to pass resolutions without holding meetings. Because this methodology does not require unanimity, and will be preferable because it saves the costs (in both time and money terms) of holding meetings, it is expected to be widely used. However, in practice it will not override the need for meetings entirely.

Directors' meetings

8761 Any of the company's directors is empowered to call a board meeting. Furthermore, the company secretary is obliged to call a meeting if requested to do so by a director. There is no specific notice period required, beyond that it should be reasonable. In addition, notice must be given to all directors. If any directors do not receive proper notice of a board meeting, the decisions taken will not be valid.

8762 In general, a board meeting can be held informally, but a casual meeting will not be sufficient if all parties do not agree to treat it as a meeting. Board meetings can be conducted by telephone or other electronic means such as video conferencing and web camera if the articles allow for these methods and any requirements are followed. For this reason the articles of many companies (and the new model articles) now incorporate powers to permit remote participation in board meetings.

8763 While directors may be expressly permitted by the articles to conduct business by written resolution, it may not be a suitable mechanism for dealing with non-routine matters that may require more serious discussion. However, the directors will themselves have to take a position on this. Written resolutions must be signed by all of the directors, although as a practical matter they do not actually have to sign the same piece of paper.

General meetings

8765 The following are types of general meeting:
- AGMs,
- general meetings, and
- class meetings.

The **quorum** required to be present at general meeting is usually specified in the articles. Where there is no mention in the articles, two members present personally or by proxy generally represent a quorum.

For public companies, an AGM must be held each calendar year and companies must not let more than 16 months elapse between the accounting reference date and the AGM and the next. In the notice calling the AGM it must be specified that the meeting is an AGM. From 1 October 2007, private companies will no longer have to hold AGMs unless there is a specific provision in the articles requiring one to be held. (Of course, the company may amend the articles to remove the necessity of an AGM.) 8766

For private companies **no longer holding AGMs**, the matters that would have been dealt with there can now be treated as follows: 8767
- accounts still have to be sent to members;
- directors may declare a second interim dividend (instead of recommending a final one at the AGM);
- the retirement by rotation of directors that formerly used to take place at AGMs will now no longer need to occur;
- auditors will be deemed to have been reappointed in the absence of an ordinary resolution of members to the contrary (such a resolution could be passed at a general meeting or in writing if necessary);
- members of a private company may exercise their right to require the company to hold a general meeting.

Some private companies may wish to **continue holding AGMs**. The following will need to be dealt with: 8768
- notice of meeting,
- form of proxy, and rights of proxies,
- quorum,
- chairman,
- adjournment,
- voting, and
- matters arising at the meeting.

Notice of meetings

A general meeting requires 14 clear days' notice. ("Clear" days excludes the day the notice is given and the day of the meeting itself.) The notice must state the date and time of the meeting and the nature of the business to be transacted. If any of the resolutions to be considered are special resolutions, they should be written out in full. 8769

A public company must give 21 clear days' notice of an AGM. As well as stating the required information for a general meeting, the notice must specifically state that the meeting is an AGM.

Notices must be sent to all shareholders as well as the directors and auditor. Notice may be given in hard copy form or electronically, although in order to send notices of meetings to shareholders electronically their consent is required.

MEMO POINTS Meetings can be held on short notice if the requisite number of members consent.

Types of resolutions

There are two types of resolutions: 8771

Ordinary resolutions – these require a simple majority (more than 50 percent) and are not normally required to be filed at Companies House.

Special resolutions – these require a majority of at least 75 percent and must be filed at Companies House within 15 days of the date on which they are passed. Examples are resolutions to:
- change the name,
- change the constitution,
- change the status, and
- reduce the share capital.

MEMO POINTS Before the Companies Act 2006, there were two other types of resolutions, which no longer exist in statute, namely **extraordinary** and **elective** resolutions. However, some articles may still require certain decisions to take the form of an extraordinary resolution.

8772 Under the Companies Act, **special notice** must be given by a member to the company of the member's intention to propose a particular resolution. This must be given at least 28 days before the date of the meeting. (Note that this is not the same as the notice of the meeting itself, which is sent by the company to the members.) The following types of resolutions are examples; though they require special notice by the member, they generally take the form of ordinary – and not special – resolutions:
– a resolution to remove directors;
– a resolution to appoint as auditor a person other than the retiring auditor, or to fill a casual vacancy in the office of auditor;
– a resolution to reappoint a retiring auditor who was appointed to fill a casual vacancy;
– a resolution to remove an auditor before the expiration of his term of office.

I. Directors

8775 The key changes brought about by the Companies Act 2006 relating to directors are:
– Some of the duties of directors that were previously determined by **common law** have now been **codified** in the Act.
– No **maximum age limit** for directors, and the **minimum age** is 16 years. (Directors who were not yet 16 years old on that date automatically ceased to be directors.)
– Every company must have at least one **natural person** as a director (the remaining members of the board may be corporate entities).
– Some of the rules regarding directors' loans are relaxed – making them easier to follow but without changing the effect significantly (see the chapter on related party transactions, ¶5045 *et seq.*, for a more detailed discussion).

MEMO POINTS Effective 1 October 2009, directors are no longer required to provide their home addresses for the public record.

8776 The **first appointments** of directors are made on incorporation by those setting up the company. **Subsequent** directors can be **appointed** either to fill one or more vacancies that have been left by departing directors or to increase the size of the board. Directors who are obliged to retire by rotation can also be **re-appointed**. The **procedure** for appointing directors is normally set out in the company's articles.

8777 Where **statute** requires the directors to have the authority of the shareholders to exercise a power, the articles or the appropriate resolution (as required by statute) must permit the directors to do so. Common examples of this are the requirements for authority or approval to:
– allot shares, which the shareholders can authorise directors to do either generally for a certain period of time, or on a case-by-case basis;
– disapply pre-emption rights; and
– reduce the company's share capital, or carry out an own share purchase out of capital (private companies only).

MEMO POINTS

The boards of **private companies** incorporated on or after 1 October 2009 **with only one class of shares** do not have to obtain the shareholders' authority to allot shares unless the articles require them to do so.

CHAPTER 6

Share-based payment

OUTLINE ¶¶

A. Introduction

FRS 20, "Share-based payment", provides guidance on all forms of payment that are made in shares or on the basis of the value of shares (or other equity instrument). Previously, UITF Abstract 17, "Employee share schemes", now superseded, was the applicable GAAP. Issued in April 2004, FRS 20 implements its international counterpart, IFRS 2, and requires companies to recognise in their profit or loss and financial position the effects of share-based payment transactions in which **share options** are granted to employees. 8850

More specifically, a company is obliged to reflect an expense (or, if applicable, an asset) measured at fair value in respect of its employee share option schemes, share purchase plans, and any other share-based payments (i.e., payments made in shares or other equity instruments, or by way of a cash amount based on the value of those instruments).

The **rules came into effect** as follows: 8851
- **listed** companies: in respect of accounting periods beginning on or after 1 January 2005;
- **unlisted** companies: in respect of accounting periods beginning on or after 1 January 2006.

When first issued, the rules of FRS 20 did not apply to companies reporting under **FRSSE** as existing at the time; however, the 2008 FRSSE contained applicable amendments relating to share-based payments. These, however, do not conform to those of FRS 20 in all respects (For share-based payments under FRSSE, see ¶6243.)

The **transactions** to which FRS 20 might apply can take many forms, though the following represent the three types it identifies: 8852 FRS 20 (2)
- **equity-settled** share-based payment transactions, in which the entity receives goods or services as consideration for equity instruments of the entity;
- **cash-settled** share-based payment transactions, in which the entity acquires goods or services by incurring liabilities to the supplier thereof for amounts that are based on the price (or value) of the entity's equity instruments; and

– transactions offering a **choice of cash or equity settlement** – i.e., where the entity receives or acquires goods or services and the terms of the arrangement provide one or other of the parties to the transaction to choose whether the settlement should be made in cash (or other assets) or by issuing equity instruments.

Each of these is discussed in detail in the sections below.

8853 In August 2009, the ASB issued an amendment to FRS 20 in order to maintain convergence with IFRS 2. This amendment clarifies both the scope of, and the accounting for, group cash-settled share-based payment transactions in the separate or individual financial statements of the entity receiving the goods or services when that entity has no obligation to settle the share-based payment transaction.

Under the amendments, an entity must apply the FRS 20 in accounting for all share-based payment transactions – whether or not it can specifically identify some or all of the goods received.

This amendment must be applied retrospectively for accounting periods beginning on or after 1 January 2010.

8855 Certain business combinations and arrangements do not fall within the scope of FRS 20. The following table provides a summary.

EXAMPLES OF SHARE-BASED TRANSACTIONS		
Form of transaction		**Covered by FRS 20?**
Entity receives services from employees	Pays by way of share issue	Yes
Entity receives goods or services from persons other than employees	• Pays by way of share option (or other equity instrument), or • Settles amount owing by cash (or other assets) based on the value of the entity's shares or other equity instruments, or • Equity instruments are transferred by shareholders, parent/s or other group members to supplier of these goods or services	Yes
Business combinations (e.g., acquisitions, mergers, etc)	Issues shares or other equity instruments directly as part of transaction	No
Arrangement affected by a business combination but not arising from it	Shares to be issued to employees in terms of existing contract are altered as a result of business combination	Yes
Contracts to buy or sell non-financial items	Settlement to be made in cash or other financial instruments as if they are financial instruments (including exchange of financial instruments)	No
Transactions with employees in their capacity as shareholder (e.g., where an employee receives a rights issue because he owns a particular class of share)		No

MEMO POINTS Under the amendment to FRS 20, a share-based payment transaction may be settled by another group entity (or a shareholder of any group entity) on behalf of the entity receiving or acquiring the goods or services. Unless the transaction is clearly for a purpose other than payment for goods or services supplied, FRS 20 must be applied to an entity that:

– receives goods or services when another entity in the same group (or a shareholder of any group entity) has the obligation to settle the share-based payment transaction, or

– has an obligation to settle a share-based payment transaction when another entity in the same group receives the goods or services.

B. Transactions settled by payments of equity

This discussion deals with transactions an entity settles by issuing equity instruments rather than settling with cash. 8860

In respect of such transactions, the entity is required to measure the subject of the transaction (i.e., the goods and/or services acquired) at its **fair value**, except where it cannot be determined reliably, in which case the entity must then measure the value of the goods or services by reference to the fair value of the **underlying equity** instruments granted. The value so determined will be the amount at which the transaction is recorded (i.e., by which equity is increased in the balance sheet). FRS 20 (10)

EXAMPLE A company receives goods worth £20,000 from a supplier. Instead of payment in cash, the supplier would prefer to receive shares in the enterprise. The share issue is deemed to take place at a value of £20,000 with the book entry being a debit to current assets and the credit to share capital.

1. With employees

In the majority of cases, transactions with employees are concerned with **services**, rather than goods. Payments in respect of services received are recorded in the profit and loss account as expenses. 8864

a. Recognition

The **timing** in respect of which the expense is recognised is the same as it would have been had the transaction been cash-based. 8865

b. Valuation

In practice, where services are received from employees, it is generally not possible to estimate reliably the fair value of the services received. This can be for many reasons; the most usual being that equity instruments are granted to employees as part of a remuneration package consisting of various components (cash, benefits, etc). In addition, these grants may be linked to specific bonus or incentive arrangements – in other words, the employee's future services are involved. The value of all these elements is difficult to measure. 8867

Therefore, the transaction must be valued at the fair value of the equity instruments granted. The valuation should be made at the measurement date based on **available market prices**, and taking into account any terms and conditions of the grant. 8869

Often, **market prices are not available** – for instance, it is generally not the case that options granted to employees are exactly the same as publicly traded options for which there is a market price. Therefore, the valuation will be based on an estimate of the fair value of the equity instruments in an arm's length transaction. The valuation technique should be consistent with commonly used valuation methodologies for pricing financial statements and take account of all factors that arm's length participants would normally take into account in calculating a fair price. 8871

c. Conditions attaching

With respect to share-based payments for services, **two possibilities** exist: the instruments can **vest immediately** (i.e., the employee becomes unconditionally entitled to the equity instruments), or they may vest at some future time when certain conditions have been met. 8873 FRS 20 (14)

In the former case (immediate vesting), the company should account for the instruments at the grant date.

8874 Depending on the specific nature of the vesting conditions in cases where the instruments do **not vest immediately**, the services are presumed to be received during the period ending on the date that vesting takes place and the company therefore accounts for the instrument at vesting date. Various vesting conditions are discussed below.

Continuity of employment

8875 FRS 20 (15) A vesting condition might relate purely to the requirement that an employee remains in employment for a specific period. If an employee is granted share options conditional upon completing three years' service, then the entity should presume that the services to be rendered by the employee as consideration for the share options will be received in the future, over the three-year vesting period.

Performance targets

8876 An employee may be granted share options conditional upon the achievement of a performance target. If the time of vesting depends on a **market-related condition**, any assumptions made at the grant date about the likely length of the vesting period (e.g., an assumption about when the market value of the instrument might reach a certain level) must be consistent with those used to estimate the fair value of the instrument granted.

The estimates are not adjusted subsequently, even if it should emerge that the assumptions were not reliable or had been revised.

8877 Where the condition is **not market related** (e.g., where it is dependent on reaching an **internal target** such as a sales volume), then estimates of the length of the vesting period should be adjusted in later accounting periods if it becomes clear that the vesting period is likely to differ from previous estimates.

8879 FRS 20 (19) Vesting conditions other than market conditions should not be taken into account in estimating the fair value of the shares or share options. Instead, their effect is taken into account by adjusting the number of equity instruments to be issued. Ultimately, the amount recognised for the services received will be based on the number of equity instruments that eventually vest.

In the meantime, the entity should recognise an amount for the goods or services received during the vesting period based on the best available estimate of the number of equity instruments expected to vest. On the vesting date, if the estimate does not equal the number of instruments that actually vested, an adjustment should be made.

8881 Market conditions (e.g., a target share price that triggers vesting) must be taken into account in estimating fair value. Therefore, the entity should recognise the goods or services received from the other party that satisfies all other vesting conditions (e.g., services received from an employee who has remained in service for the specified period) irrespective of whether the market condition is actually satisfied.

8883 FRS 20 (22) If options have a **reload feature**, this should not be taken into account when estimating fair value. A reload feature provides for the automatic re-granting of additional options to optionholders who exercise their options using the entity's shares instead of cash. Instead, a reload option should be accounted for as a separate option grant – if and when it takes place.

8885 In those cases where it is **impossible to make a reliable estimate** of the fair value of the instruments issued, the entity should:
– initially, measure the equity instruments at their **intrinsic value** (i.e., the difference between the fair value of the underlying shares and the price required to be paid);
– at subsequent reporting dates, including after the final settlement, recognise any **change** in intrinsic value in the profit and loss account; and
– recognise the goods or services received based on the **number of instruments** that ultimately vest.

If the instruments **are settled during the vesting period**, the company should immediately recognise the amount that would otherwise have accrued over the remainder of the vesting period. In addition, where payments are made on settlement, they are treated as a repurchase of equity – i.e., as a deduction from equity – but only up to the intrinsic value. Any excess over the intrinsic value must be recognised via the profit and loss account as an expense. 8887

d. Modifications to terms and conditions

An entity might modify the terms and conditions on which the equity instruments were granted (e.g., by re-pricing the share options). Where transactions are measured at values determined by reference to the equity instruments underlying them – whether with employees or otherwise – the entity must take into account the **nature** of the change and account for its effect. 8889 FRS 20 (26)

At a minimum, the entity must recognise the **fair value** of the equity instruments granted at the measurement date, except in instances where the equity instruments do not vest because a non-market-related vesting condition was not met. 8891

Where there have been changes that **benefit the other party** (i.e., changes that increase the fair value of the instruments concerned), the effect must also be recognised. 8893

If the entity **cancels or settles** a grant of equity during the vesting period (other than by failing to meet the vesting conditions), it must: 8895 FRS 20 (28)
- account for it as an acceleration of vesting and recognise immediately the amount that otherwise would have been recognised over the remainder of the vesting period;
- treat as a repurchase of equity any payment made on cancellation, up to the fair value of the equity instrument (with any excess being accounted for as an expense); and
- treat any new instruments granted at the same time in one of two ways:
  - where they are **regarded as a replacement** for the old instruments, the issue is accounted for in the same way as a modification to the conditions. The incremental fair value granted (the value granted as a result of the change) is the difference between the fair value of the new instruments (at date of replacement) and the fair value of the old, less any amounts previously treated as a deduction from equity;
  - where they **are not regarded as replacement** instruments, the transactions are accounted for separately.

Where an entity repurchases vested equity instruments, the payment made to the employee must be treated as a deduction from equity. To the extent that the **payment exceeds the fair value** at the repurchase date, any excess is to be recognised as an expense.

Where an option is unable to be exercised because vesting conditions are not met (e.g., if the employee leaves the employment or a performance target is not achieved), the cost of the options is reversed. However, if the **employer cancels** the options, the full value of the options is charged to the profit and loss account. Where the **employee cancels** the options (other than on leaving employment), the treatment should be the same as that for cancellations by the employer. 8896

2. With non-employees

Where **services** are received from **parties other than employees** and it is not possible to value these services fairly, the entity must base the value of these services on the value of the equity instruments granted, measured at the date that the services are rendered. 8898 FRS 20 (13)

Where the subject of the transaction is **goods**, the payment should be recorded as an asset.

8899 Under the amendments to FRS 20, where the identifiable consideration received appears to be less than the fair value of the equity instruments granted or liability incurred, this situation indicates that **unidentifiable** goods or services have been (or have yet to be) received by the entity. These unidentifiable goods or services must be measured as the difference between the fair value of the share-based payment and the fair value of any **identifiable** goods or services.

The entity must measure the unidentifiable goods or services received at the grant date. In the case of **cash-settled transactions**, the entity must re-measure the liability at the end of each reporting period until it has been settled.

C. Transactions settled by payments in cash

8900 Some transactions are settled by an entity in cash (or other assets) but the amount is determined by reference to the value of its shares (or other equity instruments). For example, a company might grant **share appreciation rights** to employees as part of their remuneration package, whereby employees will become entitled to a future cash payment (rather than an equity instrument) based on an increase in the share price from a specified level over a specified period. Or, an employer might grant the right to employees to receive a future cash payment by granting them a **redeemable right to shares** that is either mandatory (such as on cessation of employment) or at their own option.

FRS 20 (30) In respect of such transactions, the entity is required to measure the value of the goods or services acquired – and the liability incurred – at the fair value of the liability. All terms and conditions, and the extent to which the service has been rendered, are taken into account.

Until such time as the liability is settled, the entity must, at each reporting date, re-measure the fair value of the liability. Any changes should be recognised in the profit and loss account during the period concerned.

8902 Where the rights are **granted retrospectively**, e.g., where a bonus to be paid is based on the share price during a preceding period and there is no future service requirement, the services are presumed to have been received and a liability is recognised immediately.

8904 On the other hand, where the conditions relate to a **future period** (e.g., a continuing period of service), the liability is recognised over the period concerned.

D. Transactions settled by payments either of equity or in cash

8907 It is also possible for the terms of an arrangement to give the **choice** to both parties to a transaction as to whether the entity must settle the transaction by way of cash (or other assets) or by issuing equity. In other words, either the entity or the other party may make this election.

8908 FRS 20 (34) In these cases, the transaction must be accounted for as a cash-settled transaction if, and to the extent that, the entity has incurred a **liability to settle** in cash or other assets. It must account for the transaction as an equity-settled transaction if, and to the extent that, no liability has been incurred.

The accounting treatment therefore depends both on the basis of valuing the transaction as well as the party that has the right to elect how it will be settled.

In the case of the **employees in a subsidiary** company being granted **rights to equity instruments of the parent**, two possibilities exist: the rights can be granted either by the subsidiary or by the parent itself. The problem that arises is that the accounting treatment is different. If granted by the parent, the transaction is regarded as **equity-settled**. If granted by the subsidiary, the transaction is treated as **cash-settled in the subsidiary's** accounts but as **equity-settled in the group** accounts. 8909

This situation resulted in concerns that companies faced the burden – and cost – of having to calculate the cost of the share-based transaction for the subsidiary on a basis different from that at which it was measured in the group financial statements. As a result, the ASB stated in UITF Information Sheet No. 82 that it would consider an amendment exempting the group from this additional burden. However, after considering the issue, it concluded that such an amendment would result in a difference between FRS 20 and IFRS 2 (on which it is based). Although certain companies would achieve a cost saving, this would apply only to the minority of cases where the substance of the arrangement was a grant of options by the subsidiary itself. It would not affect those arrangements where the grant was made by the parent; in such cases the additional burden does not arise. It was felt, therefore, that the importance of not introducing a divergence between the UK and the international standards outweighed the cost benefit to preparers.

a. Entity grants right to elect choice of settlement to the other party

If the entity has granted the right to the other party to choose how the transaction is to be settled, it has in fact granted a **compound financial instrument** consisting of a debt component (i.e., the other party's right to receive payment in cash) and an equity component (i.e., its right to demand settlement in equity). 8910 FRS 20 (35)

For transactions with **parties other than employees**, in which the fair value of the goods or services is measured directly, the entity must measure the equity component of the compound financial instrument as follows: 8911

Fair value of goods or services received	£ xxx
Less: Fair value of debt component	xxx
Fair value of equity component	£ xxx

For other transactions – including those **with employees** – the entity must measure the fair value of the compound financial instrument as follows: 8912

Fair value of debt component	£ xxx
Add: Fair value of equity component [1]	xxx
Fair value of compound instrument	£ xxx

1. The other party must forfeit the right to receive cash in order to receive the equity instrument.

Transactions in which the other party has the choice of settlement are usually structured so that the fair value of one alternative is the same as the value of the other. For instance, the counterparty may have the choice of receiving share options or cash-settled share appreciation rights. In this case, the fair value of the equity component is zero, therefore the fair value of the compound instrument is equal to the fair value of the debt component. Similarly, where the fair values of the settlement options differ, the fair value of the equity component is usually higher than zero, so that the fair value of the compound instrument is greater than the value of the debt component. 8914

If the entity makes a cash payment instead of issuing equity, the payment is applied to settle the liability in full. By electing to receive cash, the other party forfeits the right to receive equity. 8916 FRS 20 (40)

b. Entity has right to elect choice of settlement

8918 FRS 20 (41) Where the entity has the choice of whether to settle in cash or by issuing equity, it must first determine whether it has a present obligation to settle in cash.

8919 If a **present obligation** exists, the company is obliged to treat the transaction as cash-settled. The following are the circumstances in which a present obligation is deemed to exist:
– the choice of settlement in equity has no commercial substance (e.g., the entity has no legal authority to issue shares);
– the entity has a past history or stated policy of settling in cash;
– the entity generally settles in cash when requested to do so by the other party.

8920 FRS 20 (42) Where the entity has **no such present obligation**, it must account for the transaction as an equity-settled share-based transaction (as described from ¶8860, above).

On **settlement**, the entity will account for the transaction in one of the following ways, as circumstances dictate:

FRS 20 (43)

CONDITIONS APPLYING	TREATMENT
(a) Entity elects to settle in cash.	Cash payment treated as repurchase of an equity interest (i.e., a deduction from equity, except as stated in (c), below).
(b) Entity elects to settle by issuing equity.	Transfer from one component of equity to another.
(c) Entity elects the settlement alternative with the higher fair value.	Amount of excess value given to be recognised as expense (e.g., the difference between cash paid and the value of the equity that would otherwise have been issued is transferred to expense).

8921 For accounting periods beginning on or after 1 January 2010, an amendment to FRS 20 sets out additional requirements relating to share-based payment transactions among **group** entities.

In its separate or individual financial statements, the **entity receiving goods or services** must measure the goods or services received as either an equity-settled or a cash-settled share-based payment transaction by assessing the nature of the awards granted and its own rights and obligations. Where the awards granted are the entity's own equity instruments or the entity has no obligation to settle the share-based payment transaction, the goods or services received should be measured as an equity-settled share-based transaction. In all other circumstances, the entity should measure the goods or services received as a cash-settled share-based payment transaction. The entity settling a share-based payment transaction when **another entity in the group** receives the goods or services should recognise the transaction as an equity-settled share-based payment transaction only if it is settled in the entity's own equity instruments. If it is not, the transaction should be measured as a cash-settled share-based payment transaction.

E. Disclosure

8925 FRS 20 requires entities to make such disclosures as are necessary to enable users of financial statements to understand:
– the **nature and extent** of share-based payment arrangements during the period under review,
– how the fair value of goods and services received – or the fair value of equity instruments granted – was **computed**, and

– the **effect** of share-based transactions on both its profit and loss for the period and its financial position at the reporting date.

The above requirements will be satisfied if the entity supplies the following information:

1. **Description** of each type of share-based payment arrangement during the period.
2. **Number** and weighted average exercise price of share options outstanding at the beginning and end of the period, exercisable at the end of the period, and granted, forfeited, exercised or expired during the period.
3. Weighted average share price **at the date of exercise** for those share options exercised during the period – or, where options were regularly exercised throughout the period, the weighted average share price **for the period**.
4. The range of exercise prices and weighted average **remaining contractual life** for options outstanding at the end of the period.
5. Where goods and/or services received were valued by reference to the value of equity granted, in the case of **new options**, their weighted average fair value at the measurement date including information on how the value was ascertained; in the case of **new equity instruments other than options**, the number and their weighted average fair value at the measurement date including information on how the value was ascertained; and in the case of **equity instruments changed during the period**, an explanation of the changes, the incremental fair value granted and information on **how** these were ascertained.
6. Where goods and services have been measured directly, details of how this was done.
7. Where the company has rebutted the presumption that the fair value of goods and services received can be measured reliably, a statement of this fact together with an **explanation** of how the **presumption** was **rebutted**.
8. Where goods and services did not qualify for recognition as assets, the total **expense** of share-based payment transactions in the period.
9. Total **carrying amount** of liabilities at the reporting date that arose as a result of share-based payment transactions, and the total **intrinsic value** at the end of the period for liabilities where the other party's rights had already vested by that date.

CHAPTER 7

Taxation

OUTLINE ¶¶

The calculation and presentation of the tax entries in the financial statements is dictated by the status of the company, the types and sources of income included within the accounting profits, and the nature of the costs incurred. **9000**

At the most basic level, corporate tax is an expense, related to profit on income, levied by national governments and borne by businesses. In the UK, a single corporate tax rate, dependent on the amount of profit a company makes, is charged on taxable profits. Further details of all tax issues can be found in *Tax Memo*.

There are two elements to the tax charge included in the performance statements:
- current tax; and
- deferred tax.

In addition, VAT affects most businesses, while in the context of **groups** there may also be specific tax implications.

A. Current tax

This section considers **accounting issues** relating to the following: **9005** FRS 16
- recognition, measurement and disclosure of the current (corporate) tax charge;
- taxes relating to dividends and interest, such as tax credits, withholding tax and underlying tax; and
- recoverable ACT.

The objective of tax accounting is to **recognise** taxation in a **consistent** and **transparent** manner.

1. Common terms

The term "current tax" includes the amount of tax estimated to be payable or recoverable relating to a company's profit or loss for a period, excluding the effects of deferred tax. **9007** FRS 16 (2)

Providing for current tax is an application of the matching concept. As the **tax liability**, calculated for the purposes of the financial statements, is often subject to refinement and possibly negotiation with Revenue and Customs, an adjustment is also usually required to the estimates used for previous periods. It is important to note that such adjustments should be treated as part of the current year's tax charge or credit, and not as a prior period adjustment.

9010 **Dividends** and **interest**, both payable and receivable, are often affected by the requirement to withhold tax at source.

The most common types of deducted taxes are:

1. **Withholding tax**, which is the tax paid over to the tax authorities by the payer of the income on behalf of the recipient. The table below gives examples of income from which withholding tax may be deducted, depending on the nature and location of the parties to the transaction.

Payer	Recipient	Types of income
UK	UK	Interest (unless between UK companies) Patent royalties
UK	Overseas	Interest Royalties Rent Dividends
Overseas	UK	As above, subject to rules of overseas jurisdiction

The amount chargeable to corporate tax is the gross amount of income, including withholding tax. When a UK company receives taxed income from overseas double tax relief is often claimed (¶9029). This may be sufficient to extinguish the UK corporation tax liability on that source of profit where the rate of deduction is high enough.

2. **Underlying tax** is the tax levied by the local jurisdiction on the overseas entity's profits. As dividends are paid out of taxed profits, the recipient of the dividend is indirectly suffering this tax, and double tax relief is available in some circumstances.

3. **Tax credits** are given to the non-corporate recipient of a dividend from a UK company, which can result in the dividend being tax free (unless the recipient is a higher or additional rate taxpayer). Under this imputation system, a company's profits are taxed only once, and individuals receiving a distribution of profits (usually dividends) are given credit for tax already suffered by the company. The tax credit is currently set at the rate of one-ninth of the net dividend paid, and is not repayable in any circumstances. This is extended to receipts from overseas companies in certain circumstances, the principal one being that the individual must be a minority shareholder, i.e., hold less than 10 percent of the ordinary share capital.

2. Measurement

9018 FRS 16 (14) Current tax is measured by applying the **tax rates**, which the UK authorities specify in advance, and **laws** that have been enacted or substantively enacted at the balance sheet date.

MEMO POINTS If a tax rate is set out in a Finance Bill that has been approved by the House of Commons, it is regarded as substantively enacted, and should be applied.

EXAMPLE A Ltd's accounting period ends on 31 December 20X5. The following main tax rates have been enacted:

Year to 31 March 20X5	30%
Year to 31 March 20X6	28%

A Ltd's effective tax rate is calculated as follows:

3/12 x 30%	7.5%
9/12 x 28%	21.0%
Effective rate	28.5%

a. Overview of corporation tax

Corporation tax is **charged** on taxable profits of companies under Corporation Tax Self Assessment. Under this system, the company **calculates** the corporation tax due, and completes a CT600 Tax Return, which is **submitted** to Revenue and Customs, together with a computation of the tax liability and a copy of the statutory accounts. Various factors affect the calculation of the tax charge. **9020**

Residence

The company's residence status is crucial to determining the liability to UK corporation tax. **9022**
1. **UK companies** are liable to UK corporation tax on their worldwide profits and gains, arising from any source.
2. **Other companies** may be liable to UK corporation tax, depending on the nature of their activities.

Period

Tax is levied on the results of the **accounting period**, which is usually the same as the period covered by the statutory accounts, although it cannot exceed 12 months. A **longer** period of account will be split into two accounting periods, the first being 12 months long. **9024**

Taxable profits

Corporation tax is **chargeable** on the aggregated profits from all sources, after adjustments have been made for: **9025**
- any allowable losses;
- deductions (such as charitable donations);
- non-taxable income (such as dividends that enjoy the dividend exemption); and
- disallowable items (such as business entertaining).

Taxable profits are seldom the same as the accounting profits, and this issue is addressed by deferred tax (¶9060).

Income and expenses subject to non-standard rates of tax

Income and expenses should be included in the financial statements on the basis of the amount **actually receivable or payable**, ignoring any notional tax effects of the individual items. For example, certain types of leasing transactions can result in a pre-tax loss but a post-tax profit, because certain items are allowable for tax in an amount that exceeds the accounting expense. Only the pre-tax loss should be included in the financial statements, however. **9026** FRS 16(11)

Where a company's accounts are **materially affected** by items that are subject to non-standard rates of tax, appropriate disclosure should be made.

Computation

Income from **different sources** is dealt with by various tax rules in order to calculate the tax due. A tax computation shows the profits chargeable to corporation tax and the calculation of the corporation tax charge, using the corporation tax rates applicable for the period, and is the main supporting document for the company tax return. **9027**

9028 **Format** The basic format of the computation is as follows:

	£
Trading income	X
Income from other sources	X
Income received under deduction of tax	X
Chargeable gains	X
	X
Less: Qualifying charitable donations	(X)
Profits chargeable to corporation tax (PCTCT)	X
Corporation tax thereon @ x %	X
Less: Income tax suffered at source	(X)
Less: Double tax relief	(X)
Net corporation tax payable	X

Overseas issues

9029 The **basis of taxation** for overseas income depends on the nature of the income. For example, dividends received from overseas are taxed when received, while overseas trading income is taxed on an accrued basis.

If **tax has already been suffered** (such as withholding or underlying tax) in the overseas country, double tax relief may be claimed under the terms of the relevant treaty or unilaterally under the applicable UK rules. Relief is limited by the amount of UK corporation tax levied on the overseas income.

MEMO POINTS Double tax relief for **underlying** tax normally requires the recipient to have 10 per cent voting control of the overseas entity. No such restriction applies to situations involving **withholding** tax.

Rates

9030 The rates of corporation tax are **dependent** on the **level of taxable profits** in a 12-month period, and are subject to periodic change. The financial year commences on 1 April and is denoted by the year in which it starts. For the years beginning 1 April 2010 (FY2010) and 2011 (FY2011) the rates of tax are summarised in the following table.

Taxable profits	Corporation tax rate 2010	Corporation tax rate 2011
0 to £300,000	21%	20%
£300,001 to £1,500,000	28% less relief[1]	27% less relief[1]
Over £1,500,000	28%	27%

Notes:
1. The relief is calculated as £1,500,000 less the amount of profits, multiplied by 7/400. See *Tax Memo* for full details.

If the accounting period is **shorter than 12 months**, the profit limits are pro-rated.

MEMO POINTS In the case of **associated** companies, the profit levels in the table above may be reduced. In broad terms, a company is an associate of another where one company controls the other, or both are controlled by a third party. A dormant company is not counted as an associated company for these purposes. See *Tax Memo* for further details.

Payment

9036 **Most companies** must pay corporation tax **within nine months** after the end of the accounting period. **Exceptionally**, larger companies (broadly, those with taxable profits exceeding £1.5m per annum, as adjusted for shorter periods and associated companies) must pay **quarterly instalments**. These instalments, which are payable in months 7, 10, 13 and 16 of a 12-month accounting period, require the company to estimate its current tax liability and to make payments accordingly.

b. Other taxes

Income tax

Income tax affects companies in the following ways: 9038

1. Companies must **deduct** income tax at source from certain payments and submit a form CT61 under a quarterly system. Examples of such items are annuities, interest paid to individuals and patent royalties. The **rate** of tax depends on the type of payment, with basic rate tax (20 per cent) usually being deducted.

2. Companies can claim **relief** for income tax suffered at source by set off against:

– any income tax deducted at source on payments which are disclosed on the quarter's CT61; or

– the company's corporation tax liability in the tax computation.

Advanced corporation tax (ACT)

ACT was abolished from 6 April 1999, but some companies still **retain** unrelieved ACT brought forward, the recovery of which is now limited by the shadow ACT rules. **Shadow ACT** is therefore relevant only to those companies and groups who had unrelieved surplus ACT at 6 April 1999, and is created by dividends paid after that date (being 25 percent of the dividend amount). 9040

The shadow ACT rules are complex, but in general the order of the set off (ignoring group situations) against the corporation tax liability is as follows:

– shadow ACT of the current year;
– shadow ACT carried forward from prior periods;
– carryback of shadow ACT from subsequent years; and
– real surplus ACT.

It should be noted that shadow ACT is a notional concept only, which does not result in any actual payments, or any actual adjustment to the corporation tax liability. Its **sole purpose** is to restrict relief of surplus ACT brought forward.

MEMO POINTS Prior to its abolition, ACT arose when dividends were paid. It was reported and paid quarterly using the CT61 system. The amount of ACT payable for the accounting period could then be offset against the corporation tax liability, subject to a limit of 20 percent of taxable profits. Where ACT remained unrelieved, otherwise known as surplus ACT, it was possible to carry it back for six years, or carry it forward indefinitely.

EXAMPLE B Ltd has surplus ACT brought forward of £50,000. B Ltd pays an interim dividend of £30,000 in June 20X7. Its taxable profits for the year ended 31 October 20X7 are £225,000. The set off is calculated as follows (ignoring any shadow ACT carried back from subsequent periods):

	£
Limit for ACT set off (£225,000 x 20%)	45,000
Amount of shadow ACT (£30,000 x 25%)	(7,500)
Capacity remaining	37,500
Set off of real surplus ACT	(37,500)
Remaining capacity	0
Surplus ACT brought forward	50,000
Set off as above	(37,500)
Surplus ACT carried forward	12,500

3. Recognition

9048 FRS 16 (5) The **general rule** is that the current tax charge should be recognised in the same performance statement as the item to which it relates, which is normally the profit and loss account.

9050 If a particular item has been recognised in the **statement of recognised gains and losses (STRGL)**, related current tax should be recognised in that statement. Examples of such items would be:
- foreign currency differences; and
- the disposal of an asset that had been previously revalued.

9052 When it is **not clear** where current tax should be recognised, a reasonable allocation between the two performance statements is appropriate.

EXAMPLE C Ltd sells a property, when the tax rate is 30%, which has been revalued by an amount of £300,000 which has all passed through the STRGL. The loss on disposal is £50,000 while the related tax charge is £75,000.
There are two possibilities for recognising current tax:
1. The tax charge is recognised only in the STRGL as it relates to the gains which have previously passed through that performance statement.
2. The tax charge is pro-rated as follows:
- a charge of £90,000 in the STRGL (£300,000 at 30%) in respect of the original revaluation surplus; and
- a credit of £15,000 in the profit and loss account (£50,000 at 30%) in respect of the book loss crystallised on disposal.

Summary:

	STRGL	**P & L**	**Total**
	£	**£**	**£**
Option 1	75,000	0	75,000
Option 2	90,000	(15,000)	75,000

9054 FRS 16 (8), (9) The amount of **dividends** payable or receivable, and **interest** payable or receivable should be stated excluding tax credits and other taxes, but including withholding taxes. For UK dividends payable or receivable, only the cash amount is included in the accounts. Overseas dividends and interest may be subject to withholding tax.

EXAMPLE A Ltd has a 1% shareholding in an overseas company, from which it receives a net dividend that is not eligible for the dividend exemption. The rate of withholding tax is 10%, and the company is liable to UK corporation tax at 30%.
The dividend income shown in the accounts will be £200, and the tax note to the profit and loss account would show the following:

	£	£
UK corporation tax		
Current tax on income for the period (200 x 30%)	60	
Double tax relief (200 × 10%)	(20)	
		40
Foreign tax		
Current tax on income for the period		20
Tax charge		60

9056 **ACT** should be recognised as an asset in the financial statements only if it is regarded as **recoverable** in the immediate and foreseeable future. Any **change** in the amount of recoverable ACT should be recognised as part of the tax expense in the profit and loss account. For example, a company may be able to recover ACT previously written off in the past, and the write back would then be recognised in the year when the ACT is recovered.

Given that ACT was abolished in 1999, it is unlikely that a company will be able to justify the recoverability of any remaining outstanding ACT in the immediate future. If this is the case then it should not be treated as an asset of the company.

B. Deferred tax

1. Purpose

Taxable profits **are rarely the same** as accounting profits, because the criteria for recognising items of income and expenses are different. Such items are often taxable or tax deductible at a different time to when they are recognised for accounting purposes, or in some cases may not be recognised or allowed at all, and the tax adjustments made to the accounting profit distort the resulting tax charge shown in the accounts. **9060** FRS 19 (2)

At the most basic level, deferred tax is the estimated amount of tax that will arise from the gap between accounting and taxable profits.

Applying the **accruals concept**, the tax charge shown in the accounts should take account of all tax consequences of income and expenses disclosed in the current period, even though those consequences may only be recognised in a later period. **9062** FRS 19 (7)

A **distinction** must however be made between differences in the accounting and tax treatment which are permanent, and those which relate to timing only.

1. **Permanent differences** arise when there are items recognised in the financial statements that will never be brought into charge to tax, or allowed as a tax deductible expense. For example, certain entertainment expenses will never be allowed as a tax deductible expense, and this difference will never resolve in the future. Such differences are irrelevant for the purposes of the deferred tax calculation.
2. **Timing differences** arise when an item is taxable or deductible in a different period to that in which it is recognised in the accounts. They are said to "originate" when they first arise, and "reverse" when they resolve in a later period.

The rationale adopted by FRS 19 is to apply the liability method, which broadly means that tax is provided for on timing differences only, in an amount that is estimated to be the liability for tax payable at some point in the future. In order to help remove the distortions to the tax charge, a provision for a deferred tax liability or a deferred tax asset is created.

The following table summarises the deferred tax treatment of certain common items: **9064** FRS 19 (2)

Item	Reference	Type of difference	Adjust for deferred tax purposes
Accelerated capital allowances	¶9066	Timing	Yes
Unrelieved tax loss	¶9074	Timing	Yes
Disallowable expenditure	¶9062	Permanent	No
Deferred expenditure	¶9080	Timing	Yes
Unpaid pension contributions	¶9082	Timing	Yes
Revaluation gain	¶9076	Timing	Yes
Intra-group profits on stock reversed on consolidation	¶9154	Timing	Yes
Unremitted income from group undertakings	¶9158	Timing	Yes

Accelerated capital allowances

Deferred tax is often relevant in respect of capital allowances, which are the tax deductible equivalent of depreciation (which is not tax deductible). An asset is commonly **depreciated at a slower rate** in the financial statements (i.e., over a longer period) than is allowed for tax purposes (in other words, the capital allowances claimed in the tax computation have **9066** FRS 19 (9) the effect of "writing off" the asset faster). This gives rise to an initial tax advantage; however, this timing difference will slowly erode over time, and ultimately resolve when the asset is sold, because an adjustment will be made in the tax computation to reverse the excess capital allowances previously given.

EXAMPLE A Ltd purchases plant for £10,000 on 1 January 20X1 which qualifies for capital allowances on a 20% reducing balance basis, and is depreciated at 15% per annum on a straight-line basis. The company has a 31 December year end.
The following timing differences will arise up to 31 December 20X3:

	20X1	20X2	20X3	Total
	£	£	£	£
Depreciation charge	1,500	1,500	1,500	4,500
Capital allowances	2,000	1,600	1,280	4,880
Timing differences:				
Originating/ (reversing)	500	100	(220)	380

In 20X4, A Ltd sells the plant for £6,000, when the net book value is £5,500, giving an accounting profit on disposal of £500. For tax purposes, the maximum capital allowances which should have been given are only £4,000 (£10,000 – £6,000), so a balancing charge of £880 is required.

	20X4
	£
Profit on disposal	(500)
Balancing charge	880
Timing differences:	
Originating/(reversing)	(380)

9068 With the **effluxion of time**, as the accumulated depreciation charge converges with the cumulative capital allowances claimed, the deferred tax liability will be released.

EXAMPLE A company purchases an asset for £10,000 and depreciates it over three years. The asset qualifies for the annual investment allowance at 100%. The company uses the asset for four years before scrapping it.

	Year 1	Year 2	Year 3	Year 4
	£	£	£	£
Depreciation charge	3,333	3,333	3,333	0
Capital allowances	10,000	0	0	0
Timing differences:				
Originating/(reversing)	6,666	(3,333)	(3,333)	0

The timing differences have reversed by Year 4, because in that time the asset has been fully depreciated and all possible capital allowances have been claimed.

9070 Even where an asset is **not depreciated**, deferred tax should still be provided on the timing difference that arises when capital allowances are claimed. An example of such an asset is plant included within an investment property (¶1900).

9072 Certain types of capital **allowances are retained** by the company even when the asset is sold for a profit, depending on the length of time the asset has been held. For example, business property renovation allowances cannot be withdrawn once a set period of ownership has elapsed (currently 7 years). From acquisition, deferred tax should still be recognised on such an asset, as the company should not anticipate holding the asset for the requisite period. After the period has expired, however, the allowances claimed become a permanent difference and the deferred tax that has previously been recognised should be reversed.

EXAMPLE B Ltd acquires an investment property (which is not depreciated) on 1 January 2XX1 for £800,000, and it qualifies for business property renovation allowances, being used as an office for the 7 year period. By 31 December 2XX7, allowances of £800,000 have been claimed in the tax computation. Deferred tax has been provided for this timing difference, and is now reversed at 31 December as the allowances can no longer be clawed back.

Unrelieved tax losses

Trading losses can be used in the following ways: 9074
- set off in the current year against other profits and chargeable gains;
- carried back to set against the profits of the prior accounting period; or
- carried forward to set against profits of the same trade.

Where **set off** can occur in the current year or by way of carryback, the appropriate reduction is made to the current tax charge. Where set off is not available, and the losses are carried forward, deferred tax comes into play, because the losses, when utilised, may lead to an eventual tax reduction or even refund. This constitutes a timing difference.

The use of **capital losses** is more restricted, so deferred tax is rarely provided as a consequence (¶9100).

Revaluation gain

Normally revaluation gains **do not give rise** to a deferred tax adjustment. However, by 9076 FRS 19 (12), (14)
exception deferred tax is provided **if**:
- the revaluation gain is recognised in the profit and loss account (such as for marked-to-market gains revalued to fair value); or
- there is a binding agreement to sell the asset at the balance sheet date and the resulting profit or loss has been recognised.

MEMO POINTS Very often **marked-to-market** items are taxed at the same time as they are recognised in the accounts; as a result no timing difference arises.

Rollover relief, which is available only for certain types of trading assets, defers the tax charge resulting from a sale when the proceeds are reinvested in a replacement asset. When rollover relief is expected to be obtained, no deferred tax should be recognised, although related disclosure is required. 9078

MEMO POINTS 1. The rolled over **tax charge will crystallise** when the replacement asset is sold, although it is possible for another rollover claim to be made, which could then defer the resulting tax charge again.
2. **Holdover relief**, which merely postpones the capital gain for a maximum of ten years, is available in certain situations, and creates a timing difference, which requires deferred tax to be provided.

Deferred expenditure

Where expenditure is allowed for tax in the year that it is incurred, but for accounting purposes there is a delay in recognition, a deferred tax liability will arise. Examples include capitalised interest costs, and expense prepayments. 9080

Pension liabilities

For **accounting purposes**, contributions to pension schemes are recognised on the accruals basis while the **rule for tax purposes** is that contributions paid wholly and exclusively for the purposes of the business to registered schemes are allowed in the period in which they are made (i.e., cash basis). 9082

Where there have been **special payments** to a pension fund (such as lump sum payments to make up a shortfall), tax relief may be spread according to specific rules that will not necessarily be the same as for accounting purposes. This will have deferred tax implications.

The **relief** is spread where the **excess payment** amounts to:
- more than 210% of the previous years contribution; and
- £500,000 or more.

The **excess payment** is the amount by which the special payment exceeds 110% of the previous year's contribution and it is spread as follows:

Amount	Spread over
≤ £500,000	N/A
£500,001 – £999,999	2 years
£1,000,000 – £1,999,999	3 years
≥ £2,000,000	4 years

Payments are deducted evenly over the periods. If a period is less than 12 months, the deduction is restricted accordingly.

A deferred tax asset will result where contributions paid are less then the pension cost shown in the accounts. (See further ¶9100.)

2. Measurement

9085 FRS 19 (37) Deferred tax is measured using the average tax rates that are expected to apply when the timing differences reverse, based on the tax rates that have been enacted, or substantively enacted, by the balance sheet. **In practice** current tax rates are often used, as they are invariably the only rates that have been enacted.

If future profits are expected to increase, it is prudent to use the standard rate of corporation tax.

EXAMPLE Continuing the example at ¶9066, an average tax rate of 28% applies throughout the period. The associated deferred tax balances would be:

	20X1	20X2	20X3	20X4
	£	£	£	£
Timing difference	500	100	(220)	(380)
Tax rate	28%	28%	28%	28%
Deferred tax liability increase/(decrease)	140	28	(62)	(106)
Deferred tax balance	140	168	106	0

Discounting

9087 FRS 19 (42) To reflect the **time value of money**, it is possible to discount a deferred tax liability, although this is not usually undertaken due to the increased complexity of calculation.

In making the decision whether to discount the deferred tax liability, the **following factors** should be considered:
- materiality;
- whether transparency outweighs the costs of performing the discounting calculations; and
- whether there is established industry practice which may influence the comparability of the accounts with those of other industry incumbents.

Discounting should be **applied** consistently, although care should be taken not to discount deferred tax provisions relating to timing differences that have already been discounted, such as defined benefit pension balances.

9090 The **period** of discounting should run until the timing differences completely reverse. For example, the relevant period for accelerated capital allowances is the time taken for the depreciation charge to catch up with the cumulative capital allowances. All future movements in the accelerated capital allowances and depreciation charges should be scheduled out on a yearly basis, taking account of future depreciation rates. No account should be taken of timing differences that might arise on fixed assets expected to be purchased in the future.

EXAMPLE A Ltd acquires plant for £80,000, which is depreciated over 8 years on a straight-line basis. For ease of calculation, assume the plant qualifies for capital allowances on a 20% reducing

balance basis, and that the average tax rate is 30%. At the beginning of Year 9, the asset is obsolete and scrapped. For tax purposes, a balancing allowance is claimed.
The original timing difference at the balance sheet date is calculated as follows:

	£
Net book value at end of year of acquisition	70,000
Tax written down value	(64,000)
Originating timing difference	6,000
Deferred tax liability (6,000 @ 30%)	1,800

The resulting undiscounted deferred tax liability/(asset) will be:

Number of years from B/S date	Depreciation charge (£)	Capital allowances (£)	Timing difference (£)	Deferred tax movement (£)	Undiscounted deferred tax liability/(asset) (£)
0					1,800
1	10,000	12,800	2,800	840	2,640
2	10,000	10,240	240	72	2,712
3	10,000	8,192	(1,808)	(542)	2,170
4	10,000	6,554	(3,446)	(1,034)	1,136
5	10,000	5,243	(4,757)	(1,427)	(291)
6	10,000	4,194	(5,806)	(1,742)	(2,033)
7	10,000	3,355	(6,645)	(1,994)	(4,027)
8	0	13,422	13,422	4,027	0
Total	70,000	64,000	6,000	1,800	

The discount **rate** must be the post-tax yield on government bonds, with equivalent maturity dates and currency to those of the deferred tax balance, at the balance sheet date. The **pre-tax yield** on government bonds can be obtained from the financial press, classified as follows: **9092**
- periods up to five years;
- between five and ten years;
- between ten and fifteen years; and
- over fifteen years.

The appropriate yield should be chosen to match the period of discounting required.

The **post-tax yield** is then calculated using an estimate of the tax payable by the company holding such a bond, based on enacted or substantively enacted tax rates and laws.

EXAMPLE The following government bonds are shown in the financial press:

Redemption period		Pre-tax yield	Post-tax yield (assuming tax at 30%)
3 years	$6.66\% \times \frac{(100-30)}{100}$	6.66%	4.66%
4 years	$6.51\% \times \frac{(100-30)}{100}$	6.51%	4.56%

It should then be applied to the scheduled out timing differences. **9094**

EXAMPLE Combining the examples at ¶9090 and ¶9092, A Ltd's deferred tax liability for Years 3 and 4 is calculated as follows:

	Year 3	Year 4
Number of years from balance sheet date (n)	3	4
Undiscounted deferred tax liability	£2,170	£1,136
Post-tax yield (P)	4.66%	4.56%
Discount factor $\frac{1}{(1+P)^n}$	$\frac{1}{(1+0.0466)^3}$ = 0.8723	$\frac{1}{(1+0.0456)^4}$ = 0.8366
	£2,170 × 0.8723 =	£1,136 × 0.8366 =
Discounted deferred tax	£1,893	£950

3. Recognition

9096 FRS 19 (34) The deferred tax charge or credit is **usually** recognised in the profit and loss account, **unless** it relates to an item that has been recognised in the STRGL (¶4300). As with current tax, a reasonable allocation between the two performance statements may be appropriate in certain circumstances.

9098 FRS 19 (7) Any deferred tax liabilities or assets which arise from timing differences should be **provided for** in full, subject to certain criteria.

Deferred tax assets

9100 FRS 19 (23) The **basic rule** is that a deferred tax asset may only be recognised if there is sufficient evidence that it is likely to be recoverable at the balance sheet date.

Where both a **deferred tax liability and asset exist** at the balance sheet date, arising on different items, it can be assumed that the asset is recoverable, as the reversal of the deferred tax liability will give rise to eventual taxable profits.

Where **the deferred tax asset cannot be fully set off** against a deferred tax liability, other evidence should be considered in deciding whether to recognise an asset, and this would include profits:
- that arise within the same entity and jurisdiction as the income or expenditure giving rise to the deferred tax asset;
- generated in the same period as the deferred tax asset is expected to reverse; and
- against which the tax loss will be set in a loss carry back or carry forward claim.

MEMO POINTS 1. If there are any doubts about the company's **going concern** status, a deferred tax asset should not be recognised.
2. The recovery of a deferred tax asset arising from a **capital loss** is restricted because there must be plans to sell an asset which will result in a capital gain, to offset the loss.

EXAMPLE C Ltd believes that it will make taxable profits of £100,000 in the foreseeable future. At the balance sheet date, a deferred tax asset of £40,000 exists.
Assuming an average tax rate of 30%, the deferred tax asset provided in the accounts should be £30,000 (£100,000 x 30%), and so £10,000 is unrecognised.

9102 Overall, the **existence of unrelieved tax losses** at the balance sheet date normally indicates a doubtful future profit position, and a deferred tax asset would not therefore normally be recognised. An exception arises if the losses result from an identifiable and non-recurring cause, such as an arson attack, when profits are expected to resume in future periods, and the deferred tax asset may well be recoverable.

MEMO POINTS When considering **suitable profits**, tax planning can also be taken into account, for instance:
- restricting future capital allowances claims to utilise tax losses; and
- switching from tax free to taxable investments.

9104 FRS 19 (23) The **recognised amount** of the deferred tax asset at each balance sheet date should be assessed annually, and where circumstances have changed, the recoverability of the asset should be reconsidered. Where future profitability is less than expected, the asset may be impaired. Alternatively, a previously unrecognised asset may be assessed as recoverable, and require inclusion in the current year's accounts as a change in accounting estimate.

EXAMPLE D Ltd made a trading loss of £200,000 in 20X4, and due to continuing production problems, no deferred tax asset was recognised in 20X4. D Ltd made further losses of £40,000 in 20X5.
In 20X6, the company started to reap the benefits of a capital reinvestment programme, and profits of £90,000 were made. Similar profits are expected in future years.
Assuming £150,000 of the trading loss is still carried forward at 20X6, after offset against the current year profits, D Ltd recognises a deferred tax asset of £45,000 (£150,000 x 30%) in 20X6. The credit to the profit and loss account is recognised as a current item relating to 20X6.

C. Disclosure and presentation

1. Current tax

Any particular accounting policy adopted in relation to current tax should be disclosed. 9110 FRS 18 (55)

The following items must be included in the **note accompanying the tax charge** in the performance statements: 9112
a. details of special circumstances that affect the tax liability for the current year or following year; and
b. the following amounts should be stated in "tax on profit on ordinary activities" allocated between UK corporation tax and foreign tax:
- amount of the charge for UK corporation tax;
- amount of the UK corporation tax ignoring double tax relief;
- amount of the charge for UK income tax;
- amount of overseas tax;
- changes in the amount of recoverable ACT;
- tax attributable to the group share of profits from associated companies and joint ventures; and
- adjustments required in respect of prior periods.

A **common way** of setting out the tax note to support the entry in the performance statements, which also complies with statutory requirements, is shown in the following pro forma. 9114 FRS 16 (Appendix. I)

	£	£
Current tax		
UK corporation tax		
Current tax on income for the period	X	
Adjustments in respect of prior periods	X	
Irrecoverable ACT	X	
	X	
Double tax relief	(X)	
		X
Foreign tax		
Current tax on income for the period	X	
Adjustments in respect of prior periods	X	
		X
Tax on profit on ordinary activities		X

The **corporation tax balance** due to or from Revenue and Customs is disclosed within either: 9116
- social security and other taxes (¶3216); or
- other debtors, if the tax is recoverable.

Many companies choose to disclose corporation tax in the balance sheet as a separate subcategory of creditors.

Any corporation tax **payable more than 12 months** after the balance sheet date should be disclosed within "creditors: amounts falling due after more than one year".

2. Deferred tax

Presentation in the profit and loss account

9120 FRS 19 (59) The deferred tax charge should be included within the heading "tax on profit or loss on ordinary activities".

Deferred tax balance

9122 FRS 19 (55), (56) This balance (except deferred tax relating to defined benefit pensions) is **usually disclosed** separately in the balance sheet within either:
- provisions for liabilities and charges (for a net deferred tax liability); or
- debtors (for a net deferred tax asset).

Deferred tax **debit and credit balances** should be offset within the above headings only if they relate to taxes levied by the same authority, and arise in the same company or group. Otherwise a separate presentation is required.

FRS 19 (58) Separate disclosure **on the face of the balance sheet** is required if the amounts are so material that readers may misinterpret the financial statements in the absence of such disclosure. (For example, the balance sheet shows net current assets of £10,000, of which £20,000 relates to a deferred tax asset.)

MEMO POINTS For **defined benefit pension schemes**, FRS 17 requires the deferred tax relating to the defined benefit asset or liability to be offset against the defined benefit asset or liability (¶8468).

Accounting policy

9124 FRS 18 (55) The accounting policy adopted in relation to deferred tax should **specifically** mention the following:
- the basis of recognition for deferred tax, taking account of timing differences which have originated and not reversed by the balance sheet date; and
- whether discounting has been used.

EXAMPLE **B Ltd**
Accounting policies
Deferred taxation

The payment of taxation is deferred or accelerated because of timing differences between the treatment of certain items for accounting and taxation purposes. Full provision for deferred taxation is made under the liability method, on all timing differences that have arisen, but not reversed by the balance sheet date, unless such provision is not permitted by FRS 19.
Deferred tax is measured at the rates that are expected to apply in the periods when the timing differences are expected to reverse, based on the tax rates and law enacted at the balance sheet date.
Where gains or losses are recognised in the statement of total recognised gains and losses, the related taxation is also taken directly to that statement.
In accordance with FRS 19, deferred taxation is not provided for:
- revaluation gains on land and buildings, unless there is a binding contract to sell them at the balance sheet date; and
- gains on the sale of non-monetary assets, where on the basis of all available evidence it is more likely than not that the taxable gain will be rolled over into the replacement assets.

The company has adopted a policy of discounting deferred tax assets and liabilities to reflect the time value of money, using a discount rate equivalent to the post-tax yield that could be obtained at the balance sheet date on government bonds with similar maturity dates and currencies. The increase or decrease in the discount deducted in arriving at the deferred tax balance is included in the deferred tax charge or credit in the profit and loss account.

Detailed disclosure

Performance statements

The notes to the financial statements should disclose the amount of deferred tax charged or credited within: **9126**
1. Tax on ordinary activities in the **profit and loss account**, identifying the following components, where material:
a. changes in deferred tax balances (before discounting where applicable) arising from:
– the origination and reversal of timing differences;
– changes in tax rates and laws; and
– adjustments to the estimated recoverable amount of deferred tax assets arising in previous periods; and
b. where applicable, changes in the amounts of discount deducted in arriving at the deferred tax balance.
2. Tax charged or credited directly in the **STRGL** for the period, separately disclosing the main components including those in 1.a. above.

Balance sheet

The notes should disclose the following: **9128**

General

a. the total deferred tax balance (before discounting, where applicable) showing the amount recognised for each significant timing difference separately;
b. the impact of discounting on, and the discounted amount of, deferred tax balance; and
c. the movement between the opening and closing net deferred tax balance, analysing separately:
– the amount charged or credited in the profit and loss account for the period;
– the amount charged or credited directly in the STRGL for the period; and
– movements arising from the acquisition or disposal of businesses.

Deferred tax asset

In relation to a deferred tax asset, the amount of the asset should be disclosed, and the nature of the evidence supporting its recognition if:
a. the recoverability of the deferred tax asset is dependent on future taxable profits in excess of those arising from the reversal of deferred tax liabilities; and
b. the reporting entity has suffered a loss in either the current or preceding period in the tax jurisdiction to which the deferred tax asset relates.

Circumstances affecting current and future tax charges

The notes to the financial statements should highlight circumstances that affect the current and total tax charges or credits in future periods, to include:
a. a reconciliation of the current tax charge (or credit) on ordinary activities to the current tax charge that would result from applying a standard rate of tax to the profit on ordinary activities before tax;
b. for assets which have been revalued (including where the market value has only been disclosed in the accounts), and assuming these were sold at the values shown:
– an estimate of the tax that could be payable or recoverable;
– an explanation of the circumstances in which the tax would crystallise; and
– an indication of the amount of tax that may become payable or recoverable in the foreseeable future;
c. for an asset which has been sold, or is the subject of a binding agreement to sell, and rollover relief is expected to be claimed:
– the conditions which will need to be met for rollover relief to be available; and
– an estimate of the tax which would crystallise if those conditions were not met;
d. the amount of any unrecognised deferred tax asset and the circumstances in which the asset would be recovered; and

e. for any other deferred tax which has not been recognised:
– the nature of the unrecognised amounts;
– the circumstances in which the tax would become payable or recoverable; and
– an indication of the amount that may become payable or recoverable in the foreseeable future.

MEMO POINTS The **standard rate of tax** for an overseas group of companies may not be the usual UK rate.

9130 FRS 19 (Appendix. II) The **interaction of the current tax and deferred tax** disclosures are best illustrated by the following example. Discounting has been ignored.

EXAMPLE **1. Tax on profit on ordinary activities (profit and loss note)**

a. Analysis of charge in period

	£'000	£'000
Current tax:		
UK corporation tax on profits of the period	40	
Adjustments in respect of previous periods	4	
		44
Foreign tax		12
Total current tax (note 1.b.)		56
Deferred tax:		
Origination and reversal of timing differences	67	
Effect of increased tax rate on opening liability	12	
Total deferred tax (note 2.)		79
Tax on profit on ordinary activities		135

b. Factors affecting tax charge for the period

Profit on ordinary activities before tax	361
Profit on ordinary activities multiplied by standard rate of corporation tax in the UK of 30%	108
Effects of:	
Expenses not deductible for tax purposes	21
Capital allowances in excess of depreciation	(56)
Utilisation of tax losses	(14)
Rollover relief on profit on disposal of property	(10)
Higher tax rates on overseas earnings	3
Adjustments to tax charge in respect of previous periods	4
Current tax charge for period	56

c. Factors that may affect future tax charges

Based on current capital investment plans, the company expects to continue to be able to claim capital allowances in excess of depreciation in future years but at a slightly lower level than in the current year. The company has now used all brought forward tax losses, which have significantly reduced tax payments in recent years.

No provision has been made for deferred tax on gains recognised on revaluing property to its market value, or on the sale of properties where potentially taxable gains have been rolled over into replacement assets. Such tax would become payable only if the property were sold without it being possible to claim rollover relief. The total amount unprovided for is £20,000, and at present it is not considered likely that any tax will become payable in the foreseeable future.

2. Provision for deferred tax (balance sheet note)

	£'000
Accelerated capital allowances	316
Pensions contributions accrued	(10)
Provision for deferred tax	306
Provision at start of period	227
Deferred tax charge in profit and loss account for period (note 1.a.)	79
Provision at end of period	306

If **discounting** was undertaken, the following amendments to the example in ¶9130 would be needed. 9132

EXAMPLE **1. Tax on profit on ordinary activities (profit and loss note)**

a. Analysis of charge in period

	£'000	£'000
Current tax:		
UK corporation tax on profits of the period	40	
Adjustments in respect of previous periods	4	
		44
Foreign tax		12
Total current tax		56
Deferred tax:		
Origination and reversal of timing differences	67	
(Increase)/reduction in discount	(6)	
Effect of increased tax rate on opening liability	12	
Total deferred tax (note 2.)		73
Tax on profit on ordinary activities		129

2. Provision for deferred tax (balance sheet note)

	£'000
Accelerated capital allowances	316
Pensions contributions accrued	(10)
Undiscounted provision for deferred tax	306
Discount	(45)
Discounted provision for deferred tax	261
Provision at start of period	188
Deferred tax charge in profit and loss account for period (note 1.a.)	73
Provision at end of period	261

Disclosures relating to the STRGL

The material components of the tax charged or credited directly to the STRGL should be disclosed in the same manner as for the profit and loss account (¶4319). 9134 FRS 19 (60)

EXAMPLE **Statement of recognised gains and losses**

	£'000
Profit earned for ordinary shareholders for the year	340
Currency translation differences on foreign current investments	(23)
Taxation on translation differences	(12)
Total recognised gains and losses for the year	305

Provision for deferred tax (balance sheet note)

	£'000
Provision at start of period	200
Currency translation adjustment	(3)
Deferred tax charge in profit and loss account for period	80
Other movements	5
Provision at end of period	282

D. Value Added Tax

General principles

9140 SSAP 5 (1) to (4) **Income and expenditure** should be stated net of VAT as the accounts should reflect the role of the company as a collector of VAT only. By **exception**, VAT is included within expenditure because it cannot be reclaimed in the following situations:
- the company is not registered for VAT;
- some or all of the activities of the company may be exempt for VAT purposes, which affects the recoverability of input VAT; and
- certain types of expenditure, such as business entertaining, incur VAT which cannot be recovered.

Turnover should always be stated net of VAT. If a company wishes to show turnover inclusive of VAT, then the VAT element must be shown as a deduction to arrive at the turnover figure net of VAT charged.

9141 SSAP 5 (5) The balance of **VAT due** to be paid or recovered from Revenue and Customs should be included as a creditor or debtor in the financial statements as appropriate, and does not require separate disclosure.

9143 SSAP 5 (6) If the company is **committed** to certain expenditure, such as the acquisition of a building, and will not be able to recover the related VAT, an appropriate disclosure should be made within a note on capital commitments.

Irrecoverable VAT relating to fixed assets should be included within each particular asset's cost.

Use of small business VAT schemes

9144 A small company may choose to use cash accounting, annual accounting or the flat rate scheme, all of which have implications for the financial statements.

9145 **Cash accounting** Under the cash accounting scheme, VAT is not payable or refundable until income is received and expenses are paid. This means that the **balance** shown as due to/from Revenue and Customs **in the accounts** will not agree to the amount shown on the relevant VAT return, even if the financial year end and VAT year end coincide.

9146 **Annual accounting** The annual accounting scheme allows only one VAT return a year to be submitted, and VAT payments can be made in instalments based on the previous year's liability. Again this means that the **balance** shown as due to/from Revenue and Customs **in the accounts** will not agree to the amount shown on the VAT return.

9147 **Flat rate scheme** This scheme allows a very small company (with turnover of up to £150,000) to ignore all the usual VAT rules, and apply a set percentage (dependent on trade sector) to turnover which becomes the amount due to Revenue and Customs.

The **amount payable** is the only entry in the balance sheet VAT account, and is deducted from turnover. All expenses are shown gross, with the exception of capital assets costing more than £2,000, when input VAT can still be recovered.

EXAMPLE Mr A is using the flat rate scheme, and his flat rate percentage is 10 percent.
He has net VATable turnover of £60,000 in a VAT quarter, and incurs expenses of £40,000 (including VAT).
Mr A's gross turnover is £72,000 (60,000 x 1.200)
The amount due to Revenue and Customs is £7,200 (72,000 x 10%)

On a very simple level, Mr A's profit and loss is as follows:

Turnover	720500 - 7,200	64,800
Expenses		(40,000)
Profit		£24,800

For a full discussion of VAT matters, please refer to our sister publication, *VAT Memo*.

E. Group aspects

Corporation tax reliefs

There are three important levels of **group relationship** for corporation tax, being 51 percent groups, 75 percent groups and consortia. The table summarises the tax consequences of each type of group: 9150

Type of group	Definition	Tax consequences
51%	A company owns more than 50% of the share capital of another company.	– affects the rate of tax payable (¶9030); – instalment payments will be due on lower profits; – no deduction of tax on intra-group charges and interest; – surplus shadow ACT must be allocated around the group before set off of real ACT.
75%	A company holds, or is entitled to at least 75% of all of the following: – ordinary share capital; – distributable profits; and – assets on a winding up. Ultimate parent must be entitled to at least 75% of sub-subsidiary.	– trading losses and certain other amounts may be group relieved; – tax refunds can be surrendered between group members.
75% (CG)	As above, with ultimate parent beneficially entitled to at least 50% of sub-subsidiary	– assets can be passed around the group without creating a tax charge; – rollover relief can be claimed on a group basis.
Consortium	20 or fewer companies each own at least 5%, and jointly at least 75%, of the ordinary share capital of another company.	– surrender of certain losses between the consortium company and the members.

The most common timing difference to affect groups is loss relief. Where **losses are group relieved**, the claimant company may pay an amount up to the amount of loss to the loss-making company, with no tax consequences. For a wholly owned subsidiary, payment for group losses is probably optional, but where minority interests are involved, payment is almost certainly required. 9152

The **amount of payment** may vary between none at all, and an amount representing the full amount of the loss surrendered. In any event, sufficient information should be clearly disclosed in the accounts of both the surrendering company and claimant company as shown in the table below. 9153

Amount of payment made for group relief	Claimant company	Surrendering company
None	Full explanation of the loss received and its effect on the tax charge.	Surrendered losses are not taken into account for the purposes of deferred tax. Disclose full financial impact.
Amount of tax saved	Included in tax charge in profit and loss account as "amount payable in respect of tax saved by group relief".	Credited to profit and loss account. Disclose full financial impact.
Amount of loss surrendered	Reduce profit before tax by amount paid as "amount payable in respect of group relief".	Increase profit before tax by amount received as "contribution receivable from group".

EXAMPLE E Ltd surrenders its trading loss of £150,000 to its 100% parent company, F Ltd. E Ltd's accounting loss is £130,000, and £20,000 of tax adjustments are made. F Ltd makes an accounting profit of £500,000, and the tax charge after claiming group relief is £93,000. F Ltd has timing differences of £40,000 upon which deferred tax is provided. The prevailing rate of tax is 30%.

1. If F Ltd makes a **payment of £45,000** to E Ltd, the following disclosures will be made:

E Ltd	£
Loss on ordinary activities before taxation	(130,000)
Taxation:	
UK corporation tax @ 30%	0
Amount received from group company in respect of group relief	45,000
Deferred tax (20,000 x 30%)	(6,000)
Loss for the financial period	(91,000)

Taxation note
Losses have been surrendered to a group company in return for consideration of £45,000. There are no tax losses available to carry forward, and deferred tax of £6,000 has been provided in respect of timing differences included in the surrendered losses.

F Ltd	£
Profit on ordinary activities before taxation	500,000
Taxation:	
UK corporation tax @ 30%	(93,000)
Amount payable to group company in respect of tax saved by group relief	(45,000)
Deferred tax (40,000 x 30%)	(12,000)
Profit for the financial period	350,000

Taxation note
A payment of £45,000 has been made in respect of the corporation tax saving resulting from a group relief claim.

2. If F Ltd makes a **payment of £150,000** to E Ltd instead, the following disclosures will result:

E Ltd	£
Operating loss	(130,000)
Contribution received from group company	150,000
Profit on ordinary activities before taxation	20,000
Taxation:	
UK corporation tax @ 30%	0
Deferred tax (20,000 x 30%)	(6,000)
Profit for the financial period	14,000

Taxation note
Losses have been surrendered to a group company in return for consideration of £150,000. There are no tax losses available to carry forward, and deferred tax of £6,000 has been provided in respect of timing differences included in the surrendered losses.

F Ltd	£
Operating profit	500,000
Amount payable to group company in respect of group relief	(150,000)
Profit on ordinary activities before taxation	350,000
Taxation:	
UK corporation tax @ 30%	(93,000)
Deferred tax (40,000 x 30%)	(12,000)
Profit for the financial period	245,000

Taxation note
A payment of £150,000 has been made in respect of group losses claimed.

Consolidated accounts

On consolidation, the group's position must be viewed as a whole. While the **individual tax charges** of each group member will be aggregated in the group accounts, the tax effect of consolidation adjustments must also be included. Such **adjustments** give rise to timing differences for the group which must be recognised by deferred tax. Examples would include: 9154
- alignment of accounting policies; and
- elimination of intra-group transactions.

EXAMPLE A Ltd sells stock to B Ltd, a subsidiary, for £100,000. The profit included in this price is £20,000, which must be eliminated on consolidation. Taking the tax rate as 30%, A Ltd would have accounted for current tax of £6,000 in relation to the profit from this stock.
In the group accounts, a deferred tax asset of £6,000 should be recognised to cancel out A Ltd's current tax charge.

When a **fair value adjustment** is made for an acquisition, it is treated as if it is a timing difference in the acquired company's accounts. The most common type of fair value adjustment is on property, and as this would be treated as a revaluation (¶9076), in most instances no deferred tax provision is required. 9156

Unremitted earnings from group undertakings

Where tax could be payable on the **future receipt** of past earnings of a subsidiary, associate or joint venture (taking account of any double taxation relief), deferred tax should be recognised to the extent that: 9158
- dividends have been accrued as receivable; or
- a binding agreement has been entered into so that past earnings will be distributed in the future.

VAT

Groups of companies where **common control** exists may apply to be treated as a single taxable person for VAT. Only companies with a fixed establishment in the UK can be included within a **group registration**. The representative company in the group will deal with all the VAT administration, and only this company needs to include a VAT liability or debtor in the balance sheet. 9160

F. Comparison with IFRS

The International Accounting Standards Board views the **balance sheet** as the statement of primary importance, for both current and deferred tax. 9165

Current tax

9167 IAS 12 (12) IAS 12 requires a liability to be recognised if there is an unpaid balance of tax relating to current and previous periods. Tax balances **must be presented** separately on the face of the balance sheet. Where current tax relates to items that have been charged or credited to equity (such as on revaluation of an asset), it should also be charged or credited directly to equity (through the revaluation reserve).

Deferred tax

9170 IAS 12 (15), (69) IAS 12 requires deferred tax to be recognised on a full provision basis but under a **different method** to FRS 19, known as the temporal method. This method accounts for the temporary difference between an asset's value for tax purposes (otherwise known as its tax base) and its book value in the accounts. In essence this means that any difference, including permanent differences and those arising from revaluation, will require a deferred tax provision, unless specifically excepted by IAS 12. This can lead to a significant rise in deferred tax liabilities when moving from FRS 19 to IAS 12.

9172 The main differences between FRS 19 and IAS 12 in relation to **recognition** are summarised below:

Issue	Recognition by FRS 19	Recognition by IAS 12
Revaluation of non-monetary assets (¶9076)	Provision required if: – asset is revalued on marked-to-market basis; or – a binding agreement to sell the asset has been entered into, and no rollover relief will be claimed.	Provision required in any event.
Sale of assets where gain might be rolled over into replacement assets (¶9078)	Provision is not required unless rollover is not expected to be obtained.	Provision is required, measured as the difference between the sold asset's tax base and the replacement asset's actual cost.
Discounting (¶9087)	Allowed with required disclosures.	Prohibited.
Presentation of deferred tax balance (¶9122)	On face of balance sheet only if material.	On face of balance sheet in any event.
Unrealised intra-group profits are eliminated on consolidation (e.g., stock supplied between group members) (¶9154)	Provision is required on the timing difference i.e. where the profit has been taxed, but not recognised in the consolidated financial statements. The provision is measured using the supplying company's rate of tax.	Provision is required on the difference between the carrying value of the stock in the group balance sheet and the higher tax base (the cost paid by the receiving company). The receiving company's rate of tax is used.
Adjustments to recognise assets and liabilities at their fair values on the acquisition of a business (¶9156)	Deferred tax should only be provided for on fair value adjustments if these were timing differences for the acquired business. No provision would be made for the revaluing of non-monetary assets to market value. No provision is required in respect of acquired goodwill.	Provision is made for all differences between fair value and tax base for all assets and liabilities. No provision is required for the temporary difference arising on the recognition of non-deductible goodwill. If the acquirer can use its own tax losses against the profits of the acquired business, a deferred tax asset should be recognised.

Issue	Recognition by FRS 19	Recognition by IAS 12
Unremitted earnings of subsidiaries, associates and joint ventures (¶9158)	Provision required in respect of accrued dividends or a binding agreement to distribute past earnings.	Provision required in all circumstances for associates. For other entities, a provision should be made if: – the timing of the remittance is not controlled by the parent; or – remittance is probable in the foreseeable future.
Exchange differences on translation of financial statements	No timing difference, so no deferred tax provision required.	Deferred tax provided on the difference between the book value (at historic exchange rate) and the revalued amount (at the exchange rate ruling at the balance sheet date).

The **disclosure requirements** are broadly similar, with the main differences being: 9174

Subject of disclosure	Disclosure required by FRS 19	Disclosure required by IAS 12
Temporary differences	Not required	Aggregate amount associated with investments in subsidiaries, branches, associates and joint ventures for which deferred tax liabilities have not been recognised.
Discontinued operations	Not required	Separate disclosure of related tax expense.
Discounting	Explanation of the effects of discounting.	Not required.
Circumstances affecting tax charges	General explanation of circumstances which are affecting the current tax charges or may affect the future tax charges.	Not required.
Reconciliation of actual tax charge to the expected charge	Reconciliation of the current tax charge to the amount expected using the standard rate of tax.	Reconciliation of the total tax charge (current and deferred tax) to the amount expected using the standard rate of tax.
Deferred tax on revalued gains	Circumstances in which deferred tax relating to revaluation and rolled over gains would become payable and an indication of the amounts that are expected to become payable in the foreseeable future.	Not required.

CHAPTER 8

Preparation and filing of financial statements

OUTLINE ¶¶

This chapter sets out the general principles for keeping accounting records and the general rules for the preparation, filing and publication of financial statements. The filing exemptions available to specific types of company are also covered. **9300**

In general, the Companies Act 2006 incorporates the provisions contained in the 1985 Act, as well as a number of **new provisions** and powers pertaining to the preparation and filing of financial statements. One set of provisions has been developed for small companies and another for large and medium-sized entities.

MEMO POINTS 1. The terms "**Accounts" and "Financial Statements**" can be used interchangeably, despite these terms having specific meanings under the Companies Act and Accounting Standards. In practice, "Accounts" are considered to include the balance sheet and profit and loss account, as well as the other "primary statements" required by the accounting standards (e.g. cash flow statement).
2. "**Financial statements**" is the terminology adopted by the ASB in its "Statements of Accounting Standards", and represents a complete set of documents, including the annual accounts and other specified explanatory material, such as the notes to the accounts, the directors' report and the OFR.
3. The requirements covering the preparation and filing of accounts for **dormant companies** are covered in ¶6400 and for **overseas companies** in ¶7700.
4. In 2007 the Government issued **three important financial reporting regulations** under the Companies Act 2006:

i. the Companies Act (Amendment) (Accounts and Reports) Regulations 2008, which increased the financial thresholds for small and medium-sized companies, and the audit exemption thresholds.
ii. the Large and Medium-Sized Companies and Groups (Accounts and Reports) Regulations 2008; and
iii. the Small Companies and Groups (Accounts and Directors' Reports) Regulations. These regulations cover the form and content of a company's accounts and reports under Schedule 15 of CA 2006. These provisions replace those contained in Schedule 7 of the CA 1985 and are effective for accounting periods beginning on or after 6 April 2008.
5. The Department of Business, Innovation and Skills (BIS) has published general guidance on the changes to the accounting and reporting regime under CA 2006. The department has also issued draft Companies Act 2006 (Accounts, Reports and Audit) Regulations 2009 with revised **filing and auditing requirements** covering Corporate Governance Statements for listed companies.

A. Preparation of annual financial statements

9301 Companies are required to prepare annual financial statements, the form and content of which are underpinned by a comprehensive regulatory framework, comprising mandatory and advisory elements, collectively referred to as GAAP (Generally Accepted Accounting Practice). **Mandatory sources** include the requirements of the Companies Act 2006, the Financial Reporting Standards (FRSs), Statements of Standard Accounting Practice (SSAPs), Statements of Recommended Practice (SORPs) and UITF Abstracts.

Advisory sources include Financial Reporting Exposure Drafts (FREDs) and Technical Releases from professional bodies such as the ICAEW and the ACCA.

Listed companies must also meet the accounting and disclosure requirements of International Financial Reporting Standards (IFRS) and intepretations as well as the Listing Rules. The IFRS regime is also underpinned by developments in EU law. For **other entities**, special legislation may also apply, governing the nature of their accounting records (e.g. charities, banks, insurance companies). For parent companies at the financial year-end the directors must prepare consolidated financial statements unless subject to the **small company regime**, under which consolidated accounts are optional.

MEMO POINTS 1. The European Parliament (EP) has in principle agreed changes to European Union (EU) accounting rules that could **exempt micro-companies** in the UK from preparing annual accounts. These amendments still have to be ratified by the EU Council and would only apply if the UK regulatory authorities agreed to grant the exemption, and apply to companies meeting two of the following criteria:
– a balance sheet total of less than £500,000;
– net turnover under £1,000,000; or
– an average of 10 employees during the financial year.
2. Micro-companies will still need to maintain proper accounting records and prepare financial reports for shareholders and HMRC.
3. Group accounts are prepared under Section 404 Companies Act (Group accounts) 2006, Schedule 6 SI 2008/409 or IFRS (IAS 1).

1. General legal framework

9302 This section **contains an overview** of the general legal framework governing the preparation of accounts, including determination of the accounting reference date and the general composition of accounting records.

MEMO POINTS The **provisions in Part 15** of the Companies Act 2006 **replace** Part 7 of the 1985 Act relating to accounts and financial reports. The provisions have been recast with those relevant to small companies appearing first. The Secretary of State can now issue regulations tailored to the requirements of different types (and size) of company.

Companies, whether trading or not, must prepare in addition to the underlying accounting records, for each financial year: 9303
- a balance sheet;
- a profit and loss account (unless dormant);
- a statement of recognised gains and losses (STRGL) where applicable;
- a cash flow statement, (unless exempted by FRS 1);
- a statement of directors' responsibilities; and
- notes to the accounts.

These elements form the "accounts" or financial statements, which should be accompanied by a **directors' report** (including an enhanced business review) and, unless the company is exempt, an auditor's report. Statutory accounts must be approved by the board of directors and circulated to the shareholders, before being filed at Companies House.

Listed companies should also produce an Operating and Financial Review (OFR). The general disclosure requirements for listed companies are also more extensive than for non-listed companies, due to the requirements of IFRS and the Listings Rules.

Overview of form and content of accounts

The form and content of the balance sheet, profit and loss account and accompanying notes **must comply with** the provisions of the Companies Act, which allows a choice between two balance sheet formats and four profit and loss formats. Once the **directors have adopted a format**, it should be consistently applied in subsequent years, unless there are special reasons for a change. Particulars of any change should be disclosed and the underlying reasons explained in a note to the accounts. Details on the choice of profit and loss and balance sheet formats are shown in ¶350 and ¶984 respectively. 9304

The financial statements **must show a true and fair view** of the company's financial affairs at the balance sheet date. Where the directors have departed from the accounting or disclosure requirements of the Companies Act or an FRS and invoked the true and fair view override, details of the circumstances involved should be given in the notes to the accounts.

MEMO POINTS Under the Companies Act 2006, the format of group accounts will be set out in regulations (see ¶9300 memo point).

Accounting reference date (ARD)

All companies must prepare annual accounts that report on the performance and activities of the company during the financial year, which starts on the day after the end of the previous financial year, or in the case of a new company, on the day of incorporation. Even though the ARD is set on incorporation it can be changed, as can subsequent accounting periods. 9306

The **ARD for a new company** represents the period between the date of incorporation (not the first day of trading) and the first anniversary, of the last day in the month the company was incorporated. For example, if the company was incorporated on 15 September 2009, its ARD would be set at 30 September, and the first accounts would cover the period from this date to 30 September 2010.

MEMO POINTS An **accounting reference period** (ARP) is a more precise term for financial year and ends on the accounting reference date or up to seven days either side of the ARD, if this is more convenient. For new companies accounts must be prepared for a period of at least 6 months, with a maximum of 18.

Changing the ARD An ARD can be obtained notifying the Registrar of Companies, by completing the relevant form available from Companies House. However, the change can only be made to the current or previous ARD and the new ARD must be registered before the filing deadline for the accounts has passed. If the **filing deadline has been missed**, a company cannot then apply to the Registrar to change the ARD. 9307

9308 **Restrictions on changing the ARD** A company may change its ARD by **shortening** the ARP as often as they like, and by as many months. However, there are restrictions on **extending** ARPs, as follows:
1. An ARD cannot be extended beyond 18 months from the start of the accounting period.
2. A company may not extend the ARD more than once every 5 years, unless either of the following apply:
- the company is subject to an administration order; or
- the Secretary of State has ordered the extension; or
- the company is aligning its reference date with that of a subsidiary or parent company established within the European Economic Area (EEA).

MEMO POINTS The European Economic Area (EEA) comprises the 27 countries that make up the European Union plus Iceland, Norway and Liechtenstein.

9309 In addition to meeting the requirements of the Companies Act, a listed company must also notify a Regulated Information Service of any change in its ARD. If the new ARD is longer than 14 months, the company must prepare and publish a second interim report covering the period up to the end of the old ARD or a date at least 6 months prior to the end of the new ARD. These rules apply to companies listed on the AIM and PLUS-markets.

MEMO POINTS Currently there are 7 providers that act as Regulated Information Service providers for companies making regulatory announcements: details of which can be found on the FSA website.

Underlying accounting records

9310 **All companies** are required to keep accounting records sufficient to show and explain the company's transactions. The records must disclose with reasonable accuracy, the financial position of the company at any one time and enable the directors to ensure that the balance sheet and profit and loss account comply with the requirements of the Companies Act.

9312 The **books of prime entry** in which a business records its transactions normally comprise:
- Sales day book;
- Sales returns book;
- Purchase day book;
- Purchase returns book;
- Cash books;
- Debtors ledger;
- Creditors ledger;
- Journals;
- Asset registers; and
- General ledger.

9314 The **accounting records must contain** the following information:
- the daily transactions involving monies received and expended by the company and the supporting reasons thereof; and
- a record of the assets and liabilities of the company (including transaction dates).

For **companies trading goods** additional records are required:
- details of the stock held by the company at the financial year-end;
- details of capital expenditure and major contracts; and
- statements of all goods sold and purchased, detailing the buyers in sufficient detail to enable their identification.

Retention of accounting records

9316 sec 388 (4) CA 2006 Accounting records **must be retained** from the date they are prepared, this being 3 years for a **private company** and 6 years for a **public company**. This is subject to any provision contained in the rules made under the Insolvency Act 1986, or the requirements of other statutes such as the VAT legislation. For instance, companies that are **registered for VAT** must retain their records and accounts for six years, unless a shorter period has been agreed with Customs and Excise.

In practice, many companies will keep their accounting records for a longer period to cover the possibility of any retrospective revenue enquiries.

MEMO POINTS Companies subject to the money laundering regulations are required to retain accounting records relating to the relevant customers for the duration of the client relationship + 5 years.

A company's **accounting records** should be kept at its **registered office** or such other place as the directors see fit, and should be available at all times for inspection by the company's authorised officers. This requirement also applies to overseas subsidiaries of UK companies. If a company registered in the UK keeps its accounting records overseas, then certain accounts and returns are required to be sent to a place in the UK and be open for inspection. 9317

If a company **fails to comply** with any of the provisions for retaining accounts, then a director or officer of the company guilty of such an offence is liable to imprisonment or a fine, or both (see also ¶9370).

The Companies Act also requires of companies, the **retention of certain statutory books and records** at the registered office, including: 9318
- the register of directors and secretaries;
- the register of charges;
- register of directors' share and debenture interests of group companies;
- memorandum and articles of association;
- the minute books detailing general meetings of the company; and
- the register of members, debenture holders.

Accounting records **may be stored** on microfilm or digital formats which are acceptable to Customs and Excise, except that prior approval should be sought.

2. Approval of financial statements

The **board of directors must approve** the annual financial statements, which must carry the signature of one director on the face of the balance sheet and state the name of the signatory. The directors' report must also be signed by a director or the company secretary. The copy of the directors' report and the balance sheet filed with the Registrar of Companies must bear an original signature and any copies laid before the company at the annual general meeting must also state the name of the signatory. Group financial statements should also be signed by the same director. 9320

The **date on which the financial statements** are approved should be disclosed in the financial statements and represents the date, up to which the directors are responsible for disclosing material post-balance sheet events (¶5700).

MEMO POINTS Small companies are no longer required to have a company secretary.

Persons entitled to receive financial statements

A copy of the financial statements, directors' report and audit report, must be dispatched to every member and debenture holder of the company, although some companies are not required to deliver an audit report (e.g. dormant companies). 9322

The financial statements sent to members are usually the same as those filed with the Registrar of Companies, except for the following:
- **small and medium-sized companies** are entitled to certain disclosure exemptions in the accounts filed with Companies House; and
- **listed companies** need not send copies of financial statements to those members who elect not to receive them. Summary financial statements may be sent instead.

Laying of financial statements at the AGM

9323 The directors **must present copies of** the annual report and accounts, together with the audit report and directors' report before the annual general meeting (AGM) of the members of the company. This is known as laying the accounts before members. Copies of the annual report should be sent to the members not less than 21 days before the date of the AGM. The time period for laying financial statements is the same as for filing accounts at Companies House (see ¶9350). Where directors fail in their obligation to lay accounts may be guilty of an offence subject to penalty.

Under the Companies Act 2006 **private companies are no longer obligated** to hold an AGM or lay financial statements before a general meeting, unless this requirement is specified in the company's articles of association (CA 2006 section 423). Public quoted companies must notify members, prior to the AGM of an ordinary resolution to approve the directors' remuneration report.

9324 **Members of a private company** may elect not to lay accounts and reports before shareholders at the AGM. Where this is the case, a company must send:

1. a copy of the accounts and reports to members, not less than 28 days before the end of the period allowed for laying and delivering financial statements. This is normally 10 months after the last day of the relevant accounting reference period.

2. a notice informing the members of their right to request the laying of accounts and reports at the AGM. This option is not available to public companies.

Companies may **electronically dispatch** accounts and reports to members who elect to receive them. Accounts published on a website are also deemed to be dispatched electronically, provided the members have been notified of the publication.

MEMO POINTS Under the new Companies Act, the timescale for laying accounts will be unchanged (s424 CA 2006).

3. Specific requirements

Groups

9326
sec 400 CA 2006

A company **that is a parent company** at the end of a financial year, should prepare consolidated financial statements for the group that comply with the Companies Act, unless it qualifies for one of the exemptions from preparation of group accounts given in the Act. A parent company's individual profit and loss account can be omitted from the consolidated accounts in certain situations, although it must be approved by the board of directors or signed on behalf of the board by a director. This topic is covered in greater detail in ¶6556. All companies in the group should have the same financial year as the parent company. Should **the dates differ**, then the parent company must consolidate accounts for accounting periods that end before its own, as long as the time difference does not exceed three months. Where this is the case the subsidiary must prepare interim accounts for the required accounting period.

9327 A **small parent company** that has prepared individual accounts for its members, using the special provisions of the Companies Act relating to shorter-form accounts (see ¶9344), can also elect to prepare group accounts. These accounts must contain a statement above the signature on the balance sheet, stating that they have been prepared in accordance with the special provisions of Part 15 Companies Act 2006, applicable to small companies.

A **small group** cannot file abbreviated accounts. Where a **medium-sized company** prepares group accounts, they must be full group accounts.

The **formats** of accounts must follow the relevant Schedules of the Companies Act depending on the size of the group.

Exemption from preparation of group accounts A parent company need not prepare group accounts (or send them to the Registrar), where the group of which it is the parent, is small or medium-sized and is not an ineligible group. 9328

MEMO POINTS The qualifying **criteria for classification** as a small or medium-sized group is contained in ¶6000.

The **exemption is not available** if the parent company was at any time during the financial year, one of the following:
- a public company;
- a banking or insurance company;
- an authorised person under the Financial Services and Market Act 2000; or
- a member of an ineligible group.

Ineligible groups A group qualifies as ineligible if any of its members is one of the following: 9329
- a public company or body corporate lawfully able to issues shares or debentures to the public;
- a banking institution so authorised under the Banking Act 1987;
- an insurance company so authorised under the Insurance Companies Act 1982; or
- a person permitted under the Financial Services and Market Act 2000 to carry on a regulated activity under that Act.

Subsidiary companies

Subsidiary companies incorporated in the UK are subject to the requirements to prepare, file and publish annual financial statements as other companies, although there are special rules that govern the disclosures required. 9330

Additional disclosures Subsidiary companies are required to provide additional disclosures relating to the following: 9331
a. guarantees and financial commitments undertaken for group undertakings (i.e. parent undertaking, fellow subsidiary or one of its own subsidiaries);
b. details of **where copies of the group accounts** referred to above can be obtained and if unincorporated, the principal place of business;
c. information on **parent undertakings** covering:
- the name and country of incorporation of the ultimate parent company;
- the parent undertaking of the largest group of companies for which group accounts are prepared, of which the reporting company is a member; or
- the parent undertaking of the smallest group of which the company is a member, for which accounts are prepared.

The disclosures required under (a) above cover any charge on the assets of the business, contingent liabilities, pension commitments and other significant commitments not provided for, such as capital expenditure.

Qualifying partnerships

A partnership will be classified as a qualifying partnership (i.e. limited partnership) if each of its members is a limited company. The members of a qualifying partnership are required to prepare annual financial statements which must be audited. 9335 SI 1993/1820

The financial statements prepared by a qualifying partnership **usually contain the following**:
- a directors' report;
- a profit and loss account;
- a STRGL;
- a reconciliation of movements in partners' accounts; and
- disclosures required by the Companies Act 2006 and the relevant accounting standards.

A qualifying partnership **must prepare accounts for a period** not exceeding 18 months. Where the accounting period is not specified in the partnership agreement, the partnership accounts 9337

must be drawn up for each 12 month period ending on 31 March in each year. The **partnership accounts** must be prepared within a period of 9 months of the end of the financial year and delivered to Companies House. For more detail on the **special filing requirements** that could apply see ¶9390. The topic of qualifying partnerships is covered in ¶7600.

9338 **Exemptions** A limited partnership (see also ¶9393) qualifying as small or medium sized may be entitled to prepare financial statements in accordance with the FRSSE, or to file abbreviated accounts.

B. Publication of financial statements

9340 The Companies Act stipulates the requirements that **companies must comply with** when publishing their financial statements, including the following:
- Statutory accounts (see ¶9302);
- Abbreviated financial statements for small and medium-sized companies (see ¶9382);
- Preliminary results for listed companies (see ¶5400);
- Interim results for listed companies (¶5500);
- Auditors report;
- Shorter-form financial statements for small companies; and
- Non-statutory financial information.

9344 **Shorter-form financial statements** In general, **the formats** for shorter-form accounts **do not differ greatly** from the full financial statements. The accounting requirements for small companies preparing shorter-form financial statements are considered in Part 8 Chapter 1.

If the company prepares shorter-form financial statements, they must be authorised by the board of directors, laid before the company in general meeting and filed with the Registrar of Companies. Instead of preparing shorter-form financial statements, a company may also elect to prepare abbreviated financial statements.

9348 **Non-statutory financial information** Where a company publishes non-statutory accounts, **a statement must be appended** explaining:
- that the accounts are not the statutory accounts of the company;
- whether the statutory accounts have been delivered to the Registrar; and
- confirmation or not that the auditors have reported on the accounts and whether the report was qualified. If qualified, the reasons for the qualification should be given.

Non-statutory accounts are deemed for the purposes of the Companies Act, to be any financial information for the financial year that is or purports to be, a balance sheet of a company or a group.

Where an **unlimited company** not required to publish statutory accounts, publishes non-statutory financial information, this should be accompanied by a statement confirming the non-publication of statutory accounts.

Electronic communications

9349 Under the Companies Act 2006 companies are being encouraged to improve electronic communications with shareholders. With shareholder permission, entities can now distribute annual reports, interim financial statements and AGM notices electronically. **Quoted companies** are expected to publish financial information of their website. Electronic communications must be dispatched to the address supplied by the member. Failure to comply with the regulations covering electronic communication of financial statements will leave the company (and its officers) liable for an offence under section 425 of the Companies Act 2006. A company must make its financial statements available at least 21 days before the AGM.

Public companies can send electronic communications to holders of its listed securities as permitted under The UKLA Listings Rules and Disclosure and Transparency Rules.

MEMO POINTS Electronic communications includes Fax, CD-ROM, E-Mail, and websites.

C. Filing of financial statements

The **directors of all companies** have obligations to file annual financial statements, including where appropriate a directors' report (¶4500) and auditor's report, with the Registrar of Companies within certain time limits. **Special provisions** apply to entities that shorten their accounting reference period (see ¶9306 and ¶9358). Small or medium-sized companies qualify for reduced filing requirements. The balance sheet and directors' report must be signed by a director on behalf of the board and the auditors' report must contain the name of the auditors, and where this is an audit firm, the name of the senior auditor. **9350**

The Registrar can enforce the filing requirements through a set of **filing deadlines** backed up by a **penalty regime**. An overview of the filing exemptions available to specific types of company is also given below.

MEMO POINTS 1. In order to comply with the **self-assessment rules** contained in the Finance Act, a company must submit to HMRC, along with its corporation tax return, a full set of financial statements, including a directors' report.
2. HMRC have confirmed that from April 2011, all company tax returns and financial statements for accounting periods ending on or after 31 March 2010, must be filed online, using the XBRL format. A plan for simultaneous (dual) on-line filing at Companies House and with HMRC is currently being developed. This ruling is independent of the filing requirements of Companies House.

Filing requirements for quoted companies The annual financial statements filed with the Registrar should include the following: **9351**
- a copy of the company's individual financial statements and consolidated financial statements where appropriate;
- a signed copy of the directors' report;
- a copy of the directors' remuneration report; and
- a copy of the auditors' report on the financial statements including the directors' remuneration report.

Filing obligations for small companies The annual financial statements filed with the Registrar must include the following minimum requirements: **9352** secs. 445-6 CA 2006
- a copy of the company's balance sheet and notes to the financial statements sent to members; and
- a copy of the auditors' report on the financial statements, unless exempt from audit and the directors have taken advantage of this exemption under section 444 of the Companies Act 2006.

Where the directors **take advantage of the exemption** from delivering a copy of the company's profit and loss account or the directors' report, the balance sheet must contain a statement that the company's accounts have been prepared in accordance with the provisions covering entities subject to the small companies regime.

Where a company submits **abbreviated accounts** to the Registrar of Companies these must include a balance sheet, profit and loss account, auditors' report (except where the company is exempt from audit under section 449 CA 2006) and notes prepared in line with SI 2008/409 Sch. 4 and Regulation 6. A statement must be included in the balance sheet to the effect that the accounts have been prepared in accordance with the small companies regime. An entity qualified to adopt the small companies regime, or that would be were it not an ineligible group, is permitted to claim the small companies exemption covering the **directors' report** (s415 CA 2006) **9352-1**

9352-2 The filing requirements for medium sized companies are the same as for large companies with the exception of the directors' remuneration report. Where medium sized entities submit abbreviated accounts these must be prepared in accordance with SI 2008/410 Reg. 4 "The Large and Medium sized Companies and Groups (Reports and Accounts) Regulations 2008 along with a special auditors' report (unless the company is exempt form audit), required under section 449 CA 2006.

1. Filing requirements

9353 secs. 441-2 CA 2006 The financial statements **are required to show** the registered number of the company, in a prominent position, usually on the first page. If any of these documents are in a language other than English then the directors should annex a certified translation.

Financial statements may be submitted in a foreign currency; namely, the local currency of the economic environment in which the company operates and generates cash flows.

Time limits

9354 There are **general time limits** that apply to the majority of companies for the filing of their financial statements:
- **private companies** – 9 months from the ARP;
- **public companies** – 6 months from the ARP.

The table illustrates the dates by which accounts must be delivered to the Registrar of Companies, although December and March are generally speaking the most popular dates.

End of relevant accounting period (ARP)	Delivery deadline-Private companies	Delivery deadline-Public companies
Jan 31	Oct 30	Jul 31
Feb 28	Nov 28	Aug 28
Mar 31	Dec 31	Sep 30

If the company's accounting period **does not end** on the last day of a month, then the period allowed for filing the financial statements ends on the **corresponding day** in the appropriate month. For example, a public company with an accounting reference date of 15 August has until 15 February following, to file its accounts. If a filing deadline expires on a Sunday or Bank Holiday the law still requires accounts to be filed by that date.

MEMO POINTS The **corresponding date rule** has also been repealed. Where there is no corresponding date, then the last day of the month will apply (e.g. 9 months from 30 April will be the 31 January following).

Initial registration

9356 For a newly formed company whose initial ARP is **longer than twelve months**, the maximum time period allowed for filing the accounts, is the later of:
- **private companies** – 21 months from the date of incorporation or 3 months from the ARP;
- **public companies** – 18 months from the date of incorporation or 3 months from the ARP.

The accounts must be delivered to the Registrar of Companies.

Event	Private Ltd.	Public Plc
First accounting reference period	**1 January 2009 to 30 June 2010**	**1 January 2009 to 30 June 2010**
21 months from the date of incorporation	30 September 2010	N/A
18 months from the date of incorporation	N/A	30 June 2010
3 Months from end of accounting reference period	30 September 2010	30 September 2010

A company that has **shortened its ARP** during its initial accounting period, is still subject to the normal 6 and 9 month time periods for public and private companies, with an alternative filing date (if later) being three months from the date the Registrar receives notice, to shorten the ARP. 9358

Example – shortening the ARD Event	Private Limited	Public Plc
Original accounting reference date	**31 December 2009**	**31 December 2009**
Date of notice to Registrar requesting shortening of accounting reference period	31 March 2010	31 March 2010
Shortened accounting reference period	**1 January 2009 to 31 October 2009**	**1 January 2009 to 31 October 2009**
9 months from end of amended accounting reference period	31 July 2010	N/A
6 months from end of amended accounting reference period	N/A	30 April 2010
3 months from date of notice to Registrar	30 June 2010	30 June 2010

Extensions to the time limits

The Secretary of State can extend the filing period, if deemed appropriate on the basis of an application made prior to the expiry of the period. The need to finalise significant **legal disputes** or **the loss of accounting records**, are examples of the type of extenuating circumstances for which the registrar may grant an extension. An application must be made, detailing the reasons for the required extension and the additional time needed. The period may be extended for as long as the Registrar so decides and specifies in the notice. 9360

For companies incorporated in **England and Wales**, an application should be made to the Secretary of State for Trade and Industry at the companies' administration section at Companies House (Cardiff). In **Scotland**, the application should be to the Secretary of State for Trade and Industry at Companies House (Edinburgh).

Rejected accounts

Documents and forms sent to Companies House are scanned and stored in electronic form and the original documents archived. There are a number of quality guidelines for the delivery of documents which are set out below. 9362

Documents rejected by the Registrar will be returned to the company for **amendment in the following instances**:
– the accounts fail to comply with the accounting or disclosure requirements of the Companies Act;
– the documents are incomplete (e.g. not signed by a director or name of signatory not stated, company registration number or pages missing, typographical errors etc); or
– the accounts do not meet the submission guidelines stipulated by the Registrar of Companies.

Where the Registrar rejects financial statements, **because they are defective** in respect of the accounting or disclosure requirements of the Act, the directors must follow the revision of defective accounts rules, which are discussed below (see ¶9365).

Rejection of accounts is **not a valid excuse** for the late filing of the corrected accounts, which must be delivered to the registrar before the normal filing deadline. Failure to do so will result in a late filing penalty.

MEMO POINTS 1. The **submission guidelines** are as follows:
a. Each document delivered to the Registrar must state prominently, the registered number of the company;

b. Documents should be on A4 plain white paper weighing between 80gsm and 100gsm with a matt finish;
c. Document text should be black, clear, legible, and of uniform density; and
d. Facsimile copies of documents will not be accepted for registration and Companies House can reject documents that cannot be captured electronically.
An acceptable copy must be delivered to the Registrar **within 14 days** of the notice, otherwise the original is treated as not having been delivered. Photocopies of the financial statements are not deemed acceptable as are prints produced on a dot matrix printer or glossy colour-printed documents.
2. Companies House has confirmed that 11% of annual financial statements submitted to them between January 2010 and June 2010 were rejected, as they had either omitted compulsory information or contained simple errors. Companies House has reiterated that accounts submitted prior to the filing deadline and subsequently rejected and then resubmitted after the deadline will still incur a late filing penalty.

Revision of defective accounts

9365 **Liability for approving** defective financial statements lies with every director of the company who approved them, unless a director can prove that they have taken reasonable steps to prevent their approval.

Under the Companies Act, the are **two remedies** for the revision of defective accounts; namely:
- voluntary revision by the directors; and
- an appointee of the Secretary of State making an application to the courts, requiring the directors to revise the accounts.

Revision of defective financial statements (both voluntary and involuntary) should take place within the statutory time limits, otherwise the normal penalty rules apply.

9366 **Voluntary revision** Where the directors of a company have prepared financial statements that do not appear to comply with the requirements of the Companies Act, they may prepare revised financial statements. If the accounts or reports have already been laid before the company at the AGM or delivered to the Registrar of Companies, the revisions should be confined to the correction of those parts of the financial statements that do not comply with the Act.
The directors **can elect to either**:
- prepare a set of new financial statements; or
- opt for a partial revision requiring only a supplementary note to the original financial statements.

Voluntary revision is permitted under SI 2008/373 "The Companies (Revision of Defective Accounts and Reports) Regulations 2008". The revised financial statements must be approved by the board and signed by a director. Where supplemenatry notes are prepared these should also be authorised by a director.
Where the **original accounts have already been sent to the members**, laid before the company in general meeting or sent to the Registrar of Companies, the revised accounts must include a note of the following:
- that the revised financial statements replace the original financial statements;
- that the accounts have been prepared to the same date as the original accounts;
- the reasons for the revision;
- details of any significant changes to the original financial statements submitted.

Where the original financial statements have been **revised by supplementary note**, the following information is required:
- a note confirming that the accounts have been revised and where the revisions apply; and
- confirmation that the revised financial statements have been made up to the same date as the original and not the revision date.

9367 **Involuntary revision** The Secretary of State has empowered the Financial Reporting Review Panel (FRRP) to request directors to revise their accounts where appropriate.

Penalty regime

The penalty regime consists of a system of late filing penalties and default fines for company directors. If the accounts are delivered late, the Registrar will impose an **automatic filing penalty** which will not be waived, even if the accounts are delayed in the post. 9370

Late filing penalties are imposed under civil law whereas a **failure to file accounts** is a criminal offence. The penalty regime is designed to encourage directors to file accounts on time, as they must provide statutory information for the public record. It is possible that a civil penalty and a default fine could be payable if a set of accounts are not filed on time. The penalties are set out in SI 2008/497 "The Companies (Late Filing Penalties) Regulations 2008 and are based on a sliding scale that reflects the delay from the statutory filing date and the actual date the accounts are delivered to the Registrar. The **penalty regime for public companies** is more draconian, with fines effectively doubled for late filing in consecutive years. In addition, the penalty periods have been shortened in order to encourage more effective compliance.

Civil law filing penalties There is an **automatic civil penalty** for late filing. 9372

The severity of the penalty will be determined by reference to whether the company is public or private, as well as to the delay between the actual filing date and the required filing deadline. It is the date of receipt by the Registrar which is important, not the date of posting. The scales of automatic fixed civil penalties are as set out in the table below.

Length of period (months)	Private company	Public company
1 month or less	£150	£750
More than 1 month but less than 3 months	£375	£1500
More than 3 months but less than 6 months	£750	£3000
More than 6 months	£1500	£7500

These penalties are similar to those imposed on directors, for failing to lay accounts and reports before the company in a general meeting, within the legal time limits outlined in ¶9354.

If the accounts are delivered late, an invoice is issued automatically to the company's registered office address. If the penalty is not paid, it will be referred to collection agents and if the fine remains unpaid, **legal action may be taken** in the form of a County Court Judgement or a Sheriff Court decree against the company.

In the example below, the statutory filing date for a private company falls on a bank holiday. However as the registrar will not take delivery of the accounts until the following day, the first of September, an automatic late filing penalty will be triggered. The Registrar can waive the late filing penalty but only in exceptional circumstances. 9374

Event	Private Company (9 months)	Pubic Company (6 months)
Accounting reference date (ARD)	31 October 2009	31 December 2009
Statutory filing deadline	30 July 2010	30 June 2010
Actual filing date	3 August 2010	3 July 2010
Filing penalty	**£150**	**£750**

Neglecting to file accounts is a criminal offence which can result in directors being fined personally in the criminal courts. In addition, the Registrar may take steps to strike the company off the register of companies. Where a filing deadline has been missed, the registrar will serve notice on the directors of the company, requiring compliance with the filing requirements within 14 days. Where the directors fail to respond to the Registrar's new deadline, 9375 the Registrar may take the matter further by instituting legal proceedings (as may a member or creditor), in order to enforce compliance by a date which will be specified in the court order. All the costs relating to the application shall be borne by the directors. Directors that consistently breach the filing deadlines can be disqualified under the Company Directors (Disqualification) Act 1986 (e.g. three defaults over a five year period).

9376 Where **directors are persistently in default** of their obligations to file accounts and other returns with the Registrar, they may be disqualified from being a company director. The directors are also liable to receive a criminal record and a fine for each offence to be determined by the court.

If a **company is restored to the register** after being struck-off and dissolved, then it is regarded as having continued to exist as though it had never been struck off. Accounts filed, including those covering periods while the company was dissolved, will be subject to late filing penalties.

In cases of non-compliance, every partner in a qualifying partnership or every director of a company that is a partner, may be prosecuted and fined up to £5,000.

2. Permissible filing (disclosure) exemptions

9380 There are a number of filing exemptions covering groups, intermediate parents, unincorporated companies and qualifying partnerships.

Small and medium-sized companies

9382 Eligible small and medium-sized companies may qualify for some, or all of the exemptions allowing them to file **abbreviated accounts** (¶6000). In addition, **dormant companies** and certain categories of small company are not required to appoint an auditor or obtain a directors' report. In these cases, an auditor's report is not required.

It should be noted that abbreviated accounts are not the same as "shorter-form" accounts, which small companies may prepare for their shareholders. If a small company chooses not to prepare abbreviated accounts, it may however file "shorter-form" accounts. However, if a small or medium-sized company files abbreviated accounts, a complete set of accounts or shorter-form accounts must still be presented to members.

MEMO POINTS 1. Under the Companies Act 2006, the abbreviated balance sheet **must be accompanied by** a statement confirming it has been prepared under the small companies regime. The format and content of the balance sheet will be set out in regulations to be published at a later date.
2. For medium-sized companies, the exemption from disclosing turnover in abbreviated profit and loss accounts delivered to the Registrar of Companies, has been removed.

Group companies

9384 A parent company must prepare **consolidated accounts** (group accounts) and file them with the registrar, except if a group qualifies as a small or medium-sized group or is an ineligible group (see ¶9326 –¶9329).

MEMO POINTS The exemption available to the parent of a medium-sized group, with regard to preparing group accounts has been abolished under the Companies Act 2006. The date this provision takes effect is yet to be determined.

Subsidiary companies that are also parent companies

9385 A subsidiary company that is itself a parent company, is in **certain circumstances exempt** under the Companies Act from preparing and filing consolidated financial statements. The exemption does not apply, if the subsidiary company is listed on a stock exchange in the European Union. However, a copy of the consolidated financial statements of the **ultimate parent company** must be attached to the company's individual financial statements delivered to the Registrar.

The **above exemption** (from filing group accounts) **applies in the following situations**: 9386
1. The company must be a wholly-owned subsidiary of a parent undertaking registered in the EU.
2. Where such a parent holds more than 50% of the shares in the company, and no notice has been served on the subsidiary company by minority interests, to prepare consolidated financial statements.
3. The subsidiary is included in the consolidated financial statements of a larger group compiled by an EU parent to the same date, or an earlier date in the same financial year and those financial statements are drawn up and audited. In addition, the parent's annual report must be compiled in compliance with the EU 7th Directive.
4. Where the subsidiary files the following copies with the Registrar of Companies:
– the group financial statements; or
– the group's annual report and auditor's report. These submissions must be within the time period permitted for the subsidiary to file its individual accounts. If the parent company accounts are not in English, a copy translated into English must also be filed.
5. Where the subsidiary discloses the following in its financial statements:
– the fact that it has taken advantage of the above filing exemption;
– the identity of the EU parent company preparing the group accounts;
– the country of incorporation of the parent undertaking, if not the UK and where the parent does not have a business establishment the UK; or
– where the parent is an unincorporated undertaking, the address of the parent company's principal place of business.

Unlimited companies

The **directors** of an unlimited company **are not required to file a copy** of the company's financial statements with the Registrar of Companies, where it was not at any time during the relevant accounting reference period: 9388 SI 220/589
– a subsidiary of a limited undertaking;
– a parent of a limited undertaking;
– a banking or insurance company or the parent company of such;
– subject to rights exercisable by or on behalf of two or more limited undertakings which, if exercised by one of them would make the company its subsidiary; or
– a qualifying company within the meaning of the meaning of the SI 2008/569 "The Partnerships (Accounts) Regulations 2008".

If an unlimited company **publishes non-statutory financial statements**, they must include a statement that the company is exempt from the requirement to deliver statutory financial statements. Where an unlimited company is exempt from filing its financial statements under section 448 of the Companies Act 2006, the accounts will have been prepared under Part 15 of the same act and approved by the board.

Qualifying partnerships (undertakings)

The **members** of a qualifying partnership **are required** to prepare annual financial statements for that partnership, which must be audited as if the partnership were a company formed under the Companies Act. Each member company must attach a copy of these financial statements to its own financial statements delivered to the Registrar. 9390

The **members** of a qualifying partnership **are exempt from this requirement** if the partnership is accounted for in the consolidated financial statements of: SI 2008/569 Reg.5
– a member of the partnership established under the law of a EC member state; or
– a parent undertaking of such a member, which is established under the law of an EU member state.

Where **advantage is taken of this exemption**, it must be disclosed in the notes to the consolidated financial statements and the accounts must be prepared on a consolidated basis, under the law of the member state in accordance with the EU 7th Company Law Directive. If this exemption is employed, any member of the partnership must disclose on request, the name of at least one member or parent undertaking in whose group accounts, the partnership accounts are consolidated.

9391 **Special requirements** apply where a qualifying partnership locates its head office in the Great Britain and each of the partners is either one of the following:
- an undertaking similar to a limited company incorporated outside the United Kingdom or other EEA state; or
- an undertaking similar to an unlimited company or partnership formed under the law of such a country with each of its members a limited or similar undertaking.

9392 The **special requirements** are as follows:
- the partnership must provide copies of the latest accounts for inspection to members of the public, without charge at the head office of the partnership, together with a certified translation if the original is not in English; and
- each member of the partnership must supply a copy of the latest accounts to any person so requesting them, complete with a translation where the original is not in English.

Limited liability partnerships

9393 The Limited Liability Partnership Regulations 2001/2008/2009 effectively bring LLPs under the same regime as limited companies (i.e. the Companies Act 1985 and 2006), for the purposes of the production, auditing and filing of financial statements. The Companies Act regime is however, subject to numerous modifications set out in Schedule 1 to the Regulations, that reflect the differing structures between LLPs and companies. A **revised SORP for LLPs** was issued in 2006 and 2010 to reflect changes made to UK accounting standards.

MEMO POINTS A limited liability partnership **should not be confused** with a qualifying partnership, which is a traditional limited partnership, whose members are all limited companies or similar and which are subject to their own regime. LLPs are covered in greater detail in Part 9 Chapter 6.

CHAPTER 9

Not for Profit Organisations

OUTLINE ¶¶

Not for profit organisations is an umbrella term covering general charities and other organisations such as clubs and associations, community interest companies or higher education institutes. This chapter **focuses primarily on charities** and in particular the requirements of the Statement of Recommended Practice (SORP) and the Charities Act 2006. The SORP is compatible with the requirements of company law and accounting standards and is the key source of accounting guidance for charities. However, although the SORP represents best practice, its adoption is not compulsory. **9500**

9501 Charities that choose **not to adopt the SORP** must continue to comply with the specific requirements of the Companies Acts, the Charities Act and accounting standards, as discussed in this book. Where **a separate SORP exists** for a particular class of charities (e.g. Registered Social Landlords or Higher Education Institutions), the trustees of the charity should apply the recommendations of that SORP. International Accounting Standards (IFRS) do not apply to charitable companies, although the Charity SORP will be continually reviewed to reflect changes to UK accounting standards, including those amendments arising out of the convergence process.

SECTION 1

Charities

9502 This section covers the registration and reporting thresholds for charities in **England and Wales**.

A "charity" **is defined as** an institution created exclusively for charitable purposes and may be unincorporated and administered by trustees or take the form of a charitable company run by its directors. Currently there are over 180,000 registered charities in the United Kingdom, the majority of which are unincorporated.

Smaller charities meeting certain threshold criteria **have the option** of preparing cash-based accounts, or adopting the reporting frameworks available to small or medium-sized companies. Some **special charities**, such as religious organisations, are now required under the Charities Act 2006 to register when income exceeds the registration threshold. The Charities Act has also created a legal framework for new legal formats such as Charitable Incorporated Organisations (CIOs) and Community Interest Companies.

MEMO POINTS The Charities Act 2006 requires all charities to adopt aims which are visibly for the public benefit. The Charity Commission provides guidance on how charities can satisfy the key criteria.

9503 **All charities** in England and Wales are required by law to produce an annual report and accounts and to make them available on request. The requirement to file annual accounts and a **Trustees' Annual Report** with the Charity Commission applies to all registered charities with a gross annual income exceeding £25,000. Furthermore, charities whose gross income exceeds £10,000 in the financial year, must also send an **Annual Return** to the Charity Commission. All the above documents must be filed within 10 months of the end of the financial year. An **audit or independent examination** is required by charities whose gross income exceeds 25,000 in the full financial year, unless stipulated by the charity's governing document.

Charity Commission – registration thresholds

9504 Charities in **England and Wales** with an annual income exceeding £5,000 must register with the Charity Commission, although charities with an annual income of less than this can still register voluntarily. The threshold is designed to reduce the administrative burden on small charities. Charities in Scotland and Northern Ireland must register with their own charity regulators. Charities that are part of a larger organisation are only required to register if they are an independent local branch that control its own funds.

9505 Prior to the Charities Act 2006, certain charities were not required to register with the Charity Commission, because they were regulated by other public sector bodies known as the "**Principal Regulator**", such as the Financial Services Agency (FSA).

However, if **a suitable regulator is not available** the charity will now have to register with the commission, although initially only those charities with an annual income exceeding £100,000 will be affected. The income threshold is expected to apply for at least five years, after which it will be reviewed.

MEMO POINTS 1. Examples of principal regulators include the Department for Culture, Media and Sport and the Higher Education and Funding Council for England. 2. Charities in Scotland must register with The Office of the Scottish Charity Regulator, based in Dundee. 3. Charities in Northern Ireland must register with The Charity Commission for Northern Ireland based in Belfast.

Special charities such as religious organisations or armed forces charities were previously exempt from registering with the Commission. These excepted charities as they are termed, will now come under the jurisdiction of the Commission although only those entities with an annual income exceeding £100,000 will be required to formally register. **Voluntary registration** is also permitted. 9506

MEMO POINTS 1. Although **excepted charities** do not need to register with the Charity Commission they do come under its jurisdiction, and their charitable activities can be investigated if there is cause for concern. Charities may be excepted by Order or Regulation or a registered place of worship. Examples include churches and charitable service funds of the armed forces.
2. **Exempt charities** are not regulated by the Charity Commission but are supervised by another organisation or body such as the Higher Education Funding Council. Examples include universities, museums and foundation schools.

Reporting options – thresholds

The current income thresholds are set out in the table below. 9509

Income thresholds	Accounts	Reporting options
Charities (non-companies) whose gross income is less than £250,000	Choice of preparing either:	
	a. Cash-based accounts (see ¶9680); or	Use format developed by Charity Commission (see ¶9940)
	b. Accrual accounts	Adoption of SORP prohibited
Charities (non-companies) whose gross income exceeds £250,000	Preparation of accrual accounts is compulsory	Choice of FRSSE, SORP or GAAP – as above
Charitable companies	Must prepare accrual accounts irrespective of the gross income threshold	Choice of FRSSE, SORP or GAAP – depending on whether the charity qualifies as a small or medium-sized company

MEMO POINTS 1. The **thresholds** are subject to periodic review.
2. Where accounting periods **are shorter or longer than 12 months**, the thresholds should be adjusted accordingly.
3. A summary of the **legislative framework** covering charities in the United Kingdom is given in Appendix I.
4. The **Charities Act** received Royal Assent in November 2006.
5. Charities often undertake trading activities through companies that they control and as such a parent charity is legally required to prepare own entity accounts. The publication of **group accounts** is designed to improve transparency concerning the full range of activities performed by the charity and the resources it controls.

SECTION 2

Application of the Charity SORP

The charity SORP has been developed within the framework of the UK financial reporting system, in order to provide clarification for the charity sector on the applicability of the accounting standards and enhance the quality of charity accounts. 9510

This section covers the structure of charity accounts and a detailed review of the accounting treatment required under the SORP. The **accounting recommendations** of the SORP **apply to** accounts prepared on an accruals basis, which is the case for the majority of charities.

Structure of charity accounts

9512 Charities differ greatly in structure. However, the accounts should detail how money and assets entrusted to the charity have been utilised during the year and the balance on each type of fund at the end of the accounting period. The structure of charity financial statements are summarised in the table below and considered in detail in the sections that follow.

Report	Content	Ref
I. A Statement of Financial Activities (SOFA)	Highlights incoming resources and resources committed, reconciled to changes in funds. The SOFA is based on a columnar format if more than one fund is involved	¶9514
Ia. Income and Expenditure Account	Where legally required (certain charitable companies)	¶9694
II. Balance Sheet	Highlights assets, liabilities and different fund categories used by the charity	¶9570
III. Notes to the Accounts	Detailing accounting policies and explanation of material items	¶9624
IV. Cash Flow Statement	Where required in accordance with the accounting standards	¶9660
V. Trustees' Annual Report	Supplements information in the primary statements – reflects impact of material transactions and commitments. Provides information on structure, corporate governance, and details of charity's objectives and key performance indicators not measurable in monetary terms.	¶9664

A. Statement of Financial Activities

9514 The Statement of Financial Activities (SOFA) provides information on the **sources and application of revenues** utilised by the charity, to meet its stated objectives and shows whether there has been a net inflow or outflow of resources. The SOFA should also contain a reconciliation of movements in the charity's funds.

The SOFA is designed to include all the gains and losses of a charity that would normally be found in the profit and loss account and STRGL, as required under FRS 3.

Format

9515 The format and activity categories of the SOFA are set out in the example below and expanded on in the following section.

Statement of Financial Activities (SOFA)	Aggregate of Unrestricted funds	Aggregate of Restricted funds	Aggregate of Endowment funds	Total funds	Prior year-total funds
1. Incoming resources					
Incoming resources from generated funds					
- Voluntary income					
- Activities for generating funds					
- Investment income					
Incoming resources from charitable activities					

Statement of Financial Activities (SOFA)	Aggregate of Unrestricted funds	Aggregate of Restricted funds	Aggregate of Endowment funds	Total funds	Prior year-total funds
Other incoming resources					
Total incoming resources					
2. Resources expended					
Costs of generating funds (fundraising)					
- Costs of generating voluntary income					
- Fundraising trading: cost of goods sold and other costs					
– Investment Management costs					
Cost of undertaking charitable activities					
Governance costs					
Other resources expended					
Total resources expended					
Net incoming/ outgoing resources before transfers					
3. Transfers					
- Gross transfers between funds					
Net incoming resources before other recognised gains and losses					
4. Other recognised gains/losses					
- Gains on revaluation of fixed assets for charity's own use					
- Gains/losses on investment assets					
- Actuarial gains/losses on defined benefit pension schemes					
Net movement in funds					
5. Reconciliation of funds					
Total funds brought forward					
Total funds carried forward					

MEMO POINTS Where a charity has **discontinued (or undertaken new) operations**, the accounts should distinguish between continuing, discontinued and acquired operations by activity. This requirement does not apply to the development or termination of projects within a specific activity.

Type of funds

9518 A charity will often have **several individual funds** comprising a particular category. Where material, more detail can be given in the notes to the accounts or additional columns can be added to the SOFA.

9519 **Endowment funds** Capital funds that cannot be converted into income by the trustees are known as endowment funds and must generally be held indefinitely, although the underlying assets can be exchanged or may be subject to depreciation or impairment. An exchange of assets can include simply a change of investment or the replacing of one asset with a similar asset.

Where trustees have the power to convert endowment funds into expendable income, these funds are termed **"expendable endowments"**. The fund must be invested to produce income used to further the objectives of the charity.

Certain expenses can be deducted from endowment funds such as related investment management fees, valuation fees etc. Where the trust deeds state the contrary or there are insufficient funds in the endowment, the costs can be charged against other funds held by the charity.

9520 **Restricted funds** Restricted funds **can only be used** for a particular purpose and must be accounted for separately. These funds may be set up by a donor, or through public appeals or a legal process. Restricted funds can be income funds expendable at the discretion of the trustees or capital funds, where the assets are retained by the charity. The terms and conditions attached to the restricted funds will vary according to the individual charity.

9521 **Unrestricted funds (General funds)** Unrestricted funds can be used at the discretion of the trustees to further the objectives of the charity. A **part of the fund** may still be designated for specific purposes, although this is an administrative classification only, or to make up any shortfall on a restricted fund. Where funds are used to construct or improve a building on land classified as an endowment asset, this expenditure should be classified as part of the permanent endowment.

1. Incoming resources

9522 Charity SORP (96)-(97) Incoming resources arise from **different types of transactions** ranging from the provision of goods or services to the receipt of unrestricted grants or donations. Guidance on how the different types of incoming resources in the charity sector should be recognised and recorded in the financial statements and how accounting principles and standards should be applied, is given in the following section.

The main **disclosure requirements** are covered in ¶9624.

a. Type of incoming resources from generated funds

9524 The **principal types** of incoming resources **can broadly be classified** as voluntary income, fundraising activities and investment income, each of which is considered below.

Voluntary income

9526 Voluntary income **is defined as** gifts that do not generate a financial return for the donor, such as legacies, gifts in kind and donated services. Disclosure should be made of activities representing voluntary income, linked where possible to an analysis of the supporting costs incurred. This information should be provided either on the face of the SOFA or in the notes to the accounts.

Legacies 1. Legacies that are **not payable immediately** should not be classified as receiv- 9528
able until all the criteria attached to the payment of the particular legacy have been met (e.g. death of a life tenant). The value of the incoming resource is then determined and recognised at that date.
2. Where **entitlement** to the legacy **is in doubt** due to legal disputes, then the resource should not be recognised until such time as the legal situation is resolved.
3. **Payments on account** from a legacy are treated as receivable. When payments on account have been agreed prior to the end of the financial year, but actually received after the balance sheet date, they should be accrued in the SOFA and the balance sheet.

Gifts in kind Gifts in kind can be classified as per the following table. 9529

The **general rule** is that the amount at which gifts in kind are recognised in the SOFA should either be a reasonable estimate of their gross value on the open market or, in the case of second-hand goods donated for resale, the amount actually realised.

Type	Recognition
1. Stock given to a charity for distribution	Recognise as an incoming resource (under voluntary income), when an equivalent amount has been included under resources expended, to reflect the distribution of the stock
2. Assets given to a charity for its own use (e.g. property)	Recognise as an incoming resource in the SOFA – plus within the relevant fixed asset category in the balance sheet
3. Gift made on trust for later conversion into cash – for subsequent expenditure by the charity	Two possible accounting treatments: **a.** Gift should be recognised when received and value adjusted on subsequent realisation **b.** Where option (a) is not practical, a gift is recognised only in accounting period when the asset is sold (e.g. second-hand items donated for resale).

Donated services A charity could receive aid through donated resources such as services 9530
or favourable loan arrangements. **Examples** of donated services include services provided free by individuals such as accountants, lawyers or tradesmen.

Type	Recognition
Donations	**Should only be recognised** in the SOFA when the benefits to the charity are quantifiable, and are based on prices the charity would expect to pay in the open market for an equivalent service.
When donated services are recognised	Then **an equivalent amount** must also be included as expenditure in the SOFA. However, a distinction must be drawn between this and time given by volunteers which should not be included in the SOFA.
Disclosure requirements	The notes to the SOFA should cover an analysis of donated services or facilities such as loaned assets and the valuation bases adopted. Donated services (e.g. type, value) **relating to volunteer services** not included in SOFA, should be disclosed in the Trustees' Annual Report.

Activities for generating funds (trading and fundraising)

e category "activities for generating funds" (non-donated funds) includes the trading and 9532
ne generating activities of the charity such as:
raising events (e.g. appeals, jumble sales, concerts);

- sponsorships, lotteries;
- income from letting property temporarily surplus to operational requirements; and
- income from charity shops through selling donated goods.

MEMO POINTS The income from selling donated goods legally, represents the realisation of a donation and is recognised under this category as it is similar to a trading activity. **Recognition is based on** an assessment of the balance of activities. For instance, where a charity shop sells primarily donated goods but also a small amount of goods produced in-house, it would be acceptable to recognise all as "shop income" under "activities for generating funds".

Investment income

9533 Investment income **includes** dividends, rents and interest **but excludes** investment gains or losses.

The accounting treatment for investment income from subsidiary undertakings is covered in ¶9712.

b. Incoming resources from direct charitable activities

9534 This category covers incoming resources **representing payment for goods and services**, provided for the benefit of the charity's beneficiaries and includes trading activities and conditional grants that are similar in nature to income from trading and fundraising.

An analysis of the main incoming resources from charitable activities should be given in the notes to the SOFA. This analysis should be linked to resources expended on charitable activities.

Charity SORP (145) **Examples** of incoming resources from charitable activities **include**:
- sale of goods or services as part of direct charitable activities;
- sale of goods or services provided by beneficiaries of the charity (e.g. paintings by disabled artists);
- letting of non-investment property;
- specific grants for activities provided by the charity; and
- contractual payments from local authorities or government for the provision of services (e.g. fees for respite care).

c. Recognition criteria

9540 All incoming resources must meet the general criteria in order to be recognised in the financial statements. The trustees may also need to consider additional factors specific to each type of funding as set out in the tables below.

Incoming resources earned by the charity and its agents and volunteers, should be reported gross.

9541 Charity SORP (94) **General criteria** Incoming resources **can only be recognised** in the SOFA, when the effect of a transaction or other event is to increase the assets of the charity. This in turn is dependant on whether:
- there is an entitlement arising from control over rights (e.g. legal arrangements, terms, jurisdiction, trust or contract law) to an incoming resource;
- it is certain the incoming resource will be received;
- it can be reliably measured in monetary terms; and
- the funding is dependent on specific contractual or performance related conditions or use is restricted.

Additional criteria depending on type of incoming resource 9542

Contracts	Recognition criteria
Goods/services	Where provided by the charity in return for a fee – recognise in the SOFA.
Payments in advance	Where the income is received in advance of a provision of goods or services – no entitlement until goods provided. The income should be deferred and disclosed as a liability in the balance sheet.
Membership subscriptions (life, annual)	1. If subscription purchases rights to services or benefits, the incoming resource should be recognised as the service is provided. 2. Membership income can be pro-rated over the subscription term. 3. Where the substance of a subscription is a donation, recognise on same basis as donations (see table below).
Long-term contracts	Recognise incoming resources when entitlement to consideration obtained. Assess fair value of goods/services provided at reporting date relative to total fair value of contract. Additional guidance provided in Application Note G – revenue recognition on long-term contracts.
Grants	
Non-conditional grants	1. Recognition of a non-conditional grant should not be deferred. 2. This requirement also applies when the grant is **received in advance** and the timing of the related expenditure is at the discretion of the charity.
Conditional grants – general	1. Where the **conditions to be met are within the charity's control** and there is evidence that they will be met, the income can be recognised. 2. Where **uncertainty exists**, the incoming resource should not be recognised but deferred as a liability, until it is certain the conditions will be met (i.e. matched funding, planning permission). 3. A condition allowing for the **recovery by the donor** of any unused part of a grant does not prevent recognition. The liability is recognised when the repayment becomes due.
Conditional grants – Donor imposed restrictions	Where resources should be expended in a given time period this restricts a charity's use of these resources. 1. Where grant must be expended by a specified future date – account for as a **deferred income** and recognise as a liability until resources are expended. 2. Where **conditions prevent recognition** of an incoming resource, a contingent asset should be disclosed where it is probable the conditions will be met at some point.
Grants provided for asset purchase	Incoming resources are recognised in the SOFA when received and not deferred over the life of the asset. 1. **Restricted grants** – account for as restricted funds. Treatment of fixed assets depends on individual case – i.e. terms of agreement may require asset to be held in a restricted fund. 2. **Unrestricted grants** – a designated fund can be established reflecting the book value of the asset, which is then depreciated over the UEL of the asset.
C. Donations	
The categories are the same as for grants	The rules are generally the same as for grants.

Contracts	Recognition criteria
D. Funds collected by or for third parties	
On behalf of a third party	When incoming resources are collected on behalf of a third party, the intermediary charity should not recognise the funds in the SOFA. **The exception is** where intermediary charity can control the resources prior to transferring them to the third party (see also ¶9607).
Funds collected by third parties	Where funds are collected by third parties on the charity's behalf, recognition is based on type of income. Proceeds should be reported net of any expenses.

2. Resources expended

9546 Charity SORP (149) The SOFA provides the framework for the recognition and analysis of the resources expended by the charity. Additionally, **where material**, an analysis should be provided of sub-activities, programmes, projects and other initiatives that support the principal activities of the charity.

Charities expend resources in a variety of ways including meeting contractual liabilities and payment of grants or donations. The SORP provides guidance on how these **different types of transactions** should be recognised in **accruals based accounts** and how the accounting standards and principles should be applied. In cash based accounts, the recognition of resources expended is based on the actual physical outflow of cash resources from the charity.

a. Type of resources expended

9550 This section considers the recognition and accounting treatment of the costs of generating funds from different sources.

Cost by type	Definition/examples	Additional requirements
A. Cost of generating funds	The costs of generating funds **should exclude** trading costs related to the provision of goods and services, and any subsequent negotiation or monitoring required under the terms of a performance related grant or contract.	Where the costs **are material**, additional information should be given in the notes to the SOFA, and where possible matched to the analysis of income.
- Voluntary income	Represents the costs incurred in generating monetary gifts made to the charity. **Examples include**: – producing advertising, marketing and direct mail; – maintaining a database; – door to door collections; – generating sponsorship; – legacy development; and – start-up costs for new fundraising activities.	

Cost by type	Definition/examples	Additional requirements
- Fundraising	Covers expenses incurred through selling for charitable purposes, either donated or purchased goods, or the provision of non-charitable services intended to generate income. **Examples include**: – the direct costs of goods sold or services provided; – other related trading costs (e.g. staff costs, premises, support costs); or – licensing (e.g. charity logos).	
- Investment management costs	Includes the costs of: – portfolio management; – investment advice; – administration of investments; and – rent collection, property repairs and maintenance charges.	**1**. Where management fees have been deducted by external investment managers, the charity should show the investment income gross with fees charged to the appropriate cost category (e.g. the costs associated with endowment fund investments should be charged to the respective endowment fund in the SOFA). **2**. The cost of disposing of investments are excluded from this category and usually netted-off against the disposal proceeds.
B. Costs of undertaking charitable activities	Covers the resources expended by charities conducting their charitable activities (e.g. delivery of goods and services) as opposed to the costs of the initial fundraising.	Resources expended by charities in undertaking their charitable activities should be analysed on the face of the SOFA or in the notes to the accounts (see example below).
- Grant funding	Includes grants made to individuals (e.g. educational, bursaries) as well as institutional grants (e.g. research projects).	The costs associated with grant funding activities include: – costs resulting from the decision to award a grant; – subsequent monitoring costs; or – related general management and administration costs (e.g. budgeting, payroll, IT).
- Support costs	Include the costs of supporting income generation and supporting the governance of the charity. **Examples include** the costs of general management accounting and administration and information technology support.	**1**. Details of the total support costs incurred and cost allocation should be given in the notes to the accounts. **2**. Where the support costs are material, information on the apportionment bases adopted should also be given.
- Governance costs	Defined as costs incurred by the charity in meeting its statutory reporting requirements including: – internal or external audits; – legal advice for trustees; – trustee meetings; or – preparation of statutory accounts.	

Support costs In charging support costs to different activities the **following principles** should be applied; namely that expenditure should where possible, be allocated direct to a specific activity and shared costs (e.g. staff costs, depreciation) should be apportioned on a justifiable and consistent basis. 9554

There are a **number of bases** that can be used to allocate costs to different activities within a charity including:
- usage per activity;
- per capita (i.e. the number of people employed within an activity);
- a time basis (e.g. staff work on different activities – timesheets); or
- floor area occupied per activity.

b. Recognition criteria

9556 Charity SORP (148)
Liabilities are recognised as resources expended when there is a "legal or constructive obligation" (see the note below), committing the charity to the expenditure. The criteria for recognising resources expended by type are set out below.

9558 Charity SORP (150)-(156)
Contract for supply Where a charity enters into a contract for the supply of goods or services, expenditure is recognised once the supplier has delivered the goods or provided the service.

9559
Grants **a.** Expenditure on **performance related grants** should be classified as resources expended, to the extent that the grant recipient has provided the contracted level of services or goods, and satisfied all other conditions that are linked to the grant (e.g. number of meals provided or a time-based service).
b. Grants related to a specific purpose are known as **restricted grants** (e.g. two-year research programme) and should be recognised as a liability when a constructive obligation is incurred to make a grant payment.
c. Under **non-performance related grants** and other expenditure relating directly to charitable activities, an "exchange for consideration" does not arise, as a contractual relationship with the grant beneficiary is not created. However, the charity may still have a liability which should be recognised, arising from a legal or constructive obligation.

MEMO POINTS 1. A **constructive obligation** exists, where events have created a valid expectation in others, that the charity will meet its obligations such as giving a specific commitment to provide goods, services or grant funding and has confirmed this with the beneficiary or grant recipient. However, the **recognition of any such liability** could also depend on any specific conditions attached to such commitments. A liability should be recognised when such conditions fall outside the control of the charity. Where the conditions have not been fulfilled, the expenditure could be avoided at the discretion of the charity and as such a liability should not be realised.
2. A **liability that has not been accrued** because certain conditions have not been met should normally be recognised as a contingent liability.
3. Where **subsequent events** make the recognition of a liability no longer appropriate, the liability should be cancelled by crediting the relevant expenditure account in the SOFA. Separate disclosure is required in the notes to the SOFA.

3. Transfers between funds

9560 Charity SORP (214)
Transfers **between different types of funds** should be shown here in the SOFA, including:
- capital funds moved from an endowment fund to an income fund;
- restricted assets released and reallocated to unrestricted income funds;
- assets transferred to cover a deficit on a restricted fund; or
- the value of a fixed asset transferred from a restricted to an unrestricted fund, when the asset has been purchased from a restricted fund donation.

9561
Material transfers should not be netted-off but shown gross on the face of the SOFA and details of material transfers between funds should be provided in the notes to the accounts.

4. Other recognised gains and losses

Gains or losses arising on the disposal, revaluation or impairment of fixed assets, held for investment purposes or for the own use of the charity, should form part of the particular fund in which the asset is held, at the time the profit or loss is determined. 9562

Category of gain or loss	Recognition	Accounting treatment
Gains or losses on fixed assets (charity's own use, non-investment)	1. Revaluation	Include in gains and losses on revaluations of fixed assets.
	2. Disposal	Gains on disposal – include under "Other incoming resources". Losses on disposal – treat as additional depreciation and charge to resources expended section in the SOFA.
	3. Impairment	Impairment losses – same treatment as for losses on disposal.
Gains or losses on investment assets (including property)		Recognised under gains or losses on the revaluation and disposal of fixed assets – single row in the SOFA
Actuarial gains or losses on defined benefit pension schemes		Disclose separately in the gains or losses section of the SOFA

B. Balance sheet

The balance sheet provides a summary of the charity's assets at the end of the financial year and how the assets are divided between different funds. The balance sheet should also highlight **which resources have legal restrictions** attached to their use or that have been designated for a specific use. 9570

Structure

The format of the asset, liability and fund headings are set out in the table below. Charities may adopt a columnar presentation in the balance sheet, analysed between each fund group. **Where the columnar method** of presentation is not adopted then the assets and liabilities constituting each fund should be analysed in the notes to the accounts. 9572

The order in which the categories of funds are presented will vary according to the preference of the individual charity.

Balance Sheet	Total Funds	Prior Year Funds
1. Fixed assets:		
Intangible assets		
Tangible assets		
Heritage assets		
Investment assets		
Programme related investments		
Total fixed assets		
2. Current assets:		
- Stocks and work-in-progress		
- Debtors		

Balance Sheet	Total Funds	Prior Year Funds
- Investments		
- Cash at bank and in hand		
Total current assets		
3. Liabilities		
Creditors: Amounts falling due within one year		
Net current assets and liabilities		
Total assets less current liabilities		
Creditors: Amounts falling due after more than one year		
Provisions for liabilities and charges		
4. Defined benefit pension scheme asset or liability		
5. The funds of the charity:		
- Endowment funds		
- Restricted income funds		
- Unrestricted income funds		
- Share capital		
- Revaluation reserve		
- Pension reserve		
Total unrestricted funds		
Total charity funds		

1. Assets and liabilities

9580 The accounting requirements for intangible and tangible fixed assets, heritage assets and investment assets are covered in this section.

a. Fixed assets

Intangible fixed assets

9581 Where a charity has an intangible fixed asset (e.g. licence, brand) which does not meet the recognition criteria under FRS 10 (see ¶1018), it should not be included in the primary statements but details of the asset should be given in the notes to the accounts.

Tangible fixed assets

9582 Tangible fixed assets should be capitalised on initial acquisition at cost or valuation. Subsequent expenditure which enhances the performance of tangible fixed assets should also be capitalised. Tangible fixed assets are treated in greater detail in ¶1200 with charity specific issues covered below.

Tangible fixed assets (other than investments)	Accounting treatment
General rules	1. Cost of acquisition including directly attributable costs 2. Fixed assets acquired in full or part from grant proceeds – should be included at acquisition cost and not netted off 3. Donated assets – include at value at date of donation. Also included in the SOFA under incoming resources.

Tangible fixed assets (other than investments)	Accounting treatment
Depreciation	See ¶1444.
Revaluation	The **general rule** is that where a revaluation policy is adopted it must be applied to all assets in a particular classification (see also ¶1352). The **exception to the rule** is that where assets **are donated or capitalised** as a result of a change in accounting policy, the initial valuation is not deemed a revaluation. This means that other assets in this group/class need not be revalued. Where a charity adopts a policy of revaluation – revaluation must be updated regularly (see ¶1374-¶1440).
Impairment	Impairment is measured according to the process outlined in ¶1562-¶1568. 1. **Impairment losses** should be recognised in accordance with FRS 11 (see ¶1670) – treat as additional depreciation and include in the SOFA. Asset then depreciated over revised UEL. 2. **Valuation measures** based on service delivery or replacement cost may be appropriate as charities often hold assets for other reasons than generating cash flows. "Value in use" based on future cash flows would be an inappropriate valuation measure.

Mixed use assets There are a **number of rules** applicable to fixed assets used for both investment and functional purposes. 9583

The **classification** of mixed use assets on the balance sheet **is determined by** the primary use of the asset and the extent to which the uses are separable.

The **following criteria** should be adopted:

1. Land and buildings held primarily for charity use but which is **part leased at a commercial rent** should be accounted for as a functional fixed asset, provided the asset is primarily used for charitable purposes.
2. Land and buildings **held** primarily **for investment purposes** should be accounted for within fixed asset investments.
3. Land and associated buildings held **for both investment and functional purposes** should be apportioned and analysed in the balance sheet between functional and investment assets.

Disclosures Tangible fixed assets can be analysed in the notes to the accounts using the broad categories set out in the example in ¶1522. The example can be adjusted to reflect other narrower classes, more appropriate to the reporting requirements of individual charities, and to summarise changes in the values of each class of tangible fixed assets through a reconciliation of the opening and closing balances. 9584

Heritage assets

Heritage assets **are defined as** assets of historical, artistic or scientific importance held to further the preservation, conservation and educational activities of charities. These assets include land, buildings, collections, exhibits or artefacts and are often central to the objectives of the charity such as supporting education in the arts (galleries) and sciences (museums). 9586

Assets **used by the charity as administrative offices** or as part of a property investment portfolio or works of art and antiques retained as a store of wealth, should not be classified as heritage assets (see also ¶1330).

EXAMPLE

1. The Woodland Trust holds land relating to the preservation and enhancement of forests throughout the UK, including many areas of natural beauty and scientific interest.

2. The National Trust for England, Wales and Northern Ireland seeks to preserve and protect the coastline, countryside and specific historical buildings, for future generations through active management and conservation.

9588

Heritage assets	Accounting issues/recognition
1. Newly purchased	**Initially recognised** at cost in accordance with FRS 15 (¶1226).
2. Valuation issues	Heritage buildings, structures or sites **present different valuation issues**, such as: 1. Determining the service potential of a unique building or structure, in terms of its heritage value (e.g. medieval castles, archaeological sites, monuments). 2. Valuing donated heritage assets where rarely sold on the open market. 3. Assets that are part purchased/part donated and that are capable of reliable measurement as should gifts and lifetime transfers which are usually valued for inheritance tax purposes. 4. Specialised buildings – use depreciated replacement cost (¶1400).
3. Acquired in the past but not capitalised (prior to 2001)	**Are excluded from balance sheet where**: – reliable cost information is not available; – conventional valuation techniques are not suitable; – costs of analysing past accounting records too onerous compared with additional benefit derived by users of accounts from this information.

9590 FRS 30 **Disclosures** A separate line for heritage assets is required on the balance sheet, with additional information given in the notes to the accounts, including:
- an analysis or description of the age, scale and nature of heritage assets;
- details of cost, additions, and disposals during the year;
- where assets are not capitalised, a description of the assets; and
- the accounting policy note covering measurement bases and capitalisation policy.

MEMO POINTS The ASB has issued FRS 30 "Heritage assets" (see ¶1330). The standard is designed to improve the consistency and transparency of the financial reporting of heritage assets, covering entities such as museums and organisations that own and manage landscapes or buildings for their environmental and historical qualities. FRS 30 includes enhanced disclosure requirements for heritage assets, whether reported in the balance sheet or not. The detailed disclosure requirements cover the nature and value of heritage assets held, as well as the stewardship policies adopted, including development, preservation and disposal of assets. The new standard also includes guidance regarding the requirement for regular impairment reviews.

Investment assets

9592 Investment assets **are classified separately** within fixed assets, **except where the charity** does not intend to reinvest the sale proceeds, in which case the asset should be reclassified as a current asset. Investment assets should be recorded in the balance sheet at market value or best estimate of market value. Changes in value in the year, whether realised or not, should be reported in the SOFA under "gains or losses on investment assets".

Investments **that are traded freely** such as shares on a recognised stock exchange will have a readily ascertainable price. Where no such market exists the trustees must adopt other measures. One such example is the valuation of shares in an unlisted company, which may be valued according to the underlying net assets or earnings of the company or the dividend record. In the case of properties, the trustees may undertake new valuations where material movements in value are expected.

Programme related investment activities

9594 Programme related activities (also termed social investments) support directly the activities of the charity. The primary motivation for these investments is not financial, but to further the objectives of the charity. **Examples include** loans to individual beneficiaries (e.g. housing deposits) or to other charities (e.g. regeneration projects).

The **general rules** for accounting for programme related investment activities are as follows: 9596
1. Programme related activities should be disclosed separately within the investments category, from those investments expected to generate a financial return for the charity.
2. These investments should be accounted for at the amount invested less repayments or impairment losses (e.g. loans, equity).
3. Where **loans** are subsequently converted to grants they should be reclassified and charged to charitable activities.
4. **Gains made on disposal** of a programme related investment should be set-off against any prior impairment losses, then included as a gain on disposal of fixed assets for the charity's own use and recorded under "other incoming resources".

b. Current assets

Current assets **should normally be recognised** at lower of cost or net realisable value. The headings may be adapted to meet the requirements of individual charities. For instance, debtors can be further classified as follows: 9604
- trade debtors;
- amounts due from subsidiary and associated undertakings;
- other debtors; and
- prepayments and accrued income.

Where **long-term debtors are material** in terms of total net current assets, they should be listed separately in the balance sheet.

c. Current liabilities and long-term creditors

Current liabilities are recorded at settlement value. The balance sheet headings may be expanded or adapted to meet the requirements of the individual charity or reflect the type of creditor. The totals for short-term and long-term creditors should be separately analysed in the notes to the accounts for: 9606
- loans and overdrafts;
- trade creditors;
- amounts due to subsidiary and associated undertakings;
- other creditors; and
- accruals and deferred income.

Where the charity **acts as an agent** for another charity or organisation, then any assets held (and associated liabilities) should be separately identified in the notes to the accounts but not included in the balance sheet. Sufficient detail should be given in order that the exact relationship and nature of the transactions between the funding partner, the intermediary and the funding recipient is clear. 9607

Where the charity is **the intermediary and principal**, then assets and associated liabilities should be included in the balance sheet.

Provisions for Liabilities

Provisions for liabilities **are defined as** the best estimate of the expenditure required to discharge the present obligation at the balance sheet date. The debit entry is to the SOFA in line with the recognition criteria set out in ¶9550. 9608 Charity SORP (321)

Due consideration should be given to any further uncertainties that could affect the total obligation, and in addition provisions should be regularly reviewed and adjusted where appropriate.

The **general rules** are as follows:
1. **Provisions no longer required** to discharge a financial obligation should be credited to the resources expended category in the SOFA, where it was originally charged.

2. Where a charity has purposely **set aside part of its unrestricted funds** for a specific future purpose, the intention to spend funds is not recognised as a provision for a liability in the financial statements. In this instance, it is usual for the charity to set up a specific fund.
3. **Accrued provisions** to be paid over a number of years should be discounted at the balance sheet date to their present value. The discount rate should reflect the time value of money and attendant risks.

2. Defined benefit pension schemes

9612 An asset or liability derived from a surplus or deficit in a defined pension scheme is included in this category and disclosed on the face of the balance sheet.

A charity **must create a pension reserve** when there is a surplus (asset) or deficit (liability) on a defined pension scheme. Where the pension reserve relates only to unrestricted funds then the reserve itself forms part of the unrestricted funds. Likewise, where the pension asset or liability forms part of a restricted fund, then the pension reserve will also form part of the restricted fund, subject to certain criteria being met.

A detailed treatment of this topic relating to charities is beyond the scope of this chapter. The application of FRS 17 "Retirement Benefits" in general and the required accounting treatment and disclosures are set out in ¶8410.

3. Types of charity fund

9614 The **definitions of** endowment funds and restricted and unrestricted funds are given in ¶9518 and the main disclosure requirements are covered in ¶9630. Other types of fund include share capital and the revaluation reserve.

9618 **Share capital** Some charities are constituted with a share capital such as Industrial and Provident Societies or incorporated as companies under the Companies Act. Typically, the share capital is for a nominal amount. Furthermore, as owners are prevented from benefiting from share ownership, any capital contributed effectively forms part of the unrestricted funds of the charity. Share capital must be shown separately on the balance sheet.

9619 **Revaluation Reserve** Charities incorporated as companies must detail in the revaluation reserve, in terms of unrestricted funds, any differences between the historic cost of fixed assets and the revalued amounts.

C. Notes to the accounts

9624 The trustees are obliged to prepare accounts that give a true and fair view of the resources and financial commitments of the charity at the end of the financial year, which could result in more detailed disclosures than those recommended by the Charity SORP. This section outlines the disclosure requirements covering accounting policies, individual funds and other key disclosures not already covered in Section 2.

1. Accounting policies

9626
FRS 18 (17)

The notes to the financial statements should detail the accounting policies selected and confirm that they are consistent with the Charity SORP, the accounting standards, and the Companies Acts.

The **notes should state** the following, **where applicable**:
1. That the historic cost basis of accounting has been adopted except for investments which are included at market value.
2. Where a branch has been omitted from the accounts (see ¶9720), the reasons justifying this policy.
3. Details of changes to policies that result in material adjustments to prior-periods.
4. The reasons for any material departures from the accounting standards.
5. The reasons for any material departures from the Charity SORP, including:
- how the accounting treatment differs from the SORP;
- the reasons why the trustees adopted this accounting treatment; and
- an estimate of the financial effect on the accounts of the policy adopted.

Additional disclosures are also required of accounting policies relevant to **material amounts** in the financial statements, as set out in the table below. **9628** Charity SORP (361)

Accounting policy	Policy disclosures required
Incoming resources	Policy for each individual type of incoming resource, for example: – basis of recognition of gifts in kind and donated services + methods of valuation; – recognition criteria for grants receivable including for fixed assets; – whether endowment funds are restricted or unrestricted; – whether incoming resources are deferred and the reasons why; – details of legacies deemed receivable; and – whether incoming resources have been included in the SOFA net of expenditure.
Resources expended	– Policy for recognition of liabilities including constructive obligations; – Provisions – and the point at which a provision is deemed binding (e.g. grants); – Policy for including costs within certain activity categories in resources expended; – Methods and principles of allocating or apportioning costs to different activity categories (i.e. based on staff time, salaries).
Asset policy	Capitalisation policy for fixed assets including: – for each class of asset, whether they are included at cost, valuation or revaluation; – the valuation (revaluation) methods and bases used; – the value below which assets not capitalised; – depreciation methods and rates; – details of impaired assets (e.g. reviews); and – any differences between carrying value and market value of assets (non-investments).
Investments	Policy of inclusion at market value except where: – investments are not listed on a recognised stock exchange; – investment properties; or – investments in subsidiary undertakings. Policy on dealing with investment gains or losses in the SOFA.
Other policy notes	Policies for recognition relating to: – types of fund held by the charity including policies for inter-fund transfers; – pension costs and pension assets and liabilities; – foreign exchange gains or losses; – finance and operating leases; – stocks and work-in-progress; – treatment of exceptional items; and – taxation.

2. Details of individual funds

9630 Information on the structure of the charity's funds should be given in the notes to the accounts, **differentiating between**:
- unrestricted income funds (general and designated);
- restricted income funds;
- permanent endowment; and
- expendable endowments.

The trustees must decide on the most appropriate presentation for the charity **depending on the complexity of the funds** and their structure. Additional information should be given of any individual material funds as illustrated in the table below.

Fund name	Fund balances b/fwd £	Incoming resources £	Outgoing resources £	Transfers £	Gains and losses £	Fund balances c/fwd £
Fund 1						
Fund 2						
Fund 3						
Other Funds						
Total Funds						

9631 **Additional disclosures** include:
- an analysis of assets and liabilities representing each type of fund where a columnar balance sheet is not adopted;
- details of the purpose of each fund and any restrictions imposed on its use;
- separate disclosure of funds in deficit, material transfers between funds; and
- allocations to designated funds with the accompanying reasons.

9632 **Analysis of net movement in funds** The net movement in funds represents the increase or decrease in resources available to a charity. Charities often provide information on the:
- total net movement in funds at the end of the financial year;
- net endowment receipts for the year;
- net expenditure on additions to fixed assets (i.e. cost less any disposal proceeds); or
- net investment in programme related investments.

3. Other important disclosure requirements

Investment assets

9633 The disclosure requirements for investment assets (in addition to the accounting policy adopted) include:

1. The **total value of investments** held at the end of the financial year by type of investment; namely:
- investment properties;
- investments listed on a recognised stock exchange, including unit trusts and open-ended investment companies;
- investments in subsidiary companies; or
- other unlisted securities.

Where material this should be segmented into UK and overseas investments.

2. Details of **programme related investments** held as equity loan or other investments, that support the charity's core activities.

3. Additional information on **material investments** relative to the size of the investment portfolio.
4. Details of **valuations** (e.g. name of valuer, basis of valuation).
5. The value of assets held in **different classes of funds**.
6. **Changes in value** of investment assets – a reconciliation of opening and closing book values using the format set out in the table below.

Investments – reconciliation of opening and closing book values	£
Carrying value (market value) at beginning of year	
Add: Additions to investments at cost	
Less: Disposals at carrying value	
Add/deduct net gain/(loss) on revaluation	
Carrying value (market value) at end of year	

Grant funding The **required disclosures** in the notes to the accounts should include: 9634
– an explanation of how the grants further the objectives of the charity;
– the support costs associated with the grants;
– the total amount of grants payable to individuals and institutions;
– an analysis of grants by type of activity (e.g. medical research, social projects, performing arts, educational); or
– for institutional grants, the name of the institution, and the total value and purpose of grants made.

EXAMPLE **Grant expenditure in furtherance of the Group's objectives**

	2010 £'000	2009 £'000
Grants payable in the year (see below)	16,685	7,095
Increase in provision for funding of endowment chairs	6,000	4,500
Write back of under-utilised grants	(3,250)	(2,100)
Unwinding of discount on provision for endowment chairs and fellowships	1,250	950
Total	**20,685**	**10,445**

Grants awarded
During the year, grant making committees made new grant awards for medical research for up to ten years as follows:

Grants awarded	2010		2009	
	£'000	No. of grants		No. of grants
Clinical Trials Committee	13,100	35		19
Tobacco Advisory Group	185	8	135	6
Behavioural Science Committee	3,400	20	1,800	13
Total	**16,685**	**63**	**7,095**	**38**

The large increase in new grants awarded for up to ten years is due to the renewal of one of the major grantees funded on a ten year term, coupled with the strategic increase in clinical research trials. The sums disclosed are payable over the term of the awards.

Costs of undertaking charitable activities

The required disclosures could be presented as shown in the example below with the totals reconciling to the SOFA. 9640

Resources expended – analysis by programme	Activity – direct £	Grant funding of activity £ See ¶9634/¶9550	Support costs £ See ¶9550	Total £
Programme 1				
Programme 2				
Programme 3				
Total				

9644 **Financial derivatives** Where charities use financial derivatives to cover the risk associated with their operations (forward currency contracts), investments or borrowing (interest rate hedging), the following disclosures are required:
- details on number and type of financial instruments used;
- impact of the risks associated with the underlying asset or liability; and
- an indication of the costs/benefits of holding derivative products.

9646 **Loan Liabilities** Details should be given of any material assets that are **subject to a mortgage or charge** given as security for a loan or other liability including:
- the amount of the loan or liability; and
- its proportion to the value of the asset subject to the mortgage or charge.

Details should also be given of the principal, interest and repayment terms of inter-fund loans and loans to trading subsidiaries.

Provisions for liabilities

9647 There are a number of required disclosures, **including details of**:
- all material provisions for liabilities and charges accrued in the balance sheet;
- material binding commitments relating to specific charitable projects, that have not been accrued, including timing; other binding commitments such as operating leases; and
- provisions arising from legal or constructive obligations (see ¶9559) should be analysed in the balance sheet between liabilities due within one year and those after one year.

A **distinction should also be drawn** in the notes to the accounts between commitments recorded in the balance sheet as liabilities and other proposed expenditure that has not been accrued for, detailing:
- the total commitments outstanding at the beginning and end of the financial year;
- amounts charged in the year to the SOFA; and
- material reductions in provisions due to changes in value of commitments.

When it is probable that there will be a future outflow of resources to settle a liability previously recognised as a **contingent liability**, the sum should be accrued in the accounts.

9648 **Contingent Assets** Contingent assets **are not recognised in the financial statements**, because this could result in recognition of resources that may never be realised. Once an inflow of economic resources is certain they are recorded in the SOFA as an incoming resource and in the balance sheet as a debtor.

The **required disclosures** are:
- details of material contingent assets;
- the nature of each contingency;
- the uncertainties expected to affect the contingency event; and
- where no estimate has been made, the reasons why.

9650 **Guarantees** Details of any material guarantees given by the charity should be detailed in the notes to the accounts.

Related party transactions The **general rule** is that transactions between a charity and its trustees should always be regarded as material and disclosed. Each type of related party transaction should be separately disclosed. Examples include remuneration paid to each charity trustee and pension arrangements and the authority for such payments. 9651

For **material transactions**, irrespective of whether they have been conducted at "arm's length" or not, the following disclosures are also required:
- name of related party;
- nature of the relationship;
- amounts involved, written-off, or outstanding;
- provisions for doubtful debts; and
- the authority for such payments.

Details of the **aggregate expenses** (e.g. travel, subsistence) paid to trustees for services given to the charity, either through reimbursement or an allowance, should also be disclosed. Where the transactions are similar, the disclosures can be aggregated.

Staff costs and emoluments The charity should give the following disclosures in the notes; namely: 9652
- costs of employing staff including seconded and temporary staff;
- total costs should be split between gross wages and salaries, national insurance costs and pension costs; and
- the average number of staff employed during the financial year.

For **charities subject to a statutory audit**, additional information should be given including:
- the numbers of employees earning £60,000 (including taxable benefits but excluding employer pension costs) and above in bands of £10,000 (e.g. £70,000); and
- for higher paid employees, the contributions made in the year to **defined contribution schemes** and defined benefit schemes.

Advisory costs The charity should provide details of sums paid to auditors, tax advisors, legal advisors, and for consultancy or marketing expertise. 9653

Ex-gratia payments Disclosures are required of ex-gratia payments including significant payments or non-monetary benefits. Where the trustees of the charity require the authority of the Court, the Attorney General or the Charity Commission, this fact must be disclosed. 9654

D. Cash flow statement

Charities **that do not qualify** as a small company (see ¶9509) are required to prepare a cash flow statement. Cash flow statements should comply with the requirements of FRS 1, which is covered in greater detail in ¶4000. The **specific requirements** in relation to charities are dealt with below. 9660

1. The **analysis of cash movements** should reflect the charity's operations as reported in the SOFA. The starting point is normally, the "net incoming/outgoing resources before other recognised gains or losses" (see ¶9515).
2. **Movements in endowments** should not be included in "cash flows from operating activities" but treated as increases or decreases in the financing section as follows:
a. cash donations to endowment funds should be treated as additions to endowments; and
b. the receipts and payments from the acquisition and disposal of investments should be shown gross under "capital expenditure and financial investments". A single line should be included in this section showing the net movement in cash flows relating to endowment investments. A corresponding row showing the same should be included in the financing section, reflecting the cash movements in and out of the endowment fund.

9661 The **disclosure requirements** of FRS 1 apply to charities with the most common being as follows:
1. Cash movements should be reconciled to the appropriate opening and closing balance sheet amounts; and
2. A reconciliation of "cash flows from operating activities" within the cash flow statement to the "net incoming resources/expenditure" row in the SOFA.

E. Trustees' Annual Report

9664 The Trustees' Annual Report (TAR) **must provide** a review of the management structure of the charity as well as its objectives, activities, funding requirements and performance over the financial year. A TAR **must be filed** by all registered charities whose gross income or total expenditure exceeds £25,000. Charities **not subject to** a statutory audit can produce an abbreviated TAR, the framework for which is set out in ¶9670. Additional disclosures are required by **larger charities** whose gross income exceeds £250,000 as they are subject to a statutory audit.

9665 The **legal requirement** for a TAR and its contents differ, according to the different charity reporting frameworks that apply within the separate legal jurisdictions in the UK (see appendix 1). Legal requirements and the Charity SORP do not limit the inclusion of other information within the TAR, such as a chairman's report or operating and financial review (OFR). The TAR should be attached to the financial statements. The deadline for filing the TAR with the Charities Commission is 10 months after the end of the financial year. **Charitable companies** must prepare a Directors' Report. A separate TAR is not required as long as the statutory Directors' Report contains all the information required in the TAR.

MEMO POINTS The TAR can now be submitted online via the Charities Commission Website.

9666 **Purpose** The purpose of the TAR is to discharge the charity's trustees' duty of public accountability and stewardship through the provision of information concerning:
– the progress made by the charity against its stated objectives;
– its financial position at the end of the financial year; and
– a review of its plans for the future.

9670 The Charity Commission has published new guidance for charity trustees, covering disclosures in the TAR, and in particular, the new requirements for **public benefit reporting**. The TAR must include a statement by the trustees confirming their compliance with section 4 of the Charities Act 2006, regarding the public benefit guidance published by the charity commission.

MEMO POINTS Two key principles underpin the notion of public benefit; namely that there must be an identifiable benefit and this must accrue to the public or section of the public.

Small charities that are **not subject to a statutory audit**, may limit the disclosures to a summary of the main achievements of the charity during the year. The public benefit reporting requirements are also less stringent.

The disclosure requirements for **larger charities** have been expanded to include a more detailed review of significant activities and strategy, including how the aims and objectives of the charity have been met. Additional disclosures are required for larger charities (depending on the size and complexity) as set out in the following table. **All charities** must confirm that they have considered the latest guidance on public benefit reporting.

Category	Small charities	Larger charities – additional disclosures
Administrative details	Include: name and registration number of charity, address of principal office, names of principal trustees.	1. Names of trustees in office at the date the TAR approved (First 50 Trustees only, including the principal officers such as the treasurer); 2. Where a trustee is a body corporate the names of the directors should be disclosed; 3. The name of the Chief Executive Officer or senior staff members; and 4. The names and addresses of principal advisors (e.g. bankers, solicitors).
Structure, governance and management	How charity is organised – decision making process. Method of recruiting trustees	Degree of detail dependent on size & complexity of charity. **Examples include**: – the nature of the governing document (e.g. trust deed, memorandum or articles of association, Royal Charter); – how the charity is constituted (e.g. limited company, unincorporated association, trustees incorporated as a body); – any related charities (subsidiaries) or organisations it cooperates with and their impact on operating policies; and – the major risks facing the charity and systems and procedures for managing the risks.
Objectives and activities	As set out in the governing document	Strategy review Means of achieving stated objectives Significant activities, programmes, projects
Performance review	Summary of the main activities and achievements of the charity (and any subsidiaries) during the financial year versus stated objectives	1. A summary of key performance indicators or benchmarks; 2. Details of material fundraising activities; 3. Information on material expenditures related to current and future income generation; 4. Details of performance of material investments held by the charity; and 5. A review of stakeholder relationships (e.g. employees, beneficiaries).
Financial review	Overview of the financial position of the charity and its subsidiaries as well as a statement of the principal financial policies. Details of any material funds in deficit and underlying reasons.	1. Level of reserves retained, the reasons why, and timescales governing expenditure; 2. Details of funds in deficit and reasons plus correction policies adopted; 3. Principal sources of funding; 4. How charity expenditure has furthered the key objectives of the charity; 5. For material investments, the investment policy and objectives including environmental or ethical investments; 6. Details of performance versus objectives.
Funds held as a Custodian Trustee	Details of assets held in this respect. Names and objectives of the charity (charities) on whose behalf the assets are held Security arrangements – safe custody and segregation of assets.	As for small charities

SECTION 3

Small charities, charitable companies and groups

A. Accounting for Smaller Charities

9678 Charities meeting the **threshold requirements** set out in ¶9509 can elect to produce cash-based receipts and payments accounts, although the charity SORP cannot be applied in this case. This **option is not available to** charitable companies who must prepare accruals accounts.

Smaller charities may also take advantage of a number of reporting concessions (including adoption of the FRSSE for accruals based accounts) when preparing financial reports.

MEMO POINTS Small charities with an annual income of less than £5,000 are not required to register with the charity commission (see ¶9504)

Cash-based receipts and payments accounts

9680 For **very small charities** with simple organisational structures and no principal assets except cash and deposit accounts, cash-based receipts and payments accounts will suffice, containing a summary of monies received and expended during the year and a list of assets at the end of the year. The issue of recognition is confined only to physical cash receipts and payments.

MEMO POINTS The Charity Commission has produced a format for preparing cash-based accounts which is set out in Appendix II.

FRSSE

9682 Charities meeting the threshold requirements for small companies and producing accrual accounts are free to adopt the FRSSE, **except where** this conflicts with the SORP, which takes preference.

The FRSSE is not applicable to charities producing cash-based accounts.

9683 A charity **adopting the FRSSE** will meet most of the requirements of the Charity SORP **except** in the following areas:
– investments including properties must be stated at market value.
– the profit and loss account and STRGL is replaced by the SOFA.
– foreign exchange gains or losses must be shown in the gains or losses section of the SOFA as the FRSSE **permits these differences** to be taken to reserves.

A charity should apply the accounting practice and disclosure requirements required by the accounting standards and the Charity SORP in relation to consolidated accounts.

B. Charitable companies

9690 In adopting the SORP, charitable companies meet most **but not all of the requirements** of the Companies Act and accounting standards, as they are not replicated in full. Charitable companies, irrespective of size, **must prepare** accrual based accounts. One of the best known examples of a charitable company is Cancer Research UK. A new legal form of charitable company known as a Charitable Incorporated Organisation has been introduced.

There are a number of **additional requirements** for charitable companies; namely that they must: 9692
1. Comply with the Companies Acts concerning the form and content of accounts, plus directors' report.
2. Apply the Companies Act financial statement formats and adapt headings and sub-headings where the special nature of the company's business so requires.
3. Include the names of its directors in the annual report as no exemption is permitted.
4. Give details of any material departures from the Charity SORP.
5. Disclose specific information relating to the revaluation reserve.
6. Where required, provide a summary income and expenditure account.

Summary income and expenditure account In a **minority of cases**, a charity may be required to prepare a summary income and expenditure account in addition to the SOFA; namely where: 9694
- the income and expenditure account cannot be identified within the SOFA due to the structure and headings adopted; or
- certain items are subject to challenge such as movements on endowment funds during the year.

Where a summary income and expenditure account is required, it should be derived from and cross-referenced to the corresponding figures in the SOFA. **A distinction need not be drawn between** unrestricted and restricted funds, but the accounting basis adopted must be the same as that for the SOFA, with a separate analysis of continuing operations, acquisitions and discontinued operations covering:
- gross income from all sources;
- transfers from endowment funds to income expendable;
- total income;
- total expenditure from the charity's income funds; and
- net income or expenditure for the year.

Revaluation reserve Charitable companies must give details of the revaluation reserve in respect of their unrestricted funds, on the face of the balance sheet. Where permitted under FRS 11 and FRS 15 (¶1348), impairment losses and downward revaluations can be off-set against the revaluation reserve. 9696

Charitable incorporated organisations (CIO)

Charities opting for a **corporate structure** have to register both as charities and companies and are subject to the regulatory requirements of both Companies House and the Charities Commission. 9697

The Charities Act 2006 created a new vehicle for these charities called "**The Charitable Incorporated Organisation" (CIO)**, which retains the advantages of a corporate structure such as reduced personal liability for trustees, whilst dispensing with the burden of dual recognition. This corporate form is now available to new charities wishing to register in England and Wales and to existing charities wishing to convert to this format. The Charity Commission is currently developing a model constitution for CIOs, following consultation and parliamentary approval.

CIOs have a number of **special features** that differentiate them from other forms of Not For Profit Organisations. 9698

Category	Special features
Single registration	CIOs report directly to the Charities Commission (and not Companies House, or the FSA). Recognised as separate legal entities and their members enjoy limited liability.
Accounting requirements	Less onerous than for companies – small CIOs can prepare receipts and payments accounts

Category	Special features
Filing requirements	Accounting and reporting and filing requirements are less onerous than those for companies in general
Constitution and governance	Governance reporting requirements less extensive than for companies. CIOs have simpler constitutional forms and there is a choice of formats and administration, available to suit organisations of all sizes.

9699 **Conversion to a CIO** Existing companies, already registered as charities or community interest companies, will be allowed to convert to CIOs through a **special conversion process**. Other types of charity (not incorporated) will also be able to convert to a CIO by setting up a new entity that subsequently acquires the existing charity's assets.

However, charitable companies or regulated societies with a share capital, including partly paid shares, will not be able to apply for conversion to a CIO. Whilst the Charities Act 2006 established a legal framework for CIOs, the detailed provisions will be developed by the Office of the Third Sector, in the form of regulations. However, it is expected that the thresholds that apply to non-company charities will also apply to CIOs, along with the accounting and reporting framework contained in the Charities Act 1993.

MEMO POINTS Plans to extend this conversion process to Industrial and Provident Societies are being considered.

C. Group accounting

9700 The SORP contains **additional requirements** for charities that may result from the specific nature of the legal or operating structures adopted, such as the consolidation of subsidiary undertakings and accounting for associates and joint ventures.

1. Consolidation of subsidiaries

9702 Charity SORP (384) A parent charity should prepare consolidated accounts for all its subsidiaries, **except where one of a small number of exemptions apply** as follows:

1. The gross income of the group, after consolidation adjustments, does not exceed the threshold for a statutory charity audit (£250,000).
2. The results of the subsidiary are immaterial relative to the size of the group.
3. A subsidiary is incorporated but subject to winding-up proceedings.

The **exemptions granted under FRS 2** permitting subsidiaries exclusion from consolidation (see ¶6570) are unlikely to apply to a charitable group.

9703 The **principles and methods** of consolidation are covered in more detail in ¶6570, and are applicable irrespective of whether the parent charity and its subsidiaries are incorporated or not. Although charities use subsidiaries for both profit and non-profit activities (e.g. non-trading or investment purposes), the distinction does not in itself determine whether or not consolidation is appropriate.

In general, the following **consolidation rules apply**:
- consolidation should be on a line-by-line basis (similar items matched);
- resources, whether incoming and expended should be shown gross; and
- all intra-group transactions should be cancelled.

9704 The **majority of unincorporated charitable subsidiaries** are aggregated within the accounts of the parent charity, as they are normally either restricted funds or endowment funds.

However, **where a charity controls another charitable entity** whose remit is wider than that of the parent charity, then consolidation will depend on the ability of the parent to control ("tests for control") the subsidiary.

Tests for control

Subsidiary undertakings **can be identified by** the measure of control enjoyed by one party over another, in the context of voting rights, participating interests and the exercise of dominant influence. 9706

Control arises in the following instances:
- the charity trustees, members or employees of the parent charity have the right to appoint or remove, the majority of the trustees of the charity; or
- the governing document of the subsidiary charity gives the parent charity's trustees or employees the right to direct or control the subsidiary charity.

Condition	Applying the test
Where the **parent is able to direct and benefit** from the activities of the subsidiary	Tests of control are met and the charitable subsidiary should be consolidated
Where the objectives of the subsidiary charity are **narrower** than those of the parent	Tests of control are met and the charitable subsidiary should be consolidated and accounted for in the restricted fund columns in the consolidated accounts
Where the objectives of the subsidiary charity are **substantially different** to those of the parent.	"Tests of control" will not be met – and the subsidiary should not be consolidated

Dominant influence may also be less formal. For instance, charities may be formed to support an established charity, and although they may remain a separate legal entity, they may be heavily influenced as to the timing and nature of this support. Where evidence of dominant influence exists, the criteria for consolidation should be deemed as having been met. 9708

A **similar type of relationship** to that of a parent and subsidiary undertaking arises where a parent charity transacting with another undertaking, retains the **risks and rewards** of the transaction. **An example is** a quasi-subsidiary, where assets are transferred to another entity, but the parent continues to use them and bears the costs of maintaining them. These undertakings should be accounted for in accordance with FRS 5 "Reporting the Substance of Transactions". 9710

Investment income

Where a parent charity receives investment income from **subsidiary undertakings**, the following accounting treatment is required: 9712

1. Payments to a charity by its subsidiary undertakings and dividend entitlements (other than amounts receivable by the charity for provision of goods and services) should be treated as incoming resources under investment income in the parent charity's accounts; and
2. Material gift aid payments from subsidiary undertakings must be separately disclosed in investment income in the SOFA.

Filing of accounts

In England and Wales it is a **statutory requirement** under the Charities Act 2006, that individual charity accounts be filed with the Charity Commission. Therefore, where the group and parent charity's accounts are consolidated, separate balance sheets and SOFAs should be provided for both the parent and the group. 9714

Where consolidated accounts **are filed without a SOFA** for the parent charity, details should be provided in the notes to the financial statements of gross income/turnover and the results of the parent charity. Furthermore, the group accounts should still contain the balance sheet for the parent charity.

Disclosures

9716 The key disclosure requirements **for subsidiary undertakings** should be given in the notes to the consolidated financial statements as follows:
- segmental information on the activities of material subsidiaries, including name, shareholding, aggregate amount of assets, liabilities and funds and a summary of turnover and profit or loss for the year;
- policy note covering the method of consolidation;
- details of excluded subsidiaries;
- aggregate amount of total investment in subsidiary undertakings;
- details of minority interests held in subsidiaries and restrictions placed on group activities;
- details of subsidiary undertaking excluded from consolidation; and
- details of funds and reserves retained by subsidiaries other than funds available for use in supporting a charity's objectives.

2. Branches

9720 A charity can operate and **raise funds through** branches, **which are defined as** entities or administrative bodies set up to undertake a particular aspect of the charity's work (e.g. geographical, specific type of fundraising). The branch may also:
- form part of the administrative structure of a reporting charity;
- represent a restricted fund or an endowment fund; or
- be a legal entity separate from the reporting charity.

9722 The most **common characteristics** of a branch are that it:
- uses the name of the reporting charity in its title;
- raises funds exclusively for the reporting charity and its own local needs;
- is covered by the reporting charity's registration number for tax purposes (i.e. tax relief);
- acts as a local representative for the reporting charity; and
- receives marketing and other support from the reporting charity (i.e. staff, funding).

9724 **Consolidation rules** The following rules also apply:
1. Branches **should be consolidated** with the accounts of the parent charity.
2. Where both the reporting charity and individual branches **are companies**, each entity must prepare financial statements. Consolidated accounts should be prepared in accordance with the rules outlined in ¶9690.
3. Where a branch **is not a separate legal entity**, its accounts must be consolidated with those of the parent charity.
4. Some charities may be termed branches within a particular organisational structure or network. However, where the branch **has a considerable degree of administrative autonomy** from the reporting charity, as set out in its founding document, it should not be consolidated and separate accounts should be prepared for submission to the regulatory authorities.

Accounting treatment

9728 1. **Inter-branch** transactions and **parent-branch** transactions should be eliminated on consolidation.
2. All **assets and liabilities** of a branch should be incorporated into the parent charity's balance sheet.
3. Funds raised by the branch for **the general charitable purposes** of the reporting charity, are accounted for as unrestricted funds in the parent charity's accounts.

4. Funds raised by the branch for **specific charitable purposes** of the reporting charity, are accounted for as restricted funds in the parent charity's accounts.
5. Where **a branch is a separate charity** and retains funds for general branch purposes, these should be accounted for as restricted funds in the reporting charity's accounts.

3. Associates and joint ventures (arrangements)

For the purposes of consolidated accounts, there are a number of additional accounting requirements where a charity has associates, joint ventures and joint arrangements. The **rules governing classification** of an entity or arrangement are covered in ¶7300, as is the accounting treatment and disclosure requirements for associates and joint arrangements. **9730**

Associates

A definition of "associates" is given in ¶7320. **9732**

Where a charity has a long-term **participating interest** (see ¶7326) in another undertaking and exercises **significant influence** (see ¶7338) over its operating and financial policies, it should be classified as an associate. Participating interest and significant influence are presumed where a charity holds 20% + of the voting rights in an entity, unless proved to the contrary.

EXAMPLE A large charity provided grants and advice and expertise to a small charity operating in a related area. The charity also nominated a trustee to sit on the board of the recipient charity, under a formal agreement to help formulate strategy and objectives. In this example, should the recipient charity be classified as an associate?
Yes. The recipient charity should be consolidated as it is small relative to the donor charity and the provision of expertise is linked to a formal agreement to exercise significant influence, through directing or influencing its financial and operating policies. If the donor charity had only provided expertise without attempting to influence policy, then associate status would not be appropriate.

Accounting treatment Associates are accounted for using the **net equity method** (see ¶7366). The following rules also apply: **9734**
1. The consolidated SOFA of the charity should show the net interest in the results for the year in the associates, as a separate row after "the net incoming/ (resources expended) before transfers".
2. In the balance sheet, the net interest in associates should be shown as a separate row within fixed asset investments.
3. If a charity's rights to the associate's assets are restricted, this should be accounted for in the valuation.

Joint ventures (arrangements)

A definition of "joint ventures" is given in ¶7410. **9736**

Where a charity holds 20% + of the voting rights in another legal undertaking, but where control is shared with other partners, the investment should be classified as a joint venture. Charities may also undertake joint arrangements covering shared activities without a separate legal entity being established.

Joint ventures should be accounted for using the **gross equity method** (see ¶7438). The charity should also declare:
– its share of the gross incoming resources for joint ventures on the face of the SOFA, on a line by line basis;
– the net interest in the results of joint ventures as a separate row after "net incoming resources/resources expended"; and
– in the balance sheet, the share of gross assets and liabilities should be shown with a linked presentation within fixed asset investments.

9738 **Joint arrangements** For joint arrangements, the charity's share of the incoming resources and resources expended should be included in the financial statements. In general, the accounting treatment is the same as for branches. Where the charity is liable for an obligation, it should accrue that part of the obligation for which it is responsible (contingent liability), with the remainder to be met by the other parties to the arrangement.

Disclosures

9739 The general disclosure requirements for associates and joint arrangements are covered in ¶7494.

The following **additional disclosures** are required for charities:
- name of organisation;
- the parent charity's shareholding and other interests;
- details of associate or joint venture activity;
- parent charity's share of results covering gross income resources by type, cost of generating funds;
- expenditure on charitable activities, and expenses on governance;
- gains or losses on investments;
- share of any unrealised gains on fixed assets;
- liabilities analysed between less than one year and more than one year;
- types of funds managed by the charity;
- contingent liabilities and other commitments, including those made by the charity to a joint arrangement; and
- its share of pre and post-tax results.

For **joint arrangements**, details should be given of the obligations/commitments made by the charity to the arrangement.

D. Audit and independent examination thresholds

9744 The Charities Act 2006 has simplified the rules stipulating when an external professional audit is required, as set out in the table below. Charitable companies that were exempt from audit under the Companies Act will now be covered by this Act.

Gross annual income thresholds	
1. Non-charitable companies	**Audit/examination requirements**
Less than £25,000	Independent examination not required
Between £25,000 and £500,000	Independent examination required. If income is above 250k, the examiner must be qualified.
£500,000 + or total net assets in excess of 3.6m + gross annual income of £250,000 +	Full audit required
2. Charitable companies	**Audit/examination requirements**
Gross income less than £500,000 + net assets less than £3.6m	Independent examination by a qualified person
£500,000 + or B/S total (3.6m +)	Full audit required

MEMO POINTS 1. The Audit Practices Board has issued a bulletin (APB PN 105 – Bulletin 2009/1) covering the type of audit reports required by UK charities. The bulletin reflects changes introduced under the Companies Act 2006 and the Charities Act 2006 and supplements the guidance contained in Practice Note 11 "The Audit of UK Charities". The Bulletin provides advice and examples on the wording of an auditor's report, that reflects the increasing complexity of the legal environment in which charities operate. Copies of the bulletin can be downloaded from the APB website.

2. The APB has also issued Bulletin 2009/3 (APB PN 109) updating its illustrative examples of auditors' reports, to show the interaction between charity legislation and the Companies Act 2006.

SECTION 4

Registered social landlords

A. Introduction

Registered social landlords, like any other accounting entity, are required to present their financial statements in accordance with companies legislation and the various elements of GAAP. As with most specialised sectors, additional rules and regulations apply together with – and sometimes instead of – the general rules. For instance, the Housing Corporation in England, under powers conferred upon it by the Housing Act 1996, makes a General Determination of the accounting requirements applicable to social landlords. Similarly, other jurisdictions issue their own General Determinations or Orders. **9750**

The format of the financial statements of a registered social landlord is, in the first place, dependent on the requirements of these Determinations/Orders – as follows: **9752**

Location	Applicable Determination/Order	Effective on/after
England	The 2006 Determination	1 January 2006
Scotland	The Scottish 2007 Order	1 April 2007
Wales	The Accounting requirements for Social Landlords Registered in Wales – General Determination	21 March 2000
Northern Ireland	The Northern Ireland 1993 Order	1 April 1993

In addition, to recommend **preferred accounting treatments** and achieve consistency, three bodies – the National Housing Federation, Community Housing Cymru, and the Scottish Federation of Housing Associations – have jointly issued a SORP, "Accounting by Registered Social Landlords 2008". An updated version was published in October 2010. The most significant areas of technical amendment concern:

– **component accounting and works to existing properties**, and
– **business combinations**, particularly the treatment of non-exchange transactions and negative goodwill.

The main requirement of the SORP is that the financial statements should show a true and fair view.

MEMO POINTS The relationship between the Determination/Order and the SORP is that the former represents the **legal requirements** while the latter represents the **recommended practice**.

The notes to the accounts are required to state whether the financial statements have been prepared in accordance with applicable accounting standards and statements of recommended practice. The SORP should therefore be regarded as the applicable statement. **9754**

MEMO POINTS Where a social landlord is a charity **registered with one of the social housing regulatory bodies**, it must follow the SORP for registered social landlords rather than the Charities SORP because the latter specifically notes that, where a more specialised SORP exists, it should be followed.

B. Scope

9758 The SORP applies to the financial statements of all registered social housing providers, charitable and non-charitable, except for co-ownership societies (see ¶9760 for definition).

Any additional accounting practices set out in the 2010 SORP should be applied to accounting periods beginning on or after 1 April 2011 (though earlier adoption is encouraged).

C. Definitions

9760 For convenience, selected terms, with specific relevance to the SORP, are defined below. A comprehensive list of definitions can be found in the SORP.

Carrying value: the amount at which a balance sheet item is shown in the accounts.

Class of properties: a category of property assets having a similar nature, function or use in the business of a social landlord.

Co-ownership society: a social landlord registered with the Financial Services Authority, the rules of which provide that:
(1) membership is restricted to tenants or prospective tenants and preclude the granting of tenancies to anyone other than members, and
(2) members are entitled, on ceasing to be members, to a sum calculated on the value of the relevant housing accommodation.

First tranche disposal: the initial portion of a shared ownership property sold to the lessee (in Scotland, this is sold to a "sharing owner", rather than a lessee).

Homebuy: a programme of loans to purchasers currently funded by the Welsh Assembly Government; in England, New Build HomeBuy was launched by the Department for Communities and Local Government as one of its three new low-cost ownership products under the HomeBuy initiative.

Housing properties: properties held by social landlords primarily for the purpose of housing.

Impairment: a reduction in the recoverable amount of a fixed asset below its carrying value.

Registered social landlord: a social landlord which is registered in one of the registers maintained by: the Tenant Services Authority or the Welsh Assembly Government for Wales under the Housing Act 1996 as amended; Scottish Housing Regulator under the Housing (Scotland) Act 2001; or the Department for Social Development (Northern Ireland) under the Housing (Northern Ireland) Order 1992. Under current legislation in Northern Ireland, these are only housing associations.

Shared ownership: housing schemes in which the social landlord has granted a shared ownership lease as defined in section 622 of the Housing Act 1985 (in England, Wales and Northern Ireland) and, in Scotland, schemes approved in accordance with Scottish Homes guidance note 2000/05 and allowable under article 58 of the Housing (Scotland) Act 2001.

D. Presentation of financial statements

9764 All financial statements must include:
1. an **income and expenditure** account,
2. a **balance sheet**,
3. a **statement of total recognised surpluses and deficits** or a **note of historical cost surpluses and deficits** (if different),

4. a **cash flow** statement,
5. **notes** to the accounts,

and each is discussed in turn below.

In accordance with FRS 28, **comparative figures** for the preceding accounting period must be given in respect of all items in the financial statements.

1. Income and expenditure account

The following is the layout of a typical income and expenditure account, and is consistent with Format 1 of the Companies Act. **9766**

Income and Expenditure Account for the year ended 31 December 2X10

	2X10	2X09
	£ 000	£ 000
Turnover[1]	XXX	XXX
Less: Operating costs[2]	XX	XX
Operating surplus	XXX	XXX
Profit/(loss) on sale of fixed assets	X	-
Interest payable	-	(X)
Other financing income/(costs)	X	X
Surplus on ordinary activities before taxation	XX	XX
Tax on surplus on ordinary activities	X	X
Surplus for the year	XX	XX

[1] **Turnover** – Turnover should be disclosed as set out in the Determination/Order; the requirements vary with the size of the social landlord and range and level of its activities. Turnover should represent income receivable net of rent and service-charge losses from voids. However, rent and service-charge losses from bad debts should be included within operating costs.

[2] **Operating costs** – Disclosure of the breakdown of operating costs varies according to the size of the landlord and the range and level of its activities.

Proceeds from **first tranche disposals** (i.e., the initial portion of a shared ownership property sold to the lessee) must be accounted for in the income and expenditure account of the period in which the disposal occurs. So too must **surpluses on disposal** be recognised there. **Cost of sales** includes costs of executing the sale including marketing and a proportion of those overall costs of bringing the asset to its saleable condition. **9768**

Sales proceeds for the first tranche sales only should be shown in **turnover**. The split between completed shared ownership properties and those under construction should be shown in a **note to the accounts** – as should the split between completed shared ownership properties and those that are work in progress. **9770**

Subsequent tranche disposals are accounted for in the income and expenditure account of the period in which the disposal occurs, at the difference between the corresponding tranche proportion of the net sale proceeds and the net carrying value. **9772**

The changes relating to shared ownership sales introduced by the 2008 SORP constitute a change in accounting policy and a prior-period adjustment must be disclosed. **9774**

2. Balance sheet

The following is the layout of a typical balance sheet, and is consistent with the General Determination 2006 issued by the Housing Corporation. **9776**

Balance Sheet at 31 December 2X10

	2X10		2X09	
	£ 000	£ 000	£ 000	£ 000
Fixed assets				
Housing properties at valuation/cost	XX		XX	
Social Housing Grant	(X)		(X)	
Other capital grants	(X)		(X)	
Net book value of housing properties		**XX**		**XX**
Intangible fixed assets	X		X	
Fixed asset investments	X		X	
Homebuy loan	X		X	
Homebuy grant	(X)		(X)	
		XX		XX
Other fixed assets		X		X
Total fixed assets		**XX**		**XX**
Current assets				
Debtors	X		X	
Investments	X		X	
Cash at bank and in hand	X		X	
Creditors: amounts falling due within one year	(X)		(X)	
Net current assets excluding pension asset		**XX**		**XX**
Pension asset		X		X
Net current assets including pension asset		**XX**		**XX**
Total assets less current liabilities		**XX**		**XX**
Creditors: amounts falling due after more than one year	X		X	
Other long-term creditors	X		X	
Provisions for liabilities and charges	X		X	
Capital and reserves				
Revaluation reserves		XX		XX
Designated reserves		XX		XX
Restricted reserves		XX		XX
Revenue reserve		XX		XX
Pension reserve		XX		XX
		XX		XX

Housing properties

9778 Housing properties should be shown in the notes and analysed by class (e.g., **held for letting**, **shared ownership**, and **other**). Completed schemes and properties under construction should be separately disclosed by class.

9780 All shared ownership properties, including those under construction, should be split between fixed and current assets. The split is made according to the percentage of the property to be sold under a first tranche sale, shown on initial recognition as a current asset, the remainder being fixed. The value at initial recognition should be allocated to current assets (first tranche sales) and fixed assets (sales of subsequent tranches) in proportion to the share of equity sold.

MEMO POINTS This treatment should not be followed if a surplus would result on the disposal of the current asset that would exceed the expected overall surplus.

Social housing grants (SHG) receivable should be set against the applicable fixed asset, unless the grant (or any element of it) is given specifically in respect of revenue items (see also ¶9794). 9782

Properties developed for outright sale and those developed for sale to other bodies are treated as **current assets** – and shown at the lower of cost or net realisable value. 9784

Housing property book values Housing properties should be disclosed in the balance sheet at historical cost less SHG and depreciation or at current value on balance sheet date ("valuation"). Where properties are at historical cost, any impairment must be provided for. Detailed reviews for impairment should be carried out only when there is an indication that impairment has occurred. Where impairment is indicated, it is measured as follows: 9786

Carrying value (historical or "valuation")		XXX
Less: the higher of:		
(1) Net realisable value	XX	
or (2) Value in use	XX	XX
		XXX

Impairments resulting from a major reduction in the service potential of the property should be recognised in the **income and expenditure account**, while those that reflect general changes in price should, if the properties are shown at valuation, be recognised in the statement of total recognised surpluses and deficits to the extent that the value falls to depreciated historical cost. Further impairments are recognised in the income and expenditure account.

The **depreciable amount of housing properties** is written off in the income and expenditure in a manner that reflects the pattern over their useful economic life. 9788

Depreciation is based on the amount at which properties are carried in the balance sheet. Freehold land should not be depreciated; therefore land and buildings are treated separately for depreciation purposes.

At the end of each reporting period the **useful economic life** of properties should be reviewed and, if expectations are found to have changed materially, the carrying amount must be depreciated over the remaining useful economic life.

If the **residual values** of properties are material, they should be reviewed at the end of each balance sheet period; changes should be accounted for over the properties' remaining useful lives unless they have been impaired.

Where properties are held at a **valuation** and depreciation is required, a transfer should be made from the revaluation reserve to a **revenue reserve**. The transfer should be the difference between actual depreciation charged and depreciation calculated on historical cost. This should be shown in the notes as a movement between reserves.

Development costs of properties should be capitalised, but only those costs directly attributable to bringing the properties into working condition should be added to the purchase price to arrive at the total cost. No further costs should be capitalised once the properties are substantially complete and ready for use. 9790

Interest on capital borrowed to **finance a development**, to the extent that it relates to the period of development, may be capitalised. The amount of interest capitalised should be disclosed in the notes as a deduction from total interest paid during the period.

Component accounting and works to existing properties The 2010 SORP proposed clearer guidance on the applicability of component accounting when accounting for works to existing properties. Social landlords should in general follow FRS 15 in deciding which items are capitalised, and which should be charged against income. 9791

Items representing works to existing properties should be charged to the income and expenditure account unless they result in an enhancement of the economic benefits of the property (in other words, an increase in the net rental stream over the life of the property).
Under FRS 15, landlords should capitalise works to existing properties in the following three circumstances:
– where a component of the tangible fixed asset that has been treated separately for depreciation purposes and depreciated over its individual useful economic life is replaced or restored;
– where the subsequent expenditure provides an enhancement of the economic benefits of the tangible fixed asset in excess of the previously assessed standard of performance;
– where the subsequent expenditure relates to a major inspection or overhaul of a tangible fixed asset that restores the economic benefits of the asset that have been consumed by the entity and have already been reflected in depreciation.

Any works that do not replace a component or result in an enhancement of economic benefits should be charged against income – for instance, expenditure incurred to ensure the property is able to **maintain its existing level** of net rental income or the standard of performance envisaged when the asset was first acquired or constructed.

MEMO POINTS Social landlords should make sure that their accounting policy for works to existing properties is made clear, and how amounts to be capitalised are determined (including a table of components capitalised and their estimated useful lives for depreciation purposes).

9792 Where a housing property comprises **two or more major components** with substantially different useful economic lives, each component must be accounted for – and depreciated – separately. Component accounting, if adopted, must be applied consistently to all assets in the same class. Land should always be dealt with as a separate asset.

Component accounting is not applicable where the rights and obligations in respect of improving the property fall to leaseholders or tenants.

Social housing grants (SHG)

9794 SHG awarded as a contribution to the capital costs of a social landlord should, where the properties concerned are shown at historical cost, be shown as a deduction from this cost on the face of the balance sheet. Furthermore, SHG should be shown separately from other grants even if the treatment of the other grants is the same (i.e., also treated as a deduction from the cost of housing properties).

If a scheme has reached the point at which a further tranche of SHG is receivable, but has not been received, the amount receivable at balance sheet date should be shown in debtors. In situations where SHG received in relation to a development programme exceeds development expenditure, the amount should be included in creditors.

Investments

9796 How to **classify** investments depends on the intention: if it is to realise the investment in the short term, without reinvesting the sales proceeds in the long term, the investments are current assets.
Investments other than housing properties should be shown at market value, but if this cannot be determined, the board should give its best estimate of market value. Where investments are **revalued upwards**, this should be reported in the statement of total recognised surpluses and deficits (and not the income and expenditure account). The credit should be allocated to a separate **investment revaluation reserve**.

Provisions

9798 Provisions should be raised in circumstances where a liability actually exists but where there is some **uncertainty** as to the timing or sums involved or to the identity of the creditor.

Where there is an **onerous contract** (defined at ¶3275) it should be measured and recognised as a provision.

Deferred tax

Social landlords should recognise deferred tax in respect of all **timing differences** that have not reversed by balance sheet date. 9800

3. Statement of total recognised surpluses and deficits and/or Note of historical cost surpluses and deficits

The following are example layouts of the two statements. 9810

Statement of total recognised surpluses and deficits
For the year ended at 31 December 2X10

	2X10	2X09
	£ 000	£ 000
Surplus for the year	XX	XX
Unrealised surplus/(deficit) on revaluation of housing properties	X	X
Deferred tax	(X)	(X)
Unrealised surplus/(deficit) on investments	X	(X)
Actual return less expected return on pension scheme assets	X	X
Experience gains and losses arising on scheme liabilities	X	X
Effect of changes in actuarial assumptions	(X)	(X)
Total recognised surpluses and deficits for the year	XX	XX
	X	–
Total surpluses and deficits recognised since last reporting period	XX	XX

MEMO POINTS If there are no recognised surpluses or losses other than those included in the income and expenditure account, this fact should be disclosed on the face of that statement and a *Statement of total recognised surpluses and deficits* need not be presented.

The note of historical cost surpluses and deficits takes the following form: 9812

Note of historical cost surpluses and deficits
For the year ended at 31 December 2X10

	2X10	2X09
	£ 000	£ 000
Reported surplus on ordinary activities before taxation	X	X
Realisation of property revaluation surpluses in previous years [1]	X	X
Difference between historical cost depreciation and actual depreciation calculated on revaluation amount	X	X
Historical cost surplus on ordinary activities before taxation	X	(X)
Historical cost surplus for the year after taxation and extraordinary items	X	X

[1] Applies only to social landlords engaged in property sales.

4. Cash flow statement

A cash flow statement must be produced by: 9820
- all developing social landlords,
- all social landlords managing more than 500 units, and
- if required by FRS 1.

A sample cash flow statement is shown below:

Cash Flow Statement for the year ended 31 December 2X10

	2X10		2X09	
	£ 000	£ 000	£ 000	£ 000
Net cash flow from operating activities				
Returns on investment and servicing of finance				
Interest received	X		X	
Interest paid	(X)		(X)	
Net cash outflows from returns on investment and servicing of finance		X		X
Taxation				
Corporation tax paid	(X)		(X)	
less: grants received	X		X	
Net cash outflow from taxation		(X)		(X)
Capital expenditure and financial investment				
Acquisition and construction of properties	(X)		(X)	
Purchase of other fixed assets	(X)		(X)	
Capital grants received	X		X	
Sales of properties	X		X	
Sales of other fixed assets	X		X	
Net cash outflow from capital expenditure		(X)		(X)
Net cash outflow before use of liquid resources and financing		(X)		(X)
Management of liquid resources		(X)		(X)
Financing				
Loan advances received	X		X	
Loan principal repayments	(X)		(X)	
Loan redemption payments	(X)		(X)	
Net cash outflow from financing		X		X
Increase in cash in the period		X		X

MEMO POINTS Only the headings shown in bold type are required to be disclosed on the face of the cash flow statement. Other items may be shown by way of note.

5. Notes to the accounts

9824 The following specific treatments are recommended by the SORP and are in addition to the general requirements of GAAP.

Accounting policies

9826 For all material items, accounting policies must be adopted that:
– are considered most appropriate to the particular circumstances and give a true and fair view;
– ensure that financial statements are prepared on the accruals basis (except for the cash flow statement) as a going concern (unless the social landlord is being liquidated or has ceased trading or where either of these is unavoidable);
– are consistent with GAAP (i.e., accounting standards, UITF abstracts and legislation); in addition, specific mention should be made as to whether the statements have been prepared in accordance with the SORP (if they have not, reasons should be given);
– are reviewed periodically to ensure their continued appropriateness (where changes are made to accounting policies adopted, details as to why the new ones are considered more appropriate, together with the effect on both the current and the prior years).

Related parties

Relationships between parents and subsidiaries must be disclosed irrespective of whether there have been transactions between those related parties. 9830

If a social landlord is controlled by another party, the relationship should be disclosed. The name of that party and, if different, that of the ultimate controlling party should also be disclosed. Where the controlling party is not known, that fact should be disclosed.

FRS 8 requires material transactions between the reporting entity and a related party to be disclosed, even in cases where a price is not charged. Such disclosures are to include: 9832
a) the names of the parties,
b) a description of the relationship between the parties,
c) a description of the transaction/s,
d) the amounts involved,
e) any other elements of the transaction/s necessary for an understanding of the financial statements,
f) amounts due to or from related parties at the balance sheet date and the provisions for doubtful debts due from such parties,
g) amounts written off in the period in respect of debts due to or from related parties.

Similar items may be disclosed in aggregate except where separate disclosure is necessary for an understanding of the effects of related party transactions on the financial statements of the entity. 9834

In normal circumstances, the disclosure of details of rents and year-end arrears of tenant board members are not required – unless the levels or policies in respect of tenant board members are not on normal commercial terms (or where they differ materially from those relating to non-board members). In such cases, disclosures are required.

MEMO POINTS All board members are related parties. If some members of the board are also tenants, leaseholders or other customers of the social landlord, that fact should be noted. In addition, a statement that their tenancies are on normal commercial terms, and that they cannot use their position to their advantage, must, if appropriate, also be made. Similarly, if some board members are also councillors or employees of related public or commercial entities, or of local authorities, this must be disclosed together with a statement that any transactions with such entities are made at arm's length and on normal commercial terms.

Share capital

Because the rights conferred by the share capital of social landlords are generally subject to limitations, such shares are not ordinarily defined as financial instruments under FRS 25. 9836

The following disclosure should therefore be made in respect of these limitations:
– the absence of rights to a dividend
– the absence of any provision for redemption
– the absence of any provision for a distribution on winding up
– voting rights.

MEMO POINTS If it is the case that voting rights are not restricted, consideration should be given as to whether classification as debt or equity, in accordance with FRS 25, is appropriate in the circumstances.

Cash balances

Cash deposits charged as security for loans are unavailable for general use. These should be disclosed in the notes. 9838

Housing Loans

Housing loans should be split and reflected in the notes according to amounts falling due based on the lender's earliest repayment date as follows: 9840
– less than one year (or on demand),
– one year or more but less than two,

– two years or more but less than five,
– five years or more.

If any debt has a **legal nature** different from normal debts (e.g., subordinated debt), this fact should be noted.

If **loans** have been **redeemed**, the full cost of any redemption penalty should be recognised in the income and expenditure account (if material, as a separate item).

9842 Where social landlords participate in **Homebuy schemes** (in Scotland: Homestart schemes) the loans should be treated as a fixed asset investment and carried at historical cost.

6. Operating and financial review (OFR) and board report

9844 Social landlords managing more than 5,000 units should, as a matter of **best practice**, publish an OFR with the financial statements. Smaller landlords are **encouraged** to do likewise.

9845 The **purpose** of the OFR is to help users in their assessment of the social landlord's future performance by setting out the board's analysis of its business. As such, it should focus on those matters the board considers to be significant to the business as a whole, and should discuss:
– the **nature** of the business, its **objectives**, and the **strategies** adopted to achieve them;
– the **performance** of the social landlord and the main influences on performance, including the possible effect of known trends and risks;
– the **financial position** (including capital structure and treasury policy) and factors likely to affect that position.

The OFR may be of particular relevance to social landlord's funders and supporters but is of interest to a wide range of users – e.g., tenants, service users, local authorities, business partners.

9846 To ensure **reliability**, the information in the OFR should be neutral, complete, free from bias, and even-handed. Similarly, to ensure **comparability**, the disclosures should be sufficient to allow users to compare information given with similar information in respect of previous periods, but also with respect to other social landlords or bodies providing social housing. Comparability will also be enhanced if the **financial and non-financial measures** underpinning the OFR (see ¶4721) are adopted universally.

SECTION 5

Higher education institutions

9850 Higher education institutions (HEFE) are established under Royal Charter, Act of Parliament or other statutory instruments. The main activities are teaching, research and ancillary activities such as the provision of student accommodation, catering, medical and conference facilities. Teaching covers full and part-time courses, training and continuing vocational and recreational education for adults.

Higher education institutions encompass universities and colleges that differ in their size and complexity and although the majority have **charitable status**, they still fall outside the scope of the Charities SORP. This is because the HEFE sector has certain financial and reporting issues that are different from other charities, and as such, a specific SORP has been developed for this sector.

9852 In general, the financial statements of all UK HEFE institutions should be prepared on a similar basis to other corporate organisations, following all relevant accounting standards and abstracts. In addition, these institutions must meet any additional requirements of the

Higher Education SORP, UK Funding Bodies (e.g. Research council), charity regulators, and other stakeholders.

Where an institution or its subsidiary **is registered as a company**, the financial statements should be prepared in accordance with the Companies Act. Where a **subsidiary undertaking** is registered as a company, the financial statements should also comply with the disclosure requirements of the Charity SORP.

In the UK, the number of students enrolling at universities and colleges of higher education is on the increase at both undergraduate and post-graduate level, as well as across the age demographic. As a consequence, there has been a significant increase in tuition fee income, particularly from increasing numbers of overseas students. However, the bulk of the income at the disposal of the HEFEs still comes from research grants and contracts. As a consequence, these institutions have in recent years, started to develop increasingly diverse income streams in an attempt to reduce dependence on public funding. 9853

A. Income recognition

Educational institutions typically receive income from **three principal sources** as set out in the table below. 9860 HEFE SORP (9)

The **general rule** is that revenue should only be recognised when a "right to consideration exists", based on the performance of a contractual obligation. Payments received in advance of the contractual criteria being met should be accounted for in the balance sheet as liabilities. HEFE SORP (50-51)

MEMO POINTS Income recognition in general is covered by UITF Abstract 40 "Revenue recognition and service contracts" and Application Note G to FRS 5 "Revenue Recognition" (see ¶520 for more detail).

9862

Category	Description	Type of income
Generated income	Tuition fees, commercial based research services, consultancy, conference and accommodation facilities, and catering.	Unrestricted
Public funding	Public funds (direct grants from specific funding bodies, research council grants, non-UK public sector bodies, and government departments or agencies)	Restricted/unrestricted
Donated income	Bequests, endowments and donations.	Restricted/unrestricted

1. Generated income

Generated income can be applied at the discretion of the educational institute. 9864

Type of generated income	Income recognition
Normal tuition fees	Recognised when right to consideration exists and contractual performance has occurred. Rebates: Determine the substance of the transaction. Where fees are reduced or the right of consideration to do so exists, income shown net.
Rental income	Rents generated from university/college student accommodation; – accommodation provided for summer conferences, courses, seminars and other adult education courses.
Retail	Revenues from student canteens, restaurants, shops etc.
Consultancy income	Consultancy services including training courses for private enterprises

2. Public funds

9865 Public funds include direct grants from specific funding bodies, research council grants, non-UK public sector bodies, and government departments or agencies. The range of grants is often diverse and reflects changes in the research priorities by governments. These grants can either be unrestricted or awarded with conditions attached (restricted).

3. Donated income

9866 HEFE SORP (137-140) Donated income includes bequests, endowments and other types of donations (e.g. telemarketing appeal monies). Donated income can also be classified as either "restricted" or "unrestricted", based on a distinction made in the HEFE SORP.

Each donation or other fundraising income must be reviewed to assess the general conditions or specific criteria attached to them, as different accounting treatments will apply.

Income **donated without restrictions** should be recorded in the income and expenditure account.

a. Restricted funds

9868 Income may be designated for specific purposes by a grant funding body or donor and can include research grants, contracts and restricted endowment income or charitable donations. The most common type of restricted funds is an endowment, which can be further sub-classified into expendable and permanent endowments.

HEFE SORP (138) Restricted income is only credited to the income and expenditure account when the terms for receipt of the income have been met.

Where the donation is given for a **specific purpose**, the donation should not be accumulated but utilised as soon as practically possible. Where expenditure exceeds the donation, general funds should be added, as it is an underlying principle of charity law that income is spent within a reasonable period of time.

However, where the institution has **material donations** in the form of legacies etc, which have not been recognised in their income and expenditure account, details should be given in the notes to the accounts.

Expendable endowment funds

9870 HEFE SORP (147) Endowment funds are a **form of charitable trust** to be maintained for the benefit of the educational institution for a specific purpose. As such these funds are categorised as restricted.

Expendable funds **differ from permanent endowment funds** in that the trustees can convert the endowed capital into income if required. Should this happen, the relevant amount should be transferred from endowment funds to the general reserve. Expendable endowment funds should be distinguished from permanent endowment funds on the face of the balance sheet.

Permanent endowment funds

9872 HEFE SORP (145) Permanent endowment funds typically comprise a capital part, which is invested to produce a constant income stream, and an accumulated income fund. The capital part of the endowment fund must be **permanently maintained** and protected.

The assets making up the endowment fund take the form of cash, bonds, equities or investment property and land. In some cases the trust could also be responsible for maintaining a specific asset such as a historic building.

The value of endowment assets must equal the total of endowment funds shown in reserves, thereby matching assets and funds.

Permanent endowment funds **must not be used** to cover general expenditure or award grants to third parties. This differentiates them from expendable endowment funds. The **exception to this rule** is costs related to professional investment management fees for assets held in the fund. Income generated by the fund can however, be used for more general purposes depending on the wishes of the donor or reinvested to grow the fund.

Asset exchange However, the **concept of "permanence"** does not mean that the assets held in the endowment cannot be exchanged or a different mix of assets held. The assets may also be subject to depreciation or impairment. 9874 HEFE SORP (146)

Exchange is taken to mean:

– the replacing of an asset with another of similar value; or

– the application of sale proceeds of freehold land and buildings for the purchase or upgrade of other properties.

Management of investments

Income from investments and increases or decreases in capital arising from the realisation or revaluation of investments held in endowment funds, should be accounted for as set out in the table below. 9878

HEFE SORP (113)

Category	Accounting treatment
Income from fixed asset investments, endowment assets or current asset investments	1. Income recorded in the income and expenditure account, under the category "Endowments and investment income" 2. Where income is generated by investments held in restricted funds – credit the income and expenditure account as a credit when donor conditions have been met 3. **Income earned in excess** of that which should be used for the purposes specified by the fund, should be transferred from the income and expenditure account to accumulated income within endowment funds in the balance sheet, as the institution should not utilise this income for its general purposes
Listed investments held as fixed assets or endowments	Record at market value
Fixed asset investment revaluations	Increase = Credit revaluation reserve via STRGL Decrease = Debit income and expenditure account to the extent it is not covered by a previous revaluation surplus
Current asset investments including listed investments	Recorded at lower of cost or NRV
Endowment asset revaluations	Increase/decrease in value of endowment assets = debit/credit endowment asset and credit/debit the endowment fund. Also show in STRGL
Gains or losses on sale of fixed assets	Gains/losses should be retained in the endowment fund in the balance sheet
Investment properties	Land and buildings – record in balance sheet at market valuation. No depreciation charged
Investments in subsidiaries	Show at cost, subject to a review for impairment
Investments in associates	Record in the consolidated balance sheet at attributable share of net assets

b. Summary

A summary of the different accounting treatments applicable to charitable donations in this sector are set out in the table below. 9890

HEFE SORP (136)

Unrestricted (General)	Accounting treatment
Income expendable	Record as a donation in the Income and Expenditure Account
Capital element must be preserved	Permanent endowment – balance sheet
Restricted (Specific)	
Expendable only when certain **donor specified criteria** met (expendable endowment fund)	Create a expendable endowment – balance sheet
Capital element maintained + but income earned thereon is expendable only on donor specified purposes	Record as a permanent endowment fund – balance sheet
Donation for purchase/construction of **fixed assets**	Recognise as a deferred capital grant in the balance sheet. The deferred capital grant should be released to income and expenditure account over estimated useful economic life of asset.
Donation for purchase of land	For purchase of land – retain in deferred capital grant fund until purchase complete – then released and credited to the income and expenditure account as a donation in other income
Where institution has **power to expend capital part** of the endowment fund	Account for as an endowment fund

B. Specific accounting issues

Bursaries and scholarships

9894 Bursaries and scholarships represent payments to students from the institution's own funds, depending on certain criteria. As such bursaries/scholarships should be accounted for gross, as expenditure is netted-off fee income. Where these are paid from endowment funds, special accounting and disclosure requirements apply.

Agency arrangements

9896 Where the institution is acting as an agent it will not normally be exposed to the risks and benefits associated with a given transaction. The **general rule** is that, where an institution distributes funds to third parties on behalf of a funding authority, and has no beneficial interest or related risk, then this income should be excluded from the institutions income and expenditure account.

However, any **commissions received** whilst acting as an agent should be included as income. Disclosure is by way of a memorandum note, showing movements on agency funds during the year and any unspent balances at the year end.

Tangible fixed assets

9898 Where an institution has **inherited fixed assets** (e.g. from a local authority), these assets should be included in the balance sheet at valuation on the date of receipt.

Donated tangible fixed assets should be valued and credited to deferred capital grants with the debit to the relevant fixed asset category of the balance sheet.

Future valuations should reflect the accounting policy adopted by the institution under FRS 15. In **exceptional circumstances** where a reliable valuation cannot be obtained, or the cost of so doing is prohibitive, the asset may be excluded from capitalisation.

Land that is donated to the institution should also be valued but the credit should be to the income and expenditure account as a donation in other income.

MEMO POINTS The accounting treatment for tangible fixed assets in general, including heritage assets, is dealt with in some detail in Part 3 Chapter 4.

Website development costs

Website design and content costs should not be capitalised. The exception is where HEFEs have designed a website to provide specific training courses or course modules, or for specific research projects. As such, any design or content costs can be capitalised in accordance with UITF Abstract 29 "Website development costs", and amortised over the useful economic life of the project. 9900 HEFE SORP (107)

Where there is uncertainty over the viability or duration of the course or project, then all costs should be expensed as incurred. Maintenance and operating costs should also be charged to the income and expenditure account as incurred.

C. Disclosure requirements

Funding bodies normally issue an annual accounts direction requiring an institution's accounts to be prepared in accordance with the higher education SORP, as well as detailing any additional disclosures required in excess of those outlined in the SORP and UK GAAP in general. 9910

Every educational institution should prepare: 9912 HEFE SORP (15)
- annual financial statements prepared on an accruals basis (see ¶9302);
- analysis of income and major expenditure in the accounting period (see example below);
- a statement of responsibilities of the governing body (governance) (see example below);
- assets and liabilities classified in accordance with the HEFE SORP;
- details of its working capital position and investment performance;
- an Operating and Financial Review (OFR) (see ¶4700). The OFR may also take the form of a treasurer's report, members' report, directors' report or report of the governing body and cover accounting policies, segmental reporting, fund peformance etc; and
- an independent auditors' report.

EXAMPLE **Casterbridge University**
Income and expenditure account (extract)

	Note	2010	2009
Income		**£'000**	**£'000**
Funding council grants	1	117.0	107.8
Academic fees and support grants	2	112.4	101.6
Research grants and contacts	3	78.2	66.1
Other operating income	4	43.6	41.9
Endowment income and interest	5	31.2	21.5
Total income		**382.4**	**345.9**
Expenditure			
Staff costs		220.1	200.0
Depreciation		12.5	10.9
Other operating expenses		147.2	139.7
Interest payable		3.5	3.3
Total expenditure		**383.3**	**353.9**
Deficit for the year		**(0.9)**	**(8.0)**

Notes

1. Funding council grants	**HEFC £'000**	**TTA £'000**	**Total £'000**
Recurrent grants	103.2	2.0	105.2
Specific grants	6.5	0.9	7.4
Deferred capital grants released in year			
– buildings	1.8	-	1.8
– equipment	2.6	-	2.6
Total from funding councils	**114.1**	**2.9**	**117.0**

2. Academic fees and support grants	
Full-time credit bearing sources-home fees	33.0
Full-time credit bearing courses-international	50.4
Part-time credit bearing courses	2.2
Other teaching contracts	21.7
Non credit bearing courses and other fees	5.1
Total	**112.4**

3. Research grants and contracts	
Research councils	34.4
UK based charities	10.1
Other grants and contracts	33.7
Total	78.2

4. Other operating income	
Residences, catering and conferences	30.2
Other services rendered	4.1
Health authorities	7.6
Other income	1.7
Total	**43.6**

5. Endowment income and interest	
Transferred from specific endowments	14.7
Income from general endowments and investments	11.6
Other interest receivable	4.9
Total	31.2

Governance

9914 HEFE institutions are required by the HEFE SORP to produce a statement of corporate governance, based on guidance issued by the various funding bodies and the British Universities Finance Directors' Group. The statement should include details of internal control systems (e.g. management structure) and how these are linked to the objectives of the institution and implemented across the organisation (see example).

The subject of corporate governance in general is covered in more detail in ¶5200.

EXAMPLE **Casterbridge University**
Notes to the accounts

Governance procedures-statement of responsibilities
The University is a corporation formed by Royal Charter with charitable status. The University is governed by an executive council, responsible for the administration and financial management of the educational institution.
The University is committed to **best practice in corporate governance**. The University Council notes the Combined Code on Corporate Governance and the HEFCE Accounts Direction requirements. In addition the University abides by the Governance Code of Practice and General Principles published by the Committee of University Chairman. The Council is the governing body of the institution and in exercising its role and powers undertakes to meet the obligations placed on the institution by the Founding Charter of the University.
The following provisions contain the **primary functions and responsibilities** of the Council, as envisaged in the Charter:
– to **approve the strategic plan** for the university including long term business and academic plans;

- to be the **principal financial authority** of the institution and to ensure that accounts are maintained;
- to exercise overall responsibility for the university's **assets and properties**;
- to **act as trustee** for any bequest, gift or endowment, made to further the aims of the university;
- to **appoint the head of the institution** to act as Chief Executive in all academic and financial matters;
- to receive **indicators of financial performance** against approved plans; and
- to ensure that **control, monitoring and assurance systems** (internal control systems) are in place and functioning.

The Council is made up of the Chancellor and Vice Chancellor as well as representatives from the Strategy and Planning Committee, the Finance Committee, the Audit Committee and the Equality and Diversity Committee. Day to day management of the university is conducted by the Management Board.
The internal control system is operated by the internal audit function which is based on HEFCE Code of Practice, supported by executive managers within the university.

Other key disclosures

9918

Category	Disclosure requirements
Accounting policies	Covering income recognition: specific endowments, donations, reserves, surplus donations etc, treatment of fixed assets, foreign currencies, stock etc.
Segmental reporting	Where institutions have significant activities in other segments such as a university press or geographical operations (overseas campuses).
Charitable funds	For each material fund: - assets and liabilities; - income and expenditure; - details of fund size, restrictions imposed and purpose of fund; and - details of material transfers between charitable funds.
Endowment funds	The capital value of endowment funds plus details of any accumulated income not yet applied for designated purposes of the fund. Where the sums involved are material in relation to the institution's financial position, disclosure should be on face of the balance sheet under heading: endowment funds.

EXAMPLE **Casterbridge University**
Notes to the accounts

Accounting policies
The financial statements have been prepared under the historical cost convention, as modified by the revaluation of endowment asset investments, and in accordance with both SORP Accounting for Further and Higher Education Institutions and applicable accounting standards. They conform to the guidance published by the Higher Education Funding Council for England.
In accordance with FRS 18 "Accounting Policies", these accounting policies have been reviewed by the Audit Committee and are considered appropriate to the University's activities.

Income recognition
Income from specific endowments, donations, research grants and contracts is recognised where the expenditure has been incurred together with any related contributions towards overhead costs. Unspent endowments are shown as endowment reserves on the balance sheet, whilst unspent donations are recognised as deferred income. All other income is credited to the income and expenditure account on a receivable basis.

SECTION 6

Clubs and associations

9920 In general, clubs and associations can be defined as a number of persons who voluntarily join together to promote a common social or economic purpose. Working men's clubs in particular, have played an important role in local society from the late 19th century onwards. Although there is no legal obligation to incorporate, the majority of these organisations choose this option.

MEMO POINTS There is no legal definition of a club, association or society and as such the terms are used interchangeably in this chapter. The accounting requirements for building societies and credit unions are outside the scope of this book.

A. Type of clubs and associations

9921 Clubs and societies comprise many different types and may or may not be incorporated, as either as a limited company under the Companies Act, a Community Interest Company (CIC), an Industrial and Provident or Friendly Society. In comparison, proprietary clubs, such as night clubs and casinos, must incorporate under the Companies Act.

Incorporated	Clubs & associations	Legal framework
Industrial and provident societies	working men's clubs, political associations – the Royal British Legion, sports clubs, social clubs, agricultural societies, retail and wholesale cooperatives (e.g. workers cooperatives), Friendly societies (new registrations only).	Industrial and Provident Societies Act 1965-78 Administered by the FSA
Friendly societies	savings, insurance, private healthcare services, critical illness cover.	Friendly Society Act 1974 (No new registrations permitted)
Community interest companies (¶9926)	profit for public good – community theatre groups – educational support for disadvantaged children	The Companies (Audit, Investigations & Community Enterprise) Act 2004 + Community Interest Company Regulations 2005
Unincorporated – Private members clubs	social groups-small scale, shared interests, trade associations, political clubs, allotment societies, sports clubs and literary societies	Not recognised as a legal entity. Register with the Charities Commission

MEMO POINTS Clubs run for profit such as proprietary clubs (e.g. night clubs and casinos) are registered under the following legislation: The Companies Act, The Gambling Act 2005 and the Licensing Act 2003.

Industrial and provident societies

9922 Industrial and provident societies are mutual, incorporated societies and must register under the Industrial and Provident Societies Act 1965 (IPSA Act 1965). At present there are in excess of 8,000 societies and 3,000 clubs registered under this Act, categorised according to the nature of their activity, as set out in the table below. Societies run for the benefit of a community, must provide services for people other than their members and reinvest any surplus profit in the organisation.

MEMO POINTS New legislation in the form of the Co-operative and Community Benefit and Societies and Credit Union Act 2010 has received Royal Assent. This legislation represents the latest in a series of measures designed to reform and modernise the regulatory position of NFP organisations providing financial services, namely those organisations with mutual status and whose classifications reflect their industrial origins, such as industrial and provident societies and credit unions. The Act introduces a number of new requirements including:
- the renaming of Industrial and Provident Societies as either co-operative societies or community benefit societies;
- extending the application of the Company Directors Disqualification Act 1986 to these types of NFP entities; and
- giving the Treasury powers to apply to industrial and provident societies, with appropriate modifications, company law covering the investigation of companies, company names and dissolution and restoration to the register.

This legislation received Royal Assent on 18 March 2010 but has not yet come into force.

Registration A number of conditions must be met before registration under the IPSA Act 1965 is permitted: namely; 9923
- the society must be carrying on a business (e.g. a working men's club);
- it must be a bona fide co-operative society;
- it must satisfy the Registrar of Industrial and Provident Societies that the business is being run for the benefit of the community; and
- there must be special reasons why an organisation should be registered under this Act rather than the Companies Act.

Regulated activities A society is responsible for considering whether any of its activities are regulated activities, (e.g. provision of financial services) under s19 of the Financial Services and Markets Act 2000 (FSMA). If so, the society must apply for authorisation from the FSA. As such, members of these societies will not have access to the Financial Ombudsman Service (FOS) or the Financial Services Compensation Scheme (FSCS). 9924

Members of societies which are both registered under the Industrial and Provident Societies Act 1965 and regulated by the FSA, because they are authorised to conduct financial services business under FSMA, will have access to the FOS and the FSCS. In addition, borrowers from societies which have Consumer Credit Licences, will have access to the FOS on issues relating to their loans.

MEMO POINTS 1. The registration function operated by the FSA is separate from its role as regulator of the financial services industry in the UK.
2. However, the majority of societies registered under the Industrial and Provident Societies Act 1965 are not regulated by the FSA under FSMA.

Friendly societies

A friendly society, otherwise known as a mutual society or benevolent society, typically provides insurance, pensions, savings and loan facilities, or cooperative banking services. Friendly societies are composed of people who join together for a common financial or social purpose, providing financial and social services to individuals, often according to their religious or political affiliations. Friendly societies **are registered under** the Friendly Societies Act 1974. Historically, these types of societies have played a very important role and although many of these societies still exist today, their numbers are in decline. 9925

Registrations are now normally made under the Industrial and Provident Societies Act 1965 as no new registrations are permitted under the Friendly Societies Act 1974. Other friendly societies have developed as large mutually-run financial institutions (e.g. insurance companies), and have lost any social and ceremonial aspect they may have had; whilst others have taken on a more charitable or social aspect.

Community interest companies (CICs)

A Community Interest Company (CIC) was introduced under the Companies (Audit, Investigations and Community Enterprise) Act 2004, and is **designed for social enterprises** that 9926 plan to utilise their profits and assets for a designated public good. CICs are relatively easy to set up, with all the flexibility and certainty of the company form, but with some **special features** to ensure they operate for the benefit of the community, rather than the need to maximise profit for shareholders.

CICs cover a wide range of social and environmental activities, operate in all parts of the economy, are diverse in character and include local community enterprises, social firms, and mutual organisations (e.g. co-operatives).

A CIC is not permitted to register as a charity but a charity can own a CIC, in which the profits are then directed into the charity. **Existing entities**, including charities, can convert to a CIC, by passing a special resolution amending their memorandum and articles of association. Charities can convert to a CIC, but will lose their charitable status in so doing.

CICs are subject to a **community interest test** and an **asset lock**, and must be approved by and continuously monitored by a special regulator.

9927 **Registration** A CIC must register under one of the following **legal regimes**:
- a company limited by guarantee;
- a private limited company; or
- a public limited company.

The CIC format appeals to charities that want to separate their trading activities and pursuit of profit for the social good, from their philanthropic activities. Charities can run **trading operations**, although there is no guarantee that profits can be sheltered from tax. New charities may prefer to register as CICs where they intend to trade and hold property, although they must balance the advantages of a flexible corporate structure against the loss of tax concessions available to registered charities.

On registration, the company must submit a **Community Interest Statement** signed by all the directors, setting out the scope of its activities and how these will benefit the community.

9928 **Regulation** CICs are subject to the supervision of the Office of the Regulator of Community Interest Companies and must file an **annual CIC Report**, containing details of stakeholders, directors remuneration, dividends, asset transfers etc. CICs are restricted by an "asset lock", which places conditions on the transfer of assets, dividend payments or disposal of assets on dissolution. CICs can pay directors a salary in contrast to charities, where trustees are not remunerated. A company can **cease to trade** as a CIC by either dissolving the company or converting to a charity.

Unincorporated clubs and associations

9929 Although **the majority of clubs are legally incorporated** there is still a significant number of smaller clubs that are not. Unregistered clubs have no separate legal status, but must still operate within a legal framework. Some clubs are registered under the Industrial Societies Acts (e.g. employees' social clubs and canteens), whilst others, if selling alcohol, must be registered under the Licensing Act 2003. Examples of such clubs include political associations, theatre clubs and sports clubs.

Each club must decide on its own set of rules and governance procedures. All the members are jointly entitled to a share of the club's property. The clubs have unlimited liability and the members are liable for any debts incurred in equal shares. Club members need to ensure that they are aware of their obligations in the event the club or association is wound up. Unincorporated clubs and associations generally elect a management committee, that is authorised to enter into contracts on the members' behalf and legal actions can be brought in the name of the club by the committee. The authority for signing contracts and division of powers, should be set out in the rules governing the club.

B. Accounting requirements

The accounting and audit requirements for the majority of clubs and associations can be found in the Industrial and Provident Societies Act 1965 and the Friendly Societies Act 1974. Whilst these Acts do not specify the exact form and content of the accounts, clubs are required to prepare a profit and loss account and balance sheet that comply with the requirements of UK GAAP. In addition, the **FSA has issued guidance** on the preparation of accounting statements. Where the accounts do not comply with these guidance notes, an annual return obtainable from the Registrar of Companies must be completed. Where accounts are prepared for a period **less or more than 12 months**, the turnover should be pro-rated after deducting any discounts or VAT. The accounts must be signed by the secretary of the society and two other committee members. 9930

MEMO POINTS The majority of clubs and societies meet the size criteria for reporting under the FRSSE.

Accounting records

All societies and clubs must maintain proper accounting records. The majority of clubs and associations are cash businesses that keep manual or simple computer records, for recording income and expenditure. A number of **accounting controls** should be in place to ensure the protection of the clubs assets. Each club must be able to demonstrate that its accounting records are detailed and accurately present a true picture of the club's financial activities. 9931

Accounting records	Basic information required
Cash book	Show different types of income, with zero rated or exempt VAT items clearly identified. Income from non-members (e.g. rental income from conferences, functions etc) should also be analysed separately, to demonstrate compliance with the rules for mutuality. A summary of general income controls is given in the table below.
Fixed asset register	Details of categories of asset, residual values, depreciation, NBV
Wages/Salaries	P11 for each staff member, Tax paid + NI Other PAYE forms (P46)
Goods received	Records of deliveries, bar stocks, invoices etc.

9932

Income by type	Controls
Subscription/membership fees	Joining fees, annual subscriptions, life membership fees reconciled to register of members
Bar income	Records of bar takings should be retained, including till rolls, till readings etc. Regular cash reconciliations should be the norm, with variances between receipts and cash banked examined. Till records should be scrutinised and any amendments checked and authorised.
Fruit (gaming) machines	Controls should cover readings, cash collected. Machines should be emptied by an officer or club member as required by the Gambling Act. Unusual patterns (high number of jackpots etc.) should be investigated.
Ticket income	Ticket sales (e.g. fundraising events) reconciled to income received
Raffles, bingo, lotteries	Records of prize monies, ticket sales must be kept
Other income	Room hire, sponsorship jukebox, cigarette machines etc. Same controls needed as for fruit machines

Taxation There are a number of taxation issues affecting clubs and associations, with perhaps the most complex involving VAT. 9933

The principal VAT issue concerning clubs and associations is whether they are involved in a business activity, and if so, what is the exact nature of the income they receive. This will in turn dictate the VAT arrangements. A business activity is principally one involving a supply made in return for a consideration (although not necessarily a profit).

A club is deemed to undertake a business activity when it provides services to:
– members including: benefits, in return for subscriptions or a separate charge (e.g. admission fees); or
– non-members, in return for a charge (e.g. catering, social etc.)

Lobbying for a political or public/charitable cause or receipt of donations for which no benefits/services are supplied in return, does not constitute a business activity.

MEMO POINTS 1. The **statutory definition** of a business activity has been developed via case law. HMRC have also given an interpretation of what constitutes a business activity.
2. Small clubs and associations may use one of the VAT schemes designed for small businesses such as cash accounting, the flat rate scheme or annual accounting.
3. If there is a **mixture of taxable and non-taxable supplies**, VAT registration may be an option under which the club would be partially exempt and able to recover some of its input tax. Non-taxable supplies could include club subscriptions which might might be classified as a donation, and therefore outside the scope of VAT. In other cases, there might be a package of benefits, some of which are deemed a supply, thereby resulting in a mixed supply. However, this area can be complex and so specialist advice sought be sought. For **a more detailed assessment** of the type of VAT issues facing clubs and association see *VAT Memo*.
4. The **VAT registration threshold** is currently £70,000.
5. HMRC have announced a new policy concerning VAT exemptions for sports clubs, following a recent decision handed down by the European Court of Justice. This judgment effectively extends the exemption to supplies of sports services to members' clubs, in contrast to UK legislation, which currently restricts the exemption to individuals. However, HMRC have advised that the exemption will only apply to supplies and services to non-profit making clubs required by the members for sporting purposes. The change became effective from September 2010.

Audit requirements

9933-1 Every society must be audited by a qualified auditor, unless it can claim exemption under the Deregulation (Industrial and Provident Society) Order 1996. The income and expenditure account should not be published until an audit has been conducted, and it should be accompanied by an audit report, except where the society has taken advantage of the exemptions available, as set out below.

If any of the above requirements have not been complied with this should be mentioned in the audit report, which should be drawn up in accordance with SAS 600.

9934 **Audit objective** The auditor is required to report whether the accounts give a true and fair view of the society's affairs at the balance sheet date and that:
– the accounts comply with the requirements of the relevant legislation;
– the society has kept proper records and books of accounts;
– a system of internal controls is in place to cover transactions and prevent fraud and misuse of assets; and
– the accounts tally with the underlying accounting records.

9935 **Exemption from a full audit** A society is exempt from having an audit if:
– the value of its assets and liabilities at the previous year-end did not exceed in aggregate £2.8m;
– its turnover for the preceding year did not exceed £5.6m.
– a resolution supported by at least 80% of members, in favour of not having an audit, is passed at the AGM.

Under SI 2006/265 there were a number of amendments made to the Friendly and Industrial and Provident Societies Act 1968, including higher audit exemption thresholds thereby bringing them into line with those currently applicable to companies.

A society will not be able to take advantage of the exemptions if at any time during the financial period in question, it was one of the following:

1. For societies registered under the Industrial and Provident Societies Act 1965:
- a credit union;
- a housing association;
- it is or has a subsidiary; or
- holds deposits other than in the form of withdrawal share capital.

2. Societies registered under the Friendly Societies Act 1974, that hold deposits other than in the form of withdrawal share capital.

Appendix I

Legislative framework for – United Kingdom

9940

Country	Relevant Acts governing charities	Charity authority –registration/ supervision	Preparation and filing of Accounts
England and Wales	Charities Act 2006 (Part V1) Companies Acts 1985, 1989 and 2006 The Industrial and Provident Societies Act 1965 to 2002	Charity Commission for England and Wales	All charities are required to prepare accounts, except exempt charities that follow relevant legislation or other SORPs. Trustee's Annual Report and Accounts must be filed by all registered charities whose gross income or total expenditure exceeds £10,000.
Scotland	Law Reform (Misc. Provisions) (Scotland) Act 1990 and regulations made under The Charity Accounts (Scotland) Amendment Regulations 2007. Charitable companies – Companies Act 2006, Charity + Trustee Investments (Scotland) Act 2005 The Charities and Benevolent Fundraising (Scotland) Regulations 2009. The Protection of Charities Assets (Exemption) and the Charity Test (Specified Bodies) (Scotland) Amendment Order 2008	Office of the Scottish Charity Regulator (OSCR)	1. No statutory requirement to file accounts. 2. Accounts prepared by non-company charities subject to the 1990 Act, which requires an Income and Expenditure Account. 3. The 2006/7 Regulations and the SORP require specific disclosures.
Northern Ireland	Charities Act (NI) 2008	The Charity Commission for Northern Ireland –supported by the Department for Social Development (DSD).	1. No registration of charities in NI 2. Section 27 of the Charities Act (NI) requires the trustees of a charity to prepare accounts 3. No requirement to file accounts except where requested by the Department for Social Development.

Appendix II

Sample format – Receipts and payments accounts

9942

Receipts and payments accounts

Name of charity: ... The Equal/Unequal Pay Trust...
Registered number: ...2223334...
Financial year ending on: ...31 December 2010...

A. Unrestricted funds

See ¶9521 for a definition.

	Receipts	Examples	20X9	20X8
A1a	Donations, legacies and other similar receipts	Donations Legacy		
A1b	Operating activities to further charity's objectives	Local authority grant		
A1c	Operating activities to generate funds	Fundraising events		
A1d	Investment income receipts	Deposit interest		
	Sub total (A1c-A1d)			
A1e	Other receipts	Sale of computer equipment		
	Total receipts			

	Payments		20X9	20X8
A2a	For generating funds	Fetes Concerts Fundraising		
A2b	Charitable payments 1. Grants 2. Charitable activities 3. Support costs 4. Management and administration	 Individual grants Staff costs Expenses for volunteers Office overheads Trustee meetings		
	Sub-total (A2a-A2b)			
A2c	Other payments	Furniture for day centre		
	Total payments			
(A1-A2)	**Net of receipts/payments**			
(A3)	**Cash funds b/fwd**			
(A1-A2 + A3)	**Cash funds c/fwd**			

B. Restricted income funds

See ¶9520 for a definition

	Receipts	Examples	20X9	20X8
B1a	Donations, legacies and other similar receipts	Mini-bus grant First-aid equipment grant		
B1b	Operating activities to further charity's objectives			
B1c	Operating activities to generate funds			
B1d	Investment income receipts			
	Sub total (B1c-B1d)			
B1e	Other receipts			
	Total receipts			

	Payments	Examples	20X9	20X8
B2a	For generating grants	Cost of appeal		
B2b	Charitable payments 1. Grants payable 2. Charitable activities 3. Support costs 4. Management and administration			
	Sub-total (B2a-B2b)			
B2c	Other payments	Mini-bus purchase First-aid equipment		
	Total payments (B2a + B2b + B2c)			
(B1-B2)	**Net of receipts/(payments)**			
(B3)	**Cash funds b/fwd**			
(B1-B2 + B3)	**Cash funds c/fwd**			

C. Endowment funds

See ¶9519 for a definition

	Receipts	Examples	20X9	20X8
C1a	Donations, legacies and other similar receipts	Jubilee appeal		
C1b	Other receipts			
	Total receipts			

	Payments	Examples	20X9	20X8
C2a	Payments to income funds			
C2b	Payments for managing investment funds			
C2c	Payments for purchase of investments and other assets			
(C2a + C2b + C2c)	**Total payments**			
(C1-C2)	**Net of receipts/(payments)**			
(C3)	**Cash funds b/fwd**			
(C1-C2 + C3)	**Cash funds c/fwd**			

D. Statement of Assets and Liabilities at the year end

	Cash funds (Examples)	**Unrestricted funds**	**Restricted funds**	**Endowment funds**
D1a	Current account			
	Deposit account			
	Total cash funds			

	Other monetary assets (Examples)	**Unrestricted funds**	**Restricted funds**	**Endowment funds**
D1b	Income tax rebate			
	Local authority grant			

	Investment assets (Examples)	**Relevant fund (Optional)**	**Cost**	**Current value (Optional)**
D1c	Common investment funds	Endowment		

	Assets retained for the Charity's own use (Examples)	**Relevant fund**	**Cost (Optional)**	**Current value (Optional)**
D1d	Furniture – day centre	Endowment		
	Computer equipment	Unrestricted		
	Mini-bus	Restricted		

	Liabilities (Examples)	**Relevant fund**	**Cost (Optional)**	**When due (Optional)**
D2	Alarm call system	Unrestricted		
	PAYE + NIC	Unrestricted		

Signed by one or two trustees on behalf of all the trustees (Optional – see section…of notes)

1… Name (Print)…

2… Name (Print)…

Date of approval…

PART 11

General information

General information

OUTLINE ¶¶

I. Model Financial Statements

Following is a model Annual Report for a hypothetical company, The Example Company Limited. 9945

The annual report has been prepared for illustrative purposes only and shows typical disclosures and formats. While it serves as a guide to layout and style, a single example obviously cannot cater to all situations (and therefore it should not be used as a checklist). Similarly, the suggested disclosures do not necessarily apply to all companies.

Please note that the dates used in these model statements (years ending in **2X10** and **2X09**) are not intended to correspond with the actual calendar years 2010 and 2009; they merely reflect a current year and a previous year.

The Example Company Limited does not apply fair value accounting rules (and does not apply FRS 23, or relevant sections of FRS 25, FRS 26, and FRS 29). The company probably meets the size criteria of a medium-sized company. 9946

THE EXAMPLE COMPANY LIMITED

ANNUAL REPORT
AND ACCOUNTS
2X10

Directors
Mr A (Chairman)
Ms B (Managing Director)
Mr C
Mr D

Secretary
Mr E

Registered Office
125 Any Street
Anytown
AN1 0WN
England

Registered Number
012345678900
England and Wales

Auditors
True, Fair and Partners
125 Accountancy Square
Anytown
AN5 8YZ

THE EXAMPLE COMPANY LIMITED

REPORT OF THE DIRECTORS

The Directors present their Annual Report on the affairs of the Company, together with the accounts and the auditors' report for the year ended 5 April 2X10.

Principal activity

The principal activity of the company during the year under review was the manufacture and distribution of electronic components.

Business review

Sales turnover in the year under review was £xxxx compared with £xxxx in the previous year. Sales turnover reflected the continued demand for the company's products and services. Trading margins were xx.x % (2X09 – xx.x %) reflecting more competitive market conditions experienced during the financial year than previously.

[The above is an example of a review in the simplest of circumstances. The review should cover the following:

- *a fair review of the company's business, and*
- *a description of the principal risks and uncertainties facing the company.*

The review required is a balanced and comprehensive analysis of:

- *the development and performance of the company's business during the financial year; and*
- *the company's position at the end of that year, consistent with the size of the business and its complexity.*

The review must, to the extent necessary for an understanding of the development, performance or position of the business, include:

- *analysis using financial key performance indicators; and*
- *where appropriate, analysis using other key performance indicators, including information relating to environmental and employee matters.*]

Future developments

[An indication should be given of the likely future developments in the company's business.]

Financial risk management

The company's operations expose it to a variety of financial risks that include the effects of changes in debt market prices, credit risk, liquidity risk and interest rate risk. The company has in place a risk management programme that seeks to limit the adverse effects on the financial performance of the company by monitoring levels of debt finance and the related finance costs.

In order to ensure stability of cash out flows and hence manage interest rate risk, the company has a policy of maintaining 90 percent of its debt (2X09 – 90 percent) at fixed rates. The company seeks to minimise the risk of uncertain funding in its operations by borrowing within a spread of maturity periods. Given the size and nature of operations, the company's policy is to operate with 50 percent of its debt being repayable within one year. At the year end, 53 percent (2X09 – 49 percent) of debt was repayable within one year. The company does not use derivative financial instruments to manage interest rate costs and no hedge accounting is applied.

Given the size of the company, the directors have not delegated the responsibility of monitoring financial risk management to a sub-committee. The policies set by the board of directors are implemented by the company's finance department. The department has a policy and procedures manual that sets our specific guidelines to manage interest rate risk, credit risk, and circumstances in which it would be appropriate to use financial instruments to manage these.

Price risk

The company is exposed to commodity price risk as a result of its operations. However, given their size, the costs of managing exposure to commodity price risk exceed any potential benefits. The directors will revisit this policy should the company's operations change in size or nature. The company has no exposure to equity securities price risk, as it holds no listed or other equity investments.

Credit risk

The company has implemented policies that require appropriate credit checks on potential customers before sales are made. Where debt finance is used, this is subject to pre-approval by the board of directors, and such approval is limited to financial institutions with an AA rating or better. The amount of exposure to any individual counterparty is subject to a limit, which is reassessed annually by the board.

Liquidity risk

The company actively maintains a mixture of long-term and short-term debt finance that is designed to ensure that the company has sufficient available funds for operations and planned expansions.

Interest rate cash flow risk

The company has both interest-bearing assets and interest-bearing liabilities. Interest-bearing assets include only government securities and cash balances, all of which earn interest at fixed rates. The company has a policy of maintaining debt at fixed rate to ensure certainty of future interest cash flows. The directors will revisit this policy should the company's operations change in size or nature.

[*Note: This disclosure is not required where the information is not material for the assessment of the company's assets, liabilities, financial position and profit or loss. In addition, there is an exemption for small companies from making these disclosures*.]

Results and dividends

Turnover for the year was £xxx (2X09 – £xxx). Profit before taxation and goodwill was £xxx (2X09 – £xxx). Profit before taxation was £xxx (2X09 – £xxx).

The Directors have proposed a final ordinary dividend of x pence per share, which, together with the interim dividend of x pence, make a total for the year of x pence (2X09 – x pence). The Company will pay the final ordinary dividend on 30 April 2X10 to shareholders on the register at the close of business on 22 March 2X10.

Directors

The directors in office during the year, and their interests in the company's issued ordinary share capital, were as follows:

	Number of Ordinary shares of £1	
	2X10	**2X09**
Mr A	xxx	xxx
Ms B	xxx	xxx
Mr C	xxx	xxx
Mr D	xxx	xxx
Ms E	-	xxx

Ms E retired as a director on 15 January 2X10.

Ms B and Mr D retire by rotation at the Annual General Meeting, and, being eligible, offer themselves for re-election. Their service contracts can be terminated by either party giving not less than twelve months' notice in writing.

Statement of directors' responsibilities The directors are responsible for preparing the directors' report and the financial statements in accordance with applicable law and regulations.

Company law requires the directors to prepare financial statements for each financial year. Under that law, the directors have elected to prepare the financial statements in accordance with United Kingdom Generally Accepted Accounting Practice. Under company law, the directors must not approve the financial statements unless they give a true and fair view of the state of affairs of the company and of the profit or loss of the company for that period. In preparing those financial statements, the directors are required to:

- select suitable accounting policies and then apply them consistently;
- make judgements and estimates that are reasonable and prudent;
- state whether applicable UK accounting standards have been followed, subject to any material departures disclosed and explained in the financial statements; and
- prepare the financial statements on the going concern basis unless it is inappropriate to presume that the company will continue in business.

The directors are responsible for keeping proper accounting records which disclose with reasonable accuracy at any time the financial position of the company and enable them to ensure that the financial statements comply with the Companies Act 2006. They are also responsible for safeguarding the assets of the company and hence for taking reasonable steps for the prevention and detection of fraud and other irregularities.

Political and charitable contributions

During the year, the company made a political contribution to the *X* Party of £xx and various charitable contributions totalling £xx.

Events since the balance sheet date

There have been no significant events since 5 April 2X10.

Differences between market and balance sheet value of land

In the opinion of the directors, the difference between the market value and balance sheet value of land is not significant.

Supplier payment policy

Company policy is to set terms of payment when agreeing each transaction with suppliers, clearly explain payment procedures, consistently settle bills within contract terms and extend terms only with prior agreement. The Company operates systems for promptly advising suppliers of, and resolving, queried and contested items.

Trade creditors of the Company at 5 April 2X10 were equivalent to 35 days' purchases (2X09 – 45 days'), based on average daily amount invoiced by suppliers during the year.

Employee involvement

Quarterly meetings are held between senior management and employee representatives to discuss matters of concern. Employees are kept well informed about the progress and position of the Company by means of regular departmental meetings, newsletters, journals and, as part of an initiative introduced during the year, the intranet.

An employee share scheme, which is open to all full-time employees, is operated.

Equal opportunities The Company is committed to the principle of equal opportunity in employment and to ensuring that no applicant or employee receives less favourable treatment on the grounds of gender, race, age, colour, nationality, religion, HIV status, disability, sexuality, or unrelated criminal convictions or other unjustified requirements or conditions.

The Company applies employment policies that are fair and equitable and that ensure entry into, and progression within, the Company determined solely by application of job criteria, personal ability and competency.

Disabled persons The Company gives full consideration to applications for employment from disabled persons where the requirements of the job can be adequately fulfilled by a handicapped or disabled person. Where existing employees become disabled, it is the Company's policy to provide continuing employment under normal terms and conditions.

Disclosure of information to auditors

[*The report must contain a statement that – in the case of each of the directors who are directors at the date of the approval of the report – the following applies*:

- *so far as the director is aware, there is no relevant audit information of which the company's auditor is unaware; and*
- *he has taken all the steps that he ought to have taken as a director in order to make himself aware of any relevant audit information and to establish that the company's auditor is aware of that information*.]

Auditors

The auditors, True, Fair and Partners, have signified their willingness to continue in office and a resolution to re-appoint them as auditors will be proposed at the Annual General Meeting.

125 Any Street
Anytown
AN1 0WN
England
(registered office)

By order of the Board
[*Name of signatory & Signature*]
...
Director
[*Date*]

THE EXAMPLE COMPANY LIMITED

INDEPENDENT AUDITORS' REPORT TO THE MEMBERS OF THE EXAMPLE COMPANY LIMITED

We have audited the financial statements of The Example Company Limited for the year ended 5 April 2X10, comprising the Profit and Loss Account, the Balance Sheet, the Cash Flow Statement, the Statement of Total Recognised Gains and Losses and the related notes numbered 1 to 18. The financial reporting framework that has been applied in their preparation is applicable law and United Kingdom accounting standards (United Kingdom Generally Accepted Accounting Practice).

Respective responsibilities of directors and auditors

As explained more fully in the Directors' Responsibilities Statement set out on page *x*, the directors are responsible for the preparation of the financial statements and for being satisfied that they give a true and fair view. Our responsibility is to audit the financial statements in accordance with applicable law and International Standards on Auditing (UK and Ireland). Those standards require us to comply with the Auditing Practices Board's Ethical Standards for Auditors.

Scope of the audit of the financial statements

An audit involves obtaining evidence about the amounts and disclosures in the financial statements sufficient to give reasonable assurance that the financial statements are free from material misstatement, whether caused by fraud or error. This includes an assessment of: whether the accounting policies are appropriate to the company's circumstances and have been consistently applied and adequately disclosed; the reasonableness of significant accounting estimates made by the directors; and the overall presentation of the financial statements. [*For periods ending on or after 23 March 2011, add the following*] In addition, we read all the financial and non-financial information in the [*describe the annual report*] to identify material inconsistencies with the audited financial statements. If we become aware of any apparent material misstatements or inconsistencies we consider the implications for our report.

Opinion on financial statements

In our opinion the financial statements:
- give a true and fair view of the company's affairs as at 5 April 2X10 and of the profit for the year then ended;
- have been properly prepared in accordance with United Kingdom Generally Accepted Accounting Practice; and
- have been prepared in accordance with the requirements of the Companies Act 2006.

Opinion on other matter prescribed by the Companies Act 2006

In our opinion the information given in the Directors' Report for the financial year for which the financial statements are prepared is consistent with the financial statements.

Matters on which we are required to report by exception

We have nothing to report in respect of the following matters where the Companies Act 2006 requires us to report to you if, in our opinion:
- adequate accounting records have not been kept, or returns adequate for our audit have not been received from branches not visited by us; or
- the financial statements are not in agreement with the accounting records and returns; or
- certain disclosures of directors' remuneration specified by law are not made; or
- we have not received all the information and explanations we require for our audit.

[Signature]

John Smith (Senior Statutory Auditor)

For and on behalf of True, Fair and Partners

Chartered Accountants and Statutory Auditors

Anytown

[Date]

THE EXAMPLE COMPANY LIMITED

PROFIT AND LOSS ACCOUNT
FOR THE YEAR ENDED 5 APRIL 2X10

	Notes	2X10 £	2X09 £
Turnover	2	xxx, xxx	xxx, xxx
Cost of sales		xxx, xxx	xxx, xxx
Gross profit		xxx, xxx	xxx, xxx
Distribution costs		xxx, xxx	xxx, xxx
Administrative expenses		xxx, xxx	xxx, xxx
Operating profit (loss)	3	xxx, xxx	(xxx, xxx)
Loss on disposal of fixed assets		xxx, xxx	xxx, xxx
Income from investments		xxx, xxx	xxx, xxx
Interest payable		xxx, xxx	xxx, xxx
Profit (loss) on ordinary activities before taxation		xxx, xxx	(xx, xxx)
Taxation		xx, xxx	x, xxx
Profit (loss) for the financial year after taxation		xxx, xxx	(xxx, xxx)
Dividends	4	xx, xxx	xx, xxx
Retained profit (loss) for the financial year		xxx, xxx	(xx, xxx)
Retained profit at 6 April 2X09 (2X08)		xxx, xxx	xxx, xxx
Retained profit at 5 April 2X10 (2X09)		£xxx, xxx	£xxx, xxx

The Company's turnover and expenses all relate to continuing operations for both the current and the prior year.

THE EXAMPLE COMPANY LIMITED

BALANCE SHEET AT 5 APRIL 2X10

	Notes	2X10 £	2X09 £
Fixed assets			
Intangible fixed assets	5	xxx, xxx	xxx, xxx
Tangible fixed assets	6	xxx, xxx	xxx, xxx
Listed investments	7	xxx, xxx	xxx, xxx
		xxx, xxx	xxx, xxx
Current assets			
Stocks	8	xxx, xxx	xxx, xxx
Debtors	9	xxx, xxx	xxx, xxx
Cash at bank and in hand		xxx, xxx	xxx, xxx
		xxx, xxx	xxx, xxx
Creditors – amounts falling due within one year	10	(xxx, xxx)	(xxx, xxx)
Net current assets		xxx, xxx	xxx, xxx
Total assets less current liabilities		xxx, xxx	xxx, xxx
Creditors – amounts falling due after one year	11	(xxx, xxx)	(xxx, xxx)
Net assets		£xxx, xxx	£xxx, xxx
Capital and reserves			
Called-up share capital	12	xxx, xxx	xxx, xxx
Share premium account	13	xxx, xxx	xxx, xxx
Revaluation reserve	13	xxx, xxx	xxx, xxx
Profit and loss account	13	xxx, xxx	xxx, xxx
Total shareholders' funds	14	£xxx, xxx	£xxx, xxx

THE EXAMPLE COMPANY LIMITED

STATEMENT OF TOTAL RECOGNISED GAINS AND LOSSES FOR THE YEAR ENDED 5 APRIL 2X10

	2X10 £	2X09 £
Profit for the year after taxation	xxx, xxx	xxx, xxx
Unrealised surplus on revaluation of property	xxx, xxx	xxx, xxx
Total recognised gains relating to the year	£xxx, xxx	£xxx, xxx

There are no material differences between the profit on ordinary activities before taxation and the retained profit for the financial year stated above and their historical cost equivalents.

[The Statement of Total Recognised Gains and Losses should be shown as a primary statement with the same prominence as other primary statements. However, it could also be shown underneath – and on the same page as – the profit and loss account.]

THE EXAMPLE COMPANY LIMITED

CASH FLOW STATEMENT
FOR THE YEAR ENDED 5 APRIL 2X10

	2X10 £	2X09 £
Net cash inflow from operating activities	xxx, xxx	xxx, xxx
Returns on investments and servicing of finance:		
Interest paid	(x, xxx)	(x, xxx)
Interest received	x, xxx	x, xxx
Taxation	(xx, xxx)	(xx, xxx)
Capital expenditure:		
Payments to acquire intangible fixed assets	(xx, xxx)	(xx, xxx)
Payments to acquire tangible fixed assets	(xx, xxx)	(xx, xxx)
Receipts from sale of tangible fixed assets	(xx, xxx)	(xx, xxx)
Capital expenditure	(xx, xxx)	(xx, xxx)
Equity dividends paid	(xx, xxx)	(xx, xxx)
Cash outflow before use of liquid resources and financing	xxx, xxx	xxx, xxx
Management of liquid resources	(xx, xxx)	(xx, xxx)
Financing:		
Issue of ordinary share capital	xx, xxx	xx, xxx
Expenses paid in connection with share issue	(x, xxx)	(x, xxx)
Increase in cash in the financial year	£xx, xxx	£xx, xxx

THE EXAMPLE COMPANY LIMITED

NOTES TO THE ACCOUNTS AT 5 APRIL 2X10

1 Accounting policies

Basis of accounting

The accounts have been prepared on a going concern basis, under the historical cost convention as modified by the revaluation of certain tangible fixed assets and in accordance with the Companies Act 2006 and applicable accounting standards in the United Kingdom. The principal accounting policies are set out below.

Turnover

Turnover represents net invoiced sales of goods, excluding VAT.

Tangible fixed assets

Depreciation is provided, after taking account of any grants receivable, at the following annual rates in order to write off each asset over its estimated useful life:

Freehold buildings – 2% on cost or revalued amounts

Plant and machinery – 15% on cost

Fixtures and fittings – 10% on cost

Motor vehicles – 25% on cost

No depreciation is provided on freehold land.

Stocks

Stocks and work in progress are valued at the lower of cost and net realisable value, after allowing for obsolete and slow-moving items. Cost includes all direct expenditure and an appropriate proportion of fixed and variable overheads.

Deferred taxation

Deferred tax arises as a result of including items of income and expenditure in taxation computations in periods different from those in which they are included in the company's accounts. Deferred tax is provided in full on timing differences which result in an obligation to pay more, or less, tax at a future date, at the average tax rates that are expected to apply when the timing differences reverse, based on current tax rates and laws.

Deferred tax is not provided on timing differences arising from the revaluation of fixed assets where there is no commitment to sell the asset.

Research and development

Expenditure on research and development is written off in the year in which it is incurred.

Foreign currencies

Assets and liabilities in foreign currencies are translated into sterling at the rates of exchange ruling at the balance sheet date. Transactions in foreign currencies are translated into sterling at the rate of exchange ruling at the date of the transaction. Exchange differences are taken into account in arriving at the operating profit.

Leased assets

Rentals applicable to operating leases where substantially all of the benefits and risks of ownership remain with the lessor are charged against profit as incurred.

Assets held under finance leases and hire purchase contracts are capitalised and depreciated over their useful lives. The corresponding lease or hire purchase obligation is treated in the balance sheet as a liability. The interest element of rental obligations is charged to the profit and loss account over the period of the lease at a constant proportion of the outstanding balance of capital repayments.

Pension costs

Contributions in respect of the company's defined contribution pension scheme are charged to the profit and loss account for the year in which they are payable to the scheme. Differences between contributions payable and contributions actually paid in the year are shown as either accruals or prepayments at the year end.

2 Turnover

Turnover, all of which originates in the United Kingdom, comprises retail and wholesale sales, net of returns, and is shown exclusive of value added tax and discounts allowed.

3 Operating profit (loss)

The operating profit (2X09 – loss) is stated after charging:

	2X10 £	2X09 £
Amortisation of intangible fixed assets	xxx, xxx	xxx, xxx
Auditors' remuneration	xxx, xxx	xxx, xxx
Depreciation of tangible fixed assets	xxx, xxx	xxx, xxx
Directors' emoluments	xxx, xxx	xxx, xxx
Pension costs	xxx, xxx	xxx, xxx

4 Dividends

	2X10 £	2X09 £
Non-equity preference dividend	xx, xxx	xx, xxx
Ordinary shares	xx, xxx	xx, xxx

5 Intangible fixed assets

	Goodwill £	Other £	Total £
Cost			
At beginning of year	xxx, xxx	xxx, xxx	xxx, xxx
Additions	-	xxx, xxx	xxx, xxx
(Disposals)	-	(xx, xxx)	(xx, xxx)
At end of year	xxx, xxx	xxx, xxx	xxx, xxx
Amortisation			
At beginning of year	xxx, xxx	xxx, xxx	xxx, xxx
Charge for the year	x, xxx	x, xxx	xx, xxx
(On disposals – written back)	–	(x, xxx)	(x, xxx)
At end of year	xxx, xxx	xxx, xxx	xxx, xxx
Net book values			
At end of year	xxx, xxx	xxx, xxx	xxx, xxx
At end of previous year	xxx, xxx	xxx, xxx	xxx, xxx

6 Tangible fixed assets

	Freehold land and buildings	Motor vehicles	Fixtures and equipment	Total
	£	£	£	£
Cost				
At beginning of year	xxx, xxx	xxx, xxx	xxx, xxx	xxx, xxx
Additions	xxx, xxx	xxx, xxx	xxx, xxx	xxx, xxx
(Disposals)	(xx, xxx)	(xx, xxx)	(xx, xxx)	(xx, xxx)
At end of year	xxx, xxx	xxx, xxx	xxx, xxx	xxx, xxx
Depreciation				
At beginning of year	xxx, xxx	xxx, xxx	xxx, xxx	xxx, xxx
Charge for the year	xxx, xxx	xxx, xxx	xxx, xxx	xxx, xxx
(On disposals – written back)	(xx, xxx)	(xx, xxx)	(xx, xxx)	(xx, xxx)
At end of year	xxx, xxx	xxx, xxx	xxx, xxx	xxx, xxx
Net book values				
At end of year	xxx, xxx	xxx, xxx	xxx, xxx	xxx, xxx
At end of previous year	xxx, xxx	xxx, xxx	xxx, xxx	xxx, xxx

The net book value of fixtures and equipment includes £xxx (2X09 – £xxx) in respect of assets held under finance leases. The amount of depreciation in respect of these assets was £xxx for the year (2X09 – £xxx).

7 Listed investments

Listed investments consist of investments listed on the London Stock Exchange.

	2X10	2X09
	£	£
Cost		
At beginning of year	xxx, xxx	xxx, xxx
Additions/(disposals)	xx, xxx	(xx, xxx)
At end of year	xxx, xxx	xxx, xxx

8 Stocks

	2X10	2X09
	£	£
Work in progress	xxx, xxx	xxx, xxx
Finished goods and goods for resale	xx, xxx	xx, xxx
	xxx, xxx	xxx, xxx

9 Debtors

	2X10	2X09
	£	£
Trade debtors	xxx, xxx	xxx, xxx
Prepayments and accrued income	xx, xxx	xx, xxx
Other	xx, xxx	xx, xxx
	xxx, xxx	xxx, xxx

Other debtors include an amount of £xxx (2X09 – £xxx) falling due after more than one year.

10 Creditors – amounts falling due within one year

	2X10 £	2X09 £
Obligations under finance leases and hire purchase contracts	xxx, xxx	xxx, xxx
Bank loans	xxx, xxx	xxx, xxx
Other loans	xxx, xxx	xxx, xxx
Trade creditors	xxx, xxx	xxx, xxx
Corporation tax	xxx, xxx	xxx, xxx
Value added tax	xxx, xxx	xxx, xxx
Payroll taxes and social security	xxx, xxx	xxx, xxx
Accruals	xxx, xxx	xxx, xxx
Proposed dividend	xxx, xxx	xxx, xxx
	xxx, xxx	xxx, xxx

Finance leases are secured against specific assets.
Bank loans are secured by fixed and floating charges over the company's assets.
Other loans of £xxx comprise guaranteed loan notes, which attract interest of 2.85%. All loan notes are redeemable at par and are repayable in December 2X10.

11 Creditors – amounts falling due after one year

	2X10 £	2X09 £
Obligations under finance leases and hire purchase contracts	xxx, xxx	xxx, xxx
Other loans	xxx, xxx	xxx, xxx
Secured bank loans	xxx, xxx	xxx, xxx
	xxx, xxx	xxx, xxx

The Company's borrowings are repayable as follows:

On demand or within one year

Hire purchase and finance leases £xxx (2X09 – £xxx)

Loans and overdrafts £xxx (2X09 – £xxx)

Between one and two years

Hire purchase and finance leases £xxx (2X09 – £xxx)

Other loans £xxx (2X09 – £xxx)

Between two and five years

Hire purchase and finance leases £xxx (2X09- £xxx)

Loans £xxx (2X09 – £xxx)

12 Called-up share capital

	2X10 £	2X09 £
Allotted, called-up and fully paid		
60,000 (2X09 – 50,000) ordinary "A" shares of £x each	xx, xxx	xx, xxx
6,000 ordinary non-voting "B" shares of £x each	xx, xxx	xx, xxx
	xxx, xxx	xxx, xxx

During the year, 10,000 ordinary "A" shares of £x were allotted and fully paid at a premium of £1.50 per share.

13 Reserves

	Share Premium	Revaluation Reserve	Profit and Loss
	£	£	£
At beginning of year	xx, xxx	xx, xxx	xx, xxx
Share issue during year	x, xxx	-	-
Retained profit for the year	–	–	xx, xx
	xx, xxx	xx, xxx	xx, xxx

14 Shareholders' funds

Analysis of shareholders' funds	2X10	2X09
	£	£
Equity	xx, xxx	xx, xxx
Total shareholders' funds	xx, xxx	xx, xxx

[*In this example, the company has only ordinary shares in issue. However, had there been non-equity shares in addition, e.g., preference shares, the non-equity element of shareholders' funds would be shown here, together with a description of the underlying shares. Such a disclosure might take the following form*:

Shareholders' funds attributable to non-equity interests comprise 25,000 5 % preference shares of £1 each at par value. Dividends, which are cumulative, are payable annually at 5% net of tax credit. The shares are redeemable at par, solely at the company's option. In the event of winding up, these shares have a priority over ordinary shares to the extent of their par value and any arrears in respect of dividends. Except when dividends are in arrears, these shares carry no vote.]

Reconciliation of movements on shareholders' funds	2X10	2X09
	£	£
Profit for the year after tax	xx, xxx	xx, xxx
Less: Dividends	xx, xxx	xx, xxx
	xx, xxx	xx, xxx
Other recognised gains for the year	xx, xx	xx, xx
Share capital issued	xx, xx	-
	xx, xx	xx, xx
Opening shareholders' funds at beginning of year	xx, xx	xx, xx
Shareholders' funds at end of year	xx, xx	xx, xx

15 Contingent liability

A claim for damages amounting to £xx, xxx has been served on the company in respect of a road traffic accident involving one of the company's delivery vehicles. The directors have sought legal advice on the basis on which the other company is contesting the case, which is considered to be without foundation. Consequently, no provision has been made in the accounts.

16 Commitments

Capital commitments

At 5 April 2X10, capital expenditure commitments were as follows:

	2X10	2X09
	£	£
Contracted but not provided for	xx, xxx	xx, xxx

Pension commitments

The company operates a defined contribution pension scheme on behalf of its directors and certain employees. The assets of the scheme and those of the company are held separately. The scheme is administered in an independent fund. The annual commitment under this scheme is for contributions of £xx, xxx (2X09 – £xx, xxx).

Lease commitments – operating leases

At year end, the company had annual commitments of £xx, xxx (2X09 – £x, xxx) under non-cancellable operating leases.

17 Related party transactions

Loan to director

During the year Mr D was granted a short-term loan in respect of the purchase of a residence. Indebtedness on the loan was as follows:

Liability at beginning of year	£ Nil
Maximum liability during the year	£xx, xxx
Liability at end of year	£xx, xxx

The loan is repayable on 5 June 2X12. Interest, at the rate of x % per annum, is payable upon repayment. At 5 April 2X10 no interest was due and unpaid.

Material interests of directors

During the year the company purchased goods to the value of £xx, xxx (2X09 – £xx, xxx) from A.N. Other Company Limited, a company in which Mr A is materially interested as a shareholder. The purchases were made on a normal trading basis.

Controlling party

Ms B, a director, together with members of her close family, control the company by virtue of a controlling interest (directly or indirectly) of 58.5% of the issued ordinary share capital.

18 Post balance sheet events

On 18 July 2X10 the company acquired the net assets of Competitor Limited, for a consideration of £xx, xxx, which has been financed by a secured loan, repayable over six years.

II. Lists

9950

Financial Reporting Standards		¶¶
FRS 1	Cash flow statements	4000
FRS 2	Accounting for subsidiary undertakings	6558+
FRS 3	Reporting financial performance	4300
FRS 4	Capital instruments	3001
FRS 5	Reporting the substance of transactions	110
FRS 6	Acquisitions and mergers	6800
FRS 7	Fair values in acquisition accounting	6866
FRS 8	Related party disclosures	5000
FRS 9	Associates and joint ventures	7300
FRS 10	Goodwill and intangible assets	1000
FRS 11	Impairment of fixed assets and goodwill	1550
FRS 12	Provisions, contingent liabilities and contingent assets	3250
FRS 13	Derivatives and other financial instruments: disclosures	3000
FRS 14	Earnings per share (superseded by FRS 22)	600
FRS 15	Tangible fixed assets	1210
FRS 16	Current tax	9005
FRS 17	Retirement benefits	8400
FRS 18	Accounting policies	5
FRS 19	Deferred tax	9120
FRS 20	Share-based payment	8850
FRS 21	Events after the balance sheet date	5700
FRS 22	Earnings per share (replacing FRS 14)	600
FRS 23	The effects of changes in foreign exchange rates	8382
FRS 24	Financial reporting in hyperinflationary economies	8387
FRS 25	Financial instruments: disclosure and presentation	3000
FRS 26	Financial instruments: measurement	3000
FRS 27	Life assurance	
FRS 28	Corresponding amounts	472
FRS 29	Financial instruments: disclosures	3000
FRS 30	Heritage assets	9586
FRSSE	Financial Reporting Standard for Smaller Entities	6000, 9682 (charities)

9960

Statements of Standard Accounting Practice	
SSAP 4	Accounting for government grants
SSAP 5	Accounting for value added tax
SSAP 9	Stocks and long-term contracts
SSAP 13	Accounting for research and development
SSAP 17	Accounting for post balance sheet events
SSAP 19	Accounting for investment properties
SSAP 20	Foreign currency translation
SSAP 21	Accounting for leases and hire purchase contracts Guidance notes on SSAP 21
SSAP 24	Accounting for pension costs
SSAP 25	Segmental reporting

9990

ASB Statements	
Although they are definitive pronouncements, ASB statements are not accounting standards and their requirements are therefore not mandatory.	
Principles and procedures	
Explanations or descriptions of the ASB's principles and procedures	• Statement of aims • Foreword to accounting standards • Foreword to UITF abstracts • Statement of principles for financial reporting • SORPs: policy and code of practice
Best practice statements	
A formulation and development of best practice for types of financial reporting that are outside the statutory annual accounts	• Operating and financial review • Interim reports • Preliminary announcements • Retirement benefits: Disclosures

9991

International Accounting Standards		¶¶
IAS 1	Presentation of financial statements	
IAS 2	Inventories	2165
IAS 7	Cash flow statements	4250
IAS 8	Net profit or loss for the period, fundamental errors and changes in accounting policies	540
IAS 10	Events after the Balance Sheet date	5754
IAS 11	Construction contracts	2376
IAS 12	Income taxes	9167
IAS 14	Segmental reporting	840
IAS 16	Property, plant and equipment	1532
IAS 17	Leases	3520
IAS 18	Revenues	540
IAS 19	Employee Benefits	8630
IAS 20	Accounting for government grants and disclosures of government assistance	7994
IAS 21	The Effects of Changes in Foreign Exchange Rates	8390
IAS 23	Borrowing costs	1532
IAS 24	Related party disclosures	5110
IAS 26	Accounting and reporting by retirement benefits plans	
IAS 27	Consolidated financial statements and accounting for investments in subsidiary	6594
IAS 28	Accounting for investment in associates	7532
IAS 29	Financial reporting in hyperinflationary economies	8399
IAS 31	Financial reporting of interest in joint ventures	7535
IAS 32	Financial instruments: disclosures and presentation	
IAS 33	Earnings per share	
IAS 34	Interim financial reporting	5620
IAS 36	Impairment of assets	1714
IAS 37	Provisions, contingent liabilities and contingent assets	
IAS 38	Intangible assets	1130
IAS 39	Financial instruments: recognition and measurement	
IAS 40	Investment income	1924
IAS 41	Agriculture	

9992

International Financial Reporting Standards		¶¶
IFRS 1	First-time Adoption of International Financial Reporting Standards	
IFRS 2	Share-based Payment	8850
IFRS 3	Business Combinations	7072
IFRS 4	Insurance Contracts	
IFRS 5	Non-current Assets Held for Sale and Discontinued Operations	6597
IFRS 6	Exploration for and Evaluation of Mineral Resources	
IFRS 7	Financial Instruments: Disclosures	
IFRS 8	Operating Segments	
IFRS 9	Financial Instruments	

Index

Using the index

Numbers refer to paragraphs.

Entries that duplicate the Outline at the head of each chapter are not repeated in the index; refer instead to the main entry in respect of individual subjects.

The symbol + following a paragraph number indicates that the subject is dealt with in the series of paragraphs beginning with that number.

The following abbreviations are used extensively and, in some cases, solely in the index.

P&L	Profit and loss/profit and loss account	**corp**	Corporate/corporation
R&D	Research and development	**iro**	In respect of
SMEs	Small and/or medium-sized entities	**ito**	In terms of

B

C

D

E

F

G

M

N

O

S

U

Composition réalisée par NORD COMPO